W9-BWZ-931

The State of the Union Messages of the Presidents of the United States

Volume III

The State of the Union Messages of the Presidents

1790-1966

★★★

with an introduction by

ARTHUR M. SCHLESINGER

Editor: Fred L. Israel

VOLUME

III

1905–1966

NEW YORK
CHELSEA HOUSE · ROBERT HECTOR
PUBLISHERS
1966

Library of Congress Catalogue Card Number: 66-20309
Printed in the United States of America

Preface

Volume III begins with Theodore Roosevelt's fifth annual message and concludes with Lyndon Johnson's third. At the turn of the century Presidents Roosevelt, Taft and Wilson were concerned about the growing trusts and how the Republic could cope with the formidable problems posed by the widening disparity between the rich and the poor. The rapid growth of cities and surging tides of immigration increased the class tensions of a society plunging into industrialization. But the advent of World War I temporarily arrested the reform impulse. In his second State of the Union message delivered on December 8, 1914, Wilson promised that "we will not ask our young men to spend the best years of their lives making soldiers of themselves." The following year, however, the President called for "more adequate national defense" including "a force of four hundred thousand disciplined citizens." And by 1917, the war, which the United States had now entered, became according to Wilson, "just and holy." Wilson had spoken of a new day dawning for democracy but the harsh realities of the peace treaties embittered many. The "just and holy" conflict was followed by a sharp election repudiation of Wilsonian idealism. After being involved in a horrible war, the nation had grown tired of crusades to "make the world safe for democracy." Presidents Harding and Coolidge concentrated on domestic affairs and the "return to normalcy." Their State of the Union messages stressed economy in government and tax reductions. "The wealth of our country is not public wealth," said Coolidge, "but private wealth. . . . No right exists to levy on a dollar, or to order the expenditure of a dollar of the money of the people, except for a necessary purpose duly authorized by the Constitution." President Hoover and Franklin Roosevelt's early messages are devoted to plans for ending the economic depression which began when the bottom dropped from the stock market in October 1929. Roosevelt's vigorous assertion of national leadership sharply contrasts with Hoover's statement that "economic depression cannot be cured by legislative action or Executive pronouncement." Roosevelt's concern over domestic problems, however, is overshadowed by the coming of World War II. For three years American servicemen fought to defeat the Axis powers in Europe, Africa, and Asia. The war had required a mighty effort and the nation successfully met the challenge. The difficulties of transition from the controlled economy of war to the relatively free economy of peace were many. President Truman's messages impressively deal with his attempts to continue the work of Roosevelt in the domestic field while constructively helping the rest of the world to restore peace, stability, and freedom. The dilemma of living in a land of plenty and a world of peril engage the messages of Eisenhower, Kennedy, and

Johnson. At home, these presidents were concerned with using the national affluence to insure realization of the American dream and abroad they acknowledged the command of Isaiah to undo the heavy burdens and let the oppressed go free.

My colleague Dr. James Watts, Jr. assisted me in preparing the comprehensive index at the end of this volume. I am deeply grateful to Dr. Watts, and I wish also to thank Mary F. McCarthy for her editorial and proofreading help and Jack Oppenheim for his encouraging support. We have sought to include every significant event and policy in our nation's history. It is our hope that this index, conceptual and analytic, will offer firm guidelines toward understanding the growth of the nation as seen through the annual reports of the Presidents of the United States.

I wish to express our special appreciation to the New York Public Library for its help with official documents and for the cooperation of its Photographic Division in processing much of the material in the Third Volume.

Fred L. Israel

Contents

WARREN G. HARDING
March 4, 1921 to August 2, 1923

CALVIN COOLIDGE (First Term)
August 3, 1923 to March 4, 1925

CALVIN COOLIDGE (Second Term)
March 4, 1925 to March 4, 1929

HERBERT C. HOOVER 1929–1933

FRANKLIN D. ROOSEVELT (First Term) 1933–1937

The State of the Union Messages of the Presidents of the United States

Volume III

Theodore Roosevelt

March 4, 1905 to March 4, 1909

(Second Term)

FIFTH ANNUAL MESSAGE.

WHITE HOUSE, *Dec. 5, 1905*

To the Senate and House of Representatives:

The people of this country continue to enjoy great prosperity. Undoubtedly there will be ebb and flow in such prosperity, and this ebb and flow will be felt more or less by all members of the community, both by the deserving and the undeserving. Against the wrath of the Lord the wisdom of man cannot avail; in time of flood or drought human ingenuity can but partially repair the disaster. A general failure of crops would hurt all of us. Again, if the folly of man mars the general well-being, then those who are innocent of the folly will have to pay part of the penalty incurred by those who are guilty of the folly. A panic brought on by the speculative folly of part of the business community would hurt the whole business community. But such stoppage of welfare, though it might be severe, would not be lasting. In the long run the one vital factor in the permanent prosperity of the country is the high individual character of the average American worker, the average American citizen, no matter whether his work be mental or manual, whether he be farmer or wage-worker, business man or professional man.

In our industrial and social system the interests of all men are so closely intertwined that in the immense majority of cases a straight-dealing man who by his efficiency, by his ingenuity and industry, benefits himself must also benefit others. Normally the man of great productive capacity who becomes rich by guiding the labor of many other men does so by enabling them to produce more than they could produce without his guidance; and both he and they share in the benefit, which comes also to the public at large. The superficial fact that the sharing may be unequal must never blind us to the underlying fact that there is this sharing, and that the benefit comes in some degree to each man concerned. Normally the wage-worker, the man of small means, and the average consumer, as well as the average producer, are all alike helped by making conditions such that the man of exceptional business ability receives an exceptional reward for his ability. Something can be done by legislation to help the general prosperity; but no such help of a permanently beneficial character can be given to the less able and less fortunate, save as the results of a policy which shall inure to the advantage of all industrious and efficient people who act decently; and this is only another way of saying that any benefit which comes to the less able and less fortunate must of necessity come even more to the more able and more fortunate. If, therefore, the less fortunate man is moved by envy of his more fortunate brother to strike at the conditions under which they have both, though unequally, prospered, the result will assuredly be that while danger may come to the one struck at, it will visit with an even heavier load the one who strikes the blow. Taken as a whole we must all go up or down together.

Yet, while not merely admitting, but insisting upon this, it is also true that where there is no governmental restraint or supervision some of the exceptional men use their energies not in ways that are for the common good, but in ways which tell against this common good. The fortunes amassed through corporate organization are now so large, and vest such power in those that wield them, as to make it a matter of necessity to give to the sovereign—that is, to the Government, which represents the people as a whole—some effective power of supervision over their corporate use. In order to insure a healthy social and industrial life, every big corporation should be held responsible by, and be accountable to, some sovereign strong enough to control its conduct. I am in no sense hostile to corporations. This is an age of combination, and any effort to prevent all combination will be not only useless, but in the end vicious, because of the contempt for law which the failure to enforce law inevitably produces. We should, moreover, recognize in cordial and ample fashion the immense good effected by corporate agencies in a country such as ours, and the wealth of intellect, energy, and fidelity devoted to their service, and therefore normally to the service of the public, by their officers and directors. The corporation has come to stay, just as the trade union has come to stay. Each can do and has done great good. Each should be favored so long as it does good. But each should be sharply checked where it acts against law and justice.

So long as the finances of the Nation are kept upon an honest basis no other question of internal economy with which the Congress has the power to deal begins to approach in importance the matter of endeavoring to secure proper industrial conditions under which the individuals —and especially the great corporations—doing an interstate business are to act. The makers of our National Constitution provided especially that the regulation of interstate commerce should come within the sphere of the General Government. The arguments in favor of their taking this stand were even then overwhelming. But they are far stronger today, in view of the enormous development of great business agencies, usually corporate in form. Experience has shown conclusively that it is useless to try to get any adequate regulation and supervision of these great corporations by State action. Such regulation and supervision can only be effectively exercised by a sovereign whose jurisdiction is coextensive with the field of work of the corporations—that is, by the National Government. I believe that this regulation and supervision can be obtained by the enactment of law by the Congress. If this proves impossible, it will certainly be necessary ultimately to confer in fullest form such power upon the National Government by a proper amendment of the Constitution. It would obviously be unwise to endeavor to secure such an amendment until it is certain that the result cannot be obtained under the Constitution as it now is. The laws of the Congress and of the several States hitherto, as passed upon by the courts, have resulted more often in showing that the States have no power in the matter than that the National Government has power; so that there at present exists a very unfortunate condition of things, under which these great corporations doing an interstate business occupy the position of subjects without a sovereign, neither any State Government nor the National Government having effective control over them. Our steady aim should be by legislation, cautiously and carefully undertaken, but resolutely persevered in, to assert the sovereignty of the National Government by affirmative action.

This is only in form an innovation. In substance it is merely a restoration; for from the earliest time such regulation of industrial activities has been recognized in the action of the lawmaking bodies; and all that I propose is to meet the changed conditions in such manner as will prevent the Commonwealth abdicating the power it has always possessed not only in this country, but also in England before and since this country became a separate Nation.

It has been a misfortune that the National laws on this subject have hitherto been of a negative or prohibitive rather than an affirmative kind, and still more that they have in part sought to prohibit what could not be effectively prohibited, and have in part in their prohibitions confounded what should be allowed and what should not be allowed. It is generally useless to try to prohibit all restraint on competition, whether this restraint be reasonable or unreasonable; and where it is not useless it is generally hurtful. Events have shown that it is not possible adequately to secure the enforcement of any law of this kind by incessant appeal to the courts. The Department of Justice has for the last four years devoted more attention to the enforcement of the anti-trust legislation than to anything else. Much has been accomplished, particularly marked has been the moral effect of the prosecutions; but it is increasingly evident that there will be a very insufficient beneficial result in the way of economic change. The successful prosecution of one device to evade the law immediately develops another device to accomplish the same purpose. What is needed is not sweeping prohibition of every arrangement, good or bad, which may tend to restrict competition, but such adequate supervision and regulation as will prevent any restriction of competition from being to the detriment of the public—as well as such supervision and regulation as will prevent other abuses in no way connected with restriction of competition. Of these abuses, perhaps the chief, although by no means the only one, is overcapitalization—generally itself the result of dishonest promotion—

because of the myriad evils it brings in its train; for such overcapitalization often means an inflation that invites business panic; it always conceals the true relation of the profit earned to the capital actually invested, and it creates a burden of interest payments which is a fertile cause of improper reduction in or limitation of wages; it damages the small investor, discourages thrift, and encourages gambling and speculation; while perhaps worst of all is the trickiness and dishonesty which it implies—for harm to morals is worse than any possible harm to material interests, and the debauchery of politics and business by great dishonest corporations is far worse than any actual material evil they do the public. Until the National Government obtains, in some manner which the wisdom of the Congress may suggest, proper control over the big corporations engaged in interstate commerce—that is, over the great majority of the big corporations—it will be impossible to deal adequately with these evils.

I am well aware of the difficulties of the legislation that I am suggesting, and of the need of temperate and cautious action in securing it. I should emphatically protest against improperly radical or hasty action. The first thing to do is to deal with the great corporations engaged in the business of interstate transportation. As I said in my message of December 6 last, the immediate and most pressing need, so far as legislation is concerned, is the enactment into law of some scheme to secure to the agents of the Government such supervision and regulation of the rates charged by the railroads of the country engaged in interstate traffic as shall summarily and effectively prevent the imposition of unjust or unreasonable rates. It must include putting a complete stop to rebates in every shape and form. This power to regulate rates, like all similar powers over the business world, should be exercised with moderation, caution, and self-restraint; but it should exist, so that it can be effectively exercised when the need arises.

The first consideration to be kept in mind is that the power should be affirmative and should be given to some administrative body created by the Congress. If given to the present Interstate Commerce Commission, or to a reorganized Interstate Commerce Commission, such commission should be made unequivocally administrative. I do not believe in the Government interfering with private business more than is necessary. I do not believe in the Government undertaking any work which can with propriety be left in private hands. But neither do I believe in the Government flinching from overseeing any work when it becomes evident that abuses are sure to obtain therein unless there is governmental supervision. It is not my province to indicate the exact terms of the law which should be enacted; but I call the attention of the Congress to certain existing conditions with which it is desirable to deal. In my judgment the most important provision which such law should contain is that conferring upon some competent administrative body the power to decide, upon the case being brought before it, whether a given rate prescribed by a railroad is reasonable and just, and if it is found to be unreasonable and unjust, then, after full investigation of the complaint, to prescribe the limit of rate beyond which it shall not be lawful to go—the maximum reasonable rate, as it is commonly called—this decision to go into effect within a reasonable time and to obtain from thence onward, subject to review by the courts. It sometimes happens at present not that a rate is too high but that a favored shipper is given too low a rate. In such case the commission would have the right to fix this already established minimum rate as the maximum; and it would need only one or two such decisions by the commission to cure railroad companies of the practice of giving improper minimum rates. I call your attention to the fact that my proposal is not to give the commission power to initiate or originate rates generally, but to regulate a rate already fixed or originated by the roads, upon complaint and after investigation. A heavy penalty should be exacted from any corporation which fails to respect an order of the commission. I regard this power to establish a maximum rate as being essential to any scheme of real reform in the matter of railway regulation. The first necessity is to secure it; and unless it is granted to the commission there is little use in touching the subject at all.

Illegal transactions often occur under the forms of law. It has often occurred that a shipper has been told by a traffic officer to buy a large quantity of some commodity and then after it has been bought an open reduction is made in the rate to take effect immediately, the arrangement resulting to the profit of one shipper and the one railroad and to the damage of all their competitors; for it must not be forgotten that the big shippers are at least as much to blame as any railroad in the matter of rebates. The law should make it clear so that nobody can fail to understand that any kind of commission paid on freight shipments, whether in this form or in the form of fictitious damages, or of a concession, a free pass, reduced passenger rate, or payment of brokerage, is illegal. It is worth while considering whether it would not be wise to confer on the Government the right of civil action against the beneficiary of a rebate for at least twice the value of the rebate; this would help stop what is really blackmail. Elevator allowances should be stopped, for they have now grown to such an extent that they are demoralizing and are used as rebates.

The best possible regulation of rates would, of course, be that regulation secured by an honest agreement among the railroads themselves to carry out the law. Such a general agreement would, for instance, at once put a stop to the efforts of any one big shipper or big railroad to discriminate against or secure advantages over some rival; and such agreement would make the railroads themselves agents for enforcing the law. The power vested in the Government to put a stop to agreements to the detriment of the public should, in my judgment, be accompanied by power to permit, under specified conditions and careful supervision, agreements clearly in the interest of the public. But, in my judgment, the necessity for giving this further power is by no means as great as the necessity for giving the commission or administrative body the other powers I have enumerated above; and it may well be inadvisable to attempt to vest this particular power in the commission or other administrative body until it already possesses and is exercising what I regard as by far the most important of all the powers I recommend—as indeed the vitally important power—that to fix a given maximum rate, which rate, after the lapse of a reasonable time, goes into full effect, subject to review by the courts.

All private-car lines, industrial roads, refrigerator charges, and the like should be expressly put under the supervision of the Interstate Commerce Commission or some similar body so far as rates, and agreements practically affecting rates, are concerned. The private car owners and the owners of industrial railroads are entitled to a fair and reasonable compensation on their investment, but neither private cars nor industrial railroads nor spur tracks should be utilized as devices for securing preferential rates. A rebate in icing charges, or in mileage, or in a division of the rate for refrigerating charges is just as pernicious as a rebate in any other way. No lower rate should apply on goods imported than actually obtains on domestic goods from the American seaboard to destination except in cases where water competition is the controlling influence. There should be publicity of the accounts of common carriers; no common carrier engaged in interstate business should keep any books or memoranda other than those reported pursuant to law or regulation, and these books or memoranda should be open to the inspection of the Government. Only in this way can violations or evasions of the law be surely detected. A system of examination of railroad accounts should be provided similar to that now conducted into the National banks by the bank examiners; a few first-class railroad accountants, if they had proper direction and proper authority to inspect books and papers, could accomplish much in preventing willful violations of the law. It would not be necessary for them to examine into the accounts of any railroad unless for good reasons they were directed to do so by the Interstate Commerce Commission. It is greatly to be desired that some way might be found by which an agreement as to transportation within a State intended to operate as a fraud upon the Federal interstate commerce laws could be brought under the jurisdiction of the Federal authorities. At present it occurs that large shipments of interstate traffic are controlled by concessions on purely State business, which of course amounts to an evasion of the law. The commission should have power to enforce fair treatment by the great trunk lines of lateral and branch lines.

I urge upon the Congress the need of providing for expeditious action by the Interstate Commerce Commission in all these matters, whether in regulating rates for transportation or for storing or for handling property or commodities in transit. The history of the cases litigated under the present commerce act shows that its efficacy has been to a great degree destroyed by the weapon of delay, almost the most formidable weapon in the hands of those whose purpose it is to violate the law.

Let me most earnestly say that these recommendations are not made in any spirit of hostility to the railroads. On ethical grounds, on grounds of right, such hostility would be intolerable; and on grounds of mere National self-interest we must remember that such hostility would tell against the welfare not merely of some few rich men, but of a multitude of small investors, a multitude of railway employes, wage workers, and most severely against the interest of the public as a whole. I believe that on the whole our railroads have done well and not ill; but the railroad men who wish to do well should not be exposed to competition with those who have no such desire, and the only way to secure this end is to give to some Government tribunal the power to see that justice is done by the unwilling exactly as it is gladly done by the willing. Moreover, if some Government body is given increased power the effect will be to furnish authoritative answer on behalf of the railroad whenever irrational clamor against it is raised, or whenever charges made against it are disproved. I ask this legislation not only in the interest of the public but in the interest of the honest railroad man and the honest shipper alike, for it is they who are chiefly jeoparded by the practices of their dishonest competitors. This legislation should be enacted in a spirit as remote as possible from hysteria and rancor. If we of the American body politic are true to the traditions we have inherited we shall always scorn any effort to make us hate any man because he is rich, just as much as we should scorn any effort to make us look down upon or treat contemptuously any man because he is poor. We judge a man by his conduct—that is, by his character—and not by his wealth or intellect. If he makes his fortune honestly, there is no just cause of quarrel with him. Indeed, we have nothing but the kindliest feelings of admiration for the successful business man who behaves decently, whether he has made his success by building or managing a railroad or by shipping goods over that railroad. The big railroad men and big shippers are simply Americans of the ordinary type who have developed to an extraordinary degree certain great business qualities. They are neither better nor worse than their fellow-citizens of smaller means. They are merely more able in certain lines and therefore exposed to certain peculiarly strong temptations. These temptations have not sprung newly into being; the exceptionally successful among mankind have always been exposed to them; but they have grown amazingly in power as a result of the extraordinary development of industrialism along new lines, and under these new conditions, which the law-makers of old could not foresee and therefore could not provide against, they have become so serious and menacing as to demand entirely new remedies. It is in the interest of the best type of railroad man and the best type of shipper no less than of the public that there should be Governmental supervision and regulation of these great business operations, for the same reason that it is in the interest of the corporation which wishes to treat its employes aright that there should be an effective Employers' Liability act, or an effective system of factory laws to prevent the abuse of women and children. All such legislation frees the corporation that wishes to do well from being driven into doing ill, in order to compete with its rival, which prefers to do ill. We desire to set up a moral standard. There can be no delusion more fatal to the Nation than the delusion that the standard of profits, of business prosperity, is sufficient in judging any business or political question—from rate legislation to municipal government. Business success, whether for the individual or for the Nation, is a good thing only so far as it is accompanied by and develops a high standard of conduct—honor, integrity, civic courage. The kind of business prosperity that blunts the standard of honor, that puts an inordinate value on mere wealth, that makes a man ruthless and conscienceless in trade, and weak and cowardly in citizenship, is not a good thing at all, but a very bad thing for the Nation. This Government stands for manhood first and for business only as an adjunct of manhood.

The question of transportation lies at the root of all industrial success, and the revolution in transportation which has taken place during the last half century has been the most important factor in the growth of the new industrial conditions. Most emphatically we do not wish to see the man of great talents refused the reward for his talents. Still less do we wish to see him penalized but we do desire to see the system of railroad transportation so handled that the strong man shall be given no advantage over the weak man. We wish to insure as fair treatment for the small town as for the big city; for the small shipper as for the big shipper. In the old days the highway of commerce, whether by water or by a road on land, was open to all; it belonged to the public and the traffic along it was free. At present the railway is this highway, and we must do our best to see that it is kept open to all on equal terms. Unlike the old highway it is a very difficult and complex thing to manage, and it is far better that it should be managed by private individuals than by the Government. But it can only be so managed on condition that justice is done the public. It is because, in my judgment, public ownership of railroads is highly undesirable and would probably in this country entail far-reaching disaster, but I wish to see such supervision and regulation of them in the interest of the public as will make it evident that there is no need for public ownership. The opponents of Government regulation dwell upon the difficulties to be encountered and the intricate and involved nature of the problem. Their contention is true. It is a complicated and delicate problem, and all kinds of difficulties are sure to arise in connection with any plan of solution, while no plan will bring all the benefits hoped for by its more optimistic adherents. Moreover, under any healthy plan the benefits will develop gradually and not rapidly. Finally, we must clearly understand that the public servants who are to do this peculiarly responsible and delicate work must themselves be of the highest type both as regards integrity and efficiency. They must be well paid, for otherwise able men cannot in the long run be secured; and they must possess a lofty probity which will revolt as quickly at the thought of pandering to any gust of popular prejudice against rich men as at the thought of anything even remotely resembling subserviency to rich men. But while I fully admit the difficulties in the way, I do not for a moment admit that these difficulties warrant us in stopping in our effort to secure a wise and just system. They should have no other effect than to spur us on to the exercise of the resolution, the even-handed justice, and the fertility of resource, which we like to think of as typically American, and which will in the end achieve good results in this as in other fields of activity. The task is a great one and underlies the task of dealing with the whole industrial problem. But the fact that it is a great problem does not warrant us in shrinking from the attempt to solve it. At present we face such utter lack of supervision, such freedom from the restraints of law, that excellent men have often been literally forced into doing what they deplored because otherwise they were left at the mercy of unscrupulous competitors. To rail at and assail the men who have done as they best could under such conditions accomplishes little. What we need to do is to develop an orderly system, and such a system can only come through the gradually increased exercise of the right of efficient Government control.

In my annual message to the Fifty-eighth Congress, at its third session, I called attention to the necessity for legislation requiring the use of block signals upon railroads engaged in interstate commerce. The number of serious collisions upon unblocked roads that have occurred within the past year adds force to the recommendation then made. The Congress should provide, by appropriate legislation, for the introduction of block signals upon all railroads engaged in interstate commerce at the earliest practicable date, as a measure of increased safety to the traveling public.

Through decisions of the Supreme Court of the United States and the lower Federal courts in cases brought before them for adjudication the safety appliance law has been materially strengthened, and the Government has been enabled to secure its effective enforcement in almost all cases, with the result that the condition of railroad equipment throughout the country is much improved and railroad employes perform their duties under safer conditions than heretofore. The Government's most effective aid in arriving at this result has been its inspection service, and that these improved conditions are not more general is due to the insufficient number of inspectors employed. The inspection service has fully demonstrated its usefulness, and in appropriating for its maintenance the Congress should make provision for an increase in the number of inspectors.

The excessive hours of labor to which railroad employes in train service are in many cases subjected is also a matter which may well engage the serious attention of the Congress. The strain, both mental and physical, upon those who are engaged in the movement and operation of railroad trains under modern conditions is perhaps greater than that which exists in any other industry, and if there are any reasons for limiting by law the hours of labor in any employment, they certainly apply with peculiar force to the employment of those upon whose vigilance and alertness in the performance of their duties the safety of all who travel by rail depends.

In my annual message to the Fifty-seventh Congress, at its second session, I recommended the passage of an employers' liability law for the District of Columbia and in our navy yards. I renewed that recommendation in my message to the Fifty-eighth Congress, at its second session, and further suggested the appointment of a commission to make a comprehensive study of employers' liability, with a view to the enactment of a wise and Constitutional law covering the subject, applicable to all industries within the scope of the Federal power. I hope that such a law will be prepared and enacted as speedily as possible.

The National Government has, as a rule, but little occasion to deal with the formidable group of problems connected more or less directly with what is known as the labor question, for in the great majority of cases these problems must be dealt with by the State and municipal authorities, and not by the National Government. The National Government has control of the District of Columbia, however, and it should see to it that the City of Washington is made a model city in all respects, both as regards parks, public playgrounds, proper regulation of the system of housing, so as to do away with the evils of alley tenements, a proper system of education, a proper system of dealing with truancy and juvenile offenders, a proper handling of the charitable work of the District. Moreover, there should be proper factory laws to prevent all abuses in the employment of women and children in the District. These will be useful chiefly as object lessons, but even this limited amount of usefulness would be of real National value.

There has been demand for depriving courts of the power to issue injunctions in labor disputes. Such special limitation of the equity powers of our courts would be most unwise. It is true that some judges have misused this power; but this does not justify a denial of the power any more than an improper exercise of the power to call a strike by a labor leader would justify the denial of the right to strike. The remedy is to regulate the procedure by requiring the judge to give due notice to the adverse parties before granting the writ, the hearing to be ex parte if the adverse party does not appear at the time and place ordered. What is due notice must depend upon the facts of the case; it should not be used as a pretext to permit violation of law or the jeopardizing of life or property. Of course, this would not authorize the issuing of a restraining order or injunction in any case in which it is not already authorized by existing law.

I renew the recommendation I made in my last annual message for an investigation by the Department of Commerce and Labor of general labor conditions, especial attention to be paid to the conditions of child labor and child-labor legislation in the several States. Such an investigation should take into account the various problems with which the question of child labor is connected. It is true that these problems can be actually met in most cases only by the States themselves, but it would be well for the Nation to endeavor to secure and publish comprehensive information as to the conditions of the labor of children in the different States, so as to spur up those that are behindhand and to secure approximately uniform legislation of a high character among the several States. In such a Republic as ours the one thing that we cannot afford to neglect is the problem of turning out decent citizens. The future of the Nation depends upon the citizenship of the generations to come; the children of today are those who tomorrow will shape the destiny of our land, and we cannot afford to neglect them. The Legislature of Colorado has recommended that the National Government provide some general measure for the protection from abuse of children and dumb animals throughout the United States. I lay the matter before you for what I trust will be your favorable consideration.

The Department of Commerce and Labor should also make a thorough investigation of the conditions of women in industry. Over five million American women are now engaged in gainful occupations; yet there is an almost complete dearth of data upon which to base any trustworthy conclusions as regards a subject as important as it is vast and complicated. There is need of full knowledge on which to base action looking toward State and municipal legislation for the protection of working women. The introduction of women into industry is working change and disturbance in the domestic and social life of the Nation. The decrease in marriage, and especially in the birth rate, has been coincident with it. We must face accomplished facts, and the adjustment of factory conditions must be made, but surely it can be made with less friction and less harmful effects on family life than is now the case. This whole matter in reality forms one of the greatest sociological phenomena of our time; it is a social question of the first importance, of far greater importance than any merely political or economic question can be, and to solve it we need ample data, gathered in a sane and scientific spirit in the course of an exhaustive investigation.

In any great labor disturbance not only are employer and employe interested, but a third party—the general public. Every considerable labor difficulty in which interstate commerce is involved should be investigated by the Government and the facts officially reported to the public.

The question of securing a healthy, self-respecting, and mutually sympathetic attitude as between employer and employe, capitalist and wage-worker, is a difficult one. All phases of the labor problem prove difficult when approached. But the underlying principles, the root principles, in accordance with which the problem must be solved are entirely simple. We can get justice and right dealing only if we put as of paramount importance the principle of treating a man on his worth as a man rather than with reference to his social position, his occupation or the class to which he belongs. There are selfish and brutal men in all ranks of life. If they are capitalists their selfishness and brutality may take the form of hard indifference to suffering, greedy disregard of every moral restraint which interferes with the accumulation of wealth, and cold-blooded exploitation of the weak; or, if they are laborers, the form of laziness, of sullen envy of the more fortunate, and of willingness to perform deeds of murderous violence. Such conduct is just as reprehensible in one case as in the other, and all honest and farseeing men should join in warring against it wherever it becomes manifest. Individual capitalist and individual wage-worker, corporation and union, are alike entitled to the protection of the law, and must alike obey the law. Moreover, in addition to mere obedience to the law, each man, if he be really a good citizen, must show broad sympathy for his neighbor and genuine desire to look at any question arising between them from the standpoint of that neighbor no less than from his own, and to this end it is essential that capitalist and wage-worker should consult freely one with the other, should each strive to bring closer the day when both shall realize that they are properly partners and not enemies. To approach the questions which inevitably arise between them solely from the standpoint which treats each side in the mass as the enemy of the other side in the mass is both wicked and foolish. In the past the most direful among the influences which have brought about the downfall of republics has ever been the growth of the class spirit, the growth of the spirit which tends to make a man subordinate the welfare of the public as a whole to the welfare of the particular class to which he belongs, the substitution of loyalty to a class for loyalty to the Nation. This inevitably brings about a tendency to treat each man not on his merits as an individual, but on his position as belonging to a certain class in the community. If such a spirit grows up in this Republic it will ultimately prove fatal to us, as in the past it has proved fatal to every community in which it has become dominant. Unless we continue to keep a quick and lively sense of the great fundamental truth that our concern is with the individual worth of the individual man, this Government cannot permanently hold the place which it has achieved among the nations. The vital lines of cleavage among our people do not correspond, and indeed run at right angles to, the lines of cleavage which divide occupation from occupation, which divide wage-workers from capitalists, farmers from bankers, men of small means from men of large means, men who live in the towns from men who live in the country; for the vital line of cleavage is the line which divides the honest man who tries to do well by his neighbor from the dishonest man who does ill by his neighbor. In other words, the standard we should establish is the standard of conduct, not the standard of occupation, of means, or of social position. It is the man's moral quality, his attitude toward the great questions which concern all humanity, his cleanliness of life, his power to do his duty toward himself and toward others, which really count; and if we substitute for the standard of personal judgment which treats each man according to his merits, another standard in accordance with which all men of one class are favored and all men of another class discriminated against, we shall do irreparable damage to the body politic. I believe that our people are too sane, too self-respecting, too fit for self-government, ever to adopt such an attitude. This Government is not and never shall be government by a plutocracy. This Government is not and never shall be government by a mob. It shall continue to be in the future what it has been in the past, a Government based on the theory that each man, rich or poor, is to be treated simply and solely on his worth as a man, that all his personal and property rights are to be safeguarded, and that he is neither to wrong others nor to suffer wrong from others.

The noblest of all forms of government is self-government; but it is also the most difficult. We who possess this priceless boon, and who desire to hand it on to our children and our children's children, should ever bear in mind the thought so finely expressed by Burke: "Men are qualified for civil liberty in exact proportion to their disposition to put moral chains upon their own appetites; in proportion as they are disposed to listen to the counsels of the wise and good in preference to the flattery of knaves. Society cannot exist unless a controlling power upon will and appetite be placed somewhere, and the less of it there be within the more there must be without. It is ordained in the eternal constitution of things that men of intemperate minds cannot be free. Their passions forge their fetters."

The great insurance companies afford striking examples of corporations whose business has extended so far beyond the jurisdiction of the States which created them as to preclude strict enforcement of supervision and regulation by the parent States. In my last annual message I recommended "that the Congress carefully consider whether the power of the Bureau of Corporations cannot constitutionally be extended to cover interstate transactions in insurance."

Recent events have emphasized the importance of an early and exhaustive consideration of this question, to see whether it is not possible to furnish better safeguards than the several States have been able to furnish against corruption of the flagrant kind which has been exposed. It has been only too clearly shown that certain of the men at the head of these large corporations take but small note of the ethical distinction between honesty and dishonesty; they draw the line only this side of what may be called law-honesty, the kind of honesty necessary in order to avoid falling into the clutches of the law. Of course the only complete remedy for this condition must be found in an aroused public conscience, a higher sense of ethical conduct in the community at large, and especially among business men and in the great profession of the law, and in the growth of a spirit which condemns all dishonesty, whether in rich man or in poor man, whether it takes the shape of bribery or of blackmail. But much can be done by legislation which is not only drastic but practical. There is need of a far stricter and more uniform regulation of the vast insurance interests of this country. The United States should in this respect follow the policy of other nations by providing adequate national supervision of commercial interests which are clearly national in character. My predecessors have repeatedly recognized that the foreign business of these companies is an important part of our foreign commercial relations. During the administrations of Presidents Cleveland, Harrison, and McKinley the State Department exercised its influence, through diplomatic channels, to prevent unjust discrimination by foreign countries against American insurance companies. These negotiations illustrated the propriety of the Congress recognizing the National character of insurance, for in the absence of Federal legislation the State Department could only give expression to the wishes of the authorities of the several States, whose policy was ineffective through want of uniformity.

I repeat my previous recommendation that the Congress should also consider whether the Federal Government has any power or owes any duty with respect to domestic transactions in insurance of an interstate character. That State supervision has proved inadequate is generally conceded. The burden upon insurance companies, and therefore their policy holders, of conflicting regulations of many States, is unquestioned, while but little effective check is imposed upon any able and unscrupulous man who desires to exploit the company in his own interest at the expense of the policy holders and of the public. The inability of a State to regulate effectively insurance corporations created under the laws of other States and transacting the larger part of their business elsewhere is also clear. As a remedy for this evil of conflicting, ineffective, and yet burdensome regulations there has been for many years a widespread demand for Federal supervision. The Congress has already recognized that interstate insurance may be a proper subject for Federal legislation, for in creating the Bureau of Corporations it authorized it to publish and supply useful information concerning interstate corporations, "including corporations engaged in insurance." It is obvious that if the compilation of statistics be the limit of the Federal power it is wholly ineffective to regulate this form of commercial intercourse between the States, and as the insurance business has outgrown in magnitude the possibility of adequate State supervision, the Congress should carefully consider whether further legislation can be had. What is said above applies with equal force to fraternal and benevolent organizations which contract for life insurance.

There is more need of stability than of the attempt to attain an ideal perfection in the methods of raising revenue; and the shock and strain to the business world certain to attend any serious change in these methods render such change inadvisable unless for grave reason. It is not possible to lay down any general rule by which to determine the moment when the reasons for will outweigh the reasons against such a change. Much must depend, not merely on the needs, but on the desires, of the people as a whole; for needs and desires are not necessarily identical. Of course, no change can be made on lines beneficial to, or desired by, one section or one State only. There must be something like a general agreement among the citizens of the several States, as represented in the Congress, that the change is needed and desired in the interest of the people, as a whole; and there should then be a sincere, intelligent, and disinterested effort to make it in such shape as will combine, so far as possible, the maximum of good to the people at large with the minimum of necessary disregard for the special interests of localities or classes. But in time of peace the revenue must on the average, taking a series of years together, equal the expenditures or else the revenues must be increased. Last year there was a deficit. Unless our expenditures can be kept within the revenues then our revenue laws must be readjusted. It is as yet too early to attempt to outline what shape such a readjustment should take, for it is as yet too early to say whether there will be need for it. It should be considered whether it is not desirable that the tariff laws should provide for applying as against or in favor of any other nation maximum and minimum tariff rates established by the Congress, so as to secure a certain reciprocity of treatment between other nations and ourselves. Having in view even larger considerations of policy than those of a purely economic nature, it would, in my judgment, be well to endeavor to bring about closer commercial connections with the other peoples of this continent. I am happy to be able to announce to you that Russia now treats us on the most-favored-nation basis.

I earnestly recommend to Congress the need of economy and to this end of a rigid scrutiny of appropriations. As examples merely, I call your attention to one or two specific matters. All unnecessary offices should be abolished. The Commissioner of the General Land Office recommends the abolishment of the office of Receiver of Public Moneys for the United States Land Office. This will effect a saving of about a quarter of a million dollars a year. As the business of the Nation grows, it is inevitable that there should be from time to time a legitimate increase in the number of officials, and this fact renders it all the more important that when offices become unnecessary they should be abolished. In the public printing also a large saving of public money can be made. There is a constantly growing tendency to publish masses of unimportant information. It is probably not unfair to say that many tens of thousands of volumes are published at which no human being ever looks and for which there is no real demand whatever.

Yet, in speaking of economy, I must in no wise be understood as advocating the false economy which is in the end the worst extravagance. To cut down on the navy, for instance, would be a crime against the Nation. To fail to push forward all work on the Panama Canal would be as great a folly.

In my message of December 2, 1902, to the Congress I said:

"Interest rates are a potent factor in business activity, and in order that these rates may be equalized to meet the varying needs of the seasons and of widely separated communities, and to prevent the recurrence of financial stringencies, which injuriously affect legitimate business, it is necessary that there should be an element of elasticity in our monetary system. Banks are the natural servants of commerce, and, upon them should be placed, as far as practicable, the burden of furnishing and maintaining a circulation adequate to supply the needs of our diversified industries and of our domestic and foreign commerce; and the issue of this should be so regulated that a sufficient supply should be always available for the business interests of the country."

Every consideration of prudence demands the addition of the element of elasticity to our currency system. The evil does not consist in an inadequate volume of money, but in the rigidity of this volume, which does not respond as it should to the varying needs of communities and of seasons. Inflation must be avoided; but some provision should be made that will insure a larger volume of money during the Fall and Winter months than in the less active seasons of the year; so that the currency will contract against speculation, and will expand for the needs of legitimate business. At present the Treasury Department is at irregularly recurring intervals obliged, in the interest of the business world—that is, in the interests of the American public—to try to avert financial crises by providing a remedy which should be provided by Congressional action.

At various times I have instituted investigations into the organization and conduct of the business of the executive departments. While none of these inquiries have yet progressed far enough to warrant final conclusions, they have already confirmed and emphasized the general impression that the organization of the departments is often faulty in principle and wasteful in results, while many of their business methods are antiquated and inefficient. There is every reason why our executive governmental machinery should be at least as well planned, economical, and efficient as the best machinery of the great business organizations, which at present is not the case. To make it so is a task of complex detail and essentially executive in its nature; probably no legislative body, no matter how wise and able, could undertake it with reasonable prospect of success. I recommend that the Congress consider this subject with a view to provide by legislation for the transfer, distribution, consolidation, and assignment of duties and executive organizations or parts of organizations, and for the changes in business methods, within or between the several departments, that will best promote the economy, efficiency, and high character of the Government work.

In my last annual message I said:

"The power of the Government to protect the integrity of the elections of its own officials is inherent and has been recognized and affirmed by repeated declarations of the Supreme Court. There is no enemy of free government more dangerous and none so insidious as the corruption of the electorate. No one defends or excuses corruption, and it would seem to follow that none would oppose vigorous measures to eradicate it. I recommend the enactment of a law directed against bribery and corruption in Federal elections. The details of such a law may be safely left to the wise discretion of the Congress, but it should go as far as under the Constitution it is possible to go, and should include severe penalties against him who gives or receives a bribe intended to influence his act or opinion as an elector; and provisions for the publication not only of the expenditures for nominations and elections of all candidates, but also of all contributions received and expenditures made by political committees."

I desire to repeat this recommendation. In political campaigns in a country as large and populous as ours it is inevitable that there should be much expense of an entirely legitimate kind. This, of course, means that many contributions, and some of them of large size, must be made, and, as a matter of fact, in any big political contest such contributions are always made to both sides. It is entirely proper both to give and receive them, unless there is an improper motive connected with either gift or reception. If they are extorted by any kind of pressure or promise, express or implied, direct or indirect, in the way of favor or immunity, then the giving or receiving becomes not only improper but criminal. It will undoubtedly be difficult, as a matter of practical detail, to shape an act which shall guard with reasonable certainty against such misconduct; but if it is possible to secure by law the full and verified publication in detail of all the sums contributed to and expended by the candidates or committees of any political parties, the result cannot but be wholesome. All contributions by corporations to any political committee or for any political purpose should be forbidden by law; directors should not be permitted to use stockholders' money for such purposes; and, moreover, a prohibition of this kind would be, as far as it went, an effective method of stopping the evils aimed at in corrupt practices acts. Not only should both the National and the several State Legislatures forbid any officer of a corporation from using the money of the corporation in or about any election, but they should also forbid such use of money in connection with any legislation save by the employment of counsel in public manner for distinctly legal services.

The first conference of nations held at The Hague in 1899, being unable to dispose of all the business before it, recommended the consideration and settlement of a number of important questions by another conference to be called subsequently and at an early date. These questions were the following: (1) The rights and duties of neutrals;

(2) the limitation of the armed forces on land and sea, and of military budgets; (3) the use of new types and calibres of military and naval guns; (4) the inviolability of private property at sea in times of war; (5) the bombardment of ports, cities, and villages by naval forces. In October, 1904, at the instance of the Interparliamentary Union, which, at a conference held in the United States, and attended by the lawmakers of fifteen different nations, had reiterated the demand for a second conference of nations, I issued invitations to all the powers signatory to The Hague Convention to send delegates to such a conference, and suggested that it be again held at The Hague. In its note of December 16, 1904, the United States Government communicated to the representatives of foreign governments its belief that the conference could be best arranged under the provisions of the present Hague treaty.

From all the powers acceptance was received, coupled in some cases with the condition that we should wait until the end of the war then waging between Russia and Japan. The Emperor of Russia, immediately after the treaty of peace which so happily terminated this war, in a note presented to the President on September 13, through Ambassador Rosen, took the initiative in recommending that the conference be now called. The United States Government in response expressed its cordial acquiescence, and stated that it would, as a matter of course, take part in the new conference and endeavor to further its aims. We assume that all civilized governments will support the movement, and that the conference is now an assured fact. This Government will do everything in its power to secure the success of the conference, to the end that substantial progress may be made in the cause of international peace, justice, and good will.

This renders it proper at this time to say something as to the general attitude of this Government toward peace. More and more war is coming to be looked upon as in itself a lamentable and evil thing. A wanton or useless war, or a war of mere aggression—in short, any war begun or carried on in a conscienceless spirit, is to be condemned as a peculiarly atrocious crime against all humanity. We can, however, do nothing of permanent value for peace unless we keep ever clearly in mind the ethical element which lies at the root of the problem. Our aim is righteousness. Peace is normally the hand-maiden of rightousness; but when peace and righteousness conflict then a great and upright people can never for a moment hesitate to follow the path which leads toward righteousness, even though that path also leads to war. There are persons who advocate peace at any price; there are others who, following a false analogy, think that because it is no longer necessary in civilized countries for individuals to protect their rights with a strong hand, it is therefore unnecessary for nations to be ready to defend their rights. These persons would do irreparable harm to any nation that adopted their principles, and even as it is they seriously hamper the cause which they advocate by tending to render it absurd in the eyes of sensible and patriotic men. There can be no worse foe of mankind in general, and of his own country in particular, than the demagogue of war, the man who in mere folly or to serve his own selfish ends continually rails at and abuses other nations, who seeks to excite his countrymen against foreigners on insufficient pretexts, who excites and inflames a perverse and aggressive national vanity, and who may on occasions wantonly bring on conflict between his nation and some other nation. But there are demagogues of peace just as there are demagogues of war, and in any such movement as this for The Hague conference it is essential not to be misled by one set of extremists any more than by the other. Whenever it is possible for a nation or an individual to work for real peace, assuredly it is failure of duty not so to strive, but if war is necessary and righteous then either the man or the nation shrinking from it forfeits all title to self-respect. We have scant sympathy with the sentimentalist who dreads oppression less than physical suffering, who would prefer a shameful peace to the pain and toil sometimes lamentably necessary in order to secure a righteous peace. As yet there is only a partial and imperfect analogy between international law and internal or municipal law, because there is no sanction of force for executing the former while there is in the case of the latter. The private citizen is protected in his rights by the law, because the law rests in the last resort upon force exercised through the forms of law. A man does not have to defend his rights with his own hand, because he can call upon the police, upon the sheriff's posse, upon the militia, or in certain extreme cases upon the army, to defend him. But there is no such sanction of force for international law. At present there could be no greater calamity than for the free peoples, the enlightened, independent, and peace-loving peoples, to disarm while yet leaving it open to any barbarism or despotism to remain armed. So long as the world is as unorganized as now the armies and navies of those peoples who on the whole stand for justice, offer not only the best, but the only possible, security for a just peace. For instance, if the United States alone, or in company only with the other nations that on the whole tend to act justly, disarmed, we might sometimes avoid bloodshed, but we would cease to be of weight in securing the peace of justice—the real peace for which the most law-abiding and high-minded men must at times be willing to fight. As the world is now, only that nation is equipped for peace that knows how to fight, and that will not shrink from fighting if ever the conditions become such that war is demanded in the name of the highest morality.

So much it is emphatically necessary to say in order both that the position of the United States may not be misunderstood, and that a genuine effort to bring nearer the day of the peace of justice among the nations may not be hampered by a folly which, in striving to achieve the impossible, would render it hopeless to attempt the achievement of the practical. But, while recognizing most clearly all above set forth, it remains our clear duty to strive in every practicable way to bring nearer the time when the sword shall not be the arbiter among nations. At present the practical thing to do is to try to minimize the number of cases in which it must be the arbiter, and to offer, at least to all civilized powers, some substitute for war which will be available in at least a considerable number of instances. Very much can be done through another Hague conference in this direction, and I most earnestly urge that this Nation do all in its power to try to further the movement and to make the result of the decisions of The Hague conference effective. I earnestly hope that the conference may be able to devise some way to make arbitration between nations the customary way of settling international disputes in all save a few classes of cases, which should themselves be as sharply defined and rigidly limited as the present governmental and social development of the world will permit. If possible, there should be a general arbitration treaty negotiated among all the nations represented at the conference. Neutral rights and property should be protected at sea as they are protected on land. There should be an international agreement to this purpose and a similar agreement defining contraband of war.

During the last century there has been a distinct diminution in the number of wars between the most civilized nations. International relations have become closer and the development of The Hague tribunal is not only a symptom of this growing closeness of relationship, but is a means by which the growth can be furthered. Our aim should be from time to time to take such steps as may be possible toward creating something like an organization of the civilized nations, because as the world becomes more highly organized the need for navies and armies will diminish. It is not possible to secure anything like an immediate disarmament, because it would first be necessary to settle what peoples are on the whole a menace to the rest of mankind, and to provide against the disarmament of the rest being turned into a movement which would really chiefly benefit these obnoxious peoples; but it may be possible to exercise some check upon the tendency to swell indefinitely the budgets for military expenditure. Of course such an effort could succeed only if it did not attempt to do too much; and if it were undertaken in a spirit of sanity as far removed as possible from a merely hysterical pseudo-philanthropy. It is worth while pointing out that since the end of the insurrection in the Philippines this

Nation has shown its practical faith in the policy of disarmament by reducing its little army one-third. But disarmament can never be of prime importance; there is more need to get rid of the causes of war than of the implements of war.

I have dwelt much on the dangers to be avoided by steering clear of any mere foolish sentimentality because my wish for peace is so genuine and earnest; because I have a real and great desire that this second Hague conference may mark a long stride forward in the direction of securing the peace of justice throughout the world. No object is better worthy the attention of enlightened statesmanship than the establishment of a surer method than now exists of securing justice as between nations, both for the protection of the little nations and for the prevention of war between the big nations. To this aim we should endeavor not only to avert bloodshed, but, above all, effectively to strengthen the forces of right. The Golden Rule should be, and as the world grows in morality it will be, the guiding rule of conduct among nations as among individuals; though the Golden Rule must not be construed, in fantastic manner, as forbidding the exercise of the police power. This mighty and free Republic should ever deal with all other States, great or small, on a basis of high honor, respecting their rights as jealously as it safeguards its own.

One of the most effective instruments for peace is the Monroe Doctrine as it has been and is being gradually developed by this Nation and accepted by other nations. No other policy could have been as efficient in promoting peace in the Western Hemisphere and in giving to each nation thereon the chance to develop along its own lines. If we had refused to apply the doctrine to changing conditions it would now be completely outworn, would not meet any of the needs of the present day, and, indeed, would probably by this time have sunk into complete oblivion. It is useful at home, and is meeting with recognition abroad because we have adapted our application of it to meet the growing and changing needs of the hemisphere. When we announce a policy such as the Monroe Doctrine we thereby commit ourselves to the consequences of the policy, and those consequences from time to time alter. It is out of the question to claim a right and yet shirk the responsibility for its exercise. Not only we, but all American republics who are benefited by the existence of the doctrine, must recognize the obligations each nation is under as regards foreign peoples no less than its duty to insist upon its own rights.

That our rights and interests are deeply concerned in the maintenance of the doctrine is so clear as hardly to need argument. This is especially true in view of the construction of the Panama Canal. As a mere matter of self-defense we must exercise a close watch over the approaches to this canal; and this means that we must be thoroughly alive to our interests in the Caribbean Sea.

There are certain essential points which must never be forgotten as regards the Monroe Doctrine. In the first place we must as a Nation make it evident that we do not intend to treat it in any shape or way as an excuse for aggrandizement on our part at the expense of the republics to the south. We must recognize the fact that in some South American countries there has been much suspicion lest we should interpret the Monroe Doctrine as in some way inimical to their interests, and we must try to convince all the other nations of this continent once and for all that no just and orderly Government has anything to fear from us. There are certain republics to the south of us which have already reached such a point of stability, order, and prosperity that they themselves, though as yet hardly consciously, are among the guarantors of this doctrine. These republics we now meet not only on a basis of entire equality, but in a spirit of frank and respectful friendship, which we hope is mutual. If all of the republics to the south of us will only grow as those to which I allude have already grown, all need for us to be the especial champions of the doctrine will disappear, for no stable and growing American Republic wishes to see some great non-American military power acquire territory in its neighborhood. All that this country desires is that the other republics on this continent shall be happy and prosperous; and they cannot be happy and prosperous unless they maintain order within their boundaries and behave with a just regard for their obligations toward outsiders. It must be understood that under no circumstances will the United States use the Monroe Doctrine as a cloak for territorial aggression. We desire peace with all the world, but perhaps most of all with the other peoples of the American Continent. There are, of course, limits to the wrongs which any self-respecting nation can endure. It is always possible that wrong actions toward this Nation, or toward citizens of this Nation, in some State unable to keep order among its own people, unable to secure justice from outsiders, and unwilling to do justice to those outsiders who treat it well, may result in our having to take action to protect our rights; but such action will not be taken with a view to territorial aggression, and it will be taken at all only with extreme reluctance and when it has become evident that every other resource has been exhausted.

Moreover, we must make it evident that we do not intend to permit the Monroe Doctrine to be used by any nation on this Continent as a shield to protect it from the consequences of its own misdeeds against foreign nations. If a republic to the south of us commits a tort against a foreign nation, such as an outrage against a citizen of that nation, then the Monroe Doctrine does not force us to interfere to prevent punishment of the tort, save to see that the punishment does not assume the form of territorial occupation in any shape. The case is more difficult when it refers to a contractual obligation. Our own Government has always refused to enforce such contractual obligations on behalf of its citizens by an appeal to arms. It is much to be wished that all foreign governments would take the same view. But they do not; and in consequence we are liable at any time to be brought face to face with disagreeable alternatives. On the one hand, this country would certainly decline to go to war to prevent a foreign government from collecting a just debt; on the other hand, it is very inadvisable to permit any foreign power to take possession, even temporarily, of the custom houses of an American Republic in order to enforce the payment of its obligations; for such temporary occupation might turn into a permanent occupation. The only escape from these alternatives may at any time be that we must ourselves undertake to bring about some arrangement by which so much as possible of a just obligation shall be paid. It is far better that this country should put through such an arrangement, rather than allow any foreign country to undertake it. To do so insures the defaulting republic from having to pay debt of an improper character under duress, while it also insures honest creditors of the republic from being passed by in the interest of dishonest or grasping creditors. Moreover, for the United States to take such a position offers the only possible way of insuring us against a clash with some foreign power. The position is, therefore, in the interest of peace as well as in the interest of justice. It is of benefit to our people; it is of benefit to foreign peoples; and most of all it is really of benefit to the people of the country concerned.

This brings me to what should be one of the fundamental objects of the Monroe Doctrine. We must ourselves in good faith try to help upward toward peace and order those of our sister republics which need such help. Just as there has been a gradual growth of the ethical element in the relations of one individual to another, so we are, even though slowly, more and more coming to recognize the duty of bearing one another's burdens, not only as among individuals, but also as among nations.

Santo Domingo, in her turn, has now made an appeal to us to help her, and not only every principle of wisdom but every generous instinct within us bids us respond to the appeal. It is not of the slightest consequence whether we grant the aid needed by Santo Domingo as an incident to the wise development of the Monroe Doctrine or because we regard the case of Santo Domingo as standing wholly by itself, and to be treated as such, and not on general principles or with any reference to the Monroe Doctrine. The important point is to give the needed aid, and the case is certainly sufficiently peculiar to deserve to be judged purely on its own merits. The conditions in Santo Domingo have for a number of years grown from bad to worse until a year ago all society was on the verge of dissolution. Fortunately, just at this time a ruler sprang up in Santo Domingo, who, with his colleagues, saw the dangers threatening their country and appealed to the friendship of the only great and powerful neighbor who possessed the power, and as they hoped also the will to help them. There was imminent danger of foreign intervention. The previous rulers of Santo Domingo had recklessly incurred debts, and owing to her internal disorders she had ceased to be able to provide means of paying the debts. The patience of her foreign creditors had become exhausted, and at least two foreign nations were on the point of intervention, and were only prevented from intervening by the unofficial assurance of this Government that it would itself strive to help Santo Domingo in her hour of need. In the case of one of these nations, only the actual opening of negotiations to this end by our Government prevented the seizure of territory in Santo Domingo by a European power. Of the debts incurred some were just, while some were not of a character which really renders it obligatory on or proper for Santo Domingo to pay them in full. But she could not pay any of them unless some stability was assured her Government and people.

Accordingly, the Executive Department of our Government negotiated a treaty under which we are to try to help the Dominican people to straighten out their finances. This treaty is pending before the Senate. In the meantime a temporary arrangement has been made which will last until the Senate has had time to take action upon the treaty. Under this arrangement the Dominican Government has appointed Americans to all the important positions in the customs service. and they are seeing to the honest collection of the revenues, turning over 45 per cent. to the Government for running expenses and putting the other 55 per cent. into a safe depository for equitable division in case the treaty shall be ratified, among the various creditors, whether European or American.

The Custom Houses offer well-nigh the only sources of revenue in Santo Domingo, and the different revolutions usually have as their real aim the obtaining of these Custom Houses. The mere fact that the Collectors of Customs are Americans, that they are performing their duties with efficiency and honesty, and that the treaty is pending in the Senate gives a certain moral power to the Government of Santo Domingo which it has not had before. This has completely discouraged all revolutionary movement, while it has already produced such an increase in the revenues that the Government is actually getting more from the 45 per cent. that the American Collectors turn over to it than it got formerly when it took the entire revenue. It is enabling the poor, harassed people of Santo Domingo once more to turn their attention to industry and to be free from the cure of interminable revolutionary disturbance. It offers to all bona-fide creditors, American and European, the only really good chance to obtain that to which they are justly entitled, while it in return gives to Santo Domingo the only opportunity of defense against claims which it ought not to pay, for now if it meets the views of the Senate we shall ourselves thoroughly examine all these claims, whether American or foreign, and see that none that are improper are paid. There is, of course, opposition to the treaty from dishonest creditors, foreign and American, and from the professional revolutionists of the island itself. We have already reason to believe that some of the creditors who do not dare expose their claims to honest scrutiny are endeavoring to stir up sedition in the island and opposition to the treaty. In the meantime, I have exercised the authority vested in me by the joint resolution of the Congress to prevent the introduction of arms into the island for revolutionary purposes.

Under the course taken, stability and order and all the benefits of peace are at last coming to Santo Domingo, danger of foreign intervention has been suspended, and there is at last a prospect that all creditors will get justice, no more and no less. If the arrangement is terminated by the failure of the treaty chaos will follow; and if chaos follows, sooner or later this Government may be involved in serious difficulties with foreign Governments over the island, or else may be forced itself to intervene in the island in some unpleasant fashion. Under the proposed treaty the independence of the island is scrupulously respected, the danger of violation of the Monroe Doctrine by the intervention of foreign powers vanishes, and the interference of our Government is minimized, so that we shall only act in conjunction with the Santo Domingo authorities to secure the proper administration of the customs, and therefore to secure the payment of just debts and to secure the Dominican Government against demands for unjust debts. The proposed method will give the people of Santo Domingo the same chance to move onward and upward which we have already given to the people of Cuba. It will be doubly to our discredit as a Nation if we fail to take advantage of this chance; for it will be of damage to ourselves, and it will be of incalculable damage to Santo Domingo. Every consideration of wise policy, and, above all, every consideration of large generosity, bids us meet the request of Santo Domingo as we are now trying to meet it.

We cannot consider the question of our foreign policy without at the same time treating of the Army and the Navy. We now have a very small army indeed, one well-nigh infinitesimal when compared with the army of any other large nation. Of course the army we do have should be as nearly perfect of its kind and for its size as is possible. I do not believe that any army in the world has a better average of enlisted men or a better type of junior officer; but the army should be trained to act effectively in a mass. Provision should be made by sufficient appropriations for manœuvers of a practical kind, so that the troops may learn how to take care of themselves under actual service conditions; every march, for instance, being made with the soldier loaded exactly as he would be in active campaign. The Generals and Colonels would thereby have opportunity of handling regiments, brigades, and divisions, and the commissary and medical departments would be tested in the field. Provision should be made for the exercise at least of a brigade and by preference of a division in marching and embarking at some point on our coast and disembarking at some other point and continuing its march. The number of posts in which the army is kept in time of peace should be materially diminished and the posts that are left made correspondingly larger. No local interests should be allowed to stand in the way of assembling the greater part of the troops which would at need form our field armies in stations of such size as will permit the best training to be given to the personnel of all grades, including the high officers and staff officers. To accomplish this end we must have not company or regimental garrisons, but brigade and division garrisons. Promotion by mere seniority can never result in a thoroughly efficient corps of officers in the higher ranks unless there accompanies it a vigorous weeding-out process. Such a weeding-out process—that is, such a process of selection—is a chief feature of the four years' course of the young officer at West Point. There is no good reason why it should stop immediately upon his graduation. While at West Point he is dropped unless he comes up to a certain standard of excellence, and when he graduates he takes rank in the army according to his rank of graduation. The results are good at West Point; and there should be in the army itself something that will achieve the same end. After a certain age has been reached the average officer is unfit to do good work below a certain grade. Provision should be made for the promotion of exceptionally meritorious men over the heads of their comrades and for the retirement of all men who have reached a given age without getting beyond a given rank; this age of retirement of course changing from rank to rank. In both the army and the navy there should be some principle of selection, that is, of promotion for merit, and there should be a resolute effort to eliminate the aged officers of reputable character who possess no special efficiency.

There should be an increase in the coast artillery force, so that our coast fortifications can be in some degree adequately manned. There is special need for an increase and reorganization of the Medical Department of the army. In both the army and navy there must be the same thorough training for duty in the staff corps as in the fighting line. Only by such training in advance can we be sure that in actual war field operations and those at sea will be carried on successfully. The importance of this was shown conclusively in the Spanish-American and the Russo-Japanese wars. The work of the medical departments in the Japanese army and navy is especially worthy of study. I renew my recommendation of January 9, 1905, as to the Medical Department of the army and call attention to the equal importance of the needs of the staff corps of the navy. In the Medical Department of the navy the first in importance is the reorganization of the Hospital Corps, on the lines of the Gallinger bill, (S. 3,984, February 1, 1904), and the reapportionment of the different grades of the medical officers to meet service requirements. It seems advisable also that medical officers of the army and navy should have similar rank and pay in their respective grades, so that their duties can be carried on without friction when they are brought together. The base hospitals of the navy should be put in condition to meet modern requirements and hospital ships be provided. Unless we now provide with ample forethought for the medical needs of the army and navy appalling suffering of a preventable kind is sure to occur if ever the country goes to war. It is not reasonable to expect successful administration in time of war of a department which lacks a third of the number of officers necessary to perform the medical service in time of peace. We need men who are not merely doctors; they must be trained in the administration of military medical service.

Our navy must, relatively to the navies of other nations, always be of greater size than our army. We have most wisely continued for a number of years to build up our navy, and it has now reached a fairly high standard of efficiency. This standard of efficiency must not only be maintained, but increased. It does not seem to be necessary, however, that the navy should—at least in the immediate future—be increased beyond the present number of units. What is now clearly necessary is to substitute efficient for inefficient units as the latter become worn out or as it becomes apparent that they are useless. Probably the result would be attained by adding a single battleship to our navy each year, the superseded or outworn vessels being laid up or broken up as they are thus replaced. The four single-turret monitors built immediately after the close of the Spanish war, for instance, are vessels which would be of but little use in the event of war. The money spent upon them could have been more usefully spent in other ways. Thus it would have been far better never to have built a single one of these monitors and to have put the money into an ample supply of reserve guns. Most of the smaller cruisers and gunboats, though they serve a useful purpose so far as they are needed for international police work, would not add to the strength of our navy in a conflict with a serious foe. There is urgent need of providing a large increase in the number of officers, and especially in the number of enlisted men.

Recent naval history has emphasized certain lessons which ought not to, but which do, need emphasis. Seagoing torpedo boats or destroyers are indispensable, not only for making night attacks by surprise upon an enemy, but even in battle for finishing already crippled ships. Under exceptional circumstances submarine boats would doubtless be of use. Fast scouts are needed. The main strength of the navy, however, lies, and can only lie, in the great battleships, the heavily armored, heavily gunned vessels which decide the mastery of the seas. Heavy-armed cruisers also play a most useful part, and unarmed cruisers, if swift enough, are very useful as scouts. Between antagonists of approximately equal prowess the comparative perfection of the instruments of war will ordinarily determine the fight. But it is, of course, true that the man behind the gun, the man in the engine room, and the man in the conning tower, considered not only individually, but especially with regard to the way in which they work together, are even more important than the weapons with which they work. The most formidable battleship is, of course, helpless against even a light cruiser if the men aboard it are unable to hit anything with their guns, and thoroughly well-handled cruisers may count seriously in an engagement with much superior vessels, if the men aboard the latter are ineffective, whether from lack of training or from any other cause. Modern warships are most formidable mechanisms when well handled, but they are utterly useless when not well handled, and they cannot be handled at all without long and careful training. This training can under no circumstance be given when once war has broken out. No fighting ship of the first class should ever be laid up save for necessary repairs, and her crew should be kept constantly exercised on the high seas, so that she may stand at the highest point of perfection. To put a new and untrained crew upon the most powerful battleship and send it out to meet a formidable enemy is not only to invite, but to insure, disaster and disgrace. To improvise crews at the outbreak of a war, so far as the serious fighting craft are concerned, is absolutely hopeless. If the officers and men are not thoroughly skilled in, and have not been thoroughly trained to, their duties, it would be far better to keep the ships in port during hostilities than to send them against a formidable opponent, for the result could only be that they would be either sunk or captured. The marksmanship of our navy is now on the whole in a gratifying condition, and there has been a great improvement in fleet practice. We need additional seamen; we need a large store of reserve guns; we need sufficient money for ample target practice, ample practice of every kind at sea. We should substitute for comparatively inefficient types—the old third-class battleship Texas, the single-turreted monitors above mentioned, and, indeed, all the monitors and some of the old cruisers—efficient, modern seagoing vessels. Seagoing torpedo-boat destroyers should be substituted for some of the smaller torpedo boats. During the present Congress there need be no additions to the aggregate number of units of the navy. Our navy, though very small relatively to the navies of other nations, is for the present sufficient in point of numbers for our needs, and while we must constantly strive to make its efficiency higher, there need be no additions to the total of ships now built and building, save in the way of substitution as above outlined. I recommend the report of the Secretary of the Navy to the careful consideration of the Congress, especially with a view to the legislation therein advocated.

During the past year evidence has accumulated to confirm the expressions contained in my last two annual messages as to the importance of revising by appropriate legislation our system of naturalizing aliens. I appointed last March a commission to make a careful examination of our naturalization laws, and to suggest appropriate measures to avoid the notorious abuses resulting from the improvident or unlawful granting of citizenship. This commission, composed of an officer of the Department of State, of the Department of Justice, and of the Department of Commerce and Labor, has discharged the duty imposed upon it, and has submitted a report, which will be transmitted to the Congress for its consideration, and, I hope, for its favorable action.

The distinguishing recommendations of the commission are:

First—A Federal Bureau of Naturalization, to be established in the Department of Commerce and Labor, to supervise the administration of the naturalization laws and to receive returns of naturalizations pending and accomplished.

Second—Uniformity of naturalization certificates, fees to be charged, and procedure.

Third—More exacting qualifications for citizenship.

Fourth—The preliminary declaration of intention to be abolished and no alien to be naturalized until at least ninety days after the filing of his petition.

Fifth—Jurisdiction to naturalize aliens to be confined to United States district courts and to such State courts as have jurisdiction in civil actions in which the amount in controversy is unlimited; in cities of over 100,000 inhabitants the United States district courts to have exclusive jurisdiction in the naturalization of the alien residents of such cities.

In my last message I asked the attention of the Congress to the urgent need of action to make our criminal law more effective; and I most earnestly request that you pay heed to the report of the Attorney General on this subject. Centuries ago it was especially needful to throw every safeguard round the accused. The danger then was lest he should be wronged by the State. The danger is now exactly the reverse. Our laws and customs tell immensely in favor of the criminal and against the interests of the public he has wronged. Some antiquated and outworn rules which once safeguarded the threatened rights of private citizens, now merely work harm to the general body politic. The criminal law of the United States stands in urgent need of revision. The criminal process of any court of the United States should run throughout the entire territorial extent of our country. The delays of the criminal law, no less than of the civil, now amount to a very great evil.

There seems to be no statute of the United States which provides for the punishment of a United States Attorney or other officer of the Government who corruptly agrees to wrongfully do or wrongfully refrain from doing any act when the consideration for such corrupt agreement is other than one possessing money value. This ought to be remedied by appropriate legislation. Legislation should also be enacted to cover explicitly, unequivocally, and beyond question breach of trust in the shape of prematurely divulging official secrets by an officer or employe of the United States, and to provide a suitable penalty therefor. Such officer or employe owes the duty to the United States to guard carefully and not to divulge or in any manner use, prematurely, information which is accessible to the officer or employe by reason of his official position. Most breaches of public trust are already covered by the law, and this one should be. It is impossible, no matter how much care is used, to prevent the occasional appointment to the public service of a man who when tempted proves unfaithful; but every means should be provided to detect and every effort made to punish the wrongdoer. So far as in my power each and every such wrongdoer shall be relentlessly hunted down; in no instance in the past has he been spared; in no instance in the future shall he be spared. His crime is a crime against every honest man in the Nation, for it is a crime against the whole body politic. Yet in dwelling on such misdeeds it is unjust not to add that they are altogether exceptional, and that on the whole the employes of the Government render upright and faithful service to the people. There are exceptions, notably in one or two branches of the service, but at no time in the Nation's history has the public service of the Nation taken as a whole stood on a higher plane than now, alike as regards honesty and as regards efficiency.

Once again I call your attention to the condition of the public land laws. Recent developments have given new urgency to the need for such changes as will fit these laws to actual present conditions. The honest disposal and right use of the remaining public lands is of fundamental importance. The iniquitous methods by which the monopolizing of the public lands is being brought about under the present laws are becoming more generally known, but the existing laws do not furnish effective remedies. The recommendations of the Public Lands Commission upon this subject are wise and should be given effect.

The creation of small irrigated farms under the Reclamation act is a powerful offset to the tendency of certain other laws to foster or permit monopoly of the land. Under that act the construction of great irrigation works has been proceeding rapidly and successfully, the lands reclaimed are eagerly taken up, and the prospect that the policy of National irrigation will accomplish all that was expected of it is bright. The act should be extended to include the State of Texas.

The Reclamation act derives much of its value from the fact that it tends to secure the greatest possible number of homes on the land, and to create communities of freeholders, in part by settlement on public lands, in part by forcing the subdivision of large private holdings before they can get water from Government irrigation works. The law requires that no right to the use of water for land in private ownership shall be sold for a tract exceeding 160 acres to any one land owner. This provision has excited active and powerful hostility, but the success of the law itself depends on the wise and firm enforcement of it. We cannot afford to substitute tenants for freeholders on the public domain.

The greater part of the remaining public lands can not be irrigated. They are at present and will probably always be of greater value for grazing than for any other purpose. This fact has led to the grazing homestead of 640 acres in Nebraska and to the proposed extension of it to other States. It is argued that a family can not be supported on 160 acres of arid grazing land. This is obviously true, but neither can a family be supported on 640 acres of much of the land to which it is proposed to apply the grazing homestead. To establish universally any such arbitrary limit would be unwise at the present time. It would probably result on the one hand in enlarging the holdings of some of the great land owners, and on the other in needless suffering and failure on the part of a very considerable proportion of the bona fide settlers who give faith to the implied assurance of the Government that such an area is sufficient. The best use of the public grazing lands requires the careful examination and classification of these lands in order to give each settler land enough to support his family and no more. While this work is being done, and until the lands are settled, the Government should take control of the open range, under reasonable regulations suited to local needs, following the general policy already in successful operation on the forest reserves. It is probable that the present grazing value of the open public range is scarcely more than half what it once was or what it might easily be again under careful regulation.

The forest policy of the Administration appears to enjoy the unbroken support of the people. The great users of timber are themselves forwarding the movement for forest preservation. All organized opposition to the forest preserves in the West has disappeared. Since the consolidation of all Government forest work in the National Forest Service there has been a rapid and notable gain in the usefulness of the forest reserves to the people and in public appreciation of their value. The National parks within or adjacent to forest reserves should be transferred to the charge of the Forest Service also.

The National Government already does something in connection with the construction and maintenance of the great system of levees along the lower course of the Mississippi; in my judgment it should do much more.

To the spread of our trade in peace and the defense of our flag in war a great and prosperous merchant marine is indispensable. We should have ships of our own and seamen of our own to convey our goods to neutral markets, and in case of need to re-inforce our battle line. It cannot but be a source of regret and uneasiness to us that the lines of communication with our sister republics of South America should be chiefly under foreign control. It is not a good thing that American merchants and manufacturers should have to send their goods and letters to South America via Europe if they wish security and dispatch. Even on the Pacific, where our ships have held their own better than on the Atlantic, our merchant flag is now threatened through the liberal aid bestowed by other Governments on their own steam lines. I ask your earnest consideration of the report with which the Merchant Marine Commission has followed its long and careful inquiry.

I again heartily commend to your favorable consideration the tercentennial celebration at Jamestown, Va. Appreciating the desirability of this commemoration, the Congress passed an act, March 3, 1905, authorizing in the year 1907, on and near the waters of Hampton Roads, in the State of Virginia, an international naval, marine, and military celebration in honor of this event. By the authority vested in me by this act, I have made proclamation of said celebration, and have issued, in conformity with its instructions, invitations to all the nations of the earth to participate, by sending their naval vessels and such military organizations as may be practicable. This celebration would fail of its full purpose unless it were enduring in its results and commensurate with the importance of the event to be celebrated, the event from which our Nation dates its birth. I earnestly hope that this celebration, already indorsed by the Congress of the United States, and by the Legislatures of sixteen States since the action of the Congress, will receive such additional aid at your hands as will make it worthy of the great event it is intended to celebrate, and thereby enable the Government of the United States to make provision for the exhibition of its own resources, and likewise enable our people who have undertaken the work of such a celebration to provide suitable and proper entertainment and instruction in the historic events of our country for all who may visit the exposition and to whom we have tendered our hospitality.

It is a matter of unmixed satisfaction once more to call attention to the excellent work of the Pension Bureau; for the veterans of the civil war have a greater claim upon us than any other class of our citizens. To them, first of all among our people, honor is due.

Seven years ago my lamented predecessor, President McKinley, stated that the time had come for the Nation to care for the graves of the Confederate dead. I recommend that the Congress take action toward this end. The first need is to take charge of the graves of the Confederate dead who died in Northern prisons.

The question of immigration is of vital interest to this country. In the year ending June 30, 1905, there came to the United States 1,026,000 alien immigrants. In other words, in the single year that has just elapsed there came to this country a greater number of people than came here during the one hundred and sixty-nine years of our Colonial life which intervened between the first landing at Jamestown and the Declaration of Independence. It is clearly shown in the report of the Commissioner General of Immigration that while much of this enormous immigration is undoubtedly healthy and natural, a considerable proportion is undesirable from one reason or another; moreover, a considerable proportion of it, probably a very large proportion, including most of the undesirable class, does not come here of its own initiative, but because of the activity of the agents of the great transportation companies. These agents are distributed throughout Europe, and by the offer of all kinds of inducements they wheedle and cajole many immigrants, often against their best interest, to come here. The most serious obstacle we have to encounter in the effort to secure a proper regulation of the immigration to these shores arises from the determined opposition of the foreign steamship lines who have no interest whatever in the matter save to increase the returns on their capital by carrying masses of immigrants hither in the steerage quarters of their ships.

As I said in my last message to the Congress, we cannot have too much immigration of the right sort and we should have none whatever of the wrong sort. Of course, it is desirable that even the right kind of immigration should be properly distributed in this country. We need more of such immigration for the South; and special effort should be made to secure it. Perhaps it would be possible to limit the number of immigrants allowed to come in any one year to New York and other Northern cities, while leaving unlimited the number allowed to come to the South; always provided, however, that a stricter effort is made to see that only immigrants of the right kind come to our country anywhere. In actual practice it has proved so difficult to enforce the immigration laws where long stretches of frontier marked by an imaginary line alone intervene between us and our neighbors that I recommend that no immigrants be allowed to come in from Canada and Mexico save natives of the two countries themselves. As much as possible should be done to distribute the immigrants upon the land and keep them away from the congested tenement-house districts of the great cities. But distribution is a palliative, not a cure. The prime need is to keep out all immigrants who will not make good American citizens. The laws now existing for the exclusion of undesirable immigrants should be strengthened. Adequate means should be adopted, enforced by sufficient penalties, to compel steamship companies engaged in the passenger business to observe in good faith the law which forbids them to encourage or solicit immigration to the United States. Moreover, there should be a sharp limitation imposed upon all vessels coming to our ports as to the number of immigrants in ratio to the tonnage which each vessel can carry. This ratio should be high enough to insure the coming hither of as good a class of aliens as possible. Provision should be made for the surer punishment of those who induce aliens to come to this country under promise or assurance of employment. It should be made possible to inflict a sufficiently heavy penalty on any employer violating this law to deter him from taking the risk. It seems to me wise that there should be an international conference held to deal with this question of immigration, which has more than a merely National significance; such a conference could, among other things, enter at length into the methods for securing a thorough inspection of would-be immigrants at the ports from which they desire to embark before permitting them to embark.

In dealing with this question it is unwise to depart from the old American tradition and to discriminate for or against any man who desires to come here and become a citizen, save on the ground of that man's fitness for citizenship. It is our right and duty to consider his moral and social quality. His standard of living should be such that he will not, by pressure of competition, lower the standard of living of our own wage-workers; for it must ever be a prime object of our legislation to keep high their standard of living. If the man who seeks to come here is from the moral and social standpoint of such a character as to bid fair to add value to the community he should be heartily welcomed. We cannot afford to pay heed to whether he is of one creed or another, of one nation, or another. We cannot afford to consider whether he is Catholic or Protestant, Jew or Gentile; whether he is Englishman or Irishman, Frenchman or German, Japanese, Italian, Scandinavian, Slav, or Magyar. What we should desire to find out is the individual quality of the individual man. In my judgment, with this end in view, we shall have to prepare through our own agents a far more rigid inspection in the countries from which the immigrants come. It will be a great deal better to have fewer immigrants, but all of the right kind, than a great number of immigrants, many of whom are necessarily of the wrong kind. As far as possible we wish to limit the immigration to this country to persons who propose to become citizens of this country, and we can well afford to insist upon adequate scrutiny of the character of those who are thus proposed for future citizenship. There should be an increase in the stringency of the laws to keep out insane, idiotic, epileptic, and pauper immigrants. But this is by no means enough. Not merely the Anarchist, but every man of Anarchistic tendencies, all violent and disorderly people, all people of bad character, the incompetent, the lazy, the vicious, the physically unfit, defective, or degenerate should be kept out. The stocks out of which American citizenship is to be built should be strong and healthy, sound in body, mind, and character. If it be objected that the Government agents would not always select well, the answer is that they would certaintly select better than do the agents and brokers of foreign steamship companies, the people who now do whatever selection is done.

The questions arising in connection with Chinese immigration stand by themselves. The conditions in China are such that the entire Chinese coolie class, that is, the class of Chinese laborers, skilled and unskilled, legitimately come under the head of undesirable immigrants to this country, because of their numbers, the low wages for which they work, and their low standard of living. Not only is it to the interest of this country to keep them out, but the Chinese authorities do not desire that they should be admitted. At present their entrance is prohibited by laws amply adequate to accomplish this purpose. These laws have been, are being, and will be, thoroughly enforced. The violations of them are so few in number as to be infinitesimal and can be entirely disregarded. There is no serious proposal to alter the immigration law as regards the Chinese laborer, skilled or unskilled, and there is no excuse for any man feeling or affecting to feel the slightest alarm on the subject.

But in the effort to carry out the policy of excluding Chinese laborers, Chinese coolies, grave injustice and wrong have been done by this Nation to the people of China, and therefore ultimately to this Nation itself. Chinese students, business and professional men of all kinds—not only merchants, but bankers, doctors, manufacturers, professors, travelers, and the like—should be encouraged to come here, and treated on precisely the same footing that we treat students, business men, travelers, and the like of other nations. Our laws and treaties should be framed, not so as to put these people in the excepted classes, but to state that we will admit all Chinese, except Chinese of the coolie class, Chinese skilled or unskilled laborers. There would not be the least danger that any such provision would result in any relaxation of the law about laborers. These will, under all conditions, be kept out absolutely. But it will be more easy to see that both justice and courtesy are shown, as they ought to be shown, to other Chinese, if the law or treaty is framed as above suggested. Examinations should be completed at the port of departure from China. For this purpose there should be provided a more adequate Consular Service in China than we now have. The appropriations both for the offices of the Consuls and for the office forces in the consulates should be increased.

As a people we have talked much of the open door in China, and we expect, and quite rightly intend to insist upon, justice being shown us by the Chinese. But we cannot expect to receive equity unless we do equity. We cannot ask the Chinese to do to us what we are unwilling to do to them. They would have a perfect right to exclude our laboring men if our laboring men threatened to come into their country in such numbers as to jeopardize the well-being of the Chinese population; and as, mutatis mutandis, these were the conditions with which Chinese immigration actually brought this people face to face, we had and have a perfect right, which the Chinese Government in no way contests, to act as we have acted in the matter of restricting coolie immigration. That this right exists for each country was explicitly acknowledged in the last treaty between the two countries. But we must treat the Chinese student, traveler, and business man in a spirit of the broadest justice and courtesy if we expect similar treatment to be accorded to our own people of similar rank who go to China. Much trouble has come during the past Summer from the organized boycott against American goods which has been started in China. The main factor in producing this boycott has been the resentment felt by the students and business people of China, by all the Chinese leaders, against the harshness of our law toward educated

Chinamen of the professional and business classes.

This Government has the friendliest feeling for China and desires China's well-being. We cordially sympathize with the announced purpose of Japan to stand for the integrity of China. Such an attitude tends to the peace of the world.

The civil service law has been on the statute books for twenty-two years. Every President and a vast majority of heads of departments who have been in office during that period have favored a gradual extension of the merit system. The more thoroughly its principles have been understood, the greater has been the favor with which the law has been regarded by administration officers. Any attempt to carry on the great executive departments of the Government without this law would inevitably result in chaos. The Civil Service Commissioners are doing excellent work, and their compensation is inadequate considering the service they perform.

The statement that the examinations are not practical in character is based on a misapprehension of the practice of the Commission. The departments are invariably consulted as to the requirements desired and as to the character of questions that shall be asked. General invitations are frequently sent out to all heads of departments asking whether any changes in the scope or character of examinations are required. In other words, the departments prescribe the requirements and qualifications desired, and the Civil Service Commission co-operates with them in securing persons with these qualifications and insuring open and impartial competition. In a large number of examinations (as, for example, those for trades positions), there are no educational requirements whatever, and a person who can neither read nor write may pass with a high average. Vacancies in the service are filled with reasonable expedition, and the machinery of the Commission, which reaches every part of the country, is the best agency that has yet been devised for finding people with the most suitable qualifications for the various offices to be filled. Written competitive examinations do not make an ideal method for filling positions, but they do represent an immeasurable advance upon the "spoils" method, under which outside politicians really make the appointments nominally made by the executive officers, the appointees being chosen by the politicians in question, in the great majority of cases, for reasons totally unconnected with the needs of the service or of the public.

Statistics gathered by the Census Bureau show that the tenure of office in the Government service does not differ materially from that enjoyed by employes of large business corporations. Heads of executive departments and members of the Commission have called my attention to the fact that the rule requiring a filing of charges and three days' notice before an employe could be separated from the service for inefficiency has served no good purpose whatever, because that is not a matter upon which a hearing of the employe found to be inefficient can be of any value, and in practice the rule providing for such notice and hearing has merely resulted in keeping in a certain number of incompetents, because of the reluctance of the heads of departments and bureau chiefs to go through the required procedure. Experience has shown that this rule is wholly ineffective to save any man, if a superior for improper reasons wishes to remove him, and is mischievous because it sometimes serves to keep in the service incompetent men not guilty of specific wrongdoing. Having these facts in view the rule has been amended by providing that where the inefficiency or incapacity comes within the personal knowledge of the head of a department the removal may be made without notice, the reasons therefor being filed and made a record of the department. The absolute right of the removal rests where it always has rested, with the head of a department; any limitation of this absolute right results in grave injury to the public service. The change is merely one of procedure; it was much needed, and it is producing good results.

The civil service law is being energetically and impartially enforced, and in the large majority of cases complaints of violations of either the law or rules are discovered to be unfounded. In this respect this law compares very favorably with any other Federal statute. The question of politics in the appointment and retention of the men engaged in merely ministerial work has been practically eliminated in almost the entire field of Government employment covered by the civil service law. The action of the Congress in providing the commission with its own force instead of requiring it to rely on detailed clerks has been justified by the increased work done at a smaller cost to the Government. I urge upon the Congress a careful consideration of the recommendations contained in the annual report of the commission.

Our copyright laws urgently need revision. They are imperfect in definition, confused and inconsistent in expression; they omit provision for many articles which, under modern reproductive processes are entitled to protection; they impose hardships upon the copyright proprietor which are not essential to the fair protection of the public; they are difficult for the courts to interpret and impossible for the Copyright Office to administer with satisfaction to the public. Attempts to improve them by amendment have been frequent, no less than twelve acts for the purpose having been passed since the Revised Statutes. To perfect them by further amendment seems impracticable. A complete revision of them is essential. Such a revision, to meet modern conditions, has been found necessary in Germany, Austria, Sweden, and other foreign countries, and bills embodying it are pending in England and the Australian colonies. It has been urged here, and proposals for a commission to undertake it have, from time to time, been pressed upon the Congress. The inconveniences of the present conditions being so great, an attempt to frame appropriate legislation has been made by the Copyright Office, which has called conferences of the various interests especially and practically concerned with the operation of the copyright laws. It has secured from them suggestions as to the changes necessary; it has added from its own experience and investigations, and it has drafted a bill which embodies such of these changes and additions as, after full discussion and expert criticism, appeared to be sound and safe. In form this bill would replace the existing insufficient and inconsistent laws by one general copyright statute. It will be presented to the Congress at the coming session. It deserves prompt consideration.

I recommend that a law be enacted to regulate inter-State commerce in misbranded and adulterated foods, drinks, and drugs. Such law would protect legitimate manufacture and commerce, and would tend to secure the health and welfare of the consuming public. Traffic in food-stuffs which have been debased or adulterated so as to injure health or to deceive purchasers should be forbidden.

The law forbidding the emission of dense black or gray smoke in the city of Washington has been sustained by the courts. Something has been accomplished under it, but much remains to be done if we would preserve the capital city from defacement by the smoke nuisance. Repeated prosecutions under the law have not had the desired effect. I recommend that it be made more stringent by increasing both the minimum and maximum fine; by providing for imprisonment in cases of repeated violation, and by affording the remedy of injunction against the continuation of the operation of plants which are persistent offenders. I recommend, also, an increase in the number of inspectors, whose duty it shall be to detect violations of the act.

I call your attention to the generous act of the State of California in conferring upon the United States Government the ownership of the Yosemite Valley and the Mariposa Big Tree Grove. There should be no delay in accepting the gift, and appropriations should be made for the including thereof in the Yosemite National Park, and for the care and policing of the park. California has acted most wisely, as well as with great magnanimity, in the matter. There are certain mighty natural features of our land which should be preserved in perpetuity for our children and our children's children. In my judgment, the Grand Canyon of the Colorado should be made into a National park. It is greatly to be wished that the State of New York should copy as regards Niagara what the State of California has done as regards the Yosemite. Nothing should be allowed to interfere with the preservation of Niagara Falls in all their beauty and majesty. If the State cannot see to this, then it is earnestly to be wished that she should be willing to turn it over to the National Government, which should in such case (if possible, in conjunction with the Canadian Government) assume the burden and responsibility of preserving unharmed Niagara Falls; just as it should gladly assume a similar burden and responsibility for the Yosemite National Park, and as it has already assumed them for the Yellowstone National Park. Adequate provision should be made by the Congress for the proper care and supervision of all these National parks. The boundaries of the Yellowstone National Park should be extended to the south and east, to take in such portions of the abutting forest reservations as will enable the Government to protect the elk on their Winter range.

The most characteristic animal of the Western plains was the great, shaggy-maned wild ox, the bison, commonly known as buffalo. Small fragments of herds exist in a domesticated state here and there, a few of them in the Yellowstone Park. Such a herd as that on the Flathead Reservation should not be allowed to go out of existence. Either on some reservation or on some forest reserve like the Wichita reserve and game refuge provision should be made for the preservation of such a herd. I believe that the scheme would be of economic advantage, for the robe of the buffalo is of high market value, and the same is true of the robe of the crossbred animals.

I call your especial attention to the desirability of giving to the members of the Life Saving Service pensions such as are given to firemen and policemen in all our great cities. The men in the Life Saving Service continually and in the most matter of fact way do deeds such as make Americans proud of their country. They have no political influence, and they live in such remote places that the really heroic services they continually render receive the scantiest recognition from the public. It is unjust for a great nation like this to permit these men to become totally disabled or to meet death in the performance of their hazardous duty and yet to give them no sort of reward. If one of them serves thirty years of his life in such a position he should surely be entitled to retire on half pay, as a fireman or policeman does, and if he becomes totally incapacitated through accident or sickness, or loses his health in the discharge of his duty, he or his family should receive a pension just as any soldier should. I call your attention with especial earnestness to this matter because it appeals not only to our judgment but to our sympathy; for the people on whose behalf I ask it are comparatively few in number, render incalculable service of a particularly dangerous kind, and have no one to speak for them.

During the year just past, the phase of the Indian question which has been most sharply brought to public attention is the larger legal significance of the Indian's induction into citizenship. This has made itself manifest not only in a great access of litigation in which the citizen Indian figures as a party defendant and in a more widespread disposition to levy local taxation upon his personalty, but in a decision of the United States Supreme Court which struck away the main prop on which has hitherto rested the Government's benevolent effort to protect him against the evils of intemperance. The court holds, in effect, that when an Indian becomes, by virtue of an allotment of land to him, a citizen of the State in which his land is situated, he passes from under Federal control in such matters as this, and the acts of the Congress prohibiting the sale or gift to him of intoxicants become substantially inoperative. It is gratifying to note that the States and municipalities of the West which have most at stake in the welfare of the Indians are taking up this subject and are trying to supply, in a measure at least, the abdication of its trusteeship forced upon the Federal Government. Nevertheless, I would urgently press upon the attention of the Congress the question whether some amendment of the internal revenue laws might not be of aid in prosecuting those malefactors, known in the Indian country as "bootleggers," who are engaged at once in defrauding the United States Treasury of taxes and, what is far more important, in debauching the Indians by carrying liquors illicitly into territory still completely under Federal jurisdiction.

Among the crying present needs of the Indians are more day schools situated in the midst of their settlements, more effective instruction in the industries pursued on their own farms, and a more liberal extension of the field-matron service, which means the education of the Indian women in the arts of home making. Until the mothers are well started in the right direction we cannot reasonably expect much from the children who are soon to form an integral part of our American citizenship. Moreover the excuse continually advanced by male adult Indians for refusing offers of remunerative employment at a distance from their homes is that they dare not leave their families too long out of their sight. One effectual remedy for this state of things is to employ the minds and strengthen the moral fibre of the Indian women—the end to which the work of the field matron is especially directed. I trust that the Congress will make its appropriations for Indian day schools and field matrons as generous as may consist with the other pressing demands upon its providence.

During the last year the Philippine Islands have been slowly recovering from the series of disasters which, since American occupation, have greatly reduced the amount of agricultural products below what was produced in Spanish times. The war, the rinderpest, the locusts, the drought, and the cholera have been united as causes to prevent a return of the prosperity much needed in the islands. The most serious is the destruction by the rinderpest of more than 75 per cent. of the draught cattle, because it will take several years of breeding to restore the necessary number of these indispensable aids to agriculture. The commission attempted to supply by purchase from adjoining countries the needed cattle, but the experiments made were unsuccessful. Most of the cattle imported were unable to withstand the change of climate and the rigors of the voyage and died from other diseases than rinderpest.

The income of the Philippine Government has necessarily been reduced by reason of the business and agricultural depression in the islands, and the Government has been obliged to exercise great economy to cut down its expenses, to reduce salaries, and in every way to avoid a deficit. It has adopted an internal revenue law, imposing taxes on cigars, cigarettes, and distilled liquors, and abolishing the old Spanish industrial taxes. The law has not operated as smoothly as was hoped, and although its principle is undoubtedly correct, it may need amendments for the purpose of reconciling the people to its provisions. The income derived from it has partly made up for the reduction in customs revenue.

There has been a marked increase in the number of Filipinos employed in the civil service, and a corresponding decrease in the number of Americans. The Government in every one of its departments has been rendered more efficient by elimination of undesirable material and the promotion of deserving public servants.

Improvements of harbors, roads, and bridges continue, although the cutting down of the revenue forbids the expenditure of any great amount from current income for these purposes. Steps are being taken, by advertisement for competitive bids, to secure the construction and maintenance of 1,000 miles of railway by private corporations under the recent enabling legislation of the Congress. The transfer of the friar lands, in accordance with the contract made some two years ago, has been completely effected, and the purchase money paid. Provision has just been made by statute for the speedy settlement in a special proceeding in the Supreme Court of controversies over the possession and title of church buildings and rectories arising between the Roman Catholic Church and schismatics claiming under ancient municipalities. Negotiations and hearings for the settlement of the amount due to the Roman Catholic Church for rent and occupation of churches and rectories by the army of the United States are in progress, and it is hoped a satisfactory conclusion may be submitted to the Congress before the end of the session.

Tranquillity has existed during the past year throughout the Archipelago, except in the Province of Cavite, the Province of Batangas, and the Province of Samar, and in the Island of Jolo among the Moros. The Jolo disturbance was put an end to by several sharp and short engagements, and now peace prevails in the Moro Province. Cavite, the mother of ladrones in the Spanish times, is so permeated with the traditional sympathy of the people for ladronism as to make it difficult to stamp out the disease. Batangas was only disturbed by reason of the fugitive ladrones from Cavite, Samar was thrown into disturbance by the uneducated and partly savage peoples living in the mountains, who, having been given by the municipal code more power than they were able to exercise discreetly, elected municipal officers who abused their trusts, compelled the people raising hemp to sell it at a much less price than it was worth, and by their abuses drove their people into resistance to constituted authority. Cavite and Samar are instances of reposing too much confidence in the self-governing power of a people. The disturbances have all now been suppressed, and it is hoped that with these lessons local governments can be formed which will secure quiet and peace to the deserving inhabitants. The incident is another proof of the fact that if there has been any error as regards giving self-government in the Philippines it has been in the direction of giving it too quickly, not too slowly. A year from next April the first legislative assembly for the islands will be held On the sanity and self-restraint of this body much will depend so far as the future self-government of the islands is concerned.

The most encouraging feature of the whole situation has been the very great interest taken by the common people in education and the great increase in the number of enrolled students in the public schools. The increase was from 300,000 to half a million pupils. The average attendance is about 70 per cent. The only limit upon the number of pupils seems to be the capacity of the government to furnish teachers and school houses.

The agricultural conditions of the islands enforce more strongly than ever the argument in favor of reducing the tariff on the products of the Philippine Islands entering the United States. I earnestly recommend that the tariff now imposed by the Dingley bill upon the products of the Philippine Islands be entirely removed, except the tariff on sugar and tobacco, and that that tariff be reduced to 25 per cent. of the present rates under the Dingley act; that after July 1, 1909, the tariff upon tobacco and sugar produced in the Philippine Islands be entirely removed, and that free trade between the islands and the United States in the products of each country then be provided for by law.

A statute in force, enacted April 15, 1904, suspends the operation of the coastwise laws of the United States upon the trade between the Philippine Islands and the United States until July 1, 1906. I earnestly recommend that this suspension be postponed until July 1, 1909. I think it of doubtful utility to apply the coastwise laws to the trade between the United States and the Philippines under any circumstances, because I am convinced that it will do no good whatever to American bottoms, and will only interfere and be an obstacle to the trade between the Philippines and the United States, but if the coastwise law must be thus applied, certainly it ought not to have effect until free trade is enjoyed between the people of the United States and the people of the Philippine Islands in their respective products.

I do not anticipate that free trade between the islands and the United States will produce a revolution in the sugar and tobacco production of the Philippine Islands. So primitive are the methods of agriculture in the Philippine Islands, so slow is capital in going to the islands, so many difficulties surround a large agricultural enterprise in the islands, that it will be many, many years before the products of those islands will have any effect whatever upon the markets of the United States. The problem of labor is also a formidable one with the sugar and tobacco producers in the islands. The best friends of the Filipino people and the people themselves are utterly opposed to the admission of Chinese coolie labor. Hence the only solution is the training of Filipino labor, and this will take a long time. The enactment of a law by the Congress of the United States making provision for free trade between the islands and the United States, however, will be of great importance from a political and sentimental standpoint; and, while its actual benefit has doubtless been exaggerated by the people of the islands, they will accept this measure of justice as an indication that the people of the United States are anxious to aid the people of the Philippine Islands in every way, and especially in the agricultural development of their archipelago. It will aid the Filipinos without injuring interests in America.

In my judgment immediate steps should be taken for the fortification of Hawaii. This is the most important point in the Pacific to fortify in order to conserve the interests of this country. It would be hard to overstate the importance of this need. Hawaii is too heavily taxed. Laws should be enacted setting aside for a period of, say, twenty years 75 per cent. of the internal revenue and customs receipts from Hawaii as a special fund to be expended in the islands for educational and public buildings, and for harbor improvements and military and naval defenses. It cannot be too often repeated that our aim must be to develop the territory of Hawaii on traditional American lines. That territory has serious commercial and industrial problems to reckon with; but no measure of relief can be considered which looks to legislation admitting Chinese and restricting them by statute to field labor and domestic service. The status of servility can never again be tolerated on American soil. We cannot concede that the proper solution of its problems is special legislation admitting to Hawaii a class of laborers denied admission to the other States and Territories. There are obstacles, and great obstacles, in the way of building up a representative American community in the Hawaiian Islands; but it is not in the American character to give up in the face of difficulty. Many an American Commonwealth has been built up against odds equal to those that now confront Hawaii.

No merely half-hearted effort to meet its problems as other American communities have met theirs can be accepted as final. Hawaii shall never become a territory in which a governing class of rich planters exists by means of coolie labor. Even if the rate of growth of the Territory is thereby rendered slower, the growth must only take place by the admission of immigrants fit in the end to assume the duties and burdens of full American citizenship. Our aim must be to develop the Territory on the same basis of stable citizenship as exists on this continent.

I earnestly advocate the adoption of legislation which will explicitly confer American citizenship on all citizens of Porto Rico. There is, in my judgment, no excuse for failure to do this. The harbor of San Juan should be dredged and improved. The expenses of the Federal Court of Porto Rico should be met from the Federal Treasury and not from the Porto Rican treasury. The elections in Porto Rico should take place every four years, and the Legislature should meet in session every two years. The present form of government in Porto Rico, which provides for the appointment by the President of the members of the Executive Council or upper house of the Legislature, has proved satisfactory and has inspired confidence in property owners and investors. I do not deem it advisable at the present time to change this form in any material feature. The problems and needs of the island are industrial and commercial rather than political.

I wish to call the attention of the Congress to one question which affects our insular possessions generally; namely, the need of an increased liberality in the treatment of the whole franchise question in these islands. In the proper desire to prevent the islands being exploited by speculators and to have them develop in the interests of their own people an error has been made in refusing to grant sufficiently liberal terms to induce the investment of American capital in the Philippines and in Porto Rico. Elsewhere in this message I have spoken strongly against the jealousy of mere wealth, and especially of corporate wealth as such. But it is particularly regrettable to allow any such jealousy to be developed when we are dealing either with our insular or with foreign affairs. The big corporation has achieved its present position in the business world simply because it is the most effective instrument in business competition. In foreign affairs we cannot afford to put our people at a disadvantage with their competitors by in any way discriminating against the efficiency of our business organizations. In the same way we cannot afford to allow our insular possessions to lag behind in industrial development from any twisted jealousy of business success. It is, of course, a mere truism to say that the business interests of the islands will only be developed if it becomes the financial interest of somebody to develop them. Yet this development is one of the things most earnestly to be wished for in the interest of the islands themselves. We have been paying all possible heed to the political and educational interests of the islands, but, important though these objects are, it is not less important that we should favor their industrial development. The Government can in certain ways help this directly, as by building good roads; but the fundamental and vital help must be given through the development of the industries of the islands, and a most efficient means to this end is to encourage big American corporations to start industries in them, and this means to make it advantageous for them to do so. To limit the ownership of mining claims, as has been done in the Philippines, is absurd. In both the Philippines and Porto Rico the limit of holdings of land should be largely raised.

I earnestly ask that Alaska be given an elective delegate. Some person should be chosen who can speak with authority of the needs of the Territory. The Government should aid in the construction of a railroad from the Gulf of Alaska to the Yukon River, in American territory. In my last two messages I advocated certain additional action on behalf of Alaska. I shall not now repeat those recommendations, but I shall lay all my stress upon the one recommendation of giving to Alaska some one authorized to speak for it. I should prefer that the delegate was made elective, but if this is not deemed wise, then make him appointive. At any rate, give Alaska some person whose business it shall be to speak with authority on her behalf to the Congress. The natural resources of Alaska are great. Some of the chief needs of the peculiarly energetic, self-reliant, and typically American white population of Alaska were set forth in my last message. I also earnestly ask your attention to the needs of the Alaskan Indians. All Indians who are competent should receive the full rights of American citizenship. It is, for instance, a gross and indefensible wrong to deny to such hard-working, decent-living Indians as the Metlakahtlas the right to obtain licenses as captains, pilots, and engineers; the right to enter mining claims, and to profit by the homestead law. These particular Indians are civilized and are competent and entitled to be put on the same basis with the white men round about them.

I recommend that Indian Territory and Oklahoma be admitted as one State and that New Mexico and Arizona be admitted as one State. There is no obligation upon us to treat territorial subdivisions, which are matters of convenience only, as binding us on the question of admission to Statehood. Nothing has taken up more time in the Congress during the past few years than the question as to the Statehood to be granted to the four Territories above mentioned, and after careful consideration of all that has been developed in the discussions of the question, I recommend that they be immediately admitted as two States. There is no justification for further delay; and the advisability of making the four Territories into two States has been clearly established.

In some of the Territories the legislative assemblies issue licenses for gambling. The Congress should by law forbid this practice, the harmful results of which are obvious at a glance.

The treaty between the United States and the Republic of Panama, under which the construction of the Panama Canal was made possible, went into effect with its ratification by the United States Senate on February 23, 1904. The canal properties of the French Canal Company were transferred to the United States on April 23, 1904, on payment of $40,000,000 to that company. On April 1, 1905, the Commission was reorganized, and it now consists of Theodore P. Shonts, Chairman; Charles E. Magoon, Benjamin M. Harrod, Rear Admiral Mordecai T. Endicott, Brig. Gen. Peter C. Hains, and Col. Oswald H. Ernst. John F. Stevens was appointed Chief Engineer on July 1 last. Active work in canal construction, mainly preparatory, has been in progress for less than a year and a half. During that period two points about the canal have ceased to be open to debate: First, the question of route; the canal will be built on the Isthmus of Panama. Second, the question of feasibility; there are no physical obstacles on this route that American engineering skill will not be able to overcome without serious difficulty, or that will prevent the completion of the canal within a reasonable time and at a reasonable cost. This is virtually the unanimous testimony of the engineers who have investigated the matter for the Government.

The point which remains unsettled is the question of type, whether the canal shall be one of several locks above sea level, or at sea level with a single tide lock. On this point I hope to lay before the Congress at an early day the findings of the Advisory Board of American and European Engineers, that at my invitation have been considering the subject, together with the report of the Commission thereon, and such comments thereon or recommendations in reference thereto as may seem necessary.

The American people is pledged to the speediest possible construction of a canal adequate to meet the demands which the commerce of the world will make upon it, and I appeal most earnestly to the Congress to aid in the fulfillment of the pledge. Gratifying progress has been made during the past year, and especially during the past four months. The greater part of the necessary preliminary work has been done. Actual work of excavation could be begun only on a limited scale till the Canal Zone was made a healthful place to live in and to work in. The Isthmus had to be sanitated first. This task has been so thoroughly accomplished that yellow fever has been virtually extirpated from the Isthmus and general health conditions vastly improved. The same methods which converted the island of Cuba from a pest hole, which menaced the health of the world, into a healthful place of abode, have been applied on the Isthmus with satisfactory results. There is no reason to doubt that when the plans for water supply, paving, and sewerage of Panama and Colon and the large labor camps have been fully carried out, the Isthmus will be, for the tropics, an unusually healthy place of abode. The work is so far advanced now that the health of all those employed in canal work is as well guarded as it is on similar work in this country and elsewhere.

In addition to sanitating the Isthmus, satisfactory quarters are being provided for employes and an adequate system of supplying them with wholesome food at reasonable prices has been created. Hospitals have been established and equipped that are without their superiors of their kind anywhere. The country has thus been made fit to work in, and provision has been made for the welfare and comfort of those who are to do the work. During the past year a large portion of the plant with which the work is to be done has been ordered. It is confidently believed that by the middle of the approaching year a sufficient proportion of this plant will have been installed to enable us to resume the work of excavation on a large scale.

What is needed now and without delay is an appropriation by the Congress to meet the current and accruing expenses of the commission. The first appropriation of $10,000,000, out of the $135,000,000 authorized by the Spooner act, was made three years ago. It is nearly exhausted. There is barely enough of it remaining to carry the commission to the end of the year. Unless the Congress shall appropriate before that time all work must cease. To arrest progress for any length of time now, when matters are advancing so satisfactorily, would be deplorable. There will be no money with which to meet pay roll obligations and none with which to meet bills coming due for materials and supplies; and there will be demoralization of the forces, here and on the Isthmus, now working so harmoniously and effectively, if there is delay in granting an emergency appropriation. Estimates of the amount necessary will be found in the accompanying reports of the Secretary of War and the commission.

I recommend more adequate provision than has been made heretofore for the work of the Department of State. Within a few years there has been a very great increase in the amount and importance of the work to be done by that department, both in Washington and abroad. This has been caused by the great increase of our foreign trade, the increase of wealth among our people, which enables them to travel more generally than heretofore, the increase of American capital which is seeking investment in foreign countries, and the growth of our power and weight in the councils of the civilized world. There has been no corresponding increase of facilities for doing the work afforded to the department having charge of our foreign relations.

Neither at home nor abroad is there a sufficient working force to do the business properly. In many respects the system which was adequate to the work of twenty-five years or even ten years ago, is inadequate now, and should be changed. Our Consular force should be classified, and appointments should be made to the several classes, with authority to the Executive to assign the members of each class to duty at such posts as the interests of the service require, instead of the appointments being made as at present to specified posts. There should be an adequate inspection service, so that the department may be able to inform itself how the business of each Consulate is being done, instead of depending upon casual private information or rumor. The fee system should be entirely abolished, and a due equivalent made in salary to the officers who now eke out their subsistence by means of fees. Sufficient provision should be made for a clerical force in every Consulate, composed entirely of Americans, instead of the insufficient provision now made, which compels the employment of great numbers of citizens of foreign countries whose services can be obtained for less money. At a large part of our Consulates the office quarters and the clerical force are inadequate to the performance of the onerous duties imposed by the recent provisions of our immigration laws as well as by our increasing trade. In many parts of the world the lack of suitable quarters for our embassies, legations, and Consulates detracts from the respect in which our officers ought to be held, and seriously impairs their weight and influence.

Suitable provision should be made for the expense of keeping our diplomatic officers more fully informed of what is being done from day to day in the progress of our diplomatic affairs with other countries. The lack of such information, caused by insufficient appropriations available for cable tolls and for clerical and messenger service, frequently puts our officers at a great disadvantage and detracts from their usefulness. The salary list should be readjusted. It does not now correspond either to the importance of the service to be rendered and the degrees of ability and experience required in the different positions, or to the differences in the cost of living. In many cases the salaries are quite inadequate.

SIXTH ANNUAL MESSAGE.

WHITE HOUSE, *Dec. 3, 1906*

To the Senate and House of Representatives:

As a nation we still continue to enjoy a literally unprecedented prosperity; and it is probable that only reckless speculation and disregard of legitimate business methods on the part of the business world can materially mar this prosperity.

No Congress in our time has done more good work of importance than the present Congress. There were several matters left unfinished at your last session, however, which I most earnestly hope you will complete before your adjournment.

I again recommend a law prohibiting all corporations from contributing to the campaign expenses of any party. Such a bill has already past one House of Congress. Let individuals contribute as they desire; but let us prohibit in effective fashion all corporations from making contributions for any political purpose, directly or indirectly.

Another bill which has just past one House of the Congress and which it is urgently necessary should be enacted into law is that conferring upon the Government the right of appeal in criminal cases on questions of law. This right exists in many of the States; it exists in the District of Columbia by act of the Congress. It is of course not proposed that in any case a verdict for the defendant on the merits should be set aside. Recently in one district where the Government had indicted certain persons for conspiracy in connection with rebates, the court sustained the defendant's demurrer; while in another jurisdiction an indictment for conspiracy to obtain rebates has been sustained by the court, convictions obtained under it, and two defendants sentenced to imprisonment. The two cases referred to may not be in real conflict with each other, but it is unfortunate that there should even be an apparent conflict. At present there is no way by which the Government can cause such a conflict, when it occurs, to be solved by an appeal to a higher court; and the wheels of justice are blocked without any real decision of the question. I can not too strongly urge the passage of the bill in question. A failure to pass it will result in seriously hampering the Government in its effort to obtain justice, especially against wealthy individuals or corporations who do wrong; and may also prevent the Government from obtaining justice for wage-workers who are not themselves able effectively to contest a case where the judgment of an inferior court has been against them. I have specifically in view a recent decision by a district judge leaving railway employees without remedy for violation of a certain so-called labor statute. It seems an absurdity to permit a single district judge, against what may be the judgment of the immense majority of his colleagues on the bench, to declare a law solemnly enacted by the Congress to be "unconstitutional," and then to deny to the Government the right to have the Supreme Court definitely decide the question.

It is well to recollect that the real efficiency of the law often depends not upon the passage of acts as to which there is great public excitement, but upon the passage of acts of this nature as to which there is not much public excitement, because there is little public understanding of their importance, while the interested parties are keenly alive to the desirability of defeating them. The importance of enacting into law the particular bill in question is further increased by the fact that the Government has now definitely begun a policy of resorting to the criminal law in those trust and interstate commerce cases where such a course offers a reasonable chance of success. At first, as was proper, every effort was made to enforce these laws by civil proceedings; but it has become increasingly evident that the action of the Government in finally deciding, in certain cases, to undertake criminal proceedings was justifiable; and tho there have been some conspicuous failures in these cases, we have had many successes, which have undoubtedly had a deterrent effect upon evil-doers, whether the penalty inflicted was in the shape of fine or imprisonment—and penalties of both kinds have already been inflicted by the courts. Of course, where the judge can see his way to inflict the penalty of imprisonment the deterrent effect of the punishment on other offenders is increased; but sufficiently heavy fines accomplish much. Judge Holt, of the New York district court, in a recent decision admirably stated the need for treating with just severity offenders of this kind. His opinion runs in part as follows:

'The Government's evidence to establish the defendant's guilt was clear, conclusive, and undisputed. The case was a flagrant one. The transactions which took place under this illegal contract were very large; the amounts of rebates returned were considerable; and the amount of the rebate itself was large, amounting to more than one-fifth of the entire tariff charge for the transportation of merchandise from this city to Detroit. It is not too much to say, in my opinion, that if this business was carried on for a considerable time on that basis—that is, if this discrimination in favor of this particular shipper was made with an 18 instead of a 23 cent rate and the tariff rate was maintained as against their competitors—the result might be and not improbably would be that their competitors would be driven out of business. This crime is one which in its nature is deliberate and premeditated. I think over a fortnight elapsed between the date of Palmer's letter requesting the reduced rate and the answer of the railroad company deciding to grant it, and then for months afterwards this business was carried on and these claims for rebates submitted month after month and checks in payment of them drawn month after month. Such a violation of the law, in my opinion, in its essential nature, is a very much more heinous act than the ordinary common, vulgar crimes which come before criminal courts constantly for punishment and which arise from sudden passion or temptation. This crime in this case was committed by men of education and of large business experience, whose standing in the community was such that they might have been expected to set an example of obedience to law, upon the maintenance of which alone in this country the security of their property depends. It was committed on behalf of a great railroad corporation, which, like other railroad corporations, has received gratuitously from the State large and valuable privileges for the public's convenience and its own, which performs quasi public functions and which is charged with the highest obligation in the transaction of its business to treat the citizens of this country alike, and not to carry on its business with unjust discriminations between different citizens or different classes of citizens. This crime in its nature is one usually done with secrecy, and proof of which it is very difficult to obtain. The interstate commerce act was past in 1887, nearly twenty years ago. Ever since that time complaints of the granting of rebates by railroads have been common, urgent, and insistent, and altho the Congress has repeatedly past legislation endeavoring to put a stop to this evil, the difficulty of obtaining proof upon which to bring prosecution in these cases is so great that this is the first case that has ever been brought in this court, and, as I am informed, this case and one recently brought in Philadelphia are the only cases that have ever been brought in the eastern part of this country. In fact, but few cases of this kind have ever been brought in this country, East or West. Now, under these circumstances, I am forced to the conclusion, in a case in which the proof is so clear and the facts are so flagrant, it is the duty of the court to fix a penalty which shall in some degree be commensurate with the gravity of the offense. As between the two defendants, in my opinion, the principal penalty should be imposed on the corporation. The traffic manager in this case, presumably, acted without any advantage to himself and without any interest in the transaction, either by the direct authority or in accordance with what he understood to be the policy or the wishes of his employer.

"The sentence of this court in this case is, that the defendant Pomeroy, for each of the six offenses upon which he has been convicted, be fined the sum of $1,000, making six fines, amounting in all to the sum of $6,000; and the defendant, The New York Central and Hudson River Railroad Company, for each of the six crimes of which it has been convicted, be fined the sum of $18,000, making six fines amounting in the aggregate to the sum of $108,000, and judgment to that effect will be entered in this case."

In connection with this matter, I would like to call attention to the very unsatisfactory state of our criminal law, resulting in large part from the habit of setting aside the judgments of inferior courts on technicalities absolutely unconnected with the merits of the case, and where there is no attempt to show that there has been any failure of substantial justice. It would be well to enact a law providing something to the effect that:

No judgment shall be set aside or new trial granted in any cause, civil or criminal, on the ground of misdirection of the jury or the improper admission or rejection of evidence, or for error as to any matter of pleading or procedure unless, in the opinion of the court to which the application is made, after an examination of the entire cause, it shall affirmatively appear that the error complained of has resulted in a miscarriage of justice.

In my last message I suggested the enactment of a law in connection with the issuance of injunctions, attention having been sharply drawn to the matter by the demand that the right of applying injunctions in labor cases should be wholly abolished. It is at least doubtful whether a law abolishing altogether the use of injunctions in such cases would stand the test of the courts; in which case of course the legislation would be ineffective. Moreover, I believe it would be wrong altogether to prohibit the use of injunctions. It is criminal to permit sympathy for criminals to weaken our hands in upholding the law; and if men seek to destroy life or property by mob violence there should be no impairment of the power of the courts to deal with them in the most summary and effective way possible. But so far as possible the abuse of the power should be provided against by some such law as I advocated last year.

In this matter of injunctions there is lodged in the hands of the judiciary a necessary power which is nevertheless subject to the possibility of grave abuse. It is a power that should be exercised with extreme care and should be subject to the jealous scrutiny of all men, and condemnation should be meted out as much to the judge who fails to use it boldly when necessary as to the judge who uses it wantonly or oppressively. Of course a judge strong enough to be fit for his office will enjoin any resort to violence or intimidation, especially by conspiracy, no matter what his opinion may be of the rights of the original quarrel. There must be no hesitation in dealing with disorder. But there must likewise be no such abuse of the injunctive power as is implied in forbidding laboring men to strive for their own betterment in peaceful and lawful ways; nor must the injunction be used merely to aid some big corporation in carrying out schemes for its own aggrandizement. It must be remembered that a preliminary injunction in a labor case, if granted without adequate proof (even when authority can be found to support the conclusions of law on which it is founded), may often settle the dispute between the parties; and therefore if improperly granted may do irreparable wrong. Yet there are many judges who assume a matter-of-course granting of a preliminary injunction to be the ordinary and proper judicial disposition of such cases; and there have undoubtedly been flagrant wrongs committed by judges in connection with labor disputes even within the last few years, altho I think much less often than in former years. Such judges by their unwise action immensely strengthen the hands of those who are striving entirely to do away with the power of injunction; and therefore such careless use of the injunctive process tends to threaten its very existence, for if the American people ever become convinced that this process is habitually abused, whether in matters affecting labor or in matters affecting corporations, it will be well-nigh impossible to prevent its abolition.

It may be the highest duty of a judge at any given moment to disregard, not merely the wishes of individuals of great political or financial power, but the overwhelming tide of public sentiment; and the judge who does thus disregard public sentiment when it is wrong, who brushes aside the plea of any special interest when the pleading is not founded on righteousness, performs the highest service to the country. Such a judge is deserving of all honor; and all honor can not be paid to this wise and fearless judge if we permit the growth of an absurd convention which would forbid any criticism of the judge of another type, who shows himself timid in the presence of arrogant disorder, or who on insufficient grounds grants an injunction that does grave injustice, or who in his capacity as a construer, and therefore in part a maker, of the law, in flagrant fashion thwarts the cause of decent government. The judge has a power over which no review can be exercised; he himself sits in review upon the acts of both the executive and legislative branches of the Government; save in the most extraordinary cases he is amenable only at the bar of public opinion; and it is unwise to maintain that public opinion in reference to a man with such power shall neither be exprest nor led.

The best judges have ever been foremost to disclaim any immunity from criticism. This has been true since the days of the great English Lord Chancellor Parker, who said: "Let all people be at liberty to know what I found my judgment upon; that, so when I have given it in any cause, others may be at liberty to judge of *me*." The proprieties of the case were set forth with singular clearness and good temper by Judge W. H. Taft, when a United States circuit judge, eleven years ago, in 1895:

"The opportunity freely and publicly to criticize judicial action is of vastly more importance to the body politic than the immunity of courts and judges from unjust aspersions and attack. Nothing tends more to render judges careful in their decisions and anxiously solicitous to do exact justice than the consciousness that every act of theirs is to be subjected to the intelligent scrutiny and candid criticism of their fellow-men. Such criticism is beneficial in proportion as it is fair, dispassionate, discriminating, and based on a knowledge of sound legal principles. The comments made by learned text writers and by the acute editors of the various law reviews upon judicial decisions are therefore highly useful. Such critics constitute more or less impartial tribunals of professional opinion before which each judgment is made to stand or fall on its merits, and thus exert a strong influence to secure uniformity of decision. But non-professional criticism also is by no means without its uses, even if accompanied, as it often is, by a direct attack upon the judicial fairness and motives of the occupants of the bench; for if the law is but the essence of common sense, the protest of many average men may evidence a defect in a judicial conclusion, tho based on the nicest legal reasoning and profoundest learning. The two important elements of moral character in a judge are an earnest desire to reach a just conclusion and courage to enforce it. In so far as fear of public comment does not affect the courage of a judge, but only spurs him on to search his conscience and to reach the result which approves itself to his inmost heart such comment serves a useful purpose. There are few men, whether they are judges for life or for a shorter term, who do not prefer to earn and hold the respect of all, and who can not be reached and made to pause and deliberate by hostile public criticism. In the case of judges having a life tenure, indeed, their very independence makes the right freely to comment on their decisions of greater importance, because it is the only practical and available instrument in the hands of a free people to keep such judges alive to the reasonable demands of those they serve.

"On the other hand, the danger of destroying the proper influence of judicial decisions by creating unfounded prejudices against the courts justifies and requires that unjust attacks shall be met and answered. Courts must ultimately rest their defense upon the inherent strength of the opinions they deliver as the ground for their conclusions and must trust to the calm and deliberate judgment of all the people as their best vindication."

There is one consideration which should be taken into account by the good people who carry a sound proposition to an excess in objecting to any criticism of a judge's decision. The instinct of the American people as a whole is sound in this matter. They will not subscribe to the doctrine that any public servant is to be above all criticism. If the best citizens, those most competent to express their judgment in such matters, and above all those belonging to the great and honorable profession of the bar, so profoundly influential in American life, take the position that there shall be no criticism of a judge under any circumstances, their view will not be accepted by the American people as a whole. In such event the people will turn to, and tend to accept as justifiable, the intemperate and improper criticism uttered by unworthy agitators. Surely it is a misfortune to leave to such critics a function, right, in itself, which they are certain to abuse. Just and temperate criticism, when necessary, is a safeguard against the acceptance by the people as a whole of that intemperate antagonism towards the judiciary which must be combated by every right-thinking man, and which, if it became widespread among the people at large, would constitute a dire menace to the Republic.

In connection with the delays of the law, I call your attention and the attention of the Nation to the prevalence of crime among us, and above all to the epidemic of lynching and mob violence that springs up, now in one part of our country, now in another. Each section, North, South, East, or West, has its own faults; no section can with wisdom spend its time jeering at the faults of another section; it should be busy trying to amend its own shortcomings. To deal with the crime of corruption it is necessary to have an awakened public conscience, and to supplement this by whatever legislation will add speed and certainty in the execution of the law. When we deal with lynching even more is necessary. A great many white men are lynched, but the crime is peculiarly frequent in respect to black men. The greatest existing cause of lynching is the perpetration, especially by black men, of the hideous crime of rape—the most abominable in all the category of crimes, even worse than murder. Mobs frequently avenge the commission of this crime by themselves torturing to death the man committing it; thus avenging in bestial fashion a bestial deed, and reducing themselves to a level with the criminal.

Lawlessness grows by what it feeds upon; and when mobs begin to lynch for rape they speedily extend the sphere of their operations and lynch for many other kinds of crimes, so that two-thirds of the lynchings are not for rape at all; while a considerable proportion of the individuals lynched are innocent of all crime. Governor Candler, of Georgia, stated on one occasion some years ago: "I can say of a verity that I have, within the last month, saved the lives of half a dozen innocent negroes who were pursued by the mob, and brought them to trial in a court of law in which they were acquitted." As Bishop Galloway, of Mississippi, has finely said: "When the rule of a mob obtains, that which distinguishes a high civilization is surrendered. The mob which lynches a negro charged with rape will in a little while lynch a white man suspected of crime. Every Christian patriot in America needs to lift up his voice in loud and eternal protest against the mob spirit that is threatening the integrity of this Republic." Governor Jelks, of Alabama, has recently spoken as follows: "The lynching of any person for whatever crime is inexcusable anywhere—it is a defiance of orderly government; but the killing of innocent people under any provocation is infinitely more horrible; and yet innocent people are likely to die when a mob's terrible lust is once aroused. The lesson is this: No good citizen can afford to countenance a defiance of the statutes, no matter what the provocation. The innocent frequently suffer, and, it is my observation, more usually suffer than the guilty. The white people of the South indict the whole colored race on the ground that even the better elements lend no assistance whatever in ferreting out criminals of their own color. The respectable colored people must learn not to harbor their criminals, but to assist the officers in bringing them to justice. This is the larger crime, and it provokes such atrocious offenses as the one at Atlanta. The two races can never get on until there is an understanding on the part of both to make common cause with the law-abiding against criminals of any color."

Moreover, where any crime committed by a member of one race against a member of another race is avenged in such fashion that it seems as if not the individual criminal, but the whole race, is attacked, the result is to exasperate to the highest degree race feeling. There is but one safe rule in dealing with black men as with white men; it is the same rule that must be applied in dealing with rich men and poor men; that is, to treat each man, whatever his color, his creed, or his social position, with even-handed justice on his real worth as a man.

White people owe it quite as much to themselves as to the colored race to treat well the colored man who shows by his life that he deserves such treatment; for it is surely the highest wisdom to encourage in the colored race all those individuals who are honest, industrious, law-abiding, and who therefore make good and safe neighbors and citizens. Reward or punish the individual on his merits as an individual. Evil will surely come in the end to both races if we substitute for this just rule the habit of treating all the members of the race, good and bad, alike. There is no question of "social equality" or "negro domination" involved; only the question of relentlessly punishing bad men, and of securing to the good man the right to his life, his liberty, and the pursuit of his happiness as his own qualities of heart, head, and hand enable him to achieve it.

Every colored man should realize that the worst enemy of his race is the negro criminal, and above all the negro criminal who commits the dreadful crime of rape; and it should be felt as in the highest degree an offense against the whole country, and against the colored race in particular, for a colored man to fail to help the officers of the law in hunting down with all possible earnestness and zeal every such infamous offender. Moreover, in my judgment, the crime of rape should always be punished with death, as is the case with murder; assault with intent to commit rape should be made a capital crime, at least in the discretion of the court; and provision should be made by which the punishment may follow immediately upon the heels of the offense; while the trial should be so conducted that the victim need not be wantonly shamed while giving testimony, and that the least possible publicity shall be given to the details.

The members of the white race on the other hand should understand that every lynching represents by just so much a loosening of the bands of civilization; that the spirit of lynching inevitably throws into prominence in the community all the foul and evil creatures who dwell therein. No man can take part in the torture of a human being without having his own moral nature permanently lowered. Every lynching means just so much moral deterioration in all the children who have any knowledge of it, and therefore just so much additional trouble for the next generation of Americans.

Let justice be both sure and swift; but let it be justice under the law, and not the wild and crooked savagery of a mob.

There is another matter which has a direct bearing upon this matter of lynching and of the brutal crime which sometimes calls it forth and at other times merely furnishes the excuse for its existence. It is out of the question for our people as a whole permanently to rise by treading down any of their own number. Even those who themselves for the moment profit by such maltreatment of their fellows will in the long run also suffer. No more shortsighted policy can be imagined than, in the fancied interest of one class, to prevent the education of another class. The free public school, the chance for each boy or girl to get a good elementary education, lies at the foundation of our whole political situation. In every community the poorest citizens, those who need the schools most, would be deprived of them if they only received school facilities proportioned to the taxes they paid. This is as true of one portion of our country as of another. It is as true for the negro as for the white man. The white man, if he is wise, will decline to allow the negroes in a mass to grow to manhood and womanhood without education. Unquestionably education such as is obtained in our public schools does not do everything towards making a man a good citizen; but it does much. The lowest and most brutal criminals, those for instance who commit the crime of rape, are in the great majority men who have had either no education or very little; just as they are almost invariably men who own no property; for the man who puts money by out of his earnings, like the man who acquires education, is usually lifted above mere brutal criminality. Of course the best type of education for the colored man, taken as a whole, is such education as is conferred in schools like Hampton and Tuskegee; where the boys and girls, the young men and young women, are trained industrially as well as in the ordinary public school branches. The graduates of these schools turn out well in the great majority of cases, and hardly any of them become criminals, while what little criminality there is never takes the form of that brutal violence which invites lynch law. Every graduate of these schools—and for the matter of that every other colored man or woman—who leads a life so useful and honorable as to win the good will and respect of those whites whose neighbor he or she is, thereby helps the whole colored race as it can be helped in no other way; for next to the negro himself, the man who can do most to help the negro is his white neighbor who lives near him; and our steady effort should be to better the relations between the two. Great tho the benefit of these schools has been to their colored pupils and to the colored people, it may well be questioned whether the benefit has not been at least as great to the white people among whom these colored pupils live after they graduate.

Be it remembered, furthermore, that the individuals who, whether from folly, from evil temper, from greed for office, or in a spirit of mere base demagogy, indulge in the inflammatory and incendiary speeches and writings which tend to arouse mobs and to bring about lynching, not only thus excite the mob, but also tend by what criminologists call "suggestion," greatly to increase the likelihood of a repetition of the very crime against which they are inveighing. When the mob is composed of the people of one race and the man lynched is of another race, the men who in their speeches and writings either excite or justify the action tend, of course, to excite a bitter race feeling and to cause the people of the opposite race to lose sight of the abominable act of the criminal himself; and in addition, by the prominence they give to the hideous deed they undoubtedly tend to excite in other brutal and depraved natures thoughts of committing it. Swift, relentless, and orderly punishment under the law is the only way by which criminality of this type can permanently be supprest.

In dealing with both labor and capital, with the questions affecting both corporations and trades unions, there is one matter more important to remember than aught else, and that is the infinite harm done by preachers of mere discontent. These are the men who seek to excite a violent class hatred against all men of wealth. They seek to turn wise and proper movements for the better control of corporations and for doing away with the abuses connected with wealth, into a campaign of hysterical excitement and falsehood in which the aim is to inflame to madness the brutal passions of mankind. The sinister demagogs and foolish visionaries who are always eager to undertake such a campaign of destruction sometimes seek to associate themselves with those working for a genuine reform in governmental and social methods, and sometimes masquerade as such reformers. In reality they are the worst enemies of the cause they profess to advocate, just as the purveyors of sensational slander in newspaper or magazine are the worst enemies of all men who are engaged in an honest effort to better what is bad in our social and governmental conditions. To preach hatred of the rich man as such, to carry on a campaign of slander and invective against him, to seek to mislead and inflame to madness honest men whose lives are hard and who have not the kind of mental training which will permit them to appreciate the danger in the doctrines preached—all this is to commit a crime against the body politic and to be false to every worthy principle and tradition of American national life. Moreover, while such preaching and such agitation may give a livelihood and a certain notoriety to some of those who take part in it, and may result in the temporary political success of others, in the long run every such movement will either fail or else will provoke a violent reaction, which will itself result not merely in undoing the mischief wrought by the demagog and the agitator, but also in undoing the good that the honest reformer, the true upholder of popular rights, has painfully and laboriously achieved. Corruption is never so rife as in communities where the demagog and the agitator bear full sway, because in such communities all moral bands become loosened, and hysteria and sensationalism replace the spirit of sound judgment and fair dealing as between man and man.. In sheer revolt against the squalid anarchy thus produced men are sure in the end to turn toward any leader who can restore order, and then their relief at being free from the intolerable burdens of class hatred, violence, and demagogy is such that they can not for some time be aroused to indignation against misdeeds by men of wealth; so that they permit a new growth of the very abuses which were in part responsible for the original outbreak. The one hope for success for our people lies in a resolute and fearless, but sane and cool-headed, advance along the path marked out last year by this very Congress. There must be a stern refusal to be misled into following either that base creature who appeals and panders to the lowest instincts and passions in order to arouse one set of Americans against their fellows, or that other creature, equally base but no baser, who in a spirit of greed, or to accumulate or add to an already huge fortune, seeks to exploit his fellow-Americans with callous disregard to their welfare of soul and body. The man who debauches others in order to obtain a high office stands on an evil equality of corruption with the man who debauches others for financial profit; and when hatred is sown the crop which springs up can only be evil.

The plain people who think—the mechanics, farmers, merchants, workers with head or hand, the men to whom American traditions are dear, who love their country and try to act decently by their neighbors, owe it to themselves to remember that the most damaging blow that can be given popular government is to elect an unworthy and sinister agitator on a platform of violence and hypocrisy. Whenever such an issue is raised in this country nothing can be gained by flinching from it, for in such case democracy is itself on trial, popular self-government under republican forms is itself on trial. The triumph of the mob is just as evil a thing as the triumph of the plutocracy, and to have escaped one danger avails nothing whatever if we succumb to the other. In the end the honest man, whether rich or poor, who earns his own living and tries to deal justly by his fellows, has as much to fear from the insincere and unworthy demagog, promising much and performing nothing, or else performing nothing but evil, who would set on the mob to plunder the rich, as from the crafty corruptionist, who, for his own ends, would permit the common people to be exploited by the very wealthy. If we ever let this Government fall into the hands of men of either of these two classes, we shall show ourselves false to America's past. Moreover, the demagog and the corruptionist often work hand in hand. There are at this moment wealthy reactionaries of such obtuse morality that they regard the public servant who prosecutes them when they violate the law, or who seeks to make them bear their proper share of the public burdens, as being even more objectionable than the violent agitator who hounds on the mob to plunder the rich. There is nothing to choose between such a reactionary and such an agitator; fundamentally they are alike in their selfish disregard of the rights of others; and it is natural that they should join in opposition to any movement of which the aim is fearlessly to do exact and even justice to all.

I call your attention to the need of passing the bill limiting the number of hours of employment of railroad employees. The measure is a very moderate one and I can conceive of no serious objection to it. Indeed, so far as it is in our power, it should be our aim steadily to reduce the number of hours of labor, with as a goal the general introduction of an eight-hour day. There are industries in which it is not possible that the hours of labor should be reduced; just as there are communities not far enough advanced for such a movement to be for their good, or, if in the Tropics, so situated that there is no analogy between their needs and ours in this matter. On the Isthmus of Panama, for instance, the conditions are in every way so different from what they are here that an eight-hour day would be absurd; just as it is absurd, so far as the Isthmus is concerned, where white labor can not be employed, to bother as to whether the necessary work is done by alien black men or by alien yellow men. But the wageworkers of the United States are of so high a grade that alike from the merely industrial standpoint and from the civic standpoint it should be our object to do what we can in the direction of securing the general observance of an eight-hour day. Until recently the eight-hour law on our Federal statute books has been very scantily observed. Now, however, largely thru the instrumentality of the Bureau of Labor, it is being rigidly enforced, and I shall speedily be able to say whether or not there is need of further legislation in reference thereto; for our purpose is to see it obeyed in spirit no less than in letter. Half holidays during summer should be established for Government employees; it is as desirable for wageworkers who toil with their hands as for salaried officials whose labor is mental that there should be a reasonable amount of holiday.

The Congress at its last session wisely provided for a truant court for the District of Columbia; a marked step in advance on the path of properly caring for the children. Let me again urge that the Congress provide for a thoro investigation of the conditions of child labor and of the labor of women in the United States. More and more our people are growing to recognize the fact that the questions which are not merely of industrial but of social importance outweigh all others; and these two questions most emphatically come in the category of those which affect in the most far-reaching way the home life of the Nation. The horrors incident to the employment of young children in factories or at work anywhere are a blot on our civilization. It is true that each State must ultimately settle the question in its own way; but a thoro official investigation of the matter, with the results published broadcast, would greatly help toward arousing the public conscience and securing unity of State action in the matter. There is, however, one law on the subject which should be enacted immediately, because there is no need for an investigation in reference thereto, and the failure to enact it is discreditable to the National Government. A drastic and thorogoing child-labor law should be enacted for the District of Columbia and the Territories.

Among the excellent laws which the Congress past at the last session was an employers' liability law. It was a marked step in advance to get the recognition of employers' liability on the statute books; but the law did not go far enough. In spite of all precautions exercised by employers there are unavoidable accidents and even deaths involved in nearly every line of business connected with the mechanic arts. This inevitable sacrifice of life may be reduced to a minimum, but it can not be completely eliminated. It is a great social injustice to compel the employee, or rather the family of the killed or disabled victim, to bear the entire burden of such an inevitable sacrifice. In other words, society shirks its duty by laying the whole cost on the victim, whereas the injury comes from what may be called the legitimate risks of the trade. Compensation for accidents or deaths due in any line of industry to the actual conditions under which that industry is carried on, should be paid by that portion of the community for the benefit of which the industry is carried on—that is, by those who profit by the industry. If the entire trade risk is placed upon the employer he will promptly and properly add it to the legitimate cost of production and assess it proportionately upon the consumers of his commodity. It is therefore clear to my mind that the law should place this entire "risk of a trade" upon the employer. Neither the Federal law, nor, as far as I am informed, the State laws dealing with the question of employers' liability are sufficiently thorogoing. The Federal law should of course include employees in navy-yards, arsenals, and the like.

The commission appointed by the President October 16, 1902, at the request of both the anthracite coal operators and miners, to inquire into, consider, and pass upon the questions in controversy in connection with the strike in the anthracite regions of Pennsylvania and the causes out of which the controversy arose, in their report, findings, and award exprest the belief "that the State and Federal governments should provide the machinery for what may be called the compulsory investigation of controversies between employers and employees when they arise." This expression of belief is deserving of the favorable consideration of the Congress and the enactment of its provisions into law. A bill has already been introduced to this end.

Records show that during the twenty years from January 1, 1881, to December 31, 1900, there were strikes affecting 117,509 establishments, and 6,105,694 employees were thrown out of employment. During the same period there were 1,005 lockouts, involving nearly 10,000 establishments, throwing over one million people out of employment. These strikes and lockouts involved an estimated loss to employees of $307,000,000 and to employers of $143,000,000, a total of $450,000,000. The public suffered directly and indirectly probably as great additional loss. But the money loss, great as it was, did not measure the anguish and suffering endured by the wives and children of employees whose pay stopt when their work stopt, or the disastrous effect of the strike or lockout upon the business of employers, or the increase in the cost of products and the inconvenience and loss to the public.

Many of these strikes and lockouts would not have occurred had the parties to the dispute been required to appear before an unprejudiced body representing the nation and, face to face, state the reasons for their contention. In most instances the dispute would doubtless be found to be due to a misunderstanding by each of the other's rights, aggravated by an unwillingness of either party to accept as true the statements of the other as to the justice or injustice of the matters in dispute. The exercise of a judicial spirit by a disinterested body representing the Federal Government, such as would be provided by a commission on conciliation and arbitration, would tend to create an atmosphere of friendliness and conciliation between contending parties; and the giving each side an equal opportunity to present fully its case in the presence of the other would prevent many disputes from developing into serious strikes or lockouts, and, in other cases, would enable the commission to persuade the opposing parties to come to terms.

In this age of great corporate and labor combinations, neither employers nor employees should be left completely at the mercy of the stronger party to a dispute, regardless of the righteousness of their respective claims. The proposed measure would be in the line of securing recognition of the fact that in many strikes the public has itself an interest which can not wisely be disregarded; an interest not merely of general convenience, for the question of a just and proper public policy must also be considered. In all legislation of this kind it is well to advance cautiously, testing each step by the actual results; the step proposed can surely be safely taken, for the decisions of the commission would not bind the parties in legal fashion, and yet would give a chance for public opinion to crystallize and thus to exert its full force for the right.

It is not wise that the Nation should alienate its remaining coal lands. I have temporarily withdrawn from settlement all the lands which the Geological Survey has indicated as containing, or in all probability containing, coal. The question, however, can be properly settled only by legislation, which in my judgment should provide for the withdrawal of these lands from sale or from entry, save in certain especial circumstances. The ownership would then remain in the United States, which should not, however, attempt to work them, but permit them to be worked by private individuals under a royalty system, the Government keeping such control as to permit it to see that no excessive price was charged consumers. It would, of course, be as necessary to supervise the rates charged by the common carriers to transport the product as the rates charged by those who mine it; and the supervision must extend to the conduct of the common carriers, so that they shall in no way favor one competitor at the expense of another. The withdrawal of these coal lands would constitute a policy analogous to that which has been followed in withdrawing the forest lands from ordinary settlement. The coal, like the forests, should be treated as the property of the public and its disposal should be under conditions which would inure to the benefit of the public as a whole.

The present Congress has taken long strides in the direction of securing proper supervision and control by the National Government over corporations engaged in interstate business—and the enormous majority of corporations of any size are engaged in interstate business. The passage of the railway rate bill, and only to a less degree the passage of the pure food bill, and the provision for increasing and rendering more effective national control over the beef-packing industry, mark an important advance in the proper direction. In the short session it will perhaps be difficult to do much further along this line; and it may be best to wait until the laws have been in operation for a number of months before endeavoring to increase their scope, because only operation will show with exactness their merits and their shortcomings and thus give opportunity to define what further remedial legislation is needed. Yet in my judgment it will in the end be advisable in connection with the packing house inspection law to provide for putting a date on the label and for charging the cost of inspection to the packers. All these laws have already justified their enactment. The interstate commerce law, for instance, has rather amusingly falsified the predictions, both of those who asserted that it would ruin the railroads and of those who asserted that it did not go far enough and would accomplish nothing. During the last five months the railroads have shown increased earnings and some of them unusual dividends; while during the same period the mere taking effect of the law has produced an unprecedented, a hitherto unheard of, number of voluntary reductions in freights and fares by the railroads. Since the founding of the Commission there has never been a time of equal length in which anything like so many reduced tariffs have been put into effect. On August 27, for instance, two days before the new law went into effect, the Commission received notices of over five thousand separate tariffs which represented reductions from previous rates.

It must not be supposed, however, that with the passage of these laws it will be possible to stop progress along the line of increasing the power of the National Government over the use of capital in interstate commerce. For example, there will ultimately be need of enlarging the powers of the Interstate Commerce Commission along several different lines, so as to give it a larger and more efficient control over the railroads.

It can not too often be repeated that experience has conclusively shown the impossibility of securing by the actions of nearly half a hundred different State legislatures anything but ineffective chaos in the way of dealing with the great corporations which do not operate exclusively within the limits of any one State. In some method, whether by a national license law or in other fashion, we must exercise, and that at an early date, a far more complete control than at present over these great corporations—a control that will among other things prevent the evils of excessive overcapitalization, and that will compel the disclosure by each big corporation of its stockholders and of its properties and business, whether owned directly or thru subsidiary or affiliated corporations. This will tend to put a stop to the securing of inordinate profits by favored individuals at the expense whether of the general public, the stockholders, or the wageworkers. Our effort should be not so much to prevent consolidation as such, but so to supervise and control it as to see that it results in no harm to the people. The reactionary or ultraconservative apologists for the misuse of wealth assail the effort to secure such control as a step toward socialism. As a matter of fact it is these reactionaries and ultraconservatives who are themselves most potent in increasing socialistic feeling. One of the most efficient methods of averting the consequences of a dangerous agitation, which is 80 per cent wrong, is to remedy the 20 per cent of evil as to which the agitation is well founded. The best way to avert the very undesirable move for the government ownership of railways is to secure by the Government on behalf of the people as a whole such adequate control and regulation of the great interstate common carriers as will do away with the evils which give rise to the agitation against them. So the proper antidote to the dangerous and wicked agitation against the men of wealth as such is to secure by proper legislation and executive action the abolition of the grave abuses which actually do obtain in connection with the business use of wealth under our present system—or rather no system—of failure to exercise any adequate control at all. Some persons speak as if the exercise of such governmental control would do away with the freedom of individual initiative and dwarf individual effort. This is not a fact. It would be a veritable calamity to fail to put a premium upon individual initiative, individual capacity and effort; upon the energy, character, and foresight which it is so important to encourage in the individual. But as a matter of fact the deadening and degrading effect of pure socialism, and especially of its extreme form communism, and the destruction of individual character which they would bring about, are in part achieved by the wholly unregulated competition which results in a single individual or corporation rising at the expense of all others until his or its rise effectually checks all competition and reduces former competitors to a position of utter inferiority and subordination.

In enacting and enforcing such legislation as this Congress already has to its credit, we are working on a coherent plan, with the steady endeavor to secure the needed reform by the joint action of the moderate men, the plain men who do not wish anything hysterical or dangerous, but who do intend to deal in resolute common-sense fashion with the real and great evils of the present system. The reactionaries and the violent extremists show symptoms of joining hands against us. Both assert, for instance, that, if logical, we should go to government ownership of railroads and the like; the reactionaries, because on such an issue they think the people would stand with them, while the extremists care rather to preach discontent and agitation than to achieve solid results. As a matter of fact, our position is as remote from that of the Bourbon reactionary as from that of the impracticable or sinister visionary. We hold that the Government should not conduct the business of the nation, but that it should exercise such supervision as will insure its being conducted in the interest of the nation. Our aim is, so far as may be, to secure, for all decent, hard working men, equality of opportunity and equality of burden.

The actual working of our laws has shown that the effort to prohibit all combination, good or bad, is noxious where it is not ineffective. Combination of capital like combination of labor is a necessary element of our present industrial system. It is not possible completely to prevent it; and if it were possible, such complete prevention would do damage to the body politic. What we need is not vainly to try to prevent all combination, but to secure such rigorous and adequate control and supervision of the combinations as to prevent their injuring the public, or existing in such form as inevitably to threaten injury—for the mere fact that a combination has secured practically complete control of a necessary of life would under any circumstances show that such combination was to be presumed to be adverse to the public interest. It is unfortunate that our present laws should forbid all combinations, instead of sharply discriminating between those combinations which do good and those combinations which do evil. Rebates, for instance, are as often due to the pressure of big shippers (as was shown in the investigation of the Standard Oil Company and as has been shown since by the investigation of the tobacco and sugar trusts) as to the initiative of big railroads. Often railroads would like to combine for the purpose of preventing a big shipper from maintaining improper advantages at the expense of small shippers and of the general public. Such a combination, instead of being forbidden by law, should be favored. In other words, it should be permitted to railroads to make agreements, provided these agreements were sanctioned by the Interstate Commerce Commission and were published. With these two conditions complied with it is impossible to see what harm such a combination could do to the public at large. It is a public evil to have on the statute books a law incapable of full enforcement because both judges and juries realize that its full enforcement would destroy the business of the country; for the result is to make decent railroad men violators of the law against their will, and to put a premium on the behavior of the wilful wrongdoers. Such a result in turn tends to throw the decent man and the wilful wrongdoer into close association, and in the end to drag down the former to the latter's level; for the man who becomes a lawbreaker in one way unhappily tends to lose all respect for law and to be willing to break it in many ways. No more scathing condemnation could be visited upon a law than is contained in the words of the Interstate Commerce Commission when, in commenting upon the fact that the numerous joint traffic associations do technically violate the law, they say: "The decision of the United States Supreme Court in the Trans-Missouri case and the Joint Traffic Association case has produced no practical effect upon the railway operations of the country. Such associations, in fact, exist now as they did before these decisions, and with the same general effect. In justice to all parties, we ought probably to add that it is difficult to see how our interstate railways could be operated with due regard to the interest of the shipper and the railway without concerted action of the kind afforded thru these associations."

This means that the law as construed by the Supreme Court is such that the business of the country can not be conducted without breaking it. I recommend that you give careful and early consideration to this subject, and if you find the opinion of the Interstate Commerce Commission justified, that you amend the law so as to obviate the evil disclosed.

The question of taxation is difficult in any country, but it is especially difficult in ours with its Federal system of government. Some taxes should on every ground be levied in a small district for use in that district. Thus the taxation of real estate is peculiarly one for the immediate locality in which the real estate is found. Again, there is no more legitimate tax for any State than a tax on the franchises conferred by that State upon street railroads and similar corporations which operate wholly within the State boundaries, sometimes in one and sometimes in several municipalities or other minor divisions of the State. But there are many kinds of taxes which can only be levied by the General Government so as to produce the best results, because, among other reasons, the attempt to impose them in one particular State too often results merely in driving the corporation or individual affected to some other locality or other State. The National Government has long derived its chief revenue from a tariff on imports and from an internal or excise tax. In addition to these there is every reason why, when next our system of taxation is revised, the National Government should impose a graduated inheritance tax, and, if possible, a graduated income tax. The man of great wealth owes a peculiar obligation to the State, because he derives special advantages from the mere existence of government. Not only should he recognize this obligation in the way he leads his daily life and in the way he earns and spends his money, but it should also be recognized by the way in which he pays for the protection the State gives him. On the one hand, it is desirable that he should assume his full and proper share of the burden of taxation; on the other hand, it is quite as necessary that in this kind of taxation, where the men who vote the tax pay but little of it, there should be clear recognition of the danger of inaugurating any such system save in a spirit of entire justice and moderation. Whenever we, as a people, undertake to remodel our taxation system along the lines suggested, we must make it clear beyond peradventure that our aim is to distribute the burden of supporting the Government more equitably than at present; that we intend to treat rich man and poor man on a basis of absolute equality, and that we regard it as equally fatal to true democracy to do or permit injustice to the one as to do or permit injustice to the other.

I am well aware that such a subject as this needs long and careful study in order that the people may become familiar with what is proposed to be done, may clearly see the necessity of proceeding with wisdom and self-restraint, and may make up their minds just how far they are willing to go in the matter; while only trained legislators can work out the project in necessary detail. But I feel that in the near future our national legislators should enact a law providing for a graduated inheritance tax by which a steadily increasing rate of duty should be put upon all moneys or other valuables coming by gift, bequest, or devise to any individual or corporation. It may be well to make the tax heavy in proportion as the individual benefited is remote of kin. In any event, in my judgment the pro rata of the tax should increase very heavily with the increase of the amount left to any one individual after a certain point has been reached It is most desirable to encourage thrift and ambition, and a potent source of thrift and ambition is the desire on the part of the breadwinner to leave his children well off. This object can be attained by making the tax very small on moderate amounts of property left; because the prime object should be to put a constantly increasing burden on the inheritance of those swollen fortunes which it is certainly of no benefit to this country to perpetuate.

There can be no question of the ethical propriety of the Government thus determining the conditions upon which any gift or inheritance should be received. Exactly how far the inheritance tax would, as an incident, have the effect of limiting the transmission by devise or gift of the enormous fortunes in question it is not necessary at present to discuss. It is wise that progress in this direction should be gradual. At first a permanent national inheritance tax, while it might be more substantial than any such tax has hitherto been, need not approximate, either in amount or in the extent of the increase by graduation, to what such a tax should ultimately be.

This species of tax has again and again been imposed, altho only temporarily, by the National Government. It was first imposed by the act of July 6, 1797, when the makers of the Constitution were alive and at the head of affairs. It was a graduated tax; tho small in amount, the rate was increased with the amount left to any individual, exceptions being made in the case of certain close kin. A similar tax was again imposed by the act of July 1, 1862; a minimum sum of one thousand dollars in personal property being excepted from taxation, the tax then becoming progressive according to the remoteness of kin. The war-revenue act of June 13, 1898, provided for an inheritance tax on any sum exceeding the value of ten thousand dollars, the rate of the tax increasing both in accordance with the amounts left and in accordance with the legatee's remoteness of kin. The Supreme Court has held that the succession tax imposed at the time of the Civil War was not a direct tax but an impost or excise which was both constitutional and valid. More recently the Court, in an opinion delivered by Mr. Justice White, which contained an exceedingly able and elaborate discussion of the powers of the Congress to impose death duties, sustained the constitutionality of the inheritance-tax feature of the war-revenue act of 1898.

In its incidents, and apart from the main purpose of raising revenue, an income tax stands on an entirely different footing from an inheritance tax; because it involves no question of the perpetuation of fortunes swollen to an unhealthy size. The question is in its essence a question of the proper adjustment of burdens to benefits. As the law now stands it is undoubtedly difficult to devise a national income tax which shall be constitutional. But whether it is absolutely impossible is another question; and if possible it is most certainly desirable. The first purely income-tax law was past by the Congress in 1861, but the most important law dealing with the subject was that of 1894. This the court held to be unconstitutional.

The question is undoubtedly very intricate, delicate, and troublesome. The decision of the court was only reached by one majority. It is the law of the land, and of course is accepted as such and loyally obeyed by all good citizens. Nevertheless, the hesitation evidently felt by the court as a whole in coming to a conclusion, when considered together with the previous decisions on the subject, may perhaps indicate the possibility of devising a constitutional income-tax law which shall substantially accomplish the results aimed at. The difficulty of amending the Constitution is so great that only real necessity can justify a resort thereto. Every effort should be made in dealing with this subject, as with the subject of the proper control by the National Government over the use of corporate wealth in interstate business, to devise legislation which without such action shall attain the desired end; but if this fails, there will ultimately be no alternative to a constitutional amendment.

It would be impossible to overstate (tho it is of course difficult quantitatively to measure) the effect upon a nation's growth to greatness of what may be called organized patriotism, which necessarily includes the substitution of a national feeling for mere local pride; with as a resultant a high ambition for the whole country. No country can develop its full strength so long as the parts which make up the whole each put a feeling of loyalty to the part above the feeling of loyalty to the whole. This is true of sections and it is just as true of classes. The industrial and agricultural classes must work together, capitalists and wageworkers must work together, if the best work of which the country is capable is to be done. It is probable that a thoroly efficient system of education comes next to the influence of patriotism in bringing about national success of this kind. Our federal form of government, so fruitful of advantage to our people in certain ways, in other ways undoubtedly limits our national effectiveness. It is not possible, for instance, for the National Government to take the lead in technical industrial education, to see that the public school system of this country develops on all its technical, industrial, scientific, and commercial sides. This must be left primarily to the several States. Nevertheless, the National Government has control of the schools of the District of Columbia, and it should see that these schools promote and encourage the fullest development of the scholars in both commercial and industrial training. The commercial training should in one of its branches deal with foreign trade. The industrial training is even more important. It should be one of our prime objects as a Nation, so far as feasible, constantly to work toward putting the mechanic, the wageworker who works with his hands, on a higher plane of efficiency and reward, so as to increase his effectiveness in the economic world, and the dignity, the remuneration, and the power of his position in the social world. Unfortunately, at present the effect of some of the work in the public schools is in the exactly opposite direction. If boys and girls are trained merely in literary accomplishments, to the total exclusion of industrial, manual, and technical training, the tendency is to unfit them for industrial work and to make them reluctant to go into it, or unfitted to do well if they do go into it. This is a tendency which should be strenuously combated. Our industrial development depends largely upon technical education, including in this term all industrial education, from that which fits a man to be a good mechanic, a good carpenter, or blacksmith, tc that which fits a man to do the greatest engineering feat. The skilled mechanic, the skilled workman, can best become such by technical industrial education. The far-reaching usefulness of institutes of technology and schools of mines or of engineering is now universally acknowledged, and no less far-reaching is the effect of a good building or mechanical trades school, a textile, or watch-making, or engraving school. All such training must develop not only manual dexterity but industrial intelligence. In international rivalry this country does not have to fear the competition of pauper labor as much as it has to fear the educated labor of specially trained competitors; and we should have the education of the hand, eye, and brain which will fit us to meet such competition.

In every possible way we should help the wageworker who toils with his hands and who must (we hope in a constantly increasing measure) also toil with his brain. Under the Constitution the National Legislature can do but little of direct importance for his welfare save where he is engaged in work which permits it to act under the interstate commerce clause of the Constitution; and this is one reason why I so earnestly hope that both the legislative and judicial branches of the Government will construe this clause of the Constitution in the broadest possible manner. We can, however, in such a matter as industrial training, in such a matter as child labor and factory laws, set an example to the States by enacting the most advanced legislation that can wisely be enacted for the District of Columbia.

The only other persons whose welfare is as vital to the welfare of the whole country as is the welfare of the wageworkers are the tillers of the soil, the farmers. It is a mere truism to say that no growth of cities, no growth of wealth, no industrial development can atone for any falling off in the character and standing of the farming population. During the last few decades this fact has been recognized with ever-increasing clearness. There is no longer any failure to realize that farming, at least in certain branches, must become a technical and scientific profession. This means that there must be open to farmers the chance for technical and scientific training, not theoretical merely but of the most severely practical type. The farmer represents a peculiarly high type of American citizenship, and he must have the same chance to rise and develop as other American citizens have. Moreover, it is exactly as true of the farmer, as it is of the business man and the wageworker, that the ultimate success of the Nation of which he forms a part must be founded not alone on material prosperity but upon high moral, mental, and physical development. This education of the farmer—self-education by preference, but also education from the outside, as with all other men—is peculiarly necessary here in the United States, where the frontier conditions even in the newest States have now nearly vanished, where there must be a substitution of a more intensive system of cultivation for the old wasteful farm management, and where there must be a better business organization among the farmers themselves.

Several factors must cooperate in the improvement of the farmer's condition. He must have the chance to be educated in the widest possible sense—in the sense which keeps ever in view the intimate relationship between the theory of education and the facts of life. In all education we should widen our aims. It is a good thing to produce a certain number of trained scholars and students; but the education superintended by the State must seek rather to produce a hundred good citizens than merely one scholar, and it must be turned now and then from the class book to the study of the great book of nature itself. This is especially true of the farmer, as has been pointed out again and again by all observers most competent to pass practical judgment on the problems of our country life. All students now realize that education must seek to train the executive powers of young people and to confer more real significance upon the phrase "dignity of labor," and to prepare the pupils so that, in addition to each developing in the highest degree his individual capacity for work, they may together help create a right public opinion, and show in many ways social and cooperative spirit. Organization has become necessary in the business world; and it has accomplished much for good in the world of labor. It is no less necessary for farmers. Such a movement as the grange movement is good in itself and is capable of a well-nigh infinite further extension for good so long as it is kept to its own legitimate business. The benefits to be derived by the association of farmers for mutual advantage are partly economic and partly sociological.

Moreover, while in the long run voluntary efforts will prove more efficacious than government assistance, while the farmers must primarily do most for themselves, yet the Government can also do much. The Department of Agriculture has broken new ground in many directions, and year by year it finds how it can improve its methods and develop fresh usefulness. Its constant effort is to give the governmental assistance in the most effective way; that is, thru associations of farmers rather than to or thru individual farmers. It is also striving to coordinate its work with the agricultural departments of the several States, and so far as its own work is educational to coordinate it with the work of other educational authorities. Agricultural education is necessarily based upon general education, but our agricultural educational institutions are wisely specializing themselves, making their courses relate to the actual teaching of the agricultural and kindred sciences to young country people or young city people who wish to live in the country.

Great progress has already been made among farmers by the creation of farmers' institutes, of dairy associations, of breeders' associations, horticultural associations, and the like. A striking example of how the Government and the farmers can cooperate is shown in connection with the menace offered to the cotton growers of the Southern States by the advance of the boll weevil. The Department is doing all it can to organize the farmers in the threatened districts, just as it has been doing all it can to organize them in aid of its work to eradicate the cattle fever tick in the South. The Department can and will cooperate with all such associations, and it must have their help if its own work is to be done in the most efficient style.

Much is now being done for the States of the Rocky Mountains and Great Plains thru the development of the national policy of irrigation and forest preservation; no Government policy for the betterment of our internal conditions has been more fruitful of good than this. The forests of the White Mountains and Southern Appalachian regions should also be preserved; and they can not be unless the people of the States in which they lie, thru their representatives in the Congress, secure vigorous action by the National Government.

I invite the attention of the Congress to the estimate of the Secretary of War for an appropriation to enable him to begin the preliminary work for the construction of a memorial amphitheater at Arlington. The Grand Army of the Republic in its national encampment has urged the erection of such an amphitheater as necessary for the proper observance of Memorial Day and as a fitting monument to the soldier and sailor dead buried there. In this I heartily concur and commend the matter to the favorable consideration of the Congress.

I am well aware of how difficult it is to pass a constitutional amendment. Nevertheless in my judgment the whole question of marriage and divorce should be relegated to the authority of the National Congress. At present the wide differences in the laws of the different States on this subject result in scandals and abuses; and surely there is nothing so vitally essential to the welfare of the nation, nothing around which the nation should so bend itself to throw every safeguard, as the home life of the average citizen. The change would be good from every standpoint. In particular it would be good because it would confer on the Congress the power at once to deal radically and efficiently with polygamy; and this should be done whether or not marriage and divorce are dealt with. It is neither safe nor proper to leave the question of polygamy to be dealt with by the several States. Power to deal with it should be conferred on the National Government.

When home ties are loosened; when men and women cease to regard a worthy family life, with all its duties fully performed, and all its responsibilities lived up to, as the life best worth living; then evil days for the commonwealth are at hand. There are regions in our land, and classes of our population, where the birth rate has sunk below the death rate. Surely it should need no demonstration to show that wilful sterility is, from the standpoint of the nation, from the standpoint of the human race, the one sin for which the penalty is national death, race death; a sin for which there is no atonement; a sin which is the more dreadful exactly in proportion as the men and women guilty thereof are in other respects, in character, and bodily and mental powers, those whom for the sake of the state it would be well to see the fathers and mothers of many healthy children, well brought up in homes made happy by their presence. No man, no woman, can shirk the primary duties of life, whether for love of ease and pleasure, or for any other cause, and retain his or her self-respect.

Let me once again call the attention of the Congress to two subjects concerning which I have frequently before communicated with them. One is the question of developing American shipping. I trust that a law embodying in substance the views, or a major part of the views, expressed in the report on this subject laid before the House at its last session will be past. I am well aware that in former years objectionable measures have been proposed in reference to the encouragement of American shipping; but it seems to me that the proposed measure is as nearly unobjectionable as any can be. It will of course benefit primarily our seaboard States, such as Maine, Louisiana, and Washington; but what benefits part of our people in the end benefits all; just as Government aid to irrigation and forestry in the West is really of benefit, not only to the Rocky Mountain States, but to all our country. If it prove impracticable to enact a law for the encouragement of shipping generally, then at least provision should be made for better communication with South America, notably for fast mail lines to the chief South American ports. It is discreditable to us that our business people, for lack of direct communication in the shape of lines of steamers with South America, should in that great sister continent be at a disadvantage compared to the business people of Europe.

I especially call your attention to the second subject, the condition of our currency laws. The national bank act has ably served a great purpose in aiding the enormous business development of the country;

and within ten years there has been an increase in circulation per capita from $21.41 to $33.08. For several years evidence has been accumulating that additional legislation is needed. The recurrence of each crop season emphasizes the defects of the present laws. There must soon be a revision of them, because to leave them as they are means to incur liability of business disaster. Since your body adjourned there has been a fluctuation in the interest on call money from 2 per cent to 30 per cent; and the fluctuation was even greater during the preceding six months. The Secretary of the Treasury had to step in and by wise action put a stop to the most violent period of oscillation. Even worse than such fluctuation is the advance in commercial rates and the uncertainty felt in the sufficiency of credit even at high rates. All commercial interests suffer during each crop period. Excessive rates for call money in New York attract money from the interior banks into the speculative field; this depletes the fund that would otherwise be available for commercial uses, and commercial borrowers are forced to pay abnormal rates; so that each fall a tax, in the shape of increased interest charges, is placed on the whole commerce of the country.

The mere statement of these facts shows that our present system is seriously defective. There is need of a change. Unfortunately, however, many of the proposed changes must be ruled from consideration because they are complicated, are not easy of comprehension, and tend to disturb existing rights and interests. We must also rule out any plan which would materially impair the value of the United States 2 per cent bonds now pledged to secure circulation, the issue of which was made under conditions peculiarly creditable to the Treasury. I do not press any especial plan. Various plans have recently been proposed by expert committees of bankers. Among the plans which are possibly feasible and which certainly should receive your consideration is that repeatedly brought to your attention by the present Secretary of the Treasury, the essential features of which have been approved by many prominent bankers and business men. According to this plan national banks should be permitted to issue a specified proportion of their capital in notes of a given kind, the issue to be taxed at so high a rate as to drive the notes back when not wanted in legitimate trade. This plan would not permit the issue of currency to give banks additional profits, but to meet the emergency presented by times of stringency.

I do not say that this is the right system. I only advance it to emphasize my belief that there is need for the adoption of some system which shall be automatic and open to all sound banks, so as to avoid all possibility of discrimination and favoritism. Such a plan would tend to prevent the spasms of high money and speculation which now obtain in the New York market; for at present there is too much currency at certain seasons of the year, and its accumulation at New York tempts bankers to lend it at low rates for speculative purposes; whereas at other times when the crops are being moved there is urgent need for a large but temporary increase in the currency supply. It must never be forgotten that this question concerns business men generally quite as much as bankers; especially is this true of stockmen, farmers, and business men in the West; for at present at certain seasons of the year the difference in interest rates between the East and the West is from 6 to 10 per cent, whereas in Canada the corresponding difference is but 2 per cent. Any plan must, of course, guard the interests of western and southern bankers as carefully as it guards the interests of New York or Chicago bankers; and must be drawn from the standpoints of the farmer and the merchant no less than from the standpoints of the city banker and the country banker.

The law should be amended so as specifically to provide that the funds derived from customs duties may be treated by the Secretary of the Treasury as he treats funds obtained under the internal-revenue laws. There should be a considerable increase in bills of small denominations. Permission should be given banks, if necessary under settled restrictions, to retire their circulation to a larger amount than three millions a month.

I most earnestly hope that the bill to provide a lower tariff for or else absolute free trade in Philippine products will become a law. No harm will come to any American industry; and while there will be some small but real material benefit to the Filipinos, the main benefit will come by the showing made as to our purpose to do all in our power for their welfare. So far our action in the Philippines has been abundantly justified, not mainly and indeed not primarily because of the added dignity it has given us as a nation by proving that we are capable honorably and efficiently to bear the international burdens which a mighty people should bear, but even more because of the immense benefit that has come to the people of the Philippine Islands. In these islands we are steadily introducing both liberty and order, to a greater degree than their people have ever before known. We have secured justice. We have provided an efficient police force, and have put down ladronism. Only in the islands of Leyte and Samar is the authority of our Government resisted and this by wild mountain tribes under the superstitious inspiration of fakirs and pseudo-religious leaders. We are constantly increasing the measure of liberty accorded the islanders, and next spring, if conditions warrant, we shall take a great stride forward in testing their capacity for self-government by summoning the first Filipino legislative assembly; and the way in which they stand this test will largely determine whether the self-government thus granted will be increased or decreased; for if we have erred at all in the Philippines it has been in proceeding too rapidly in the direction of granting a large measure of self-government. We are building roads. We have, for the immeasurable good of the people, arranged for the building of railroads. Let us also see to it that they are given free access to our markets. This nation owes no more imperative duty to itself and mankind than the duty of managing the affairs of all the islands under the American flag—the Philippines, Porto Rico, and Hawaii—so as to make it evident that it is in every way to their advantage that the flag should fly over them.

American citizenship should be conferred on the citizens of Porto Rico. The harbor of San Juan in Porto Rico should be dredged and improved. The expenses of the federal court of Porto Rico should be met from the Federal Treasury. The administration of the affairs of Porto Rico, together with those of the Philippines, Hawaii, and our other insular possessions, should all be directed under one executive department; by preference the Department of State or the Department of War.

The needs of Hawaii are peculiar; every aid should be given the islands; and our efforts should be unceasing to develop them along the lines of a community of small freeholders, not of great planters with coolie-tilled estates. Situated as this Territory is, in the middle of the Pacific, there are duties imposed upon this small community which do not fall in like degree or manner upon any other American community. This warrants our treating it differently from the way in which we treat Territories contiguous to or surrounded by sister Territories or other States, and justifies the setting aside of a portion of our revenues to be expended for educational and internal improvements therein. Hawaii is now making an effort to secure immigration fit in the end to assume the duties and burdens of full American citizenship, and whenever the leaders in the various industries of those islands finally adopt our ideals and heartily join our administration in endeavoring to develop a middle class of substantial citizens, a way will then be found to deal with the commercial and industrial problems which now appear to them so serious. The best Americanism is that which aims for stability and permanency of prosperous citizenship, rather than immediate returns on large masses of capital.

Alaska's needs have been partially met, but there must be a complete reorganization of the governmental system, as I have before indicated to you. I ask your especial attention to this. Our fellow-citizens who dwell on the shores of Puget Sound with characteristic energy are arranging to hold in Seattle the Alaska Yukon Pacific Exposition. Its special aims include the upbuilding of Alaska and the development of American commerce on the Pacific Ocean. This exposition, in its purposes and scope, should appeal not only to the people of the Pacific slope, but to the people of the United States at large. Alaska since it was bought has yielded to the Government eleven millions of dollars of revenue, and has produced nearly three hundred millions of dollars in gold, furs, and fish. When properly developed it will become in large degree a land of homes. The countries bordering the Pacific Ocean have a population more numerous than that of all the countries of Europe; their annual foreign commerce amounts to over three billions of dollars, of which the share of the United States is some seven hundred millions of dollars. If this trade were thoroly understood and pushed by our manufacturers and producers, the industries not only of the Pacific slope, but of all our country, and particularly of our cotton-growing States, would be greatly benefited. Of course, in order to get these benefits, we must treat fairly the countries with which we trade.

It is a mistake, and it betrays a spirit of foolish cynicism, to maintain that all international governmental action is, and must ever be, based upon mere selfishness, and that to advance ethical reasons for such action is always a sign of hypocrisy. This is no more necessarily true of the action of governments than of the action of individuals. It is a sure sign of a base nature always to ascribe base motives for the actions of others. Unquestionably no nation can afford to disregard proper considerations of self-interest, any more than a private individual can so do. But it is equally true that the average private individual in any really decent community does many actions with reference to other men in which he is guided, not by self-interest, but by public spirit, by regard for the rights of others, by a disinterested purpose to do good to others, and to raise the tone of the community as a whole. Similarly, a really great nation must often act, and as a matter of fact often does act, toward other nations in a spirit not in the least of mere self-interest, but paying heed chiefly to ethical reasons; and as the centuries go by this disinterestedness in international action, this tendency of the individuals comprizing a nation to require that nation to act with justice toward its neighbors, steadily grows and strengthens. It is neither wise nor right for a nation to disregard its own needs, and it is foolish—and may be wicked—to think that other nations will disregard theirs. But it is wicked for a nation only to regard its own interest, and foolish to believe that such is the sole motive that actuates any other nation. It should be our steady aim to raise the ethical standard of national action just as we strive to raise the ethical standard of individual action.

Not only must we treat all nations fairly, but we must treat with justice and good will all immigrants who come here under the law. Whether they are Catholic or Protestant, Jew or Gentile; whether they come from England or Germany, Russia, Japan, or Italy, matters nothing. All we have a right to question is the man's conduct. If he is honest and upright in his dealings with his neighbor and with the State, then he is entitled to respect and good treatment. Especially do we need to remember our duty to the stranger within our gates. It is the sure mark of a low civilization, a low morality, to abuse or discriminate against or in any way humiliate such stranger who has come here lawfully and who is conducting himself properly. To remember this is incumbent on every American citizen, and it is of course peculiarly incumbent on every Government official, whether of the nation or of the several States.

I am prompted to say this by the attitude of hostility here and there assumed toward the Japanese in this country. This hostility is sporadic and is limited to a very few places. Nevertheless, it is most discreditable to us as a people, and it may be fraught with the gravest consequences to the nation. The friendship between the United States and Japan has been continuous since the time, over half a century ago, when Commodore Perry, by his expedition to Japan, first opened the islands to western civilization. Since then the growth of Japan has been literally astounding. There is not only nothing to parallel it, but nothing to approach it in the history of civilized mankind. Japan has a glorious and ancient past. Her civilization is older than that of the nations of northern Europe—the nations from whom the people of the United States have chiefly sprung. But fifty years ago Japan's development was still that of the Middle Ages. During that fifty years the progress of the country in every walk in life has been a marvel to mankind, and she now stands as one of the greatest of civilized nations; great in the arts of war and in the arts of peace; great in military, in industrial, in artistic development and achievement. Japanese soldiers and sailors have shown themselves equal in combat to any of whom history makes note. She has produced great generals and mighty admirals; her fighting men, afloat and ashore, show all the heroic courage, the unquestioning, unfaltering loyalty, the splendid indifference to hardship and death, which marked the Loyal Ronins; and they show also that they possess the highest ideal of patriotism. Japanese artists of every kind see their products eagerly sought for in all lands. The industrial and commercial development of Japan has been phenomenal; greater than that of any other country during the same period. At the same time the advance in science and philosophy is no less marked. The admirable management of the Japanese Red Cross during the late war, the efficiency and humanity of the Japanese officials, nurses, and doctors, won the respectful admiration of all acquainted with the facts. Thru the Red Cross the Japanese people sent over $100,000 to the sufferers of San Francisco, and the gift was accepted with gratitude by our people. The courtesy of the Japanese, nationally and individually, has become proverbial. To no other country has there been such an increasing number of visitors from this land as to Japan. In return, Japanese have come here in great numbers. They are welcome, socially and intellectually, in all our colleges and institutions of higher learning, in all our professional and social bodies. The Japanese have won in a single generation the right to stand abreast of the foremost and most enlightened peoples of Europe and America; they have won on their own merits and by their own exertions the right to treatment on a basis of full and frank equality. The overwhelming mass of our people cherish a lively regard and respect for the people of Japan, and in almost every quarter of the Union the stranger from Japan is treated as he deserves; that is, he is treated as the stranger from any part of civilized Europe is and deserves to be treated. But here and there a most unworthy feeling has manifested itself toward the Japanese—the feeling that has been shown in shutting them out from the common schools in San Francisco, and in mutterings against them in one or two other places, because of their efficiency as workers. To shut them out from the public schools is a wicked absurdity, when there are no first-class colleges in the land, including the universities and colleges of California, which do not gladly welcome Japanese students and on which Japanese students do not reflect credit. We have as much to learn from Japan as Japan has to learn from us; and no nation is fit to teach unless it is also willing to learn. Thruout Japan Americans are well treated, and any failure on the part of Americans at home to treat the Japanese with a like courtesy and consideration is by just so much a confession of inferiority in our civilization.

Our nation fronts on the Pacific, just as it fronts on the Atlantic. We hope to play a constantly growing part in the great ocean of the Orient. We wish, as we ought to wish, for a great commercial development in our dealings with Asia; and it is out of the question that we should permanently have such development unless we freely and gladly extend to other nations the same measure of justice and good treatment which we expect to receive in return. It is only a very small body of our citizens that act badly. Where the Federal Government has power it will deal summarily with any such. Where the several States have power I earnestly ask that they also deal wisely and promptly with such conduct, or else this small body of wrongdoers may bring shame upon the great mass of their innocent and right-thinking fellows—that is, upon our nation as a whole. Good manners should be an international no less than an individual attribute. I ask fair treatment for the Japanese as I would ask fair treatment for Germans or Englishmen, Frenchmen, Russians, or Italians. I ask it as due to humanity and civilization. I ask it as due to ourselves because we must act uprightly toward all men.

I recommend to the Congress that an act be past specifically providing for the naturalization of Japanese who come here intending to become American citizens. One of the great embarrassments attending the performance of our international obligations is the fact that the Statutes of the United States are entirely inadequate. They fail to give to the National Government sufficiently ample power, thru United States courts and by the use of the Army and Navy, to protect aliens in the rights secured to them under solemn treaties which are the law of the land. I therefore earnestly recommend that the criminal and civil statutes of the United States be so amended and added to as to enable the President, acting for the United States Government, which is responsible in our international relations, to enforce the rights of aliens under treaties. Even as the law now is something can be done by the Federal Government toward this end, and in the matter now before me affecting the Japanese everything that it is in my power to do will be done, and all of the forces, military and civil, of the United States which I may lawfully employ will be so employed. There should, however, be no particle of doubt as to the power of the National Government completely to perform and enforce its own obligations to other nations. The mob of a single city may at any time perform acts of lawless violence against some class of foreigners which would plunge us into war. That city by itself would be powerless to make defense against the foreign power thus assaulted, and if independent of this Government it would never venture to perform or permit the performance of the acts complained of. The entire power and the whole duty to protect the offending city or the offending community lies in the hands of the United States Government. It is unthinkable that we should continue a policy under which a given locality may be allowed to commit a crime against a friendly nation, and the United States Government limited, not to preventing the commission of the crime, but, in the last resort, to defending the people who have committed it against the consequences of their own wrongdoing.

Last August an insurrection broke out in Cuba which it speedily grew evident that the existing Cuban Government was powerless to quell. This Government was repeatedly asked by the then Cuban Government to intervene, and finally was notified by the President of Cuba that he intended to resign; that his decision was irrevocable; that none of the other constitutional officers would consent to carry on the Government, and that he was powerless to maintain order. It was evident that chaos was impending, and there was every probability that if steps were not immediately taken by this Government to try to restore order the representatives of various European nations in the island would apply to their respective governments for armed intervention in order to protect the lives and property of their citizens. Thanks to the preparedness of our Navy, I was able immediately to send enough ships to Cuba to prevent the situation from becoming hopeless; and I furthermore dispatched to Cuba the Secretary of War and the Assistant Secretary of State, in order that they might grapple with the situation on the ground. All efforts to secure an agreement between the contending factions, by which they should themselves come to an amicable understanding and settle upon some modus vivendi—some provisional government of their own—failed. Finally the President of the Republic resigned. The quorum of Congress assembled failed by deliberate purpose of its members, so that there was no power to act on his resignation, and the Government came to a halt. In accordance with the so-called Platt amendment, which was embodied in the constitution of Cuba, I thereupon proclaimed a provisional government for the island, the Secretary of War acting as provisional governor until he could be replaced by Mr. Magoon, the late minister to Panama and governor of the Canal Zone on the Isthmus; troops were sent to support them and to relieve the Navy, the expedition being handled with most satisfactory speed and efficiency. The insurgent chiefs immediately agreed that their troops should lay down their arms and disband; and the agreement was carried out. The provisional government has left the personnel of the old government and the old laws, so far as might be, unchanged, and will thus administer the island for a few months until tranquillity can be restored, a new election properly held, and a new government inaugurated. Peace has come in the island; and the harvesting of the sugar-cane crop, the great crop of the island, is about to proceed.

When the election has been held and the new government inaugurated in peaceful and orderly fashion the provisional government will come to an end. I take this opportunity of expressing upon behalf of the American people, with all possible solemnity, our most earnest hope that the people of Cuba will realize the imperative need of preserving justice and keeping order in the Island. The United States wishes nothing of Cuba except that it shall prosper morally and materially, and wishes nothing of the Cubans save that they shall be able to preserve order among themselves and therefore to preserve their independence. If the elections become a farce, and if the insurrectionary habit becomes confirmed in the Island, it is absolutely out of the question that the Island should continue independent; and the United States, which has assumed the sponsorship before the civilized world for Cuba's career as a nation, would again have to intervene and to see that the government was managed in such orderly fashion as to secure the safety of life and property. The path to be trodden by those who exercise self-government is always hard, and we should have every charity and patience with the Cubans as they tread this difficult path. I have the utmost sympathy with, and regard for, them; but I most earnestly adjure them solemnly to weigh their responsibilities and to see that when their new government is started it shall run smoothly, and with freedom from flagrant denial of right on the one hand, and from insurrectionary disturbances on the other.

The Second International Conference of American Republics, held in Mexico in the years 1901-2, provided for the holding of the third conference within five years, and committed the fixing of the time and place and the arrangements for the conference to the governing board of the Bureau of American Republics, composed of the representatives of all the American nations in Washington. That board discharged the duty imposed upon it with marked fidelity and painstaking care, and upon the courteous invitation of the United States of Brazil the conference was held at Rio de Janeiro, continuing from the 23d of July to the 29th of August last. Many subjects of common interest to all the American nations were discust by the conference, and the conclusions reached, embodied in a series of resolutions and proposed conventions, will be laid before you upon the coming in of the final report of the American delegates. They contain many matters of importance relating to the extension of trade, the increase of communication, the smoothing away of barriers to free intercourse, and the promotion of a better knowlege and good understanding between the different countries represented. The meetings of the conference were harmonious and the conclusions were reached with substantial unanimity. It is interesting to observe that in the successive conferences which have been held the representatives of the different American nations have been learning to work together effectively, for, while the First Conference in Washington in 1889, and the Second Conference in Mexico in 1901-2, occupied many months, with much time wasted in an unregulated and fruitless discussion, the Third Conference at Rio exhibited much of the facility in the practical dispatch of business which characterizes permanent deliberative bodies, and completed its labors within the period of six weeks originally allotted for its sessions.

Quite apart from the specific value of the conclusions reached by the conference, the example of the representatives of all the American nations engaging in harmonious and kindly consideration and discussion of subjects of common interest is itself of great and substantial value for the promotion of reasonable and considerate treatment of all international questions. The thanks of this country are due to the Government of Brazil and to the people of Rio de Janeiro for the generous hospitality with which our delegates, in common with the others, were received, entertained, and facilitated in their work.

Incidentally to the meeting of the conference, the Secretary of State visited the city of Rio de Janeiro and was cordially received by the conference, of which he was made an honorary president. The announcement of his intention to make this visit was followed by most courteous and urgent invitations from nearly all the countries of South America to visit them as the guest of their Governments. It was deemed that by the acceptance of these invitations we might appropriately express the real respect and friendship in which we hold our sister Republics of the southern continent, and the Secretary, accordingly, visited Brazil, Uruguay, Argentina, Chile, Peru, Panama, and Colombia. He refrained from visiting Paraguay, Bolivia, and Ecuador only because the distance of their capitals from the seaboard made it impracticable with the time at his disposal. He carried with him a message of peace and friendship, and of strong desire for good understanding and mutual helpfulness; and he was everywhere received in the spirit of his message. The members of government, the press, the learned professions, the men of business, and the great masses of the people united everywhere in emphatic response to his friendly expressions and in doing honor to the country and cause which he represented.

In many parts of South America there has been much misunderstanding of the attitude and purposes of the United States towards the other American Republics. An idea had become prevalent that our assertion of the Monroe Doctrine implied, or carried with it, an assumption of superiority, and of a right to exercise some kind of protectorate over the countries to whose territory that doctrine applies. Nothing could be farther from the truth. Yet that impression continued to be a serious barrier to good understanding, to friendly intercourse, to the introduction of American capital and the extension of American trade. The impression was so widespread that apparently it could not be reached by any ordinary means.

It was part of Secretary Root's mission to dispel this unfounded impression, and there is just cause to believe that he has succeeded. In an address to the Third Conference at Rio on the 31st of July—an address of such note that I send it in, together with this message—he said:

"We wish for no victories but those of peace; for no territory except our own; for no sovereignty except the sovereignty over ourselves. We deem the independence and equal rights of the smallest and weakest member of the family of nations entitled to as much respect as those of the greatest empire, and we deem the observance of that respect the chief guaranty of the weak against the oppression of the strong. We neither claim nor desire any rights or privileges or powers that we do not freely concede to every American Republic. We wish to increase our prosperity, to extend our trade, to grow in wealth, in wisdom, and in spirit, but our conception of the true way to accomplish this is not to pull down others and profit by their ruin, but to help all friends to a common prosperity and a common growth, that we may all become greater and stronger together. Within a few months for the first time the recognized possessors of every foot of soil upon the American continents can be and I hope will be represented with the acknowledged rights of equal sovereign states in the great World Congress at The Hague. This will be the world's formal and final acceptance of the declaration that no part of the American continents is to be deemed subject to colonization. Let us pledge ourselves to aid each other in the full performance of the duty to humanity which that accepted declaration implies, so that in time the weakest and most unfortunate of our Republics may come to march with equal step by the side of the stronger and more fortunate. Let us help each other to show that for all the races of men the liberty for which we have fought and labored is the twin sister of justice and peace. Let us unite in creating and maintaining and making effective an all-American public opinion, whose power shall influence international conduct and prevent international wrong, and narrow the causes of war, and forever preserve our free lands from the burden of such armaments as are massed behind the frontiers of Europe, and bring us ever nearer to the perfection of ordered liberty. So shall come security and prosperity, production and trade, wealth, learning, the arts, and happiness for us all."

These words appear to have been received with acclaim in every part of South America. They have my hearty approval, as I am sure they will have yours, and I can not be wrong in the conviction that they correctly represent the sentiments of the whole American people. I can not better characterize the true attitude of the United States in its assertion of the Monroe Doctrine than in the words of the distinguished former minister of foreign affairs of Argentina, Doctor Drago, in his speech welcoming Mr. Root at Buenos Ayres. He spoke of—

"The traditional policy of the United States (which) without accentuating superiority or seeking preponderance, condemned the oppression of the nations of this part of the world and the control of their destinies by the great Powers of Europe."

It is gratifying to know that in the great city of Buenos Ayres, upon the arches which spanned the streets, entwined with Argentine and American flags for the reception of our representative, there were emblazoned not only the names of Washington and Jefferson and Marshall, but also, in appreciative recognition of their services to the cause of South American independence, the names of James Monroe, John Quincy Adams, Henry Clay, and Richard Rush. We take especial pleasure in the graceful courtesy of the Government of Brazil, which has given to the beautiful and stately building first used for the meeting of the conference the name of "Palacio Monroe." Our grateful acknowledgments are due to the Governments and the people of all the countries visited by the Secretary of State for the courtesy, the friendship, and the honor shown to our country in their generous hospitality to him.

In my message to you on the 5th of December, 1905, I called your attention to the embarrassment that might be caused to this Government by the assertion by foreign nations of the right to collect by force of arms contract debts due by American republics to citizens of the collecting nation, and to the danger that the process of compulsory collection might result in the occupation of territory tending to become permanent. I then said:

"Our own Government has always refused to enforce such contractual obligations on behalf of its citizens by an appeal to arms. It is much to be wisht that all foreign governments would take the same view."

This subject was one of the topics of consideration at the conference at Rio and a resolution was adopted by that conference recommending to the respective governments represented "to consider the advisability of asking the Second Peace Conference at The Hague to examine the question of the compulsory collection of public debts, and, in general, means tending to diminish among nations conflicts of purely pecuniary origin."

This resolution was supported by the representatives of the United States in accordance with the following instructions:

"It has long been the established policy of the United States not to use its armed forces for the collection of ordinary contract debts due to its citizens by other governments. We have not considered the use of force for such a purpose consistent with that respect for the independent sovereignty of other members of the family of nations which is the most important principle of international law and the chief protection of weak nations against the oppression of the strong. It seems to us that the practise is injurious in its general effect upon the relations of nations and upon the welfare of weak and disordered states, whose development ought to be encouraged in the interests of civilization; that it offers frequent temptation to bullying and oppression and to unnecessary and unjustifiable warfare. We regret that other powers, whose opinions and sense of justice we esteem highly, have at times taken a different view and have permitted themselves, tho we believe with reluctance, to collect such debts by force. It is doubtless true that the non-payment of public debts may be accompanied by such circumstances of fraud and wrongdoing or violation of treaties as to justify the use of force. This Government would be glad to see an international consideration of the subject which shall discriminate between such cases and the simple nonperformance of a contract with a private person, and a resolution in favor of reliance upon peaceful means in cases of the latter class.

"It is not felt, however, that the conference at Rio should undertake to make such a discrimination or to resolve upon such a rule.

Most of the American countries are still debtor nations, while the countries of Europe are the creditors. If the Rio conference, therefore, were to take such action it would have the appearance of a meeting of debtors resolving how their creditors should act, and this would not inspire respect. The true course is indicated by the terms of the program, which proposes to request the Second Hague Conference, where both creditors and debtors will be assembled, to consider the subject."

Last June trouble which had existed for some time between the Republics of Salvador, Guatemala, and Honduras culminated in war—a war which threatened to be ruinous to the countries involved and very destructive to the commercial interests of Americans, Mexicans, and other foreigners who are taking an important part in the development of these countries. The thoroly good understanding which exists between the United States and Mexico enabled this Government and that of Mexico to unite in effective mediation between the warring Republics; which mediation resulted, not without long-continued and patient effort, in bringing about a meeting of the representatives of the hostile powers on board a United States warship as neutral territory, and peace was there concluded; a peace which resulted in the saving of thousands of lives and in the prevention of an incalculable amount of misery and the destruction of property and of the means of livelihood. The Rio Conference past the following resolution in reference to this action:

"That the Third International American Conference shall address to the Presidents of the United States of America and of the United States of Mexico a note in which the conference which is being held at Rio expresses its satisfaction at the happy results of their mediation for the celebration of peace between the Republics of Guatemala, Honduras, and Salvador."

This affords an excellent example of one way in which the influence of the United States can properly be exercised for the benefit of the peoples of the Western Hemisphere; that is, by action taken in concert with other American republics and therefore free from those suspicions and prejudices which might attach if the action were taken by one alone. In this way it is possible to exercise a powerful influence toward the substitution of considerate action in the spirit of justice for the insurrectionary or international violence which has hitherto been so great a hindrance to the development of many of our neighbors. Repeated examples of united action by several or many American republics in favor of peace, by urging cool and reasonable, instead of excited and belligerent, treatment of international controversies, can not fail to promote the growth of a general public opinion among the American nations which will elevate the standards of international action, strengthen the sense of international duty among governments, and tell in favor of the peace of mankind.

I have just returned from a trip to Panama and shall report to you at length later on the whole subject of the Panama Canal.

The Algeciras Convention, which was signed by the United States as well as by most of the powers of Europe, supersedes the previous convention of 1880, which was also signed both by the United States and a majority of the European powers. This treaty confers upon us equal commercial rights with all European countries and does not entail a single obligation of any kind upon us, and I earnestly hope it may be speedily ratified. To refuse to ratify it would merely mean that we forfeited our commercial rights in Morocco and would not achieve another object of any kind. In the event of such refusal we would be left for the first time in a hundred and twenty years without any commercial treaty with Morocco; and this at a time when we are everywhere seeking new markets and outlets for trade.

The destruction of the Pribilof Islands fur seals by pelagic sealing still continues. The herd which, according to the surveys made in 1874 by direction of the Congress, numbered 4,700,000, and which, according to the survey of both American and Canadian commissioners in 1891, amounted to 1,000,000, has now been reduced to about 180,000. This result has been brought about by Canadian and some other sealing vessels killing the female seals while in the water during their annual pilgrimage to and from the south, or in search of food. As a rule the female seal when killed is pregnant, and also has an unweaned pup on land, so that, for each skin taken by pelagic sealing, as a rule, three lives are destroyed—the mother, the unborn offspring, and the nursing pup, which is left to starve to death. No damage whatever is done to the herd by the carefully regulated killing on land; the custom of pelagic sealing is solely responsible for all of the present evil, and is alike indefensible from the economic standpoint and from the standpoint of humanity.

In 1896 over 16,000 young seals were found dead from starvation on the Pribilof Islands. In 1897 it was estimated that since pelagic sealing began upward of 400,000 adult female seals had been killed at sea, and over 300,000 young seals had died of starvation as the result. The revolting barbarity of such a practise, as well as the wasteful destruction which it involves, needs no demonstration and is its own condemnation. The Bering Sea Tribunal, which sat in Paris in 1893, and which decided against the claims of the United States to exclusive jurisdiction in the waters of Bering Sea and to a property right in the fur seals when outside of the three-mile limit, determined also upon certain regulations which the Tribunal considered sufficient for the proper protection and preservation of the fur seal in, or habitually resorting to, the Bering Sea. The Tribunal by its regulations established a close season, from the 1st of May to the 31st of July, and excluded all killing in the waters within 60 miles around the Pribilof Islands. They also provided that the regulations which they had determined upon, with a view to the protection and preservation of the seals, should be submitted every five years to new examination, so as to enable both interested Governments to consider whether, in the light of past experience, there was occasion for any modification thereof.

The regulations have proved plainly inadequate to accomplish the object of protection and preservation of the fur seals, and for a long time this Government has been trying in vain to secure from Great Britain such revision and modification of the regulations as were contemplated and provided for by the award of the Tribunal of Paris.

The process of destruction has been accelerated during recent years by the appearance of a number of Japanese vessels engaged in pelagic sealing. As these vessels have not been bound even by the inadequate limitations prescribed by the Tribunal of Paris, they have paid no attention either to the close season or to the sixty-mile limit imposed upon the Canadians, and have prosecuted their work up to the very islands themselves. On July 16 and 17 the crews from several Japanese vessels made raids upon the island of St. Paul, and before they were beaten off by the very meager and insufficiently armed guard, they succeeded in killing several hundred seals and carrying off the skins of most of them. Nearly all the seals killed were females and the work was done with frightful barbarity. Many of the seals appear to have been skinned alive and many were found half skinned and still alive. The raids were repelled only by the use of firearms, and five of the raiders were killed, two were wounded, and twelve captured, including the two wounded. Those captured have since been tried and sentenced to imprisonment. An attack of this kind had been wholly unlookt for, but such provision of vessels, arms, and ammunition will now be made that its repetition will not be found profitable.

Suitable representations regarding the incident have been made to the Government of Japan, and we are assured that all practicable measures will be taken by that country to prevent any recurrence of the outrage. On our part, the guard on the island will be increased and better equipped and organized, and a better revenue-cutter patrol service about the islands will be established; next season a United States war vessel will also be sent there.

We have not relaxed our efforts to secure an agreement with Great Britain for adequate protection of the seal herd, and negotiations with Japan for the same purpose are in progress.

The laws for the protection of the seals within the jurisdiction of the United States need revision and amendment. Only the islands of St. Paul and St. George are now, in terms, included in the Government reservation, and the other islands are also to be included. The landing of aliens as well as citizens upon the islands, without a permit from the Department of Commerce and Labor, for any purpose except in case of stress of weather or for water, should be prohibited under adequate penalties. The approach of vessels for the excepted purposes should be regulated. The authority of the Government agents on the islands should be enlarged, and the chief agent should have the powers of a committing magistrate. The entrance of a vessel into the territorial waters surrounding the islands with intent to take seals should be made a criminal offense and cause of forfeiture. Authority for seizures in such cases should be given and the presence on any such vessel of seals or sealskins, or the paraphernalia for taking them, should be made *prima facie* evidence of such intent. I recommend what legislation is needed to accomplish these ends; and I commend to your attention the report of Mr. Sims, of the Department of Commerce and Labor, on this subject.

In case we are compelled to abandon the hope of making arrangements with other governments to put an end to the hideous cruelty now incident to pelagic sealing, it will be a question for your serious consideration how far we should continue to protect and maintain the seal herd on land with the result of continuing such a practise, and whether it is not better to end the practice by exterminating the herd ourselves in the most humane way possible.

In my last message I advised you that the Emperor of Russia had taken the initiative in bringing about a second peace conference at The Hague. Under the guidance of Russia the arrangement of the preliminaries for such a conference has been progressing during the past year. Progress has necessarily been slow, owing to the great number of countries to be consulted upon every question that has arisen. It is a matter of satisfaction that all of the American Republics have now, for the first time, been invited to join in the proposed conference.

The close connection between the subjects to be taken up by the Red Cross Conference held at Geneva last summer and the subjects which naturally would come before The Hague Conference made it apparent that it was desirable to have the work of the Red Cross Conference completed and considered by the different powers before the meeting at The Hague. The Red Cross Conference ended its labors on the 6th day of July, and the revised and amended convention, which was signed by the American delegates, will be promptly laid before the Senate.

By the special and highly appreciated courtesy of the Governments of Russia and the Netherlands, a proposal to call The Hague Conference together at a time which would conflict with the Conference of the American Republics at Rio de Janeiro in August was laid aside. No other date has yet been suggested. A tentative program for the conference has been proposed by the Government of Russia, and the subjects which it enumerates are undergoing careful examination and consideration in preparation for the conference.

It must ever be kept in mind that war is not merely justifiable, but imperative, upon honorable men, upon an honorable nation, where peace can only be obtained by the sacrifice of conscientious conviction or of national welfare. Peace is normally a great good, and normally it coincides with righteousness; but it is righteousness and not peace which should bind the conscience of a nation as it should bind the conscience of an individual; and neither a nation nor an individual can surrender conscience to another's keeping. Neither can a nation, which is an entity, and which does not die as individuals die, refrain from taking thought for the interest of the generations that are to come, no less than for the interest of the generation of to-day; and no public men have a right, whether from shortsightedness, from selfish indifference, or from sentimentality, to sacrifice national interests which are vital in character. A just war is in the long run far better for a nation's soul than the most prosperous peace obtained by acquiescence in wrong or injustice. Moreover, tho it is criminal for a nation not to prepare for war, so that it may escape the dreadful consequences of being defeated in war, yet it must always be remembered that even to be defeated in war may be far better than not to have fought at all. As has been well and finely said, a beaten nation is not necessarily a disgraced nation; but the nation or man is disgraced if the obligation to defend right is shirked.

We should as a nation do everything in our power for the cause of honorable peace. It is morally as indefensible for a nation to commit a wrong upon another nation, strong or weak, as for an individual thus to wrong his fellows. We should do all in our power to hasten the day when there shall be peace among the nations—a peace based upon justice and not upon cowardly submission to wrong. We can accomplish a good deal in this direction, but we can not accomplish everything, and the penalty of attempting to do too much would almost inevitably be to do worse than nothing; for it must be remembered that fantastic extremists are not in reality leaders of the causes which they espouse, but are ordinarily those who do most to hamper the real leaders of the cause and to damage the cause itself. As yet there is no likelihood of establishing any kind of international power, of whatever sort, which can effectively check wrongdoing, and in these circumstances it would be both a foolish and an evil thing for a great and free nation to deprive itself of the power to protect its own rights and even in exceptional cases to stand up for the rights of others. Nothing would more promote iniquity, nothing would further defer the reign upon earth of peace and righteousness, than for the free and enlightened peoples which, tho with much stumbling and many shortcomings, nevertheless strive toward justice, deliberately to render themselves powerless while leaving every despotism and barbarism armed and able to work their wicked will. The chance for the settlement of disputes peacefully, by arbitration, now depends mainly upon the possession by the nations that mean to do right of sufficient armed strength to make their purpose effective.

The United States Navy is the surest guarantor of peace which this country possesses. It is earnestly to be wisht that we would profit by the teachings of history in this matter. A strong and wise people will study its own failures no less than its triumphs, for there is wisdom to be learned from the study of both, of the mistake as well as of the success. For this purpose nothing could be more instructive than a rational study of the war of 1812, as it is told, for instance, by Captain Mahan. There was only one way in which that war could have been avoided. If during the preceding twelve years a navy relatively as strong as that which this country now has had been built up, and an army provided relatively as good as that which the country now has, there never would have been the slightest necessity of fighting the war; and if the necessity had arisen the war would under such circumstances have ended with our speedy and overwhelming triumph. But our people during those twelve years refused to make any preparations whatever, regarding either the Army or the Navy. They saved a million or two of dollars by so doing; and in mere money paid a hundredfold for each million they thus saved during the three years of war which followed—a war which brought untold suffering upon our people, which at one time threatened the gravest national disaster, and which, in spite of the necessity of waging it, resulted merely in what was in effect a drawn battle, while the balance of defeat and triumph was almost even.

I do not ask that we continue to increase our Navy. I ask merely that it be maintained at its present strength; and this can be done only if we replace the obsolete and outworn ships by new and good ones, the equals of any afloat in any navy. To stop building ships for one year means that for that year the Navy goes back instead of forward. The old battle ship Texas, for instance, would now be of little service in a stand-up fight with a powerful adversary. The old double-turret monitors have outworn their usefulness, while it was a waste of money to build the modern single-turret monitors. All these ships should be replaced by others; and this can be done by a well-settled program of providing for the building each year of at least one first-class battle ship equal in size and speed to any that any nation is at the same time building; the armament presumably to consist of as large a number as possible of very heavy guns of one caliber, together with smaller guns to repel torpedo attack; while there should be heavy armor, turbine engines, and in short, every modern device. Of course, from time to time, cruisers, colliers, torpedo-boat destroyers or torpedo boats, will have to be built also. All this, be it remembered, would not increase our Navy, but would merely keep it at its present strength. Equally of course, the ships will be absolutely useless if the men aboard them are not so trained that they can get the best possible service out of the formidable but delicate and complicated mechanisms intrusted to their care. The marksmanship of our men has so improved during the last five years that I deem it within bounds to say that the Navy is more than twice as efficient, ship for ship, as half a decade ago. The Navy can only attain proper efficiency if enough officers and men are provided, and if these officers and men are given the chance (and required to take advantage of it) to stay continually at sea and to exercise the fleets singly and above all in squadron, the exercise to be of every kind and to include unceasing practise at the guns, conducted under conditions that will test marksmanship in time of war.

In both the Army and the Navy there is urgent need that everything possible should be done to maintain the highest standard for the personnel, alike as regards the officers and the enlisted men. I do not believe that in any service there is a finer body of enlisted men and of junior officers than we have in both the Army and the Navy, including the Marine Corps. All possible encouragement to the enlisted men should be given, in pay and otherwise, and everything practicable done to render the service attractive to men of the right type. They should be held to the strictest discharge of their duty, and in them a spirit should be encouraged which demands not the mere performance of duty, but the performance of far more than duty, if it conduces to the honor and the interest of the American nation; and in return the amplest consideration should be theirs.

West Point and Annapolis already turn out excellent officers. We do not need to have these schools made more scholastic. On the contrary we should never lose sight of the fact that the aim of each school is to turn out a man who shall be above everything else a fighting man. In the Army in particular it is not necessary that either the cavalry or infantry officer should have special mathematical ability. Probably in both schools the best part of the education is the high standard of character and of professional morale which it confers.

But in both services there is urgent need for the establishment of a principle of selection which will eliminate men after a certain age if they can not be promoted from the subordinate ranks, and which will bring into the higher ranks fewer men, and these at an earlier age. This principle of selection will be objected to by good men of mediocre capacity, who are fitted to do well while young in the lower positions, but who are not fitted to do well when at an advanced age they come into positions of command and of great responsibility. But the desire of these men to be promoted to positions which they are not competent to fill should not weigh against the interest of the Navy and the country. At present our men, especially in the Navy, are kept far too long in the junior grades, and then, at much too advanced an age, are put quickly thru the senior grades, often not attaining to these senior grades until they are too old to be of real use in them; and if they are of real use, being put thru them so quickly that little benefit to the Navy comes from their having been in them at all.

The Navy has one great advantage over the Army in the fact that the officers of high rank are actually trained in the continual performance of their duties; that is, in the management of the battle ships and armored cruisers gathered into fleets. This is not true of the army officers, who rarely have corresponding chances to exercise command over troops under service conditions. The conduct of the Spanish war showed the lamentable loss of life, the useless extravagance, and the inefficiency certain to result, if during peace the high officials of the War and Navy Departments are praised and rewarded only if they save money at no matter what cost to the efficiency of the service, and if the higher officers are given no chance whatever to exercise and practise command. For years prior to the Spanish war the Secretaries of War were praised chiefly if they practised economy; which economy, especially in connection with the quartermaster, commissary, and medical departments, was directly responsible for most of the mismanagement that occurred in the war itself—and parenthetically be it observed that the very people who clamored for the misdirected economy in the first place were foremost to denounce the mismanagement, loss, and suffering which were primarily due to this same misdirected economy and to the lack of preparation it involved. There should soon be an increase in the number of men for our coast defenses; these men should be of the right type and properly trained; and there should therefore be an increase of pay for certain skilled grades, especially in the coast artillery. Money should be appropriated to permit troops to be massed in body and exercised in maneuvers, particularly in marching. Such exercise during the summer just past has been of incalculable benefit to the Army and should under no circumstances be discontinued. If on these practise marches and in these maneuvers elderly officers prove unable to bear the strain, they should be retired at once, for the fact is conclusive as to their unfitness for war; that is, for the only purpose because of which they should be allowed to stay in the service. It is a real misfortune to have scores of small company or regimental posts scattered thruout the country; the Army should be gathered in a few brigade or division posts; and the generals should be practised in handling the men in masses. Neglect to provide for all of this means to incur the risk of future disaster and disgrace.

The readiness and efficiency of both the Army and Navy in dealing with the recent sudden crisis in Cuba illustrate afresh their value to the Nation. This readiness and efficiency would have been very much less had it not been for the existence of the General Staff in the Army and the General Board in the Navy; both are essential to the proper development and use of our military forces afloat and ashore. The troops that were sent to Cuba were handled flawlessly. It was the swiftest mobilization and dispatch of troops over sea ever accomplished by our Government. The expedition landed completely equipped and ready for immediate service, several of its organizations hardly remaining in Havana over night before splitting up into detachments and going to their several posts. It was a fine demonstration of the value and efficiency of the General Staff. Similarly, it was owing in large part to the General Board that the Navy was able at the outset to meet the Cuban crisis with such instant efficiency; ship after ship appearing on the shortest notice at any threatened point, while the Marine Corps in particular performed indispensable service. The Army and Navy War Colleges are of incalculable value to the two services, and they cooperate with constantly increasing efficiency and importance.

The Congress has most wisely provided for a National Board for the promotion of rifle practise. Excellent results have already come from this law, but it does not go far enough. Our Regular Army is so small that in any great war we would have to trust mainly to volunteers; and in such event these volunteers should already know how to shoot; for if a soldier has the fighting edge, and ability to take care of himself in the open, his efficiency on the line of battle is almost directly proportionate to excellence in marksmanship. We should establish shooting galleries in all the large public and military schools, should maintain national target ranges in different parts of the country, and should in every way encourage the formation of rifle clubs thruout all parts of the land. The little Republic of Switzerland offers us an excellent example in all matters connected with building up an efficient citizen soldiery.

SEVENTH ANNUAL MESSAGE.

WHITE HOUSE, *Dec. 3, 1907*

To the Senate and House of Representatives:

No nation has greater resources than ours, and I think it can be truthfully said that the citizens of no nation possess greater energy and industrial ability. In no nation are the fundamental business conditions sounder than in ours at this very moment; and it is foolish, when such is the case, for people to hoard money instead of keeping it in sound banks; for it is such hoarding that is the immediate occasion of money stringency. Moreover, as a rule, the business of our people is conducted with honesty and probity, and this applies alike to farms and factories, to railroads and banks, to all our legitimate commercial enterprises.

In any large body of men, however, there are certain to be some who are dishonest, and if the conditions are such that these men prosper or commit their misdeeds with impunity, their example is a very evil thing for the community. Where these men are business men of great sagacity and of temperament both unscrupulous and reckless, and where the conditions are such that they act without supervision or control and at first without effective check from public opinion, they delude many innocent people into making investments or embarking in kinds of business that are really unsound. When the misdeeds of these successfully dishonest men are discovered, suffering comes not only upon them, but upon the innocent men whom they have misled. It is a painful awakening, whenever it occurs; and, naturally, when it does occur those who suffer are apt to forget that the longer it was deferred the more painful it would be. In the effort to punish the guilty it is both wise and proper to endeavor so far as possible to minimize the distress of those who have been misled by the guilty. Yet it is not possible to refrain because of such distress from striving to put an end to the misdeeds that are the ultimate causes of the suffering, and, as a means to this end, where possible to punish those responsible for them. There may be honest differences of opinion as to many governmental policies; but surely there can be no such differences as to the need of unflinching perseverance in the war against successful dishonesty.

In my Message to the Congress on December 5, 1905, I said:

"If the folly of man mars the general well-being, then those who are innocent of the folly will have to pay part of the penalty incurred by those who are guilty of the folly. A panic brought on by the speculative folly of part of the business community would hurt the whole business community; but such stoppage of welfare, though it might be severe, would not be lasting. In the long run, the one vital factor in the permanent prosperity of the country is the high individual character of the average American worker, the average American citizen, no matter whether his work be mental or manual, whether he be farmer or wage-worker, business man or professional man.

"In our industrial and social system the interests of all men are so closely intertwined that in the immense majority of cases a straight-dealing man, who by his efficiency, by his ingenuity and industry, benefits himself, must also benefit others. Normally, the man of great productive capacity who becomes rich by guiding the labor of many other men does so by enabling them to produce more than they could produce without his guidance; and both he and they share in the benefit, which comes also to the public at large. The superficial fact that the sharing may be unequal must never blind us to the underlying fact that there is this sharing, and that the benefit comes in some degree to each man concerned. Normally, the wageworker, the man of small means, and the average consumer, as well as the average producer, are all alike helped by making conditions such that the man of exceptional business ability receives an exceptional reward for his ability Something can be done by legislation to help the general prosperity; but no such help of a permanently beneficial character can be given to the less able and less fortunate save as the results of a policy which shall inure to the advantage of all industrious and efficient people who act decently; and this is only another way of saying that any benefit which comes to the less able and less fortunate must of necessity come even more to the more able and more fortunate. If, therefore, the less fortunate man is moved by envy of his more fortunate brother to strike at the conditions under which they have both, though unequally, prospered, the result will assuredly be that while damage may come to the one struck at, it will visit with an even heavier load the one who strikes the blow. Taken as a whole, we must all go up or go down together.

"Yet, while not merely admitting, but insisting upon this, it is also true that where there is no governmental restraint or supervision some of the exceptional men use their energies, not in ways that are for the common good, but in ways which tell against this common good. The fortunes amassed through corporate organization are now so large, and vest such power in those that wield them, as to make it a matter of necessity to give to the sovereign—that is, to the Government, which represents the people as a whole—some effective power of supervision over their corporate use. In order to insure a healthy social and industrial life, every big corporation should be held responsible by, and be accountable to, some sovereign strong enough to control its conduct. I am in no sense hostile to corporations. This is an age of combination, and any effort to prevent all combination will be not only useless, but in the end vicious, because of the contempt for law which the failuure to enforce law inevitably produces. We should, moreover, recognize in cordial and ample fashion the immense good effected by corporate agencies in a country such as ours, and the wealth of intellect, energy, and fidelity devoted to their service, and therefore normally to the service of the public, by their officers and directors. The corporation has come to stay, just as the trade union has come to stay. Each can do and has done great good. Each should be favored so long as it does good. But each should be sharply checked where it acts against law and justice.

"* * * The makers of our National Constitution provided especially that the regulation of interstate commerce should come within the sphere of the General Government. The arguments in favor of their taking this stand were even then overwhelming. But they are far stronger to-day, in view of the enormous development of great business agencies, usually corporate in form. Experience has shown conclusively that it is useless to try to get any adequate regulation and supervision of these great corporations by State action. Such regulation and supervision can only be effectively exercised by a sovereign whose jurisdiction is coextensive with the field of work of the corporations —that is, by the National Government. I believe that this regulation and supervision can be obtained by the enactment of law by the Congress. * * * Our steady aim should be by legislation, cautiously and carefully undertaken, but resolutely persevered in, to assert the sovereignty of the National Government by affirmative action.

"This is only in form an innovation. In substance it is merely a restoration; for from the earliest time such regulation of industrial activities has been recognized in the action of the lawmaking bodies; and all that I propose is to meet the changed conditions in such manner as will prevent the Commonwealth abdicating the power it has always possessed, not only in this country, but also in England before and since this country became a separate nation.

"It has been a misfortune that the National laws on this subject have hitherto been of a negative or prohibitive rather than an affirmative kind, and still more that they have in part sought to prohibit what could not be effectively prohibited, and have in part in their prohibitions confounded what should be allowed and what should not be allowed. It is generally useless to try to prohibit all restraint on competition, whether this restraint be reasonable or unreasonable; and where it is not useless it is generally hurtful. * * * The successful prosecution of one device to evade the law immediately develops another device to accomplish the same purpose. What is needed is not sweeping prohibition of every arrangement, good or bad, which may tend to restrict competition, but such adequate supervision and regulation as will prevent any restriction of competition from being to the detriment of the public, as well as such supervision and regulation as will prevent other abuses in no way connected with restriction of competition."

I have called your attention in these quotations to what I have already said because I am satisfied that it is the duty of the National Government to embody in action the principles thus expressed.

No small part of the trouble that we have comes from carrying to an extreme the national virtue of self-reliance, of independence in initiative and action. It is wise to conserve this virtue and to provide for its fullest exercise, compatible with seeing that liberty does not become a liberty to wrong others. Unfortunately, this is the kind of liberty that the lack of all effective regulation inevitably breeds. The founders of the Constitution provided that the National Government should have complete and sole control of interstate commerce. There was then practically no interstate business save such as was conducted by water, and this the National Government at once proceeded to regulate in thoroughgoing and effective fashion. Conditions have now so wholly changed that the interstate commerce by water is insignificant compared with the amount that goes by land, and almost all big business concerns are now engaged in interstate commerce. As a result, it can be but partially and imperfectly controlled or regulated by the action of any one of the several States; such action inevitably tending to be either too drastic or else too lax, and in either case ineffective for purposes of justice. Only the National Government can in thoroughgoing fashion exercise the needed control. This does not mean that there should be any extension of Federal authority, for such authority already exists under the Constitution in amplest and most far-reaching form; but it does mean that there should be an extension of Federal activity. This is not advocating centralization. It is merely looking facts in the face, and realizing that centralization in business has already come and can not be avoided or undone, and that the public at large can only protect itself from certain evil effects of this business centralization by providing better methods for the exercise of control through the authority already centralized in the National Government by the Constitution itself. There must be no halt in the healthy constructive course of action which this Nation has elected to pursue, and has steadily pursued, during the last six years, as shown both in the legislation of the Congress and the administration of the law by the Department of Justice. The most vital need is in connection with the railroads. As to these, in my judgment there should now be either a national incorporation act or a law licensing railway companies to engage in interstate commerce upon certain conditions. The law should be so framed as to give to the Interstate Commerce Commission power to pass upon the future issue of securities, while ample means should be provided to enable the Commission, whenever in its judgment it is necessary, to make a physical valuation of any railroad. As I stated in my Message to the Congress a year ago, railroads should be given power to enter into agreements, subject to these argreements being made public in minute detail and to the consent of the Interstate Commerce Commission being first obtained. Until the National Government assumes proper control of interstate commerce, in the exercise of the authority it already possesses, it will be impossible either to give to or to get from the railroads full justice. The railroads and all other great corporations will do well to recognize that this control must come; the only question is as to what governmental body can most wisely exercise it. The courts will determine the limits within which the Federal authority can exercise it, and there will still remain ample work within each State for the railway commission of that State; and the National Interstate Commerce Commission will work in harmony with the several State commissions, each within its own province, to achieve the desired end.

Moreover, in my judgment there should be additional legislation looking to the proper control of the great business concerns engaged in interstate business, this control to be exercised for their own benefit and prosperity no less than for the protection of investors and of the general public. As I have repeatedly said in Messages to the Congress and elsewhere, experience has definitely shown not merely the unwisdom but the futility of endeavoring to put a stop to all business combinations. Modern industrial conditions are such that combination is not only necessary but inevitable. It is so in the world of business just as it is so in the world of labor, and it is as idle to desire to put an end to all corporations, to all big combinations of capital, as to desire to put an end to combinations of labor. Corporation and labor union alike have come to stay. Each if properly managed is a source of good and not evil. Whenever in either there is evil, it should be promptly held to account; but it should receive hearty encouragement so long as it is properly managed. It is profoundly immoral to put or keep on the statute books a law, nominally in the interest of public morality. that really puts a premium upon public immorality, by undertaking to forbid honest men from doing what must be done under modern business conditions, so that the law itself provides that its own infraction must be the condition precedent upon business success. To aim at the accomplishment of too much usually means the accomplishment of too little, and often the doing of positive damage. In my Message to the Congress a year ago, in speaking of the antitrust laws, I said:

"The actual working of our laws has shown that the effort to prohibit all combination, good or bad, is noxious where it is not ineffective. Combination of capital, like combination of labor, is a necessary element in our present industrial system. It is not possible completely to prevent it; and if it were possible, such complete prevention would do damage to the body politic. What we need is not vainly to try to prevent all combination, but to secure such rigorous and adequate control and supervision of the combinations as to prevent their injuring the public, or existing in such forms as inevitably to threaten injury. * * * It is unfortunate that our present laws should forbid all combinations instead of sharply discriminating between those combinations which do evil. * * * Often railroads would like to combine for the purpose of preventing a big shipper from maintaining improper advantages at the expense of small shippers and of the general public. Such a combination, instead of being forbidden by law, should be favored. * * * It is a public evil to have on the statute books a law incapable of full enforcement, because both judges and juries realize that its full enforcement would destroy the business of the country; for the result is to make decent men violators of the law against their will, and to put a premium on the behavior of the willful wrongdoers. Such a result in turn tends to throw the decent man and the willful wrongdoer into close association, and in the end to drag down the former to the latter's level; for the man who becomes a lawbreaker in one way unhappily tends to lose all respect for law and to be willing to break it in many ways. No more scathing condemnation could be visited upon a law than is contained in the words of the Interstate Commerce Commission when, in commenting upon the fact that the numerous joint traffic associations do technically violate the law, they say: 'The decision of the United States Supreme Court in the Trans-Missouri case and the Joint Traffic Association case has produced no practical effect upon the railway operations of the country. Such associations, in fact, exist now as they did before these decisions, and with the same general effect. In justice to all parties, we ought probably to add that it is difficult to see how our interstate railways could be operated with due regard to the interest of the shipper and the railway without concerted action of the kind afforded through these asociations.'

"This means that the law as construed by the Supreme Court is such that the business of the country can not be conducted without breaking it."

As I have elsewhere said:

'All this is substantially what I have said over and over again. Surely it ought not to be necessary to say that it in no shape or way represents any hostility to corporations as such. On the contrary, it means a frank recognition of the fact that combinations of capital, like combinations of labor, are a natural result of modern conditions and of our National development. As far as in my ability lies my endeavor is and will be to prevent abuse of power by either and to favor both so long as they do well. The aim of the National Government is quite as much to favor and protect honest corporations, honest business men of wealth, as to bring to justice those individuals and corporations representing dishonest methods. Most certainly there will be no relaxation by the Government authorities in the effort to get at any great railroad wrecker—any man who by clever swindling devices robs investors, oppresses wage-workers, and does injustice to the general public. But any such move as this is in the interest of honest railway operators, of honest corporations, and of those who, when they invest their small savings in stocks and bonds, wish to be assured that these will represent money honestly expended for legitimate business purposes. To confer upon the National Government the power for which I ask would be a check upon overcapitalization and upon the clever gamblers who benefit by overcapitalization. But it alone would mean an increase in the value, an increase in the safety of the stocks and bonds of law-abiding, honestly managed railroads, and would render it far easier to market their securities. I believe in proper publicity. There has been complaint of some of the investigations recently carried on, but those who complain should put the blame where it belongs—upon the misdeeds which are done in darkness and not upon the investigations which brought them to light. The Administration is responsible for turning on the light, but it is not responsible for what the light showed. I ask for full power to be given the Federal Government, because no single State can by legislation effectually cope with these powerful corporations engaged in interstate commerce, and, while doing them full justice, exact from them in return full justice to others. The conditions of railroad activity, the conditions of our immense interstate commerce, are such as to make the Central Government alone competent to exercise full supervision and control.

"The grave abuses in individual cases of railroad management in the past represent wrongs not merely to the general public, but, above all, wrongs to fair-dealing and honest corporations and men of wealth, because they excite a popular anger and distrust which from the very nature of the case tends to include in the sweep of its resentment good and bad alike. From the standpoint of the public I can not too earnestly say that as soon as the natural and proper resentment aroused by these abuses becomes indiscriminate and unthinking, it also becomes not merely unwise and unfair, but calculated to defeat the very ends which those feeling it have in view. There has been plenty of dishonest work by corporations in the past. There will not be the slightest let-up in the effort to hunt down and punish every dishonest man. But the bulk of our business is honestly done. In the natural indignation the people feel over the dishonesty, it is essential that they should not lose their heads and get drawn into an indiscriminate raid upon all corporations, all people of wealth, whether they do well or ill. Out of any such wild movement good will not come, can not come, and never has come. On the contrary, the surest way to invite reaction is to follow the lead of either demagogue or visionary in a sweeping assault upon property values and upon public confidence, which would work incalculable damage in the business world and would produce such distrust of the agitators that in the revulsion the distrust would extend to honest men who, in sincere and same fashion, are trying to remedy the evils."

The antitrust law should not be repealed; but it should be made both more efficient and more in harmony with actual conditions. It should be so amended as to forbid only the kind of combination which does harm to the general public, such amendment to be accompanied by, or to be an incident of, a grant of supervisory power to the Government over these big concerns engaged in interstate business. This should be accompanied by provision for the compulsory publication of accounts and the subjection of books and papers to the inspection of the Government officials. A beginning has already been made for such supervision by the establishment of the Bureau of Corporations.

The antitrust law should not prohibit combinations that do no injustice to the public, still less those the existence of which is on the whole of benefit to the public. But even if this feature of the law were abolished, there would remain as an equally objectionable feature the difficulty and delay now incident to its enforcement. The Government must now submit to irksome and repeated delay before obtaining a final decision of the courts upon proceedings instituted, and even a favorable decree may mean an empty victory. Moreover, to attempt to control these corporations by lawsuits means to impose upon both the Department of Justice and the courts an impossible burden; it is not feasible to carry on more than a limited number of such suits. Such a law to be really effective must of course be administered by an executive body, and not merely by means of lawsuits. The design should be to prevent the abuses incident to the creation of unhealthy and improper combinations, instead of waiting until they are in existence and then attempting to destroy them by civil or criminal proceedings.

A combination should not be tolerated if it abuse the power acquired by combination to the public detriment. No corporation or association of any kind should be permitted to engage in foreign or interstate commerce that is formed for the purpose of, or whose operations create, a monopoly or general control of the production, sale, or distribution of any one or more of the prime necessities of life or articles of general use and necessity. Such combinations are against public policy; they violate the common law; the doors of the courts are closed to those who are parties to them, and I believe the Congress can close the channels of interstate commerce against them for its protection. The law should make its prohibitions and permissions as clear and definite as possible, leaving the least possible room for arbitrary action, or allegation of such action, on the part of the Executive, or of divergent interpretations by the courts. Among the points to be aimed at should be the prohibition of unhealthy competition, such as by rendering service at an actual loss for the purpose of crushing out competition, the prevention of inflation of capital, and the prohibition of a corporation's making exclusive trade with itself a condition of having any trade with itself. Reasonable agreements between, or combinations of, corporations should be permitted, provided they are submitted to and approved by some appropriate Government body.

The Congress has the power to charter corporations to engage in interstate and foreign commerce, and a general law can be enacted under the provisions of which existing corporations could take out Federal charters and new Federal corporations could be created. An essential provision of such a law should be a method of predetermining by some Federal board or commission whether the applicant for a Federal charter was an association or combination within the restrictions of the Federal law. Provision should also be made for complete publicity in all matters affecting the public and complete protection to the investing public and the shareholders in the matter of issuing corporate securities. If an incorporation law is not deemed advisable, a license act for big interstate corporations might be enacted; or a combination of the two might be tried. The supervision established might be analogous to that now exercised over national banks. At least, the antitrust act should be supplemented by specific prohibitions of the methods which experience has shown have been of most service in enabling monopolistic combinations to crush out competition. The real owners of a corporation should be compelled to do business in their own name. The right to hold stock in other corporations should hereafter be denied to interstate corporations, unless on approval by the Government officials, and a prerequisite to such approval should be the listing with the Government of all owners and stockholders, both by the corporation owning such stock and by the corporation in which such stock is owned.

To confer upon the National Government, in connection with the amendment I advocate in the antitrust law, power of supervision over big business concerns engaged in interstate commerce, would benefit them as it has benefited the national banks. In the recent business crisis it is noteworthy that the institutions which failed were institutions which were not under the supervision and control of the National Government. Those which were under National control stood the test.

National control of the kind above advocated would be to the benefit of every well-managed railway. From the standpoint of the public there is need for additional tracks, additional terminals, and improvements in the actual handling of the railroads, and all this as rapidly as possible. Ample, safe, and speedy transportation facilities are even more necessary than cheap transportation. Therefore, there is need for the investment of money which will provide for all these things while at the same time securing as far as is possible better wages and shorter hours for their employees. Therefore, while there must be just and reasonable regulation of rates, we should be the first to protest against any arbitrary and unthinking movement to cut them down without the fullest and most careful consideration of all interests concerned and of the actual needs of the situation. Only a special body of men acting for the National Government under authority conferred upon it by the Congress ic competent to pass judgment on such a matter.

Those who fear, from any reason, the extension of Federal activity will do well to study the history not only of the national banking act but of the pure-food law, and notably the meat inspection law recently enacted. The pure-food law was opposed so violently that its passage was delayed for a decade; yet it has worked unmixed and immediate good. The meat inspection law was even more violently assailed; and the same men who now denounce the attitude of the National Government in seeking to oversee and control the workings of interstate common carriers and business concerns, then asserted that we were "discrediting and ruining a great American industry." Two years have not elapsed, and already it has become evident that the great benefit the law confers upon the public is accompanied by an equal benefit to the reputable packing establishments. The latter are better off under the law than they were without it. The benefit to interstate common carriers and business concerns from the legislation I advocate would be equally marked.

Incidentally, in the passage of the pure-food law the action of the various State food and dairy commissioners showed in striking fashion how much good for the whole people results from the hearty cooperation of the Federal and State officials in securing a given reform. It is primarily to the action of these State commissioners that we owe the enactment of this law; for they aroused the people, first to demand the enactment and enforcement of State laws on the subject, and then the enactment of the Federal law, without which the State laws were largely ineffective. There must be the closest cooperation between the National and State governments in administering these laws.

In my Message to the Congress a year ago I spoke as follows of the currency:

"I especially call your attention to the condition of our currency laws. The national-bank act has ably served a great purpose in aiding the enormous business development of the country, and within ten years there has been an increase in circulation per capita from $21.41 to $33.08. For several years evidence has been accumulating that additional legislation is needed. The recurrence of each crop season emphasizes the defects of the present laws. There must soon be a revision of them, because to leave them as they are means to incur liability of business disaster. Since your body adjourned there has been a fluctuation in the interest on call money from 2 per cent to 30 per cent, and the fluctuation was even greater during the preceding six months. The Secretary of the Treasury had to step in and by wise action put a stop to the most violent period of oscillation. Even worse than such fluctuation is the advance in commercial rates and the uncertainty felt in the sufficiency of credit even at high rates. All commercial interests suffer during each crop period. Excessive rates for call money in New York attract money from the interior banks into the speculative field. This depletes the fund that would otherwise be available for commercial uses, and commercial borrowers are forced to pay abnormal rates, so that each fall a tax, in the shape of increased interest charges, is placed on the whole commerce of the country.

"The mere statement of these facts shows that our present system is seriously defective. There is need of a change. Unfortunately, however, many of the proposed changes must be ruled from consideration because they are complicated, are not easy of comprehension, and tend to disturb existing rights and interests. We must also rule out any plan which would materially impair the value of the United States 2 per cent bonds now pledged to secure circulation, the issue of which was made under conditions peculiarly creditable to the Treasury. I do not press any especial plan. Various plans have recently been proposed by expert committees of bankers. Among the plans which are possibly feasible and which certainly should receive your consideration is that repeatedly brought to your attention by the present Secretary of the Treasury, the essential features of which have been approved by many prominent bankers and business men. According to this plan national banks should be permitted to issue a specified proportion of their capital in notes of a given kind, the issue to be taxed at so high a rate as to drive the notes back when not wanted in legitimate trade. This plan would not permit the issue of currency to give banks additional profits, but to meet the emergency presented by times of stringency.

"I do not say that this is the right system. I only advance it to emphasize my belief that there is need for the adoption of some system which shall be automatic and open to all sound banks, so as to avoid all possibility of discrimination and favoritism. Such a plan would tend to prevent the spasms of high money and speculation which now obtain in the New York market; for at present there is too much currency at certain seasons of the year, and its accumulation at New York tempts bankers to lend it at low rates for speculative purposes; whereas at other times when the crops are being moved there is urgent need for a large but temporary increase in the currency supply. It must never be forgotten that this question concerns business men generally quite as much as bankers; especially is this true of stockmen, farmers, and business men in the West; for at present at certain seasons of the year the difference in interest rates between the East and the West is from 6 to 10 per cent, whereas in Canada the corresponding difference is but 2 per cent. Any plan must, of course, guard the interests of western and southern bankers as carefully as it guards the interests of New York or Chicago bankers, and must be drawn from the standpoints of the farmer and the merchant no less than from the standpoints of the city banker and the country banker."

I again urge on the Congress the need of immediate attention to this matter. We need a greater elasticity in our currency; provided, of course, that we recognize the even greater need of a safe and secure currency. There must always be the most rigid examination by the National authorities. Provision should be made for an emergency currency. The emergency issue should, of course, be made with an effective guaranty, and upon conditions carefully prescribed by the Government. Such emergency issue must be based on adequate securities approved by the Government, and must be issued under a heavy tax. This would permit currency being issued when the demand for it was urgent, while securing its requirement as the demand fell off. It is worth investigating to determine whether officers and directors of national banks should ever be allowed to loan to themselves. Trust companies should be subject to the same supervision as banks; legislation to this effect should be enacted for the District of Columbia and the Territories.

Yet we must also remember that even the wisest legislation on the subject can only accomplish a certain amount. No legislation can by any possibility guarantee the business community against the results of speculative folly any more than it can guarantee an individual against the results of his extravagance. When an individual mortgages his house to buy an automobile he invites disaster; and when wealthy men, or men who pose as such, or are unscrupulously or foolishly eager to become such, indulge in reckless speculation—especially if it is accompanied by dishonesty—they jeopardize not only their own future but the future of all their innocent fellow-citizens, for they expose the whole business community to panic and distress.

The income account of the Nation is in a most satisfactory condition. For the six fiscal years ending with the 1st of July last, the total expenditures and revenues of the National Government, exclusive of the postal revenues and expenditures, were, in round numbers, revenues, $3,465,000,0000, and expenditures, $3,275,000,000. The net excess of income over expenditures, including in the latter the fifty millions expended for the Panama Canal, was one hundred and ninety million dollars for the six years, an average of about thirty-one millions a year. This represents an approximation between income and outgo which it would be hard to improve. The satisfactory working of the present tariff law has been chiefly responsible for this excellent showing. Nevertheless, there is an evident and constantly growing feeling among our people that the time is rapidly approaching when our system of revenue legislation must be revised.

This country is definitely committed to the protective system and any effort to uproot it could not but cause widespread industrial disaster. In other words, the principle of the present tariff law could not with wisdom be changed. But in a country of such phenomenal growth as ours it is probably well that every dozen years or so the tariff laws should be carefully scrutinized so as to see that no excessive or improper benefits are conferred thereby, that proper revenue is provided, and that our foreign trade is encouraged. There must always be as a minimum a tariff which will not only allow for the collection of an ample revenue but which will at least make good the difference in cost of production here and abroad; that is, the difference in the labor cost here and abroad, for the well-being of the wage-worker must ever be a cardinal point of American policy. The question should be approached purely from a business standpoint; both the time and the manner of the change being such as to arouse the minimum of agitation and disturbance in the business world, and to give the least play for selfish and factional motives. The sole consideration should be to see that the sum total of changes represents the public good. This means that the subject can not with wisdom be dealt with in the year preceding a Presidential election, because as a matter of fact experience has conclusively shown that at such a time it is impossible to get men to treat it from the standpoint of the public good. In my judgment the wise time to deal with the matter is immediately after such election.

When our tax laws are revised the question of an income tax and an inheritance tax should receive the careful attention of our legislators. In my judgment both of these taxes should be part of our system of Federal taxation. I speak diffidently about the income tax because one scheme for an income tax was declared unconstitutional by the Supreme Court; while in addition it is a difficult tax to administer in its practical working, and great care would have to be exercised to see that it was not evaded by the very men whom it was most desirable to have taxed, for if so evaded it would, of course, be worse than no tax at all; as the least desirable of all taxes is the tax which bears heavily upon the honest as compared with the dishonest man. Nevertheless, a graduated income tax of the proper type would be a desirable feature of Federal taxation, and it is to be hoped that one may be devised which the Supreme Court will declare constitutional. The inheritance tax, however, is both a far better method of taxation, and far more important for the purpose of having the fortunes of the country bear in proportion to their increase in size a corresponding increase and burden of taxation. The Government has the absolute right to decide as to the terms upon which a man shall receive a bequest or devise from another, and this point in the devolution of property is especially appropriate for the imposition of a tax. Laws imposing such taxes have repeatedly been placed upon the National statute books and as repeatedly declared constitutional by the courts; and these laws contained the progressive principle, that is, after a certain amount is reached the bequest or gift, in life or death, is increasingly burdened and the rate of taxation is increased in proportion to the remoteness of blood of the man receiving the bequest. These principles are recognized already in the leading civilized nations of the world. In Great Britain all the estates worth $5,000 or less are practically exempt from death duties, while the increase is such that when an estate exceeds five millions of dollars in value and passes to a distant kinsman or stranger in blood the Government receives all told an amount equivalent to nearly a fifth of the whole estate. In France so much of an inheritance as exceeds $10,000,000 pays over a fifth to the State if it passes to a distant relative. The German law is especially interesting to us because it makes the inheritance tax an imperial measure while allotting to the individual States of the Empire a portion of the proceeds and permitting them to impose taxes in addition to those imposed by the Imperial Government. Small inheritances are exempt, but the tax is so sharply progressive that when the inheritance is still not very large, provided it is not an agricultural or a forest land, it is taxed at the rate of 25 per cent if it goes to distant relatives. There is no reason why in the United States the National Government should not impose inheritance taxes in addition to those imposed by the States, and when we last had an inheritance tax about one-half of the States levied such taxes concurrently with the National Government, making a combined maximum rate, in some cases as high as 25 per cent. The French law has one feature which is to be heartily commended. The progressive principle is so applied that each higher rate is imposed only on the excess above the amount subject to the next lower rate; so that each increase of rate will apply only to a certain amount above a certain maximum. The tax should if possible be made to bear more heavily upon those residing without the country than within it. A heavy progressive tax upon a very large fortune is in no way such a tax upon thrift or industry as a like would be on a small fortune. No advantage comes either to the country as a whole or to the individuals inheriting the money by permitting the transmission in their entirety of the enormous fortunes which would be affected by such a tax; and as an incident to its function of revenue raising, such a tax would help to preserve a measurable equality of opportunity for the people of the generations growing to manhood. We have not the slightest sympathy with that socialistic idea which would try to put laziness, thriftlessness and inefficiency on a par with industry, thrift and efficiency; which would strive to break up not merely private property, but what is far more important, the home, the chief prop upon which our whole civilization stands. Such a theory, if ever adopted, would mean the ruin of the entire country—a ruin which would bear heaviest upon the weakest, upon those least able to shift for themselves. But proposals for legislation such as this herein advocated are directly opposed to this class of socialistic theories. Our aim is to recognize what Lincoln pointed out: The fact that there are some respects in which men are obviously not equal; but also to insist that there should be an equality of self-respect and of mutual respect, an equality of rights before the law, and at least an approximate equality in the conditions under which each man obtains the chance to show the stuff that is in him when compared to his fellows.

A few years ago there was loud complaint that the law could not be invoked against wealthy offenders. There is no such complaint now. The course of the Department of Justice during the last few years has been such as to make it evident that no man stands above the law, that no corporation is so wealthy that it can not be held to account. The Department of Justice has been as prompt to proceed against the wealthiest malefactor whose crime was one of greed and cunning as to proceed against the agitator who incites to brutal violence. Everything that can be done under the existing law, and with the existing state of public opinion, which so profoundly influences both the courts and juries, has been done. But the laws themselves need strengthening in more than one important point; they should be made more definite, so that no honest man can be led unwittingly to break them, and so that the real wrongdoer can be readily punished.

Moreover, there must be the public opinion back of the laws or the laws themselves will be of no avail. At present, while the average juryman undoubtedly wishes to see trusts broken up, and is quite ready to fine the corporation itself, he is very reluctant to find the facts proven beyond a reasonable doubt when it comes to sending to jail a member of the business community for indulging in practices which are profoundly unhealthy, but which, unfortunately, the business community has grown to recognize as well-nigh normal. Both the present condition of the law and the present temper of juries render it a task of extreme difficulty to get at the real wrongdoer in any such case, especially by imprisonment. Yet it is from every standpoint far preferable to punish the prime offender by imprisonment rather than to fine the corporation, with the attendant damage to stockholders.

The two great evils in the execution of our criminal laws to-day are sentimentality and technicality. For the latter the remedy must come from the hands of the legislatures, the courts, and the lawyers. The other must depend for its cure upon the gradual growth of a sound public opinion which shall insist that regard for the law and the demands of reason shall control all other influences and emotions in the jury box. Both of these evils must be removed or public discontent with the criminal law will continue.

Instances of abuse in the granting of injunctions in labor disputes continue to occur, and the resentment in the minds of those who feel that thelr rights are being invaded and their liberty of action and of speech unwarrantably restrained continues likewise to grow. Much of the attack on the use of the process of injunction is wholly without warrant; but I am constrained to express the belief that for some of it there is warrant. This question is becoming more and more one of prime importance, and unless the courts will themselves deal with it in effective manner, it is certain ultimately to demand some form of legislative action. It would be most unfortunate for our social welfare if we should permit many honest and law-abiding citizens to feel that they had just cause for regarding our courts with hostility. I earnestly commend to the attention of the Congress this matter, so that some way may be devised which will limit the abuse of injunctions and protect those rights which from time to time it unwarrantably invades. Moreover, discontent is often expressed with the use of the process of injunction by the courts, not only in labor disputes, but where State laws are concerned. I refrain from discussion of this question as I am informed that it will soon receive the consideration of the Supreme Court.

The Federal courts must of course decide ultimately what are the respective spheres of State and Nation in connection with any law, State or National, and they must decide definitely and finally in matters affecting individual citizens, not only as to the rights and wrongs of labor but as to the rights and wrongs of capital; and the National Government must always see that the decision of the court is put into effect. The process of injunction is an essential adjunct of the court's doing its work well; and as preventive measures are always better than remedial, the wise use of this process is from every standpoint commendable. But where it is recklessly or unnecessarily used, the abuse should be censured, above all by the very men who are properly anxious to prevent any effort to shear the courts of this necessary power. The court's decision must be final; the protest is only against the conduct of individual juudges in needlessly anticipating such final decision, or in the tyrannical use of what is nominally a temporary injunction to accomplish what is in fact a permanent decision.

The loss of life and limb from railroad accidents in this country has become appalling. It is a subject of which the National Government should take supervision. It might be well to begin by providing for a Federal inspection of interstate railroads somewhat along the lines of Federal inspection of steamboats, although not going so far; perhaps at first all that it would be necessary to have would be some officer whose duty would be to investigate all accidents on interstate railroads and report in detail the causes thereof. Such an officer should make it his business to get into close touch with railroad operating men so as to become thoroughly familiar with every side of the question, the idea being to work along the lines of the present steamboat inspection law.

The National Government should be a model employer. It should demand the highest quality of service from each of its employees and it should care for all of them properly in return. Congress should adopt legislation providing limited but definite compensation for accidents to all workmen within the scope of the Federal power, including employees of navy yards and arsenals. In other words, a model employers' liability act, far-reaching and thoroughgoing, should be enacted which should apply to all positions, public and private, over which the National Government has jurisdiction. The number of accidents to wage-workers, including those that are preventable and those that are not, has become appalling in the mechanical, manufacturing, and transportation operations of the day. It works grim hardship to the ordinary wage-worker and his family to have the effect of such an accident fall solely upon him; and, on the other hand, there are whole classes of attorneys who exist only by inciting men who may or may not have been wronged to undertake suits for negligence. As a matter of fact a suit for negligence is generally an inadequate remedy for the person injured, while it often causes altogether disproportionate annoyance to the employer. The law should be made such that the payment for accidents by the employer would be automatic instead of being a matter for lawsuits. Workmen should receive certain and definite compensation for all accidents in industry irrespective of negligence. The employer is the agent of the public and on his own responsibililty and for his own profit he serves the public. When he starts in motion agencies which create risks for others, he should take all the ordinary and extraordinary risks involved; and the risk he thus at the moment assumes will ultimately be assumed, as it ought to be, by the general public. Only in this way can the shock of the accident be diffused, instead of falling upon the man or woman least able to bear it, as is now the case. The community at large should share the burdens as well as the benefits of industry. By the proposed law, employers would gain a desirable certainty of obligation and get rid of litigation to determine it, while the workman and his family would be relieved from a crushing load. With such a policy would come increased care, and accidents would be reduced in number. The National laws providing for employers' liability on railroads engaged in interstate commerce and for safety appliances, as well as for diminishing the hours any employee of a railroad should be permitted to work, should all be strengthened wherever in actual practice they have shown weakness; they should be kept on the statute books in thoroughgoing form.

The constitutionality of the employers' liability act passed by the preceding Congress has been carried before the courts. In two jurisdictions the law has been declared unconstitutional, and in three jurisdictions its constitutionality has been affirmed. The question has been carried to the Supreme Court, the case has been heard by that tribunal, and a decision is expected at an early date. In the event that the court should affirm the constitutionality of the act, I urge further legislation along the lines advocated in my Message to the preceding Congress. The practice of putting the entire burden of loss to life or limb upon the victim or the victim's family is a form of social injustice in which the United States stands in unenviable prominence. In both our Federal and State legislation we have, with few exceptions, scarcely gone farther than the repeal of the fellow-servant principle of the old law of liability, and in some of our States even this slight modification of a completely outgrown principle has not yet been secured. The legislation of the rest of the industrial world stands out in striking contrast to our backwardness in this respect. Since 1895 practically every country of Europe, together with Great Britain, New Zealand, Australia, British Columbia, and the Cape of Good Hope has enacted legislation embodying in one form or another the complete recognition of the principle which places upon the employer the entire trade risk in the various lines of industry. I urge upon the Congress the enactment of a law which will at the same time bring Federal legislation up to the standard already established by all the European countries, and which will serve as a stimulus to the various States to perfect their legislation in this regard.

The Congress should consider the extension of the eight-hour law. The constitutionality of the present law has recently been called into question, and the Supreme Court has decided that the existing legislation is unquestionably within the powers of the Congress. The principle of the eight-hour day should as rapidly and as far as practicable be extended to the entire work carried on by the Government; and the present law should be amended to embrace contracts on those public works which the present wording of the act has been construed to exclude. The general introduction of the eight-hour day should be the goal toward which we should steadily tend, and the Government should set the example in this respect.

Strikes and lockouts, with their attendant loss and suffering, continue to increase. For the five years ending December 31, 1905, the number of strikes was greater than those in any previous ten years and was double the number in the preceding five years. These figures indicate the increasing need of providing some machinery to deal with this class of disturbance in the interest alike of the employer, the employee, and the general public. I renew my previous recommendation that the Congress favorably consider the matter of creating the machinery for compulsory investigation of such industrial controversies as are of sufficient magnitude and of sufficient concern to the people of the country as a whole to warrant the Federal Government in taking action.

The need for some provision fo rsuch investigation was forcibly illustrated during the past summer. A strike of telegraph operators seriously interfered with telegraphic communication, causing great damage to business interests and serious inconvenience to the general public. Appeals were made to me from many parts of the country, from city councils, from boards of trade, from chambers of commerce, and from labor organizations, urging that steps be taken to terminate the strike. Everything that could with any propriety be done by a representative of the Government was done, without avail, and for weeks the public stood by and suffered without recourse of any kind. Had the machinery existed and had there been authority for compulsory investigation of the dispute, the public would have been placed in possession of the merits of the controversy, and public opinion would probably have brought about a prompt adjustment.

Each successive step creating machinery for the adjustment of labor difficulties must be taken with caution, but we should endeavor to make progress in this direction.

The provisions of the act of 1898 creating the chairman of the Interstate Commerce Commission and the Commissioner of Labor a board of mediation in controversies between interstate railroads and their employees has, for the first time, been subjected to serious tests within the past year, and the wisdom of the experiment has been fully demonstrated. The creation of a board for compulsory investigation in cases where mediation fails and arbitration is rejected is the next logical step in a progressive program.

It is certain that for some time to come there will be a constant increase absolutely, and perhaps relatively, of those among our citizens who dwell in cities or towns of some size and who work for wages. This means that there will be an ever-increasing need to consider the problems inseparable from a great industrial civilization. Where an immense and complex business, especially in those branches relating to manufacture and transportation, is transacted by a large number of capitalists who employ a very much larger number of wage-earners, the former tend more and more to combine into corporations and the latter into unions. The relations of the capitalist and wage-worker to one another, and of each to the general public, are not always easy to adjust; and to put them and keep them on a satisfactory basis is one of the most important and one of the most delicate tasks before our whole civilization. Much of the work for the accomplishment of this end must be done by the individuals concerned themselves, whether singly or in combination; and the one fundamental fact that must never be lost track of is that the character of the average man, whether he be a man of means or a man who works with his hands, is the most important factor in solving the problem aright. But it is almost equally important to remember that without good laws it is also impossible to reach the proper solution. It is idle to hold that without good laws evils such as child labor, as the over-working of women, as the failure to protect employees from loss of life or limb, can be effectively reached, any more than the evils of rebates and stock-watering can be reached without good laws. To fail to stop these practices by legislation means to force honest men into them, because otherwise the dishonest who surely will take advantage of them will have everything their own way. If the States will correct these evils, well and good; but the Nation must stand ready to aid them.

No question growing out of our rapid and complex industrial development is more important than that of the employment of women and children. The presence of women in industry reacts with extreme directness upon the character of the home and upon family life, and the conditions surrounding the employment of children bear a vital relation to our future citizenship. Our legislation in those areas under the control of the Congress is very much behind the legislation of our more progressive States. A thorough and comprehensive measure should be adopted at this session of the Congress relating to the employment of women and children in the District of Columbia and the Territories. The investigation into the condition of women and children wage-earners recently authorized and directed by the Congress is now being carried on in the various States, and I recommend that the appropriation made last year for beginning this work be renewed, in order that we may have the thorough and comprehensive investigation which the subject demands. The National Government has as an ultimate resort for control of child labor the use of the interstate commerce clause to prevent the products of child labor from entering into interstate commerce. But before using this it ought certainly to enact model laws on the subject for the Territories under its own immediate control.

There is one fundamental proposition which can be laid down as regards all these matters, namely: While honesty by itself will not solve the problem, yet the insistence upon honesty—not merely technical honesty, but honesty in purpose and spirit—is an essential element in arriving at a right conclusion. Vice in its cruder and more archaic forms shocks everybody; but there is very urgent need that public opinion should be just as severe in condemnation of the vice which hides itself behind class or professional loyalty, or which denies that it is vice if it can escape conviction in the courts. The public and the representatives of the public, the high officials, whether on the bench or in executive or legislative positions, need to remember that often the most dangerous criminals, so far as the life of the Nation is concerned, are not those who commit the crimes known to and condemned by the popular conscience for centuries, but those who commit crimes only rendered possible by the complex conditions of our modern industrial life. It makes not a particle of difference whether these crimes are committed by a capitalist or by a laborer, by a leading banker or manufacturer or railroad man, or by a leading representative of a labor union. Swindling in stocks, corrupting legislatures, making fortunes by the inflation of securities, by wrecking railroads, by destroying competitors through rebates—these forms of wrongdoing in the capitalist, are far more infamous than any ordinary form of embezzlement or forgery; yet it is a matter of extreme difficulty to secure the punishment of the man most guilty of them, most responsible for them. The business man who condones such conduct stands on a level with the labor man who deliberately supports a corrupt demagogue and agitator, whether head of a union or head of some municipality, because he is said to have "stood by the union." The members of the business community, the educators, or clergymen, who condone and encourage the first kind of wrongdoing, are no more dangerous to the community, but are morally even worse, than the labor men who are guilty of the second type of wrongdoing, because less is to be pardoned those who have no such excuse as is furnished either by ignorance or by dire need.

When the Department of Agriculture was founded there was much sneering as to its usefulness. No Department of the Government, however, has more emphatically vindicated its usefulness, and none save the Post-Office Department comes so continually and intimately into touch with the people. The two citizens whose welfare is in the aggregate most vital to the welfare of the Nation, and therefore to the welfare of all other citizens, are the wage-worker who does manual labor and the tiller of the soil, the farmer. There are, of course, kinds of labor where the work must be purely mental, and there are other kinds of labor where, under existing conditions, very little demand indeed is made upon the mind, though I am glad to say that the proportion of men engaged in this kind of work is diminishing. But in any community with the solid, healthy qualities which make up a really great nation the bulk of the people should do work which calls for the exercise of both body and mind. Progress can not permanently exist in the abandonment of physical labor, but in the development of physical labor, so that it shall represent more and more the work of the trained mind in the trained body. Our school system is gravely defective in so far as it puts a premium upon mere literary training and tends therefore to train the boy away from the farm and the workshop. Nothing is more needed than the best type of industrial school, the school for mechanical industries in the city, the school for practically teaching agriculture in the country. The calling of the skilled tiller of the soil, the calling of the skilled mechanic, should alike be recognized as professions, just as emphatically as the callings of lawyer, doctor, merchant, or clerk. The schools recognize this fact and it should equally be recognized in popular opinion. The young man who has the farsightedness and courage to recognize it and to get over the idea that it makes a difference whether what he earns is called salary or wages, and who refuses to enter the crowded field of the so-called professions, and takes to constructive industry instead, is reasonably sure of an ample reward in earnings, in health, in opportunity to marry early, and to establish a home with a fair amount of freedom from worry. It should be one of our prime objects to put both the farmer and the mechanic on a higher plane of efficiency and reward, so as to increase their effectiveness in the economic world, and therefore the dignity, the remuneration, and the power of their positions in the social world.

No growth of cities, no growth of wealth, can make up for any loss in either the number or the character of the farming population. We of the United States should realize this above almost all other peoples. We began our existence as a nation of farmers, and in every great crisis of the past a peculiar dependence has had to be placed upon the farming population; and this dependence has hitherto been justified. But it can not be justified in the future if agriculture is permitted to sink in the scale as compared with other employments. We can not afford to lose that preeminently typical American, the farmer who owns his own medium-sized farm. To have his place taken by either a class of small peasant proprietors, or by a class of great landlords with tenant-farmed estates would be a veritable calamity. The growth ot our cities is a good thing but only in so far as it does not mean a growth at the expense of the country farmer. We must welcome the rise of physical sciences in their application to agricultural practices, and we must do all we can to render country conditions more easy and pleasant. There are forces which now tend to bring about both these results, but they are, as yet, in their infancy. The National Government through the Department of Agriculture should do all it can by joining with the State governments and with independent associations of farmers to encourage the growth in the open farming country of such institutional and social movements as will meet the demand of the best type of farmers, both for the improvement of their farms and for the betterment of the life itself. The Department of Agriculture has in many places, perhaps especially in certain districts of the South, accomplished an extraordinary amount by cooperating with and teaching the farmers through their associations, on their own soil, how to increase their income by managing their farms better than they were hitherto managed. The farmer must not lose his independence, his initiative, his rugged self-reliance, yet he must learn to work in the heartiest cooperation with his fellows, exactly as the business man has learned to work; and he must prepare to use to constantly better advantage the knowledge that can be obtained from agricultural colleges, while he must insist upon a practical curriculum in the schools in which his children are taught. The Department of Agriculture and the Department of Commerce and Labor both deal with the fundamental needs of our people in the production of raw material and its manufacture and distribution, and, therefore, with the welfare of those who produce it in the raw state, and of those who manufacture and distribute it. The Department of Commerce and Labor has but recently been founded but has already justified its existence; while the Department of Agriculture yields to no other in the Government in the practical benefits which it produces in proportion to the public money expended. It must continue in the future to deal with growing crops as it has dealt in the past, but it mnst still further extend its field of usefulness hereafter by dealing with live men, through a far-reaching study and treatment of the problems of farm life alike from the industrial and economic and social standpoint. Farmers must cooperate with one another and with the Government, and the Government can best give its aid through associations of farmers, so as to deliver to the farmer the large body of agricultural knowledge which has been accumulated by the National and State governments and by the agricultural colleges and schools.

The grain producing industry of the country, one of the most important in the United States, deserves special consideration at the hands of the Congress. Our grain is sold almost exclusively by grades. To secure satisfactory results in our home markets and to facilitate our trade abroad, these grades should approximate the highest degree of uniformity and certainty. The present diverse methods of inspection and grading throughout the country under different laws and boards, result in confusion and lack of uniformity, destroying that confidence which is necessary for healthful trade. Complaints against the present methods have continued for years and they are growing in volume and intensity, not only in this country but abroad. I therefore suggest to the Congress the advisability of a National system of inspection and grading of grain entering into interstate and foreign commerce as a remedy for the present evils.

The conservation of our natural resources and their proper use constitute the fundamental problem which underlies almost every other problem of our National life. We must maintain for our civilization the adequate material basis without which that civilization can not exist. We must show foresight, we must look ahead. As a nation we not only enjoy a wonderful measure of present prosperity but if this prosperity is used aright it is an earnest of future success such as no other nation will have. The reward of foresight for this Nation is great and easily foretold. But there must be the look ahead, there must be a realization of the fact that to waste, to destroy, our natural resources, to skin and exhaust the land instead of using it so as to increase its usefulness, will result in undermining in the days of our children the very prosperity which we ought by right to hand down to them amplified and developed. For the last few years, through several agencies, the Government has been endeavoring to get our people to look ahead and to substitute a planned and orderly development of our resources in place of a haphazard striving for immediate profit. Our great river systems should be developed as National water highways, the Mississippi, with its tributaries, standing first in importance, and the Columbia second, although there are many others of importance on the Pacific, the Atlantic and the Gulf slopes. The National Government should undertake this work, and I hope a beginning will be made in the present Congress; and the greatest of all our rivers, the Mississippi, should receive especial attention. From the Great Lakes to the mouth of the Mississippi there should be a deep waterway, with deep waterways leading from it to the East and the West. Such a waterway would practically mean the extension of our coast line into the very heart of our country. It would be of incalculable benefit to our people. If begun at once it can be carried through in time appreciably to relieve the congestion of our great freight-carrying lines of railroads. The work should be systematically and continuously carried forward in accordance with some well-conceived plan. The main streams should be improved to the highest point of efficiency before the improvement of the branches is attempted; and the work should be kept free from every taint of recklessness or jobbery. The inland waterways which lie just back of the whole eastern and southern coasts should likewise be developed. Moreover, the development of our waterways involves many other important water problems, all of which should be considered as part of the same general scheme. The

Government dams should be used to produce hundreds of thousands of horsepower as an incident to improving navigation; for the annual value of the unused water-power of the United States perhaps exceeds the annual value of the products of all our mines. As an incident to creating the deep waterways down the Mississippi, the Government should build along its whole lower length levees which taken together with the control of the headwaters, will at once and forever put a complete stop to all threat of floods in the immensely fertile Delta region. The territory lying adjacent to the Mississippi along its lower course will thereby become one of the most prosperous and populous, as it already is one of the most fertile, farming regions in all the world. I have appointed an Inland Waterways Commission to study and outline a comprehensive scheme of development along all the lines indicated. Later I shall lay its report before the Congress.

Irrigation should be far more extensively developed than at present, not only in the States of the Great Plains and the Rocky Mountains, but in many others, as, for instance, in large portions of the South Atlantic and Gulf States, where it should go hand in hand with the reclamation of swamp land. The Federal Government should seriously devote itself to this task, realizing that utilization of waterways and water-power, forestry, irrigation, and the reclamation of lands threatened with overflow, are all interdependent parts of the same problem. The work of the Reclamation Service in developing the larger opportunities of the western half of our country for irrigation is more important than almost any other movement. The constant purpose of the Government in connection with the Reclamation Service has been to use the water resources of the public lands for the ultimate greatest good of the greatest number; in other words, to put upon the land permanent home-makers, to use and develop it for themselves and for their children and children's children. There has been, of course, opposition to this work; opposition from some interested men who desire to exhaust the land for their own immediate profit without regard to the welfare of the next generation, and opposition from honest and well-meaning men who did not fully understand the subject or who did not look far enough ahead. This opposition is, I think, dying away, and our people are understanding that it would be utterly wrong to allow a few individuals to exhaust for their own temporary personal profit the resources which ought to be developed through use so as to be conserved for the permanent common advantage of the people as a whole.

The effort of the Government to deal with the public land has been based upon the same principle as that of the Reclamation Service. The land law system which was designed to meet the needs of the fertile and well-watered regions of the Middle West has largely broken down when applied to the dryer regions of the Great Plains, the mountains, and much of the Pacific slope, where a farm of 160 acres is inadequate for self-support. In these regions the system lent itself to fraud, and much land passed out of the hands of the Government without passing into the hands of the home-maker. The Department of the Interior and the Department of Justice joined in prosecuting the offenders against the law; and they have accomplished much, while where the administration of the law has been defective it has been changed. But the laws themselves are defective. Three years ago a public lands commission was appointed to scrutinize the law, and defects, and recommend a remedy. Their examination specifically showed the existence of great fraud upon the public domain, and their recommendations for changes in the law were made with the design of conserving the natural resources of every part of the public lands by putting it to its best use. Especial attention was called to the prevention of settlement by the passage of great areas of public land into the hands of a few men, and to the enormous waste caused by unrestricted grazing upon the open range. The recommendations of the Public Lands Commission are sound, for they are especially in the interest of the actual home-maker; and where the small home-maker can not at present utilize the land they provide that the Government shall keep control of it so that it may not be monopolized by a few men. The Congress has not yet acted upon these recommendations; but they are so just and proper, so essential to our National welfare, that I feel confident, if the Congress will take time to consider them, that they will ultimately be adopted.

Some such legislation as that proposed is essential in order to preserve the great stretches of public grazing land which are unfit for cultivation under present methods and are valuable only for the forage which they supply. These stretches amount in all to some 300,000,000 acres, and are open to the free grazing of cattle, sheep, horses and goats, without restriction. Such a system, or lack of system, means that the range is not so much used as wasted by abuse. As the West settles the range becomes more and more over-grazed. Much of it can not be used to advantage unless it is fenced, for fencing is the only way by which to keep in check the owners of nomad flocks which roam hither and thither, utterly destroying the pastures and leaving a waste behind so that their presence is incompatible with the presence of home-makers. The existing fences are all illegal. Some of them represent the improper exclusion of actual settlers, actual home-makers, from territory which is usurped by great cattle companies. Some of them represent what is in itself a proper effort to use the range for those upon the land, and to prevent its use by nomadic outsiders. All these fences, those that are hurtful and those that are beneficial, are alike illegal and must come down. But it is an outrage that the law should necessitate such action on the part of the Administration. The unlawful fencing of public lands for private grazing must be stopped, but the necessity which occasioned it must be provided for. The Federal Government should have control of the range, whether by permit or lease, as local necessities may determine. Such control could secure the great benefit of legitimate fencing, while at the same time securing and promoting the settlement of the country. In some places it may be that the tracts of range adjacent to the homesteads of actual settlers should be allotted to them severally or in common for the summer grazing of their stock. Elsewhere it may be that a lease system would serve the purpose; the leases to be temporary and subject to the rights of settlement, and the amount charged being large enough merely to permit of the efficient and beneficial control of the range by the Government, and of the payment to the county of the equivalent of what it would otherwise receive in taxes. The destruction of the public range will continue until some such laws as these are enacted. Fully to prevent the fraud in the public lands which, through the joint action of the Interior Department and the Department of Justice, we have been endeavoring to prevent, there must be further legislation, and especially a sufficient appropriation to permit the Department of the Interior to examine certain classes of entries on the ground before they pass into private ownership. The Government should part with its title only to the actual home-maker, not to the profit-maker who does not care to make a home.. Our prime object is to secure the rights and guard the interests of the small ranchman, the man who plows and pitches hay for himself. It is this small ranchman, this actual settler and home-maker, who in the long run is most hurt by permitting thefts of the public land in whatever form.

Optimism is a good characteristic, but if carried to an excess it becomes foolishness. We are prone to speak of the resources of this country as inexhaustible; this is not so. The mineral wealth of the country, the coal, iron, oil, gas, and the like, does not reproduce itself, and therefore is certain to be exhausted ultimately; and wastefulness in dealing with it to-day means that our descendants will feel the exhaustion a generation or two before they otherwise would. But there are certain other forms of waste which could be entirely stopped—the waste of soil by washing, for instance, which is among the most dangerous of all wastes now in progress in the United States, is easily preventable, so that this present enormous loss of fertility is entirely unnecessary. The preservation or replacement of the forests is one of the most important means of preventing this loss. We have made a beginning in forest preservation, but it is only a beginning. At present lumbering is the fourth greatest industry in the United States; and yet, so rapid has been the rate of exhaustion of timber in the United States in the past, and so rapidly is the remainder being exhausted, that the country is unquestionably on the verge of a timber famine which will be felt in every household in the land. There has already been a rise in the price of lumber, but there is certain to be a more rapid and heavier rise in the future. The present annual consumption of lumber is certainly three times as great as the annual growth; and if the consumption and growth continue unchanged, practically all our lumber will be exhausted in another generation, while long before the limit to complete exhaustion is reached the growing scarcity will make itself felt in many blighting ways upon our National welfare. About 20 per cent of our forested territory is now reserved in National forests; but these do not include the most valuable timber lands, and in any event the proportion is too small to expect that the reserves can accomplish more than a mitigation of the trouble which is ahead for the nation. Far more drastic action is needed. Forests can be lumbered so as to give to the public the full use of their mercantile timber without the slightest detriment to the forest, any more than it is a detriment to a farm to furnish a harvest; so that there is no parallel between forests and mines, which can only be completely used by exhaustion. But forests, if used as all our forests have been used in the past and as most of them are still used, will be either wholly destroyed, or so damaged that many decades have to pass before effective use can be made of them again. All these facts are so obvious that it is extraordinary that it should be necessary to repeat them. Every business man in the land, every writer in the newspapers, every man or woman of an ordinary school education, ought to be able to see that immense quantities of timber are used in the country, that the forests which supply this timber are rapidly being exhausted, and that, if no change takes place, exhaustion will come comparatively soon, and that the effects of it will be felt severely in the every-day life of our people. Surely, when these facts are so obvious, there should be no delay in taking preventive measures. Yet we seem as a nation to be willing to proceed in this matter with happy-go-lucky indifference even to the immediate future. It is this attitude which permits the self-interest of a very few persons to weigh for more than the ultimate interest of all our people. There are persons who find it to their immense pecuniary benefit to destroy the forests by lumbering. They are to be blamed for thus sacrificing the future of the Nation as a whole to their own self-interest of the moment; but heavier blame attaches to the people at large for permitting such action, whether in the White Mountains, in the southern Alleghenies, or in the Rockies and Sierras. A big lumbering company, impatient for immediate returns and not caring to look far enough ahead, will often deliberately destroy all the good timber in a region, hoping afterwards to move on to some new country. The shiftless man of small means, who does not care to become an actual home-maker but would like immediate profit, will find it to his advantage to take up timber land simply to turn it over to such a big company, and leave it valueless for future settlers. A big mine owner, anxious only to develop his mine at the moment, will care only to cut all the timber that he wishes without regard to the future—probably not looking ahead to the condition of the country when the forests are exhausted, any more than he does to the condition when the mine is worked out. I do not blame these men nearly as much as I blame the supine public opinion, the indifferent public opinion, which permits their action to go unchecked. Of course to check the waste of timber means that there must be on the part of the public the acceptance of a temporary restriction in the lavish use of the timber, in order to prevent the total loss of this use in the future. There are plenty of men in public and private life who actually advocate the continuance of the present system of unchecked and wasteful extravagance, using as an argument the fact that to check it will of course mean interference with the ease and comfort of certain people who now get lumber at less cost than they ought to pay, at the expense of the future generations. Some of these persons actually demand that the present forest reserves be thrown open to destruction, because, forsooth, they think that thereby the price of lumber could be put down again for two or three or more years. Their attitude is precisely like that of an agitator protesting against the outlay of money by farmers on manure and in taking care of their farms generally. Undoubtedly, if the average farmer were content absolutely to ruin his farm, he could for two or three years avoid spending any money on it, and yet make a good deal of money out of it. But only a savage would, in his private affairs, show such reckless disregard of the future; yet it is precisely this reckless disregard of the future which the opponents of the forestry system are now endeavoring to get the people of the United States to show. The only trouble with the movement for the preservation of our forests is that it has not gone nearly far enough, and was not begun soon enough. It is a most fortunate thing, however, that we began it when we did. We should acquire in the Appalachian and White Mountain regions all the forest lands that it is possible to acquire for the use of the Nation. These lands, because they form a National asset, are as emphatically national as the rivers which they feed, and which flow through so many States before they reach the ocean.

There should be no tariff on any forest product grown in this country; and, in especial, there should be no tariff on wood pulp; due notice of the change being of course given to those engaged in the business so as to enable them to adjust themselves to the new conditions.

The repeal of the duty on wood pulp should if possible be accompanied by an agreement with Canada that there shall be no export duty on Canadian pulp wood.

In the eastern United States the mineral fuels have already passed into the hands of large private owners, and those of the West are rapidly following. It is obvious that these fuels should be conserved and not wasted, and it would be well to protect the people against unjust and extortionate prices, so far as that can still be done. What has been accomplished in the great oil fields of the Indian Territory by the action of the Administration, offers a striking example of the good results of such a policy. In my judgment the Government should have the right to keep the fee of the coal, oil, and gas fields in its own possession and to lease the rights to develop them under proper regulations; or else, if the Congress will not adopt this method, the coal deposits should be sold under limitations, to conserve them as public utilities, the right to mine coal being separated from the title to the soil. The regulations should permit coal lands to be worked in sufficient quantity by the several corporations. The present limitations have been absurd, excessive, and serve no useful purpose, and often render it necessary that there should be either fraud or close abandonment of the work of getting out the coal.

Work on the Panama Canal is proceeding in a highly satisfactory manner. In March last, John F. Stevens, chairman of the Commission and chief engineer, resigned, and the Commission was reorganized and constituted as follows: Lieut. Col. George W. Goethals, Corps. of Engineers, U. S. Army, chairman and chief engineer; Maj. D. D. Gaillard, Corps of Engineers, U. S. Army; Maj. William L. Sibert, Corps of Engineers, U. S. Army; Civil Engineer H. H. Rousseau, U. S. Navy; Mr. J. C. S. Blackburn; Col. W. C. Gorgas, U. S. Army, and Mr. Jackson Smith, Commissioners. This change of authority and direction went into effect on April 1, without causing a perceptible check to the progress of the work. In March the total excavation in the Culebra Cut, where effort was chiefly concentrated, was 815,270 cubic yards. In April this was increased to 879,527 cubic yards. There was a considerable decrease in the output for May and June owing partly to the advent of the rainy season and partly to temporary trouble with the steam shovel men over the question of wages. This trouble was settled satisfactorily to all parties and in July the total excavation advanced materially and in August the grand total from all points in the canal prism by steam shovels and dredges exceeded all previous United States records, reaching 1,274,404 cubic yards. In September this record was eclipsed and a total of 1,517,412 cubic yards was removed. Of this amount 1,481,307 cubic yards were from the canal prism and 36,105 cubic yards were from accessory works.. These results were achieved in the rainy season with a rainfall in August of 11.89 inches and in September of 11.65 inches. Finally, in October, the record was again eclipsed, the total excavation being 1,868,729 cubic yards; a truly extraordinary record, especially in view of the heavy rainfall, which was 17.1 inches. In fact, experience during the last two rainy seasons demonstrates that the rains are a less serious obstacle to progress than has hitherto been supposed.

Work on the locks and dams at Gatun, which began actively in March last, has advanced so far that it is thought that masonry work on the locks can be begun within fifteen months. In order to remove all doubt as to the satisfactory character of the foundations for the locks of the Canal, the Secretary of War requested three eminent civil engineers, of special experience in such construction, Alfred Noble, Frederic P. Stearns and John R. Freeman, to visit the Isthmus and make thorough personal investigations of the sites. These gentlemen went to the Isthmus in April and by means of test pits which had been dug for the purpose, they inspected the proposed foundations, and also examined the borings that had been made. In their report to the Secretary of War, under date of May 2, 1907, they said: "We found that all of the locks, of the dimensions now propesed, will rest upon rock of such character that it will furnish a safe and stable foundation." Subsequent new borings, conducted by the present Commission, have fully confirmed this verdict. They show that the locks will rest on rock for their entire length. The cross section of the dam and method of construction will be such as to insure against any slip or sloughing off. Similar examination of the foundations of the locks and dams on the Pacific side are in progress. I believe that the locks should be made of a width of 120 feet.

Last winter bids were requested and received for doing the work of canal construction by contract. None of them was found to be satisfactory and all were rejected. It is the unanimous opinion of the present Commission that the work can be done better, more cheaply, and more quickly by the Government than by private contractors. Fully 80 per cent of the entire plant needed for construction has been purchased or contracted for; machine shops have been erected and equipped for making all needed repairs to the plant; many thousands of employees have been secured; an effective organization has been perfected; a recruiting system is in operation which is capable of furnishing more labor than can be used advantageously; employees are well sheltered and well fed; salaries paid are satisfactory, and the work is not only going forward smoothly, but it is producing results far in advance of the most sanguine anticipations. Under these favorable conditions, a change in the method of prosecuting the work would be unwise and unjustifiable, for it would inevitably disorganize existing conditions, check progress, and increase the cost and lengthen the time of completing the Canal.

The chief engineer and all his professional associates are firmly convinced that the 85 feet level lock canal which they are constructing is the best that could be desired. Some of them had doubts on this point when they went to the Isthmus. As the plans have developed under their direction their doubts have been dispelled. While they may decide upon changes in detail as construction advances they are in hearty accord in approving the general plan. They believe that it provides a canal not only adequate to all demands that will be made upon it but superior in every way to a sea level canal. I concur in this belief.

I commend to the favorable consideration of the Congress a postal savings bank system, as recommended by the Postmaster-General. The primary object is to encourage among our people economy and thrift and by the use of postal savings banks to give them an opportunity to husband their resources, particularly those who have not the facilities at hand for depositing their money in savings banks. Viewed, however, from the experience of the past few weeks, it is evident that the advantages of such an institution are still more far-reaching. Timid depositors have withdrawn their savings for the time being from national banks, trust companies, and savings banks; individuals have hoarded their cash and the workingmen their earnings; all of which money has been withheld and kept in hiding or in safe deposit box to the detriment of prosperity. Through the agency of the postal savings banks such money would be restored to the channels of trade, to the mutual benefit of capital and labor.

I further commend to the Congress the consideration of the Postmaster-General's recommendation for an extension of the parcel post, especially on the rural routes. There are now 38,215 rural routes, serving nearly 15,000,000 people who do not have the advantages of the inhabitants of cities in obtaining their supplies. These recommendations have been drawn up to benefit the farmer and the country storekeeper; otherwise, I should not favor them, for I believe that it is good policy for our Government to do everything possible to aid the small town and the country district. It is desirable that the country merchant should not be crushed out.

The fourth-class postmasters' convention has passed a very strong resolution in favor of placing the fourth-class postmasters under the civil-service law. The Administration has already put into effect the policy of refusing to remove any fourth-class postmasters save for reasons connected with the good of the service; and it is endeavoring so far as possible to remove them from the domain of partisan politics. It would be a most desirable thing to put the fourth-class postmasters in the classified service. It is possible that this might be done without

Congressional action, but, as the matter is debatable, I earnestly recommend that the Congress enact a law providing that they be included under the civil-service law and put in the classified service.

Oklahoma has become a State, standing on a full equality with her elder sisters, and her future is assured by her great natural resources. The duty of the National Government to guard the personal and property rights of the Indians within her borders remains of course unchanged.

I reiterate my recommendations of last year as regards Alaska. Some form of local self-government should be provided, as simple and inexpensive as possible; it is impossible for the Congress to devote the necessary time to all the little details of necessary Alaskan legislation. Road building and railway building should be encouraged. The Governor of Alaska should begiven an ample appropriation wherewith to organize a force to preserve the public peace. Whisky selling to the natives should be made a felony. The coal land laws should be changed so as to meet the peculiar needs of the Territory. This should be attended to at once; for the present laws permit individuals to locate large areas of the public domain for speculative purposes; and cause an immense amount of trouble, fraud, and litigation. There should be another judicial division established. As early as possible lighthouses and buoys should be established as aids to navigation, especially in and about Prince William Sound, and the survey of the coast completed. There is need of liberal appropriations for lighting and buoying the southern coast and improving the aids to navigation in southeastern Alaska. One of the great industries of Alaska, as of Puget Sound and the Columbia, is salmon fishing. Gradually, by reason of lack of proper laws, this industry is being ruined; it should now be taken in charge, and effectively protected, by the United States Government.

The courage and enterprise of the citizens of the far Northwest in their projected Alaskan-Yukon-Pacific Exposition, to be held in 1909, should receive liberal encouragement. This exposition is not sentimental in its conception, but seeks to exploit the natural resources of Alaska and to promote the commerce, trade, and industry of the Pacific States with their neighboring States and with our insular possessions and the neighboring countries of the Pacific. The exposition asks no loan from the Congress but seeks appropriations for National exhibits and exhibits of the western dependencies of the General Government. The State of Washington and the city of Seattle have shown the characteristic western enterprise in large donations for the conduct of this exposition in which other States are lending generous assistance.

The unfortunate failure of the shipping bill at the last session or the last Congress was followed by the taking off of certain Pacific steamships, which has greatly hampered the movement of passengers between Hawaii and the mainland. Unless the Congress is prepared by positive encouragement to secure proper facilities in the way of shipping between Hawaii and the mainland, then the coastwise shipping laws should be so far relaxed as to prevent Hawaii suffering as it is now suffering. I again call your attention to the capital importance from every standpoint of making Pearl Harbor available for the largest deep water vessels, and of suitably fortifying the island.

The Secretary of War has gone to the Philippines. On his return I shall submit to you his report on the islands.

I again recommend that the rights of citizenship be conferred upon the people of Porto Rico.

A bureau of mines should be created under the control and direction ot the Secretary of the Interior; the bureau to have power to collect statistics and make investigations in all matters pertaining to mining and particularly to the accidents and dangers of the industry. If this can not now be done, at least additional appropriations should be given the Interior Department to be used for the study of mining conditions, for the prevention of fraudulent mining schemes, for carrying on the work of mapping the mining districts, for studying methods for minimizing the accidents and dangers in the industry; in short, to aid in all proper ways the development of the mining industry.

I strongly recommend to the Congress to provide funds for keeping up the Hermitage, the home of Andrew Jackson; these funds to be used through the existing Hermitage Association for the preservation of a historic building which should ever be dear to Americans.

I further recommend that a naval monument be established in the Vicksburg National Park. This national park gives a unique opportunity for commemorating the deeds of those gallant men who fought on water, no less than of those who fought on land, in the great civil war.

Legislation should be enacted at the present session of the Congress for the Thirteenth Census. The establishment of the permanent Census Bureau affords the opportunity for a better census than we have ever had, but in order to realize the full advantage of the permanent organization, ample time must be given for preparation.

There is a constantly growing interest in this country in the question of the public health. At last the public mind is awake to the fact that many diseases, notably tuberculosis, are National scourges. The work of the State and city boards of health should be supplemented by a constantly increasing interest on the part of the National Government. The Congress has already provided a bureau of public health and has provided for a hygienic laboratory. There are other valuable laws relating to the public health connected with the various departments. This whole branch of the Government should be strengthened and aided in every way.

I call attention to two Government commissions which I have appointed and which have already done excellent work. The first of these has to do with the organization of the scientific work of the Government, which has grown up wholly without plan and is in consequence so unwisely distributed among the Executive Departments that much of its effect is lost for the lack of proper coordination. This commission's chief object is to introduce a planned and orderly development and operation in the place of the ill-assorted and often ineffective grouping and methods of work which have prevailed. This can not be done without legislation, nor would it be feasible to deal in detail with so complex an administrative problem by specific provisions of law. I recommend that the President be given authority to concentrate related lines of work and reduce duplication by Executive order through transfer and consolidation of lines of work.

The second committee, that on Department methods, was instructed to investigate and report upon the changes needed to place the conduct of the executive force of the Government on the most economical and effective basis in the light of the best modern business practice. The committee has made very satisfactory progress. Antiquated practices and bureaucratic ways have been abolished, and a general renovation of departmental methods has been inaugurated. All that can be done by Executive order has already been accomplished or will be put into effect in the near future. The work of the main committee and its several assistant committees has produced a wholesome awakening on the part of the great body of officers and employees engaged in Government work. In nearly every Department and office there has been a careful self-inspection for the purpose of remedying any defects before they could be made the subject of adverse criticism. This has led individuals to a wider study of the work on which they were engaged, and this study has resulted in increasing their efficiency in their respective lines of work. There are recommendations of special importance from the committee on the subject of personnel and the classification of salaries which will require legislative action before they can be put into effect. It is my intention to submit to the Congress in the near future a special message on those subjects.

Under our form of government voting is not merely a right but a duty, and, moreover, a fundamental and necessary duty if a man is to be a good citizen. It is well to provide that corporations shall not contribute to Presidential or National campaigns, and furthermore to provide for the publication of both contributions and expenditures. There is, however, always danger in laws of this kind, which from their very nature are difficult of enforcement; the danger being lest they be obeyed only by the honest, and disobeyed by the unscrupulous, so as to act only as a penalty upon honest men. Moreover, no such law would hamper an unscrupulous man of unlimited means from buying his own way into office. There is a very radical measure which would, I believe, work a substantial improvement in our system of conducting a campaign, although I am well aware that it will take some time for people so to familiarize themselves with such a proposal as to be willing to consider its adoption. The need for collecting large campaign funds would vanish if Congress provided an appropriation for the proper and legitimate expenses of each of the great national parties, an appropriation ample enough to meet the necessity for thorough organization and machinery, which requires a large expenditure of money. Then the stipulation should be made that no party receiving campaign funds from the Treasury should accept more than a fixed amount from any individual subscriber or donor; and the necessary publicity for receipts and expenditures could without difficulty be provided.

There should be a National gallery of art established in the capital city of this country. This is important not merely to the artistic but to the material welfare of the country; and the people are to be congratulated on the fact that the movement to establish such a gallery is taking definite form under the guidance of the Smithsonian Institution. So far from there being a tariff on works of art brought into the country, their importation should be encouraged in every way. There have been no sufficient collections of objects of art by the Government, and what collections have been acquired are scattered and are generally placed in unsuitable and imperfectly lighted galleries.

The Biological Survey is quietly working for the good of our agricultural interests, and is an excellent example of a Government bureau which conducts original scientific research the findings of which are of much practical utility. For more than twenty years it has studied the food habits of birds and mammals that are injurious or beneficial to agriculture, horticulture, and forestry; has distributed illustrated bulletins on the subject, and has labored to secure legislative protection for the beneficial species. The cotton boll-weevil, which has recently overspread the cotton belt of Texas and is steadily extending its range, is said to cause an annual loss of about $3,000,000. The Biological Survey has ascertained and gives wide publicity to the fact that at least 43 kinds of birds prey upon this destructive insect. It has discovered that 57 species of birds feed upon scale-insects—dreaded enemies of the fruit grower. It has shown that woodpeckers as a class, by destroying the larvæ of wood-boring insects, are so essential to tree life that it is doubtful if our forests could exist without them. It has shown that cuckoos and orioles are the natural enemies of the leaf-eating caterpillars that destroy our shade and fruit trees; that our quails and sparrows consume annually hundreds of tons of seeds of noxious weeds; that hawks and owls as a class (excepting the few that kill poultry and game birds) are markedly beneficial, spending their lives in catching grasshoppers, mice, and other pests that prey upon the products of husbandry. It has conducted field experiments for the purpose of devising and perfecting simple methods for holding in check the hordes of destructive rodents—rats, mice, rabbits, gophers, prairie dogs, and ground squirrels—which annually destroy crops worth many millions of dollars; and it has published practical directions for the destruction of wolves and coyotes on the stock ranges of the West, resulting during the past year in an estimated saving of cattle and sheep valued at upwards of a million dollars.

It has inaugurated a system of inspection at the principal ports of entry on both Atlantic and Pacific coasts by means of which the introduction of noxious mammals and birds is prevented, thus keeping out the mongoose and certain birds which are as much to be dreaded as the previously introduced English sparrow and the house rats and mice.

In the interest of game protection it has cooperated with local officials in every State in the Union, has striven to promote uniform legislation in the several States, has rendered important service in enforcing the Federal law regulating interstate traffic in game, and has shown how game protection may be made to yield a large revenue to the State—a revenue amounting in the case of Illinois to $128,000 in a single year.

The Biological Survey has explored the faunas and floras of America with reference to the distribution of animals and plants; it has defined and mapped the natural life areas—areas in which, by reason of prevailing climatic conditions, certain kinds of animals and plants occur—and has pointed out the adaptability of these areas to the cultivation of particular crops. The results of these investigations are not only of high educational value but are worth each year to the progressive farmers of the country many times the cost of maintaining the Survey, which, it may be added, is exceedingly small. I recommend to Congress that this bureau, whose usefulness is seriously handicapped by lack of funds, be granted an appropriation in some degree commensurate with the importance of the work it is doing.

I call your especial attention to the unsatisfactory condition of our foreign mail service, which, because of the lack of American steamship lines is now largely done through foreign lines, and which, particularly so far as South and Central America are concerned, is done in a manner which constitutes a serious barrier to the extension of our commerce.

The time has come, in my judugment, to set to work seriously to make our ocean mail service correspond more closely with our recent commercial and political development. A beginning was made by the ocean mail act of March 3, 1891, but even at that time the act was known to be inadequate in various particulars. Since that time events have moved rapidly in our history. We have acquired Hawaii, the Philippines, and lesser islands in the Pacific. We are steadily prosecuting the great work of uniting at the Isthmus the waters of the Atlantic and the Pacific. To a greater extent than seemed probable even a dozen years ago, we may look to an American future on the sea worthy of the traditions of our past. As the first step in that direction, and the step most feasible at the present time, I recommend the extension of the ocean mail act of 1891. This act has stood for some years free from successful criticism of its principle and purpose. It was based on theories of the obligations of a great maritime nation, undisputed in our own land and followed by other nations since the beginning of steam navigation. Briefly those theories are, that it is the duty of a first-class Power so far as practicable to carry its ocean mails under its own flag; that the fast ocean steamships and their crews, required for such mail service, are valuable auxiliaries to the sea power of a nation. Furthermore, the construction of such steamships insures the maintenance in an efficient condition of the shipyards in which our battleships must be built.

The expenditure of public money for the performance of such necessary functions of government is certainly warranted, nor is it necessary to dwell upon the incidental benefits to our foreign commerce, to the shipbuilding industry, and to ship owning and navigation which will accompany the discharge of these urgent public duties, though they, too, should have weight.

The only serious question is whether at this time we can afford to improve our ocean mail service as it should be improved. All doubt on this subject is removed by the reports of the Post-Office Department. For the fiscal year ended June 30, 1907, that Department estimates that the postage collected on the articles exchanged with foreign countries other than Canada and Mexico amounted to $6,579,043.48, or $3,637,226.81 more than the net cost of the service exclusive of the cost of transporting the articles between the United States exchange postoffices and the United States postoffices at which they were mailed or delivered. In other words, the Government of the United States, having assumed a monopoly of carrying the mails for the people, is making a profit of over $3,600,000 by rendering a cheap and inefficient service. That profit I believe should be devoted to strengthening our maritime power in those directions where it will best promote our prestige. The country is familiar with the facts of our maritime impotence in the harbors of the great and friendly Republics of South America. Following the failure of the shipbuilding bill we lost our only American line of steamers to Australasia, and that loss on the Pacific has become a serious embarrassment to the people of Hawaii, and has wholly cut off the Samoan islands from regular communication with the Pacific coast. Puget Sound, in the year, has lost over half (four out of seven) of its American steamers trading with the Orient.

We now pay under the act of 1891 $4 a statute mile outward to 20-knot American mail steamships, built according to naval plans, available as cruisers, and manned by Americans. Steamships of that speed are confined exclusively to trans-Atlantic trade with New York. To steamships of 16 knots or over only $2 a mile can be paid, and it is steamships of this speed and type which are needed to meet the requirements of mail service to South America, Asia (including the Philippines), and Australia. I strongly recommend, therefore, a simple amendment to the ocean mail act of 1891 which shall authorize the Postmaster-General in his discretion to enter into contracts for the transportation of mails to the Republics of South America, to Asia, the Philippines, and Australia at a rate not to exceed $4 a mile for steamships of 16 knots speed or upwards, subject to the restrictions and obligations of the act of 1891. The profit of $3,600,000 which has been mentioned will fully cover the maximum annual expenditure involved in this recommendation, and it is believed will in time establish the lines so urgently needed. The proposition involves no new principle, but permits the efficient discharge of public functions now inadequately performed or not performed at all.

Not only there is not now, but there never has been, any other nation in the world so wholly free from the evils of militarism as is ours. There never has been any other large nation, not even China, which for so long a period has had relatively to its numbers so small a regular army as has ours. Never at any time in our history has this Nation suffered from militarism or been in the remotest danger of suffering from militarism. Never at any time of our history has the Regular Army been of a size which caused the slightest appreciable tax upon the tax-paying citizens of the Nation. Almost always it has been too small in size and underpaid. Never in our entire history has the Nation suffered in the least particular because too much care has been given to the Army, too much prominence given it, too much money spent upon it, or because it has been too large. But again and again we have suffered because enough care has not been given to it, because it has been too small, because there has not been sufficient preparation in advance for possible war. Every foreign war in which we have engaged has cost us many times the amount which, if wisely expended during the preceding years of peace on the Regular Army, would have insured the war ending in but a fraction of the time and but for a fraction of the cost that was actually the case. As a Nation we have always been shortsighted in providing for the efficiency of the Army in time of peace. It is nobody's especial interest to make such provision and no one looks ahead to war at any period, no matter how remote, as being a serious possibility; while an improper economy, or rather niggardliness, can be practiced at the expense of the Army with the certainty that those practicing it will not be called to account therefor, but that the price will be paid by the unfortunate persons who happen to be in office when a war does actually come.

I think it is only lack of foresight that troubles us, not any hostility to the Army. There are, of course, foolish people who denounce any care of the Army or Navy as "militarism," but I do not think that these people are numerous. This country has to contend now, and has had to contend in the past, with many evils, and there is ample scope for all who would work for reform. But there is not one evil that now exists, or that ever has existed in this country, which is, or ever has been, owing in the smallest part to militarism. Declamation against militarism has no more serious place in an earnest and intelligent movement for righteousness in this country than declamation against the worship of Baal or Astaroth. It is declamation against a non-existent evil, one which never has existed in this country, and which has not the slightest chance of appearing here. We are glad to help in any movement for international peace, but this is because we sincerely believe that it is our duty to help all such movements provided they are sane and rational, and not because there is any tendency toward militarism on our part which needs to be cured. The evils we have to fight are those in connection with industrialism, not militarism. Industry is always necessary, just as war is sometimes necessary. Each has its price, and industry in the United States now exacts, and has always exacted, a far heavier toll of death than all our wars put together. The statistics of the railroads of this country for the year ended June 30, 1906, the last contained in the annual statistical report of the Interstate Commerce Commission, show in that one year a total of 108,324 casualties to persons, of which 10,618 represent the number of persons killed. In that wonderful hive of human activity, Pittsburg, the deaths due to industrial accidents in 1906 were 919, all the result of accidents in mills, mines or on railroads. For the entire country, therefore, it is safe to say that the deaths due to industrial accidents aggregate in the neighborhood of twenty thousand a year. Such a record makes the death rate in all our foreign wars utterly trivial by comparison. The number of deaths in battle in all the foreign wars put together, for the last century and a quarter, aggregate considerably less than one year's death record for our industries. A mere glance at these figures is sufficient to show the absurdity of the outcry against militarism.

But again and again in the past our little Regular Army has rendered service literally vital to the country, and it may at any time have to do so in the future. Its standard of efficiency and instruction is higher now than ever in the past. But it is too small. There are not enough officers; and it is impossible to secure enough enlisted men. We should maintain in peace a fairly complete skeleton of a large army. A great and long-continued war would have to be fought by volunteers. But months would pass before any large body of efficient volunteers could be put in the field, and our Regular Army should be large enough to meet any immediate need. In particular it is essential that we should possess a number of extra officers trained in peace to perform efficiently the duties urgently required upon the breaking out of war.

The Medical Corps should be much larger than the needs of our Regular Army in war. Yet at present it is smaller than the needs of the service demand even in peace. The Spanish war occurred less than ten years ago. The chief loss we suffered in it was by disease among the regiments which never left the country. At the moment the Nation seemed deeply impressed by this fact; yet seemingly it has already been forgotten, for not the slightest effort has been made to prepare a medical corps of sufficient size to prevent the repetition of the same disaster on a much larger scale if we should ever be engaged in a serious conflict. The trouble in the Spanish war was not with the then existing officials of the War Department; it was with the representatives of the people as a whole who, for the preceding thirty years, had declined to make the necessary provision for the Army. Unless ample provision is now made by Congress to put the Medical Corps where it should be put disaster in the next war is inevitable, and the responsibility will not lie with those then in charge of the War Department, but with those who now decline to make the necessary provision. A well organized medical corps, thoroughly trained before the advent of war in all the important administrative duties of a military sanitary corps, is essential to the efficiency of any large army, and especially of a large volunteer army. Such knowledge of medicine and surgery as is possessed by the medical profession generally will not alone suffice to make an efficient military surgeon. He must have, in addition, knowledge of the administration and sanitation of large field hospitals and camps, in order to safeguard the health and lives of men intrusted in great numbers to his care. A bill has long been pending before the Congress for the reorganization of the Medical Corps; its passage is urgently needed.

But the Medical Department is not the only department for which increased provision should be made. The rate of pay for the officers should be greatly increased; there is no higher type of citizen than the American regular officer, and he should have a fair reward for his admirable work. There should be a relatively even greater increase in the pay for the enlisted men. In especial provision should be made for establishing grades equivalent to those of warrant officers in the Navy which should be open to the enlisted men who serve sufficiently long and who do their work well. Inducements should be offered sufficient to encourage really good men to make the Army a life occupation. The prime needs of our present Army is to secure and retain competent noncommissioned officers. This difficulty rests fundamentally on the question of pay. The noncommissioned officer does not correspond with an unskilled laborer; he corresponds to the best type of skilled workman or to the subordinate official in civil institutions. Wages have greatly increased in outside occupations in the last forty years and the pay of the soldier, like the pay of the officers, should be proportionately increased. The first sergeant of a company, if a good man, must be one of such executive and administrative ability, and such knowledge of his trade, as to be worth far more than we at present pay him. The same is true of the regimental sergeant major. These men should be men who had fully resolved to make the Army a life occupation and they should be able to look forward to ample reward; while only men properly qualified should be given a chance to secure these final rewards. The increase over the present pay need not be great in the lower grades for the first one or two enlistments, but the increase should be marked for the noncommissioned officers of the upper grades who serve long enough to make it evident that they intend to stay permanently in the Army, while additional pay should be given for high qualifications in target practice. The position of warrant officer should be established and there should be not only an increase of pay, but an increase of privileges and allowances and dignity, so as to make the grade open to noncommissioned officers capable of filling them desirably from every standpoint. The rate of desertion in our Army now in time of peace is alarming. The deserter should be treated by public opinion as a man guilty of the greatest crime; while on the other hand the man who serves steadily in the Army should be treated as what he is, that is, as preeminently one of the best citizens of this Republic. After twelve years' service in the Army my own belief is that the man should be given a preference according to his ability for certain types of office over all civilian applicants without examination. This should also apply, of course, to the men who have served twelve years in the Navy. A special corps should be provided to do the manual labor now necessarily demanded of the privates themselves.

Among the officers there should be severe examinations to weed out the unfit up to the grade of major. From that position on appointments should be solely by selection and it should be understood that a man of merely average capacity could never get beyond the position of major, while every man who serves in any grade a certain length of time prior to promotion to the next grade without getting the promotion to the next grade should be forthwith retired. The practice marches and field maneuvers of the last two or three years have been invaluable to the Army. They should be continued and extended. A rigid and not a perfunctory examination of physical capacity has been provided for the higher grade officers. This will work well. Unless an officer has a good physique, unless he can stand hardship, ride well, and walk fairly, he is not fit for any position, even after he has become a colonel. Before he has become a colonel the need for physical fitness in the officers is almost as great as in the enlisted man. I hope speedily to see introduced into the Army a far more rigid and thoroughgoing test of horsemanship for all field officers than at present. There should be a Chief of Cavalry just as there is a Chief of Artillery.

Perhaps the most important of all legislation needed for the benefit of the Army is a law to equalize and increase the pay of officers and enlisted men of the Army, Navy, Marine Corps, and Revenue-Cutter Service. Such a bill has been prepared, which it is hoped will meet with your favorable consideration. The next most essential measure is to authorize a number of extra officers as mentioned above. To make the Army more attractive to enlisted men, it is absolutely essential to create a service corps, such as exists in nearly every modern army in the world, to do the skilled and unskilled labor, inseparably connected with military administration, which is now exacted, without just compensation, of enlisted men who voluntarily entered the Army to do service of an altogether different kind. There are a number of other laws necessary to so organize the Army as to promote its efficiency and facilitate its rapid expansion in time of war; but the above are the most important.

It was hoped The Hague Conference might deal with the question of the limitation of armaments. But even before it had assembled informal inquiries had developed that as regards naval armaments, the only ones in which this country had any interest, it was hopeless to try to devise any plan for which there was the slightest possibility of securing the assent of the nations gathered at The Hague. No plan was even proposed which would have had the assent of more than one first class Power outside of the United States. The only plan that seemed at all feasible, that of limiting the size of battleships, met with no favor at all. It is evident, therefore, that it is folly for this Nation to base any hope of securing peace on any international agreement as to the limitations of armaments. Such being the fact it would be most unwise for us to stop the upbuilding of our Navy. To build one battleship of the best and most advanced type a year would barely keep our fleet up to its present force. This is not enough. In my judgment, we should this year provide for four battleships. But it is idle to build battleships unless in addition to providing the men, and the means for thorough training, we provide the auxiliaries for them, unless we provide docks, the coaling stations, the colliers and supply ships that they need. We are extremely deficient in coaling stations and docks on the Pacific, and this deficiency should not longer be permitted to exist. Plenty of torpedo boats and destroyers should be built. Both on the Atlantic and Pacific coasts, fortifications of the best type should be provided for all our greatest harbors.

We need always to remember that in time of war the Navy is not to be used to defend harbors and sea-coast cities; we should perfect our system of coast fortifications. The only efficient use for the Navy is for offense. The only way in which it can efficiently protect our own coast against the possible action of a foreign navy is by destroying that foreign navy. For defense against a hostile fleet which actually attacks them, the coast cities must depend upon their forts, mines, torpedoes, submarines, and torpedo boats and destroyers. All of these together are efficient for defensive purposes, but they in no way supply the place of a thoroughly efficient navy capable of acting on the offensive; for parrying never yet won a fight. It can only be won by hard hitting, and an aggressive sea-going navy alone can do this hard hitting of the offensive type. But the forts and the like are necessary so that the Navy may be footloose. In time of war there is sure to be demand, under pressure, of fright, for the ships to be scattered so as to defend all kind of ports. Under penalty of terrible disaster, this demand must be refused. The ships must be kept together, and their objective made the enemies' fleet. If fortifications are sufficiently strong, no modern navy will venture to attack them, so long as the foe has in existence a hostile navy of anything like the same size or efficiency. But unless there exists such a navy then the fortifications are powerless by themselves to secure the victory. For of course the mere deficiency means that any resolute enemy can at his leisure combine all his forces upon one point with the certainty that he can take it.

Until our battle fleet is much larger than at present it should never be split into detachments so far apart that they could not in event of emergency be speedily united. Our coast line is on the Pacific just as much as on the Atlantic. The interests of California, Oregon, and Washington are as emphatically the interests of the whole Union as those of Maine and New York, of Louisiana and Texas. The battle fleet should now and then be moved to the Pacific, just as at other times it should be kept in the Atlantic. When the Isthmian Canal is built the transit of the battle fleet from one ocean to the other will be comparatively easy. Until it is built I earnestly hope that the battle fleet will be thus shifted between the two oceans every year or two. The marksmanship on all our ships has improved phenomenally during the last five years. Until within the last two or three years it was not possible to train a battle fleet in squadron maneuvers under service conditions, and it is only during these last two or three years that the training under these conditions has become really effective. Another and most necessary stride in advance is now being taken. The battle fleet is about starting by the Straits of Magellan to visit the Pacific coast.. Sixteen battleships are going under the command of Rear-Admiral Evans, while eight armored cruisers and two other battleships will meet him at San Francisco, whither certain torpedo destroyers are also going. No fleet of such size has ever made such a voyage, and it will be of very great educational use to all engaged in it.. The only way by which to teach officers and men how to handle the fleet so as to meet every possible strain and emergency in time of war is to have them practice under similar conditions in time of peace. Moreover, the only way to find out our actual needs is to perform in time of peace whatever maneuvers might be necessary in time of war. After war is declared it is too late to find out the needs; that means to invite disaster. This trip to the Pacific will show what some of our needs are and will enable us to provide for them. The proper place for an officer to learn his duty is at sea, and the only way in which a navy can ever be made efficient is by practice at sea, under all the conditions which would have to be met if war existed.

I bespeak the most liberal treatment for the officers and enlisted men of the Navy. It is true of them, as likewise of the officers and enlisted men of the Army, that they form a body whose interests should be close to the heart of every good American. In return the most rigid performance of duty should be exacted from them. The reward should be ample when they do their best; and nothing less than their best should be tolerated. It is idle to hope for the best results when the men in the senior grades come to those grades late in life and serve too short a time in them. Up to the rank of lieutenant-commander promotion in the Navy should be as now, by seniority, subject, however, to such rigid tests as would eliminate the unfit. After the grade of lieutenant-commander, that is, when we come to the grade of command rank, the unfit should be eliminated in such manner that only the conspicuously fit would remain, and sea service should be a principal test of fitness. Those who are passed by should, after a certain length of service in their respective grades, be retired. Of a given number of men it may well be that almost all would make good lieutenants and most of them good lieutenant-commanders, while only a minority be fit to be captains, and but three or four to be admirals. Those who object to promotion otherwise than by mere seniority should reflect upon the elementary fact that no business in private life could be successfully managed if those who enter at the lowest rungs of the ladder should each in turn, if he lived, become the head of the firm, its active director, and retire after he had held the position a few months. On its face such a scheme is an absurdity. Chances for improper favoritism can be minimized by a properly formed board; such as the board of last June, which did such conscientious and excellent work in elimination.

If all that ought to be done can not now be done, at least let a beginning be made. In my last three annual Messages, and in a special Message to the last Congress, the necessity for legislation that will cause officers of the line of the Navy to reach the grades of captain and rear-admiral at less advanced ages and which will cause them to have more sea training and experience in the highly responsible duties of those grades, so that they may become thoroughly skillful in handling battleships, divisions, squadrons, and fleets in action, has been fully explained and urgently recommended. Upon this subject the Secretary of the Navy has submitted detailed and definite recommendations which have received my approval, and which, if enacted into law, will accomplish what is immediately necessary, and will, as compared with existing law, make a saving of more than five millions of dollars during the next seven years. The navy personnel act of 1899 has accomplished all that was expected of it in providing satisfactory periods of service in the several subordinate grades, from the grade of ensign to the grade of lieutenant-commander, but the law is inadequate in the upper grades and will continue to be inadequate on account of the expansion of the personnel since its enactment. Your attention is invited to the following quotations from the report of the personnel board of 1906, of which the Assistant Secretary of the Navy was president:

"Congress has authorized a considerable increase in the number of midshipmen at the Naval Academy, and these midshipmen upon graduation are promoted to ensign and lieutenant (junior-grade). But no provision has been made for a corresponding increase in the upper grades, the result being that the lower grades will become so congested that a midshipman now in one of the lowest classes at Annapolis may possibly not be promoted to lieutenant until he is between 45 and 50 years of age. So it will continue under the present law, congesting at the top and congesting at the bottom. The country fails to get from the officers of the service the best that is in them by not providing opportunity for their normal development and training. The board believes that this works a serious detriment to the efficiency of the Navy and is a real menace to the public safety."

As stated in my special Message to the last Congress: "I am firmly of the opinion that unless the present conditions of the higher commissioned personnel is rectified by judicious legislation the future of our Navy will be gravely compromised." It is also urgently necessary to increase the efficiency of the Medical Corps of the Navy. Special legislation to this end has already been proposed; and I trust it may be enacted without delay.

It must be remembered that everything done in the Navy to fit it to do well in time of war must be done in time of peace. Modern wars are short; they do not last the length of time requisite to build a battleship; and it takes longer to train the officers and men to do well on a battleship than it takes to build it. Nothing effective can be done for the Navy once war has begun, and the result of the war, if the combatants are otherwise equally matched, will depend upon which power has prepared best in time of peace. The United States Navy is the best guaranty the Nation has that its honor and interest will not be neglected; and in addition it offers by far the best insurance for peace that can by human ingenuity be devised.

I call attention to the report of the official Board of Visitors to the Naval Academy at Annapolis which has been forwarded to the Congress. The report contains this paragraph:

"Such revision should be made of the courses of study and methods of conducting and marking examinations as will develop and bring out the average all-round ability of the midshipman rather than to give him prominence in any one particular study. The fact should be kept in mind that the Naval Academy is not a university but a school, the primary object of which is to educate boys to be efficient naval officers. Changes in curriculum, therefore, should be in the direction of making the course of instruction less theoretical and more practical. No portion of any future class should be graduated in advance of the full four years' course, and under no circumstances should the standard of instruction be lowered. The Academy in almost all of its departments is now magnificently equipped, and it would be very unwise to make the course of instruction less exacting than it is to-day."

Acting upon this suggestion I designated three seagoing officers, Capt. Richard Wainwright, Commander Robert S. Griffin, and Lieut. Commander Albert L. Key, all graduates of the Academy, to investigate conditions and to recommend to me the best method of carrying into effect this general recommendation. These officers performed the duty promptly and intelligently, and, under the personal direction of

Capt. Charles J. Badger, Superintendent of the Academy, such of the proposed changes as were deemed to be at present advisable were put into effect at the beginning of the academic year, October 1, last. The results, I am confident, will be most beneficial to the Academy, to the midshipmen, and to the Navy.

In foreign affairs this country's steady policy is to behave toward other nations as a strong and self-respecting man should behave toward the other men with whom he is brought into contact.. In other words, our aim is disinterestedly to help other nations where such help can be wisely given without the appearance of meddling with what does not concern us; to be careful to act as a good neighbor; and at the same time, in good-natured fashion, to make it evident that we do not intend to be imposed upon.

The Second International Peace Conference was convened at The Hague on the 15th of June last and remained in session until the 18th of October. For the first time the representatives of practically all the civilized countries of the world united in a temperate and kindly discussion of the methods by which the causes of war might be narrowed and its injurious effects reduced.

Although the agreements reached in the Conference did not in any direction go to the length hoped for by the more sanguine, yet in many directions important steps were taken, and upon every subject on the programme there was such full and considerate discussion as to justify the belief that substantial progress has been made toward further agreements in the future. Thirteen conventions were agreed upon embodying the definite conclusions which had been reached, and resolutions were adopted marking the progress made in matters upon which agreement was not yet sufficiently complete to make conventions practicable.

The delegates of the United States were instructed to favor an agreement for obligatory arbitration, the establishment of a permanent court of arbitration to proceed judicially in the hearing and decision of international causes, the prohibition of force for the collection of contract debts alleged to be due from governments to citizens of other countries until after arbitration as to the justice and amount of the debt and the time and manner of payment, the immunity of private property at sea, the better definition of the rights of neutrals, and, in case any measure to that end should be introduced, the limitation of armaments.

In the field of peaceful disposal of international differences several important advances were made. First, as to obligatory arbitration. Although the Conference failed to secure a unanimous agreement upon the details of a convention for obligatory arbitration, it did resolve as follows:

"It is unanimous: (1) In accepting the principle for obligatory arbitration; (2) In declaring that certain differences, and notably those relating to the interpretation and application of international conventional stipulations are susceptible of being submitted to obligatory arbitration without any restriction."

In view of the fact that as a result of the discussion the vote upon the definite treaty of obligatory arbitration, which was proposed, stood 32 in favor to 9 against the adoption of the treaty, there can be little doubt that the great majority of the countries of the world have reached a point where they are now ready to apply practically the principles thus unanimously agreed upon by the Conference.

The second advance, and a very great one, is the agreement which relates to the use of force for the collection of contract debts. Your attention is invited to the paragraphs upon this subject in my Message of December, 1906, and to the resolution of the Third American Conference at Rio in the summer of 1906. The convention upon this subject adopted by the Conference substantially as proposed by the American delegates is as follows: :

"In order to avoid between nations armed conflicts of a purely pecuniary origin arising from contractual debts claimed of the government of one country by the government of another country to be due to its nationals, the signatory Powers agree not to have recourse to armed force for the collection of such contractual debts.

"However, this stipulation shall not be applicable when the debtor State refuses or leaves unanswered an offer to arbitrate, or, in case of acceptance, makes it impossible to formulate the terms of submission, or, after arbitration, fails to comply with the award rendered.

"It is further agreed that arbitration here contemplated shall be in conformity, as to procedure, with Chapter III of the Convention for the Pacific Settlement of International Disputes adopted at The Hague, and that it shall determine, in so far as there shall be no agreement between the parties, the justice and the amount of the debt, the time and mode of payment thereof."

Such a provision would have prevented much injustice and extortion in the past, and I cannot doubt that its effect in the future will be most salutary.

A third advance has been made in amending and perfecting the convention of 1899 for the voluntary settlement of international disputes, and particularly the extension of those parts of that convention which relate to commissions of inquiry. The existence of those provisions enabled the Governments of Great Britain and Russia to avoid war, notwithstanding great public excitement, at the time of the Dogger Bank incident, and the new convention agreed upon by the Conference gives practical effect to the experience gained in that inquiry.

Substantial progress was also made towards the creation of a permanent judicial tribunal for the determination of international causes. There was very full discussion of the proposal for such a court and a general agreement was finally reached in favor of its creation. The Conference recommended to the signatory Powers the adoption of a draft upon which it agreed for the organization of the court, leaving to be determined only the method by which the judges should be selected. This remaining unsettled question is plainly one which time and good temper will solve.

A further agreement of the first importance was that for the creation of an international prize court. The constitution, organization and procedure of such a tribunal were provided for in detail. Anyone who recalls the injustices under which this country suffered as a neutral power during the early part of the last century can not fail to see in this provision for an international prize court the great advance which the world is making towards the substitution of the rule of reason and justice in place of simple force. Not only will the international prize court be the means of protecting the interests of neutrals, but it is in itself a step towards the creation of the more general court for the hearing of international controversies to which reference has just been made. The organization and action of such a prize court can not fail to accustom the different countries to the submission of international questions to the decision of an international tribunal, and we may confidently expect the results of such submission to bring about a general agreement upon the enlargement of the practice.

Numerous provisions were adopted for reducing the evil effects of war and for defining the rights and duties of neutrals.

The Conference also provided for the holding of a third Conference within a period similar to that which elapsed between the First and Second Conferences.

The delegates of the United States worthily represented the spirit of the American people and maintained with fidelity and ability the policy of our Government upon all the great questions discussed in the Conference.

The report of the delegation, together with authenticated copies of the conventions signed, when received, will be laid before the Senate for its consideration.

When we remember how difficult it is for one of our own legislative bodies, composed of citizens of the same country, speaking the same language, living under the same laws, and having the same customs, to reach an agreement, or even to secure a majority upon any difficult and important subject which is proposed for legislation, it becomes plain that the representatives of forty-five different countries, speaking many different languages, accustomed to different methods of procedure, with widely diverse interests, who discussed so many different subjects and reached agreements upon so many, are entitled to grateful appreciation for the wisdom, patience, and moderation with which they have discharged their duty. The example of this temperate discussion, and the agreements and the efforts to agree, among representatives of all the nations of the earth, acting with universal recognition of the supreme obligation to promote peace, can not fail to be a powerful influence for good in future international relations.

A year ago in consequence of a revolutionary movement in Cuba which threatened the immediate return to chaos of the island, the United States intervened, sending down an army and establishing a provisional government under Governor Magoon. Absolute quiet and prosperity have returned to the island because of this action. We are now taking steps to provide for elections in the island and our expectation is within the coming year to be able to turn the island over again to a government chosen by the people thereof. Cuba is at our doors. It is not possible that this Nation should permit Cuba again to sink into the condition from which we rescued it. All that we ask of the Cuban people is that they be prosperous, that they govern themselves so as to bring content, order and progress to their island, the Queen of the Antilles; and our only interference has been and will be to help them achieve these results.

An invitation has been extended by Japan to the Government and people of the United States to participate in a great national exposition to be held at Tokyo from April 1 to October 31, 1912, and in which the principal countries of the world are to be invited to take part. This is an occasion of special interest to all the nations of the world, and peculiarly so to us; for it is the first instance in which such a great national exposition has been held by a great power dwelling on the Pacific; and all the nations of Europe and America will, I trust, join in helping to success this first great exposition ever held by a great nation of Asia. The geographical relations of Japan and the United States as the possessors of such large portions of the coasts of the Pacific, the intimate trade relations already existing between the two countries, the warm friendship which has been maintained between them without break since the opening of Japan to intercourse with the western nations, and her increasing wealth and production, which we regard with hearty goodwill and wish to make the occasion of mutually beneficial commerce, all unite in making it eminently desirable that this invitation should be accepted. I heartily recommend such legislation as will provide in generous fashion for the representation of this Government and its people in the proposed exposition. Action should be taken now. We are apt to underestimate the time necessary for preparation in such cases. The invitation to the French Exposition of 1900 was brought to the attention of the Congress by President Cleveland in December, 1895; and so many are the delays necessary to such proceedings that the period of four years and a half which then intervened before the exposition proved none too long for the proper preparation of the exhibits.

The adoption of a new tariff by Germany, accompanied by conventions for reciprocal tariff concessions between that country and most of the other countries of continental Europe, led the German Government to give the notice necessary to terminate the reciprocal commercial agreement with this country proclaimed July 13, 1900. The notice was to take effect on the 1st of March, 1906, and in default of some other arrangements this would have left the exports from the United States to Germany subject to the general German tariff duties, from 25 to 50 per cent higher than the conventional duties imposed upon the goods of most of our competitors for German trade.

Under a special agreement made between the two Governments in February, 1906, the German Government postponed the operation of their notice until the 30th of June, 1907. In the meantime, deeming it to be my duty to make every possible effort to prevent a tariff war between the United States and Germany arising from misunderstanding by either country of the conditions existing in the other, and acting upon the invitation of the German Government, I sent to Berlin a commission composed of competent experts in the operation and administration of the customs tariff, from the Departments of the Treasury and Commerce and Labor. This commission was engaged for several months in conference with a similar commission appointed by the German Government, under instructions, so far as practicable, to reach a common understanding as to all the facts regarding the tariffs of the United States and Germany material and relevant to the trade relations between the two countries. The commission reported, and upon the basis of the report, a further temporary commercial agreement was entered into by the two countries, pursuant to which, in the exercise of the authority conferred upon the President by the third section of the tariff act of July 24, 1897, I extended the reduced tariff rates provided for in that section to champagne and all other sparkling wines, and pursuant to which the German conventional or minimum tariff rates were extended to about 96½ per cent of all the exports from the United States to Germany. This agreement is to remain in force until the 30th of June, 1908, and until six months after notice by either party to terminate it.

The agreement and the report of the commission on which it is based will be laid before the Congress for its information.

This careful examination into the tariff relations between the United States and Germany involved an inquiry into certain of our methods of administration which had been the cause of much complaint on the part of German exporters. In this inquiry I became satisfied that certain vicious and unjustifiable practices had grown up in our customs administration, notably the practice of determining values of imports upon detective reports never disclosed to the persons whose interests were affected. The use of detectives, though often necessary, tends towards abuse, and should be carefully guarded. Under our practice as I found it to exist in this case, the abuse had become gross and discreditable. Under it, instead of seeking information as to the market value of merchandise from the well-known and respected members of the commercial community in the country of its production, secret statements were obtained from informers and discharged employees and business rivals, and upon this kind of secret evidence the values of imported goods were frequently raised and heavy penalties were frequently imposed upon importers who were never permitted to know what the evidence was and who never had an opportunity to meet it. It is quite probable that this system tended towards an increase of the duties collected upon imported goods, but I conceive it to be a violation of law to exact more duties than the law provides, just as it is a violation to admit goods upon the payment of less than the legal rate of duty. This practice was repugnant to the spirit of American law and to American sense of justice. In the judgment of the most competent experts of the Treasury Department and the Department of Commerce and Labor it was wholly unnecessary for the due collection of the customs revenues, and the attempt to defend it merely illustrates the demoralization which naturally follows from a long continued course of reliance upon such methods. I accordingly caused the regulations governing this branch of the customs service to be modified so that values are determined upon a hearing in which all the parties interested have an opportunity to be heard and to know the evidence against them. Moreover our Treasury agents are accredited to the government of the country in which they seek information, and in Germany receive the assistance of the quasi-official chambers of commerce in determining the actual market value of goods, in accordance with what I am advised to be the true construction of the law.

These changes of regulations were adapted to the removal of such manifest abuses that I have not felt that they ought to be confined to our relations with Germany; and I have extended their operation to all other countries which have expressed a desire to enter into similar administrative relations.

I ask for authority to re-form the agreement with China under which the indemnity of 1900 was fixed, by remitting and cancelling the obligation of China for the payment of all that part of the stipulated indemnity which is in excess of the sum of eleven million, six hundred and fifty-five thousand, four hundred and ninety-two dollars and sixty-nine cents, and interest at four per cent. After the rescue of the foreign legations in Peking during the Boxer troubles in 1900 the Powers required from China the payment of equitable indemnities to the several nations, and the final protocol under which the troops were withdrawn, signed at Peking, September 7, 1901, fixed the amount of this indemnity allotted to the United States at over $20,000,000, and China paid, up to and including the 1st day of June last, a little over $6,000,000. It was the first intention of this Government at the proper time, when all claims had been presented and all expenses ascertained as fully as possible, to revise the estimates and account, and as a proof of sincere friendship for China voluntarily to release that country from its legal liability for all payments in excess of the sum which should prove to be necessary for actual indemnity to the United States and its citizens.

This Nation should help in every practicable way in the education of the Chinese people, so that the vast and populous Empire of China may gradually adapt itself to modern conditions. One way of doing this is by promoting the coming of Chinese students to this country and making it attractive to them to take courses at our universities and higher educational institutions. Our educators should, so far as possible, take concerted action toward this end.

On the courteous invitation of the President of Mexico, the Secretary of State visited that country in September and October and was received everywhere with the greatest kindness and hospitality.

He carried from the Government of the United States to our southern neighbor a message of respect and good will and of desire for better acquaintance and increasing friendship. The response from the Government and the people of Mexico was hearty and sincere. No pains were spared to manifest the most friendly attitude and feeling toward the United States.

In view of the close neighborhood of the two countries the relations which exist between Mexico and the United States are just cause for gratification. We have a common boundary of over 1,500 miles from the Gulf of Mexico to the Pacific. Much of it is marked only by the shifting waters of the Rio Grande. Many thousands of Mexicans are residing upon our side of the line and it is estimated that over 40,000 Americans are resident in Mexican territory and that American investments in Mexico amount to over seven hundred million dollars. The extraordinary industrial and commercial prosperity of Mexico has been greatly promoted by American enterprise, and Americans are sharing largely in its results. The foreign trade of the Republic already exceeds $240,000,000 per annum, and of this two-thirds both of exports and imports are exchanged with the United States. Under these circumstances numerous questions necessarily arise between the two countries. These questions are always approached and disposed of in a spirit of mutual courtesy and fair dealing. Americans carrying on business in Mexico testify uniformly to the kindness and consideration with which they are treated and their sense of the security of their property and enterprises under the wise administration of the great statesman who has so long held the office of Chief Magistrate of that Republic.

The two Governments have been uniting their efforts for a considerable time past to aid Central America in attaining the degree of peace and order which have made possible the prosperity of the northern ports of the Continent. After the peace between Guatemala, Honduras, and Salvador, celebrated under the circumstances described in my last Message, a new war broke out between the Republics of Nicaragua, Honduras, and Salvador. The effort to compose this new difficulty has resulted in the acceptance of the joint suggestion of the Presidents of Mexico and of the United States for a general peace conference between all the countries of Central America. On the 17th day of September last a protocol was signed between the representatives of the five Central American countries accredited to this Government agreeing upon a conference to be held in the City of Washington "in order to devise the means of preserving the good relations among said Republics and bringing about permanent peace in those countries." The protocol includes the expression of a wish that the Presidents of the United States and Mexico should appoint "representatives to lend their good and impartial offices in a purely friendly way toward the realization of the objects of the conference." The conference is now in session and will have our best wishes and, where it is practicable, our friendly assistance.

One of the results of the Pan American Conference at Rio Janeiro in the summer of 1906 has been a great increase in the activity and usefulness of the International Bureau of American Republics. That institution, which includes all the American Republics in its membership and brings all their representatives together, is doing a really valuable work in informing the people of the United States about the other Republics and in making the United States known to them. Its action is now limited by appropriations determined when it was doing a work on a much smaller scale and rendering much less valuable service. I recommend that the contribution of this Government to the expenses of the Bureau be made commensurate with its increased work.

EIGHTH ANNUAL MESSAGE

WHITE HOUSE, *Dec. 8, 1908.*

To the Senate and House of Representatives:

FINANCES.

The financial standing of the Nation at the present time is excellent, and the financial management of the Nation's interests by the Government during the last seven years has shown the most satisfactory results. But our currency system is imperfect, and it is earnestly to be hoped that the Currency Commission will be able to propose a thoroughly good system which will do away with the existing defects.

During the period from July 1, 1901, to September 30, 1908, there was an increase in the amount of money in circulation of $902,991,399. The increase in the per capita during this period was $7.06. Within this time there were several occasions when it was necessary for the Treasury Department to come to the relief of the money market by purchases or redemptions of United States bonds; by increasing deposits in national banks; by stimulating additional issues of national bank notes, and by facilitating importations from abroad of gold. Our imperfect currency system has made these proceedings necessary, and they were effective until the monetary disturbance in the fall of 1907 immensely increased the difficulty of ordinary methods of relief. By the middle of November the available working balance in the Treasury had been reduced to approximately $5,000,000. Clearing house associations throughout the country had been obliged to resort to the expedient of issuing clearing house certificates, to be used as money. In this emergency it was determined to invite subscriptions for $50,000,000 Panama Canal bonds, and $100,000,000 three per cent certificates of indebtedness authorized by the act of June 13, 1898. It was proposed to re-deposit in the national banks the proceeds of these issues, and to permit their use as a basis for additional circulating notes of national banks. The moral effect of this procedure was so great that it was necessary to issue only $24,631,980 of the Panama Canal bonds and $15,436,500 of the certificates of indebtedness.

During the period from July 1, 1901, to September 30, 1908, the balance between the net ordinary receipts and the net ordinary expenses of the Government showed a surplus in the four years

1902, 1903, 1906 and 1907, and a deficit in the years 1904, 1905, 1908 and a fractional part of the fiscal year 1909. The net result was a surplus of $99,283,413.54. The financial operations of the Government during this period, based upon these differences between receipts and expenditures, resulted in a net reduction of the interest-bearing debt of the United States from $987,141,040 to $897,253,990, notwithstanding that there had been two sales of Panama Canal bonds amounting in the aggregate to $54,631,980, and an issue of three per cent certificates of indebtedness under the act of June 13, 1898, amounting to $15,436,500. Refunding operations of the Treasury Department under the act of March 14, 1900, resulted in the conversion into two per cent consols of 1930 of $200,309,400 bonds bearing higher rates of interest. A decrease of $8,687,956 in the annual interest charge resulted from these operations.

In short, during the seven years and three months there has been a net surplus of nearly one hundred millions of receipts over expenditures, a reduction of the interest-bearing debt by ninety millions, in spite of the extraordinary expense of the Panama Canal, and a saving of nearly nine millions on the annual interest charge. This is an exceedingly satisfactory showing, especially in view of the fact that during this period the Nation has never hesitated to undertake any expenditure that it regarded as necessary. There have been no new taxes and no increase of taxes; on the contrary, some taxes have been taken off; there has been a reduction of taxation.

CORPORATIONS.

As regards the great corporations engaged in interstate business, and especially the railroad, I can only repeat what I have already again and again said in my messages to the Congress. I believe that under the interstate clause of the Constitution the United States has complete and paramount right to control all agencies of interstate commerce, and I believe that the National Government alone can exercise this right with wisdom and effectiveness so as both to secure justice from, and to do justice to, the great corporations which are the most important factors in modern business. I believe that it is worse than folly to attempt to prohibit all combinations as is done by the Sherman anti-trust law, because such a law can be enforced only imperfectly and unequally, and its enforcement works almost as much hardship as good. I strongly advocate that instead of an unwise effort to prohibit all combinations there shall be substituted a law which shall expressly permit combinations which are in the interest of the public, but shall at the same time give to some agency of the National Government full power of control and supervision over them. One of the chief features of this control should be securing entire publicity in all matters which the public has a right to know, and furthermore, the power, not by judicial but by executive action, to prevent or put a stop to every form of improper favoritism or other wrongdoing.

The railways of the country should be put completely under the Interstate Commerce Commission and removed from the domain of the anti-trust law. The power of the Commission should be made thoroughgoing, so that it could exercise complete supervision and control over the issue of securities as well as over the raising and lowering of rates. As regards rates, at least, this power should be summary. The power to investigate the financial operations and accounts of the railways has been one of the most valuable features in recent legislation. Power to make combinations and traffic agreements should be explicitly conferred upon the railroads, the permission of the Commission being first gained and the combination or agreement being published in all its details. In the interest of the public the representatives of the public should have complete power to see that the railroads do their duty by the public, and as a matter of course this power should also be exercised so as to see that no injustice is done to the railroads. The shareholders, the employees and the shippers all have interests that must be guarded. It is to the interest of all of them that no swindling stock speculation should be allowed, and that there should be no improper issuance of securities. The guiding intelligences necessary for the successful building and successful management of railroads should receive ample remuneration; but no man should be allowed to make money in connection with railroads out of fraudulent over-capitalization and kindred stock-gambling performances; there must be no defrauding of investors, oppression of the farmers and business men who ship freight, or callous disregard of the rights and needs of the employees. In addition to this the interests of the shareholders, of the employees, and of the shippers should all be guarded as against one another. To give any one of them undue and improper consideration is to do injustice to the others. Rates must be made as low as is compatible with giving proper returns to all the employees of the railroad, from the highest to the lowest, and proper returns to the shareholders; but they must not, for instance, be reduced in such fashion as to necessitate a cut in the wages of the employees or the abolition of the proper and legitimate profits of honest shareholders.

Telegraph and telephone companies engaged in interstate business should be put under the jurisdiction of the Interstate Commerce Commission.

It is very earnestly to be wished that our people, through their representatives, should act in this matter. It is hard to say whether most damage to the country at large would come from entire failure on the part of the public to supervise and control the actions of the great corporations, or from the exercise of the necessary governmental power in a way which would do injustice and wrong to the corporations. Both the preachers of an unrestricted individualism, and the preachers of an oppression which would deny to able men of business the just reward of their initiative and business sagacity, are advocating policies that would be fraught with the gravest harm to the whole country. To permit every lawless capitalist, every law-defying corporation, to take any action, no matter how iniquitous, in the effort to secure an improper profit and to build up privilege, would be ruinous to the Republic and would mark the abandonment of the effort to secure in the industrial world the spirit of democratic fair dealing. On the other hand, to attack these wrongs in that spirit of demagogy which can see wrong only when committed by the man of wealth, and is dumb and blind in the presence of wrong committed against men of property or by men of no property, is exactly as evil as corruptly to defend the wrongdoing of men of wealth. The war we wage must be waged against misconduct, against wrongdoing wherever it is found; and we must stand heartily for the rights of every decent man, whether he be a man of great wealth or a man who earns his livelihood as a wage-worker or a tiller of the soil.

It is to the interest of all of us that there should be a premium put upon individual initiative and individual capacity, and an ample reward for the great directing intelligences alone competent to manage the great business operations of to-day. It is well to keep in mind that exactly as the anarchist is the worst enemy of liberty and the reactionary the worst enemy of order, so the men who defend the rights of property have most to fear from the wrongdoers of great wealth, and the men who are championing popular rights have most to fear from the demagogues who in the name of popular rights would do wrong to and oppress honest business men, honest men of wealth; for the success of either type of wrongdoer necessarily invites a violent reaction against the cause the wrongdoer nominally upholds. In point of danger to the Nation there is nothing to choose between on the one hand the corruptionist, the bribe-giver, the bribe-taker, the man who employs his great talent to swindle his fellow-citizens on a large scale, and, on the other hand, the preacher of class hatred, the man who, whether from ignorance or from willingness to sacrifice his country to his ambition, persuades well-meaning but wrong-headed men to try to destroy the instruments upon which our prosperity mainly rests. Let each group of men beware of and guard against the shortcomings to which that group is itself most liable. Too often we see the business community in a spirit of unhealthy class consciousness deplore the effort to hold to account under the law the wealthy men who in their management of great corporations, whether railroads, street railways, or other industrial enterprises, have behaved in a way that revolts the conscience of the plain, decent people.

Such an attitude can not be condemned too severely, for men of property should recognize that they jeopardize the rights of property when they fail heartily to join in the effort to do away with the abuses of wealth. On the other hand, those who advocate proper control on behalf of the public, through the State, of these great corporations, and of the wealth engaged on a giant scale in business operations, must ever keep in mind that unless they do scrupulous justice to the corporation, unless they permit ample profit, and cordially encourage capable men of business so long as they act with honesty, they are striking at the root of our national wellbeing; for in the long run, under the mere pressure of material distress, the people as a whole would probably go back to the reign of an unrestricted individualism rather than submit to a control by the State so drastic and so foolish, conceived in a spirit of such unreasonable and narrow hostility to wealth, as to prevent business operations from being profitable, and therefore to bring ruin upon the entire business community, and ultimately upon the entire body of citizens.

The opposition to Government control of these great corporations makes its most effective effort in the shape of an appeal to the old doctrine of State's rights. Of course there are many sincere men who now believe in unrestricted individualism in business, just as there were formerly many sincere men who believed in slavery—that is, in the unrestricted right of an individual to own another individual. These men do not by themselves have great weight, however. The effective fight against adequate Government control and supervision of individual, and especially of corporate, wealth engaged in interstate business is chiefly done under cover; and especially under cover of an appeal to State's rights. It is not at all infrequent to read in the same speech a denunciation of predatory wealth fostered by special privilege and defiant of both the public welfare and law of the land, and a denunciation of centralization in the Central Government of the power to deal with this centralized and organized wealth. Of course the policy set forth in such twin denunciations amounts to absolutely nothing, for the first half is nullified by the second half. The chief reason, among the many sound and compelling reasons, that led to the formation of the National Government was the absolute need that the Union, and not the several States, should deal with interstate and foreign commerce; and the power to deal with interstate commerce was granted absolutely and plenarily to the Central Government and was exercised completely as regards the only instruments of interstate commerce known in those days—the waterways, the highroads, as well as the partnerships of individuals who then conducted all of what business there was. Interstate commerce is now chiefly conducted by railroads; and the great corporation has supplanted the mass of small partnerships or individuals. The proposal to make the National Government supreme over, and therefore to give it complete control over, the railroads and other instruments of interstate commerce is merely a proposal to carry out to the letter one of the prime purposes, if not the prime purpose, for which the Constitution was founded. It does not represent centralization. It represents merely the acknowledgment of the patent fact that centralization has already come in business. If this irresponsible outside business power is to be controlled in the interest of the general public it can only be controlled in one way—by giving adequate power of control to the one sovereignty capable of exercising such power—the National Government. Forty or fifty separate state governments can not exercise that power over corporations doing business in most or all of them; first, because they absolutely lack the authority to deal with interstate business in any form; and second, because of the inevitable conflict of authority sure to arise in the effort to enforce different kinds of state regulation, often inconsistent with one another and sometimes oppressive in themselves. Such divided authority can not regulate commerce with wisdom and effect. The Central Government is the only power which, without oppression, can nevertheless thoroughly and adequately control and supervise the large corporations. To abandon the effort for National control means to abandon the effort for all adequate control and yet to render likely continual bursts of action by State legislatures, which can not achieve the purpose sought for, but which can do a great deal of damage to the corporation without conferring any real benefit on the public.

I believe that the more farsighted corporations are themselves coming to recognize the unwisdom of the violent hostility they have displayed during the last few years to regulation and control by the National Government of combinations engaged in interstate business. The truth is that we who believe in this movement of asserting and exercising a genuine control, in the public interest, over these great corporations have to contend against two sets of enemies, who, though nominally opposed to one another, are really allies in preventing a proper solution of the problem. There are, first, the big corporation men, and the extreme individualists among business men, who genuinely believe in utterly unregulated business—that is, in the reign of plutocracy; and, second, the men who, being blind to the economic movements of the day, believe in a movement of repression rather than of regulation of corporations, and who denounce both the power of the railroads and the exercise of the Federal power which alone can really control the railroads. Those who believe in efficient national control, on the other hand, do not in the least object to combinations; do not in the least object to concentration in business administration. On the contrary, they favor both, with the all important proviso that there shall be such publicity about their workings, and such thoroughgoing control over them, as to insure their being in the interest, and not against the interest, of the general public. We do not object to the concentration of wealth and administration; but we do believe in the distribution of the wealth in profits to the real owners, and in securing to the public the full benefit of the concentrated administration. We believe that with concentration in administration there can come both the advantage of a larger ownership and of a more equitable distribution of profits, and at the same time a better service to the commonwealth. We believe that the administration should be for the benefit of the many; and that greed and rascality, practiced on a large scale, should be punished as relentlessly as if practiced on a small scale.

We do not for a moment believe that the problem will be solved by any short and easy method. The solution will come only by pressing various concurrent remedies. Some of these remedies must lie outside the domain of all government. Some must lie outside the domain of the Federal Government. But there is legislation which the Federal Government alone can enact and which is absolutely vital in order to secure the attainment of our purpose. Many laws are needed. There should be regulation by the National Government of the great interstate corporations, including a simple method of account keeping, publicity, supervision of the issue of securities, abolition of rebates, and of special privileges. There should be short time franchises for all corporations engaged in public business; including the corporations which get power from water rights. There should be National as well as State guardianship of mines and forests. The labor legislation hereinafter referred to should concurrently be enacted into law.

To accomplish this, means of course a certain increase in the use of—not the creation of—power, by the Central Government. The power already exists; it does not have to be created; the only question is whether it shall be used or left idle—and meanwhile the corporations over which the power ought to be exercised will not remain idle. Let those who object to this increase in the use of the only power available, the national power, be frank, and admit openly that they propose to abandon any effort to control the great business corporations and to exercise supervision over the accumulation and distribution of wealth; for such supervision and control can only come through this particular kind of increase of power. We no more believe in that empiricism which demands absolutely unrestrained individualism than we do in that empiricism which clamors for a deadening socialism which would destroy all individual initiative and would ruin the country with a completeness that not even an unrestrained individualism itself could achieve

The danger to American democracy lies not in the least in the concentration of administrative power in responsible and accountable hands. It lies in having the power insufficiently concentrated, so that no one can be held responsible to the people for its use. Concentrated power is palpable, visible, responsible, easily reached, quickly held to account. Power scattered through many administrators, many legislators, many men who work behind and through legislators and administrators, is impalpable, is unseen, is irresponsible, can not be reached, can not be held to account. Democracy is in peril wherever the administration of political power is scattered among a variety of men who work in secret, whose very names are unknown to the common people. It is not in peril from any man who derives authority from the people, who exercises it in sight of the people, and who is from time to time compelled to give an account of its exercise to the people.

LABOR.

There are many matters affecting labor and the status of the wage-worker to which I should like to draw your attention, but an exhaustive discussion of the problem in all its aspects is not now necessary. This administration is nearing its end; and, moreover, under our form of government the solution of the problem depends upon the action of the States as much as upon the action of the Nation. Nevertheless, there are certain considerations which I wish to set before you, because I hope that our people will more and more keep them in mind. A blind and ignorant resistance to every effort for the reform of abuses and for the readjustment of society to modern industrial conditions represents not true conservatism, but an incitement to the wildest radicalism; for wise radicalism and wise conservatism go hand in hand, one bent on progress, the other bent on seeing that no change is made unless in the right direction. I believe in a steady effort, or perhaps it would be more accurate to say in steady efforts in many different directions, to bring about a condition of affairs under which the men who work with hand or with brain, the laborers, the superintendents, the men who produce for the market and the men who find a market for the articles produced, shall own a far greater share than at present of the wealth they produce, and be enabled to invest it in the tools and instruments by which all work is carried on. As far as possible I hope to see a frank recognition of the advantages conferred by machinery, organization, and division of labor, accompanied by an effort to bring about a larger share in the ownership by wage-worker of railway, mill and factory. In farming, this simply means that we wish to see the farmer own his own land; we do not wish to see the farms so large that they become the property of absentee landlords who farm them by tenants, nor yet so small that the farmer becomes like a European peasant. Again, the depositors in our savings banks now number over one-tenth of our entire population. These are all capitalists, who through the savings banks loan their money to the workers—that is, in many cases to themselves—to carry on their various industries. The more we increase their number, the more we introduce the principles of cooperation into our industry. Every increase in the number of small stockholders in corporations is a good thing, for the same reasons; and where the employees are the stockholders the result is particularly good. Very much of this movement must be outside of anything that can be accomplished by legislation; but legislation can do a good deal. Postal savings banks will make it easy for the poorest to keep their savings in absolute safety. The regulation of the national highways must be such that they shall serve all people with equal justice. Corporate finances must be supervised so as to make it far safer than at present for the man of small means to invest his money in stocks. There must be prohibition of child labor, diminution of woman labor, shortening of hours of all mechanical labor; stock watering should be prohibited, and stock gambling so far as is possible discouraged. There should be a progressive inheritance tax on large fortunes. Industrial education should be encouraged. As far as possible we should lighten the burden of taxation on the small man. We should put a premium upon thrift, hard work, and business energy; but these qualities cease to be the main factors in accumulating a fortune long before that fortune reaches a point where it would be seriously affected by any inheritance tax such as I propose. It is eminently right that the Nation should fix the terms upon which the great fortunes are inherited. They rarely do good and they often do harm to those who inherit them in their entirety.

PROTECTION FOR WAGEWORKERS.

The above is the merest sketch, hardly even a sketch in outline, of the reforms for which we should work. But there is one matter with which the Congress should deal at this session. There should no longer be any paltering with the question of taking care of the wageworkers who, under our present industrial system, become killed, crippled, or worn out as part of the regular incidents of a given business. The majority of wageworkers must have their rights secured for them by State action; but the National Government should legislate in thoroughgoing and far-reaching fashion not only for all employees of the National Government, but for all persons engaged in interstate commerce. The object sought for could be achieved to a measurable degree, as far as those killed or crippled are concerned, by proper employers' liability laws. As far as concerns those who have been worn out, I call your attention to the fact that definite steps toward providing old-age pensions have been taken in many of our private industries. These may be indefinitely extended through voluntary association and contributory schemes, or through the agency of savings banks, as under the recent Massachusetts plan. To strengthen these practical measures should be our immediate duty; it is not at present necessary to consider the larger and more general governmental schemes that most European governments have found themselves obliged to adopt.

Our present system, or rather no system, works dreadful wrong, and is of benefit to only one class of people—the lawyers. When a workman is injured what he needs is not an expensive and doubtful lawsuit, but the certainty of relief through immediate administrative action. The number of accidents which result in the death or crippling of wageworkers, in the Union at large, is simply appalling; in a very few years it runs up a total far in excess of the aggregate of the dead and wounded in any modern war. No academic theory about "freedom of contract" or "constitutional liberty to contract" should be permitted to interfere with this and similar movements. Progress in civilization has everywhere meant a limitation and regulation of contract. I call your especial attention to the bulletin of the Bureau of Labor which gives a statement of the methods of treating the unemployed in European countries, as this is a subject which in Germany, for instance, is treated in connection with making provision for worn-out and crippled workmen.

Pending a thoroughgoing investigation and action there is certain legislation which should be enacted at once. The law, passed at the last session of the Congress, granting compensation to certain classes of employees of the Government, should be extended to include all employees of the Government and should be made more liberal in its terms. There is no good ground for the distinction made in the law between those engaged in hazardous occupations and those not so engaged. If a man is injured or killed in any line of work, it was hazardous in his case. Whether 1 per cent or 10 per cent of those following a given occupation actually suffer injury or death ought not to have any bearing on the question of their receiving compensation. It is a grim logic which says to an injured employee or to the dependents of one killed that he or they are entitled to no compensation because very few people other than he have been injured or killed in that occupation. Perhaps one of the most striking omissions in the law is that it does not embrace peace officers and others whose lives may be sacrificed in enforcing the laws of the United States. The terms of the act providing compensation should be made more liberal than in the present act. A year's compensation is not adequate for a wage-earner's family in the event of his death by accident in the course of his employment. And in the event of death occurring, say, ten or eleven months after the accident, the family would only receive as compensation the equivalent of one or two months' earnings. In this respect the generosity of the United States towards its employees compares most unfavorably with that of every country in Europe—even the poorest.

The terms of the act are also a hardship in prohibiting payment in cases where the accident is in any way due to the negligence of the employee. It is inevitable that daily familiarity with danger will lead men to take chances that can be construed into negligence. So well is this recognized that in practically all countries in the civilized world, except the United States, only a great degree of negligence acts as a bar to securing compensation. Probably in no other respect is our legislation, both State and National, so far behind practically the entire civilized world as in the matter of liability and compensation for accidents in industry. It is humiliating that at European international congresses on accidents the United States should be singled out as the most belated among the nations in respect to employers' liability legislation. This Government is itself a large employer of labor, and in its dealings with its employees it should set a standard in this country which would place it on a par with the most progressive countries in Europe. The laws of the United States in this respect and the laws of European countries have been summarized in a recent Bulletin of the Bureau of Labor, and no American who reads this summary can fail to be struck by the great contrast between our practices and theirs—a contrast not in any sense to our credit.

The Congress should without further delay pass a model employers' liability law for the District of Columbia. The employers' liability act recently declared unconstitutional, on account of apparently including in its provisions employees engaged in intrastate commerce as well as those engaged in interstate commerce, has been held by the local courts to be still in effect so far as its provisions apply to the District of Columbia. There should be no ambiguity on this point. If there is any doubt on the subject, the law should be reenacted with special reference to the District of Columbia. This act, however, applies only to employees of common carriers. In all other occupations the liability law of the District is the old common law. The severity and injustice o fthe common law in this matter has been in some degree or another modified in the majority of our States, and the only jurisdiction under the exclusive control of the Congress should be ahead and not behind the States of the Union in this respect. A comprehensive employers' liability law should be passed for the District of Columbia.

I renew my recommendation made in a previous message that half-holidays be granted during summer to all wageworkers in Government employ.

I also renew my recommendation that the principle of the eight-hour day should as rapidly and as far as practicable be extended to the entire work being carried on by the Government; the present law should be amended to embrace contracts on those public works which the present wording of the act seems to exclude.

THE COURTS.

I most earnestly urge upon the Congress the duty of increasing the totally inadequate salaries now given to our Judges. On the whole there is no body of public servants who do as valuable work, nor whose moneyed reward is so inadequate compared to their work. Beginning with the Supreme Court, the Judges should have their salaries doubled. It is not befitting the dignity of the Nation that its most honored public servants should be paid sums so small compared to what they would earn in private life that the performance of public service by them implies an exceedingly heavy pecuniary sacrifice.

It is earnestly to be desired that some method should be devised for doing away with the long delays which now obtain in the administration of justice, and which operate with peculiar severity against persons of small means, and favor only the very criminals whom it is most desirable to punish. These long delays in the final decisions of cases make in the aggregate a crying evil; and a remedy should be devised. Much of this intolerable delay is due to improper regard paid to technicalities which are a mere hindrance to justice. In some noted recent cases this over-regard for technicalities has resulted in a striking denial of justice, and flagrant wrong to the body politic.

At the last election certain leaders of organized labor made a violent and sweeping attack upon the entire judiciary of the country, an attack couched in such terms as to include the most upright, honest and broad-minded judges, no less than those of narrower mind and more restricted outlook. It was the kind of attack admirably fitted to prevent any successful attempt to reform abuses of the judiciary, because it gave the champions of the unjust judge their eagerly desired opportunity to shift their ground into a championship of just judges who were unjustly assailed. Last year, before the House Committee on the Judiciary, these same labor leaders formulated their demands, specifying the bill that contained them, refusing all compromise, stating they wished the principle of that bill or nothing. They insisted on a provision that in a labor dispute no injunction should issue except to protect a property right, and specifically provided that the right to carry on business should not be construed as a property right; and in a second provision their bill made legal in a labor dispute any act or agreement by or between two or more persons that would not have been unlawful if done by a single person. In other words, this bill legalized blacklisting and boycotting in every form, legalizing, for instance, those forms of the secondary boycott which the anthracite coal strike commission so unreservedly condemned; while the right to carry on a business was explicitly taken out from under that protection which the law throws over property. The demand was made that there should be trial by jury in contempt cases, thereby most seriously impairing the authority of the courts. All this represented a course of policy which, if carried out, would mean the enthronement of class privilege in its crudest and most brutal form, and the destruction of one of the most essential functions of the judiciary in all civilized lands.

The violence of the crusade for this legislation, and its complete failure, illustrate two truths which it is essential our people should learn. In the first place, they ought to teach the workingman, the laborer, the wageworker, that by demanding what is improper and impossible he plays into the hands of his foes. Such a crude and vicious attack upon the courts, even if it were temporarily successful, would inevitably in the end cause a violent reaction and would band the great mass of citizens together, forcing them to stand by all the judges, competent and incompetent alike, rather than to see the wheels of justice stopped. A movement of this kind can ultimately result in nothing but damage to those in whose behalf it is nominally undertaken. This is a most healthy truth, which it is wise for all our people to learn. Any movement based on that class hatred which at times assumes the name of "class consciousness" is certain ultimately to fail, and if it temporarily succeeds, to do far-reaching damage. "Class consciousness," where it is merely another name for the odious vice of class selfishness, is equally noxious whether in an employer's association or in a workingman's association. The movement in question was one in which the appeal was made to all workingmen to vote primarily, not as American citizens, but as individuals of a certain class in society. Such an appeal in the first place revolts the more high-minded and far-sighted among the persons to whom it is addressed, and in the second place tends to arouse a strong antagonism among all other classes of citizens, whom it therefore tends to unite against the very organization on whose behalf it is issued. The result is therefore unfortunate from every standpoint. This healthy truth, by the way, will be learned by the socialists if they ever succeed in establishing in this country an important national party based on such class consciousness and selfish class interest.

The wageworkers, the workingmen, the laboring men of the country, by the way in which they repudiated the effort to get them to cast their votes in response to an appeal to class hatred, have emphasized their sound patriotism and Americanism. The whole country has cause to feel pride in this attitude of sturdy independence, in this uncompromising insistence upon acting simply as good citizens, as good Americans, without regard to fancied—and improper—class interests. Such an attitude is an object-lesson in good citizenship to the entire nation.

But the extreme reactionaries, the persons who blind themselves to the wrongs now and then committed by the courts on laboring men, should also think seriously as to what such a movement as this portends. The judges who have shown themselves able and willing effectively to check the dishonest activity of the very rich man who works iniquity by the mismanagement of corporations, who have shown themselves alert to do justice to the wageworker, and sympathetic with the needs of the mass of our people, so that the dweller in the tenement houses, the man who practices a dangerous trade, the man who is crushed by excessive hours of labor, feel that their needs are understood by the courts—these judges are the real bulwark of the courts; these judges, the judges of the stamp of the President-elect, who have been fearless in opposing labor when it has gone wrong, but fearless also in holding to strict account corporations that work iniquity, and far-sighted in seeing that the workingman gets his rights, are the men of all others to whom we owe it that the appeal for such violent and mistaken legislation has fallen on deaf ears, that the agitation for its passage proved to be without substantial basis. The courts are jeopardized primarily by the action of those Federal and State judges who show inability or unwillingness to put a stop to the wrongdoing of very rich men under modern industrial conditions, and inability or unwillingness to give relief to men of small means or wageworkers who are crushed down by these modern industrial conditions; who, in other words, fail to understand and apply the needed remedies for the new wrongs produced by the new and highly complex social and industrial civilization which has grown up in the last half century.

The rapid changes in our social and industrial life which have attended this rapid growth have made it necessary that, in applying to concrete cases the great rule of right laid down in our Constitution, there should be a full understanding and appreciation of the new conditions to which the rules are to be applied. What would have been an infringement upon liberty half a century ago may be the necessary safeguard of liberty to-day. What would have been an injury to property then may be necessary to the enjoyment of property now. Every judicial decision involves two terms—one, as interpretation of the law; the other, the understanding of the facts to which it is to be applied. The great mass of our judicial officers are, I believe, alive to those changes of conditions which so materially affect the performance of their judicial duties. Our judicial system is sound and effective at core, and it remains, and must ever be maintained, as the safeguard of those principles of liberty and justice which stand at the foundation of American institutions; for, as Burke finely said, when liberty and justice are separated, neither is safe. There are, however, some members of the judicial body who have lagged behind in their understanding of these great and vital changes in the body politic, whose minds have never been opened to the new applications of the old principles made necessary by the new conditions. Judges of this stamp do lasting harm by their decisions, because they convince poor men in need of protection that the courts of the land are profoundly ignorant of and out of sympathy with their needs, and profoundly indifferent or hostile to any proposed remedy. To such men it seems a cruel mockery to have any court decide against them on the ground that it desires to preserve "liberty" in a purely technical form, by withholding liberty in any real and constructive sense. It is desirable that the legislative body should possess, and wherever necessary exercise, the power to determine whether in a given case employers and employees are not on an equal footing, so that the necessities of the latter compel them to submit to such exactions as to hours and conditions of labor as unduly to tax their strength; and only mischief can result when such determination is upset on the ground that there must be no "interference with the liberty to contract"—often a merely academic "liberty," the exercise of which is the negation of real liberty.

There are certain decisions by various courts which have been exceedingly detrimental to the rights of wageworkers. This is true of all the decisions that decide that men and women are, by the Constitution, "guaranteed their liberty" to contract to enter a dangerous occupation, or to work an undesirable or improper number of hours, or to work in unhealthy surroundings; and therefore can not recover damages when maimed in that occupation and can not be forbidden to work what the legislature decides is an excessive number of hours, or to carry on the work under conditions which the legislature decides to be unhealthy. The most dangerous occupations are often the poorest paid and those where the hours of work are longest; and in many cases those who go into them are driven by necessity so great that they have practically no alternative. Decisions such as those alluded to above nullify the legislative effort to protect the wageworkers who most need protection from those employers who take advantage of their grinding need. They halt or hamper the movement for securing better and more equitable conditions of labor. The talk about preserving to the misery-hunted beings who make contracts for such service their "liberty" to make them, is either to speak in a spirit of heartless irony or else to show an utter lack of knowledge of the conditions of life among the great masses of our fellow-countrymen, a lack which unfits a judge to do good service just as it would unfit any executive or legislative officer.

There is also, I think, ground for the belief that substantial injustice is often suffered by employees in consequence of the custom of courts issuing temporary injunctions without notice to them, and punishing them for contempt of court in instances where, as a matter of fact, they have no knowledge of any proceedings. Outside of organized labor there is a widespread feeling that this system often works great injustice to wageworkers when their efforts to better their working condition result in industrial disputes. A temporary injunction procured ex parte may as a matter of fact have all the effect of a permanent injunction in causing disaster to the wageworkers' side in such a dispute. Organized labor is chafing under the unjust restraint which comes from repeated resort to this plan of procedure. Its discontent has been unwisely expressed, and often improperly expressed, but there is a sound basis for it, and the orderly and law-abiding people of a community would be in a far stronger position for upholding the courts if the undoubtedly existing abuses could be provided against.

Such proposals as those mentioned above as advocated by the extreme labor leaders contain the vital error of being class legislation of the most offensive kind, and even if enacted into law I believe that the law would rightly be held unconstitutional. Moreover, the labor people are themselves now beginning to invoke the use of the power of injunction. During the last ten years, and within my own knowledge, at least fifty injunctions have been obtained by labor unions in New York City alone, most of them being to protect the union label (a "property right"), but some being obtained for other reasons against employers. The power of injunction is a great equitable remedy, which should on no account be destroyed. But safeguards should be erected against its abuse. I believe that some such provisions as those I advocated a year ago for checking the abuse of the issuance of temporary injunctions should be adopted. In substance, provision should be made that no injunction or temporary restraining order issue otherwise than on notice, except where irreparable injury would otherwise result; and in such case a hearing on the merits of the order should be had within a short fixed period, and, if not then continued after hearing, it should forthwith lapse. Decisions should be rendered immediately, and the chance of delay minimized in every way. Moreover, I believe that the procedure should be sharply defined, and the judge required minutely to state the particulars both of his action and of his reasons therefor, so that the Congress can, if it desires, examine and investigate the same.

The chief lawmakers in our country may be, and often are, the judges, because they are the final seat of authority. Every time they interpret contract, property, vested rights, due process of law, liberty, they necessarily enact into law parts of a system of social philosophy; and as such interpretation is fundamental, they give direction to all law-making. The decisions of the courts on economic and social questions depend upon their economic and social philosophy; and for the peaceful progress of our people during the twentieth century we shall owe most to those judges who hold to a twentieth century economic and social philosophy and not to a long outgrown philosophy, which was itself the product of primitive economic conditions. Of course a judge's views on progressive social philosophy are entirely second in importance to his possession of a high and fine character; which means the possession of such elementary virtues as honesty, courage, and fairmindedness. The judge who owes his election to pandering to demagogic sentiments or class hatreds and prejudices, and the judge who owes either his election or his appointment to the money or the favor of a great corporation, are alike unworthy to sit on the bench, are alike traitors to the people; and no profundity of legal learning, or correctness of abstract conviction on questions of public policy, can serve as an offset to such shortcomings. But it is also true that judges, like executives and legislators, should hold sound views on the questions of public policy which are of vital interest to the people.

The legislators and executives are chosen to represent the people in enacting and administering the laws. The judges are not chosen to represent the people in this sense. Their function is to interpret the laws. The legislators are responsible for the laws; the judges for the spirit in which they interpret and enforce the laws. We stand aloof from the reckless agitators who would make the judges mere pliant tools of popular prejudice and passion; and we stand aloof from those equally unwise partisans of reaction and privilege who deny the proposition that, inasmuch as judges are chosen to serve the interests of the whole people, they should strive to find out what those interests are, and, so far as they conscientiously can, should strive to give effect to popular conviction when deliberately and duly expressed by the lawmaking body. The courts are to be highly commended and staunchly upheld when they set their faces against wrongdoing or tyranny by a majority; but they are to be blamed when they fail to recognize under a government like ours the deliberate judgment of the majority as to a matter of legitimate policy, when duly expressed by the legislature. Such lawfully expressed and deliberate judgment should be given effect by the courts, save in the extreme and exceptional cases where there has been a clear violation of a constitutional provision. Anything like frivolity or wantonness in upsetting such clearly taken governmental action is a grave offense against the Republic. To protest against tyranny, to protect minorities from oppression, to nullify an act committed in a spasm of popular fury, is to render a service to the Republic. But for the courts to arrogate to themselves functions which properly belong to the legislative bodies is all wrong, and in the end works mischief. The people should not be permitted to pardon evil and slipshod legislation on the theory that the court will set it right; they should be taught that the right way to get rid of a bad law is to have the legislature repeal it, and not to have the courts by ingenious hair-splitting nullify it. A law may be unwise and improper; but it should not for these reasons be declared unconstitutional by a strained interpretation, for the result of such action is to take away from the people at large their sense of responsibility and ultimately to destroy their capacity for orderly self restraint and self government. Under such a popular government as ours, founded on the theory that in the long run the will of the people is supreme, the ultimate safety of the Nation can only rest in training and guiding the people so that what they will shall be right, and not in devising means to defeat their will by the technicalities of strained construction.

For many of the shortcomings of justice in our country our people as a whole are themselves to blame, and the judges and juries merely bear their share together with the public as a whole. It is discreditable to us as a people that there should be difficulty in convicting murderers, or in bringing to justice men who as public servants have been guilty of corruption, or who have profited by the corruption of public servants. The result is equally unfortunate, whether due to hairsplitting technicalities in the interpretation of law by judges, to sentimentality and class consciousness on the part of juries, or to hysteria and sensationalism in the daily press. For much of this failure of justice no responsibility whatever lies on rich men as such. We who make up the mass of the people can not shift the responsibility from our own shoulders. But there is an important part of the failure which has specially to do with inability to hold to proper account men of wealth who behave badly.

The chief breakdown is in dealing with the new relations that arise from the mutualism, the interdependence of our time. Every new social relation begets a new type of wrongdoing—of sin, to use an old-fashioned word—and many years always elapse before society is able to turn this sin into crime which can be effectively punished at law. During the lifetime of the older men now alive the social relations have changed far more rapidly than in the preceding two centuries. The immense growth of corporations, of business done by associations, and the extreme strain and pressure of modern life, have produced conditions which render the public confused as to who its really dangerous foes are; and among the public servants who have not only shared this confusion, but by some of their acts have increased it, are certain judges. Marked inefficiency has been shown in dealing with corporations and in re-settling the proper attitude to be taken by the public not only towards corporations, but towards labor and towards the social questions arising out of the factory system and the enormous growth of our great cities.

The huge wealth that has been accumulated by a few individuals of recent years, in what has amounted to a social and industrial revolution, has been as regards some of these individuals made possible only by the improper use of the modern corporation. A certain type of modern corporation, with its officers and agents, its many issues of securities, and its constant consolidation with allied undertakings, finally becomes an instrument so complex as to contain a greater number of elements that, under various judicial decisions, lend themselves to fraud and oppression than any device yet evolved in the human brain. Corporations are necessary instruments of modern business. They have been permitted to become a menace largely because the governmental representatives of the people have worked slowly in providing for adequate control over them.

The chief offender in any given case may be an executive, a legislature, or a judge. Every executive head who advises violent, instead of gradual, action, or who advocates ill-considered and sweeping measures of reform (especially if they are tainted with vindictiveness and disregard for the rights of the minority) is particularly blameworthy. The several legislatures are responsible for the fact that our laws are often prepared with slovenly haste and lack of consideration. Moreover, they are often prepared, and still more frequently amended during passage, at the suggestion of the very parties against whom they are afterwards enforced. Our great clusters of corporations, huge trusts and fabulously wealthy multimillionaires, employ the very best lawyers they can obtain to pick flaws in these statutes after their passage; but they also employ a class of secret agents who seek, under the advice of experts, to render hostile legislation innocuous by making it unconstitutional, often through the insertion of what appear on their face to be drastic and sweeping provisions against the interests of the parties inspiring them; while the demagogues, the corrupt creatures who introduce blackmailing schemes to "strike" corporations, and all who demand extreme, and undesirably radical, measures, show themselves to be the worst enemies of the very public whose loud-mouthed champions they profess to be. A very striking illustration of the consequences of carelessness in the preparation of a statute was the employers' liability law of 1906. In the cases arising under that law, four out of six courts of first instance held it unconstitutional; six out of nine justices of the Supreme Court held that its subject-matter was within the province of congressional action; and four of the nine justices held it valid. It was, however, adjudged unconstitutional by a bare majority of the court—five to four. It was surely a very slovenly piece of work to frame the legislation in such shape as to leave the question open at all.

Real damage has been done by the manifold and conflicting interpretations of the interstate commerce law. Control over the great corporations doing interstate business can be effective only if it is vested with full power in an administrative department, a branch of the Federal executive, carrying out a Federal law; it can never be effective if a divided responsibility is left in both the States and the Nation; it can never be effective if left in the hands of the courts to be decided by lawsuits.

The courts hold a place of peculiar and deserved sanctity under our form of government. Respect for the law is essential to the permanence of our institutions; and respect for the law is largely conditioned upon respect for the courts. It is an offense against the Republic to say anything which can weaken this respect, save for the gravest reason and in the most carefully guarded manner. Our judges should be held in peculiar honor; and the duty of respectful and truthful comment and criticism, which should be binding when we speak of anybody, should be especially binding when we speak of them. On an average they stand above any other servants of the community, and the greatest judges have reached the high level held by those few greatest patriots whom the whole country delights to honor. But we must face the fact that there are wise and unwise judges, just as there are wise and unwise executives and legislators. When a president or a governor behaves improperly or unwisely, the remedy is easy, for his term is short; the same is true with the legislator, although not to the same degree, for he is one of many who belong to some given legislative body, and it is therefore less easy to fix his personal responsibility and hold him accountable therefor. With a judge, who, being human, is also likely to err, but whose tenure is for life, there is no similar way of holding him to responsibility. Under ordinary conditions the only forms of pressure to which he is in any way amenable are public opinion and the action of his fellow judges. It is the last which is most immediately effective, and to which we should look for the reform of abuses. Any remedy applied from without is fraught with risk. It is far better, from every standpoint, that the remedy should come from within. In no other nation in the world do the courts wield such vast and far-reaching power as in the United States. All that is necessary is that the courts as a whole should exercise this power with the farsighted wisdom already shown by those judges who scan the future while they act in the present. Let them exercise this great power not only honestly and bravely, but with wise insight into the needs and fixed purposes of the people, so that they may do justice and work equity, so that they may protect all persons in their rights, and yet break down the barriers of privilege, which is the foe of right.

FORESTS.

If there is any one duty which more than another we owe it to our children and our children's children to perform at once, it is to save the forests of this country, for they constitute the first and most important element in the conservation of the natural resources of the country. There are of course two kinds of natural resources. One is the kind which can only be used as part of a process of exhaustion; this is true of mines, natural oil and gas wells, and the like. The other, and of course ultimately by far the most important, includes the resources which can be improved in the process of wise use; the soil, the rivers, and the forests come under this head. Any really civilized nation will so use all of these three great national assets that the nation will have their benefit in the future. Just as a farmer, after all his life making his living from his farm, will, if he is an expert farmer, leave it as an asset of increased value to his son, so we should leave our national domain to our children, increased in value and not worn out. There are small sections of our own country, in the East and the West, in the Adriondacks, the White Mountains, and the Appalachians, and in the Rocky Mountains, where we can already see for ourselves the damage in the shape of permanent injury to the soil and the river systems which comes from reckless deforestation. It matters not whether this deforestation is due to the actual reckless cutting of timber, to the fires that inevitably follow such reckless cutting of timber, or to reckless and uncontrolled grazing, especially by the great migratory bands of sheep, the unchecked wandering of which over the country means destruction to forests and disaster to the small home makers, the settlers of limited means.

Shortsighted persons, or persons blinded to the future by desire to make money in every way out of the present, sometimes speak as if no great damage would be done by the reckless destruction of our forests. It is difficult to have patience with the arguments of these persons. Thanks to our own recklessness in the use of our splendid forests, we have already crossed the verge of a timber famine in this country, and no measures that we now take can, at least for many years, undo the mischief that has already been done. But we can prevent further mischief being done; and it would be in the highest degree reprehensible to let any consideration of temporary convenience or temporary cost interfere with such action, especially as regards the National Forests which the nation can *now*, at this very moment, control.

All serious students of the question are aware of the great damage that has been done in the Mediterranean countries of Europe, Asia, and Africa by deforestation. The similar damage that has been done in Eastern Asia is less well known. A recent investigation into conditions in North China by Mr. Frank N. Meyer, of the Bureau of Plant Industry of the United States Department of Agriculture, has incidentally furnished in very striking fashion proof of the ruin that comes from reckless deforestation of mountains, and of the further fact that the damage once done may prove practically irreparable. So important are these investigations that I herewith attach as an appendix to my message certain photographs showing present conditions in China. They show in vivid fashion the appalling desolation, taking the shape of barren mountains and gravel- and sand-covered plains, which immediately follows and depends upon the deforestation of the mountains. Not many centuries ago the country of northern China was one of the most fertile and beautiful spots in the entire world, and was heavily forested. We know this not only from the old Chinese records, but from the accounts given by the traveler, Marco Polo. He, for instance, mentions that in visiting the provinces of Shansi and Shensi he observed many plantations of mulberry trees. Now there is hardly a single mulberry tree in either of these provinces, and the culture of the silkworm has moved farther south, to regions of atmospheric moisture. As an illustration of the complete change in the rivers, we may take Polo's statement that a certain river, the Hun Ho, was so large and deep that merchants ascended it from the sea with heavily laden boats; today this river is simply a broad sandy bed, with shallow, rapid currents wandering hither and thither across it, absolutely unnavigable. But we do not have to depend upon written records. The dry wells, and the wells with water far below the former watermark, bear testimony to the good days of the past and the evil days of the present. Wherever the native vegetation has been allowed to remain, as, for instance, here and there around a sacred temple or imperial burying ground, there are still huge trees and tangled jungle, fragments of the glorious ancient forests. The thick, matted forest growth formerly covered the mountains to their summits. All natural factors favored this dense forest growth, and as long as it was permitted to exist the plains at the foot of the mountains were among the most fertile on the globe, and the whole country was a garden. Not the slightest effort was made, however, to prevent the unchecked cutting of the trees, or to secure reforestation. Doubtless for many centuries the tree-cutting by the inhabitants of the mountains worked but slowly in bringing about the changes that have now come to pass; doubtless for generations the inroads were scarcely noticeable. But there came a time when the forest had shrunk sufficiently to make each year's cutting a serious matter, and from that time on the destruction proceeded with appalling rapidity; for of course each year of destruction rendered the forest less able to recuperate, less able to resist next year's inroad. Mr. Meyer describes the ceaseless progress of the destruction even now, when there is so little left to destroy. Every morning men and boys go out armed with mattox or axe, scale the steepest mountain sides, and cut down and grub out, root and branch, the small trees and shrubs still to be found. The big trees disappeared centuries ago, so that now one of these is never seen save in the neighborhood of temples, where they are artificially protected; and even here it takes all the watch and care of the tree-loving priests to prevent their destruction. Each family, each community, where there is no common care exercised in the interest of all of them to prevent deforestation, finds its profit in the immediate use of the fuel which would otherwise be used by some other family or some other community. In the total absence of regulation of the matter in the interest of the whole people, each small group is inevitably pushed into a policy of destruction which can not afford to take thought for the morrow. This is just one of those matters which it is fatal to leave to unsupervised individual control. The forest can only be protected by the State, by the Nation; and the liberty of action of individuals must be conditioned upon what the State or Nation determines to be necessary for the common safety.

The lesson of deforestation in China is a lesson which mankind should have learned many times already from what has occurred in other places. Denudation leaves naked soil; then gullying cuts down to the bare rock; and meanwhile the rock-waste buries the bottom-lands. When the soil is gone, men must go; and the process does not take long.

This ruthless destruction of the forests in northern China has brought about, or has aided in bringing about, desolation, just as the destruction of the forests in central Asia aid in bringing ruin to the once rich central Asian cities; just as the destruction of the forest in northern Africa helped towards the ruin of a region that was a fertile granary in Roman days. Shortsighted man, whether barbaric, semi-civilized, or what he mistakenly regards as fully civilized, when he has destroyed the forests, has rendered certain the ultimate destruction of the land itself. In northern China the mountains are now such as are shown by the accompanying photographs, absolutely barren peaks. Not only have the forests been destroyed, but because of their destruction the soil has been washed off the naked rock. The terrible consequence is that it is impossible now to undo the damage that has been done. Many centuries would have to pass before soil would again collect, or could be made to collect, in sufficient quantity once more to support the old-time forest growth. In consequence the Mongol Desert is practically extending eastward over northern China. The climate has changed and is still changing. It has changed even within the last half century, as the work of tree destruction has been consummated. The great masses of arboreal vegetation on the mountains formerly absorbed the heat of the sun and sent up currents of cool air which brought the moisture-laden clouds lower and forced them to precipitate in rain a part of their burden of water. Now that there is no vegetation, the barren mountains, scorched by the sun, send up currents of heated air which drive away instead of attracting the rain clouds, and cause their moisture to be disseminated. In consequence, instead of the regular and plentiful rains which existed in these regions of China when the forests were still in evidence, the unfortunate inhabitants of the deforested lands now see their crops wither for lack of rainfall, while the seasons grow more and more irregular; and as the air becomes dryer certain crops refuse longer to grow at all. That everything dries out faster than formerly is shown by the fact that the level of the wells all over the land has sunk perceptibly, many of them having become totally dry. In addition to the resulting agricultural distress, the watercourses have changed. Formerly they were narrow and deep, with an abundance of clear water the year around; for the roots and humus of the forests caught the rainwater and let it escape by slow, regular seepage. They have now become broad, shallow stream beds, in which muddy water trickles in slender currents during the dry seasons, while when it rains there are freshets, and roaring muddy torrents come tearing down, bringing disaster and destruction everywhere. Moreover, these floods and freshets, which diversify the general dryness, wash away from the mountain sides, and either wash away or cover in the valleys, the rich fertile soil which it took tens of thousands of years for Nature to form; and it is lost forever, and until the forests grow again it can not be replaced. The sand and stones from the mountain sides are washed loose and come rolling down to cover the arable lands, and in consequence, throughout this part of China, many formerly rich districts are now sandy wastes, useless for human cultivation and even for pasture. The cities have been of course seriously affected, for the streams have gradually ceased to be navigable. There is testimony that even within the memory of men now living there has been a serious diminution of the rainfall of northeastern China. The level of the Sungari River in northern Manchuria has been sensibly lowered during the last fifty years, at least partly as the result of the indiscriminate cutting of the forests forming its watershed. Almost all the rivers of northern China have become uncontrollable, and very dangerous to the dwellers along their banks, as a direct result of the destruction of the forests. The journey from Pekin to Jehol shows in melancholy fashion how the soil has been washed away from whole valleys, so that they have been converted into deserts.

In northern China this disastrous process has gone on so long and has proceeded so far that no complete remedy could be applied. There are certain mountains in China from which the soil is gone so utterly that only the slow action of the ages could again restore it; although of course much could be done to prevent the still further eastward extension of the Mongolian Desert if the Chinese Government would act at once. The accompanying cuts from photographs show the inconceivable desolation of the barren mountains in which certain of these rivers rise—mountains, be it remembered, which formerly supported dense forests of larches and firs, now unable to produce any wood, and because of their condition a source of danger to the whole country. The photographs also show the same rivers after they have passed through the mountains, the beds having become broad and sandy because of the deforestation of the mountains. One of the photographs shows a caravan passing through a valley. Formerly, when the mountains were forested, it was thickly peopled by prosperous peasants. Now the floods have carried destruction all over the land and the valley is a stony desert. Another photograph shows a mountain road covered with the stones and rocks that are brought down in the rainy season from the mountains which have already been deforested by human hands. Another shows a pebbly river-bed in southern Manchuria where what was once a great stream has dried up owing to the deforestation in the mountains. Only some scrub wood is left, which will disappear within a half century. Yet another shows the effect of one of the washouts, destroying an arable mountain side, these washouts being due to the removal of all vegetation; yet in this photograph the foreground shows that reforestation is still a possibility in places.

What has thus happened in northern China, what has happened in Central Asia, in Palestine, in North Africa, in parts of the Mediterranean countries of Europe, will surely happen in our country if we do not exercise that wise forethought which should be one of the chief marks of any people calling itself civilized. Nothing should be permitted to stand in the way of the preservation of the forests, and it is criminal to permit individuals to purchase a little gain for themselves through the destruction of forests when this destruction is fatal to the wellbeing of the whole country in the future.

INLAND WATERWAYS.

Action should be begun forthwith, during the present session of the Congress, for the improvement of our inland waterways—action which will result in giving us not only navigable but navigated rivers. We have spent hundreds of millions of dollars upon these waterways, yet the traffic on nearly all of them is steadily declining. This condition is the direct result of the absence of any comprehensive and far-seeing plan of waterway improvement. Obviously we can not continue thus to expend the revenues of the Government without return. It is poor business to spend money for inland navigation unless we get it.

Inquiry into the condition of the Mississippi and its principal tributaries reveals very many instances of the utter waste caused by the methods which have hitherto obtained for the so-called "improvement" of navigation. A striking instance is supplied by the "improvement" of the Ohio, which, begun in 1824, was continued under a single plan for half a century. In 1875 a new plan was adopted and followed for a quarter of a century. In 1902 still a different plan was adopted and has since been pursued at a rate which only promises a navigable river in from twenty to one hundred years longer.

Such shortsighted, vacillating, and futile methods are accompanied by decreasing water-borne commerce and increasing traffic congestion on land, by increasing floods, and by the waste of public money. The remedy lies in abandoning the methods which have so signally failed and adopting new ones in keeping with the needs and demands of our people.

In a report on a measure introduced at the first session of the present Congress, the Secretary of War said: "The chief defect in the methods hitherto pursued lies in the absence of executive authority for originating comprehensive plans covering the country or natural divisions thereof." In this opinion I heartily concur. The present methods not only fail to give us inland navigation, but they are injurious to the army as well. What is virtually a permanent detail of the corps of engineers to civilian duty necessarily impairs the efficiency of our military establishment. The military engineers have undoubtedly done efficient work in actual construction, but they are necessarily unsuited by their training and traditions to take the broad view, and to gather and transmit to the Congress the commercial and industrial information and forecasts, upon which waterway improvement must always so largely rest. Furthermore, they have failed to grasp the great underlying fact that every stream is a unit from its source to its mouth, and that all its uses are interdependent. Prominent officers of the Engineer Corps have recently even gone so far as to assert in print that waterways are not dependent upon the conservation of the forests about their headwaters. This position is opposed to all the recent work of the scientific bureaus of the Government and to the general experience of mankind. A physician who disbelieved in vaccination would not be the right man to handle an epidemic of smallpox, nor should we leave a doctor skeptical about the transmission of yellow fever by the Stegomyia mosquito in charge of sanitation at Havana or Panama. So with the improvement of our rivers; it is no longer wise or safe to leave this great work in the hands of men who fail to grasp the essential relations between navigation and general development and to assimilate and use the central facts about our streams.

Until the work of river improvement is undertaken in a modern way it can not have results that will meet the needs of this modern nation. These needs should be met without further dilly-dallying or delay. The plan which promises the best and quickest results is that of a permanent commission authorized to coordinate the work of all the Government departments relating to waterways, and to frame and supervise the execution of a comprehensive plan. Under such a commission the actual work of construction might be entrusted to the reclamation service; or to the military engineers acting with a sufficient number of civilians to continue the work in time of war; or it might be divided between the reclamation service and the corps of engineers. Funds should be provided from current revenues if it is deemed wise—otherwise from the sale of bonds. The essential thing is that the work should go forward under the best possible plan, and with the least possible delay. We should have a new type of work and a new organization for planning and directing it. The time for playing with our waterways is past. The country demands results.

NATIONAL PARKS.

I urge that all our National parks adjacent to National forests be placed completely under the control of the forest service of the Agricultural Department, instead of leaving them as they now are, under the Interior Department and policed by the army. The Congress should provide for superintendents with adequate corps of first-class civilian scouts, or rangers, and, further, place the road construction under the superintendent instead of leaving it with the War Department. Such a change in park management would result in economy and avoid the difficulties of administration which now arise from having the responsibility of care and protection divided between different departments. The need for this course is peculiarly great in the Yellowstone Park. This, like the Yosemite, is a great wonderland, and should be kept as a national playground. In both, all wild things should be protected and the scenery kept wholly unmarred.

I am happy to say that I have been able to set aside in various parts of the country small, well-chosen tracts of ground to serve as sanctuaries and nurseries for wild creatures.

DENATURED ALCOHOL.

I had occasion in my message of May 4, 1906, to urge the passage of some law putting alcohol, used in the arts, industries, and manufactures, upon the free list—that is, to provide for the withdrawal free of tax of alcohol which is to be denatured for those purposes. The law of June 7, 1906, and its amendment of March 2, 1907, accomplished what was desired in that respect, and the use of denatured alcohol, as intended, is making a fair degree of progress and is entitled to further encouragement and support from the Congress.

PURE FOOD.

The pure food legislation has already worked a benefit difficult to overestimate.

INDIAN SERVICE.

It has been my purpose from the beginning of my administration to take the Indian Service completely out of the atmosphere of political activity, and there has been steady progress toward that end. The last remaining stronghold of politics in that service was the agency system, which had seen its best days and was gradually falling to pieces from natural or purely evolutionary causes, but, like all such survivals, was decaying slowly in its later stages. It seems clear that its extinction had better be made final now, so that the ground can be cleared for larger constructive work on behalf of the Indians, preparatory to their induction into the full measure of responsible citizenship. On November 1 only eighteen agencies were left on the roster; with two exceptions, where some legal questions seemed to stand temporarily in the way, these have been changed to superintendencies, and their heads brought into the classified civil service.

SECRET SERVICE.

Last year an amendment was incorporated in the measure providing for the Secret Service, which provided that there should be no detail from the Secret Service and no transfer therefrom. It is not too much to say that this amendment has been of benefit only, and could be of benefit only, to the criminal classes. If deliberately introduced for the purpose of diminishing the effectiveness of war against crime it could not have been better devised to this end. It forbade the practices that had been followed to a greater or less extent by the executive heads of various departments for twenty years. To these practices we owe the securing of the evidence which enabled us to drive great lotteries out of business and secure a quarter of a million of dollars in fines from their promoters. These practices have enabled us to get some of the evidence indispensable in order in connection with the theft of government land and government timber by great corporations and by individuals. These practices have enabled us to get some of the evidence indispensable in order to secure the conviction of the wealthiest and most formidable criminals with whom the Government has to deal, both those operating in violation of the anti-trust law and others. The amendment in question was of benefit to no one excepting to these criminals, and it seriously hampers the Government in the detection of crime and the securing of justice. Moreover, it not only affects departments outside of the Treasury, but it tends to hamper the Secretary of the Treasury himself in the effort to utilize the employees of his department so as to best meet the requirements of the public service. It forbids him from preventing frauds upon the customs service, from investigating irregularities in branch mints and assay offices, and has seriously crippled him. It prevents the promotion of employees in the Secret Service, and this further discourages good effort. In its present form the restriction operates only to the advantage of the criminal, of the wrongdoer. The chief argument in favor of the provision was that the Congressmen did not themselves wish to be investigated by Secret Service men. Very little of such investigation has been done in the past; but it is true that the work of the Secret Service agents was partly responsible for the indictment and conviction of a Senator and a Congressman for land frauds in Oregon. I do not believe that it is in the public interest to protect criminally in any branch of the public service, and exactly as we have again and again during the past seven years prosecuted and convicted such criminals who were in the executive branch of the Government, so in my belief we should be given ample means to prosecute them if found in the legislative branch. But if this is not considered desirable a special exception could be made in the law prohibiting the use of the Secret Service force in investigating members of the Congress. It would be far better to do this than to do what actually was done, and strive to prevent or at least to hamper effective action against criminals by the executive branch of the Government.

POSTAL SAVINGS BANKS.

I again renew my recommendation for postal savings banks, for depositing savings with the security of the Government behind them. The object is to encourage thrift and economy in the wage-earner and person of moderate means. In 14 States the deposits in savings banks as reported to the Comptroller of the Currency amount to $3,590,245,402, or 98.4 per cent of the entire deposits, while in the remaining 32 States there are only $70,308,543, or 1.6 per cent, showing conclusively that there are many localities in the United States where sufficient opportunity is not given to the people to deposit their savings. The result is that money is kept in hiding and unemployed. It is believed that in the aggregate vast sums of money would be brought into circulation through the instrumentality of the postal savings banks. While there are only 1,453 savings banks reporting to the Comptroller there are more than

61,000 post-offices, 40,000 of which are money order offices. Postal savings banks are now in operation in practically all of the great civilized countries with the exception of the United States.

PARCEL POST.

In my last annual message I commended the Postmaster-General's recommendation for an extension of the parcel post on the rural routes. The establishment of a local parcel post on rural routes would be to the mutual benefit of the farmer and the country storekeeper, and it is desirable that the routes, serving more than 15,000,000 people, should be utilized to the fullest practicable extent. An amendment was proposed in the Senate at the last session, at the suggestion of the Postmaster-General, providing that, for the purpose of ascertaining the practicability of establishing a special local parcel post system on the rural routes throughout the United States, the Postmaster-General be authorized and directed to experiment and report to the Congress the result of such experiment by establishing a special local parcel post system on rural delivery routes in not to exceed four counties in the United States for packages of fourth-class matter originating on a rural route or at the distributing post office for delivery by rural carriers. It would seem only proper that such an experiment should be tried in order to demonstrate the practicability of the proposition, especially as the Postmaster-General estimates that the revenue derived from the operation of such a system on all the rural routes would amount to many million dollars.

EDUCATION.

The share that the National Government should take in the broad work of education has not received the attention and the care it rightly deserves. The immediate responsibility for the support and improvement of our educational systems and institutions rests and should always rest with the people of the several States acting through their state and local governments, but the Nation has an opportunity in educational work which must not be lost and a duty which should no longer be neglected.

The National Bureau of Education was established more than forty years ago. Its purpose is to collect and diffuse such information "as shall aid the people of the United States in the establishment and maintenance of efficient school systems and otherwise promote the cause of education throughout the country." This purpose in no way conflicts with the educational work of the States, but may be made of great advantage to the States by giving them the fullest, most accurate, and hence the most helpful information and suggestion regarding the best educational systems. The Nation, through its broader field of activities, its wider opportunity for obtaining information from all the States and from foreign countries, is able to do that which not even the richest States can do, and with the distinct additional advantage that the information thus obtained is used for the immediate benefit of all our people.

With the limited means hitherto provided, the Bureau of Education has rendered efficient service, but the Congress has neglected to adequately supply the bureau with means to meet the educational growth of the country. The appropriations for the general work of the bureau, outside education in Alaska, for the year 1909 are but $87,500—an amount less than they were ten years ago, and some of the important items in these appropriations are less than they were thirty years ago. It is an inexcusable waste of public money to appropriate an amount which is so inadequate as to make it impossible properly to do the work authorized, and it is unfair to the great educational interests of the country to deprive them of the value of the results which can be obtained by proper appropriations.

I earnestly recommend that this unfortunate state of affairs as regards the national educational office be remedied by adequate appropriations. This recommendation is urged by the representatives of our common schools and great state universities and the leading educators, who all unite in requesting favorable consideration and action by the Congress upon this subject.

CENSUS.

I strongly urge that the request of the Director of the Census in connection with the decennial work so soon to be begun be complied with and that the appointments to the census force be placed under the civil service law, waiving the geographical requirements as requested by the Director of the Census. The supervisors and enumerators should not be appointed under the civil service law, for the reasons given by the Director. I commend to the Congress the careful consideration of the admirable report of the Director of the Census, and I trust that his recommendations will be adopted and immediate action thereon taken.

PUBLIC HEALTH

It is highly advisable that there should be intelligent action on the part of the Nation on the question of preserving the health of the country. Through the practical extermination in San Francisco of disease-bearing rodents our country has thus far escaped the bubonic plague. This is but one of the many achievements of American health officers; and it shows what can be accomplished with a better organization than at present exists. The dangers to public health from food adulteration and from many other sources, such as the menace to the physical, mental and moral development of children from child labor, should be met and overcome. There are numerous diseases, which are now known to be preventable, which are, nevertheless, not prevented. The recent International Congress on Tuberculosis has made us painfully aware of the inadequacy of American public health legislation. This Nation can not afford to lag behind in the world-wide battle now being waged by all civilized people with the microscopic foes of mankind, nor ought we longer to ignore the reproach that this Government takes more pains to protect the lives of hogs and of cattle than of human beings.

REDISTRIBUTION OF BUREAUS.

The first legislative step to be taken is that for the concentration of the proper bureaus into one of the existing departments. I therefore urgently recommend the passage of a bill which shall authorize a redistribution of the bureaus which shall best accomplish this end.

GOVERNMENT PRINTING OFFICE.

I recommend that legislation be enacted placing under the jurisdiction of the Department of Commerce and Labor the Government Printing Office. At present this office is under the combined control, supervision, and administrative direction of the President and of the Joint Committee on Printing of the two Houses of the Congress. The advantage of having the 4,069 employees in this office and the expenditure of the $5,761,377.57 appropriated therefor supervised by an executive department is obvious, instead of the present combined supervision.

SOLDIERS' HOMES.

All Soldiers' Homes should be placed under the complete jurisdiction and control of the War Department.

INDEPENDENT BUREAUS AND COMMISSIONS.

Economy and sound business policy require that all existing independent bureaus and commissions should be placed under the jurisdiction of appropriate executive departments. It is unwise from every standpoint, and results only in mischief, to have any executive work done save by the purely executive bodies, under the control of the President; and each such executive body should be under the immediate supervision of a Cabinet Minister.

STATEHOOD.

I advocate the immediate admission of New Mexico and Arizona as States. This should be done at the present session of the Congress. The people of the two Territories have made it evident by their votes that they will not come in as one State. The only alternative is to admit them as two, and I trust that this will be done without delay.

INTERSTATE FISHERIES.

I call the attention of the Congress to the importance of the problem of the fisheries in the interstate waters. On the Great Lakes we are now, under the very wise treaty of April 11th of this year, endeavoring to come to an international agreement for the preservation and satisfactory use of the fisheries of these waters which can not otherwise be achieved. Lake Erie, for example, has the richest fresh water fisheries in the world; but it is now controlled by the statutes of two Nations, four States, and one Province, and in this Province by different ordinances in different counties. All these political divisions work at cross purposes, and in no case can they achieve protection to the fisheries, on the one hand, and justice to the localities and individuals on the other. The case is similar in Puget Sound.

But the problem is quite as pressing in the interstate waters of the United States. The salmon fisheries of the Columbia River are now but a fraction of what they were twenty-five years ago, and what they would be now if the United States Government had taken complete charge of them by intervening between Oregon and Washington. During these twenty-five years the fishermen of each State have naturally tried to take all they could get, and the two legislatures have never been able to agree on joint action of any kind adequate in degree for the protection of the fisheries. At the moment the fishing on the Oregon side is practically closed, while there is no limit on the Washington side of any kind, and no one can tell what the courts will decide as to the very statutes under which this action and non-action result. Meanwhile very few salmon reach the spawning grounds, and probably four years hence the fisheries will amount to nothing; and this comes from a struggle between the associated, or gill-net, fishermen on the one hand, and the owners of the fishing wheels up the river. The fisheries of the Mississippi, the Ohio, and the Potomac are also in a bad way. For this there is no remedy except for the United States to control and legislate for the interstate fisheries as part of the business of interstate commerce. In this case the machinery for scientific investigation and for control already exists in the United States Bureau of Fisheries. In this as in similar problems the obvious and simple rule should be followed of having those matters which no particular State can manage taken in hand by the United States; problems which in the seesaw of conflicting State legislatures are absolutely unsolvable are easy enough for Congress to control.

FISHERIES AND FUR SEALS.

The federal statute regulating interstate traffic in game should be extended to include fish. New federal fish hatcheries should be established. The administration of the Alaskan fur-seal service should be vested in the Bureau of Fisheries.

FOREIGN AFFAIRS.

This Nation's foreign policy is based on the theory that right must be done between nations precisely as between individuals, and in our actions for the last ten years we have in this matter proven our faith by our deeds. We have behaved, and are behaving, towards other nations as in private life an honorable man would behave towards his fellows.

LATIN-AMERICAN REPUBLICS.

The commercial and material progress of the twenty Latin-American Republics is worthy of the careful attention of the Congress. No other section of the world has shown a greater proportionate development of its foreign trade during the last ten years and none other has more special claims on the interest of the United States. It offers to-day probably larger opportunities for the legitimate expansion of our commerce than any other group of countries. These countries will want our products in greatly increased quantities, and we shall correspondingly need theirs. The International Bureau of the American Republics is doing a useful work in making these nations and their resources better known to us, and in acquainting them not only with us as a people and with our purposes towards them, but with what we have to exchange for their goods. It is an international institution supported by all the governments of the two Americas.

PANAMA CANAL.

The work on the Panama Canal is being done with a speed, efficiency and entire devotion to duty which make it a model for all work of the kind. No task of such magnitude has ever before been undertaken by any nation; and no task of the kind has ever been better performed. The men on the isthmus, from Colonel Goethals and his fellow commissioners through the entire list of employees who are faithfully doing their duty, have won their right to the ungrudging respect and gratitude of the American people.

OCEAN MAIL LINERS.

I again recommend the extension of the ocean mail act of 1891 so that satisfactory American ocean mail lines to South America, Asia, the Philippines, and Australiasia may be established. The creation of such steamship lines should be the natural corollary of the voyage of the battle fleet. It should precede the opening of the Panamal Canal. Even under favorable conditions several years must elapse before such lines can be put into operation. Accordingly I urge that the Congress act promptly where foresight already shows that action sooner or later will be inevitable.

HAWAII.

I call particular attention to the Territory of Hawaii. The importance of those islands is apparent, and the need of improving their condition and developing their resources is urgent. In recent years industrial conditions upon the islands have radically changed. The importation of coolie labor has practically ceased, and there is now developing such a diversity in agricultural products as to make possible a change in the land conditions of the Territory, so that an opportunity may be given to the small land owner similar to that on the mainland. To aid these changes, the National Government must provide the necessary harbor improvements on each island, so that the agricultural products can be carried to the markets of the world. The coastwise shipping laws should be amended to meet the special needs of the islands, and the alien contract labor law should be so modified in its application to Hawaii as to enable American and Europen labor to be brought thither.

We have begun to improve Pearl Harbor for a naval base and to provide the necessary military fortifications for the protection of the islands, but I can not too strongly emphasize the need of appropriations for these purposes of such an amount as will within the shortest possible time make those islands practically impregnable. It is useless to develop the industrial conditions of the islands and establish there bases of supply for our naval and merchant fleets unless we insure, as far as human ingenuity can, their safety from foreign seizure.

One thing to be remembered with all our fortifications is that it is almost useless to make them impregnable from the sea if they are left open to land attack. This is true even of our own coast, but it is doubly true of our insular possessions. In Hawaii, for instance, it is worse than useless to establish a naval station unless we establish it behind fortifications so strong that no landing force can take them save by regular and long-continued siege operations.

THE PHILIPPINES.

Real progress toward self-government is being made in the Philippine Islands. The gathering of a Philippine legislative body and Philippine assembly marks a process absolutely new in Asia, not only as regards Asiatic colonies of European powers but as regards Asiatic possessions of other Asiatic powers; and, indeed, always excepting the striking and wonderful example afforded by the great Empire of Japan, it opens an entirely new departure when compared with anything which has happened among Asiatic powers which are their own masters. Hitherto this Philippine legislature has acted with moderation and self-restraint, and has seemed in practical fashion to realize the eternal truth that there must always be government, and that the only way in which any body of individuals can escape the necessity of being governed by outsiders is to show that they are able to restrain themselves, to keep down wrongdoing and disorder. The Filipino people, through their officials, are therefore making real steps in the direction of self-government. I hope and believe that these steps mark the beginning of a course which will continue till the Filipinos become fit to decide for themselves whether they desire to be an independent nation. But it is well for them (and well also for those Americans who during the past decade have done so much damage to the Filipinos by agitation for an immediate independence for which they were totally unfit) to remember that self-government depends, and must depend, upon the Filipinos themselves. All we can do is to give them the opportunity to develop the capacity for self-government. If we had followed the advice of the foolish doctrinaires who wished us at any time during the last ten years to turn the Filipino people adrift, we should have shirked the plainest possible duty and have inflicted a lasting wrong upon the Filipino people. We have acted in exactly the opposite spirit. We have given the Filipinos constitutional government—a government based upon justice—and we have shown that we have governed them for their good and not for our aggrandizement. At the present time, as during the past ten years, the inexorable logic of facts shows that this government must be supplied by us and not by them. We must be wise and generous; we must help the Filipinos to master the difficult art of self-control, which is simply another name for self-government. But we can not give them self-government save in the sense of governing them so that gradually they may, if they are able, learn to govern themselves. Under the present system of just laws and sympathetic administration, we have every reason to believe that they are gradually acquiring the character which lies at the basis of self-government, and for which, if it be lacking, no system of laws, no paper constitution, will in any wise serve as a substitute. Our people in the Philippines have achieved what may legitimately be called a marvelous success in giving to them a government which marks on the part of those in authority both the necessary understanding of the people and the necessary purpose to serve them disinterestedly and in good faith. I trust that within a generation the time will arrive when the Philippines can decide for themselves whether it is well for them to become independent, or to continue under the protection of a strong and disinterested power, able to guarantee to the islands order at home and protection from foreign invasion. But no one can prophesy the exact date when it will be wise to consider independence as a fixed and definite policy. It would be worse than folly to try to set down such a date in advance, for it must depend upon the way in which the Philippine people themselves develop the power of self-mastery.

PORTO RICO

I again recommend that American citizenship be conferred upon the people of Porto Rico.

CUBA.

In Cuba our occupancy will cease in about two months' time; the Cubans have in orderly manner elected their own governmental authorities, and the island will be turned over to them. Our occupation on this occasion has lasted a little over two years, and Cuba has thriven and prospered under it. Our earnest hope and one desire is that the people of the island shall now govern themselves with justice, so that peace and order may be secure. We will gladly help them to this end; but I would solemnly warn them to remember the great truth that the only way a people can permanently avoid being governed from without is to show that they both can and will govern themselves from within.

JAPANESE EXPOSITION.

The Japanese Government has postponed until 1917 the date of the great international exposition, the action being taken so as to insure ample time in which to prepare to make the exposition all that it should be made. The American commissioners have visited Japan and the postponement will merely give ampler opportunity for America to be represented at the exposition. Not since the first international exposition has there been one of greater importance than this will be, marking as it does the fiftieth anniversary of the ascension to the throne of the Emperor of Japan. The extraordinary leap to a foremost place among the nations of the world made by Japan during this half century is something unparalleled in all previous history. This exposition will fitly commemorate and signalize the giant progress that has been achieved. It is the first exposition of its kind that has ever been held in Asia. The United States, because of the ancient friendship between the two peoples, because each of us fronts on the Pacific, and because of the growing commercial relations between this country and Asia, takes a peculiar interest in seeing the exposition made a success in every way.

I take this opportunity publicly to state my appreciation of the way in which in Japan, in Australia, in New Zealand, and in all the States of South America, the battle fleet has been received on its practice voyage around the world. The American Government can not too strongly express its appreciation of the abounding and generous hospitality shown our ships in every port they visited.

THE ARMY.

As regards the Army I call attention to the fact that while our junior officers and enlisted men stand very high, the present system of promotion by seniority results in bringing into the higher grades many men of mediocre capacity who have but a short time to serve. No man should regard it as his vested right to rise to the highest rank in the Army any more than in any other profession. It is a curious and by no means creditable fact that there should be so often a failure on the part of the public and its representatives to understand the great need, from the standpoint of the service and the Nation, of refusing to promote respectable, elderly incompetents. The higher places should be given to the most deserving men without regard to seniority; at least seniority should be treated as only one consideration. In the stress of modern industrial competition no business firm could succeed if those responsible for its management were chosen simply on the ground that they were the oldest people in its employment; yet this is the course advocated as regards the Army, and required by law for all grades except those of general officer. As a matter of fact, all of the best officers in the highest ranks of the Army are those who have attained their present position wholly or in part by a process of selection.

The scope of retiring boards should be extended so that they could consider general unfitness to command for any cause, in order to secure a far more rigid enforcement than at present in the elimination of officers for mental, physical or temperamental disabilities. But this plan is recommended only if the Congress does not see fit to provide what in my judgment is far better; that is, for selection in promotion, and for elimination for age. Officers who fail to attain a certain rank by a certain age should be retired—for instance, if a man should not attain field rank by the time he is 45 he should of course be placed on the retired list. General officers should be selected as at present, and one-third of the other promotions should be made by selection, the selection to be made by the President or the Secretary of War from a list of at least two candidates proposed for each vacancy by a board of officers from the arm of the service from which the promotion is to be made. A bill is now before the Congress having for its object to secure the promotion of officers to various grades at reasonable ages through a process of selection, by boards of officers, of the least efficient for retirement with a percentage of their pay depending upon length of service. The bill, although not accomplishing all that should be done, is a long step in the right direction; and I earnestly recommend its passage, or that of a more completely effective measure.

The cavalry arm should be reorganized upon modern lines. This is an arm in which it is peculiarly necessary that the field officers should not be old. The cavalry is much more difficult to form than infantry, and it should be kept up to the maximum both in efficiency and in strength, for it can not be made in a hurry. At present both infantry and artillery are too few in number for our needs. Especial attention should be paid to development of the machine gun. A general service corps should be established. As things are now the average soldier has far too much labor of a nonmilitary character to perform.

NATIONAL GUARD.

Now that the organized militia, the National Guard, has been incorporated with the Army as a part of the national forces, it behooves the Government to do every reasonable thing in its power to perfect its efficiency. It should be assisted in its instruction and otherwise aided more liberally than heretofore. The continuous services of many well-trained regular officers will be essential in this connection. Such officers must be specially trained at service schools best to qualify them as instructors of the National Guard. But the detailing of officers for training at the service schools and for duty with the National Guard entails detaching them from their regiments which are already greatly depleted by detachment of officers for assignment to duties prescribed by acts of the Congress.

A bill is now pending before the Congress creating a number of extra officers in the Army, which if passed, as it ought to be, will enable more officers to be trained as instructors of the National Guard and assigned to that duty. In case of war it will be of the utmost importance to have a large number of trained officers to use for turning raw levies into good troops.

There should be legislation to provide a complete plan for organizing the great body of volunteers behind the Regular Army and National Guard when war has come. Congressional assistance should be given those who are endeavoring to promote rifle practice so that our men, in the services or out of them, may know how to use the rifle. While teams representing the United States won the rifle and revolver championships of the world against all comers in England this year, it is unfortunately true that the great body of our citizens shoot less and less as time goes on. To meet this we should encourage rifle practice among schoolboys, and indeed among all classes, as well as in the military services, by every means in our power. Thus, and not otherwise, may we be able to assist in preserving the peace of the world. Fit to hold our own against the strong nations of the earth, our voice for peace will carry to the ends of the earth. Unprepared, and therefore unfit, we must sit dumb and helpless to defend ourselves, protect others, or preserve peace. The first step—in the direction of preparation to avert war if possible, and to be fit for war if it should come—is to teach our men to shoot.

THE NAVY.

I approve the recommendations of the General Board for the increase of the Navy, calling especial attention to the need of additional destroyers and colliers, and, above all, of the four battleships. It is desirable to complete as soon as possible a squadron of eight battleships of the best existing type. The *North Dakota, Delaware, Florida,* and *Utah* will form the first division of this squadron. The four vessels proposed will form the second division. It will be an improvement on the first, the ships being of the heavy, single caliber, all big gun type. All the vessels should have the same tactical qualities—that is, speed and turning circle—and as near as possible these tactical qualities should be the same as in the four vessels before named now being built.

I most earnestly recommend that the General Board be by law turned into a General Staff. There is literally no excuse whatever for continuing the present bureau organization of the Navy. The Navy should be treated as a purely military organization, and everything should be subordinated to the one object of securing military efficiency. Such military efficiency can only be guaranteed in time of war if there is the most thorough previous preparation in time of peace—a preparation, I may add, which will in all probability prevent any need of war. The Secretary must be supreme, and he should have as his official advisers a body of line officers who should themselves have the power to pass upon and coordinate all the work and all the proposals of the several bureaus. A system of promotion by merit, either by selection or by exclusion, or by both processes, should be introduced. It is out of the question, if the present principle of promotion by mere seniority is kept, to expect to get the best results from the higher officers. Our men come too old, and stay for too short a time, in the high command positions.

Two hospital ships should be provided. The actual experience of the hospital ship with the fleet in the Pacific has shown the invaluable work which such a ship does, and has also proved that it is well to have it kept under the command of a medical officer. As was to be expected, all of the anticipations of trouble from such a command have proved completely baseless. It is as absurd to put a hospital ship under a line officer as it would be to put a hospital on shore under such a command. This ought to have been realized before, and there is no excuse for failure to realize it now.

Nothing better for the Navy from every standpoint has ever occurred than the cruise of the battle fleet around the world. The improvement of the ships in every way has been extraordinary, and they have gained far more experience in battle tactics than they would have gained if they had stayed in the Atlantic waters. The American people have cause for profound gratification, both in view of the excellent condition of the fleet as shown by this cruise, and in view of the improvement the cruise has worked in this already high condition. I do not believe that there is any other service in the world in which the average of character and efficiency in the enlisted men is as high as is now the case in our own. I believe that the same statement can be made as to our officers, taken as a whole; but there must be a reservation made in regard to those in the highest ranks—as to which I have already spoken—and in regard to those who have just entered the service; because we do not now get full benefit from our excellent naval school at Annapolis. It is absurd not to graduate the midshipmen as ensigns; to keep them for two years in such an anomalous position as at present the law requires is detrimental to them and to the service. In the academy itself, every first classman should be required in turn to serve as petty officer and officer; his ability to discharge his duties as such should be a prerequisite to his going into the line, and his success in commanding should largely determine his standing at graduation. The Board of Visitors should be appointed in January, and each member should be required to give at least six days' service, only from one to three days' to be performed during June week, which is the least desirable time for the board to be at Annapolis so far as benefiting the Navy by their observations is concerned.

William Howard Taft

March 4, 1909 to March 4, 1913

FIRST ANNUAL MESSAGE

THE WHITE HOUSE, *December 7, 1909.*

To the Senate and House of Representatives:

The relations of the United States with all foreign governments have continued upon the normal basis of amity and good understanding, and are very generally satisfactory.

EUROPE.

Pursuant to the provisions of the general treaty of arbitration concluded between the United States and Great Britain, April 4, 1908, a special agreement was entered into between the two countries on January 27, 1909, for the submission of questions relating to the fisheries on the North Atlantic Coast to a tribunal to be formed from members of the Permanent Court of Arbitration at The Hague.

In accordance with the provisions of the special agreement the printed case of each Government was, on October 4 last, submitted to the other and to the Arbitral Tribunal at The Hague, and the counter case of the United States is now in course of preparation.

The American rights under the fisheries article of the Treaty of 1818 have been a cause of difference between the United States and Great Britain for nearly seventy years. The interests involved are of great importance to the American fishing industry, and the final settlement of the controversy will remove a source of constant irritation and complaint. This is the first case involving such great international questions which has been submitted to the Permanent Court of Arbitration at The Hague.

The treaty between the United States and Great Britain concerning the Canadian International boundary, concluded April 11, 1908, authorizes the appointment of two commissioners to define and mark accurately the international boundary line between the United States and the Dominion of Canada in the waters of the Passamaquoddy Bay, and provides for the exchange of briefs within the period of six months. The briefs were duly presented within the prescribed period, but as the commissioners failed to agree within six months after the exchange of the printed statements, as required by the treaty, it has now become necessary to resort to the arbitration provided for in the article.

The International Fisheries Commission appointed pursuant to and under the authority of the Convention of April 11, 1908, between the United States and Great Britain, has completed a system of uniform and common international regulations for the protection and preservation of the food fishes in international boundary waters of the United States and Canada.

The regulations will be duly submitted to Congress with a view to the enactment of such legislation as will be necessary under the convention to put them into operation.

The Convention providing for the settlement of international differences between the United States and Canada, including the apportionment between the two countries of certain of the boundary waters and the appointment of commissioners to adjust certain other questions, signed on the 11th day of January, 1909, and to the ratification of which the Senate gave its advice and consent on March 3, 1909, has not yet been ratified on the part of Great Britain.

Commissioners have been appointed on the part of the United States to act jointly with Commissioners on the part of Canada in examining into the question of obstructions in the St. John River between Maine and New Brunswick, and to make recommendations for the regulation of the uses thereof, and are now engaged in this work.

Negotiations for an international conference to consider and reach an arrangement providing for the preservation and protection of the fur seals in the North Pacific are in progress with the Governments of Great Britain, Japan, and Russia. The attitude of the Governments interested leads me to hope for a satisfactory settlement of this question as the ultimate outcome of the negotiations.

The Second Peace Conference recently held at The Hague adopted a convention for the establishment of an International Prize Court upon the joint proposal of delegations of the United States, France, Germany and Great Britain. The law to be observed by the Tribunal in the decision of prize cases was, however, left in an uncertain and therefore unsatisfactory state. Article 7 of the Convention provided that the Court was to be governed by the provisions of treaties existing between the belligerents, but that " in the absence of such provisions, the court shall apply the rules of international law. If no generally recognized rule exists, the court shall give judgment in accordance with the general principles of justice and equity." As, however, many questions in international maritime law are understood differently and therefore interpreted differently in various countries, it was deemed advisable not to intrust legislative powers to the proposed court, but to determine the rules of law properly applicable in a Conference of the representative maritime nations. Pursuant to an invitation of Great Britain a conference was held at London from December 2, 1908, to February 26, 1909, in which the following Powers participated: the United States, Austria-Hungary, France, Germany, Great Britain, Italy, Japan, the Netherlands, Russia and Spain. The conference resulted in the Declaration of London, unanimously agreed to and signed by the participating Powers, concerning among other matters, the highly important subjects of blockade, contraband, the destruction of neutral prizes, and continuous voyages.

The declaration of London is an eminently satisfactory codification of the international maritime law, and it is hoped that its reasonableness and fairness will secure its general adoption, as well as remove one of the difficulties standing in the way of the establishment of an International Prize Court.

Under the authority given in the sundry civil appropriation act, approved March 4, 1909, the United States was represented at the International Conference on Maritime Law at Brussels. The Conference met on the 28th of September last and resulted in the signature *ad referendum* of a convention for the unification of certain regulations with regard to maritime assistance and salvage and a convention for the unification of certain rules with regard to collisions at sea.

Two new projects of conventions which have not heretofore been considered in a diplomatic conference, namely, one concerning the limitation of the responsibility of shipowners, and the other concerning marine mortgages and privileges, have been submitted by the Conference to the different governments.

The Conference adjourned to meet again on April 11, 1910.

The International Conference for the purpose of promoting uniform legislation concerning letters of exchange, which was called by the Government of the Netherlands to meet at The Hague in September, 1909, has been postponed to meet at that capital in June, 1910. The United States will be appropriately represented in this Conference under the provision therefor already made by Congress.

The cordial invitation of Belgium to be represented by a fitting display of American progress in the useful arts and inventions at the World's Fair to be held at Brussels in 1910 remains to be acted upon by the Congress. Mindful of the advantages to accrue to our artisans and producers in competition with their Continental rivals, I renew the recommendation heretofore made that provision be made for acceptance of the invitation and adequate representation in the Exposition.

The question arising out of the Belgian annexation of the Independent State of the Congo, which has so long and earnestly preoccupied the attention of this Government and enlisted the sympathy of our best citizens, is still open, but in a more hopeful stage. This Government was among the foremost in the great work of uplifting the uncivilized regions of Africa and urging the extension of the benefits of civilization, education, and fruitful open commerce to that vast domain, and is a party to treaty engagements of all the interested powers designed to carry out that great duty to humanity. The way to better the original and adventitious conditions, so burdensome to the natives and so destructive to their development, has been pointed out, by observation and experience, not alone of American representatives, but by cumulative evidence from all quarters and by the investigations of Belgian Agents. The announced programmes of reforms, striking at many of the evils known to exist, are an augury of better things. The attitude of the United States is one of benevolent encouragement, coupled with a hopeful trust that the good work, responsibly undertaken and zealously perfected to the accomplishment of the results so ardently desired, will soon justify the wisdom that inspires them and satisfy the demands of humane sentiment throughout the world.

A convention between the United States and Germany, under which the nonworking provisions of the German patent law are made inapplicable to the patents of American citizens, was concluded on February 23, 1909, and is now in force. Negotiations for similar conventions looking to the placing of American inventors on the same footing as nationals have recently been initiated with other European governments whose laws require the local working of foreign patents.

Under an appropriation made at the last session of the Congress, a commission was sent on American cruisers to Monrovia to investigate the interests of the United States and its citizens in Liberia. Upon its arrival at Monrovia the commission was enthusiastically received, and during its stay in Liberia was everywhere met with the heartiest expressions of good will for the American Government and people and the hope was repeatedly expressed on all sides that this Government might see its way clear to do something to relieve the critical position of the Republic arising in a measure from external as well as internal and financial embarrassments.

The Liberian Government afforded every facility to the Commission for ascertaining the true state of affairs. The Commission also had conferences with representative citizens, interested foreigners and the representatives of foreign governments in Monrovia. Visits were made to various parts of the Republic and to the neighboring British colony of Sierra Leone, where the Commission was received by and conferred with the Governor.

It will be remembered that the interest of the United States in the Republic of Liberia springs from the historical fact of the foundation of the Republic by the colonization of American citizens of the African race. In an early treaty with Liberia there is a provision under which the United States may be called upon for advice or assistance. Pursuant to this provision and in the spirit of the moral relationship of the United States to Liberia, that Republic last year asked this Government to lend assistance in the solution of certain of their national problems, and hence the Commission was sent.

The report of our commissioners has just been completed and is now under examination by the Department of State. It is hoped that there may result some helpful measures, in which case it may be my duty again to invite your attention to this subject.

The Norwegian Government, by a note addressed on January 26, 1909, to the Department of State, conveyed an invitation to the Government of the United States to take part in a conference which it is understood will be held in February or March, 1910, for the purpose of devising means to remedy existing conditions in the Spitzbergen Islands.

This invitation was conveyed under the reservation that the question of altering the status of the islands as countries belonging to no particular State, and as equally open to the citizens and subjects of all States, should not be raised.

The European Powers invited to this Conference by the Government of Norway were Belgium, Denmark, France, Germany, Great Britain, Russia, Sweden and the Netherlands.

The Department of State, in view of proofs filed with it in 1906, showing the American possession, occupation, and working of certain coal-bearing lands in Spitzbergen, accepted the invitation under the reservation above stated, and under the further reservation that all interests in those islands already vested should be protected and that there should be equality of opportunity for the future. It was further pointed out that membership in the Conference on the part of the United States was qualified by the consideration that this Government would not become a signatory to any conventional arrangement concluded by the European members of the Conference which would imply contributory participation by the United States in any obligation or responsibility for the enforcement of any scheme of administration which might be devised by the Conference for the islands.

THE NEAR EAST.

His Majesty Mehmed V, Sultan of Turkey, recently sent to this country a special embassy to announce his accession. The quick transition of the Government of the Ottoman Empire from one of retrograde tendencies to a constitutional government with a Parliament and with progressive modern policies of reform and public improvement is one of the important phenomena of our times. Constitutional government seems also to have made further advance in Persia. These events have turned the eyes of the world upon the Near East. In that quarter the prestige of the United States has spread widely through the peaceful influence of American schools, universities and missionaries. There is every reason why we should obtain a greater share of the commerce of the Near East since the conditions are more favorable now than ever before.

LATIN AMERICA.

One of the happiest events in recent Pan-American diplomacy was the pacific, independent settlement by the Governments of Bolivia and Peru of a boundary difference between them, which for some weeks threatened to cause war and even to entrain embitterments affecting other republics less directly concerned. From various quarters, directly or indirectly concerned, the intermediation of the United States was sought to assist in a solution of the controversy. Desiring at all times to abstain from any undue mingling in the affairs of sister republics and having faith in the ability of the Governments of Peru and Bolivia themselves to settle their differences in a manner staisfactory to themselves which, viewed with magnanimity, would assuage all embitterment, this Government steadily abstained from being drawn into the controversy and was much gratified to find its confidence justified by events.

On the 9th of July next there will open at Buenos Aires the Fourth Pan-American Conference. This conference will have a special meaning to the hearts of all Americans, because around its date are clustered the anniversaries of the independence of so many of the American republics. It is not necessary for me to remind the Congress of the political, social and commercial importance of these gatherings. You are asked to make liberal appropriation for our participation. If this be granted, it is my purpose to appoint a distinguished and representative delegation, qualified fittingly to represent this country and to deal with the problems of intercontinental interest which will there be discussed.

The Argentine Republic will also hold from May to November, 1910, at Buenos Aires, a great International Agricultural Exhibition in which the United States has been invited to participate. Considering the rapid growth of the trade of the United States with the Argentine Republic and the cordial relations existing between the two nations, together with the fact that it provides an opportunity to show deference to a sister republic on the occasion of the celebration of its national independence, the proper Departments of this Government are taking steps to apprise the interests concerned of the opportunity afforded by this Exhibition, in which appropriate participation by this country is so desirable. The designation of an official representative is also receiving consideration.

To-day, more than ever before, American capital is seeking investment in foreign countries, and American products are more and more generally seeking foreign markets. As a consequence, in all countries there are American citizens and American interests to be protected, on occasion, by their Government. These movements of men, of capital, and of commodities bring peoples and governments closer together and so form bonds of peace and mutual dependency, as they must also naturally sometimes make passing points of friction. The resultant situation inevitably imposes upon this Government vastly increased responsibilities. This Administration, through the Department of State and the foreign service, is lending all proper support to legitimate and beneficial American enterprises in foreign countries, the degree of such support being measured by the national advantages to be expected. A citizen himself can not by contract or otherwise divest himself of the right, nor can this Government escape the obligation, of his protection in his personal and property rights when these are unjustly infringed in a foreign country. To avoid ceaseless vexations it is proper that in considering whether American enterprise should be encouraged or supported in a particular country, the Government should give full weight not only to the national, as opposed to the individual benefits to accrue, but also to the fact whether or not the Government of the country in question is in its administration and in its diplomacy faithful to the principles of moderation, equity and justice upon which alone depend international credit, in diplomacy as well as in finance.

The Pan-American policy of this Government has long been fixed in its principles and remains unchanged. With the changed circumstances of the United States and of the Republics to the south of us, most of which have great natural resources, stable government and progressive ideals, the apprehension which gave rise to the Monroe Doctrine may be said to have nearly disappeared, and neither the doctrine as it exists nor any other doctrine of American policy should be permitted to operate for the perpetuation of irresponsible government, the escape of just obligations, or the insidious allegation of dominating ambitions on the part of the United States.

Beside the fundamental doctrines of our Pan-American policy there have grown up a realization of political interests, community of institutions and ideals, and a flourishing commerce. All these bonds will be greatly strengthened as time goes on and increased facilities, such as the great bank soon to be established in Latin America, supply the means for building up the colossal intercontinental commerce of the future.

My meeting with President Diaz and the greeting exchanged on both American and Mexican soil served, I hope, to signalize the close and cordial relations which so well bind together this Republic and the great Republic immediately to the south, between which there is so vast a network of material interests.

I am happy to say that all but one of the cases which for so long vexed our relations with Venezuela have been settled within the past few months and that, under the enlightened régime now directing the Government of Venezuela, provision has been made for arbitration of the remaining case before The Hague Tribunal.

On July 30, 1909, the Government of Panama agreed, after considerable negotiation, to indemnify the relatives of the American officers and sailors who were brutally treated, one of them having, indeed, been killed by the Panaman police this year.

The sincere desire of the Government of Panama to do away with a situation where such an accident could occur is manifest in the recent request in compliance with which this Government has lent the services of an officer of the Army to be employed by the Government of Panama as Instructor of Police.

The sanitary improvements and public works undertaken in Cuba prior to the present administration of that Government, in the success of which the United States is interested under the treaty, are reported to be making good progress and since the Congress provided for the continuance of the reciprocal commercial arrangement between Cuba and the United States assurance has been received that no negotiations injuriously affecting the situation will be undertaken without consultation.

The collection of the customs of the Dominican Republic through the general receiver of customs appointed by the President of the United States in accordance with the convention of February 8, 1907, has proceeded in an uneventful and satisfactory manner. The customs receipts have decreased owing to disturbed political and economic conditions and to a very natural curtailment of imports in view of the anticipated revision of the Dominican tariff schedule. The payments to the fiscal agency fund for the service of the bonded debt of the Republic, as provided by the convention, have been regularly and promptly made, and satisfactory progress has been made in carrying out the provisions of the convention looking towards the completion of the adjustment of the debt and the acquirement by the Dominican Government of certain concessions and monopolies which have been a burden to the commerce of the country. In short, the receivership has demonstrated its ability, even under unfavorable economic and political conditions, to do the work for which it was intended.

This Government was obliged to intervene diplomatically to bring about arbitration or settlement of the claim of the Emery Company against Nicaragua, which it had long before been agreed should be arbitrated. A settlement of this troublesome case was reached by the signature of a protocol on September 18, 1909.

Many years ago diplomatic intervention became necessary to the protection of the interests in the American claim of Alsop and Company against the Government of Chile. The Government of Chile had frequently admitted obligation in the case and had promised this Government to settle. There had been two abortive attempts to do so through arbitral commissions, which failed through lack of jurisdiction. Now, happily, as the result of the recent diplomatic negotiations, the Governments of the United States and of Chile, actuated by the sincere desire to free from any strain those cordial and friendly relations upon which both set such store, have agreed by a protocol to submit the controversy to definitive settlement by His Britannic Majesty, Edward VII.

Since the Washington Conventions of 1907 were communicated to the Government of the United States as a consulting and advising party, this Government has been almost continuously called upon by one or another, and in turn by all the five Central American Republics, to exert itself for the maintenance of the Conventions. Nearly every complaint has been against the Zelaya Government of Nicaragua, which has kept Central America in constant tension or turmoil. The responses made to the representations of Central American Republics, as due from the United States on account of its relation to the Washington Conventions, have been at all times conservative and have avoided, so far as possible, any semblance of interference, although it is very apparent that the considerations of geographic proximity to the Canal Zone and of the very substantial American interests in Central America give to the United States a special position in the zone of these Republics and the Caribbean Sea.

I need not rehearse here the patient efforts of this Government to promote peace and welfare among these Republics, efforts which are fully appreciated by the majority of them who are loyal to their true interests. It would be no less unnecessary to rehearse here the sad tale of unspeakable barbarities and oppression alleged to have been committed by the Zelaya Government. Recently two Americans were put to death by order of President Zelaya himself. They were reported to have been regularly commissioned officers in the organized forces of a revolution which had continued many weeks and was in control of about half of the Republic, and as such, according to the modern enlightened practice of civilized nations, they were entitled to be dealt with as prisoners of war.

At the date when this message is printed this Government has terminated diplomatic relations with the Zelaya Government, for reasons made public in a communication to the former Nicaraguan chargé d'affaires, and is intending to take such future steps as may be found most consistent with its dignity, its duty to American interests, and its moral obligations to Central America and to civilization. It may later be necessary for me to bring this subject to the attention of the Congress in a special message.

The International Bureau of American Republics has carried on an important and increasing work during the last year. In the exercise of its peculiar functions as an international agency, maintained by all the American Republics for the development of Pan-American commerce and friendship, it has accomplished a great practical good which could be done in the same way by no individual department or bureau of one government, and is therefore deserving of your liberal support. The fact that it is about to enter a new building, erected through the munificence of an American philanthropist and the contributions of all the American nations, where both its efficiency of administration and expense of maintenance will naturally be much augmented, further entitles it to special consideration.

THE FAR EAST.

In the Far East this Government preserves unchanged its policy of supporting the principle of equality of opportunity and scrupulous respect for the integrity of the Chinese Empire, to which policy are pledged the interested Powers of both East and West.

By the Treaty of 1903 China has undertaken the abolition of likin with a moderate and proportionate raising of the customs tariff along with currency reform. These reforms being of manifest advantage to foreign commerce as well as to the interests of China, this Government is endeavoring to facilitate these measures and the needful acquiescence of the treaty Powers. When it appeared that Chinese likin revenues were to be hypothecated to foreign bankers in connection with a great railway project, it was obvious that the Governments whose nationals held this loan would have a certain direct interest in the question of the carrying out by China of the reforms in question. Because this railroad loan represented a practical and real application of the open door policy through cooperation with China by interested Powers as well as because of its relations to the reforms referred to above, the Administration deemed American participation to be of great national interest.

Happily, when it was as a matter of broad policy urgent that this opportunity should not be lost, the indispensable instrumentality presented itself when a group of American bankers, of international reputation and great resources, agreed at once to share in the loan upon precisely such terms as this Government should approve. The chief of those terms was that American railway material should be upon an exact equality with that of the other nationals joining in the loan in the placing of orders for this whole railroad system. After months of negotiation the equal participation of Americans seems at last assured. It is gratifying that Americans will thus take their share in this extension of these great highways of trade, and to believe that such activities will give a real impetus to our commerce and will prove a practical corollary to our historic policy in the Far East.

The Imperial Chinese Government in pursuance of its decision to devote funds from the portion of the indemnity remitted by the United States to the sending of students to this country has already completed arrangements for carrying out this purpose, and a considerable body of students have arrived to take up their work in our schools and universities. No one can doubt the happy effect that the associations formed by these representative young men will have when they return to take up their work in the progressive development of their country.

The results of the Opium Conference held at Shanghai last spring at the invitation of the United States have been laid before the Government. The report shows that China is making remarkable progress and admirable efforts toward the eradication of the opium evil and that the Governments concerned have not allowed their commercial interests to interfere with a helpful cooperation in this reform. Collateral investigations of the opium question in this country lead me to recommend that the manufacture, sale and use of opium and its derivatives in the United States should be so far as possible more rigorously controlled by legislation.

In one of the Chinese-Japanese Conventions of September 4 of this year there was a provision which caused considerable public apprehension in that upon its face it was believed in some quarters to seek to establish a monopoly of mining privileges along the South Manchurian and Antung-Mukden Railroads, and thus to exclude Americans from a wide field of enterprise, to take part in which they were by treaty with China entitled. After a thorough examination of the Conventions and of the several contextual documents, the Secretary of State reached the conclusion that no such monopoly was intended or accomplished. However, in view of the widespread discussion of this question, to confirm the view it had reached, this Government made inquiry of the Imperial Chinese and Japanese

Governments and received from each official assurance that the provision had no purpose inconsistent with the policy of equality of opportunity to which the signatories, in common with the United States, are pledged.

Our traditional relations with the Japanese Empire continue cordial as usual. As the representative of Japan, His Imperial Highness Prince Kuni visited the Hudson-Fulton Celebration. The recent visit of a delegation of prominent business men as guests of the chambers of commerce of the Pacific slope, whose representatives had been so agreeably received in Japan, will doubtless contribute to the growing trade across the Pacific, as well as to that mutual understanding which leads to mutual appreciation. The arrangement of 1908 for a cooperative control of the coming of laborers to the United States has proved to work satisfactorily. The matter of a revision of the existing treaty between the United States and Japan which is terminable in 1912 is already receiving the study of both countries.

The Department of State is considering the revision in whole or in part, of the existing treaty with Siam, which was concluded in 1856, and is now, in respect to many of its provisions, out of date.

THE DEPARTMENT OF STATE.

I earnestly recommend to the favorable action of the Congress the estimates submitted by the Department of State and most especially the legislation suggested in the Secretary of State's letter of this date whereby it will be possible to develop and make permanent the reorganization of the Department upon modern lines in a manner to make it a thoroughly efficient instrument in the furtherance of our foreign trade and of American interests abroad. The plan to have Divisions of Latin-American and Far Eastern Affairs and to institute a certain specialization in business with Europe and the Near East will at once commend itself. These politico-geographical divisions and the detail from the diplomatic or consular service to the Department of a number of men, who bring to the study of complicated problems in different parts of the world practical knowledge recently gained on the spot, clearly is of the greatest advantage to the Secretary of State in foreseeing conditions likely to arise and in conducting the great variety of correspondence and negotiation. It should be remembered that such facilities exist in the foreign offices of all the leading commercial nations and that to deny them to the Secretary of State would be to place this Government at a great disadvantage in the rivalry of commercial competition.

The consular service has been greatly improved under the law of April 5, 1906, and the Executive Order of June 27, 1906, and I commend to your consideration the question of embodying in a statute the principles of the present Executive Order upon which the efficiency of our consular service is wholly dependent.

In modern times political and commercial interests are interrelated, and in the negotiation of commercial treaties, conventions and tariff agreements, the keeping open of opportunities and the proper support of American enterprises, our diplomatic service is quite as important as the consular service to the business interests of the country. Impressed with this idea and convinced that selection after rigorous examination, promotion for merit solely and the experience only to be gained through the continuity of an organized service are indispensable to a high degree of efficiency in the diplomatic service, I have signed an Executive Order as the first step toward this very desirable result. Its effect should be to place all secretaries in the diplomatic service in much the same position as consular officers are now placed and to tend to the promotion of the most efficient to the grade of minister, generally leaving for outside appointments such posts of the grade of ambassador or minister as it may be expedient to fill from without the service. It is proposed also to continue the practice instituted last summer of giving to all newly appointed secretaries at least one month's thorough training in the Department of State before they proceed to their posts. This has been done for some time in regard to the consular service with excellent results.

Under a provision of the Act of August 5, 1909, I have appointed three officials to assist the officers of the Government in collecting information necessary to a wise administration of the tariff act of August 5, 1909. As to questions of customs administration they are cooperating with the officials of the Treasury Department and as to matters of the needs and the exigencies of our manufacturers and exporters, with the Department of Commerce and Labor, in its relation to the domestic aspect of the subject of foreign commerce. In the study of foreign tariff treatment they will assist the Bureau of Trade Relations of the Department of State. It is hoped thus to coordinate and bring to bear upon this most important subject all the agencies of the Government which can contribute anything to its efficient handling.

As a consequence of Section 2 of the tariff act of August 5, 1909, it becomes the duty of the Secretary of State to conduct as diplomatic business all the negotiations necessary to place him in a position to advise me as to whether or not a particular country unduly discriminates against the United States in the sense of the statute referred to. The great scope and complexity of this work, as well as the obligation to lend all proper aid to our expanding commerce, is met by the expansion of the Bureau of Trade Relations as set forth in the estimates for the Department of State.

OTHER DEPARTMENTS.

I have thus in some detail described the important transactions of the State Department since the beginning of this Administration for the reason that there is no provision either by statute or custom for a formal report by the Secretary of State to the President or to Congress, and a Presidential message is the only means by which the condition of our foreign relations is brought to the attention of Congress and the public.

In dealing with the affairs of the other Departments, the heads of which all submit annual reports, I shall touch only those matters that seem to me to call for special mention on my part without minimizing in any way the recommendations made by them for legislation affecting their respective Departments, in all of which I wish to express my general concurrence.

GOVERNMENT EXPENDITURES AND REVENUES.

Perhaps the most important question presented to this Administration is that of economy in expenditures and sufficiency of revenue. The deficit of the last fiscal year, and the certain deficit of the current year, prompted Congress to throw a greater responsibility on the Executive and the Secretary of the Treasury than had heretofore been declared by statute. This declaration imposes upon the Secretary of the Treasury the duty of assembling all the estimates of the Executive Departments, bureaus, and offices, of the expenditures necessary in the ensuing fiscal year, and of making an estimate of the revenues of the Government for the same period; and if a probable deficit is thus shown, it is made the duty of the President to recommend the method by which such deficit can be met.

The report of the Secretary shows that the ordinary expenditures for the current fiscal year ending June 30, 1910, will exceed the estimated receipts by $34,075,620. If to this deficit is added the sum to be disbursed for the Panama Canal, amounting to $38,000,000, and $1,000,000 to be paid on the public debt, the deficit of ordinary receipts and expenditures will be increased to a total deficit of $73,075,620. This deficit the Secretary proposes to meet by the proceeds of bonds issued to pay the cost of constructing the Panama Canal. I approve this proposal.

The policy of paying for the construction of the Panama Canal, not out of current revenue, but by bond issues, was adopted in the Spooner Act of 1902, and there seems to be no good reason for departing from the principle by which a part at least of the burden of the cost of the canal shall fall upon our posterity who are to enjoy it; and there is all the more reason for this view because the actual cost to date of the canal, which is now half done and which will be completed January 1, 1915, shows that the cost of engineering and construction will be $297,766,000, instead of $139,705,200, as originally estimated. In addition to engineering and construction, the other expenses, including sanitation and government, and the amount paid for the properties, the franchise, and the privilege of building the canal, increase the cost by $75,435,000, to a total of $375,201,000. The increase in the cost of engineering and construction is due to a substantial enlargement of the plan of construction by widening the canal 100 feet in the Culebra cut and by increasing the dimensions of the locks, to the underestimate of the quantity of the work to be done under the original plan, and to an underestimate of the cost of labor and materials both of which have greatly enhanced in price since the original estimate was made.

In order to avoid a deficit for the ensuing fiscal year, I directed the heads of Departments in the preparation of their estimates to make them as low as possible consistent with imperative governmental necessity. The result has been, as I am advised by the Secretary of the Treasury, that the estimates for the expenses of the Government for the next fiscal year ending June 30, 1911, are less than the appropriations for this current fiscal year by $42,818,000. So far as the Secretary of the Treasury is able to form a judgment as to future income, and compare it with the expenditures for the next fiscal year ending June 30, 1911, and excluding payments on account of the Panama Canal, which will doubtless be taken up by bonds, there will be a surplus of $35,931,000.

In the present estimates the needs of the Departments and of the Government have been cut to the quick, so to speak, and any assumption on the part of Congress, so often made in times past, that the estimates have been prepared with the expectation that they may be reduced, will result in seriously hampering proper administration.

The Secretary of the Treasury points out what should be carefully noted in respect to this reduction in governmental expenses for the next fiscal year, that the economies are of two kinds—first, there is a saving in the permanent administration of the Departments, bureaus, and offices of the Government; and, second, there is a present reduction in expenses by a postponement of projects and improvements that ultimately will have to be carried out, but which are now delayed with the hope that additional revenue in the future will permit their execution without producing a deficit.

It has been impossible in the preparation of estimates greatly to reduce the cost of permanent administration. This can not be done without a thorough reorganization of bureaus, offices, and departments. For the purpose of securing information which may enable the executive and the legislative branches to unite in a plan for the permanent reduction of the cost of governmental administration, the Treasury Department has instituted an investigation by one of the most skilled expert accountants in the United States. The result of his work in two or three bureaus, which, if extended to the entire Government, must occupy two or more years, has been to show much room for improvement and opportunity for substantial reductions in the cost and increased efficiency of administration. The object of the investigation is to devise means to increase the average efficiency of each employee. There is great room for improvement toward this end, not only by the reorganization of bureaus and departments and in the avoidance of duplication, but also in the treatment of the individual employee.

Under the present system it constantly happens that two employees receive the same salary when the work of one is far more difficult and important and exacting than that of the other. Superior ability is not rewarded or encouraged. As the classification is now entirely by salary, an employee often rises to the highest class while doing the easiest work, for which alone he may be fitted. An investigation ordered by my predecessor resulted in the recommendation that the civil service be reclassified according to the kind of work, so that the work requiring most application and knowledge and ability shall receive most compensation. I believe such a change would be fairer to the whole force and would permanently improve the personnel of the service.

More than this, every reform directed toward the improvement in the average efficiency of government employees must depend on the ability of the Executive to eliminate from the government service those who are inefficient from any cause, and as the degree of efficiency in all the Departments is much lessened by the retention of old employees who have outlived their energy and usefulness, it is indispensable to any proper system of economy that provision be made so that their separation from the service shall be easy and inevitable. It is impossible to make such provision unless there is adopted a plan of civil pensions.

Most of the great industrial organizations, and many of the well-conducted railways of this country, are coming to the conclusion that a system of pensions for old employees, and the substitution therefor of younger and more energetic servants, promotes both economy and efficiency of administration.

I am aware that there is a strong feeling in both Houses of Congress, and possibly in the country, against the establishment of civil pensions, and that this has naturally grown out of the heavy burden of military pensions, which it has always been the policy of our Government to assume; but I am strongly convinced that no other practical solution of the difficulties presented by the superannuation of civil servants can be found than that of a system of civil pensions.

The business and expenditures of the Government have expanded enormously since the Spanish war, but as the revenues have increased in nearly the same proportion as the expenditures until recently, the attention of the public, and of those responsible for the Government, has not been fastened upon the question of reducing the cost of administration. We can not, in view of the advancing prices of living, hope to save money by a reduction in the standard of salaries paid. Indeed, if any change is made in that regard, an increase rather than a decrease will be necessary; and the only means of economy will be in reducing the number of employees and in obtaining a greater average of efficiency from those retained in the service.

Close investigation and study needed to make definite recommendations in this regard will consume at least two years. I note with much satisfaction the organization in the Senate of a Committee on Public Expenditures, charged with the duty of conducting such an investigation, and I tender to that committee all the assistance which the executive branch of the Government can possibly render.

FRAUDS IN THE COLLECTION OF CUSTOMS.

I regret to refer to the fact of the discovery of extensive frauds in the collections of the customs revenue at New York City, in which a number of the subordinate employees in the weighing and other departments were directly concerned, and in which the beneficiaries were the American Sugar Refining Company and others. The frauds consisted in the payment of duty on underweights of sugar. The Government has recovered from the American Sugar Refining Company all that it is shown to have been defrauded of. The sum was received in full of the amount due, which might have been recovered by civil suit against the beneficiary of the fraud, but there was an express reservation in the contract of settlement by which the settlement should not interfere with, or prevent the criminal prosecution of everyone who was found to be subject to the same.

Criminal prosecutions are now proceeding against a number of the Government officers. The Treasury Department and the Department of Justice are exerting every effort to discover all the wrongdoers, including the officers and employees of the companies who may have been privy to the fraud. It would seem to me that an investigation of the frauds by Congress at present, pending the probing by the Treasury Department and the Department of Justice, as proposed, might by giving immunity and otherwise prove an embarrassment in securing conviction of the guilty parties.

MAXIMUM AND MINIMUM CLAUSE IN TARIFF ACT.

Two features of the new tariff act call for special reference. By virtue of the clause known as the "Maximum and Minimum" clause, it is the duty of the Executive to consider the laws and practices of other countries with reference to the importation into those countries of the products and merchandise of the United States, and if the Executive finds such laws and practices not to be *unduly discriminatory* against the United States, the minimum duties provided in the bill are to go into force. Unless the President makes such a finding, then the maximum duties provided in the bill, that is, an increase of twenty-five per cent. *ad valorem* over the minimum duties, are to be in force. Fear has been expressed that this power conferred and duty imposed on the Executive is likely to lead to a tariff war. I beg to express the hope and belief that no such result need be anticipated.

The discretion granted to the Executive by the terms "unduly discriminatory" is wide. In order that the maximum duty shall be charged against the imports from a country, it is necessary that he shall find on the part of that country not only discriminations in its laws or the practice under them against the trade of the United States, but that the discriminations found shall be undue; that is, without good and fair reason. I conceive that this power was reposed in the President with the hope that the maximum duties might never be applied in any case, but that the power to apply them would enable the President and the State Department through friendly negotiation to secure the elimination from the laws and the practice under them of any foreign country of that which is unduly discriminatory. No one is seeking a tariff war or a condition in which the spirit of retaliation shall be aroused.

USES OF THE NEW TARIFF BOARD.

The new tariff law enables me to appoint a tariff board to assist me in connection with the Department of State in the administration of the minimum and maximum clause of the act and also to assist officers of the Government in the administration of the entire law. An examination of the law and an understanding of the nature of the facts which should be considered in discharging the functions imposed upon the Executive show that I have the power to direct the tariff board to make a comprehensive glossary and encyclopedia of the terms used and articles embraced in the tariff law, and to secure information as to the cost of production of such goods in this country and the cost of their production in foreign countries. I have therefore appointed a tariff board consisting of three members and have directed them to perform all the duties above described. This work will perhaps take two or three years, and I ask from Congress a continuing annual appropriation equal to that already made for its prosecution. I believe that the work of this board will be of prime utility and importance whenever Congress shall deem it wise again to readjust the customs duties. If the facts secured by the tariff board are of such a character as to show generally that the rates of duties imposed by the present tariff law are excessive under the principles of protection as described in the platform of the successful party at the late election, I shall not hesitate to invite the attention of Congress to this fact and to the necessity for action predicated thereon. Nothing, however, halts business and interferes with the course of prosperity so much as the threatened revision of the tariff, and until the facts are at hand, after careful and deliberate investigation, upon which such revision can properly be undertaken, it seems to me unwise to attempt it. The amount of misinformation that creeps into arguments *pro* and *con* in respect to tariff rates is such as to require the kind of investigation that I have directed the tariff board to make, an investigation undertaken by it wholly without respect to the effect which the facts may have in calling for a readjustment of the rates of duty.

WAR DEPARTMENT.

In the interest of immediate economy and because of the prospect of a deficit, I have required a reduction in the estimates of the War Department for the coming fiscal year, which brings the total estimates down to an amount forty-five millions less than the corresponding estimates for last year. This could only be accomplished by cutting off new projects and suspending for the period of one year all progress in military matters. For the same reason I have directed that the Army shall not be recruited up to its present authorized strength. These measures can hardly be more than temporary—to last until our revenues are in better condition and until the whole question of the expediency of adopting a definite military policy can be submitted to Congress, for I am sure that the interests of the military establishment are seriously in need of careful consideration by Congress. The laws regulating the organization of our armed forces in the event of war need to be revised in order that the organization can be modified so as to produce a force which would be more consistently apportioned throughout its numerous branches. To explain the circumstances upon which this opinion is based would necessitate a lengthy discussion, and I postpone it until the first convenient opportunity shall arise to send to Congress a special message upon this subject.

The Secretary of War calls attention to a number of needed changes in the Army in all of which I concur, but the point upon which I place most emphasis is the need for an elimination bill providing a method by which the merits of officers shall have some effect upon their advancement and by which the advancement of all may be accelerated by the effective elimination of a definite proportion of the least efficient. There are in every army, and certainly in ours, a number of officers who do not violate their duty in any such way as to give reason for a court-martial or dismissal, but who do not show such aptitude and skill and character for high command as to justify their remaining in the active service to be Promoted. Provision should be made by which they may be retired on a certain proportion of their pay, increasing with their length of service at the time of retirement. There is now a personnel law for the Navy which itself needs amendment and to which I shall make further reference. Such a law is needed quite as much for the Army.

The coast defenses of the United States proper are generally all that could be desired, and in some respects they are rather more elaborate than under present conditions are needed to stop an enemy's fleet from entering the harbors defended. There is, however, one place where additional defense is badly needed, and that is at the mouth of Chesapeake Bay, where it is proposed to make an artificial island for a fort which shall prevent an enemy's fleet from entering this most important strategical base of operations on the whole Atlantic and Gulf coasts. I hope that appropriate legislation will be adopted to secure the construction of this defense.

The military and naval joint board have unanimously agreed that it would be unwise to make the large expenditures which at one time were contemplated in the establishment of a naval base and station in the Philippine Islands, and have expressed their judgment, in which I fully concur, in favor of making an extensive naval base at Pearl Harbor, near Honolulu, and not in the Philippines. This does not dispense with the necessity for the comparatively small appropriations required to finish the proper coast defenses in the Philippines now under construction on the island of Corregidor and elsewhere or to complete a suitable repair station and coaling supply station at Olongapo, where is the floating dock "Dewey." I hope that this recommendation of the joint board will end the discussion as to the comparative merits of Manila Bay and Olongapo as naval stations, and will lead to prompt measures for the proper equipment and defense of Pearl Harbor.

THE NAVY.

The return of the battle-ship fleet from its voyage around the world, in more efficient condition than when it started, was a noteworthy event of interest alike to our citizens and the naval authorities of the world. Besides the beneficial and far-reaching effect on our personal and diplomatic relations in the countries which the fleet visited, the marked success of the ships in steaming around the world in all weathers on schedule time has increased respect for our Navy and has added to our national prestige.

Our enlisted personnel recruited from all sections of the country is young and energetic and representative of the national spirit. It is, moreover, owing to its intelligence, capable of quick training into the modern man-of-warsman. Our officers are earnest and zealous in their profession, but it is a regrettable fact that the higher officers are old for the responsibilities of the modern navy, and the admirals do not arrive at flag rank young enough to obtain adequate training in their duties as flag officers. This need for reform in the Navy has been ably and earnestly presented to Congress by my predecessor, and I also urgently recommend the subject for consideration.

Early in the coming session a comprehensive plan for the reorganization of the officers of all corps of the Navy will be presented to Congress, and I hope it will meet with action suited to its urgency.

Owing to the necessity for economy in expenditures, I have directed the curtailment of recommendations for naval appropriations so that they are thirty-eight millions less than the corresponding estimates of last year, and the request for new naval construction is limited to two first-class battle ships and one repair vessel.

The use of a navy is for military purposes, and there has been found need in the Department of a military branch dealing directly with the military use of the fleet. The Secretary of the Navy has also felt the lack of responsible advisers to aid him in reaching conclusions and deciding important matters between coordinate branches of the Department. To secure these results he has inaugurated a tentative plan involving certain changes in the organization of the Navy Department, including the navy-yards, all of which have been found by the Attorney-General to be in accordance with law. I have approved the execution of the plan proposed because of the greater efficiency and economy it promises.

The generosity of Congress has provided in the present Naval Observatory the most magnificent and expensive astronomical establishment in the world. It is being used for certain naval purposes which might easily and adequately be subserved by a small division connected with the Naval Department at only a fraction of the cost of the present Naval Observatory. The official Board of Visitors established by Congress and appointed in 1901 expressed its conclusion that the official head of the observatory should be an eminent astronomer appointed by the President by and with the advice and consent of the Senate, holding his place by a tenure at least as permanent as that of the Superintendent of the Coast Survey or the head of the Geological Survey, and not merely by a detail of two or three years' duration. I fully concur in this judgment, and urge a provision by law for the appointment of such a director.

It may not be necessary to take the observatory out of the Navy Department and put it into another department in which opportunity for scientific research afforded by the observatory would seem to be more appropriate, though I believe such a transfer in the long run is the best policy. I am sure, however, I express the desire of the astronomers and those learned in the kindred sciences when I urge upon Congress that the Naval Observatory be now dedicated to science under control of a man of science who can, if need be, render all the service to the Navy Department which this observatory now renders, and still furnish to the world the discoveries in astronomy that a great astronomer using such a plant would be likely to make.

DEPARTMENT OF JUSTICE.

EXPEDITION IN LEGAL PROCEDURE

The deplorable delays in the administration of civil and criminal law have received the attention of committees of the American Bar Association and of many State Bar Associations, as well as the considered thought of judges and jurists. In my judgment, a change in judicial procedure, with a view to reducing its expense to private litigants in civil cases and facilitating the dispatch of business and final decision in both civil and criminal cases, constitutes the greatest need in our American institutions. I do not doubt for one moment that much of the lawless violence and cruelty exhibited in lynchings is directly due to the uncertainties and injustice growing out of the delays in trials, judgments, and the executions thereof by our courts. Of course these remarks apply quite as well to the administration of justice in State courts as to that in Federal courts, and without making invidious distinction it is perhaps not too much to say that, speaking generally, the defects are less in the Federal courts than in the State courts. But they are very great in the Federal courts. The expedition with which business is disposed of both on the civil and the criminal side of English courts under modern rules of procedure makes the delays in our courts seem archaic and barbarous. The procedure in the Federal courts should furnish an example for the State courts. I presume it is impossible, without an amendment to the Constitution, to unite under one form of action the proceedings at common law and proceedings in equity in the Federal courts, but it is certainly not impossible by a statute to simplify and make short and direct the procedure both at law and in equity in those courts. It is not impossible to cut down still more than it is cut down, the jurisdiction of the Supreme Court so as to confine it almost wholly to statutory and constitutional questions. Under the present statutes the equity and admiralty procedure in the Federal courts is under the control of the Supreme Court, but in the pressure of business to which that court is subjected, it is impossible to hope that a radical and proper reform of the Federal equity procedure can be brought about. I therefore recommend legislation providing for the appointment by the President of a commission with authority to examine the law and equity procedure of the Federal courts of first instance, the law of appeals from those courts to the courts of appeals and to the Supreme Court, and the costs imposed in such procedure upon the private litigants and upon the public treasury and make recommendation with a view to simplifying and expediting the procedure as far as possible and making it as inexpensive as may be to the litigant of little means.

INJUNCTIONS WITHOUT NOTICE.

The platform of the successful party in the last election contained the following:

"The Republican party will uphold at all times the authority and integrity of the courts, State and Federal, and will ever insist that their powers to enforce their process and to protect life, liberty, and property shall be preserved inviolate. We believe, however, that the rules of procedure in the Federal courts with respect to the issuance of the writ of injunction should be more accurately defined by statute, and that no injunction or temporary restraining order should be issued without notice, except where irreparable injury would result from delay, in which case a speedy hearing thereafter should be granted."

I recommend that in compliance with the promise thus made, appropriate legislation be adopted. The ends of justice will best be met and the chief cause of complaint against ill-considered injunctions without notice will be removed by the enactment of a statute forbidding hereafter the issuing of any injunction or restraining order, whether temporary or permanent, by any Federal court, without previous notice and a reasonable opportunity to be heard on behalf of the parties to be enjoined; unless it shall appear to the satisfaction of the court that the delay necessary to give such notice and hearing would result in irreparable injury to the complainant and unless also the court shall from the evidence make a written finding, which shall be spread upon the court minutes, that immediate and irreparable injury is likely to ensue to the complainant, and shall define the injury, state why it is irreparable, and shall also endorse on the order issued the date and the hour of the issuance of the order. Moreover, every such injunction or restraining order issued without previous notice and opportunity by the defendant to be heard should by force of the statute expire and be of no effect after seven days from the issuance thereof or within any time less than that period which the court may fix, unless within such seven days or such less period, the injunction or order is extended or renewed after previous notice and opportunity to be heard.

My judgment is that the passage of such an act which really embodies the best practice in equity and is very like the rule now in force in some courts will prevent the issuing of ill-advised orders of injunction without notice and will render such orders when issued much less objectionable by the short time in which they may remain effective.

ANTI-TRUST AND INTERSTATE COMMERCE LAWS.

The jurisdiction of the General Government over interstate commerce has led to the passage of the so-called "Sherman Anti-trust Law" and the "Interstate Commerce Law" and its amendments. The developments in the operation of those laws, as shown by indictments, trials, judicial decisions, and other sources of information, call for a discussion and some suggestions as to amendments. These I prefer to embody in a special message instead of including them in the present communication, and I shall avail myself of the first convenient opportunity to bring these subjects to the attention of Congress.

JAIL OF THE DISTRICT OF COLUMBIA.

My predecessor transmitted to the Congress a special message on January 11, 1909, accompanying the report of Commissioners theretofore appointed to investigate the jail, workhouse, etc., in the District of Columbia, in which he directed attention to the report as setting forth vividly, "the really outrageous conditions in the workhouse and jail."

The Congress has taken action in pursuance of the recommendations of that report and of the President, to the extent of appropriating funds and enacting the necessary legislation for the establishment of a workhouse and reformatory. No action, however, has been taken by the Congress with respect to the jail, the conditions of which are still antiquated and insanitary. I earnestly recommend the passage of a sufficient appropriation to enable a thorough remodeling of that institution to be made without delay. It is a reproach to the National Government that almost under the shadow of the Capitol Dome prisoners should be confined in a building destitute of the ordinary decent appliances requisite to cleanliness and sanitary conditions.

POST-OFFICE DEPARTMENT.

SECOND-CLASS MAIL MATTER.

The deficit every year in the Post-Office Department is largely caused by the low rate of postage of 1 cent a pound charged on second-class mail matter, which includes not only newspapers, but magazines and miscellaneous periodicals. The actual loss growing out of the transmission of this second-class mail matter at 1 cent a pound amounts to about $63,000,000 a year. The average cost of the transportation of this matter is more than 9 cents a pound.

It appears that the average distance over which newspapers are delivered to their customers is 291 miles, while the average haul of magazines is 1,049, and of miscellaneous periodicals 1,128 miles. Thus, the average haul of the magazine is three and one-half times and that of the miscellaneous periodical nearly four times the haul of the daily newspaper, yet all of them pay the same postage rate of 1 cent a pound. The statistics of 1907 show that second-class mail matter constituted 63.91 per cent. of the weight of all the mail, and yielded only 5.19 per cent. of the revenue.

The figures given are startling, and show the payment by the Government of an enormous subsidy to the newspapers, magazines, and periodicals, and Congress may well consider whether radical steps should not be taken to reduce the deficit in the Post-Office Department caused by this discrepancy between the actual cost of transportation and the compensation exacted therefor.

A great saving might be made, amounting to much more than half of the loss, by imposing upon magazines and periodicals a higher rate of postage. They are much heavier than newspapers, and contain a much higher proportion of advertising to reading matter, and the average distance of their transportation is three and a half times as great.

The total deficit for the last fiscal year in the Post-Office Department amounted to $17,500,000. The branches of its business which it did at a loss were the second-class mail service, in which the loss, as already said, was $63,000,000, and the free rural delivery, in which the loss was $28,000,000. These losses were in part offset by the profits of the letter postage and other sources of income. It would seem wise to reduce the loss upon second-class mail matter, at least to the extent of preventing a deficit in the total operations of the Post-Office.

I commend the whole subject to Congress, not unmindful of the spread of intelligence which a low charge for carrying newspapers and periodicals assists. I very much doubt, however, the wisdom of a policy which constitutes so large a subsidy and requires additional taxation to meet it.

POSTAL SAVINGS BANKS.

The second subject worthy of mention in the Post-Office Department is the real necessity and entire practicability of establishing postal savings banks. The successful party at the last election declared in favor of postal savings banks, and although the proposition finds opponents in many parts of the country, I am convinced that the people desire such banks, and am sure that when the banks are furnished they will be productive of the utmost good. The postal savings banks are not constituted for the purpose of creating competition with other banks. The rate of interest upon deposits to which they would be limited would be so small as to prevent their drawing deposits away from other banks.

I believe them to be necessary in order to offer a proper inducement to thrift and saving to a great many people of small means who do not now have banking facilities, and to whom such a system would offer an opportunity for the accumulation of capital. They will furnish a satisfactory substitute, based on sound principle and actual successful trial in nearly all the countries of the world, for the system of government guaranty of deposits now being adopted in several western States, which with deference to those who advocate it seems to me to have in it the seeds of demoralization to conservative banking and certain financial disaster.

The question of how the money deposited in postal savings banks shall be invested is not free from difficulty, but I believe that a satisfactory provision for this purpose was inserted as an amendment to the bill considered by the Senate at its last session. It has been proposed to delay the consideration of legislation establishing a postal savings bank until after the report of the Monetary Commission. This report is likely to be delayed, and properly so, because of the necessity for careful deliberation and close investigation. I do not see why the one should be tied up with the other. It is understood that the Monetary Commission have looked into the systems of banking which now prevail abroad, and have found that by a control there exercised in respect to reserves and the rates of exchange by some central authority panics are avoided. It is not apparent that a system of postal savings banks would in any way interfere with a change to such a system here. Certainly in most of the countries of Europe where control is thus exercised by a central authority, postal savings banks exist and are not thought to be inconsistent with a proper financial and banking system.

SHIP SUBSIDY.

Following the course of my distinguished predecessor, I earnestly recommend to Congress the consideration and passage of a ship subsidy bill, looking to the establishment of lines between our Atlantic seaboard and the eastern coast of South America, as well as lines from the west coast of the United States to South America. China, Japan, and the Philippines. The profits on foreign mails are perhaps a sufficient measure of the expenditures which might first be tentatively applied to this method of inducing American capital to undertake the establishment of American lines of steamships in those directions in which we now feel it most important that we should have means of transportation controlled in the interest of the expansion of our trade. A bill of this character has once passed the House and more than once passed the Senate, and I hope that at this session a bill framed on the same lines and with the same purposes may become a law.

INTERIOR DEPARTMENT.

NEW MEXICO AND ARIZONA.

The successful party in the last election in its national platform declared in favor of the admission as separate States of New Mexico and Arizona, and I recommend that legislation appropriate to this end be adopted. I urge, however, that care be exercised in the preparation of the legislation affecting each Territory to secure deliberation in the selection of persons as members of the convention to draft a constitution for the incoming State, and I earnestly advise that such constitution after adoption by the convention shall be submitted to the people of the Territory for their approval at an election in which the sole issue shall be the merits of the proposed constitution, and if the constitution is defeated by popular vote means shall be provided in the enabling act for a new convention and the drafting of a new constitution. I think it vital that the issue as to the merits of the constitution should not be mixed up with the selection of State officers, and that no election of State officers should be had until after the constitution has been fully approved and finally settled upon.

ALASKA.

With respect to the Territory of Alaska, I recommend legislation which shall provide for the appointment by the President of a governor and also of an executive council, the members of which shall during their term of office reside in the Territory, and which shall have legislative powers sufficient to enable it to give to the Territory local laws adapted to its present growth. I strongly deprecate legislation looking to the election of a Territorial legislature in that vast district. The lack of permanence of residence of a large part of the present population and the small number of the people who either permanently or temporarily reside in the district as compared with its vast expanse and the variety of the interests that have to be subserved, make it altogether unfitting in my judgment to provide for a popular election of a legislative body. The present system is not adequate and does not furnish the character of local control that ought to be there. The only compromise it seems to me which may give needed local legislation and secure a conservative government is the one I propose.

CONSERVATION OF NATIONAL RESOURCES.

In several Departments there is presented the necessity for legislation looking to the further conservation of our national resources, and the subject is one of such importance as to require a more detailed and extended discussion than can be entered upon in this communication. For that reason I shall take an early opportunity to send a special message to Congress on the subject of the improvement of our waterways, upon the reclamation and irrigation of arid, semiarid, and swamp lands; upon the preservation of our forests and the reforesting of suitable areas; upon the reclassification of the public domain with a view of separating from agricultural settlement mineral, coal, and phosphate lands and sites belonging to the Government bordering on streams suitable for the utilization of water power.

DEPARTMENT OF AGRICULTURE.

I commend to your careful consideration the report of the Secretary of Agriculture as showing the immense sphere of usefulness which that Department now fills and the wonderful addition to the wealth of the nation made by the farmers of this country in the crops of the current year.

DEPARTMENT OF COMMERCE AND LABOR.

THE LIGHT-HOUSE BOARD.

The Light-House Board now discharges its duties under the Department of Commerce and Labor. For upwards of forty years this Board has been constituted of military and naval officers and two or three men of science, with such an absence of a duly constituted executive head that it is marvelous what work has been accomplished. In the period of construction the energy and enthusiasm of all the members prevented the inherent defects of the system from interfering greatly with the beneficial work of the Board, but now that the work is chiefly confined to maintenance and repair, for which purpose the country is divided into sixteen districts, to which are assigned an engineer officer of the Army and an inspector of the Navy, each with a light-house tender and the needed plant for his work, it has become apparent by the frequent friction that arises, due to the absence of any central independent authority, that there must be a complete reorganization of the Board. I concede the advantage of keeping in the system the rigidity of discipline that the presence of naval and military officers in charge insures, but unless the presence of such officers in the Board can be made consistent with a responsible executive head that shall have proper authority, I recommend the transfer of control over the light-houses to a suitable civilian bureau. This is in accordance with the judgment of competent persons who are familiar with the workings of the present system. I am confident that a reorganization can be effected which shall avoid the recurrence of friction between members, instances of which have been officially brought to my attention, and that by such reorganization greater efficiency and a substantial reduction in the expense of operation can be brought about.

CONSOLIDATION OF BUREAUS.

I request Congressional authority to enable the Secretary of Commerce and Labor to unite the Bureaus of Manufactures and Statistics. This was recommended by a competent committee appointed in the previous administration for the purpose of suggesting changes in the interest of economy and efficiency, and is requested by the Secretary.

THE WHITE SLAVE TRADE.

I greatly regret to have to say that the investigations made in the Bureau of Immigration and other sources of information lead to the view that there is urgent necessity for additional legislation and greater executive activity to suppress the recruiting of the ranks of prostitutes from the streams of immigration into this country—an evil which, for want of a better name, has been called "The White Slave Trade." I believe it to be constitutional to forbid, under penalty, the transportation of persons for purposes of prostitution across national and state lines; and by appropriating a fund of $50,000 to be used by the Secretary of Commerce and Labor for the employment of special inspectors it will be possible to bring those responsible for this trade to indictment and conviction under a federal law.

BUREAU OF HEALTH.

For a very considerable period a movement has been gathering strength, especially among the members of the medical profession, in favor of a concentration of the instruments of the National Government which have to do with the promotion of public health. In the nature of things, the Medical Department of the Army and the Medical Department of the Navy must be kept separate. But there seems to be no reason why all the other bureaus and offices in the General Government which have to do with the public health or subjects akin thereto should not be united in a bureau to be called the "Bureau of Public Health." This would necessitate the transfer of the Marine-Hospital Service to such a bureau. I am aware that there is wide field in respect to the public health committed to the States in which the Federal Government can not exercise jurisdiction, but we have seen in the Agricultural Department the expansion into widest usefulness of a department giving attention to agriculture when that subject is plainly one over which the States properly exercise direct jurisdiction. The opportunities offered for useful research and the spread of useful information in regard to the cultivation of the soil and the breeding of stock and the solution of many of the intricate problems in progressive agriculture have demonstrated the wisdom of establishing that department. Similar reasons, of equal force, can be given for the establishment of a bureau of health that shall not only exercise the police jurisdiction of the Federal Government respecting quarantine, but which shall also afford an opportunity for investigation and research by competent experts into questions of health affecting the whole country, or important sections thereof, questions which, in the absence of Federal governmental work, are not likely to be promptly solved.

CIVIL SERVICE COMMISSION.

The work of the United States Civil Service Commission has been performed to the general satisfaction of the executive officers with whom the Commission has been brought into official communication. The volume of that work and its variety and extent have under new laws, such as the Census Act, and new Executive orders, greatly increased. The activities of the Commission required by the statutes have reached to every portion of the public domain.

The accommodations of the Commission are most inadequate for its needs. I call your attention to its request for increase in those accommodations as will appear from the annual report for this year.

POLITICAL CONTRIBUTIONS.

I urgently recommend to Congress that a law be passed requiring that candidates in elections of Members of the House of Representatives, and committees in charge of their candidacy and campaign, file in a proper office of the United States Government a statement of the contributions received and of the expenditures incurred in the campaign for such elections and that similar legislation be enacted in respect to all other elections which are constitutionally within the control of Congress

FREEDMAN'S SAVINGS AND TRUST COMPANY.

Recommendations have been made by my predecessors that Congress appropriate a sufficient sum to pay the balance—about 38 per cent.—of the amounts due depositors in the Freedman's Savings and Trust Company. I renew this recommendation, and advise also that a proper limitation be prescribed fixing a period within which the claims may be presented, that assigned claims be not recognized, and that a limit be imposed on the amount of fees collectible for services in presenting such claims.

SEMI-CENTENNIAL OF NEGRO FREEDOM.

The year 1913 will mark the fiftieth anniversary of the issuance of the Emancipation Proclamation granting freedom to the negroes. It seems fitting that this event should be properly celebrated. Already a movement has been started by prominent negroes, encouraged by prominent white people and the press. The South especially is manifesting its interest in this movement.

It is suggested that a proper form of celebration would be an exposition to show the progress the negroes have made, not only during their period of freedom, but also from the time of their coming to this country.

I heartily indorse this proposal, and request that the Executive be authorized to appoint a preliminary commission of not more than seven persons to consider carefully whether or not it is wise to hold such an exposition, and if so, to outline a plan for the enterprise. I further recommend that such preliminary commission serve without salary, except as to their actual expenses, and that an appropriation be made to meet such expenses.

CONCLUSION.

I have thus, in a message compressed as much as the subjects will permit, referred to many of the legislative needs of the country, with the exceptions already noted. Speaking generally, the country is in a high state of prosperity. There is every reason to believe that we are on the eve of a substantial business expansion, and we have just garnered a harvest unexampled in the market value of our agricultural products. The high prices which such products bring mean great prosperity for the farming community, but on the other hand they mean a very considerably increased burden upon those classes in the community whose yearly compensation does not expand with the improvement in business and the general prosperity. Various reasons are given for the high prices. The proportionate increase in the output of gold, which to-day is the chief medium of exchange and is in some respects a measure of value, furnishes a substantial explanation of at least a part of the increase in prices. The increase in population and the more expensive mode of living of the people, which have not been accompanied by a proportionate increase in acreage production, may furnish a further reason. It is well to note that the increase in the cost of living is not confined to this country, but prevails the world over, and that those who would charge increases in prices to the existing protective tariff must meet the fact that the rise in prices has taken place almost wholly in those products of the factory and farm in respect to which there has been either no increase in the tariff or in many instances a very considerable reduction.

SECOND ANNUAL MESSAGE.

THE WHITE HOUSE, *December 6, 1910.*

To the Senate and House of Representatives:

During the past year the foreign relations of the United States have continued upon a basis of friendship and good understanding.

ARBITRATION.

The year has been notable as witnessing the pacific settlement of two important international controversies before the Permanent Court of The Hague.

The arbitration of the Fisheries dispute between the United States and Great Britain, which has been the source of nearly continuous diplomatic correspondence since the Fisheries Convention of 1818, has given an award which is satisfactory to both parties. This arbitration is particularly noteworthy not only because of the eminently just results secured, but also because it is the first arbitration held under the general arbitration treaty of April 4, 1908, between the United States and Great Britain, and disposes of a controversy the settlement of which has resisted every other resource of diplomacy, and which for nearly ninety years has been the cause of friction between two countries whose common interest lies in maintaining the most friendly and cordial relations with each other.

The United States was ably represented before the tribunal. The complicated history of the questions arising made the issue depend, more than ordinarily in such cases, upon the care and skill with which our case was presented, and I should be wanting in proper recognition of a great patriotic service if I did not refer to the lucid historical analysis of the facts and the signal ability and force of the argument —six days in length—presented to the Court in support of our case by Mr. Elihu Root. As Secretary of State, Mr. Root had given close study to the intricate facts bearing on the controversy, and by diplomatic correspondence had helped to frame the issues. At the solicitation of the Secretary of State and myself, Mr. Root, though burdened by his duties as Senator from New York, undertook the preparation of the case as leading counsel, with the condition imposed by himself that, in view of his position as Senator, he should not receive any compensation.

The Tribunal constituted at The Hague by the Governments of the United States and Venezuela has completed its deliberations and has rendered an award in the case of the Orinoco Steamship Company against Venezuela. The award may be regarded as satisfactory since it has, pursuant to the contentions of the United States, recognized a number of important principles making for a judicial attitude in the determining of international disputes.

In view of grave doubts which had been raised as to the constitutionality of The Hague Convention for the establishment of an International Prize Court, now before the Senate for ratification, because of that provision of the Convention which provides that there may be an appeal to the proposed Court from the decisions of national courts, this government proposed in an Identic Circular Note addressed to those Powers who had taken part in the London Maritime Conference, that the powers signatory to the Convention, if confronted with such difficulty, might insert a reservation to the effect that appeals to the International Prize Court in respect to decisions of its national tribunals, should take the form of a direct claim for compensation; that the proceedings thereupon to be taken should be in the form of a trial *de novo,* and that judgment of the Court should consist of compensation for the illegal capture, irrespective of the decision of the national court whose judgment had thus been internationally involved. As the result of an informal discussion it was decided to provide such procedure by means of a separate protocol which should be ratified at the same time as the Prize Court Convention itself.

Accordingly, the Government of the Netherlands, at the request of this Government, proposed under date of May 24, 1910, to the powers signatory to The Hague Convention, the negotiation of a supplemental protocol embodying stipulations providing for this alternative procedure. It is gratifying to observe that this additional protocol is being signed without objection, by the powers signatory to the original convention, and there is every reason to believe that the International Prize Court will be soon established.

The Identic Circular Note also proposed that the International Prize Court when established should be endowed with the functions of an Arbitral Court of Justice under and pursuant to the recommendation adopted by the last Hague Conference. The replies received from the various powers to this proposal inspire the hope that this also may be accomplished within the reasonably near future.

It is believed that the establishment of these two tribunals will go a long way toward securing the arbitration of many questions which have heretofore threatened and, at times, destroyed the peace of nations.

PEACE COMMISSION.

Appreciating these enlightened tendencies of modern times, the Congress at its last session passed a law providing for the appointment of a commission of five members "to be appointed by the President of the United States to consider the expediency of utilizing existing international agencies for the purpose of limiting the armaments of the nations of the world by international agreement, and of constituting the combined navies of the world an international force for the preservation of universal peace, and to consider and report upon any other means to diminish the expenditures of government for military purposes and to lessen the probabilities of war."

I have not as yet made appointments to this Commission because I have invited and am awaiting the expressions of foreign governments as to their willingness to cooperate with us in the appointment of similar commissions or representatives who would meet with our commissioners and by joint action seek to make their work effective.

GREAT BRITAIN AND CANADA.

Several important treaties have been negotiated with Great Britain in the past twelve months. A preliminary diplomatic agreement has been reached regarding the arbitration of pecuniary claims which each Government has against the other. This agreement, with the schedules of claims annexed, will, as soon as the schedules are arranged, be submitted to the Senate for approval.

An agreement between the United States and Great Britain with regard to the location of the international boundary line between the United States and Canada in Passamaquoddy Bay and to the middle of Grand Manan Channel was reached in a Treaty concluded May 21, 1910, which has been ratified by both Governments and proclaimed, thus making unnecessary the arbitration provided for in the previous treaty of April 11, 1908.

The Convention concluded January 11, 1909, between the United States and Great Britain providing for the settlement of international differences between the United States and Canada including the apportionment between the two countries of certain of the boundary waters and the appointment of Commissioners to adjust certain other questions has been ratified by both Governments and proclaimed.

The work of the International Fisheries Commission appointed in 1908, under the treaty of April 11, 1908, between Great Britain and the United States, has resulted in the formulation and recommendation of uniform regulations governing the fisheries of the boundary waters of Canada and the United States for the purpose of protecting and increasing the supply of food fish in such waters. In completion of this work, the regulations agreed upon require congressional legislation to make them effective and for their enforcement in fulfillment of the treaty stipulations.

PORTUGAL.

In October last the monarchy in Portugal was overthrown, a provisional Republic was proclaimed, and there was set up a de facto Government which was promptly recognized by the Government of the United States for purposes of ordinary intercourse pending formal recognition by this and other Powers of the Governmental entity to be duly established by the national sovereignty.

LIBERIA.

A disturbance among the native tribes of Liberia in a portion of the Republic during the early part of this year resulted in the sending, under the Treaty of 1862, of an American vessel of war to the disaffected district, and the Liberian authorities, assisted by the good offices of the American Naval Officers, were able to restore order. The negotiations which have been undertaken for the amelioration of the conditions found in Liberia by the American Commission, whose report I transmitted to Congress on March 25 last, are being brought to conclusion, and it is thought that within a short time practical measures of relief may be put into effect through the good offices of this Government and the cordial cooperation of other governments interested in Liberia's welfare.

THE NEAR EAST.

TURKEY.

To return the visit of the Special Embassy announcing the accession of His Majesty Mehemet V, Emperor of the Ottomans, I sent to Constantinople a Special Ambassador who, in addition to this mission of ceremony, was charged with the duty of expressing to the Ottoman Government the value attached by the Government of the United States to increased and more important relations between the countries and the desire of the United States to contribute to the larger economic and commercial development due to the new régime in Turkey.

The rapid development now beginning in that ancient empire and the marked progress and increased commercial importance of Bulgaria, Roumania, and Servia make it particularly opportune that the possibilities of American commerce in the Near East should receive due attention.

MONTENEGRO.

The National Skoupchtina having expressed its will that the Principality of Montenegro be raised to the rank of Kingdom, the Prince of Montenegro on August 15 last assumed the title of King of Montenegro. It gave me pleasure to accord to the new kingdom the recognition of the United States.

THE FAR EAST.

The center of interest in Far Eastern affairs during the past year has again been China.

It is gratifying to note that the negotiations for a loan to the Chinese Government for the construction of the trunk railway lines from Hankow southward to Canton and westward through the Yangtse Valley, known as the Hukuang Loan, were concluded by the representatives of the various financial groups in May last and the results approved by their respective governments. The agreement, already initialed by the Chinese Government, is now awaiting formal ratification. The basis of the settlement of the terms of this loan was one of exact equality between America, Great Britain, France, and Germany in respect to financing the loan and supplying materials for the proposed railways and their future branches.

The application of the principle underlying the policy of the United States in regard to the Hukuang Loan, viz., that of the internationalization of the foreign interest in such of the railways of China as may be financed by foreign countries, was suggested on a broader scale by the Secretary of State in a proposal for internationalization and commercial neutralization of all the railways of Manchuria. While the principle which led to the proposal of this Government was generally admitted by the powers to whom it was addressed, the Governments of Russia and Japan apprehended practical difficulties in the execution of the larger plan which prevented their ready adherence. The question of constructing the Chinchow-Aigun railway by means of an international loan to China is, however, still the subject of friendly discussion by the interested parties.

The policy of this Government in these matters has been directed by a desire to make the use of American capital in the development of China an instrument in the promotion of China's welfare and material prosperity without prejudice to her legitimate rights as an independent political power.

This policy has recently found further exemplification in the assistance given by this Government to the negotiations between China and a group of American bankers for a loan of $50,000,000 to be employed chiefly in currency reform. The confusion which has from ancient times existed in the monetary usages of the Chinese has been one of the principal obstacles to commercial intercourse with that people. The United States in its Treaty of 1903 with China obtained a pledge from the latter to introduce a uniform national coinage, and the following year, at the request of China, this Government sent to Peking a member of the International Exchange Commission, to discuss with the Chinese Government the best methods of introducing the reform. In 1908 China sent a Commissioner to the United States to consult with American financiers as to the possibility of securing a large loan with which to inaugurate the new currency system, but the death of Their Majesties, the Empress Dowager and the Emperor of China, interrupted the negotiations, which were not resumed until a few months ago, when this Government was asked to communicate to the bankers concerned the request of China for a loan of $50,000,000 for the purpose under review. A preliminary agreement between the American group and China has been made covering the loan.

For the success of this loan and the contemplated reforms which are of the greatest importance to the commercial interests of the United States and the civilized world at large, it is realized that an expert will be necessary, and this Government has received assurances from China that such an adviser, who shall be an American, will be engaged.

It is a matter of interest to Americans to note the success which is attending the efforts of China to establish gradually a system of representative government. The provincial assemblies were opened in October, 1909, and in October of the present year a consultative body, the nucleus of the future national parliament, held its first session at Peking.

The year has further been marked by two important international agreements relating to Far Eastern affairs. In the Russo-Japanese Agreement relating to Manchuria, signed July 4, 1910, this Government was gratified to note an assurance of continued peaceful conditions in that region and the reaffirmation of the policies with respect to China to which the United States together with all other interested powers are alike solemnly committed.

The treaty annexing Korea to the Empire of Japan, promulgated August 29, 1910, marks the final step in a process of control of the ancient empire by her powerful neighbor that has been in progress for several years past. In communicating the fact of annexation the Japanese Government gave to the Government of the United States assurances of the full protection of the rights of American citizens in Korea under the changed conditions.

Friendly visits of many distinguished persons from the Far East have been made during the year. Chief among these were Their Imperial Highnesses Princes Tsai-tao and Tsai-Hsun of China; and His Imperial Highness Prince Higashi Fushimi, and Prince Tokugawa, President of the House of Peers of Japan. The Secretary of War has recently visited Japan and China in connection with his tour to the Philippines, and a large delegation of American business men are at present traveling in China. This exchange of friendly visits has had the happy effect of even further strengthening our friendly international relations.

LATIN AMERICA.

During the past year several of our southern sister Republics celebrated the one hundredth anniversary of their independence. In honor of these events, special embassies were sent from this country to Argentina, Chile, and Mexico, where the gracious reception and splendid hospitality extended them manifested the cordial relations and friendship existing between those countries and the United States, relations which I am happy to believe have never before been upon so high a plane and so solid a basis as at present.

The Congressional commission appointed under a concurrent resolution to attend the festivities celebrating the centennial anniversary of Mexican independence, together with a special ambassador, were received with the highest honors and with the greatest cordiality, and returned with the report of the bounteous hospitality and warm reception of President Diaz and the Mexican people, which left no doubt of the desire of the immediately neighboring Republic to continue the mutually beneficial and intimate relations which I feel sure the two governments will ever cherish.

At the Fourth Pan-American Conference which met in Buenos Aires during July and August last, after seven weeks of harmonious deliberation, three conventions were signed providing for the regulation of trade-marks, patents, and copyrights, which when ratified by the different Governments, will go far toward furnishing to American authors, patentees, and owners of trade-marks the protection needed in localities where heretofore it has been either lacking or inadequate. Further, a convention for the arbitration of pecuniary claims was signed and a number of important resolutions passed. The Conventions will in due course be transmitted to the Senate, and the report of the Delegation of the United States will be communicated to the Congress for its information. The special cordiality between representative men from all parts of America which was shown at this Conference cannot fail to react upon and draw still closer the relations between the countries which took part in it.

The International Bureau of American Republics is doing a broad and useful work for Pan American commerce and comity. Its duties were much enlarged by the International Conference of American States at Buenos Aires and its name was shortened to the more practical and expressive term of Pan American Union. Located now in its new building, which was specially dedicated April 26 of this year to the development of friendship, trade and peace among the American nations, it has improved instrumentalities to serve the twenty-two republics of this hemisphere.

I am glad to say that the action of the United States in its desire to remove imminent danger of war between Peru and Ecuador growing out of a boundary dispute, with the cooperation of Brazil and the Argentine Republic as joint mediators with this Government, has already resulted successfully in preventing war. The Government of Chile, while not one of the mediators, lent effective aid in furtherance of a preliminary agreement likely to lead on to an amicable settlement, and it is not doubted that the good offices of the mediating Powers and the conciliatory cooperation of the Governments directly interested will finally lead to a removal of this perennial cause of friction between Ecuador and Peru. The inestimable value of cordial cooperation between the sister republics of America for the maintenance of peace in this hemisphere has never been more clearly shown than in this mediation, by which three American Governments have given to this hemisphere the honor of first invoking the most far-reaching provisions of The Hague Convention for the pacific settlement of international disputes.

There has been signed by the representatives of the United States and Mexico a protocol submitting to the United States-Mexican Boundary Commission (whose membership for the purpose of this case is to be increased by the addition of a citizen of Canada) the question of sovereignty over the Chamizal Tract which lies within the present physical boundaries of the city of El Paso, Tex. The determination of this question will remove a source of no little annoyance to the two Governments.

The Republic of Honduras has for many years been burdened with a heavy bonded debt held in Europe, the interest on which long ago fell in arrears. Finally conditions were such that it became imperative to refund the debt and place the finances of the Republic upon a sound basis. Last year a group of American bankers undertook to do this and to advance funds for railway and other improvements contributing directly to the country's prosperity and commerce—an arrangement which has long been desired by this Government. Negotiations to this end have been under way for more than a year and it is now confidently believed that a short time will suffice to conclude an arrangement which will be satisfactory to the foreign creditors, eminently advantageous to Honduras, and highly creditable to the judgment and foresight of the Honduranean Government. This is much to be desired since, as recognized by the Washington Conventions, a strong Honduras would tend immensely to the progress and prosperity of Central America.

During the past year the Republic of Nicaragua has been the scene of internecine struggle. General Zelaya, for seventeen years the absolute ruler of Nicaragua, was throughout his career the disturber of Central America and opposed every plan for the promotion of peace and friendly relations between the five republics. When the people of Nicaragua were finally driven into rebellion by his lawless exactions, he violated the laws of war by the unwarranted execution of two American citizens who had regularly enlisted in the ranks of the revolutionists. This and other offenses made it the duty of the American Government to take measures with a view to ultimate reparation and for the safeguarding of its interests. This involved the breaking off of all diplomatic relations with the Zelaya Government for the reasons laid down in a communication from the Secretary of State, which also notified the contending factions in Nicaragua that this Government would hold each to strict accountability for outrages on the rights of American citizens. American forces were sent to both coasts of Nicaragua to be in readiness should occasion arise to protect Americans and their interests, and remained there until the war was over and peace had returned to that unfortunate country. These events, together with Zelaya's continued exactions, brought him so clearly to the bar of public opinion that he was forced to resign and to take refuge abroad.

In the above-mentioned communication of the Secretary of State to the Chargé d'Affaires of the Zelaya Government, the opinion was expressed that the revolution represented the wishes of the majority of the Nicaraguan people. This has now been proved beyond doubt by the fact that since the complete overthrow of the Madriz Government and the occupation of the capital by the forces of the revolution, all factions have united to maintain public order and as a result of discussion with an Agent of this Government, sent to Managua at the request of the Provisional Government, comprehensive plans are being made for the future welfare of Nicaragua, including the rehabilitation of public credit. The moderation and conciliatory spirit shown by the various factions give ground for the confident hope that Nicaragua will soon take its rightful place among the law-abiding and progressive countries of the world.

It gratifies me exceedingly to announce that the Argentine Republic some months ago placed with American manufacturers a contract for the construction of two battle-ships and certain additional naval equipment. The extent of this work and its importance to the Argentine Republic make the placing of the bid an earnest of friendly feeling toward the United States.

TARIFF NEGOTIATIONS.

The new tariff law, in section 2, respecting the maximum and minimum tariffs of the United States, which provisions came into effect on April 1, 1910, imposed upon the President the responsibility of determining prior to that date whether or not any undue discrimination existed against the United States and its products in any country of the world with which we sustained commercial relations.

In the case of several countries instances of apparent undue discrimination against American commerce were found to exist. These discriminations were removed by negotiation. Prior to April 1, 1910, when the maximum tariff was to come into operation with respect to importations from all those countries in whose favor no proclamation applying the minimum tariff should be issued by the President, one hundred and thirty-four such proclamations were issued. This series of proclamations embraced the entire commercial world, and hence the minimum tariff of the United States has been given universal application, thus testifying to the satisfactory character of our trade relations with foreign countries.

Marked advantages to the commerce of the United States were obtained through these tariff settlements. Foreign nations are fully cognizant of the fact that under section 2 of the tariff act the President is required, whenever he is satisfied that the treatment accorded by them to the products of the United States is not such as to entitle them to the benefits of the minimum tariff of the United States, to withdraw those benefits by proclamation giving ninety days' notice, after which the maximum tariff will apply to their dutiable products entering the United States. In its general operation this section of the tariff law has thus far proved a guaranty of continued commercial peace, although there are unfortunately instances where foreign governments deal arbitrarily with American interests within their jurisdiction in a manner injurious and inequitable.

The policy of broader and closer trade relations with the Dominion of Canada which was initiated in the adjustment of the maximum and minimum provisions of the Tariff Act of August, 1909, has proved mutually beneficial. It justifies further efforts for the readjustment of the commercial relations of the two countries so that their commerce may follow the channels natural to contiguous countries and be commensurate with the steady expansion of trade and industry on both sides of the boundary line. The reciprocation on the part of the Dominion Government of the sentiment which was expressed by this Government was followed in October by the suggestion that it would be glad to have the negotiations, which had been temporarily suspended during the summer, resumed. In accordance with this suggestion the Secretary of State, by my direction, dispatched two representatives of the Department of State as special commissioners to Ottawa to confer with representatives of the Dominion Government. They were authorized to take such steps for formulating a reciprocal trade agreement as might be necessary and to receive and consider any propositions which the Dominion Government might care to submit.

Pursuant to the instructions issued conferences were held by these commissioners with officials of the Dominion Government at Ottawa in the early part of November.

The negotiations were conducted on both sides in a spirit of mutual accommodation. The discussion of the common commercial interests of the two countries had for its object a satisfactory basis for a trade arrangement which offers the prospect of a freer interchange for the products of the United States and of Canada. The conferences were adjourned to be resumed in Washington in January, when it is hoped that the aspiration of both Governments for a mutually advantageous measure of reciprocity will be realized.

FOSTERING FOREIGN TRADE.

All these tariff negotiations, so vital to our commerce and industry, and the duty of jealously guarding the equitable and just treatment of our products, capital, and industry abroad devolve upon the Department of State.

The Argentine battle-ship contracts, like the subsequent important one for Argentine railway equipment, and those for Cuban Government vessels, were secured for our manufacturers largely through the good offices of the Department of State.

The efforts of that Department to secure for citizens of the United States equal opportunities in the markets of the world and to expand American commerce have been most successful. The volume of business obtained in new fields of competition and upon new lines is already very great and Congress is urged to continue to support the Department of State in its endeavors for further trade expansion.

Our foreign trade merits the best support of the Government and the most earnest endeavor of our manufacturers and merchants, who, if they do not already in all cases need a foreign market, are certain soon to become dependent on it. Therefore, now is the time to secure a strong position in this field.

AMERICAN BRANCH BANKS ABROAD.

I cannot leave this subject without emphasizing the necessity of such legislation as will make possible and convenient the establishment of American banks and branches of American banks in foreign countries. Only by such means can our foreign trade be favorably financed, necessary credits be arranged, and proper avail be made of commercial opportunities in foreign countries, and most especially in Latin America.

AID TO OUR FOREIGN MERCHANT MARINE.

Another instrumentality indispensable to the unhampered and natural development of American commerce is merchant marine. All maritime and commercial nations recognize the importance of this factor. The greatest commercial nations, our competitors, jealously foster their merchant marine. Perhaps nowhere is the need for rapid and direct mail, passenger and freight communication quite so urgent as between the United States and Latin America. We can secure in no other quarter of the world such immediate benefits in friendship and commerce as would flow from the establishment of direct lines of communication with the countries of Latin America adequate to meet the requirements of a rapidly increasing appreciation of the reciprocal dependence of the countries of the Western Hemisphere upon each other's products, sympathies and assistance.

I alluded to this most important subject in my last annual message; it has often been before you and I need not recapitulate the reasons for its recommendation. Unless prompt action be taken the completion of the Panama Canal will find this the only great commercial nation unable to avail in international maritime business of this great improvement in the means of the world's commercial intercourse.

Quite aside from the commercial aspect, unless we create a merchant marine, where can we find the seafaring population necessary as a natural naval reserve and where could we find, in case of war, the transports and subsidiary vessels without which a naval fleet is arms without a body? For many reasons I cannot too strongly urge upon the Congress the passage of a measure by mail subsidy or other subvention adequate to guarantee the establishment and rapid development of an American merchant marine, and the restoration of the American flag to its ancient place upon the seas.

Of course such aid ought only to be given under conditions of publicity of each beneficiary's business and accounts which would show that the aid received was needed to maintain the trade and was properly used for that purpose.

FEDERAL PROTECTION TO ALIENS.

With our increasing international intercourse, it becomes incumbent upon me to repeat more emphatically than ever the recommendation which I made in my Inaugural Address that Congress shall at once give to the Courts of the United States jurisdiction to punish as a crime the violation of the rights of aliens secured by treaty with the United States, in order that the general government of the United States shall be able, when called upon by a friendly nation, to redeem its solemn promise by treaty to secure to the citizens or subjects of that nation resident in the United States, freedom from violence and due process of law in respect to their life, liberty and property.

MERIT SYSTEM FOR DIPLOMATIC AND CONSULAR SERVICE.

I also strongly commend to the favorable action of the Congress the enactment of a law applying to the diplomatic and consular service the principles embodied in Section 1753 of the Revised Statutes of the United States, in the Civil Service Act of January 16, 1883, and the Executive Orders of June 27, 1906, and of November 26, 1909. The excellent results which have attended the partial application of Civil Service principles to the diplomatic and consular services are an earnest of the benefit to be wrought by a wider and more permanent extension of those principles to both branches of the foreign service. The marked improvement in the consular service during the four years since the principles of the Civil Service Act were applied to that service in a limited way, and the good results already noticeable from a similar application of civil service principles to the diplomatic service a year ago, convince me that the enactment into law of the general principles of the existing executive regulations could not fail to effect further improvement of both branches of the foreign service, offering as it would by its assurance of permanency of tenure and promotion on merit, an inducement for the entry of capable young men into the service and an incentive to those already in to put forth their best efforts to attain and maintain that degree of efficiency which the interests of our international relations and commerce demand.

GOVERNMENT OWNERSHIP OF OUR EMBASSY AND LEGATION PREMISES.

During many years past appeals have been made from time to time to Congress in favor of Government ownership of embassy and legation premises abroad. The arguments in favor of such ownership have been many and oft repeated and are well known to the Congress. The acquisition by the Government of suitable residences and offices for its diplomatic officers, especially in the capitals of the Latin-American States and of Europe, is so important and necessary to an improved diplomatic service that I have no hesitation in urging upon the Congress the passage of some measure similar to that favorably reported by the House Committee on Foreign Affairs on February 14, 1910 (Report No. 438), that would authorize the gradual and annual acquisition of premises for diplomatic use.

The work of the Diplomatic Service is devoid of partisanship; its importance should appeal to every American citizen and should receive the generous consideration of the Congress.

TREASURY DEPARTMENT.

ESTIMATES FOR NEXT YEAR'S EXPENSES.

Every effort has been made by each department chief to reduce the estimated cost of his department for the ensuing fiscal year ending June 30, 1912. I say this in order that Congress may understand that these estimates thus made present the smallest sum which will maintain the departments, bureaus, and offices of the Government and meet its other obligations under existing law, and that a cut of these estimates would result in embarrassing the executive branch of the Government in the performance of its duties. This remark does not apply to the river and harbor estimates, except to those for expenses of maintenance and the meeting of obligations under authorized contracts, nor does it apply to the public building bill nor to the navy building program. Of course, as to these Congress could withhold any part or all of the estimates for them without interfering with the discharge of the ordinary obligations of the Government or the performance of the functions of its departments, bureaus, and offices.

A FIFTY-TWO MILLION CUT.

The final estimates for the year ending June 30, 1912, as they have been sent to the Treasury, on November 29 of this year, for the ordinary expenses of the Government, including those for public buildings, rivers and harbors, and the navy building program, amount to $630,494,013.12. This is $52,964,887.36 less than the appropriations for the fiscal year ending June 30, 1911. It is $16,883,153.44 less than the total estimates, including supplemental estimates submitted to Congress by the Treasury for the year 1911, and is $5,574,659.39 less than the original estimates submitted by the Treasury for 1911.

These figures do not include the appropriations for the Panama Canal, the policy in respect to which ought to be, and is, to spend as much each year as can be economically and effectively expended in order to complete the Canal as promptly as possible, and, therefore, the ordinary motive for cutting down the expense of the Government does not apply to appropriations for this purpose. It will be noted that the estimates for the Panama Canal for the ensuing year are more than fifty-six millions of dollars, an increase of twenty millions over the amount appropriated for this year—a difference due to the fact that the estimates for 1912 include something over nineteen millions for the fortification of the Canal. Against the estimated expenditures of $630,494,013.12, the Treasury has estimated receipts for next year $680,000,000, making a probable surplus of ordinary receipts over ordinary expenditures of about $50,000,000.

A table showing in detail the estimates and the comparisons referred to follows. (See next page.)

TYPICAL ECONOMIES.

The Treasury Department is one of the original departments of the Government. With the changes in the monetary system made from time to time and with the creation of national banks, it was thought necessary to organize new bureaus and divisions which were added in a somewhat haphazard way and resulted in a duplication of duties which might well now be ended. This lack of system and economic coordination has attracted the attention of the head of that Department who has been giving his time for the last two years, with the aid of experts and by consulting his bureau chiefs, to its reformation. He has abolished four hundred places in the civil service without at all injuring its efficiency. Merely to illustrate the character of the reforms that are possible, I shall comment on some of the specific changes that are being made, or ought to be made by legislative aid.

AUDITING SYSTEM.

The auditing system in vogue is as old as the Government and the methods used are antiquated. There are six Auditors and seven Assistant Auditors for the nine departments, and under the present system the only function which the Auditor of a department exercises is to determine, on accounts presented by disbursing officers, that the object of the expenditure was within the law and the appropriation made by Congress for the purpose on its face, and that the calculations in the accounts are correct. He does not examine the merits of the transaction or determine the reasonableness of the price paid for the articles purchased, nor does he furnish any substantial check upon disbursing officers and the heads of departments or bureaus with sufficient promptness to enable the Government to recoup itself in full measure for unlawful expenditure. A careful plan is being devised and will be presented to Congress with the recommendation that the force of auditors and employees under them be greatly reduced, thereby effecting substantial economy. But this economy will be small compared with the larger economy that can be effected by consolidation and change of methods. The possibilities in this regard have been shown in the reduction of expenses and the importance of methods and efficiency in the office of the Auditor for the Post Office Department, who, without in the slightest degree impairing the comprehensiveness and efficiency of his work, has cut down the expenses of his office $120,000 a year.

CUSTOMS COLLECTION.

Again, in the collection of the revenues, especially the customs revenues, a very great improvement has been effected, and further improvements are contemplated. By the detection of frauds in weighing sugar, upwards of $3,400,000 have been recovered from the beneficiaries of the fraud, and an entirely new system free from the possibilities of such abuse has been devised. The Department has perfected the method of collecting duties at the Port of New York so as to save the Government upwards of ten or eleven million dollars; and the same spirit of change and reform has been infused into the other customs offices of the country.

The methods used at many places are archaic. There would seem to be no reason at all why the Surveyor of the Port, who really acts for the Collector, should not be a subordinate of the Collector at a less salary and directly under his control, and there is but little reason for the existence of the Naval Officer, who is a kind of local auditor. His work is mainly an examination of accounts which is conducted again in Washington and which results in no greater security to the Government. The Naval Officers in the various ports are Presidential appointees, many of them drawing good salaries, and those offices should be abolished or with reduced force made part of the central auditing system.

There are entirely too many customs districts and too many customs collectors. These districts should be consolidated and the collectors in charge of them, who draw good salaries, many of them out of pro-

Statement of estimates of appropriations for the fiscal years 1912 and 1911, and of appropriations for 1911, showing increases and decreases.

	Final estimates for 1912 as of November 29.	Original estimates submitted by the Treasury for 1911.	Total estimates for 1911 including supplementals.	Appropriations for 1911.	Increase (+) and decrease (−), 1912 estimates against 1911 total estimates.	Increase (+) and decrease (−), 1912 estimates against 1911 appropriations.	Increase (+) and decrease (−), 1911 estimates against 1911 appropriations.
Legislative	$13,426,805.73	$13,169,679.70	$13,169,679.70	$12,938,048.00	+ $257,126.03	+ $488,757.73	+ $231,631.70
Executive	998,170.00	472,270.00	722,270.00	870,750.00	+ 275,900.00	+ 127,420.00	− 148,480.00
State Department	4,875,576.41	4,576,301.41	4,749,801.41	5,046,701.41	+ 125,775.00	− 171,125.00	− 296,900.00
Treasury Department:							
Treasury Department proper	68,735,451.00	69,865,240.00	70,393,543.75	69,973,434.61	− 1,658,092.75	− 1,237,983.61	+ 420,109.14
Public buildings and works	11,864,545.60	6,198,365.60	7,101,465.60	5,565,164.00	+ 4,763,080.00	+ 6,299,381.60	+ 1,536,301.60
Territorial governments	202,150.00	287,350.00	292,350.00	282,600.00	− 90,200.00	− 80,450.00	+ 9,750.00
Independent offices	2,638,695.12	2,400,695.12	2,492,695.12	2,128,695.12	+ 146,000.00	+ 510,000.00	+ 364,000.00
District of Columbia	13,602,785.90	11,884,928.49	12,108,878.49	11,440,345.99	+ 1,493,907.41	+ 2,162,439.91	+ 668,532.50
War Department:							
War Department proper	120,104,260.12	124,165,656.28	125,717,204.77	122,322,178.12	− 5,612,944.65	− 2,217,918.00	+ 3,395,026.65
Rivers and harbors	28,232,438.00	28,232,465.00	28,232,465.00	49,390,541.50	− 27.00	−21,158,103.50	−21,158,076.50
Navy Department:							
Navy Department proper	116,101,730.24	117,029,914.38	119,768,860.83	119,596,870.46	− 3,667,130.59	− 3,495,140.22	+ 171,990.37
New navy building program	12,840,428.00	12,844,122.00	12,844,122.00	14,790,122.00	− 3,694.00	− 1,949,694.00	− 1,946,000.00
Interior Department	189,151,875.00	191,224,182.90	193,948,582.02	214,754,278.00	− 4,796,707.02	−25,602,403.00	−20,805,695.98
Post-Office Department proper	1,697,490.00	1,695,690.00	1,695,690.00	2,085,005.33	+ 1,800.00	− 387,515.33	− 389,315.33
Deficiency in postal revenues	....	10,634,122.63	10,634,122.63	10,634,122.63	−10,634,122.65	−10,634,122.63	....
Department of Agriculture	19,681,066.00	17,681,136.00	17,753,931.24	17,821,836.00	+ 1,927,134.76	+ 1,859,230.00	− 67,904.76
Department of Commerce and Labor	16,276,970.00	14,187,913.00	15,789,271.00	14,169,969.32	+ 487,699.00	+ 2,107,000.68	+ 1,619,301.68
Department of Justice	10,063,576.00	9,518,640.00	9,962,233.00	9,648,237.99	+ 101,343.00	+ 415,338.01	+ 313,995.01
Total ordinary	630,494,013.12	636,068,672.51	647,377,166.56	683,458,900.48	−16,883,153.44	−52,964 887.36	−36,081,733.92
Panama Canal	56,920,847.69	48,063,524.70	52,063,524 70	37,855,000.00	+ 4,857,322.99	+19,065,847.69	+14,208,524.70
Total	687,414,860.81	684,132,197.21	699,440,691.26	721,313,900.48	−12 025,830.45	−33,899,039.67	−21,873,209.22

portion to the collections made, should be abolished or treated as mere branch offices, in accordance with the plan of the Treasury Department, which will be presented for the consideration of Congress. As an illustration, the cost of collecting $1 of revenue at typical small ports like the port of York, Me., was $50.04. At the port of Annapolis, Md., it cost $309.41 to collect $1 of revenue; at Natchez, $52.76; at Alexandria, Va., $122.49.

It is not essential to the preventing of smuggling that customs districts should be increased in number. The violation of the customs laws can be quite as easily prevented, and much more economically, by the revenue-cutter service and by the use of the special agent traveling force of the Treasury Department. A reorganization of the special customs agents has been perfected with a view to retaining only those who have special knowledge of the customs laws, regulations, and usual methods of evasion, and with this improvement, there will be no danger to the Government from the recommended consolidation and abolition of customs districts.

An investigation of the appraising system now in vogue in New York City has shown a sacrifice of the interests of the Government by under-appraisement, which is in the course of being remedied by reorganization and the employment of competent experts. Prosecutions have been instituted growing out of the frauds there discovered and are now awaiting hearing in the Federal Courts.

Very great improvements have been made in respect to the mints and assay offices. Diminished appropriations have been asked for those whose continuance is unnecessary, and this year's estimate of expenses is $326,000 less than two years ago. There is an opportunity for further saving in the abolition of several mints and assay offices that have now become unnecessary. Modern machinery has been installed there, more and better work has been done, and the appropriations have been consequently diminished.

In the Bureau of Engraving and Printing, great economies have been effected. Useless divisions have been abolished with the result of saving $440,000 this year in the total expenses of the Bureau despite increased business.

The Treasurer's office and that of the Division of Public Moneys in part cover the same functions and this is also true of the office of the Register and the Division of Loans and Currency. Plans for the elimination of the duplication in these offices will be presented to Congress.

COMPTROLLER OF THE CURRENCY.

The office of the Comptroller of the Currency is one most important in the preservation of proper banking methods in the national banking system of the United States, and the present Comptroller has impressed his subordinates with the necessity of so conducting their investigations as to establish the principle that every bank failure is unnecessary because proper inspection and notice of threatening conditions to the responsible directors and officers can prevent it.

PUBLIC BUILDINGS.

In our public buildings we still suffer from the method of appropriation, which has been so much criticised in connection with our rivers and harbors. Some method should be devised for controlling the supply of public buildings, so that they will harmonize with the actual needs of the Government. Then, when it comes to the actual construction, there has been in the past too little study of the building plans and sites with a view to the actual needs of the Government. Post-Office buildings which are in effect warehouses for the economical handling of transportation of thousands of tons of mail have been made monumental structures, and often located far from the convenient and economical spot. In the actual construction of the buildings, a closer scrutiny of the methods employed by the Government architects or by architects employed by the Government have resulted in decided economies. It is hoped that more time will give opportunity for a more thorough reorganization. The last public building bill carried authorization for the ultimate expenditure of $33,011,500 and I approved it because of the many good features it contained, just as I approved the river and harbor bill, but it was drawn upon a principle that ought to be abandoned. It seems to me that the wiser method of preparing a public building bill would be the preparation of a report by a commission of Government experts whose duty it should be to report to Congress the Government's needs in the way of the construction of public buildings in every part of the country, just as the Army Engineers make report with reference to the utility of proposed improvements in rivers and harbors, with the added function which I have recommended for the Army Engineers of including in their recommendation the relative importance of the various projects found to be worthy of approval and execution.

REVENUES.

As the Treasury Department is the one through which the income of the Government is collected and its expenditures are disbursed, this seems a proper place to consider the operation of the existing tariff bill, which became a law August 6, 1909. As an income-producing measure, the existing tariff bill has never been exceeded by any customs bill in the history of the country.

The corporation excise tax, proportioned to the net income of every business corporation in the country, has worked well. The tax has been easily collected. Its prompt payment indicates that the incidence of the tax has not been heavy. It offers, moreover, an opportunity for knowledge by the Government of the general condition and business of all corporations, and that means by far the most important part of the business of the country. In the original act provision was made for the publication of returns. This provision was subsequently amended by Congress, and the matter left to the regulation of the President. I have directed the issue of the needed regulations, and have made it possible for the public generally to know from an examination of the record, the returns of all corporations, the stock of which is listed on any public stock exchange or is offered for sale to the general public by advertisement or otherwise. The returns of those corporations whose stock is not so listed or offered for sale are directed to be open to the inspection and examination of creditors and stockholders of the corporation whose record is sought. The returns of all corporations are subject to the inspection of any government officer or to the examination of any court, in which the return made by the corporation is relevant and competent evidence.

THE PAYNE TARIFF ACT.

The schedules of the rates of duty in the Payne tariff act have been subjected to a great deal of criticism, some of it just, more of it unfounded, and to much misrepresentation. The act was adopted in pursuance of a declaration by the party which is responsible for it that a customs bill should be a tariff for the protection of home industries, the measure of the protection to be the difference between the cost of producing the imported article abroad and the cost of producing it at home, together with such addition to that difference as might give a reasonable profit to the home producer. The chief criticism of this tariff is a charge that in respect to a number of the schedules the declared measure was not followed, but a higher difference retained or inserted by way of undue discrimination in favor of certain industries and manufactures. Little, if any, of the criticism of the tariff has been directed against the protective principle above stated.

TARIFF BOARD.

The time in which the tariff was prepared undoubtedly was so short as to make it impossible for the Congress and its experts to acquire all the information necessary strictly to conform to the declared measure. In order to avoid criticism of this kind in the future and for the purpose of more nearly conforming to the party promise, Congress at its last session made provision at my request for the continuance of a board created under the authority of the maximum and minimum clause of the tariff bill, and authorized this board to expend the money appropriated under my direction for the ascertainment of the cost of production at home and abroad of the various articles included in the schedules of the tariff. The tariff board thus appointed and authorized has been diligent in preparing itself for the necessary investigations. The hope of those who have advocated the use of this board for tariff purposes is that the question of the rate of a duty imposed shall become more of a business question and less of a political question, to be ascertained by experts of long training and accurate knowledge. The halt in business and the shock to business, due to the announcement that a new tariff bill is to be prepared and put in operation, will be avoided by treating the schedules one by one as occasion shall arise for a change in the rates of each, and only after a report upon the schedule by the tariff board competent to make such report. It is not likely that the board will be able to make a report during the present session of Congress on any of the schedules, because a proper examination involves an enormous amount of detail and a great deal of care; but I hope to be able at the opening of the new Congress, or at least during the session of that Congress, to bring to its attention the facts in regard to those schedules in the present tariff that may prove to need amendment. The carrying out of this plan, of course, involves the full cooperation of Congress in limiting the consideration in tariff matters to one schedule at a time, because if a proposed amendment to a tariff bill is to involve a complete consideration of all the schedules and another revision, then we shall only repeat the evil from which the business of this country has in times past suffered most grievously by stagnation and uncertainty, pending a resettlement of a law affecting all business directly or indirectly. I can not too much emphasize the importance and benefit of the plan above proposed for the treatment of the tariff. It facilitates the removal of noteworthy defects in an important law without a disturbance of business prosperity, which is even more important to the happiness and the comfort of the people than the elimination of instances of injustice in the tariff.

The inquiries which the members of the Tariff Board made during the last summer into the methods pursued by other Governments with reference to the fixing of tariffs and the determination of their effect upon trade, show that each Government maintains an office or bureau, the officers and employees of which have made their life work the study of tariff matters, of foreign and home prices and cost of articles imported, and the effect of the tariff upon trade, so that whenever a change is thought to be necessary in the tariff law this office is the source of the most reliable information as to the propriety of the change and its effect. I am strongly convinced that we need in this Government just such an office, and that it can be secured by making the Tariff Board already appointed a permanent tariff commission, with such duties, powers, and emoluments as it may seem wise to Congress to give. It has been proposed to enlarge the board from three to five. The present number is convenient, but I do not know that an increase of two members would be objectionable.

Whether or not the protective policy is to be continued, and the degree of protection to be accorded to our home industries, are questions which the people must decide through their chosen representatives; but whatever policy is adopted, it is clear that the necessary legislation should be based on an impartial, thorough, and continuous study of the facts.

BANKING AND CURRENCY REFORM.

The method of impartial scientific study by experts as a preliminary to legislation, which I hope to see ultimately adopted as our fixed national policy with respect to the tariff, rivers and harbors, waterways, and public buildings, is also being pursued by the nonpartisan Monetary Commission of Congress. An exhaustive and most valuable study of the banking and currency systems of foreign countries has been completed.

A comparison of the business methods and institutions of our powerful and successful commercial rivals with our own is sure to be of immense value. I urge upon Congress the importance of a nonpartisan and disinterested study and consideration of our banking and currency system. It is idle to dream of commercial expansion, and of the development of our national trade on a scale that measures up to our matchless opportunities, unless we can lay a solid foundation in a sound and enduring banking and currency system. The problem is not partisan, is not sectional—it is national.

WAR DEPARTMENT.

The War Department has within its jurisdiction the management of the Army, and, in connection therewith, the coast defenses; the government of the dependencies of the Philippines and of Porto Rico; the recommendation of plans for the improvement of harbors and waterways, and their execution when adopted; and, by virtue of an executive order, the supervision of the construction of the Panama Canal.

The Army of the United States is a small body compared with the total number of people for the preservation of whose peace and good order it is a last resource. The Army now numbers about 80,000 men, of whom about 18,000 are engaged in the Coast Artillery and detailed to the management and use of the guns in the forts and batteries that protect our coasts. The rest of the Army, or about 60,000, is the mobile part of our national forces and is divided into 31 regiments of infantry, including the Porto Rican regiment, 15 regiments of cavalry, 6 regiments of field artillery, a corps of ordnance, of engineers, and of signal, a quartermaster's department, a commissary department, and a medical corps.

The general plan for an army of the United States at peace should be that of a skeleton organization with an excess of trained officers and thus capable of rapid enlargement by enlistments, to be supplemented in emergency by the national militia and a volunteer force. In some measure this plan has been adopted in the very large proportion of cavalry and field artillery as compared with infantry in the present army and on a peace basis. An infantry force can be trained in six months; a cavalry or a light artillery force not under one and one-half or two years; hence the importance of having ready a larger number of the more skilled soldiers.

The militia system, for which Congress by the Constitution is authorized to provide, was developed by the so-called Dick law, under which the discipline, the tactics, the drill, the rank, the uniform, and the various branches of the militia are assimilated as far as possible to those of the Regular Army. Under the militia law, as the Constitution provides, the Governors of the States appoint the militia officers, but, by appropriations from Congress, States have been induced to comply with the rules of assimilation between the Regular Army and the militia, so that now there is a force, the efficiency of which differs in different States, which could be incorporated under a single command with the Regular Army, and which for some time each year receives the benefit of drill and maneuvers with conditions approximating actual military service, under the supervision of Regular Army officers.

In the Army of the United States, in addition to the regular forces and the militia forces which may be summoned to the defense of the Nation by the President, there is also the volunteer force, which made up a very large part of the army in the Civil War, and which in any war of long continuance would become its most important constituent. There is an act which dates from the Civil War, known as the Volunteer Act, which makes provision for the enlistment of volunteers in the Army of the United States in time of war. This was found to be so defective in the Philippine War that a special act for the organization of volunteer regiments to take part in that war was adopted, and it was much better adapted to the necessities of the case. There is now pending in Congress a bill repealing the present Volunteer Act and making provision for the organization of volunteer forces in time of war, which is admirably adapted to meet the exigencies which would be then presented. The passage of the bill would not entail a dollar's expense upon the Government at this time, or in the future, until war comes, but when war does come the methods therein directed are in accordance with the best military judgment as to what they ought to be, and the act would prevent the necessity for the discussion of new legislation and the delays incident to its consideration and adoption. I earnestly urge the passage of this Volunteer Bill.

I further recommend that Congress establish a commission to determine as early as practicable a comprehensive policy for the organization, mobilization and administration of the Regular Army, the organized militia, and the volunteer forces in the event of war.

NEED FOR ADDITIONAL OFFICERS.

One of the great difficulties in the prompt organization and mobilization of militia and volunteer forces is the absence of competent officers of the rank of captain to teach the new army, by the unit of the company, the business of being soldiers and of taking care of themselves so as to render effective service. This need of army officers can only be supplied by provisions of law authorizing the appointment of a greater number of army officers than are needed to supply the commands of regular army troops now enlisted in the service. There are enough regular army officers to command the troops now enlisted, but Congress has authorized, and the Department has followed the example of Congress and exercised the authority conferred by detailing these army officers to duty other than that of the command of troops. For instance, there are a large number of army officers assigned to duty with military colleges or in colleges in which military training is given. Then a large number of officers are assigned to General Staff duty, and there are various other places to which army officers can be and are legally assigned, which take them away from their regiments and companies. In order that the militia of each State should be properly drilled and made more like the regular army, regular army officers should be detailed to assist the Adjutant-General of each State in the supervision of the state militia; but this is impossible unless provision is made by Congress for a very considerable increase in the number of company and field officers of the Army. A bill is pending in Congress for this purpose, and I earnestly hope that, in the interest of the proper development of a republican army, an army, small in the time of peace but possible of prompt and adequate enlargement in time of war, shall become possible under the laws of the United States.

PROPOSED INCREASE IN ARMY ENGINEERS.

A bill, the strong argument for which can be based on the ground quite similar to that of the increased officers bill, is a bill for the increase of sixty in the Army Engineers. The Army Engineers are largely employed in the expenditure of the moneys appropriated for the improvement of rivers and harbors and in the construction of the Panama Canal. This, in addition to their military duties, which include the building of fortifications both on our coasts and in our dependencies, requires many more engineers than the Army has, and public works, civil and military, are, therefore, much delayed. I earnestly recommend the passage of this bill, which passed the House at the last session and is now pending in the Senate.

FORTIFICATIONS.

I have directed that the estimates for appropriation for the improvement of coast defenses in the United States should be reduced to a minimum, while those for the completion of the needed fortifications at Corregidor in the Philippine Islands and at Pearl Harbor in the Hawaiian Islands should be expedited as much as possible. The proposition to make Olongapo and Subig Bay the naval base for the Pacific was given up, and it is to be treated merely as a supply station, while the fortifications in the Philippines are to be largely confined to Corregidor Island and the adjacent islands which command entrance to Manila Bay and which are being rendered impregnable from land and sea attack. The Pacific Naval base has been transferred to Pearl Harbor in the Hawaiian Islands. This necessitates the heavy fortification of the harbor and the establishment of an important military station near Honolulu. I urge that all the estimates made by the War Department for these purposes be approved by Congressional appropriation.

PHILIPPINE ISLANDS.

During the last summer, at my request, the Secretary of War visited the Philippine Islands and has described his trip in his report. He found the Islands in a state of tranquillity and growing prosperity, due largely to the change in the tariff laws, which has opened the markets of America to the products of the Philippines, and has opened the Philippine markets to American manufactures. The rapid increase in the trade between the two countries is shown in the following table:

Philippine exports, fiscal years 1908–1910.

[Exclusive of gold and silver.]

Fiscal year.	To—		Total.
	United States.	Other countries.	
1908	$10,323,233	$22,493,334	$32,816,567
1909	10,215,331	20,778,232	30,993,563
1910	18,741,771	21,122,398	39,864,169

NOTE.—Latest monthly returns show exports for the year ending August, 1910, to the United States $20,035,902, or 49 per cent of the $41,075,738 total, against $11,-031,275 to the United States, or 34 per cent of the $32,183,871 total for the year ending August, 1909.

Philippine imports, fiscal years 1908–1910.
[Exclusive of gold and silver and government supplies.]

Fiscal year.	From—		Total.
	United States.	Other countries.	
1908	$5,079,487	$25,838,870	$30,918,357
1909	4,691,770	23,100,627	27,792,397
1910	10,775,301	26,292,329	37,067,630

NOTE.—Latest monthly returns show imports for the year ending August, 1910, from the United States $11,615,982, or 30 per cent of the $39,025,667 total, against $5,193,419 from the United States, or 18 per cent of the $28,948,011 total for the year ending August, 1909.

PORTO RICO.

The year has been one of prosperity and progress in Porto Rico. Certain political changes are embodied in the bill "To Provide a Civil Government for Porto Rico and for other Purposes," which passed the House of Representatives on June 15, 1910, at the last session of Congress, and is now awaiting the action of the Senate.

The importance of those features of this bill relating to public health and sanitation can not be overestimated.

The removal from politics of the judiciary by providing for the appointment of the municipal judges is excellent, and I recommend that a step further be taken by providing therein for the appointment of secretaries and marshals of these courts.

The provision in the bill for a partially elective senate, the number of elective members being progressively increased, is of doubtful wisdom, and the composition of the senate as provided in the bill when introduced in the House, seems better to meet conditions existing in Porto Rico. This is an important measure, and I recommend its early consideration and passage.

RIVERS AND HARBORS.

I have already expressed my opinion to Congress in respect to the character of the river and harbor bills which should be enacted into law; and I have exercised as much power as I could under the law in directing the Chief of Engineers to make his report to Congress conform to the needs of the committee framing such a bill in determining which of the proposed improvements is the more important and ought to be completed first, and promptly.

PANAMA CANAL.

At the instance of Colonel Goethals, the Army Engineer officer in charge of the work on the Panama Canal, I have just made a visit to the Isthmus to inspect the work done and to consult with him on the ground as to certain problems which are likely to arise in the near future. The progress of the work is most satisfactory. If no unexpected obstacle presents itself, the canal will be completed well within the time fixed by Colonel Goethals, to wit, January 1, 1915, and within the estimate of cost, $375,000,000.

Press reports have reached the United States from time to time giving accounts of slides of earth of very large yardage in the Culebra Cut and elsewhere along the line, from which it might be inferred that the work has been much retarded and that the time of completion has been necessarily postponed.

The report of Doctor Hayes, of the Geological Survey, whom I sent within the last month to the Isthmus to make an investigation, shows that this section of the Canal Zone is composed of sedimentary rocks of rather weak structure and subject to almost immediate disintegration when exposed to the air. Subsequent to the deposition of these sediments, igneous rocks, harder and more durable, have been thrust into them, and being cold at the time of their intrusion united but indifferently with the sedimentary rock at the contacts. The result of these conditions is that as the cut is deepened, causing unbalanced pressures, slides from the sides of the cut have occurred. These are in part due to the flowing of surface soil and decomposed sedimentary rocks upon inclined surfaces of the underlying undecomposed rock and in part by the crushing of structurally weak beds under excessive pressure. These slides occur on one side or the other of the cut through a distance of 4 or 5 miles, and now that their character is understood, allowance has been made in the calculations of yardage for the amount of slides which will have to be removed and the greater slope that will have to be given to the bank in many places in order to prevent their recurrence. Such allowance does not exceed ten millions of yards. Considering that the number of yards removed from this cut on an average of each month through the year is 1,300,000, and that the total remaining to be excavated, including slides, is about 30,000,000 yards, it is seen that this addition to the excavation does not offer any great reason for delay.

While this feature of the material to be excavated in the cut will not seriously delay or obstruct the construction of a canal of the lock type, the increase of excavation due to such slides in the cut made 85 feet deeper for a sea-level canal would certainly have been so great as to delay its completion to a time beyond the patience of the American people.

FORTIFY THE CANAL.

Among questions arising for present solution is whether the Canal shall be fortified. I have already stated to the Congress that I strongly favor fortification and I now reiterate this opinion and ask your consideration of the subject in the light of the report already before you made by a competent board.

If, in our discretion, we believe modern fortifications to be necessary to the adequate protection and policing of the Canal, then it is our duty to construct them. We have built the Canal. It is our property. By convention we have indicated our desire for, and indeed undertaken, its universal and equal use. It is also well known that one of the chief objects in the construction of the Canal has been to increase the military effectiveness of our Navy.

Failure to fortify the Canal would make the attainment of both these aims depend upon the mere moral obligations of the whole international public—obligations which we would be powerless to enforce and which could never in any other way be absolutely safeguarded against a desperate and irresponsible enemy.

CANAL TOLLS.

Another question which arises for consideration and possible legislation is the question of tolls in the Canal. This question is necessarily affected by the probable tonnage which will go through the Canal. It is all a matter of estimate, but one of the government commission in 1900 investigated the question and made a report. He concluded that the total tonnage of the vessels employed in commerce that could use the Isthmian Canal in 1914 would amount to 6,843,805 tons net register, and that this traffic would increase 25.1 per cent per decade; that it was not probable that all the commerce included in the totals would at once abandon the routes at present followed and make use of the new Canal, and that it might take some time, perhaps two years, to readjust trade with reference to the new conditions which the Canal would establish. He did not include, moreover, the tonnage of war vessels, although it is to be inferred that such vessels would make considerable use of the Canal. In the matter of tolls he reached the conclusion that a dollar a net ton would not drive business away from the Canal, but that a higher rate would do so.

In determining what the tolls should be we certainly ought not to insist that they should at once amount to enough to pay the interest on the investment of $400,000,000 which the United States has made in the construction of the Canal. We ought not to do this, first, because the benefit to be derived by the United States from this expenditure is not to be measured solely by a return upon the investment. If it were, then the construction might well have been left to private enterprise. It was because an adequate return upon the money invested could not be expected immediately, or in the near future, and because there were peculiar political advantages to be derived from the construction of the Canal that it fell to the Government to advance the money and perform the work.

In addition to the benefit to our naval strength, the Canal greatly increases the trade facilities of the United States. It will undoubtedly cheapen the rates of transportation in all freight between the Eastern and Western seaboard. Then, if we are to have a world canal, and if we are anxious that the world's trade shall use it, we must recognize that we have an active competitor in the Suez Canal and that there are other means of carriage between the two oceans—by the Tehuantepec Railroad and by other railroads and freight routes in Central America.

In all these cases the question whether the Panama Canal is to be used and its tonnage increased will be determined mainly by the charge for its use. My own impression is that the tolls ought not to exceed $1 per net ton. On January 1, 1911, the tolls in the Suez Canal are to be 7 francs and 25 centimes for 1 net ton by Suez Canal measurement, which is a modification of Danube measurement. A dollar a ton will secure under the figures above a gross income from the Panama Canal of nearly $7,000,000. The cost of maintenance and operation is estimated to exceed $3,000,000. Ultimately, of course, with the normal increase in trade, we hope the income will approximate the interest charges upon the investment. The inquiries already made of the Chief Engineer of the Canal show that the present consideration of this question is necessary in order that the commerce of the world may have time to adjust itself to the new conditions resulting from the opening of this new highway. On the whole I should recommend that within certain limits the President be authorized to fix the tolls of the Canal and adjust them to what seems to be commercial necessity.

MAINTENANCE OF CANAL.

The next question that arises is as to the maintenance, management, and general control of the canal after its completion. It should be premised that it is an essential part of our navy establishment to have the coal, oil and other ship supplies, a dry dock, and repair shops, conveniently located with reference to naval vessels passing through the canal. Now, if the Government, for naval purposes, is to undertake to furnish these conveniences to the navy, and they are conveniences equally required by commercial vessels, there would seem to be strong reasons why the Government should take over and include in its management the furnishing, not only to the navy but to the public, dry-dock and repair-shop facilities, and the sale of coal, oil, and other ship supplies.

The maintenance of a lock canal of this enormous size in a sparsely populated country and in the tropics, where the danger from disease is always present, requires a large and complete and well-trained organization with full police powers, exercising the utmost care. The visitor to the canal who is impressed with the wonderful freedom from tropical diseases on the Isthmus must not be misled as to the constant vigilance that is needed to preserve this condition. The vast machinery of the locks, the necessary amount of dredging, the preservation of the banks of the canal from slides, the operation and the maintenance of the equipment of the railway—will all require a force, not, of course, to be likened in any way to the present organization for construction, but a skilled body of men who can keep in a state of usefulness this great instrument of commerce. Such an organization makes it easy to include within its functions the furnishing of dry-dock, fuel, repairs and supply facilities to the trade of the world. These will be more essential at the Isthmus of Panama than they are at Port Said or Suez, because there are no depots for coal, supplies, and other commercial necessities within thousands of miles of the Isthmus.

Another important reason why these ancillary duties may well be undertaken by the Government is the opportunity for discrimination between patrons of the canal that is offered where private concessions are granted for the furnishing of these facilities. Nothing would create greater prejudice against the canal than the suspicion that certain lines of traffic were favored in the furnishing of supplies or that the supplies were controlled by any large interest that might have a motive for increasing the cost of the use of the canal. It may be added that the termini are not ample enough to permit the fullest competition in respect to the furnishing of these facilities and necessities to the world's trade even if it were wise to invite such competition and the granting of the concession would necessarily, under these circumstances, take on the appearance of privilege or monopoly.

PROHIBITION OF RAILROAD OWNERSHIP OF CANAL STEAMERS.

I can not close this reference to the canal without suggesting as a wise amendment to the interstate commerce law a provision prohibiting interstate commerce railroads from owning or controlling ships engaged in the trade through the Panama Canal. I believe such a provision may be needed to save to the people of the United States the benefits of the competition in trade between the eastern and western seaboards which this canal was constructed to secure.

DEPARTMENT OF JUSTICE.

The duties of the Department of Justice have been greatly increased by legislation of Congress enacted in the interest of the general welfare of the people and extending its activities into avenues plainly within its constitutional jurisdiction, but which it has not been thought wise or necessary for the General Government heretofore to occupy.

I am glad to say that under the appropriations made for the Department, the Attorney-General has so improved its organization that a vast amount of litigation of a civil and criminal character has been disposed of during the current year. This will explain the necessity for slightly increasing the estimates for the expenses of the Department. His report shows the recoveries made on behalf of the Government, of duties fraudulently withheld, public lands improperly patented, fines and penalties for trespass, prosecutions and convictions under the antitrust law, and prosecutions under the interstate-commerce law. I invite especial attention to the prosecutions under the Federal law of the so-called "bucket shops," and of those schemes to defraud in which the use of the mail is an essential part of the fraudulent conspiracy, prosecutions which have saved ignorant and weak members of the public and are saving them hundreds of millions of dollars. The violations of the antitrust law present perhaps the most important litigation before the Department, and the number of cases filed shows the activity of the Government in enforcing that statute.

NATIONAL INCORPORATION.

In a special message last year I brought to the attention of Congress the propriety and wisdom of enacting a general law providing for the incorporation of industrial and other companies engaged in interstate commerce, and I renew my recommendation in that behalf.

PAYMENT OF JUST CLAIMS.

I invite the attention of Congress to the great number of claims which, at the instance of Congress, have been considered by the Court of Claims and decided to be valid claims against the Government. The delay that occurs in the payment of the money due under the claims injures the reputation of the Government as an honest debtor, and I earnestly recommend that those claims which come to Congress with the judgment and approval of the Court of Claims should be promptly paid.

REFORM IN JUDICIAL PROCEDURE.

One great crying need in the United States is cheapening the cost of litigation by simplifying judicial procedure and expediting final judgment. Under present conditions the poor man is at a woeful disadvantage in a legal contest with a corporation or a rich opponent. The necessity for the reform exists both in the United States courts and in all State courts. In order to bring it about, however, it naturally falls to the General Government by its example to furnish a model to all States. A legislative commission appointed by joint resolution of Congress to revise the procedure in the United States courts has as yet made no report.

Under the law the Supreme Court of the United States has the power and is given the duty to frame the equity rules of procedure which are to obtain in the Federal courts of first instance. In view of the heavy burden of pressing litigation which that Court has had to carry, with one or two of its members incapacitated through ill health, it has not been able to take up problems of improving the equity procedure, which has practically remained the same since the organization of the Court in 1789. It is reasonable to expect that with all the vacancies upon the Court filled, it will take up the question of cheapening and simplifying the procedure in equity in the courts of the United States. The equity business is much the more important in the Federal courts, and I may add much the more expensive. I am strongly convinced that the best method of improving judicial procedure at law is to empower the Supreme Court to do it through the medium of the rules of the court, as in equity. This is the way in which it has been done in England, and thoroughly done. The simplicity and expedition of procedure in the English courts today make a model for the reform of other systems.

Several of the Lord Chancellors of England and of the Chief Justices have left their lasting impress upon the history of their country by their constructive ability in proposing and securing the passage of remedial legislation effecting law reforms. I can not conceive any higher duty that the Supreme Court could perform than in leading the way to a simplification of procedure in the United States courts.

RELIEF OF SUPREME COURT FROM UNNECESSARY APPEALS.

No man ought to have, as a matter of right, a review of his case by the Supreme Court. He should be satisfied by one hearing before a court of first instance and one review by a court of appeals. The proper and chief usefulness of a Supreme Court, and especially of the Supreme Court of the United States, is, in the cases which come before it, so to expound the law, and especially the fundamental law —the Constitution—as to furnish precedents for the inferior courts in future litigation and for the executive officers in the construction of statutes and the performance of their legal duties. Therefore, any provisions for review of cases by the Supreme Court that cast upon that Court the duty of passing on questions of evidence and the construction of particular forms of instruments, like indictments, or wills, or contracts, decisions not of general application or importance, merely clog and burden the Court and render more difficult its higher function, which makes it so important a part of the framework of our Government. The Supreme Court is now carrying an unnecessary burden of appeals of this kind, and I earnestly urge that it be removed.

The statutes respecting the review by the Supreme Court of the United States of decisions of the Court of Appeals of the District of Columbia ought to be so amended as to place that court in the same position with respect to the review of its decisions as that of the various United States Circuit Courts of Appeals. The act of March 2, 1907, authorizing appeals by the Government from certain judgments in criminal cases where the defendant has not been put in jeopardy, within the meaning of the Constitution, should be amended so that such appeals should be taken to the Circuit Courts of Appeals instead of to the Supreme Court in all cases except those involving the construction of the Constitution or the constitutionality of a statute, with the same power in the Supreme Court to review on *certiorari* as is now exercised by that court over determinations of the several Circuit Courts of Appeals. Appeals in copyright cases should reach final judgment in the courts of appeals instead of the Supreme Court as now. The decision of the courts of appeals should be made final also in all cases wnerein jurisdiction rests on both diverse citizenship and the existence of a federal question, and not as now be reviewable in the Supreme Court when the case involves more than one thousand dollars. Appeals from the United States Court in Porto Rico should run to the Circuit Court of Appeals of the third circuit instead of to the Supreme Court. These suggested changes would, I am advised, relieve the Supreme Court of the consideration of about 100 cases annually.

The American Bar Association has had before it the question of reducing the burden of litigation involved in reversals on review and new trials or re-hearings and in frivolous appeals in habeas corpus and criminal cases. Their recommendations have been embodied in bills now pending in Congress. The recommendations are not radical, but they will accomplish much if adopted into law, and I earnestly recommend the passage of the bills embodying them.

INJUNCTION BILL.

I wish to renew my urgent recommendation made in my last Annual Message in favor of the passage of a law which shall regulate the issuing of injunctions in equity without notice in accordance with the best practice now in vogue in the courts of the United States. I regard this of especial importance, first because it has been promised, and second because it will deprive those who now complain of certain alleged abuses in the improper issuing of injunctions without notice of any real ground for further amendment and will take away all semblance of support for the extremely radical legislation they propose, which will be most pernicious if adopted, will sap the foundations of judicial power, and legalize that cruel social instrument, the secondary boycott.

JUDICIAL SALARIES.

I further recommend to Congress the passage of the bill now pending for the increase in the salaries of the Federal Judges, by which the Chief Justice of the United States shall receive $17,500 and the Associate Justices of the Supreme Court $17,000; the Circuit Judges constituting the Circuit Court of Appeals shall receive $10,000, and the District Judges $9,000. These judges exercise a wise jurisdiction and their duties require of them a profound knowledge of the law, great ability in the dispatch of business, and care and delicacy in the exercise of their jurisdiction so as to avoid conflict whenever possible between the Federal and the State courts. The positions they occupy ought to be filled by men who have shown the greatest ability in their professional work at the bar, and it is the poorest economy possible for the Government to pay salaries so low for judicial service as not to be able to command the best talent of the legal profession in every part of the country. The cost of living is such, especially in the large cities, that even the salaries fixed in the proposed bill will enable the incumbents to accumulate little, if anything, to support their families after their death. Nothing is so important to the preservation of our country and its beloved institutions as the maintenance of the independence of the judiciary, and next to the life tenure an adequate salary is the most material contribution to the maintenance of independence on the part of our Judges.

POST-OFFICE DEPARTMENT.

POSTAL SAVINGS BANKS.

At its last session Congress made provision for the establishment of savings banks by the Post-Office Department of this Government, by which, under the general control of trustees, consisting of the Postmaster-General, the Secretary of the Treasury and the Attorney-General, the system could be begun in a few cities and towns, and enlarged to cover within its operations as many cities and towns and as large a part of the country as seemed wise. The initiation and establishment of such a system has required a great deal of study on the part of the experts in the Post-Office and Treasury Departments, but a system has now been devised which is believed to be more economical and simpler in its operation than any similar system abroad. Arrangements have been perfected so that savings banks will be opened in some cities and towns on the 1st of January, and there will be a gradual extension of the benefits of the plan to the rest of the country.

WIPING OUT OF POSTAL DEFICIT.

As I have said, the Post-Office Department is a great business department, and I am glad to note the fact that under its present management principles of business economy and efficiency are being applied. For many years there has been a deficit in the operations of the Post-Office Department which has been met by appropriation from the Treasury. The appropriation estimated for last year from the Treasury over and above the receipts of the Department was $17,500,000. I am glad to record the fact that of that $17,500,000 estimated for, $11,500,000 were saved and returned to the Treasury. The personal efforts of the Postmaster-General secured the effective cooperation of the thousands of postmasters and other postal officers throughout the country in carrying out his plans of reorganization and retrenchment. The result is that the Postmaster-General has been able to make his estimate of expenses for the present year so low as to keep within the amount the postal service is expected to earn. It is gratifying to report that the reduction in the deficit has been accomplished without any curtailment of postal facilities. On the contrary the service has been greatly extended during the year in all its branches. A principle which the Postmaster-General has recommended and sought to have enforced in respect to all appointments has been that those appointees who have rendered good service should be reappointed. This has greatly strengthened the interest of postmasters throughout the country in maintaining efficiency and economy in their offices, because they believed generally that this would secure for them a further tenure.

EXTENSION OF THE CLASSIFIED SERVICE.

Upon the recommendation of the Postmaster-General, I have included in the classified service all assistant postmasters, and I believe that this giving a secure tenure to those who are the most important subordinates of Postmasters will add much to the efficiency of their offices and an economical administration. A large number of the fourth-class postmasters are now in the classified service. I think it would be wise to put in the classified service the first, second, and third class postmasters. It is more logical to do this than to classify the fourth-class postmasters, for the reason that the fourth-class post-offices are invariably small, and the postmasters are necessarily men who must combine some other business with the postmastership, whereas the first, second, and third class postmasters are paid a sufficient amount to justify the requirement that they shall have no other business and that they shall devote their attention to their post-office duties. To classify first, second, and third class postmasters would require the passage of an act changing the method of their appointment so as to take away the necessity for the advice and consent of the Senate. I am aware that this is inviting from the Senate a concession in respect to its quasi executive power that is considerable, but I believe it to be in the interest of good administration and efficiency of service. To make this change would take the postmasters out of politics; would relieve Congressmen who now are burdened with the necessity of making recommendations for these places of a responsibility that must be irksome and can create nothing but trouble; and it would result in securing from postmasters greater attention to business, greater fidelity, and consequently greater economy and efficiency in the post-offices which they conduct.

THE FRANKING PRIVILEGE.

The unrestricted manner in which the franking privilege is now being used by the several branches of the Federal service and by Congress has laid it open to serious abuses, a fact clearly established through investigations recently instituted by the Department. While it has been impossible without a better control of franking to determine the exact expense to the Government of this practice, there can be no doubt that it annually reaches into the millions. It is believed that many abuses of the franking system could be prevented, and consequently a marked economy effected, by supplying through the agencies of the postal service special official envelopes and stamps for the free mail of the Government, all such envelopes and stamps to be issued on requisition to the various branches of the Federal service requiring them, and such records to be kept of all official stamp supplies as will enable the Post-Office Department to maintain a proper postage account covering the entire volume of free Government mail. As the first step in the direction of this reform, special stamps and stamped envelopes have been provided for use instead of franks in the free transmission of the official mail resulting from the business of the new postal savings system. By properly recording the issuance of such stamps and envelopes accurate records can be kept of the cost to the Government of handling the postal savings mail, which is certain to become an important item of expense and one that should be separately determined. In keeping with this plan it is hoped that Congress will authorize the substitution of special official stamps and stamped envelopes for the various forms of franks now used to carry free of postage the vast volume of Departmental and Congressional mail matter. During the past year methods of accounting similar to those employed in the most progressive of our business establishments have been introduced in the postal service and nothing has so impeded the Department's plan in this regard as the impossibility of determining with any exactness how far the various expenses of the postal service are increased by the present unrestricted use of the franking privilege. It is believed that the adoption of a more exact method of dealing with this problem as proposed will prove to be of tremendous advantage in the work of placing the postal service on a strictly businesslike basis.

SECOND-CLASS MAIL MATTER.

In my last Annual Message I invited the attention of Congress to the inadequacy of the postal rate imposed upon second-class mail matter in so far as that includes magazines, and showed by figures prepared by experts of the Post-Office Department that the Government was rendering a service to the magazines, costing many millions in excess of the compensation paid. An answer was attempted to this by the representatives of the magazines, and a reply was filed to this answer by the Post-Office Department. The utter inadequacy of the answer, considered in the light of the reply of the Post-Office Department, I think must appeal to any fair-minded person. Whether the answer was all that could be said in behalf of the magazines is another question. I agree that the question is one of fact; but I insist that if the fact is as the experts of the Post-Office Department show, that we are furnishing to the owners of magazines a service worth millions more than they pay for it, then justice requires that the rate should be increased. The increase in the receipts of the Department resulting from this change may be devoted to increasing the usefulness of the Department in establishing a parcels post and in reducing the cost of first-class postage to one cent. It has been said by the Postmaster-General that a fair adjustment might be made under which the advertising part of the magazine should be charged for at a different and higher rate from that of the reading matter. This would relieve many useful magazines that are not circulated at a profit, and would not shut them out from the use of the mails by a prohibitory rate.

PARCELS POST.

With respect to the parcels post, I respectfully recommend its adoption on all rural-delivery routes, and that 11 pounds—the international limit—be made the limit of carriage in such post, and this, with a view to its general extension when the income of the Post-Office will permit it and the Postal Savings Banks shall have been fully established.

The same argument is made against the parcels post that was made against the postal savings bank—that it is introducing the Government into a business which ought to be conducted by private persons, and is paternalism. The Post-Office Department has a great plant and a great organization, reaching into the most remote hamlet of the United States, and with this machinery it is able to do a great many things economically that if a new organization were necessary it would be impossible to do without extravagant expenditure. That is the reason why the postal savings bank can be carried on at a small additional cost, and why it is possible to incorporate at a very inconsiderable expense a parcels post in the rural-delivery system. A general parcels post will involve a much greater outlay.

NAVY DEPARTMENT.

REORGANIZATION.

In the last annual report of the Secretary of the Navy and in my Annual Message, attention was called to the new detail of officers in the Navy Department by which officers of flag rank were assigned to duty as Aides to the Secretary in respect to naval operations, personnel, inspection, and material. This change was a substantial compliance with the recommendation of the Commission on Naval Reorganization, headed by Mr. Justice Moody, and submitted to President Roosevelt on February 26, 1909. Through the advice of this committee of line officers, the Secretary is able to bring about a proper coordination of all the branches of the naval department with greater military efficiency. The Secretary of the Navy recommends that this new organization be recognized by legislation and thus made permanent. I concur in the recommendation.

LEGISLATIVE RECOMMENDATIONS.

The Secretary, in view of the conclusions of a recent Court of Inquiry on certain phases of Marine Corps administration, recommends that the Major-General Commandant of the Marine Corps be appointed for a four years' term, and that officers of the Adjutant and Inspector's department be detailed from the line. He also asks for legislation to improve the conditions now existing in the personnel of officers of the Navy, particularly with regard to the age and experience of flag officers and captains, and points out that it is essential to the highest efficiency of the Navy that the age of our officers be reduced and that flag officers, particularly, should gain proper experience as flag officers, in order to enable them to properly command fleets. I concur in the Secretary's recommendations.

COVERING OF NAVAL SUPPLY FUND INTO TREASURY.

I commend to your attention the report of the Secretary on the change in the system of cost accounting in navy-yards, and also to the history of the naval supply fund and the present conditions existing in regard to that matter. Under previous practice and what now seems to have been an erroneous construction of the law, the supply fund of the navy was increased from $2,700,000 to something over $14,-000,000, and a system of accounting was introduced which prevented the striking of a proper balance and a knowledge of the exact cost of maintaining the naval establishment. The system has now been abandoned and a Naval Supply Account established by law July 1, 1910. The Naval Supply fund of $2,700,000 is now on deposit in the Treasury to the credit of the Department. The Secretary recommends that the Naval Supply Account be made permanent by law and that the $2,700,000 of the naval supply fund be covered into the Treasury as unnecessary, and I ask for legislative authority to do this. This sum when covered into the Treasury will be really a reduction in the recorded Naval cost for this year.

ESTIMATES AND BUILDING PROGRAM.

The estimates of the Navy Department are $5,000,000 less than the appropriations for the same purpose last year, and included in this is the building program of the same amount as that submitted for your consideration last year. It is merely carrying out the plan of building two battleships a year, with a few needed auxiliary vessels. I earnestly hope that this program will be adopted.

ABOLITION OF NAVY-YARDS.

The Secretary of the Navy has given personal examination to every navy-yard and has studied the uses of the navy-yards with reference to the necessities of our fleet. With a fleet considerably less than half the size of that of the British navy, we have shipyards more than double the number, and there are several of these shipyards, expensively equipped with modern machinery, which after investigation the Secretary of the Navy believes to be entirely useless for naval purposes. He asks authority to abandon certain of them and to move their machinery to other places where it can be made of use.

In making these recommendations the Secretary is following directly along progressive lines which have been adopted in our great commercial and manufacturing consolidations in this country; that is, of dismantling unnecessary and inadequate plants and discontinuing their existence where it has been demonstrated that it is unprofitable to continue their maintenance at an expense not commensurate to their product.

GUANTANAMO PROPER NAVAL BASE.

The Secretary points out that the most important naval base in the West Indies is Guantanamo, in the southeastern part of Cuba. Its geographical situation is admirably adapted to protect the commercial paths to the Panama Canal, and he shows that by the expenditure of less than half a million dollars, with the machinery which he shall take from other navy-yards, he can create a naval station at Guantanamo of sufficient size and equipment to serve the purpose of an emergency naval base. I earnestly join in the recommendation that he be given the authority which he asks. I am quite aware that such action is likely to arouse local opposition; but I conceive it to be axiomatic that in legislating in the interest of the Navy, and for the general protection of the country by the Navy, mere local pride or pecuniary interest in the establishment of a navy-yard or station ought to play no part. The recommendation of the Secretary is based upon the judgment of impartial naval officers, entirely uninfluenced by any geographical or sectional considerations.

JOHN PAUL JONES.

I unite with the Secretary in the recommendation that an appropriation be made to construct a suitable crypt at Annapolis for the custody of the remains of John Paul Jones.

PEARY.

The complete success of our country in Arctic exploration should not remain unnoticed. For centuries there has been friendly rivalry in this field of effort between the foremost nations and between the bravest and most accomplished men. Expeditions to the unknown North have been encouraged by enlightened governments and deserved honors have been granted to the daring men who have conducted them. The unparalleled accomplishment of an American in reaching the North Pole, April 6, 1909, approved by critical examination of the most expert scientists, has added to the distinction of our navy, to which he belongs, and reflects credit upon his country. His unique success has received generous acknowledgment from scientific bodies and institutions of learning in Europe and America. I recommend fitting recognition by Congress of the great achievement of Robert Edwin Peary.

DEPARTMENT OF THE INTERIOR.

APPEALS TO COURT IN LAND CASES.

The Secretary of the Interior recommends a change of the law in respect to the procedure in adjudicating claims for lands, by which appeals can be taken from the decisions of the Department to the Court of Appeals of the District of Columbia for a judicial consideration of the rights of the claimant. This change finds complete analogy in the present provision for appeals from the decisions of the Commissioner of Patents. The judgments of the court in such cases would be of decisive value to land claimants generally and to the Department of the Interior in the administration of the law, would enable claimants to bring into Court the final consideration of issues as to the title to Government land and would, I think, obviate a good deal of the subsequent litigation that now arises in our Western courts. The bill is pending, I believe, in the House, having been favorably reported from the Committee on Public Lands, and I recommend its enactment.

ARREARS WIPED OUT.

One of the difficulties in the Interior Department and in the Land Office has been the delays attendant upon the consideration by the Land Office and the Secretary of the Interior of claims for patents of public lands to individuals. I am glad to say that under the recent appropriations of the Congress and the earnest efforts of the Secretary and his subordinates, these arrears have been disposed of, and the work of the Department has been brought more nearly up to date in respect to the pending business than ever before in its history. Economies have been effected where possible without legislative assistance, and these are shown in the reduced estimates for the expenses of the Department during the current fiscal year and during the year to come.

CONSERVATION.

The subject of the conservation of the public domain has commanded the attention of the people within the last two or three years.

AGRICULTURAL LANDS.

There is no need for radical reform in the methods of disposing of what are really agricultural lands. The present laws have worked well. The enlarged homestead law has encouraged the successful farming of lands in the semiarid regions.

RECLAMATION.

The total sum already accumulated in the fund provided by the act for the reclamation of arid lands is about $69,449,058.76, and of this, all but $6,241,058.76 has been allotted to the various projects, of which there are thirty. Congress at its last session provided for the issuing of certificates of indebtedness not exceeding twenty millions of dollars, to be redeemed from the reclamation fund when the proceeds of lands sold and from the water-rents should be sufficient. Meantime, in accordance with the provisions of the law, I appointed a board of army engineers to examine the projects and to ascertain which are feasible and worthy of completion. That board has made a report upon the subject, which I shall transmit in a separate message within a few days.

CONSERVATION ADDRESS.

In September last a conservation Congress was held at St. Paul, at which I delivered an address on the subject of conservation so far as it was within the jurisdiction and possible action of the Federal Government. In that address I assembled from the official records the statistics and facts as to what had been done in this behalf in the administration of my predecessor and in my own, and indicated the legislative measures which I believed to be wise in order to secure the best use, in the public interest, of what remains of our National domain. There was in this address a very full discussion of the reasons which led me to the conclusions stated. For the purpose of saving in an official record a comprehensive résumé of the statistics and facts gathered with some difficulty in that address, and to avoid their repetition in the body of this message, I venture to make the address an accompanying appendix. The statistics are corrected to November 15th last.

SPECIFIC RECOMMENDATIONS.

For the reasons stated in the conservation address, I recommend:

First, that the limitation now imposed upon the Executive which forbids his reserving more forest lands in Oregon, Washington, Idaho, Montana, Colorado, and Wyoming, be repealed.

Second, that the coal deposits of the Government be leased after advertisement inviting competitive bids, for terms not exceeding fifty years, with a minimum rental and royalties upon the coal mined, to be readjusted every ten or twelve years, and with conditions as to maintenance which will secure proper mining, and as to assignment which will prevent combinations to monopolize control of the coal in any one district or market. I do not think that coal measures under 2,500 acres of surface would be too large an amount to lease to any one lessee.

The Secretary of the Interior thinks there are difficulties in the way of leasing public coal lands, which objections he has set forth in his report, the force of which I freely concede. I entirely approved his stating at length in his report the objections in order that the whole subject may be presented to Congress, but after a full consideration I favor a leasing system and recommend it.

Third, that the law should provide the same separation in respect to government phosphate lands of surface and mineral rights that now obtains in coal lands and that power to lease such lands upon terms and limitations similar to those above recommended for coal leases, with an added condition enabling the Government to regulate, and if need be to prohibit, the export to foreign countries of the product.

Fourth, that the law should allow a prospector for oil or gas to have the right to prospect for two years over a certain tract of government land, the right to be evidenced by a license for which he shall pay a small sum; and that upon discovery, a lease may be granted upon terms securing a minimum rental and proper royalties to the Government, and also the conduct of the oil or gas well in accord with the best method for husbanding the supply of oil in the district. The period of the leases should not be as long as those of coal, but they should contain similar provisions as to assignment to prevent monopolistic combinations.

Fifth, that water-power sites be directly leased by the Federal Government, after advertisement and bidding, for not exceeding fifty years upon a proper rental and with a condition fixing rates charged to the public for units of electric power, both rental and rates to be readjusted equitably every ten years by arbitration or otherwise, with suitable provisions against assignment to prevent monopolistic combinations. Or, that the law shall provide that upon application made by the authorities of the State where the water-power site is situated, it may be patented to the State on condition that the State shall dispose of it under terms like those just described, and shall enforce those terms, or upon failure to comply with the condition the water-power site and all the plant and improvement on the site shall be forfeited and revert to the United States, the President being given the power to declare the forfeiture and to direct legal proceedings for its enforcement. Either of these methods would, I think, accomplish the proper public purpose in respect to water-power sites, but one or the other should be promptly adopted.

NECESSITY FOR PROMPT ACTION.

I earnestly urge upon Congress that at this session general conservation legislation of the character indicated be adopted. At its last session this Congress took most useful and proper steps in the cause of conservation by allowing the Executive, through withdrawals, to suspend the action of the existing laws in respect to much of the public domain. I have not thought that the danger of disposing of coal lands in the United States under the present laws in large quantities was so great as to call for their withdrawal, because under the present provisions it is reasonably certain that the Government will receive the real value of the land. But, in respect to oil lands, or phosphate lands, and of gas lands in the United States, and in respect to coal lands in Alaska, I have exercised the full power of withdrawal with the hope that the action of Congress would follow promptly and prevent that tying up of the resources of the country in the western and less settled portion and in Alaska, which means stagnation and retrogression.

The question of conservation is not a partisan one, and I sincerely hope that even in the short time of the present session consideration may be given to those questions which have now been much discussed, and that action may be taken upon them.

ALASKA.

With reference to the government of Alaska, I have nothing to add to the recommendations I made in my last message on the subject. I am convinced that the migratory character of the population, its unequal distribution, and its smallness of number, which the new census shows to be about 50,000, in relation to the enormous expanse of the territory, make it altogether impracticable to give to those people who are in Alaska to-day and may not be there a year hence, the power to elect a legislature to govern an immense territory to which they have a relation so little permanent. It is far better for the development of the territory that it be committed to a commission to be appointed by the Executive, with limited legislative powers sufficiently broad to meet the local needs, than to continue the present insufficient government with few remedial powers, or to make a popular government where there is not proper foundation upon which to rest it.

The suggestion that the appointment of a commission will lead to the control of the government by corporate or selfish and exploiting interests has not the slightest foundation in fact. Such a government worked well in the Philippines, and would work well in Alaska, and those who are really interested in the proper development of that territory for the benefit of the people who live in it and the benefit of the people of the United States, who own it, should support the institution of such a government.

ALASKAN RAILWAYS.

I have been asked to recommend that the credit of the Government be extended to aid the construction of railroads in Alaska. I am not ready now to do so. A great many millions of dollars have already been expended in the construction of at least two railroads, and if laws be passed providing for the proper development of the resources of Alaska, especially for the opening up of the coal lands, I believe that the capital already invested will induce the investment of more capital, sufficient to complete the railroads building, and to furnish cheap coal not only to Alaska but to the whole Pacific coast. The passage of a law permitting the leasing of government coal lands in Alaska after public competition, and the appointment of a commission for the government of the territory, with enabling powers to meet the local needs, will lead to an improvement in Alaska and the development of her resources that is likely to surprise the country.

NATIONAL PARKS.

Our national parks have become so extensive and involve so much detail of action in their control that it seems to me there ought to be legislation creating a bureau for their care and control. The greatest natural wonder of this country and the surrounding territory should be included in another national park. I refer to the Grand Canyon of the Colorado.

PENSIONS.

The uniform policy of the Government in the matter of granting pensions to those gallant and devoted men who fought to save the life of the Nation in the perilous days of the great Civil War, has always been of the most liberal character. Those men are now rapidly passing away. The best obtainable official statistics show that they are dying at the rate of something over three thousand a month, and, in view of their advancing years, this rate must inevitably, in proportion, rapidly increase. To the man who risked everything on the field of battle to save the Nation in the hour of its direst need, we owe a debt which has not been and should not be computed in a begrudging or parsimonious spirit. But while we should be actuated by this spirit to the soldier himself, care should be exercised not to go to absurd lengths, or distribute the bounty of the Government to classes of persons who may, at this late day, from a mere mercenary motive, seek to obtain some legal relation with an old veteran now tottering on the brink of the grave. The true spirit of the pension laws is to be found in the noble sentiments expressed by Mr. Lincoln in his last inaugural address, wherein, in speaking of the Nation's duty to its soldiers when the struggle should be over, he said we should " care for him who shall have borne the battle, and for his widow and orphans."

DEPARTMENT OF AGRICULTURE.

VALUE OF THIS YEAR'S CROPS.

The report of the Secretary of Agriculture invites attention to the stupendous value of the agricultural products of this country, amounting in all to $8,926,000,000 for this year. This amount is larger than that of 1909 by $305,000,000. The existence of such a crop indicates a good prospect for business throughout the country. A notable change for the better is commented upon by the Secretary in the fact that the South, especially in those regions where the boll weevil has interfered with the growth of cotton, has given more attention to the cultivation of corn and other cereals, so that there is a greater diversification of crops in the South than ever before—and all to the great advantage of that section.

DEPARTMENT ACTIVITIES.

The report contains a most interesting account of the activities of the Department in its various bureaus, showing how closely the agricultural progress in this country is following along the lines of improvement recommended by the Department through its publications and the results of its experiment stations in every State, and by the instructions given through the agricultural schools aided by the Federal Government and following the general curriculum urged by the head and bureau chiefs of the Department.

The activities of the Department have been greatly increased by the enactment of recent legislation, by the pure-food act, the meat-inspection act, the cattle-transportation act, and the act concerning the interstate shipment of game. This department is one of those the scope of whose action is constantly widening, and therefore it is impossible under existing legislation to reduce the cost and their estimates below those of preceding years.

FARMERS' INCOME AND COST OF LIVING.

An interesting review of the results of an examination made by the Department into statistics and prices, shows that on the average since 1891, farm products have increased in value 72 per cent while the things which the farmer buys for use have increased but 12 per cent, an indication that present conditions are favorable to the farming community.

FOREST SERVICE.

I have already referred to the forests of the United States and their extent, and have urged, as I do again, the removal of the limitation upon the power of the Executive to reserve other tracts of land in six Western States in which withdrawal for this purpose is now forbidden. The Secretary of Agriculture gives a very full description of the disastrous fires that occurred during the last summer in the national forests. A drought more intense than any recorded in the history of the West had introduced a condition into the forests which made fires almost inevitable, and locomotive sparks, negligent campers, and in some cases incendiaries furnished the needed immediate cause. At one time the fires were so extended that they covered a range of a hundred miles, and the Secretary estimates that standing timber of the value of 25 millions of dollars was destroyed. Seventy-six persons in the employ of the Forest Service were killed and many more injured, and I regret to say that there is no provision in the law by which the expenses for their hospital treatment or of their interment could be met out of public funds. The Red Cross contributed a thousand dollars, and the remainder of the necessary expenses was made up by private contribution, chiefly from the force of the Forest Service and its officials. I recommend that suitable legislation be adopted to enable the Secretary of Agriculture to meet the moral obligations of the Government in this respect.

APPROPRIATION FOR FIRE FIGHTING.

The specific fund for fighting fires was only about $135,000, but there existed discretion in the Secretary in case of an emergency to apply other funds in his control to this purpose, and he did so to the extent of nearly a million of dollars, which will involve the presentation of a deficiency estimate for the current fiscal year of over $900,000. The damage done was not therefore due to the lack of an appropriation by Congress available to meet the emergency, but the difficulty of fighting it lay in the remote points where the fires began and where it was impossible with the roads and trails as they now exist promptly to reach them. Proper protection necessitates, as the Secretary points out, the expenditure of a good deal more money in the development of roads and trails in the forests, the establishment of lookout stations, and telephone connection between them and places where assistance can be secured.

REFORESTATION.

The amount of reforestation shown in the report of the Forest Service—only about 15,000 acres as compared with the 150 millions of acres of national forests—seems small, and I am glad to note that in this regard the Secretary of Agriculture and the chief of the Forest Service are looking forward to far greater activity in the use of available Government land for this purpose. Progress has been made in learning by experiment the best methods of reforesting. Congress is appealed to now by the Secretary of Agriculture to make the appropriations needed for enlarging the usefulness of the Forest Service in this regard. I hope that Congress will approve and adopt the estimate of the Secretary for this purpose.

DEPARTMENT OF COMMERCE AND LABOR.

The Secretary of the Department of Commerce and Labor has had under his immediate supervision the application of the merit system of promotion to a large number of employees, and his discussion of this method of promotions based on actual experience, I commend to the attention of Congress.

THE CENSUS BUREAU.

The taking of the census has proceeded with promptness and efficiency. The Secretary believes, and I concur, that it will be more thorough and accurate than any census which has heretofore been taken, but it is not perfect. The motive that prompts men with a false civic pride to induce the padding of census returns in order to increase the population of a particular city has been strong enough to lead to fraud in respect to a few cities in this country, and I have directed the Attorney-General to proceed with all the vigor possible against those who are responsible for these frauds. They have been discovered and they will not interfere with the accuracy of the census, but it is of the highest importance that official inquiry of this sort should not be embarrassed by fraudulent conspiracies in some private or local interest.

BUREAU OF LIGHT-HOUSES.

The reorganization of the Light-House Board has effected a very considerable saving in the administration, and the estimates for that service for the present year are $428,000 less than for the preceding year. In addition, three tenders, for which appropriations were made, are not being built because they are not at present needed for the service. The Secretary is now asking for a large sum for the addition of lights and other aids to the commerce of the seas, including a number in Alaska. The trade along that coast is becoming so important that I respectfully urge the necessity for following his recommendation.

BUREAU OF CORPORATIONS.

The Commissioner of Corporations has just completed the first part of a report on the lumber industry in the United States. This part does not find the existence of a trust or combination in the manufacture of lumber. The Commissioner does find, however, a condition in the ownership of the standing timber of the United States, other than the Government timber, that calls for serious attention. The direct investigation made by the Commissioner covered an area which contains 80 per cent of the privately owned timber of the country. His report shows that one-half of the timber in this area is owned by 200 individuals and corporations; that 14 per cent is owned by 3 corporations, and that there is very extensive interownership of stock, as well as other circumstances, all pointing to friendly relations among those who own a majority of this timber, a relationship which might lead to a combination for the maintenance of a price that would be very detrimental to the public interest, and would create the necessity of removing all tariff obstacles to the free importations of lumber from other countries.

BUREAU OF FISHERIES.

I am glad to note in the Secretary's report the satisfactory progress which is being made in respect to the preservation of the seals of the Pribiloff Islands. Very active steps are being taken by the Department of State to secure an arrangement which shall protect the Pribiloff herd from the losses due to pelagic sealing. Meantime the Government has secured seal pelts of the bachelor seals (the killing of which does not interfere with the maintenance of the herd), from the sale of which next month it is expected to realize about $450,000, a sum largely in excess of the rental paid by the lessee of the Government under the previous contract.

COAST AND GEODETIC SURVEY.

The Coast and Geodetic Survey has been engaged in surveying the coasts of the Philippine archipelago. This is a heavy work, because of the extended character of the coast line in those Islands, but I am glad to note that about half of the needed survey has been completed. So large a part of the coast line of the archipelago has been unsurveyed as to make navigation in the neighborhood of a number of the islands, and especially on the east side, particularly dangerous.

BUREAU OF LABOR.

The Commissioner of Labor has been actively engaged in composing the differences between employers and employees engaged in interstate transportation, under the Erdman Act, jointly with the Chairman of the Interstate Commerce Commission. I can not speak in too high terms of the success of these two officers in conciliation and settlement of controversies which, but for their interposition, would have resulted disastrously to all interests.

TAX ON PHOSPHOROUS MATCHES.

I invite attention to the very serious injury caused to all those who are engaged in the manufacture of phosphorous matches. The diseases incident to this are frightful, and as matches can be made from other materials entirely innocuous, I believe that the injurious manufacture could be discouraged and ought to be discouraged by the imposition of a heavy federal tax. I recommend the adoption of this method of stamping out a very serious abuse.

EIGHT-HOUR LAW.

Since 1868 it has been the declared purpose of this Government to favor the movement for an eight-hour day by a provision of law that none of the employees employed by or *on behalf* of the Government should work longer than eight hours in every twenty-four. The first declaration of this view was not accompanied with any penal clause or with any provision for its enforcement, and, though President Grant by a proclamation twice attempted to give it his sanction and to require the officers of the Government to carry it out, the purpose of the framers of the law was ultimately defeated by a decision of the Supreme Court holding that the statute as drawn was merely a direction of the Government to its agents and did not invalidate a contract made in behalf of the Government which provided in the contract for labor for a day of longer hours than eight. Thereafter, in 1892, the present eight-hour law was passed, which provides that the services and employment of all laborers and mechanics who are now or may hereafter be employed by the Government of the United States, by the District of Columbia, or by any contractor or subcontractor on any of the public works of the United States and of the said District of Columbia is hereby restricted to eight hours in any one calendar day. This law has been construed to limit the application of the requirement to those who are directly employed by the Government or to those who are employed upon public works situate upon land owned by the United States. This construction prevented its application to government battle ships and other vessels built in private shipyards and to heavy guns and armor plate contracted for and made at private establishments.

PENDING BILL.

The proposed act provides that no laborer or mechanic doing any part of the work contemplated by a contract with the United States in the employ of the contractor or any subcontractor shall be required or permitted to work more than eight hours a day in any one calendar day.

It seems to me from the past history that the Government has been committed to a policy of encouraging the limitation of the day's work to eight hours in all works of construction initiated by itself, and it seems to me illogical to maintain a difference between government work done on government soil and government work done in a private establishment, when the work is of such large dimensions and involves the expenditure of much labor for a considerable period, so that the private manufacturer may adjust himself and his establishment to the special terms of employment that he must make with his workmen for this particular job. To require, however, that every small contract of manufacture entered into by the Government should be carried out by the contractor with men working at eight hours would be to impose an intolerable burden upon the Government by limiting its sources of supply and excluding altogether the great majority of those who would otherwise compete for its business.

The proposed act recognizes this in the exceptions which it makes to contracts

"for transportation by land or water, for the transmission of intelligence, and for such materials or articles as may usually be bought in the open market whether made to conform to particular specifications or not, or for the purchase of supplies by the Government, whether manufactured to conform to particular specifications or not."

SUBSTITUTE FOR PENDING BILL.

I recommend that instead of enacting the proposed bill, the meaning of which is not clear and definite and might be given a construction embarrassing to the public interest, the present act be enlarged by providing that public works shall be construed to include not only buildings and work upon public ground, but also ships, armor, and large guns when manufactured in private yards or factories.

PROVISION FOR SUSPENSION IN EMERGENCIES BY PRESIDENT.

One of the great difficulties in enforcing this eight-hour law is that its application under certain emergencies becomes exceedingly oppressive and there is a great temptation to subordinate officials to evade it. I think that it would be wiser to allow the President, by Executive order, to declare an emergency in special instances in which the limitation might not apply and, in such cases, to permit the payment by the Government of extra compensation for the time worked each day in excess of eight hours. I may add that my suggestions in respect to this legislation have the full concurrence of the Commissioner of Labor.

WORKMEN'S COMPENSATION.

In view of the keen, widespread interest now felt in the United States in a system of compensation for industrial accidents to supplant our present thoroughly unsatisfactory system of employers' liability (a subject the importance of which Congress has already recognized by the appointment of a commission), I recommend that the International Congress on Industrial Insurance be invited to hold its meeting in 1913 in Washington, and that an appropriation of $10,000 be made to cover the necessary expenses of organizing and carrying on the meeting.

BUREAU OF IMMIGRATION.

DISTRIBUTING IMMIGRANTS.

The immigration into this country is increasing each year. A large part of it comes through the immigrant station at Ellis Island in the City of New York. An examination of the station and the methods pursued satisfies me that a difficult task is there performed by the commissioner and his force with common sense, the strictest fairness, and with the most earnest desire to enforce the law equitably and mercifully. It has been proposed to enlarge the accommodations so as to allow more of the immigrants to come by that port. I do not think it wise policy to do this. I have no objection to—on the contrary, I recommend—the construction of additional buildings for the purpose of facilitating a closer and more careful examination of each immigrant as he comes in, but I deprecate the enlargement of the buildings and of the force for the purpose of permitting the examination of more immigrants per day than are now examined. If it is understood that no more immigrants can be taken in at New York than are now taken in, and the steamship companies thus are given a reason and a motive for transferring immigrants to other ports, we can be confident that they will be better distributed through the country and that there will not be that congestion in the City of New York which does not make for the better condition of the immigrant or increase his usefulness as a new member of this community. Everything which tends to send the immigrants west and south into rural life helps the country.

AMENDMENTS RECOMMENDED.

I concur with the Secretary in his recommendations as to the amendments to the immigration law in increasing the fine against the companies for violation of the regulations, and in giving greater power to the commissioner to enforce more care on the part of the steamship companies in accepting immigrants. The recommendation of the Secretary, in which he urges that the law may be amended so as to discourage the separation of families, is, I think, a good one.

MISCELLANEOUS SUBJECTS NOT INCLUDED IN DEPARTMENTS.

BUREAU OF HEALTH.

In my message of last year I recommended the creation of a Bureau of Health, in which should be embraced all those Government agencies outside of the War and Navy Departments which are now directed toward the preservation of public health or exercise functions germane to that subject. I renew this recommendation. I greatly regret that the agitation in favor of this bureau has aroused a counteragitation against its creation, on the ground that the establishment of such a bureau is to be in the interest of a particular school of medicine. It seems to me that this assumption is wholly unwarranted, and that those responsible for the Government can be trusted to secure in the personnel of the bureau the appointment of representatives of all recognized schools of medicine, and in the management of the bureau entire freedom from narrow prejudice in this regard.

THE IMPERIAL VALLEY PROJECT.

By an act passed by Congress the President was authorized to expend a million dollars to construct the needed work to prevent injury to the lands of the Imperial Valley from the overflow of the Colorado River. I appointed a competent engineer to examine the locality and to report a plan for construction. He has done so. In order to complete the work it is necessary to secure the consent of Mexico, for part of the work must be constructed in Mexican territory. Negotiations looking to the securing of such authority are quite near success. The Southern Pacific Railroad Company proposes to assist us in the work by lending equipment and by the transportation of material at cost price, and it is hoped that the work may be completed before any danger shall arise from the spring floods in the river. The work is being done under the supervision of the Secretary of the Interior and his consulting engineer, General Marshall, late Chief of Engineers, now retired.

This leads me to invite the attention of Congress to the claim made by the Southern Pacific Railroad Company for an amount expended in a similar work of relief called for by a flood and great emergency. This work, as I am informed, was undertaken at the request of my predecessor and under promise to reimburse the railroad company. It seems to me the equity of this claim is manifest, and the only question involved is the reasonable value of the work done. I recommend the payment of the claim in a sum found to be just.

DISTRICT OF COLUMBIA.

CHARACTER OF GOVERNMENT.

The government of the District of Columbia is a good government. The police force, while perhaps it might be given, or acquire, more military discipline in bearing and appearance, is nevertheless an efficient body of men, free from graft, and discharges its important duties in this capital of the nation effectively. The parks and the streets of the city and the District are generally kept clean and in excellent condition. The Commissioners of the District have its affairs well in hand, and, while not extravagant, are constantly looking to those municipal improvements that are expensive but that must be made in a modern growing city like Washington. While all this is true, nevertheless the fact that Washington is governed by Congress, and that the citizens are not responsible and have no direct control through popular election in District matters, properly subjects the government to inquiry and criticism by its citizens, manifested through the public press and otherwise; such criticism should command the careful attention of Congress. Washington is the capital of the nation and its maintenance as a great and beautiful city under national control, every lover of his country has much at heart; and it should present in every way a model in respect of economy of expenditure, of sanitation, of tenement reform, of thorough public instruction, of the proper regulation of public utilities, of sensible and extended charities, of the proper care of criminals and of youth needing reform, of healthful playgrounds and opportunity for popular recreation, and of a beautiful system of parks. I am glad to think that progress is being made in all these directions, but I venture to point out certain specific improvements toward these ends which Congress in its wisdom might adopt. Speaking generally, I think there ought to be more concentration of authority in respect to the accomplishment of some of these purposes with more economy of expenditure.

PUBLIC PARKS.

Attention is invited to the peculiar situation existing in regard to the parks of Washington. The park system proper, comprising some 343 different areas, is under the Office of Public Buildings and Grounds, which, however, has nothing to do with the control of Rock Creek Park, the Zoological Park, the grounds of the Department of Agriculture, the Botanic Garden, the grounds of the Capitol, and other public grounds which are regularly open to the public and ought to be part of the park system. Exclusive of the grounds of the Soldiers' Home and of Washington Barracks, the public grounds used as parks in the District of Columbia comprise over 3,100 acres, under ten different controlling officials or bodies. This division of jurisdiction is most unfortunate.

Large sums of money are spent yearly in beautifying and keeping in good condition these parks and the grounds connected with Government buildings and institutions. The work done on all of them is of the same general character—work for which the Office of Public Buildings and Grounds has been provided by Congress with a special organization and equipment, which are lacking for the grounds not under that office. There can be no doubt that if all work of care and improvement upon the grounds belonging to the United States in the District of Columbia were put, as far as possible, under one responsible head, the result would be not only greater efficiency and economy in the work itself, but greater harmony in the development of the public parks and gardens of the city.

Congress at its last session provided for two more parks, called the Meridian Hill and Montrose parks, and the District Commissioners have also included in their estimates a sum to be used for the acquisition of much needed park land adjoining the Zoological Park, known as the Klingle Ford tract. The expense of these three parks, included in the estimates of the Commissioners, aggregates $900,000. I think it would lead to economy if the improvement and care of all these parks and other public grounds above described should be transferred to the Office of Public Buildings and Grounds, which has an equipment well and economically adapted to carrying out the public purpose in respect to improvements of this kind.

To prevent encroachments upon the park area it is recommended that the erection of any permanent structure on any lands in the District of Columbia belonging to the United States be prohibited except by specific authority of Congress.

THE DISTRICT OF COLUMBIA IN VIRGINIA.

I have already in previous communications to Congress referred to the importance of acquiring for the District of Columbia at least a part of the territory on the other side of the Potomac in Virginia which was originally granted for the District by the State of Virginia, and then was retroceded by act of Congress in 1846. It is very evident from conferences that I have had with the Senators and Representatives from Virginia that there is no hope of a regranting by the State of the land thus given back; and I am frank to say that in so far as the tract includes the town of Alexandria and land remote from the Potomac River there would be no particular advantage in bringing that within national control. But the land which lies along the Potomac River above the railroad bridge and across the Potomac, including Arlington Cemetery, Fort Myer, the Government experiment farm, the village of Rosslyn, and the Palisades of the Potomac, reaching to where the old District line intersects the river, is very sparsely settled and could be admirably utilized for increasing the system of the parks of Washington. It has been suggested to me by the same Virginia Senators and Representatives that if the Government were to acquire for a government park the land above described, which is not of very great value, the present law of Virginia would itself work the creation of federal jurisdiction over it, and if that were not complete enough, the legislature of Virginia would in all probability so enlarge the jurisdiction as to enable Congress to include it within the control of the government of the District of Columbia and actually make it a part of Washington. I earnestly recommend that steps be taken to carry out this plan.

PUBLIC UTILITIES.

There are a sufficient number of corporations enjoying the use of public utilities in the District of Columbia to justify and require the enactment of a law providing for their supervision and regulation in the public interest consistent with the vested rights secured to them by their charters. A part of these corporations, to wit, the street railways, have been put under the control of the Interstate Commerce Commission, but that Commission recommends that the power be taken from it, and intimates broadly that its other and more important duties make it impossible for it to give the requisite supervision. It seems to me wise to place this general power of supervision and regulation in the District Commissioners. It is said that their present duties are now absorbing and would prevent the proper discharge by them of these new functions, but their present jurisdiction brings them so closely and frequently in contact with these corporations and makes them to know in such detail how the corporations are discharging their duties under the law and how they are serving the public interest that the Commissioners are peculiarly fitted to do this work, and I hope that Congress will impose it upon them by intrusting them with powers in respect to such corporations similar to those of the public utilities commission of New York City or similar boards in Massachusetts.

SCHOOL SYSTEM.

I do not think the present control of the school system of Washington commends itself as the most efficient and economical and thorough instrument for the carrying on of public instruction.

The cost of education in the District of Columbia is excessive as compared with the cost in other cities of similar size, and it is not apparent that the results are in general more satisfactory. The average cost per pupil per day in Washington is about 38 cents, while the average cost in 13 other American cities fairly comparable with Washington in population and standard of education is about 25.5 cents. For each dollar spent in salaries of school teachers and officers in the District about 4.4 days of instruction per pupil are given, while in the 13 cities above referred to each dollar expended for salaries affords on the average 6.8 days of instruction. For the current fiscal year the estimates of the Board of Education amounted to about three-quarters of the entire revenue locally collected for District purposes.

If I may say so, there seems to be a lack of definite plan in the expansion of the school system and the erection of new buildings and of proper economy in the use of these buildings that indicates the necessity for the concentration of control. All plans for improvement and expansion in the school system are with the School Board, while the limitation of expenses is with the District Commissioners. I think it would be much better to put complete control and responsibility in the District Commissioners, and then provide a board of school visitors, to be appointed by the Supreme Court of the District or by the

President, from the different school districts of Washington, who, representing local needs, shall meet and make recommendations to the Commissioners and to the Superintendent of Education—an educator of ability and experience who should be an appointee of and responsible to the District Commissioners.

PERMANENT IMPROVEMENTS.

Among other items for permanent improvements appearing in the District estimates for 1912 is one designed to substitute for Willow Tree Alley, notorious in the records of the Police and Health Departments, a playground with a building containing baths, a gymnasium, and other helpful features, and I hope Congress will approve this estimate. Fair as Washington seems with her beautiful streets and shade trees, and free, as the expanse of territory which she occupies would seem to make her, from slums and insanitary congestion of population, there are centers in the interior of squares where the very poor, and the criminal classes as well, huddle together in filth and noisome surroundings, and it is of primary importance that these nuclei of disease and suffering and vice should be removed, and that there should be substituted for them small parks as breathing spaces, and model tenements having sufficient air space and meeting other hygienic requirements. The estimate for the reform of Willow Tree Alley, the worst of these places in the city, is the beginning of a movement that ought to attract the earnest attention and support of Congress, for Congress can not escape its responsibility for the existence of these human pest holes.

The estimates for the District of Columbia for the fiscal year 1912 provide for the repayment to the United States of $616,000, one-fourth of the floating debt that will remain on June 30, 1911. The bonded debt will be reduced in 1912 by about the same amount.

The District of Columbia is now in an excellent financial condition. Its own share of indebtedness will, it is estimated, be less than $6,000,000 on June 30, 1912, as compared with about $9,000,000 on June 30, 1909.

The bonded debt, owed half and half by the United States and the District, will be extinguished by 1924, and the floating debt of the District probably long before that time.

The revenues have doubled in the last ten years, while the population during the same period has increased but 18.78 per cent. It is believed that, if due economy be practiced, the District can soon emerge from debt, even while financing its permanent improvements with reasonable rapidity from current revenues.

To this end, I recommend the enactment into law of a bill now before Congress—and known as the Judson Bill—which will insure the gradual extinguishment of the District's debt, while at the same time requiring that the many permanent improvements needed to complete a fitting capital city shall be carried on from year to year and at a proper rate of progress with funds derived from the rapidly increasing revenues.

FREEDMEN'S BANK.

I renew my recommendation that the claims of the depositors in the Freedmen's Bank be recognized and paid by the passage of the pending bill on that subject.

NEGRO EXPOSITION.

I also renew my recommendation that steps be taken looking to the holding of a Negro exposition in celebration of the fiftieth anniversary of the issuing by Mr. Lincoln of the Emancipation Proclamation.

CIVIL SERVICE COMMISSION.

The Civil Service Commission has continued its useful duties during the year. The necessity for the maintenance of the provisions of the civil service law was never greater than to-day. Officers responsible for the policy of the Administration, and their immediate personal assistants or deputies, should not be included within the classified service; but in my judgment, public opinion has advanced to the point where it would support a bill providing a secure tenure during efficiency for all purely administrative officials. I entertain the profound conviction that it would greatly aid the cause of efficient and economical government, and of better politics if Congress could enact a bill providing that the Executive shall have the power to include in the classified service all local offices under the Treasury Department, the Department of Justice, the Post-Office Department, the Interior Department, and the Department of Commerce and Labor, appointments to which now require the confirmation of the Senate, and that upon such classification the advice and consent of the Senate shall cease to be required in such appointments. By their certainty of tenure, dependent on good service, and by their freedom from the necessity for political activity, these local officers would be induced to become more efficient public servants.

The civil service law is an attempt to solve the problem of the proper selection of those who enter the service. A better system under that law for promotions ought to be devised, but, given the selected employee, there remains still the question of promoting his efficiency and his usefulness to the Government, and that can be brought about only by a careful comparison of unit work done by the individual and a pointing out of the necessity for improvement in this regard where improvement is possible.

INQUIRY INTO ECONOMY AND EFFICIENCY.

The increase in the activities and in the annual expenditures of the Federal Government has been so rapid and so great that the time has come to check the expansion of government activities in new directions until we have tested the economy and efficiency with which the Government of to-day is being carried on. The responsibility rests upon the head of the Administration. He is held accountable by the public, and properly so. Despite the unselfish and patriotic efforts of the heads of departments and others charged with responsibility of government, there has grown up in this country a conviction that the expenses of government are too great. The fundamental reason for the existence undetected of waste, duplication, and bad management is the lack of prompt, accurate information. The president of a private corporation doing so vast a business as the Government transacts would, through competent specialists, maintain the closest scrutiny on the comparative efficiency and the comparative costs in each division or department of the business. He would know precisely what the duties and the activities of each bureau or division are in order to prevent overlapping. No adequate machinery at present exists for supplying the President of the United States with such information respecting the business for which he is responsible. For the first time in the history of the Government, Congress in the last session supplied this need and made an appropriation to enable the President to inquire into the economy and efficiency of the executive departments, and I am now assembling an organization for that purpose.

At the outset I find comparison between departments and bureaus impossible for the reason that in no two departments are the estimates and expenditures displayed and classified alike. The first step is to reduce all to a common standard for classification and judgment, and this work is now being done. When it is completed, the foundation will be laid for a businesslike national budget, and for such a just comparison of the economy and efficiency with which the several bureaus and divisions are conducted as will enable the President and the heads of Departments to detect waste, eliminate duplication, encourage the intelligent and effective civil servants whose efforts too often go unnoticed, and secure the public service at the lowest possible cost.

The Committees on Appropriations of Congress have diligently worked to reduce the expenses of government and have found their efforts often blocked by lack of accurate information containing a proper analysis of requirements and of actual and reasonable costs. The result of this inquiry should enable the Executive in his communications to Congress to give information to which Congress is entitled and which will enable it to promote economy.

My experience leads me to believe that while Government methods are much criticised, the bad results—if we do have bad results—are not due to a lack of zeal or willingness on the part of the civil servants. On the contrary, I believe that a fine spirit of willingness to work exists in the personnel, which, if properly encouraged, will produce results equal to those secured in the best managed private enterprises. In handling Government expenditure the aim is not profit—the aim is the maximum of public service at the minimum of cost. We wish to reduce the expenditures of the Government, and we wish to save money to enable the Government to go into some of the beneficial projects which we are debarred from taking up now because we ought not to increase our expenditures.

I have requested the head of each Department to appoint committees on economy and efficiency in order to secure full cooperation in the movement by the employees of the Government themselves.

At a later date I shall send to Congress a special message on this general subject.

I urge the continuance of the appropriation of $100,000 requested for the fiscal year 1912.

CIVIL SERVICE RETIREMENT.

It is impossible to proceed far in such an investigation without perceiving the need of a suitable means of eliminating from the service the superannuated. This can be done in one of two ways, either by straight civil pension or by some form of contributory plan.

Careful study of experiments made by foreign governments shows that three serious objections to the civil pension payable out of the public treasury may be brought against it by the taxpayer, the administrative officer, and the civil employee, respectively. A civil pension is bound to become an enormous, continuous, and increasing tax on the public exchequer; it is demoralizing to the service since it makes difficult the dismissal of incompetent employees after they have partly earned their pension; and it is disadvantageous to the main body of employees themselves since it is always taken into account in fixing salaries and only the few who survive and remain in the service until pensionable age receive the value of their deferred pay. For this reason, after a half century of experience under a most liberal pension system, the civil servants of England succeeded, about a year ago, in having the system so modified as to make it virtually a contributory plan with provision for refund of their theoretical contributions.

The experience of England and other countries shows that neither can a contributory plan be successful, human nature being what it is, which does not make provision for the return of contributions, with interest, in case of death or resignation before pensionable age. Followed to its logical conclusion this means that the simplest and most independent solution of the problem for both employee and the Government is a compulsory savings arrangement, the employee to set aside from his salary a sum sufficient, with the help of a liberal rate of interest from the Government, to purchase an adequate annuity for him on retirement, this accumulation to be inalienably his and claimable if he leaves the service before reaching the retirement age or by his heirs in case of his death. This is the principle upon which the Gillett bill now pending is drawn.

The Gillett bill, however, goes further and provides that the Government shall contribute to the pension fund of those employees who are now so advanced in age that their personal contributions will not be sufficient to create their annuities before reaching the retirement age. In my judgment this provision should be amended so that the annuities of those employees shall be paid out of the salaries appropriated for the positions vacated by retirement, and that the difference between the annuities thus granted and the salaries may be used for the employment of efficient clerks at the lower grades. If the bill can be thus amended I recommend its passage, as it will initiate a valuable system and ultimately result in a great saving in the public expenditures.

INTERSTATE COMMERCE COMMISSION.

There has not been time to test the benefit and utility of the amendments to the interstate commerce law contained in the act approved June 18, 1910. The law as enacted did not contain all the features which I recommended. It did not specifically denounce as unlawful the purchase by one of two parallel and competing roads of the stock of the other. Nor did it subject to the restraining influence of the Interstate Commerce Commission the power of corporations engaged in operating interstate railroads to issue new stock and bonds; nor did it authorize the making of temporary agreements between railroads, limited to thirty days, fixing the same rates for traffic between the same places.

I do not press the consideration of any of these objects upon Congress at this session. The object of the first provision is probably generally covered by the antitrust law. The second provision was in the act referred to the consideration of a commission to be appointed by the Executive and to report upon the matter to Congress. That commission has been appointed, and is engaged in the investigation and consideration of the question submitted under the law. It consists of President Arthur T. Hadley, of Yale University, as chairman; Frederick Strauss, Frederick N. Judson, Walter L. Fisher, and Prof. B. H. Meyer, with William E. S. Griswold as secretary.

The third proposal led to so much misconstruction of its object, as being that of weakening the effectiveness of the antitrust law, that I am not disposed to press it for further consideration. It was intended to permit railroad companies to avoid useless rate cutting by a mere temporary acquiescence in the same rates for the same service over competing railroads, with no obligation whatever to maintain those rates for any time.

SAFETY APPLIANCES AND PROVISIONS.

The protection of railroad employees from personal injury is a subject of the highest importance and demands continuing attention. There have been two measures pending in Congress, one for the supervision of boilers and the other for the enlargement of dangerous clearances. Certainly some measures ought to be adopted looking to a prevention of accidents from these causes. It seems to me that with respect to boilers a bill might well be drawn requiring and enforcing by penalty a proper system of inspection by the railway companies themselves which would accomplish our purpose. The entire removal of outside clearances would be attended by such enormous expense that some other remedy must be adopted. By act of May 6, 1910, the Interstate Commerce Commission is authorized and directed to investigate accidents, to report their causes and its recommendations. I suggest that the Commission be requested to make a special report as to injuries from outside clearances and the best method of reducing them.

VALUATION OF RAILROADS.

The Interstate Commerce Commission has recommended appropriations for the purpose of enabling it to enter upon a valuation of all railroads. This has always been within the jurisdiction of the Commission, but the requisite funds have been wanting. Statistics of the value of each railroad would be valuable for many purposes, especially if we ultimately enact any limitations upon the power of the interstate railroads to issue stocks and bonds, as I hope we may. I think, therefore, that in order to permit a correct understanding of the facts, it would be wise to make a reasonable appropriation to enable the Interstate Commerce Commission to proceed with due dispatch to the valuation of all railroads. I have no doubt that railroad companies themselves can and will greatly facilitate this valuation and make it much less costly in time and money than has been supposed.

FRAUDULENT BILLS OF LADING.

Forged and fraudulent bills of lading purporting to be issued against cotton, some months since, resulted in losses of several millions of dollars to American and foreign banking and cotton interests. Foreign bankers then notified American bankers that, after October 31, 1910, they would not accept bills of exchange drawn against bills of lading for cotton issued by American railroad companies, unless American bankers would guarantee the integrity of the bills of lading. The American bankers rightly maintained that they were not justified in giving such guarantees, and that, if they did so, the United States would be the only country in the world whose bills were so discredited, and whose foreign trade was carried on under such guaranties.

The foreign bankers extended the time at which these guaranties were demanded until December 31, 1910, relying upon us for protection in the meantime, as the money which they furnish to move our cotton crop is of great value to this country.

For the protection of our own people and the preservation of our credit in foreign trade, I urge upon Congress the immediate enactment of a law under which one who, in good faith, advances money or credit upon a bill of lading issued by a common carrier upon an interstate or foreign shipment can hold the carrier liable for the value of the goods described in the bill at the valuation specified in the bill, at least to the extent of the advances made in reliance upon it. Such liability exists under the laws of many of the States. I see no objection to permitting two classes of bills of lading to be issued: (1) Those under which a carrier shall be absolutely liable, as above suggested, and (2) those with respect to which the carrier shall assume no liability except for the goods actually delivered to the agent issuing the bill. The carrier might be permitted to make a small separate specific charge in addition to the rate of transportation for such guaranteed bill, as an insurance premium against loss from the added risk, thus removing the principal objection which I understand is made by the railroad companies to the imposition of the liability suggested, viz., that the ordinary transportation rate would not compensate them for the liability assumed by the absolute guaranty of the accuracy of the bills of lading.

I further recommend that a punishment of fine and imprisonment be imposed upon railroad agents and shippers for fraud or misrepresentation in connection with the issue of bills of lading issued upon interstate and foreign shipments.

GENERAL CONCLUSION AS TO INTERSTATE COMMERCE AND ANTITRUST LAW.

Except as above, I do not recommend any amendment to the interstate-commerce law as it stands. I do not now recommend any amendment to the anti-trust law. In other words, it seems to me that the existing legislation with reference to the regulation of corporations and the restraint of their business has reached a point where we can stop for a while and witness the effect of the vigorous execution of the laws on the statute books in restraining the abuses which certainly did exist and which roused the public to demand reform. If this test develops a need for further legislation, well and good, but until then let us execute what we have. Due to the reform movements of the present decade, there has undoubtedly been a great improvement in business methods and standards. The great body of business men of this country, those who are responsible for its commercial development, now have an earnest desire to obey the law and to square their conduct of business to its requirements and limitations. These will doubtless be made clearer by the decisions of the Supreme Court in cases pending before it. It is in the interest of all the people of the country that for the time being the activities of government, in addition to enforcing earnestly and impartially the existing laws, should be directed to economy of administration, to the enlargement of opportunities for foreign trade, to the conservation and improvement of our agricultural lands and our other natural resources, to the building up of home industries, and to the strengthening of confidence of capital in domestic investment.

THIRD ANNUAL MESSAGE.

PART I.

[On the Anti-Trust Statute.]

THE WHITE HOUSE, *December 5, 1911.*

To the Senate and House of Representatives:

This message is the first of several which I shall send to Congress during the interval between the opening of its regular session and its adjournment for the Christmas holidays. The amount of information to be communicated as to the operations of the Government, the number of important subjects calling for comment by the Executive, and the transmission to Congress of exhaustive reports of special commissions, make it impossible to include in one message of a reasonable length a discussion of the topics that ought to be brought to the attention of the National Legislature at its first regular session.

THE ANTI-TRUST LAW—THE SUPREME COURT DECISIONS.

In May last the Supreme Court handed down decisions in the suits in equity brought by the United States to enjoin the further maintenance of the Standard Oil Trust and of the American Tobacco Trust, and to secure their dissolution. The decisions are epoch-making and serve to advise the business world authoritatively of the scope and operation of the anti-trust act of 1890. The decisions do not depart in any substantial way from the previous decisions of the court in construing and applying this important statute, but they clarify those decisions by further defining the already admitted exceptions to the literal construction of the act. By the decrees, they furnish a useful precedent as to the proper method of dealing with the capital and property of illegal trusts. These decisions suggest the need and wisdom of additional or supplemental legislation to make it easier for the entire business community to square with the rule of action and legality thus finally established and to preserve the benefit, freedom, and spur of reasonable competition without loss of real efficiency or progress.

NO CHANGE IN THE RULE OF DECISION—MERELY IN ITS FORM OF EXPRESSION.

The statute in its first section declares to be illegal "every contract, combination in the form of trust or otherwise, or conspiracy, in restraint of trade or commerce among the several States or with foreign nations," and in the second, declares guilty of a misdemeanor "every person who shall monopolize or attempt to monopolize or combine or conspire with any other person to monopolize any part of the trade or commerce of the several States or with foreign nations."

In two early cases, where the statute was invoked to enjoin a transportation rate agreement between interstate railroad companies, it was held that it was no defense to show that the agreement as to rates complained of was reasonable at common law, because it was said that the statute was directed against all contracts and combinations in restraint of trade whether reasonable at common law or not. It was plain from the record, however, that the contracts complained of in those cases would not have been deemed reasonable at common law. In subsequent cases the court said that the statute should be given a reasonable construction and refused to include within its inhibition, certain contractual restraints of trade which it denominated as incidental or as indirect.

These cases of restraint of trade that the court excepted from the operation of the statute were instances which, at common law, would have been called reasonable. In the Standard Oil and Tobacco cases, therefore, the court merely adopted the tests of the common law, and in defining exceptions to the literal application of the statute, only substituted for the test of being incidental or indirect, that of being reasonable, and this, without varying in the slightest the actual scope and effect of the statute. In other words, all the cases under the statute which have now been decided would have been decided the same way if the court had originally accepted in its construction the rule at common law.

It has been said that the court, by introducing into the construction of the statute common-law distinctions, has emasculated it. This is obviously untrue. By its judgment every contract and combination in restraint of interstate trade made with the purpose or necessary effect of controlling prices by stifling competition, or of establishing in whole or in part a monopoly of such trade, is condemned by the statute. The most extreme critics can not instance a case that ought to be condemned under the statute which is not brought within its terms as thus construed.

The suggestion is also made that the Supreme Court by its decision in the last two cases has committed to the court the undefined and unlimited discretion to determine whether a case of restraint of trade is within the terms of the statute. This is wholly untrue. A reasonable restraint of trade at common law is well understood and is clearly defined. It does not rest in the discretion of the court. It must be limited to accomplish the purpose of a lawful main contract to which, in order that it shall be enforceable at all, it must be incidental. If it exceed the needs of that contract, it is void.

The test of reasonableness was never applied by the court at common law to contracts or combinations or conspiracies in restraint of trade whose purpose was or whose necessary effect would be to stifle competition, to control prices, or establish monopolies. The courts never assumed power to say that such contracts or combinations or conspiracies might be lawful if the parties to them were only moderate in the use of the power thus secured and did not exact from the public too great and exorbitant prices. It is true that many theorists, and others engaged in business violating the statute, have hoped that some such line could be drawn by courts; but no court of authority has ever attempted it. Certainly there is nothing in the decisions of the latest two cases from which such a dangerous theory of judicial discretion in enforcing this statute can derive the slightest sanction.

FORCE AND EFFECTIVENESS OF STATUTE A MATTER OF GROWTH.

We have been twenty-one years making this statute effective for the purposes for which it was enacted. The Knight case was discouraging and seemed to remit to the States the whole available power to attack and suppress the evils of the trusts. Slowly, however, the error of that judgment was corrected, and only in the last three or four years has the heavy hand of the law been laid upon the great illegal combinations that have exercised such an absolute dominion over many of our industries. Criminal prosecutions have been brought and a number are pending, but juries have felt averse to convicting for jail sentences, and judges have been most reluctant to impose such sentences on men of respectable standing in society whose offense has been regarded as merely statutory. Still, as the offense becomes better understood and the committing of it partakes more of studied and deliberate defiance of the law, we can be confident that juries will convict individuals and that jail sentences will be imposed.

THE REMEDY IN EQUITY BY DISSOLUTION.

In the Standard Oil case the Supreme and Circuit Courts found the combination to be a monopoly of the interstate business of refining, transporting, and marketing petroleum and its products, effected and maintained through thirty-seven different corporations, the stock of which was held by a New Jersey company. It in effect commanded the dissolution of this combination, directed the transfer and *pro rata* distribution by the New Jersey company of the stock held by it in the thirty-seven corporations to and among its stockholders; and the corporations and individual defendants were enjoined from conspiring or combining to restore such monopoly; and all agreements between the subsidiary corporations tending to produce or bring about further violations of the act were enjoined.

In the Tobacco case, the court found that the individual defendants, twenty-nine in number, had been engaged in a successful effort to acquire complete dominion over the manufacture, sale, and distribution of tobacco in this country and abroad, and that this had been done by combinations made with a purpose and effect to stifle competition, control prices, and establish a monopoly, not only in the manufacture of tobacco, but also of tin-foil and licorice used in its manufacture and of its products of cigars, cigarettes, and snuffs. The tobacco suit presented a far more complicated and difficult case than the Standard Oil suit for a decree which would effectuate the will of the court and end the violation of the statute. There was here no single holding company as in the case of the Standard Oil Trust. The main company was the American Tobacco Company, a manufacturing, selling, and holding company. The plan adopted to destroy the combination and restore competition involved the redivision of the capital and plants of the whole trust between some of the companies constituting the trust and new companies organized for the purposes of the decree and made parties to it, and numbering, new and old, fourteen.

SITUATION AFTER READJUSTMENT.

The American Tobacco Company (old), readjusted capital, $92,000,000; the Liggett & Meyers Tobacco Company (new), capital, $67,000,000; the P. Lorillard Company (new), capital, $47,000,000; and the R. J. Reynolds Tobacco Company (old), capital, $7,525,000, are chiefly engaged in the manufacture and sale of chewing and smoking tobacco and cigars. The former one tin-foil company is divided into two, one of $825,000 capital and the other of $400,000. The one snuff company is divided into three companies, one with a capital of $15,000,000, another with a capital of $8,000,000, and a third with a capital of $8,000,000. The licorice companies are two, one with a capital of $5,758,300 and another with a capital of $2,000,000. There is, also, the British-American Tobacco Company, a British corporation, doing business abroad with a capital of $26,000,000, the Porto Rican Tobacco Company, with a capital of $1,800,000, and the corporation of United Cigar Stores, with a capital of $9,000,000.

Under this arrangement, each of the different kinds of business will be distributed between two or more companies with a division of the prominent brands in the same tobacco products, so as to make competition not only possible but necessary. Thus the smoking-tobacco business of the country is divided so that the present independent companies have 21.39 per cent, while the American Tobacco Company will have 33.08 per cent, the Liggett & Meyers 20.05 per cent, the Lorillard Company 22.82 per cent, and the Reynolds Company 2.66 per cent. The stock of the other thirteen companies, both preferred and common, has been taken from the defendant American Tobacco Company and has been distributed among its stockholders. All covenants restricting competition have been declared null and further performance of them has been enjoined. The preferred stock of the different companies has now been given voting power which was denied it under the old organization. The ratio of the preferred stock to the common was as 78 to 40. This constitutes a very decided change in the character of the ownership and control of each company.

In the original suit there were twenty-nine defendants who were charged with being the conspirators through whom the illegal combination acquired and exercised its unlawful dominion. Under the decree these defendants will hold amounts of stock in the various distributee companies ranging from 41 per cent as a maximum to 28½ per cent as a minimum, except in the case of one small company, the Porto Rican Tobacco Company, in which they will hold 45 per cent. The twenty-nine individual defendants are enjoined for three years from buying any stock except from each other, and the group is thus prevented from extending its control during that period. All parties to the suit, and the new companies who are made parties, are enjoined perpetually from in any way effecting any combination between any of the companies in violation of the statute by way of resumption of the old trust. Each of the fourteen companies is enjoined from acquiring stock in any of the others. All these companies are enjoined from having common directors or officers, or common buying or selling agents, or common offices, or lending money to each other.

SIZE OF NEW COMPANIES.

Objection was made by certain independent tobacco companies that this settlement was unjust because it left companies with very large capital in active business, and that the settlement that would be effective to put all on an equality would be a division of the capital and plant of the trust into small fractions in amount more nearly equal to that of each of the independent companies. This contention results from a misunderstanding of the anti-trust law and its purpose. It is not intended thereby to prevent the accumulation of large capital in business enterprises in which such a combination can secure reduced cost of production, sale, and distribution. It is directed against such an aggregation of capital only when its purpose is that of stifling competition, enhancing or controlling prices, and establishing a monopoly. If we shall have by the decree defeated these purposes and restored competition between the large units into which the capital and plant have been divided, we shall have accomplished the useful purpose of the statute.

CONFISCATION NOT THE PURPOSE OF THE STATUTE.

It is not the purpose of the statute to confiscate the property and capital of the offending trusts. Methods of punishment by fine or imprisonment of the individual offenders, by fine of the corporation or by forfeiture of its goods in transportation, are provided, but the proceeding in equity is a specific remedy to stop the operation of the trust by injunction and prevent the future use of the plant and capital in violation of the statute.

EFFECTIVENESS OF DECREE.

I venture to say that not in the history of American law has a decree more effective for such a purpose been entered by a court than that against the Tobacco Trust. As Circuit Judge Noyes said in his judgment approving the decree:

"The extent to which it has been necessary to tear apart this combination and force it into new forms with the attendant burdens ought to demonstrate that the Federal anti-trust statute is a drastic statute which accomplishes effective results; which so long as it stands on the statute books must be obeyed, and which can not be disobeyed without incurring far-reaching penalties. And, on the other hand, the successful reconstruction of this organization should teach that the effect of enforcing this statute is not to destroy, but to reconstruct; not to demolish, but to re-create in accordance with the conditions which the Congress has declared shall exist among the people of the United States."

COMMON STOCK OWNERSHIP.

It has been assumed that the present *pro rata* and common ownership in all these companies by former stockholders of the trust would insure a continuance of the same old single control of all the companies into which the trust has by decree been disintegrated. This is erroneous and is based upon the assumed inefficacy and innocuousness of judicial injunctions. The companies are enjoined from cooperation or combination; they have different managers, directors, purchasing and sales agents. If all or many of the numerous stockholders, reaching into the thousands, attempt to secure concerted action of the companies with a view to the control of the market, their number is so large that such an attempt could not well be concealed, and its prime movers and all its participants would be at once subject to contempt proceedings and imprisonment of a summary character. The immediate result of the present situation will necessarily be activity by all the companies under different managers, and then competition must follow, or there will be activity by one company and stagnation by another. Only a short time will inevitably lead to a change in ownership of the stock, as all opportunity for continued cooperation must disappear. Those critics who speak of this disintegration in the trust as a mere change of garments have not given consideration to the inevitable working of the decree and understand little the personal danger of attempting to evade or set at naught the solemn injunction of a court whose object is made plain by the decree and whose inhibitions are set forth with a detail and comprehensiveness unexampled in the history of equity jurisprudence.

VOLUNTARY REORGANIZATIONS OF OTHER TRUSTS AT HAND.

The effect of these two decisions has led to decrees dissolving the combination of manufacturers of electric lamps, a southern wholesale grocers' association, an interlocutory decree against the Powder Trust with directions by the circuit court compelling dissolution, and other combinations of a similar history are now negotiating with the Department of Justice looking to a disintegration by decree and reorganization in accordance with law. It seems possible to bring about these reorganizations without general business disturbance.

MOVEMENT FOR REPEAL OF THE ANTI-TRUST LAW.

But now that the anti-trust act is seen to be effective for the accomplishment of the purpose of its enactment, we are met by a cry from many different quarters for its repeal. It is said to be obstructive of business progress, to be an attempt to restore old-fashioned methods of destructive competition between small units, and to make impossible those useful combinations of capital and the reduction of the cost of production that are essential to continued prosperity and normal growth.

In the recent decisions the Supreme Court makes clear that there is nothing in the statute which condemns combinations of capital or mere bigness of plant organized to secure economy in production and a reduction of its cost. It is only when the purpose or necessary effect of the organization and maintenance of the combination or the aggregation of immense size are the stifling of competition, actual and potential, and the enhancing of prices and establishing a monopoly, that the statute is violated. Mere size is no sin against the law. The merging of two or more business plants necessarily eliminates competition between the units thus combined, but this elimination is in contravention of the statute only when the combination is made for purpose of ending this particular competition in order to secure control of, and enhance, prices and create a monopoly.

LACK OF DEFINITENESS IN THE STATUTE.

The complaint is made of the statute that it is not sufficiently definite in its description of that which is forbidden, to enable business men to avoid its violation. The suggestion is, that we may have a combination of two corporations, which may run on for years, and that subsequently the Attorney General may conclude that it was a violation of the statute, and that which was supposed by the combiners to be innocent then turns out to be a combination in violation of the statute. The answer to this hypothetical case is that when men attempt to amass such stupendous capital as wili enable them to suppress competition, control prices and establish a monopoly, they know the purpose of their acts. Men do not do such a thing without having it clearly in mind. If what they do is merely for the purpose of reducing the cost of production, without the thought of suppressing competition by use of the bigness of the plant they are creating, then they can not be convicted at the time the union is made, nor can they be convicted later, unless it happen that later on they conclude to suppress competition and take the usual methods for doing so, and thus establish for themselves a monopoly. They can, in such a case, hardly complain if the motive which subsequently is disclosed is attributed by the court to the original combination.

NEW REMEDIES SUGGESTED.

Much is said of the repeal of this statute and of constructive legislation intended to accomplish the purpose and blaze a clear path for honest merchants and business men to follow. It may be that such a plan will be evolved, but I submit that the discussions which have been brought out in recent days by the fear of the continued execution of the anti-trust law have produced nothing but glittering generalities and have offered no line of distinction or rule of action as definite and as clear as that which the Supreme Court itself lays down in enforcing the statute.

SUPPLEMENTAL LEGISLATION NEEDED—NOT REPEAL OR AMENDMENT.

I see no objection—and indeed I can see decided advantages—in the enactment of a law which shall describe and denounce methods of competition which are unfair and are badges of the unlawful purpose denounced in the anti-trust law. The attempt and purpose to suppress a competitor by underselling him at a price so unprofitable as to drive him out of business, or the making of exclusive contracts with customers under which they are required to give up association with other manufacturers, and numerous kindred methods for stifling competition and effecting monopoly, should be described with sufficient accuracy in a criminal statute on the one hand to enable the Government to shorten its task by prosecuting single misdemeanors instead of an entire conspiracy, and, on the other hand, to serve the purpose of pointing out more in detail to the business community what must be avoided.

FEDERAL INCORPORATION RECOMMENDED.

In a special message to Congress on January 7, 1910, I ventured to point out the disturbance to business that would probably attend the dissolution of these offending trusts. I said:

"But such an investigation and possible prosecution of corporations whose prosperity or destruction affects the comfort not only of stockholders but of millions of wage earners, employees, and associated tradesmen must necessarily tend to disturb the confidence of the business community, to dry up the now flowing sources of capital from its places of hoarding, and produce a halt in our present prosperity that will cause suffering and strained circumstances among the innocent many for the faults of the guilty few. The question which I wish in this message to bring clearly to the consideration and discussion of Congress is whether, in order to avoid such a possible business danger, something can not be done by which these business combinations may be offered a means, without great financial disturbance, of changing the character, organization, and extent of their business into one within the lines of the law under Federal control and supervision, securing compliance with the anti-trust statute.

"Generally, in the industrial combinations called 'trusts,' the principal business is the sale of goods in many States and in foreign markets; in other words, the interstate and foreign business far exceeds the business done in any one State. This fact will justify the Federal Government in granting a Federal charter to such a combination to make and sell in interstate and foreign commerce the products of useful manufacture under such limitations as will secure a compliance with the anti-trust law. It is possible so to frame a statute that while it offers protection to a Federal company against harmful, vexatious, and unnecessary invasion by the States, it shall subject it to reasonable taxation and control by the States with respect to its purely local business. * * *

"Corporations organized under this act should be prohibited from acquiring and holding stock in other corporations (except for special reasons, upon approval by the proper Federal authority), thus avoiding the creation under national auspices of the holding company with subordinate corporations in different States, which has been such an effective agency in the creation of the great trusts and monopolies.

"If the prohibition of the anti-trust act against combinations in restraint of trade is to be effectively enforced, it is essential that the National Government shall provide for the creation of national corporations to carry on a legitimate business throughout the United States. The conflicting laws of the different States of the Union with respect to foreign corporations make it difficult, if not impossible, for one corporation to comply with their requirements so as to carry on business in a number of different States."

I renew the recommendation of the enactment of a general law providing for the voluntary formation of corporations to engage in trade and commerce among the States and with foreign nations. Every argument which was then advanced for such a law, and every explanation which was at that time offered to possible objections, have been confirmed by our experience since the enforcement of the anti-trust statute has resulted in the actual dissolution of active commercial organizations.

It is even more manifest now than it was then that the denunciation of conspiracies in restraint of trade should not and does not mean the denial of organizations large enough to be intrusted with our interstate and foreign trade. It has been made more clear now than it was then that a purely negative statute like the anti-trust law may well be supplemented by specific provisions for the building up and regulation of legitimate national and foreign commerce.

GOVERNMENT ADMINISTRATIVE EXPERTS NEEDED TO AID COURTS IN TRUST DISSOLUTIONS.

The drafting of the decrees in the dissolution of the present trusts, with a view to their reorganization into legitimate corporations, has made it especially apparent that the courts are not provided with the administrative machinery to make the necessary inquiries preparatory to reorganization, or to pursue such inquiries, and they should be empowered to invoke the aid of the Bureau of Corporations in determining the suitable reorganization of the disintegrated parts. The circuit court and the Attorney General were greatly aided in framing the decree in the Tobacco Trust dissolution by an expert from the Bureau of Corporations.

FEDERAL CORPORATION COMMISSION PROPOSED.

I do not set forth in detail the terms and sections of a statute which might supply the constructive legislation permitting and aiding the formation of combinations of capital into Federal corporations. They should be subject to rigid rules as to their organization and procedure, including effective publicity, and to the closest supervision as to the issue of stock and bonds by an executive bureau or commission in the Department of Commerce and Labor, to which in times of doubt they might well submit their proposed plans for future business. It must be distinctly understood that incorporation under Federal law could not exempt the company thus formed and its incorporators and managers from prosecution under the anti-trust law for subsequent illegal conduct, but the publicity of its procedure and the opportunity for frequent consultation with the bureau or commission in charge of the incorporation as to the legitimate purpose of its transactions would offer it as great security against successful prosecutions for violations of the law as would be practical or wise.

Such a bureau or commission might well be invested also with the duty already referred to, of aiding courts in the dissolution and recreation of trusts within the law. It should be an executive tribunal of the dignity and power of the Comptroller of the Currency or the Interstate Commerce Commission, which now exercise supervisory power over important classes of corporations under Federal regulation.

The drafting of such a Federal incorporation law would offer ample opportunity to prevent many manifest evils in corporate management to-day, including irresponsibility of control in the hands of the few who are not the real owners.

INCORPORATION VOLUNTARY.

I recommend that the Federal charters thus to be granted shall be voluntary, at least until experience justifies mandatory provisions. The benefit to be derived from the operation of great businesses under the protection of such a charter would attract all who are anxious to keep within the lines of the law. Other large combinations that fail to take advantage of the Federal incorporation will not have a right to complain if their failure is ascribed to unwillingness to submit their transactions to the careful official scrutiny, competent supervision, and publicity attendant upon the enjoyment of such a charter.

ONLY SUPPLEMENTAL LEGISLATION NEEDED.

The opportunity thus suggested for Federal incorporation, it seems to me, is suitable constructive legislation needed to facilitate the squaring of great industrial enterprises to the rule of action laid down by the anti-trust law. This statute as construed by the Supreme Court must continue to be the line of distinction for legitimate business. It must be enforced, unless we are to banish individualism from all business and reduce it to one common system of regulation or control of prices like that which now prevails with respect to public utilities, and which when applied to all business would be a long step toward State socialism.

IMPORTANCE OF THE ANTI-TRUST ACT.

The anti-trust act is the expression of the effort of a freedom-loving people to preserve equality of opportunity. It is the result of the confident determination of such a people to maintain their future growth by preserving uncontrolled and unrestricted the enterprise of the individual, his industry, his ingenuity, his intelligence, and his independent courage.

For twenty years or more this statute has been upon the statute book. All knew its general purpose and approved. Many of its violators were cynical over its assumed impotence. It seemed impossible of enforcement. Slowly the mills of the courts ground, and only gradually did the majesty of the law assert itself. Many of its statesmen-authors died before it became a living force, and they and others saw the evil grow which they had hoped to destroy. Now its efficacy is seen; now its power is heavy; now its object is near achievement. Now we hear the call for its repeal on the plea that it interferes with business prosperity, and we are advised in most general terms, how by some other statute and in some other way the evil we are just stamping out can be cured, if we only abandon this work of twenty years and try another experiment for another term of years.

It is said that the act has not done good. Can this be said in the face of the effect of the Northern Securities decree? That decree was in no way so drastic or inhibitive in detail as either the Standard Oil decree or the Tobacco decree; but did it not stop for all time the then powerful movement toward the control of all the railroads of the country in a single hand? Such a one-man power could not have been a healthful influence in the Republic, even though exercised under the general supervision of an interstate commission.

Do we desire to make such ruthless combinations and monopolies lawful? When all energies are directed, not toward the reduction of the cost of production for the public benefit by a healthful competition, but toward new ways and means for making permanent in a few hands the absolute control of the conditions and prices prevailing in the whole field of industry, then individual enterprise and effort will be paralyzed and the spirit of commercial freedom will be dead.

PART II.

[On Foreign Relations.]

THE WHITE HOUSE, *December 7, 1911.*

To the Senate and House of Representatives:

The relations of the United States with other countries have continued during the past twelve months upon a basis of the usual good will and friendly intercourse.

ARBITRATION.

The year just passed marks an important general movement on the part of the Powers for broader arbitration. In the recognition of the manifold benefits to mankind in the extension of the policy of the settlement of international disputes by arbitration rather than by war, and in response to a widespread demand for an advance in that direction on the part of the people of the United States and of Great Britain and of France, new arbitration treaties were negotiated last spring with Great Britain and France, the terms of which were designed, as expressed in the preamble of these treaties, to extend the scope and obligations of the policy of arbitration adopted in our present treaties with those Governments. To pave the way for this treaty with the United States, Great Britain negotiated an important modification in its alliance with Japan, and the French Government also expedited the negotiations with signal good will. The new treaties have been submitted to the Senate and are awaiting its advice and consent to their ratification. All the essentials of these important treaties have long been known, and it is my earnest hope that they will receive prompt and favorable action.

CLAIM OF ALSOP & CO. SETTLED.

I am glad to report that on July 5 last the American claim of Alsop & Co. against the Government of Chile was finally disposed of by the decision of His Britannic Majesty George V, to whom, as *amiable compositeur,* the matter had been referred for determination. His Majesty made an award of nearly $1,000,000 to the claimants, which was promptly paid by Chile. The settlement of this controversy has happily eliminated from the relations between the Republic of Chile and the United States the only question which for two decades had given the two foreign offices any serious concern and makes possible the unobstructed development of the relations of friendship which it has been the aim of this Government in every possible way to further and cultivate.

ARBITRATIONS—PANAMA AND COSTA RICA—COLOMBIA AND HAITI.

In further illustration of the practical and beneficent application of the principle of arbitration and the underlying broad spirit of conciliation, I am happy to advert to the part of the United States in facilitating amicable settlement of disputes which menaced the peace between Panama and Costa Rica and between Haiti and the Dominican Republic.

Since the date of their independence, Colombia and Costa Rica had been seeking a solution of a boundary dispute, which came as an heritage from Colombia to the new Republic of Panama, upon its beginning life as an independent nation. Although the disputants had submitted this question for decision to the President of France under the terms of an arbitration treaty, the exact interpretation of the provisions of the award rendered had been a matter of serious disagreement between the two countries, both contending for widely different lines even under the terms of the decision. Subsequently and since 1903 this boundary question had been the subject of fruitless diplomatic negotiations between the parties. In January, 1910, at the request of both Governments the agents representing them met in conference at the Department of State and subsequently concluded a protocol submitting this long-pending controversy to the arbitral judgment of the Chief Justice of the United States, who consented to act in this capacity. A boundary commission, according to the international agreement, has now been appointed, and it is expected that the arguments will shortly proceed and that this long-standing dispute will be honorably and satisfactorily terminated.

Again, a few months ago it appeared that the Dominican Republic and Haiti were about to enter upon hostilities because of complications growing out of an acrimonious boundary dispute which the efforts of many years had failed to solve. The Government of the United States, by a friendly interposition of good offices, succeeded in prevailing upon the parties to place their reliance upon some form of pacific settlement. Accordingly, on the friendly suggestion of this Government, the two Governments empowered commissioners to meet at Washington in conference at the State Department in order to arrange the terms of submission to arbitration of the boundary controversy.

CHAMIZAL ARBITRATION NOT SATISFACTORY.

Our arbitration of the Chamizal boundary question with Mexico was unfortunately abortive, but with the earnest efforts on the part of both Governments which its importance commands, it is felt that an early practical adjustment should prove possible.

LATIN AMERICA.

VENEZUELA.

During the past year the Republic of Venezuela celebrated the one hundredth anniversary of its independence. The United States sent, in honor of this event, a special embassy to Caracas, where the cordial reception and generous hospitality shown it were most gratifying as a further proof of the good relations and friendship existing between that country and the United States.

MEXICO.

The recent political events in Mexico received attention from this Government because of the exceedingly delicate and difficult situation created along our southern border and the necessity for taking measures properly to safeguard American interests. The Government of the United States, in its desire to secure a proper observance and enforcement of the so-called neutrality statutes of the Federal Government, issued directions to the appropriate officers to exercise a diligent and vigilant regard for the requirements of such rules and laws. Although a condition of actual armed conflict existed, there was no official recognition of belligerency involving the technical neutrality obligations of international law.

On the 6th of March last, in the absence of the Secretary of State, I had a personal interview with Mr. Wilson, the ambassador of the

United States to Mexico, in which he reported to me that the conditions in Mexico were much more critical than the press dispatches disclosed; that President Diaz was on a volcano of popular uprising; that the small outbreaks which had occurred were only symptomatic of the whole condition; that a very large per cent of the people were in sympathy with the insurrection; that a general explosion was probable at any time, in which case he feared that the 40,000 or more American residents in Mexico might be assailed, and that the very large American investments might be injured or destroyed.

After a conference with the Secretary of War and the Secretary of the Navy, I thought it wise to assemble an Army division of full strength at San Antonio, Tex., a brigade of three regiments at Galveston, a brigade of Infantry in the Los Angeles district of southern California, together with a squadron of battleships and cruisers and transports at Galveston, and a small squadron of ships at San Diego. At the same time, through our representative at the City of Mexico, I expressed to President Diaz the hope that no apprehensions might result from unfounded conjectures as to these military maneuvers, and assured him that they had no significance which should cause concern to his Government.

The mobilization was effected with great promptness, and on the 15th of March, through the Secretary of War and the Secretary of the Navy, in a letter addressed to the Chief of Staff, I issued the following instructions:

It seems my duty as Commander in Chief to place troops in sufficient number where, if Congress shall direct that they enter Mexico to save American lives and property, an effective movement may be promptly made. Meantime, the movement of the troops to Texas and elsewhere near the boundary, accompanied with sincere assurances of the utmost goodwill toward the present Mexican Government and with larger and more frequent patrols along the border to prevent insurrectionary expeditions from American soil, will hold up the hands of the existing Government and will have a healthy moral effect to prevent attacks upon Americans and their property in any subsequent general internecine strife. Again, the sudden mobilization of a division of troops has been a great test of our Army and full of useful instruction, while the maneuvers that are thus made possible can occupy the troops and their officers to great advantage.

The assumption by the press that I contemplate intervention on Mexican soil to protect American lives or property is of course gratuitous, because I seriously doubt whether I have such authority under any circumstances, and if I had I would not exercise it without express congressional approval. Indeed, as you know, I have already declined, without Mexican consent, to order a troop of Cavalry to protect the breakwater we are constructing just across the border in Mexico at the mouth of the Colorado River to save the Imperial Valley, although the insurrectos had scattered the Mexican troops and were taking our horses and supplies and frightening our workmen away. My determined purpose, however, is to be in a position so that when danger to American lives and property in Mexico threatens and the existing Government is rendered helpless by the insurrection, I can promptly execute congressional orders to protect them, with effect.

Meantime, I send you this letter, through the Secretary, to call your attention to some things in connection with the presence of the division in the Southwest which have doubtless occurred to you, but which I wish to emphasize.

In the first place, I want to make the mobilization a first-class training for the Army, and I wish you would give your time and that of the War College to advising and carrying out maneuvers of a useful character, and plan to continue to do this during the next three months. By that time we may expect that either Ambassador Wilson's fears will have been realized and chaos and its consequences have ensued, or that the present Government of Mexico will have so readjusted matters as to secure tranquillity—a result devoutly to be wished. The troops can then be returned to their posts. I understood from you in Washington that Gen. Aleshire said that you could probably meet all the additional expense of this whole movement out of the present appropriations if the troops continue in Texas for three months. I sincerely hope this is so. I observe from the newspapers that you have no blank cartridges, but I presume that this is an error, or that it will be easy to procure those for use as soon as your maneuvers begin.

Second. Texas is a State ordinarily peaceful, but you can not put 20,000 troops into it without running some risk of a collision between the people of that State, and especially the Mexicans who live in Texas near the border and who sympathize with the insurrectos, and the Federal soldiers. For that reason I beg you to be as careful as you can to prevent friction of any kind. We were able in Cuba, with the army of pacification there of something more than 5,000 troops, to maintain them for a year without any trouble, and I hope you can do the same thing in Texas. Please give your attention to this, and advise all the officers in command of the necessity for very great circumspection in this regard.

Third. One of the great troubles in the concentration of troops is the danger of disease, and I suppose that you have adopted the most modern methods for preventing and, if necessary, for stamping out epidemics. That is so much a part of a campaign that it hardly seems necessary for me to call attention to it.

Finally, I wish you to examine the question of the patrol of the border and put as many troops on that work as is practicable, and more than are now engaged in it, in order to prevent the use of our borderland for the carrying out of the insurrection. I have given assurances to the Mexican ambassador on this point.

I sincerely hope that this experience will always be remembered by the Army and Navy as a useful means of education, and I should be greatly disappointed if it resulted in any injury or disaster to our forces from any cause. I have taken a good deal of responsibility in ordering this mobilization, but I am ready to answer for it if only you and those under you use the utmost care to avoid the difficulties which I have pointed out.

You may have a copy of this letter made and left with Gen. Carter and such other generals in command as you may think wise and necessary to guide them in their course, but to be regarded as confidential.

I am more than happy to here record the fact that all apprehensions as to the effect of the presence of so large a military force in Texas proved groundless; no disturbances occurred; the conduct of the troops was exemplary and the public reception and treatment of them was all that could have been desired, and this notwithstanding the presence of a large number of Mexican refugees in the border territory.

From time to time communications were received from Ambassador Wilson, who had returned to Mexico, confirming the view that the massing of American troops in the neighborhood had had good effect. By dispatch of April 3, 1911, the ambassador said:

The continuing gravity of the situation here and the chaos that would ensue should the constitutional authorities be eventually overthrown, thus greatly increasing the danger to which American lives and property are already subject, confirm the wisdom of the President in taking those military precautions which, making every allowance for the dignity and the sovereignty of a friendly state, are due to our nationals abroad.

Charged as I am with the responsibility of safeguarding these lives and property, I am bound to say to the department that our military dispositions on the frontier have produced an effective impression on the Mexican mind and may, at any moment, prove to be the only guaranties for the safety of our nationals and their property. If it should eventuate that conditions here require more active measures by the President and Congress, sporadic attacks might be made upon the lives and property of our nationals, but the ultimate result would be order and adequate protection.

The insurrection continued and resulted in engagements between the regular Mexican troops and the insurgents, and this along the border, so that in several instances bullets from the contending forces struck American citizens engaged in their lawful occupations on American soil.

Proper protests were made against these invasions of American rights to the Mexican authorities. On April 17, 1911, I received the following telegram from the governor of Arizona:

As a result of to-day's fighting across the international line, but within gunshot range of the heart of Douglas, five Americans wounded on this side of the line. Everything points to repetition of these casualties on to-morrow, and while the Federals seem disposed to keep their agreement not to fire into Douglas, the position of the insurrectionists is such that when fighting occurs on the east and southeast of the intrenchments people living in Douglas are put in danger of their lives. In my judgment radical measures are needed to protect our innocent people, and if anything can be done to stop the fighting at Agua Prieta the situation calls for such action. It is impossible to safeguard the people of Douglas unless the town be vacated. Can anything be done to relieve situation, now acute?

After a conference with the Secretary of State, the following telegram was sent to Governor Sloan, on April 18, 1911, and made public:

Your dispatch received. Have made urgent demand upon Mexican Government to issue instructions to prevent firing across border by Mexican federal troops, and am waiting reply. Meantime I have sent direct warning to the Mexican and insurgent forces near Douglas. I infer from your dispatch that both parties attempt to heed the warning, but that in the strain and exigency of the contest wild bullets still find their way into Douglas. The situation might justify me in ordering our troops to cross the border and attempt to stop the fighting, or to fire upon both combatants from the American side. But if I take this step, I must face the possibility of resistance and greater bloodshed, and also the danger of having our motives misconstrued and misrepresented, and of thus inflaming Mexican popular indignation against many thousand Americans now in Mexico and jeopardizing their lives and property. The pressure for general intervention under such conditions it might not be practicable to resist. It is impossible to foresee or reckon the consequences of such a course, and we must use the greatest self-restraint to avoid it. Pending my urgent representation to the Mexican Government, I can not therefore order the troops at Douglas to cross the border, but I must ask you and the local authorities, in case the same danger recurs, to direct the people of Douglas to place themselves where bullets can not reach them and thus avoid casualty. I am loath to endanger Americans in Mexico, where they are necessarily exposed, by taking a radical step to prevent injury to Americans on our side of the border who can avoid it by a temporary inconvenience.

I am glad to say that no further invasion of American rights of any substantial character occurred.

The presence of a large military and naval force available for prompt action, near the Mexican border, proved to be most fortunate under the somewhat trying conditions presented by this invasion of American rights. Had no movement theretofore taken place, and because of these events it had been necessary then to bring about the mobilization, it must have had sinister significance. On the other hand, the presence of the troops before and at the time of the unfortunate killing and wounding of American citizens at Douglas, made clear that the restraint exercised by our Government in regard to this occurrence was not due to lack of force or power to deal with it promptly and aggressively, but was due to a real desire to use every means possible to avoid direct intervention in the affairs of our neighbor, whose friendship we valued and were most anxious to retain.

The policy and action of this Government were based upon an earnest friendliness for the Mexican people as a whole, and it is a matter of gratification to note that this attitude of strict impartiality as to all factions in Mexico and of sincere friendship for the neighboring nation, without regard for party allegiance, has been generally recognized and has resulted in an even closer and more sympathetic understanding between the two Republics and a warmer regard one for the other. Action to suppress violence and restore tranquillity throughout the Mexican Republic was of peculiar interest to this Government, in that it concerned the safeguarding of American life and property in that country. The Government of the United States had occasion to accord permission for the passage of a body of Mexican rurales through Douglas, Arizona, to Tia Juana, Mexico, for the suppression of general lawlessness which had for some time existed in the region of northern Lower California. On May 25, 1911, President Diaz resigned, Señor de la Barra was chosen provisional President. Elections for President and Vice President were thereafter held throughout the Republic, and Señor Francisco I. Madero was formally declared elected on October 15 to the chief magistracy. On November 6 President Madero entered upon the duties of his office.

Since the inauguration of President Madero a plot has been unearthed against the present Government, to begin a new insurrection. Pursuing the same consistent policy which this administration has adopted from the beginning, it directed an investigation into the conspiracy charged, and this investigation has resulted in the indictment of Gen. Bernardo Reyes and others and the seizure of a number of officers and men and horses and accoutrements assembled upon the soil of Texas for the purpose of invading Mexico. Similar proceedings had been taken during the insurrection against the Diaz Government resulting in the indictments and prosecution of persons found to be engaged in violating the neutrality laws of the United States in aid of that uprising.

The record of this Government in respect of the recognition of constituted authority in Mexico therefore is clear.

CENTRAL AMERICA—HONDURAS AND NICARAGUA TREATIES PROPOSED.

As to the situation in Central America, I have taken occasion in the past to emphasize most strongly the importance that should be attributed to the consummation of the conventions between the Republics of Nicaragua and of Honduras and this country, and I again earnestly recommend that the necessary advice and consent of the Senate be accorded to these treaties, which will make it possible for these Central American Republics to enter upon an era of genuine economic national development. The Government of Nicaragua which has already taken favorable action on the convention, has found it necessary, pending the exchange of final ratifications, to enter into negotiations with American bankers for the purpose of securing a temporary loan to relieve the present financial tension. In connection with this temporary loan and in the hope of consummating, through the ultimate operation of the convention, a complete and lasting economic regeneration, the Government of Nicaragua has also decided to engage an American citizen as collector general of customs. The claims commission on which the services of two American citizens have been sought, and the work of the American financial adviser should accomplish a lasting good of inestimable benefit to the prosperity, commerce, and peace of the Republic. In considering the ratification of the conventions with Nicaragua and Honduras, there rests with the United States the heavy responsibility of the fact that their rejection here might destroy the progress made and consign the Republics concerned to still deeper submergence in bankruptcy, revolution, and national jeopardy.

PANAMA.

Our relations with the Republic of Panama, peculiarly important, due to mutual obligations and the vast interests created by the canal, have continued in the usual friendly manner, and we have been glad to make appropriate expression of our attitude of sympathetic interest in the endeavors of our neighbor in undertaking the development of the rich resources of the country. With reference to the internal political affairs of the Republic, our obvious concern is in the maintenance of public peace and constitutional order, and the fostering of the general interests created by the actual relations of the two countries, without the manifestation of any preference for the success of either of the political parties.

THE PAN AMERICAN UNION.

The Pan American Union, formerly known as the Bureau of American Republics, maintained by the joint contributions of all the American nations, has during the past year enlarged its practical work as an international organization, and continues to prove its usefulness as an agency for the mutual development of commerce, better acquaintance, and closer intercourse between the United States and her sister American republics.

THE FAR EAST.

THE CHINESE LOANS.

The past year has been marked in our relations with China by the conclusion of two important international loans, one for the construction of the Hukuang railways, the other for carrying out of the currency reform to which China was pledged by treaties with the United States, Great Britain, and Japan, of which mention was made in my last annual message.

It will be remembered that early in 1909 an agreement was consummated among British, French, and German financial groups whereby they proposed to lend the Chinese Government funds for the construction of railways in the Provinces of Hunan and Hupeh, reserving for their nationals the privilege of engineering the construction of the lines and of furnishing the materials required for the work. After negotiations with the Governments and groups concerned an agreement was reached whereby American, British, French, and German nationals should participate upon equal terms in this important and useful undertaking. Thereupon the financial groups, supported by their respective Governments, began negotiations with the Chinese Government which terminated in a loan to China of $30,000,000, with the privilege of increasing the amount to $50,000,000. The cooperative construction of these trunk lines should be of immense advantage, materially and otherwise, to China and should greatly facilitate the development of the bountiful resources of the Empire. On the other hand, a large portion of these funds is to be expended for materials, American products having equal preference with those of the other three lending nations, and as the contract provides for branches and extensions subsequently to be built on the same terms the opportunities for American materials will reach considerable proportions.

Knowing the interest of the United States in the reform of Chinese currency, the Chinese Government, in the autumn of 1910, sought the assistance of the American Government to procure funds with which to accomplish that all-important reform. In the course of the subsequent negotiations there was combined with the proposed currency loan one for certain industrial developments in Manchuria, the two loans aggregating the sum of $50,000,000. While this was originally to be solely an American enterprise, the American Government, consistently with its desire to secure a sympathetic and practical cooperation of the great powers toward maintaining the principle of equality of opportunity and the administrative integrity of China, urged the Chinese Government to admit to participation in the currency loan the associates of the American group in the Hukuang loan. While of immense importance in itself, the reform contemplated in making this loan is but preliminary to other and more comprehensive fiscal reforms which will be of incalculable benefit to China and foreign interests alike, since they will strengthen the Chinese Empire and promote the rapid development of international trade.

NEUTRAL FINANCIAL ADVISER.

When these negotiations were begun, it was understood that a financial adviser was to be employed by China in connection with the reform, and in order that absolute equality in all respects among the lending nations might be scrupulously observed, the American Government proposed the nomination of a neutral adviser, which was agreed to by China and the other Governments concerned. On September 28, 1911, Dr. Vissering, president of the Dutch Java Bank and a financier of wide experience in the Orient, was recommended to the Chinese Government for the post of monetary adviser.

Especially important at the present, when the ancient Chinese Empire is shaken by civil war incidental to its awakening to the many influences and activities of modernization, are the cooperative policy of good understanding which has been fostered by the international projects referred to above and the general sympathy of view among all the Powers interested in the Far East. While safeguarding the interests of our nationals, this Government is using its best efforts in continuance of its traditional policy of sympathy and friendship toward the Chinese Empire and its people, with the confident hope for their economic and administrative development, and with the constant disposition to contribute to their welfare in all proper ways consistent with an attitude of strict impartiality as between contending factions.

For the first time in the history of the two countries, a Chinese cruiser, the *Haichi,* under the command of Admiral Ching, recently visited New York, where the officers and men were given a cordial welcome.

NEW JAPANESE TREATY.

The treaty of commerce and navigation between the United States and Japan, signed in 1894, would by a strict interpretation of its provisions have terminated on July 17, 1912. Japan's general treaties with the other powers, however, terminated in 1911, and the Japanese Government expressed an earnest desire to conduct the negotiations for a new treaty with the United States simultaneously with its negotiations with the other powers. There were a number of important questions involved in the treaty, including the immigration of laborers, revision of the customs tariff, and the right of Americans to hold real estate in Japan. The United States consented to waive all technicalities and to enter at once upon negotiations for a new treaty on the understanding that there should be a continuance throughout the life of the treaty of the same effective measures for the restriction of immigration of laborers to American territory which had been in operation with entire satisfaction to both Governments since 1908.

The Japanese Government accepted this basis of negotiation, and a new treaty was quickly concluded, resulting in a highly satisfactory settlement of the other questions referred to.

A satisfactory adjustment has also been effected of the questions growing out of the annexation of Korea by Japan.

The recent visit of Admiral Count Togo to the United States as the Nation's guest afforded a welcome opportunity to demonstrate the friendly feeling so happily existing between the two countries.

SIAM.

There has been a change of sovereigns in Siam and the American minister at Bangkok was accredited in a special capacity to represent the United States at the coronation ceremony of the new King.

EUROPE AND THE NEAR EAST.

In Europe and the Near East, during the past twelve-month, there has been at times considerable political unrest. The Moroccan question, which for some months was the cause of great anxiety, happily appears to have reached a stage at which it need no longer be regarded with concern. The Ottoman Empire was occupied for a period by strife in Albania and is now at war with Italy. In Greece and the Balkan countries the disquieting potentialities of this situation have been more or less felt. Persia has been the scene of a long internal struggle. These conditions have been the cause of uneasiness in European diplomacy, but thus far without direct political concern to the United States.

In the war which unhappily exists between Italy and Turkey this Government has no direct political interest, and I took occasion at the suitable time to issue a proclamation of neutrality in that conflict. At the same time all necessary steps have been taken to safeguard the personal interests of American citizens and organizations in so far as affected by the war.

COMMERCE WITH THE NEAR EAST.

In spite of the attendant economic uncertainties and detriments to commerce, the United States has gained markedly in its commercial standing with certain of the nations of the Near East. Turkey, especially, is beginning to come into closer relations with the United States through the new interest of American manufacturers and exporters in the possibilities of those regions, and it is hoped that foundations are being laid for a large and mutually beneficial exchange of commodities between the two countries. This new interest of Turkey in American goods is indicated by the fact that a party of prominent merchants from a large city in Turkey recently visited the United States to study conditions of manufacture and export here, and to get into personal touch with American merchants, with a view to cooperating more intelligently in opening up the markets of Turkey and the adjacent countries to our manufactures. Another indication of this new interest of America in the commerce of the Near East is the recent visit of a large party of American merchants and manufacturers to central and eastern Europe, where they were entertained by prominent officials and organizations of the large cities, and new bonds of friendship and understanding were established which can not but lead to closer and greater commercial interchange.

CORONATION OF KING GEORGE V.

The 22d of June of the present year marked the coronation of His Britannic Majesty King George V. In honor of this auspicious occasion I sent a special embassy to London. The courteous and cordial welcome extended to this Government's representatives by His Majesty and the people of Great Britain has further emphasized the strong bonds of friendship happily existing between the two nations.

SETTLEMENT OF LONG-STANDING DIFFERENCES WITH GREAT BRITAIN.

As the result of a determined effort on the part of both Great Britain and the United States to settle all of their outstanding differences a number of treaties have been entered into between the two countries in recent years, by which nearly all of the unsettled questions between them of any importance have either been adjusted by agreement or arrangements made for their settlement by arbitration. A number of the unsettled questions referred to consist of pecuniary claims presented by each country against the other, and in order that as many of these claims as possible should be settled by arbitration a special agreement for that purpose was entered into between the two Governments on the 18th day of August, 1910, in accordance with Article II of the general arbitration treaty with Great Britain of April 4, 1908. Pursuant to the provisions of this special agreement a schedule of claims has already been agreed upon, and the special agreement, together with this schedule, received the approval of the Senate when submitted to it for that purpose at the last session of Congress. Negotiations between the two Governments for the preparation of an additional schedule of claims are already well advanced, and it is my intention to submit such schedule as soon as it is agreed upon to the Senate for its approval, in order that the arbitration proceedings may be undertaken at an early date. In this connection the attention of Congress is particularly called to the necessity for an appropriation to cover the expense incurred in submitting these claims to arbitration.

PRESENTATION TO GERMANY OF REPLICA OF VON STEUBEN STATUE.

In pursuance of the act of Congress, approved June 23, 1910, the Secretary of State and the Joint Committee on the Library entered into a contract with the sculptor, Albert Jaegers, for the execution of a bronze replica of the statue of Gen. von Steuben erected in Washington, for presentation to His Majesty the German Emperor and the German nation in recognition of the gift of the statue of Frederick the Great made by the Emperor to the people of the United States.

The presentation was made on September 2 last by representatives whom I commissioned as the special mission of this Government for the purpose.

The German Emperor has conveyed to me by telegraph, on his own behalf and that of the German people, an expression of appreciative thanks for this action of Congress.

RUSSIA.

By direction of the State Department, our ambassador to Russia has recently been having a series of conferences with the minister of foreign affairs of Russia, with a view to securing a clearer understanding and construction of the treaty of 1832 between Russia and the United States and the modification of any existing Russian regulations which may be found to interfere in any way with the full recognition of the rights of American citizens under this treaty. I believe that the Government of Russia is addressing itself seriously to the need of changing the present practice under the treaty and that sufficient progress has been made to warrant the continuance of these conferences in the hope that there may soon be removed any justification of the complaints of treaty violation now prevalent in this country.

I expect that immediately after the Christmas recess I shall be able to make a further communication to Congress on this subject.

LIBERIA.

Negotiations for the amelioration of conditions found to exist in Liberia by the American commission, undertaken through the Department of State, have been concluded and it is only necessary for certain formalities to be arranged in securing the loan which it is hoped will place that republic on a practical financial and economic footing.

RECOGNITION OF PORTUGUESE REPUBLIC.

The National Constituent Assembly, regularly elected by the vote of the Portuguese people, having on June 19 last unanimously proclaimed a republican form of government, the official recognition of the Government of the United States was given to the new Republic in the afternoon of the same day.

SPITZBERGEN ISLANDS.

Negotiations for the betterment of conditions existing in the Spitzbergen Islands and the adjustment of conflicting claims of American citizens and Norwegian subjects to lands in that archipelago are still in progress.

INTERNATIONAL CONVENTIONS AND CONFERENCES.

INTERNATIONAL PRIZE COURT.

The supplementary protocol to The Hague convention for the establishment of an international prize court, mentioned in my last annual message, embodying stipulations providing for an alternative procedure which would remove the constitutional objection to that part of The Hague convention which provides that there may be an appeal to the proposed court from the decisions of national courts, has received the signature of the governments parties to the original convention and has been ratified by the Government of the United States, together with the prize court convention.

The deposit of the ratifications with the Government of the Netherlands awaits action by the powers on the declaration, signed at London on February 26, 1909, of the rules of international law to be recognized within the meaning of article 7 of The Hague convention for the establishment of an International Prize Court.

FUR-SEAL TREATY.

The fur-seal controversy, which for nearly twenty-five years has been the source of serious friction between the United States and the powers bordering upon the north Pacific Ocean, whose subjects have been permitted to engage in pelagic sealing against the fur-seal herds having their breeding grounds within the jurisdiction of the United States, has at last been satisfactorily adjusted by the conclusion of the north Pacific sealing convention entered into between the United States, Great Britain, Japan, and Russia on the 7th of July last. This convention is a conservation measure of very great importance, and if it is carried out in the spirit of reciprocal concession and advantage upon which it is based, there is every reason to believe that not only will it result in preserving the fur-seal herds of the north Pacific Ocean and restoring them to their former value for the purposes of commerce, but also that it will afford a permanently satisfactory settlement of a question the only other solution of which seemed to be the total destruction of the fur seals. In another aspect, also, this convention is of importance in that it furnishes an illustration of the feasibility of securing a general international game law for the protection of other mammals of the sea, the preservation of which is of importance to all the nations of the world.

LEGISLATION NECESSARY.

The attention of Congress is especially called to the necessity for legislation on the part of the United States for the purpose of fulfilling the obligations assumed under this convention, to which the Senate gave its advice and consent on the 24th day of July last.

PROTECTION OF INDUSTRIAL PROPERTY UNION.

The conference of the International Union for the Protection of Industrial Property, which, under the authority of Congress, convened at Washington on May 16, 1911, closed its labors on June 2, 1911, by the signature of three acts, as follows:

(1) A convention revising the Paris convention of March 20, 1883, for the protection of industrial property, as modified by the additional act signed at Brussels on December 14, 1900;

(2) An arrangement to replace the arrangement signed at Madrid on April 14, 1891, for the international registration of trade-marks, and the additional act with regard thereto signed at Brussels on December 14, 1900; and

(3) An arrangement to replace the arrangement signed at Madrid on April 14, 1891, relating to the repression of false indication of production of merchandise.

The United States is a signatory of the first convention only, and this will be promptly submitted to the Senate.

INTERNATIONAL OPIUM COMMISSION.

In a special message transmitted to the Congress on the 11th of January, 1911, in which I concurred in the recommendations made by the Secretary of State in regard to certain needful legislation for the control of our interstate and foreign traffic in opium and other menacing drugs, I quoted from my annual message of December 7, 1909, in which I announced that the results of the International Opium Commission held at Shanghai in February, 1909, at the invitation of the United States, had been laid before this Government; that the report of that commission showed that China was making remarkable progress and admirable efforts toward the eradication of the opium evil; that the interested governments had not permitted their commercial interests to prevent their cooperation in this reform; and, as a result of collateral investigations of the opium question in this country, I recommended that the manufacture, sale, and use of opium in the United States should be more rigorously controlled by legislation

Prior to that time and in continuation of the policy of this Government to secure the cooperation of the interested nations, the United States proposed an international opium conference with full powers for the purpose of clothing with the force of international law the resolutions adopted by the above-mentioned commission, together with their essential corollaries. The other powers concerned cordially responded to the proposal of this Government, and, I am glad to be able to announce, representatives of all the powers assembled in conference at The Hague on the first of this month.

Since the passage of the opium-exclusion act, more than twenty States have been animated to modify their pharmacy laws and bring them in accord with the spirit of that act, thus stamping out, to a measure, the intrastate traffic in opium and other habit-forming drugs. But, although I have urged on the Congress the passage of certain measures for Federal control of the interstate and foreign traffic in these drugs, no action has yet been taken. In view of the fact that there is now sitting at The Hague so important a conference, which has under review the municipal laws of the different nations for the mitigation of their opium and other allied evils, a conference which will certainly deal with the international aspects of these evils, it seems to me most essential that the Congress should take immediate action on the anti-narcotic legislation to which I have already called attention by a special message.

BUENOS AIRES CONVENTIONS.

The four important conventions signed at the Fourth Pan American Conference at Buenos Aires, providing for the regulation of trademarks, patents, and copyrights, and for the arbitration of pecuniary claims, have, with the advice and consent of the Senate, been ratified on the part of the United States and the ratifications have been deposited with the Government of the Argentine Republic in accordance with the requirements of the conventions. I am not advised that similiar action has been taken by any other of the signatory governments.

INTERNATIONAL ARRANGEMENT TO SUPPRESS OBSCENE PUBLICATIONS.

One of the notable advances in international morality accomplished in recent years was an arrangement entered into on April 13th of the present year between the United States and other powers for the repression of the circulation of obscene publications.

FOREIGN TRADE RELATIONS OF THE UNITED STATES.

In my last annual message I referred to the tariff negotiations of the Department of State with foreign countries in connection with the application, by a series of proclamations, of the minimum tariff of the United States to importations from the several countries, and I stated that, in its general operation, section 2 of the new tariff law had proved a guaranty of continued commercial peace, although there were, unfortunately, instances where foreign governments dealt arbitrarily with American interests within their jurisdiction in a manner injurious and inequitable. During the past year some instances of discriminatory treatment have been removed, but I regret to say that there remain a few cases of differential treatment adverse to the commerce of the United States. While none of these instances now appears to amount to undue discrimination in the sense of section 2 of the tariff law of August 5, 1909, they are all exceptions to that complete degree of equality of tariff treatment that the Department of State has consistently sought to obtain for American commerce abroad.

While the double tariff feature of the tariff law of 1909 has been amply justified by the results achieved in removing former and preventing new, undue discriminations against American commerce, it is believed that the time has come for the amendment of this feature of the law in such way as to provide a graduated means of meeting varying degrees of discriminatory treatment of American commerce in foreign countries as well as to protect the financial interests abroad of American citizens against arbitrary and injurious treatment on the part of foreign governments through either legislative or administrative measures.

It would seem desirable that the maximum tariff of the United States should embrace within its purview the free list, which is not the case at the present time, in order that it might have reasonable significance to the governments of those countries from which the importations into the United States are confined virtually to articles on the free list.

RECORD OF HIGHEST AMOUNT OF FOREIGN TRADE.

The fiscal year ended June 30, 1911, shows great progress in the development of American trade. It was noteworthy as marking the highest record of exports of American products to foreign countries, the valuation being in excess of $2,000,000,000. These exports showed a gain over the preceding year of more than $300,000,000.

FACILITIES FOR FOREIGN TRADE FURNISHED BY JOINT ACTION OF DEPARTMENT OF STATE AND OF COMMERCE AND LABOR.

There is widespread appreciation expressed by the business interests of the country as regards the practical value of the facilities now offered by the Department of State and the Department of Commerce and Labor for the furtherance of American commerce. Conferences with their officers at Washington who have an expert knowledge of trade conditions in foreign countries and with consular officers and commercial agents of the Department of Commerce and Labor who, while on leave of absence, visit the principal industrial centers of the United States, have been found of great value. These trade conferences are regarded as a particularly promising method of governmental aid in foreign trade promotion. The Department of Commerce and Labor has arranged to give publicity to the expected arrival and the itinerary of consular officers and commercial agents while on leave in the United States, in order that trade organizations may arrange for conferences with them.

As I have indicated, it is increasingly clear that to obtain and maintain that equity and substantial equality of treatment essential to the flourishing foreign trade, which becomes year by year more important to the industrial and commercial welfare of the United States, we should have a flexibility of tariff sufficient for the give and take of negotiation by the Department of State on behalf of our commerce and industry.

CRYING NEED FOR AMERICAN MERCHANT MARINE.

I need hardly reiterate the conviction that there should speedily be built up an American merchant marine. This is necessary to assure favorable transportation facilities to our great ocean-borne commerce as well as to supplement the Navy with an adequate reserve of ships and men. It would have the economic advantage of keeping at home part of the vast sums now paid foreign shipping for carrying American goods. All the great commercial nations pay heavy subsidies to their merchant marine, so that it is obvious that without some wise aid from the Congress the United States must lag behind in the matter of merchant marine in its present anomalous position.

EXTENSION OF AMERICAN BANKING TO FOREIGN COUNTRIES.

Legislation to facilitate the extension of American banks to foreign countries is another matter in which our foreign trade needs assistance.

CHAMBERS OF FOREIGN COMMERCE SUGGESTED.

The interests of our foreign commerce are nonpartisan, and as a factor in prosperity are as broad as the land. In the dissemination of useful information and in the coordination of effort certain unofficial associations have done good work toward the promotion of foreign commerce. It is cause for regret, however, that the great number of such associations and the comparative lack of cooperation between them fails to secure an efficiency commensurate with the public interest. Through the agency of the Department of Commerce and Labor, and in some cases directly, the Department of State transmits to reputable business interests information of commercial opportunities, supplementing the regular published consular reports. Some central organization in touch with associations and chambers of commerce throughout the country and able to keep purely American interests in closer touch with different phases of commercial affairs would, I believe, be of great value. Such organization might be managed by a committee composed of a small number of those now actively carrying on the work of some of the larger associations, and there might be added to the committee, as members ex officio, one or two officials of the Department of State and one or two officials from the Department of Commerce and Labor and representatives of the appropriate committees of Congress. The authority and success of such an organization would evidently be enhanced if the Congress should see fit to prescribe its scope and organization through legislation which would give to it some such official standing as that, for example, of the National Red Cross.

With these factors and the continuance of the foreign-service establishment (departmental, diplomatic, and consular) upon the high plane where it has been placed by the recent reorganization this Government would be abreast of the times in fostering the interests of its foreign trade, and the rest must be left to the energy and enterprise of our business men.

IMPROVEMENT OF THE FOREIGN SERVICE.

The entire foreign-service organization is being improved and developed with especial regard to the requirements of the commercial interests of the country. The rapid growth of our foreign trade makes it of the utmost importance that governmental agencies through which that trade is to be aided and protected should possess a high degree of efficiency. Not only should the foreign representatives be maintained upon a generous scale in so far as salaries and establishments are concerned, but the selection and advancement of officers should be definitely and permanently regulated by law so that the service shall not fail to attract men of high character and ability. The experience of the past few years with a partial application of civil-service rules to the Diplomatic and Consular Service leaves no doubt in my mind of the wisdom of a wider and more permanent extension of those principles to both branches of the foreign service. The men selected for appointment by means of the existing executive regulations have been of a far higher average of intelligence and ability than the men appointed before the regulations were promulgated. Moreover, the feeling that under the existing rules there is reasonable hope for permanence of tenure during good behavior and for promotion for meritorious service has served to bring about a zealous activity in the interests of the country, which never before existed or could exist. It is my earnest conviction that the enactment into law of the general principles of the existing regulations can not fail to effect further improvement in both branches of the foreign service by providing greater inducement for young men of character and ability to seek a career abroad in the service of the Government, and an incentive to those already in the service to put forth greater efforts to attain the high standards which the successful conduct of our international relations and commerce requires.

I therefore again commend to the favorable action of the Congress the enactment of a law applying to the diplomatic and consular service the principles embodied in section 1753 of the Revised Statutes of the United States, in the civil-service act of January 16, 1883, and the Executive orders of June 27, 1906, and of November 26, 1909. In its consideration of this important subject I desire to recall to the attention of the Congress the very favorable report made on the Lowden bill for the improvement of the foreign service by the Foreign Affairs Committee of the House of Representatives. Available statistics show the strictness with which the merit system has been applied to the foreign service during recent years and the absolute nonpartisan selection of consuls and diplomatic-service secretaries who, indeed, far from being selected with any view to political consideration, have actually been chosen to a disproportionate extent from States which would have been unrepresented in the foreign service under the system which it is to be hoped is now permanently obsolete. Some legislation for the perpetuation of the present system of examinations and promotions upon merit and efficiency would be of greatest value to our commerical and international interests.

PART III.

THE WHITE HOUSE, *December 20, 1911.*

To the Senate and House of Representatives:

In my annual message to Congress, December, 1909, I stated that under section 2 of the act of August 5, 1909, I had appointed a Tariff Board of three members to cooperate with the State Department in the administration of the maximum and minimum clause of that act, to make a glossary or encyclopedia of the existing tariff so as to render its terms intelligible to the ordinary reader, and then to investigate industrial conditions and costs of production at home and abroad with a view to determining to what extent existing tariff rates actually exemplify the protective principle, viz., that duties should be made adequate, and only adequate, to equalize the difference in cost of production at home and abroad.

I further stated that I believed these investigations would be of great value as a basis for accurate legislation, and that I should from time to time recommend to Congress the revision of certain schedules in accordance with the findings of the Board.

In the last session of the Sixty-first Congress a bill creating a permanent Tariff Board of five members, of whom not more than three should be of the same political party, passed each House, but failed of enactment because of slight differences on which agreement was not reached before adjournment. An appropriation act provided that the permanent Tariff Board, if created by statute, should report to Congress on Schedule K in December, 1911.

Therefore, to carry out so far as lay within my power the purposes of this bill for a permanent Tariff Board, I appointed in March, 1911, a board of five, adding two members of such party affiliation as would have fulfilled the statutory requirement, and directed them to make a report to me on Schedule K of the tariff act in December of this year.

In my message of August 17, 1911, accompanying the veto of the wool bill, I said that, in my judgment, Schedule K should be revised and the rates reduced. My veto was based on the ground that, since the Tariff Board would make, in December, a detailed report on wool and wool manufactures, with special reference to the relation of the existing rates of duties to relative costs here and abroad, public policy and a fair regard to the interests of the producers and the manufacturers on the one hand and of the consumers on the other demanded that legislation should not be hastily enacted in the absence of such information; that I was not myself possessed at that time of adequate knowledge of the facts to determine whether or not the proposed act was in accord with my pledge to support a fair and reasonable protective policy; that such legislation might prove only temporary and inflict upon a great industry the evils of continued uncertainty.

I now herewith submit a report of the Tariff Board on Schedule K. The board is unanimous in its findings. On the basis of these findings I now recommend that the Congress proceed to a consideration of this schedule with a view to its revision and a general reduction of its rates.

The report shows that the present method of assessing the duty on raw wool—this is, by a specific rate on the grease pound (i. e., unscoured)—operates to exclude wools of high shrinkage in scouring but fine quality from the American market and thereby lessens the range of wools available to the domestic manufacturer; that the duty on scoured wool of 33 cents per pound is prohibitory and operates to exclude the importation of clean, low-priced foreign wools of inferior grades, which are nevertheless valuable material for manufacturing, and which can not be imported in the grease because of their heavy shrinkage. Such wools, if imported, might be used to displace the cheap substitutes now in use.

To make the preceding paragraph a little plainer, take the instance of a hundred pounds of first-class wool imported under the present duty, which is 11 cents a pound. That would make the duty on the hundred pounds $11. The merchantable part of the wool thus imported is the weight of the wool of this hundred pounds after scouring. If the wool shrinks 80 per cent, as some wools do, then the duty in such a case would amount to $11 on 20 pounds of scoured wool. This, of course, would be prohibitory. If the wool shrinks only 50 per cent, it would be $11 on 50 pounds of wool, and this is near to the average of the great bulk of wools that are imported from Australia, which is the principal source of our imported wool.

These discriminations could be overcome by assessing a duty in ad valorem terms, but this method is open to the objection, first, that it increases administrative difficulties and tends to decrease revenue through undervaluation; and, second, that as prices advance, the ad valorem rate increases the duty per pound at the time when the consumer most needs relief and the producer can best stand competition; while if prices decline the duty is decreased at the time when the consumer is least burdened by the price and the producer most needs protection.

Another method of meeting the difficulty of taxing the grease pound is to assess a specific duty on grease wool in terms of its scoured content. This obviates the chief evil of the present system, namely, the discrimination due to different shrinkages, and thereby tends greatly to equalize the duty. The board reports that this method is feasible in practice and could be administered without great expense. The scoured content of the wool is the basis on which users of wool make their calculations, and a duty of this kind would fit the usages of the trade. One effect of this method of assessment would be that, regardless of the rate of duty, there would be an increase in the supply and variety of wool by making available to the American market wools of both low and fine quality now excluded.

The report shows in detail the difficulties involved in attempting to state in categorical terms the cost of wool production and the great differences in cost as between different regions and different types of wool. It is found, however, that, taking all varieties in account, the average cost of production for the whole American clip is higher than the cost in the chief competing country by an amount somewhat less than the present duty.

The report shows that the duties on noils, wool wastes, and shoddy, which are adjusted to the rate of 33 cents on scoured wool are prohibitory in the same measure that the duty on scoured wool is prohibitory. In general, they are assessed at rates as high as, or higher than, the duties paid on the clean content of wools actually imported. They should be reduced and so adjusted to the rate on wool as to bear their proper proportion to the real rate levied on the actual wool imports.

The duties on many classes of wool manufacture are prohibitory and greatly in excess of the difference in cost of production here and abroad.

This is true of tops, of yarns (with the exception of worsted yarns of a very high grade), and of low and medium grade cloth of heavy weight.

On tops up to 52 cents a pound in value, and on yarns of 65 cents in value, the rate is 100 per cent with correspondingly higher rates for lower values. On cheap and medium grade cloths, the existing rates frequently run to 150 per cent and on some cheap goods to over 200 per cent. This is largely due to that part of the duty which is levied ostensibly to compensate the manufacturer for the enhanced cost of his raw material due to the duty on wool. As a matter of fact, this compensatory duty, for numerous classes of goods, is much in excess of the amount needed for strict compensation.

On the other hand, the findings show that the duties which run to such high ad valorem equivalents are prohibitory, since the goods are not imported, but that the prices of domestic fabrics are not raised by the full amount of duty. On a set of 1-yard samples of 16 English fabrics, which are completely excluded by the present tariff rates, it was found that the total foreign value was $41.84; the duties which would have been assessed had these fabrics been imported, $76.90; the foreign value plus the amount of the duty, $118.74; or a nominal duty of 183 per cent. In fact, however, practically identical fabrics of domestic make sold at the same time at $69.75, showing an enhanced price over the foreign market value of but 67 per cent.

Although these duties do not increase prices of domestic goods by anything like their full amount, it is none the less true that such prohibitive duties eliminate the possibility of foreign competition, even in time of scarcity; that they form a temptation to monopoly and conspiracies to control domestic prices; that they are much in excess of the difference in cost of production here and abroad, and that they should be reduced to a point which accords with this principle.

The findings of the board show that in this industry the actual manufacturing cost, aside from the question of the price of materials, is much higher in this country than it is abroad; that in the making of yarn and cloth the domestic woolen or worsted manufacturer has in general no advantage in the form of superior machinery or more efficient labor to offset the higher wages paid in this country. The findings show that the cost of turning wool into yarn in this country is about double that in the leading competing country, and that the cost of turning yarn into cloth is somewhat more than double. Under the protective policy a great industry, involving the welfare of hundreds of thousands of people, has been established despite these handicaps.

In recommending revision and reduction, I therefore urge that action be taken with these facts in mind, to the end that an important and established industry may not be jeopardized.

The Tariff Board reports that no equitable method has been found to levy purely specific duties on woolen and worsted fabrics and that, excepting for a compensatory duty, the rate must be ad valorem on such manufactures. It is important to realize, however, that no flat ad valorem rate on such fabrics can be made to work fairly and effectively. Any single rate which is high enough to equalize the difference in manufacturing cost at home and abroad on highly finished goods involving such labor would be prohibitory on cheaper goods, in which the labor cost is a smaller proportion of the total value. Conversely, a rate only adequate to equalize this difference on cheaper goods would remove protection from the fine-goods manufacture, the increase in which has been one of the striking features of the trade's development in recent years. I therefore recommend that in any revision the importance of a graduated scale of ad valorem duties on cloths be carefully considered and applied.

I venture to say that no legislative body has ever had presented to it a more complete and exhaustive report than this on so difficult and complicated a subject as the relative costs of wool and woolens the world over. It is a monument to the thoroughness, industry, impartiality, and accuracy of the men engaged in its making. They were chosen from both political parties but have allowed no partisan spirit to prompt or control their inquiries. They are unanimous in their findings. I feel sure that after the report has been printed and studied the value of such a compendium of exact knowledge in respect to this schedule of the tariff will convince all of the wisdom of making such a board permanent in order that it may treat each schedule of the tariff as it has treated this, and then keep its bureau of information up to date with current changes in the economic world.

It is no part of the function of the Tariff Board to propose rates of duty. Their function is merely to present findings of fact on which rates of duty may be fairly determined in the light of adequate knowledge in accord with the economic policy to be followed. This is what the present report does.

The findings of fact by the board show ample reason for the revision downward of Schedule K, in accord with the protective principle, and present the data as to relative costs and prices from which may be determined what rates will fairly equalize the difference in production costs. I recommend that such revision be proceeded with at once.

PART IV.

[On the financial condition of the treasury, needed banking and currency reform, and departmental questions.]

THE WHITE HOUSE, *December 21, 1911.*

To the Senate and House of Representatives:

The financial condition of the Government, as shown at the close of the last fiscal year, June 30, 1911, was very satisfactory. The ordinary receipts into the general fund, excluding postal revenues, amounted to $701,372,374.99, and the disbursements from the general fund for current expenses and capital outlays, excluding postal and Panama Canal disbursements, including the interest on the public debt, amounted to $654,137,907.89, leaving a surplus of $47,234,377.10.

The postal revenue receipts amounted to $237,879,823.60, while the payments made for the postal service from the postal revenues amounted to $237,660,705.48, which left a surplus of postal receipts over disbursements of $219,118.12, the first time in 27 years in which a surplus occurred.

The interest-bearing debt of the United States June 30, 1911, amounted to $915,353,190. The debt on which interest had ceased amounted to $1,879,830.26, and the debt bearing no interest, including greenbacks, national bank notes to be redeemed, and fractional currency, amounted to $386,751,917.43, or a total of interest and non-interest bearing debt amounting to $1,303,984,937.69.

The actual disbursements, exclusive of those for the Panama Canal and for the postal service for the year ending June 30, 1911, were $654,137,997.89. The actual disbursements for the year ending June 30, 1910, exclusive of the Panama Canal and the postal service disbursements, were $659,705,391.08, making a decrease of $5,567,393.19 in yearly expenditures in the year 1911 under that of 1910. For the year ending June 30, 1912, the estimated receipts, exclusive of the postal revenues, are $666,000,000, while the total estimates, exclusive of those for the Panama Canal and the postal expenditures payable from the postal revenues, amount to $645,842,799.34. This is a decrease in the 1912 estimates from that of the 1911 estimates of $1,534,367.22.

For the year ending June 30, 1913, the estimated receipts, exclusive of the postal revenues, are $667,000,000, while the total estimated appropriations, exclusive of the Panama Canal and postal disbursements payable from postal revenues, will amount to $637,920,803.35. This is a decrease in the 1913 estimates from that of the 1912 estimates of $7,921,995.99.

As to the postal revenues, the expansion of the business in that department, the normal increase in the Post Office and the extension of the service, will increase the outlay to the sum of $260,938,463; but as the department was self-sustaining this year the Postmaster General is assured that next year the receipts will at least equal the expenditures, and probably exceed them by more than the surplus of this year. It is fair and equitable, therefore, in determining the economy with which the Government has been run, to exclude the transactions of a department like the Post Office Department, which relies for its support upon its receipts. In calculations heretofore made for comparison of economy in each year, it has been the proper custom only to include in the statement the deficit in the Post Office Department which was paid out of the Treasury.

A calculation of the actual increase in the expenses of Government arising from the increase in the population and the general expansion of governmental functions, except those of the Post Office, for a number of years shows a normal increase of about 4 per cent a year. By directing the exercise of great care to keep down the expenses and the estimates we have succeeded in reducing the total disbursements each year.

THE CREDIT OF THE UNITED STATES.

The credit of this Government was shown to be better than that of any other Government by the sale of the Panama Canal 3 per cent bonds. These bonds did not give their owners the privilege of using them as a basis for bank-note circulation, nor was there any other privilege extended to them which would affect their general market value. Their sale, therefore, measured the credit of the Government. The premium which was realized upon the bonds made the actual interest rate of the transaction 2.909 per cent.

EFFICIENCY AND ECONOMY IN THE TREASURY DEPARTMENT.

In the Treasury Department the efficiency and economy work has been kept steadily up. Provision is made for the elimination of 134 positions during the coming year. Two hundred and sixty-seven statutory positions were eliminated during the last year in the office of the Treasury in Washington, and 141 positions in the year 1910, making an elimination of 542 statutory positions since March 4, 1909; and this has been done without the discharge of anybody, because the normal resignations and deaths have been equal to the elimination of the places, a system of transfers having taken care of the persons whose positions were dropped out. In the field service of the department, too, 1,259 positions have been eliminated down to the present time, making a total net reduction of all Treasury positions to the number of 1,801. Meantime the efficiency of the work of the department has increased.

MONETARY REFORM.

A matter of first importance that will come before Congress for action at this session is monetary reform. The Congress has itself arranged an early introduction of this great question through the report of its Monetary Commission. This commission was appointed to recommend a solution of the banking and currency problems so long confronting the Nation and to furnish the facts and data necessary to enable the Congress to take action. The commission was appointed when an impressive and urgent popular demand for legislative relief suddenly arose out of the distressing situation of the people caused by the deplorable panic of 1907. The Congress decided that while it could not give immediately the relief required, it would provide a commission to furnish the means for prompt action at a later date.

In order to do its work with thoroughness and precision this commission has taken some time to make its report. The country is undoubtedly hoping for as prompt action on the report as the convenience of the Congress can permit. The recognition of the gross imperfections and marked inadequacy of our banking and currency system even in our most quiet financial periods is of long standing; and later there has matured a recognition of the fact that our system is responsible for the extraordinary devastation, waste, and business paralysis of our recurring periods of panic. Though the members of the Monetary Commission have for a considerable time been working in the open, and while large numbers of the people have been openly working with them, and while the press has largely noted and discussed this work as it has proceeded, so that the report of the commission promises to represent a national movement, the details of the report are still being considered. I can not, therefore, do much more at this time than commend the immense importance of monetary reform, urge prompt consideration and action when the commission's report is received, and express my satisfaction that the plan to be proposed promises to embrace main features that, having met the approval of a great preponderance of the practical and professional opinion of the country, are likely to meet equal approval in Congress.

It is exceedingly fortunate that the wise and undisputed policy of maintaining unchanged the main features of our banking system rendered it at once impossible to introduce a central bank; for a central bank would certainly have been resisted, and a plan into which it could have been introduced would probably have been defeated. But as a central bank could not be a part of the only plan discussed or considered, that troublesome question is eliminated. And ingenious and novel as the proposed National Reserve Association appears, it simply is a logical outgrowth of what is best in our present system, and is, in fact, the fulfillment of that system.

Exactly how the management of that association should be organized is a question still open. It seems to be desirable that the banks which would own the association should in the main manage it. It will be an agency of the banks to act for them, and they can be trusted better than anybody else chiefly to conduct it. It is mainly bankers' work. But there must be some form of Government supervision and ultimate control, and I favor a reasonable representation of the Government in the management. I entertain no fear of the introduction of politics or of any undesirable influences from a properly measured Government representation.

I trust that all banks of the country possessing the requisite standards will be placed upon a footing of perfect equality of opportunity. Both the National system and the State system should be fairly recognized, leaving them eventually to coalesce if that shall prove to be their tendency. But such evolution can not develop impartially if the banks of one system are given or permitted any advantages of opportunity over those of the other system. And I trust also that the new legislation will carefully and completely protect and assure the individuality and the independence of each bank, to the end that any tendency there may ever be toward a consolidation of the money or banking power of the Nation shall be defeated.

It will always be possible, of course, to correct any features of the new law which may in practice prove to be unwise; so that while this law is sure to be enacted under conditions of unusual knowledge and authority, it also will include, it is well to remember, the possibility of future amendment.

With the present prospects of this long-awaited reform encouraging us, it would be singularly unfortunate if this monetary question should by any chance become a party issue. And I sincerely hope it will not. The exceeding amount of consideration it has received from the people of the Nation has been wholly nonpartisan; and the Congress set its nonpartisan seal upon it when the Monetary Commission was appointed. In commending the question to the favorable consideration of Congress, I speak for, and in the spirit of, the great number of my fellow citizens who without any thought of party or partisanship feel with remarkable earnestness that this reform is necessary to the interests of all the people.

THE WAR DEPARTMENT.

There is now before Congress a bill, the purpose of which is to increase the efficiency and decrease the expense of the Army. It contains four principal features: First, a consolidation of the General Staff with the Adjutant General's and the Inspector General's Departments; second, a consolidation of the Quartermaster's Department with the Subsistence and the Pay Departments; third, the creation of an Army Service Corps; and fourth, an extension of the enlistment period from three to five years.

With the establishment of an Army Service Corps, as proposed in the bill, I am thoroughly in accord and am convinced that the establishment of such a corps will result in a material economy and a very great increase of efficiency in the Army. It has repeatedly been recommended by me and my predecessors. I also believe that a consolidation of the Staff Corps can be made with a resulting increase in efficiency and economy, but not along the lines provided in the bill under consideration.

I am opposed to any plan the result of which would be to break up or interfere with the essential principles of the detail system in the Staff Corps established by the act of February 2, 1901, and I am opposed to any plan the result of which would be to give to the officer selected as Chief of Staff or to any other member of the General Staff Corps greater permanency of office than he now has. Under the existing law neither the Chief of Staff nor any other member of the General Staff Corps can remain in office for a period of more than four years, and there must be an interval of two years between successive tours of duty.

The bill referred to provides that certain persons shall become permanent members of the General Staff Corps, and that certain others are subject to redetail without an interval of two years. Such provision is fraught with danger to the welfare of the Army, and would practically nullify the main purpose of the law creating the General Staff.

In making the consolidations no reduction should be made in the total number of officers of the Army, of whom there are now too few to perform the duties imposed by law. I have in the past recommended an increase in the number of officers by 600 in order to provide sufficient officers to perform all classes of staff duty and to reduce the number of line officers detached from their commands. Congress at the last session increased the total number of officers by 200, but this is not enough. Promotion in the line of the Army is too slow. Officers do not attain command rank at an age early enough properly to exercise it. It would be a mistake further to retard this already slow promotion by throwing back into the line of the Army a number of high-ranking officers to be absorbed as is provided in the proposed plan of consolidation.

Another feature of the bill which I believe to be a mistake is the proposed increase in the term of enlistment from three to five years. I believe it would be better to enlist men for six years, release them at the end of three years from active service, and put them in reserve for the remaining three years. Reenlistments should be largely confined to the noncommissioned officers and other enlisted men in the skilled grades. This plan, by the payment of a comparatively small compensation during the three years of reserve, would keep a large body of men at the call of the Government, trained and ready for service, and able to meet any exigency.

The Army of the United States is in good condition. It showed itself able to meet an emergency in the successful mobilization of an army division of from 15,000 to 20,000 men, which took place along the border of Mexico during the recent disturbances in that country. The marvelous freedom from the ordinary camp diseases of typhoid fever and measles is referred to in the report of the Secretary of War, and shows such an effectiveness in the sanitary regulations and treatment of the Medical Corps, and in the discipline of the Army itself, as to invoke the highest commendation.

MEMORIAL AMPHITHEATER AT ARLINGTON.

I beg to renew my recommendation of last year that the Congress appropriate for a memorial amphitheater at Arlington, Va., the funds required to construct it upon the plans already approved.

THE PANAMA CANAL.

The very satisfactory progress made on the Panama Canal last year has continued, and there is every reason to believe that the canal will be completed as early as the 1st of July, 1913, unless something unforeseen occurs. This is about 18 months before the time promised by the engineers.

We are now near enough the completion of the canal to make it imperatively necessary that legislation should be enacted to fix the method by which the canal shall be maintained and controlled and the zone governed. The fact is that to-day there is no statutory law by authority of which the President is maintaining the government of the zone. Such authority was given in an amendment to the Spooner Act, which expired by the terms of its own limitation some years ago. Since that time the government has continued, under the advice of the Attorney General that in the absence of action by Congress, there is necessarily an implied authority on the part of the Executive to maintain a government in a territory in which he has to see that the laws are executed. The fact that we have been able thus to get along during the important days of construction without legislation expressly formulating the government of the zone, or delegating the creation of it to the President, is not a reason for supposing that we may continue the same kind of a government after the construction is finished. The implied authority of the President to maintain a civil government in the zone may be derived from the mandatory direction given him in the original Spooner Act, by which he was commanded to build the canal; but certainly, now that the canal is about to be completed and to be put under a permanent management, there ought to be specific statutory authority for its regulation and control and for the government of the zone, which we hold for the chief and main purpose of operating the canal.

I fully concur with the Secretary of War that the problem is simply the management of a great public work, and not the government of a local republic; that every provision must be directed toward the successful maintenance of the canal as an avenue of commerce, and that all provisions for the government of those who live within the zone should be subordinate to the main purpose.

The zone is 40 miles long and 10 miles wide. Now, it has a population of 50,000 or 60,000, but as soon as the work of construction is completed, the towns which make up this population will be deserted, and only comparatively few natives will continue their residence there. The control of them ought to approximate a military government. One judge and two justices of the peace will be sufficient to attend to all the judicial and litigated business there is. With a few fundamental laws of Congress, the zone should be governed by the orders of the President, issued through the War Department, as it is to-day. Provisions can be made for the guaranties of life, liberty, and property, but beyond those, the government should be that of a military reservation, managed in connection with this great highway of trade.

FURNISHING SUPPLIES AND REPAIRS.

In my last annual message I discussed at length the reasons for the Government's assuming the task of furnishing to all ships that use the canal, whether our own naval vessels or others, the supplies of coal and oil and other necessities with which they must be replenished either before or after passing through the canal, together with the dock facilities and repairs of every character. This it is thought wise to do through the Government, because the Government must establish for itself, for its own naval vessels, large depots and dry docks and warehouses, and these may easily be enlarged so as to secure to the world public using the canal reasonable prices and a certainty that there will be no discrimination between those who wish to avail themselves of such facilities.

TOLLS.

I renew my recommendation with respect to the tolls of the canal that within limits, which shall seem wise to Congress, the power of fixing tolls be given to the President. In order to arrive at a proper conclusion, there must be some experimenting, and this can not be done if Congress does not delegate the power to one who can act expeditiously.

POWER EXISTS TO RELIEVE AMERICAN SHIPPING.

I am very confident that the United States has the power to relieve from the payment of tolls any part of our shipping that Congress deems wise. We own the canal. It was our money that built it. We have the right to charge tolls for its use. Those tolls must be the same to everyone; but when we are dealing with our own ships, the practice of many Governments of subsidizing their own merchant vessels is so well established in general that a subsidy equal to the tolls, an equivalent remission of tolls, can not be held to be a discrimination in the use of the canal. The practice in the Suez Canal makes this clear. The experiment in tolls to be made by the President would doubtless disclose how great a burden of tolls the coastwise trade between the Atlantic and the Pacific coast could bear without preventing its usefulness in competition with the transcontinental railroads. One of the chief reasons for building the canal was to set up this competition and to bring the two shores closer together as a practical trade problem. It may be that the tolls will have to be wholly remitted. I do not think this is the best principle, because I believe that the cost of such a Government work as the Panama Canal ought to be imposed gradually but certainly upon the trade which it creates and makes possible. So far as we can, consistent with the development of the world's trade through the canal, and the benefit which it was intended to secure to the east and west coastwise trade, we ought to labor to secure from the canal tolls a sufficient amount ultimately to meet the debt which we have assumed and to pay the interest.

THE PHILIPPINE ISLANDS.

In respect to the Philippines, I urgently join in the recommendation of the Secretary of War that the act of February 6, 1905, limiting the indebtedness that may be incurred by the Philippine Government for the construction of public works, be increased from $5,000,000 to $15,000,000. The finances of that Government are in excellent condition. The maximum sum mentioned is quite low as compared with the amount of indebtedness of other governments with similar resources, and the success which has attended the expenditure of the $5,000,000 in the useful improvements of the harbors and other places in the Islands justifies and requires additional expenditures for like purposes.

NATURALIZATION.

I also join in the recommendation that the legislature of the Philippine Islands be authorized to provide for the naturalization of Filipinos and others who by the present law are treated as aliens, so as to enable them to become citizens of the Philippine Islands.

FRIARS' LANDS.

Pending an investigation by Congress at its last session, through one of its committees, into the disposition of the friars' lands, Secretary Dickinson directed that the friars' lands should not be sold in excess of the limits fixed for the public lands until Congress should pass upon the subject or should have concluded its investigation. This order has been an obstruction to the disposition of the lands, and I expect to direct the Secretary of War to return to the practice under the opinion of the Attorney General which will enable us to dispose of the lands much more promptly, and to prepare a sinking fund with which to meet the $7,000,000 of bonds issued for the purchase of the lands. I have no doubt whatever that the Attorney General's construction was a proper one, and that it is in the interest of everyone that the land shall be promptly disposed of. The danger of creating a monopoly of ownership in lands under the statutes as construed is nothing. There are only two tracts of 60,000 acres each unimproved and in remote Provinces that are likely to be disposed of in bulk, and the rest of the lands are subject to the limitation that they shall be first offered to the present tenants and lessors who hold them in small tracts.

RIVERS AND HARBORS.

The estimates for the river and harbor improvements reach $32,-000,000 for the coming year. I wish to urge that whenever a project has been adopted by Congress as one to be completed, the more money which can be economically expended in its construction in each year, the greater the ultimate economy. This has especial application to the improvement of the Mississippi River and its large branches. It seems to me that an increase in the amount of money now being annually expended in the improvement of the Ohio River which has been formally adopted by Congress would be in the interest of the public. A similar change ought to be made during the present Congress, in the amount to be appropriated for the Missouri River. The engineers say that the cost of the improvement of the Missouri River from Kansas City to St. Louis, in order to secure 6 feet as a permanent channel, will reach $20,000,000. There have been at least three recommendations from the Chief of Engineers that if the improvement be adopted, $2,000,000 should be expended upon it annually. This particular improvement is especially entitled to the attention of Congress, because a company has been organized in Kansas City, with a capital of $1,000,000, which has built steamers and barges, and is actually using the river for transportation in order to show what can be done in the way of affecting rates between Kansas City and St. Louis, and in order to manifest their good faith and confidence in respect of the improvement. I urgently recommend that the appropriation for this improvement be increased from $600,000, as recommended now in the completion of a contract, to $2,000,000 annually, so that the work may be done in 10 years.

WATERWAY FROM THE LAKES TO THE GULF.

The project for a navigable waterway from Lake Michigan to the mouth of the Illinois River, and thence via the Mississippi to the Gulf of Mexico, is one of national importance. In view of the work already accomplished by the Sanitary District of Chicago, an agency of the State of Illinois, which has constructed the most difficult and costly stretch of this waterway and made it an asset of the Nation, and in view of the fact that the people of Illinois have authorized the expenditure of $20,000,000 to carry this waterway 62 miles farther to Utica, I feel that it is fitting that this work should be supplemented by the Government, and that the expenditures recommended by the special board of engineers on the waterway from Utica to the mouth of the Illinois River be made upon lines which while providing a waterway for the Nation should otherwise benefit that State to the fullest extent. I recommend that the term of service of said special board of engineers be continued, and that it be empowered to reopen the question of the treatment of the lower Illinois River, and to negotiate with a properly constituted commission representing the State of Illinois, and to agree upon a plan for the improvement of the lower Illinois River and upon the extent to which the United States may properly cooperate with the State of Illinois in securing the construction of a navigable waterway from Lockport to the mouth of the Illinois River in conjunction with the development of water power by that State between Lockport and Utica.

THE DEPARTMENT OF JUSTICE.

Removal of clerks of Federal courts.

The report of the Attorney General shows that he has subjected to close examination the accounts of the clerks of the Federal courts; that he has found a good many which disclose irregularities or dishonesty; but that he has had considerable difficulty in securing an effective prosecution or removal of the clerks thus derelict. I am certainly not unduly prejudiced against the Federal courts, but the fact is that the long and confidential relations which grow out of the tenure for life on the part of the judge and the practical tenure for life on the part of the clerk are not calculated to secure the strictness of dealing by the judge with the clerk in respect to his fees and accounts which assures in the clerk's conduct a freedom from overcharges and carelessness. The relationship between the judge and the clerk makes it ungracious for members of the bar to complain of the clerk or for department examiners to make charges against him to be heard by the court, and an order of removal of a clerk and a judgment for the recovery of fees are in some cases reluctantly entered by the judge. For this reason I recommend an amendment to the law whereby the President shall be given power to remove the clerks for cause. This provision need not interfere with the right of the judge to appoint his clerk or to remove him.

French spoliation awards.

In my last message, I recommended to Congress that it authorize the payment of the findings or judgments of the Court of Claims in the matter of the French spoliation cases. There has been no appropriation to pay these judgments since 1905. The findings and awards were obtained after a very bitter fight, the Government succeeding in about 75 per cent of the cases. The amount of the awards ought, as a matter of good faith on the part of the Government, to be paid.

EMPLOYERS' LIABILITY AND WORKMEN'S COMPENSATION COMMISSION.

The limitation of the liability of the master to his servant for personal injuries to such as are occasioned by his fault has been abandoned in most civilized countries and provision made whereby the employee injured in the course of his employment is compensated for his loss of working ability irrespective of negligence. The principle upon which such provision proceeds is that accidental injuries to workmen in modern industry, with its vast complexity and inherent dangers arising from complicated machinery and the use of the great forces of steam and electricity, should be regarded as risks of the industry and the loss borne in some equitable proportion by those who for their own profit engage therein. In recognition of this the last Congress authorized the appointment of a commission to investigate the subject of employers' liability and workmen's compensation and to report the result of their investigations, through the President, to Congress. This commission was appointed and has been at work, holding hearings, gathering data, and considering the subject, and it is expected will be able to report by the first of the year, in accordance with the provisions of the law. It is hoped and expected that the commission will suggest legislation which will enable us to put in the place of the present wasteful and sometimes unjust system of employers' liability a plan of compensation which will afford some certain and definite relief to all employees who are injured in the course of their employment in those industries which are subject to the regulating power of Congress.

MEASURES TO PREVENT DELAY AND UNNECESSARY COST OF LITIGATION.

In promotion of the movement for the prevention of delay and unnecessary cost, in litigation, I am glad to say that the Supreme Court has taken steps to reform the present equity rules of the Federal courts, and that we may in the near future expect a revision of them which will be a long step in the right direction.

The American Bar Association has recommended to Congress several bills expediting procedure, one of which has already passed the House unanimously, February 6, 1911. This directs that no judgment should be set aside or reversed, or new trial granted, unless it appears to the court, after an examination of the entire cause, that the error complained of has injuriously affected the substantial rights of the parties, and also provides for the submission of issues of fact to a jury, reserving questions of law for subsequent argument and decision. I hope this bill will pass the Senate and become law, for it will simplify the procedure at law.

Another bill to amend chapter 11 of the Judicial Code, in order to avoid errors in pleading, was presented by the same association, and one enlarging the jurisdiction of the Supreme Court so as to permit that court to examine, upon a writ of error, all cases in which any right or title is claimed under the Constitution, or any statute or treaty of the United States, whether the decision in the court below has been against the right or title or in its favor. Both these measures are in the interest of justice and should be passed.

POST OFFICE.

At the beginning of the present administration in 1909 the postal service was in arrears to the extent of $17,479,770.47. It was very much the largest deficit on record. In the brief space of two years this has been turned into a surplus of $220,000, which has been accomplished without curtailment of the postal facilities, as may be seen by the fact that there have been established 3,744 new post offices; delivery by carrier has been added to the service in 186 cities; 2,516 new rural routes have been established, covering 60,000 miles; the force of postal employees has been increased in these two years by more than 8,000, and their average annual salary has had a substantial increase.

POSTAL-SAVINGS SYSTEM.

On January 3, 1911, postal-savings depositories were established experimentally in 48 States and Territories. After three months' successful operation the system was extended as rapidly as feasible to the 7,500 post offices of the first, second, and third classes constituting the presidential grade. By the end of the year practically all of these will have been designated and then the system will be extended to all fourth-class post offices doing a money-order business.

In selecting post offices for depositories consideration was given to the efficiency of the postmasters and only those offices where the ratings were satisfactory to the department have been designated. Withholding designation from postmasters with unsatisfactory ratings has had a salutary effect on the service.

The deposits have kept pace with the extension of the system. Amounting to only $60,652 at the end of the first month's operation in the experimental offices, they increased to $679,310 by July, and now after 11 months of operation have reached a total of $11,000,000. This sum is distributed among 2,710 banks and protected under the law by bonds deposited with the Treasurer of the United States.

Under the method adopted for the conduct of the system certificates are issued as evidence of deposits, and accounts with depositors are kept by the post offices instead of by the department. Compared with the practice in other countries of entering deposits in pass books and keeping at the central office a ledger account with each depositor, the use of the certificate has resulted in great economy of administration.

The depositors thus far number approximately 150,000. They include 40 nationalities, native Americans largely predominating and English and Italians coming next.

The first conversion of deposits into United States bonds bearing interest at the rate of 2½ per cent occurred on July 1, 1911, the amount of deposits exchanged being $41,900, or a little more than 6 per cent of the total outstanding certificates of deposit on June 30. Of this issue, bonds to the value of $6,120 were in coupon form and $35,780 in registered form.

PARCEL POST.

Steps should be taken immediately for the establishment of a rural parcel post. In the estimates of appropriations needed for the maintenance of the postal service for the ensuing fiscal year an item of $150,000 has been inserted to cover the preliminary expense of establishing a parcel post on rural mail routes, as well as to cover an investigation having for its object the final establishment of a general parcel post on all railway and steamboat transportation routes. The department believes that after the initial expenses of establishing the system are defrayed and the parcel post is in full operation on the rural routes it will not only bring in sufficient revenue to meet its cost, but also a surplus that can be utilized in paying the expenses of a parcel post in the City Delivery Service.

It is hoped that Congress will authorize the immediate establishment of a limited parcel post on such rural routes as may be selected, providing for the delivery along the routes of parcels not exceeding eleven pounds, which is the weight limit for the international parcel post, or at the post office from which such route emanates, or on another route emanating from the same office. Such preliminary service will prepare the way for the more thorough and comprehensive inquiry contemplated in asking for the appropriation mentioned, enable the department to gain definite information concerning the practical operation of a general system, and at the same time extend the benefit of the service to a class of people who, above all others, are specially in need of it.

The suggestion that we have a general parcel post has awakened great opposition on the part of some who think that it will have the effect to destroy the business of the country storekeeper. Instead of doing this, I think the change will greatly increase business for the benefit of all. The reduction in the cost of living it will bring about ought to make its coming certain.

THE NAVY DEPARTMENT.

On the 2d of November last, I reviewed the fighting fleet of battleships and other vessels assembled in New York Harbor, consisting of 24 battleships, 2 armored cruisers, 2 cruisers, 22 destroyers, 12 torpedo boats, 8 submarines, and other attendant vessels, making 98 vessels of all classes, of a tonnage of 576,634 tons. Those who saw the fleet were struck with its preparedness and with its high military efficiency. All Americans should be proud of its personnel.

The fleet was deficient in the number of torpedo destroyers, in cruisers, and in colliers, as well as in large battleship cruisers, which are now becoming a very important feature of foreign navies, notably the British, German, and Japanese.

The building plan for this year contemplates two battleships and two colliers. This is because the other and smaller vessels can be built much more rapidly in case of emergency than the battleships, and we certainly ought to continue the policy of two battleships a year until after the Panama Canal is finished and until in our first line and in our reserve line we can number 40 available vessels of proper armament and size.

The reorganization of the Navy and the appointment of four aids to the Secretary have continued to demonstrate their usefulness. It would be difficult now to administer the affairs of the Navy without the expert counsel and advice of these aids, and I renew the recommendation which I made last year, that the aids be recognized by statute.

It is certain that the Navy, with its present size, should have admirals in active command higher than rear admirals. The recognized grades in order are: Admiral of the fleet, admiral, vice admiral, and rear admiral. Our great battleship fleet is commanded by a rear admiral, with four other rear admirals under his orders. This is not as it should be, and when questions of precedence arise between our naval officers and those of European navies, the American rear admiral, though in command of ten times the force of a foreign vice admiral, must yield precedence to the latter. Such an absurdity ought not to prevail, and it can be avoided by the creation of two or three positions of flag rank above that of rear admiral.

I attended the opening of the new training school at North Chicago, Ill., and am glad to note the opportunity which this gives for drawing upon young men of the country from the interior, from farms, stores, shops, and offices, which insures a high average of intelligence and character among them, and which they showed in the very wonderful improvement in discipline and drill which only a few short weeks' presence at the naval station had made.

I invite your attention to the consideration of the new system of detention and of punishment for Army and Navy enlisted men which has obtained in Great Britain, and which has made greatly for the better control of the men. We should adopt a similar system here.

Like the Treasury Department and the War Department, the Navy Department has given much attention to economy in administration, and has cut down a number of unnecessary expenses and reduced its estimates except for construction and the increase that that involves.

I urge upon Congress the necessity for an immediate increase of 2,000 men in the enlisted strength of the Navy, provided for in the estimates. Four thousand more are now needed to man all the available vessels.

There are in the service to-day about 47,750 enlisted men of all ratings.

Careful computation shows that in April, 1912, 49,166 men will be required for vessels in commission, and 3,000 apprentice seamen should be kept under training at all times.

ABOLITION OF NAVY YARDS.

The Secretary of the Navy has recommended the abolition of certain of the smaller and unnecessary navy yards, and in order to furnish a complete and comprehensive report has referred the question of all navy yards to the joint board of the Army and Navy. This board will shortly make its report and the Secretary of the Navy advises me that his recommendations on the subject will be presented early in the coming year. The measure of economy contained in a proper handling of this subject is so great and so important to the interests of the Nation that I shall present it to Congress as a separate subject apart from my annual message. Concentration of the necessary work for naval vessels in a few navy yards on each coast is a vital necessity if proper economy in Government expenditures is to be attained.

AMALGAMATION OF STAFF CORPS IN THE NAVY.

The Secretary of the Navy is striving to unify the various corps of the Navy to the extent possible and thereby stimulate a Navy spirit as distinguished from a corps spirit. In this he has my warm support.

All officers are to be naval officers first and specialists afterwards. This means that officers will take up at least one specialty, such as ordnance, construction, or engineering. This is practically what is done now, only some of the specialists, like the pay officers and naval constructors, are not of the line. It is proposed to make them all of the line.

All combatant corps should obviously be of the line. This necessitates amalgamating the pay officers and also those engaged in the technical work of producing the finished ship. This is at present the case with the single exception of the naval constructors, whom it is now proposed to amalgamate with the line.

COUNCIL OF NATIONAL DEFENSE.

I urge again upon Congress the desirability of establishing the council of national defense. The bill to establish this council was before Congress last winter, and it is hoped that this legislation will pass during the present session. The purpose of the council is to determine the general policy of national defense and to recommend to Congress and to the President such measures relating to it as it shall deem necessary and expedient.

No such machinery is now provided by which the readiness of the Army and Navy may be improved and the programs of military and naval requirements shall be coordinated and properly scrutinized with a view of the necessities of the whole Nation rather than of separate departments.

DEPARTMENTS OF AGRICULTURE AND COMMERCE AND LABOR.

For the consideration of matters which are pending or have been disposed of in the Agricultural Department and in the Department of Commerce and Labor, I refer to the very excellent reports of the Secretaries of those departments. I shall not be able to submit to Congress until after the Christmas holidays the question of conservation of our resources arising in Alaska and the West and the question of the rate for second-class mail matter in the Post Office Department.

COMMISSION ON EFFICIENCY AND ECONOMY.

The law does not require the submission of the reports of the Commission on Economy and Efficiency until the 31st of December. I shall therefore not be able to submit a report of the work of that commission until the assembling of Congress after the holidays.

CIVIL RETIREMENT AND CONTRIBUTORY PENSION SYSTEM.

I have already advocated, in my last annual message, the adoption of a civil-service retirement system, with a contributory feature to it so as to reduce to a minimum the cost to the Government of the pensions to be paid. After considerable reflection, I am very much opposed to a pension system that involves no contribution from the employees. I think the experience of other governments justifies this view; but the crying necessity for some such contributory system, with possibly a preliminary governmental outlay, in order to cover the initial cost and to set the system going at once while the contributions are accumulating, is manifest on every side. Nothing will so much promote the economy and efficiency of the Government as such a system.

ELIMINATION OF ALL LOCAL OFFICES FROM POLITICS.

I wish to renew again my recommendation that all the local offices throughout the country, including collectors of internal revenue, collectors of customs, postmasters of all four classes, immigration commissioners and marshals, should be by law covered into the classified service, the necessity for confirmation by the Senate be removed, and the President and the others, whose time is now taken up in distributing this patronage under the custom that has prevailed since the beginning of the Government in accordance with the recommendation of the Senators and Congressmen of the majority party, should be relieved from this burden. I am confident that such a change would greatly reduce the cost of administering the Government, and that it would add greatly to its efficiency. It would take away the power to use the patronage of the Government for political purposes. When officers are recommended by Senators and Congressmen from political motives and for political services rendered, it is impossible to expect that while in office the appointees will not regard their tenure as more or less dependent upon continued political service for their patrons, and no regulations, however stiff or rigid, will prevent this, because such regulations, in view of the method and motive for selection, are plainly inconsistent and deemed hardly worthy of respect.

FOURTH ANNUAL MESSAGE.

Part I.

[On Our Foreign Relations.]

THE WHITE HOUSE, *December 3, 1912.*

To the Senate and House of Representatives:

The foreign relations of the United States actually and potentially affect the state of the Union to a degree not widely realized and hardly surpassed by any other factor in the welfare of the whole Nation. The position of the United States in the moral, intellectual, and material relations of the family of nations should be a matter of vital interest to every patriotic citizen. The national prosperity and power impose upon us duties which we can not shirk if we are to be true to our ideals. The tremendous growth of the export trade of the United States has already made that trade a very real factor in the industrial and commercial prosperity of the country. With the development of our industries the foreign commerce of the United States must rapidly become a still more essential factor in its economic welfare. Whether we have a farseeing and wise diplomacy and are not recklessly plunged into unnecessary wars, and whether our foreign policies are based upon an intelligent grasp of present-day world conditions and a clear view of the potentialities of the future, or are governed by a temporary and timid expediency or by narrow views befitting an infant nation, are questions in the alternative consideration of which must convince any thoughtful citizen that no department of national polity offers greater opportunity for promoting the interests of the whole people on the one hand, or greater chance on the other of permanent national injury, than that which deals with the foreign relations of the United States.

The fundamental foreign policies of the United States should be raised high above the conflict of partisanship and wholly dissociated from differences as to domestic policy. In its foreign affairs the United States should present to the world a united front. The intellectual, financial, and industrial interests of the country and the publicist, the wage earner, the farmer, and citizen of whatever occupation must cooperate in a spirit of high patriotism to promote that national solidarity which is indispensable to national efficiency and to the attainment of national ideals.

The relations of the United States with all foreign powers remain upon a sound basis of peace, harmony, and friendship. A greater insistence upon justice to American citizens or interests wherever it may have been denied and a stronger emphasis of the need of mutuality in commercial and other relations have only served to strengthen our friendships with foreign countries by placing those friendships upon a firm foundation of realities as well as aspirations.

Before briefly reviewing the more important events of the last year in our foreign relations, which it is my duty to do as charged with their conduct and because diplomatic affairs are not of a nature to make it appropriate that the Secretary of State make a formal annual report, I desire to touch upon some of the essentials to the safe management of the foreign relations of the United States and to endeavor, also, to define clearly certain concrete policies which are the logical modern corollaries of the undisputed and traditional fundamentals of the foreign policy of the United States.

REORGANIZATION OF THE STATE DEPARTMENT

At the beginning of the present administration the United States, having fully entered upon its position as a world power, with the responsibilities thrust upon it by the results of the Spanish-American War, and already engaged in laying the groundwork of a vast foreign trade upon which it should one day become more and more dependent, found itself without the machinery for giving thorough attention to, and taking effective action upon, a mass of intricate business vital to American interests in every country in the world.

The Department of State was an archaic and inadequate machine lacking most of the attributes of the foreign office of any great modern power. With an appropriation made upon my recommendation by the Congress on August 5, 1909, the Department of State was completely reorganized. There were created Divisions of Latin-American Affairs and of Far Eastern, Near Eastern, and Western European Affairs. To these divisions were called from the foreign service diplomatic and consular officers possessing experience and knowledge gained by actual service in different parts of the world and thus familiar with political and commercial conditions in the regions concerned. The work was highly specialized. The result is that where previously this Government from time to time would emphasize in its foreign relations one or another policy, now American interests in every quarter of the globe are being cultivated with equal assiduity. This principle of politico-geographical division possesses also the good feature of making possible rotation between the officers of the departmental, the diplomatic, and the consular branches of the foreign service, and thus keeps the whole diplomatic and consular establishments under the Department of State in close touch and equally inspired with the aims and policy of the Government. Through the newly created Division of Information the foreign service is kept fully informed of what transpires from day to day in the international relations of the country, and contemporary foreign comment affecting American interests is promptly brought to the attention of the department. The law offices of the department were greatly strengthened. There were added foreign-trade advisers to cooperate with the diplomatic and consular bureaus and the politico-geographical divisions in the innumerable matters where commercial diplomacy or consular work calls for such special knowledge. The same officers, together with the rest of the new organization, are able at all times to give to American citizens accurate information as to conditions in foreign countries with which they have business and likewise to cooperate more effectively with the Congress and also with the other executive departments.

MERIT SYSTEM IN CONSULAR AND DIPLOMATIC CORPS

Expert knowledge and professional training must evidently be the essence of this reorganization. Without a trained foreign service there would not be men available for the work in the reorganized Department of State. President Cleveland had taken the first step toward introducing the merit system in the foreign service. That had been followed by the application of the merit principle, with excellent results, to the entire consular branch. Almost nothing, however, had been done in this direction with regard to the Diplomatic Service. In this age of commercial diplomacy it was evidently of the first importance to train an adequate personnel in that branch of the service. Therefore, on November 26, 1909, by an Executive order I placed the Diplomatic Service up to the grade of secretary of embassy, inclusive, upon exactly the same strict nonpartisan basis of the merit system, rigid examination for appointment and promotion only for efficiency, as had been maintained without exception in the Consular Service.

STATISTICS AS TO MERIT AND NONPARTISAN CHARACTER OF APPOINTMENTS

How faithful to the merit system and how nonpartisan has been the conduct of the Diplomatic and Consular Services in the last four years may be judged from the following: Three ambassadors now serving held their present rank at the beginning of my administration. Of the ten ambassadors whom I have appointed, five were by promotion from the rank of minister. Nine ministers now serving held their present rank at the beginning of my administration. Of the thirty ministers whom I have appointed, eleven were promoted from the lower grades of the foreign service or from the Department of State. Of the nineteen missions in Latin America, where our relations are close and our interest is great, fifteen chiefs of mission are service men, three having entered the service during this administration. Thirty-seven secretaries of embassy or legation who have received their initial appointments after passing successfully the required examination were chosen for ascertained fitness, without regard to political affiliations. A dearth of candidates from Southern and Western States has alone made it impossible thus far completely to equalize all the States' representations in the foreign service. In the effort to equalize the representation of the various States in the Consular Service I have made sixteen of the twenty-nine new appointments as consul which have occurred during my administration from the Southern States. This is 55 per cent. Every other consular appointment made, including the promotion of eleven young men from the consular assistant and student interpreter corps, has been by promotion or transfer, based solely upon efficiency shown in the service.

In order to assure to the business and other interests of the

United States a continuance of the resulting benefits of this reform, I earnestly renew my previous recommendations of legislation making it permanent along some such lines as those of the measure now pending in Congress.

LARGER PROVISION FOR EMBASSIES AND LEGATIONS AND FOR OTHER EXPENSES OF OUR FOREIGN REPRESENTATIVES RECOMMENDED

In connection with legislation for the amelioration of the foreign service, I wish to invite attention to the advisability of placing the salary appropriations upon a better basis. I believe that the best results would be obtained by a moderate scale of salaries, with adequate funds for the expense of proper representation, based in each case upon the scale and cost of living at each post, controlled by a system of accounting, and under the general direction of the Department of State.

In line with the object which I have sought of placing our foreign service on a basis of permanency, I have at various times advocated provision by Congress for the acquisition of Government-owned buildings for the residence and offices of our diplomatic officers, so as to place them more nearly on an equality with similar officers of other nations and to do away with the discrimination which otherwise must necessarily be made, in some cases, in favor of men having large private fortunes. The act of Congress which I approved on February 17, 1911, was a right step in this direction. The Secretary of State has already made the limited recommendations permitted by the act for any one year, and it is my hope that the bill introduced in the House of Representatives to carry out these recommendations will be favorably acted on by the Congress during its present session.

In some Latin-American countries the expense of government-owned legations will be less than elsewhere, and it is certainly very urgent that in such countries as some of the Republics of Central America and the Caribbean, where it is peculiarly difficult to rent suitable quarters, the representatives of the United States should be justly and adequately provided with dignified and suitable official residences. Indeed, it is high time that the dignity and power of this great Nation should be fittingly signalized by proper buildings for the occupancy of the Nation's representatives everywhere abroad.

DIPLOMACY A HAND MAID OF COMMERCIAL INTERCOURSE AND PEACE

The diplomacy of the present administration has sought to respond to modern ideas of commercial intercourse. This policy has been characterized as substituting dollars for bullets. It is one that appeals alike to idealistic humanitarian sentiments, to the dictates of sound policy and strategy, and to legitimate commercial aims. It is an effort frankly directed to the increase of American trade upon the axiomatic principle that the Government of the United States shall extend all proper support to every legitimate and beneficial American enterprise abroad. How great have been the results of this diplomacy, coupled with the maximum and minimum provision of the tariff law, will be seen by some consideration of the wonderful increase in the export trade of the United States. Because modern diplomacy is commercial, there has been a disposition in some quarters to attribute to it none but materialistic aims. How strikingly erroneous is such an impression may be seen from a study of the results by which the diplomacy of the United States can be judged.

SUCCESSFUL EFFORTS IN PROMOTION OF PEACE

In the field of work toward the ideals of peace this Government negotiated, but to my regret was unable to consummate, two arbitration treaties which set the highest mark of the aspiration of nations toward the substitution of arbitration and reason for war in the settlement of international disputes. Through the efforts of American diplomacy several wars have been prevented or ended. I refer to the successful tripartite mediation of the Argentine Republic, Brazil, and the United States between Peru and Ecuador; the bringing of the boundary dispute between Panama and Costa Rica to peaceful arbitration; the staying of warlike preparations when Haiti and the Dominican Republic were on the verge of hostilities; the stopping of a war in Nicaragua; the halting of internecine strife in Honduras. The Government of the United States was thanked for its influence toward the restoration of amicable relations between the Argentine Republic and Bolivia. The diplomacy of the United States is active in seeking to assuage the remaining ill-feeling between this country and the Republic of Colombia. In the recent civil war in China the United States successfully joined with the other interested powers in urging an early cessation of hostilities. An agreement has been reached between the Governments of Chile and Peru whereby the celebrated Tacna-Arica dispute, which has so long embittered international relations on the west coast of South America, has at last been adjusted. Simultaneously came the news that the boundary dispute between Peru and Ecuador had entered upon a stage of amicable settlement. The position of the United States in reference to the Tacna-Arica dispute between Chile and Peru has been one of nonintervention, but one of friendly influence and pacific counsel throughout the period during which the dispute in question has been the subject of interchange of views between this Government and the two Governments immediately concerned. In the general easing of international tension on the west coast of South America the tripartite mediation, to which I have referred, has been a most potent and beneficent factor.

CHINA

In China the policy of encouraging financial investment to enable that country to help itself has had the result of giving new life and practical application to the open-door policy. The consistent purpose of the present administration has been to encourage the use of American capital in the development of China by the promotion of those essential reforms to which China is pledged by treaties with the United States and other powers. The hypothecation to foreign bankers in connection with certain industrial enterprises, such as the Hukuang railways, of the national revenues upon which these reforms depended, led the Department of State early in the administration to demand for American citizens participation in such enterprises, in order that the United States might have equal rights and an equal voice in all questions pertaining to the disposition of the public revenues concerned. The same policy of promoting international accord among the powers having similar treaty rights as ourselves in the matters of reform, which could not be put into practical effect without the common consent of all, was likewise adopted in the case of the loan desired by China for the reform of its currency. The principle of international cooperation in matters of common interest upon which our policy had already been based in all of the above instances has admittedly been a great factor in that concert of the powers which has been so happily conspicuous during the perilous period of transition through which the great Chinese nation has been passing.

CENTRAL AMERICA NEEDS OUR HELP IN DEBT ADJUSTMENT

In Central America the aim has been to help such countries as Nicaragua and Honduras to help themselves. They are the immediate beneficiaries. The national benefit to the United States is two-fold. First, it is obvious that the Monroe doctrine is more vital in the neighborhood of the Panama Canal and the zone of the Caribbean than anywhere else. There, too, the maintenance of that doctrine falls most heavily upon the United States. It is therefore essential that the countries within that sphere shall be removed from the jeopardy involved by heavy foreign debt and chaotic national finances and from the ever-present danger of international complications due to disorder at home. Hence the United States has been glad to encourage and support American bankers who were willing to lend a helping hand to the financial rehabilitation of such countries because this financial rehabilitation and the protection of their customhouses from being the prey of would-be dictators would remove at one stroke the menace of foreign creditors and the menace of revolutionary disorder.

The second advantage of the United States is one affecting chiefly all the southern and Gulf ports and the business and industry of the South. The Republics of Central America and the Caribbean possess great natural wealth. They need only a measure of stability and the means of financial regeneration to enter upon an era of peace and prosperity, bringing profit and happiness to themselves and at the same time creating conditions sure to lead to a flourishing interchange of trade with this country.

I wish to call your especial attention to the recent occurrences in Nicaragua, for I believe the terrible events recorded there during the revolution of the past summer—the useless loss of life, the devastation of property, the bombardment of defenseless cities, the killing and wounding of women and children, the torturing of noncombatants to exact contributions, and the suffering of thousands of human beings—might have been averted had the Department of State, through approval of the loan convention by the Senate, been permitted to carry out its now well-developed policy of encouraging the extending of financial aid to weak Central American States with the primary objects of avoiding just such revolutions by assisting those Republics to rehabilitate their finances, to establish their currency on a stable basis, to remove the customhouses from the danger of revolutions by arranging for their secure administration, and to establish reliable banks.

During this last revolution in Nicaragua, the Government of that Republic having admitted its inability to protect American life and property against acts of sheer lawlessness on the part of the malcontents, and having requested this Government to assume that office, it became necessary to land over 2,000 marines and bluejackets in Nicaragua. Owing to their presence the constituted Government of Nicaragua was free to devote its attention wholly to its internal troubles, and was thus enabled to stamp out the rebellion in a short space of time. When the Red Cross supplies sent to Granada had been exhausted, 8,000 persons having been given food in one day upon the arrival of the American forces, our men supplied other unfortunate, needy Nicaraguans from their own haversacks. I wish to congratulate the officers and men of the United States navy and Marine Corps who took part in reestablishing order in Nicaragua upon their splendid conduct, and to record with sorrow the death of seven American marines and bluejackets. Since the reestablishment of peace and order, elections have been held amid conditions of quiet and tranquility. Nearly all the American marines have now been withdrawn. The country should soon be on the road to recovery. The only apparent danger now threatening Nicaragua arises from the shortage of funds. Although American bankers have already rendered assistance, they may naturally be loath to advance a loan adequate to set the country upon its feet without the support of some such convention as that of June, 1911, upon which the Senate has not yet acted.

ENFORCEMENT OF NEUTRALITY LAWS

In the general effort to contribute to the enjoyment of peace by those Republics which are near neighbors of the United States, the administration has enforced the so-called neutrality statutes with a new vigor, and those statutes were greatly strengthened in restricting the exportation of arms and munitions by the joint resolution of last March. It is still a regrettable fact that certain American ports are made the rendezvous of professional revolutionists and others engaged in intrigue against the peace of those Republics. It must be admitted that occasionally a revolution in this region is justified as a real popular movement to throw off the shackles of a vicious and tyrannical government. Such was the Nicaraguan revolution against the Zelaya régime. A nation enjoying our liberal institutions can not escape sympathy with a true popular movement, and one so well justified. In very many cases, however, revolutions in the Republics in question have no basis in principle, but are due merely to the machinations of conscienceless and ambitious men, and have no effect but to bring new suffering and fresh burdens to an already oppressed people. The question whether the use of American ports as *foci* of revolutionary intrigue can be best dealt with by a further amendment to the neutrality statutes or whether it would be safer to deal with special cases by special laws is one worthy of the careful consideration of the Congress.

VISIT OF SECRETARY KNOX TO CENTRAL AMERICA AND THE CARIBBEAN

Impressed with the particular importance of the relations between the United States and the Republics of Central America and the Caribbean region, which of necessity must become still more intimate by reason of the mutual advantages which will be presented by the opening of the Panama Canal, I directed the Secretary of State last February to visit these Republics for the purpose of giving evidence of the sincere friendship and good will which the Government and people of the United States bear toward them. Ten Republics were visited. Everywhere he was received with a cordiality of welcome and a generosity of hospitality such as to impress me deeply and to merit our warmest thanks. The appreciation of the Governments and people of the countries visited, which has been appropriately shown in various ways, leaves me no doubt that his visit will conduce to that closer union and better understanding between the United States and those Republics which I have had it much at heart to promote.

OUR MEXICAN POLICY

For two years revolution and counter-revolution has distraught the neighboring Republic of Mexico. Brigandage has involved a great deal of depredation upon foreign interests. There have constantly recurred questions of extreme delicacy. On several occasions very difficult situations have arisen on our frontier. Throughout this trying period, the policy of the United States has been one of patient nonintervention, steadfast recognition of constituted authority in the neighboring nation, and the exertion of every effort to care for American interests. I profoundly hope that the Mexican nation may soon resume the path of order, prosperity, and progress. To that nation in its sore troubles, the sympathetic friendship of the United States has been demonstrated to a high degree. There were in Mexico at the beginning of the revolution some thirty or forty thousand American citizens engaged in enterprises contributing greatly to the prosperity of that Republic and also benefiting the important trade between the two countries. The investment of American capital in Mexico has been estimated at $1,000,000,000. The responsibility of endeavoring to safeguard those interests and the dangers inseparable from propinquity to so turbulent a situation have been great, but I am happy to have been able to adhere to the policy above outlined—a policy which I hope may be soon justified by the complete success of the Mexican people in regaining the blessings of peace and good order.

AGRICULTURAL CREDITS

A most important work, accomplished in the past year by the American diplomatic officers in Europe, is the investigation of the agricultural credit system in the European countries. Both as a means to afford relief to the consumers of this country through a more thorough development of agricultural resources and as a means of more sufficiently maintaining the agricultural population, the project to establish credit facilities for the farmers is a concern of vital importance to this Nation. No evidence of prosperity among well-established farmers should blind us to the fact that lack of capital is preventing a development of the Nation's agricultural resources and an adequate increase of the land under cultivation; that agricultural production is fast falling behind the increase in population; and that, in fact, although these well-established farmers are maintained in increasing prosperity because of the natural increase in population, we are not developing the industry of agriculture. We are not breeding in proportionate numbers a race of independent and independence-loving landowners, for a lack of which no growth of cities can compensate. Our farmers have been our mainstay in times of crisis, and in future it must still largely be upon their stability and common sense that this democracy must rely to conserve its principles of self-government.

The need of capital which American farmers feel to-day had been experienced by the farmers of Europe, with their centuries-old farms, many years ago. The problem had been successfully solved in the Old World and it was evident that the farmers of this country might profit by a study of their systems. I therefore ordered, through the Department of State, an investigation to be made by the diplomatic officers in Europe, and I have laid the results of this investigation before the governors of the various States with the hope that they will be used to advantage in their forthcoming meeting.

INCREASE OF FOREIGN TRADE

In my last annual message I said that the fiscal year ended June 30, 1911, was noteworthy as marking the highest record of exports of American products to foreign countries. The fiscal year 1912 shows that this rate of advance has been maintained, the total domestic exports having a valuation approximately of $2,200,000,000, as compared with a fraction over $2,000,000,000 the previous year. It is also significant that manufactured and partly manufactured articles continue to be the chief commodities forming the volume of our augmented exports, the demands of our own people for consumption requiring that an increasing proportion of our abundant agricultural products be kept at home. In the fiscal year 1911 the exports of articles in the various stages of manufacture, not including foodstuffs partly or wholly manufactured, amounted approximately to $907,500,000. In the fiscal year 1912 the total was nearly $1,022,-000,000, a gain of $114,000,000.

ADVANTAGE OF MAXIMUM AND MINIMUM TARIFF PROVISION

The importance which our manufactures have assumed in the commerce of the world in competition with the manufactures of other countries again draws attention to the duty of this Government to use its utmost endeavors to secure impartial treatment for American products in all markets. Healthy commercial rivalry in international intercourse is best assured by the possession of proper means for protecting and promoting our foreign trade. It is natural that competitive countries should view with some concern this steady expansion of our commerce. If in some instance the measures taken by them to meet it are not entirely equitable, a remedy should be found. In former messages I have described the negotiations of the Department of State with foreign Governments for the adjustment of the maximum and minimum tariff as provided in section 2 of the tariff law of 1909. The advantages secured by the adjustment of our trade relations under this law have continued during the last year, and some additional cases of discriminatory treatment of which we had reason to complain have been removed. The Department of State has for the first time in the history of this country obtained substantial most-favored-nation treatment from all the countries of the world. There are, however, other instances which, while apparently not constituting undue discrimination in the sense of section 2, are nevertheless exceptions to the complete equity of tariff treatment for American products that the Department of State consistently has sought to obtain for American commerce abroad.

NECESSITY FOR SUPPLEMENTARY LEGISLATION

These developments confirm the opinion conveyed to you in my annual message of 1911, that while the maximum and minimum provision of the tariff law of 1909 has been fully justified by the success achieved in removing previously existing undue discriminations against American products, yet experience has shown that this feature of the law should be amended in such way as to provide a fully effective means of meeting the varying degrees of discriminatory treatment of American commerce in foreign countries still encountered, as well as to protect against injurious treatment on the part of foreign Governments, through either legislative or administrative measures, the financial interests abroad of American citizens whose enterprises enlarge the market for American commodities.

I can not too strongly recommend to the Congress the passage of some such enabling measure as the bill which was recommended by the Secretary of State in his letter of December 13, 1911. The object of the proposed legislation is, in brief, to enable the Executive to apply, as the case may require, to any or all commodities, whether or not on the free list from a country which discriminates against the United States, a graduated scale of duties up to the maximum of 25 per cent *ad valorem* provided in the present law. Flat tariffs are out of date. Nations no longer accord equal tariff treatment to all other nations irrespective of the treatment from them received. Such a flexible power at the command of the Executive would serve to moderate any unfavorable tendencies on the part of those countries from which the importations into the United States are substantially confined to articles on the free list as well as of the countries which find a lucrative market in the United States for their products under existing customs rates. It is very necessary that the American Government should be equipped with weapons of negotiation adapted to modern economic conditions, in order that we may at all times be in a position to gain not only technically just but actually equitable treatment for our trade, and also for American enterprise and vested interests abroad.

BUSINESS SECURED TO OUR COUNTRY BY DIRECT OFFICIAL EFFORT

As illustrating the commercial benefits of the Nation derived from the new diplomacy and its effectiveness upon the material as well as the more ideal side, it may be remarked that through direct official efforts alone there have been obtained in the course of this administration, contracts from foreign Governments involving an expenditure of $50,000,000 in the factories of the United States. Consideration of this fact and some reflection upon the necessary effects of a scientific tariff system and a foreign service alert and equipped to cooperate with the business men of America carry the conviction that the gratifying increase in the export trade of this country is, in substantial amount, due to our improved governmental methods of protecting and stimulating it. It is germane to these observations to remark that in the two years that have elapsed since the successful negotiation of our new treaty with Japan, which at the time seemed to present so many practical difficulties, our export trade to that country has increased at the rate of over $1,000,000 a month. Our exports to Japan for the year ended June 30, 1910, were $21,959,310, while for the year ended June 30, 1912, the exports were $53,478,046, a net increase in the sale of American products of nearly 150 per cent.

SPECIAL CLAIMS ARBITRATION WITH GREAT BRITAIN

Under the special agreement entered into between the United States and Great Britain on August 18, 1910, for the arbitration of outstanding pecuniary claims, a schedule of claims and the terms of submission have been agreed upon by the two Governments, and together with the special agreement were approved by the Senate on July 19, 1911, but in accordance with the terms of the agreement they did not go into effect until confirmed by the two Governments by an exchange of notes, which was done on April 26 last. Negotiations are still in progress for a supplemental schedule of claims to be submitted to arbitration under this agreement, and meanwhile the necessary preparations for the arbitration of the claims included in the first schedule have been undertaken and are being carried on under the authority of an appropriation made for that purpose at the last session of Congress. It is anticipated that the two Governments will be prepared to call upon the arbitration tribunal, established under this agreement, to meet at Washington early next year to proceed with this arbitration.

FUR SEAL TREATY AND NEED FOR AMENDMENT OF OUR STATUTE

The act adopted at the last session of Congress to give effect to the fur-seal convention of July 7, 1911, between Great Britain, Japan, Russia, and the United States provided for the suspension of all land killing of seals on the Pribilof Islands for a period of five years, and an objection has now been presented to this provision by the other parties in interest, which raises the issue as to whether or not this prohibition of land killing is inconsistent with the spirit, if not the letter, of the treaty stipulations. The justification of establishing this close season depends, under the terms of the convention, upon how far, if at all, it is necessary for protecting and preserving the American fur-seal herd and for increasing its number. This is a question requiring examination of the present condition of the herd and the treatment which it needs in the light of actual experience and scientific investigation. A careful examination of the subject is now being made, and this Government will soon be in possession of a considerable amount of new information about the American seal herd, which has been secured during the past season and will be of great value in determining this question; and if it should appear that there is any uncertainty as to the real necessity for imposing a close season at this time I shall take an early opportunity to address a special message to Congress on this subject, in the belief that this Government should yield on this point rather than give the slightest ground for the charge that we have been in any way remiss in observing our treaty obligations.

FINAL SETTLEMENT OF NORTH ATLANTIC FISHERIES DISPUTE

On the 20th of July last an agreement was concluded between the United States and Great Britain adopting, with certain modifications, the rules and method of procedure recommended in the award rendered by the North Atlantic Coast Fisheries Arbitration Tribunal on September 7, 1910, for the settlement hereafter, in accordance with the principles laid down in the award, of questions arising with reference to the exercise of the American fishing liberties under Article I of the treaty of October 20, 1818, between the United States and Great Britain. This agreement received the approval of the Senate on August 1 and was formally ratified by the two Governments on November 15 last. The rules and a method of procedure embodied in the award provided for determining by an impartial tribunal the reasonableness of any new fishery regulations on the treaty coasts of Newfoundland and Canada before such regulations could be enforced against American fishermen exercising their treaty liberties on those coasts, and also for determining the delimitation of bays on such coasts more than 10 miles wide, in accordance with the definition adopted by the tribunal of the meaning of the word "bays" as used in the treaty. In the subsequent negotiations between the two Governments, undertaken for the purpose of giving practical effect to these rules and methods of procedure, it was found that certain modifications therein were desirable from the point of view of both Governments, and these negotiations have finally resulted in the agreement above mentioned by which the award recommendations as modified by mutual consent of the two Governments are finally adopted and made effective, thus bringing this century-old controversy to a final conclusion, which is equally beneficial and satisfactory to both Governments.

IMPERIAL VALLEY AND MEXICO

In order to make possible the more effective performance of the work necessary for the confinement in their present channel of the waters of the lower Colorado River, and thus to protect the people of the Imperial Valley, as well as in order to reach with the Government of Mexico an understanding regarding the distribution of the waters of the Colorado River, in which both Governments are much interested, negotiations are going forward with a view to the establishment of a preliminary Colorado River commission, which shall have the powers necessary to enable it to do the needful work and with authority to study the question of the equitable distribution of the waters. There is every reason to believe that an understanding upon this point will be reached and that an agreement will be signed in the near future.

CHAMIZAL DISPUTE

In the interest of the people and city of El Paso this Government has been assiduous in its efforts to bring to an early settlement the long-standing Chamizal dispute with Mexico. Much has been accomplished, and while the final solution of the dispute is not immediate, the favorable attitude lately assumed by the Mexican Government encourages the hope that this troublesome question will be satisfactorily and definitively settled at an early day.

INTERNATIONAL COMMISSION OF JURISTS

In pursuance of the convention of August 23, 1906, signed at the Third Pan American Conference, held at Rio de Janeiro, the International Commission of Jurists met at that capital during the month of last June. At this meeting 16 American Republics were represented, including the United States, and comprehensive plans for the future work of the commission were adopted. At the next meeting fixed for June, 1914, committees already appointed are instructed to report regarding topics assigned to them.

OPIUM CONFERENCE—UNFORTUNATE FAILURE OF OUR GOVERNMENT TO ENACT RECOMMENDED LEGISLATION

In my message on foreign relations communicated to the two Houses of Congress December 7, 1911, I called especial attention to the assembling of the Opium Conference at The Hague, to the fact that that conference was to review all pertinent municipal laws relating to the opium and allied evils, and certainly all international rules regarding these evils, and to the fact that it seemed to me most essential that the Congress should take immediate action on the antinarcotic legislation before the Congress, to which I had previously called attention by a special message.

The international convention adopted by the conference conforms almost entirely to the principles contained in the proposed antinarcotic legislation which has been before the last two Congresses. It was most unfortunate that this Government, having taken the initiative in the international action which eventuated in the important international opium convention, failed to do its share in the great work by neglecting to pass the necessary legislation to correct the deplorable narcotic evils in the United States as well as to redeem international pledges upon which it entered by virtue of the abovementioned convention. The Congress at its present session should enact into law those bills now before it which have been so carefully drawn up in collaboration between the Department of State and the other executive departments, and which have behind them not only the moral sentiment of the country, but the practical support of all the legitimate trade interests likely to be affected. Since the international convention was signed, adherence to it has been made by several European States not represented at the conference at The Hague and also by seventeen Latin-American Republics.

EUROPE AND THE NEAR EAST

The war between Italy and Turkey came to a close in October last by the signature of a treaty of peace, subsequently to which the Ottoman Empire renounced sovereignty over Cyrenaica and Tripolitania in favor of Italy. During the past year the Near East has unfortunately been the theater of constant hostilities. Almost simultaneously with the conclusion of peace between Italy and Turkey and their arrival at an adjustment of the complex questions at issue between them, war broke out between Turkey on the one hand and Bulgaria, Greece, Montenegro, and Servia on the other. The United

States has happily been involved neither directly nor indirectly with the causes or questions incident to any of these hostilities and has maintained in regard to them an attitude of absolute neutrality and of complete political disinterestedness. In the second war in which the Ottoman Empire has been engaged the loss of life and the consequent distress on both sides have been appalling, and the United States has found occasion, in the interest of humanity, to carry out the charitable desires of the American people, to extend a measure of relief to the sufferers on either side through the impartial medium of the Red Cross. Beyond this the chief care of the Government of the United States has been to make due provision for the protection of its national resident in belligerent territory. In the exercise of my duty in this matter I have dispatched to Turkish waters a special-service squadron, consisting of two armored cruisers, in order that this Government may if need be bear its part in such measures as it may be necessary for the interested nations to adopt for the safeguarding of foreign lives and property in the Ottoman Empire in the event that a dangerous situation should develop. In the meanwhile the several interested European powers have promised to extend to American citizens the benefit of such precautionary or protective measures as they might adopt, in the same manner in which it has been the practice of this Government to extend its protection to all foreign residents in those countries of the Western Hemisphere in which it has from time to time been the task of the United States to act in the interest of peace and good order. The early appearance of a large fleet of European warships in the Bosphorus apparently assured the protection of foreigners in that quarter, where the presence of the American *stationnaire* the U. S. S. *Scorpion* sufficed, under the circumstances, to represent the United States. Our cruisers were thus left free to act if need be along the Mediterranean coasts should any unexpected contingency arise affecting the numerous American interests in the neighborhood of Smyrna and Beirut.

SPITZBERGEN

The great preponderance of American material interests in the subarctic island of Spitzbergen, which has always been regarded politically as "no man's land," impels this Government to a continued and lively interest in the international dispositions to be made for the political governance and administration of that region. The conflict of certain claims of American citizens and others is in a fair way to adjustment, while the settlement of matters of administration, whether by international conference of the interested powers or otherwise, continues to be the subject of exchange of views between the Governments concerned.

LIBERIA

As a result of the efforts of this Government to place the Government of Liberia in position to pay its outstanding indebtedness and to maintain a stable and efficient government, negotiations for a loan of $1,700,000 have been successfully concluded, and it is anticipated that the payment of the old loan and the issuance of the bonds of the 1912 loan for the rehabilitation of the finances of Liberia will follow at an early date, when the new receivership will go into active operation. The new receivership will consist of a general receiver of customs designated by the Government of the United States and three receivers of customs designated by the Governments of Germany, France, and Great Britain, which countries have commercial interests in the Republic of Liberia.

In carrying out the understanding between the Government of Liberia and that of the United States, and in fulfilling the terms of the agreement between the former Government and the American bankers, three competent ex-army officers are now effectively employed by the Liberian Government in reorganizing the police force of the Republic, not only to keep in order the native tribes in the hinterland but to serve as a necessary police force along the frontier. It is hoped that these measures will assure not only the continued existence but the prosperity and welfare of the Republic of Liberia. Liberia possesses fertility of soil and natural resources, which should insure to its people a reasonable prosperity. It was the duty of the United States to assist the Republic of Liberia in accordance with our historical interest and moral guardianship of a community founded by American citizens, as it was also the duty of the American Government to attempt to assure permanence to a country of much sentimental and perhaps future real interest to a large body of our citizens.

MOROCCO

The legation at Tangier is now in charge of our consul general, who is acting as chargé d'affaires, as well as caring for our commercial interests in that country. In view of the fact that many of the foreign powers are now represented by chargés d'affaires it has not been deemed necessary to appoint at the present time a minister to fill a vacancy occurring in that post.

THE FAR EAST

The political disturbances in China in the autumn and winter of 1911–12 resulted in the abdication of the Manchu rulers on February 12, followed by the formation of a provisional republican government empowered to conduct the affairs of the nation until a permanent government might be regularly established. The natural sympathy of the American people with the assumption of republican principles by the Chinese people was appropriately expressed in a concurrent resolution of Congress on April 17, 1912. A constituent assembly, composed of representatives duly chosen by the people of China in the elections that are now being held, has been called to meet in January next to adopt a permanent constitution and organize the Government of the nascent Republic. During the formative constitutional stage and pending definite action by the assembly, as expressive of the popular will, and the hoped-for establishment of a stable republican form of government, capable of fulfilling its international obligations, the United States is, according to precedent, maintaining full and friendly *de facto* relations with the provisional Government.

The new condition of affairs thus created has presented many serious and complicated problems, both of internal rehabilitation and of international relations, whose solution it was realized would necessarily require much time and patience. From the beginning of the upheaval last autumn it was felt by the United States, in common with the other powers having large interests in China, that independent action by the foreign Governments in their own individual interests would add further confusion to a situation already complicated. A policy of international cooperation was accordingly adopted in an understanding, reached early in the disturbances, to act together for the protection of the lives and property of foreigners if menaced, to maintain an attitude of strict impartiality as between the contending factions, and to abstain from any endeavor to influence the Chinese in their organization of a new form of government. In view of the seriousness of the disturbances and their general character, the American minister at Peking was instructed at his discretion to advise our nationals in the affected districts to concentrate at such centers as were easily accessible to foreign troops or men of war. Nineteen of our naval vessels were stationed at various Chinese ports, and other measures were promptly taken for the adequate protection of American interests.

It was further mutually agreed, in the hope of hastening an end to hostilities, that none of the interested powers would approve the making of loans by its nationals to either side. As soon, however, as a united provisional Government of China was assured, the United States joined in a favorable consideration of that Government's request for advances needed for immediate administrative necessities and later for a loan to effect a permanent national reorganization. The interested Governments had already, by common consent, adopted, in respect to the purposes, expenditure, and security of any loans to China made by their nationals, certain conditions which were held to be essential, not only to secure reasonable protection for the foreign investors, but also to safeguard and strengthen China's credit by discouraging indiscriminate borrowing and by insuring the application of the funds toward the establishment of the stable and effective government necessary to China's welfare. In June last representative banking groups of the United States, France, Germany, Great Britain, Japan, and Russia formulated, with the general sanction of their respective Governments, the guaranties that would be expected in relation to the expenditure and security of the large reorganization loan desired by China, which, however, have thus far proved unacceptable to the provisional Government.

SPECIAL MISSION OF CONDOLENCE TO JAPAN

In August last I accredited the Secretary of State as special ambassador to Japan, charged with the mission of bearing to the imperial family, the Government, and the people of that Empire the sympathetic message of the American Commonwealth on the sad occasion of the death of His Majesty the Emperor Mutsuhito, whose long and benevolent reign was the greater part of Japan's modern history. The kindly reception everywhere accorded to Secretary Knox showed that his mission was deeply appreciated by the Japanese nation and emphasized strongly the friendly relations that have for so many years existed between the two peoples.

SOUTH AMERICA

Our relations with the Argentine Republic are most friendly and cordial. So, also, are our relations with Brazil, whose Government has accepted the invitation of the United States to send two army officers to study at the Coast Artillery School at Fort Monroe. The long-standing Alsop claim, which had been the only hindrance to the healthy growth of the most friendly relations between the United States and Chile, having been eliminated through the submission of the question to His Britannic Majesty King George V as "amiable compositeur," it is a cause of much gratification to me that our relations with Chile are now established upon a firm basis of growing friendship. The Chilean Government has placed an officer of the United States Coast Artillery in charge of the Chilean Coast Artillery School, and has shown appreciation of American methods by confiding to an American firm important work for the Chilean coast defenses.

Last year a revolution against the established Government of Ecuador broke out at the pricipal port of that Republic. Previous to this occurrence the chief American interest in Ecuador, represented by the Guayaquil & Quito Railway Co., incorporated in the United States, had rendered extensive transportation and other services on account to the Ecuadorian Government, the amount of which ran into a sum which was steadily increasing and which the Ecuadorian Government had made no provision to pay, thereby threatening to crush out the very existence of this American enterprise. When tranquillity had been restored to Ecuador as a result of the triumphant progress of the Government forces from Quito, this Government interposed its good offices to the end that the American interests in Ecuador might be saved from complete extinction. As a part of the arrangement which was reached between the parties, and at the request of the Government of Ecuador, I have consented to name an arbitrator, who, acting under the terms of the railroad contract, with an arbitrator named by the Ecuadorian Government, will pass upon the claims that have arisen since the arrangement reached through the action of a similar arbitral tribunal in 1908.

In pursuance of a request made some time ago by the Ecuadorian Government, the Department of State has given much attention to the problem of the proper sanitation of Guayaquil. As a result a detail of officers of the Canal Zone will be sent to Guayaquil to recommend measures that will lead to the complete permanent sanitation of this plague and fever infected region of that Republic, which has for so long constituted a menace to health conditions on the Canal Zone. It is hoped that the report which this mission will furnish will point out a way whereby the modicum of assistance which the United States may properly lend the Ecuadorian Government may be made effective in ridding the west coast of South America of a focus of contagion to the future commercial current passing through the Panama Canal.

In the matter of the claim of John Celestine Landreau against the Government of Peru, which claim arises out of certain contracts and transactions in connection with the discovery and exploitation of guano, and which has been under discussion between the two Governments since 1874, I am glad to report that as the result of prolonged negotiations, which have been characterized by the utmost friendliness and good will on both sides, the Department of State has succeeded in securing the consent of Peru to the arbitration of the claim, and that the negotiations attending the drafting and signature of a protocol submitting the claim to an arbitral tribunal are proceeding with due celerity.

An officer of the American Public Health Service and an American sanitary engineer are now on the way to Iquitos, in the employ of the Peruvian Government, to take charge of the sanitation of that river port. Peru is building a number of submarines in this country, and continues to show every desire to have American capital invested in the Republic.

In July the United States sent undergraduate delegates to the Third International Students Congress held at Lima, American students having been for the first time invited to one of these meetings.

The Republic of Uruguay has shown its appreciation of American agricultural and other methods by sending a large commission to this country and by employing many American experts to assist in building up agricultural and allied industries in Uruguay.

Venezuela is paying off the last of the claims the settlement of which was provided for by the Washington protocols, including those of American citizens. Our relations with Venezuela are most cordial, and the trade of that Republic with the United States is now greater than with any other country.

CENTRAL AMERICA AND THE CARIBBEAN

During the past summer the revolution against the administration which followed the assassination of President Caceres a year ago last November brought the Dominican Republic to the verge of administrative chaos, without offering any guaranties of eventual stability in the ultimate success of either party. In pursuance of the treaty relations of the United States with the Dominican Republic, which were threatened by the necessity of suspending the operation under American administration of the customhouses on the Haitian frontier, it was found necessary to dispatch special commissioners to the island to reestablish the customhouses and with a guard sufficient to insure needed protection to the customs administration. The efforts which have been made appear to have resulted in the restoration of normal conditions throughout the Republic. The good offices which the commissioners were able to exercise were instrumental in bringing the contending parties together and in furnishing a basis of adjustment which it is hoped will result in permanent benefit to the Dominican people.

Mindful of its treaty relations, and owing to the position of the Government of the United States as mediator between the Dominican Republic and Haiti in their boundary dispute, and because of the further fact that the revolutionary activities on the Haitian-Dominican frontier had become so active as practically to obliterate the line of demarcation that had been heretofore recognized pending the definitive settlement of the boundary in controversy, it was found necessary to indicate to the two island Governments a provisional *de facto* boundary line. This was done without prejudice to the rights or obligations of either country in a final settlement to be reached by arbitration. The tentative line chosen was one which, under the circumstances brought to the knowledge of this Government, seemed to conform to the best interests of the disputants

The border patrol which it had been found necessary to reestablish for customs purposes between the two countries was instructed provisionally to observe this line.

The Republic of Cuba last May was in the throes of a lawless uprising that for a time threatened the destruction of a great deal of valuable property—much of it owned by Americans and other foreigners—as well as the existence of the Government itself. The armed forces of Cuba being inadequate to guard property from attack and at the same time properly to operate against the rebels, a force of American marines was dispatched from our naval station at Guantanamo into the Province of Oriente for the protection of American and other foreign life and property. The Cuban Government was thus able to use all its forces in putting down the outbreak, which it succeeded in doing in a period of six weeks. The presence of two American warships in the harbor of Habana during the most critical period of this disturbance contributed in great measure to allay the fears of the inhabitants, including a large foreign colony.

There has been under discussion with the Government of Cuba for some time the question of the release by this Government of its leasehold rights at Bahia Honda, on the northern coast of Cuba, and the enlargement, in exchange therefor, of the naval station which has been established at Guantanamo Bay, on the south. As the result of the negotiations thus carried on an agreement has been reached between the two Governments providing for the suitable enlargement of the Guantanamo Bay station upon terms which are entirely fair and equitable to all parties concerned.

At the request alike of the Government and both political parties in Panama, an American commission undertook supervision of the recent presidential election in that Republic, where our treaty relations, and, indeed, every geographical consideration, make the maintenance of order and satisfactory conditions of peculiar interest to the Government of the United States. The elections passed without disorder, and the new administration has entered upon its functions.

The Government of Great Britain has asked the support of the United States for the protection of the interests of British holders of the foreign bonded debt of Guatemala. While this Government is hopeful of an arrangement equitable to the British bondholders, it is naturally unable to view the question apart from its relation to the broad subject of financial stability in Central America, in which the policy of the United States does not permit it to escape a vital interest. Through a renewal of negotiations between the Government of Guatemala and American bankers, the aim of which is a loan for the rehabilitation of Guatemalan finances, a way appears to be open by which the Government of Guatemala could promptly satisfy any equitable and just British claims, and at the same time so improve its whole financial position as to contribute greatly to the increased prosperity of the Republic and to redound to the benefit of foreign investments and foreign trade with that country. Failing such an arrangement, it may become impossible for the Government of the United States to escape its obligations in connection with such measures as may become necessary to exact justice to legitimate foreign claims.

In the recent revolution in Nicaragua, which, it was generally admitted, might well have resulted in a general Central American conflict but for the intervention of the United States, the Government of Honduras was especially menaced; but fortunately peaceful conditions were maintained within the borders of that Republic. The financial condition of that country remains unchanged, no means having been found for the final adjustment of pressing outstanding foreign claims. This makes it the more regrettable that the financial convention between the United States and Honduras has thus far failed of ratification. The Government of the United States continues to hold itself ready to cooperate with the Government of Honduras, which it is believed, can not much longer delay the meeting of its foreign obligations, and it is hoped at the proper time American bankers will be willing to cooperate for this purpose.

NECESSITY FOR GREATER GOVERNMENTAL EFFORT IN RETENTION AND EXPANSION OF OUR FOREIGN TRADE

It is not possible to make to the Congress a communication upon the present foreign relations of the United States so detailed as to convey an adequate impression of the enormous increase in the importance and activities of those relations. If this Government is really to preserve to the American people that free opportunity in foreign markets which will soon be indispensable to our prosperity, even greater efforts must be made. Otherwise the American merchant, manufacturer, and exporter will find many a field in which American trade should logically predominate preempted through the more energetic efforts of other governments and other commercial nations.

There are many ways in which through hearty cooperation the legislative and executive branches of this Government can do much. The absolute essential is the spirit of united effort and singleness of purpose. I will allude only to a very few specific examples of action which ought then to result. America can not take its proper place in the most important fields for its commercial activity and enterprise unless we have a merchant marine. American commerce and enterprise can not be effectively fostered in those fields unless we have good American banks in the countries referred to. We need American newspapers in those countries and proper means for public information about them. We need to assure the permanency of a trained foreign service. We need legislation enabling the members of the foreign service to be systematically brought in direct contact with the industrial, manufacturing, and exporting interests of this country in order that American business men may enter the foreign field with a clear perception of the exact conditions to be dealt with and the officers themselves may prosecute their work with a clear idea of what American industrial and manufacturing interests require.

CONCLUSION

Congress should fully realize the conditions which obtain in the world as we find ourselves at the threshold of our middle age as a Nation. We have emerged full grown as a peer in the great concourse of nations. We have passed through various formative periods. We have been self-centered in the struggle to develop our domestic resources and deal with our domestic questions. The Nation is now too matured to continue in its foreign relations those temporary expedients natural to a people to whom domestic affairs are the sole concern. In the past our diplomacy has often consisted, in normal times, in a mere assertion of the right to international existence. We are now in a larger relation with broader rights of our own and obligations to others than ourselves. A number of great guiding principles were laid down early in the history of this Government. The recent task of our diplomacy has been to adjust those principles to the conditions of to-day, to develop their corollaries, to find practical applications of the old principles expanded to meet new situations. Thus are being evolved bases upon which can rest the superstructure of policies which must grow with the destined progress of this Nation. The successful conduct of our foreign relations demands a broad and a modern view. We can not meet new questions nor build for the future if we confine ourselves to outworn dogmas of the past and to the perspective appropriate at our emergence from colonial times and conditions. The opening of the Panama Canal will mark a new era in our international life and create new and world-wide conditions which, with their vast correlations and consequences, will obtain for hundreds of years to come. We must not wait for events to overtake us unawares. With continuity of purpose we must deal with the problems of our external relations by a diplomacy modern, resourceful, magnanimous, and fittingly expressive of the high ideals of a great nation.

Part II.

[On Fiscal, Judicial, Military and Insular Affairs.]

THE WHITE HOUSE, *December 6, 1912.*

To the Senate and House of Representatives:

On the 3d of December I sent a message to the Congress, which was confined to our foreign relations. The Secretary of State makes no report to the President or to Congress, and a review of the history of the transactions of the State Department in one year must therefore be included by the President in his annual message or Congress will not be fully informed of them. A full discussion of all the transactions of the Government, with a view to informing the Congress of the important events of the year and recommending new legislation, requires more space than one message of reasonable length affords. I have therefore adopted the course of sending three or four messages during the first ten days of the session, so as to include reference to the more important matters that should be brought to the attention of the Congress.

BUSINESS CONDITIONS

The condition of the country with reference to business could hardly be better. While the four years of the administration now drawing to a close have not developed great speculative expansion or a wide field of new investment, the recovery and progress made from the depressing conditions following the panic of 1907 have been steady and the improvement has been clear and easily traced in the statistics. The business of the country is now on a solid basis. Credits are not unduly extended, and every phase of the situation seems in a state of preparedness for a period of unexampled prosperity. Manufacturing concerns are running at their full capacity and the demand for labor was never so constant and growing. The foreign trade of the country for this year will exceed $4,000,000,000, while the balance in our favor—that of the excess of exports over imports—will exceed $500,000,000. More than half our exports are manufactures or partly manufactured material, while our exports of farm products do not show the same increase because of domestic consumption. It is a year of bumper crops; the total money value of farm products will exceed $9,500,000,000. It is a year when the bushel or unit price of agricultural products has gradually fallen, and yet the total value of the entire crop is greater by over $1,000,000,000 than we have known in our history.

CONDITION OF THE TREASURY

The condition of the Treasury is very satisfactory. The total interest-bearing debt is $963,777,770, of which $134,631,980 constitute the Panama Canal loan. The noninterest-bearing debt is $378,301,-284.90, including $346,681,016 of greenbacks. We have in the Treasury $150,000,000 in gold coin as a reserve against the outstanding greenbacks; and in addition we have a cash balance in the Treasury as a general fund of $167,152,478.99, or an increase of $26,975,552 over the general fund last year.

RECEIPTS AND EXPENDITURES

For three years the expenditures of the Government have decreased under the influence of an effort to economize. This year presents an apparent exception. The estimate by the Secretary of the Treasury of the ordinary receipts, exclusive of postal revenues, for the year ending June 30, 1914, indicates that they will amount to $710,-000,000. The sum of the estimates of the expenditures for that same year, exclusive of Panama Canal disbursements and postal disbursements payable from postal revenues, is $732,000,000, indicating a deficit of $22,000,000. For the year ending June 30, 1913, similarly estimated receipts were $667,000,000, while the total corresponding estimate of expenditures for that year, submitted through the Secretary of the Treasury to Congress, amounted to $656,000,000. This shows an increase of $76,000,000 in the estimates for 1914 over the total estimates of 1913. This is due to an increase of $25,000,000 in the estimate for rivers and harbors for the next year on projects and surveys authorized by Congress; to an increase under the new pension bill of $32,500,000; and to an increase in the estimates for expenses of the Navy Department of $24,000,000. The estimate for the Navy Department for the year 1913 included two battleships. Congress made provision for only one battleship, and therefore the Navy Department has deemed it necessary and proper to make an estimate which includes the first year's expenditure for three battleships in addition to the amount required for work on the uncompleted ships now under construction. In addition to the natural increase in the expenditures for the uncompleted ships, and the additional battleship estimated for, the other increases are due to the pay required for 4,000 or more additional enlisted men in the Navy; and to this must be added the additional cost of construction imposed by the change in the eight-hour law which makes it applicable to ships built in private shipyards.

With the exceptions of these three items, the estimates show a reduction this year below the total estimates for 1913 of more than $5,000,000.

The estimates for Panama Canal construction for 1914 are $17,-000,000 less than for 1913.

OUR BANKING AND CURRENCY SYSTEM

A time when panics seem far removed is the best time for us to prepare our financial system to withstand a storm. The most crying need this country has is a proper banking and currency system. The existing one is inadequate, and everyone who has studied the question admits it.

It is the business of the National Government to provide a medium, automatically contracting and expanding in volume, to meet the needs of trade. Our present system lacks the indispensable quality of elasticity.

The only part of our monetary medium that has elasticity is the bank-note currency. The peculiar provisions of the law requiring national banks to maintain reserves to meet the call of the depositors operates to increase the money stringency when it arises rather than to expand the supply of currency and relieve it. It operates upon each bank and furnishes a motive for the withdrawal of currency from the channels of trade by each bank to save itself, and offers no inducement whatever for the use of the reserve to expand the supply of currency to meet the exceptional demand.

After the panic of 1907 Congress realized that the present system was not adapted to the country's needs and that under it panics were possible that might properly be avoided by legislative provision. Accordingly a monetary commission was appointed which made a report in February, 1912. The system which they recommended involved a National Reserve Association, which was, in certain of its faculties and functions, a bank, and which was given through its governing authorities the power, by issuing circulating notes for approved commercial paper, by fixing discounts, and by other methods of transfer of currency, to expand the supply of the monetary medium where it was most needed to prevent the export or hoarding of gold and generally to exercise such supervision over the supply of money in every part of the country as to prevent a stringency and a panic. The stock in this association was to be distributed to the banks of the whole United States, State and National, in a mixed proportion to bank units and to capital stock paid in. The control of the association was vested in a board of directors to be elected by representatives of the banks, except certain ex-officio directors, three Cabinet officers, and the Comptroller of the Currency. The President was to appoint the governor of the association from three persons to be selected by the directors, while the two deputy governors were to be elected by the board of directors. The details of the plan were worked out with great care and ability, and the plan in general seems to me to furnish the basis for a proper solution of our present difficulties. I feel that the Government might very properly be given a greater voice in the executive committee of the board of directors without danger of injecting politics into its management, but I think the federation system of banks is a good one, provided proper precautions are taken to prevent banks of large capital from absorbing power through ownership of stock in other banks. The objections to a central bank it seems to me are obviated if the ownership of the reserve association is distributed among all the banks of a country in which banking is free. The earnings of the reserve association are limited in percentage to a reasonable and fixed amount, and the profits over and above this are to be turned into the Government Treasury. It is quite probable that still greater security against control by money centers may be worked into the plan.

Certain it is, however, that the objections which were made in the past history of this country to a central bank as furnishing a monopoly of financial power to private individuals, would not apply to an association whose ownership and control is so widely distributed and is divided between all the banks of the country, State and National, on the one hand, and the Chief Executive through three department heads and his Comptroller of the Currency, on the other. The ancient hostility to a national bank, with its branches, in which is concentrated the privilege of doing a banking business and carrying on the financial transactions of the Government, has prevented the establishment of such a bank since it was abolished in the Jackson Administration. Our present national banking law has obviated objections growing out of the same cause by providing a free banking system in which any set of stockholders can establish a national bank if they comply with the conditions of law. It seems to me that the National Reserve Association meets the same objection in a similar way; that is, by giving to each bank, State and National, in accordance with its size, a certain share in the stock of the reserve association, nontransferable and only to be held by the bank while it performs its functions as a partner in the reserve association.

The report of the commission recommends provisions for the imposition of a graduated tax on the expanded currency of such a character as to furnish a motive for reducing the issue of notes whenever their presence in the money market is not required by the exigencies of trade. In other words, the whole system has been worked out with the greatest care. Theoretically it presents a plan that ought to command support. Practically it may require modification in various of its provisions in order to make the security against abuses by combinations among the banks impossible. But in the face of the crying necessity that there is for improvement in our present system, I urgently invite the attention of Congress to the proposed plan and the report of the commission, with the hope that an earnest consideration may suggest amendments and changes within the general plan which will lead to its adoption for the benefit of the country. There is no class in the community more interested in a safe and sane banking and currency system, one which will prevent panics and automatically furnish in each trade center the currency needed in the carrying on of the business at that center, than the wage earner. There is no class in the community whose experience better qualifies them to make suggestions as to the sufficiency of a currency and banking system than the bankers and business men. Ought we, therefore, to ignore their recommendations and reject their financial judgment as to the proper method of reforming our financial system merely because of the suspicion which exists against them in the minds of many of our fellow citizens? Is it not the duty of Congress to take up the plan suggested, examine it from all standpoints, give impartial consideration to the testimony of those whose experience ought to fit them to give the best advice on the subject, and then to adopt some plan which will secure the benefits desired?

A banking and currency system seems far away from the wage earner and the farmer, but the fact is that they are vitally interested in a safe system of currency which shall graduate its volume to the amount needed and which shall prevent times of artificial stringency that frighten capital, stop employment, prevent the meeting of the pay roll, destroy local markets, and produce penury and want.

THE TARIFF

I have regarded it as my duty in former messages to the Congress to urge the revision of the tariff upon principles of protection. It was my judgment that the customs duties ought to be revised downward, but that the reduction ought not to be below a rate which would represent the difference in the cost of production between the article in question at home and abroad, and for this and other reasons I vetoed several bills which were presented to me in the last session of this Congress. Now that a new Congress has been elected on a platform of a tariff for revenue only rather than a protective tariff, and is to revise the tariff on that basis, it is needless for me to occupy the time of this Congress with arguments or recommendations in favor of a protective tariff.

Before passing from the tariff law, however, known as the Payne tariff law of August 5, 1909, I desire to call attention to section 38 of that act, assessing a special excise tax on corporations. It contains a provision requiring the levy of an additional 50 per cent to the annual tax in cases of neglect to verify the prescribed return or to file it before the time required by law. This additional charge of 50 per cent operates in some cases as a harsh penalty for what may have been a mere inadvertence or unintentional oversight, and the law should be so amended as to mitigate the severity of the charge in such instances. Provision should also be made for the refund of additional taxes heretofore collected because of such infractions in those cases where the penalty imposed has been so disproportionate to the offense as equitably to demand relief.

BUDGET

The estimates for the next fiscal year have been assembled by the Secretary of the Treasury and by him transmitted to Congress. I purpose at a later day to submit to Congress a form of budget prepared for me and recommended by the President's Commission on Economy and Efficiency, with a view of suggesting the useful and informing character of a properly framed budget.

WAR DEPARTMENT

The War Department combines within its jurisdiction functions which in other countries usually occupy three departments. It not only has the management of the Army and the coast defenses, but its jurisdiction extends to the government of the Philippines and of Porto Rico and the control of the receivership of the customs revenues of the Dominican Republic; it also includes the recommendation of all plans for the improvement of harbors and waterways and their execution when adopted; and, by virtue of an Executive order, the supervision of the construction of the Panama Canal.

ARMY REORGANIZATION

Our small Army now consists of 83,809 men, excluding the 5,000 Philippine scouts. Leaving out of consideration the Coast Artillery force, whose position is fixed in our various seacoast defenses, and the present garrisons of our various insular possessions, we have to-day within the continental United States a mobile Army of only about 35,000 men. This little force must be still further drawn upon to supply the new garrisons for the great naval base which is being established at Pearl Harbor, in the Hawaiian Islands, and to protect the locks now rapidly approaching completion at Panama. The forces remaining in the United States are now scattered in nearly 50 posts, situated for a variety of historical reasons in 24 States. These posts contain only fractions of regiments, averaging less than 700 men each. In time of peace it has been our historical policy to administer these units separately by a geographical organization. In other words, our Army in time of peace has never been a united organization but merely scattered groups of companies, battalions, and regiments, and the first task in time of war has been to create out of these scattered units an Army fit for effective teamwork and cooperation.

To the task of meeting these patent defects, the War Department has been addressing itself during the past year. For many years we had no officer or division whose business it was to study these problems and plan remedies for these defects. With the establishment of the General Staff nine years ago a body was created for this purpose. It has, necessarily, required time to overcome, even in its own personnel, the habits of mind engendered by a century of lack of method, but of late years its work has become systematic and effective, and it has recently been addressing itself vigorously to these problems.

A comprehensive plan of Army reorganization was prepared by the War College Division of the General Staff. This plan was thoroughly discussed last summer at a series of open conferences held by the Secretary of War and attended by representatives from all branches of the Army and from Congress. In printed form it has been distributed to Members of Congress and throughout the Army and the National Guard, and widely through institutions of learning and elsewhere in the United States. In it, for the first time, we have a tentative chart for future progress.

Under the influence of this study definite and effective steps have been taken toward Army reorganization so far as such reorganization lies within the Executive power. Hitherto there has been no difference of policy in the treatment of the organization of our foreign garrisons from those of troops within the United States. The difference of situation is vital, and the foreign garrison should be prepared to defend itself at an instant's notice against a foe who may command the sea. Unlike the troops in the United States, it can not count upon reinforcements or recruitment. It is an outpost upon which will fall the brunt of the first attack in case of war. The historical policy of the United States of carrying its regiments during time of peace at half strength has no application to our foreign garrisons. During the past year this defect has been remedied as to the Philippines garrison. The former garrison of 12 reduced regiments has been replaced by a garrison of 6 regiments at full strength, giving fully the same number of riflemen at an estimated economy in cost of maintenance of over $1,000,000 per year. This garrison is to be permanent. Its regimental units, instead of being transferred periodically back and forth from the United States, will remain in the islands. The officers and men composing these units will, however, serve a regular tropical detail as usual, thus involving no greater hardship upon the personnel and greatly increasing the effectiveness of the garrison. A similar policy is proposed for the Hawaiian and Panama garrisons as fast as the barracks for them are completed. I strongly urge upon Congress that the necessary appropriations for this purpose should be promptly made. It is, in my opinion, of first importance that these national outposts, upon which a successful home defense will, primarily, depend, should be finished and placed in effective condition at the earliest possible day.

THE HOME ARMY

Simultaneously with the foregoing steps the War Department has been proceeding with the reorganization of the Army at home. The formerly disassociated units are being united into a tactical organization of three divisions, each consisting of two or three brigades of Infantry and, so far as practicable, a proper proportion of divisional Cavalry and Artillery. Of course, the extent to which this reform can be carried by the Executive is practically limited to a paper organization. The scattered units can be brought under a proper organization, but they will remain physically scattered until Congress supplies the necessary funds for grouping them in more concentrated posts. Until that is done the present difficulty of drilling our scattered groups together, and thus training them for the proper team play, can not be removed. But we shall, at least, have an Army which will know its own organization and will be inspected by its proper commanders, and to which, as a unit, emergency orders can be issued in time of war or other emergency. Moreover, the organization, which in many respects is necessarily a skeleton, will furnish a guide for future development. The separate regiments and companies will know the brigades and divisions to which they belong. They will be maneuvered together whenever maneuvers are established by Congress, and the gaps in their organization will show the pattern into which can be filled new troops as the Nation grows and a larger Army is provided.

REGULAR ARMY RESERVE

One of the most important reforms accomplished during the past year has been the legislation enacted in the Army appropriation bill of last summer, providing for a Regular Army reserve. Hitherto our national policy has assumed that at the outbreak of war our regiments would be immediately raised to full strength. But our laws have provided no means by which this could be accomplished, or by which the losses of the regiments when once sent to the front could be repaired. In this respect we have neglected the lessons learned by other nations. The new law provides that the soldier, after serving four years with colors, shall pass into a reserve for three years. At his option he may go into the reserve at the end of three years, remaining there for four years. While in the reserve he can be called to active duty only in case of war or other national emergency, and when so called and only in such case will receive a stated amount of pay for all of the period in which he has been a member of the reserve. The legislation is imperfect, in my opinion, in certain particulars, but it is a most important step in the right direction, and I earnestly hope that it will be carefully studied and perfected by Congress.

THE NATIONAL GUARD

Under existing law the National Guard constitutes, after the Regular Army, the first line of national defense. Its organization, discipline, training, and equipment, under recent legislation, have been assimilated, as far as possible, to those of the Regular Army, and its practical efficiency, under the effect of this training, has very greatly increased. Our citizen soldiers under present conditions have reached a stage of development beyond which they can not reasonably be asked to go without further direct assistance in the form of pay from the Federal Government. On the other hand, such pay from the National Treasury would not be justified unless it produced a proper equivalent in additional efficiency on the part of the National Guard. The Organized Militia to-day can not be ordered outside of the limits of the United States, and thus can not lawfully be used for general military purposes. The officers and men are ambitious and eager to make themselves thus available and to become an efficient national reserve of citizen soldiery. They are the only force of trained men, other than the Regular Army, upon which we can rely. The so-called militia pay bill, in the form agreed on between the authorities of the War Department and the representatives of the National Guard, in my opinion adequately meets these conditions and offers a proper return for the pay which it is proposed to give to the National Guard. I believe that its enactment into law would be a very long step toward providing this Nation with a first line of citizen soldiery, upon which its main reliance must depend in case of any national emergency. Plans for the organization of the National Guard into tactical divisions, on the same lines as those adopted for the Regular Army, are being formulated by the War College Division of the General Staff.

NATIONAL VOLUNTEERS

The National Guard consists of only about 110,000 men. In any serious war in the past it has always been necessary, and in such a war in the future it doubtless will be necessary, for the Nation to depend, in addition to the Regular Army and the National Guard, upon a large force of volunteers. There is at present no adequate provision of law for the raising of such a force. There is now pending in Congress, however, a bill which makes such provision, and which I believe is admirably adapted to meet the exigencies which would be presented in case of war. The passage of the bill would not entail a dollar's expense upon the Government at this time or in the future until war comes. But if war comes the methods therein directed are in accordance with the best military judgment as to what they ought to be, and the act would prevent the necessity for a discussion of any legislation and the delays incident to its consideration and adoption. I earnestly urge its passage.

CONSOLIDATION OF THE SUPPLY CORPS

The Army appropriation act of 1912 also carried legislation for the consolidation of the Quartermaster's Department, the Subsistence Department, and the Pay Corps into a single supply department, to be known as the Quartermaster's Corps. It also provided for the organization of a special force of enlisted men, to be known as the Service Corps, gradually to replace many of the civilian employees engaged in the manual labor necessary in every army. I believe that both of these enactments will improve the administration of our military establishment. The consolidation of the supply corps has already been effected, and the organization of the service corps is being put into effect.

All of the foregoing reforms are in the direction of economy and efficiency. Except for the slight increase necessary to garrison our outposts in Hawaii and Panama, they do not call for a larger Army, but they do tend to produce a much more efficient one. The only substantial new appropriations required are those which, as I have pointed out, are necessary to complete the fortifications and barracks at our naval bases and outposts beyond the sea.

PORTO RICO

Porto Rico continues to show notable progress, both commercially and in the spread of education. Its external commerce has increased 17 per cent over the preceding year, bringing the total value up to $92,631,886, or more than five times the value of the commerce of the island in 1901. During the year 160,657 pupils were enrolled in the public schools, as against 145,525 for the preceding year, and as compared with 26,000 for the first year of American administration. Special efforts are under way for the promotion of vocational and industrial training, the need of which is particularly pressing in the island. When the bubonic plague broke out last June, the quick and efficient response of the people of Porto Rico to the demands of modern sanitation was strikingly shown by the thorough campaign which was instituted against the plague and the hearty public opinion which supported the Government's efforts to check its progress and to prevent its recurrence.

The failure thus far to grant American citizenship continues to be the only ground of dissatisfaction. The bill conferring such citizenship has passed the House of Representatives and is now awaiting the action of the Senate. I am heartily in favor of the passage of this bill. I believe that the demand for citizenship is just, and that it is amply earned by sustained loyalty on the part of the inhabitants of the island. But it should be remembered that the demand must be, and in the minds of most Porto Ricans is, entirely disassociated from any thought of statehood. I believe that no substantial approved public opinion in the United States or in Porto Rico contemplates statehood for the island as the ultimate form of relations between us. I believe that the aim to be striven for is the fullest possible allowance of legal and fiscal self-government, with American citizenship as to the bond between us; in other words, a relation analogous to the present relation between Great Britain and such self-governing colonies as Canada and Australia. This would conduce to the fullest and most self-sustaining development of Porto Rico, while at the same time it would grant her the economic and political benefits of being under the American flag.

PHILIPPINES

A bill is pending in Congress which revolutionizes the carefully worked out scheme of government under which the Philippine Islands are now governed and which proposes to render them virtually autonomous at once and absolutely independent in eight years. Such a proposal can only be founded on the assumption that we have now discharged our trusteeship to the Filipino people and our responsibility for them to the world, and that they are now prepared for self-government as well as national sovereignty. A thorough and unbiased knowledge of the facts clearly shows that these assumptions are absolutely without justification. As to this, I believe that there is no substantial difference of opinion among any of those who have had the responsibility of facing Philippine problems in the administration of the islands, and I believe that no one to whom the future of this people is a responsible concern can countenance a policy fraught with the direst consequences to those on whose behalf it is ostensibly urged.

In the Philippine Islands we have embarked upon an experiment unprecedented in dealing with dependent people. We are developing there conditions exclusively for their own welfare. We found an archipelago containing 24 tribes and races, speaking a great variety of languages, and with a population over 80 per cent of which could neither read nor write. Through the unifying forces of a common education, of commercial and economic development, and of gradual participation in local self-government we are endeavoring to evolve a homogeneous people fit to determine, when the time arrives, their own destiny. We are seeking to arouse a national spirit and not, as under the older colonial theory, to suppress such a spirit. The character of the work we have been doing is keenly recognized in the Orient, and our success thus far followed with not a little envy by those who, initiating the same policy, find themselves hampered by conditions grown up in earlier days and under different theories of administration. But our work is far from done. Our duty to the Filipinos is far from discharged. Over half a million Filipino students are now in the Philippine schools helping to mold the men of the future into a homogeneous people, but there still remain more than a million Filipino children of school age yet to be reached. Freed from American control the integrating forces of a common education and a common language will cease and the educational system now well started will slip back into inefficiency and disorder.

An enormous increase in the commercial development of the islands has been made since they were virtually granted full access to our markets three years ago, with every prospect of increasing development and diversified industries. Freed from American control such development is bound to decline. Every observer speaks of the great progress in public works for the benefit of the Filipinos, of harbor improvements, of roads and railways, of irrigation and artesian wells, public buildings, and better means of communication. But large parts of the islands are still unreached, still even unexplored, roads and railways are needed in many parts, irrigation systems are still to be installed, and wells to be driven. Whole villages and towns are still without means of communication other than almost impassable roads and trails. Even the great progress in sanitation, which has successfully suppressed smallpox, the bubonic plague, and Asiatic cholera, has found the cause of and a cure for beriberi, has segregated the lepers, has helped to make Manila the most healthful city in the Orient, and to free life throughout the whole archipelago from its former dread diseases, is nevertheless incomplete in many essentials of permanence in sanitary policy. Even more remains to be accomplished. If freed from American control sanitary progress is bound to be arrested and all that has been achieved likely to be lost.

Concurrent with the economic, social, and industrial development of the islands has been the development of the political capacity of the people. By their progressive participation in government the Filipinos are being steadily and hopefully trained for self-government. Under Spanish control they shared in no way in the government. Under American control they have shared largely and increasingly. Within the last dozen years they have gradually been given complete autonomy in the municipalities, the right to elect two-thirds of the provincial governing boards and the lower house of the insular legislature. They have four native members out of nine members of the commission, or upper house. The chief justice and two justices of the supreme court, about one-half of the higher judicial positions, and all of the justices of the peace are natives. In the classified civil service the proportion of Filipinos increased from 51 per cent in 1904 to 67 per cent in 1911. Thus to-day all the municipal employees, over 90 per cent of the provincial employees, and 60 per cent of the officials and employees of the central government are Filipinos. The ideal which has been kept in mind in our political guidance of the islands has been *real* popular self-government and not mere paper independence. I am happy to say that the Filipinos have done well enough in the places they have filled and in the discharge of the political power with which they have been intrusted to warrant the belief that they can be educated and trained to complete self-government. But the present satisfactory results are due to constant support and supervision at every step by Americans.

If the task we have undertaken is higher than that assumed by other nations, its accomplishment must demand even more patience. We must not forget that we found the Filipinos wholly untrained in government. Up to our advent all other experience sought to repress rather than encourage political power. It takes long time and much experience to ingrain political habits of steadiness and efficiency. Popular self-government ultimately must rest upon common habits of thought and upon a reasonably developed public opinion. No such foundations for self-government, let alone independence, are now present in the Philippine Islands. Disregarding even their racial heterogeneity and the lack of ability to think as a nation, it is sufficient to point out that under liberal franchise privileges only about 3 per cent of the Filipinos vote and only 5 per cent of the people are said to read the public press. To confer independence upon the Filipinos now is, therefore, to subject the great mass of their people to the dominance of an oligarchical and, probably, exploiting minority. Such a course will be as cruel to those people as it would be shameful to us.

Our true course is to pursue steadily and courageously the path we have thus far followed; to guide the Filipinos into self-sustaining pursuits; to continue the cultivation of sound political habits through education and political practice; to encourage the diversification of industries, and to realize the advantages of their industrial education by conservatively approved cooperative methods, at once checking the dangers of concentrated wealth and building up a sturdy, independent citizenship. We should do all this with a disinterested endeavor to secure for the Filipinos economic independence and to fit them for complete self-government, with the power to decide eventually, according to their own largest good, whether such self-government shall be accompanied by independence. A present declaration even of future independence would retard progress by the dissension and disorder it would arouse. On our part it would be a disingenuous attempt, under the guise of conferring a benefit on them, to relieve ourselves from the heavy and difficult burden which thus far we have been bravely and consistently sustaining. It would be a disguised policy of scuttle. It would make the helpless Filipino the football of oriental politics, under the protection of a guaranty of their independence, which we would be powerless to enforce.

REGULATION OF WATER POWER

There are pending before Congress a large number of bills proposing to grant privileges of erecting dams for the purpose of creating water power in our navigable rivers. The pendency of these bills has brought out an important defect in the existing general dam act. That act does not, in my opinion, grant sufficient power to the Federal Government in dealing with the construction of such dams to exact protective conditions in the interest of navigation. It does not permit the Federal Government, as a condition of its permit, to require that a part of the value thus created shall be applied to the further general improvement and protection of the stream. I believe this to be one of the most important matters of internal improvement now confronting the Government. Most of the navigable rivers of this country are comparatively long and shallow. In order that they may be made fully useful for navigation there has come into vogue a method of improvement known as canalization, or the slack-water method, which consists in building a series of dams and locks, each of which will create a long pool of deep navigable water. At each of these dams there is usually created also water power of commercial value. If the water power thus created can be made available for the further improvement of navigation in the stream, it is manifest that the improvement will be much more quickly effected on the one hand, and, on the other, that the burden on the general taxpayers of the country will be very much reduced. Private interests seeking permits to build water-power dams in navigable streams usually urge that they thus improve navigation, and that if they do not impair navigation they should be allowed to take for themselves the entire profits of the water-power development. Whatever they may do by way of relieving the Government of the expense of improving navigation should be given due consideration, but it must be apparent that there may be a profit beyond a reasonably liberal return upon the private investment which is a potential asset of the Government in carrying out a comprehensive policy of waterway development. It is no objection to the retention and use of such an asset by the Government that a comprehensive waterway policy will include the protection and development of the other public uses of water, which can not and should not be ignored in making and executing plans for the protection and development of navigation. It is also equally clear that inasmuch as the water power thus created is or may be an incident of a general scheme of waterway improvement within the constitutional jurisdiction of the Federal Government, the regulation of such water power lies also within that jurisdiction. In my opinion constructive statesmanship requires that legislation should be enacted which will permit the development of navigation in these great rivers to go hand in hand with the utilization of this by-product of water power, created in the course of the same improvement, and that the general dam act should be so amended as to make this possible. I deem it highly important that the Nation should adopt a consistent and harmonious treatment of these water-power projects, which will preserve for this purpose their value to the Government, whose right it is to grant the permit. Any other policy is equivalent to throwing away a most valuable national asset.

THE PANAMA CANAL

During the past year the work of construction upon the canal has progressed most satisfactorily. About 87 per cent of the excavation work has been completed, and more than 93 per cent of the concrete for all the locks is in place. In view of the great interest which has been manifested as to some slides in the Culebra Cut, I am glad to say that the report of Col. Goethals should allay any apprehension on this point. It is gratifying to note that none of the slides which occurred during this year would have interfered with the passage of the ships had the canal, in fact, been in operation, and when the slope pressures will have been finally adjusted and the growth of vegetation will minimize erosion in the banks of the cut, the slide problem will be practically solved and an ample stability assured for the Culebra Cut.

Although the official date of the opening has been set for January 1, 1915, the canal will, in fact, from present indications, be opened for shipping during the latter half of 1913. No fixed date can as yet be set, but shipping interests will be advised as soon as assurances can be given that vessels can pass through without unnecessary delay.

Recognizing the administrative problem in the management of the canal, Congress in the act of August 24, 1912, has made admirable provisions for executive responsibility in the control of the canal and the government of the Canal Zone. The problem of most efficient organization is receiving careful consideration, so that a scheme of organization and control best adapted to the conditions of the canal may be formulated and put in operation as expeditiously as possible. Acting under the authority conferred on me by Congress, I have, by Executive proclamation, promulgated the following schedule of tolls for ships passing through the canal, based upon the thorough report of Emory R. Johnson, special commissioner on traffic and tolls:

1. On merchant vessels carrying passengers or cargo, $1.20 per net vessel ton—each 100 cubic feet—of actual earning capacity.

2. On vessels in ballast without passengers or cargo, 40 per cent less than the rate of tolls for vessels with passengers or cargo.

3. Upon naval vessels, other than transports, colliers, hospital ships, and supply ships, 50 cents per displacement ton.

4. Upon Army and Navy transports, colliers, hospital ships, and supply ships, $1.20 per net ton, the vessels to be measured by the same rules as are employed in determining the net tonnage of merchant vessels.

Rules for the determination of the tonnage upon which toll charges are based are now in course of preparation and will be promulgated in due season.

PANAMA CANAL TREATY

The proclamation which I have issued in respect to the Panama Canal tolls is in accord with the Panama Canal act passed by this Congress August 24, 1912. We have been advised that the British Government has prepared a protest against the act and its enforcement in so far as it relieves from the payment of tolls American ships engaged in the American coastwise trade on the ground that it violates British rights under the Hay-Pauncefote treaty concerning the Panama Canal. When the protest is presented, it will be promptly considered and an effort made to reach a satisfactory adjustment of any differences there may be between the two Governments.

WORKMEN'S COMPENSATION ACT

The promulgation of an efficient workmen's compensation act, adapted to the particular conditions of the zone, is awaiting adequate appropriation by Congress for the payment of claims arising thereunder. I urge that speedy provision be made in order that we may install upon the zone a system of settling claims for injuries in best accord with modern humane, social, and industrial theories.

PROMOTION FOR COL. GOETHALS

As the completion of the canal grows nearer, and as the wonderful executive work of Col. Goethals becomes more conspicuous in the eyes of the country and of the world, it seems to me wise and proper to make provision by law for such reward to him as may be commensurate with the service that he has rendered to his country. I suggest that this reward take the form of an appointment of Col. Goethals as a major general in the Army of the United States, and that the law authorizing such appointment be accompanied with a provision permitting his designation as Chief of Engineers upon the retirement of the present incumbent of that office.

NAVY DEPARTMENT

The Navy of the United States is in a greater state of efficiency and is more powerful than it has ever been before, but in the emulation which exists between different countries in respect to the increase of naval and military armaments this condition is not a permanent one. In view of the many improvements and increases by foreign Governments the slightest halt on our part in respect to new construction throws us back and reduces us from a naval power of the first rank and places us among the nations of the second rank. In the past 15 years the Navy has expanded rapidly and yet far less rapidly than our country. From now on reduced expenditures in the Navy means reduced military strength. The world's history has shown the importance of sea power both for adequate defense and for the support of important and definite policies.

I had the pleasure of attending this autumn a mobilization of the Atlantic Fleet, and was glad to observe and note the preparedness of the fleet for instant action. The review brought before the President and the Secretary of the Navy a greater and more powerful collection of vessels than had ever been gathered in American waters. The condition of the fleet and of the officers and enlisted men and of the equipment of the vessels entitled those in authority to the greatest credit.

I again commend to Congress the giving of legislative sanction to the appointment of the naval aids to the Secretary of the Navy. These aids and the council of aids appointed by the Secretary of the Navy to assist him in the conduct of his department have proven to be of the highest utility. They have furnished an executive committee of the most skilled naval experts, who have coordinated the action of the various bureaus in the Navy, and by their advice have enabled the Secretary to give an administration at the same time economical and most efficient. Never before has the United States had a Navy that compared in efficiency with its present one, but never before have the requirements with respect to naval warfare been higher and more exacting than now. A year ago Congress refused to appropriate for more than one battleship. In this I think a great mistake of policy was made, and I urgently recommend that this Congress make up for the mistake of the last session by appropriations authorizing the construction of three battleships, in addition to destroyers, fuel ships, and the other auxiliary vessels as shown in the building program of the general board. We are confronted by a condition in respect to the navies of the world which requires us, if we would maintain our Navy as an insurance of peace, to augment our naval force by at least two battleships a year and by battle cruisers, gunboats, torpedo destroyers, and submarine boats in a proper proportion. We have no desire for war. We would go as far as any nation in the world to avoid war, but we are a world power. Our population, our wealth, our definite policies, our responsibilities in the Pacific and the Atlantic, our defense of the Panama Canal, together with our enormous world trade and our missionary outposts on the frontiers of civilization, require us to recognize our position as one of the foremost in the family of nations, and to clothe ourselves with sufficient naval power to give force to our reasonable demands, and to give weight to our influence in those directions of progress that a powerful Christian nation should advocate.

I observe that the Secretary of the Navy devotes some space to a change in the disciplinary system in vogue in that branch of the service. I think there is nothing quite so unsatisfactory to either the Army or the Navy as the severe punishments necessarily inflicted by court-martial for desertions and purely military offenses, and I am glad to hear that the British have solved this important and difficult matter in a satisfactory way. I commend to the consideration of Congress the details of the new disciplinary system, and recommend that laws be passed putting the same into force both in the Army and the Navy.

I invite the attention of Congress to that part of the report of the Secretary of the Navy in which he recommends the formation of a naval reserve by the organization of the ex-sailors of the Navy.

I repeat my recommendation made last year that proper provision should be made for the rank of the commander in chief of the squadrons and fleets of the Navy. The inconvenience attending the necessary precedence that most foreign admirals have over our own whenever they meet in official functions ought to be avoided. It impairs the prestige of our Navy and is a defect that can be very easily removed.

DEPARTMENT OF JUSTICE

This department has been very active in the enforcement of the law. It has been better organized and with a larger force than ever before in the history of the Government. The prosecutions which have been successfully concluded and which are now pending testify to the effectiveness of the departmental work.

The prosecution of trusts under the Sherman antitrust law has gone on without restraint or diminution, and decrees similar to those entered in the Standard Oil and the Tobacco cases have been entered in other suits, like the suits against the Powder Trust and the Bathtub Trust. I am very strongly convinced that a steady, consistent course in this regard, with a continuing of Supreme Court decisions upon new phases of the trust question not already finally decided is going to offer a solution of this much-discussed and troublesome issue in a quiet, calm, and judicial way, without any radical legislation changing the governmental policy in regard to combinations now denounced by the Sherman antitrust law. I have already recommended as an aid in this matter legislation which would declare unlawful certain well-known phases of unfair competition in interstate trade, and I have also advocated voluntary national incorporation for the larger industrial enterprises, with provision for a closer supervision by the Bureau of Corporations, or a board appointed for the purpose, so as to make more certain compliance with the antitrust law on the one hand and to give greater security to the stockholders against possible prosecutions on the other. I believe, however, that the orderly course of litigation in the courts and the regular prosecution of trusts charged with the violation of the antitrust law is producing among business men a clearer and clearer perception of the line of distinction between business that is to be encouraged and business that is to be condemned, and that in this quiet way the question of trusts can be settled and competition retained as an economic force to secure reasonableness in prices and freedom and independence in trade.

REFORM OF COURT PROCEDURE

I am glad to bring to the attention of Congress the fact that the Supreme Court has radically altered the equity rules governing the procedure on the equity side of all Federal courts, and though, as these changes have not been yet put in practice so as to enable us to state from actual results what the reform will accomplish, they are of such a character that we can reasonably prophesy that they will greatly reduce the time and cost of litigation in such courts. The court has adopted many of the shorter methods of the present English procedure, and while it may take a little while for the profession to accustom itself to these methods, it is certain greatly to facilitate litigation. The action of the Supreme Court has been so drastic and so full of appreciation of the necessity for a great reform in court procedure that I have no hesitation in following up this action with a recommendation which I foreshadowed in my message of three years ago, that the sections of the statute governing the procedure in the Federal courts on the common-law side should be so amended as to give to the Supreme Court the same right to make rules of procedure in common law as they have, since the beginning of the court, exercised in equity. I do not doubt that a full consideration of the subject will enable the court while giving effect to the substantial differences in right and remedy between the system of common law and the system of equity so to unite the two procedures into the form of one civil action and to shorten the procedure in such civil action as to furnish a model to all the State courts exercising concurrent jurisdiction with the Federal courts of first instance.

Under the statute now in force the common-law procedure in each Federal court is made to conform to the procedure in the State in which the court is held. In these days, when we should be making progress in court procedure, such a conformity statute makes the Federal method too dependent upon the action of State legislatures. I can but think it a great opportunity for Congress to intrust to the highest tribunal in this country, evidently imbued with a strong spirit in favor of a reform of procedure, the power to frame a model code of procedure, which, while preserving all that is valuable and necessary of the rights and remedies at common law and in equity, shall lessen the burden of the poor litigant to a minimum in the expedition and cheapness with which his cause can be fought or defended through Federal courts to final judgment.

WORKMAN'S COMPENSATION ACT

The workman's compensation act reported by the special commission appointed by Congress and the Executive, which passed the Senate and is now pending in the House, the passage of which I have in previous messages urged upon Congress, I venture again to call to its attention. The opposition to it which developed in the Senate, but which was overcome by a majority in that body, seemed to me to grow out rather of a misapprehension of its effect than of opposition to its principle. I say again that I think no act can have a better effect directly upon the relations between the employer and employee than this act applying to railroads and common carriers of an interstate character, and I am sure that the passage of the act would greatly relieve the courts of the heaviest burden of litigation that they have, and would enable them to dispatch other business with a speed never before attained in courts of justice in this country.

Part III.

[Concerning the Work of the Departments of the Post Office, Interior, Agriculture, and Commerce and Labor and District of Columbia.]

THE WHITE HOUSE, *December 19, 1912.*

To the Senate and House of Representatives:

This is the third of a series of messages in which I have brought to the attention of the Congress the important transactions of the Government in each of its departments during the last year and have discussed needed reforms.

HEADS OF DEPARTMENTS SHOULD HAVE SEATS ON THE FLOOR OF CONGRESS

I recommend the adoption of legislation which shall make it the duty of heads of departments—the members of the President's Cabinet—at convenient times to attend the session of the House and the Senate, which shall provide seats for them in each House, and give them the opportunity to take part in all discussions and to answer questions of which they have had due notice. The rigid holding apart of the executive and the legislative branches of this Government has not worked for the great advantage of either. There has been much lost motion in the machinery, due to the lack of cooperation and interchange of views face to face between the representatives of the Executive and the Members of the two legislative branches of the Government. It was never intended that they should be separated in the sense of not being in constant effective touch and relationship to each other. The legislative and the executive each performs its own appropriate function, but these functions must be coordinated. Time and time again debates have arisen in each House upon issues which the information of a particular department head would have enabled him, if present, to end at once by a simple explanation or statement. Time and time again a forceful and earnest presentation of facts and arguments by the representative of the Executive whose duty it is to enforce the law would have brought about a useful reform by amendment, which in the absence of such a statement has failed of passage. I do not think I am mistaken in saying that the presence of the members of the Cabinet on the floor of each House would greatly contribute to the enactment of beneficial legislation. Nor would this in any degree deprive either the legislative or the executive of the independence which separation of the two branches has been intended to promote. It would only facilitate their co-operation in the public interest.

On the other hand, I am sure that the necessity and duty imposed upon department heads of appearing in each House and in answer to searching questions, of rendering upon their feet an account of what they have done, or what has been done by the administration, will spur each member of the Cabinet to closer attention to the details of his department, to greater familiarity with its needs, and to greater care to avoid the just criticism which the answers brought out in questions put and discussions arising between the Members of either House and the members of the Cabinet may properly evoke.

Objection is made that the members of the administration having no vote could exercise no power on the floor of the House, and could not assume that attitude of authority and control which the English parliamentary Government have and which enables them to meet the responsibilities the English system thrusts upon them. I agree that in certain respects it would be more satisfactory if members of the Cabinet could at the same time be Members of both Houses, with voting power, but this is impossible under our system; and while a lack of this feature may detract from the influence of the department chiefs, it will not prevent the good results which I have described above both in the matter of legislation and in the matter of administration. The enactment of such a law would be quite within the power of Congress without constitutional amendment, and it has such possibilities of usefulness that we might well make the experiment, and if we are disappointed the misstep can be easily retraced by a repeal of the enabling legislation.

This is not a new proposition. In the House of Representatives, in the Thirty-eighth Congress, the proposition was referred to a select committee of seven Members. The committee made an extensive report, and urged the adoption of the reform. The report showed that our history had not been without illustration of the necessity and the examples of the practice by pointing out that in early days Secretaries were repeatedly called to the presence of either House for consultation, advice, and information. It also referred to remarks of Mr. Justice Story in his Commentaries on the Constitution, in which he urgently presented the wisdom of such a change. This report is to be found in Volume I of the Reports of Committees of the First Session of the Thirty-eighth Congress, April 6, 1864.

Again, on February 4, 1881, a select committee of the Senate recommended the passage of a similar bill, and made a report, in which, while approving the separation of the three branches, the executive, legislative, and judicial, they point out as a reason for the proposed change that, although having a separate existence, the branches are "to cooperate, each with the other, as the different members of the human body must cooperate, with each other in order to form the figure and perform the duties of a perfect man."

The report concluded as follows:

This system will require the selection of the strongest men to be heads of departments and will require them to be well equipped with the knowledge of their offices. It will also require the strongest men to be the leaders of Congress and participate in debate. It will bring these strong men in contact, perhaps into conflict, to advance the public weal, and thus stimulate their abilities and their efforts, and will thus assuredly result to the good of the country.

If it should appear by actual experience that the heads of departments in fact have not time to perform the additional duty imposed on them by this bill, the force in their offices should be increased or the duties devolving on them personally should be diminished. An undersecretary should be appointed to whom could be confided that routine of administration which requires only order and accuracy. The principal officers could then confine their attention to those duties which require wise discretion and intellectual activity. Thus they would have abundance of time for their duties under this bill. Indeed, your committee believes that the public interest would be subserved if the Secretaries were relieved of the harassing cares of distributing clerkships and closely supervising the mere machinery of the departments. Your committee believes that the adoption of this bill and the effective execution of its provisions will be the first step toward a sound civil-service reform which will secure a larger wisdom in the adoption of policies and a better system in their execution.

(Signed) GEO. H. PENDLETON.
W. B. ALLISON.
D. W. VOORHEES.
J. G. BLAINE.
M. C. BUTLER.
JOHN J. INGALLS.
O. H. PLATT.
J. T. FARLEY.

It would be difficult to mention the names of higher authority in the practical knowledge of our Government than those which are appended to this report.

POSTAL SAVINGS BANK SYSTEM

The Postal Savings Bank System has been extended so that it now includes 4,004 fourth-class post offices, as well as 645 branch offices and stations in the larger cities. There are now 12,812 depositories at which patrons of the system may open accounts. The number of depositors is 300,000 and the amount of their deposits is approximately $28,000,000, not including $1,314,140 which has been withdrawn by depositors for the purpose of buying postal savings bonds. Experience demonstrates the value of dispensing with the pass-book and introducing in its place a certificate of deposit. The gross income of the postal savings system for the fiscal year ending June 30, 1913, will amount to $700,000 and the interest payable to depositors to $300,000. The cost of supplies, equipment, and salaries is $700,000. It thus appears that the system lacks $300,000 a year of paying interest and expenses. It is estimated, however, that when the deposits have reached the sum of $50,000,000, which at the present rate they soon will do, the system will be self-sustaining. By law the postal savings funds deposited at each post office are required to be redeposited in local banks. State and national banks to the number of 7,357 have qualified as depositories for these funds. Such deposits are secured by bonds aggregating $54,000,000. Of this amount, $37,000,000 represent municipal bonds.

PARCEL POST

In several messages I have favored and recommended the adoption of a system of parcel post. In the postal appropriation act of last year a general system was provided and its installation was directed by the 1st of January. This has entailed upon the Post Office Department a great deal of very heavy labor, but the Postmaster General informs me that on the date selected, to wit, the 1st of January, near at hand, the department will be in readiness to meet successfully the requirements of the public.

CLASSIFICATION OF POSTMASTERS

A trial, during the past three years, of the system of classifying fourth-class postmasters in that part of the country lying between the Mississippi River on the west, Canada on the north, the Atlantic Ocean on the east, and Mason and Dixon's line on the south has been sufficiently satisfactory to justify the postal authorities in recommending the extension of the order to include all the fourth-class postmasters in the country. In September, 1912, upon the suggestion of the Postmaster General, I directed him to prepare an order which should put the system in effect, except in Alaska, Guam, Hawaii, Porto Rico, and Samoa. Under date of October 15 I issued such an order which affected 36,000 postmasters. By the order the post offices were divided into groups A and B. Group A includes all postmasters whose compensation is $500 or more, and group B those whose compensation is less than that sum. Different methods are pursued in the selection of the postmasters for group A and group B. Criticism has been made of this order on the ground that the motive for it was political. Nothing could be further from the truth.

The order was made before the election and in the interest of efficient public service. I have several times requested Congress to give me authority to put first-, second-, and third-class postmasters, and all other local officers, including internal-revenue officers, customs officers, United States marshals, and the local agents of the other departments under the classification of the civil-service law by taking away the necessity for confirming such appointments by the Senate. I deeply regret the failure of Congress to follow these recommendations. The change would have taken out of politics practically every local officer and would have entirely cured the evils growing out of what under the present law must always remain a remnant of the spoils system.

COMPENSATION TO RAILWAYS FOR CARRYING MAILS

It is expected that the establishment of a parcel post on January 1st will largely increase the amount of mail matter to be transported by the railways, and Congress should be prompt to provide a way by which they may receive the additional compensation to which they will be entitled. The Postmaster General urges that the department's plan for a complete readjustment of the system of paying the railways for carrying the mails be adopted, substituting space for weight as the principal factor in fixing compensation. Under this plan it will be possible to determine without delay what additional payment should be made on account of the parcel post. The Postmaster General's recommendation is based on the results of a far-reaching investigation begun early in the administration with the object of determining what it costs the railways to carry the mails. The statistics obtained during the course of the inquiry show that while many of the railways, and particularly the large systems, were making profits from mail transportations, certain of the lines were actually carrying the mails at a loss. As a result of the investigation the department, after giving the subject careful consideration, decided to urge the abandonment of the present plan of fixing compensation on the basis of the weight of the mails carried, a plan that has proved to be exceedingly expensive and in other respects unsatisfactory. Under the method proposed the railway companies will annually submit to the department reports showing what it costs them to carry the mails, and this cost will be apportioned on the basis of the car space engaged, payment to be allowed at the rate thus determined in amounts that will cover the cost and a reasonable profit. If a railway is not satisfied with the manner in which the department apportions the cost in fixing compensation, it is to have the right, under the new plan, of appealing to the Interstate Commerce Commission. This feature of the proposed law would seem to insure a fair treatment of the railways. It is hoped that Congress will give the matter immediate attention and that the method of compensation recommended by the department or some other suitable plan will be promptly authorized.

DEPARTMENT OF THE INTERIOR

The Interior Department, in the problems of administration included within its jurisdiction, presents more difficult questions than any other. This has been due perhaps to temporary causes of a political character, but more especially to the inherent difficulty in the performance of some of the functions which are assigned to it. Its chief duty is the guardianship of the public domain and the disposition of that domain to private ownership under homestead, mining, and other laws, by which patents from the Government to the individual are authorized on certain conditions. During the last decade the public seemed to become suddenly aware that a very large part of its domain had passed from its control into private ownership, under laws not well adapted to modern conditions, and also that in the doing of this the provisions of existing law and regulations adopted in accordance with law had not been strictly observed, and that in the transfer of title much fraud had intervened, to the pecuniary benefit of dishonest persons. There arose thereupon a demand for conservation of the public domain, its protection against fraudulent diminution, and the preservation of that part of it from private acquisition which it seemed necessary to keep for future public use. The movement, excellent in the intention which prompted it, and useful in its results, has nevertheless had some bad effects, which the western country has recently been feeling and in respect of which there is danger of a reaction toward older abuses unless we can attain the golden mean, which consists in the prevention of the mere exploitation of the public domain for private purposes while at the same time facilitating its development for the benefit of the local public.

The land laws need complete revision to secure proper conservation on the one hand of land that ought to be kept in public use and, on the other hand, prompt disposition of those lands which ought to be disposed in private ownership or turned over to private use by properly guarded leases. In addition to this there are not enough officials in our Land Department with legal knowledge sufficient promptly to make the decisions which are called for. The whole land-laws system should be reorganized, and not until it is reorganized, will decisions be made as promptly as they ought, or will men who have earned title to public land under the statute receive their patents within a reasonably short period. The present administration has done what it could in this regard, but the necessity for reform and change by a revision of the laws and an increase and reorganization of the force remains, and I submit to Congress the wisdom of a full examination of this subject, in order that a very large and important part of our people in the West may be relieved from a just cause of irritation.

I invite your attention to the discussion by the Secretary of the Interior of the need for legislation with respect to mining claims, leases of coal lands in this country and in Alaska, and for similar disposition of oil, phosphate, and potash lands, and also to his discussion of the proper use to be made of water-power sites held by the Government. Many of these lands are now being withheld from use by the public under the general withdrawal act which was passed by the last Congress. That act was not for the purpose of disposing of the question, but it was for the purpose of preserving the lands until the question could be solved. I earnestly urge that the matter is of the highest importance to our western fellow citizens and ought to command the immediate attention of the legislative branch of the Government.

Another function which the Interior Department has to perform is that of the guardianship of Indians. In spite of everything which has been said in criticism of the policy of our Government toward the Indians, the amount of wealth which is now held by it for these wards per capita shows that the Government has been generous; but the management of so large an estate, with the great variety of circumstances that surround each tribe and each case, calls for the exercise of the highest business discretion, and the machinery provided in the Indian Bureau for the discharge of this function is entirely inadequate. The position of Indian commissioner demands the exercise of business ability of the first order, and it is difficult to secure such talent for the salary provided.

The condition of health of the Indian and the prevalence in the tribes of curable diseases has been exploited recently in the press. In a message to Congress at its last session I brought this subject to its attention and invited a special appropriation, in order that our facilities for overcoming diseases among the Indians might be properly increased, but no action was then taken by Congress on the subject, nor has such appropriation been made since.

The commission appointed by authority of the Congress to report on proper method of securing railroad development in Alaska is formulating its report, and I expect to have an opportunity before the end of this session to submit its recommendations.

DEPARTMENT OF AGRICULTURE

The far-reaching utility of the educational system carried on by the Department of Agriculture for the benefit of the farmers of our country calls for no elaboration. Each year there is a growth in the variety of facts which it brings out for the benefit of the farmer, and each year confirms the wisdom of the expenditure of the appropriations made for that department.

PURE-FOOD LAW

The Department of Agriculture is charged with the execution of the pure-food law. The passage of this encountered much opposition from manufacturers and others who feared the effect upon their business of the enforcement of its provisions. The opposition aroused the just indignation of the public, and led to an intense sympathy with the severe and rigid enforcement of the provisions of the new law. It had to deal in many instances with the question whether or not products of large business enterprises, in the form of food preparations, were deleterious to the public health; and while in a great majority of instances this issue was easily determinable, there were not a few cases in which it was hard to draw the line between a useful and a harmful food preparation. In cases like this when a decision involved the destruction of great business enterprises representing the investment of large capital and the expenditure of great energy and ability, the danger of serious injustice was very considerable in the enforcement of a new law under the spur of great public indignation. The public officials charged with executing the law might do injustice in heated controversy through unconscious pride of opinion and obstinacy of conclusion. For this reason President Roosevelt felt justified in creating a board of experts, known as the Remsen Board, to whom in cases of much importance an appeal might be taken and a review had of a decision of the Bureau of Chemistry in the Agricultural Department. I heartily agree that it was wise to create this board in order that injustice might not be done. The questions which arise are not generally those involving palpable injury to health, but they are upon the narrow and doubtful line in respect of which it is better to be in some error not dangerous than to be radically destructive. I think that the time has come for Congress to recognize the necessity for some such tribunal of appeal and to make specific statutory provision for it. While we are struggling to suppress an evil of great proportions like that of impure food, we must provide machinery in the law itself to prevent its becoming an instrument of oppression, and we ought to enable those whose business is threatened with annihilation to have some tribunal and some form of appeal in which they have a complete day in court.

AGRICULTURAL CREDITS

I referred in my first message to the question of improving the system of agricultural credits. The Secretary of Agriculture has made an investigation into the matter of credits in this country, and I commend a consideration of the information which through his agents he has been able to collect. It does not in any way minimize the importance of the proposal, but it gives more accurate information upon some of the phases of the question than we have heretofore had.

DEPARTMENT OF COMMERCE AND LABOR

I commend to Congress an examination of the report of the Secretary of Commerce and Labor, and especially that part in which he discusses the office of the Bureau of Corporations, the value to commerce of a proposed trade commission, and the steps which he has taken to secure the organization of a national chamber of commerce. I heartily commend his view that the plan of a trade commission which looks to the fixing of prices is altogether impractical and ought not for a moment to be considered as a possible solution of the trust question.

The trust question in the enforcement of the Sherman antitrust law is gradually solving itself, is maintaining the principle and restoring the practice of competition, and if the law is quietly but firmly enforced, business will adjust itself to the statutory requirements, and the unrest in commercial circles provoked by the trust discussion will disappear.

PANAMA-PACIFIC INTERNATIONAL EXPOSITION

In conformity with a joint resolution of Congress, an Executive proclamation was issued last February, inviting the nations of the world to participate in the Panama-Pacific International Exposition to be held at San Francisco to celebrate the construction of the Panama Canal. A sympathetic response was immediately forthcoming, and several nations have already selected the sites for their buildings. In furtherance of my invitation, a special commission visited European countries during the past summer, and received assurance of hearty cooperation in the task of bringing together a universal industrial, military, and naval display on an unprecedented scale. It is evident that the exposition will be an accurate mirror of the world's activities as they appear 400 years after the date of the discovery of the Pacific Ocean.

It is the duty of the United States to make the nations welcome at San Francisco and to facilitate such acquaintance between them and ourselves as will promote the expansion of commerce and familiarize the world with the new trade route through the Panama Canal. The action of the State governments and individuals assures a comprehensive exhibit of the resources of this country and of the progress of the people. This participation by State and individuals should be supplemented by an adequate showing of the varied and unique activities of the National Government. The United States can not with good grace invite foreign governments to erect buildings and make expensive exhibits while itself refusing to participate. Nor would it be wise to forego the opportunity to join with other nations in the inspiring interchange of ideas tending to promote intercourse, friendship, and commerce. It is the duty of the Government to foster and build up commerce through the canal, just as it was the duty of the Government to construct it.

I earnestly recommend the appropriation at this session of such a sum as will enable the United States to construct a suitable building, install a governmental exhibit, and otherwise participate in the Panama-Pacific International Exposition in a manner commensurate with the dignity of a nation whose guests are to be the people of the world. I recommend also such legislation as will facilitate the entry of material intended for exhibition and protect foreign exhibitors against infringement of patents and the unauthorized copying of patterns and designs. All aliens sent to San Francisco to construct and care for foreign buildings and exhibits should be admitted without restraint or embarrassment.

THE DISTRICT OF COLUMBIA AND THE CITY OF WASHINGTON

The city of Washington is a beautiful city, with a population of 352,936, of whom 98,667 are colored. The annual municipal budget is about $14,000,000. The presence of the National Capital and other governmental structures constitutes the chief beauty and interest of the city. The public grounds are extensive, and the opportunities for improving the city and making it still more attractive are very great. Under a plan adopted some years ago, one half the cost of running the city is paid by taxation upon the property, real and personal, of the citizens and residents, and the other half is borne by the General Government. The city is expanding at a remarkable rate, and this can only be accounted for by the coming here from other parts of the country of well-to-do people who, having finished their business careers elsewhere, build and make this their permanent place of residence.

On the whole, the city as a municipality is very well governed. It is well lighted, the water supply is good, the streets are well paved, the police force is well disciplined, crime is not flagrant, and while it has purlieus and centers of vice, like other large cities, they are not exploited, they do not exercise any influence or control in the government of the city, and they are suppressed in as far as it has been found practicable. Municipal graft is inconsiderable. There are interior courts in the city that are noisome and centers of disease and the refuge of criminals, but Congress has begun to clean these out, and progress has been made in the case of the most notorious of these, which is known as "Willow Tree Alley." This movement should continue.

The mortality for the past year was at the rate of 17.80 per 1,000 of both races; among the whites it was 14.61 per thousand, and among the blacks 26.12 per thousand. These are the lowest mortality rates ever recorded in the District.

One of the most crying needs in the government of the District is a tribunal or public authority for the purpose of supervising the corporations engaged in the operation of public utilities. Such a bill is pending in Congress and ought to pass. Washington should show itself under the direction of Congress to be a city with a model form of government, but as long as such authority over public utilities is withheld from the municipal government, it must always be defective.

Without undue criticism of the present street railway accommodations, it can be truly said that under the spur of a public utilities commission they might be substantially improved.

While the school system of Washington perhaps might be bettered in the economy of its management and the distribution of its buildings, its usefulness has nevertheless greatly increased in recent years, and it now offers excellent facilities for primary and secondary education.

From time to time there is considerable agitation in Washington in favor of granting the citizens of the city the franchise and constituting an elective government. I am strongly opposed to this change. The history of Washington discloses a number of experiments of this kind, which have always been abandoned as unsatisfactory. The truth is this is a city governed by a popular body, to wit, the Congress of the United States, selected from the people of the United States, who own Washington. The people who come here to live do so with the knowledge of the origin of the city and the restrictions, and therefore voluntarily give up the privilege of living in a municipality governed by popular vote. Washington is so unique in its origin and in its use for housing and localizing the sovereignty of the Nation that the people who live here must regard its peculiar character and must be content to subject themselves to the control of a body selected by all the people of the Nation. I agree that there are certain inconveniences growing out of the government of a city by a national legislature like Congress, and it would perhaps be possible to lessen these by the delegation by Congress to the District Commissioners of greater legislative power for the enactment of local laws than they now possess, especially those of a police character.

Every loyal American has a personal pride in the beauty of Washington and in its development and growth. There is no one with a proper appreciation of our Capital City who would favor a niggardly policy in respect to expenditures from the National Treasury to add to the attractiveness of this city, which belongs to every citizen of the entire country, and which no citizen visits without a sense of pride of ownership. We have had restored by a Commission of Fine Arts, at the instance of a committee of the Senate, the original plan of the French engineer L'Enfant for the city of Washington, and we know with great certainty the course which the improvement of Washington should take. Why should there be delay in making this improvement in so far as it involves the extension of the parking system and the construction of greatly needed public buildings? Appropriate buildings for the State Department, the Department of Justice, and the Department of Commerce and Labor have been projected, plans have been approved, and nothing is wanting but the appropriations for the beginning and completion of the structures. A hall of archives is also badly needed, but nothing has been done toward its construction, although the land for it has long been bought and paid for. Plans have been made for the union of Potomac Park with the valley of Rock Creek and Rock Creek Park, and the necessity for the connection between the Soldiers' Home and Rock Creek Park calls for no comment. I ask again why there should be delay in carrying out these plans We have the money in the Treasury, the plans are national in their scope, and the improvement should be treated as a national project. The plan will find a hearty approval throughout the country. I am quite sure, from the information which I have, that, at comparatively small expense, from that part of the District of Columbia which was retroceded to Virginia, the portion including the Arlington estate, Fort Myer, and the palisades of the Potomac can be acquired by purchase and the jurisdiction of the State of Virginia over this land ceded to the Nation. This ought to be done.

The construction of the Lincoln Memorial and of a memorial bridge from the base of the Lincoln Monument to Arlington would be an appropriate and symbolic expression of the union of the North and the South at the Capital of the Nation. I urge upon Congress the appointment of a commission to undertake these national improvements, and to submit a plan for their execution; and when the plan has been submitted and approved, and the work carried out, Washington will really become what it ought to be—the most beautiful city in the world.

Woodrow Wilson

March 4, 1913 to March 4, 1921

FIRST ANNUAL MESSAGE.

[Delivered at a Joint Session of the two Houses of Congress, December 2, 1913.]

Gentlemen of the Congress:

In pursuance of my constitutional duty to "give to the Congress information of the state of the Union," I take the liberty of addressing you on several matters which ought, as it seems to me, particularly to engage the attention of your honorable bodies, as of all who study the welfare and progress of the Nation.

I shall ask your indulgence if I venture to depart in some degree from the usual custom of setting before you in formal review the many matters which have engaged the attention and called for the action of the several departments of the Government or which look to them for early treatment in the future, because the list is long, very long, and would suffer in the abbreviation to which I should have to subject it. I shall submit to you the reports of the heads of the several departments, in which these subjects are set forth in careful detail, and beg that they may receive the thoughtful attention of your committees and of all Members of the Congress who may have the leisure to study them. Their obvious importance, as constituting the very substance of the business of the Government, makes comment and emphasis on my part unnecessary.

The country, I am thankful to say, is at peace with all the world, and many happy manifestations multiply about us of a growing cordiality and sense of community of interest among the nations, foreshadowing an age of settled peace and good will. More and more readily each decade do the nations manifest their willingness to bind themselves by solemn treaty to the processes of peace, the processes of frankness and fair concession. So far the United States has stood at the front of such negotiations. She will, I earnestly hope and confidently believe, give fresh proof of her sincere adherence to the cause of international friendship by ratifying the several treaties of arbitration awaiting renewal by the Senate. In addition to these, it has been the privilege of the Department of State to gain the assent, in principle, of no less than 31 nations, representing four-fifths of the population of the world, to the negotiation of treaties by which it shall be agreed that whenever differences of interest or of policy arise which can not be resolved by the ordinary processes of diplomacy they shall be publicly analyzed, discussed, and reported upon by a tribunal chosen by the parties before either nation determines its course of action.

There is only one possible standard by which to determine controversies between the United States and other nations, and that is compounded of these two elements: Our own honor and our obligations to the peace of the world. A test so compounded ought easily to be made to govern both the establishment of new treaty obligations and the interpretation of those already assumed.

There is but one cloud upon our horizon. That has shown itself to the south of us, and hangs over Mexico. There can be no certain prospect of peace in America until Gen. Huerta has surrendered his usurped authority in Mexico; until it is understood on all hands, indeed, that such pretended governments will not be countenanced or dealt with by the Government of the United States. We are the friends of constitutional government in America; we are more than its friends, we are its champions; because in no other way can our neighbors, to whom we would wish in every way to make proof of our friendship, work out their own development in peace and liberty. Mexico has no Government. The attempt to maintain one at the City of Mexico has broken down, and a mere military despotism has been set up which has hardly more than the semblance of national authority. It originated in the usurpation of Victoriano Huerta, who, after a brief attempt to play the part of constitutional President, has at last cast aside even the pretense of legal right and declared himself dictator. As a consequence, a condition of affairs now exists in Mexico which has made it doubtful whether even the most elementary and fundamental rights either of her own people or of the citizens of other countries resident within her territory can long be successfully safeguarded, and which threatens, if long continued, to imperil the interests of peace, order, and tolerable life in the lands immediately to the south of us. Even if the usurper had succeeded in his purposes, in despite of the constitution of the Republic and the rights of its people, he would have set up nothing but a precarious and hateful power, which could have lasted but a little while, and whose eventual downfall would have left the country in a more deplorable condition than ever. But he has not succeeded. He has forfeited the respect and the moral support even of those who were at one time willing to see him succeed. Little by little he has been completely isolated. By a little every day his power and prestige are crumbling and the collapse is not far away. We shall not, I believe, be obliged to alter our policy of watchful waiting. And then, when the end comes, we shall hope to see constitutional order restored in distressed Mexico by the concert and energy of such of her leaders as prefer the liberty of their people to their own ambitions.

I turn to matters of domestic concern. You already have under consideration a bill for the reform of our system of banking and currency, for which the country waits with impatience, as for something fundamental to its whole business life and necessary to set credit free from arbitrary and artificial restraints. I need not say how earnestly

I hope for its early enactment into law. I take leave to beg that the whole energy and attention of the Senate be concentrated upon it till the matter is successfully disposed of. And yet I feel that the request is not needed—that the Members of that great House need no urging in this service to the country.

I present to you, in addition, the urgent necessity that special provision be made also for facilitating the credits needed by the farmers of the country. The pending currency bill does the farmers a great service. It puts them upon an equal footing with other business men and masters of enterprise, as it should; and upon its passage they will find themselves quit of many of the difficulties which now hamper them in the field of credit. The farmers, of course, ask and should be given no special privilege, such as extending to them the credit of the Government itself. What they need and should obtain is legislation which will make their own abundant and substantial credit resources available as a foundation for joint, concerted local action in their own behalf in getting the capital they must use. It is to this we should now address ourselves.

It has, singularly enough, come to pass that we have allowed the industry of our farms to lag behind the other activities of the country in its development. I need not stop to tell you how fundamental to the life of the Nation is the production of its food. Our thoughts may ordinarily be concentrated upon the cities and the hives of industry, upon the cries of the crowded market place and the clangor of the factory, but it is from the quiet interspaces of the open valleys and the free hillsides that we draw the sources of life and of prosperity, from the farm and the ranch, from the forest and the mine. Without these every street would be silent, every office deserted, every factory fallen into disrepair. And yet the farmer does not stand upon the same footing with the forester and the miner in the market of credit. He is the servant of the seasons. Nature determines how long he must wait for his crops, and will not be hurried in her processes. He may give his note, but the season of its maturity depends upon the season when his crop matures, lies at the gates of the market where his products are sold. And the security he gives is of a character not known in the broker's office or as familiarly as it might be on the counter of the banker.

The Agricultural Department of the Government is seeking to assist as never before to make farming an efficient business, of wide co-operative effort, in quick touch with the markets for foodstuffs. The farmers and the Government will henceforth work together as real partners in this field, where we now begin to see our way very clearly and where many intelligent plans are already being put into execution. The Treasury of the United States has, by a timely and well-considered distribution of its deposits, facilitated the moving of the crops in the present season and prevented the scarcity of available funds too often experienced at such times. But we must not allow ourselves to depend upon extraordinary expedients. We must add the means by which the farmer may make his credit constantly and easily available and command when he will the capital by which to support and expand his business. We lag behind many other great countries of the modern world in attempting to do this. Systems of rural credit have been studied and developed on the other side of the water while we left our farmers to shift for themselves in the ordinary money market. You have but to look about you in any rural district to see the result, the handicap and embarrassment which have been put upon those who produce our food.

Conscious of this backwardness and neglect on our part, the Congress recently authorized the creation of a special commission to study the various systems of rural credit which have been put into operation in Europe, and this commission is already prepared to report. Its report ought to make it easier for us to determine what methods will be best suited to our own farmers. I hope and believe that the committees of the Senate and House will address themselves to this matter with the most fruitful results, and I believe that the studies and recently formed plans of the Department of Agriculture may be made to serve them very greatly in their work of framing appropriate and adequate legislation. It would be indiscreet and presumptuous in anyone to dogmatize upon so great and many-sided a question, but I feel confident that common counsel will produce the results we must all desire.

Turn from the farm to the world of business which centers in the city and in the factory, and I think that all thoughtful observers will agree that the immediate service we owe the business communities of the country is to prevent private monopoly more effectually than it has yet been prevented. I think it will be easily agreed that we should let the Sherman anti-trust law stand, unaltered, as it is, with its debatable ground about it, but that we should as much as possible reduce the area of that debatable ground by further and more explicit legislation; and should also supplement that great act by legislation which will not only clarify it but also facilitate its administration and make it fairer to all concerned. No doubt we shall all wish, and the country will expect, this to be the central subject of our deliberations during the present session; but it is a subject so many-sided and so deserving of careful and discriminating discussion that I shall take the liberty of addressing you upon it in a special message at a later date than this. It is of capital importance that the business men of this country should be relieved of all uncertainties of law with regard to their enterprises and investments and a clear path indicated which they can travel without anxiety. It is as important that they should be relieved of embarrassment and set free to prosper as that private monopoly should be destroyed. The ways of action should be thrown wide open.

I turn to a subject which I hope can be handled promptly and without serious controversy of any kind. I mean the method of selecting nominees for the Presidency of the United States. I feel confident that I do not misinterpret the wishes or the expectations of the country when I urge the prompt enactment of legislation which will provide for primary elections throughout the country at which the voters of the several parties may choose their nominees for the Presidency without the intervention of nominating conventions. I venture the suggestion that this legislation should provide for the retention of party conventions, but only for the purpose of declaring and accepting the verdict of the primaries and formulating the platforms of the parties; and I suggest that these conventions should consist not of delegates chosen for this single purpose, but of the nominees for Congress, the nominees for vacant seats in the Senate of the United States, the Senators whose terms have not yet closed, the national committees, and the candidates for the Presidency themselves, in order that platforms may be framed by those responsible to the people for carrying them into effect.

These are all matters of vital domestic concern, and besides them, outside the charmed circle of our own national life in which our affections command us, as well as our consciences, there stand out our obligations toward our territories over sea. Here we are trustees. Porto Rico, Hawaii, the Philippines, are ours, indeed, but not ours to do what we please with. Such territories, once regarded as mere possessions, are no longer to be selfishly exploited; they are part of the domain of public conscience and of serviceable and enlightened statesmanship. We must administer them for the people who live in them and with the same sense of responsibility to them as toward our own people in our domestic affairs. No doubt we shall successfully enough bind Porto Rico and the Hawaiian Islands to ourselves by ties of justice and interest and affection, but the performance of our duty toward the Philippines is a more difficult and debatable matter. We can satisfy the obligations of generous justice toward the people of Porto Rico by giving them the ample and familiar rights and privileges accorded our own citizens in our own territories and our obligations toward the people of Hawaii by perfecting the provisions for self-government already granted them, but in the Philippines we must go further. We must hold steadily in view their ultimate independence, and we must move toward the time of that independence as steadily as the way can be cleared and the foundations thoughtfully and permanently laid.

Acting under the authority conferred upon the President by Congress, I have already accorded the people of the islands a majority in both houses of their legislative body by appointing five instead of four native citizens to the membership of the commission. I believe that in this way we shall make proof of their capacity in counsel and their sense of responsibility in the exercise of political power, and that the success of this step will be sure to clear our view for the steps which are to follow. Step by step we should extend and perfect the system of self-government in the islands, making test of them and modifying them as experience discloses their successes and their failures; that we should more and more put under the control of the native citizens of the archipelago the essential instruments of their life, their local instrumentalities of government, their schools, all the common interests of their communities, and so by counsel and experience set up a government which all the world will see to be suitable to a people whose affairs are under their own control. At last, I hope and believe, we are beginning to gain the confidence of the Filipino peoples. By their counsel and experience, rather than by our own, we shall learn how best to serve them and how soon it will be possible and wise to withdraw our supervision. Let us once find the path and set out with firm and confident tread upon it and we shall not wander from it or linger upon it.

A duty faces us with regard to Alaska which seems to me very pressing and very imperative; perhaps I should say a double duty, for it concerns both the political and the material development of the Territory. The people of Alaska should be given the full Territorial form of government, and Alaska, as a storehouse, should be unlocked. One key to it is a system of railways. These the Government should itself build and administer, and the ports and terminals it should itself control in the interest of all who wish to use them for the service and development of the country and its people.

But the construction of railways is only the first step; is only thrusting in the key to the storehouse and throwing back the lock and opening the door. How the tempting resources of the country are to be exploited is another matter, to which I shall take the liberty of from time to time calling your attention, for it is a policy which must be worked out by well-considered stages, not upon theory, but upon lines of practical expediency. It is part of our general problem of conservation. We have a freer hand in working out the problem in Alaska than in the States of the Union; and yet the principle and object are the same, wherever we touch it. We must use the resources of the country, not lock them up. There need be no conflict or jealousy as between State and Federal authorities, for there can be no essential difference of purpose between them. The resources in question must be used, but not destroyed or wasted;

used, but not monopolized upon any narrow idea of individual rights as against the abiding interests of communities. That a policy can be worked out by conference and concession which will release these resources and yet not jeopard or dissipate them, I for one have no doubt; and it can be done on lines of regulation which need be no less acceptable to the people and governments of the States concerned than to the people and Government of the Nation at large, whose heritage these resources are. We must bend our counsels to this end. A common purpose ought to make agreement easy.

Three or four matters of special importance and significance I beg that you will permit me to mention in closing.

Our Bureau of Mines ought to be equipped and empowered to render even more effectual service than it renders now in improving the conditions of mine labor and making the mines more economically productive as well as more safe. This is an all-important part of the work of conservation; and the conservation of human life and energy lies even nearer to our interests than the preservation from waste of our material resources.

We owe it, in mere justice to the railway employees of the country, to provide for them a fair and effective employers' liability act; and a law that we can stand by in this matter will be no less to the advantage of those who administer the railroads of the country than to the advantage of those whom they employ. The experience of a large number of the States abundantly proves that.

We ought to devote ourselves to meeting pressing demands of plain justice like this as earnestly as to the accomplishment of political and economic reforms. Social justice comes first. Law is the machinery for its realization and is vital only as it expresses and embodies it.

An international congress for the discussion of all questions that affect safety at sea is now sitting in London at the suggestion of our own Government. So soon as the conclusions of that congress can be learned and considered we ought to address ourselves, among other things, to the prompt alleviation of the very unsafe, unjust, and burdensome conditions which now surround the employment of sailors and render it extremely difficult to obtain the services of spirited and competent men such as every ship needs if it is to be safely handled and brought to port.

May I not express the very real pleasure I have experienced in co-operating with this Congress and sharing with it the labors of common service to which it has devoted itself so unreservedly during the past seven months of uncomplaining concentration upon the business of legislation? Surely it is a proper and pertinent part of my report on "the state of the Union" to express my admiration for the diligence, the good temper, and the full comprehension of public duty which has already been manifested by both the Houses; and I hope that it may not be deemed an impertinent intrusion of myself into the picture if I say with how much and how constant satisfaction I have availed myself of the privilege of putting my time and energy at their disposal alike in counsel and in action.

SECOND ANNUAL MESSAGE.

[Delivered at a Joint Session of the two Houses of Congress, December 8, 1914.]

GENTLEMEN OF THE CONGRESS:

The session upon which you are now entering will be the closing session of the Sixty-third Congress, a Congress, I venture to say, which will long be remembered for the great body of thoughtful and constructive work which it has done, in loyal response to the thought and needs of the country. I should like in this address to review the notable record and try to make adequate assessment of it; but no doubt we stand too near the work that has been done and are ourselves too much part of it to play the part of historians toward it.

Our program of legislation with regard to the regulation of business is now virtually complete. It has been put forth, as we intended, as a whole, and leaves no conjecture as to what is to follow. The road at last lies clear and firm before business. It is a road which it can travel without fear or embarrassment. It is the road to ungrudged, unclouded success. In it every honest man, every man who believes that the public interest is part of his own interest, may walk with perfect confidence.

Moreover, our thoughts are now more of the future than of the past. While we have worked at our tasks of peace the circumstances of the whole age have been altered by war. What we have done for our own land and our own people we did with the best that was in us, whether of character or of intelligence, with sober enthusiasm and a confidence in the principles upon which we were acting which sustained us at every step of the difficult undertaking; but it is done. It has passed from our hands. It is now an established part of the legislation of the country. Its usefulness, its effects will disclose themselves in experience. What chiefly strikes us now, as we look about us during these closing days of a year which will be forever memorable in the history of the world, is that we face new tasks, have been facing them these six months, must face them in the months to come,—face them without partisan feeling, like men who have forgotten everything but a common duty and the fact that we are representatives of a great people whose thought is not of us but of what America owes to herself and to all mankind in such circumstances as these upon which we look amazed and anxious.

War has interrupted the means of trade not only but also the processes of production. In Europe it is destroying men and resources wholesale and upon a scale unprecedented and appalling. There is reason to fear that the time is near, if it be not already at hand, when several of the countries of Europe will find it difficult to do for their people what they have hitherto been always easily able to do,—many essential and fundamental things. At any rate, they will need our help and our manifold services as they have never needed them before; and we should be ready, more fit and ready than we have ever been.

It is of equal consequence that the nations whom Europe has usually supplied with innumerable articles of manufacture and commerce of which they are in constant need and without which their economic development halts and stands still can now get only a small part of what they formerly imported and eagerly look to us to supply their all but empty markets. This is particularly true of our own neighbors, the States, great and small, of Central and South America. Their lines of trade have hitherto run chiefly athwart the seas, not to our ports but to the ports of Great Britain and of the older continent of Europe. I do not stop to inquire why, or to make any comment on probable causes. What interests us just now is not the explanation but the fact, and our duty and opportunity in the presence of it. Here are markets which we must supply, and we must find the means of action. The United States, this great people for whom we speak and act, should be ready, as never before, to serve itself and to serve mankind; ready with its resources, its energies, its forces of production, and its means of distribution.

It is a very practical matter, a matter of ways and means. We have the resources, but are we fully ready to use them? And, if we can make ready what we have, have we the means at hand to distribute it? We are not fully ready; neither have we the means of distribution. We are willing, but we are not fully able. We have the wish to serve and to serve greatly, generously; but we are not prepared as we should be. We are not ready to mobilize our resources at once. We are not prepared to use them immediately and at their best, without delay and without waste.

To speak plainly, we have grossly erred in the way in which we have stunted and hindered the development of our merchant marine. And now, when we need ships, we have not got them. We have year after year debated, without end or conclusion, the best policy to pursue with regard to the use of the ores and forests and water powers of our national domain in the rich States of the West, when we should have acted; and they are still locked up. The key is still turned upon them, the door shut fast at which thousands of vigorous men, full of initiative, knock clamorously for admittance. The water power of our navigable streams outside the national domain also, even in the eastern States, where we have worked and planned for generations, is still not used as it might be, because we will and we won't; because the laws we have made do not intelligently balance encouragement against restraint. We withhold by regulation.

I have come to ask you to remedy and correct these mistakes and omissions, even at this short session of a Congress which would certainly seem to have done all the work that could reasonably be expected of it. The time and the circumstances are extraordinary, and so must our efforts be also.

Fortunately, two great measures, finely conceived, the one to unlock, with proper safeguards, the resources of the national domain, the other to encourage the use of the navigable waters outside that domain for the generation of power, have already passed the House of Representatives and are ready for immediate consideration and action by the Senate. With the deepest earnestness I urge their prompt passage. In them both we turn our backs upon hesitation and makeshift and formulate a genuine policy of use and conservation, in the best sense of those words. We owe the one measure not only to the people of that great western country for whose free and systematic development, as it seems to me, our legislation has done so little, but also to the people of the Nation as a whole; and we as clearly owe the other fulfillment of our repeated promises that the water power of the country should in fact as well as in name be put at the disposal of great industries which can make economical and profitable use of it, the rights of the public being adequately guarded the while, and monopoly in the use prevented. To have begun such measures and not completed them would indeed mar the record of this great Congress very seriously. I hope and confidently believe that they will be completed.

And there is another great piece of legislation which awaits and should receive the sanction of the Senate: I mean the bill which gives a larger measure of self-government to the people of the Philippines. How better, in this time of anxious questioning and perplexed policy, could we show our confidence in the principles of liberty, as the source as well as the expression of life, how better could we demonstrate our own self-possession and steadfastness in the courses of justice and disinterestedness than by thus going calmly forward to fulfill our promises to a dependent people, who will now look more anxiously than ever to see whether we have indeed the liberality, the unselfishness, the courage, the faith we have boasted and professed. I can not believe that the Senate will let this great measure of constructive justice await the action of another Congress. Its passage would nobly crown the record of these two years of memorable labor.

But I think that you will agree with me that this does not complete the toll of our duty. How are we to carry our goods to the empty markets of which I have spoken if we have not the ships? How are we to build up a great trade if we have not the certain and constant means of transportation upon which all profitable and useful commerce depends? And how are we to get the ships if we wait for the trade to develop without them? To correct the many mistakes by which we have discouraged and all but destroyed the merchant marine of the country, to retrace the steps by which we have, it seems almost deliberately, withdrawn our flag from the seas, except where, here and there, a ship of war is bidden carry it or some wandering yacht displays it, would take a long time and involve many detailed items of legislation, and the trade which we ought immediately to handle would disappear or find other channels while we debated the items.

The case is not unlike that which confronted us when our own continent was to be opened up to settlement and industry, and we needed long lines of railway, extended means of transportation prepared beforehand, if development was not to lag intolerably and wait interminably. We lavishly subsidized the building of transcontinental railroads. We look back upon that with regret now, because the subsidies led to many scandals of which we are ashamed; but we know that the railroads had to be built, and if we had it to do over again we should of course build them, but in another way. Therefore I propose another way of providing the means of transportation, which must precede, not tardily follow, the development of our trade with our neighbor states of America. It may seem a reversal of the natural order of things, but it is true, that the routes of trade must be actually opened—by many ships and regular sailings and moderate charges—before streams of merchandise will flow freely and profitably through them.

Hence the pending shipping bill, discussed at the last session but as yet passed by neither House. In my judgment such legislation is imperatively needed and can not wisely be postponed. The Government must open these gates of trade, and open them wide; open them before it is altogether profitable to open them, or altogether reasonable to ask private capital to open them at a venture. It is not a question of the Government monopolizing the field. It should take action to make it certain that transportation at reasonable rates will be promptly provided, even where the carriage is not at first profitable; and then, when the carriage has become sufficiently profitable to attract and engage private capital, and engage it in abundance, the Government ought to withdraw. I very earnestly hope that the Congress will be of this opinion, and that both Houses will adopt this exceedingly important bill.

The great subject of rural credits still remains to be dealt with, and it is a matter of deep regret that the difficulties of the subject have seemed to render it impossible to complete a bill for passage at this session. But it can not be perfected yet, and therefore there are no other constructive measures the necessity for which I will at this time call your attention to; but I would be negligent of a very manifest duty were I not to call the attention of the Senate to the fact that the proposed convention for safety at sea awaits its confirmation and that the limit fixed in the convention itself for its acceptance is the last day of the present month. The conference in which this convention originated was called by the United States; the representatives of the United States played a very influential part indeed in framing the provisions of the proposed convention; and those provisions are in themselves for the most part admirable. It would hardly be consistent with the part we have played in the whole matter to let it drop and go by the board as if forgotten and neglected. It was ratified in May by the German Government and in August by the Parliament of Great Britain. It marks a most hopeful and decided advance in international civilization. We should show our earnest good faith in a great matter by adding our own acceptance of it.

There is another matter of which I must make special mention, if I am to discharge my conscience, lest it should escape your attention. It may seem a very small thing. It affects only a single item of appropriation. But many human lives and many great enterprises hang upon it. It is the matter of making adequate provision for the survey and charting of our coasts. It is immediately pressing and exigent in connection with the immense coast line of Alaska, a coast line greater than that of the United States themselves, though it is also very important indeed with regard to the older coasts of the continent. We can not use our great Alaskan domain, ships will not ply thither, if those coasts and their many hidden dangers are not thoroughly surveyed and charted. The work is incomplete at almost every point. Ships and lives have been lost in threading what were supposed to be well-known main channels. We have not provided adequate vessels or adequate machinery for the survey and charting. We have used old vessels that were not big enough or strong enough and which were so nearly unseaworthy that our inspectors would not have allowed private owners to send them to sea. This is a matter which, as I have said, seems small, but is in reality very great. Its importance has only to be looked into to be appreciated.

Before I close may I say a few words upon two topics, much discussed out of doors, upon which it is highly important that our judgments should be clear, definite, and steadfast?

One of these is economy in government expenditures. The duty of economy is not debatable. It is manifest and imperative. In the appropriations we pass we are spending the money of the great people whose servants we are,—not our own. We are trustees and responsible stewards in the spending. The only thing debatable and upon which we should be careful to make our thought and purpose clear is the kind of economy demanded of us. I assert with the greatest confidence that the people of the United States are not jealous of the amount their Government costs if they are sure that they get what they need and desire for the outlay, that the money is being spent for objects of which they approve, and that it is being applied with good business sense and management.

Governments grow, piecemeal, both in their tasks and in the means by which those tasks are to be performed, and very few Governments are organized, I venture to say, as wise and experienced business men would organize them if they had a clean sheet of paper to write upon. Certainly the Government of the United States is not. I think that it is generally agreed that there should be a systematic reorganization and reassembling of its parts so as to secure greater efficiency and effect considerable savings in expense. But the amount of money saved in that way would, I believe, though no doubt considerable in itself, running, it may be, into the millions, be relatively small,—small, I mean, in proportion to the total necessary outlays of the Government. It would be thoroughly worth effecting, as every saving would, great or small. Our duty is not altered by the scale of the saving. But my point is that the people of the United States do not wish to curtail the activities of this Government; they wish, rather, to enlarge them; and with every enlargement, with the mere growth, indeed, of the country itself, there must come, of course, the inevitable increase of expense. The sort of economy we ought to practice may be effected, and ought to be effected, by a careful study and assessment of the tasks to be performed; and the money spent ought to be made to yield the best possible returns in efficiency and achievement. And, like good stewards, we should so account for every dollar of our appropriations as to make it perfectly evident what it was spent for and in what way it was spent.

It is not expenditure but extravagance that we should fear being criticized for; not paying for the legitimate enterprise and undertakings of a great Government whose people command what it should do, but adding what will benefit only a few or pouring money out for what need not have been undertaken at all or might have been postponed or better and more economically conceived and carried out. The Nation is not niggardly; it is very generous. It will chide us only if we forget for whom we pay money out and whose money it is we pay. These are large and general standards, but they are not very difficult of application to particular cases.

The other topic I shall take leave to mention goes deeper into the principles of our national life and policy. It is the subject of national defense.

It can not be discussed without first answering some very searching questions. It is said in some quarters that we are not prepared for war. What is meant by being prepared? Is it meant that we are not ready upon brief notice to put a nation in the field, a nation of men trained to arms? Of course we are not ready to do that; and we shall never be in time of peace so long as we retain our present political principles and institutions. And what is it that it is suggested we should be prepared to do? To defend ourselves against attack? We have always found means to do that, and shall find them whenever it is necessary without calling our people away from their necessary tasks to render compulsory military service in times of peace.

Allow me to speak with great plainness and directness upon this great matter and to avow my convictions with deep earnestness. I have tried to know what America is, what her people think, what they are, what they most cherish and hold dear. I hope that some of their finer passions are in my own heart,—some of the great conceptions and desires which gave birth to this Government and which have made the voice of this people a voice of peace and hope and liberty among the peoples of the world, and that, speaking my own thoughts, I shall, at least in part, speak theirs also, however faintly and inadequately, upon this vital matter.

We are at peace with all the world. No one who speaks counsel based on fact or drawn from a just and candid interpretation of realities can say that there is reason to fear that from any quarter our independence or the integrity of our territory is threatened. Dread of the power of any other nation we are incapable of. We are not jealous of rivalry in the fields of commerce or of any other peaceful achievement. We mean to live our own lives as we will; but we mean also to let live. We are, indeed, a true friend to all the nations of the world, because we threaten none, covet the possessions of none, desire the overthrow of none. Our friendship can be accepted and is accepted without reservation, because it is offered in a spirit and for a purpose which no one need ever question or suspect. Therein lies our greatness. We are the champions of peace and of concord. And we should be very jealous of this distinction which we have sought to earn. Just now we should be particularly jealous of it because it is our dearest present hope that this character and reputation may presently, in God's providence, bring us an opportunity such as has seldom been vouchsafed any nation, the opportunity to counsel and obtain peace in the world and reconciliation and a healing settlement of many a matter that has cooled and interrupted the friendship of nations. This is the time above all others when we should wish and resolve to keep our strength by self-possession, our influence by preserving our ancient principles of action.

From the first we have had a clear and settled policy with regard to military establishments. We never have had, and while we retain our present principles and ideals we never shall have, a large standing army. If asked, Are you ready to defend yourselves? we reply, Most assuredly, to the utmost; and yet we shall not turn America into a military camp. We will not ask our young men to spend the best years of their lives making soldiers of themselves. There is another sort of energy in us. It will know how to declare itself and make itself effective should occasion arise. And especially when half the world is on fire we shall be careful to make our moral insurance against the spread of the conflagration very definite and certain and adequate indeed.

Let us remind ourselves, therefore, of the only thing we can do or will do. We must depend in every time of national peril, in the future as in the past, not upon a standing army, nor yet upon a reserve army, but upon a citizenry trained and accustomed to arms. It will be right enough, right American policy, based upon our accustomed principles and practices, to provide a system by which every citizen who will volunteer for the training may be made familiar with the use of modern arms, the rudiments of drill and maneuver, and the maintenance and sanitation of camps. We should encourage such training and make it a means of discipline which our young men will learn to value. It is right that we should provide it not only, but that we should make it as attractive as possible, and so induce our young men to undergo it at such times as they can command a little freedom and can seek the physical development they need, for mere health's sake, if for nothing more. Every means by which such things can be stimulated is legitimate, and such a method smacks of true American ideas. It is right, too, that the National Guard of the States should be developed and strengthened by every means which is not inconsistent with our obligations to our own people or with the established policy of our Government. And this, also, not because the time or occasion specially calls for such measures, but because it should be our constant policy to make these provisions for our national peace and safety.

More than this carries with it a reversal of the whole history and character of our polity. More than this, proposed at this time, permit me to say, would mean merely that we had lost our self-possession, that we had been thrown off our balance by a war with which we have nothing to do, whose causes can not touch us, whose very existence affords us opportunities of friendship and disinterested service which should make us ashamed of any thought of hostility or fearful preparation for trouble. This is assuredly the opportunity for which a people and a government like ours were raised up, the opportunity not only to speak but actually to embody and exemplify the counsels of peace and amity and the lasting concord which is based on justice and fair and generous dealing.

A powerful navy we have always regarded as our proper and natural means of defense; and it has always been of defense that we have thought, never of aggression or of conquest. But who shall tell us now what sort of navy to build? We shall take leave to be strong upon the seas, in the future as in the past; and there will be no thought of offense or of provocation in that. Our ships are our natural bulwarks. When will the experts tell us just what kind we should construct—and when will they be right for ten years together, if the relative efficiency of craft of different kinds and uses continues to change as we have seen it change under our very eyes in these last few months?

But I turn away from the subject. It is not new. There is no new need to discuss it. We shall not alter our attitude toward it because some amongst us are nervous and excited. We shall easily and sensibly agree upon a policy of defense. The question has not changed its aspects because the times are not normal. Our policy will not be for an occasion. It will be conceived as a permanent and settled thing, which we will pursue at all seasons, without haste and after a fashion perfectly consistent with the peace of the world, the abiding friendship of states, and the unhampered freedom of all with whom we deal. Let there be no misconception. The country has been misinformed. We have not been negligent of national defense. We are not unmindful of the great responsibility resting upon us. We shall learn and profit by the lesson of every experience and every new circumstance; and what is needed will be adequately done.

I close, as I began, by reminding you of the great tasks and duties of peace which challenge our best powers and invite us to build what will last, the tasks to which we can address ourselves now and at all times with free-hearted zest and with all the finest gifts of constructive wisdom we possess. To develop our life and our resources; to supply our own people, and the people of the world as their need arises, from the abundant plenty of our fields and our marts of trade to enrich the commerce of our own States and of the world with the products of our mines, our farms, and our factories, with the creations of our thought and the fruits of our character,—this is what will hold our attention and our enthusiasm steadily, now and in the years to come, as we strive to show in our life as a nation what liberty and the inspirations of an emancipated spirit may do for men and for societies, for individuals, for states, and for mankind.

THIRD ANNUAL MESSAGE

[Delivered at a Joint Session of the Two Houses of Congress, December 7, 1915.]

GENTLEMEN OF THE CONGRESS: Since I last had the privilege of addressing you on the state of the Union the war of nations on the other side of the sea, which had then only begun to disclose its portentous proportions, has extended its threatening and sinister scope until it has swept within its flame some portion of every quarter of the globe, not excepting our own hemisphere, has altered the whole face of international affairs, and now presents a prospect of reorganization and reconstruction such as statesmen and peoples have never been called upon to attempt before.

We have stood apart, studiously neutral. It was our manifest duty to do so. Not only did we have no part or interest in the policies which seem to have brought the conflict on; it was necessary, if a universal catastrophe was to be avoided, that a limit should be set to the sweep of destructive war and that some part of the great family of nations should keep the processes of peace alive, if only to prevent collective economic ruin and the breakdown throughout the world of the industries by which its populations are fed and sustained. It was manifestly the duty of the self-governed nations of this hemisphere to redress, if possible, the balance of economic loss and confusion in the other, if they could do nothing more. In the day of readjustment and recuperation we earnestly hope and believe that they can be of infinite service.

In this neutrality, to which they were bidden not only by their separate life and their habitual detachment from the politics of Europe but also by a clear perception of international duty, the states of America have become conscious of a new and more vital community of interest and moral partnership in affairs, more clearly conscious of the many common sympathies and interests and duties which bid them stand together.

There was a time in the early days of our own great nation and of the republics fighting their way to independence in Central and South America when the government of the United States looked upon itself as in some sort the guardian of the republics to the south of her as against any encroachments or efforts at political control from the other side of the water; felt it its duty to play the part even without invitation from them; and I think that we can claim that the task was undertaken with a true and disinterested enthusiasm for the freedom of the Americas and the unmolested self-government of her independent peoples. But it was always difficult to maintain such a rôle without offense to the pride of the peoples whose freedom of action we sought to protect, and without provoking serious misconceptions of our motives, and every thoughtful man of affairs must welcome the altered circumstances of the new day in whose light we now stand, when there is no claim of guardianship or thought of wards but, instead, a full and honorable association as of partners between ourselves and our neighbors, in the interest of all America, north and south. Our concern for the independence and prosperity of the states of Central and South America is not altered. We retain unabated the spirit that has inspired us throughout the whole life of our government and which was so frankly put into words by President Monroe. We still mean always to make a common cause of national independence and of political liberty in America. But that purpose is now better understood so far as it concerns ourselves. It is known not to be a selfish purpose. It is known to have in it no thought of taking advantage of any government in this hemisphere or playing its political fortunes for our own benefit. All the governments of America stand, so far as we are concerned, upon a footing of genuine equality and unquestioned independence.

We have been put to the test in the case of Mexico, and we have stood the test. Whether we have benefited Mexico by the course we have pursued remains to be seen. Her fortunes are in her own hands. But we have at least proved that we will not take advantage of her in her distress and undertake to impose upon her an order and government of our own choosing. Liberty is often a fierce and intractable thing, to which no bounds can be set, and to which no bounds of a few men's choosing ought ever to be set. Every American who has drunk at the true fountains of principle and tradition must subscribe without reservation to the high doctrine of the Virginia Bill of Rights, which in the great days in which our government was set up was everywhere amongst us accepted as the creed of free men. That doctrine is, "That government is, or ought to be, instituted for the common benefit, protection, and security of the people, nation, or community"; that "of all the various modes and forms of government, that is the best which is capable of producing the greatest degree of happiness and safety, and is most effectually secured against the danger of maladministration; and that, when any government shall be found inadequate or contrary to these purposes, a majority of the community hath an indubitable, inalienable, and indefeasible right to reform, alter, or abolish it, in such manner as shall be judged most conducive to the public weal." We have unhesitatingly applied that heroic principle to the case of Mexico, and now hopefully await the rebirth of the troubled Republic, which had so much of which to purge itself and so little sympathy from any outside quarter in the radical but necessary process. We will aid and befriend Mexico, but we will not coerce her; and our course with regard to her ought to be sufficient proof to all America that we seek no political suzerainty or selfish control.

The moral is, that the states of America are not hostile rivals but coöperating friends, and that their growing sense of community of interest, alike in matters political and in matters economic, is likely to give them a new significance as factors in international affairs and in the political history of the world. It presents them as in a very deep and true sense a unit in world affairs, spiritual partners, standing together because thinking together, quick with common sympathies and common ideals. Separated they are subject to all the cross currents of the confused politics of a world of hostile rivalries; united in spirit and purpose they cannot be disappointed of their peaceful destiny.

This is Pan-Americanism. It has none of the spirit of empire in it. It is the embodiment, the effectual embodiment, of the spirit of law and independence and liberty and mutual service.

A very notable body of men recently met in the City of Washington, at the invitation and as the guests of this Government, whose deliberations are likely to be looked back to as marking a memorable turning point in the history of America. They were representative spokesmen of the several independent states of this hemisphere and were assembled to discuss the financial and commercial relations of the republics of the two continents which nature and political fortune have so intimately linked together. I earnestly recommend to your perusal the reports of their proceedings and of the actions of their committees. You will get from them, I think, a fresh conception of the ease and intelligence and advantage with which Americans of both continents may draw together in practical coöperation and of what the material foundations of this hopeful partnership of interest must consist,—of how we should build them and of how necessary it is that we should hasten their building.

There is, I venture to point out, an especial significance just now attaching to this whole matter of drawing the Americans together in bonds of honorable partnership and mutual advantage because of the economic readjustments which the world must inevitably witness within the next generation, when peace shall have at last resumed its healthful tasks. In the performance of these tasks I believe the Americas to be destined to play their parts together. I am interested to fix your attention on this prospect now because unless you take it within your view and permit the full significance of it to command your thought I cannot find the right light in which to set forth the particular matter that lies at the very font of my whole thought as I address you to-day. I mean national defense.

No one who really comprehends the spirit of the great people for whom we are appointed to speak can fail to perceive that their passion is for peace, their genius best displayed in the practice of the arts of peace. Great democracies are not belligerent. They do not seek or desire war. Their thought is of individual liberty and of the free labor that supports life and the uncensored thought that quickens it. Conquest and dominion are not in our reckoning, or agreeable to our principles. But just because we demand unmolested development and the undisturbed government of our own lives upon our own principles of right and liberty, we resent, from whatever quarter it may come, the aggression we ourselves will not practice. We insist upon security in prosecuting our self-chosen lines of national development. We do more than that. We demand it also for others. We do not confine our enthusiasm for individual liberty and free national development to the incidents and movements of affairs which affect only ourselves. We feel it wherever there is a people that tries to walk in these difficult paths of independence and right. From the first we have made common cause with all partisans of liberty on this side the sea, and have deemed it as important that our neighbors should be free from all outside domination as that we ourselves should be; have set America aside as a whole for the uses of independent nations and political freemen.

Out of such thoughts grow all our policies. We regard war merely as a means of asserting the rights of a people against aggression. And we are as fiercely jealous of coercive or dictatorial power within our own nation as of aggression from without. We will not maintain a standing army except for uses which are as necessary in times of peace as in times of war; and we shall always see to it that our military peace establishment is no larger than is actually and continuously needed for the uses of days in which no enemies move against us. But we do believe in a body of free citizens ready and sufficient to take care of themselves and of the governments which they have set up to serve them. In our constitutions themselves we have commanded that "the right of the people to keep and bear arms shall not be infringed," and our confidence has been that our safety in times of danger would lie in the rising of the nation to take care of itself, as the farmers rose at Lexington.

But war has never been a mere matter of men and guns. It is a thing of disciplined might. If our citizens are ever to fight effectively upon a sudden summons, they must know how modern fighting is done, and what to do when the summons comes to render themselves immediately available and immediately effective. And the government must be their servant in this matter, must supply them with the training they need to take care of themselves and of it. The military arm of their government, which they will not allow to direct them, they may properly use to serve them and make their independence secure,—and not their own independence merely but the rights also of those with whom they have made common cause, should they also be put in jeopardy. They must be fitted to play the great rôle in the world, and particularly in this hemisphere, for which they are qualified by principle and by chastened ambition to play.

It is with these ideals in mind that the plans of the Department of War for more adequate national defense were conceived which will be laid before you, and which I urge you to sanction and put into effect as soon as they can be properly scrutinized and discussed. They seem to me the essential first steps, and they seem to me for the present sufficient.

They contemplate an increase of the standing force of the regular army from its present strength of five thousand and twenty-three officers and one hundred and two thousand nine hundred and eighty-five enlisted men of all services to a strength of seven thousand one hundred and thirty-six officers and one hundred and thirty-four thousand seven hundred and seven enlisted men, or 141,843, all told, all services, rank and file, by the addition of fifty-two companies of coast artillery, fifteen companies of engineers, ten regiments of infantry, four regiments of field artillery, and four aero squadrons, besides seven hundred and fifty officers required for a great variety of extra service, especially the all important duty of training the citizen force of which I shall presently speak, seven hundred and ninety-two non-commissioned officers for service in drill, recruiting and the like, and the necessary quota of enlisted men for the Quartermaster Corps, the Hospital Corps, the Ordnance Department, and other similar auxiliary services. These are the additions necessary to render the army adequate for its present duties, duties which it has to perform not only upon our own continental coasts and borders and at our interior army posts, but also in the Philippines, in the Hawaiian Islands, at the Isthmus, and in Porto Rico.

By way of making the country ready to assert some part of its real power promptly and upon a larger scale, should occasion arise, the plan also contemplates supplementing the army by a force of four hundred thousand disciplined citizens, raised in increments of one hundred and thirty-three thousand a year throughout a period of three years. This it is proposed to do by a process of enlistment under which the serviceable men of the country would be asked to bind themselves to serve with the colors for purposes of training for short periods throughout three years, and to come to the colors at call at any time throughout an additional "furlough" period of three years. This force of four hundred thousand men would be provided with personal accoutrements as fast as enlisted and their equipment for the field made ready to be supplied at any time. They would be assembled for training at stated intervals at convenient places in association with suitable units of the regular army. Their period of annual training would not necessarily exceed two months in the year.

It would depend upon the patriotic feeling of the younger men of the country whether they responded to such a call to service or not. It would depend upon the patriotic spirit of the employers of the country whether they made it possible for the younger men in their employ to respond under favorable conditions or not. I, for one, do not doubt the patriotic devotion either of our young men or of those who give them employment,—those for whose benefit and protection they would in fact enlist. I would look forward to the success of such an experiment with entire confidence.

At least so much by way of preparation for defense seems to me to be absolutely imperative now. We cannot do less.

The programme which will be laid before you by the Secretary of the Navy is similarly conceived. It involves only a shortening of the time within which plans long matured shall be carried out; but it does make definite and explicit a programme which has heretofore been only implicit, held in the minds of the Committees on Naval Affairs and disclosed in the debates of the two Houses but nowhere formulated or formally adopted. It seems to me very clear that it will be to the advantage of the country for the Congress to adopt a comprehensive plan for putting the navy upon a final footing of strength and efficiency and to press that plan to completion within the next five years. We have always looked to the navy of the country as our first and chief line of defense; we have always seen it to be our manifest course of prudence to be strong on the seas. Year by year we have been creating a navy which now ranks very high indeed among the navies of the maritime nations. We should now definitely determine how we shall complete what we have begun, and how soon.

The programme to be laid before you contemplates the construction within five years of ten battleships, six battle cruisers, ten scout cruisers, fifty destroyers, fifteen fleet submarines, eighty-five coast submarines, four gunboats, one hospital ship, two ammunition ships, two fuel oil ships, and one repair ship. It is proposed that of this number we shall the first year provide for the construction of two battleships, two battle cruisers, three scout cruisers, fifteen destroyers, five fleet submarines, twenty-five coast submarines, two gunboats, and one hospital ship; the second year, two battleships, one scout cruiser, ten destroyers, four fleet submarines, fifteen coast submarines, one gunboat, and one fuel oil ship; the third year, two battleships, one battle cruiser, two scout cruisers, five destroyers, two fleet submarines, and fifteen coast submarines; the fourth year, two battleships, two battle cruisers, two scout cruisers, ten destroyers, two fleet submarines, fifteen coast submarines, one ammunition ship, and one fuel oil ship; and the fifth year, two battleships, one battle cruiser, two scout cruisers, ten destroyers, two fleet submarines, fifteen coast submarines, one gunboat, one ammunition ship, and one repair ship.

The Secretary of the Navy is asking also for the immediate addition to the personnel of the navy of seven thousand five hundred sailors, twenty-five hundred apprentice seamen, and fifteen hundred marines. This increase would be sufficient to care for the ships which are to be completed within the fiscal year 1917 and also for the number of men which must be put in training to man the ships which will be completed early in 1918. It is also necessary that the number of midshipmen at the Naval academy at Annapolis should be increased by at least three hundred in order that the force of officers should be more rapidly added to; and authority is asked to appoint, for engineering duties only, approved graduates of engineering colleges, and for service in the aviation corps a certain number of men taken from civil life.

If this full programme should be carried out we should have built or building in 1921, according to the estimates of survival and standards of classification followed by the General Board of the Department, an effective navy consisting of twenty-seven battleships of the first line, six battle cruisers, twenty-five battleships of the second line, ten armored cruisers, thirteen scout cruisers, five first class cruisers, three second class cruisers, ten third class cruisers, one hundred and eight destroyers, eighteen fleet submarines, one hundred and fifty-seven coast submarines, six monitors, twenty gunboats, four supply ships, fifteen fuel ships, four transports, three tenders to torpedo vessels, eight vessels of special types, and two ammunition ships. This would be a navy fitted to our needs and worthy of our traditions.

But armies and instruments of war are only part of what has to be considered if we are to provide for the supreme matter of national self-sufficiency and security in all its aspects. There are other great matters which will be thrust upon our attention whether we will or not. There is, for example, a very pressing question of trade and shipping involved in this great problem of national adequacy. It is necessary for many weighty reasons of national efficiency and development that we should have a great merchant marine. The great merchant fleet we once used to make us rich, that great body of sturdy sailors who used to carry our flag into every sea, and who were the pride and often the bulwark of the nation, we have almost driven out of existence by inexcusable neglect and indifference and by a hopelessly blind and provincial policy of so-called economic protection. It is high time we repaired our mistake and resumed our commercial independence on the seas.

For it is a question of independence. If other nations go to war or seek to hamper each other's commerce, our merchants, it seems, are at their mercy, to do with as they please. We must use their ships, and use them as they determine. We have not ships enough of our own. We cannot handle our own commerce on the seas. Our independence is provincial, and is only on land and within our own borders. We are not likely to be permitted to use even the ships of other nations in rivalry of their own trade, and are without means to extend our commerce even where the doors are wide open and our goods desired. Such a situation is not to be endured. It is of capital importance not only that the United States should be its own carrier on the seas and enjoy the economic independence which only an adequate merchant marine would give it, but also that the American hemisphere as a whole should enjoy a like independence and self-sufficiency, if it is not to be drawn into the tangle of European affairs. Without such independence the whole question of our political unity and self-determination is very seriously clouded and complicated indeed.

Moreover, we can develop no true or effective American policy without ships of our own,—not ships of war, but ships of peace, carrying goods and carrying much more: creating friendships and rendering indispensable services to all interests on this side the water. They must move constantly back and forth between the Americas. They are the only shuttles that can weave the delicate fabric of sympathy, comprehension, confidence, and mutual dependence in which we wish to clothe our policy of America for Americans.

The task of building up an adequate merchant marine for America private capital must ultimately undertake and achieve, as it has undertaken and achieved every other like task amongst us in the past, with admirable enterprise, intelligence, and vigor; and it seems to me a manifest dictate of wisdom that we should promptly remove every legal obstacle that may stand in the way of this much to be desired revival of our old independence and should facilitate in every possible way the building, purchase, and American registration of ships. But capital cannot accomplish this great task of a sudden. It must embark upon it by degrees, as the opportunities of trade develop. Something must be done at once; done to open routes and develop opportunities where they are as yet undeveloped; done to open the arteries of trade where the currents have not yet learned to run,—especially between the two American continents, where they are, singularly enough, yet to be created and quickened; and it is evident that only the government can undertake such beginnings and assume the initial financial risks. When the risk has passed and private capital begins to find its way in sufficient abundance into these new channels, the government may withdraw. But it cannot omit to begin. It should take the first steps, and should take them at once. Our goods must not lie piled up at our ports and stored upon side tracks in freight cars which are daily needed on the roads; must not be left without means of transport to any foreign quarter. We must not await the permission of foreign ship-owners and foreign governments to send them where we will.

With a view to meeting these pressing necessities of our commerce and availing ourselves at the earliest possible moment of the present unparalleled opportunity of linking the two Americas together in bonds of mutual interest and service, an opportunity which may never return again if we miss it now, proposals will be made to the present Congress for the purchase or construction of ships to be owned and directed by the government similar to those made to the last Congress, but modified in some essential particulars. I recommend these proposals to you for your prompt acceptance with the more confidence because every month that has elapsed since the former proposals were made has made the necessity for such action more and more manifestly imperative. That need was then foreseen; it is now acutely felt and everywhere realized by those for whom trade is waiting but who can find no conveyance for their goods. I am not so much interested in the particulars of the programme as I am in taking immediate advantage of the great opportunity which awaits us if we will but act in this emergency. In this matter, as in all others, a spirit of common counsel should prevail, and out of it should come an early solution of this pressing problem.

There is another matter which seems to me to be very intimately associated with the question of national safety and preparation for defense. That is our policy towards the Philippines and the people of Porto Rico. Our treatment of them and their attitude towards us are manifestly of the first consequence in the development of our duties in the world and in getting a free hand to perform those duties. We must be free from every unnecessary burden or embarrassment; and there is no better way to be clear of embarrassment than to fulfil our promises and promote the interests of those dependent on us to the utmost. Bills for the alteration and reform of the government of the Philippines and for rendering fuller political justice to the people of Porto Rico were submitted to the sixty-third Congress. They will be submitted also to you. I need not particularize their details. You are most of you already familiar with them. But I do recommend them to your early adoption with the sincere conviction that there are few measures you could adopt which would more serviceably clear the way for the great policies by which we wish to make good, now and always, our right to lead in enterprises of peace and good will and economic and political freedom.

The plans for the armed forces of the nation which I have outlined, and for the general policy of adequate preparation for mobilization and defense, involve of course very large additional expenditures of money,—expenditures which will considerably exceed the estimated revenues of the government. It is made my duty by law, whenever the estimates of expenditure exceed the estimates of revenue, to call the attention of the Congress to the fact and suggest any means of meeting the deficiency that it may be wise or possible for me to suggest. I am ready to believe that it would be my duty to do so in any case; and I feel particularly bound to speak of the matter when it appears that the deficiency will arise directly out of the adoption by the Congress of measures which I myself urge it to adopt. Allow me, therefore, to speak briefly of the present state of the Treasury and of the fiscal problems which the next year will probably disclose.

On the thirtieth of June last there was an available balance in the general fund of the Treasury of $104,170,105.78. The total estimated receipts for the year 1916, on the assumption that the emergency revenue measure passed by the last Congress will not be extended beyond its present limit, the thirty-first of December, 1915, and that the present duty of one cent per pound on sugar will be discontinued after the first of May, 1916, will be $670,365,500. The balance of June last and these estimated revenues come, therefore, to a grand total of $774,535,605.78. The total estimated disbursements for the present fiscal year, including twenty-five millions for the Panama Canal, twelve millions for probable deficiency appropriations, and fifty thousand dollars for miscellaneous debt redemptions, will be $753,891,000; and the balance in the general fund of the Treasury will be reduced to $20,644,605.78. The emergency revenue act, if continued beyond its present time limitation, would produce, during the half year then remaining, about forty-one millions. The duty of one cent per pound on sugar, if continued, would produce during the two months of the fiscal year remaining after the first of May, about fifteen millions. These two sums, amounting together to fifty-six millions, if added to the revenues of the second half of the fiscal year, would yield the Treasury at the end of the year an available balance of $76,644,605.78.

The additional revenues required to carry out the programme of military and naval preparation of which I have spoken, would, as at present estimated, be for the fiscal year 1917, $93,800,000. Those figures, taken with the figures for the present fiscal year which I have already given, disclose our financial problem for the year 1917. Assuming that the taxes imposed by the emergency revenue act and the present duty on sugar are to be discontinued, and that the balance at the close of the present fiscal year will be only $20,644,605.78, that the disbursements for the Panama Canal will again be about twenty-five millions, and that the additional expenditures for the army and navy are authorized by the Congress, the deficit in the general fund of the Treasury on the thirtieth of June, 1917, will be nearly two hundred and thirty-five millions. To this sum at least fifty millions should be added to represent a safe working balance for the Treasury, and twelve millions to include the usual deficiency estimates in 1917; and these additions would make a total deficit of some two hundred and ninety-seven millions. If the present taxes should be continued throughout this year and the next, however, there would be a balance in the Treasury of some seventy-six and a half millions at the end of the present fiscal year, and a deficit at the end of the next year of only some fifty millions, or, reckoning in sixty-two millions for deficiency appropriations and a safe Treasury balance at the end of the year, a total deficit of some one hundred and twelve millions. The obvious moral of the figures is that it is a plain counsel of prudence to continue all of the present taxes or their equivalents, and confine ourselves to the problem of providing one hundred and twelve millions of new revenue rather than two hundred and ninety-seven millions.

How shall we obtain the new revenue? We are frequently reminded that there are many millions of bonds which the Treasury is authorized under existing law to sell to reimburse the sums paid out of current revenues for the construction of the Panama Canal; and it is true that bonds to the amount of approximately $222,000,000 are now available for that purpose. Prior to 1913, $134,631,980 of these bonds had actually been sold to recoup the expenditures at the Isthmus; and now constitute a considerable item of the public debt. But I, for one, do not believe that the people of this country approve of postponing the payment of their bills. Borrowing money is short-sighted finance. It can be justified only when permanent things are to be accomplished which many generations will certainly benefit by and which it seems hardly fair that a single generation should pay for. The objects we are now proposing to spend money for cannot be so classified, except in the sense that everything wisely done may be said to be done in the interest of posterity as well as in our own. It seems to me a clear dictate of prudent statesmanship and frank finance that in what we are now, I hope, about to undertake we should pay as we go. The people of the country are entitled to know just what burdens of taxation they are to carry, and to know from the outset, now. The new bills should be paid by internal taxation.

To what sources, then, shall we turn? This is so peculiarly a question which the gentlemen of the House of Representatives are expected under the Constitution to propose an answer to that you will hardly expect me to do more than discuss it in very general terms. We should be following an almost universal example of modern governments if we were to draw the greater part or even the whole of the revenues we need from the income taxes. By somewhat lowering the present limits of exemption and the figure at which the surtax shall begin to be imposed, and by increasing, step by step throughout the present graduation, the surtax itself, the income taxes as at present apportioned would yield sums sufficient to balance the books of the Treasury at the end of the fiscal year 1917 without anywhere making the burden unreasonably or oppressively heavy. The precise reckonings are fully and accurately set out in the report of the Secretary of the Treasury which will be immediately laid before you.

And there are many additional sources of revenue which can justly be resorted to without hampering the industries of the country or putting any too great charge upon individual expenditure. A tax of one cent per gallon on gasoline and naphtha would yield, at the present estimated production, $10,000,000; a tax of fifty cents per horse power on automobiles and internal explosion engines, $15,000,000; a stamp tax on bank cheques, probably $18,000,000; a tax of twenty-five cents per ton on pig iron, $10,000,000; a tax of twenty-five cents per ton on fabricated iron and steel, probably $10,000,000. In a country of great industries like this it ought to be easy to distribute the burdens of taxation without making them anywhere bear too heavily or too exclusively upon any one set of persons or undertakings. What is clear is, that the industry of this generation should pay the bills of this generation.

I have spoken to you to-day, Gentlemen, upon a single theme, the thorough preparation of the nation to care for its own security and to make sure of entire freedom to play the impartial rôle in this hemisphere and in the world which we all believe to have been providentially assigned to it. I have had in my mind no thought of any immediate or particular danger arising out of our relations with other nations. We are at peace with all the nations of the world, and there is reason to hope that no question in controversy between this and other Governments will lead to any serious breach of amicable relations, grave as some differences of attitude and policy have been and may yet turn out to be. I am sorry to say that the gravest threats against our national peace and safety have been uttered within our own borders. There are citizens of the United States,

I blush to admit, born under other flags but welcomed under our generous naturalization laws to the full freedom and opportunity of America, who have poured the poison of disloyalty into the very arteries of our national life; who have sought to bring the authority and good name of our Government into contempt, to destroy our industries wherever they thought it effective for their vindictive purposes to strike at them, and to debase our politics to the uses of foreign intrigue. Their number is not great as compared with the whole number of those sturdy hosts by which our nation has been enriched in recent generations out of virile foreign stock; but it is great enough to have brought deep disgrace upon us and to have made it necessary that we should promptly make use of processes of law by which we may be purged of their corrupt distempers. America never witnessed anything like this before. It never dreamed it possible that men sworn into its own citizenship, men drawn out of great free stocks such as supplied some of the best and strongest elements of that little, but how heroic, nation that in a high day of old staked its very life to free itself from every entanglement that had darkened the fortunes of the older nations and set up a new standard here,—that men of such origins and such free choices of allegiance would ever turn in malign reaction against the Government and people who had welcomed and nurtured them and seek to make this proud country once more a hotbed of European passion. A little while ago such a thing would have seemed incredible. Because it was incredible we made no preparation for it. We would have been almost ashamed to prepare for it, as if we were suspicious of ourselves, our own comrades and neighbors! But the ugly and incredible thing has actually come about and we are without adequate federal laws to deal with it. I urge you to enact such laws at the earliest possible moment and feel that in doing so I am urging you to do nothing less than save the honor and self-respect of the nation. Such creatures of passion, disloyalty, and anarchy must be crushed out. They are not many, but they are infinitely malignant, and the hand of our power should close over them at once. They have formed plots to destroy property, they have entered into conspiracies against the neutrality of the Government, they have sought to pry into every confidential transaction of the Government in order to serve interests alien to our own. It is possible to deal with these things very effectually. I need not suggest the terms in which they may be dealt with.

I wish that it could be said that only a few men, misled by mistaken sentiments of allegiance to the governments under which they were born, had been guilty of disturbing the self-possession and misrepresenting the temper and principles of the country during these days of terrible war, when it would seem that every man who was truly an American would instinctively make it his duty and his pride to keep the scales of judgment even and prove himself a partisan of no nation but his own. But it cannot. There are some men among us, and many resident abroad who, though born and bred in the United States and calling themselves Americans, have so forgotten themselves and their honor as citizens as to put their passionate sympathy with one or the other side in the great European conflict above their regard for the peace and dignity of the United States. They also preach and practice disloyalty. No laws, I suppose, can reach corruptions of the mind and heart; but I should not speak of others without also speaking of these and expressing the even deeper humiliation and scorn which every self-possessed and thoughtfully patriotic American must feel when he thinks of them and of the discredit they are daily bringing upon us.

While we speak of the preparation of the nation to make sure of her security and her effective power we must not fall into the patent error of supposing that her real strength comes from armaments and mere safeguards of written law. It comes, of course, from her people, their energy, their success in their undertakings, their free opportunity to use the natural resources of our great home land and of the lands outside our continental borders which look to us for protection, for encouragement, and for assistance in their development; from the organization and freedom and vitality of our economic life. The domestic questions which engaged the attention of the last Congress are more vital to the nation in this its time of test than at any other time. We cannot adequately make ready for any trial of our strength unless we wisely and promptly direct the force of our laws into these all-important fields of domestic action. A matter which it seems to me we should have very much at heart is the creation of the right instrumentalities by which to mobilize our economic resources in any time of national necessity. I take it for granted that I do not need your authority to call into systematic consultation with the directing officers of the army and navy men of recognized leadership and ability from among our citizens who are thoroughly familiar, for example, with the transportation facilities of the country and therefore competent to advise how they may be coördinated when the need arises, those who can suggust the best way in which to bring about prompt coöperation among the manufacturers of the country, should it be necessary, and those who could assist to bring the technical skill of the country to the aid of the Government in the solution of particular problems of defense. I only hope that if I should find it feasible to constitute such an advisory body the Congress would be willing to vote the small sum of money that would be needed to defray the expenses that would probably be necessary to give it the clerical and administrative machinery with which to do serviceable work.

What is more important is, that the industries and resources of the country should be available and ready for mobilization. It is the more imperatively necessary, therefore, that we should promptly devise means for doing what we have not yet done: that we should give intelligent federal aid and stimulation to industrial and vocational education, as we have long done in the large field of our agricultural industry; that, at the same time that we safeguard and conserve the natural resources of the country we should put them at the disposal of those who will use them promptly and intelligently, as was sought to be done in the admirable bills submitted to the last Congress from its committees on the public lands, bills which I earnestly recommend in principle to your consideration; that we should put into early operation some provision for rural credits which will add to the extensive borrowing facilities already afforded the farmer by the Reserve Bank Act, adequate instrumentalities by which long credits may be obtained on land mortgages; and that we should study more carefully than they have hitherto been studied the right adaptation of our economic arrangements to changing conditions.

Many conditions about which we have repeatedly legislated are being altered from decade to decade, it is evident, under our very eyes, and are likely to change even more rapidly and more radically in the days immediately ahead of us, when peace has returned to the world and the nations of Europe once more take up their tasks of commerce and industry with the energy of those who must bestir themselves to build anew. Just what these changes will be no one can certainly foresee or confidently predict. There are no calculable, because no stable, elements in the problem. The most we can do is to make certain that we have the necessary instrumentalities of information constantly at our service so that we may be sure that we know exactly what we are dealing with when we come to act, if it should be necessary to act at all. We must first certainly know what it is that we are seeking to adapt ourselves to. I may ask the privilege of addressing you more at length on this important matter a little later in your session.

In the meantime may I make this suggestion? The transportation problem is an exceedingly serious and pressing one in this country. There has from time to time of late been reason to fear that our railroads would not much longer be able to cope with it successfully, as at present equipped and coördinated. I suggest that it would be wise to provide for a commission of inquiry to ascertain by a thorough canvass of the whole question whether our laws as at present framed and administered are as serviceable as they might be in the solution of the problem. It is obviously a problem that lies at the very foundation of our efficiency as a people. Such an inquiry ought to draw out every circumstance and opinion worth considering and we need to know all sides of the matter if we mean to do anything in the field of federal legislation.

No one, I am sure, would wish to take any backward step. The regulation of the railways of the country by federal commission has had admirable results and has fully justified the hopes and expectations of those by whom the policy of regulation was originally proposed. The question is not what should we undo? It is, whether there is anything else we can do that would supply us with effective means, in the very process of regulation, for bettering the conditions under which the railroads are operated and for making them more useful servants of the country as a whole. It seems to me that it might be the part of wisdom, therefore, before further legislation in this field is attempted, to look at the whole problem of coördination and efficiency in the full light of a fresh assessment of circumstance and opinion, as a guide to dealing with the several parts of it.

For what we are seeking now, what in my mind is the single thought of this message, is national efficiency and security. We serve a great nation. We should serve it in the spirit of its peculiar genius. It is the genius of common men for self-government, industry, justice, liberty and peace. We should see to it that it lacks no instrument, no facility or vigor of law, to make it sufficient to play its part with energy, safety, and assured success. In this we are no partisans but heralds and prophets of a new age.

FOURTH ANNUAL MESSAGE.

[Delivered at a Joint Session of the Two Houses of Congress, December 5, 1916.]

GENTLEMEN OF THE CONGRESS—In fulfilling at this time the duty laid upon me by the Constitution of communicating to you from time to time information of the state of the Union and recommending to your consideration such legislative measures as may be judged necessary and expedient, I shall continue the practice, which I hope has been acceptable to you, of leaving to the reports of the several heads of the executive departments the elaboration of the detailed needs of the public service and confine myself to those matters of more general public policy with which it seems necessary and feasible to deal at the present session of the Congress.

I realize the limitations of time under which you will necessarily act at this session and shall make my suggestions as few as possible; but there were some things left undone at the last session which there will now be time to complete and which it seems necessary in the interest of the public to do at once.

In the first place, it seems to me imperatively necessary that the earliest possible consideration and action should be accorded the remaining measures of the program of settlement and regulation which I had occasion to recommend to you at the close of your last session in view of the public dangers disclosed by the unaccommodated difficulties which then existed, and which still unhappily continue to exist, between the railroads of the country and their locomotive engineers, conductors and trainmen.

I then recommended:

First, immediate provision for the enlargement and administrative reorganization of the Interstate Commerce Commission along the lines embodied in the bill recently passed by the House of Representatives and now awaiting action by the Senate; in order that the Commission may be enabled to deal with the many great and various duties now devolving upon it with a promptness and thoroughness which are, with its present constitution and means of action, practically impossible.

Second, the establishment of an eight-hour day as the legal basis alike of work and wages in the employment of all railway employes who are actually engaged in the work of operating trains in interstate transportation.

Third, the authorization of the appointment by the President of a small body of men to observe actual results in experience of the adoption of the eight-hour day in railway transportation alike for the men and for the railroads.

Fourth, explicit approval by the Congress of the consideration by the Interstate Commerce Commission of an increase of freight rates to meet such additional expenditures by the railroads as may have been rendered necessary by the adoption of the eight-hour day and which have not been offset by administrative readjustments and economies, should the facts disclosed justify the increase.

Fifth, an amendment of the existing Federal statute which provides for the mediation, conciliation and arbitration of such controversies as the present by adding to it a provision that, in case the methods of accommodation now provided for should fail, a full public investigation of the merits of every such dispute shall be instituted and completed before a strike or lockout may lawfully be attempted.

And, sixth, the lodgment in the hands of the Executive of the power, in case of military necessity, to take control of such portions and such rolling stock of the railways of the country as may be required for military use and to operate them for military purposes, with authority to draft into the military service of the United States such train crews and administrative officials as the circumstances require for their safe and efficient use.

The second and third of these recommendations the Congress immediately acted on: it established the eight-hour day as the legal basis of work and wages in train service and it authorized the appointment of a commission to observe and report upon the practical results, deeming these the measures most immediately needed; but it postponed action upon the other suggestions until an opportunity should be offered for a more deliberate consideration of them.

The fourth recommendation I do not deem it necessary to renew. The power of the Interstate Commerce Commission to grant an increase of rates on the ground referred to is indisputably clear and a recommendation by the Congress with regard to such a matter might seem to draw in question the scope of the commission's authority or its inclination to do justice when there is no reason to doubt either.

The other suggestions—the increase in the Interstate Commerce Commission's membership and in its facilities for performing its manifold duties; the provision for full public investigation and assessment of industrial disputes, and the grant to the Executive of the power to control and operate the railways when necessary in time of war or other like public necessity—I now very earnestly renew.

The necessity for such legislation is manifest and pressing. Those who have entrusted us with the responsibility and duty of serving and safeguarding them in such matters would find it hard, I believe, to excuse a failure to act upon these grave matters or any unnecessary postponement of action upon them.

Not only does the Interstate Commerce Commission now find it practically impossible, with its present membership and organization, to perform its great functions promptly and thoroughly, but it is not unlikely that it may presently be found advisable to add to its duties still others equally heavy and exacting. It must first be perfected as an administrative instrument.

The country cannot and should not consent to remain any longer exposed to profound industrial disturbances for lack of additional means of arbitration and conciliation which the Congress can easily and promptly supply.

And all will agree that there must be no doubt as to the power of the Executive to make immediate and uninterrupted use of the railroads for the concentration of the military forces of the nation wherever they are needed and whenever they are needed.

This is a program of regulation, prevention and administrative efficiency which argues its own case in the mere statement of it. With regard to one of its items, the increase in the efficiency of the Interstate Commerce Commission, the House of Representatives has already acted; its action needs only the concurrence of the Senate.

I would hesitate to recommend, and I dare say the Congress would hesitate to act upon the suggestion should I make it, that any man in any occupation should be obliged by law to continue in an employment which he desired to leave.

To pass a law which forbade or prevented the individual workman to leave his work before receiving the approval of society in doing so would be to adopt a new principle into our jurisprudence, which I take it for granted we are not prepared to introduce.

But the proposal that the operation of the railways of the country shall not be stopped or interrupted by the concerted action of organized bodies of men until a public investigation shall have been instituted, which shall make the whole question at issue plain for the judgment of the opinion of the nation, is not to propose any such principle.

It is based upon the very different principle that the concerted action of powerful bodies of men shall not be permitted to stop the industrial processes of the nation, at any rate before the nation shall have had an opportunity to acquaint itself with the merits of the case as between employe and employer, time to form its opinion upon an impartial statement of the merits, and opportunity to consider all practicable means of conciliation or arbitration.

I can see nothing in that proposition but the justifiable safeguarding by society of the necessary processes of its very life. There is nothing arbitrary or unjust in it unless it be arbitrarily and unjustly done. It can and should be done with a full and scrupulous regard for the interests and liberties of all concerned as well as for the permanent interests of society itself.

Three matters of capital importance await the action of the Senate which have already been acted upon by the House of Representatives; the bill which seeks to extend greater freedom of combination to those engaged in promoting the foreign commerce of the country than is now thought by some to be legal under the terms of the laws against monopoly; the bill amending the present organic law of Porto Rico; and the bill proposing a more thorough and systematic regulation of the expenditure of money in elections, commonly called the Corrupt Practices Act.

I need not labor my advice that these measures be enacted into law. Their urgency lies in the manifest circumstances which render their adoption at this time not only opportune but necessary. Even delay would seriously jeopard the interests of the country and of the Government.

Immediate passage of the bill to regulate the expenditure of money in elections may seem to be less necessary than the immediate enactment of the other measures to which I refer, because at least two years will elapse before another election in which Federal offices are to be filled; but it would greatly relieve the public mind if this important matter were dealt with while the circumstances and the dangers to the public morals of the present method of obtaining and spending campaign funds stand clear under recent observation, and the methods of expenditure can be frankly studied in the light of present experience; and a delay would have the further very serious disadvantage of postponing action until another election was at hand and some special object connected with it might be thought to be in the mind of those who urged it. Action can be taken now with facts for guidance and without suspicion of partisan purpose.

I shall not argue at length the desirability of giving a freer hand in the matter of combined and concerted effort to those who shall undertake the essential enterprise of building up our export trade. That enterprise will presently, will immediately assume, has indeed already assumed a magnitude unprecedented in our experience. We have not the necessary instrumentalities for its prosecution; it is deemed to be doubtful whether they could be created upon an adequate scale under our present laws.

We should clear away all legal obstacles and create a basis of undoubted law for it which will give freedom without permitting unregulated license. The thing must be done now, because the opportunity is here and may escape us if we hesitate or delay.

The argument for the proposed amendments of the organic law of Porto Rico is brief and conclusive. The present laws governing the island and regulating the rights and privileges of its people are not just. We have created expectations of extended privilege which we have not satisfied. There is uneasiness among the people of the island and even a suspicious doubt with regard to our intentions concerning them which the adoption of the pending measure would happily remove. We do not doubt what we wish to do in any essential particular. We ought to do it at once.

At the last session of the Congress a bill was passed by the Senate which provides for the promotion of vocational and industrial education, which is of vital importance to the whole country because it concerns a matter, too long neglected, upon which the thorough industrial preparation of the country for the critical years of economic development immediately ahead of us in very large measure depends.

May I not urge its early and favorable consideration by the House of Representatives and its early enactment into law? It contains plans which affect all interests and all parts of the country, and I am sure that there is no legislation now pending before the Congress whose passage the country awaits with more thoughtful approval or greater impatience to see a great and admirable thing set in the way of being done.

There are other matters already advanced to the stage of conference between the two houses of which it is not necessary that I should speak.

Some practicable basis of agreement concerning them will no doubt be found and action taken upon them.

Inasmuch as this is, gentlemen, probably the last occasion I shall have to address the Sixty-fourth Congress, I hope that you will permit me to say with what genuine pleasure and satisfaction I have co-operated with you in the many measures of constructive policy with which you have enriched the legislative annals of the country. It has been a privilege to labor in such company. I take the liberty of congratulating you upon the completion of a record of rare serviceableness and distinction.

FIFTH ANNUAL ADDRESS.

[Delivered to Joint Session of Congress, December 4, 1917.]

GENTLEMEN OF THE CONGRESS: Eight months have elapsed since I last had the honor of addressing you. They have been months crowded with events of immense and grave significance for us. I shall not undertake to detail or even to summarize those events. The practical particulars of the part we have played in them will be laid before you in the reports of the executive departments. I shall discuss only our present outlook upon these vast affairs, our present duties, and the immediate means of accomplishing the objects we shall hold always in view.

I shall not go back to debate the causes of the war. The intolerable wrongs done and planned against us by the sinister masters of Germany have long since become too grossly obvious and odious to every true American to need to be rehearsed. But I shall ask you to consider again and with a very grave scrutiny our objectives and the measures by which we mean to attain them; for the purpose of discussion here in this place is action, and our action must move straight toward definite ends. Our object is, of course, to win the war; and we shall not slacken or suffer ourselves to be diverted until it is won. But it is worth while asking and answering the question, When shall we consider the war won?

From one point of view it is not necessary to broach this fundamental matter. I do not doubt that the American people know what the war is about and what sort of an outcome they will regard as a realization of their purpose in it.

As a nation we are united in spirit and intention. I pay little heed to those who tell me otherwise. I hear the voices of dissent—who does not? I hear the criticism and the clamor of the noisily thoughtless and troublesome. I also see men here and there fling themselves in impotent disloyalty against the calm, indomitable power of the Nation. I hear men debate peace who understand neither its nature nor the way in which we may attain it with uplifted eyes and unbroken spirits. But I know that none of these speaks for the Nation. They do not touch the heart of anything. They may safely be left to strut their uneasy hour and be forgotten.

But from another point of view I believe that it is necessary to say plainly what we here at the seat of action consider the war to be for and what part we mean to play in the settlement of its searching issues. We are the spokesmen of the American people, and they have a right to know whether their purpose is ours. They desire peace by the overcoming of evil, by the defeat once for all of the sinister forces that interrupt peace and render it impossible, and they wish to know how closely our thought runs with theirs and what action we propose. They are impatient with those who desire peace by any sort of compromise—deeply and indignantly impatient—but they will be equally impatient with us if we do not make it plain to them what our objectives are and what we are planning for in seeking to make conquest of peace by arms.

I believe that I speak for them when I say two things: First, that this intolerable thing of which the masters of Germany have shown us the ugly face, this menace of combined intrigue and force which we now see so clearly as the German power, a thing without conscience or honor or capacity for covenanted peace, must be crushed and, if it be not utterly brought to an end, at least shut out from the friendly intercourse of the nations; and second, that when this thing and its power are indeed defeated and the time comes that we can discuss peace—when the German people have spokesmen whose word we can believe and when those spokesmen are ready in the name of their people to accept the common judgment of the nations as to what shall henceforth be the bases of law and of covenant for the life of the world—we shall be willing and glad to pay the full price for peace, and pay it ungrudgingly.

We know what that price will be. It will be full, impartial justice—justice done at every point and to every nation that the final settlement must affect, our enemies as well as our friends.

You catch, with me, the voices of humanity that are in the air. They grow daily more audible, more articulate, more persuasive, and they come from the hearts of men everywhere. They insist that the war shall not end in vindictive action of any kind; that no nation or people shall be robbed or punished because the irresponsible rulers of a single country have themselves done deep and abominable wrong. It is this thought that has been expressed in the formula, "No annexations, no contributions, no punitive indemnities."

Just because this crude formula expresses the instinctive judgment as to right of plain men everywhere, it has been made diligent use of by the masters of German intrigue to lead the people of Russia astray—and the people of every other country their agents could reach—in order that a premature peace might be brought about before autocracy has been taught its final and convincing lesson and the people of the world put in control of their own destinies.

But the fact that a wrong use has been made of a just idea is no reason why a right use should not be made of it. It ought to be brought under the patronage of its real friends. Let it be said again that autocracy must first be shown the utter futility of its claim to power or leadership in the modern world. It is impossible to apply any standard of justice so long as such forces are unchecked and undefeated as the present masters of Germany command. Not until that has been done can right be set up as arbiter and peacemaker among the nations. But when that has been done—as, God willing, it assuredly will be—we shall at last be free to do an unprecedented thing, and this is the time to avow our purpose to do it. We shall be free to base peace on generosity and justice, to the exclusions of all selfish claims to advantage even on the part of the victors.

Let there be no misunderstanding. Our present and immediate task is to win the war and nothing shall turn us aside from it until it is accomplished. Every power and resource we possess, whether of men, of money, or of materials, is being devoted and will continue to be devoted to that purpose until it is achieved. Those who desire to bring peace about before that purpose is achieved I counsel to carry their advice elsewhere. We will not entertain it. We shall regard the war as won only when the German people say to us, through properly accredited representatives, that they are ready to agree to a settlement based upon justice and reparation of the wrongs their rulers have done. They have done a wrong to Belgium which must be repaired. They have established a power over other lands and peoples than their own—over the great empire of Austria-Hungary, over hitherto free Balkan states, over Turkey and within Asia—which must be relinquished.

Germany's success by skill, by industry, by knowledge, by enterprise we did not grudge or oppose, but admired, rather. She had built up for herself a real empire of trade and influence, secured by the peace of the world. We were content to abide by the rivalries of manufacture, science and commerce that were involved for us in her success, and stand or fall as we had or did not have the brains and the initiative to surpass her. But at the moment when she had conspicuously won her triumphs of peace she threw them away, to establish in their stead what the world will no longer permit to be established, military and political domination by arms, by which to oust where she could not excel the rivals she most feared and hated. The peace we make must remedy that wrong. It must deliver the once fair lands and happy peoples of

Belgium and Northern France from the Prussian conquest and the Prussian menace, but it must deliver also the peoples of Austria-Hungary, the peoples of the Balkans and the peoples of Turkey, alike in Europe and Asia, from the impudent and alien dominion of the Prussian military and commercial autocracy.

We owe it, however, to ourselves, to say that we do not wish in any way to impair or to rearrange the Austro-Hungarian Empire. It is no affair of ours what they do with their own life, either industrially or politically. We do not purpose or desire to dictate to them in any way. We only desire to see that their affairs are left in their own hands, in all matters, great or small. We shall hope to secure for the peoples of the Balkan peninsula and for the people of the Turkish Empire the right and opportunity to make their own lives safe, their own fortunes secure against oppression or injustice and from the dictation of foreign courts or parties.

And our attitude and purpose with regard to Germany herself are of a like kind. We intend no wrong against the German Empire, no interference with her internal affairs. We should deem either the one or the other absolutely unjustifiable, absolutely contrary to the principles we have professed to live by and to hold most sacred throughout our life as a nation.

The people of Germany are being told by the men whom they now permit to deceive them and to act as their masters that they are fighting for the very life and existence of their empire, a war of desperate self-defense against deliberate aggression. Nothing could be more grossly or wantonly false, and we must seek by the utmost openness and candor as to our real aims to convince them of its falseness. We are in fact fighting for their emancipation from the fear, along with our own—from the fear as well as from the fact of unjust attack by neighbors or rivals or schemers after world empire. No one is threatening the existence or the independence of the peaceful enterprise of the German Empire.

The worst that can happen to the detriment of the German people is this, that if they should still, after the war is over, continue to be obliged to live under ambitious and intriguing masters interested to disturb the peace of the world, men or classes of men whom the other peoples of the world could not trust, it might be impossible to admit them to the partnership of nations which must henceforth guarantee the world's peace. That partnership must be a partnership of peoples, not a mere partnership of governments. It might be impossible, also, in such untoward circumstances, to admit Germany to the free economic intercourse which must inevitably spring out of the other partnerships of a real peace. But there would be no aggression in that; and such a situation, inevitable, because of distrust, would in the very nature of things sooner or later cure itself, by processes which would assuredly set in.

The wrongs, the very deep wrongs, committed in this war will have to be righted. That, of course. But they cannot and must not be righted by the commission of similar wrongs against Germany and her allies. The world will not permit the commission of similar wrongs as a means of reparation and settlement. Statesmen must by this time have learned that the opinion of the world is everywhere wide awake and fully comprehends the issues involved. No representative of any self-governed nation will dare disregard it by attempting any such covenants of selfishness and compromise as were entered into at the Congress of Vienna. The thought of the plain people here and everywhere throughout the world, the people who enjoy no privilege and have very simple and unsophisticated standards of right and wrong, is the air all governments must henceforth breathe if they would live.

It is in the full disclosing light of that thought that all policies must be received and executed in this midday hour of the world's life. German rulers have been able to upset the peace of the world only because the German people were not suffered under their tutelage to share the comradeship of the other peoples of the world either in thought or in purpose. They were allowed to have no opinion of their own which might be set up as a rule of conduct for those who exercised authority over them. But the Congress that concludes this war will feel the full strength of the tides that run now in the hearts and consciences of free men everywhere. Its conclusions will run with those tides.

All those things have been true from the very beginning of this stupendous war; and I cannot help thinking that if they had been made plain at the very outset the sympathy and enthusiasm of the Russian people might have been once for all enlisted on the side of the Allies, suspicion and distrust swept away, and a real and lasting union of purpose effected. Had they believed these things at the very moment of their revolution, and had they been confirmed in that belief since, the sad reverses which have recently marked the progress of their affairs towards an ordered and stable government of free men might have been avoided. The Russian people have been poisoned by the very same falsehoods that have kept the German people in the dark, and the poison has been administered by the very same hand. The only possible antidote is the truth. It cannot be uttered too plainly or too often.

From every point of view, therefore, it has seemed to be my duty to speak these declarations of purpose, to add these specific interpretations to what I took the liberty of saying to the Senate in January. Our entrance into the war has not altered out attitude towards the settlement that must come when it is over.

When I said in January that the nations of the world were entitled not only to free pathways upon the sea, but also to assured and unmolested access to those pathways, I was thinking, and I am thinking now, not of the smaller and weaker nations alone which need our countenance and support, but also of the great and powerful nations and of our present enemies as well as our present associates in the war. I was thinking, and am thinking now, of Austria herself, among the rest, as well as of Serbia and of Poland.

Justice and equality of rights can be had only at a great price. We are seeking permanent, not temporary, foundations for the peace of the world, and must seek them candidly and fearlessly. As always, the right will prove to be the expedient.

What shall we do, then, to push this great war of freedom and justice to its righteous conclusion? We must clear away with a thorough hand all impediments to success, and we must make every adjustment of law that will facilitate the full and free use of our whole capacity and force as a fighting unit.

One very embarrassing obstacle that stands in our way is that we are at war with Germany but not with her allies. I, therefore, very earnestly recommend that the Congress immediately declare the United States in a state of war with Austria-Hungary. Does it seem strange to you that this should be the conclusion of the argument I have just addressed to you? It is not. It is in fact the inevitable logic of what I have said. Austria-Hungary is for the time being not her own mistress but simply the vassal of the German Government.

We must face the facts as they are and act upon them without sentiment in this stern business. The Government of Austria and Hungary is not acting upon its own initiative or in response to the wishes and feelings of its own peoples, but as the instrument of another nation. We must meet its force with our own and regard the Central Powers as but one. The war can be successfully conducted in no other way.

The same logic would lead also to a declaration of war against Turkey and Bulgaria. They also are the tools of Germany, but they are mere tools and do not yet stand in the direct path of our necessary action. We shall go wherever the necessities of this war carry us, but it seems to me that we should go only where immediate and practical considerations lead us, and not heed any others.

The financial and military measures which must be adopted will suggest themselves as the war and its undertakings develop, but I will take the liberty of proposing to you certain other acts of legislation which seem to me to be needed for the support of the war and for the release of our whole force and energy.

It will be necessary to extend in certain particulars the legislation of the last session with regard to alien enemies, and also necessary, I believe, to create a very definite and particular control over the entrance and departure of all persons into and from the United States.

Legislation should be enacted defining as a criminal offense every wilful violation of the presidential proclamation relating to alien enemies promulgated under section 4067 of the revised statutes and providing appropriate punishments; and women, as well as men, should be included under the terms of the acts placing restraints upon alien enemies.

It is likely that as time goes on many alien enemies will be willing to be fed and housed at the expense of the Government in the detention camps, and it would be the purpose of the legislation I have suggested to confine offenders among them in the penitentiaries and other similar institutions where they could be made to work as other criminals do.

Recent experience has convinced me that the Congress must go further in authorizing the Government to set limits to prices. The law of supply and demand, I am sorry to say, has been replaced by the law of unrestrained selfishness. While we have eliminated profiteering in several branches of industry, it still runs impudently rampant in others. The farmers, for example, complain with a great deal of justice that, while the regulation of food prices restricts their incomes, no restraints are placed upon the prices of most of the things they must themselves purchase; and similar inequities obtain on all sides.

It is imperatively necessary that the consideration of the full use of the water power of the country, and also of the consideration of the systematic and yet economical development of such of the natural resources of the country as are still under the control of the Federal Government should be immediately resumed and affirmatively and constructively dealt with at the earliest possible moment. The pressing need of such legislation is daily becoming more obvious.

The legislation proposed at the last session with regard to regulated combinations among our exporters in order to provide for our foreign trade a more effective organization and method of co-operation ought by all means to be completed at this session.

And I beg that the members of the House of Representatives will permit me to express the opinion that it will be impossible to deal in any but a very wasteful and extravagant fashion with the enormous appropriations of the public moneys which must continue to be made if the war is to be properly sustained, unless the House will consent to return to its former practice of initiating and preparing all appropriation bills through a single committee, in order that responsibility may be centered, expenditures standardized and made uniform, and waste and duplication as much as possible avoided.

Additional legislation may also become necessary before the present Congress again adjourns in order to effect the most efficient co-ordination and operation of the railways and other transportation systems of the country; but to that I shall, if circumstances should demand, call the attention of Congress upon another occasion.

If I have overlooked anything that ought to be done for the more effective conduct of the war, your own counsels will supply the omission. What I am perfectly clear about is that in the present session of the Congress our whole attention and energy should be concentrated on the vigorous, rapid and successful prosecution of the great task of winning the war.

We can do this with all the greater zeal and enthusiasm because we know that for us this is a war of high principle, debased by no selfish ambition of conquest or spoiliation; because we know, and all the world knows, that we have been forced into it to save the very institutions we live under from corruption and destruction. The purpose of the Central Powers strikes straight at the very heart of everything we believe in; their methods of warfare outrage every principle of humanity and of knightly honor; their intrigue has corrupted the very thought and spirit of many of our people; their sinister and secret diplomacy has sought to take our very territory away from us and disrupt the union of the states. Our safety would be at an end, our honor forever sullied and brought into contempt, were we to permit their triumph. They are striking at the very existence of democracy and liberty.

It is because it is for us a war of high, disinterested purpose, in which all the free peoples of the world are banded together for the vindication of right, a war for the preservation of our nation, of all that it has held dear, of principle and of purpose, that we feel ourselves doubly constrained to propose for its outcome only that which is righteous and of irreproachable intention, for our foes as well as for our friends. The cause being just and holy, the settlement must be of like motive and equality. For this we can fight, but for nothing less noble or less worthy of our traditions. For this cause we entered the war and for this cause will we battle until the last gun is fired.

I have spoken plainly because this seems to me the time when it is most necessary to speak plainly, in order that all the world may know that, even in the heat and ardor of the struggle and when our whole thought is of carrying the war through to its end, we have not forgotten any ideal or principle for which the name of America has been held in honor among the nations and for which it has been our glory to contend in the great generations that went before us. A supreme moment of history has come. The eyes of the people have been opened and they see. The hand of God is laid upon the nations. He will show them favor, I devoutly believe, only if they rise to the clear heights of His own justice and mercy.

SIXTH ANNUAL ADDRESS.

[Delivered to Joint Session of Congress, December 2, 1918.]

Gentlemen of the Congress: The year that has elapsed since I last stood before you to fulfil my constitutional duty to give to the Congress from time to time information on the state of the Union has been so crowded with great events, great processes, and great results that I cannot hope to give you an adequate picture of its transactions or of the far-reaching changes which have been wrought in the life of our nation and of the world. You have yourselves witnessed these things, as I have. It is too soon to assess them; and we who stand in the midst of them and are part of them are less qualified than men of another generation will be to say what they mean, or even what they have been. But some great outstanding facts are unmistakable and constitute, in a sense, part of the public business with which it is our duty to deal. To state them is to set the stage for the legislative and executive action which must grow out of them and which we have yet to shape and determine.

A year ago we had sent 145,918 men overseas. Since then we have sent 1,950,513, an average of 162,542 each month, the number in fact rising, in May last, to 245,951, in June to 278,760, in July to 307,182, and continuing to reach similar figures in August and September,—in August 289,570 and in September 257,438. No such movement of troops ever took place before, across three thousand miles of sea, followed by adequate equipment and supplies, and carried safely through extraordinary dangers of attack,—dangers which were alike strange and infinitely difficult to guard against. In all this movement only seven hundred and fifty-eight men were lost by enemy attack,—six hundred and thirty of whom were upon a single English transport which was sunk near the Orkney Islands.

I need not tell you what lay back of this great movement of men and material. It is not invidious to say that back of it lay a supporting organization of the industries of the country and of all its productive activities more complete, more thorough in method and effective in result, more spirited and unanimous in purpose and effort than any other great belligerent had been able to effect. We profited greatly by the experience of the nations which had already been engaged for nearly three years in the exigent and exacting business, their every resource and every executive proficiency taxed to the utmost. We were their pupils. But we learned quickly and acted with a promptness and a readiness of cooperation that justify our great pride that we were able to serve the world with unparalleled energy and quick accomplishment.

But it is not the physical scale and executive efficiency of preparation, supply, equipment and despatch that I would dwell upon, but the mettle and quality of the officers and men we sent over and of the sailors who kept the seas, and the spirit of the nation that stood behind them. No soldiers or sailors ever proved themselves more quickly ready for the test of battle or acquitted themselves with more splendid courage and achievement when put to the test. Those of us who played some part in directing the great processes by which the war was pushed irresistibly forward to the final triumph may now forget all that and delight our thoughts with the story of what our men did. Their officers understood the grim and exacting task they had undertaken and performed it with an audacity, efficiency, and unhesitating courage that touch the story of convoy and battle with imperishable distinction at every turn, whether the enterprise were great or small, —from their great chiefs, Pershing and Sims, down to the youngest lieutenant; and their men were worthy of them,—such men as hardly need to be commanded, and go to their terrible adventure blithely and with the quick intelligence of those who know just what it is they would accomplish. I am proud to be the fellow-countryman of men of such stuff and valor. Those of us who stayed at home did our duty; the war could not have been won or the gallant men who fought it given their opportunity to win it otherwise; but for many a long day we shall think ourselves "accurs'd we were not there, and hold our manhoods cheap while any speaks that fought" with these at St. Mihiel or Thierry. The memory of those days of triumphant battle will go with these fortunate men to their graves; and each will have his favorite memory. "Old men forget; yet all shall be forgot, but he'll remember with advantages what feats he did that day!"

What we all thank God for with deepest gratitude is that our men went in force into the line of battle just at the critical moment when the whole fate of the world seemed to hang in the balance and threw their fresh strength into the ranks of freedom in time to turn the whole tide and sweep of the fateful struggle,—turn it once for all, so that thenceforth it was back, back, back for their enemies, always back, never again forward! After that it was only a scant four months before the commanders of the Central Empires knew themselves beaten; and now their very empires are in liquidation!

And throughout it all how fine the spirit of the nation was: what unity of purpose, what untiring zeal! What elevation of purpose ran through all its splendid display of strength, its untiring accomplishment! I have said that those of us who stayed at home to do the work of organization and supply will always wish that we had been with the men whom we sustained by our labor; but we can never be ashamed. It has been an inspiring thing to be here in the midst of fine men who had turned aside from every private interest of their own and devoted the whole of their trained capacity to the tasks that supplied the sinews of the whole great undertaking! The patriotism, the unselfishness, the thoroughgoing devotion and distinguished capacity that marked their toilsome labors, day after day, month after month, have made them fit mates and comrades of the men in the trenches and on the sea. And not the men here in Washington only. They have but directed the vast achievement. Throughout innumerable factories, upon innumerable farms, in the depths of coal mines and iron mines and copper mines, wherever the stuffs of industry were to be obtained and prepared, in the shipyards, on the railways, at the docks, on the sea, in every labor that was needed to sustain the battle lines, men have vied with each other to do their part and do it well. They can look any man-at-arms in the face, and say, We also strove to win and gave the best that was in us to make our fleets and armies sure of their triumph!

And what shall we say of the women,—of their instant intelligence, quickening every task that they touched; their capacity for organization and cooperation, which gave their action discipline and enhanced the effectiveness of everything they attempted; their aptitude at tasks to which they had never before set their hands; their utter self-sacrifice alike in what they did and in what they gave? Their contribution to the great result is beyond appraisal. They have added a new lustre to the annals of American womanhood.

The least tribute we can pay them is to make them the equals of men in political rights as they have proved themselves their equals in every field of practical work they have entered, whether for themselves or for their country. These great days of completed achievement would be sadly marred were we to omit that act of justice. Besides the immense practical services they have rendered the women of the country have been the moving spirits in the systematic economies by which our people have voluntarily assisted to supply the suffering peoples of the world and the armies upon every front with food and everything else that we had that might serve the common cause. The details of such a story can never be fully written, but we carry them at our hearts and thank God that we can say that we are the kinsmen of such.

And now we are sure of the great triumph for which every sacrifice was made. It has come, come in its completeness, and with the pride and inspiration of these days of achievement quick within us, we turn to the tasks of peace again,—a peace secure against the violence of irresponsible monarchs and ambitious military coteries and made ready for a new order, for new foundations of justice and fair dealing.

We are about to give order and organization to this peace not only for ourselves but for the other peoples of the world as well, so far as they will suffer us to serve them. It is international justice that we seek, not domestic safety merely. Our thoughts have dwelt of late upon Europe, upon Asia, upon the near and the far East, very little upon the acts of peace and accommodation that wait to be performed at our own doors. While we are adjusting our relations with the rest of the world is it not of capital importance that we should clear away all grounds of misunderstanding with our immediate neighbors and give proof of the friendship we really feel? I hope that the members of the Senate will permit me to speak once more of the unratified treaty of friendship and adjustment with the Republic of Colombia. I very earnestly urge upon them an early and favorable action upon that vital matter. I believe that they will feel, with me, that the stage of affairs is now set for such action as will be not only just but generous and in the spirit of the new age upon which we have so happily entered.

So far as our domestic affairs are concerned the problem of our return to peace is a problem of economic and industrial readjustment. That problem is less serious for us than it may turn out to be for the nations which have suffered the disarrangements and the losses of war longer than we. Our people, moreover, do not wait to be coached and led. They know their own business, are quick and resourceful at every readjustment, definite in purpose, and self-reliant in action. Any leading strings we might seek to put them in would speedily become hopelessly tangled because they would pay no attention to them and go their own way. All that we can do as their legislative and executive servants is to mediate the process of change here, there, and elsewhere as we may. I have heard much counsel as to the plans that should be formed and personally conducted to a happy consummation, but from no quarter have I seen any general scheme of "reconstruction" emerge which I thought it likely we could force our spirited business men and self-reliant laborers to accept with due pliancy and obedience.

While the war lasted we set up many agencies by which to direct the industries of the country in the services it was necessary for them to render, by which to make sure of an abundant supply of the materials needed, by which to check undertakings that could for the time be dispensed with and stimulate those that were most serviceable in war, by which to gain for the purchasing departments of the Government a certain control over the prices of essential articles and materials, by which to restrain trade with alien enemies, make the most of the available shipping, and systematize financial transactions, both public and private, so that there would be no unnecessary conflict or confusion,—by which, in short, to put every material energy of the country in harness to draw the common load and make of us one team in the accomplishment of a great task. But the moment we knew the armistice to have been signed we took the harness off. Raw materials upon which the Government had kept its hand for fear there should not be enough for the industries that supplied the armies have been released and put into the general market again. Great industrial plants whose whole output and machinery had been taken over for the uses of the Government have been set free to return to the uses to which they were put before the war. It has not been possible to remove so readily or so quickly the control of foodstuffs and of shipping, because the world has still to be fed from our granaries and the ships are still needed to send supplies to our men overseas and to bring the men back as fast as the disturbed conditions on the other side of the water permit; but even there restraints are being relaxed as much as possible and more and more as the weeks go by.

Never before have there been agencies in existence in this country which knew so much of the field of supply, of labor, and of industry as the War Industries Board, the War Trade Board, the Labor Department, the Food Administration, and the Fuel Administration have known since their labors became thoroughly systematized; and they have not been isolated agencies; they have been directed by men who represented the permanent Departments of the Government and so have been the centres of unified and cooperative action. It has been the policy of the Executive, therefore, since the armistice was assured (which is in effect a complete submission of the enemy) to put the knowledge of these bodies at the disposal of the business men of the country and to offer their intelligent mediation at every point and in every matter where it was desired. It is surprising how fast the process of return to a peace footing has moved in the three weeks since the fighting stopped. It promises to outrun any inquiry that may be instituted and any aid that may be offered. It will not be easy to direct it any better than it will direct itself. The American business man is of quick initiative.

The ordinary and normal processes of private initiative will not, however, provide immediate employment for all of the men of our returning armies. Those who are of trained capacity, those who are skilled workmen, those who have acquired familiarity with established businesses, those who are ready and willing to go to the farms, all those whose aptitudes are known or will be sought out by employers will find no difficulty, it is safe to say, in finding place and employment. But there will be others who will be at a loss where to gain a livelihood unless pains are taken to guide them and put them in the way of work. There will be a large floating residuum of labor which should not be left wholly to shift for itself. It seems to me important, therefore, that the development of public works of every sort should be promptly resumed, in order that opportunities should be created for unskilled labor in particular, and that plans should be made for such developments of our unused lands and our natural resources as we have hitherto lacked stimulation to undertake.

I particularly direct your attention to the very practical plans which the Secretary of the Interior has developed in his annual report and before your Committees for the reclamation of arid, swamp, and cut-over lands which might, if the States were willing and able to cooperate, redeem some three hundred million acres of land for cultivation. There are said to be fifteen or twenty million acres of land in the West, at present arid, for whose reclamation water is available, if properly conserved. There are about two hundred and thirty million acres from which the forests have been cut but which have never yet been cleared for the plow and which lie waste and desolate. These lie scattered all over the Union. And there are nearly eighty million acres of land that lie under swamps or subject to periodical overflow or too wet for anything but grazing, which it is perfectly feasible to drain and protect and redeem. The Congress can at once direct thousands of the returning soldiers to the reclamation of the arid lands which it has already undertaken, if it will but enlarge the plans and appropriations which it has entrusted to the Department of the Interior. It is possible in dealing with our unused land to effect a great rural and agricultural development which will afford the best sort of opportunity to men who want to help themselves; and the Secretary of the Interior has thought the possible methods out in a way which is worthy of your most friendly attention.

I have spoken of the control which must yet for a while, perhaps for a long while, be exercised over shipping because of the priority of service to which our forces overseas are entitled and which should also be accorded the shipments which are to save recently liberated peoples from starvation and many devasted regions from permanent ruin. May I not say a special word about the needs of Belgium and northern France? No sums of money paid by way of indemnity will serve of themselves to save them from hopeless disadvantage for years to come. Something more must be done than merely find the money. If they had money and raw materials in abundance to-morrow they could not resume their place in the industry of the world to-morrow,—the very important place they held before the flame of war swept across them. Many of their factories are razed to the ground. Much of their machinery is destroyed or has been taken away. Their people are scattered and many of their best workmen are dead. Their markets will be taken by others, if they are not in some special way assisted to rebuild their factories and replace their lost instruments of manufacture. They should not be left to the vicissitudes of the sharp competition for materials and for industrial facilities which is now to set in. I hope, therefore, that the Congress will not be unwilling, if it should become necessary, to grant to some such agency as the War Trade Board the right to establish priorities of export and supply for the benefit of these people whom we have been so happy to assist in saving from the German terror and whom we must not now thoughtlessly leave to shift for themselves in a pitiless competitive market.

For the steadying and facilitation of our own domestic business readjustments nothing is more important than the immediate determination of the taxes that are to be levied for 1918, 1919, and 1920. As much of the burden of taxation must be lifted from business as sound methods of financing the Government will permit, and those who conduct the great essential industries of the country must be told as exactly as possible what obligations to the Government they will be expected to meet in the years immediately ahead of them. It will be of serious consequence to the country to delay removing all uncertainties in this matter a single day longer than the right processes of debate justify. It is idle to talk of successful and confident business reconstruction before those uncertainties are resolved.

If the war had continued it would have been necessary to raise at least eight billion dollars by taxation payable in the year 1919; but the war has ended and I agree with the Secretary of the Treasury that it will be safe to reduce the amount to six billions. An immediate rapid decline in the expenses of the Government is not to be looked for. Contracts made for war supplies will, indeed, be rapidly cancelled and liquidated, but their immediate liquidation will make heavy drains on the Treasury for the months just ahead of us. The maintenance of our forces on the other side of the sea is still necessary. A considerable proportion of those forces must remain in Europe during the period of occupation, and those which are brought home will be transported and demobilized at heavy expense for months to come. The interest on our war debt must of course be paid and provision made for the retirement of the obligations of the Government which represent it. But these demands will of course fall much below what a continuation of military operations would have entailed and six billions should suffice to supply a sound foundation for the financial operations of the year.

I entirely concur with the Secretary of the Treasury in recommending that the two billions needed in addition to the four billions provided by existing law be obtained from the profits which have accrued and shall accrue from war contracts and distinctively war business, but that these taxes be confined to the war profits accruing in 1918, or in 1919 from business originating in war contracts. I urge your acceptance of his recommendation that provision be made now, not subsequently, that the taxes to be paid in 1920 should be reduced from six to four billions. Any arrangements less definite than these would add elements of doubt and confusion to the critical period of industrial readjustment through which the country must now immediately pass, and which no true friend of the nation's essential business interests can afford to be responsible for creating or prolonging. Clearly determined conditions, clearly and simply charted, are indispensable to the economic revival and rapid industrial development which may confidently be expected if we act now and sweep all interrogation points away.

I take it for granted that the Congress will carry out the naval programme which was undertaken before we entered the war. The

Secretary of the Navy has submitted to your Committees for authorization that part of the programme which covers the building plans of the next three years. These plans have been prepared along the lines and in accordance with the policy which the Congress established, not under the exceptional conditions of the war, but with the intention of adhering to a definite method of development for the navy. I earnestly recommend the uninterrupted pursuit of that policy. It would clearly be unwise for us to attempt to adjust our programmes to a future world policy as yet undetermined.

The question which causes me the greatest concern is the question of the policy to be adopted towards the railroads. I frankly turn to you for counsel upon it. I have no confident judgment of my own. I do not see how any thoughtful man can have who knows anything of the complexity of the problem. It is a problem which must be studied, studied immediately, and studied without bias or prejudice. Nothing can be gained by becoming partisans of any particular plan of settlement.

It was necessary that the administration of the railways should be taken over by the Government so long as the war lasted. It would have been impossible otherwise to establish and carry through under a single direction the necessary priorities of shipment. It would have been impossible otherwise to combine maximum production at the factories and mines and farms with the maximum possible car supply to take the products to the ports and markets; impossible to route troop shipments and freight shipments without regard to the advantage or disadvantage of the roads employed; impossible to subordinate, when necessary, all questions of convenience to the public necessity; impossible to give the necessary financial support to the roads from the public treasury. But all these necessities have now been served, and the question is, What is best for the railroads and for the public in the future?

Exceptional circumstances and exceptional methods of administration were not needed to convince us that the railroads were not equal to the immense tasks of transportation imposed upon them by the rapid and continuous development of the industries of the country. We knew that already. And we knew that they were unequal to it partly because their full cooperation was rendered impossible by law and their competition made obligatory, so that it has been impossible to assign to them severally the traffic which could best be carried by their respective lines in the interest of expedition and national economy.

We may hope, I believe, for the formal conclusion of the war by treaty by the time Spring has come. The twenty-one months to which the present control of the railways is limited after formal proclamation of peace shall have been made will run at the farthest, I take it for granted, only to the January of 1921. The full equipment of the railways which the federal administration had planned could not be completed within any such period. The present law does not permit the use of the revenues of the several roads for the execution of such plans except by formal contract with their directors, some of whom will consent while some will not, and therefore does not afford sufficient authority to undertake improvements upon the scale upon which it would be necessary to undertake them. Every approach to this difficult subject-matter of decision brings us face to face, therefore, with this unanswered question: What is it right that we should do with the railroads, in the interest of the public and in fairness to their owners?

Let me say at once that I have no answer ready. The only thing that is perfectly clear to me is that it is not fair either to the public or to the owners of the railroads to leave the question unanswered and that it will presently become my duty to relinquish control of the roads, even before the expiration of the statutory period, unless there should appear some clear prospect in the meantime of a legislative solution. Their release would at least produce one element of a solution, namely certainty and a quick stimulation of private initiative.

I believe that it will be serviceable for me to set forth as explicitly as possible the alternative courses that lie open to our choice. We can simply release the roads and go back to the old conditions of private management, unrestricted competition, and multiform regulation by both state and federal authorities; or we can go to the opposite extreme and establish complete government control, accompanied, if necessary, by actual government ownership; or we can adopt an intermediate course of modified private control, under a more unified and affirmative public regulation and under such alterations of the law as will permit wasteful competition to be avoided and a considerable degree of unification of administration to be effected, as, for example, by regional corporations under which the railways of definable areas would be in effect combined in single systems.

The one conclusion that I am ready to state with confidence is that it would be a disservice alike to the country and to the owners of the railroads to return to the old conditions unmodified. Those are conditions of restraint without development. There is nothing affirmative or helpful about them. What the country chiefly needs is that all its means of transportation should be developed, its railways, its waterways, its highways, and its countryside roads. Some new element of policy, therefore, is absolutely necessary,—necessary for the service of the public, necessary for the release of credit to those who are administering the railways, necessary for the protection of their security holders. The old policy may be changed much or little, but surely it cannot wisely be left as it was. I hope that the Congress will have a complete and impartial study of the whole problem instituted at once and prosecuted as rapidly as possible. I stand ready and anxious to release the roads from the present control and I must do so at a very early date if by waiting until the statutory limit of time is reached I shall be merely prolonging the period of doubt and uncertainty which is hurtful to every interest concerned.

I welcome this occasion to announce to the Congress my purpose to join in Paris the representatives of the governments with which we have been associated in the war against the Central Empires for the purpose of discussing with them the main features of the treaty of peace. I realize the great inconveniences that will attend my leaving the country, particularly at this time, but the conclusion that it was my paramount duty to go has been forced upon me by considerations which I hope will seem as conclusive to you as they have seemed to me.

The Allied governments have accepted the bases of peace which I outlined to the Congress on the eighth of January last, as the Central Empires also have, and very reasonably desire my personal counsel in their interpretation and application, and it is highly desirable that I should give it in order that the sincere desire of our Government to contribute without selfish purpose of any kind to settlements that will be of common benefit to all the nations concerned may be made fully manifest. The peace settlements which are now to be agreed upon are of transcendent importance both to us and to the rest of the world, and I know of no business or interest which should take precedence of them. The gallant men of our armed forces on land and sea have consciously fought for the ideals which they knew to be the ideals of their country; I have sought to express those ideals; they have accepted my statements of them as the substance of their own thought and purpose, as the associated governments have accepted them; I owe it to them to see to it, so far as in me lies, that no false or mistaken interpretation is put upon them, and no possible effort omitted to realize them. It is now my duty to play my full part in making good what they offered their life's blood to obtain. I can think of no call to service which could transcend this.

I shall be in close touch with you and with affairs on this side the water, and you will know all that I do. At my request, the French and English governments have absolutely removed the censorship of cable news which until within a fortnight they had maintained and there is now no censorship whatever exercised at this end except upon attempted trade communications with enemy countries. It has been necessary to keep an open wire constantly available between Paris and the Department of State and another between France and the Department of War. In order that this might be done with the least possible interference with the other uses of the cables, I have temporarily taken over the control of both cables in order that they may be used as a single system. I did so at the advice of the most experienced cable officials, and I hope that the results will justify my hope that the news of the next few months may pass with the utmost freedom and with the least possible delay from each side of the sea to the other.

May I not hope, Gentlemen of the Congress, that in the delicate tasks I shall have to perform on the other side of the sea, in my efforts truly and faithfully to interpret the principles and purposes of the country we love, I may have the encouragement and the added strength of your united support? I realize the magnitude and difficulty of the duty I am undertaking; I am poignantly aware of its grave responsibilities. I am the servant of the nation. I can have no private thought or purpose of my own in performing such an errand. I go to give the best that is in me to the common settlements which I must now assist in arriving at in conference with the other working heads of the associated governments. I shall count upon your friendly countenance and encouragement. I shall not be inaccessible. The cables and the wireless will render me available for any counsel or service you may desire of me, and I shall be happy in the thought that I am constantly in touch with the weighty matters of domestic policy with which we shall have to deal. I shall make my absence as brief as possible and shall hope to return with the happy assurance that it has been possible to translate into action the great ideals for which America has striven.

SEVENTH ANNUAL MESSAGE.

[This was the first of President Wilson's annual messages to Congress to be read instead of delivered in person, the President being confined to the White House by illness.]

THE WHITE HOUSE, *December 2, 1919.*

TO THE SENATE AND HOUSE OF REPRESENTATIVES:

I sincerely regret that I cannot be present at the opening of this session of the Congress. I am thus prevented from presenting in as direct a way as I could wish the many questions that are pressing for solution at this time. Happily, I have had the advantage of the advice of the heads of the several executive departments who have kept in close touch with affairs in their detail and whose thoughtful recommendations I earnestly second.

In the matter of the railroads and the readjustment of their affairs growing out of Federal control, I shall take the liberty at a later date of addressing you.

I hope that Congress will bring to a conclusion at this session legislation looking to the establishment of a budget system. That there should be one single authority responsible for the making of all appropriations and that appropriations should be made not independently of each other, but with reference to one single comprehensive plan of expenditure properly related to the nation's income, there can be no doubt. I believe the burden of preparing the budget must, in the nature of the case, if the work is to be properly done and responsibility concentrated instead of divided, rest upon the executive. The budget so prepared should be submitted to and approved or amended by a single committee of each House of Congress and no single appropriation should be made by the Congress, except such as may have been included in the budget prepared by the executive or added by the particular committee of Congress charged with the budget legislation.

Another and not less important aspect of the problem is the ascertainment of the economy and efficiency with which the moneys appropriated are expended. Under existing law the only audit is for the purpose of ascertaining whether expenditures have been lawfully made within the appropriations. No one is authorized or equipped to ascertain whether the money has been spent wisely, economically and effectively. The auditors should be highly trained officials with permanent tenure in the Treasury Department, free of obligations to or motives of consideration for this or any subsequent administration, and authorized and empowered to examine into and make report upon the methods employed and the results obtained by the executive departments of the Government. Their reports should be made to the Congress and to the Secretary of the Treasury.

I trust that the Congress will give its immediate consideration to the problem of future taxation. Simplification of the income and profits taxes has become an immediate necessity. These taxes performed indispensable service during the war. They must, however, be simplified, not only to save the taxpayer inconvenience and expense, but in order that his liability may be made certain and definite.

With reference to the details of the Revenue Law, the Secretary of the Treasury and the Commissioner of Internal Revenue will lay before you for your consideration certain amendments necessary or desirable in connection with the administration of the law—recommendations which have my approval and support. It is of the utmost importance that in dealing with this matter the present law should not be disturbed so far as regards taxes for the calendar year 1920, payable in the calendar year 1921. The Congress might well consider whether the higher rates of income and profits taxes can in peace times be effectively productive of revenue, and whether they may not, on the contrary, be destructive of business activity and productive of waste and inefficiency. There is a point at which in peace times high rates of income and profits taxes discourage energy, remove the incentive to new enterprises, encourage extravagant expenditures and produce industrial stagnation with consequent unemployment and other attendant evils.

The problem is not an easy one. A fundamental change has taken place with reference to the position of America in the world's affairs. The prejudice and passions engendered by decades of controversy between two schools of political and economic thought,—the one believers in protection of American industries, the other believers in tariff for revenue only,—must be subordinated to the single consideration of the public interest in the light of utterly changed conditions. Before the war America was heavily the debtor of the rest of the world and the interest payments she had to make to foreign countries on American securities held abroad, the expenditures of American travelers abroad and the ocean freight charges she had to pay to others, about balanced the value of her pre-war favorable balance of trade. During the war America's exports have been greatly stimulated, and increased prices have increased their value. On the other hand, she has purchased a large proportion of the American securities previously held abroad, has loaned some $9,000,000,000 to foreign governments, and has built her own ships. Our favorable balance of trade has thus been greatly increased and Europe has been deprived of the means of meeting it heretofore existing. Europe can have only three ways of meeting the favorable balance of trade in peace times: by imports into this country of gold or of goods, or by establishing new credits. Europe is in no position at the present time to ship gold to us nor could we contemplate large further imports of gold into this country without concern. The time has nearly passed for international governmental loans and it will take time to develop in this country a market for foreign securities. Anything, therefore, which would tend to prevent foreign countries from settling for our exports by shipments of goods into this country could only have the effect of preventing them from paying for our exports and therefore of preventing the exports from being made. The productivity of the country, greatly stimulated by the war, must find an outlet by exports to foreign countries, and any measures taken to prevent imports will inevitably curtail exports, force curtailment of production, load the banking machinery of the country with credits to carry unsold products and produce industrial stagnation and unemployment. If we want to sell, we must be prepared to buy. Whatever, therefore, may have been our views during the period of growth of American business concerning tariff legislation, we must now adjust our own economic life to a changed condition growing out of the fact that American business is full grown and that America is the greatest capitalist in the world.

No policy of isolation will satisfy the growing needs and opportunities of America. The provincial standards and policies of the past, which have held American business as if in a strait-jacket, must yield and give way to the needs and exigencies of the new day in which we live, a day full of hope and promise for American business, if we will but take advantage of the opportunities that are ours for the asking. The recent war has ended our isolation and thrown upon us a great duty and responsibility. The United States must share the expanding world market. The United States desires for itself only equal opportunity with the other nations of the world, and that through the process of friendly cooperation and fair competition the legitimate interests of the nations concerned may be successfully and equitably adjusted.

There are other matters of importance upon which I urged action at the last session of Congress which are still pressing for solution. I am sure it is not necessary for me again to remind you that there is one immediate and very practicable question resulting from the war which we should meet in the most liberal spirit. It is a matter of recognition and relief to our soldiers. I can do no better than to quote from my last message urging this very action:

"We must see to it that our returning soldiers are assisted in every practicable way to find the places for which they are fitted in the daily work of the country. This can be done by developing and maintaining upon an adequate scale the admirable organization created by the Department of Labor for placing men seeking work; and it can also be done, in at least one very great field, by creating new opportunities for individual enterprise. The Secretary of the Interior has pointed out the way by which returning soldiers may be helped to find and take up land in the hitherto undeveloped regions of the country which the Federal Government has already prepared, or can readily prepare, for cultivation and also on many of the cut-over or neglected areas which lie within the limits of the older states; and I once more take the liberty of recommending very urgently that his plans shall receive the immediate and substantial support of the Congress."

In the matter of tariff legislation, I beg to call your attention to the statements contained in my last message urging legislation with reference to the establishment of the chemical and dyestuffs industry in America:

"Among the industries to which special consideration should be given is that of the manufacture of dyestuffs and related chemicals. Our complete dependence upon German supplies before the war made the interruption of trade a cause of exceptional economic disturbance. The close relation between the manufacture of dyestuffs, on the one hand, and of explosive and poisonous gases, on the other, moreover, has given the industry an exceptional significance and value. Although the United States will gladly and unhesitatingly join in the programme of international disarmament, it will, nevertheless, be a policy of obvious prudence to make certain of the successful maintenance of many strong and well-equipped chemical plants. The German chemical industry, with which we will be brought into competition, was and may well be again, a thoroughly knit monopoly capable of exercising a competition of a peculiarly insidious and dangerous kind."

During the war the farmer performed a vital and willing service to the nation. By materially increasing the production of his land, he supplied America and the Allies with the increased amounts of food necessary to keep their immense armies in the field. He indispensably helped to win the war. But there is now scarcely less need of increasing the production in food and the necessaries of life. I ask the Congress to consider means of encouraging effort along these lines. The importance of doing everything possible to promote production along economical lines, to improve marketing, and to make rural life more attractive and healthful, is obvious. I would urge approval of the plans already proposed to the Congress by the Secretary of Agriculture, to secure the essential facts required for the proper study of this question, through the proposed enlarged programmes for farm management studies and crop estimates. I would urge, also, the continuance of Federal participation in the building of good roads, under the terms of existing law and under the direction of present agencies; the need of further action on the part of the States and the Federal Government to preserve and develop our forest resources, especially through the practice of better forestry methods on private holdings and the extension of the publicly owned forests; better support for country schools and the more definite direction of their courses of study along lines related to rural problems; and fuller provision for sanitation in rural districts and the building up of needed hospital and medical facilities in these localities. Perhaps the way might be cleared for many of these desirable reforms by a fresh, comprehensive survey made of rural conditions by a conference composed of representatives of the farmers and of the agricultural agencies responsible for leadership.

I would call your attention to the widespread condition of political restlessness in our body politic. The causes of this unrest, while various and complicated, are superficial rather than deep-seated. Broadly, they arise from or are connected with the failure on the part of our Government to arrive speedily at a just and permanent peace permitting return to normal conditions, from the transfusion of radical theories from seething European centers pending such delay, from heartless profiteering resulting in the increase of the cost of living, and lastly from the machinations of passionate and malevolent agitators. With the return to normal conditions, this unrest will rapidly disappear. In the meantime, it does much evil. It seems to me that in dealing with this situation Congress should not be impatient or drastic but should seek rather to remove the causes. It should endeavor to bring our country back speedily to a peace basis, with ameliorated living conditions under the minimum of restrictions upon personal liberty that is consistent with our reconstruction problems. And it should arm the Federal Government with power to deal in its criminal courts with those persons who by violent methods would abrogate our time-tested institutions. With the free expression of opinion and with the advocacy of orderly political change, however fundamental, there must be no interference, but towards passion and malevolence tending to incite crime and insurrection under guise of political evolution there should be no leniency. Legislation to this end has been recommended by the Attorney General and should be enacted. In this direct connection, I would call your attention to my recommendations on August 8th, pointing out legislative measures which would be effective in controlling and bringing down the present cost of living, which contributes so largely to this unrest. On only one of these recommendations has the Congress acted. If the Government's campaign is to be effective, it is necessary that the other steps suggested should be acted on at once.

I renew and strongly urge the necessity of the extension of the present Food Control Act as to the period of time in which it shall remain in operation. The Attorney General has submitted a bill providing for an extension of this Act for a period of six months. As it now stands, it is limited in operation to the period of the war and becomes inoperative upon the formal proclamation of peace. It is imperative that it should be extended at once. The Department of Justice has built up extensive machinery for the purpose of enforcing its provisions; all of which must be abandoned upon the conclusion of peace unless the provisions of this Act are extended.

During this period the Congress will have an opportunity to make similar permanent provisions and regulations with regard to all goods destined for interstate commerce and to exclude them from interstate shipment, if the requirements of the law are not compiled with. Some such regulation is imperatively necessary. The abuses that have grown up in the manipulation of prices by the withholding of foodstuffs and other necessaries of life cannot otherwise be effectively prevented. There can be no doubt of either the necessity of the legitimacy of such measures.

As I pointed out in my last message, publicity can accomplish a great deal in this campaign. The aims of the Government must be clearly brought to the attention of the consuming public, civic organizations and state officials, who are in a position to lend their assistance to our efforts. You have made available funds with which to carry on this campaign, but there is no provision in the law authorizing their expenditure for the purpose of making the public tully informed about the efforts of the Government. Specific recommendation has been made by the Attorney General in this regard. I would strongly urge upon you its immediate adoption, as it constitutes one of the preliminary steps to this campaign.

I also renew my recommendation that the Congress pass a law regulating cold storage as it is regulated, for example, by the laws of the State of New Jersey, which limit the time during which goods may be kept in storage, prescribe the method of disposing of them if kept beyond the permitted period, and require that goods released from storage shall in all cases bear the date of their receipt. It would materially add to the serviceability of the law, for the purpose we now have in view, if it were also prescribed that all goods released from storage for interstate shipment should have plainly marked upon each package the selling or market price at which they went into storage. By this means the purchaser would always be able to learn what profits stood between him and the producer or the wholesale dealer.

I would also renew my recommendation that all goods destined for interstate commerce should in every case, where their form or package makes it possible, be plainly marked with the price at which they left the hands of the producer.

We should formulate a law requiring a Federal license of all corporations engaged in interstate commerce and embodying in the license, or in the conditions under which it is to be issued, specific regulations designed to secure competitive selling and prevent unconscionable profits in the method of marketing. Such a law would afford a welcome opportunity to effect other much needed reforms in the business of interstate shipment and in the methods of corporations which are engaged in it; but for the moment I confine my recommendations to the object immediately in hand, which is to lower the cost of living.

No one who has observed the march of events in the last year can fail to note the absolute need of a definite programme to bring about an improvement in the conditions of labor. There can be no settled conditions leading to increased production and a reduction in the cost of living if labor and capital are to be antagonists instead of partners. Sound thinking and an honest desire to serve the interests of the whole nation, as distinguished from the interests of a class, must be applied to the solution of this great and pressing problem. The failure of other nations to consider this matter in a vigorous way has produced bitterness and jealousies and antagonisms, the food of radicalism. The only way to keep men from agitating against grievances is to remove the grievances. An unwillingness even to discuss these matters produces only dissatisfaction and gives comfort to the extreme elements in our country which endeavor to stir up disturbances in order to provoke governments to embark upon a course of retaliation and repression. The seed of revolution is repression. The remedy for these things must not be negative in character. It must be constructive. It must comprehend the general interest. The real antidote for the unrest which manifests itself is not suppression, but a deep consideration of the wrongs that beset our national life and the application of a remedy.

Congress has already shown its willingness to deal with these industrial wrongs by establishing the eight-hour day as the standard in every field of labor. It has sought to find a way to prevent child labor. It has served the whole country by leading the way in developing the means of preserving and safeguarding lives and health in dangerous industries. It must now help in the difficult task of finding a method that will bring about a genuine democratization of industry, based upon the full recognition of the right of those who work, in whatever rank, to participate in some organic way in every decision which directly affects their welfare. It is with this purpose in mind that I called a conference to meet in Washington on December 1st, to consider these problems in all their broad aspects, with the idea of bringing about a better understanding between these two interests.

The great unrest throughout the world, out of which has emerged a demand for an immediate consideration of the difficulties between capital and labor, bids us put our own house in order. Frankly, there can be no permanent and lasting settlements between capital and labor which do not recognize the fundamental concepts for which labor has been struggling through the years. The whole world gave its recognition and endorsement to these fundamental purposes in the League of Nations. The statesmen gathered at Versailles recognized the fact that world stability could not be had by reverting to industrial standards and conditions against which the average workman of the world had revolted. It is, therefore, the task of the statesmen of this new day of change and readjustment to recognize world conditions and to seek to bring about, through legislation, conditions that will mean the ending of age-long antagonisms between capital and labor and that will hopefully lead to the building up of a comradeship which will result not only in greater contentment among the mass of workmen but also bring about a greater production and a greater prosperity to business itself.

To analyze the particulars in the demands of labor is to admit the justice of their complaint in many matters that lie at their basis. The workman demands an adequate wage, sufficient to permit him to live in comfort, unhampered by the fear of poverty and want in his old age. He demands the right to live and the right to work amidst sanitary surroundings, both in home and in workshop, surroundings that develop and do not retard his own health and well-being; and the right to provide for his children's wants in the matter of health and education. In other words, it is his desire to make the conditions of his life and the lives of those dear to him tolerable and easy to bear.

The establishment of the principles regarding labor laid down in the covenant of the League of Nations offers us the way to industrial peace and conciliation. No other road lies open to us. Not to pursue this one is longer to invite enmities, bitterness, and antagonisms which in the end only lead to industrial and social disaster. The unwilling workman is not a profitable servant. An employee whose industrial life is hedged about by hard and unjust conditions, which he did not create and over which he has no control, lacks that fine spirit of enthusiasm and volunteer effort which are the necessary ingredients of a great producing entity. Let us be frank about this solemn matter. The evidences of world-wide unrest which manifest themselves in violence throughout the world bid us pause and consider the means to be found to stop the spread of this contagious thing before it saps the very vitality of the nation itself. Do we gain strength by withholding the remedy? Or is it not the business of statesmen to treat these manifestations of unrest which meet us on every hand as evidences of an economic disorder and to apply constructive remedies wherever necessary, being sure that in the application of the remedy we touch not the vital tissues of our industrial and economic life? There can be no recession of the tide of unrest until constructive instrumentalities are set up to stem that tide.

Governments must recognze the right of men collectively to bargain for humane objects that have at their base the mutual protection and welfare of those engaged in all industries. Labor must not be longer treated as a commodity. It must be regarded as the activity of human beings, possessed of deep yearnings and desires. The business man gives his best thought to the repair and replenishment of his machinery, so that its usefulness will not be impaired and its power to produce may always be at its height and kept in full vigor and motion. No less regard ought to be paid to the human machine, which after all propels the machinery of the world and is the great dynamic force that lies back of all industry and progress. Return to the old standards of wage and industry in employment are unthinkable. The terrible tragedy of war which has just ended and which has brought the world to the verge of chaos and disaster would be in vain if there should ensue a return to the conditions of the past. Europe itself, whence has come the unrest which now holds the world at bay, is an example of standpatism in these vital human matters which America might well accept as an example, not to be followed but studiously to be avoided. Europe made labor the differential, and the price of it all is enmity and antagonism and prostrated industry. The right of labor to live in peace and comfort must be recognized by governments and America should be the first to lay the foundation stones upon which industrial peace shall be built.

Labor not only is entitled to an adequate wage, but capital should receive a reasonable return upon its investment and is entitled to protection at the hands of the Government in every emergency. No Government worthy of the name can "play" these elements against each other, for there is a mutuality of interest between them which the Government must seek to express and to safeguard at all cost.

The right of individuals to strike is inviolate and ought not to be interfered with by any process of Government, but there is a predominant right and that is the right of the Government to protect all of its people and to assert its power and majesty against the challenge of any class. The Government, when it asserts that right, seeks not to antagonize a class but simply to defend the right of the whole people as against the irreparable harm and injury that might be done by the attempt by any class to usurp a power that only Government itself has a right to exercise as a protection to all.

In the matter of international disputes which have led to war, statesmen have sought to set up as a remedy arbitration for war. Does this not point the way for the settlement of industrial disputes, by the establishment of a tribunal, fair and just alike to all, which will settle industrial disputes which in the past have led to war and disaster? America, witnessing the evil consequences which have followed out of such disputes between these contending forces, must not admit itself impotent to deal with these matters by means of peaceful processes. Surely, there must be some method of bringing together in a council of peace and amity these two great interests, out of which will come a happier day of peace and cooperation, a day that will make men more hopeful and enthusiastic in their various tasks, that will make for more comfort and happiness in living and a more tolerable condition among all classes of men. Certainly human intelligence can devise some acceptable tribunal for adjusting the differences between capital and labor.

This is the hour of test and trial for America. By her prowess and strength, and the indomitable courage of her soldiers, she demonstrated her power to vindicate on foreign battlefields her conceptions of liberty and justice. Let not her influence as a mediator between capital and labor be weakened and her own failure to settle matters of purely domestic concern be proclaimed to the world. There are those in this country who threaten direct action to force their will upon a majority. Russia today, with its blood and terror, is a painful object lesson of the power of minorities. It makes little difference what minority it is; whether capital or labor, or any other class; no sort of privilege will ever be permitted to dominate this country. We are a partnership or nothing that is worth while. We are a democracy, where the majority are the masters, or all the hopes and purposes of the men who founded this government have been defeated and forgotten. In America there is but one way by which great reforms can be accomplished and the relief sought by classes obtained, and that is through the orderly processes of representative government. Those who would propose any other method of reform are enemies of this country. America will not be daunted by threats nor lose her composure or calmness in these distressing times. We can afford, in the midst of this day of passion and unrest, to be self-contained and sure. The instrument of all reform in America is the ballot. The road to economic and social reform in America is the straight road of justice to all classes and conditions of men. Men have but to follow this road to realize the full fruition of their objects and purposes. Let those beware who would take the shorter road of disorder and revolution. The right road is the road of justice and orderly process.

EIGHTH ANNUAL MESSAGE.

[Read Before Congress on December 7, 1920.]

GENTLEMEN OF THE CONGRESS:

When I addressed myself to performing the duty laid upon the President by the Constitution to present to you an annual report on the state of the Union, I found my thought dominated by an immortal sentence of Abraham Lincoln's—"Let us have faith that right makes might, and in that faith let us dare to do our duty as we understand it"—a sentence immortal because it embodies in a form of utter simplicity and purity the essential faith of the nation, the faith in which it was conceived, and the faith in which it has grown to glory and power. With that faith and the birth of a nation founded upon it came the hope into the world that a new order would prevail throughout the affairs of mankind, an order in which reason and right would take precedence over covetousness and force; and I believe that I express the wish and purpose of every thoughtful American when I say that this sentence marks for us in the plainest manner the part we should play alike in the arrangement of our domestic affairs and in our exercise of influence upon the affairs of the world.

By this faith, and by this faith alone, can the world be lifted out of its present confusion and despair. It was this faith which prevailed over the wicked force of Germany. You will remember that the beginning of the end of the war came when the German people found themselves face to face with the conscience of the world and realized that right was everywhere arrayed against the wrong that their government was attempting to perpetrate. I think, therefore, that it is true to say that this was the faith which won the war. Certainly this is the faith with which our gallant men went into the field and out upon the seas to make sure of victory.

This is the mission upon which Democracy came into the world. Democracy is an assertion of the right of the individual to live and to be treated justly as against any attempt on the part of any combination of individuals to make laws which will overburden him or which will destroy his equality among his fellows in the matter of right or privilege; and I think we all realize that the day has come when Democracy is being put upon its final test. The Old World is just now suffering from a wanton rejection of the principle of democracy and a substitution of the principle of autocracy as asserted in the name, but without the authority and sanction, of the multitude. This is the time of all others when Democracy should prove its purity and its spiritual power to prevail. It is surely the manifest destiny of the United States to lead in the attempt to make this spirit prevail.

There are two ways in which the United States can assist to accomplish this great object. First, by offering the example within her own borders of the will and power of Democracy to make and enforce laws which are unquestionably just and which are equal in their administration—laws which secure its full right to Labor and yet at the same time safeguard the integrity of property, and particularly of that property which is devoted to the development of industry and the increase of the necessary wealth of the world. Second, by standing for right and justice as toward individual nations. The law of Democracy is for the protection of the weak, and the influence of every democracy in the world should be for the protection of the weak nation, the nation which is struggling toward its right and toward its proper recognition and privilege in the family of nations.

The United States cannot refuse this role of champion without putting the stigma of rejection upon the great and devoted men who brought its government into existence and established it in the face of almost universal opposition and intrigue, even in the face of wanton force, as, for example, against the Orders in Council of Great Britain and the arbitrary Napoleonic decrees which involved us in what we know as the War of 1812.

I urge you to consider that the display of an immediate disposition on the part of the Congress to remedy any injustices or evils that may have shown themselves in our own national life will afford the most effectual offset to the forces of chaos and tyranny which are playing so disastrous a part in the fortunes of the free peoples of more than one part of the world. The United States is of necessity the sample democracy of the world, and the triumph of Democracy depends upon its success.

Recovery from the disturbing and sometimes disastrous effects of the late war has been exceedingly slow on the other side of the water, and has given promise, I venture to say, of early completion only in our own fortunate country; but even with us the recovery halts and is impeded at times, and there are immediately serviceable acts of legislation which it seems to me we ought to attempt, to assist that recovery and prove the indestructible recuperative force of a great government of the people. One of these is to prove that a great democracy can keep house as successfully and in as business-like a fashion as any other government. It seems to me that the first step toward providing this is to supply ourselves with a systematic method of handling our estimates and expenditures and bringing them to the point where they will not be an unnecessary strain upon our income or necessitate unreasonable taxation; in other words, a workable budget system. And I respectfully suggest that two elements are essential to such a system—namely, not only that the proposal of appropriations should be in the hands of a single body, such as a single appropriations committee in each house of the Congress, but also that this body should be brought into such cooperation with the Departments of the Government and with the Treasury of the United States as would enable it to act upon a complete conspectus of the needs of the Government and the resources from which it must draw its income.

I reluctantly vetoed the budget bill passed by the last session of the

Congress because of a constitutional objection. The House of Representatives subsequently modified the bill in order to meet this objection. In the revised form, I believe that the bill, coupled with action already taken by the Congress to revise its rules and procedure, furnishes the foundation for an effective national budget system. I earnestly hope, therefore, that one of the first steps to be taken by the present session of the Congress will be to pass the budget bill.

The nation's finances have shown marked improvement during the last year. The total ordinary receipts of $6,694,000,000 for the fiscal year 1920 exceeded those for 1919 by $1,542,000,000, while the total net ordinary expenditures decreased from $18,514,000,000 to $6,403,000,000. The gross public debt, which reached its highest point on August 31, 1919, when it was $26,596,000,000, had dropped on November 30, 1920, to $24,175,000,000.

There has also been a marked decrease in holdings of government war securities by the banking institutions of the country, as well as in the amount of bills held by the Federal Reserve Banks secured by government war obligations. This fortunate result has relieved the banks and left them freer to finance the needs of Agriculture, Industry, and Commerce. It has been due in large part to the reduction of the public debt, especially of the floating debt, but more particularly to the improved distribution of government securities among permanent investors. The cessation of the Government's borrowings, except through short-term certificates of indebtedness, has been a matter of great consequence to the people of the country at large, as well as to the holders of Liberty Bonds and Victory Notes, and has had an important bearing on the matter of effective credit control.

The year has been characterized by the progressive withdrawal of the Treasury from the domestic credit market and from a position of dominant influence in that market. The future course will necessarily depend upon the extent to which economies are practiced and upon the burdens placed upon the Treasury, as well as upon industrial developments and the maintenance of tax receipts at a sufficiently high level. The fundamental fact which at present dominates the Government's financial situation is that seven and a half billions of its war indebtedness mature within the next two and a half years. Of this amount, two and a half billions are floating debt and five billions, Victory Notes and War Savings Certificates. The fiscal program of the Government must be determined with reference to these maturities. Sound policy demands that Government expenditures be reduced to the lowest amount which will permit the various services to operate efficiently and that Government receipts from taxes and salvage be maintained sufficiently high to provide for current requirements, including interest and sinking fund charges on the public debt, and at the same time retire the floating debt and part of the Victory Loan before maturity.

With rigid economy, vigorous salvage operations, and adequate revenues from taxation, a surplus of current receipts over current expenditures can be realized and should be applied to the floating debt. All branches of the Government should cooperate to see that this program is realized. I cannot overemphasize the necessity of economy in Government appropriations and expenditures and the avoidance by the Congress of practices which take money from the Treasury by indefinite or revolving fund appropriations. The estimates for the present year show that over a billion dollars of expenditures were authorized by the last Congress in addition to the amounts shown in the usual compiled statements of appropriations. This strikingly illustrates the importance of making direct and specific appropriations. The relation between the current receipts and current expenditures of the Government during the present fiscal year, as well as during the last half of the last fiscal year, has been disturbed by the extraordinary burdens thrown upon the Treasury by the Transportation Act, in connection with the return of the railroads to private control. Over $600,000,000 has already been paid to the railroads under this act—$350,000,000 during the present fiscal year; and it is estimated that further payments aggregating possibly $650,000,000 must still be made to the railroads during the current year. It is obvious that these large payments have already seriously limited the Government's progress in retiring the floating debt.

Closely connected with this, it seems to me, is the necessity for an immediate consideration of the revision of our tax laws. Simplification of the income and profits taxes has become an immediate necessity. These taxes performed an indispensable service during the war. The need for their simplification, however, is very great, in order to save the taxpayer inconvenience and expense and in order to make his liability more certain and definite. Other and more detailed recommendations with regard to taxes will no doubt be laid before you by the Secretary of the Treasury and the Commissioner of Internal Revenue.

It is my privilege to draw to the attention of Congress for very sympathetic consideration the problem of providing adequate facilities for the care and treatment of former members of the military and naval forces who are sick and disabled as the result of their participation in the war. These heroic men can never be paid in money for the service they patriotically rendered the nation. Their reward will lie rather in realization of the fact that they vindicated the rights of their country and aided in safeguarding civilization. The nation's gratitude must be effectively revealed to them by the most ample provision for their medical care and treatment as well as for their vocational training and placement. The time has come when a more complete program can be formulated and more satisfactorily administered for their treatment and training, and I earnestly urge that the Congress give the matter its early consideration. The Secretary of the Treasury and the Board for Vocational Education will outline in their annual reports proposals covering medical care and rehabilitation which I am sure will engage your earnest study and commend your most generous support.

Permit me to emphasize once more the need for action upon certain matters upon which I dwelt at some length in my message to the second session of the Sixty-sixth Congress. The necessity, for example, of encouraging the manufacture of dyestuffs and related chemicals; the importance of doing everything possible to promote agricultural production along economic lines, to improve agricultural marketing, and to make rural life more attractive and healthful; the need for a law regulating cold storage in such a way as to limit the time during which goods may be kept in storage, prescribing the method of disposing of them if kept beyond the permitted period, and requiring goods released from storage in all cases to bear the date of their receipt. It would also be most serviceable if it were provided that all goods released from cold storage for interstate shipment should have plainly marked upon each package the selling or market price at which they went into storage, in order that the purchaser might be able to learn what profits stood between him and the producer or the wholesale dealer. Indeed, it would be very serviceable to the public if all goods destined for interstate commerce were made to carry upon every packing case whose form made it possible a plain statement of the price at which they left the hands of the producer. I respectfully call your attention also to the recommendations of the message referred to with regard to a federal license for all corporations engaged in interstate commerce.

In brief, the immediate legislative need of the time is the removal of all obstacles to the realization of the best ambitions of our people in their several classes of employment and the strengthening of all instrumentalities by which difficulties are to be met and removed and justice dealt out, whether by law or by some form of mediation and conciliation. I do not feel it to be my privilege at present to suggest the detailed and particular methods by which these objects may be attained, but I have faith that the inquiries of your several committees will discover the way and the method.

In response to what I believe to be the impulse of sympathy and opinion throughout the United States, I earnestly suggest that the Congress authorize the Treasury of the United States to make to the struggling government of Armenia such a loan as was made to several of the Allied governments during the war, and I would also suggest that it would be desirable to provide in the legislation itself that the expenditure of the money thus loaned should be under the supervision of a commission, or at least a commissioner, from the United States in order that revolutionary tendencies within Armenia itself might not be afforded by the loan a further tempting opportunity.

Allow me to call your attention to the fact that the people of the Philippine Islands have succeeded in maintaining a stable government since the last action of the Congress in their behalf, and have thus fulfilled the condition set by the Congress as precedent to a consideration of granting independence to the Islands. I respectfully submit that this condition precedent having been fulfilled, it is now our liberty and our duty to keep our promise to the people of those islands by granting them the independence which they so honorably covet.

I have not so much laid before you a series of recommendations, gentlemen, as sought to utter a confession of faith, of the faith in which I was bred and which it is my solemn purpose to stand by until my last fighting day. I believe this to be the faith of America, the faith of the future, and of all the victories which await national action in the days to come, whether in America or elsewhere.

Warren G. Harding

March 4, 1921 to August 2, 1923

FIRST ANNUAL MESSAGE.

Dec. 6, 1921

MR. SPEAKER AND MEMBERS OF THE CONGRESS: It is a very gratifying privilege to come to the Congress with the Republic at peace with all the nations of the world. More, it is equally gratifying to report that our country is not only free from every impending menace of war, but there are growing assurances of the permanency of the peace which we so deeply cherish.

For approximately ten years we have dwelt amid menaces of war or as participants in war's actualities, and the inevitable aftermath, with its disordered conditions, has added to the difficulties of government which adequately can not be appraised except by those who are in immediate contact and know the responsibilities. Our tasks would be less difficult if we had only ourselves to consider, but so much of the world was involved, the disordered conditions are so well-nigh universal, even among nations not engaged in actual warfare, that no permanent readjustments can be effected without consideration of our inescapable relationship to world affairs in finance and trade. Indeed, we should be unworthy of our best traditions if we were unmindful of social, moral, and political conditions which are not of direct concern to us, but which do appeal to the human sympathies and the very becoming interest of a people blest with our national good fortune.

It is not my purpose to bring to you a program of world restoration. In the main such a program must be worked out by the nations more directly concerned. They must themselves turn to the heroic remedies for the menacing conditions under which they are struggling, then we can help, and we mean to help. We shall do so unselfishly because there is compensation in the consciousness of assisting, selfishly because the commerce and international exchanges in trade, which marked our high tide of fortunate advancement, are possible only when the nations of all continents are restored to stable order and normal relationship.

In the main the contribution of this Republic to restored normalcy in the world must come through the initiative of the executive branch of the Government, but the best of intentions and most carefully considered purposes would fail utterly if the sanction and the cooperation of Congress were not cheerfully accorded.

I am very sure we shall have no conflict of opinion about constitutional duties or authority. During the anxieties of war, when necessity seemed compelling, there were excessive grants of authority and an extraordinary concentration of powers in the Chief Executive. The repeal of war-time legislation and the automatic expirations which attended the peace proclamations have put an end to these emergency excesses, but I have the wish to go further than that. I want to join you in restoring, in the most cordial way, the spirit of coordination and cooperation, and that mutuality of confidence and respect which is necessary in representative popular government.

Encroachment upon the functions of Congress or attempted dictation of its policy are not to be thought of, much less attempted, but there is an insistent call for harmony of purpose and concord of action to speed the solution of the difficult problems confronting both the legislative and executive branches of the Government.

It is worth while to make allusion here to the character of our Government, mindful as one must be that an address to you is no less a message to all our people, for whom you speak most intimately. Ours is a popular Government through political parties. We divide along political lines, and I would ever have it so. I do not mean that partisan preferences should hinder any public servant in the performance of a conscientious and patriotic official duty. We saw partisan lines utterly obliterated when war imperiled, and our faith in the Republic was riveted anew. We ought not to find these partisan lines obstructing the expeditious solution of the urgent problems of peace.

Granting that we are fundamentally a representative popular Government, with political parties the governing agencies, I believe the political party in power should assume responsibility, determine upon policies in the conference which supplements conventions and election campaigns, and then strive for achievement through adherence to the accepted policy.

There is vastly greater security, immensely more of the national viewpoint, much larger and prompter accomplishment where our divisions are along party lines, in the broader and loftier sense, than to divide geographically, or according to pursuits, or personal following. For a century and a third, parties have been charged with responsibility and held to strict accounting. When they fail, they are relieved of authority; and the system has brought us to a national eminence no less than a world example.

Necessarily legislation is a matter of compromise. The full ideal is seldom attained. In that meeting of minds necessary to insure results, there must and will be accommodations and compromises, but in the estimate of convictions and sincere purposes the supreme responsibility to national interest must not be ignored. The shield to the high-minded public servant who adheres to party policy is manifest, but the higher purpose is the good of the Republic as a whole.

It would be ungracious to withhold acknowledgment of the really large volume and excellent quality of work accomplished by the extraordinary session of Congress which so recently adjourned. I am not unmindful of the very difficult tasks with which you were called to deal, and no one can ignore the insistent conditions which, during recent years, have called for the continued and almost exclusive attention of your membership to public work. It would suggest insincerity if I expressed complete accord with every expression recorded in your roll calls, but we are all agreed about the difficulties and the inevitable divergence of opinion in seeking the reduction, amelioration and readjustment of the burdens of taxation. Later on, when other problems are solved, I shall make some recommendations about renewed consideration of our tax program, but for the immediate time before us we must be content with the billion dollar reduction in the tax draft upon the people, and diminished irritations, banished uncertainty and improved methods of collection. By your sustainment of the rigid economies already inaugurated, with hoped-for extension of these economies and added efficiencies in administration, I believe further reductions may be enacted and hindering burdens abolished.

In these urgent economies we shall be immensely assisted by the budget system for which you made provision in the extraordinary session. The first budget is before you. Its preparation is a signal achievement, and the perfection of the system, a thing impossible in the few months available for its initial trial, will mark its enactment as the beginning of the greatest reformation in governmental practices since the beginning of the Republic.

There is pending a grant of authority to the administrative branch of the Government for the funding and settlement of our vast foreign loans growing out of our grant of war credits. With the hands of the executive branch held impotent to deal with these debts we are hindering urgent readjustments among our debtors and accomplishing nothing for ourselves. I think it is fair for the Congress to assume that the executive branch of the Government would adopt no major policy in dealing with these matters which would conflict with the purpose of Congress in authorizing the loans, certainly not without asking congressional approval, but there are minor problems incident to prudent loan transactions and the safeguarding of our interests which can not even be attempted without this authorization. It will be helpful to ourselves and it will improve conditions among our debtors if funding and the settlement of defaulted interest may be negotiated.

The previous Congress, deeply concerned in behalf of our merchant marine, in 1920 enacted the existing shipping law, designed for the upbuilding of the American merchant marine. Among other things provided to encourage our shipping on the world's seas, the Executive was directed to give notice of the termination of all existing commercial treaties in order to admit of reduced duties on imports carried in American bottoms. During the life of the act no Executive has complied with this order of the Congress. When the present administration came into responsibility it began an early inquiry into the failure to execute the expressed purpose of the Jones Act. Only one conclusion has been possible. Frankly, Members of House and Senate, eager as I am to join you in the making of an American merchant marine commensurate with our commerce, the denouncement of our commercial treaties would involve us in a chaos of trade relationships and add indescribably to the confusion of the already disordered commercial world. Our power to do so is not disputed, but power and ships, without comity of relationship, will not give us the expanded trade which is inseparably linked with a great merchant marine. Moreover, the applied reduction of duty, for which the treaty denouncements were necessary, encouraged only the carrying of dutiable imports to our shores, while the tonnage which unfurls the flag on the seas is both free and dutiable, and the cargoes which make a nation eminent in trade are outgoing, rather than incoming.

It is not my thought to lay the problem before you in detail to-day. It is desired only to say to you that the executive branch of the Government, uninfluenced by the protest of any nation, for none has been made, is well convinced that your proposal, highly intended and heartily supported here, is so fraught with difficulties and so marked by tendencies to discourage trade expansion, that I invite your tolerance of noncompliance for only a few weeks until a plan may be presented which contemplates no greater draft upon the Public Treasury, and which, though yet too crude to offer it to-day, gives such promise of expanding our merchant marine, that it will argue its own approval. It is enough to say to-day that we are so possessed of ships, and the American intention to establish a merchant marine is so unalterable, that a plan of reimbursement, at no other cost than is contemplated in the existing act, will appeal to the pride and encourage the hope of all the American people.

There is before you the completion of the enactment of what has been termed a " permanent " tariff law, the word " permanent " being used to distinguish it from the emergency act which the Congress expedited early in the extraordinary session, and which is the law to-day. I can not too strongly urge an early completion of this necessary legislation. It is needed to stabilize our industry at home; it is essential to make more definite our trade relations abroad. More, it is vital to the preservation of many of our own industries which contribute so notably to the very lifeblood of our Nation.

There is now, and there always will be, a storm of conflicting opinion about any tariff revision. We can not go far wrong when we base our tariffs on the policy of preserving the productive activities which enhance employment and add to our national prosperity.

Again comes the reminder that we must not be unmindful of world conditions, that peoples are struggling for industrial rehabilitation and that we can not dwell in industrial and commercial exclusion and at the same time do the just thing in aiding world reconstruction and readjustment. We do not seek a selfish aloofness, and we could not profit by it, were it possible. We recognize the necessity of buying wherever we sell, and the permanency of trade lies in its acceptable exchanges. In our pursuit of markets we must give as well as receive. We can not sell to others who do not produce, nor can we buy unless we produce at home. Sensible of every obligation of humanity, commerce and finance, linked as they are in the present world condition, it is not to be argued that we need destroy ourselves to be helpful to others. With all my heart I wish restoration to the peoples blighted by the awful World War, but the process of restoration does not lie in our acceptance of like conditions. It were better to remain on firm ground, strive for ample employment and high standards of wage at home, and point the way to balanced budgets, rigid economies, and resolute, efficient work as the necessary remedies to cure disaster.

Everything relating to trade, among ourselves and among nations, has been expanded, excessive, inflated, abnormal, and there is a madness in finance which no American policy alone will cure. We are a creditor Nation, not by normal processes, but made so by war. It is not an unworthy selfishness to seek to save ourselves, when the processes of that salvation are not only not denied to others, but commended to them. We seek to undermine for others no industry by which they subsist; we are obligated to permit the undermining of none of our own which make for employment and maintained activities.

Every contemplation, it little matters in which direction one turns, magnifies the difficulty of tariff legislation, but the necessity of the revision is magnified with it. Doubtless we are justified in seeking a more flexible policy than we have provided heretofore. I hope a way will be found to make for flexibility and elasticity, so that rates may be adjusted to meet unusual and changing conditions which can not be accurately anticipated. There are problems incident to unfair practices, and to exchanges which madness in money have made almost unsolvable. I know of no manner in which to effect this flexibility other than the extension of the powers of the Tariff Commission, so that it can adapt itself to a scientific and wholly just administration of the law.

I am not unmindful of the constitutional difficulties. These can be met by giving authority to the Chief Executive, who could proclaim additional duties to meet conditions which the Congress may designate.

At this point I must disavow any desire to enlarge the Executive's powers or add to the responsibilities of the office. They are already too large. If there were any other plan I would prefer it.

The grant of authority to proclaim would necessarily bring the Tariff Commission into new and enlarged activities, because no Executive could discharge such a duty except upon the information acquired and recommendations made by this commission. But the plan is feasible, and the proper functioning of the board would give us a better administration of a defined policy than ever can be made possible by tariff duties prescribed without flexibility.

There is a manifest difference of opinion about the merits of American valuation. Many nations have adopted delivery valuation as the basis for collecting duties; that is, they take the cost of the imports delivered at the port of entry as the basis for levying duty. It is no radical departure, in view of varying conditions and the disordered state of money values, to provide for American valuation, but there can not be ignored the danger of such a valuation, brought to the level of our own production costs, making our tariffs prohibitive. It might do so in many instances where imports ought to be encouraged. I believe Congress ought well consider the desirability of the only promising alternative, namely, a provision authorizing proclaimed American valuation, under prescribed conditions, on any given list of articles imported.

In this proposed flexibility, authorizing increases to meet conditions so likely to change, there should also be provision for decreases. A rate may be just to-day, and entirely out of proportion six months from to-day. If our tariffs are to be made equitable, and not necessarily burden our imports and hinder our trade abroad, frequent adjustment will be necessary for years to come. Knowing the impossibility of modification by act of Congress for any one or a score of lines without involving a long array of schedules, I think we shall go a long ways toward stabilization, if there is recognition of the Tariff Commission's fitness to recommend urgent changes by proclamation.

I am sure about public opinion favoring the early determination of our tariff policy. There have been reassuring signs of a business revival from the deep slump which all the world has been experiencing. Our unemployment, which gave us deep concern only a few weeks ago, has grown encouragingly less, and new assurances and renewed confidence will attend the congressional declaration that American industry will be held secure.

Much has been said about the protective policy for ourselves making it impossible for our debtors to discharge their obligations to us. This is a contention not now pressing for decision. If we must choose between a people in idleness pressing for the payment of indebtedness, or a people resuming the normal ways of employment and carrying the credit, let us choose the latter. Sometimes we appraise largest the human ill most vivid in our minds. We have been giving, and are giving now, of our influence and appeals to minimize the likelihood of war and throw off the crushing burdens of armament. It is all very earnest, with a national soul impelling. But a people unemployed, and gaunt with hunger, face a situation quite as disheartening as war, and our greater obligation to-day is to do the Government's part toward resuming productivity and promoting fortunate and remunerative employment.

Something more than tariff protection is required by American agriculture. To the farmer has come the earlier and the heavier burdens of readjustment. There is actual depression in our agricultural industry, while agricultural prosperity is absolutely essential to the general prosperity of the country.

Congress has sought very earnestly to provide relief. It has promptly given such temporary relief as has been possible, but the call is insistent for the permanent solution. It is inevitable that large crops lower the prices and short crops advance them. No legislation can cure that fundamental law. But there must be some economic solution for the excessive variation in returns for agricultural production.

It is rather shocking to be told, and to have the statement strongly supported, that 9,000,000 bales of cotton, raised on American plantations in a given year, will actually be worth more to the producers than 13,000,000 bales would have been. Equally shocking is the statement that 700,000,000 bushels of wheat, raised by American farmers, would bring them more money than a billion bushels. Yet these are not exaggerated statements. In a world where there are tens of millions who need food and clothing which they can not get, such a condition is sure to indict the social system which makes it possible.

In the main the remedy lies in distribution and marketing. Every proper encouragement should be given to the cooperative marketing programs. These have proven very helpful to the cooperating communities in Europe. In Russia the cooperative community has become the recognized bulwark of law and order, and saved individualism from engulfment in social paralysis. Ultimately they will be accredited with the salvation of the Russian State.

There is the appeal for this experiment. Why not try it? No one challenges the right of the farmer to a larger share of the consumer's pay for his product, no one disputes that we can not live without the farmer. He is justified in rebelling against the transportation cost. Given a fair return for his labor, he will have less occasion to appeal for financial aid; and given assurance that his labors shall not be in vain, we reassure all the people of a production sufficient to meet our National requirement and guard against disaster.

The base of the pyramid of civilization which rests upon the soil is shrinking through the drift of population from farm to city. For a generation we have been expressing more or less concern about this tendency. Economists have warned and statesmen have deplored. We thought for a time that modern conveniences and the more intimate contact would halt the movement, but it has gone steadily on. Perhaps only grim necessity will correct it, but we ought to find a less drastic remedy.

The existing scheme of adjusting freight rates has been favoring the basing points, until industries are attracted to some centers and repelled from others. A great volume of uneconomic and wasteful transportation has attended, and the cost increased accordingly. The grain-milling and meat-packing industries afford ample illustration, and the attending concentration is readily apparent. The menaces in concentration are not limited to the retarding influences on agriculture. Manifestly the conditions and terms of railway transportation ought not be permitted to increase this undesirable tendency. We have a just pride in our great cities, but we shall find a greater pride in the Nation, which has a larger distribution of its population into the country, where comparatively self-sufficient smaller communities may blend agricultural and manufacturing interests in harmonious helpfulness and enhanced good fortune. Such a movement contemplates no destruction of things wrought, of investments made, or wealth involved. It only looks to a general policy of transportation, of distributed industry, and of highway construction, to encourage the spread of our population and restore the proper balance between city and country. The problem may well have your earnest attention.

It has been perhaps the proudest claim of our American civilization that in dealing with human relationships it has constantly moved toward such justice in distributing the product of human energy that it has improved continuously the economic status of the mass of people. Ours has been a highly productive social organization. On the way up from the elemental stages of society we have eliminated slavery and serfdom and are now far on the way to the elimination of poverty.

Through the eradication of illiteracy and the diffusion of education mankind has reached a stage where we may fairly say that in the

United States equality of opportunity has been attained, though all are not prepared to embrace it. There is, indeed, a too great divergence between the economic conditions of the most and the least favored classes in the community. But even that divergence has now come to the point where we bracket the very poor and the very rich together as the least fortunate classes. Our efforts may well be directed to improving the status of both.

While this set of problems is commonly comprehended under the general phrase "Capital and labor," it is really vastly broader. It is a question of social and economic organization. Labor has become a large contributor, through its savings, to the stock of capital; while the people who own the largest individual aggregates of capital are themselves often hard and earnest laborers. Very often it is extremely difficult to draw the line of demarcation between the two groups; to determine whether a particular individual is entitled to be set down as laborer or as capitalist. In a very large proportion of cases he is both, and when he is both he is the most useful citizen.

The right of labor to organize is just as fundamental and necessary as is the right of capital to organize. The right of labor to negotiate, to deal with and solve its particular problems in an organized way, through its chosen agents, is just as essential as is the right of capital to organize, to maintain corporations, to limit the liabilities of stockholders. Indeed, we have come to recognize that the limited liability of the citizen as a member of a labor organization closely parallels the limitation of liability of the citizen as a stockholder in a corporation for profit. Along this line of reasoning we shall make the greatest progress toward solution of our problem of capital and labor.

In the case of the corporation which enjoys the privilege of limited liability of stockholders, particularly when engaged in the public service, it is recognized that the outside public has a large concern which must be protected; and so we provide regulations, restrictions, and in some cases detailed supervision. Likewise in the case of labor organizations, we might well apply similar and equally well-defined principles of regulation and supervision in order to conserve the public's interests as affected by their operations.

Just as it is not desirable that a corporation shall be allowed to impose undue exactions upon the public, so it is not desirable that a labor organization shall be permitted to exact unfair terms of employment or subject the public to actual distresses in order to enforce its terms. Finally, just as we are earnestly seeking for procedures whereby to adjust and settle political differences between nations without resort to war, so we may well look about for means to settle the differences between organized capital and organized labor without resort to those forms of warfare which we recognize under the name of strikes, lockouts, boycotts, and the like.

As we have great bodies of law carefully regulating the organization and operations of industrial and financial corporations, as we have treaties and compacts among nations which look to the settlement of differences without the necessity of conflict in arms, so we might well have plans of conference, of common counsel, of mediation, arbitration, and judicial determination in controversies between labor and capital. To accomplish this would involve the necessity to develop a thoroughgoing code of practice in dealing with such affairs. It might be well to frankly set forth the superior interest of the community as a whole to either the labor group or the capital group. With rights, privileges, immunities, and modes of organization thus carefully defined, it should be possible to set up judicial or quasi judicial tribunals for the consideration and determination of all disputes which menace the public welfare.

In an industrial society such as ours the strike, the lockout, and the boycott are as much out of place and as disastrous in their results as is war or armed revolution in the domain of politics. The same disposition to reasonableness, to conciliation, to recognition of the other side's point of view, the same provision of fair and recognized tribunals and processes, ought to make it possible to solve the one set of questions as easily as the other. I believe the solution is possible.

The consideration of such a policy would necessitate the exercise of care and deliberation in the construction of a code and a charter of elemental rights, dealing with the relations of employer and employee. This foundation in the law, dealing with the modern conditions of social and economic life, would hasten the building of the temple of peace in industry which a rejoicing nation would acclaim.

After each war, until the last, the Government has been enabled to give homes to its returned soldiers, and a large part of our settlement and development has attended this generous provision of land for the Nation's defenders.

There is yet unreserved approximately 200,000,000 acres in the public domain, 20,000,000 acres of which are known to be susceptible of reclamation and made fit for homes by provision for irrigation.

The Government has been assisting in the development of its remaining lands, until the estimated increase in land values in the irrigated sections is full $500,000,000, and the crops of 1920 alone on these lands are estimated to exceed $100,000,000. Under the law authorizing these expenditures for development the advances are to be returned, and it would be good business for the Government to provide for the reclamation of the remaining 20,000,000 acres, in addition to expediting the completion of projects long under way.

Under what is known as the coal and gas lease law, applicable also to deposits of phosphates and other minerals on the public domain, leases are now being made on the royalty basis, and are producing large revenues to the Government. Under this legislation, 10 per centum of all royalties is to be paid directly to the Federal Treasury, and of the remainder 50 per centum is to be used for reclamation of arid lands by irrigation, and 40 per centum is to be paid to the States, in which the operations are located, to be used by them for school and road purposes.

These resources are so vast, and the development is affording so reliable a basis of estimate, that the Interior Department expresses the belief that ultimately the present law will add in royalties and payments to the treasuries of the Federal Government and the States containing these public lands a total of $12,000,000,000. This means, of course, an added wealth of many times that sum. These prospects seem to afford every justification of Government advances in reclamation and irrigation.

Contemplating the inevitable and desirable increase of population, there is another phase of reclamation full worthy of consideration. There are 79,000,000 acres of swamp and cut-over lands which may be reclaimed and made as valuable as any farm lands we possess. These acres are largely located in Southern States, and the greater proportion is owned by the States or by private citizens. Congress has a report of the survey of this field for reclamation, and the feasibility is established. I gladly commend Federal aid, by way of advances, where State and private participation is assured.

Home making is one of the greater benefits which government can bestow. Measures are pending embodying this sound policy to which we may well adhere. It is easily possible to make available permanent homes which will provide, in turn, for prosperous American families, without injurious competition with established activities, or imposition on wealth already acquired.

While we are thinking of promoting the fortunes of our own people I am sure there is room in the sympathetic thought of America for fellow human beings who are suffering and dying of starvation in Russia. A severe drought in the Valley of the Volga has plunged 15,000,000 people into grievous famine. Our voluntary agencies are exerting themselves to the utmost to save the lives of children in this area, but it is now evident that unless relief is afforded the loss of life will extend into many millions. America can not be deaf to such a call as that.

We do not recognize the government of Russia, nor tolerate the propaganda which emanates therefrom, but we do not forget the traditions of Russian friendship. We may put aside our consideration of all international politics and fundamental differences in government. The big thing is the call of the suffering and the dying. Unreservedly I recommend the appropriation necessary to supply the American Relief Administration with 10,000,000 bushels of corn and 1,000,000 bushels of seed grains, not alone to halt the wave of death through starvation, but to enable spring planting in areas where the seed grains have been exhausted temporarily to stem starvation.

The American Relief Administration is directed in Russia by former officers of our own armies, and has fully demonstrated its ability to transport and distribute relief through American hands without hindrance or loss. The time has come to add the Government's support to the wonderful relief already wrought out of the generosity of the American private purse.

I am not unaware that we have suffering and privation at home. When it exceeds the capacity for the relief within the States concerned, it will have Federal consideration. It seems to me we should be indifferent to our own heart promptings, and out of accord with the spirit which acclaims the Christmastide, if we do not give out of our national abundance to lighten this burden of woe upon a people blameless and helpless in famine's peril.

There are a full score of topics concerning which it would be becoming to address you, and on which I hope to make report at a later time. I have alluded to the things requiring your earlier attention. However, I can not end this limited address without a suggested amendment to the organic law.

Many of us belong to that school of thought which is hesitant about altering the fundamental law. I think our tax problems, the tendency of wealth to seek nontaxable investment, and the menacing increase of public debt, Federal, State and municipal—all justify a proposal to change the Constitution so as to end the issue of nontaxable bonds. No action can change the status of the many billions outstanding, but we can guard against future encouragement of capital's paralysis, while a halt in the growth of public indebtedness would be beneficial throughout our whole land.

Such a change in the Constitution must be very thoroughly considered before submission. There ought to be known what influence it will have on the inevitable refunding of our vast national debt, how it will operate on the necessary refunding of State and municipal debt, how the advantages of Nation over State and municipality, or the contrary, may be avoided. Clearly the States would not ratify to their own apparent disadvantage. I suggest the consideration because the drift of wealth into nontaxable securities is hindering the flow of large capital to our industries, manufacturing, agricultural, and carrying, until we are discouraging the very activities which make our wealth.

Agreeable to your expressed desire and in complete accord with the purposes of the executive branch of the Government, there is in Washington, as you happily know, an International Conference now most earnestly at work on plans for the limitation of armament, a naval holiday, and the just settlement of problems which might develop into causes of international disagreement.

It is easy to believe a world-hope is centered on this Capital City. A most gratifying world-accomplishment is not improbable.

SECOND ANNUAL MESSAGE.

Dec. 8, 1922

MEMBERS OF THE CONGRESS:

So many problems are calling for solution that a recital of all of them, in the face of the known limitations of a short session of Congress, would seem to lack sincerity of purpose. It is four years since the World War ended, but the inevitable readjustment of the social and economic order is not more than barely begun. There is no acceptance of pre-war conditions anywhere in the world. In a very general way humanity harbors individual wishes to go on with war-time compensations for production, with pre-war requirements in expenditure. In short, everyone, speaking broadly, craves readjustment for everybody except himself, while there can be no just and permanent readjustment except when all participate.

The civilization which measured its strength of genius and the power of science and the resources of industries, in addition to testing the limits of man power and the endurance and heroism of men and women—that same civilization is brought to its severest test in restoring a tranquil order and committing humanity to the stable ways of peace.

If the sober and deliberate appraisal of pre-war civilization makes it seem a worth-while inheritance, then with patience and good courage it will be preserved. There never again will be precisely the old order; indeed, I know of no one who thinks it to be desirable. For out of the old order came the war itself, and the new order, established and made secure, never will permit its recurrence.

It is no figure of speech to say we have come to the test of our civilization. The world has been passing—is to-day passing—through a great crisis. The conduct of war itself is not more difficult than the solution of the problems which necessarily follow. I am not speaking at this moment of the problem in its wider aspect of world rehabilitation or of international relationships. The reference is to our own social, financial, and economic problems at home. These things are not to be considered solely as problems apart from all international relationship, but every nation must be able to carry on for itself, else its international relationship will have scant importance.

Doubtless our own people have emerged from the World War tumult less impaired than most belligerent powers; probably we have made larger progress toward reconstruction. Surely we have been fortunate in diminishing unemployment, and our industrial and business activities, which are the lifeblood of our material existence, have been restored as in no other reconstruction period of like length in the history of the world. Had we escaped the coal and railway strikes, which had no excuse for their beginning and less justification for their delayed settlement, we should have done infinitely better. But labor was insistent on holding to the war heights, and heedless forces of reaction sought the pre-war levels, and both were wrong. In the folly of conflict our progress was hindered, and the heavy cost has not yet been fully estimated. There can be neither adjustment nor the penalty of the failure to readjust in which all do not somehow participate.

The railway strike accentuated the difficulty of the American farmer. The first distress of readjustment came to the farmer, and it will not be a readjustment fit to abide until he is relieved. The distress brought to the farmer does not affect him alone. Agricultural ill fortune is a national ill fortune. That one-fourth of our population which produces the food of the Republic and adds so largely to our export commerce must participate in the good fortunes of the Nation, else there is none worth retaining.

Agriculture is a vital activity in our national life. In it we had our beginning, and its westward march with the star of the empire has reflected the growth of the Republic. It has its vicissitudes which no legislation will prevent, its hardships for which no law can provide escape. But the Congress can make available to the farmer the financial facilities which have been built up under Government aid and supervision for other commercial and industrial enterprises. It may be done on the same solid fundamentals and make the vitally important agricultural industry more secure, and it must be done.

This Congress already has taken cognizance of the misfortune which precipitate deflation brought to American agriculture. Your measures of relief and the reduction of the Federal reserve discount rate undoubtedly saved the country from widespread disaster. The very proof of helpfulness already given is the strongest argument for the permanent establishment of widened credits, heretofore temporarily extended through the War Finance Corporation.

The Farm Loan Bureau, which already has proven its usefulness through the Federal land banks, may well have its powers enlarged to provide ample farm production credits as well as enlarged land credits. It is entirely practical to create a division in the Federal land banks to deal with production credits, with the limitations of time so adjusted to the farm turnover as the Federal reserve system provides for the turnover in the manufacturing and mercantile world. Special provision must be made for live-stock production credits, and the limit of land loans may be safely enlarged. Various measures are pending before you, and the best judgment of Congress ought to be expressed in a prompt enactment at the present session.

But American agriculture needs more than added credit facilities. The credits will help to solve the pressing problems growing out of war-inflated land values and the drastic deflation of three years ago, but permanent and deserved agricultural good fortune depends on better and cheaper transportation.

Here is an outstanding problem, demanding the most rigorous consideration of the Congress and the country. It has to do with more than agriculture. It provides the channel for the flow of the country's commerce. But the farmer is particularly hard hit. His market, so affected by the world consumption, does not admit of the price adjustment to meet carrying charges. In the last half of the year now closing the railways, broken in carrying capacity because of motive power and rolling stock out of order, though insistently declaring to the contrary, embargoed his shipments or denied him cars when fortunate markets were calling. Too frequently transportation failed while perishable products were turning from possible profit to losses counted in tens of millions.

I know of no problem exceeding in importance this one of transportation. In our complex and interdependent modern life transportation is essential to our very existence. Let us pass for the moment the menace in the possible paralysis of such service as we have and note the failure, for whatever reason, to expand our transportation to meet the Nation's needs.

The census of 1880 recorded a population of 50,000,000. In two decades more we may reasonably expect to count thrice that number. In the three decades ending in 1920 the country's freight by rail increased from 631,000,000 tons to 2,234,000,000 tons; that is to say, while our population was increasing less than 70 per cent, the freight movement increased over 250 per cent.

We have built 40 per cent of the world's railroad mileage, and yet find it inadequate to our present requirements. When we contemplate the inadequacy of to-day it is easy to believe that the next few decades will witness the paralysis of our transportation-using social scheme or a complete reorganization on some new basis. Mindful of the tremendous costs of betterments, extensions, and expansions, and mindful of the staggering debts of the world to-day, the difficulty is magnified. Here is a problem demanding wide vision and the avoidance of mere makeshifts. No matter what the errors of the past, no matter how we acclaimed construction and then condemned operations in the past, we have the transportation and the honest investment in the transportation which sped us on to what we are, and we face conditions which reflect its inadequacy to-day, its greater inadequacy to-morrow, and we contemplate transportation costs which much of the traffic can not and will not continue to pay.

Manifestly, we have need to begin on plans to coordinate all transportation facilities. We should more effectively connect up our rail lines with our carriers by sea. We ought to reap some benefit from the hundreds of millions expended on inland waterways, proving our capacity to utilize as well as expend. We ought to turn the motor truck into a railway feeder and distributor instead of a destroying competitor.

It would be folly to ignore that we live in a motor age. The motor car reflects our standard of living and gauges the speed of our present-day life. It long ago ran down Simple Living, and never halted to inquire about the prostrate figure which fell as its victim. With full recognition of motor-car transportation we must turn it to the most practical use. It can not supersede the railway lines, no matter how generously we afford it highways out of the Public Treasury. If freight traffic by motor were charged with its proper and proportionate share of highway construction, we should find much of it wasteful and more costly than like service by rail. Yet we have paralleled the railways, a most natural line of construction, and thereby taken away from the agency of expected service much of its profitable traffic, which the taxpayers have been providing the highways, whose cost of maintenance is not yet realized.

The Federal Government has a right to inquire into the wisdom of this policy, because the National Treasury is contributing largely to this highway construction. Costly highways ought to be made to serve as feeders rather than competitors of the railroads, and the motor truck should become a coordinate factor in our great distributing system.

This transportation problem can not be waived aside. The demand for lowered costs on farm products and basic materials can not be ignored. Rates horizontally increased, to meet increased wage outlays during the war inflation, are not easily reduced. When some very moderate wage reductions were effected last summer there was a 5 per cent horizontal reduction in rates. I sought at that time, in a very informal way, to have the railway managers go before the Interstate Commerce Commission and agree to a heavier reduction on farm products and coal and other basic commodities, and leave unchanged the freight tariffs which a very large portion of the traffic was able to bear. Neither the managers nor the commission saw fit to adopt the suggestion, so we had the horizontal reduction too slight to be felt by the higher class cargoes and too little to benefit the heavy tonnage calling most loudly for relief.

Railways are not to be expected to render the most essential service in our social organization without a fair return on capital invested, but the Government has gone so far in the regulation of rates and rules of operation that it has the responsibility of pointing the way to the reduced freight costs so essential to our national welfare.

Government operation does not afford the cure. It was Government operation which brought us to the very order of things against which we now rebel, and we are still liquidating the costs of that supreme folly.

Surely the genius of the railway builders has not become extinct among the railway managers. New economies, new efficiencies in cooperation must be found. The fact that labor takes 50 to 60 per cent of total railway earnings makes limitations within which to effect economies very difficult, but the demand is no less insistent on that account.

Clearly the managers are without that intercarrier, cooperative relationship so highly essential to the best and most economical operation. They could not function in harmony when the strike threatened the paralysis of all railway transportation. The relationship of the service to public welfare, so intimately affected by State and Federal regulation, demands the effective correlation and a concerted drive to meet an insistent and justified public demand.

The merger of lines into systems, a facilitated interchange of freight cars, the economic use of terminals, and the consolidation of facilities are suggested ways of economy and efficiency.

I remind you that Congress provided a Joint Commission of Agricultural Inquiry which made an exhaustive investigation of car service and transportation, and unanimously recommended in its report of October 15, 1921, the pooling of freight cars under a central agency. This report well deserves your serious consideration. I think well of the central agency, which shall be a creation of the railways themselves, to provide, under the jurisdiction of the Interstate Commerce Commission, the means for financing equipment for carriers which are otherwise unable to provide their proportion of car equipment adequate to transportation needs. This same agency ought to point the way to every possible economy in maintained equipment and the necessary interchanges in railway commerce.

In a previous address to the Congress I called to your attention the insufficiency of power to enforce the decisions of the Railroad

Labor Board. Carriers have ignored its decisions, on the one hand, railway workmen have challenged its decisions by a strike, on the other hand.

The intent of Congress to establish a tribunal to which railway labor and managers may appeal respecting questions of wages and working conditions can not be too strongly commended. It is vitally important that some such agency should be a guaranty against suspended operation. The public must be spared even the threat of discontinued service.

Sponsoring the railroads as we do, it is an obligation that labor shall be assured the highest justice and every proper consideration of wage and working conditions, but it is an equal obligation to see that no concerted action in forcing demands shall deprive the public of the transportation service essential to its very existence. It is now impossible to safeguard public interest, because the decrees of the board are unenforceable against either employer or employee.

The Labor Board itself is not so constituted as best to serve the public interest. With six partisan members on a board of nine, three partisans nominated by the employees and three by the railway managers, it is inevitable that the partisan viewpoint is maintained throughout hearings and in decisions handed down. Indeed, the few exceptions to a strictly partisan expression in decisions thus far rendered have been followed by accusations of betrayal of the partisan interests represented. Only the public group of three is free to function in unbiased decisions. Therefore the partisan membership may well be abolished, and decisions should be made by an impartial tribunal.

I am well convinced that the functions of this tribunal could be much better carried on here in Washington. Even were it to be continued as a separate tribunal, there ought to be contact with the Interstate Commerce Commission, which has supreme authority in the rate making to which wage cost bears an indissoluble relationship. Theoretically, a fair and living wage must be determined quite apart from the employer's earning capacity, but in practice, in the railway service, they are inseparable. The record of advanced rates to meet increased wages, both determined by the Government, is proof enough.

The substitution of a labor division in the Interstate Commerce Commission, made up from its membership, to hear and decide disputes relating to wages and working conditions which have failed of adjustment by proper committees created by the railways and their employees, offers a more effective plan.

It need not be surprising that there is dissatisfaction over delayed hearings and decisions by the present board when every trivial dispute is carried to that tribunal. The law should require the railroads and their employees to institute means and methods to negotiate between themselves their constantly arising differences, limiting appeals to the Government tribunal to disputes of such character as are likely to affect the public welfare.

This suggested substitution will involve a necessary increase in the membership of the commission, probably four, to constitute the labor division. If the suggestion appeals to the Congress, it will be well to specify that the labor division shall be constituted of representatives of the four rate-making territories, thereby assuring a tribunal conversant with the conditions which obtain in the different rate-making sections of the country.

I wish I could bring to you the precise recommendation for the prevention of strikes which threaten the welfare of the people and menace public safety. It is an impotent civilization and an inadequate government which lacks the genius and the courage to guard against such a menace to public welfare as we experienced last summer. You were aware of the Government's great concern and its futile attempt to aid in an adjustment. It will reveal the inexcusable obstinacy which was responsible for so much distress to the country to recall now that, though all disputes are not yet adjusted, the many settlements which have been made were on the terms which the Government proposed in mediation.

Public interest demands that ample power shall be conferred upon the labor tribunal, whether it is the present board or the suggested substitute, to require its rulings to be accepted by both parties to a disputed question.

Let there be no confusion about the purpose of the suggested conferment of power to make decisions effective. There can be no denial of constitutional rights of either railway workmen or railway managers. No man can be denied his right to labor when and how he chooses, or cease to labor when he so elects, but, since the Government assumes to safeguard his interests while employed in an essential public service, the security of society itself demands his retirement from the service shall not be so timed and related as to effect the destruction of that service. This vitally essential public transportation service, demanding so much of brain and brawn, so much for efficiency and security, ought to offer the most attractive working conditions and the highest of wages paid to workmen in any employment.

In essentially every branch, from track repairer to the man at the locomotive throttle, the railroad worker is responsible for the safety of human lives and the care of vast property. His high responsibility might well rate high his pay within the limits the traffic will bear; but the same responsibility, plus governmental protection, may justly deny him and his associates a withdrawal from service without a warning or under circumstances which involve the paralysis of necessary transportation. We have assumed so great a responsibility in necessary regulation that we unconsciously have assumed the responsibility for maintained service; therefore the lawful power for the enforcement of decisions is necessary to sustain the majesty of government and to administer to the public welfare.

During its longer session the present Congress enacted a new tariff law. The protection of the American standards of living demanded the insurance it provides against the distorted conditions of world commerce. The framers of the law made provision for a certain flexibility of customs duties, whereby it is possible to readjust them as developing conditions may require. The enactment has imposed a large responsibility upon the Executive, but that responsibility will be discharged with a broad mindfulness of the whole business situation. The provision itself admits either the possible fallibility of rates or their unsuitableness to changing conditions. I believe the grant of authority may be promptly and discreetly exercised, ever mindful of the intent and purpose to safeguard American industrial activity, and at the same time prevent the exploitation of the American consumer and keep open the paths of such liberal exchanges as do not endanger our own productivity.

No one contemplates commercial aloofness nor any other aloofness contradictory to the best American traditions or loftiest human purposes. Our fortunate capacity for comparative self-containment affords the firm foundation on which to build for our own security, and a like foundation on which to build for a future of influence and importance in world commerce. Our trade expansion must come of capacity and of policies of righteousness and reasonableness in all our commercial relations.

Let no one assume that our provision for maintained good fortune at home, and our unwillingness to assume the correction of all the ills of the world, means a reluctance to cooperate with other peoples or to assume every just obligation to promote human advancement anywhere in the world.

War made us a creditor Nation. We did not seek an excess possession of the world's gold, and we have neither desire to profit unduly by its possession nor permanently retain it. We do not seek to become an international dictator because of its power.

The voice of the United States has a respectful hearing in international councils, bcause we have convinced the world that we have no selfish ends to serve, no old grievances to avenge, no territorial or other greed to satisfy. But the voice being heard is that of good counsel, not of dictation. It is the voice of sympathy and fraternity and helpfulness, seeking to assist but not assume for the United States burdens which nations must bear for themselves. We would rejoice to help rehabilitate currency systems and facilitate all commerce which does not drag us to the very levels of those we seek to lift up.

While I have everlasting faith in our Republic, it would be folly, indeed, to blind ourselves to our problems at home. Abusing the hospitality of our shores are the advocates of revolution, finding their deluded followers among those who take on the habiliments of an American without knowing an American soul. There is the recrudescence of hyphenated Americanism which we thought to have been stamped out when we committed the Nation, life and soul, to the World War.

There is a call to make the alien respect our institutions while he accepts our hospitality. There is need to magnify the American viewpoint to the alien who seeks a citizenship among us. There is need to magnify the national viewpoint to Americans throughout the land. More, there is a demand for every living being in the United States to respect and abide by the laws of the Republic. Let men who are rending the moral fiber of the Republic through easy contempt for the prohibition law, because they think it restricts their personal liberty, remember that they set the example and breed a contempt for law which will ultimately destroy the Republic.

Constitutional prohibition has been adopted by the Nation. It is the supreme law of the land. In plain speaking, there are conditions relating to its enforcement which savor of nation-wide scandal. It is the most demoralizing factor in our public life.

Most of our people assumed that the adoption of the eighteenth amendment meant the elimination of the question from our politics. On the contrary, it has been so intensified as an issue that many voters are disposed to make all political decisions with reference to this single question. It is distracting the public mind and prejudicing the judgment of the electorate.

The day is unlikely to come when the eighteenth amendment will be repealed. The fact may as well be recognized and our course adapted accordingly. If the statutory provisions for its enforcement are contrary to deliberate public opinion, which I do not believe, the rigorous and literal enforcement will concentrate public attention on any requisite modification. Such a course conforms with the law and saves the humiliation of the Government and the humiliation of our people before the world, and challenges the destructive forces engaged in widespread violation, official corruption, and individual demoralization.

The eighteenth amendment involves the concurrent authority of State and Federal Governments, for the enforcement of the policy it defines. A certain lack of definiteness, through division of responsibility, is thus introduced. In order to bring about a full understanding of duties and responsibilities as thus distributed, I purpose to invite the governors of the States and Territories, at an early opportunity, to a conference with the Federal Executive authority. Out of the full and free considerations which will thus be possible, it is confidently believed, will emerge a more adequate comprehension of the whole problem, and definite policies of National and State cooperation in administering the laws.

There are pending bills for the registration of the alien who has come to our shores. I wish the passage of such an act might be expedited. Life amid American opportunities is worth the cost of registration if it is worth the seeking, and the Nation has the right to know who are citizens in the making or who live among us and share our advantages while seeking to undermine our cherished institutions. This provision will enable us to guard against the abuses in immigration, checking the undesirable whose irregular coming is his first violation of our laws. More, it will facilitate the needed Americanizing of those who mean to enroll as fellow citizens.

Before enlarging the immigration quotas we had better provide registration for aliens, those now here or continually pressing for admission, and establish our examination boards abroad, to make sure of desirables only. By the examination abroad we could end the pathos at our ports, when men and women find our doors closed, after long voyages and wasted savings, because they are unfit for admission. It would be kindlier and safer to tell them before they embark.

Our program of admission and treatment of immigrants is very intimately related to the educational policy of the Republic. With illiteracy estimated at from two-tenths of 1 per cent to less than 2 per cent in 10 of the foremost nations of Europe, it rivets our attention to a serious problem when we are reminded of a 6 per cent illiteracy in the United States. The figures are based on the test which defines an illiterate as one having no schooling whatever. Remembering the wide freedom of our public schools, with compulsory attendance in many States in the Union, one is convinced that much of our excessive illiteracy comes to us from abroad, and the education of the immigrant becomes a requisite to his Americanization. It must be done if he is fittingly to exercise the duties as well as enjoy the privileges of American citizenship. Here is revealed the special field for Federal cooperation in furthering education.

From the very beginning public education has been left mainly in the hands of the States. So far as schooling youth is concerned the policy has been justified, because no responsibility can be so effective as that of the local community alive to its task. I believe in the cooperation of the national authority to stimulate, encourage, and broaden the work of the local authorities. But it is the especial obligation of the Federal Government to devise means and effectively assist in the education of the newcomer from foreign lands, so that the level of American education may be made the highest that is humanly possible.

Closely related to this problem of education is the abolition of child labor. Twice Congress has attempted the correction of the evils incident to child employment. The decision of the Supreme Court has put this problem outside the proper domain of Federal regulation until the Constitution is so amended as to give the Congress indubitable authority. I recommend the submission of such an amendment.

We have two schools of thought relating to amendment of the Constitution. One need not be committed to the belief that amendment is weakening the fundamental law, or that excessive amendment is essential to meet every ephemeral whim. We ought to amend to meet the demands of the people when sanctioned by deliberate public opinion.

One year ago I suggested the submission of an amendment so that we may lawfully restrict the issues of tax-exempt securities, and I renew that recommendation now. Tax-exempt securities are drying up the sources of Federal taxation and they are encouraging unproductive and extravagant expenditures by States and municipalities. There is more than the menace in mounting public debt, there is the dissipation of capital which should be made available to the needs of productive industry. The proposed amendment will place the State and Federal Governments and all political subdivisions on an exact equality, and will correct the growing menace of public borrowing, which if left unchecked may soon threaten the stability of our institutions.

We are so vast and so varied in our national interests that scores of problems are pressing for attention. I must not risk the wearying of your patience with detailed reference.

Reclamation and irrigation projects, where waste land may be made available for settlement and productivity, are worthy of your favorable consideration.

When it is realized that we are consuming our timber four times as rapidly as we are growing it, we must encourage the greatest possible cooperation between the Federal Government, the various States, and the owners of forest lands, to the end that protection from fire shall be made more effective and replanting encouraged.

The fuel problem is under study now by a very capable fact-finding commission, and any attempt to deal with the coal problem, of such deep concern to the entire Nation, must await the report of the commission.

There are necessary studies of great problems which Congress might well initiate. The wide spread between production costs and prices which consumers pay concerns every citizen of the Republic. It contributes very largely to the unrest in agriculture and must stand sponsor for much against which we inveigh in that familiar term—the high cost of living.

No one doubts the excess is traceable to the levy of the middleman, but it would be unfair to charge him with all responsibility before we appraise what is exacted of him by our modernly complex life. We have attacked the problem on one side by the promotion of cooperative marketing, and we might well inquire into the benefits of cooperative buying. Admittedly, the consumer is much to blame himself, because of his prodigal expenditure and his exaction of service, but Government might well serve to point the way of narrowing the spread of price, especially between the production of food and its consumption.

A superpower survey of the eastern industrial region has recently been completed, looking to unification of steam, water, and electric powers, and to a unified scheme of power distribution. The survey proved that vast economies in tonnage movement of freights, and in the efficiency of the railroads, would be effected if the superpower program were adopted. I am convinced that constructive measures calculated to promote such an industrial development—I am tempted to say, such an industrial revolution—would be well worthy the careful attention and fostering interest of the National Government.

The proposed survey of a plan to draft all the resources of the Republic, human and material, for national defense may well have your approval. I commended such a program in case of future war, in the inaugural address of March 4, 1921, and every experience in the adjustment and liquidation of war claims and the settlement of war obligations persuades me we ought to be prepared for such universal call to armed defense.

I bring you no apprehension of war. The world is abhorrent of it, and our own relations are not only free from every threatening cloud, but we have contributed our larger influence toward making armed conflict less likely.

Those who assume that we played our part in the World War and later took ourselves aloof and apart, unmindful of world obligations, give scant credit to the helpful part we assume in international relationships.

Whether all nations signatory ratify all the treaties growing out of the Washington Conference on Limitation of Armament or some withhold approval, the underlying policy of limiting naval armament has the sanction of the larger naval powers, and naval competition is suspended. Of course, unanimous ratification is much to be desired.

The four-power pact, which abolishes every probability of war on the Pacific, has brought new confidence in a maintained peace, and I can well believe it might be made a model for like assurances wherever in the world any common interests are concerned.

We have had expressed the hostility of the American people to a supergovernment or to any commitment where either a council or an assembly of leagued powers may chart our course. Treaties of armed alliance can have no likelihood of American sanction, but we believe in respecting the rights of nations, in the value of conference and consultation, in the effectiveness of leaders of nations looking each other in the face before resorting to the arbitrament of arms.

It has been our fortune both to preach and promote international understanding. The influence of the United States in bringing near the settlement of an ancient dispute between South American nations is added proof of the glow of peace in ample understanding. In Washington to-day are met the delegates of the Central American nations, gathered at the table of international understanding, to stabilize their Republics and remove every vestige of disagreement. They are met here by our invitation, not in our aloofness, and they accept our hospitality because they have faith in our unselfishness and believe in our helpfulness. Perhaps we are selfish in craving their confidence and friendship, but such a selfishness we proclaim to the world, regardless of hemisphere, or seas dividing.

I would like the Congress and the people of the Nation to believe that in a firm and considerate way we are insistent on American rights wherever they may be questioned, and deny no rights of others in the assertion of our own. Moreover we are cognizant of the world's struggles for full readjustment and rehabilitation, and we have shirked no duty which comes of sympathy, or fraternity, or highest fellowship among nations. Every obligation consonant with American ideals and sanctioned under our form of government is willingly met. When we can not support we do not demand. Our constitutional limitations do not forbid the exercise of a moral influence, the measure of which is not less than the high purposes we have sought to serve.

After all there is less difference about the part this great Republic shall play in furthering peace and advancing humanity than in the manner of playing it. We ask no one to assume responsibility for us; we assume no responsibility which others must bear for themselves, unless nationality is hopelessly swallowed up in internationalism.

Calvin Coolidge

August 3, 1923 to March 4, 1929

FIRST ANNUAL MESSAGE.

[Delivered at a Joint Session, December 6, 1923.]

Since the close of the last Congress the Nation has lost President Harding. The world knew his kindness and his humanity, his greatness and his character. He has left his mark upon history. He has made justice more certain and peace more secure. The surpassing tribute paid to his memory as he was borne across the continent to rest at last at home revealed the place he held in the hearts of the American people. But this is not the occasion for extended reference to the man or his work. In this presence, among these who knew and loved him, that is unnecessary. But we who were associated with him could not resume together the functions of our office without pausing for a moment, and in his memory reconsecrating ourselves to the service of our country. He is gone. We remain. It is our duty, under the inspiration of his example, to take up the burdens which he was permitted to lay down, and to develop and support the wise principles of government which he represented.

FOREIGN AFFAIRS.

For us peace reigns everywhere. We desire to perpetuate it always by granting full justice to others and requiring of others full justice to ourselves.

Our country has one cardinal principle to maintain in its foreign policy. It is an American principle. It must be an American policy. We attend to our own affairs, conserve our own strength, and protect the interests of our own citizens; but we recognize thoroughly our obligation to help others, reserving to the decision of our own judgment the time, the place, and the method. We realize the common bond of humanity. We know the inescapable law of service.

Our country has definitely refused to adopt and ratify the covenant of the League of Nations. We have not felt warranted in assuming the responsibilities which its members have assumed. I am not proposing any change in this policy; neither is the Senate. The incident, so far as we are concerned, is closed. The League exists as a foreign agency. We hope it will be helpful. But the United States sees no reason to limit its own freedom and independence of action by joining it. We shall do well to recognize this basic fact in all national affairs and govern ourselves accordingly.

WORLD COURT.

Our foreign policy has always been guided by two principles. The one is the avoidance of permanent political alliances which would sacrifice our proper independence. The other is the peaceful settlement of controversies between nations. By example and by treaty we have advocated arbitration. For nearly 25 years we have been a member of The Hague Tribunal, and have long sought the creation of a permanent World Court of Justice. I am in full accord with both of these policies. I favor the establishment of such a court intended to include the whole world. That is, and has long been, an American policy.

Pending before the Senate is a proposal that this Government give its support to the Permanent Court of International Justice, which is a new and somewhat different plan. This is not a partisan question. It should not assume an artificial importance. The court is merely a convenient instrument of adjustment to which we could go, but to which we could not be brought. It should be discussed with entire candor, not by a political but by a judicial method, without pressure and without prejudice. Partisanship has no place in our foreign relations. As I wish to see a court established, and as the proposal presents the only practical plan on which many nations have ever agreed, though it may not meet every desire, I therefore commend it to the favorable consideration of the Senate, with the proposed reservations clearly indicating our refusal to adhere to the League of Nations.

RUSSIA.

Our diplomatic relations, lately so largely interrupted, are now being resumed, but Russia presents notable difficulties. We have every desire to see that great people, who are our traditional friends, restored to their position among the nations of the earth. We have relieved their pitiable destitution with an enormous charity. Our Government offers no objection to the carrying on of commerce by our citizens with the people of Russia. Our Government does not propose, however, to enter into relations with another régime which refuses to recognize the sanctity of international obligations. I do not propose to barter away for the privilege of trade any of the cherished rights of humanity. I do not propose to make merchandise of any American principles. These rights and principles must go wherever the sanctions of our Government go.

But while the favor of America is not for sale, I am willing to make very large concessions for the purpose of rescuing the people of Russia. Already encouraging evidences of returning to the ancient ways of society can be detected. But more are needed. Whenever there appears any disposition to compensate our citizens who were despoiled, and to recognize that debt contracted with our Government, not by the Czar, but by the newly formed Republic of Russia; whenever the active spirit of enmity to our institutions is abated; whenever there appear works mete for repentance; our country ought to be the first to go to the economic and moral rescue of Russia. We have every desire to help and no desire to injure. We hope the time is near at hand when we can act.

DEBTS.

The current debt and interest due from foreign Governments, exclusive of the British debt of $4,600,000,000, is about $7,200,000,000. I do not favor the cancellation of this debt, but I see no objection to adjusting it in accordance with the principle adopted for the British debt. Our country would not wish to assume the rôle of an oppressive creditor, but would maintain the principle that financial obligations between nations are likewise moral obligations which international faith and honor require should be discharged.

Our Government has a liquidated claim against Germany for the expense of the army of occupation of over $255,000,000. Besides this, the Mixed Claims Commission have before them about 12,500 claims of American citizens, aggregating about $1,225,000,000. These claims have already been reduced by a recent decision, but there are valid claims reaching well toward $500,000,000. Our thousands of citizens with credits due them of hundreds of millions of dollars have no redress save in the action of our Government. These are very substantial interests, which it is the duty of our Government to protect as best it can. That course I propose to pursue.

It is for these reasons that we have a direct interest in the economic recovery of Europe. They are enlarged by our desire for the stability of civilization and the welfare of humanity. That we are making sacrifices to that end none can deny. Our deferred interest alone amounts to a million dollars every day. But recently we offered to aid with our advice and counsel. We have reiterated our desire to see France paid and Germany revived. We have proposed disarmament. We have earnestly sought to compose differences and restore peace. We shall persevere in well-doing, not by force, but by reason.

FOREIGN PAPERS.

Under the law the papers pertaining to foreign relations to be printed are transmitted as a part of this message. Other volumes of these papers will follow.

FOREIGN SERVICE.

The foreign service of our Government needs to be reorganized and improved.

FISCAL CONDITION.

Our main problems are domestic problems. Financial stability is the first requisite of sound government. We can not escape the effect of world conditions. We can not avoid the inevitable results of the economic disorders which have reached all nations. But we shall diminish their harm to us in proportion as we continue to restore our Government finances to a secure and endurable position. This we can and must do. Upon that firm foundation rests the only hope of progress and prosperity. From that source must come relief for the people.

This is being accomplished by a drastic but orderly retrenchment, which is bringing our expenses within our means. The origin of this has been the determination of the American people, the main support has been the courage of those in authority, and the effective method has been the Budget System. The result has involved real sacrifice by department heads, but it has been made without flinching. This system is a law of the Congress. It represents your will. It must be maintained, and ought to be strengthened by the example of your observance. Without a Budget System there can be no fixed responsibility and no constructive scientific economy.

This great concentration of effort by the administration and Congress has brought the expenditures, exclusive of the self-supporting Post Office Department, down to three billion dollars. It is possible, in consequence, to make a large reduction in the taxes of the people, which is the sole object of all curtailment. This is treated at greater length in the Budget message, and a proposed plan has been presented in detail in a statement by the Secretary of the Treasury which has my unqualified approval. I especially commend a decrease on earned incomes, and further abolition of admission, message, and nuisance taxes. The amusement and educational value of moving pictures ought not to be taxed. Diminishing charges against moderate incomes from investment will afford immense relief, while a revision of the surtaxes will not only provide additional money for capital investment, thus stimulating industry and employing more labor, but will not greatly reduce the revenue from that source, and may in the future actually increase it.

Being opposed to war taxes in time of peace, I am not in favor of excess-profits taxes. A very great service could be rendered through immediate enactment of legislation relieving the people of some of the burden of taxation. To reduce war taxes is to give every home a better chance.

For seven years the people have borne with uncomplaining courage the tremendous burden of national and local taxation. These must both be reduced. The taxes of the Nation must be reduced now as much as prudence will permit, and expenditures must be reduced accordingly. High taxes reach everywhere and burden everybody. They bear most heavily upon the poor. They diminish industry and commerce. They make agriculture unprofitable. They increase the rates on transportation. They are a charge on every necessary of life. Of all services which the Congress can render to the country, I have no hesitation in declaring this one to be paramount. To neglect it, to postpone it, to obstruct it by unsound proposals, is to become unworthy of public confidence and untrue to public trust. The country wants this measure to have the right of way over all others.

Another reform which is urgent in our fiscal system is the abolition of the right to issue tax-exempt securities. The existing system not only permits a large amount of the wealth of the Nation to escape its just burden but acts as a continual stimulant to municipal extravagance. This should be prohibited by constitutional amendment. All the wealth of the Nation ought to contribute its fair share to the expenses of the Nation.

TARIFF LAW.

The present tariff law has accomplished its two main objects. It has secured an abundant revenue and been productive of an abounding prosperity. Under it the country has had a very large export and import trade. A constant revision of the tariff by the Congress is disturbing and harmful. The present law contains an elastic provision authorizing the President to increase or decrease present schedules not in excess of 50 per centum to meet the difference in cost of production at home and abroad. This does not, to my mind, warrant a rewriting of the whole law, but does mean, and will be so administered, that whenever the required investigation shows that inequalities of sufficient importance exist in any schedule, the power to change them should and will be applied.

SHIPPING.

The entire well being of our country is dependent upon transportation by sea and land. Our Government during the war acquired a large merchant fleet which should be transferred, as soon as possible, to private ownership and operation under conditions which would secure two results: First, and of prime importance, adequate means for national defense; second, adequate service to American commerce. Until shipping conditions are such that our fleet can be disposed of advantageously under these conditions, it will be operated as economically as possible under such plans as may be devised from time to time by the Shipping Board. We must have a merchant marine which meets these requirements, and we shall have to pay the cost of its service.

PUBLIC IMPROVEMENTS.

The time has come to resume in a moderate way the opening of our intracoastal waterways; the control of flood waters of the Mississippi and of the Colorado Rivers; the improvement of the waterways from the Great Lakes toward the Gulf of Mexico; and the development of the great power and navigation project of the St. Lawrence River, for which efforts are now being made to secure the necessary treaty with Canada. These projects can not all be undertaken at once, but all should have the immediate consideration of the Congress and be adopted as fast as plans can be matured and the necessary funds become available. This is not incompatible with economy, for their nature does not require so much a public expenditure as a capital investment which will be reproductive, as evidenced by the marked increase in revenue from the Panama Canal. Upon these projects depend much future industrial and agricultural progress. They represent the protection of large areas from flood and the addition of a great amount of cheap power and cheap freight by use of navigation, chief of which is the bringing of ocean-going ships to the Great Lakes.

Another problem of allied character is the superpower development of the Northeastern States, consideration of which is proceeding under the direction of the Department of Commerce by joint conference with the local authorities.

RAILROADS.

Criticism of the railroad law has been directed, first, to the section laying down the rule by which rates are fixed, and providing for payment to the Government and use of excess earnings; second, to the method for the adjustment of wage scales; and third, to the authority permitting consolidations.

It has been erroneously assumed that the act undertakes to guarantee railroad earnings. The law requires that rates should be just and reasonable. That has always been the rule under which rates have been fixed. To make a rate that does not yield a fair return results in confiscation, and confiscatory rates are of course unconstitutional. Unless the Government adheres to the rule of making a rate that will yield a fair return, it must abandon rate making altogether. The new and important feature of that part of the law is the recapture and redistribution of excess rates. The constitutionality of this method is now before the Supreme Court for adjudication. Their decision should be awaited before attempting further legislation on this subject. Furthermore, the importance of this feature will not be great if consolidation goes into effect.

The settlement of railroad labor disputes is a matter of grave public concern. The Labor Board was established to protect the public in the enjoyment of continuous service by attempting to insure justice between the companies and their employees. It has been a great help, but is not altogether satisfactory to the public, the employees, or the companies. If a substantial agreement can be reached among the groups interested, there should be no hesitation in enacting such agreement into law. If it is not reached, the Labor Board may very well be left for the present to protect the public welfare.

The law for consolidations is not sufficiently effective to be expeditious. Additional legislation is needed giving authority for voluntary consolidations, both regional and route, and providing Government machinery to aid and stimulate such action, always subject to the approval of the Interstate Commerce Commission. This should authorize the commission to appoint committees for each proposed group, representing the public and the component roads, with power to negotiate with individual security holders for an exchange of their securities for those of the consolidation on such terms and conditions as the commission may prescribe for avoiding any confiscation and preserving fair values. Should this permissive consolidation prove ineffective after a limited period, the authority of the Government will have to be directly invoked.

Consolidation appears to be the only feasible method for the maintenance of an adequate system of transportation with an opportunity so to adjust freight rates as to meet such temporary conditions as now prevail in some agricultural sections. Competent authorities agree that an entire reorganization of the rate structure for freight is necessary. This should be ordered at once by the Congress.

DEPARTMENT OF JUSTICE.

As no revision of the laws of the United States has been made since 1878, a commission or committee should be created to undertake this work. The Judicial Council reports that two more district judges are needed in the southern district of New York, one in the northern district of Georgia, and two more circuit judges in the Circuit Court of Appeals of the Eighth Circuit. Legislation should be considered for this purpose.

It is desirable to expedite the hearing and disposal of cases. A commission of Federal judges and lawyers should be created to recommend legislation by which the procedure in the Federal trial courts may be simplified and regulated by rules of court, rather than by statute; such rules to be submitted to the Congress and to be in force until annulled or modified by the Congress. The Supreme Court needs legislation revising and simplifying the laws governing review by that court, and enlarging the classes of cases of too little public importance to be subject to review. Such reforms would expedite the transaction of the business of the courts. The administration of justice is likely to fail if it be long delayed.

The National Government has never given adequate attention to its prison problems. It ought to provide employment in such forms of production as can be used by the Government, though not sold to the public in competition with private business, for all prisoners who can be placed at work, and for which they should receive a reasonable compensation, available for their dependents.

Two independent reformatories are needed; one for the segregation of women, and another for the segregation of young men serving their first sentence.

The administration of justice would be facilitated greatly by including in the Bureau of Investigation of the Department of Justice a Division of Criminal Identification, where there would be collected this information which is now indispensable in the suppression of crime.

PROHIBITION.

The prohibition amendment to the Constitution requires the Congress and the President to provide adequate laws to prevent its violation. It is my duty to enforce such laws. For that purpose a treaty is being negotiated with Great Britain with respect to the right of search of hovering vessels. To prevent smuggling, the Coast Guard should be greatly strengthened, and a supply of swift power boats should be provided. The major sources of production should be rigidly regulated, and every effort should be made to suppress interstate traffic. With this action on the part of the National Government, and the cooperation which is usually rendered by municipal and State authorities, prohibition should be made effective. Free government has no greater menace than disrespect for authority and continual violation of law. It is the duty of a citizen not only to observe the law but to let it be known that he is opposed to its violation.

THE NEGRO.

Numbered among our population are some 12,000,000 colored people. Under our Constitution their rights are just as sacred as those of any other citizen. It is both a public and a private duty to protect those rights. The Congress ought to exercise all its powers of prevention and punishment against the hideous crime of lynching, of which the negroes are by no means the sole sufferers, but for which they furnish a majority of the victims.

Already a considerable sum is appropriated to give the negroes vocational training in agriculture. About half a million dollars is recommended for medical courses at Howard University to help contribute to the education of 500 colored doctors needed each year. On account of the migration of large numbers into industrial centers, it has been proposed that a commission be created, composed of members from both races, to formulate a better policy for mutual understanding and confidence. Such an effort is to be commended. Everyone would rejoice in the accomplishment of the results which it seeks. But it is well to recognize that these difficulties are to a large extent local problems which must be worked out by the mutual forbearance and human kindness of each community. Such a method gives much more promise of a real remedy than outside interference.

CIVIL SERVICE.

The maintenance and extension of the classified civil service is exceedingly important. There are nearly 550,000 persons in the executive civil service drawing about $700,000,000 of yearly compensation. Four-fifths of these are in the classified service. This method of selection of the employees of the United States is especially desirable for the Post Office Department. The Civil Service Commission has recommended that postmasters at first, second, and third class offices be classified. Such action, accompanied by a repeal of the four-year term of office, would undoubtedly be an improvement. I also recommend that the field force for prohibition enforcement be brought within the classified civil service without covering in the present membership. The best method for selecting public servants is the merit system.

PUBLIC BUILDINGS.

Many of the departments in Washington need better housing facilities. Some are so crowded that their work is impeded, others are so scattered that they lose their identity. While I do not favor at this time a general public building law, I believe it is now necessary, in accordance with plans already sanctioned for a unified and orderly system for the development of this city, to begin the carrying out of those plans by authorizing the erection of three or four buildings most urgently needed by an annual appropriation of $5,000,000.

REGULATORY LEGISLATION.

Cooperation with other maritime powers is necessary for complete protection of our coast waters from pollution. Plans for this are under way, but await certain experiments for refuse disposal. Meantime laws prohibiting spreading oil and oil refuse from vessels in our own territorial waters would be most helpful against this menace and should be speedily enacted.

Laws should be passed regulating aviation.

Revision is needed of the laws regulating radio interference.

Legislation and regulations establishing load lines to provide safe loading of vessels leaving our ports are necessary and recodification of our navigation laws is vital.

Revision of procedure of the Federal Trade Commission will give more constructive purpose to this department.

If our Alaskan fisheries are to be saved from destruction, there must be further legislation declaring a general policy and delegating the authority to make rules and regulations to an administrative body.

ARMY AND NAVY.

For several years we have been decreasing the personnel of the Army and Navy, and reducing their power to the danger point. Further reductions should not be made. The Army is a guarantee of the security of our citizens at home; the Navy is a guarantee of the security of our citizens abroad. Both of these services should be strengthened rather than weakened. Additional planes are needed for the Army, and additional submarines for the Navy. The defenses of Panama must be perfected. We want no more competitive armaments. We want no more war. But we want no weakness that invites imposition. A people who neglect their national defense are putting in jeopardy their national honor.

INSULAR POSSESSIONS.

Conditions in the insular possessions on the whole have been good. Their business has been reviving. They are being administered according to law. That effort has the full support of the administration. Such recommendations as may come from their people or their governments should have the most considerate attention.

EDUCATION AND WELFARE.

Our National Government is not doing as much as it legitimately can do to promote the welfare of the people. Our enormous material wealth, our institutions, our whole form of society, can not be considered fully successful until their benefits reach the merit of every individual. This is not a suggestion that the Government should, or could, assume for the people the inevitable burdens of existence. There is no method by which we can either be relieved of the results of our own folly or be guaranteed a successful life. There is an inescapable personal responsibility for the development of character, of industry, of thrift, and of self-control. These do not come from the Government, but from the people themselves. But the Government can and should always be expressive of steadfast determination, always vigilant, to maintain conditions under which these virtues are most likely to develop and secure recognition and reward. This is the American policy.

It is in accordance with this principle that we have enacted laws for the protection of the public health and have adopted prohibition in narcotic drugs and intoxicating liquors. For purposes of national uniformity we ought to provide, by constitutional amendment and appropriate legislation, for a limitation of child labor, and in all cases under the exclusive jurisdiction of the Federal Government a minimum wage law for women, which would undoubtedly find sufficient power of enforcement in the influence of public opinion.

Having in mind that education is peculiarly a local problem, and that it should always be pursued with the largest freedom of choice by students and parents, nevertheless, the Federal Government might well give the benefit of its counsel and encouragement more freely in this direction. If anyone doubts the need of concerted action by the States of the Nation for this purpose, it is only necessary to consider the appalling figures of illiteracy representing a condition which does not vary much in all parts of the Union. I do not favor the making of appropriations from the National Treasury to be expended directly on local education, but I do consider it a fundamental requirement of national activity which, accompanied by allied subjects of welfare, is worthy of a separate department and a place in the Cabinet. The humanitarian side of government should not be repressed, but should be cultivated.

Mere intelligence, however, is not enough. Enlightenment must be accompanied by that moral power which is the product of the home and of religion. Real education and true welfare for the people rest inevitably on this foundation, which the Government can approve and commend, but which the people themselves must create.

IMMIGRATION.

American institutions rest solely on good citizenship. They were created by people who had a background of self-government. New arrivals should be limited to our capacity to absorb them into the ranks of good citizenship. America must be kept American. For this purpose, it is necessary to continue a policy of restricted immigration. It would be well to make such immigration of a selective nature with some inspection at the source, and based either on a prior census or upon the record of naturalization. Either method would insure the admission of those with the largest capacity and best intention of becoming citizens. I am convinced that our present economic and social conditions warrant a limitation of those to be admitted. We should find additional safety in a law requiring the immediate registration of all aliens. Those who do not want to be partakers of the American spirit ought not to settle in America.

VETERANS.

No more important duty falls on the Government of the United States than the adequate care of its veterans. Those suffering disabilities incurred in the service must have sufficient hospital relief and compensation. Their dependents must be supported. Rehabilitation and vocational training must be completed. All of this service must be clean, must be prompt and effective, and it must be administered in a spirit of the broadest and deepest human sympathy. If investigation reveals any present defects of administration or need of legislation, orders will be given for the immediate correction of administration, and recommendations for legislation should be given the highest preference.

At present there are 9,500 vacant beds in Government hospitals, I recommend that all hospitals be authorized at once to receive and care for, without hospital pay, the veterans of all wars needing such care, whenever there are vacant beds, and that immediate steps be taken to enlarge and build new hospitals to serve all such cases.

The American Legion will present to the Congress a legislative program too extensive for detailed discussion here. It is a carefully matured plan. While some of it I do not favor, with much of it I am in hearty accord, and I recommend that a most painstaking effort be made to provide remedies for any defects in the administration of the present laws which their experience has revealed. The attitude of the Government toward these proposals should be one of generosity. But I do not favor the granting of a bonus.

COAL.

The cost of coal has become unbearably high. It places a great burden on our industrial and domestic life. The public welfare requires a reduction in the price of fuel. With the enormous deposits in existence, failure of supply ought not to be tolerated. Those responsible for the conditions in this industry should undertake its reform and free it from any charge of profiteering.

The report of the Coal Commission will be before the Congress. It comprises all the facts. It represents the mature deliberations and conclusions of the best talent and experience that ever made a national survey of the production and distribution of fuel. I do not favor Government ownership or operation of coal mines. The need is for action under private ownership that will secure greater continuity of production and greater public protection. The Federal Government probably has no peace-time authority to regulate wages, prices, or profits in coal at the mines or among dealers, but by ascertaining and publishing facts it can exercise great influence.

The source of the difficulty in the bituminous coal fields is the intermittence of operation which causes great waste of both capital and labor. That part of the report dealing with this problem has much significance, and is suggestive of necessary remedies. By amending the car rules, by encouraging greater unity of ownership, and possibly by permitting common selling agents for limited districts on condition that they accept adequate regulations and guarantee that competition between districts be unlimited, distribution, storage, and continuity ought to be improved.

The supply of coal must be constant. In case of its prospective interruption, the President should have authority to appoint a commission empowered to deal with whatever emergency situation might arise, to aid conciliation and voluntary arbitration, to adjust any existing or threatened controversy between the employer and the employee when collective bargaining fails, and by controlling distribution to prevent profiteering in this vital necessity. This legislation is exceedingly urgent, and essential to the exercise of national authority for the protection of the people. Those who undertake the responsibility of management or employment in this industry do so with the full knowledge that the public interest is paramount, and that to fail through any motive of selfishness in its service is such a betrayal of duty as warrants uncompromising action by the Government.

REORGANIZATION.

A special joint committee has been appointed to work out a plan for a reorganization of the different departments and bureaus of the Government more scientific and economical than the present system. With the exception of the consolidation of the War and Navy Departments and some minor details, the plan has the general sanction of the President and the Cabinet. It is important that reorganization be enacted into law at the present session.

AGRICULTURE.

Aided by the sound principles adopted by the Government, the business of the country has had an extraordinary revival. Looked at as a whole, the Nation is in the enjoyment of remarkable prosperity. Industry and commerce are thriving. For the most part agriculture is successful, eleven staples having risen in value from about $5,300,000,000 two years ago to about $7,000,000,000 for the current year. But range cattle are still low in price, and some sections of the wheat area, notably Minnesota, North Dakota, and on west, have many cases of actual distress. With his products not selling on a parity with the products of industry, every sound remedy that can be devised should be applied for the relief of the farmer. He represents a character, a type of citizenship, and a public necessity that must be preserved and afforded every facility for regaining prosperity.

The distress is most acute among those wholly dependent upon one crop. Wheat acreage was greatly expanded and has not yet been sufficiently reduced. A large amount is raised for export, which has to meet the competition in the world market of large amounts raised on land much cheaper and much more productive.

No complicated scheme of relief, no plan for Government fixing of prices, no resort to the public Treasury will be of any permanent value in establishing agriculture. Simple and direct methods put into operation by the farmer himself are the only real sources for restoration.

Indirectly the farmer must be relieved by a reduction of national and local taxation. He must be assisted by the reorganization of the freight-rate structure which could reduce charges on his production. To make this fully effective there ought to be railroad consolidations. Cheaper fertilizers must be provided.

He must have organization. His customer with whom he exchanges products of the farm for those of industry is organized, labor is organized, business is organized, and there is no way for agriculture to meet this unless it, too, is organized. The acreage of wheat is too large. Unless we can meet the world market at a profit, we must stop raising for export. Organization would help to reduce acreage. Systems of cooperative marketing created by the farmers themselves, supervised by competent management, without doubt would be of assistance, but they can not wholly solve the problem. Our agricultural schools ought to have thorough courses in the theory of organization and cooperative marketing.

Diversification is necessary. Those farmers who raise their living on their land are not greatly in distress. Such loans as are wisely needed to assist buying stock and other materials to start in this direction should be financed through a Government agency as a temporary and emergency expedient.

The remaining difficulty is the disposition of exportable wheat. I do not favor the permanent interference of the Government in this problem. That probably would increase the trouble by increasing production. But it seems feasible to provide Government assistance to exports, and authority should be given the War Finance

Corporation to grant, in its discretion, the most liberal terms of payment for fats and grains exported for the direct benefit of the farm.

MUSCLE SHOALS.

The Government is undertaking to develop a great water-power project known as Muscle Shoals, on which it has expended many million dollars. The work is still going on. Subject to the right to retake in time of war, I recommend that this property with a location for auxiliary steam plant and rights of way be sold. This would end the present burden of expense and should return to the Treasury the largest price possible to secure.

While the price is an important element, there is another consideration even more compelling. The agriculture of the Nation needs a greater supply and lower cost of fertilizer. This is now imported in large quantities. The best information I can secure indicates that present methods of power production would not be able profitably to meet the price at which these imports can be sold. To obtain a supply from this water power would require long and costly experimentation to perfect a process for cheap production. Otherwise our purpose would fail completely. It seems desirable, therefore, in order to protect and promote the public welfare, to have adequate covenants that such experimentation be made and carried on to success. The great advantage of low-priced nitrates must be secured for the direct benefit of the farmers and the indirect benefit of the public in time of peace, and of the Government in time of war. If this main object be accomplished, the amount of money received for the property is not a primary or major consideration.

Such a solution will involve complicated negotiations, and there is no authority for that purpose. I therefore recommend that the Congress appoint a small joint committee to consider offers, conduct negotiations, and report definite recommendations.

RECLAMATION.

By reason of many contributing causes, occupants of our reclamation projects are in financial difficulties, which in some cases are acute. Relief should be granted by definite authority of law empowering the Secretary of the Interior in his discretion to suspend, readjust, and reassess all charges against water users. This whole question is being considered by experts. You will have the advantage of the facts and conclusions which they may develop. This situation, involving a Government investment of more than $135,000,000, and affecting more than 30,000 water users, is serious. While relief which is necessary should be granted, yet contracts with the Government which can be met should be met. The established general policy of these projects should not be abandoned for any private control.

HIGHWAYS AND FORESTS.

Highways and reforestation should continue to have the interest and support of the Government. Everyone is anxious for good highways. I have made a liberal proposal in the Budget for the continuing payment to the States by the Federal Government of its share for this necessary public improvement. No expenditure of public money contributes so much to the national wealth as for building good roads.

Reforestation has an importance far above the attention it usually secures. A special committee of the Senate is investigating this need, and I shall welcome a constructive policy based on their report.

It is 100 years since our country announced the Monroe doctrine. This principle has been ever since, and is now, one of the main foundations of our foreign relations. It must be maintained. But in maintaining it we must not be forgetful that a great change has taken place. We are no longer a weak Nation, thinking mainly of defense, dreading foreign imposition. We are great and powerful. New powers bring new responsibilities. Our duty then was to protect ourselves. Added to that, our duty now is to help give stability to the world. We want idealism. We want that vision which lifts men and nations above themselves. These are virtues by reason of their own merit. But they must not be cloistered; they must not be impractical; they must not be ineffective.

The world has had enough of the curse of hatred and selfishness, of destruction and war. It has had enough of the wrongful use of material power. For the healing of the nations there must be good will and charity, confidence and peace. The time has come for a more practical use of moral power, and more reliance upon the principle that right makes its own might. Our authority among the nations must be represented by justice and mercy. It is necessary not only to have faith, but to make sacrifices for our faith. The spiritual forces of the world make all its final determinations. It is with these voices that America should speak. Whenever they declare a righteous purpose there need be no doubt that they will be heard. America has taken her place in the world as a Republic—free, independent, powerful. The best service that can be rendered to humanity is the assurance that this place will be maintained.

SECOND ANNUAL MESSAGE.

THE WHITE HOUSE, *December 3, 1924.*

To the Congress of the United States:

The present state of the Union, upon which it is customary for the President to report to the Congress under the provisions of the Constitution, is such that it may be regarded with encouragement and satisfaction by every American. Our country is almost unique in its ability to discharge fully and promptly all its obligations at home and abroad, and provide for all its inhabitants an increase in material resources, in intellectual vigor and in moral power. The Nation holds a position unsurpassed in all former human experience.

This does not mean that we do not have any problems. It is elementary that the increasing breadth of our experience necessarily increases the problems of our national life. But it does mean that if we will but apply ourselves industriously and honestly, we have ample powers with which to meet our problems and provide for their speedy solution. I do not profess that we can secure an era of perfection in human existence, but we can provide an era of peace and prosperity, attended with freedom and justice and made more and more satisfying by the ministrations of the charities and humanities of life.

Our domestic problems are for the most part economic. We have our enormous debt to pay, and we are paying it. We have the high cost of government to diminish, and we are diminishing it. We have a heavy burden of taxation to reduce, and we are reducing it. But while remarkable progress has been made in these directions, the work is yet far from accomplished. We still owe over $21,000,000,000, the cost of the National Government is still about $3,500,000,000, and the national taxes still amount to about $27 for each one of our inhabitants. There yet exists this enormous field for the application of economy.

In my opinion the Government can do more to remedy the economic ills of the people by a system of rigid economy in public expenditure than can be accomplished through any other action. The costs of our national and local governments combined now stand at a sum close to $100 for each inhabitant of the land. A little less than one-third of this is represented by national expenditure, and a little more than two-thirds by local expenditure. It is an ominous fact that only the National Government is reducing its debt. Others are increasing theirs at about $1,000,000,000 each year. The depression that overtook business, the disaster experienced in agriculture, the lack of employment and the terrific shrinkage in all values which our country experienced in a most acute form in 1920, resulted in no small measure from the prohibitive taxes which were then levied on all productive effort. The establishment of a system of drastic economy in public expenditure, which has enabled us to pay off about one-fifth of the national debt since 1919, and almost cut in two the national tax burden since 1921, has been one of the main causes in reestablishing a prosperity which has come to include within its benefits almost every one of our inhabitants. Economy reaches everywhere. It carries a blessing to everybody.

The fallacy of the claim that the costs of government are borne by the rich and those who make a direct contribution to the National Treasury can not be too often exposed. No system has been devised, I do not think any system could be devised, under which any person living in this country could escape being affected by the cost of our government. It has a direct effect both upon the rate and the purchasing power of wages. It is felt in the price of those prime necessities of existence, food, clothing, fuel and shelter. It would appear to be elementary that the more the Government expends the more it must require every producer to contribute out of his production to the Public Treasury, and the less he will have for his own benefit. The continuing costs of public administration can be met in only one way—by the work of the people. The higher they become, the more the people must work for the Government. The less they are, the more the people can work for themselves.

The present estimated margin between public receipts and expenditures for this fiscal year is very small. Perhaps the most important work that this session of the Congress can do is to continue a policy of economy and further reduce the cost of government, in order that we may have a reduction of taxes for the next fiscal year. Nothing is more likely to produce that public confidence which is the forerunner and the mainstay of prosperity, encourage and enlarge business opportunity with ample opportunity for employment at good wages, provide a larger market for agricultural products, and put our country in a stronger position to be able to meet the world competition in trade, than a continuing policy of economy. Of course necessary costs must be met, proper functions of the Government performed, and constant investments for capital account and reproductive effort must be carried on by our various departments. But the people must know that their Government is placing upon them no unnecessary burden.

TAXES

Everyone desires a reduction of taxes, and there is a great preponderance of sentiment in favor of taxation reform. When I approved the present tax law, I stated publicly that I did so in spite of certain provisions which I believed unwise and harmful. One of the most glaring of these was the making public of the amounts assessed against different income-tax payers. Although that damage has now been done, I believe its continuation to be detrimental to the public welfare and bound to decrease public revenues, so that it ought to be repealed.

Anybody can reduce taxes, but it is not so easy to stand in the gap and resist the passage of increasing appropriation bills which would make tax reduction impossible. It will be very easy to measure the strength of the attachment to reduced taxation by the power with which increased appropriations are resisted. If at the close of the present session the Congress has kept within the budget which I propose to present, it will then be possible to have a moderate amount of tax reduction and all the tax reform that the Congress may wish for during the next fiscal year. The country is now feeling the direct stimulus which came from the passage of the last revenue bill, and under the assurance of a reasonable system of taxation there is every prospect of an era of prosperity of unprecedented proportions. But it would be idle to expect any such results unless business can continue free from excess profits taxation and be accorded a system of surtaxes at rates which have for their object not the punishment of success or the discouragement of business, but the production of the greatest amount of revenue from large incomes. I am convinced that the larger incomes of the country would actually yield more revenue to the Government if the basis of taxation were scientifically revised downward. Moreover the effect of the present method of this taxation is to increase the cost of interest on productive enterprise and to increase the burden of rent. It is altogether likely that such reduction would so encourage and stimulate investment that it would firmly establish our country in the economic leadership of the world.

WATERWAYS

Meantime our internal development should go on. Provision should be made for flood control of such rivers as the Mississippi and the Colorado, and for the opening up of our inland waterways to commerce. Consideration is due to the project of better navigation from the Great Lakes to the Gulf. Every effort is being made to promote an agreement with Canada to build the St. Lawrence waterway. There are pending before the Congress bills for further development of the Mississippi Basin, for the taking over of the Cape Cod Canal in accordance with a moral obligation which seems to have been incurred during the war, and for the improvement of harbors on both the Pacific and the Atlantic coasts. While this last should be divested of some of its projects and we must proceed slowly, these bills in general have my approval. Such works are productive of wealth and in the long run tend to a reduction of the tax burden.

RECLAMATION

Our country has a well-defined policy of reclamation established under statutory authority. This policy should be continued and made a self-sustaining activity administered in a manner that will meet local requirements and bring our arid lands into a profitable state of cultivation as fast as there is a market for their products. Legislation is pending based on the report of the Fact Finding Commission for the proper relief of those needing extension of time in which to meet their payments on irrigated land, and for additional amendments and reforms of our reclamation laws, which are all exceedingly important and should be enacted at once.

No more important development has taken place in the last year than the beginning of a restoration of agriculture to a prosperous condition. We must permit no division of classes in this country, with one occupation striving to secure advantage over another. Each must proceed under open opportunities and with a fair prospect of economic equality. The Government can not successfully insure prosperity or fix prices by legislative fiat. Every business has its risk and its times of depression. It is well known that in the long run there will be a more even prosperity and a more satisfactory range of prices under the natural working out of economic laws than when the Government undertakes the artificial support of markets and industries. Still we can so order our affairs, so protect our own people from foreign competition, so arrange our national finances, so administer our monetary system, so provide for the extension of credits, so improve methods of distribution, as to provide a better working machinery for the transaction of the business of the Nation with the least possible friction and loss. The Government has been constantly increasing its efforts in these directions for the relief and permanent establishment of agriculture on a sound and equal basis with other business.

It is estimated that the value of the crops for this harvest year may reach $13,000,000,000, which is an increase of over $3,000,000,000 in three years. It compares with $7,100,000,000 in 1913, and if we make deduction from the figures of 1924 for the comparatively decreased value of the dollar, the yield this year still exceeds 1913 in purchasing power by over $1,000,000,000, and in this interval there has been no increase in the number of farmers. Mostly by his own effort the farmer has decreased the cost of production. A marked increase in the price of his products and some decrease in the price of his supplies has brought him about to a parity with the rest of the Nation. The crop area of this season is estimated at 370,000,000 acres, which is a decline of 3,000,000 acres from last year, and 6,000,000 acres from 1919. This has been a normal and natural application of economic laws, which has placed agriculture on a foundation which is undeniably sound and beginning to be satisfactory.

A decrease in the world supply of wheat has resulted in a very large increase in the price of that commodity. The position of all agricultural products indicates a better balanced supply, but we can not yet conclude that agriculture is recovered from the effects of the war period or that it is permanently on a prosperous basis. The cattle industry has not yet recovered and in some sections has been suffering from dry weather. Every effort must be made, both by Government activity and by private agencies, to restore and maintain agriculture to a complete normal relationship with other industries.

It was on account of past depression, and in spite of present more encouraging conditions, that I have assembled an Agricultural Conference made up of those who are representative of this great industry in both its operating and economic sides. Everyone knows that the great need of the farmer is markets. The country is not suffering on the side of production. Almost the entire difficulty is on the side of distribution. This reaches back, of course, to unit costs and diversification, and many allied subjects. It is exceedingly intricate, for our domestic and foreign trade, transportation and banking, and in fact our entire economic system, are closely related to it. In time for action at this session, I hope to report to the Congress such legislative remedies as the conference may recommend. An appropriation should be made to defray their necessary expenses.

MUSCLE SHOALS

The production of nitrogen for plant food in peace and explosives in war is more and more important. It is one of the chief sustaining elements of life. It is estimated that soil exhaustion each year is represented by about 9,000,000 tons and replenishment by 5,450,000 tons. The deficit of 3,550,000 tons is reported to represent the impairment of 118,000,000 acres of farm lands each year.

To meet these necessities the Government has been developing a water power project at Muscle Shoals to be equipped to produce nitrogen for explosives and fertilizer. It is my opinion that the support of agriculture is the chief problem to consider in connection with this property. It could by no means supply the present needs for nitrogen, but it would help and its development would encourage bringing other water powers into like use.

Several offers have been made for the purchase of this property. Probably none of them represent final terms. Much costly experimentation is necessary to produce commercial nitrogen. For that reason it is a field better suited to private enterprise than to Government operation. I should favor a sale of this property, or long-time lease, under rigid guaranties of commercial nitrogen production at reasonable prices for agricultural use. There would be a surplus of power for many years over any possibility of its application to a developing manufacture of nitrogen. It may be found advantageous to dispose of the right to surplus power separately with such reservations as will allow its gradual withdrawal and application to nitrogen manufacture. A subcommittee of the Committees on Agriculture should investigate this field and negotiate with prospective purchasers. If no advantageous offer be made, the development should continue and the plant should be dedicated primarily to the production of materials for the fertilization of the soil.

RAILWAYS

The railways during the past year have made still further progress in recuperation from the war, with large gains in efficiency and ability expeditiously to handle the traffic of the country. We have now passed through several periods of peak traffic without the car shortages which so frequently in the past have brought havoc to our agriculture and industries. The condition of many of our great freight terminals is still one of difficulty and results in imposing large costs on the public for inward-bound freight, and on the railways for outward-bound freight. Owing to the growth of our large cities and the great increase in the volume of traffic, particularly in perishables, the problem is not only difficult of solution, but in some cases not wholly solvable by railway action alone.

In my message last year I emphasized the necessity for further legislation with a view to expediting the consolidation of our railways into larger systems. The principle of Government control of rates and profits, now thoroughly imbedded in our governmental attitude toward natural monopolies such as the railways, at once eliminates the need of competition by small units as a method of rate adjustment. Competition must be preserved as a stimulus to service, but this will exist and can be increased under enlarged systems. Consequently the consolidation of the railways into larger units for the purpose of securing the substantial values to the public which will come from larger operation has been the logical conclusion of Congress in its previous enactments, and is also supported by the best opinion in the country. Such consolidation will assure not only a greater element of competition as to service, but it will afford economy in operation, greater stability in railway earnings, and more economical financing. It opens large possibilities of better equalization of rates between different classes of traffic so as to relieve undue burdens upon agricultural products and raw materials generally, which are now not possible without ruin to small units owing to the lack of diversity of traffic. It would also tend to equalize earnings in such fashion as to reduce the importance of section 15A, at which criticism, often misapplied, has been directed. A smaller number of units would offer less difficulties in labor adjustments and would contribute much to the solution of terminal difficulties.

The consolidations need to be carried out with due regard to public interest and to the rights and established life of various communities in our country. It does not seem to me necessary that we endeavor to anticipate any final plan or adhere to any artificial and unchangeable project which shall stipulate a fixed number of systems, but rather we ought to approach the problem with such a latitude of action that it can be worked out step by step in accordance with a comprehensive consideration of public interest. Whether the number of ultimate systems shall be more or less seems to me can only be determined by time and actual experience in the development of such consolidations.

Those portions of the present law contemplating consolidations are not sufficiently effective in producing expeditious action and need amplification of the authority of the Interstate Commerce Commission, particularly in affording a period for voluntary proposals to the commission and in supplying Government pressure to secure action after the expiration of such a period.

There are other proposals before Congress for amending the transportation acts. One of these contemplates a revision of the method of valuation for rate-making purposes to be followed by a renewed valuation of the railways. The valuations instituted by the Interstate Commerce Commission 10 years ago have not yet been completed. They have cost the Government an enormous sum, and they have imposed great expenditure upon the railways, most of which has in effect come out of the public in increased rates. This work should not be abandoned or supplanted until its results are known and can be considered.

Another matter before the Congress is legislation affecting the labor sections of the transportation act. Much criticism has been directed at the workings of this section and experience has shown that some useful amendment could be made to these provisions.

It would be helpful if a plan could be adopted which, while retaining the practice of systematic collective bargaining with conciliation and voluntary arbitration of labor differences, could also provide simplicity in relations and more direct local responsibility of employees and managers. But such legislation will not meet the requirements of the situation unless it recognizes the principle that the public has a right to the uninterrupted service of transportation, and therefore a right to be heard when there is danger that the Nation may suffer great injury through the interruption of operations because of labor disputes. If these elements are not comprehended in proposed legislation, it would be better to gain further experience with the present organization for dealing with these questions before undertaking a change.

SHIPPING BOARD

The form of the organization of the Shipping Board was based originally on its functions as a semijudicial body in regulation of rates. During the war it was loaded with enormous administrative duties. It has been demonstrated time and again that this form of organization results in indecision, division of opinion and administrative functions, which make a wholly inadequate foundation for the conduct of a great business enterprise. The first principle in securing the objective set out by Congress in building up the American merchant marine upon the great trade routes and subsequently disposing of it into private operation can not proceed with effectiveness until the entire functions of the board are reorganized. The immediate requirement is to transfer into the Emergency Fleet Corporation the whole responsibility of operation of the fleet and other property, leaving to the Shipping Board solely the duty of determining certain major policies which require deliberative action.

The procedure under section 28 of the merchant marine act has created great difficulty and threatened friction during the past 12 months. Its attempted application developed not only great opposition from exporters, particularly as to burdens that may be imposed upon agricultural products, but also great anxiety in the different seaports as to the effect upon their relative rate structures. This trouble will certainly recur if action is attempted under this section. It is uncertain in some of its terms and of great difficulty in interpretation.

It is my belief that action under this section should be suspended until the Congress can reconsider the entire question in the light of the experience that has been developed since its enactment.

NATIONAL ELECTIONS

Nothing is so fundamental to the integrity of a republican form of government as honesty in all that relates to the conduct of elections. I am of the opinion that the national laws governing the choice of members of the Congress should be extended to include appropriate representation of the respective parties at the ballot box and equality of representation on the various registration boards, wherever they exist.

THE JUDICIARY

The docket of the Supreme Court is becoming congested. At the opening term last year it had 592 cases, while this year it had 687 cases. Justice long delayed is justice refused. Unless the court be given power by preliminary and summary consideration to determine the importance of cases, and by disposing of those which are not of public moment reserve its time for the more extended consideration of the remainder, the congestion of the docket is likely to increase. It is also desirable that the Supreme Court should have power to improve and reform procedure in suits at law in the Federal courts through the adoption of appropriate rules. The Judiciary Committee of the Senate has reported favorably upon two bills providing for these reforms which should have the immediate favorable consideration of the Congress.

I further recommend that provision be made for the appointment of a commission, to consist of two or three members of the Federal judiciary and as many members of the bar, to examine the present criminal code of procedure and recommend to the Congress measures which may reform and expedite court procedure in the administration and enforcement of our criminal laws.

PRISON REFORM

Pending before the Congress is a bill which has already passed one House providing for a reformatory to which could be committed first offenders and young men for the purpose of segregating them from contact with hardened criminals and providing them with special training, in order to reestablish in them the power to pursue a law-abiding existence in the social and economic life of the Nation. This is a matter of so much importance as to warrant the early attention of the present session. Further provision should also be made, for a like reason, for a separate reformatory for women.

NATIONAL POLICE BUREAU

Representatives of the International Police Conference will bring to the attention of the Congress a proposal for the establishment of a national police bureau. Such action would provide a central point for gathering, compiling, and later distributing to local police authorities much information which would be helpful in the prevention and detection of crime. I believe this bureau is needed, and I recommend favorable consideration of this proposal.

DISTRICT OF COLUMBIA WELFARE

The welfare work of the District of Columbia is administered by several different boards dealing with charities and various correctional efforts. It would be an improvement if this work were consolidated and placed under the direction of a single commission.

FRENCH SPOLIATION CLAIMS

During the last session of the Congress legislation was introduced looking to the payment of the remaining claims generally referred to as the French spoliation claims. The Congress has provided for the payment of many similar claims. Those that remain unpaid have been long pending. The beneficiaries thereunder have every reason to expect payment. These claims have been examined by the Court of Claims and their validity and amount determined. The United States ought to pay its debts. I recommend action by the Congress which will permit of the payment of these remaining claims.

THE WAGE EARNER

Two very important policies have been adopted by this country which, while extending their benefits also in other directions, have been of the utmost importance to the wage earners. One of these is the protective tariff, which enables our people to live according to a better standard and receive a better rate of compensation than any people, any time, anywhere on earth, ever enjoyed. This saves the American market for the products of the American workmen. The other is a policy of more recent origin and seeks to shield our wage earners from the disastrous competition of a great influx of foreign peoples. This has been done by the restrictive immigration law. This saves the American job for the American workmen. I should like to see the administrative features of this law rendered a little more humane for the purpose of permitting those already here a greater latitude in securing admission of members of their own families. But I believe this law in principle is necessary and sound, and destined to increase greatly the public welfare. We must maintain our own economic position, we must defend our own national integrity.

It is gratifying to report that the progress of industry, the enormous increase in individual productivity through labor-saving devices, and the high rate of wages have all combined to furnish our people in general with such an abundance not only of the necessaries but of the conveniences of life that we are by a natural evolution solving our problems of economic and social justice.

THE NEGRO

These developments have brought about a very remarkable improvement in the condition of the negro race. Gradually, but surely, with the almost universal sympathy of those among whom they live, the colored people are working out their own destiny. I firmly believe that it is better for all concerned that they should be cheerfully accorded their full constitutional rights, that they should be protected from all of those impositions to which, from their position, they naturally fall a prey, especially from the crime of lynching, and that they should receive every encouragement to become full partakers in all the blessings of our common American citizenship.

CIVIL SERVICE

The merit system has long been recognized as the correct basis for employment in our civil service. I believe that first, second, and third class postmasters, and without covering in the present membership the field force of prohibition enforcement, should be brought within the classified service by statute law. Otherwise the Executive order of one administration is changed by the Executive order of another administration, and little real progress is made. Whatever its defects, the merit system is certainly to be preferred to the spoils system.

DEPARTMENTAL REORGANIZATION

One way to save public money would be to pass the pending bill for the reorganization of the various departments. This project has been pending for some time, and has had the most careful consideration of experts and the thorough study of a special congressional committee. This legislation is vital as a companion piece to the Budget law. Legal authority for a thorough reorganization of the Federal structure with some latitude of action to the Executive in the rearrangement of secondary functions would make for continuing economy in the shift of Government activities which must follow every change in a developing country. Beyond this many of the independent agencies of the Government must be placed under responsible Cabinet officials, if we are to have safeguards of efficiency, economy, and probity.

ARMY AND NAVY

Little has developed in relation to our national defense which needs special attention. Progress is constantly being made in air navigation and requires encouragement and development. Army aviators have made a successful trip around the world, for which I recommend suitable recognition through provisions for promotion, compensation, and retirement. Under the direction of the Navy a new Zeppelin has been successfully brought from Europe across the Atlantic to our own country.

Due to the efficient supervision of the Secretary of War the Army of the United States has been organized with a small body of Regulars and a moderate National Guard and Reserve. The defense test of September 12 demonstrated the efficiency of the operating plans. These methods and operations are well worthy of congressional support.

Under the limitation of armaments treaty a large saving in outlay and a considerable decrease in maintenance of the Navy has been accomplished. We should maintain the policy of constantly working toward the full treaty strength of the Navy. Careful investigation is being made in this department of the relative importance of aircraft, surface and submarine vessels, in order that we may not fail to take advantage of all modern improvements for our national defense. A special commission also is investigating the problem of petroleum oil for the Navy, considering the best policy to insure the future supply of fuel oil and prevent the threatened drainage of naval oil reserves. Legislative action is required to carry on experiments in oil shale reduction, as large deposits of this type have been set aside for the use of the Navy.

We have been constantly besought to engage in competitive armaments. Frequent reports will reach us of the magnitude of the military equipment of other nations. We shall do well to be little impressed by such reports or such actions. Any nation undertaking to maintain a military establishment with aggressive and imperialistic designs will find itself severely handicapped in the economic development of the world. I believe thoroughly in the Army and Navy, in adequate defense and preparation. But I am opposed to any policy of competition in building and maintaining land or sea armaments.

Our country has definitely relinquished the old standard of dealing with other countries by terror and force, and is definitely committed to the new standard of dealing with them through friendship and understanding. This new policy should be constantly kept in mind by the guiding forces of the Army and Navy, by the Congress and by the country at large. I believe it holds a promise of great benefit to humanity. I shall resist any attempt to resort to the old methods and the old standards. I am especially solicitous that foreign nations should comprehend the candor and sincerity with which we have adopted this position. While we propose to maintain defensive and supplementary police forces by land and sea, and to train them through inspections and maneuvers upon appropriate occasions in order to maintain their efficiency, I wish every other nation to understand that this does not express any unfriendliness or convey any hostile intent. I want the armed forces of America to be considered by all peoples not as enemies but as friends, as the contribution which is made by this country for the maintenance of the peace and security of the world.

VETERANS

With the authorization for general hospitalization of the veterans of all wars provided during the present year, the care and treatment of those who have served their country in time of peril and the attitude of the Government toward them is not now so much one of needed legislation as one of careful, generous and humane administration. It will ever be recognized that their welfare is of the first concern and always entitled to the most solicitous consideration on the part of their fellow citizens. They are organized in various associations, of which the chief and most representative is the American Legion. Through its officers the Legion will present to the Congress numerous suggestions for legislation. They cover such a wide variety of subjects that it is impossible to discuss them within the scope of this message. With many of the proposals I join in hearty approval and commend them all to the sympathetic investigation and consideration of the Congress.

FOREIGN RELATIONS

At no period in the past 12 years have our foreign relations been in such a satisfactory condition as they are at the present time. Our actions in the recent months have greatly strengthened the American policy of permanent peace with independence. The attitude which our Government took and maintained toward an adjustment of European reparations, by pointing out that it was not a political but a business problem, has demonstrated its wisdom by its actual results. We desire to see Europe restored that it may resume its productivity in the increase of industry and its support in the advance of civilization. We look with great gratification at the hopeful prospect of recuperation in Europe through the Dawes plan. Such assistance as can be given through the action of the public authorities and of our private citizens, through friendly counsel and cooperation, and through economic and financial support, not for any warlike effort but for reproductive enterprise, not to provide means for unsound government financing but to establish sound business administration, should be unhesitatingly provided.

Ultimately nations, like individuals, can not depend upon each other but must depend upon themselves. Each one must work out its own salvation. We have every desire to help. But with all our resources we are powerless to save unless our efforts meet with a constructive response. The situation in our own country and all over the world is one that can be improved only by hard work and self-denial. It is necessary to reduce expenditures, increase savings and liquidate debts. It is in this direction that there lies the greatest hope of domestic tranquillity and international peace. Our own country ought to furnish the leading example in this effort. Our past adherence to this policy, our constant refusal to maintain a military establishment that could be thought to menace the security of others, our honorable dealings with other nations whether great or small, has left us in the almost constant enjoyment of peace.

It is not necessary to stress the general desire of all the people of this country for the promotion of peace. It is the leading principle of all our foreign relations. We have on every occasion tried to cooperate to this end in all ways that were consistent with our proper independence and our traditional policies. It will be my constant effort to maintain these principles, and to reinforce them by all appropriate agreements and treaties. While we desire always to cooperate and to help, we are equally determined to be independent and free. Right and truth and justice and humanitarian efforts will have the moral support of this country all over the world. But we do not wish to become involved in the political controversies of others. Nor is the country disposed to become a member of the League of Nations or to assume the obligations imposed by its covenant.

INTERNATIONAL COURT

America has been one of the foremost nations in advocating tribunals for the settlement of international disputes of a justiciable character. Our representatives took a leading part in those conferences which resulted in the establishment of The Hague Tribunal, and later in providing for a Permanent Court of International Justice. I believe it would be for the advantage of this country and helpful to the stability of other nations for us to adhere to the protocol establishing that court upon the conditions stated in the recommendation which is now before the Senate, and further that our country shall not be bound by advisory opinions which may be rendered by the court upon questions which we have not voluntarily submitted for its judgment. This court would provide a practical and convenient tribunal before which we could go voluntarily, but to which we could not be summoned, for a determination of justiciable questions when they fail to be resolved by diplomatic negotiations.

DISARMAMENT CONFERENCE

Many times I have expressed my desire to see the work of the Washington Conference on Limitation of Armaments appropriately supplemented by further agreements for a further reduction and for the purpose of diminishing the menace and waste of the competition in preparing instruments of international war. It has been and is my expectation that we might hopefully approach other great powers for further conference on this subject as soon as the carrying out of the present reparation plan as the established and settled policy of Europe has created a favorable opportunity. But on account of proposals which have already been made by other governments for a European conference, it will be necessary to wait to see what the outcome of their actions may be. I should not wish to propose or have representatives attend a conference which would contemplate commitments opposed to the freedom of action we desire to maintain unimpaired with respect to our purely domestic policies.

INTERNATIONAL LAW

Our country should also support efforts which are being made toward the codification of international law. We can look more hopefully, in the first instance, for research and studies that are likely to be productive of results, to a cooperation among representatives of the bar and members of international law institutes and societies, than to a conference of those who are technically representative of their respective governments, although, when projects have been developed, they must go to the governments for their approval. These expert professional studies are going on in certain quarters and should have our constant encouragement and approval.

OUTLAW OF WAR

Much interest has of late been manifested in this country in the discussion of various proposals to outlaw aggressive war. I look with great sympathy upon the examination of this subject. It is in harmony with the traditional policy of our country, which is against aggressive war and for the maintenance of permanent and honorable peace. While, as I have said, we must safeguard our liberty to deal according to our own judgment with our domestic policies, we can not fail to view with sympathetic interest all progress to this desired end or carefully to study the measures that may be proposed to attain it.

LATIN AMERICA

While we are desirous of promoting peace in every quarter of the globe, we have a special interest in the peace of this hemisphere. It is our constant desire that all causes of dispute in this area may be tranquilly and satisfactorily adjusted. Along with our desire for peace is the earnest hope for the increased prosperity of our sister republics of Latin America, and our constant purpose to promote cooperation with them which may be mutually beneficial and always inspired by the most cordial friendships.

FOREIGN DEBTS

About $12,000,000,000 is due to our Government from abroad, mostly from European Governments. Great Britain, Finland, Hungary, Lithuania and Poland have negotiated settlements amounting close to $5,000,000,000. This represents the funding of over 42 per cent of the debt since the creation of the special Foreign Debt Commission. As the life of this commission is about to expire, its term should be extended. I am opposed to the cancellation of these debts and believe it for the best welfare of the world that they should be liquidated and paid as fast as possible. I do not favor oppressive measures, but unless money that is borrowed is repaid credit can not be secured in time of necessity, and there exists besides a moral obligation which our country can not ignore and no other country can evade. Terms and conditions may have to conform to differences in the financial abilities of the countries concerned, but the principle that each country should meet its obligation admits of no differences and is of universal application.

It is axiomatic that our country can not stand still. It would seem to be perfectly plain from recent events that it is determined to go forward. But it wants no pretenses, it wants no vagaries. It is determined to advance in an orderly, sound and common-sense way. It does not propose to abandon the theory of the Declaration that the people have inalienable rights which no majority and no power of government can destroy. It does not propose to abandon the practice of the Constitution that provides for the protection of these rights. It believes that within these limitations, which are imposed not by the fiat of man but by the law of the Creator, self-government is just and wise. It is convinced that it will be impossible for the people to provide their own government unless they continue to own their own property.

These are the very foundations of America. On them has been erected a Government of freedom and equality, of justice and mercy, of education and charity. Living under it and supporting it the people have come into great possessions on the material and spiritual sides of life. I want to continue in this direction. I know that the Congress shares with me that desire. I want our institutions to be more and more expressive of these principles. I want the people of all the earth to see in the American flag the symbol of a Government which intends no oppression at home and no aggression abroad, which in the spirit of a common brotherhood provides assistance in time of distress.

THIRD ANNUAL MESSAGE.

[Read to Congress on December 8, 1925.]

Members of the Congress:

In meeting the constitutional requirement of informing the Congress upon the state of the Union, it is exceedingly gratifying to report that the general condition is one of progress and prosperity. Here and there are comparatively small and apparently temporary difficulties needing adjustment and improved administrative methods, such as are always to be expected, but in the fundamentals of government and business the results demonstrate that we are going in the right direction. The country does not appear to require radical departures from the policies already adopted so much as it needs a further extension of these policies and the improvement of details. The age of perfection is still in the somewhat distant future, but it is more in danger of being retarded by mistaken Government activity than it is from lack of legislation. We are by far the most likely to accomplish permanent good if we proceed with moderation.

In our country the people are sovereign and independent, and must accept the resulting responsibilities. It is their duty to support themselves and support the Government. That is the business of the Nation, whatever the charity of the Nation may require. The functions which the Congress are to discharge are not those of local government but of National Government. The greatest solicitude should be exercised to prevent any encroachment upon the rights of the States or their various political subdivisions. Local self-government is one of our most precious possessions. It is the greatest contributing factor to the stability, strength, liberty, and progress of the Nation. It ought not to be infringed by assault or undermined by purchase. It ought not to abdicate its power through weakness or resign its authority through favor. It does not at all follow that because abuses exist it is the concern of the Federal Government to attempt their reform.

Society is in much more danger from encumbering the National Government beyond its wisdom to comprehend, or its ability to administer, than from leaving the local communities to bear their own burdens and remedy their own evils. Our local habit and custom is so strong, our variety of race and creed is so great, the Federal authority is so tenuous, that the area within which it can function successfully is very limited. The wiser policy is to leave the localities, so far as we can, possessed of their own sources of revenue and charged with their own obligations.

GOVERNMENT ECONOMY

It is a fundamental principle of our country that the people are sovereign. While they recognize the undeniable authority of the state, they have established as its instrument a Government of limited powers. They hold inviolate in their own hands the jurisdiction over their own freedom and the ownership of their own property. Neither of these can be impaired except by due process of law. The wealth of our country is not public wealth, but private wealth. It does not belong to the Government, it belongs to the people. The Government has no justification in taking private property except for a public purpose. It is always necessary to keep these principles in mind in the laying of taxes and in the making of appropriations. No right exists to levy on a dollar, or to order the expenditure of a dollar, of the money of the people, except for a necessary public purpose duly authorized by the Constitution. The power over the purse is the power over liberty.

That is the legal limitation within which the Congress can act. How it will proceed within this limitation is always a question of policy. When the country is prosperous and free from debt, when the rate of taxation is low, opportunity exists for assuming new burdens and undertaking new enterprises. Such a condition now prevails only to a limited extent. All proposals for assuming new obligations ought to be postponed, unless they are reproductive capital investments or are such as are absolutely necessary at this time. We still have an enormous debt of over $20,000,000,000, on which the interest and sinking-fund requirements are $1,320,000,000. Our appropriations for the Pension Office and the Veterans' Bureau are $600,000,000. The War and Navy Departments call for $642,000,000. Other requirements, exclusive of the Post Office, which is virtually self-sustaining, brought the appropriations for the current year up to almost $3,100,000,000. This shows an expenditure of close to $30 for every inhabitant of our country. For the average family of five it means a tax, directly or indirectly paid, of about $150 for national purposes alone. The local tax adds much more. These enormous expenditures ought not to be increased, but through every possible effort they ought to be reduced.

Only one of these great items can be ultimately extinguished.

That is the item of our war debt. Already this has been reduced by about $6,000,000,000, which means an annual saving in interest of close to $250,000,000. The present interest charge is about $820,000,000 yearly. It would seem to be obvious that the sooner this debt can be retired the more the taxpayers will save in interest and the easier it will be to secure funds with which to prosecute needed running expenses, constructions, and improvements. This item of $820,000,000 for interest is a heavy charge on all the people of the country, and it seems to me that we might well consider whether it is not greatly worth while to dispense with it as early as possible by retiring the principal debt which it is required to serve.

It has always been our policy to retire our debts. That of the Revolutionary War period, notwithstanding the additions made in 1812, was paid by 1835, and the Civil War debt within 23 years. Of the amount already paid, over $1,000,000,000 is a reduction in cash balances. That source is exhausted. Over one and two-thirds billions of dollars was derived from excess receipts. Tax reduction eliminates that. The sale of surplus war materials has been another element of our income. That is practically finished. With these eliminated, the reduction of the debt has been only about $500,000,000 each year, not an excessive sum on so large a debt.

Proposals have been made to extend the payment over a period of 62 years. If $1,000,000,000 is paid at the end of 20 years, the cost to the taxpayers is the principal and, if the interest is 4¼ per cent, a total of $1,850,000,000. If the same sum is paid at the end of 62 years, the cost is $3,635,000,000, or almost double. Here is another consideration: Compared with its purchasing power in 1913, the dollar we borrowed represented but 52 cents. As the value of our dollar increases, due to the falling prices of commodities, the burden of our debt increases. It has now risen to 63½ cents. The taxpayer will be required to produce nearly twice the amount of commodities to pay his debt if the dollar returns to the 1913 value. The more we pay while prices are high, the easier it will be.

Deflation of government after a war period is slower than deflation of business, where curtailment is either prompt and effective or disaster follows. There is room for further economy in the cost of the Federal Government, but a comparison of current expenditures with pre-war expenditures is not unfavorable to the efficiency with which Government business is now being done. The expenditures of 1916, the last pre-war year, were $742,000,000, and in 1925 over $3,500,000,000, or nearly five times as great. If we subtract expenditures for debt retirements and interest, veterans' relief, increase of pensions, and other special outlays, consisting of refunds, trust investments, and like charges, we find that the general expenditures of the Government in 1925 were slightly more than twice as large as in 1916.

As prices in 1925 were approximately 40 per cent higher than in 1916, the cost of the same Government must also have increased. But the Government is not the same. It is more expensive to collect the much greater revenue necessary and to administer our great debt. We have given enlarged and improved services to agriculture and commerce. Above all, America has grown in population and wealth. Government expenditures must always share in this growth. Taking into account the factors I have mentioned, I believe that present Federal expenses are not far out of line with pre-war expenses. We have nearly accomplished the deflation.

This does not mean that further economies will not come. As we reduce our debt our interest charges decline. There are many details yet to correct. The real improvement, however, must come not from additional curtailment of expenses, but by a more intelligent, more ordered spending. Our economy must be constructive. While we should avoid as far as possible increases in permanent current expenditures, oftentimes a capital outlay like internal improvements will result in actual constructive saving. That is economy in its best sense. It is an avoidance of waste that there may be the means for an outlay to-day which will bring larger returns to-morrow. We should constantly engage in scientific studies of our future requirements and adopt an orderly program for their service. Economy is the method by which we prepare to-day to afford the improvements of to-morrow.

A mere policy of economy without any instrumentalities for putting it into operation would be very ineffective. The Congress has wisely set up the Bureau of the Budget to investigate and inform the President what recommendations he ought to make for current appropriations. This gives a centralized authority where a general and comprehensive understanding can be reached of the sources of income and the most equitable distribution of expenditures. How well it has worked is indicated by the fact that the departmental estimates for 1922, before the budget law, were $4,068,000,000 while the Budget estimates for 1927 are $3,156,000,000. This latter figure shows the reductions in departmental estimates for the coming year made possible by the operation of the Budget system that the Congress has provided.

But it is evidently not enough to have care in making appropriations without any restraint upon expenditure. The Congress has provided that check by establishing the office of Comptroller General.

The purpose of maintaining the Budget Director and the Comptroller General is to secure economy and efficiency in Government expenditure. No better method has been devised for the accomplishment of that end. These offices can not be administered in all the various details without making some errors both of fact and of judgment. But the important consideration remains that these are the instrumentalities of the Congress and that no other plan has ever been adopted which was so successful in promoting economy and efficiency. The Congress has absolute authority over the appropriations and is free to exercise its judgment, as the evidence may warrant, in increasing or decreasing budget recommendations. But it ought to resist every effort to weaken or break down this most beneficial system of supervising appropriations and expenditures. Without it all the claim of economy would be a mere pretense.

TAXATION

The purpose of reducing expenditures is to secure a reduction in taxes. That purpose is about to be realized. With commendable promptness the Ways and Means Committee of the House has undertaken in advance of the meeting of the Congress to frame a revenue act. As the bill has proceeded through the committee it has taken on a nonpartisan character, and both Republicans and Democrats have joined in a measure which embodies many sound principles of tax reform. The bill will correct substantially the economic defects injected into the revenue act of 1924, as well as many which have remained as war-time legacies. In its present form it should provide sufficient revenue for the Government.

The excessive surtaxes have been reduced, estate tax rates are restored to more reasonable figures, with every prospect of withdrawing from the field when the States have had the opportunity to correct the abuses in their own inheritance tax laws, the gift tax and publicity section are to be repealed, many miscellaneous taxes are lowered or abandoned, and the Board of Tax Appeals and the administrative features of the law are improved and strengthened. I approve of the bill in principle. In so far as income-tax exemptions are concerned, it seems to me the committee has gone as far as it is safe to go and somewhat further than I should have gone. Any further extension along these lines would, in my opinion, impair the integrity of our income-tax system.

I am advised that the bill will be through the House by Christmas. For this prompt action the country can thank the good sense of the Ways and Means Committee in framing an economic measure upon economic considerations. If this attitude continues to be reflected through the Congress, the taxpayer will have his relief by the time his March 15th installment of income taxes is due. Nonpartisan effort means certain, quick action. Determination of a revenue law definitely, promptly and solely as a revenue law, is one of the greatest gifts a legislature can bestow upon its constituents. I commend the example of the Ways and Means Committee. If followed, it will place sound legislation upon the books in time to give the taxpayers the full benefit of tax reduction next year. This means that the bill should reach me prior to March 15.

All these economic results are being sought not to benefit the rich, but to benefit the people. They are for the purpose of encouraging industry in order that employment may be plentiful. They seek to make business good in order that wages may be good. They encourage prosperity in order that poverty may be banished from the home. They seek to lay the foundation which, through increased production, may give the people a more bountiful supply of the necessaries of life, afford more leisure for the improvement of the mind, the appreciation of the arts of music and literature, sculpture and painting, and the beneficial enjoyment of outdoor sports and recreation, enlarge the resources which minister to charity and by all these means attempting to strengthen the spiritual life of the Nation.

FOREIGN RELATIONS

The policy of our foreign relations, casting aside any suggestion of force, rests solely on the foundation of peace, good will, and good works. We have sought, in our intercourse with other nations, better understandings through conference and exchange of views as befits beings endowed with reason. The results have been the gradual elimination of disputes, the settlement of controversies, and the establishment of a firmer friendship between America and the rest of the world than has ever existed at any previous time.

The example of this attitude has not been without its influence upon other countries. Acting upon it, an adjustment was made of the difficult problem of reparations. This was the second step toward peace in Europe. It paved the way for the agreements which were drawn up at the Locarno Conference. When ratified, these will represent the third step toward peace. While they do not of themselves provide an economic rehabilitation, which is necessary for the progress of Europe, by strengthening the guaranties of peace they diminish the need for great armaments. If the energy which now goes into military effort is transferred to productive endeavor, it will greatly assist economic progress.

The Locarno agreements were made by the European countries directly interested without any formal intervention of America, although on July 3 I publicly advocated such agreements in an address made in Massachusetts. We have consistently refrained from intervening except when our help has been sought and we have felt it could be effectively given, as in the settlement of reparations and the London Conference. These recent Locarno agreements represent the success of this policy which we have been insisting ought to be adopted, of having European countries settle their own political problems without involving this country. This beginning seems to demonstrate that this policy is sound. It is exceedingly gratifying to observe this progress, which both in its method and in its result promises so much that is beneficial to the world.

When these agreements are finally adopted, they will provide guaranties of peace that make the present prime reliance upon force in some parts of Europe very much less necessary. The natural corollary to these treaties should be further international contracts for the limitation of armaments. This work was successfully begun at the Washington Conference. Nothing was done at that time concerning land forces because of European objection. Our standing army has been reduced to around 118,000, about the necessary police force for 115,000,000 people. We are not proposing to increase it, nor is it supposable that any foreign country looks with the slightest misapprehension upon our land forces. They do not menace anybody. They are rather a protection to everybody.

The question of disarming upon land is so peculiarly European in its practical aspects that our country would look with particular gratitude upon any action which those countries might take to reduce their own military forces. This is in accordance with our policy of not intervening unless the European powers are unable to agree and make request for our assistance. Whenever they are able to agree of their own accord it is especially gratifying to us, and such agreements may be sure of our sympathetic support.

It seems clear that it is the reduction of armies rather than of navies that is of the first importance to the world at the present time. We shall look with great satisfaction upon that effort and give it our approbation and encouragement. If that can be settled, we may more easily consider further reduction and limitation of naval armaments. For that purpose our country has constantly through its Executive, and through repeated acts of Congress, indicated its willingness to call such a conference. Under congressional sanction it would seem to be wise to participate in any conference of the great powers for naval limitation of armament proposed upon such conditions that it would hold a fair promise of being effective. The general policy of our country is for disarmament, and it ought not to hesitate to adopt any practical plan that might reasonably be expected to succeed. But it would not care to attend a conference which from its location or constituency would in all probability prove futile.

In the further pursuit of strengthening the bonds of peace and good will we have joined with other nations in an international conference held at Geneva and signed an agreement which will be laid before the Senate for ratification providing suitable measures for control and for publicity in international trade in arms, ammunition, and implements of war, and also executed a protocol providing for a prohibition of the use of poison gas in war, in accordance with the principles of Article 5 of the treaty relating thereto signed at the Washington Conference. We are supporting the Pan American efforts that are being made toward the codification of international law, and looking with sympathy on the investigations being conducted under philanthropic auspices of the proposal to make agreements outlawing war. In accordance with promises made at the Washington Conference, we have urged the calling of and are now represented at the Chinese Customs Conference and on the Commission on Extraterritoriality, where it will be our policy so far as possible to meet the aspirations of China in all ways consistent with the interests of the countries involved.

COURT OF INTERNATIONAL JUSTICE

Pending before the Senate for nearly three years is the proposal to adhere to the protocol establishing the Permanent Court of International Justice. A well-established line of precedents mark America's effort to effect the establishment of a court of this nature. We took a leading part in laying the foundation on which it rests in the establishment of The Hague Court of Arbitration. It is that tribunal which nominates the judges who are elected by the Council and Assembly of the League of Nations.

The proposal submitted to the Senate was made dependent upon four conditions, the first of which is that by supporting the court we do not assume any obligations under the league; second, that we may participate upon an equality with other States in the election of judges; third, that the Congress shall determine what part of the expenses we shall bear; fourth, that the statute creating the court shall not be amended without our consent; and to these I have proposed an additional condition to the effect that we are not to be bound by advisory opinions rendered without our consent.

The court appears to be independent of the league. It is true the judges are elected by the Assembly and Council, but they are nominated by the Court of Arbitration, which we assisted to create and of which we are a part. The court was created by a statute, so-called, which is really a treaty made among some forty-eight different countries, that might properly be called a constitution of the court. This statute provides a method by which the judges are chosen, so that when the Court of Arbitration nominates them and the Assembly and Council of the League elect them, they are not acting as instruments of the Court of Arbitration or instruments of the league, but as instruments of the statute.

This will be even more apparent if our representatives sit with the members of the council and assembly in electing the judges. It is true they are paid through the league though not by the league, but by the countries which are members of the league and by our country if we accept the protocol. The judges are paid by the league only in the same sense that it could be said United States judges are paid by the Congress. The court derives all its authority from the statute and is so completely independent of the league that it could go on functioning if the league were disbanded, at least until the terms of the judges expired.

The most careful provisions are made in the statute as to the qualifications of judges. Those who make the nominations are recommended to consult with their highest court of justice, their law schools and academies. The judges must be persons of high moral character, qualified to hold the highest judicial offices in that country, or be jurisconsults of recognized competence in international law. It must be assumed that these requirements will continue to be carefully met, and with America joining the countries already concerned it is difficult to comprehend how human ingenuity could better provide for the establishment of a court which would maintain its independence. It has to be recognized that independence is to a considerable extent a matter of ability, character, and personality. Some effort was made in the early beginnings to interfere with the independence of our Supreme Court. It did not succeed because of the quality of the men who made up that tribunal.

It does not seem that the authority to give advisory opinions interferes with the independence of the court. Advisory opinions in and of themselves are not harmful, but may be used in such a way as to be very beneficial because they undertake to prevent injury rather than merely afford a remedy after the injury has been done. As a principle that only implies that the court shall function when proper application is made to it. Deciding the question involved upon issues submitted for an advisory opinion does not differ materially from deciding the question involved upon issues submitted by contending parties. Up to the present time the court has given an advisory opinion when it judged it had jurisdiction, and refused to give one when it judged it did not have jurisdiction. Nothing in the work of the court has yet been an indication that this is an impairment of its independence or that its practice differs materially from the giving of like opinions under the authority of the constitutions of several of our States.

No provision of the statute seems to me to give this court any authority to be a political rather than a judicial court. We have brought cases in this country before our courts which, when they have been adjudged to be political, have been thereby dismissed. It is not improbable that political questions will be submitted to this court, but again up to the present time the court has refused to pass on political questions and our support would undoubtedly have a tendency to strengthen it in that refusal.

We are not proposing to subject ourselves to any compulsory jurisdiction. If we support the court, we can never be obliged to submit any case which involves our interests for its decision. Our appearance before it would always be voluntary, for the purpose of presenting a case which we had agreed might be presented. There is no more danger that others might bring cases before the court involving our interests which we did not wish to have brought, after we have adhered, and probably not so much, than there would be of bringing such cases if we do not adhere. I think that we would have the same legal or moral right to disregard such a finding in the one case that we would in the other.

If we are going to support any court, it will not be one that we have set up alone or which reflects only our ideals. Other nations have their customs and their institutions, their thoughts and their methods of life. If a court is going to be international, its composition will have to yield to what is good in all these various elements. Neither will it be possible to support a court which is exactly perfect, or under which we assume absolutely no obligations. If we are seeking that opportunity, we might as well declare that we are opposed to supporting any court. If any agreement is made, it will be because it undertakes to set up a tribunal which can do some of the things that other nations wish to have done. We shall not find ourselves bearing a disproportionate share of the world's burdens by our adherence, and we may as well remember that there is absolutely no escape for our country from bearing its share of the world's burdens in any case. We shall do far better service to ourselves and to others if we admit this and discharge our duties voluntarily, than if we deny it and are forced to meet the same obligations unwillingly.

It is difficult to imagine anything that would be more helpful to the world than stability, tranquillity and international justice. We may say that we are contributing to these factors independently, but others less fortunately located do not and can not make a like contribution except through mutual cooperation. The old balance of power, mutual alliances, and great military forces were not brought about by any mutual dislike for independence, but resulted from the domination of circumstances. Ultimately they were forced on us. Like all others engaged in the war whatever we said as a matter of fact we joined an alliance, we became a military power, we impaired our independence. We have more at stake than any one else in avoiding a repetition of that calamity. Wars do not spring into existence. They arise from small incidents and trifling irritations which can be adjusted by an international court. We can contribute greatly to the advancement of our ideals by joining with other nations in maintaining such a tribunal.

FOREIGN DEBTS

Gradually, settlements have been made which provide for the liquidation of debts due to our Government from foreign governments. Those made with Great Britain, Finland, Hungary, Lithuania, and Poland have already been approved by the Congress. Since the adjournment, further agreements have been entered into with Belgium, Czechoslovakia, Latvia, Esthonia, Italy, and Rumania. These 11 nations, which have already made settlements, represent $6,419,528,641 of the original principal of the loans. The principal sums without interest, still pending, are the debt of France, of

$3,340,000,000; Greece, $15,000,000; Yugoslavia, $51,000,000; Liberia, $26,000; Russia, $192,000,000, which those at present in control have undertaken openly to repudiate; Nicaragua, $84,000, which is being paid currently; and Austria, $24,000,000, on which by act of Congress a moratorium of 20 years has been granted. The only remaining sum is $12,000,000, due from Armenia, which has now ceased to exist as an independent nation.

In accordance with the settlements made, the amount of principal and interest which is to be paid to the United States under these agreements aggregates $15,200,688,253.93. It is obvious that the remaining settlements, which will undoubtedly be made, will bring this sum up to an amount which will more than equal the principal due on our present national debt. While these settlements are very large in the aggregate, it has been felt that the terms granted were in all cases very generous. They impose no undue burden and are mutually beneficial in the observance of international faith and the improvement of international credit.

Every reasonable effort will be made to secure agreements for liquidation with the remaining countries, whenever they are in such condition that they can be made. Those which have already been negotiated under the bipartisan commission established by the Congress have been made only after the most thoroughgoing and painstaking investigation, continued for a long time before meeting with the representatives of the countries concerned. It is believed that they represent in each instance the best that can be done and the wisest settlement that can be secured. One very important result is the stabilization of foreign currency, making exchange assist rather than embarrass our trade. Wherever sacrifices have been made of money, it will be more than amply returned in better understanding and friendship, while in so far as these adjustments will contribute to the financial stability of the debtor countries, to their good order, prosperity, and progress, they represent hope of improved trade relations and mutual contributions to the civilization of the world.

ALIEN PROPERTY

Negotiations are progressing among the interested parties in relation to the final distribution of the assets in the hands of the Alien Property Custodian. Our Government and people are interested as creditors; the German Government and people are interested as debtors and owners of the seized property. Pending the outcome of these negotiations, I do not recommend any affirmative legislation. For the present we should continue in possession of this property which we hold as security for the settlement of claims due to our people and our Government.

IMMIGRATION

While not enough time has elapsed to afford a conclusive demonstration, such results as have been secured indicate that our immigration law is on the whole beneficial. It is undoubtedly a protection to the wage earners of this country. The situation should, however, be carefully surveyed, in order to ascertain whether it is working a needless hardship upon our own inhabitants. If it deprives them of the comfort and society of those bound to them by close family ties, such modifications should be adopted as will afford relief, always in accordance with the principle that our Government owes its first duty to our own people and that no alien, inhabitant of another country, has any legal rights whatever under our Constitution and laws. It is only through treaty, or through residence here, that such rights accrue. But we should not, however, be forgetful of the obligations of a common humanity.

While our country numbers among its best citizens many of those of foreign birth, yet those who now enter in violation of our laws by that very act thereby place themselves in a class of undesirables. If investigation reveals that any considerable number are coming here in defiance of our immigration restrictions, it will undoubtedly create the necessity for the registration of all aliens. We ought to have no prejudice against an alien because he is an alien. The standard which we apply to our inhabitants is that of manhood, not place of birth. Restrictive immigration is to a large degree for economic purposes. It is applied in order that we may not have a larger annual increment of good people within our borders than we can weave into our economic fabric in such a way as to supply their needs without undue injury to ourselves.

NATIONAL DEFENSE

Never before in time of peace has our country maintained so large and effective a military force as it now has. The Army, Navy, Marine Corps, National Guard, and Organized Reserves represent a strength of about 558,400 men. These forces are well trained, well equipped, and high in morale.

A sound selective service act giving broad authority for the mobilization in time of peril of all the resources of the country, both persons and materials, is needed to perfect our defensive policy in accordance with our ideals of equality. The provision for more suitable housing to be paid for out of funds derived from the sale of excess lands, pending before the last Congress, ought to be brought forward and passed. Reasonable replacements ought to be made to maintain a sufficient ammunition reserve.

The Navy has the full treaty tonnage of capital ships. Work is going forward in modernizing the older ones, building aircraft carriers, additional fleet submarines, and fast scout cruisers, but we are carefully avoiding anything that might be construed as a competition in armaments with other nations. The joint Army and Navy maneuvers at Hawaii, followed by the cruise of a full Battle Fleet to Australia and New Zealand, were successfully carried out. These demonstrations revealed a most satisfactory condition of the ships and the men engaged.

Last year at my suggestion the General Board of the Navy made an investigation and report on the relation of aircraft to warships. As a result authorizations and appropriations were made for more scout cruisers and fleet submarines and for completing aircraft carriers and equipping them with necessary planes. Additional training in aviation was begun at the Military and Naval Academies. A method of coordination and cooperation of the Army and Navy and the principal aircraft builders is being perfected. At the suggestion of the Secretaries of War and Navy I appointed a special board to make a further study of the problem of aircraft.

The report of the Air Board ought to be reassuring to the country, gratifying to the service and satisfactory to the Congress. It is thoroughly complete and represents the mature thought of the best talent in the country. No radical change in organization of the service seems necessary. The Departments of War, Navy, and Commerce should each be provided with an additional assistant secretary, not necessarily with statutory duties but who would be available under the direction of the Secretary to give especial attention to air navigation. We must have an air strength worthy of America. Provision should be made for two additional brigadier generals for the Army Air Service. Temporary rank corresponding to their duties should be awarded to active flying officers in both Army and Navy.

Aviation is of great importance both for national defense and commercial development. We ought to proceed in its improvement by the necessary experiment and investigation. Our country is not behind in this art. It has made records for speed and for the excellence of its planes. It ought to go on maintaining its manufacturing plants capable of rapid production, giving national assistance to the laying out of airways, equipping itself with a moderate number of planes, and keeping an air force trained to the highest efficiency.

While I am a thorough believer in national defense and entirely committed to the policy of adequate preparation, I am just as thoroughly opposed to instigating or participating in a policy of competitive armaments. Nor does preparation mean a policy of militarizing. Our people and industries are solicitous for the cause of our country, and have great respect for the Army and Navy and for the uniform worn by the men who stand ready at all times for our protection to encounter the dangers and perils necessary to military service, but all of these activities are to be taken not in behalf of aggression but in behalf of peace. They are the instruments by which we undertake to do our part to promote good will and support stability among all peoples.

VETERANS

If any one desires to estimate the esteem in which the veterans of America are held by their fellow citizens, it is but necessary to remember that the current budget calls for an expenditure of about $650,000,000 in their behalf. This is nearly the amount of the total cost of the National Government, exclusive of the post office, before we entered the last war.

At the two previous sessions of Congress legislation affecting veterans' relief was enacted and the law liberalized. This legislation brought into being a number of new provisions tending more nearly to meet the needs of our veterans, as well as afford the necessary authority to perfect the administration of these laws.

Experience with the new legislation so far has clearly demonstrated its constructive nature. It has increased the benefits received by many and has made eligible for benefits many others. Direct disbursements to the veteran or his dependents exceeding $21,000,000 have resulted, which otherwise would not have been made. The degree of utilization of our hospitals has increased through making facilities available to the incapacitated veteran regardless of service origin of the disability. This new legislation also has brought about a marked improvement of service to the veteran.

The organizations of ex-service men have proposed additional legislative changes which you will consider, but until the new law and the modifications made at the last session of Congress are given a more thorough test further changes in the basic law should be few and made only after careful though sympathetic consideration.

The principal work now before the Veterans' Bureau is the perfection of its organization and further improvements in service. Some minor legislative changes are deemed necessary to enable the bureau to retain that high grade of professional talent essential in handling the problems of the bureau. Such changes as tend toward the improvement of service and the carrying forward to completion of the hospital construction program are recommended for the consideration of the proper committees of Congress.

With the enormous outlay that is now being made in behalf of the veterans and their dependents, with a tremendous war debt still requiring great annual expenditure, with the still high rate of taxation, while every provision should be made for the relief of the disabled and the necessary care of dependents, the Congress may well consider whether the financial condition of the Government is not such that further bounty through the enlargement of general pensions and other emoluments ought not to be postponed.

AGRICULTURE

No doubt the position of agriculture as a whole has very much improved since the depression of three and four years ago. But there are many localities and many groups of individuals, apparently through no fault of their own, sometimes due to climatic conditions and sometimes to the prevailing price of a certain crop, still in a distressing condition. This is probably temporary, but it is none the less acute. National Government agencies, the Departments of Agriculture and Commerce, the Farm Loan Board, the intermediate credit banks, and the Federal Reserve Board are all cooperating to be of assistance and relief. On the other hand, there are localities and individuals who have had one of their most prosperous years. The general price level is fair, but here again there are exceptions both ways, some items being poor while others are excellent. In spite of a lessened production the farm income for this year will be about the same as last year and much above the three preceding years.

Agriculture is a very complex industry. It does not consist of one problem, but of several. They can not be solved at one stroke. They have to be met in different ways, and small gains are not to be despised.

It has appeared from all the investigations that I have been able to make that the farmers as a whole are determined to maintain the independence of their business. They do not wish to have meddling on the part of the Government or to be placed under the inevitable restrictions involved in any system of direct or indirect price-fixing, which would result from permitting the Government to operate in the agricultural markets. They are showing a very commendable skill in organizing themselves to transact their own business through cooperative marketing, which will this year turn over about $2,500,000,000, or nearly one-fifth of the total agricultural business. In this they are receiving help from the Government. The Department of Agriculture should be strengthened in this facility, in order to be able to respond when these marketing associations want help. While it ought not to undertake undue regulation, it should be equipped to give prompt information on crop prospects, supply, demand, current receipts, imports, exports, and prices.

A bill embodying these principles, which has been drafted under the advice and with the approval of substantially all the leaders and managers in the cooperative movement, will be presented to the Congress for its enactment. Legislation should also be considered to provide for leasing the unappropriated public domain for grazing purposes and adopting a uniform policy relative to grazing on the public lands and in the national forests.

A more intimate relation should be established between agriculture and the other business activities of the Nation. They are mutually dependent and can each advance their own prosperity most by advancing the prosperity of the other. Meantime the Government will continue those activities which have resulted in an unprecedented amount of legislation and the pouring out of great sums of money during the last five years. The work for good roads, better land and water transportation, increased support for agricultural education, extension of credit facilities through the Farm Loan Boards and the intermediate credit banks, the encouragement of orderly marketing and a repression of wasteful speculation, will all be continued.

Following every other depression, after a short period the price of farm produce has taken and maintained the lead in the advance. This advance had reached a climax before the war. Everyone will recall the discussion that went on for four or five years prior to 1914 concerning the high cost of living. This history is apparently beginning to repeat itself. While wholesale prices of other commodities have been declining, farm prices have been increasing. There is every reason to suppose that a new era in agricultural prosperity lies just before us, which will probably be unprecedented.

MUSCLE SHOALS

The problem of Muscle Shoals seems to me to have assumed a place all out of proportion with its real importance. It probably does not represent in market value much more than a first-class battleship, yet it has been discussed in the Congress over a period of years and for months at a time. It ought to be developed for the production of nitrates primarily, and incidentally for power purposes. This would serve defensive, agricultural, and industrial purposes. I am in favor of disposing of this property to meet these purposes. The findings of the special commission will be transmitted to the Congress for their information. I am convinced that the best possible disposition can be made by direct authorization of the Congress. As a means of negotiation I recommend the immediate appointment of a small joint special committee chosen from the appropriate general standing committees of the House and Senate to receive bids, which when made should be reported with recommendations as to acceptance, upon which a law should be enacted, effecting a sale to the highest bidder who will agree to carry out these purposes.

If anything were needed to demonstrate the almost utter incapacity of the National Government to deal directly with an industrial and commercial problem, it has been provided by our experience with this property. We have expended vast fortunes, we have taxed everybody, but we are unable to secure results which benefit anybody. This property ought to be transferred to private management under conditions which will dedicate it to the public purpose for which it was conceived.

RECLAMATION

The National Government is committed to a policy of reclamation and irrigation which it desires to establish on a sound basis and continue in the interest of the localities concerned. Exhaustive studies have recently been made of Federal reclamation, which have resulted in improving the projects and adjusting many difficulties. About one third of the projects is in good financial condition, another third can probably be made profitable, while the other third is under unfavorable conditions. The Congress has already provided for a survey which will soon be embodied in a report. That ought to suggest a method of relief which will make unnecessary further appeals to the Congress. Unless this can be done, Federal reclamation will be considerably retarded. With the greatly increased cost of construction and operation, it has become necessary to plan in advance, by community organization and selective agriculture, methods sufficient to repay these increasing outlays.

The human and economic interests of the farmer citizens suggest that the States should be required to exert some effort and assume some responsibility, especially in the intimate, detailed, and difficult work of securing settlers and developing farms which directly profit them, but only indirectly and remotely can reimburse the Nation. It is believed that the Federal Government should continue to be the agency for planning and constructing the great undertakings needed to regulate and bring into use the rivers of the West, many of which are interstate in character, but the detailed work of creating agricultural communities and a rural civilization on the land made ready for reclamation ought to be either transferred to the State in its entirety or made a cooperative effort of the State and Federal Government.

SHIPPING

The maintenance of a merchant marine is of the utmost importance for national defense and the service of our commerce. We have a large number of ships engaged in that service. We also have a surplus supply, costly to care for, which ought to be sold. All the investigations that have been made under my direction, and those which have been prosecuted independently, have reached the conclusion that the fleet should be under the direct control of a single executive head, while the Shipping Board should exercise its judicial and regulatory functions in accordance with its original conception. The report of Henry G. Dalton, a business man of broad experience, with a knowledge of shipping, made to me after careful investigation, will be transmitted for the information of the Congress, the studies pursued under the direction of the United States Chamber of Commerce will also be accessible, and added to these will be the report of the special committee of the House.

I do not advocate the elimination of regional considerations, but it has become apparent that without centralized executive action the management of this great business, like the management of any other great business, will flounder in incapacity and languish under a division of council. A plain and unmistakable reassertion of this principle of unified control, which I have always been advised was the intention of the Congress to apply, is necessary to increase the efficiency of our merchant fleet.

COAL

The perennial conflict in the coal industry is still going on to the great detriment of the wage earners, the owners, and especially to the public. With deposits of coal in this country capable of supplying its needs for hundreds of years, inability to manage and control this great resource for the benefit of all concerned is very close to a national economic failure. It has been the subject of repeated investigation and reiterated recommendation. Yet the industry seems never to have accepted modern methods of adjusting differences between employers and employees. The industry could serve the public much better and become subject to a much more effective method of control if regional consolidations and more freedom in the formation of marketing associations, under the supervision of the Department of Commerce, were permitted.

At the present time the National Government has little or no authority to deal with this vital necessity of the life of the country. It has permitted itself to remain so powerless that its only attitude must be humble supplication. Authority should be lodged with the President and the Departments of Commerce and Labor, giving them power to deal with an emergency. They should be able to appoint temporary boards with authority to call for witnesses and documents, conciliate differences, encourage arbitration, and in case of threatened scarcity exercise control over distribution. Making the facts public under these circumstances through a statement from an authoritative source would be of great public benefit. The report of the last coal commission should be brought forward, reconsidered, and acted upon.

PROHIBITION

Under the orderly processes of our fundamental institutions the Constitution was lately amended providing for national prohibition. The Congress passed an act for its enforcement, and similar acts have been provided by most of the States. It is the law of the land. It is the duty of all who come under its jurisdiction to observe the spirit of that law, and it is the duty of the Department of Justice and the Treasury Department to enforce it. Action to prevent smuggling, illegal transportation in interstate commerce, abuse in the use of permits, and existence of sources of supply for illegal traffic is almost entirely imposed upon the Federal Government.

Through treaties with foreign governments and increased activities of the Coast Guard, revenue agents, district attorneys, and enforcement agents effort is being made to prevent these violations. But the Constitution also puts a concurrent duty on the States. We need their active and energetic cooperation, the vigilant action of their police, and the jurisdiction of their courts to assist in enforcement. I request of the people observance, of the public officers continuing efforts for enforcement, and of the Congress favorable action on the budget recommendation for the prosecution of this work.

WATERWAY DEVELOPMENT

For many years our country has been employed in plans and operations for the development of our intracoastal and inland waterways. This work along our coast is an important adjunct to our commerce. It will be carried on, together with the further opening up of our harbors, as our resources permit. The Government made an agreement during the war to take over the Cape Cod Canal, under which the owners made valuable concessions. This pledged faith of the Government ought to be redeemed.

Two other main fields are under consideration. One is the Great Lakes and St. Lawrence, including the Erie Canal. This includes stabilizing the lake level, and is both a waterway and power project. A joint commission of the United States and Canada is working on plans and surveys which will not be completed until next April. No final determination can be made, apparently, except under treaty as to the participation of both countries. The other is the Mississippi River system. This is almost entirely devoted to navigation. Work on the Ohio River will be completed in about three years. A modern channel connecting Chicago, New Orleans, Kansas City, and Pittsburgh should be laid out and work on the tributaries prosecuted. Some work is being done of a preparatory nature along the Missouri, and large expenditures are being made yearly in the lower reaches of the Mississippi and its tributaries which contribute both to flood control and navigation. Preliminary measures are being taken on the Colorado River project, which is exceedingly important for flood control, irrigation, power development, and water supply to the area concerned. It would seem to be very doubtful, however, whether it is practical to secure affirmative action of the Congress, except under a joint agreement of the several States.

The Government has already expended large sums upon scientific research and engineering investigation in promotion of this Colorado River project. The actual progress has been retarded for many years by differences among the seven States in the basin over their relative water rights and among different groups as to methods. In an attempt to settle the primary difficulty of the water rights, Congress authorized the Colorado River Commission which agreed on November 24, 1922, upon an interstate compact to settle these rights, subject to the ratification of the State legislatures and Congress. All seven States except Arizona at one time ratified, the Arizona Legislature making certain reservations which failed to meet the approval of the governor. Subsequently an attempt was made to establish the compact upon a six-State basis, but in this case California imposed reservations. There appears to be no division of opinion upon the major principles of the compact, but difficulty in separating contentions as to methods of development from the discussion of it. It is imperative that flood control be undertaken for California and Arizona, preparation made for irrigation, for power, and for domestic water.

Some or all of these questions are combined in every proposed development. The Federal Government is interested in some of these phases, State governments and municipalities and irrigation districts in others, and private corporations in still others. Because of all this difference of view it is most desirable that Congress should consider the creation of some agency that will be able to determine methods of improvement solely upon economic and engineering facts, that would be authorized to negotiate and settle, subject to the approval of Congress, the participation, rights, and obligations of each group in any particular works. Only by some such method can early construction be secured.

WATER POWER

Along with the development of navigation should go every possible encouragement for the development of our water power. While steam still plays a dominant part, this is more and more becoming an era of electricity. Once installed, the cost is moderate, has not tended greatly to increase, and is entirely free from the unavoidable dirt and disagreeable features attendant upon the burning of coal. Every facility should be extended for the connection of the various units into a superpower plant, capable at all times of a current increasing uniformity over the entire system.

RAILROADS

The railroads throughout the country are in a fair state of prosperity. Their service is good and their supply of cars is abundant. Their condition would be improved and the public better served by a system of consolidations. I recommend that the Congress authorize such consolidations under the supervision of the Interstate Commerce Commission, with power to approve or disapprove when proposed parts are excluded or new parts added. I am informed that the railroad managers and their employees have reached a substantial agreement as to what legislation is necessary to regulate and improve their relationship. Whenever they bring forward such proposals, which seem sufficient also to protect the interests of the public, they should be enacted into law.

It is gratifying to report that both the railroad managers and railroad employees are providing boards for the mutual adjustment of differences in harmony with the principles of conference, conciliation, and arbitration. The solution of their problems ought to be an example to all other industries. Those who ask the protections of civilization should be ready to use the methods of civilization.

A strike in modern industry has many of the aspects of war in the modern world. It injures labor and it injures capital. If the industry involved is a basic one, it reduces the necessary economic surplus and, increasing the cost of living, it injures the economic welfare and general comfort of the whole people. It also involves a deeper cost. It tends to embitter and divide the community into warring classes and thus weakens the unity and power of our national life.

Labor can make no permanent gains at the cost of the general welfare. All the victories won by organized labor in the past generation have been won through the support of public opinion. The manifest inclination of the managers and employees of the railroads to adopt a policy of action in harmony with these principles marks a new epoch in our industrial life.

OUTLYING POSSESSIONS

The time has come for careful investigation of the expenditures and success of the laws by which we have undertaken to administer our outlying possessions. A very large amount of money is being expended for administration in Alaska. It appears so far out of proportion to the number of inhabitants and the amount of production as to indicate cause for thorough investigation. Likewise consideration should be given to the experience under the law which governs the Philippines. From such reports as reach me there are indications that more authority should be given to the Governor General, so that he will not be so dependent upon the local legislative body to render effective our efforts to set an example of the sound administration and good government, which is so necessary for the preparation of the Philippine people for self-government under ultimate independence. If they are to be trained in these arts, it is our duty to provide for them the best that there is.

RETIREMENT OF JUDGES

The act of March 3, 1911, ought to be amended so that the term of years of service of judges of any court of the United States requisite for retirement with pay shall be computed to include not only continuous but aggregate service.

MOTHERS' AID

The Government ought always to be alert on the side of the humanities. It ought to encourage provisions for economic justice for the defenseless. It ought to extend its relief through its national and local agencies, as may be appropriate in each case, to the suffering and the needy. It ought to be charitable.

Although more than 40 of our States have enacted measures in aid of motherhood, the District of Columbia is still without such a law. A carefully considered bill will be presented, which ought to have most thoughtful consideration in order that the Congress may adopt a measure which will be hereafter a model for all parts of the Union.

CIVIL SERVICE

In 1883 the Congress passed the civil service act, which from a modest beginning of 14,000 employees has grown until there are now 425,000 in the classified service. This has removed the clerical force of the Nation from the wasteful effects of the spoils system and made it more stable and efficient. The time has come to consider classifying all postmasters, collectors of customs, collectors of internal revenue, and prohibition agents, by an act covering in those at present in office, except when otherwise provided by Executive order.

The necessary statistics are now being gathered to form the basis of a valuation of the civil service retirement fund based on current conditions of the service. It is confidently expected that this valuation will be completed in time to be made available to the Congress during the present session. It will afford definite knowledge of existing and future liabilities under the present law and determination of liabilities under any proposed change in the present law. We should have this information before creating further obligations for retirement annuities which will become liabilities to be met in the future from the money of the taxpayer.

The classification act of 1923, with the subsequent legislative action providing for adjustment of the compensation of field service positions, has operated materially to improve employment conditions in the Federal service. The administration of the act is in the hands of an impartial board, functioning without the necessity of a direct appropriation. It would be inadvisable at this time to place in other hands the administration of this act.

FEDERAL TRADE COMMISSION

The proper function of the Federal Trade Commission is to supervise and correct those practices in commerce which are detrimental to fair competition. In this it performs a useful function and should be continued and supported. It was designed also to be a help to honest business. In my message to the Sixty-eighth Congress I recommended that changes in the procedure then existing be made. Since then the commission by its own action has reformed its rules, giving greater speed and economy in the disposal of its cases and full opportunity for those accused to be heard. These changes are improvements and, if necessary, provision should be made for their permanency.

REORGANIZATION

No final action has yet been taken on the measure providing for the reorganization of the various departments. I therefore suggest that this measure, which will be of great benefit to the efficient and economical administration of the business of the Government, be brought forward and passed.

THE NEGRO

Nearly one-tenth of our population consists of the Negro race. The progress which they have made in all the arts of civilization in the last 60 years is almost beyond belief. Our country has no more loyal citizens. But they do still need sympathy, kindness, and helpfulness. They need reassurance that the requirements of the Government and society to deal out to them even-handed justice will be met. They should be protected from all violence and supported in the peaceable enjoyment of the fruits of their labor. Those who do violence to them should be punished for their crimes. No other course of action is worthy of the American people.

Our country has many elements in its population, many different modes of thinking and living, all of which are striving in their own way to be loyal to the high ideals worthy of the crown of American citizenship. It is fundamental of our institutions that they seek to guarantee to all our inhabitants the right to live their own lives under the protection of the public law. This does not include any license to injure others materially, physically, morally, to incite revolution, or to violate the established customs which have long had the sanction of enlightened society.

But it does mean the full right to liberty and equality before the law without distinction of race or creed. This condition can not be granted to others, or enjoyed by ourselves, except by the application of the principle of broadest tolerance. Bigotry is only another name for slavery. It reduces to serfdom not only those against whom it is directed, but also those who seek to apply it. An enlarged freedom can only be secured by the application of the golden rule. No other utterance ever presented such a practical rule of life.

CONCLUSION

It is apparent that we are reaching into an era of great general prosperity. It will continue only so long as we shall use it properly. After all, there is but a fixed quantity of wealth in this country at any fixed time. The only way that we can all secure more of it is to create more. The element of time enters into production. If the people have sufficient moderation and contentment to be willing to improve their condition by the process of enlarging production, eliminating waste, and distributing equitably, a prosperity almost without limit lies before us. If the people are to be dominated by selfishness, seeking immediate riches by nonproductive speculation and by wasteful quarreling over the returns from industry, they will be confronted by the inevitable results of depression and privation. If they will continue industrious and thrifty, contented with fair wages and moderate profits, and the returns which accrue from the development of our natural resources, our prosperity will extend itself indefinitely.

In all your deliberations you should remember that the purpose of legislation is to translate principles into action. It is an effort to have our country be better by doing better. Because the thoughts and ways of people are firmly fixed and not easily changed, the field within which immediate improvement can be secured is very narrow. Legislation can provide opportunity. Whether it is taken advantage of or not depends upon the people themselves. The Government of the United States has been created by the people. It is solely responsible to them. It will be most successful if it is conducted solely for their benefit. All its efforts would be of little avail unless they brought more justice, more enlightenment, more happiness and prosperity into the home. This means an opportunity to observe religion, secure education, and earn a living under a reign of law and order. It is the growth and improvement of the material and spiritual life of the Nation. We shall not be able to gain these ends merely by our own action. If they come at all, it will be because we have been willing to work in harmony with the abiding purpose of a Divine Providence.

FOURTH ANNUAL MESSAGE.

THE WHITE HOUSE, *December 7, 1926.*

Members of the Congress:

In reporting to the Congress the state of the Union, I find it impossible to characterize it other than one of general peace and prosperity. In some quarters our diplomacy is vexed with difficult and as yet unsolved problems, but nowhere are we met with armed conflict. If some occupations and areas are not flourishing, in none does there remain any acute chronic depression. What the country requires is not so much new policies as a steady continuation of those which are already being crowned with such abundant success. It can not be too often repeated that in common with all the world we are engaged in liquidating the war.

In the present short session no great amount of new legislation is possible, but in order to comprehend what is most desirable some survey of our general situation is necessary. A large amount of time is consumed in the passage of appropriation bills. If each Congress in its opening session would make appropriations to continue for two years, very much time would be saved which could either be devoted to a consideration of the general needs of the country or would result in decreasing the work of legislation.

ECONOMY

Our present state of prosperity has been greatly promoted by three important causes, one of which is economy, resulting in reduction and reform in national taxation. Another is the elimination of many kinds of waste. The third is a general raising of the standards of efficiency. This combination has brought the perfectly astonishing result of a reduction in the index price of commodities and an increase in the index rate of wages. We have secured a lowering of the cost to produce and a raising of the ability to consume. Prosperity resulting from these causes rests on the securest of all foundations. It gathers strength from its own progress.

In promoting this progress the chief part which the National Government plays lies in the field of economy. Whatever doubts may have been entertained as to the necessity of this policy and the beneficial results which would accrue from it to all the people of the Nation, its wisdom must now be considered thoroughly demonstrated. It may not have appeared to be a novel or perhaps brilliant conception, but it has turned out to be preeminently sound. It has not failed to work. It has surely brought results. It does not have to be excused as a temporary expedient adopted as the lesser evil to remedy some abuse, it is not a palliative seeking to treat symptoms, but a major operation for the eradication at the source of a large number of social diseases.

Nothing is easier than the expenditure of public money. It does not appear to belong to anybody. The temptation is overwhelming to bestow it on somebody. But the results of extravagance are ruinous. The property of the country, like the freedom of the country, belongs to the people of the country. They have not empowered their Government to take a dollar of it except for a necessary public purpose. But if the Constitution conferred such right, sound economics would forbid it. Nothing is more destructive of the progress of the Nation than Government extravagance. It means an increase in the burden of taxation, dissipation of the returns from enterprise, a decrease in the real value of wages, with ultimate stagnation and decay. The whole theory of our institutions is based on the liberty and independence of the individual. He is dependent on himself for support and therefore entitled to the rewards of his own industry. He is not to be deprived of what he earns that others may be benefited by what they do not earn. What he saves through his private effort is not to be wasted by Government extravagance.

Our national activities have become so vast that it is necessary to scrutinize each item of public expenditure if we are to apply the principle of economy. At the last session we made an immediate increase in the annual budget of more than $100,000,000 in benefits conferred on the veterans of three wars, public buildings, and river and harbor improvement. Many projects are being broached requiring further large outlays. I am convinced that it would be greatly for the welfare of the country if we avoid at the present session all commitments except those of the most pressing nature. From a reduction of the debt and taxes will accrue a wider benefit to all the people of this country than from embarking on any new enterprise. When our war debt is decreased we shall have resources for expansion. Until that is accomplished we should confine ourselves to expenditures of the most urgent necessity.

The Department of Commerce has performed a most important function in making plans and securing support of all kinds of national enterprise for the elimination of waste. Efficiency has been greatly promoted through good management and the constantly increasing cooperation of the wage earners throughout the whole realm of private business. It is my opinion that this whole development has been predicated on the foundation of a protective tariff.

TAX REDUCTION

As a result of economy of administration by the Executive and of appropriation by the Congress, the end of this fiscal year will leave a surplus in the Treasury estimated at $383,000,000. Unless otherwise ordered, such surplus is used for the retirement of the war debt. A bond which can be retired to-day for 100 cents will cost the people 104¼ cents to retire a year from now. While I favor a speedy reduction of the debt as already required by law and in accordance with the promises made to the holders of our Liberty bonds when they were issued, there is no reason why a balanced portion of surplus revenue should not be applied to a reduction of taxation. It can not be repeated too often that the enormous revenues of this Nation could not be collected without becoming a charge on all the people whether or not they directly pay taxes. Everyone who is paying for the bare necessities of food and shelter and clothing, without considering the better things of life, is indirectly paying a national tax. The nearly 20,000,000 owners of securities, the additional scores of millions of holders of insurance policies and depositors in savings banks, are all paying a national tax. Millions of individuals and corporations are making a direct contribution to the National Treasury which runs from 1½ to 25 per cent of their income, besides a number of special requirements, like automobile and admission taxes. Whenever the state of the Treasury will permit, I believe in a reduction of taxation. I think the taxpayers are entitled to it. But I am not advocating tax reduction merely for the benefit of the taxpayer; I am advocating it for the benefit of the country.

If it appeared feasible, I should welcome permanent tax reduction at this time. The estimated surplus, however, for June 30, 1928, is not much larger than is required in a going business of nearly $4,000,000,000. We have had but a few months' experience under the present revenue act and shall need to know what is developed by the returns of income produced under it, which are not required to be made until about the time this session terminates, and what the economic probabilities of the country are in the latter part of 1927, before we can reach any justifiable conclusion as to permanent tax reduction. Moreover the present surplus results from many nonrecurrent items. Meantime, it is possible to grant some real relief by a simple measure making reductions in the payments which accrue on the 15th of March and June, 1927. I am very strongly of the conviction that this is so much a purely business matter that it ought not to be dealt with in a partisan spirit. The Congress has already set the notable example of treating tax problems without much reference to party, which might well be continued. What I desire to advocate most earnestly is relief for the country from unnecessary tax burdens. We can not secure that if we stop to engage in a partisan controversy. As I do not think any change in the special taxes, or any permanent reduction is practical, I therefore urge both parties of the House Ways and Means Committee to agree on a bill granting the temporary relief which I have indicated. Such a reduction would directly affect millions of taxpayers, release large sums for investment in new enterprise, stimulating industrial production and agricultural consumption, and indirectly benefiting every family in the whole country. These are my convictions stated with full knowledge that it is for the Congress to decide whether they judge it best to make such a reduction or leave the surplus for the present year to be applied to retirement of the war debt. That also is eventually tax reduction.

PROTECTIVE TARIFF

It is estimated that customs receipts for the present fiscal year will exceed $615,000,000, the largest which were ever secured from that source. The value of our imports for the last fiscal year was $4,466,000,000, an increase of more than 71 per cent since the present tariff law went into effect. Of these imports about 65 per cent, or, roughly, $2,900,000,000, came in free of duty, which means that the

United States affords a duty-free market to other countries almost equal in value to the total imports of Germany and greatly exceeding the total imports of France. We have admitted a greater volume of free imports than any other country except England.

We are, therefore, levying duties on about $1,550,000,000 of imports. Nearly half of this, or $700,000,000, is subject to duties for the protection of agriculture and have their origin in countries other than Europe. They substantially increased the prices received by our farmers for their produce. About $300,000,000 more is represented by luxuries such as costly rugs, furs, precious stones, etc. This leaves only about $550,000,000 of our imports under a schedule of duties which is in general under consideration when there is discussion of lowering the tariff. While the duties on this small portion, representing only about 12 per cent of our imports, undoubtedly represent the difference between a fair degree of prosperity or marked depression to many of our industries and the difference between good pay and steady work or wide unemployment to many of our wage earners, it is impossible to conceive how other countries or our own importers could be greatly benefited if these duties are reduced. Those who are starting an agitation for a reduction of tariff duties, partly at least for the benefit of those to whom money has been lent abroad, ought to know that there does not seem to be a very large field within the area of our imports in which probable reductions would be advantageous to foreign goods. Those who wish to benefit foreign producers are much more likely to secure that result by continuing the present enormous purchasing power which comes from our prosperity that has increased our imports over 71 per cent in four years than from any advantages that are likely to accrue from a general tariff reduction.

AGRICULTURE

The important place which agriculture holds in the economic and social life of the Nation can not be overestimated. The National Government is justified in putting forth every effort to make the open country a desirable place to live. No condition meets this requirement which fails to supply a fair return on labor expended and capital invested. While some localities and some particular crops furnish exceptions, in general agriculture is continuing to make progress in recovering from the depression of 1921 and 1922. Animal products and food products are in a more encouraging position, while cotton, due to the high prices of past years supplemented by ideal weather conditions, has been stimulated to a point of temporary overproduction. Acting on the request of the cotton-growing interests, I appointed a committee to assist in carrying out their plans. As a result of this cooperation sufficient funds have been pledged to finance the storage and carrying of 4,000,000 bales of cotton. Whether those who own the cotton are willing to put a part of their stock into this plan depends on themselves. The Federal Government has cooperated in providing ample facilities. No method of meeting the situation would be adequate which does not contemplate a reduction of about one-third in the acreage for the coming year. The responsibility for making the plan effective lies with those who own and finance cotton and cotton lands.

The Department of Agriculture estimates the net income of agriculture for the year 1920–21 at only $375,000,000; for 1924–25, $2,656,000,000; for 1925–26, $2,757,000,000. This increase has been brought about in part by the method already referred to, of Federal tax reduction, the elimination of waste, and increased efficiency in industry. The wide gap that existed a few years ago between the index price of agricultural products and the index price of other products has been gradually closing up, though the recent depression in cotton has somewhat enlarged it. Agriculture had on the whole been going higher while industry had been going lower. Industrial and commercial activities, being carried on for the most part by corporations, are taxed at a much higher rate than farming, which is carried on by individuals. This will inevitably make industrial commodity costs high while war taxation lasts. It is because of this circumstance that national tax reduction has a very large indirect benefit upon the farmer, though it can not relieve him from the very great burden of the local taxes which he pays directly. We have practically relieved the farmer of any Federal income tax.

There is agreement on all sides that some portions of our agricultural industry have lagged behind other industries in recovery from the war and that further improvement in methods of marketing of agricultural products is most desirable. There is belief also that the Federal Government can further contribute to these ends beyond the many helpful measures taken during the last five years through the different acts of Congress for advancing the interests of the farmers.

The packers and stockyards act,
Establishing of the intermediate credit banks for agricultural purposes,
The Purnell Act for agricultural research,
The Capper-Volstead Cooperative Marketing Act,
The cooperative marketing act of 1926,
Amendments to the warehousing act,
The enlargement of the activities of the Department of Agriculture,
Enlargement of the scope of loans by the Farm Loan Board,
The tariff on agricultural products,
The large Federal expenditure in improvement of waterways and highways,
The reduction of Federal taxes,

in all comprise a great series of governmental actions in the advancement of the special interest of agriculture.

In determination of what further measures may be undertaken it seems to me there are certain pitfalls which must be avoided and our test in avoiding them should be to avoid disaster to the farmer himself.

Acting upon my recommendation, the Congress has ordered the Interstate Commerce Commission to investigate the freight-rate structure, directing that such changes shall be made in freight rates as will promote freedom of movement of agricultural products. Railroad consolidation which I am advocating would also result in a situation where rates could be made more advantageous for farm produce, as has recently been done in the revision of rates on fertilizers in the South. Additional benefit will accrue from the development of our inland waterways. The Mississippi River system carries a commerce of over 50,000,000 tons at a saving of nearly $18,000,000 annually. The Inland Waterways Corporation operates boats on 2,500 miles of navigable streams and through its relation with 165 railroads carries freight into and out of 45 States of the Union. During the past six months it has handled over 1,000,000 bushels of grain monthly and by its lower freight rates has raised the price of such grain to the farmer probably 2½ cents to 3 cents a bushel. The highway system on which the Federal Government expends about $85,000,000 a year is of vital importance to the rural regions.

The advantages to be derived from a more comprehensive and less expensive system of transportation for agriculture ought to be supplemented by provision for an adequate supply of fertilizer at a lower cost than it is at present obtainable. This advantage we are attempting to secure by the proposed development at Muscle Shoals, and there are promising experiments being made in synthetic chemistry for the production of nitrates.

A survey should be made of the relation of Government grazing lands to the livestock industry. Additional legislation is desirable more definitely to establish the place of grazing in the administration of the national forests, properly subordinated to their functions of producing timber and conserving the water supply. Over 180,000,000 acres of grazing lands are still pastured as commons in the public domain with little or no regulation. This has made their use so uncertain that it has contributed greatly to the instability of the livestock industry. Very little of this land is suited to settlement or private ownership. Some plan ought to be adopted for its use in grazing, corresponding broadly to that already successfully applied to the national forests.

The development of sound and strong cooperative associations is of fundamental importance to our agriculture. It is encouraging to note, therefore, that a vigorous and healthy growth in the cooperative movement is continuing. Cooperative associations reporting to the Department of Agriculture at the end of 1925 had on their membership rolls a total of 2,700,000 producers. Their total business in 1925 amounted to approximately $2,400,000,000, compared with $635,800,000 in 1915. Legislative action to assist cooperative associations and supplement their efforts was passed at the last session of Congress. Important credit measures were also provided by Congress in 1923 which have been of inestimable value to the cooperative associations. Although the Federal credit agencies have served agriculture well, I think it may be possible to broaden and strengthen the service of these institutions.

Attention is again directed to the surplus problem of agriculture by the present cotton situation. Surpluses often affect prices of various farm commodities in a disastrous manner, and the problem urgently demands a solution. Discussions both in and out of Congress during the past few years have given us a better understanding of the subject, and it is my hope that out of the various proposals made the basis will be found for a sound and effective solution upon which agreement can be reached. In my opinion cooperative marketing associations will be important aids to the ultimate solution of the problem. It may well be, however, that additional measures will be needed to supplement their efforts. I believe all will agree that such measures should not conflict with the best interests of the cooperatives, but rather assist and strengthen them. In working out this problem to any sound conclusion it is necessary to avoid putting the Government into the business of production or marketing or attempting to enact legislation for the purpose of price fixing. The farmer does not favor any attempted remedies that partake of these elements. He has a sincere and candid desire for assistance. If matched by an equally sincere and candid consideration of the different remedies proposed, a sound measure of relief ought to result. It is unfortunate that no general agreement has been reached by the various agricultural interests upon any of the proposed remedies. Out of the discussion of various proposals which can be had before the Committees of Agriculture some measure ought to be perfected which would be generally satisfactory.

Due to the emergency arising from a heavy tropical storm in southern Florida, I authorized the Secretary of Agriculture to use certain funds in anticipation of legislation to enable the farmers in that region to plant their crops. The department will present a bill ratifying the loans which were made for this purpose.

Federal legislation has been adopted authorizing the cooperation of the Government with States and private owners in the protection of forest lands from fire. This preventive measure is of such great importance that I have recommended for it an increased appropriation.

Another preventive measure of great economic and sanitary importance is the eradication of tuberculosis in cattle. Active work is now in progress in one-fourth of the counties of the United States to secure this result. Over 12,000,000 cattle have been under treatment, and the average degree of infection has fallen from 4.9 per cent to 2.8 per cent. The Federal Government is making substantial expenditures for this purpose.

Serious damage is threatened to the corn crop by the European corn borer. Since 1917 it has spread from eastern New England westward into Indiana and now covers about 100,000 square miles. It is one of the most formidible pests because it spreads rapidly and is exceedingly difficult of control. It has assumed a menace that is of national magnitude and warrants the Federal Government in extending its cooperation to the State and local agencies which are attempting to prevent its further spread and secure its eradication.

The whole question of agriculture needs most careful consideration. In the past few years the Government has given this subject more attention than any other and has held more consultations in relation to it than on any other subject. While the Government is not to be blamed for failure to perform the impossible, the agricultural regions are entitled to know that they have its constant solicitude and sympathy. Many of the farmers are burdened with debts and taxes which they are unable to carry. We are expending in this country many millions of dollars each year to increase farm production. We ought now to put more emphasis on the question of farm marketing. If a sound solution of a permanent nature can be found for this problem, the Congress ought not to hesitate to adopt it.

DEVELOPMENT OF WATER RESOURCES

In previous messages I have referred to the national importance of the proper development of our water resources. The great projects of extension of the Mississippi system, the protection and development of the lower Colorado River, are before Congress, and I have previously commented upon them. I favor the necessary legislation to expedite these projects. Engineering studies are being made for connecting the Great Lakes with the North Atlantic, either through an all-American canal or by way of the St. Lawrence River. These reports will undoubtedly be before the Congress during its present session. It is unnecessary to dwell upon the great importance of such a waterway not only to our mid-continental basin but to the commerce and development of practically the whole Nation. Our river and harbor improvement should be continued in accordance with the present policy. Expenditure of this character is compatible with economy; it is in the nature of capital investment. Work should proceed on the basic trunk lines if this work is to be a success. If the country will be content to be moderate and patient and permit improvements to be made where they will do the greatest general good, rather than insisting on expenditures at this time on secondary projects, our internal waterways can be made a success. If proposed legislation results in a gross manifestation of local jealousies and selfishness, this program can not be carried out. Ultimately we can take care of extensions, but our first effort should be confined to the main arteries.

Our inland commerce has been put to great inconvenience and expense by reason of the lowering of the water level of the Great Lakes. This is an international problem on which competent engineers are making reports. Out of their study it is expected that a feasible method will be developed for raising the level to provide relief for our commerce and supply water for drainage. Whenever a practical plan is presented it ought to be speedily adopted.

RECLAMATION

It is increasingly evident that the Federal Government must in the future take a leading part in the impounding of water for conservation with incidental power for the development of the irrigable lands of the arid region. The unused waters of the West are found mainly in large rivers. Works to store and distribute these have such magnitude and cost that they are not attractive to private enterprise. Water is the irreplaceable natural resource. Its precipitation can not be increased. Its storage on the higher reaches of streams, to meet growing needs, to be used repeatedly as it flows toward the seas, is a practical and prudent business policy.

The United States promises to follow the course of older irrigation countries, where recent important irrigation developments have been carried out as national undertakings. It is gratifying, therefore, that conditions on Federal reclamation projects have become satisfactory. The gross value of crops grown with water from project works increased from $110,000,000 in 1924 to $131,000,000 in 1925. The adjustments made last year by Congress relieved irrigators from paying construction costs on unprofitable land, and by so doing inspired new hope and confidence in ability to meet the payments required. Construction payments by water users last year were the largest in the history of the bureau.

The anticipated reclamation fund will be fully absorbed for a number of years in the completion of old projects and the construction of projects inaugurated in the past three years. We should, however, continue to investigate and study the possibilities of a carefully planned development of promising projects, logically of governmental concern because of their physical magnitude, immense cost, and the interstate and international problems involved. Only in this way may we be fully prepared to meet intelligently the needs of our fast-growing population in the years to come.

TRANSPORTATION

It would be difficult to conceive of any modern activity which contributes more to the necessities and conveniences of life than transportation. Without it our present agricultural production and practically all of our commerce would be completely prostrated. One of the large contributing causes to the present highly satisfactory state of our economic condition is the prompt and dependable service, surpassing all our previous records, rendered by the railroads. This power has been fostered by the spirit of cooperation between Federal and State regulatory commissions. To render this service more efficient and effective and to promote a more scientific regulation, the process of valuing railroad properties should be simplified and the primary valuations should be completed as rapidly as possible. The problem of rate reduction would be much simplified by a process of railroad consolidations. This principle has already been adopted as Federal law. Experience has shown that a more effective method must be provided. Studies have already been made and legislation introduced seeking to promote this end. It would be of great advantage if it could be taken up at once and speedily enacted. The railroad systems of the country and the convenience of all the people are waiting on this important decision.

MERCHANT MARINE

It is axiomatic that no agricultural and industrial country can get the full benefit of its own advantages without a merchant marine. We have been proceeding under the act of Congress that contemplates the establishment of trade routes to be ultimately transferred to private ownership and operation. Due to temporary conditions abroad and at home we have a large demand just now for certain types of freight vessels. Some suggestion has been made for new construction. I do not feel that we are yet warranted in entering that field. Such ships as we might build could not be sold after they are launched for anywhere near what they would cost. We have expended over $250,000,000 out of the public Treasury in recent years to make up the losses of operation, not counting depreciation or any cost whatever of our capital investment. The great need of our merchant marine is not for more ships but for more freight.

Our merchants are altogether too indifferent about using American ships for the transportation of goods which they send abroad or bring home. Some of our vessels necessarily need repairs, which should be made. I do not believe that the operation of our fleet is as economical and efficient as it could be made if placed under a single responsible head, leaving the Shipping Board free to deal with general matters of policy and regulation.

RADIO LEGISLATION

The Department of Commerce has for some years urgently presented the necessity for further legislation in order to protect radio listeners from interference between broadcasting stations and to carry out other regulatory functions. Both branches of Congress at the last session passed enactments intended to effect such regulation, but the two bills yet remain to be brought into agreement and final passage.

Due to decisions of the courts, the authority of the department under the law of 1912 has broken down; many more stations have been operating than can be accommodated within the limited number of wave lengths available; further stations are in course of construction; many stations have departed from the scheme of allocation set down by the department, and the whole service of this most important public function has drifted into such chaos as seems likely, if not remedied, to destroy its great value. I most urgently recommend that this legislation should be speedily enacted.

I do not believe it is desirable to set up further independent agencies in the Government. Rather I believe it advisable to entrust the important functions of deciding who shall exercise the privilege of radio transmission and under what conditions, the assigning of wave lengths and determination of power, to a board to be assembled whenever action on such questions becomes necessary. There should be right of appeal to the courts from the decisions of such board. The administration of the decisions of the board and the other features of regulation and promotion of radio in the public interest, together with scientific research, should remain in the Department of Commerce. Such an arrangement makes for more expert, more efficient, and more economical administration than an independent agency or board, whose duties, after initial stages, require but little attention, in which administrative functions are confused with semijudicial functions and from which of necessity there must be greatly increased personnel and expenditure.

THE WAGE EARNER

The great body of our people are made up of wage earners. Several hundred thousands of them are on the pay rolls of the United States Government. Their condition very largely is fixed by legislation. We have recently provided increases in compensation under a method of reclassification and given them the advantage of a liberal retirement system as a support for their declining years. Most of them are under the merit system, which is a guaranty of their intelligence, and the efficiency of their service is a demonstration of their loyalty. The Federal Government should continue to set a good example for all other employers.

In the industries the condition of the wage earner has steadily improved. The 12-hour day is almost entirely unknown. Skilled labor is well compensated. But there are unfortunately a multitude of workers who have not yet come to share in the general prosperity of the Nation. Both the public authorities and private enterprise should be solicitous to advance the welfare of this class. The Federal Government has been seeking to secure this end through a protective tariff, through restrictive immigration, through requiring safety devices for the prevention of accidents, through the granting of workman's compensation, through civilian vocational rehabilitation and education, through employment information bureaus, and through such humanitarian relief as was provided in the maternity and infancy legislation. It is a satisfaction to report that a more general condition of contentment exists among wage earners and the country is more free from labor disputes than it has been for years. While restrictive immigration has been adopted in part for the benefit of the wage earner, and in its entirety for the benefit of the country, it ought not to cause a needless separation of families and dependents from their natural source of support contrary to the dictates of humanity.

BITUMINOUS COAL

No progress appears to have been made within large areas of the bituminous coal industry toward creation of voluntary machinery by which greater assurance can be given to the public of peaceful adjustment of wage difficulties such as has been accomplished in the anthracite industry. This bituminous industry is one of primary necessity and bears a great responsibility to the Nation for continuity of supplies. As the wage agreements in the unionized section of the industry expire on April 1 next, and as conflicts may result which may imperil public interest, and have for many years often called for action of the Executive in protection of the public, I again recommend the passage of such legislation as will assist the Executive in dealing with such emergencies through a special temporary board of conciliation and mediation and through administrative agencies for the purpose of distribution of coal and protection of the consumers of coal from profiteering. At present the Executive is not only without authority to act but is actually prohibited by law from making any expenditure to meet the emergency of a coal famine.

JUDICIARY

The Federal courts hold a high position in the administration of justice in the world. While individual judicial officers have sometimes been subjected to just criticism, the courts as a whole have maintained an exceedingly high standard. The Congress may well consider the question of supplying fair salaries and conferring upon the Supreme Court the same rule-making power on the law side of the district courts that they have always possessed on the equity side. A bill is also pending providing for retirement after a certain number of years of service, although they have not been consecutive, which should have your favorable consideration. These faithful servants of the Government are about the last that remain to be provided for in the postwar readjustments.

BANKING

There has been pending in Congress for nearly three years banking legislation to clarify the national bank act and reasonably to increase the powers of the national banks. I believe that within the limitation of sound banking principles Congress should now and for the future place the national banks upon a fair equality with their competitors, the State banks, and I trust that means may be found so that the differences on branch-banking legislation between the Senate and the House of Representatives may be settled along sound lines and the legislation promptly enacted.

It would be difficult to overestimate the service which the Federal reserve system has already rendered to the country. It is necessary only to recall the chaotic condition of our banking organization at the time the Federal reserve system was put into operation. The old system consisted of a vast number of independent banking units, with scattered bank reserves which never could be mobilized in times of greatest need. In spite of vast banking resources, there was no coordination of reserves or any credit elasticity. As a consequence, a strain was felt even during crop-moving periods and when it was necessary to meet other seasonal and regularly recurring needs.

The Federal reserve system is not a panacea for all economic or financial ills. It can not prevent depression in certain industries which are experiencing overexpansion of production or contraction of their markets. Its business is to furnish adequate credit and currency facilities. This it has succeeded in doing, both during the war and in the more difficult period of deflation and readjustment which followed. It enables us to look to the future with confidence and to make plans far ahead, based on the belief that the Federal reserve system will exercise a steadying influence on credit conditions and thereby prevent any sudden or severe reactions from the period of prosperity which we are now enjoying. In order that these plans may go forward, action should be taken at the present session on the question of renewing the banks' charters and thereby insuring a continuation of the policies and present usefulness of the Federal reserve system.

FEDERAL REGULATION

I am in favor of reducing, rather than expanding, Government bureaus which seek to regulate and control the business activities of the people. Everyone is aware that abuses exist and will exist so long as we are limited by human imperfections. Unfortunately, human nature can not be changed by an act of the legislature. When practically the sole remedy for many evils lies in the necessity of the people looking out for themselves and reforming their own abuses, they will find that they are relying on a false security if the Government assumes to hold out the promise that it is looking out for them and providing reforms for them. This principle is preeminently applicable to the National Government. It is too much assumed that because an abuse exists it is the business of the National Government to provide a remedy. The presumption should be that it is the business of local and State governments. Such national action results in encroaching upon the salutary independence of the States and by undertaking to supersede their natural authority fills the land with bureaus and departments which are undertaking to do what it is impossible for them to accomplish and brings our whole system of government into disrespect and disfavor. We ought to maintain high standards. We ought to punish wrongdoing. Society has not only the privilege but the absolute duty of protecting itself and its individuals. But we can not accomplish this end by adopting a wrong method. Permanent success lies in local, rather than national action. Unless the locality rises to its own requirements, there is an almost irresistible impulse for the National Government to intervene. The States and the Nation should both realize that such action is to be adopted only as a last resort.

THE NEGRO

The social well-being of our country requires our constant effort for the amelioration of race prejudice and the extension to all elements of equal opportunity and equal protection under the laws which are guaranteed by the Constitution. The Federal Government especially is charged with this obligation in behalf of the colored people of the Nation. Not only their remarkable progress, their devotion and their loyalty, but our duty to ourselves under our claim that we are an enlightened people requires us to use all our power to protect them from the crime of lynching. Although violence of this kind has very much decreased, while any of it remains we can not justify neglecting to make every effort to eradicate it by law.

The education of the colored race under Government encouragement is proceeding successfully and ought to have continuing support. An increasing need exists for properly educated and trained medical skill to be devoted to the service of this race.

INSULAR POSSESSIONS

This Government holds in sacred trusteeship islands which it has acquired in the East and West Indies. In all of them the people are more prosperous than at any previous time. A system of good roads, education, and general development is in progress. The people are better governed than ever before and generally content.

In the Philippine Islands Maj. Gen. Leonard Wood has been Governor General for five years and has administered his office with tact and ability greatly to the success of the Filipino people. These are a proud and sensitive race, who are making such progress with our cooperation that we can view the results of this experiment with great satisfaction. As we are attempting to assist this race toward self-government, we should look upon their wishes with great respect, granting their requests immediately when they are right, yet maintaining a frank firmness in refusing when they are wrong. We shall measure their progress in no small part by their acceptance of the terms of the organic law under which the islands are governed and their faithful observance of its provisions. Need exists for clarifying the duties of the auditor and declaring them to be what everyone had supposed they were. We have placed our own expenditures under the supervision of the Comptroller General. It is not likely that the expenditures in the Philippine Islands need less supervision than our own. The Governor General is hampered in his selection of subordinates by the necessity of securing a confirmation, which has oftentimes driven him to the expediency of using Army officers in work for which civilian experts would be much better fitted. Means should be provided for this and such other purposes as he may require out of the revenue which this Government now turns back to the Philippine treasury.

In order that these possessions might suffer no seeming neglect, I have recently sent Col. Carmi A Thompson to the islands to make a survey in cooperation with the Governor General to suggest what might be done to improve conditions. Later, I may make a more extended report including recommendations. The economic development of the islands is very important. They ought not to be turned back to the people until they are both politically fitted for self-government and economically independent. Large areas are adaptable to the production of rubber. No one contemplates any time in the future either under the present or a more independent form of government when we should not assume some responsibility for their defense. For their economic advantage, for the employment of their people, and as a contribution to our power of defense which could not be carried on without rubber, I believe this industry should be encouraged. It is especially adapted to the Filipino people themselves, who might cultivate it individually on a small acreage. It could be carried on extensively by American capital in a way to furnish employment at good wages. I am opposed to the promotion of any policy that does not provide for absolute freedom on the part of the wage earners and do not think we should undertake to give power for large holdings of land in the islands against the opposition of the people of the locality. Any development of the islands must be solely with the first object of benefiting the people of the islands. At an early day, these possessions should be taken out from under all military control and administered entirely on the civil side of government.

NATIONAL DEFENSE

Our policy of national defense is not one of making war, but of insuring peace. The land and sea force of America, both in its domestic and foreign implications, is distinctly a peace force. It is an arm of the police power to guarantee order and the execution of the law at home and security to our citizens abroad. No self-respecting nation would neglect to provide an army and navy proportionate to its population, the extent of its territory, and the dignity of the place which it occupies in the world. When it is considered that no navy in the world, with one exception, approaches ours and none surpasses it, that our Regular Army of about 115,000 men is the equal of any other like number of troops, that our entire permanent and reserve land and sea force trained and training consists of a personnel of about 610,000, and that our annual appropriations are about $680,000,000 a year, expended under the direction of an exceedingly competent staff, it can not be said that our country is neglecting its national defense. It is true that a cult of disparagement exists, but that candid examination made by the Congress through its various committees has always reassured the country and demonstrated that it is maintaining the most adequate defensive forces in these present years that it has ever supported in time of peace.

This general policy should be kept in effect. Here and there temporary changes may be made in personnel to meet requirements in other directions. Attention should be given to submarines, cruisers, and air forces. Particular points may need strengthening, but as a whole our military power is sufficient.

The one weak place in the whole line is our still stupendous war debt. In any modern campaign the dollars are the shock troops. With a depleted treasury in the rear, no army can maintain itself in the field. A country loaded with debt is a country devoid of the first line of defense. Economy is the handmaid of preparedness. If we wish to be able to defend ourselves to the full extent of our power in the future, we shall discharge as soon as possible the financial burden of the last war. Otherwise we would face a crisis with a part of our capital resources already expended.

The amount and kind of our military equipment is preeminently a question for the decision of the Congress, after giving due consideration to the advice of military experts and the available public revenue. Nothing is more laudable than the cooperation of the agricultural and industrial resources of the country for the purpose of supplying the needs of national defense. In time of peril the people employed in these interests volunteered in a most self-sacrificing way, often at the nominal charge of a dollar a year. But the Army and Navy are not supported for the benefit of supply concerns; supply concerns are supported for the benefit of the Army and Navy. The distribution of orders on what is needed from different concerns for the purpose of keeping up equipment and organization is perfectly justified, but any attempt to prevail upon the Government to purchase beyond its needs ought not to be tolerated. It is eminently fair that those who deal with the Government should do so at a reasonable profit. However, public money is expended not that some one may profit by it, but in order to serve a public purpose.

While our policy of national defense will proceed in order that we may be independent and self-sufficient, I am opposed to engaging in any attempt at competitive armaments. No matter how much or how little some other country may feel constrained to provide, we can well afford to set the example, not of being dictated to by others, but of adopting our own standards. We are strong enough to pursue that method, which will be a most wholesome model for the rest of the world. We are eminently peaceful, but we are by no means weak. While we submit our differences with others, not to the adjudication of force, but of reason, it is not because we are unable to defend our rights. While we are doing our best to eliminate all resort to war for the purpose of settling disputes, we can not but remember that the peace we now enjoy had to be won by the sword and that if the rights of our country are to be defended we can not rely for that purpose upon anyone but ourselves. We can not shirk the responsibility, which is the first requisite of all government, of preserving its own integrity and maintaining the rights of its own citizens. It is only in accordance with these principles that we can establish any lasting foundations for an honorable and permanent peace.

It is for these reasons that our country, like any other country, proposes to provide itself with an army and navy supported by a merchant marine. Yet these are not for competition with any other power. For years we have besought nations to disarm. We have recently expressed our willingness at Geneva to enter into treaties for the limitation of all types of warships according to the ratio adopted at the Washington Conference. This offer is still pending. While we are and shall continue to be armed it is not as a menace, but rather a common assurance of tranquillity to all the peace-loving people of the world. For us to do any less would be to disregard our obligations, evade our responsibilities, and jeopardize our national honor.

VETERANS

This country, not only because it is bound by honor but because of the satisfaction derived from it, has always lavished its bounty upon its veterans. For years a service pension has been bestowed upon the Grand Army on reaching a certain age. Like provision has been made for the survivors of the Spanish War. A liberal future compensation has been granted to all the veterans of the World War. But it is in the case of the disabled and the dependents that the Government exhibits its greatest solicitude. This work is being well administered by the Veterans' Bureau. The main unfinished feature is that of hospitalization. This requirement is being rapidly met. Various veteran bodies will present to you recommendations which should have your careful consideration. At the last session we increased our annual expenditure for pensions and relief on account of the veterans of three wars. While I approve of proper relief for all suffering, I do not favor any further extension of our pension system at this time.

ALIEN PROPERTY

We still have in the possession of the Government the alien property. It has always been the policy of America to hold that private enemy property should not be confiscated in time of war. This principle we have scrupulously observed. As this property is security for the claims of our citizens and our Government, we can not relinquish it without adequate provision for their reimbursement. Legislation for the return of this property, accompanied by suitable provisions for the liquidation of the claims of our citizens and our Treasury, should be adopted. If our Government releases to foreigners the security which it holds for Americans, it must at the same time provide satisfactory safeguards for meeting American claims.

PROHIBITION

The duly authorized public authorities of this country have made prohibition the law of the land. Acting under the Constitution, the Congress and the legislatures of practically all the States have adopted legislation for its enforcement. Some abuses have arisen which require reform. Under the law the National Government has entrusted to the Treasury Department the especial duty of regulation and enforcement. Such supplementary legislation as it requires to meet existing conditions should be carefully and speedily enacted. Failure to support the Constitution and observe the law ought not to be tolerated by public opinion. Especially those in public places, who have taken their oath to support the Constitution, ought to be most scrupulous in its observance. Officers of the Department of Justice throughout the country should be vigilant in enforcing the law, but local authorities, which had always been mainly responsible for the enforcement of law in relation to intoxicating liquor, ought not to seek evasion by attempting to shift the burden wholly upon the Federal agencies. Under the Constitution the States are jointly charged with the Nation in providing for the enforcement of the prohibition amendment. Some people do not like the amendment, some do not like other parts of the Constitution, some do not like any of it. Those who entertain such sentiments have a perfect right to seek through legal methods for a change. But for any of our inhabitants to observe such parts of the Constitution as they like, while disregarding others, is a doctrine that would break down all protection of life and property and destroy the American system of ordered liberty.

FOREIGN RELATIONS

The foreign policy of this Government is well known. It is one of peace based on that mutual respect that arises from mutual regard for international rights and the discharge of international obligations. It is our purpose to promote understanding and good will between ourselves and all other people. The American people are altogether lacking in an appreciation of the tremendous good fortune that surrounds their international position. We have no traditional enemies. We are not embarrassed over any disputed territory. We have no possessions that are coveted by others; they have none that are coveted by us. Our borders are unfortified. We fear no one; no one fears us. All the world knows that the whole extent of our influence is against war and in favor of peace, against the use of force and in favor of negotiation, arbitration, and adjudication as a method of adjusting international differences. We look with disfavor upon all aggressive warfare. We are strong enough so that no one can charge us with weakness if we are slow to anger. Our place is sufficiently established so that we need not be sensitive over trifles. Our resources are large enough so that we can afford to be generous. At the same time we are a nation among nations and recognize a responsibility not only to ourselves, but in the interests of a stable and enlightened civilization, to protect and defend the international rights of our Government and our citizens.

It is because of our historical detachment and the generations of comparative indifference toward us by other nations that our public is inclined to consider altogether too seriously the reports that we are criticized abroad. We never had a larger foreign trade than at the present time. Our good offices were never more sought and the necessity for our assistance and cooperation was never more universally declared in any time of peace. We know that the sentiments which we entertain toward all other nations are those of the most sincere friendship and good will and of an unbounded desire to help, which we are perfectly willing to have judged by their fruits. In our efforts to adjust our international obligations we have met with a response which, when everything is considered, I believe history will record as a most remarkable and gratifying demonstration of the sanctity with which civilized nations undertake to discharge their mutual obligations. Debt settlements have been negotiated with practically all of those who owed us and all finally adjusted but two, which are in process of ratification. When we consider the real sacrifice that will be necessary on the part of other nations, considering all their circumstances, to meet their agreed payments, we ought to hold them in increased admiration and respect. It is true that we have extended to them very generous treatment, but it is also true that they have agreed to repay us all that we loaned to them and some interest.

A special conference on the Chinese customs tariff provided for by the treaty between the nine powers relating to the Chinese customs tariff signed at Washington on February 6, 1922, was called by the Chinese Government to meet at Peking on October 26, 1925. We participated in this conference through fully empowered delegates and, with good will, endeavored to cooperate with the other participating powers with a view to putting into effect promises made to China at the Washington conference, and considering any reasonable proposal that might be made by the Chinese Government for the revision of the treaties on the subject of China's tariff. With these aims in view the American delegation at the outset of the conference proposed to put into effect the surtaxes provided for by the Washington treaty and to proceed immediately to the negotiation of a treaty, which, among other things, was to make provision for the abolition of taxes collected on goods in transit, remove the tariff restrictions in existing treaties, and put into effect the national tariff law of China.

Early in April of the present year the central Chinese Government was ousted from power by opposing warring factions. It became impossible under the circumstances to continue the negotiations. Finally, on July 3, the delegates of the foreign powers, including those of the United States, issued a statement expressing their unanimous and earnest desire to proceed with the work of the conference at the earliest possible moment when the delegates of the Chinese Government are in a position to resume discussions with the foreign delegates of the problems before the conference. We are prepared to resume the negotiations thus interrupted whenever a Government representing the Chinese people and acting on their behalf presents itself. The fact that constant warfare between contending Chinese factions has rendered it impossible to bring these negotiations to a successful conclusion is a matter of deep regret. Throughout these conflicts we have maintained a position of the most careful neutrality. Our naval vessels in Asiatic waters, pursuant to treaty rights, have been used only for the protection of American citizens.

Silas H. Strawn, Esq., was sent to China as American commissioner to cooperate with commissioners of the other powers in the establishment of a commission to inquire into the present practice of extraterritorial jurisdiction in China, with a view to reporting to the Governments of the several powers their findings of fact in regard to these matters. The commission commenced its work in January, 1926, and agreed upon a joint report which was signed on September 16, 1926. The commission's report has been received and is being studied with a view to determining our future policy in regard to the question of extraterritorial privileges under treaties between the United States and China.

The Preparatory Commission for the Disarmament Conference met at Geneva on May 18 and its work has been proceeding almost continuously since that date. It would be premature to attempt to form a judgment as to the progress that has been made. The commission has had before it a comprehensive list of questions touching upon all aspects of the question of the limitation of armament. In the commission's discussions many differences of opinion have developed. However, I am hopeful that at least some measure of agreement will be reached as the discussions continue. The American representation on the commission has consistently tried to be helpful, and has kept before it the practical objective to which the commission is working, namely, actual agreements for the limitation of armaments. Our representatives will continue their work in that direction.

One of the most encouraging features of the commission's work thus far has been the agreement in principle among the naval experts of a majority of the powers parties to the Washington treaty limiting naval armament upon methods and standards for the comparison and further limitation of naval armament. It is needless to say that at the proper time I shall be prepared to proceed along practical lines to the conclusion of agreements carrying further the work begun at the Washington Conference in 1921.

DEPARTMENT REPORTS

Many important subjects which it is impossible even to mention in the short space of an annual message you will find fully discussed in the departmental reports. A failure to include them here is not to be taken as indicating any lack of interest, but only a disinclination to state inadequately what has been much better done in other documents.

THE CAPITAL CITY

We are embarking on an ambitious building program for the city of Washington. The Memorial Bridge is under way with all that it holds for use and beauty. New buildings are soon contemplated.

This program should represent the best that exists in the art and science of architecture. Into these structures which must be considered as of a permanent nature ought to go the aspirations of the Nation, its ideals expressed in forms of beauty. If our country wishes to compete with others, let it not be in the support of armaments but in the making of a beautiful capital city. Let it express the soul of America. Whenever an American is at the seat of his Government, however traveled and cultured he may be, he ought to find a city of stately proportion, symmetrically laid out and adorned with the best that there is in architecture, which would arouse his imagination and stir his patriotic pride. In the coming years Washington should be not only the art center of our own country but the art center of the world. Around it should center all that is best in science, in learning, in letters, and in art. These are the results that justify the creation of those national resources with which we have been favored.

AMERICAN IDEALS

America is not and must not be a country without ideals. They are useless if they are only visionary; they are only valuable if they are practical. A nation can not dwell constantly on the mountain tops. It has to be replenished and sustained through the ceaseless toil of the less inspiring valleys. But its face ought always to be turned upward, its vision ought always to be fixed on high.

We need ideals that can be followed in daily life, that can be translated into terms of the home. We can not expect to be relieved from toil, but we do expect to divest it of degrading conditions. Work is honorable; it is entitled to an honorable recompense. We must strive mightily, but having striven there is a defect in our political and social system if we are not in general rewarded with success. To relieve the land of the burdens that came from the war, to release to the individual more of the fruits of his own industry, to increase his earning capacity and decrease his hours of labor, to enlarge the circle of his vision through good roads and better transportation, to place before him the opportunity for education both in science and in art, to leave him free to receive the inspiration of religion, all these are ideals which deliver him from the servitude of the body and exalt him to the service of the soul. Through this emancipation from the things that are material, we broaden our dominion over the things that are spiritual.

FIFTH ANNUAL MESSAGE.

THE WHITE HOUSE, *December 6, 1927.*

Members of the Congress:

It is gratifying to report that for the fourth consecutive year the state of the Union in general is good. We are at peace. The country as a whole has had a prosperity never exceeded. Wages are at their highest range, employment is plentiful. Some parts of agriculture and industry have lagged; some localities have suffered from storm and flood. But such losses have been absorbed without serious detriment to our great economic structure. Stocks of goods are moderate and a wholesome caution is prevalent. Rates of interest for industry, agriculture, and government have been reduced. Savers and investors are providing capital for new construction in industry and public works. The purchasing power of agriculture has increased. If the people maintain that confidence which they are entitled to have in themselves, in each other, and in America, a comfortable prosperity will continue.

CONSTRUCTIVE ECONOMY

Without constructive economy in Government expenditures we should not now be enjoying these results or these prospects. Because we are not now physically at war, some people are disposed to forget that our war debt still remains. The Nation must make financial sacrifices, accompanied by a stern self-denial in public expenditures, until we have conquered the disabilities of our public finance. While our obligation to veterans and dependents is large and continuing, the heavier burden of the national debt is being steadily eliminated. At the end of this fiscal year it will be reduced from about $26,600,000,000 to about $17,975,000,000. Annual interest, including war savings, will have been reduced from $1,055,000,000 to $670,-000,000. The sacrifices of the people, the economy of the Government, are showing remarkable results. They should be continued for the purpose of relieving the Nation of the burden of interest and debt and releasing revenue for internal improvements and national development.

Not only the amount, but the rate, of Government interest has been reduced. Callable bonds have been refunded and paid, so that during this year the average rate of interest on the present public debt for the first time fell below 4 per cent. Keeping the credit of the Nation high is a tremendously profitable operation.

TAX REDUCTION

The immediate fruit of economy and the retirement of the public debt is tax reduction. The annual saving in interest between 1925 and 1929 is $212,000,000. Without this no bill to relieve the taxpayers would be worth proposing. The three measures already enacted leave our Government revenues where they are not oppressive.

Exemptions have been increased until 115,000,000 people make but 2,500,000 individual taxable returns, so that further reduction should be mainly for the purpose of removing inequalities. The Secretary of the Treasury has recommended a measure which would give us a much better balanced system of taxation and without oppression produce sufficient revenue. It has my complete support.

Unforeseen contingencies requiring money are always arising. Our probable surplus for June 30, 1929, is small. A slight depression in business would greatly reduce our revenue because of our present method of taxation. The people ought to take no selfish attitude of pressing for removing moderate and fair taxes which might produce a deficit. We must keep our budget balanced for each year. That is the corner stone of our national credit, the trifling price we pay to command the lowest rate of interest of any great power in the world. Any surplus can be applied to debt reduction, and debt reduction is tax reduction. Under the present circumstances it would be far better to leave the rates as they are than to enact a bill carrying the peril of a deficit. This is not a problem to be approached in a narrow or partisan spirit. All of those who participate in finding a reasonable solution will be entitled to participate in any credit that accrues from it without regard to party. The Congress has already demonstrated that tax legislation can be removed from purely political consideration into the realm of patriotic business principles.

Any bill for tax reduction should be written by those who are responsible for raising, managing, and expending the finances of the Government. If special interests, too often selfish, always uninformed of the national needs as a whole, with hired agents using their proposed beneficiaries as engines of propaganda, are permitted to influence the withdrawal of their property from taxation, we shall have a law that is unbalanced and unjust, bad for business, bad for the country, probably resulting in a deficit, with disastrous financial consequences. The Constitution has given the Members of the Congress sole authority to decide what tax measures shall be presented for approval. While welcoming information from any quarter, the Congress should continue to exercise its own judgment in a matter so vital and important to all the interests of the country as taxation.

NATIONAL DEFENSE

Being a nation relying not on force, but on fair dealing and good will, to maintain peace with others, we have provided a moderate military force in a form adapted solely to defense. It should be continued with a very generous supply of officers and with the present base of personnel, subject to fluctuations which may be temporarily desirable.

The five-year program for our air forces is in keeping with this same policy and commensurate with the notable contributions of America to the science of aeronautics. The provisions of the law lately enacted are being executed as fast as the practical difficulties of an orderly and stable development permit.

While our Army is small, prudence requires that it should be kept in a high state of efficiency and provided with such supplies as would permit of its immediate expansion. The garrison ration has lately been increased. Recommendations for an appropriation of $6,166,000 for new housing made to the previous Congress failed to pass. While most of the Army is well housed, some of it which is quartered in war-time training camps is becoming poorly housed. In the past three years $12,533,000 have been appropriated for reconstruction and repairs, and an authorization has been approved of $22,301,000 for new housing, under which $8,070,000 has already been appropriated. A law has also been passed, complying with the request of the War Department, allocating funds received from the sale of buildings and land for housing purposes. The work, however, is not completed, so that other appropriations are being recommended.

Our Navy is likewise a weapon of defense. We have a foreign commerce and ocean lines of trade unsurpassed by any other country. We have outlying territory in the two great oceans and long stretches of seacoast studded with the richest cities in the world. We are responsible for the protection of a large population and the greatest treasure ever bestowed upon any people. We are charged with an international duty of defending the Panama Canal. To meet these responsibilities we need a very substantial sea armament. It needs aircraft development, which is being provided under the five-year program. It needs submarines as soon as the department decides upon the best type of construction. It needs airplane carriers and a material addition to its force of cruisers. We can plan for the future and begin a moderate building program.

This country has put away the Old World policy of competitive armaments. It can never be relieved of the responsibility of adequate national defense. We have one treaty secured by an unprecedented attitude of generosity on our part for a limitation in naval armament. After most careful preparation, extending over months, we recently made every effort to secure a three-power treaty to the same end. We were granted much cooperation by Japan, but we were unable to come to an agreement with Great Britain. While the results of the conference were of considerable value, they were mostly of a negative character. We know now that no agreement can be reached which will be inconsistent with a considerable building program on our part. We are ready and willing to continue the preparatory investigations on the general subject of limitation of armaments which have been started under the auspices of the League of Nations.

We have a considerable cruiser tonnage, but a part of it is obsolete. Everyone knew that had a three-power agreement been reached it would have left us with the necessity of continuing our building program. The failure to agree should not cause us to build either more or less than we otherwise should. Any future treaty of limitation will call on us for more ships. We should enter on no competition. We should refrain from no needful program. It should be made clear to all the world that lacking a definite agreement, the attitude of any other country is not to be permitted to alter our own policy. It should especially be demonstrated that propaganda will not cause us to change our course. Where there is no treaty limitation, the size of the Navy which America is to have will be solely for America to determine. No outside influence should enlarge it or diminish it. But it should be known to all that our military power holds no threat of aggrandizement. It is a guaranty of peace and security at home, and when it goes abroad it is an instrument for the protection of the legal rights of our citizens under international law, a refuge in time of disorder, and always the servant of world peace. Wherever our flag goes the rights of humanity increase.

MERCHANT MARINE

The United States Government fleet is transporting a large amount of freight and reducing its drain on the Treasury. The Shipping Board is constantly under pressure, to which it too often yields, to protect private interests, rather than serve the public welfare. More attention should be given to merchant ships as an auxiliary of the Navy. The possibility of including their masters and crews in the Naval Reserve, with some reasonable compensation, should be thoroughly explored as a method of encouraging private operation of shipping. Public operation is not a success. No investigation, of which I have caused several to be made, has failed to report that it could not succeed or to recommend speedy transfer to private ownership. Our exporters and importers are both indifferent about using American ships. It should be our policy to keep our present vessels in repair and dispose of them as rapidly as possible, rather than undertake any new construction. Their operation is a burden on the National Treasury, for which we are not receiving sufficient benefits.

COMMERCIAL AVIATION

A rapid growth is taking place in aeronautics. The Department of Commerce has charge of the inspection and licensing system and the construction of national airways. Almost 8,000 miles are already completed and about 4,000 miles more contemplated. Nearly 4,400 miles are now equipped and over 3,000 miles more will have lighting and emergency landing fields by next July. Air mail contracts are expected to cover 24 of these lines. Daily airway flying is nearly 15,000 miles and is expected to reach 25,000 miles early next year. Flights for other purposes exceed 22,000 miles each day. Over 900 airports, completed and uncompleted, have been laid out. The demand for aircraft has greatly increased. The policy already adopted by the Congress is producing the sound development of this coming industry.

WESTERN HEMISPHERE AIR MAIL

Private enterprise is showing much interest in opening up aviation service to Mexico and Central and South America. We are particularly solicitous to have the United States take a leading part in this development. It is understood that the governments of our sister countries would be willing to cooperate. Their physical features, the undeveloped state of their transportation, make an air service especially adaptable to their usage. The Post Office Department should be granted power to make liberal long-term contracts for carrying our mail, and authority should be given to the Army and the Navy to detail aviators and planes to cooperate with private enterprise in establishing such mail service with the consent of the countries concerned. A committee of the Cabinet will later present a report on this subject.

GOOD ROADS

The importance and benefit of good roads is more and more coming to be appreciated. The National Government has been making liberal contributions to encourage their construction. The results and benefits have been very gratifying. National participation, however, should be confined to trunk-line systems. The national tax on automobiles is now nearly sufficient to meet this outlay. This tax is very small, and on low-priced cars is not more than $2 or $3 each year.

While the advantage of having good roads is very large, the desire for improved highways is not limited to our own country. It should and does include all the Western Hemisphere. The principal points in Canada are already accessible. We ought to lend our encouragement in any way we can for more good roads to all the principal points in this hemisphere south of the Rio Grande. It has been our practice to supply these countries with military and naval advisers, when they have requested it, to assist them in national defense. The arts of peace are even more important to them and to us. Authority should be given by law to provide them at their request with engineering advisers for the construction of roads and bridges. In some of these countries already wonderful progress is being made in road building, but the engineering features are often very exacting and the financing difficult. Private interests should look with favor on all reasonable loans sought by these countries to open such main lines of travel.

This general subject has been promoted by the Pan American Congress of Highways, which will convene again at Rio de Janeiro in July, 1928. It is desirable that the Congress should provide for the appointment of delegates to represent the Government of the United States.

CUBAN PARCEL POST

We have a temporary parcel-post convention with Cuba. The advantage of it is all on our side. During 1926 we shipped twelve times as many parcels, weighing twenty-four times as much, as we received. This convention was made on the understanding that we would repeal an old law prohibiting the importation of cigars and cigarettes in quantities less than 3,000 enacted in 1866 to discourage smuggling, for which it has long been unnecessary. This law unjustly discriminates against an important industry of Cuba. Its repeal has been recommended by the Treasury and Post Office Departments. Unless this is done our merchants and railroads will find themselves deprived of this large parcel-post business after the 1st of next March, the date of the expiration of the convention, which has been extended upon the specific understanding that it would expire at that time unless this legislation was enacted. We purchase large quantities of tobacco made in Cuba. It is not probable that our purchases would be any larger if this law was repealed, while it would be an advantage to many other industries in the United States.

INSULAR POSSESSIONS

Conditions in the Philippine Islands have been steadily improved. Contentment and good order prevail. Roads, irrigation works, harbor improvements, and public buildings are being constructed. Public education and sanitation have been advanced. The Government is in a sound financial condition. These immediate results were especially due to the administration of Gov. Gen. Leonard Wood. The six years of his governorship marked a distinct improvement in the islands and rank as one of the outstanding accomplishments of this distinguished man. His death is a loss to the Nation and the islands.

Greater progress could be made, more efficiency could be put into administration, if the Congress would undertake to expend, through its appropriating power, all or a part of the customs revenues which are now turned over to the Philippine treasury. The powers of the auditor of the islands also need revision and clarification. The government of the islands is about 98 per cent in the hands of the Filipinos. An extension of the policy of self-government will be hastened by the demonstration on their part of their desire and their ability to carry out cordially and efficiently the provisions of the organic law enacted by the Congress for the government of the islands. It would be well for a committee of the Congress to visit the islands every two years.

A fair degree of progress is being made in Porto Rico. Its agricultural products are increasing; its treasury position, which has given much concern, shows improvement. I am advised by the governor that educational facilities are still lacking. Roads are being constructed, which he represents are the first requisite for building schoolhouses. The loyalty of the island to the United States is exceedingly gratifying. A memorial will be presented to you requesting authority to have the governor elected by the people of Porto Rico. This was never done in the case of our own Territories. It is admitted that education outside of the towns is as yet very deficient. Until it has progressed further the efficiency of the government and the happiness of the people may need the guiding hand of an appointed governor. As it is not contemplated that any change should be made immediately, the general subject may well have the thoughtful study of the Congress.

PANAMA CANAL

The number of commercial ships passing through the Panama Canal has increased from 3,967 in 1923 to 5,475 in 1927. The total amount of tolls turned into the Treasury is over $166,000,000, while all the operations of the canal have yielded a surplus of about $80,000,000. In order to provide additional storage of water and give some control over the floods of the Chagres River, it is proposed to erect a dam to cost about $12,000,000 at Alhajuela. It will take some five years to complete this work.

AGRICULTURE

The past year has seen a marked improvement in the general condition of agriculture. Production is better balanced and without acute shortage or heavy surplus. Costs have been reduced and the average output of the worker increased. The level of farm prices has risen, while others have fallen, so that the purchasing power of the farmer is approaching a normal figure. The individual farmer is entitled to great credit for the progress made since 1921. He has adjusted his production and through cooperative organizations and other methods improved his marketing. He is using authenticated facts and employing sound methods which other industries are obliged to use to secure stability and prosperity. The old-fashioned haphazard system is being abandoned, economics are being applied to ascertain the best adapted unit of land, diversification is being promoted, and scientific methods are being used in production, and business principles in marketing.

Agriculture has not fully recovered from postwar depression. The fact is that economic progress never marches forward in a straight line. It goes in waves. One part goes ahead, while another halts and another recedes. Everybody wishes agriculture to prosper. Any sound and workable proposal to help the farmer will have the earnest support of the Government. Their interests are not all identical. Legislation should assist as many producers in as many regions as possible. It should be the aim to assist the farmer to work out his own salvation socially and economically. No plan will be of any permanent value to him which does not leave him standing on his own foundation.

In the past the Government has spent vast sums to bring land under cultivation. It is apparent that this has reached temporarily the saturation point. We have had a surplus of production and a poor market for land, which has only lately shown signs of improvement. The main problem which is presented for solution is one of dealing with a surplus of production. It is useless to propose a temporary expedient. What is needed is permanency and stability. Government price fixing is known to be unsound and bound to result in disaster. A Government subsidy would work out in the same way. It can not be sound for all of the people to hire some of the people to produce a crop which neither the producers nor the rest of the people want.

Price fixing and subsidy will both increase the surplus, instead of diminishing it. Putting the Government directly into business is merely a combination of subsidy and price fixing aggravated by political pressure. These expedients would lead logically to telling the farmer by law what and how much he should plant and where he should plant it, and what and how much he should sell and where he should sell it. The most effective means of dealing with surplus crops is to reduce the surplus acreage. While this can not be done by the individual farmer, it can be done through the organizations already in existence, through the information published by the Department of Agriculture, and especially through banks and others who supply credit refusing to finance an acreage manifestly too large.

It is impossible to provide by law for an assured success and prosperity for all those who engage in farming. If acreage becomes overextended, the Government can not assume responsibility for it.

The Government can, however, assist cooperative associations and other organizations in orderly marketing and handling a surplus clearly due to weather and seasonal conditions, in order to save the producer from preventable loss. While it is probably impossible to secure this result at a single step, and much will have to be worked out by trial and rejection, a beginning could be made by setting up a Federal board or commission of able and experienced men in marketing, granting equal advantages under this board to the various agricultural commodities and sections of the country, giving encouragement to the cooperative movement in agriculture, and providing a revolving loan fund at a moderate rate of interest for the necessary financing. Such legislation would lay the foundation for a permanent solution of the surplus problem.

This is not a proposal to lend more money to the farmer, who is already fairly well financed, but to lend money temporarily to experimental marketing associations which will no doubt ultimately be financed by the regularly established banks, as were the temporary operations of the War Finance Corporation. Cooperative marketing especially would be provided with means of buying or building physical properties.

The National Government has almost entirely relieved the farmer from income taxes by successive tax reductions, but State and local taxes have increased, putting on him a grievous burden. A policy of rigid economy should be applied to State and local expenditures. This is clearly within the legislative domain of the States. The Federal Government has also improved our banking structure and system of agricultural credits. The farmer will be greatly benefited by similar action in many States. The Department of Agriculture is undergoing changes in organization in order more completely to separate the research and regulatory divisions, that each may be better administered. More emphasis is being placed on the research program, not only by enlarging the appropriations for State experiment stations but by providing funds for expanding the research work of the department. It is in this direction that much future progress can be expected.

THE PROTECTIVE TARIFF

The present tariff rates supply the National Treasury with well over $600,000,000 of annual revenue. Yet, about 65 per cent of our imports come in duty free. Of the remaining 35 per cent of imports on which duties are laid about 23 per cent consists of luxuries and agricultural products, and the balance of about 12 per cent, amounting to around $560,000,000, is made up of manufactures and merchandise. As no one is advocating any material reduction in the rates on agriculture or luxuries, it is only the comparatively small amount of about $560,000,000 of other imports that are really considered in any discussion of reducing tariff rates. While this amount, duty free, would be large enough seriously to depress many lines of business in our own country, it is of small importance when spread over the rest of the world.

It is often stated that a reduction of tariff rates on industry would benefit agriculture. It would be interesting to know to what commodities it is thought this could be applied. Everything the farmer uses in farming is already on the free list. Nearly everything he sells is protected. It would seem to be obvious that it is better for the country to have the farmer raise food to supply the domestic manufacturer than the foreign manufacturer. In one case our country would have only the farmer; in the other it would have the farmer and the manufacturer. Assuming that Europe would have more money if it sold us larger amounts of merchandise, it is not certain it would consume more food, or, if it did, that its purchases would be made in this country. Undoubtedly it would resort to the cheapest market, which is by no means ours. The largest and best and most profitable market for the farmer in the world is our own domestic market. Any great increase in manufactured imports means the closing of our own plants. Nothing could be worse for agriculture.

Probably no one expects a material reduction in the rates on manufactures while maintaining the rates on agriculture. A material reduction in either would be disastrous to the farmer. It would mean a general shrinkage of values, a deflation of prices, a reduction of wages, a general depression carrying our people down to the low standard of living in our competing countries. It is obvious that this would not improve but destroy our market for imports, which is best served by maintaining our present high purchasing power under which in the past five years imports have increased 63 per cent.

FARM LOAN SYSTEM

It is exceedingly important that the Federal land and joint-stock land banks should furnish the best possible service for agriculture. Certain joint-stock banks have fallen into improper and unsound practices, resulting in the indictment of the officials of three of them. More money has been provided for examinations, and at the instance of the Treasury rules and regulations of the Federal Farm Board have been revised. Early last May three of its members resigned. Their places were filled with men connected with the War Finance Corporation, Eugene Meyer being designated as Farm Loan Commissioner. The new members have demonstrated their ability in the field of agricultural finance in the extensive operations of the War Finance Corporation. Three joint-stock banks have gone into receivership. It is necessary to preserve the public confidence in this system in order to find a market for their bonds. A recent flotation was made at a record low rate of 4 per cent. Careful supervision is absolutely necessary to protect the investor and enable these banks to exercise their chief function in serving agriculture.

MUSCLE SHOALS

The last year has seen considerable changes in the problem of Muscle Shoals. Development of other methods show that nitrates can probably be produced at less cost than by the use of hydro-electric power. Extensive investigation made by the Department of War indicates that the nitrate plants on this project are of little value for national defense and can probably be disposed of within two years. The oxidation part of the plants, however, should be retained indefinitely. This leaves this project mostly concerned with power. It should, nevertheless, continue to be dedicated to agriculture. It is probable that this desire can be best served by disposing of the plant and applying the revenues received from it to research for methods of more economical production of concentrated fertilizer and to demonstrations and other methods of stimulating its use on the farm. But in disposing of the property preference should be given to proposals to use all or part of it for nitrate production and fertilizer manufacturing.

FLOOD CONTROL

For many years the Federal Government has been building a system of dikes along the Mississippi River for protection against high water. During the past season the lower States were overcome by a most disastrous flood. Many thousands of square miles were inundated, a great many lives were lost, much livestock was drowned, and a very heavy destruction of property was inflicted upon the inhabitants. The American Red Cross at once went to the relief of the stricken communities. Appeals for contributions have brought in over $17,000,000. The Federal Government has provided services, equipment, and supplies probably amounting to about $7,000,000 more. Between $5,000,000 and $10,000,000 in addition have been provided by local railroads, the States, and their political units. Credits have been arranged by the Farm Loan Board, and three emergency finance corporations with a total capital of $3,000,000 have insured additional resources to the extent of $12,000,000. Through these means the 700,000 people in the flooded areas have been adequately supported. Provision has been made to care for those in need until after the 1st of January.

The Engineer Corps of the Army has contracted to close all breaks in the dike system before the next season of high water. A most thorough and elaborate survey of the whole situation has been made and embodied in a report with recommendations for future flood control, which will be presented to the Congress. The carrying out of their plans will necessarily extend over a series of years. They will call for a raising and strengthening of the dike system with provision for emergency spillways and improvements for the benefit of navigation.

Under the present law the land adjacent to the dikes has paid one-third of the cost of their construction. This has been a most extraordinary concession from the plan adopted in relation to irrigation, where the general rule has been that the land benefited should bear the entire expense. It is true, of course, that the troublesome waters do not originate on the land to be reclaimed, but it is also true that such waters have a right of way through that section of the country and the land there is charged with that easement. It is the land of this region that is to be benefited. To say that it is unable to bear any expense of reclamation is the same thing as saying that it is not worth reclaiming. Because of expenses incurred and charges already held against this land, it seems probable that some revision will have to be made concerning the proportion of cost which it should bear. But it is extremely important that it should pay enough so that those requesting improvements will be charged with some responsibility for their cost, and the neighborhood where works are constructed have a pecuniary interest in preventing waste and extravagance and securing a wise and economical expenditure of public funds.

It is necessary to look upon this emergency as a national disaster. It has been so treated from its inception. Our whole people have provided with great generosity for its relief. Most of the departments of the Federal Government have been engaged in the same effort. The governments of the afflicted areas, both State and municipal, can not be given too high praise for the courageous and helpful way in which they have come to the rescue of the people. If the sources directly chargeable can not meet the demand, the National Government should not fail to provide generous relief. This, however, does not mean restoration. The Government is not an insurer of its citizens against the hazard of the elements. We shall always have flood and drought, heat and cold, earthquake and wind, lightning and tidal wave, which are all too constant in their afflictions. The Government does not undertake to reimburse its citizens for loss and damage incurred under such circumstances. It is chargeable, however, with the rebuilding of public works and the humanitarian duty of relieving its citizens from distress.

The people in the flooded area and their representatives have approached this problem in the most generous and broad-minded way. They should be met with a like spirit on the part of the National Government. This is all one country. The public needs of each part must be provided for by the public at large. No required relief should be refused. An adequate plan should be adopted to prevent a recurrence of this disaster in order that the people may restore to productivity and comfort their fields and their towns.

Legislation by this Congress should be confined to our principal and most pressing problem, the lower Mississippi, considering tributaries only so far as they materially affect the main flood problem. A definite Federal program relating to our waterways was proposed when the last Congress authorized a comprehensive survey of all the important streams of the country in order to provide for their improvement, including flood control, navigation, power, and irrigation. Other legislation should wait pending a report on this survey. The recognized needs of the Mississippi should not be made a vehicle for carrying other projects. All proposals for development should stand on their own merits. Any other method would result in ill-advised conclusions, great waste of money, and instead of promoting would delay the orderly and certain utilization of our water resources.

Very recently several of the New England States have suffered somewhat similarly from heavy rainfall and high water. No reliable estimate of damage has yet been computed, but it is very large to private and public property. The Red Cross is generously undertaking what is needed for immediate relief, repair and reconstruction of houses, restocking of domestic animals, and food, clothing, and shelter. A considerable sum of money will be available through the regular channels in the Department of Agriculture for reconstruction of highways. It may be necessary to grant special aid for this purpose. Complete reports of what is required will undoubtedly be available early in the session.

INLAND NAVIGATION

The Congress in its last session authorized the general improvements necessary to provide the Mississippi waterway system with better transportation. Stabilization of the levels of the Great Lakes and their opening to the sea by an effective shipway remain to be considered. Since the last session the Board of Engineers of the War Department has made a report on the proposal for a canal through the State of New York, and the Joint Board of Engineers, representing Canada and the United States, has finished a report on the St. Lawrence River. Both of these boards conclude that the St. Lawrence project is cheaper, affords a more expeditious method of placing western products in European markets, and will cost less to operate. The State Department has requested the Canadian Government to negotiate treaties necessary to provide for this improvement. It will also be necessary to secure an agreement with Canada to put in works necessary to prevent fluctuation in the levels of the Great Lakes.

Legislation is desirable for the construction of a dam at Boulder Canyon on the Colorado River, primarily as a method of flood control and irrigation. A secondary result would be a considerable power development and a source of domestic water supply for southern California. Flood control is clearly a national problem, and water supply is a Government problem, but every other possibility should be exhausted before the Federal Government becomes engaged in the power business. The States which are interested ought to reach mutual agreement. This project is in reality their work. If they wish the Federal Government to undertake it, they should not hesitate to make the necessary concessions to each other. This subject is fully discussed in the annual report of the Secretary of the Interior. The Columbia River Basin project is being studied and will be one to be considered at some future time.

The Inland Waterways Corporation is proving successful and especially beneficial to agriculture. A survey is being made to determine its future needs. It has never been contemplated that if inland rivers were opened to navigation it would then be necessary for the Federal Government to provide the navigation. Such a request is very nearly the equivalent of a declaration that their navigation is not profitable, that the commodities which they are to carry can be taken at a cheaper rate by some other method, in which case the hundreds of millions of dollars proposed to be expended for opening rivers to navigation would be not only wasted, but would entail further constant expenditures to carry the commodities of private persons for less than cost.

The policy is well established that the Government should open public highways on land and on water, but for use of the public in their private capacity. It has put on some demonstration barge lines, but always with the expectation that if they prove profitable they would pass into private hands and if they do not prove profitable they will be withdrawn. The problems of transportation over inland waterways should be taken up by private enterprise, so that the public will have the advantage of competition in service. It is expected that some of our lines can be sold, some more demonstration work done, and that with the completion of the Ohio project a policy of private operation can be fully developed.

PROHIBITION

After more than two generations of constant debate, our country adopted a system of national prohibition under all the solemnities involved in an amendment to the Federal Constitution. In obedience to this mandate the Congress and the States, with one or two notable exceptions, have passed required laws for its administration and enforcement. This imposes upon the citizenship of the country, and especially on all public officers, not only the duty to enforce, but the obligation to observe the sanctions of this constitutional provision and its resulting laws. If this condition could be secured, all question concerning prohibition would cease. The Federal Government is making every effort to accomplish these results through careful organization, large appropriations, and administrative effort. Smuggling has been greatly cut down, the larger sources of supply for illegal sale have been checked, and by means of injunction and criminal prosecution the process of enforcement is being applied. The same vigilance on the part of local governments would render these efforts much more successful. The Federal authorities propose to discharge their obligation for enforcement to the full extent of their ability.

THE NEGRO

History does not anywhere record so much progress made in the same length of time as that which has been accomplished by the Negro race in the United States since the Emancipation Proclamation. They have come up from slavery to be prominent in education, the professions, art, science, agriculture, banking, and commerce. It is estimated that 50,000 of them are on the Government pay rolls, drawing about $50,000,000 each year. They have been the recipients of presidential appointments and their professional ability has arisen to a sufficiently high plane so that they have been intrusted with the entire management and control of the great veterans' hospital at Tuskegee, where their conduct has taken high rank. They have shown that they have been worthy of all the encouragement which they have received. Nevertheless, they are too often subjected to thoughtless and inconsiderate treatment, unworthy alike of the white or colored races. They have especially been made the target of the foul crime of lynching. For several years these acts of unlawful violence had been diminishing. In the last year they have shown an increase. Every principle of order and law and liberty is opposed to this crime. The Congress should enact any legislation it can under the Constitution to provide for its elimination.

AMERICAN INDIAN

The condition of the American Indian has much improved in recent years. Full citizenship was bestowed upon them on June 2, 1924, and appropriations for their care and advancement have been increased. Still there remains much to be done.

Notable increases in appropriations for the several major functions performed by the Department of the Interior on behalf of the Indians have marked the last five years. In that time, successive annual increases in appropriations for their education total $1,804,325; for medical care, $578,000; and for industrial advancement, $205,000; or $2,582,325 more than would have been spent in the same period on the basis of appropriations for 1923 and the preceding years.

The needs along health, educational, industrial, and social lines, however, are great, and the Budget estimates for 1929 include still further increases for Indian administration.

To advance the time when the Indians may become self-sustaining, it is my belief that the Federal Government should continue to improve the facilities for their care, and as rapidly as possible turn its responsibility over to the States.

COAL

Legislation authorizing a system of fuel administration and the appointment by the President of a Board of Mediation and Conciliation in case of actual or threatened interruption of production is needed. The miners themselves are now seeking information and action from the Government, which could readily be secured through such a board. It is believed that a thorough investigation and reconsideration of this proposed policy by the Congress will demonstrate that this recommendation is sound and should be adopted.

PETROLEUM CONSERVATION

The National Government is undertaking to join in the formation of a cooperative committee of lawyers, engineers, and public officers, to consider what legislation by the States or by the Congress can be adopted for the preservation and conservation of our supply of petroleum. This has come to be one of the main dependencies for transportation and power so necessary to our agricultural and industrial life. It is expected the report of this committee will be available for later congressional action. Meantime, the requirement that the Secretary of the Interior should make certain leases of land belonging to the Osage Indians, in accordance with the act of March 3, 1921, should be repealed. The authority to lease should be discretionary, in order that the property of the Indians may not be wasted and the public suffer a future lack of supply.

ALIEN PROPERTY

Under treaty the property held by the Alien Property Custodian was to be retained until suitable provision had been made for the satisfaction of American claims. While still protecting the American claimants, in order to afford every possible accommodation to the nationals of the countries whose property was held, the Congress has made liberal provision for the return of a large part of the property. All trusts under $10,000 were returned in full, and partial returns were made on the others. The total returned was approximately $350,000,000.

There is still retained, however, about $250,000,000. The Mixed Claims Commission has made such progress in the adjudication of claims that legislation can now be enacted providing for the return of the property, which should be done under conditions which will protect our Government and our claimants. Such a measure will be proposed, and I recommend its enactment.

RAILROAD CONSOLIDATION

In order to increase the efficiency of transportation and decrease its cost to the shipper, railroad consolidation must be secured. Legislation is needed to simplify the necessary procedure to secure such agreements and arrangements for consolidation, always under the control and with the approval of the Interstate Commerce Commission. Pending this, no adequate or permanent reorganization can be made of the freight-rate structure. Meantime, both agriculture and industry are compelled to wait for needed relief. This is purely a business question, which should be stripped of all local and partisan bias and decided on broad principles and its merits in order to promote the public welfare. A large amount of new construction and equipment, which will furnish employment for labor and markets for commodities of both factory and farm, wait on the decision of this important question. Delay is holding back the progress of our country.

Many of the same arguments are applicable to the consolidation of the Washington traction companies.

VETERANS

The care which this country has lavished on its veterans is known of all men. The yearly outlay for this purpose is about $750,000,000, or about the cost of running the Federal Government, outside of the Post Office Department, before the World War. The Congress will have before it recommendations of the American Legion, the Veterans of Foreign Wars, and other like organizations, which should receive candid consideration. We should continue to foster our system of compensation and rehabilitation, and provide hospitals and insurance. The magnitude of the undertaking is already so large that all requests calling for further expenditure should have the most searching scrutiny. Our present system of pensions is already sufficiently liberal. It was increased by the last Congress for Civil and Spanish War veterans and widows and for some dependents.

It has been suggested that the various governmental agencies now dealing with veterans' relief be consolidated. This would bring many advantages. It is recommended that the proper committees of the Congress make a thorough survey of this subject, in order to determine if legislation to secure such consolidation is desirable.

EDUCATION

For many years it has been the policy of the Federal Government to encourage and foster the cause of education. Large sums of money are annually appropriated to carry on vocational training. Many millions go into agricultural schools. The general subject is under the immediate direction of a Commissioner of Education. While this subject is strictly a State and local function, it should continue to have the encouragement of the National Government. I am still of the opinion that much good could be accomplished through the establishment of a Department of Education and Relief, into which would be gathered all of these functions under one directing member of the Cabinet.

DEPARTMENT OF LABOR

Industrial relations have never been more peaceful. In recent months they have suffered from only one serious controversy. In all others difficulties have been adjusted, both management and labor wishing to settle controversies by friendly agreement rather than by compulsion. The welfare of women and children is being especially guarded by our Department of Labor. Its Children's Bureau is in cooperation with 26 State boards and 80 juvenile courts.

Through its Bureau of Immigration it has been found that medical examination abroad has saved prospective immigrants from much hardship. Some further legislation to provide for reuniting families when either the husband or the wife is in this country, and granting more freedom for the migration of the North American Indian tribes is desirable.

The United States Employment Service has enabled about 2,000,000 men and women to gain paying positions in the last fiscal year. Particular attention has been given to assisting men past middle life and in providing field labor for harvesting agricultural crops. This has been made possible in part through the service of the Federal Board for Vocational Education, which is cooperating with the States in a program to increase the technical knowledge and skill of the wage earner.

PUBLIC BUILDINGS

Construction is under way in the country and ground has been broken for carrying out a public-building program for Washington. We have reached a time when not only the conveniences but the architectural beauty of the public buildings of the Capital City should be given much attention. It will be necessary to purchase further land and provide the required continuing appropriations.

HISTORICAL CELEBRATIONS

Provision is being made to commemorate the two hundredth anniversary of the birth of George Washington. Suggestion has been made for the construction of a memorial road leading from the Capital to Mount Vernon, which may well have the consideration of the Congress, and the commission intrusted with preparations for the celebration will undoubtedly recommend publication of the complete writings of Washington and a series of writings by different authors relating to him.

February 25, 1929, is the one hundred and fiftieth anniversary of the capture of Fort Sackville, at Vincennes, in the State of Indiana. This eventually brought into the Union what was known as the Northwest Territory, embracing the region north of the Ohio River between the Alleghenies and the Mississippi River. This expedition was led by George Rogers Clark. His heroic character and the importance of his victory are too little known and understood. They gave us not only this Northwest Territory but by means of that the prospect of reaching the Pacific. The State of Indiana is proposing to dedicate the site of Fort Sackville as a national shrine. The Federal Government may well make some provision for the erection under its own management of a fitting memorial at that point.

FOREIGN RELATIONS

It is the policy of the United States to promote peace. We are a peaceful people and committed to the settling of disputes by amicable adjustment rather than by force. We have believed that peace can best be secured by a faithful observance on our part of the principles of international law, accompanied by patience and conciliation, and requiring of others a like treatment for ourselves. We have lately had some difference with Mexico relative to the injuries inflicted upon our nationals and their property within that country. A firm adherence to our rights and a scrupulous respect for the sovereignty of Mexico, both in accordance with the law of nations, coupled with patience and forbearance, it is hoped will resolve all our differences without interfering with the friendly relationship between the two Governments.

We have been compelled to send naval and marine forces to China to protect the lives and property of our citizens. Fortunately their simple presence there has been sufficient to prevent any material loss of life. But there has been considerable loss of property. That unhappy country is torn by factions and revolutions which bid fair to last for an indefinite period. Meanwhile we are protecting our citizens and stand ready to cooperate with any government which may emerge in promoting the welfare of the people of China. They have always had our friendship, and they should especially merit our consideration in these days of their distraction and distress.

We were confronted by similar condition on a small scale in Nicaragua. Our marine and naval forces protected our citizens and their property and prevented a heavy sacrifice of life and the destruction of that country by a reversion to a state of revolution. Henry L. Stimson, former Secretary of War, was sent there to cooperate with our diplomatic and military officers in effecting a settlement between the contending parties. This was done on the assurance that we would cooperate in restoring a state of peace where our rights would be protected by giving our assistance in the conduct of the next presidential election, which occurs in a few months. With this assurance the population returned to their peace-time pursuits, with the exception of some small roving bands of outlaws.

In general, our relations with other countries can be said to have improved within the year. While having a due regard for our own affairs, the protection of our own rights, and the advancement of our own people, we can afford to be liberal toward others. Our example has become of great importance in the world. It is recognized that we are independent, detached, and can and do take a disinterested position in relation to international affairs. Our charity embraces the earth. Our trade is far flung. Our financial favors are widespread. Those who are peaceful and law-abiding realize that not only have they nothing to fear from us, but that they can rely on our moral support. Proposals for promoting the peace of the world will have careful consideration. But we are not a people who are always seeking for a sign. We know that peace comes from honesty and fair dealing, from moderation, and a generous regard for the rights of others. The heart of the Nation is more important than treaties. A spirit of generous consideration is a more certain defense than great armaments. We should continue to promote peace by our example, and fortify it by such international covenants against war as we are permitted under our Constitution to make.

AMERICAN PROGRESS

Our country has made much progress. But it has taken, and will continue to take, much effort. Competition will be keen, the temptation to selfishness and arrogance will be severe, the provocations to deal harshly with weaker peoples will be many. All of these are embraced in the opportunity for true greatness. They will be overbalanced by cooperation, by generosity, and a spirit of neighborly kindness. The forces of the universe are taking humanity in that direction. In doing good, in walking humbly, in sustaining its own people, in ministering to other nations, America will work out its own mighty destiny.

SIXTH ANNUAL MESSAGE.

THE WHITE HOUSE, *December 4, 1928.*

TO THE CONGRESS OF THE UNITED STATES:

No Congress of the United States ever assembled, on surveying the state of the Union, has met with a more pleasing prospect than that which appears at the present time. In the domestic field there is tranquillity and contentment, harmonious relations between management and wage earner, freedom from industrial strife, and the highest record of years of prosperity. In the foreign field there is peace, the good will which comes from mutual understanding, and the knowledge that the problems which a short time ago appeared so ominous are yielding to the touch of manifest friendship. The great wealth created by our enterprise and industry, and saved by our economy, has had the widest distribution among our own people, and has gone out in a steady stream to serve the charity and the business of the world. The requirements of existence have passed beyond the standard of necessity into the region of luxury. Enlarging production is consumed by an increasing demand at home and an expanding commerce abroad. The country can regard the present with satisfaction and anticipate the future with optimism.

The main source of these unexampled blessings lies in the integrity and character of the American people. They have had great faith, which they have supplemented with mighty works. They have been able to put trust in each other and trust in their Government. Their candor in dealing with foreign governments has commanded respect and confidence. Yet these remarkable powers would have been exerted almost in vain without the constant cooperation and careful administration of the Federal Government.

We have been coming into a period which may be fairly characterized as a conservation of our national resources. Wastefulness in public business and private enterprise has been displaced by constructive economy. This has been accomplished by bringing our domestic and foreign relations more and more under a reign of law. A rule of force has been giving way to a rule of reason. We have substituted for the vicious circle of increasing expenditures, increasing tax rates, and diminishing profits the charmed circle of diminishing expenditures, diminishing tax rates, and increasing profits.

Four times we have made a drastic revision of our internal revenue system, abolishing many taxes and substantially reducing almost all others. Each time the resulting stimulation to business has so increased taxable incomes and profits that a surplus has been produced. One-third of the national debt has been paid, while much of the other two-thirds has been refunded at lower rates, and these savings of interest and constant economies have enabled us to repeat the satisfying process of more tax reductions. Under this sound and healthful encouragement the national income has increased nearly 50 per cent, until it is estimated to stand well over $90,000,000,000. It has been a method which has performed the seeming miracle of leaving a much greater percentage of earnings in the hands of the taxpayers with scarcely any diminution of the Government revenue. That is constructive economy in the highest degree. It is the corner stone of prosperity. It should not fail to be continued.

This action began by the application of economy to public expenditure. If it is to be permanent, it must be made so by the repeated application of economy. There is no surplus on which to base further tax revision at this time. Last June the estimates showed a threatened deficit for the current fiscal year of $94,000,000. Under my direction the departments began saving all they could out of their present appropriations. The last tax reduction brought an encouraging improvement in business, beginning early in October, which will also increase our revenue. The combination of economy and good times now indicates a surplus of about $37,000,000. This is a margin of less than 1 per cent on our expenditures and makes it obvious that the Treasury is in no condition to undertake increases in expenditures to be made before June 30. It is necessary therefore during the present session to refrain from new appropriations for immediate outlay, or if such are absolutely required to provide for them by new revenue; otherwise, we shall reach the end of the year with the unthinkable result of an unbalanced budget. For the first time during my term of office we face that contingency. I am certain that the Congress would not pass and I should not feel warranted in approving legislation which would involve us in that financial disgrace.

On the whole the finances of the Government are most satisfactory. Last year the national debt was reduced about $906,000,000. The refunding and retirement of the second and third Liberty loans have just been brought to a successful conclusion, which will save about $75,000,000 a year in interest. The unpaid balance has been arranged in maturities convenient for carrying out our permanent debt-paying program.

The enormous savings made have not been at the expense of any legitimate public need. The Government plant has been kept up and many improvements are under way, while its service is fully manned and the general efficiency of operation has increased. We have been enabled to undertake many new enterprises. Among these are the adjusted compensation of the veterans of the World War, which is costing us $112,000,000 a year; amortizing our liability to the civil-service retirement funds, $20,000,000; increase of expenditures for rivers and harbors including flood control, $43,000,000; public buildings, $47,000,000. In 1928 we spent $50,000,000 in the adjustment of war claims and alien property. These are examples of a large list of items.

FOREIGN RELATIONS

When we turn from our domestic affairs to our foreign relations, we likewise perceive peace and progress. The Sixth International Conference of American States was held at Habana last winter. It contributed to a better understanding and cooperation among the nations. Eleven important conventions were signed and 71 resolutions passed. Pursuant to the plan then adopted, this Government has invited the other 20 nations of this hemisphere to a conference on conciliation and arbitration, which meets in Washington on December 10. All the nations have accepted and the expectation is justified that important progress will be made in methods for resolving international differences by means of arbitration.

During the year we have signed 11 new arbitration treaties, and 22 more are under negotiation.

NICARAGUA

When a destructive and bloody revolution lately broke out in Nicaragua, at the earnest and repeated entreaties of its Government I dispatched our Marine forces there to protect the lives and interests of our citizens. To compose the contending parties, I sent there Col. Henry L. Stimson, former Secretary of War and now Governor General of the Philippine Islands, who secured an agreement that warfare should cease, a national election should be held and peace should be restored. Both parties conscientiously carried out this agreement, with the exception of a few bandits who later mostly surrendered or left the country. President Diaz appointed Brig. Gen. Frank R. McCoy, United States Army, president of the election board, which included also one member of each political party.

A free and fair election has been held and has worked out so successfully that both parties have joined in requesting like cooperation from this country at the election four years hence, to which I have refrained from making any commitments, although our country must be gratified at such an exhibition of success and appreciation.

Nicaragua is regaining its prosperity and has taken a long step in the direction of peaceful self-government.

TACNA-ARICA

The long-standing differences between Chile and Peru have been sufficiently composed so that diplomatic relations have been resumed by the exchange of ambassadors. Negotiations are hopefully proceeding as this is written for the final adjustment of the differences over their disputed territory.

MEXICO

Our relations with Mexico are on a more satisfactory basis than at any time since their revolution. Many misunderstandings have been resolved and the most frank and friendly negotiations promise a final adjustment of all unsettled questions. It is exceedingly gratifying that Ambassador Morrow has been able to bring our two neighboring countries, which have so many interests in common, to a position of confidence in each other and of respect for mutual sovereign rights.

CHINA

The situation in China which a few months ago was so threatening as to call for the dispatch of a large additional force has been much composed. The Nationalist Government has established itself over the country and promulgated a new organic law announcing a program intended to promote the political and economic welfare of the people. We have recognized this Government, encouraged its progress, and have negotiated a treaty restoring to China complete tariff autonomy and guaranteeing our citizens against discriminations. Our trade in that quarter is increasing and our forces are being reduced.

GREEK AND AUSTRIAN DEBTS

Pending before the Congress is a recommendation for the settlement of the Greek debt and the Austrian debt. Both of these are comparatively small and our country can afford to be generous. The rehabilitation of these countries awaits their settlement. There would also be advantages to our trade. We could scarcely afford to be the only nation that refuses the relief which Austria seeks. The Congress has already granted Austria a long-time moratorium, which it is understood will be waived and immediate payments begun on her debt on the same basis which we have extended to other countries.

PEACE TREATY

One of the most important treaties ever laid before the Senate of the United States will be that which the 15 nations recently signed at Paris, and to which 44 other nations have declared their intention to adhere, renouncing war as a national policy and agreeing to resort only to peaceful means for the adjustment of international differences. It is the most solemn declaration against war, the most positive adherence to peace, that it is possible for sovereign nations to make. It does not supersede our inalienable sovereign right and duty of national defense or undertake to commit us before the event to any mode of action which the Congress might decide to be wise if ever the treaty should be broken. But it is a new standard in the world around which can rally the informed and enlightened opinion of nations to prevent their governments from being forced into hostile action by the temporary outbreak of international animosities. The observance of this covenant, so simple and so straightforward, promises more for the peace of the world than any other agreement ever negotiated among the nations.

NATIONAL DEFENSE

The first duty of our Government to its own citizens and foreigners within its borders is the preservation of order. Unless and until that duty is met a government is not even eligible for recognition among the family of nations. The advancement of world civilization likewise is dependent upon that order among the people of different countries which we term peace. To insure our citizens against the infringement of their legal rights at home and abroad, to preserve order, liberty, and peace by making the law supreme, we have an Army and a Navy.

Both of these are organized for defensive purposes. Our Army could not be much reduced, but does not need to be increased. Such new housing and repairs as are necessary are under way and the 5-year program in aviation is being put into effect in both branches of our service.

Our Navy, according to generally accepted standards, is deficient in cruisers. We have 10 comparatively new vessels, 22 that are old, and 8 to be built. It is evident that renewals and replacements must be provided. This matter was thoroughly canvassed at the last session of the Congress and does not need restatement. The bill before the Senate with the elimination of the time clause should be passed. We have no intention of competing with any other country. This building program is for necessary replacements and to meet our needs for defense.

The cost of national defense is stupendous. It has increased $118,000,000 in the past four years. The estimated expenditure for 1930 is $668,000,000. While this is made up of many items it is, after all, mostly dependent upon numbers. Our defensive needs do not call for any increase in the number of men in the Army or the Navy. We have reached the limit of what we ought to expend for that purpose.

I wish to repeat again for the benefit of the timid and the suspicious that this country is neither militaristic nor imperialistic. Many people at home and abroad, who constantly make this charge, are the same ones who are even more solicitous to have us extend assistance to foreign countries. When such assistance is granted, the inevitable result is that we have foreign interests. For us to refuse the customary support and protection of such interests would be in derogation of the sovereignty of this Nation. Our largest foreign interests are in the British Empire, France, and Italy. Because we are constantly solicitous for those interests, I doubt if anyone would suppose that those countries feel we harbor toward them any militaristic or imperialistic design. As for smaller countries, we certainly do not want any of them. We are more anxious than they are to have their sovereignty respected. Our entire influence is in behalf of their independence. Cuba stands as a witness to our adherence to this principle.

The position of this Government relative to the limitation of armaments, the results already secured, and the developments up to the present time are so well known to the Congress that they do not require any restatement.

VETERANS

The magnitude of our present system of veterans' relief is without precedent, and the results have been far-reaching. For years a service pension has been granted to the Grand Army and lately to the survivors of the Spanish-American War. At the time we entered the World War, however, Congress departed from the usual pension system followed by our Government. Eleven years have elapsed since our laws were first enacted, initiating a system of compensation, rehabilitation, hospitalization, and insurance for the disabled of the World War and their dependents. The administration of all the laws concerning relief has been a difficult task, but it can safely be stated that these measures have omitted nothing in their desire to deal generously and humanely. We should continue to foster this system and provide all the facilities necessary for adequate care. It is the conception of our Government that the pension roll is an honor roll. It should include all those who are justly entitled to its benefits, but exclude all others.

Annual expenditures for all forms of veterans' relief now approximate $765,000,000, and are increasing from year to year. It is doubtful if the peak of expenditures will be reached even under present legislation for some time yet to come. Further amendments to the existing law will be suggested by the American Legion, the Veterans of Foreign Wars of the United States, the Disabled American Veterans of the World War, and other like organizations, and it may be necessary for administrative purposes, or in order to remove some existing inequalities in the present law, to make further changes. I am sure that such recommendations as may be submitted to the Congress will receive your careful consideration. But because of the vast expenditure now being made each year, with every assurance that it will increase, and because of the great liberality of the existing law, the proposal of any additional legislation dealing with this subject should receive most searching scrutiny from the Congress.

You are familiar with the suggestion that the various public agencies now dealing with matters of veterans' relief be consolidated in one Government department. Some advantages to this plan seem apparent, especially in the simplification of administration and in the opportunity of bringing about a greater uniformity in the application of veterans' relief. I recommend that a survey be made by the proper committees of Congress dealing with this subject, in order to determine whether legislation to secure this consolidation is desirable.

AGRICULTURE

The past year has been marked by notable though not uniform improvement in agriculture. The general purchasing power of farm products and the volume of production have advanced. This means not only further progress in overcoming the price disparity into which agriculture was plunged in 1920–21, but also increased efficiency on the part of farmers and a well-grounded confidence in the future of agriculture.

The livestock industry has attained the best balance for many years and is prospering conspicuously. Dairymen, beef producers, and poultrymen are receiving substantially larger returns than last year. Cotton, although lower in price than at this time last year, was produced in greater volume, and the prospect for cotton incomes is favorable. But progress is never uniform in a vast and highly diversified agriculture or industry. Cash grains, hay, tobacco, and potatoes will bring somewhat smaller returns this year than last. Present indications are, however, that the gross farm income will be somewhat larger than in the crop year 1927–28, when the total was $12,253,000,000. The corresponding figure for 1926–27 was $12,127,-000,000, and in 1925–26, $12,670,000,000. Still better results would have been secured this year had there not been an undue increase in the production of certain crops. This is particularly true of potatoes, which have sold at an unremunerative price, or at a loss, as a direct result of overexpansion of acreage.

The present status of agriculture, although greatly improved over that of a few years ago, bespeaks the need of further improvement, which calls for determined effort of farmers themselves, encouraged and assisted by wise public policy. The Government has been, and must continue to be, alive to the needs of agriculture.

In the past eight years more constructive legislation of direct benefit to agriculture has been adopted than during any other period. The Department of Agriculture has been broadened and reorganized to insure greater efficiency. The department is laying greater stress on the economic and business phases of agriculture. It is lending every possible assistance to cooperative marketing associations. Regulatory and research work have been segregated in order that each field may be served more effectively.

I can not too strongly commend, in the field of fact finding, the research work of the Department of Agriculture and the State experiment stations. The department now receives annually $4,000,000 more for research than in 1921. In addition, the funds paid to the States for experimentation purposes under the Purnell Act constitute an annual increase in Federal payments to State agricultural experiment stations of $2,400,000 over the amount appropriated in 1921. The program of support for research may wisely be continued and expanded. Since 1921 we have appropriated nearly an additional $2,000,000 for extension work, and this sum is to be increased next year under authorization by the Capper-Ketcham Act.

THE SURPLUS PROBLEM

While these developments in fundamental research, regulation, and dissemination of agricultural information are of distinct help to agriculture, additional effort is needed. The surplus problem demands attention. As emphasized in my last message, the Government should assume no responsibility in normal times for crop surplus clearly due to overextended acreage. The Government should, however, provide reliable information as a guide to private effort; and in this connection fundamental research on prospective supply and demand, as a guide to production and marketing, should be encouraged. Expenditure of public funds to bring in more new land should have most searching scrutiny, so long as our farmers face unsatisfactory prices for crops and livestock produced on land already under cultivation.

Every proper effort should be made to put land to uses for which it is adapted. The reforestation of land best suited for timber production is progressing and should be encouraged, and to this end the forest taxation inquiry was instituted to afford a practical guide for public policy. Improvement has been made in grazing regulation in the forest reserves, not only to protect the ranges, but to preserve the soil from erosion. Similar action is urgently needed to protect other public lands which are now overgrazed and rapidly eroding.

Temporary expedients, though sometimes capable of appeasing the demands of the moment, can not permanently solve the surplus problem and might seriously aggravate it. Hence putting the Government directly into business, subsidies, and price fixing, and the alluring promises of political action as a substitute for private initiative, should be avoided.

The Government should aid in promoting orderly marketing and in handling surpluses clearly due to weather and seasonal conditions. As a beginning there should be created a Federal farm board consisting of able and experienced men empowered to advise producers' associations in establishing central agencies or stabilization corporations to handle surpluses, to seek more economical means of merchandising, and to aid the producer in securing returns according to the quality of his product. A revolving loan fund should be provided for the necessary financing until these agencies shall have developed means of financing their operations through regularly constituted credit institutions. Such a bill should carry authority for raising the money, by loans or otherwise, necessary to meet the expense, as the Treasury has no surplus.

Agriculture has lagged behind industry in achieving that unity of effort which modern economic life demands. The cooperative movement, which is gradually building the needed organization, is in harmony with public interest and therefore merits public encouragement.

THE RESPONSIBILITY OF THE STATES

Important phases of public policy related to agriculture lie within the sphere of the States. While successive reductions in Federal taxes have relieved most farmers of direct taxes to the National Government, State and local levies have become a serious burden. This problem needs immediate and thorough study with a view to correction at the earliest possible moment. It will have to be made largely by the States themselves.

COMMERCE

It is desirable that the Government continue its helpful attitude toward American business. The activities of the Department of Commerce have contributed largely to the present satisfactory position in our international trade, which has reached about $9,000,000,000 annually. There should be no slackening of effort in that direction. It is also important that the department's assistance to domestic commerce be continued. There is probably no way in which the Government can aid sound economic progress more effectively than by cooperating with our business men to reduce wastes in distribution.

COMMERCIAL AERONAUTICS

Continued progress in civil aviation is most gratifying. Demands for airplanes and motors have taxed both the industry and the licensing and inspection service of the Department of Commerce to their capacity. While the compulsory licensing provisions of the air commerce act apply only to equipment and personnel engaged in interstate and foreign commerce, a Federal license may be procured by anyone possessing the necessary qualifications. State legislation, local airport regulations, and insurance requirements make such a license practically indispensable. This results in uniformity of regulation and increased safety in operation, which are essential to aeronautical development. Over 17,000 young men and women have now applied for Federal air-pilot's licenses or permits. More than 80 per cent of them applied during the past year.

Our national airway system exceeds 14,000 miles in length and has 7,500 miles lighted for night operations. Provision has been made for lighting 4,000 miles more during the current fiscal year and equipping an equal mileage with radio facilities. Three-quarters of our people are now served by these routes. With the rapid growth of air mail, express, and passenger service, this new transportation medium is daily becoming a more important factor in commerce. It is noteworthy that this development has taken place without governmental subsidies. Commercial passenger flights operating on schedule have reached 13,000 miles per day.

During the next fortnight this Nation will entertain the nations of the world in a celebration of the twenty-fifth anniversary of the first successful airplane flight. The credit for this epoch-making achievement belongs to a citizen of our own country, Orville Wright.

CUBAN PARCEL POST

I desire to repeat my recommendation of an earlier message, that Congress enact the legislation necessary to make permanent the Parcel Post Convention with Cuba, both as a facility to American commerce and as a measure of equity to Cuba in the one class of goods which that country can send here by parcel post without detriment to our own trade.

"MAINE" BATTLESHIP MEMORIAL

When I attended the Pan American Conference at Habana, the President of Cuba showed me a marble statue made from the original memorial that was overturned by a storm after it was erected on the Cuban shore to the memory of the men who perished in the destruction of the battleship *Maine*. As a testimony of friendship and appreciation of the Cuban Government and people he most generously offered to present this to the United States, and I assured him of my pleasure in accepting it. There is no location in the White House for placing so large and heavy a structure, and I therefore urge the Congress to provide by law for some locality where it can be set up.

RAILROADS

In previous annual messages I have suggested the enactment of laws to promote railroad consolidation with the view of increasing the efficiency of transportation and lessening its cost to the public. While consolidations can and should be made under the present law until it is changed, yet the provisions of the act of 1920 have not been found fully adequate to meet the needs of other methods of consolidation. Amendments designed to remedy these defects have been considered at length by the respective committees of Congress and a bill was reported out late in the last session which I understand has the approval in principle of the Interstate Commerce Commission. It is to be hoped that this legislation may be enacted at an early date.

Experience has shown that the interstate commerce law requires definition and clarification in several other respects, some of which have been pointed out by the Interstate Commerce Commission in its annual reports to the Congress. It will promote the public interest to have the Congress give early consideration to the recommendations there made.

MERCHANT MARINE

The cost of maintaining the United States Government merchant fleet has been steadily reduced. We have established American flag lines in foreign trade where they had never before existed as a means of promoting commerce and as a naval auxiliary. There have been sold to private American capital for operation within the past few years 14 of these lines, which, under the encouragement of the recent legislation passed by the Congress, give promise of continued successful operation. Additional legislation from time to time may be necessary to promote future advancement under private control.

Through the cooperation of the Post Office Department and the Shipping Board long-term contracts are being made with American steamship lines for carrying mail, which already promise the construction of 15 to 20 new vessels and the gradual reestablishment of the American merchant marine as a private enterprise. No action of the National Government has been so beneficial to our shipping. The cost is being absorbed to a considerable extent by the disposal of unprofitable lines operated by the Shipping Board, for which the new law has made a market. Meanwhile it should be our policy to maintain necessary strategic lines under the Government operation until they can be transferred to private capital.

INTER-AMERICAN HIGHWAY

In my message last year I expressed the view that we should lend our encouragement for more good roads to all the principal points on this hemisphere south of the Rio Grande. My view has not changed.

The Pan American Union has recently indorsed it. In some of the countries to the south a great deal of progress is being made in road building. In others engineering features are often exacting and financing difficult. As those countries enter upon programs for road building we should be ready to contribute from our abundant experience to make their task easier of accomplishment. I prefer not to go into civil life to accomplish this end. We already furnish military and naval advisors, and following this precedent we could draw competent men from these same sources and from the Department of Agriculture.

We should provide our southern neighbors, if they request it, with such engineer advisors for the construction of roads and bridges. Private interests should look with favor upon all reasonable loans sought by these countries to open main lines of travel. Such assistance should be given especially to any project for a highway designed to connect all the countries on this hemisphere and thus facilitate intercourse and closer relations among them.

AIR MAIL SERVICE

The friendly relations and the extensive commercial intercourse with the Western Hemisphere to the south of us are being further cemented by the establishment and extension of air-mail routes. We shall soon have one from Key West, Fla., over Cuba, Haiti, and Santo Domingo to San Juan, P. R., where it will connect with another route to Trinidad. There will be another route from Key West to the Canal Zone, where connection will be made with a route across the northern coast of South America to Paramaribo. This will give us a circle around the Caribbean under our own control.. Additional connections will be made at Colon with a route running down the west coast of South America as far as Concepcion, Chile, and with the French air mail at Paramaribo running down the eastern coast of South America. The air service already spans our continent, with laterals running to Mexico and Canada, and covering a daily flight of over 28,000 miles, with an average cargo of 15,000 pounds.

WATERWAYS

Our river and harbor improvements are proceeding with vigor. In the past few years we have increased the appropriation for this regular work $28,000,000, besides what is to be expended on flood control. The total appropriation for this year was over $91,000,000. The Ohio River is almost ready for opening; work on the Missouri and other rivers is under way. In accordance with the Mississippi flood law Army engineers are making investigations and surveys on other streams throughout the country with a view to flood control, navigation, waterpower, and irrigation. Our barge lines are being operated under generous appropriations, and negotiations are developing relative to the St. Lawrence waterway. To secure the largest benefits from all these waterways joint rates must be established with the railroads, preferably by agreement, but otherwise as a result of congressional action.

We have recently passed several river and harbor bills. The work ordered by the Congress, not yet completed, will cost about $243,-

000,000, besides the hundreds of millions to be spent on the Mississippi flood way. Until we can see our way out of this expense no further river and harbor legislation should be passed, as expenditures to put it into effect would be four or five years away.

IRRIGATION OF ARID LANDS

For many years the Federal Government has been committed to the wise policy of reclamation and irrigation. While it has met with some failures due to unwise selection of projects and lack of thorough soil surveys, so that they could not be placed on a sound business basis, on the whole the service has been of such incalculable benefit in so many States that no one would advocate its abandonment. The program to which we are already committed, providing for the construction of new projects authorized by Congress and the completion of old projects, will tax the resources of the reclamation fund over a period of years. The high cost of improving and equipping farms adds to the difficulty of securing settlers for vacant farms on Federal projects.

Readjustments authorized by the reclamation relief act of May 25, 1926, have given more favorable terms of repayment to settlers. These new financial arrangements and the general prosperity on irrigation projects have resulted in increased collections by the Department of the Interior of charges due the reclamation fund. Nevertheless, the demand for still smaller yearly payments on some projects continues. These conditions should have consideration in connection with any proposed new projects.

COLORADO RIVER

For several years the Congress has considered the erection of a dam on the Colorado River for flood-control, irrigation, and domestic water purposes, all of which may properly be considered as Government functions. There would be an incidental creation of water power which could be used for generating electricity. As private enterprise can very well fill this field, there is no need for the Government to go into it. It is unfortunate that the States interested in this water have been unable to agree among themselves. Nevertheless, any legislation should give every possible safeguard to the present and prospective rights of each of them.

The Congress will have before it the detailed report of a special board appointed to consider the engineering and economic feasibility of this project. From the short summary which I have seen of it, I judge they consider the engineering problems can be met at somewhat increased cost over previous estimates. They prefer the Black Canyon site. On the economic features they are not so clear and appear to base their conclusions on many conditions which can not be established with certainty. So far as I can judge, however, from the summary, their conclusions appear sufficiently favorable, so that I feel warranted in recommending a measure which will protect the rights of the States, discharge the necessary Government functions, and leave the electrical field to private enterprise.

MUSCLE SHOALS

The development of other methods of producing nitrates will probably render this plant less important for that purpose than formerly. But we have it, and I am told it still provides a practical method of making nitrates for national defense and farm fertilizers. By dividing the property into its two component parts of power and nitrate plants it would be possible to dispose of the power, reserving the right to any concern that wished to make nitrates to use any power that might be needed for that purpose. Such a disposition of the power plant can be made that will return in rental about $2,000,000 per year. If the Congress would grant the Secretary of War authority to lease the nitrate plant on such terms as would insure the largest production of nitrates, the entire property could begin to function. Such a division, I am aware, has never seemed to appeal to the Congress. I should also gladly approve a bill granting authority to lease the entire property for the production of nitrates.

I wish to avoid building another dam at public expense. Future operators should provide for that themselves. But if they were to be required to repay the cost of such dam with the prevailing commercial rates for interest, this difficulty will be considerably lessened. Nor do I think this property should be made a vehicle for putting the United States Government indiscriminately into the private and retail field of power distribution and nitrate sales.

CONSERVATION

The practical application of economy to the resources of the country calls for conservation. This does not mean that every resource should not be developed to its full degree, but it means that none of them should be wasted. We have a conservation board working on our oil problem. This is of the utmost importance to the future well-being of our people in this age of oil-burning engines and the general application of gasoline to transportation. The Secretary of the Interior should not be compelled to lease oil lands of the Osage Indians when the market is depressed and the future supply is in jeopardy.

While the area of lands remaining in public ownership is small, compared with the vast area in private ownership, the natural resources of those in public ownership are of immense present and future value. This is particularly true as to minerals and water power. The proper bureaus have been classifying these resources to the end that they may be conserved. Appropriate estimates are being submitted, in the Budget, for the further prosecution of this important work.

IMMIGRATION

The policy of restrictive immigration should be maintained. Authority should be granted the Secretary of Labor to give immediate preference to learned professions and experts essential to new industries. The reuniting of families should be expedited. Our immigration and naturalization laws might well be codified.

WAGE EARNER

In its economic life our country has rejected the long accepted law of a limitation of the wage fund, which led to pessimism and despair because it was the doctrine of perpetual poverty, and has substituted for it the American conception that the only limit to profits and wages is production, which is the doctrine of optimism and hope because it leads to prosperity. Here and there the councils of labor are still darkened by the theory that only by limiting individual production can there be any assurance of permanent employment for increasing numbers, but in general, management and wage earner alike have become emancipated from this doom and have entered a new era in industrial thought which has unleashed the productive capacity of the individual worker with an increasing scale of wages and profits, the end of which is not yet. The application of this theory accounts for our widening distribution of wealth. No discovery ever did more to increase the happiness and prosperity of the people.

Since 1922 increasing production has increased wages in general 12.9 per cent, while in certain selected trades they have run as high as 34.9 per cent and 38 per cent. Even in the boot and shoe shops the increase is over 5 per cent and in woolen mills 8.4 per cent, although these industries have not prospered like others. As the rise in living costs in this period is negligible, these figures represent real wage increases.

The cause of constructive economy requires that the Government should cooperate with private interests to eliminate the waste arising from industrial accidents. This item, with all that has been done to reduce it, still reaches enormous proportions with great suffering to the workman and great loss to the country.

WOMEN AND CHILDREN

The Federal Government should continue its solicitous care for the 8,500,000 women wage earners and its efforts in behalf of public health, which is reducing infant mortality and improving the bodily and mental condition of our citizens.

CIVIL SERVICE

The most marked change made in the civil service of the Government in the past eight years relates to the increase in salaries. The Board of Actuaries on the retirement act shows by its report that July 1, 1921, the average salary of the 330,047 employees subject to the act was $1,307, while on June 30, 1927, the average salary of the corresponding 405,263 was $1,969. This was an increase in six years of nearly 53 per cent. On top of this was the generous increase made at the last session of the Congress generally applicable to Federal employees and another bill increasing the pay in certain branches of the Postal Service beyond the large increase which was made three years ago. This raised the average level from $1,969 to $2,092, making an increase in seven years of over 63 per cent. While it is well known that in the upper brackets the pay in the Federal service is much smaller than in private employment, in the lower brackets, ranging well up over $3,000, it is much higher. It is higher not only in actual money paid, but in privileges granted, a vacation of 30 actual working days, or 5 weeks each year, with additional time running in some departments as high as 30 days for sick leave and the generous provisions of the retirement act. No other body of public servants ever occupied such a fortunate position.

EDUCATION

Through the Bureau of Education of the Department of the Interior the Federal Government, acting in an informative and advisory capacity, has rendered valuable service. While this province belongs peculiarly to the States, yet the promotion of education and efficiency in educational methods is a general responsibility of the Federal Government. A survey of negro colleges and universities in the United States has just been completed by the Bureau of Education through funds provided by the institutions themselves and through private sources. The present status of negro higher education was determined and recommendations were made for its advancement. This was one of the numerous cooperative undertakings of the bureau. Following the invitation of the Association of Land Grant Colleges and Universities, the Bureau of Education now has under way the survey of agricultural colleges, authorized by Congress. The purpose of the survey is to ascertain the accomplishments, the status, and the future objectives of this type of educational training. It is now proposed to undertake a survey of secondary schools, which educators insist is timely and essential.

PUBLIC BUILDINGS

We have laid out a public building program for the District of Columbia and the country at large running into hundreds of millions of dollars. Three important structures and one annex are already under way and one addition has been completed in the City of Washington. In the country sites have been acquired, many buildings are in course of construction, and some are already completed. Plans for all this work are being prepared in order that it may be carried forward as rapidly as possible. This is the greatest building program ever assumed by this Nation. It contemplates structures of utility and of beauty. When it reaches completion the people will be well served and the Federal city will be supplied with the most beautiful and stately public buildings which adorn any capital in the world.

THE AMERICAN INDIAN

The administration of Indian affairs has been receiving intensive study for several years. The Department of the Interior has been able to provide better supervision of health, education, and industrial advancement of this native race through additional funds provided by the Congress. The present cooperative arrangement existing between the Bureau of Indian Affairs and the Public Health Service should be extended. The Government's responsibility to the American Indian has been acknowledged by annual increases in appropriations to fulfill its obligations to them and to hasten the time when Federal supervision of their affairs may be properly and safely terminated. The movement in Congress and in some of the State legislatures for extending responsibility in Indian affairs to States should be encouraged. A complete participation by the Indian in our economic life is the end to be desired.

THE NEGRO

For 65 years now our negro population has been under the peculiar care and solicitude of the National Government. The progress which they have made in education and the professions, in wealth and in the arts of civilization, affords one of the most remarkable incidents in this period of world history. They have demonstrated their ability to partake of the advantages of our institutions and to benefit by a free and more and more independent existence. Whatever doubt there may have been of their capacity to assume the status granted to them by the Constitution of this Union is being rapidly dissipated. Their cooperation in the life of the Nation is constantly enlarging.

Exploiting the Negro problem for political ends is being abandoned and their protection is being increased by those States in which their percentage of population is largest. Every encouragement should be extended for the development of the race. The colored people have been the victims of the crime of lynching, which has in late years somewhat decreased. Some parts of the South already have wholesome laws for its restraint and punishment. Their example might well be followed by other States, and by such immediate remedial legislation as the Federal Government can extend under the Constitution.

PHILIPPINE ISLANDS

Under the guidance of Governor General Stimson the economic and political conditions of the Philippine Islands have been raised to a standard never before surpassed. The cooperation between his administration and the people of the islands is complete and harmonious. It would be an advantage if relief from double taxation could be granted by the Congress to our citizens doing business in the islands.

PORTO RICO

Due to the terrific storm that swept Porto Rico last September, the people of that island suffered large losses. The Red Cross and the War Department went to their rescue. The property loss is being retrieved. Sugar, tobacco, citrus fruit, and coffee, all suffered damage. The first three can largely look after themselves. The coffee growers will need some assistance, which should be extended strictly on a business basis, and only after most careful investigation. The people of Porto Rico are not asking for charity.

DEPARTMENT OF JUSTICE

It is desirable that all the legal activities of the Government be consolidated under the supervision of the Attorney General. In

1870 it was felt necessary to create the Department of Justice for this purpose. During the intervening period, either through legislation creating law officers or departmental action, additional legal positions not under the supervision of the Attorney General have been provided until there are now over 900. Such a condition is as harmful to the interest of the Government now as it was in 1870, and should be corrected by appropriate legislation.

SPECIAL GOVERNMENT COUNSEL

In order to prosecute the oil cases, I suggested and the Congress enacted a law providing for the appointment of two special counsel. They have pursued their work with signal ability, recovering all the leased lands besides nearly $30,000,000 in money, and nearly $17,000,000 in other property. They find themselves hampered by a statute, which the Attorney General construes as applying to them, prohibiting their appearing for private clients before any department. For this reason, one has been compelled to resign. No good result is secured by the application of this rule to these counsel, and as Mr. Roberts has consented to take reappointment if the rule is abrogated I recommend the passage of an amendment to the law creating their office exempting them from the general rule against taking other cases involving the Government.

PROHIBITION

The country has duly adopted the eighteenth amendment. Those who object to it have the right to advocate its modification or repeal. Meantime, it is binding upon the National and State Governments and all our inhabitants. The Federal enforcement bureau is making every effort to prevent violations, especially through smuggling, manufacture, and transportation, and to prosecute generally all violations for which it can secure evidence. It is bound to continue this policy. Under the terms of the Constitution, however, the obligation is equally on the States to exercise the power which they have through the executive, legislative, judicial, and police branches of their governments in behalf of enforcement. The Federal Government is doing and will continue to do all it can in this direction and is entitled to the active cooperation of the States.

CONCLUSION

The country is in the midst of an era of prosperity more extensive and of peace more permanent than it has ever before experienced. But, having reached this position, we should not fail to comprehend that it can easily be lost. It needs more effort for its support than the less exalted places of the world. We shall not be permitted to take our ease, but shall continue to be required to spend our days in unremitting toil. The actions of the Government must command the confidence of the country. Without this, our prosperity would be lost. We must extend to other countries the largest measure of generosity, moderation, and patience. In addition to dealing justly, we can well afford to walk humbly.

The end of government is to keep open the opportunity for a more abundant life. Peace and prosperity are not finalities; they are only methods. It is too easy under their influence for a nation to become selfish and degenerate. This test has come to the United States. Our country has been provided with the resources with which it can enlarge its intellectual, moral, and spiritual life. The issue is in the hands of the people. Our faith in man and God is the justification for the belief in our continuing success.

Herbert Hoover

March 4, 1929 to March 4, 1933

FIRST ANNUAL MESSAGE.

THE WHITE HOUSE, *December 3, 1929.*

To the Senate and House of Representatives:

The Constitution requires that the President "shall, from time to time, give to the Congress information of the state of the Union, and recommend to their consideration such measures as he shall judge necessary and expedient." In complying with that requirement I wish to emphasize that during the past year the Nation has continued to grow in strength; our people have advanced in comfort; we have gained in knowledge; the education of youth has been more widely spread; moral and spiritual forces have been maintained; peace has become more assured. The problems with which we are confronted are the problems of growth and of progress. In their solution we have to determine the facts, to develop the relative importance to be assigned to such facts, to formulate a common judgment upon them, and to realize solutions in a spirit of conciliation.

FOREIGN RELATIONS

We are not only at peace with all the world, but the foundations for future peace are being substantially strengthened. To promote peace is our long-established policy. Through the Kellogg-Briand pact a great moral standard has been raised in the world. By it fifty-four nations have covenanted to renounce war and to settle all disputes by pacific means. Through it a new world outlook has been inaugurated which has profoundly affected the foreign policies of nations. Since its inauguration we have initiated new efforts not only in the organization of the machinery of peace but also to eliminate dangerous forces which produce controversies amongst nations.

In January, 1926, the Senate gave its consent to adherence to The Court of International Justice with certain reservations. In September of this year the statute establishing the court has, by the action of the nations signatory, been amended to meet the Senate's reservations and to go even beyond those reservations to make clear that the court is a true international court of justice. I believe it will be clear to everyone that no controversy or question in which this country has or claims an interest can be passed on by the court without our consent at the time the question arises. The doubt about advisory opinions has been completely safeguarded. Our adherence to the

International Court is, as now constituted, not the slightest step toward entry into the League of Nations. As I have before indicated, I shall direct that our signature be affixed to the protocol of adherence and shall submit it for the approval of the Senate with a special message at some time when it is convenient to deal with it.

In the hope of reducing friction in the world, and with the desire that we may reduce the great economic burdens of naval armament, we have joined in conference with Great Britain, France, Italy, and Japan to be held in London in January to consider the further limitation and reduction of naval arms. We hold high hopes that success may attend this effort.

At the beginning of the present administration the neighboring State of Mexico was beset with domestic insurrection. We maintained the embargo upon the shipment of arms to Mexico but permitted the duly constituted Government to procure supplies from our surplus war stocks. Fortunately, the Mexican Government by its own strength successfully withstood the insurrection with but slight damage. Opportunity of further peaceful development is given to that country. At the request of the Mexican Government, we have since lifted the embargo on shipment of arms altogether. The two governments have taken further steps to promote friendly relationships and so solve our differences. Conventions prolonging for a period of two years the life of the general and special claims commissions have been concluded.

In South America we are proud to have had part in the settlement of the long-standing dispute between Chile and Peru in the disposal of the question of Tacna-Arica.

The work of the commission of inquiry and conciliation between Bolivia and Paraguay, in which a representative of this Government participated, has successfully terminated an incident which seemed to threaten war. The proposed plan for final settlement as suggested by the neutral governments is still under consideration.

This Government has continued its efforts to act as a mediator in boundary difficulties between Guatemala and Honduras.

A further instance of profound importance in establishing good will was the inauguration of regular air mail service between the United States and Caribbean, Central American, and South American countries.

We still have marines on foreign soil—in Nicaragua, Haiti, and China. In the large sense we do not wish to be represented abroad in such manner. About 1,600 marines remain in Nicaragua at the urgent request of that government and the leaders of all parties pending the training of a domestic constabulary capable of insuring tranquility. We have already reduced these forces materially and we are anxious to withdraw them further as the situation warrants.

In Haiti we have about 700 marines, but it is a much more difficult problem, the solution of which is still obscure. If Congress approves, I shall dispatch a commission to Haiti to review and study the matter in an endeavor to arrive at some more definite policy than at present. Our forces in China constitute 2,605 men, which we hope also further to reduce to the normal legation guard.

It is my desire to establish more firmly our understanding and relationships with the Latin American countries by strengthening the diplomatic missions to those countries. It is my hope to secure men long experienced in our Diplomatic Service, who speak the languages of the peoples to whom they are accredited, as chiefs of our diplomatic missions in these States. I shall send to the Senate at an early date the nominations of several such men.

The Congress has by numerous wise and foresighted acts in the past few years greatly strengthened the character of our representation abroad. It has made liberal provision for the establishment of suitable quarters for our foreign staffs in the different countries. In order, however, that we may further develop the most effective force in this, one of the most responsible functions of our Government, I shall recommend to the Congress more liberal appropriations for the work of the State Department. I know of no expenditure of public money from which a greater economic and moral return can come to us than by assuring the most effective conduct of our foreign relations.

NATIONAL DEFENSE

To preserve internal order and freedom from encroachment is the first purpose of government. Our Army and Navy are being maintained in a most efficient state under officers of high intelligence and zeal. The extent and expansion of their numbers and equipment as at present authorized are ample for this purpose.

We can well be deeply concerned, however, at the growing expense. From a total expenditure for national defense purposes in 1914 of $267,000,000, it naturally rose with the Great War, but receded again to $612,000,000 in 1924, when again it began to rise until during the current fiscal year the expenditures will reach to over $730,000,000, excluding all civilian services of those departments. Programs now authorized will carry it to still larger figures in future years. While the remuneration paid to our soldiers and sailors is justly at a higher rate than that of any other country in the world, and while the cost of subsistence is higher, yet the total of our expenditures is in excess of those of the most highly militarized nations of the world.

Upon the conference shortly to be held in London will depend such moderation as we can make in naval expenditure. If we shall be compelled to undertake the naval construction implied in the Washington arms treaty as well as other construction which would appear to be necessary if no international agreement can be completed, we shall be committed during the next six years to a construction expenditure of upward of $1,200,000,000 besides the necessary further increase in costs for annual upkeep.

After 1914 the various Army contingents necessarily expanded to the end of the Great War and then receded to the low point in 1924, when expansion again began. In 1914 the officers and men in our regular forces, both Army and Navy, were about 164,000, in 1924 there were about 256,000, and in 1929 there were about 250,000. Our citizens' army, however, including the National Guard and other forms of reserves, increase these totals up to about 299,000 in 1914, about 672,000 in 1924, and about 728,000 in 1929.

Under the Kellogg pact we have undertaken never to use war as an instrument of national policy. We have, therefore, undertaken by covenant to use these equipments solely for defensive purposes. From a defense point of view our forces should be proportioned to national need and should, therefore, to some extent be modified by the prospects of peace, which were never brighter than to-day.

It should be borne in mind that the improvement in the National Guard by Federal support begun in 1920 has definitely strengthened our national security by rendering them far more effective than ever heretofore. The advance of aviation has also greatly increased our effectiveness in defense. In addition to the very large program of air forces which we are maintaining in the Army and Navy, there has been an enormous growth of commercial aviation. This has provided unanticipated reserves in manufacturing capacity and in industrial and air personnel, which again adds to our security.

I recommend that Congress give earnest consideration to the possibilities of prudent action which will give relief from our continuously mounting expenditures.

FINANCES OF THE GOVERNMENT

The finances of the Government are in sound condition. I shall submit the detailed evidences and the usual recommendations in the special Budget message. I may, however, summarize our position. The public debt on June 30 this year stood at $16,931,000,000, compared to the maximum in August, 1919, of $26,596,000,000. Since June 30 it has been reduced by a further $238,000,000. In the Budget to be submitted the total appropriations recommended for the fiscal year 1931 are $3,830,445,231, as compared to $3,976,141,651 for the present fiscal year. The present fiscal year, however, includes $150,000,000 for the Federal Farm Board, as to which no estimate can as yet be determined for 1931.

Owing to the many necessary burdens assumed by Congress in previous years which now require large outlays, it is with extreme difficulty that we shall be able to keep the expenditures for the next fiscal year within the bounds of the present year. Economies in many directions have permitted some accommodation of pressing needs, the net result being an increase, as shown above, of about one-tenth of 1 per cent above the present fiscal year. We can not fail to recognize the obligations of the Government in support of the public welfare but we must coincidentally bear in mind the burden of taxes and strive to find relief through some tax reduction. Every dollar so returned fertilizes the soil of prosperity.

TAX REDUCTION

The estimate submitted to me by the Secretary of the Treasury and the Budget Director indicates that the Government will close the fiscal year 1930 with a surplus of about $225,000,000 and the fiscal year 1931 with a surplus of about $123,000,000. Owing to unusual circumstances, it has been extremely difficult to estimate future revenues with accuracy.

I believe, however, that the Congress will be fully justified in giving the benefits of the prospective surpluses to the taxpayers, particularly as ample provision for debt reduction has been made in both years through the form of debt retirement from ordinary revenues. In view of the uncertainty in respect of future revenues and the comparatively small size of the indicated surplus in 1931, relief should take the form of a provisional revision of tax rates.

I recommend that the normal income tax rates applicable to the incomes of individuals for the calendar year 1929 be reduced from 5, 3, and 1½ per cent, to 4, 2, and ½ per cent, and that the tax on the income of corporations for the calendar year 1929 be reduced from 12 to 11 per cent. It is estimated that this will result in a reduction of $160,000,000 in income taxes to be collected during the calendar year 1930. The loss in revenue will be divided approximately equally between the fiscal years 1930 and 1931. Such a program will give a measure of tax relief to the maximum number of taxpayers, with relatively larger benefits to taxpayers with small or moderate incomes.

FOREIGN DEBTS

The past year has brought us near to completion of settlements of the indebtedness of foreign governments to the United States.

The act of Congress approved February 4, 1929, authorized the settlement with the Government of Austria along lines similar to the terms of settlement offered by that Government to its other relief creditors. No agreement has yet been concluded with that government, but the form of agreement has been settled and its execution only awaits the Government of Austria securing the assent by all the other relief creditors of the terms offered. The act of Congress approved February 14, 1929, authorized the settlement with the Government of Greece, and an agreement was concluded on May 10, 1929.

The Government of France ratified the agreement with us on July 27, 1929. This agreement will shortly be before the Congress and I recommend its approval.

The only indebtedness of foreign governments to the United States now unsettled is that of Russia and Armenia.

During the past year a committee of distinguished experts under American leadership submitted a plan looking to a revision of claims against Germany by the various Governments. The United States denied itself any participation in the war settlement of general reparations and our claims are comparatively small in amount. They arise from costs of the army of occupation and claims of our private citizens for losses under awards from the Mixed Claims Commission established under agreement with the German Government. In finding a basis for settlement it was necessary for the committee of experts to request all the Governments concerned to make some contribution to the adjustment and we have felt that we should share a proportion of the concessions made.

The State and Treasury Departments will be in a position shortly to submit for your consideration a draft of an agreement to be executed between the United States and Germany providing for the payments of these revised amounts. A more extensive statement will be submitted at that time.

The total amount of indebtedness of the various countries to the United States now funded is $11,579,465,885. This sum was in effect provided by the issue of United States Government bonds to our own people. The payments of the various Governments to us on account of principal and interest for 1930 are estimated at a total of about $239,000,000, for 1931 at about $236,000,000, for 1932 at about $246,000,000. The measure of American compromise in these settlements may be appreciated from the fact that our taxpayers are called upon to find annually about $475,000,000 in interest and in addition to redeem the principal of sums borrowed by the United States Government for these purposes.

ALIEN ENEMY PROPERTY

The wise determination that this property seized in war should be returned to its owners has proceeded with considerable rapidity. Of the original seized cash and property (valued at a total of about $625,000,000), all but $111,566,700 has been returned. Most of the remainder should be disposed of during the next year.

GENERAL ECONOMIC SITUATION

The country has enjoyed a large degree of prosperity and sound progress during the past year with a steady improvement in methods of production and distribution and consequent advancement in standards of living. Progress has, of course, been unequal among industries, and some, such as coal, lumber, leather, and textiles, still lag behind. The long upward trend of fundamental progress, however, gave rise to over-optimism as to profits, which translated itself into a wave of uncontrolled speculation in securities, resulting in the diversion of capital from business to the stock market and the inevitable crash. The natural consequences have been a reduction in the consumption of luxuries and semi-necessities by those who have met with losses, and a number of persons thrown temporarily out of employment. Prices of agricultural products dealt in upon the great markets have been affected in sympathy with the stock crash.

Fortunately, the Federal reserve system had taken measures to strengthen the position against the day when speculation would break, which together with the strong position of the banks has carried the whole credit system through the crisis without impairment. The capital which has been hitherto absorbed in stock-market loans for speculative purposes is now returning to the normal channels of business. There has been no inflation in the prices of commodities; there has been no undue accumulation of goods, and foreign trade has expanded to a magnitude which exerts a steadying influence upon activity in industry and employment.

The sudden threat of unemployment and especially the recollection of the economic consequences of previous crashes under a much less secured financial system created unwarranted pessimism and fear. It was recalled that past storms of similar character had resulted in retrenchment of construction, reduction of wages, and laying off of workers. The natural result was the tendency of business agencies throughout the country to pause in their plans and proposals for continuation and extension of their businesses, and this hesitation unchecked could in itself intensify into a depression with widespread unemployment and suffering.

I have, therefore, instituted systematic, voluntary measures of cooperation with the business institutions and with State and municipal authorities to make certain that fundamental businesses of the country shall continue as usual, that wages and therefore consuming power shall not be reduced, and that a special effort shall be made to expand construction work in order to assist in equalizing other deficits in employment. Due to the enlarged sense of cooperation and responsibility which has grown in the business world during the past few years the response has been remarkable and satisfactory.

We have canvassed the Federal Government and instituted measures of prudent expansion in such work that should be helpful, and upon which the different departments will make some early recommendations to Congress.

I am convinced that through these measures we have reestablished confidence. Wages should remain stable. A very large degree of industrial unemployment and suffering which would otherwise have occurred has been prevented. Agricultural prices have reflected the returning confidence. The measures taken must be vigorously pursued until normal conditions are restored.

AGRICULTURE

The agricultural situation is improving. The gross farm income as estimated by the Department of Agriculture for the crop season 1926–27 was $12,100,000,000; for 1927–28 it was $12,300,000,000; for 1928–29 it was $12,500,000,000; and estimated on the basis of prices since the last harvest the value of the 1929–30 crop would be over $12,650,000,000. The slight decline in general commodity prices during the past few years naturally assists the farmers' buying power.

The number of farmer bankruptcies is very materially decreased below previous years. The decline in land values now seems to be arrested and rate of movement from the farm to the city has been reduced. Not all sections of agriculture, of course, have fared equally, and some areas have suffered from drought. Responsible farm leaders have assured me that a large measure of confidence is returning to agriculture and that a feeling of optimism pervades that industry.

The most extensive action for strengthening the agricultural industry ever taken by any government was inaugurated through the farm marketing act of June 15 last. Under its provisions the Federal Farm Board has been established, comprised of men long and widely experienced in agriculture and sponsored by the farm organizations of the country. During its short period of existence the board has taken definite steps toward a more efficient organization of agriculture, toward the elimination of waste in marketing, and toward the upbuilding of farmers' marketing organizations on sounder and more efficient lines. Substantial headway has been made in the organization of four of the basic commodities—grain, cotton, livestock, and wool. Support by the board to cooperative marketing organizations and other board activities undoubtedly have served to steady the farmers' market during the recent crisis and have operated also as a great stimulus to the cooperative organization of agriculture. The problems of the industry are most complex, and the need for sound organization is imperative. Yet the board is moving rapidly along the lines laid out for it in the act, facilitating the creation by farmers of farmer-owned and farmer-controlled organizations and federating them into central institutions, with a view to increasing the bargaining power of agriculture, preventing and controlling surpluses, and mobilizing the economic power of agriculture.

THE TARIFF

The special session of Congress was called to expedite the fulfillment of party pledges of agricultural relief and the tariff. The pledge of farm relief has been carried out. At that time I stated the principles upon which I believed action should be taken in respect to the tariff:

> "An effective tariff upon agricultural products, that will compensate the farmer's higher costs and higher standards of living, has a dual purpose. Such a tariff not only protects the farmer in our domestic market but it also stimulates him to diversify his crops and to grow products that he could not otherwise produce, and thus lessens his dependence upon exports to foreign markets. The great expansion of production abroad under the conditions I have mentioned renders foreign competition in our export markets increasingly serious. It seems but natural, therefore, that the American farmer, having been greatly handicapped in his foreign market by such competition from the younger expanding countries, should ask that foreign access to our domestic market should be regulated by taking into account the differences in our costs of production. * * *
>
> "In considering the tariff for other industries than agriculture, we find that there have been economic shifts necessitating a readjustment of some of the tariff schedules. Seven years of experience under the tariff bill enacted in 1922 have demonstrated the wisdom of Congress in the enactment of that measure. On the whole it has worked well. In the main our wages have been maintained at high levels; our exports and imports have steadily increased; with some exceptions our manufacturing industries have been prosperous. Nevertheless, economic changes have taken place during that time which have placed certain domestic products at a disadvantage and new industries have come into being, all of which create the necessity for some limited changes in the schedules and in the administrative clauses of the laws as written in 1922.
>
> "It would seem to me that the test of necessity for revision is, in the main, whether there has been a substantial slackening of activity in an industry during the past few years, and a consequent decrease of employment due to insurmountable competition in the products of that industry. It is not as if we were

setting up a new basis of protective duties. We did that seven years ago. What we need to remedy now is whatever substantial loss of employment may have resulted from shifts since that time. * * *

"In determining changes in our tariff we must not fail to take into account the broad interests of the country as a whole, and such interests include our trade relations with other countries."

No condition has arisen in my view to change these principles stated at the opening of the special session. I am firmly of the opinion that their application to the pending revision will give the country the kind of a tariff law it both needs and wants. It would be most helpful if action should be taken at an early moment, more especially at a time when business and agriculture are both cooperating to minimize future uncertainties. It is just that they should know what the rates are to be.

Even a limited revision requires the consideration and readjustment of many items. The exhaustive inquiries and valuable debate from men representative of all parts of the country which is needed to determine the detailed rates must necessarily be accomplished in the Congress. However perfectly this rate structure may be framed at any given time, the shifting of economic forces which inevitably occurs will render changes in some items desirable between the necessarily long intervals of congressional revision. Injustices are bound to develop, such as were experienced by the dairymen, the flaxseed producers, the glass industry, and others, under the 1922 rates. For this reason, I have been most anxious that the broad principle of the flexible tariff as provided in the existing law should be preserved and its delays in action avoided by more expeditious methods of determining the costs of production at home and abroad, with executive authority to promulgate such changes upon recommendation of the Tariff Commission after exhaustive investigation. Changes by the Congress in the isolated items such as those to which I have referred would have been most unlikely both because of the concentrations of oppositions in the country, who could see no advantage to their own industry or State, and because of the difficulty of limiting consideration by the Congress to such isolated cases.

There is no fundamental conflict between the interests of the farmer and the worker. Lowering of the standards of living of either tends to destroy the other. The prosperity of one rests upon the well-being of the other. Nor is there any real conflict between the East and the West or the North and the South in the United States. The complete interlocking of economic dependence, the common striving for social and spiritual progress, our common heritage as Americans, and the infinite web of national sentiment, have created a solidarity in a great people unparalleled in all human history. These invisible bonds should not and can not be shattered by differences of opinion growing out of discussion of a tariff.

PUBLIC BUILDINGS

Under the provisions of various acts of Congress $300,000,000 has been authorized for public buildings and the land upon which to construct them, being $75,000,000 for the District of Columbia and $225,000,000 for the country at large. Excluding $25,000,000 which is for the acquisition of land in the so-called "triangle" in this city, this public building legislation provides for a five-year program for the District of Columbia and between an eight and nine year program for the country at large. Of this sum approximately $27,400,000 was expended up to June 30 last, of which $11,400,000 has been expended in the District and $16,000,000 outside.

Even this generous provision for both the District of Columbia and the country is insufficient for most pressing governmental needs. Expensive rents and inadequate facilities are extravagance and not economy. In the District even after the completion of these projects we shall have fully 20,000 clerks housed in rented and temporary war buildings which can last but a little longer.

I therefore recommend that consideration should be given to the extension of authorizations both for the country at large and for the District of Columbia again distributed over a term of years. A survey of the need in both categories has been made by the Secretary of the Treasury and the Postmaster General. It would be helpful in the present economic situation if such steps were taken as would enable early construction work.

An expedition and enlargement of the program in the District would bring about direct economies in construction by enabling the erection of buildings in regular sequence. By maintaining a stable labor force in the city, contracts can be made on more advantageous terms.

The earlier completion of this program which is an acknowledged need would add dignity to the celebration in 1932 of the two hundredth anniversary of the birth of President Washington.

In consideration of these projects which contribute so much to dignify the National Capital I should like to renew the suggestion that the Fine Arts Commission should be required to pass upon private buildings which are proposed for sites facing upon public buildings and parks. Without such control much of the effort of the Congress in beautification of the Capital will be minimized.

THE WATERWAYS AND FLOOD CONTROL

The development of inland waterways has received new impulse from the completion during this year of the canalization of the Ohio to a uniform 9-foot depth. The development of the other segments of the Mississippi system should be expedited and with this in view I am recommending an increase in appropriations for rivers and harbors from $50,000,000 to $55,000,000 per annum which, together with about $4,000,000 per annum released by completion of the Ohio, should make available after providing for other river and harbor works a sum of from $25,000,000 to $30,000,000 per annum for the Mississippi system and thus bring it to early completion.

Conflict of opinion which has arisen over the proposed floodway from the Arkansas River to the Gulf of Mexico via the Atchafalaya River has led me to withhold construction upon this portion of the Mississippi flood control plan until it could be again reviewed by the engineers for any further recommendation to Congress. The other portions of the project are being vigorously prosecuted and I have recommended an increase in appropriations for this from $30,000,000 of the present year to $35,000,000 during the next fiscal year.

Expansion of our intracoastal waterways to effective barge depths is well warranted. We are awaiting the action of Canada upon the St. Lawrence waterway project.

HIGHWAYS

There are over 3,000,000 miles of legally established highways in the United States, of which about 10 per cent are included in the State highway systems, the remainder being county and other local roads. About 626,000 miles have been improved with some type of surfacing, comprising some 63 per cent of the State highway systems and 16 per cent of the local roads. Of the improved roads about 102,000 miles are hard surfaced, comprising about 22 per cent of the State highway systems and about 8 per cent of the local roads.

While proper planning should materially reduce the listed mileage of public roads, particularly in the agricultural districts, and turn these roads back to useful purposes, it is evident that road construction must be a long-continued program. Progress in improvement is about 50,000 miles of all types per annum, of which some 12,000 miles are of the more durable types. The total expenditures of Federal, State, and local governments last year for construction and maintenance assumed the huge total of $1,660,000,000.

Federal aid in the construction of the highway systems in conjunction with the States has proved to be beneficial and stimulating. We must ultimately give consideration to the increase of our contribution to these systems, particularly with a view to stimulating the improvement of farm-to-market roads.

POST OFFICE

Our Post Office deficit has now increased to over $80,000,000 a year, of which perhaps $14,000,000 is due to losses on ocean mail and air mail contracts. The department is making an exhaustive study of the sources of the deficit with view to later recommendation to Congress in respect to it.

The Post Office quarters are provided in part by the Federal construction, in part by various forms of rent and lease arrangements. The practice has grown up in recent years of contracting long term leases under which both rent and amortization principal cost of buildings is included. I am advised that fully 40 per cent could be saved from many such rent and lease agreements even after allowing interest on the capital required at the normal Government rate. There are also many objectionable features to some of these practices. The provision of adequate quarters for the Post Office should be put on a sound basis.

A revision of air mail rates upon a more systematic and permanent footing is necessary. The subject is under study, and if legislation should prove necessary the subject will be presented to the Congress. In the meantime I recommend that the Congress should consider the desirability of authorizing further expansion of the South American services.

COMMERCIAL AVIATION

During the past year progress in civil aeronautics has been remarkable. This is to a considerable degree due to the wise assistance of the Federal Government through the establishment and maintenance of airways by the Department of Commerce and the mail contracts from the Post Office Department. The Government-improved airways now exceed 25,000 miles—more than 14,000 miles of which will be lighted and equipped for night-flying operations by the close of the current year. Airport construction through all the States is extremely active. There are now 1,000 commercial and municipal airports in operation with an additional 1,200 proposed for early development.

Through this assistance the Nation is building a sound aviation system, operated by private enterprise. Over 6,400 planes are in commercial use, and 9,400 pilots are licensed by the Government. Our manufacturing capacity has risen to 7,500 planes per annum. The aviation companies have increased regular air transportation until it now totals 90,000 miles per day—one-fourth of which is flown by night. Mail and express services now connect our principal cities, and extensive services for passenger transportation have been inaugurated, and others of importance are imminent. American air lines now reach into Canada and Mexico, to Cuba, Porto Rico, Central America, and most of the important countries of South America.

RAILWAYS

As a whole, the railroads never were in such good physical and financial condition, and the country has never been so well served by them. The greatest volume of freight traffic ever tendered is being carried at a speed never before attained and with satisfaction to the shippers. Efficiencies and new methods have resulted in reduction in the cost of providing freight transportation, and freight rates show a continuous descending line from the level enforced by the World War.

We have, however, not yet assured for the future that adequate system of transportation through consolidations which was the objective of the Congress in the transportation act. The chief purpose of consolidation is to secure well-balanced systems with more uniform and satisfactory rate structure, a more stable financial structure, more equitable distribution of traffic, greater efficiency, and single-line instead of multiple-line hauls. In this way the country will have the assurance of better service and ultimately at lower and more even rates than would otherwise be attained. Legislation to simplify and expedite consolidation methods and better to protect public interest should be enacted.

Consideration should also be given to relief of the members of the Commission from the necessity of detailed attention to comparatively inconsequential matters which, under the existing law, must receive their direct and personal consideration. It is in the public interest that the members of the Commission should not be so pressed by minor matters that they have inadequate time for investigation and consideration of the larger questions committed to them for solution. As to many of these minor matters, the function of the Commission might well be made revisory, and the primary responsibility delegated to subordinate officials after the practice long in vogue in the executive departments.

MERCHANT MARINE

Under the impulse of the merchant marine act of 1928 the transfer to private enterprise of the Government-owned steamship lines is going forward with increasing success. The Shipping Board now operates about 18 lines, which is less than half the number originally established, and the estimate of expenditures for the coming fiscal year is based upon reduction in losses on Government lines by approximately one-half. Construction loans have been made to the amount of approximately $75,000,000 out of the revolving fund authorized by Congress and have furnished an additional aid to American shipping and further stimulated the building of vessels in American yards.

Desirous of securing the full values to the Nation of the great effort to develop our merchant marine by the merchant marine act soon after the inauguration of the present administration, I appointed an interdepartmental committee, consisting of the Secretary of Commerce, as chairman, the Secretary of the Navy, the Postmaster General, and the chairman of the Shipping Board, to make a survey of the policies being pursued under the act of 1928 in respect of mail contracts; to inquire into its workings and to advise the Postmaster General in the administration of the act.

In particular it seemed to me necessary to determine if the result of the contracts already let would assure the purpose expressed in the act, "to further develop an American merchant marine, to assure its permanence in the transportation of the foreign trade of the United States, and for other purposes," and to develop a coordinated policy by which these purposes may be translated into actualities.

In review of the mail contracts already awarded it was found that they aggregated 25 separate awards imposing a governmental obligation of a little over $12,000,000 per annum. Provision had been imposed in five of the contracts for construction of new vessels with which to replace and expand services. These requirements come to a total of 12 vessels in the 10-year period, aggregating 122,000 tons. Some other conditions in the contracts had not worked out satisfactorily.

That study has now been substantially completed and the committee has advised the desirability and the necessity of securing much larger undertakings as to service and new construction in future contracts. The committee at this time is recommending the advertising of 14 additional routes, making substantial requirements for the construction of new vessels during the life of each contract recommended. A total of 40 new vessels will be required under the contracts proposed, about half of which will be required to be built during the next three years. The capital cost of this new construction will be approximately $250,000,000, involving approximately 460,000 gross tons. Should bidders be found who will make these undertakings, it will be necessary to recommend to Congress an increase in the authorized expenditure by the Post Office of about $5,500,000 annually. It will be most advantageous to grant such an authority.

A conflict as to the administration of the act has arisen in the contention of persons who have purchased Shipping Board vessels that they are entitled to mail contracts irrespective of whether they are the lowest bidder, the Post Office, on the other hand, being required by law to let contracts in that manner. It is urgent that Congress should clarify this situation.

THE BANKING SYSTEM

It is desirable that Congress should consider the revision of some portions of the banking law.

The development of "group" and "chain" banking presents many new problems. The question naturally arises as to whether if allowed to expand without restraint these methods would dangerously concentrate control of credit, and whether they would not in any event seriously threaten one of the fundamentals of the American credit system—which is that credit which is based upon banking deposits should be controlled by persons within those areas which furnish these deposits and thus be subject to the restraints of local interest and public opinion in those areas. To some degree, however, this movement of chain or group banking is a groping for stronger support to the banks and a more secure basis for these institutions.

The growth in size and stability of the metropolitan banks is in marked contrast to the trend in the country districts, with its many failures and the losses these failures have imposed upon the agricultural community.

The relinquishment of charters of national banks in great commercial centers in favor of State charters indicates that some conditions surround the national banks which render them unable to compete with State banks; and their withdrawal results in weakening our national banking system.

It has been proposed that permission should be granted to national banks to engage in branch banking of a nature that would preserve within limited regions the local responsibility and the control of such credit institutions.

All these subjects, however, require careful investigation, and it might be found advantageous to create a joint commission embracing Members of the Congress and other appropriate Federal officials for subsequent report.

ELECTRICAL POWER REGULATION

The Federal Power Commission is now comprised of three Cabinet officers, and the duties involved in the competent conduct of the growing responsibilities of this commission far exceed the time and attention which these officials can properly afford from other important duties. I recommend that authority be given for the appointment of full-time commissioners to replace them.

It is also desirable that the authority of the commission should be extended to certain phases of power regulation. The nature of the electric utilities industry is such that about 90 per cent of all power generation and distribution is intrastate in character, and most of the States have developed their own regulatory systems as to certificates of convenience, rates, and profits of such utilities. To encroach upon their authorities and responsibilities would be an encroachment upon the rights of the States. There are cases, however, of interstate character beyond the jurisdiction of the States. To meet these cases it would be most desirable if a method could be worked out by which initial action may be taken between the commissions of the States whose joint action should be made effective by the Federal Power Commission with a reserve to act on its own motion in case of disagreement or nonaction by the States.

THE RADIO COMMISSION

I recommend the reorganization of the Radio Commission into a permanent body from its present temporary status. The requirement of the present law that the commissioners shall be appointed from specified zones should be abolished and a general provision made for their equitable selection from different parts of the country. Despite the effort of the commissioners, the present method develops a public insistence that the commissioners are specially charged with supervision of radio affairs in the zone from which each is appointed. As a result there is danger that the system will degenerate from a national system into five regional agencies with varying practices, varying policies, competitive tendencies, and consequent failure to attain its utmost capacity for service to the people as a whole.

MUSCLE SHOALS

It is most desirable that this question should be disposed of. Under present conditions the income from these plants is less than could otherwise be secured for its use, and more especially the public is not securing the full benefits which could be obtained from them.

It is my belief that such parts of these plants as would be useful and the revenues from the remainder should be dedicated for all time to the farmers of the United States for investigation and experimentation on a commercial scale in agricultural chemistry. By such means advancing discoveries of science can be systematically applied to agricultural need, and development of the chemical industry of the Tennessee Valley can be assured.

I do not favor the operation by the Government of either power or manufacturing business except as an unavoidable by-product of some other major public purpose.

Any form of settlement of this question will imply entering upon a contract or contracts for the lease of the plants either as a whole or in parts and the reservation of facilities, products, or income for agricultural purposes. The extremely technical and involved nature of such contracts dealing with chemical and electrical enterprises, added to the unusual difficulties surrounding these special plants, and the rapid commercial changes now in progress in power and synthetic nitrogen manufacture, lead me to suggest that Congress create a special commission, not to investigate and report as in the past, but with authority to negotiate and complete some sort of contract or contracts on behalf of the Government, subject, of course, to such general requirements as Congress may stipulate.

BOULDER DAM

The Secretary of the Interior is making satisfactory progress in negotiation of the very complex contracts required for the sale of the power to be generated at this project. These contracts must assure the return of all Government outlays upon the project. I recommend that the necessary funds be appropriated for the initiation of this work as soon as the contracts are in the hands of Congress.

CONSERVATION

Conservation of national resources is a fixed policy of the Government. Three important questions bearing upon conservation of the public lands have become urgent.

Conservation of our oil and gas resources against future need is a national necessity. The working of the oil permit system in development of oil and gas resources on the public domain has been subject to great abuse. I considered it necessary to suspend the issuance of such permits and to direct the review of all outstanding permits as to compliance of the holders with the law. The purpose was not only to end such abuse but to place the Government in position to review the entire subject.

We are also confronted with a major problem in conservation due to the overgrazing on public lands. The effect of overgrazing (which has now become general) is not only to destroy the ranges but by impairing the ground coverage seriously to menace the water supply in many parts of the West through quick run-off, spring floods, and autumn drought.

We have a third problem of major dimensions in the reconsideration of our reclamation policy. The inclusion of most of the available lands of the public domain in existing or planned reclamation projects largely completes the original purpose of the Reclamation Service. There still remains the necessity for extensive storage of water in the arid States which renders it desirable that we should give a wider vision and purpose to this service.

To provide for careful consideration of these questions and also of better division of responsibilities in them as between the State and Federal Governments, including the possible transfer to the States for school purposes of the lands unreserved for forests, parks, power, minerals, etc., I have appointed a Commission on Conservation of the Public Domain, with a membership representing the major public land States and at the same time the public at large. I recommend that Congress should authorize a moderate sum to defray their expenses.

SOCIAL SERVICE

The Federal Government provides for an extensive and valuable program of constructive social service, in education, home building, protection to women and children, employment, public health, recreation, and many other directions.

In a broad sense Federal activity in these directions has been confined to research and dissemination of information and experience, and at most to temporary subsidies to the States in order to secure uniform advancement in practice and methods. Any other attitude by the Federal Government will undermine one of the most precious possessions of the American people; that is, local and individual responsibility. We should adhere to this policy.

Federal officials can, however, make a further and most important contribution by leadership in stimulation of the community and voluntary agencies, and by extending Federal assistance in organization of these forces and bringing about cooperation among them.

As an instance of this character, I have recently, in cooperation with the Secretaries of Interior and Labor, laid the foundations of an exhaustive inquiry into the facts precedent to a nation-wide White House conference on child health and protection. This cooperative movement among interested agencies will impose no expense upon the Government. Similar nation-wide conferences will be called in connection with better housing and recreation at a later date.

In view of the considerable difference of opinion as to the policies which should be pursued by the Federal Government with respect to education, I have appointed a committee representative of the important educational associations and others to investigate and present recommendations. In cooperation with the Secretary of the Interior, I have also appointed a voluntary committee of distinguished membership to assist in a nation-wide movement for abolition of illiteracy.

I have recommended additional appropriations for the Federal employment service in order that it may more fully cover its cooperative work with State and local services. I have also recommended additional appropriations for the Women's and Children's Bureaus for much-needed research as to facts which I feel will prove most helpful.

PUBLIC HEALTH

The advance in scientific discovery as to disease and health imposes new considerations upon us. The Nation as a whole is vitally interested in the health of all the people; in protection from spread of contagious disease; in the relation of physical and mental disabilities to criminality; and in the economic and moral advancement which is fundamentally associated with sound body and mind. The organization of preventive measures and health education in its personal application is the province of public health service. Such organization should be as universal as public education. Its support is a proper burden upon the taxpayer. It can not be organized with success, either in its sanitary or educational phases, except under public authority. It should be based upon local and State responsibility, but I consider that the Federal Government has an obligation of contribution to the establishment of such agencies.

In the practical working out of organization, exhaustive experiment and trial have demonstrated that the base should be competent organization of the municipality, county, or other local unit. Most of our municipalities and some 400 rural counties out of 3,000 now have some such unit organization. Where highly developed, a health unit comprises at least a physician, sanitary engineer, and community nurse with the addition, in some cases, of another nurse devoted to the problems of maternity and children. Such organization gives at once a fundamental control of preventive measures and assists in community instruction. The Federal Government, through its interest in control of contagion, acting through the United States Public Health Service and the State agencies, has in the past and should in the future concern itself with this development, particularly in the many rural sections which are unfortunately far behind in progress. Some parts of the funds contributed under the Sheppard-Towner Act through the Children's Bureau of the Department of Labor have also found their way into these channels.

I recommend to the Congress that the purpose of the Sheppard-Towner Act should be continued through the Children's Bureau for a limited period of years; and that the Congress should consider the desirability of confining the use of Federal funds by the States to the building up of such county or other local units, and that such outlay should be positively coordinated with the funds expended through the United States Public Health Service directed to other phases of the same county or other local unit organization. All funds appropriated should of course be applied through the States, so that the public health program of the county or local unit will be efficiently coordinated with that of the whole State.

FEDERAL PRISONS

Closely related to crime conditions is the administration of the Federal prison system. Our Federal penal institutions are overcrowded, and this condition is daily becoming worse. The parole and probation systems are inadequate. These conditions make it impossible to perform the work of personal reconstruction of prisoners so as to prepare them for return to the duties of citizenship. In order to relieve the pressing evils I have directed the temporary transfer of the Army Disciplinary Barracks at Leavenworth to the Department of Justice for use as a Federal prison. Not only is this temporary but it is inadequate for present needs.

We need some new Federal prisons and a reorganization of our probation and parole systems; and there should be established in the Department of Justice a Bureau of Prisons with a sufficient force to deal adequately with the growing activities of our prison institutions. Authorization for the improvements should be given speedily, with initial appropriations to allow the construction of the new institutions to be undertaken at once.

IMMIGRATION

Restriction of immigration has from every aspect proved a sound national policy. Our pressing problem is to formulate a method by which the limited number of immigrants whom we do welcome shall be adapted to our national setting and our national needs.

I have been opposed to the basis of the quotas now in force and I have hoped that we could find some practical method to secure what I believe should be our real national objective; that is, fitness of the immigrant as to physique, character, training, and our need of service. Perhaps some system of priorities within the quotas could produce these results and at the same time enable some hardships in the present system to be cleared up. I recommend that the Congress should give the subject further study, in which the executive departments will gladly cooperate with the hope of discovering such method as will more fully secure our national necessities.

VETERANS

It has been the policy of our Government almost from its inception to make provision for the men who have been disabled in defense of our country. This policy should be maintained. Originally it took the form of land grants and pensions. This system continued until our entry into the World War. The Congress at that time inaugurated a new plan of compensation, rehabilitation, hospitalization, medical care and treatment, and insurance, whereby benefits were awarded to those veterans and their immediate dependents whose disabilities were attributable to their war service. The basic principle in this legislation is sound.

In a desire to eliminate all possibilities of injustice due to difficulties in establishing service connection of disabilities, these principles have been to some degree extended. Veterans whose diseases or injuries have become apparent within a brief period after the war are now receiving compensation; insurance benefits have been liberalized. Emergency officers are now receiving additional benefits. The doors of the Government's hospitals have been opened to all veterans, even though their diseases or injuries were not the result of their war service. In addition adjusted service certificates have been issued to 3,433,300 veterans. This in itself will mean an expenditure of nearly $3,500,000,000 before 1945, in addition to the $600,000,000 which we are now appropriating annually for our veterans' relief.

The administration of all laws concerning the veterans and their dependents has been upon the basis of dealing generously, humanely, and justly. While some inequalities have arisen, substantial and adequate care has been given and justice administered. Further improvement in administration may require some amendment from time to time to the law, but care should be taken to see that such changes conform to the basic principles of the legislation.

I am convinced that we will gain in efficiency, economy, and more uniform administration and better definition of national policies if the Pension Bureau, the National Home for Volunteer Soldiers, and the Veterans' Bureau are brought together under a single agency. The total appropriations to these agencies now exceed $800,000,000 per annum.

CIVIL SERVICE

Approximately four-fifths of all the employees in the executive civil service now occupy positions subject to competitive examination under the civil service law.

There are, however, still commanding opportunities for extending the system. These opportunities lie within the province of Congress and not the President. I recommend that a further step be taken by authorization that appointments of third-class postmasters be made under the civil service law.

DEPARTMENTAL REORGANIZATION

This subject has been under consideration for over 20 years. It was promised by both political parties in the recent campaign. It has been repeatedly examined by committees and commissions—congressional, executive, and voluntary. The conclusions of these investigations have been unanimous that reorganization is a necessity of sound administration; of economy; of more effective governmental policies and of relief to the citizen from unnecessary harassment in his relations with a multitude of scattered governmental agencies. But the presentation of any specific plan at once enlivens opposition from every official whose authority may be curtailed or who fears his position is imperiled by such a result; of bureaus and departments which wish to maintain their authority and activities; of citizens and their organizations who are selfishly interested, or who are inspired by fear that their favorite bureau may, in a new setting, be less subject to their influence or more subject to some other influence.

It seems to me that the essential principles of reorganization are two in number. First, all administrative activities of the same major purpose should be placed in groups under single-headed responsibility; second, all executive and administrative functions should be separated from boards and commissions and placed under individual responsibility, while quasilegislative and quasijudicial and broadly advisory functions should be removed from individual authority and assigned to boards and commissions. Indeed, these are the fundamental principles upon which our Government was founded, and they are the principles which have been adhered to in the whole development of our business structure, and they are the distillation of the common sense of generations.

For instance, the conservation of national resources is spread among eight agencies in five departments. They suffer from conflict and overlap. There is no proper development and adherence to broad national policies and no central point where the searchlight of public opinion may concentrate itself. These functions should be grouped under the direction of some such official as an assistant secretary of conservation. The particular department or cabinet officer under which such a group should be placed is of secondary importance to the need of concentration. The same may be said of educational services, of merchant marine aids, of public works, of public health, of veterans' services, and many others, the component parts of which are widely scattered in the various departments and independent agencies. It is desirable that we first have experience with these different groups in action before we create new departments. These may be necessary later on.

With this background of all previous experience I can see no hope for the development of a sound reorganization of the Government unless Congress be willing to delegate its authority over the problem (subject to defined principles) to the Executive, who should act upon approval of a joint committee of Congress or with the reservation of power of revision by Congress within some limited period adequate for its consideration.

PROHIBITION

The first duty of the President under his oath of office is to secure the enforcement of the laws. The enforcement of the laws enacted to give effect to the eighteenth amendment is far from satisfactory and this is in part due to the inadequate organization of the administrative agencies of the Federal Government. With the hope of expediting such reorganization, I requested on June 6 last that Congress should appoint a joint committee to collaborate with executive agencies in preparation of legislation. It would be helpful if it could be so appointed. The subject has been earnestly considered by the Law Enforcement Commission and the administrative officials of the Government. Our joint conclusions are that certain steps should be taken at once. First, there should be an immediate concentration of responsibility and strengthening of enforcement agencies of the Federal Government by transfer to the Department of Justice of the Federal functions of detection and to a considerable degree of prosecution, which are now lodged in the Prohibition Bureau in the Treasury; and at the same time the control of the distribution of industrial alcohol and legalized beverages should remain in the Treasury. Second, provision should be made for relief of congestion in the Federal courts by modifying and simplifying the procedure for dealing with the large volume of petty prosecutions under various Federal acts. Third, there should be a codification of the laws relating to prohibition to avoid the necessity which now exists of resorting to more than 25 statutes enacted at various times over 40 years. Technical defects in these statutes that have been disclosed should be cured. I would add to these recommendations the desirability of reorganizing the various services engaged in the prevention of smuggling into one border patrol under the Coast Guard. Further recommendations upon the subject as a whole will be developed after further examination by the Law Enforcement Commission, but it is not to be expected that any criminal law will ever be fully enforced so long as criminals exist.

The District of Columbia should be the model of city law enforcement in the Nation. While conditions here are much better than in many other cities, they are far from perfect, and this is due in part to the congestion of criminal cases in the Supreme Court of the District, resulting in long delays. Furthermore, there is need for legislation in the District supplementing the national prohibition act, more sharply defining and enlarging the duties and powers of the District Commissioners and the police of the District, and opening the way for better cooperation in the enforcement of prohibition between the District officials and the prohibition officers of the Federal Government. It is urgent that these conditions be remedied.

LAW ENFORCEMENT AND OBSERVANCE

No one will look with satisfaction upon the volume of crime of all kinds and the growth of organized crime in our country. We have pressing need so to organize our system of administering criminal justice as to establish full vigor and effectiveness. We need to reestablish faith that the highest interests of our country are served by insistence upon the swift and even-handed administration of justice to all offenders, whether they be rich or poor. That we shall effect improvement is vital to the preservation of our institutions. It is the most serious issue before our people.

Under the authority of Congress I have appointed a National Commission on Law Observance and Enforcement, for an exhaustive study of the entire problem of the enforcement of our laws and the improvement of our judicial system, including the special problems and abuses growing out of the prohibition laws. The commission has been invited to make the widest inquiry into the shortcomings of the administration of justice and into the causes and remedies for them. It has organized its work under subcommittees dealing with the many contributory causes of our situation and has enlisted the aid of investigators in fields requiring special consideration. I am confident that as a result of its studies now being carried forward it will make a notable contribution to the solution of our pressing problems.

Pending further legislation, the Department of Justice has been striving to weed out inefficiency wherever it exists, to stimulate activity on the part of its prosecuting officers, and to use increasing care in examining into the qualifications of those appointed to serve as prosecutors. The department is seeking systematically to strengthen the law enforcement agencies week by week and month by month, not by dramatic displays but by steady pressure; by removal of negligent officials and by encouragement and assistance to the vigilant. During the course of these efforts it has been revealed that in some districts causes contributing to the congestion of criminal dockets, and to delays and inefficiency in prosecutions, have been lack of sufficient forces in the offices of United States attorneys, clerks of courts, and marshals. These conditions tend to clog the machinery of justice. The last conference of senior circuit judges has taken note of them and indorsed the department's proposals for improvement. Increases in appropriations are necessary and will be asked for in order to reenforce these offices.

The orderly administration of the law involves more than the mere machinery of law enforcement. The efficient use of that machinery and a spirit in our people in support of law are alike essential. We have need for improvement in both. However much we may perfect the mechanism, still if the citizen who is himself dependent upon some laws for the protection of all that he has and all that he holds dear, shall insist on selecting the particular laws which he will obey, he undermines his own safety and that of his country. His attitude may obscure, but it can not conceal, the ugly truth that the lawbreaker, whoever he may be, is the enemy of society. We can no longer gloss over the unpleasant reality which should be made vital in the consciousness of every citizen, that he who condones or traffics with crime, who is indifferent to it and to the punishment of the criminal, or to the lax performance of official duty, is himself the most effective agency for the breakdown of society.

Law can not rise above its source in good citizenship—in what right-minded men most earnestly believe and desire. If the law is upheld only by Government officials, then all law is at an end. Our laws are made by the people themselves; theirs is the right to work for their repeal; but until repeal it is an equal duty to observe them and demand their enforcement.

I have been gratified at the awakening sense of this responsibility in our citizens during the past few months, and gratified that many instances have occurred which refuted the cynicism which has asserted that our system could not convict those who had defied the law and possessed the means to resist its execution. These things reveal a moral awakening both in the people and in officials which lies at the very foundation of the rule of law.

CONCLUSION

The test of the rightfulness of our decisions must be whether we have sustained and advanced the ideals of the American people; self-government in its foundations of local government; justice whether to the individual or to the group; ordered liberty; freedom from domination; open opportunity and equality of opportunity; the initiative and individuality of our people; prosperity and the lessening of poverty; freedom of public opinion; education; advancement of knowledge; the growth of religious spirit; the tolerance of all faiths; the foundations of the home and the advancement of peace.

SECOND ANNUAL MESSAGE.

THE WHITE HOUSE, *December 2, 1930.*

To the Senate and House of Representatives:

I have the honor to comply with the requirement of the Constitution that I should lay before the Congress information as to the state of the Union, and recommend consideration of such measures as are necessary and expedient.

Substantial progress has been made during the year in national peace and security; the fundamental strength of the Nation's economic life is unimpaired; education and scientific discovery have made advances; our country is more alive to its problems of moral and spiritual welfare.

ECONOMIC SITUATION

During the past 12 months we have suffered with other Nations from economic depression.

The origins of this depression lie to some extent within our own borders through a speculative period which diverted capital and energy into speculation rather than constructive enterprise. Had overspeculation in securities been the only force operating, we should have seen recovery many months ago, as these particular dislocations have generally readjusted themselves.

Other deep-seated causes have been in action, however, chiefly the world-wide overproduction beyond even the demand of prosperous times for such important basic commodities as wheat, rubber, coffee, sugar, copper, silver, zinc, to some extent cotton, and other raw materials. The cumulative effects of demoralizing price falls of these important commodities in the process of adjustment of production to world consumption have produced financial crises in many countries and have diminished the buying power of these countries for imported goods to a degree which extended the difficulties farther afield by creating unemployment in all the industrial nations. The political agitation in Asia; revolutions in South America and political unrest in some European States; the methods of sale by Russia of her increasing agricultural exports to European markets; and our own drought—have all contributed to prolong and deepen the depression.

In the larger view the major forces of the depression now lie outside of the United States, and our recuperation has been retarded by the unwarranted degree of fear and apprehension created by these outside forces.

The extent of the depression is indicated by the following approximate percentages of activity during the past three months as compared with the highly prosperous year of 1928:

Value of department-store sales	93% of 1928
Volume of manufacturing production	80% of 1928
Volume of mineral production	90% of 1928
Volume of factory employment	84% of 1928
Total of bank deposits	105% of 1928
Wholesale prices—all commodities	83% of 1928
Cost of living	94% of 1928

Various other indexes indicate total decrease of activity from 1928 of from 15 to 20 per cent.

There are many factors which give encouragement for the future. The fact that we are holding from 80 to 85 per cent of our normal activities and incomes; that our major financial and industrial institutions have come through the storm unimpaired; that price levels of major commodities have remained approximately stable for some time; that a number of industries are showing signs of increasing demand; that the world at large is readjusting itself to the situation; all reflect grounds for confidence. We should remember that these occasions have been met many times before, that they are but temporary, that our country is to-day stronger and richer in resources, in equipment, in skill, than ever in its history. We are in an extraordinary degree self-sustaining, we will overcome world influences and will lead the march of prosperity as we have always done hitherto.

Economic depression can not be cured by legislative action or executive pronouncement. Economic wounds must be healed by the action of the cells of the economic body—the producers and consumers themselves. Recovery can be expedited and its effects mitigated by cooperative action. That cooperation requires that every individual should sustain faith and courage; that each should maintain his self-reliance; that each and every one should search for method of improving his business or service; that the vast majority whose income is unimpaired should not hoard out of fear but should pursue their normal living and recreations; that each should seek to assist his neighbors who may be less fortunate; that each industry should assist its own employees; that each community and each State should assume its full responsibilities for organization of employment and relief of distress with that sturdiness and independence which built a great Nation.

Our people are responding to these impulses in remarkable degree.

The best contribution of government lies in encouragement of this voluntary cooperation in the community. The Government, National, State, and local, can join with the community in such programs and do its part. A year ago I, together with other officers of the Government, initiated extensive cooperative measures throughout the country.

The first of these measures was an agreement of leading employers to maintain the standards of wages and of labor leaders to use their influence against strife. In a large sense these undertakings have been adhered to and we have not witnessed the usual reductions of wages which have always heretofore marked depressions. The index of union wage scales shows them to be to-day fully up to the level of any of the previous three years. In consequence the buying power of the country has been much larger than would otherwise have been the case. Of equal importance the Nation has had unusual peace in industry and freedom from the public disorder which has characterized previous depressions.

The second direction of cooperation has been that our governments, National, State, and local, the industries and business so distribute employment as to give work to the maximum number of employees.

The third direction of cooperation has been to maintain and even extend construction work and betterments in anticipation of the future. It has been the universal experience in previous depressions that public works and private construction have fallen off rapidly with the general tide of depression. On this occasion, however, the increased authorization and generous appropriations by the Congress and the action of States and municipalities have resulted in the expansion of public construction to an amount even above that in the most prosperous years. In addition the cooperation of public utilities, railways, and other large organizations has been generously given in construction and betterment work in anticipation of future need. The Department of Commerce advises me that as a result, the volume of this type of construction work, which amounted to roughly $6,300,000,000 in 1929, instead of decreasing will show a total of about $7,000,000,000 for 1930. There has, of course, been a substantial decrease in the types of construction which could not be undertaken in advance of need.

The fourth direction of cooperation was the organization in such States and municipalities, as was deemed necessary, of committees to organize local employment, to provide for employment agencies, and to effect relief of distress.

The result of magnificent cooperation throughout the country has been that actual suffering has been kept to a minimum during the past 12 months, and our unemployment has been far less in proportion than in other large industrial countries. Some time ago it became evident that unemployment would continue over the winter and would necessarily be added to from seasonal causes and that the savings of workpeople would be more largely depleted. We have as a Nation a definite duty to see that no deserving person in our country suffers from hunger or cold. I therefore set up a more extensive organization to stimulate more intensive cooperation throughout the country. There has been a most gratifying degree of response, from governors, mayors, and other public officials, from welfare organizations, and from employers in concerns both large and small. The local communities through their voluntary agencies have assumed the duty of relieving individual distress and are being generously supported by the public.

The number of those wholly out of employment seeking for work was accurately determined by the census last April as about 2,500,000. The Department of Labor index of employment in the larger trades shows some decrease in employment since that time. The problem from a relief point of view is somewhat less than the published estimates of the number of unemployed would indicate. The intensive community and individual efforts in providing special employment outside the listed industries are not reflected in the statistical indexes and tend to reduce such published figures. Moreover, there is estimated to be a constant figure at all times of nearly 1,000,000 unemployed who are not without annual income but temporarily idle in the shift from one job to another. We have an average of about three breadwinners to each two families, so that every person unemployed does not represent a family without income. The view that the relief problems are less than the gross numbers would indicate is confirmed by the experience of several cities, which shows that the number of families in distress represents from 10 to 20 per cent of the number of the calculated unemployed. This is not said to minimize the very real problem which exists but to weigh its actual proportions.

As a contribution to the situation the Federal Government is engaged upon the greatest program of waterway, harbor, flood control, public building, highway, and airway improvement in all our history. This, together with loans to merchant shipbuilders, improvement of the Navy and in military aviation, and other construction work of the Government will exceed $520,000,000 for this fiscal year. This compares with $253,000,000 in the fiscal year 1928. The construction works already authorized and the continuation of policies in Government aid will require a continual expenditure upwards of half a billion dollars annually.

I favor still further temporary expansion of these activities in aid to unemployment during this winter. The Congress will, however, have presented to it numbers of projects, some of them under the guise of, rather than the reality of, their usefulness in the increase of employment during the depression. There are certain commonsense limitations upon any expansions of construction work. The Government must not undertake works that are not of sound economic purpose and that have not been subject to searching technical investigation, and which have not been given adequate consideration by the Congress. The volume of construction work in the Government is already at the maximum limit warranted by financial prudence as a continuing policy. To increase taxation for purposes of construction work defeats its own purpose, as such taxes directly diminish employment in private industry. Again any kind of construction requires, after its authorization, a considerable time before labor can be employed in which to make engineering, architectural, and legal preparations. Our immediate problem is the increase of employment for the next six months, and new plans which do not produce such immediate result or which extend commitments beyond this period are not warranted.

The enlarged rivers and harbors, public building, and highway plans authorized by the Congress last session, however, offer an opportunity for assistance by the temporary acceleration of construction of these programs even faster than originally planned, especially if the technical requirements of the laws which entail great delays could be amended in such fashion as to speed up acquirements of land and the letting of contracts.

With view, however, to the possible need for acceleration, we, immediately upon receiving those authorities from the Congress five months ago, began the necessary technical work in preparation for such possible eventuality. I have canvassed the departments of the Government as to the maximum amount that can be properly added to our present expenditure to accelerate all construction during the next six months, and I feel warranted in asking the Congress for an appropriation of from $100,000,000 to $150,000,000 to provide such further employment in this emergency. In connection therewith we need some authority to make enlarged temporary advances of Federal-highway aid to the States.

I recommend that this appropriation be made distributable to the different departments upon recommendation of a committee of the Cabinet and approval by the President. Its application to works already authorized by the Congress assures its use in directions of economic importance and to public welfare. Such action will imply an expenditure upon construction of all kinds of over $650,000,000 during the next twelve months.

AGRICULTURE

The world-wide depression has affected agriculture in common with all other industries. The average price of farm produce has fallen to about 80 per cent of the levels of 1928. This average is, however, greatly affected by wheat and cotton, which have participated in world-wide overproduction and have fallen to about 60 per cent of the average price of the year 1928. Excluding these commodities, the prices of all other agricultural products are about 84 per cent of those of 1928. The average wholesale prices of other primary goods, such as nonferrous metals, have fallen to 76 per cent of 1928.

The price levels of our major agricultural commodities are, in fact, higher than those in other principal producing countries, due to the combined result of the tariff and the operations of the Farm Board. For instance, wheat prices at Minneapolis are about 30 per cent higher than at Winnipeg, and at Chicago they are about 20 per cent higher than at Buenos Aires. Corn prices at Chicago are over twice as high as at Buenos Aires. Wool prices average more than 80 per cent higher in this country than abroad, and butter is 30 per cent higher in New York City than in Copenhagen.

Aside from the misfortune to agriculture of the world-wide depression we have had the most severe drought. It has affected particularly the States bordering on the Potomac, Ohio, and Lower Mississippi Rivers, with some areas in Montana, Kansas, Oklahoma, and Texas. It has found its major expression in the shortage of pasturage and a shrinkage in the corn crop from an average of about 2,800,000,000 bushels to about 2,090,000,000 bushels.

On August 14 I called a conference of the governors of the most acutely affected States, and as a result of its conclusions I appointed a national committee comprising the heads of the important Federal agencies under the chairmanship of the Secretary of Agriculture. The governors in turn have appointed State committees representative of the farmers, bankers, business men, and the Red Cross, and subsidiary committees have been established in most of the acutely affected counties. Railway rates were reduced on feed and livestock in and out of the drought areas, and over 50,000 cars of such products have been transported under these reduced rates. The Red Cross established a preliminary fund of $5,000,000 for distress relief purposes and established agencies for its administration in each county. Of this fund less than $500,000 has been called for up to this time as the need will appear more largely during the winter. The Federal Farm Loan Board has extended its credit facilities, and the Federal Farm Board has given financial assistance to all affected cooperatives.

In order that the Government may meet its full obligation toward our countrymen in distress through no fault of their own, I recommend that an appropriation should be made to the Department of Agriculture to be loaned for the purpose of seed and feed for animals. Its application should as hitherto in such loans be limited to a gross amount to any one individual, and secured upon the crop.

The Red Cross can relieve the cases of individual distress by the sympathetic assistance of our people.

FINANCES OF THE GOVERNMENT

I shall submit the detailed financial position of the Government with recommendations in the usual Budget message. I will at this time, however, mention that the Budget estimates of receipts and expenditures for the current year were formulated by the Treasury and the Budget Bureau at a time when it was impossible to forecast the severity of the business depression and have been most seriously affected by it. At that time a surplus of about $123,000,000 was estimated for this fiscal year and tax reduction which affected the fiscal year to the extent of $75,000,000 was authorized by the Congress, thus reducing the estimated surplus to about $48,000,000. Closely revised estimates now made by the Treasury and the Bureau of the Budget of the tax, postal, and other receipts for the current fiscal year indicate a decrease of about $430,000,000 from the estimate of a year ago, of which about $75,000,000 is due to tax reduction, leaving about $355,000,000 due to the depression. Moreover, legislation enacted by Congress subsequent to the submission of the Budget enlarging Federal construction work to expand employment and for increase in veterans' services and other items, have increased expenditures during the current fiscal year by about $225,000,000.

Thus the decrease of $430,000,000 in revenue and the increase of $225,000,000 in expenditure adversely change the original Budget situation by about $655,000,000. This large sum is offset by the original estimated surplus a year ago of about $123,000,000, by the application of $185,000,000 of interest payments upon the foreign debt to current expenditures, by arrangements of the Farm Board through repayments, etc., in consequence of which they reduced their net cash demands upon the Treasury by $100,000,000 in this period, and by about $67,000,000 economies and deferments brought about in the Government, thus reducing the practical effect of the change in the situation to an estimated deficit of about $180,000,000 for the present fiscal year. I shall make suggestions for handling the present-year deficit in the Budget message, but I do not favor encroachment upon the statutory reduction of the public debt.

While it will be necessary in public interest to further increase expenditures during the current fiscal year in aid to unemployment by speeding up construction work and aid to the farmers affected by the drought, I can not emphasize too strongly the absolute necessity to defer any other plans for increase of Government expenditures. The Budget for 1932 fiscal year indicates estimated expenditure of about $4,054,000,000, including postal deficit. The receipts are estimated at about $4,085,000,000 if the temporary tax reduction of last year be discontinued, leaving a surplus of only about $30,000,000. Most rigid economy is therefore necessary to avoid increase in taxes.

NATIONAL DEFENSE

Our Army and Navy are being maintained at a high state of efficiency, under officers of high training and intelligence, supported by a devoted personnel of the rank and file. The London naval treaty has brought important economies in the conduct of the Navy. The Navy Department will lay before the committees of the Congress recommendations for a program of authorization of new construction which should be initiated in the fiscal year of 1932.

LEGISLATION

This is the last session of the Seventy-first Congress. During its previous sittings it has completed a very large amount of important legislation, notably: The establishment of the Federal Farm Board; fixing congressional reapportionment; revision of the tariff, including the flexible provisions and a reorganization of the Tariff Commission; reorganization of the Radio Commission; reorganization of the Federal Power Commission; expansion of Federal prisons; reorganization of parole and probation system in Federal prisons; expansion of veterans' hospitals; establishment of disability allowances to veterans; consolidation of veteran activities; consolidation and strengthening of prohibition enforcement activities in the Department of Justice; organization of a Narcotics Bureau; large expansion of rivers and harbors improvements; substantial increase in Federal highways; enlargement of public buildings construction program; and the ratification of the London naval treaty.

The Congress has before it legislation partially completed in the last sitting in respect to Muscle Shoals, bus regulation, relief of congestion in the courts, reorganization of border patrol in prevention of smuggling, law enforcement in the District of Columbia, and other subjects.

It is desirable that these measures should be completed.

The short session does not permit of extensive legislative programs, but there are a number of questions which, if time does not permit action, I recommend should be placed in consideration by the Congress, perhaps through committees cooperating in some instances with the Federal departments, with view to preparation for subsequent action. Among them are the following subjects:

ELECTRICAL POWER

I have in a previous message recommended effective regulation of interstate electrical power. Such regulation should preserve the independence and responsibility of the States.

RAILWAYS

We have determined upon a national policy of consolidation of the railways as a necessity of more stable and more economically operated transportation. Further legislation is necessary to facilitate such consolidation. In the public interest we should strengthen the railways that they may meet our future needs.

ANTITRUST LAWS

I recommend that the Congress institute an inquiry into some aspects of the economic working of these laws. I do not favor repeal of the Sherman Act. The prevention of monopolies is of most vital public importance. Competition is not only the basis of protection to the consumer but is the incentive to progress. However, the interpretation of these laws by the courts, the changes in business, especially in the economic effects upon those enterprises closely related to the use of the natural resources of the country, make such an inquiry advisable. The producers of these materials assert that certain unfortunate results of wasteful and destructive use of these natural resources together with a destructive competition which impoverishes both operator and worker can not be remedied because of the prohibitive interpretation of the antitrust laws. The well-known condition of the bituminous coal industry is an illustration. The people have a vital interest in the conservation of their natural resources; in the prevention of wasteful practices; in conditions of destructive competition which may impoverish the producer and the wage earner; and they have an equal interest in maintaining adequate competition. I therefore suggest that an inquiry be directed especially to the effect of the workings of the antitrust laws in these particular fields to determine if these evils can be remedied without sacrifice of the fundamental purpose of these laws.

CAPITAL-GAINS TAX

It is urged by many thoughtful citizens that the peculiar economic effect of the income tax on so-called capital gains at the present rate is to enhance speculative inflation and likewise impede business recovery. I believe this to be the case and I recommend that a study be made of the economic effects of this tax and of its relation to the general structure of our income tax law.

IMMIGRATION

There is need for revision of our immigration laws upon a more limited and more selective basis, flexible to the needs of the country.

Under conditions of current unemployment it is obvious that persons coming to the United States seeking work would likely become either a direct or indirect public charge. As a temporary measure the officers issuing visas to immigrants have been, in pursuance of the law, instructed to refuse visas to applicants likely to fall into this class. As a result the visas issued have decreased from an average of about 24,000 per month prior to restrictions to a rate of about 7,000 during the last month. These are largely preferred persons under the law. Visas from Mexico are about 250 per month compared to about 4,000 previous to restrictions. The whole subject requires exhaustive reconsideration.

DEPORTATION OF ALIEN CRIMINALS

I urge the strengthening of our deportation laws so as to more fully rid ourselves of criminal aliens. Furthermore, thousands of persons have entered the country in violation of the immigration laws. The very method of their entry indicates their objectionable character, and our law-abiding foreign-born residents suffer in consequence. I recommend that the Congress provide methods of strengthening the Government to correct this abuse.

POST OFFICE

Due to deferment of Government building over many years, previous administrations had been compelled to enter upon types of leases for secondary facilities in large cities, some of which were objectionable as representing too high a return upon the value of the property. To prevent the occasion for further uneconomic leasing I recommend that the Congress authorize the building by the Government of its own facilities.

VETERANS

The Nation has generously expanded its care for veterans. The consolidation of all veterans' activities into the Veterans' Administration has produced substantial administrative economies. The consolidation also brings emphasis to the inequalities in service and allowances. The whole subject is under study by the administrator, and I recommend it should also be examined by the committees of the Congress.

SOCIAL SERVICE

I urge further consideration by the Congress of the recommendations I made a year ago looking to the development through temporary Federal aid of adequate State and local services for the health of children and the further stamping out of communicable disease, particularly in the rural sections. The advance of scientific discovery, methods, and social thought imposes a new vision in these matters. The drain upon the Federal Treasury is comparatively small. The results both economic and moral are of the utmost importance.

GENERAL

It is my belief that after the passing of this depression, when we can examine it in retrospect, we shall need to consider a number of other questions as to what action may be taken by the Government to remove possible governmental influences which make for instability and to better organize mitigation of the effect of depression. It is as yet too soon to constructively formulate such measures.

There are many administrative subjects, such as departmental reorganization, extension of the civil service, readjustment of the postal rates, etc., which at some appropriate time require the attention of the Congress.

FOREIGN RELATIONS

Our relations with foreign countries have been maintained upon a high basis of cordiality and good will.

During the past year the London naval pact was completed, approved by the Senate, and ratified by the governments concerned. By this treaty we have abolished competition in the building of warships, have established the basis of parity of the United States with the strongest of foreign powers, and have accomplished a substantial reduction in war vessels.

During the year there has been an extended political unrest in the world. Asia continues in disturbed condition, and revolutions have taken place in Brazil, Argentina, Peru, and Bolivia. Despite the jeopardy to our citizens and their property which naturally arises in such circumstances, we have, with the cooperation of the governments concerned, been able to meet all such instances without friction.

We have resumed normal relations with the new Governments of Brazil, Argentina, Peru, and Bolivia immediately upon evidence that they were able to give protection to our citizens and their property, and that they recognized their international obligations.

A commission which was supported by the Congress has completed its investigation and reported upon our future policies in respect to Haiti and proved of high value in securing the acceptance of these policies. An election has been held and a new government established. We have replaced our high commissioner by a minister and have begun the gradual withdrawal of our activities with view to complete retirement at the expiration of the present treaty in 1935.

A number of arbitration and conciliation treaties have been completed or negotiated during the year, and will be presented for

approval by the Senate.

I shall, in a special message, lay before the Senate the protocols covering the statutes of the World Court which have been revised to accord with the sense of previous Senate reservations.

THIRD ANNUAL MESSAGE.

THE WHITE HOUSE, *December 8, 1931.*

To the Senate and House of Representatives:

It is my duty under the Constitution to transmit to the Congress information on the state of the Union and to recommend for its consideration necessary and expedient measures.

The chief influence affecting the state of the Union during the past year has been the continued world-wide economic disturbance. Our national concern has been to meet the emergencies it has created for us and to lay the foundations for recovery.

If we lift our vision beyond these immediate emergencies we find fundamental national gains even amid depression. In meeting the problems of this difficult period, we have witnessed a remarkable development of the sense of cooperation in the community. For the first time in the history of our major economic depressions there has been a notable absence of public disorders and industrial conflict. Above all there is an enlargement of social and spiritual responsibility among the people. The strains and stresses upon business have resulted in closer application, in saner policies, and in better methods. Public improvements have been carried out on a larger scale than even in normal times. The country is richer in physical property, in newly discovered resources, and in productive capacity than ever before. There has been constant gain in knowledge and education; there has been continuous advance in science and invention; there has been distinct gain in public health. Business depressions have been recurrent in the life of our country and are but transitory. The Nation has emerged from each of them with increased strength and virility because of the enlightenment they have brought, the readjustments and the larger understanding of the realities and obligations of life and work which come from them.

NATIONAL DEFENSE

Both our Army and Navy have been maintained in a high state of efficiency. The ability and devotion of both officers and men sustain the highest traditions of the service. Reductions and postponements in expenditure of these departments to meet the present emergency are being made without reducing existing personnel or impairing the morale of either establishment.

The agreement between the leading naval powers for limitation of naval armaments and establishment of their relative strength and thus elimination of competitive building also implies for ourselves the gradual expansion of the deficient categories in our Navy to the parities provided in those treaties. However, none of the other nations, parties to these agreements, is to-day maintaining the full rate of construction which the treaty size of fleets would imply.

Although these agreements secured the maximum reduction of fleets which it was at that time possible to attain, I am hopeful that the naval powers, party to these agreements, will realize that establishment of relative strength in itself offers opportunity for further reduction without injury to any of them. This would be the more possible if pending negotiations are successful between France and Italy. If the world is to regain its standards of life, it must further decrease both naval and other arms. The subject will come before the General Disarmament Conference which meets in Geneva on February 2 next.

FOREIGN AFFAIRS

We are at peace with the world. We have cooperated with other nations to preserve peace. The rights of our citizens abroad have been protected.

The economic depression has continued and deepened in every part of the world during the past year. In many countries political instability, excessive armaments, debts, governmental expenditures, and taxes have resulted in revolutions, in unbalanced budgets and monetary collapse and financial panics, in dumping of goods upon world markets, and in diminished consumption of commodities.

Within two years there have been revolutions or acute social disorders in 19 countries, embracing more than half the population of the world. Ten countries have been unable to meet their external obligations. In 14 countries, embracing a quarter of the world's population, former monetary standards have been temporarily abandoned. In a number of countries there have been acute financial panics or compulsory restraints upon banking. These disturbances have many roots in the dislocations from the World War. Every one of them has reacted upon us. They have sharply affected the markets and prices of our agricultural and industrial products. They have increased unemployment and greatly embarrassed our financial and credit system.

As our difficulties during the past year have plainly originated in large degree from these sources, any effort to bring about our own recuperation has dictated the necessity of cooperation by us with other nations in reasonable effort to restore world confidence and economic stability.

Cooperation of our Federal reserve system and our banks with the central banks in foreign countries has contributed to localize and ameliorate a number of serious financial crises or moderate the pressures upon us and thus avert disasters which would have affected us.

The economic crisis in Germany and Central Europe last June rose to the dimensions of a general panic from which it was apparent that without assistance these nations must collapse. Apprehensions of such collapse had demoralized our agricultural and security markets and so threatened other nations as to impose further dangers upon us. But of highest importance was the necessity of cooperation on our part to relieve the people of Germany from imminent disasters and to maintain their important relations to progress and stability in the world. Upon the initiative of this Government a year's postponement of reparations and other intergovernmental debts was brought about. Upon our further initiative an agreement was made by Germany's private creditors providing for an extension of such credits until the German people can develop more permanent and definite forms of relief.

We have continued our policy of withdrawing our marines from Haiti and Nicaragua.

The difficulties between China and Japan have given us great concern, not alone for the maintenance of the spirit of the Kellogg-Briand Pact, but for the maintenance of the treaties to which we are a party assuring the territorial integrity of China. It is our purpose to assist in finding solutions sustaining the full spirit of those treaties.

I shall deal at greater length with our foreign relations in a later message.

THE DOMESTIC SITUATION

Many undertakings have been organized and forwarded during the past year to meet the new and changing emergencies which have constantly confronted us.

Broadly the community has cooperated to meet the needs of honest distress, and to take such emergency measures as would sustain confidence in our financial system and would cushion the violence of liquidation in industry and commerce, thus giving time for orderly readjustment of costs, inventories, and credits without panic and widespread bankruptcy. These measures have served those purposes and will promote recovery.

In these measures we have striven to mobilize and stimulate private initiative and local and community responsibility. There has been the least possible Government entry into the economic field, and that only in temporary and emergency form. Our citizens and our local governments have given a magnificent display of unity and action, initiative and patriotism in solving a multitude of difficulties and in cooperating with the Federal Government.

For a proper understanding of my recommendations to the Congress it is desirable very briefly to review such activities during the past year.

The emergencies of unemployment have been met by action in many directions. The appropriations for the continued speeding up of the great Federal construction program have provided direct and indirect aid to employment upon a large scale. By organized unity of action, the States and municipalities have also maintained large programs of public improvement. Many industries have been prevailed upon to anticipate and intensify construction. Industrial concerns and other employers have been organized to spread available work amongst all their employees, instead of discharging a portion of them. A large majority have maintained wages at as high levels as the safe conduct of their business would permit. This course has saved us from industrial conflict and disorder which have characterized all previous depressions. Immigration has been curtailed by administrative action. Upon the basis of normal immigration the decrease amounts to about 300,000 individuals who otherwise would have been added to our unemployment. The expansion of Federal employment agencies under appropriations by the Congress has proved most effective. Through the President's organization for unemployment relief, public and private agencies were successfully mobilized last winter to provide employment and other measures against distress. Similar organization gives assurance against suffering during the coming winter. Committees of leading citizens are now active at practically every point of unemployment. In the large majority they have been assured the funds necessary which, together with local government aids, will meet the situation. A few exceptional localities will be further organized. The evidence of the Public Health Service shows an actual decrease of sickness and infant and general mortality below normal years. No greater proof could be adduced that our people have been protected from hunger and cold and that the sense of social responsibility in the Nation has responded to the need of the unfortunate.

To meet the emergencies in agriculture the loans authorized by Congress for rehabilitation in the drought areas have enabled farmers to produce abundant crops in those districts. The Red Cross undertook and magnificently administered relief for over 2,500,000 drought sufferers last winter. It has undertaken this year to administer relief to 100,000 sufferers in the new drought area of certain Northwest States. The action of the Federal Farm Board in granting credits to farm cooperatives saved many of them from bankruptcy and increased their purpose and strength. By enabling farm cooperatives to cushion the fall in prices of farm products in 1930 and 1931 the Board secured higher prices to the farmer than would have been obtained otherwise, although the benefits of this action were partially defeated by continued world overproduction. Incident to this action the failure of a large number of farmers and of country banks was averted which could quite possibly have spread into a major disaster. The banks in the South have cooperated with the Farm Board in creation of a pool for the better marketing of accumulated cotton. Growers have been materially assisted by this action. Constant effort has been made to reduce overproduction in relief of agriculture and to promote the foreign buying of agricultural products by sustaining economic stability abroad.

To meet our domestic emergencies in credit and banking arising from the reaction to acute crises abroad the National Credit Association was set up by the banks with resources of $500,000,000 to support sound banks against the frightened withdrawals and hoarding. It is giving aid to reopen solvent banks which have been closed. Federal officials have brought about many beneficial unions of banks and have employed other means which have prevented many bank closings. As a result of these measures the hoarding withdrawals which had risen to over $250,000,000 per week after the British crisis have substantially ceased.

FURTHER MEASURES

The major economic forces and weaknesses at home and abroad have now been exposed and can be appraised, and the time is ripe for forward action to expedite our recovery.

Although some of the causes of our depression are due to speculation, inflation of securities and real estate, unsound foreign investments, and mismanagement of financial institutions, yet our self-contained national economy, with its matchless strength and resources, would have enabled us to recover long since but for the continued dislocations, shocks, and setbacks from abroad.

Whatever the causes may be, the vast liquidation and readjustments which have taken place have left us with a large degree of credit paralysis, which, together with the situation in our railways and the conditions abroad, are now the outstanding obstacles to recuperation. If we can put our financial resources to work and can ameliorate the financial situation in the railways, I am confident we can make a large measure of recovery independent of the rest of the world. A strong America is the highest contribution to world stability.

One phase of the credit situation is indicated in the banks. During the past year banks, representing 3 per cent of our total deposits have been closed. A large part of these failures have been caused by withdrawals for hoarding, as distinguished from the failures early in the depression where weakness due to mismanagement was the larger cause of failure. Despite their closing, many of them will pay in full. Although such withdrawals have practically ceased, yet $1,100,000,000 of currency was previously withdrawn which has still to return to circulation. This represents a large reduction of the ability of our banks to extend credit which would otherwise fertilize industry and agriculture. Furthermore, many of our bankers, in order to prepare themselves to meet possible withdrawals, have felt compelled to call in loans, to refuse new credits, and to realize upon securities, which in turn has demoralized the markets. The paralysis has been further augmented by the steady increase in recent years of the proportion of bank assets invested in long-term securities, such as mortgages and bonds. These securities tend to lose their liquidity in depression or temporarily to fall in value so that the ability of the banks to meet the shock of sudden withdrawal is greatly lessened and the restriction of all kinds of credit is thereby increased. The continuing credit paralysis has operated to accentuate the deflation and liquidation of commodities, real estate, and securities below any reasonable basis of values.

All of this tends to stifle business, especially the smaller units, and finally expresses itself in further depression of prices and values, in restriction on new enterprise, and in increased unemployment.

The situation largely arises from an unjustified lack of confidence. We have enormous volumes of idle money in the banks and in hoarding. We do not require more money or working capital—we need to put what we have to work.

The fundamental difficulties which have brought about financial strains in foreign countries do not exist in the United States. No external drain on our resources can threaten our position, because the balance of international payments is in our favor; we owe less to foreign countries than they owe to us; our industries are efficiently organized; our currency and bank deposits are protected by the greatest gold reserve in history.

Our first step toward recovery is to reestablish confidence and thus restore the flow of credit which is the very basis of our economic life.

We must put some steel beams in the foundations of our credit structure. It is our duty to apply the full strength of our Government not only to the immediate phases, but to provide security against shocks and the repetition of the weaknesses which have been proven.

The recommendations which I here lay before the Congress are designed to meet these needs by strengthening financial, industrial, and agricultural life through the medium of our existing institutions, and thus to avoid the entry of the Government into competition with private business.

FEDERAL GOVERNMENT FINANCE

The first requirement of confidence and of economic recovery is financial stability of the United States Government. I shall deal with fiscal questions at greater length in the Budget message. But I must at this time call attention to the magnitude of the deficits which have developed and the resulting necessity for determined and courageous policies. These deficits arise in the main from the heavy decrease in tax receipts due to the depression and to the increase in expenditure on construction in aid to unemployment, aids to agriculture, and upon services to veterans.

During the fiscal year ending June 30 last we incurred a deficit of about $903,000,000, which included the statutory reduction of the debt and represented an increase of the national debt by $616,000,000. Of this, however, $153,000,000 is offset by increased cash balances.

In comparison with the fiscal year 1928 there is indicated a fall in Federal receipts for the present fiscal year amounting to $1,683,000,000, of which $1,034,000,000 is in individual and corporate income taxes alone. During this fiscal year there will be an increased expenditure, as compared to 1928, on veterans of $255,000,000, and an increased expenditure on construction work which may reach $520,000,000. Despite large economies in other directions, we have an indicated deficit, including the statutory retirement of the debt, of $2,123,000,000, and an indicated net debt increase of about $1,711,000,000.

The Budget for the fiscal year beginning July 1 next, after allowing for some increase of taxes under the present laws and after allowing for drastic reduction in expenditures, still indicates a deficit of $1,417,000,000. After offsetting the statutory debt retirements this would indicate an increase in the national debt for the fiscal year 1933 of about $921,000,000.

Several conclusions are inevitable. We must have insistent and determined reduction in Government expenses. We must face a temporary increase in taxes. Such increase should not cover the whole of these deficits or it will retard recovery. We must partially finance the deficit by borrowing. It is my view that the amount of taxation should be fixed so as to balance the Budget for 1933 except for the statutory debt retirement. Such Government receipts would assure the balance of the following year's budget including debt retirement. It is my further view that the additional taxation should be imposed solely as an emergency measure terminating definitely two years from July 1 next. Such a basis will give confidence in the determination of the Government to stabilize its finance and will assure taxpayers of its temporary character. Even with increased taxation, the Government will reach the utmost safe limit of its borrowing capacity by the expenditures for which we are already obligated and the recommendations here proposed. To go further than these limits in either expenditures, taxes, or borrowing will destroy confidence, denude commerce and industry of its resources, jeopardize the financial system, and actually extend unemployment and demoralize agriculture rather than relieve it.

FEDERAL LAND BANKS

I recommend that the Congress authorize the subscription by the Treasury of further capital to the Federal land banks to be retired as provided in the original act, or when funds are available, and that repayments of such capital be treated as a fund available for further subscriptions in the same manner. It is urgent that the banks be supported so as to stabilize the market values of their bonds and thus secure capital for the farmers at low rates, that they may continue their services to agriculture and that they may meet the present situation with consideration to the farmers.

DEPOSITS IN CLOSED BANKS

A method should be devised to make available quickly to depositors some portion of their deposits in closed banks as the assets of such banks may warrant. Such provision would go far to relieve distress in a multitude of families, would stabilize values in many communities, and would liberate working capital to thousands of concerns. I recommend that measures be enacted promptly to accomplish these results and I suggest that the Congress should consider the development of such a plan through the Federal Reserve Banks.

HOME-LOAN DISCOUNT BANKS

I recommend the establishment of a system of home-loan discount banks as the necessary companion in our financial structure of the Federal Reserve Banks and our Federal Land Banks. Such action will relieve present distressing pressures against home and farm property owners. It will relieve pressures upon and give added strength to building and loan associations, savings banks, and deposit banks, engaged in extending such credits. Such action would further decentralize our credit structure. It would revive residential construction and employment. It would enable such loaning institutions more effectually to promote home ownership. I discussed this plan at some length in a statement made public November 14, last. This plan has been warmly indorsed by the recent National Conference upon Home Ownership and Housing, whose members were designated by the governors of the States and the groups interested.

RECONSTRUCTION FINANCE CORPORATION

In order that the public may be absolutely assured and that the Government may be in position to meet any public necessity, I recommend that an emergency Reconstruction Corporation of the nature of the former War Finance Corporation should be established. It may not be necessary to use such an instrumentality very extensively. The very existence of such a bulwark will strengthen confidence. The Treasury should be authorized to subscribe a reasonable capital to it, and it should be given authority to issue its own debentures. It should be placed in liquidation at the end of two years. Its purpose is that by strengthening the weak spots to thus liberate the full strength of the Nation's resources. It should be in position to facilitate exports by American agencies; make advances to agricultural credit agencies where necessary to protect and aid the agricultural industry; to make temporary advances upon proper securities to established industries, railways, and financial institutions which can not otherwise secure credit, and where such advances will protect the credit structure and stimulate employment. Its functions would not overlap those of the National Credit Corporation.

FEDERAL RESERVE ELIGIBILITY

On October 6th I issued a statement that I should recommend to the Congress an extension during emergencies of the eligibility provisions in the Federal reserve act. This statement was approved by a representative gathering of the Members of both Houses of the Congress, including members of the appropriate committees. It was approved by the officials of the Treasury Department, and I understand such an extension has been approved by a majority of the governors of the Federal reserve banks. Nothing should be done which would lower the safeguards of the system.

The establishment of the mortgage-discount banks herein referred to will also contribute to further reserve strength in the banks without inflation.

BANKING LAWS

Our people have a right to a banking system in which their deposits shall be safeguarded and the flow of credit less subject to storms. The need of a sounder system is plainly shown by the extent of bank failures. I recommend the prompt improvement of the banking laws. Changed financial conditions and commercial practices must be met. The Congress should investigate the need for separation between different kinds of banking; an enlargement of branch banking under proper restrictions; and the methods by which enlarged membership in the Federal reserve system may be brought about.

POSTAL SAVINGS BANKS

The Postal Savings deposits have increased from about $200,000,000 to about $550,000,000 during the past year. This experience has raised important practical questions in relation to deposits and investments which should receive the attention of the Congress.

RAILWAYS

The railways present one of our immediate and pressing problems. They are and must remain the backbone of our transportation system. Their prosperity is interrelated with the prosperity of all industries. Their fundamental service in transportation, the volume of their employment, their buying power for supplies from other industries, the enormous investment in their securities, particularly their bonds, by insurance companies, savings banks, benevolent and other trusts, all reflect their partnership in the whole economic fabric. Through these institutions the railway bonds are in a large sense the investment of every family. The well-maintained and successful operation and the stability of railway finances are of primary importance to economic recovery. They should have more effective opportunity to reduce operating costs by proper consolidation. As their rates must be regulated in public interest, so also approximate regulation should be applied to competing services by some authority. The methods of their regulation should be revised. The Interstate Commerce Commission has made important and far-reaching recommendations upon the whole subject, which I commend to the early consideration of the Congress.

ANTITRUST LAWS

In my message of a year ago I commented on the necessity of congressional inquiry into the economic action of the antitrust laws. There is wide conviction that some change should be made especially in the procedure under these laws. I do not favor their repeal. Such action would open wide the door to price fixing, monopoly, and destruction of healthy competition. Particular attention should be given to the industries founded upon natural resources, especially where destructive competition produces great wastes of these resources and brings great hardships upon operators, employees, and the public. In recent years there has been continued demoralization in the bituminous coal, oil, and lumber industries. I again commend the matter to the consideration of the Congress.

UNEMPLOYMENT

As an aid to unemployment the Federal Government is engaged in the greatest program of public-building, harbor, flood-control, highway, waterway, aviation, merchant and naval ship construction in all history. Our expenditures on these works during this calendar year will reach about $780,000,000 compared with $260,000,000 in 1928. Through this increased construction, through the maintenance of a full complement of Federal employees, and through services to veterans it is estimated that the Federal taxpayer is now directly contributing to the livelihood of 10,000,000 of our citizens.

We must avoid burdens upon the Government which will create more unemployment in private industry than can be gained by further expansion of employment by the Federal Government. We can now stimulate employment and agriculture more effectually and speedily through the voluntary measures in progress, through the thawing out of credit, through the building up of stability abroad, through the home loan discount banks, through an emergency finance corporation and the rehabilitation of the railways and other such directions.

I am opposed to any direct or indirect Government dole. The breakdown and increased unemployment in Europe is due in part to such practices. Our people are providing against distress from unemployment in true American fashion by a magnificent response to public appeal and by action of the local governments.

GENERAL LEGISLATION

There are many other subjects requiring legislative action at this session of the Congress. I may list the following among them:

VETERANS' SERVICES

The law enacted last March authorizing loans of 50 per cent upon adjusted-service certificates has, together with the loans made under previous laws, resulted in payments of about $1,260,000,000. Appropriations have been exhausted. The Administrator of Veterans' Affairs advises that a further appropriation of $200,000,000 is required at once to meet the obligations made necessary by existing legislation.

There will be demands for further veterans' legislation; there are inequalities in our system of veterans' relief; it is our national duty to meet our obligations to those who have served the Nation. But our present expenditure upon these services now exceeds $1,000,000,000 per annum. I am opposed to any extension of these expenditures until the country has recovered from the present situation.

ELECTRICAL-POWER REGULATION

I have recommended in previous messages the effective regulation of interstate electrical power as the essential function of the reorganized Federal Power Commission. I renew the recommendation. It is urgently needed in public protection.

MUSCLE SHOALS

At my suggestion, the Governors and Legislatures of Alabama and Tennessee selected three members each for service on a committee to which I appointed a representative of the farm organizations and two representatives of the War Department for the purpose of recommending a plan for the disposal of these properties which would be in the interest of the people of those States and the agricultural industry throughout the country. I shall transmit the recommendations to the Congress.

REORGANIZATION OF FEDERAL DEPARTMENTS

I have referred in previous messages to the profound need of further reorganization and consolidation of Federal administrative functions to eliminate overlap and waste, and to enable coordination and definition of Government policies now wholly impossible in scattered and conflicting agencies which deal with parts of the same major function. I shall lay before the Congress further recommendations upon this subject, particularly in relation to the Department of the Interior. There are two directions of such reorganization, however, which have an important bearing upon the emergency problems with which we are confronted.

SHIPPING BOARD

At present the Shipping Board exercises large administrative functions independent of the Executive. These administrative functions should be transferred to the Department of Commerce, in keeping with that single responsibility which has been the basis of our governmental structure since its foundation. There should be created in that department a position of Assistant Secretary for Merchant Marine, under whom this work and the several bureaus having to do with merchant marine may be grouped.

The Shipping Board should be made a regulatory body acting also in advisory capacity on loans and policies, in keeping with its original conception. Its regulatory powers should be amended to include regulation of coastwise shipping so as to assure stability and better service. It is also worthy of consideration that the regulation of rates and services upon the inland waterways should be assigned to such a reorganized board.

REORGANIZATION OF PUBLIC WORKS ADMINISTRATION

I recommend that all building and construction activities of the Government now carried on by many departments be consolidated into an independent establishment under the President to be known as the "Public Works Administration" directed by a Public Works Administrator. This agency should undertake all construction work in service to the different departments of the Government (except naval and military work). The services of the Corps of Army Engineers should be delegated in rotation for military duty to this administration in continuation of their supervision of river and harbor work. Great economies, sounder policies, more effective coordination to employment, and expedition in all construction work would result from this consolidation.

LAW ENFORCEMENT

I shall present some recommendations in a special message looking to the strengthening of criminal-law enforcement and improvement in judicial procedure connected therewith.

INLAND WATERWAY AND HARBOR IMPROVEMENT

These improvements are now proceeding upon an unprecedented scale. Some indication of the volume of work in progress is conveyed by the fact that during the current year over 380,000,000 cubic yards of material have been moved—an amount equal to the entire removal in the construction of the Panama Canal. The Mississippi waterway system, connecting Chicago, Kansas City, Pittsburgh, and New Orleans, will be in full operation during 1933. Substantial progress is being made upon the projects of the upper Missouri, upper Mississippi, etc.

Negotiations are now in progress with Canada for the construction of the St. Lawrence Waterway.

THE TARIFF

Wages and standards of living abroad have been materially lowered during the past year. The temporary abandonment of the gold standard by certain countries has also reduced their production costs compared to ours. Fortunately any increases in the tariff which may be necessary to protect agriculture and industry from these lowered foreign costs, or decreases in items which may prove to be excessive, may be undertaken at any time by the Tariff Commission under authority which it possesses by virtue of the tariff act of 1930. The commission during the past year has reviewed the rates upon over 254 items subject to tariff. As a result of vigorous and industrious action, it is up to date in the consideration of pending references and is prepared to give prompt attention to any further applications. This procedure presents an orderly method for correcting inequalities. I am opposed to any general congressional revision of the tariff. Such action would disturb industry, business, and agriculture. It would prolong the depression.

IMMIGRATION AND DEPORTATION

I recommend that immigration restriction now in force under administrative action be placed upon a more definite basis by law. The deportation laws should be strengthened. Aliens lawfully in the country should be protected by the issuance of a certificate of residence.

PUBLIC HEALTH

I again call attention to my previous recommendations upon this subject, particularly in its relation to children. The moral results are of the utmost importance.

CONCLUSION

It is inevitable that in these times much of the legislation proposed to the Congress and many of the recommendations of the Executive must be designed to meet emergencies. In reaching solutions we must not jeopardize those principles which we have found to be the basis of the growth of the Nation. The Federal Government must not encroach upon nor permit local communities to abandon that precious possession of local initiative and responsibility. Again, just as the largest measure of responsibility in the government of the Nation rests upon local self-government, so does the largest measure of social responsibility in our country rest upon the individual. If the individual surrenders his own initiative and responsibilities, he is surrendering his own freedom and his own liberty. It is the duty of the National Government to insist that both the local governments and the individual shall assume and bear these responsibilities as a fundamental of preserving the very basis of our freedom.

Many vital changes and movements of vast proportions are taking place in the economic world. The effect of these changes upon the future can not be seen clearly as yet. Of this, however, we are sure: Our system, based upon the ideals of individual initiative and of equality of opportunity, is not an artificial thing. Rather it is the outgrowth of the experience of America, and expresses the faith and spirit of our people. It has carried us in a century and a half to leadership of the economic world. If our economic system does not match our highest expectations at all times, it does not require revolutionary action to bring it into accord with any necessity that experience may prove. It has successfully adjusted itself to changing conditions in the past. It will do so again. The mobility of our institutions, the richness of our resources, and the abilities of our people enable us to meet them unafraid. It is a distressful time for many of our people, but they have shown qualities as high in fortitude, courage, and resourcefulness as ever in our history. With that spirit, I have faith that out of it will come a sounder life, a truer standard of values, a greater recognition of the results of honest effort, and a healthier atmosphere in which to rear our children. Ours must be a country of such stability and security as can not fail to carry forward and enlarge among all the people that abundant life of material and spiritual opportunity which it has represented among all nations since its beginning.

FOURTH ANNUAL MESSAGE.

THE WHITE HOUSE, *December 6, 1932.*

To the Senate and House of Representatives:

In accord with my constitutional duty, I transmit herewith to the Congress information upon the state of the Union together with recommendation of measures for its consideration.

Our country is at peace. Our national defense has been maintained at a high state of effectiveness. All of the executive departments of the Government have been conducted during the year with a high devotion to public interest. There has been a far larger degree of freedom from industrial conflict than hitherto known. Education and science have made further advances. The public health is to-day at its highest known level. While we have recently engaged in the aggressive contest of a national election, its very tranquillity and the acceptance of its results furnish abundant proof of the strength of our institutions.

In the face of widespread hardship our people have demonstrated daily a magnificent sense of humanity, of individual and community responsibility for the welfare of the less fortunate. They have grown in their conceptions and organization for cooperative action for the common welfare.

In the provision against distress during this winter, the great private agencies of the country have been mobilized again; the generosity of our people has again come into evidence to a degree in which all America may take great pride. Likewise the local authorities and the States are engaged everywhere in supplemental measures of relief. The provisions made for loans from the Reconstruction Finance Corporation, to States that have exhausted their own resources, guarantee that there should be no hunger or suffering from cold in the country. The large majority of States are showing a sturdy cooperation in the spirit of the Federal aid.

The Surgeon General, in charge of the Public Health Service, furnishes me with the following information upon the state of public health:

Mortality rate per 1,000 of population on an annual basis from representative States

	General	Infant
First 9 months of—		
1928	11. 9	67. 8
1929	12. 0	65. 8
1930	11. 4	62. 0
1931	11. 2	60. 0
1932	10. 6	55. 0

The sickness rates from data available show the same trends. These facts indicate the fine endeavor of the agencies which have been mobilized for care of those in distress.

ECONOMIC SITUATION

The unparalleled world-wide economic depression has continued through the year. Due to the European collapse, the situation developed during last fall and winter into a series of most acute crises. The unprecedented emergency measures enacted and policies adopted undoubtedly saved the country from economic disaster. After serving to defend the national security, these measures began in July to show their weight and influence toward improvement of conditions in many parts of the country. The following tables of current business indicators show the general economic movement during the past eleven months.

Monthly business indices with seasonal variations eliminated

[Monthly average 1923–1925=100]

Year and month	Industrial production	Factory employment	Freight-car loadings	Department store sales, value	Exports, value	Imports, value	Building contracts, all types	Industrial electric power consumption
1931								
December	74	69. 4	69	81	46	48	38	89. 1
1932								
January	72	68 1	64	78	39	42	31	93. 9
February	69	67. 8	62	78	45	41	27	98. 8
March	67	66. 4	61	72	41	37	26	88. 0
April	63	64. 3	59	80	38	36	27	82. 2
May	60	62. 1	54	73	37	34	26	82. 0
June	59	60. 0	52	71	34	36	27	78. 1
July	58	58. 3	51	67	32	27	27	79. 2
August	60	58. 8	51	66	31	29	30	73. 5
September	66	60. 3	54	70	33	32	30	84. 0
October	66	61. 1	57	70	33	32	29	84. 4

The measures and policies which have procured this turn toward recovery should be continued until the depression is passed, and then the emergency agencies should be promptly liquidated. The expansion of credit facilities by the Federal Reserve System and the Reconstruction Finance Corporation has been of incalculable value. The loans of the latter for reproductive works, and to railways for the creation of employment; its support of the credit structure through loans to banks, insurance companies, railways, building and loan associations, and to agriculture has protected the savings and insurance policies of millions of our citizens and has relieved millions of borrowers from duress; they have enabled industry and business to function and expand. The assistance given to Farm Loan Banks, the establishment of the Home Loan Banks and Agricultural Credit Associations—all in their various ramifications have placed large sums of money at the disposal of the people in protection and aid. Beyond this, the extensive organization of the country in voluntary action has produced profound results.

The following table indicates direct expenditures of the Federal Government in aid to unemployment, agriculture, and financial relief over the past four years. The sums applied to financial relief multiply themselves many fold, being in considerable measure the initial capital supplied to the Reconstruction Finance Corporation, Farm Loan Banks, etc., which will be recovered to the Treasury.

	Public works [1]	Agricultural relief and financial loans
Fiscal year ending June 30—		
1930	$410, 420, 000	$156, 100, 000
1931	574, 870, 000	196, 700, 000
1932	655, 880, 000	772, 700, 000
1933	717, 260, 000	52, 000, 000
Total	2, 358, 430, 000	1, 177, 500, 000

[1] Public Building, Highways, Rivers and Harbors and their maintenance, naval and other vessels construction, hospitals, etc.

Continued constructive policies promoting the economic recovery of the country must be the paramount duty of the Government. The result of the agencies we have created and the policies we have pursued has been to buttress our whole domestic financial structure and greatly to restore credit facilities. But progress in recovery requires another element as well—that is fully restored confidence in the future. Institutions and men may have resources and credit but unless they have confidence progress is halting and insecure.

There are three definite directions in which action by the Government at once can contribute to strengthen further the forces of recovery by strengthening of confidence. They are the necessary foundations to any other action, and their accomplishment would at once promote employment and increase prices.

The first of these directions of action is the continuing reduction of all Government expenditures, whether national, State, or local. The difficulties of the country demand undiminished efforts toward economy in government in every direction. Embraced in this problem is the unquestioned balancing of the Federal Budget. That is the first necessity of national stability and is the foundation of further recovery. It must be balanced in an absolutely safe and sure manner if full confidence is to be inspired.

The second direction for action is the complete reorganization at once of our banking system. The shocks to our economic life have undoubtedly been multiplied by the weakness of this system, and until they are remedied recovery will be greatly hampered.

The third direction for immediate action is vigorous and whole-souled cooperation with other governments in the economic field. That our major difficulties find their origins in the economic weakness of foreign nations requires no demonstration. The first need to-day is strengthening of commodity prices. That can not be permanently accomplished by artificialities. It must be accomplished by expansion in consumption of goods through the return of stability and confidence in the world at large and that in turn can not be fully accomplished without cooperation with other nations.

BALANCING THE BUDGET

I shall in due course present the Executive Budget to the Congress. It will show proposed reductions in appropriations below those enacted by the last session of the Congress by over $830,000,000. In addition I shall present the necessary Executive orders under the recent act authorizing the reorganization of the Federal Government which, if permitted to go into force, will produce still further substantial economies. These sums in reduction of appropriations will, however, be partially offset by an increase of about $250,000,000 in uncontrollable items such as increased debt services, etc.

In the Budget there is included only the completion of the Federal public works projects already undertaken or under contract. Speeding up of Federal public works during the past four years as an aid to employment has advanced many types of such improvements to the point where further expansion can not be justified in their usefulness to the Government or the people. As an aid to unemployment we should beyond the normal constructive programs substitute reproductive or so-called self-liquidating works. Loans for such purposes have been provided for through the Reconstruction Finance Corporation. This change in character of projects directly relieves the taxpayer and is capable of expansion into a larger field than the direct Federal works. The reproductive works constitute an addition to national wealth and to future employment, whereas further undue expansion of Federal public works is but a burden upon the future.

The Federal construction program thus limited to commitments and work in progress under the proposed appropriations contemplates expenditures for the next fiscal year, including naval and other vessel construction, as well as other forms of public works and maintenance, of a total of $442,769,000, as compared with $717,262,000 for the present year.

The expenditure on such items over the four years ending June 30 next will amount to $2,350,000,000, or an amount of construction work eight times as great as the cost of the Panama Canal and, except for completion of certain long-view projects, places the Nation in many directions well ahead of its requirements for some years to come. A normal program of about $200,000,000 per annum should hereafter provide for the country's necessities and will permit substantial future reduction in Federal expenditures.

I recommend that the furlough system installed last year be continued not only because of the economy produced but because, being tantamount to the "5-day week," it sets an example which should be followed by the country and because it embraces within its workings the "spread work" principle and thus serves to maintain a number of public servants who would otherwise be deprived of all income. I feel, however, in view of the present economic situation and the decrease in the cost of living by over 20 per cent, that some further sacrifice should be made by salaried officials of the Government over and above the 8⅓ per cent reduction under the furlough system. I will recommend that after exempting the first $1,000 of salary there should be a temporary reduction for one year of 11 per cent of that part of all Government salaries in excess of the $1,000 exemption, the result of which, combined with the furlough system, will average about 14.8 per cent reduction in pay to those earning more than $1,000.

I will recommend measures to eliminate certain payments in the veterans' services. I conceive these outlays were entirely beyond the original intentions of Congress in building up veterans' allowances. Many abuses have grown up from ill-considered legislation. They should be eliminated. The Nation should not ask for a reduction in allowances to men and dependents whose disabilities rise out of war service nor to those veterans with substantial service who have become totally disabled from non-war-connected causes and who are at the same time without other support. These latter veterans are a charge on the community at some point, and I feel that in view of their service to the Nation as a whole the responsibility should fall upon the Federal Government.

Many of the economies recommended in the Budget were presented at the last session of the Congress but failed of adoption. If the Economy and Appropriations Committees of the Congress in canvassing these proposed expenditures shall find further reductions which can be made without impairing essential Government services, it will be welcomed both by the country and by myself. But under no circumstances do I feel that the Congress should fail to uphold the total of reductions recommended.

Some of the older revenues and some of the revenues provided under the act passed during the last session of the Congress, particularly those generally referred to as the nuisance taxes, have not been as prolific of income as had been hoped. Further revenue is necessary in addition to the amount of reductions in expenditures recommended. Many of the manufacturers' excise taxes upon selected industries not only failed to produce satisfactory revenue, but they are in many ways unjust and discriminatory. The time has come when, if the Government is to have an adequate basis of revenue to assure a balanced Budget, this system of special manufacturers' excise taxes should be extended to cover practically all manufactures at a uniform rate, except necessary food and possibly some grades of clothing.

At the last session the Congress responded to my request for authority to reorganize the Government departments. The act provides for the grouping and consolidation of executive and administrative agencies according to major purpose, and thereby reducing the number and overlap and duplication of effort. Executive orders issued for these purposes are required to be transmitted to the Congress while in session and do not become effective until after the expiration of 60 calendar days after such transmission, unless the Congress shall sooner approve.

I shall issue such Executive orders within a few days grouping or consolidating over fifty executive and administrative agencies including a large number of commissions and "independent" agencies.

The second step, of course, remains that after these various bureaus and agencies are placed cheek by jowl into such groups, the administrative officers in charge of the groups shall eliminate their overlap and still further consolidate these activities. Therein lie large economies.

The Congress must be warned that a host of interested persons inside and outside the Government whose vision is concentrated on some particular function will at once protest against these proposals. These same sorts of activities have prevented reorganization of the Government for over a quarter of a century. They must be disregarded if the task is to be accomplished.

BANKING

The basis of every other and every further effort toward recovery is to reorganize at once our banking system. The shocks to our economic system have undoubtedly multiplied by the weakness of our financial system. I first called attention of the Congress in 1929 to this condition, and I have unceasingly recommended remedy since that time. The subject has been exhaustively investigated both by the committees of the Congress and the officers of the Federal Reserve System.

The banking and financial system is presumed to serve in furnishing the essential lubricant to the wheels of industry, agriculture, and commerce, that is, credit. Its diversion from proper use, its improper use, or its insufficiency instantly brings hardship and dislocation in economic life. As a system our banking has failed to meet this great emergency. It can be said without question of doubt that our losses and distress have been greatly augmented by its wholly inadequate organization. Its inability as a system to respond to our needs is to-day a constant drain upon progress toward recovery. In this statement I am not referring to individual banks or bankers. Thousands of them have shown distinguished courage and ability. On the contrary, I am referring to the system itself, which is so organized, or so lacking in organization, that in an emergency its very mechanism jeopardizes or paralyzes the action of sound banks and its instability is responsible for periodic dangers to our whole economic system.

Bank failures rose in 1931 to 10½ per cent of all the banks as compared to 1½ per cent of the failures of all other types of enterprise. Since January 1, 1930, we have had 4,665 banks suspend, with $3,300,000,000 in deposits. Partly from fears and drains from abroad, partly from these failures themselves (which indeed often caused closing of sound banks), we have witnessed hoarding of currency to an enormous sum, rising during the height of the crisis to over $1,600,000,000. The results from interreaction of cause and effect have expressed themselves in strangulation of credit which at times has almost stifled the Nation's business and agriculture. The losses, suffering, and tragedies of our people are incalculable. Not alone do they lie in the losses of savings to millions of homes, injury by deprival of working capital to thousands of small businesses, but also, in the frantic pressure to recall loans to meet pressures of hoarding and in liquidation of failed banks, millions of other people have suffered in the loss of their homes and farms, businesses have been ruined, unemployment increased, and farmers' prices diminished.

That this failure to function is unnecessary and is the fault of our particular system is plainly indicated by the fact that in Great Britain, where the economic mechanism has suffered far greater shocks than our own, there has not been a single bank failure during the depression. Again in Canada, where the situation has been in large degree identical with our own, there have not been substantial bank failures.

The creation of the Reconstruction Finance Corporation and the amendments to the Federal Reserve Act served to defend the Nation in a great crisis. They are not remedies; they are relief. It is inconceivable that the Reconstruction Corporation, which has extended aid to nearly 6,000 institutions and is manifestly but a temporary device, can go on indefinitely.

It is to-day a matter of satisfaction that the rate of bank failures, of hoarding, and the demands upon the Reconstruction Corporation have greatly lessened. The acute phases of the crisis have obviously passed and the time has now come when this national danger and this failure to respond to national necessities must be ended and the measures to end them can be safely undertaken. Methods of reform have been exhaustively examined. There is no reason now why solution should not be found at the present session of the Congress. Inflation of currency or governmental conduct of banking can have no part in these reforms. The Government must abide within the field of constructive organization, regulation, and the enforcement of safe practices only.

Parallel with reform in the banking laws must be changes in the Federal Farm Loan Banking system and in the Joint Stock Land Banks. Some of these changes should be directed to permanent improvement and some to emergency aid to our people where they wish to fight to save their farms and homes.

I wish again to emphasize this view—that these widespread banking reforms are a national necessity and are the first requisites for further recovery in agriculture and business. They should have immediate consideration as steps greatly needed to further recovery.

ECONOMIC COOPERATION WITH OTHER NATIONS

Our major difficulties during the past two years find their origins in the shocks from economic collapse abroad which in turn are the aftermath of the Great War. If we are to secure rapid and assured recovery and protection for the future we must cooperate with foreign nations in many measures.

We have actively engaged in a World Disarmament Conference where, with success, we should reduce our own tax burdens and the tax burdens of other major nations. We should increase political stability of the world. We should lessen the danger of war by increasing defensive powers and decreasing offensive powers of nations. We would thus open new vistas of economic expansion for the world.

We are participating in the formulation of a World Economic Conference, successful results from which would contribute much to advance in agricultural prices, employment, and business. Currency depreciation and correlated forces have contributed greatly to decrease in price levels. Moreover, from these origins rise most of the destructive trade barriers now stifling the commerce of the world. We could by successful action increase security and expand trade through stability in international exchange and monetary values. By such action world confidence could be restored. It would bring courage and stability, which will reflect into every home in our land.

The European governments, obligated to us in war debts, have requested that there should be suspension of payments due the United States on December 15 next, to be accompanied by exchange of views upon this debt question. Our Government has informed them that we do not approve of suspension of the December 15 payments. I have stated that I would recommend to the Congress methods to overcome temporary exchange difficulties in connection with this payment from nations where it may be necessary.

In the meantime I wish to reiterate that here are three great fields of international action which must be considered not in part but as a whole. They are of most vital interest to our people. Within them there are not only grave dangers if we fail in right action but there also lie immense opportunities for good if we shall succeed. Within success there lie major remedies for our economic distress and major progress in stability and security to every fireside in our country.

The welfare of our people is dependent upon successful issue of the great causes of world peace, world disarmament, and organized world recovery. Nor is it too much to say that to-day as never before the welfare of mankind and the preservation of civilization depend upon our solution of these questions. Such solutions can not be attained except by honest friendship, by adherence to agreements entered upon until mutually revised and by cooperation amongst nations in a determination to find solutions which will be mutually beneficial.

OTHER LEGISLATION

I have placed various legislative needs before the Congress in previous messages, and these views require no amplification on this occasion. I have urged the need for reform in our transportation and power regulation, in the antitrust laws as applied to our national resource industries, western range conservation, extension of Federal aid to child-health services, membership in the World Court, the ratification of the Great Lakes-St. Lawrence Seaway Treaty, revision of the bankruptcy acts, revision of Federal court procedure, and many other pressing problems.

These and other special subjects I shall where necessary deal with by special communications to the Congress.

The activities of our Government are so great, when combined with the emergency activities which have arisen out of the world crisis, that even the briefest review of them would render the annual message unduly long. I shall therefore avail myself of the fact that every detail of the Government is covered in the reports to the Congress by each of the departments and agencies of the Government.

CONCLUSION

It seems to me appropriate upon this occasion to make certain general observations upon the principles which must dominate the solution of problems now pressing upon the Nation. Legislation in response to national needs will be effective only if every such act conforms to a complete philosophy of the people's purposes and destiny. Ours is a distinctive government with a unique history and background, consciously dedicated to specific ideals of liberty and to a faith in the inviolable sanctity of the individual human spirit. Furthermore, the continued existence and adequate functioning of our government in preservation of ordered liberty and stimulation of progress depends upon the maintenance of State, local, institutional, and individual sense of responsibility. We have builded a system of individualism peculiarly our own which must not be forgotten in any governmental acts, for from it have grown greater accomplishments than those of any other nation.

On the social and economic sides, the background of our American system and the motivation of progress is essentially that we should allow free play of social and economic forces as far as will not limit equality of opportunity and as will at the same time stimulate the initiative and enterprise of our people. In the maintenance of this balance the Federal Government can permit of no privilege to any person or group. It should act as a regulatory agent and not as a participant in economic and social life. The moment the Government participates, it becomes a competitor with the people. As a competitor it becomes at once a tyranny in whatever direction it may touch. We have around us numerous such experiences, no one of which can be found to have justified itself except in cases where the people as a whole have met forces beyond their control, such as those of the Great War and this great depression, where the full powers of the Federal Government must be exerted to protect the people. But even these must be limited to an emergency sense and must be promptly ended when these dangers are overcome.

With the free development of science and the consequent multitude of inventions, some of which are absolutely revolutionary in our national life, the Government must not only stimulate the social and economic responsibility of individuals and private institutions but it must also give leadership to cooperative action amongst the people which will soften the effect of these revolutions and thus secure social transformations in an orderly manner. The highest form of self-government is the voluntary cooperation within our people for such purposes.

But I would emphasize again that social and economic solutions, as such, will not avail to satisfy the aspirations of the people unless they conform with the traditions of our race, deeply grooved in their sentiments through a century and a half of struggle for ideals of life that are rooted in religion and fed from purely spiritual springs.

Franklin D. Roosevelt

March 4, 1933 to April 12, 1945

FIRST ANNUAL MESSAGE.

JANUARY 3, 1934.

MR. PRESIDENT, MR. SPEAKER, SENATORS AND REPRESENTATIVES IN CONGRESS:

I come before you at the opening of the Regular Session of the 73rd Congress, not to make requests for special or detailed items of legislation; I come, rather, to counsel with you, who, like myself, have been selected to carry out a mandate of the whole people, in order that without partisanship you and I may cooperate to continue the restoration of our national well-being and, equally important, to build on the ruins of the past a new structure designed better to meet the present problems of modern civilization.

Such a structure includes not only the relations of industry and agriculture and finance to each other but also the effect which all of these three have on our individual citizens and on the whole people as a nation.

Now that we are definitely in the process of recovery, lines have been rightly drawn between those to whom this recovery means a return to old methods—and the number of these people is small—and those for whom recovery means a reform of many old methods, a permanent readjustment of many of our ways of thinking and therefore of many of our social and economic arrangements.

Civilization can not go back: civilization must not stand still. We have undertaken new methods. It is our task to perfect, to improve, to alter when necessary, but in all cases to go forward. To consolidate what we are doing, to make our economic and social structure capable of dealing with modern life is the joint task of the Legislative, the Judicial, and the Executive Branches of the National Government.

Without regard to party, the overwhelming majority of our people seek a greater opportunity for humanity to prosper and find happiness. They recognize that human welfare has not increased and does not increase through mere materialism and luxury, but that it does progress through integrity, unselfishness, responsibility and justice.

In the past few months, as a result of our action, we have demanded of many citizens that they surrender certain licenses to do as they please in their business relationships; but we have asked this in exchange for the protection which the State can give against exploitation by their fellow men or by combinations of their fellow men.

I congratulate this Congress upon the courage, the earnestness and the efficiency with which you met the crisis at the Special Session. It was your fine understanding of the national problem that furnished the example which the country has so splendidly followed. I venture to say that the task confronting the First Congress of 1789 was no greater than your own.

I shall not attempt to set forth either the many phases of the crisis which we experienced last March, nor the many measures which you and I undertook during the Special Session that we might initiate recovery and reform.

It is sufficient that I should speak in broad terms of the results of our common counsel.

The credit of the Government has been fortified by drastic reduction in the cost of its permanent agencies through the Economy Act.

With the two-fold purpose of strengthening the whole financial structure and of arriving eventually at a medium of exchange which will have over the years less variable purchasing and debt paying power for our people than that of the past, I have used the authority granted me to purchase all American produced gold and silver and to buy additional gold in the world markets. Careful investigation and constant study prove that in the matter of foreign exchange rates certain of our sister nations find themselves so handicapped by internal and other conditions that they feel unable at this time to enter into stabilization discussion based on permanent and world-wide objectives.

The overwhelming majority of the banks, both national and state, which reopened last spring, are in sound condition and have been brought within the protection of Federal Insurance. In the case of those banks which were not permitted to reopen, nearly 600 million dollars of frozen deposits are being restored to the depositors through the assistance of the National Government.

We have made great strides towards the objectives of the National Industrial Recovery Act, for not only have several millions of our unemployed been restored to work, but industry is organizing itself with a greater understanding that reasonable profits can be earned while at the same time protection can be assured to guarantee to labor adequate pay and proper conditions of work. Child labor is abolished. Uniform standards of hours and wages apply today to 95% of industrial employment within the field of the National Industrial Recovery Act. We seek the definite end of preventing combinations in furtherance of monopoly and in restraint of trade, while at the same time we seek to prevent ruinous rivalries within industrial groups which in many cases resemble the gang wars of the underworld and in which the real victim in every case is the public itself.

Under the authority of this Congress, we have brought the component parts of each industry together around a common table, just as we have brought problems affecting labor to a common meeting ground. Though the machinery, hurriedly devised, may need readjustment from time to time, nevertheless I think you will agree with me that we have created a permanent feature of our modernized industrial structure and that it will continue under the supervision but not the arbitrary dictation of government itself.

You recognized last spring that the most serious part of the debt burden affected those who stood in danger of losing their farms and their homes. I am glad to tell you that refinancing in both of these cases is proceeding with good success and in all probability within the financial limits set by the Congress.

But agriculture had suffered from more than its debts. Actual experience with the operation of the Agricultural Adjustment Act leads to my belief that thus far the experiment of seeking a balance between production and consumption is succeeding and has made progress entirely in line with reasonable expectations towards the restoration of farm prices to parity. I continue in my conviction that industrial progress and prosperity can only be attained by bringing the purchasing power of that portion of our population which in one form or another is dependent upon agriculture up to a level which will restore a proper balance between every section of the country and every form of work.

In this field, through carefully planned flood control, power development and land use policies, in the Tennessee Valley and in other great watersheds, we are seeking the elimination of waste, the removal of poor lands from agriculture and the encouragement of small local industries, thus furthering this principle of a better balanced national life. We recognize the great ultimate cost of the application of this rounded policy to every part of the Union. Today we are creating heavy obligations to start the work and because of the great unemployment needs of the moment. I look forward, however, to the time in the not distant future, when annual appropriations, wholly covered by current revenue, will enable the work to proceed with a national plan. Such a national plan will, in a generation or two, return many times the money spent on it; more important, it will eliminate the use of inefficient tools, conserve and increase natural resources, prevent waste, and enable millions of our people to take better advantage of the opportunities which God has given our country.

I cannot, unfortunately, present to you a picture of complete optimism regarding world affairs.

The delegation representing the United States has worked in close cooperation with the other American republics assembled at Montevideo to make that conference an outstanding success. We have, I hope, made it clear to our neighbors that we seek with them future avoidance of territorial expansion and of interference by one nation in the internal affairs of another. Furthermore, all of us are seeking the restoration of commerce in ways which will preclude the building up of large favorable trade balances by any one nation at the expense of trade debits on the part of other nations.

In other parts of the world, however, fear of immediate or future aggression and with this the spending of vast sums on armament and the continued building up of defensive trade barriers prevent any great progress in peace or trade agreements. I have made it clear that the United States cannot take part in political arrangements in Europe but that we stand ready to cooperate at any time in practicable measures on a world basis looking to immediate reduction of armaments and the lowering of the barriers against commerce.

I expect to report to you later in regard to debts owed the government and people of this country by the governments and peoples of other countries. Several nations, acknowledging the debt, have paid in small part; other nations have failed to pay. One nation—Finland—has paid the installments due this country in full.

Returning to home problems, we have been shocked by many notorious examples of injuries done our citizens by persons or groups who have been living off their neighbors by the use of methods either unethical or criminal.

In the first category—a field which does not involve violations of the letter of our laws—practices have been brought to light which have shocked those who believed that we were in the past generation raising the ethical standards of business. They call for stringent preventive or regulatory measures. I am speaking of those individuals who have evaded the spirit and purpose of our tax laws, of those high officials of banks or corporations who have grown rich at the expense of their stockholders or the public, of those reckless speculators with their own or other people's money whose operations have injured the values of the farmers' crops and the savings of the poor.

In the other category, crimes of organized banditry, cold-blooded shooting, lynching and kidnaping have threatened our security.

These violations of ethics and these violations of law call on the strong arm of government for their immediate suppression; they call also on the country for an aroused public opinion.

The adoption of the 21st Amendment should give material aid to the elimination of those new forms of crime which came from the illegal traffic in liquor.

I shall continue to regard it as my duty to use whatever means may be necessary to supplement state, local and private agencies for the relief of suffering caused by unemployment. With respect to this question, I have recognized the dangers inherent in the direct giving of relief and have sought the means to provide not mere relief, but the opportunity for useful and remunerative work. We shall, in the process of recovery, seek to move as rapidly as possible from direct relief to publicly supported work and from that to the rapid restoration of private employment.

It is to the eternal credit of the American people that this tremendous readjustment of our national life is being accomplished peacefully, without serious dislocation, with only a minimum of injustice and with a great, willing spirit of cooperation throughout the country.

Disorder is not an American habit. Self help and self control are the essence of the American tradition—not of necessity the form of that tradition, but its spirit. The program itself comes from the American people.

It is an integrated program, national in scope. Viewed in the large, it is designed to save from destruction and to keep for the future the genuinely important values created by modern society. The vicious and wasteful parts of that society we could not save if we wished; they have chosen the way of self-destruction. We would save useful mechanical invention, machine production, industrial efficiency, modern means of communication, broad education. We would save and encourage the slowly growing impulse among consumers to enter the industrial market place equipped with sufficient organization to insist upon fair prices and honest sales.

But the unnecessary expansion of industrial plants, the waste of natural resources, the exploitation of the consumers of natural monopolies, the accumulation of stagnant surpluses, child labor, and the ruthless exploitation of all labor, the encouragement of speculation with other people's money, these were consumed in the fires that they themselves kindled: we must make sure that as we reconstruct our life there be no soil in which such weeds can grow again.

We have ploughed the furrow and planted the good seed; the hard beginning is over. If we would reap the full harvest, we must cultivate the soil where this good seed is sprouting and the plant is reaching up to mature growth.

A final personal word. I know that each of you will appreciate that I am speaking no mere politeness when I assure you how much I value the fine relationship that we have shared during these months of hard and incessant work. Out of these friendly contacts we are, fortunately, building a strong and permanent tie between the legislative and executive branches of the government. The letter of the Constitution wisely declared a separation, but the impulse of common purpose declares a union. In this spirit we join once more in serving the American people.

SECOND ANNUAL MESSAGE.

THE WHITE HOUSE, *January 4, 1935.*

MR. PRESIDENT, MR. SPEAKER, MEMBERS OF THE SENATE AND OF THE HOUSE OF REPRESENTATIVES:

The Constitution wisely provides that the Chief Executive shall report to the Congress on the state of the Union, for through you, the chosen legislative representatives, our citizens everywhere may fairly judge the progress of our governing. I am confident that today, in the light of the events of the past 2 years, you do not consider it merely a trite phrase when I tell you that I am truly glad to greet you and that I look forward to common counsel, to useful cooperation, and to genuine friendships between us.

We have undertaken a new order of things; yet we progress to it under the framework and in the spirit and intent of the American Constitution. We have proceeded throughout the Nation a measurable distance on the road toward this new order. Materially, I can report to you substantial benefits to our agricultural population, increased industrial activity, and profits to our merchants. Of equal moment, there is evident a restoration of that spirit of confidence and faith which marks the American character. Let him who, for speculative profit or partisan purpose, without just warrant would seek to disturb or dispel this assurance, take heed before he assumes responsibility for any act which slows our onward steps.

Throughout the world change is the order of the day. In every nation economic problems long in the making have brought crises of many kinds for which the masters of old practice and theory were unprepared. In most nations social justice, no longer a distant ideal, has become a definite goal, and ancient governments are beginning to heed the call.

Thus the American people do not stand alone in the world in their desire for change. We seek it through tested liberal traditions, through processes which retain all of the deep essentials of that republican form of representative government first given to a troubled world by the United States.

As the various parts in the program begun in the extraordinary session of the Seventy-third Congress shape themselves in practical administration, the unity of our program reveals itself to the Nation. The outlines of the new economic order, rising from the disintegration of the old, are apparent. We test what we have done as our measures take root in the living texture of life. We see where we have built wisely and where we can do still better.

The attempt to make a distinction between recovery and reform is a narrowly conceived effort to substitute the appearance of reality for reality itself. When a man is convalescing from illness wisdom dictates not only cure of the symptoms but also removal of their cause.

It is important to recognize that while we seek to outlaw specific abuses, the American objective of today has an infinitely deeper, finer and more lasting purpose than mere repression. Thinking people in almost every country of the world have come to realize certain fundamental difficulties with which civilization must reckon. Rapid changes—the machine age, the advent of universal and rapid communication, and many other new factors have brought new problems. Succeeding generations have attempted to keep pace by reforming in piecemeal fashion this or that attendant abuse. As a result, evils overlap and reform becomes confused and frustrated. We lose sight, from time to time, of our ultimate human objectives.

Let us, for a moment, strip from our simple purpose the confusion that results from a multiplicity of detail and from millions of written and spoken words.

We find our population suffering from old inequalities, little changed by past sporadic remedies. In spite of our efforts and in spite of our talk, we have not weeded out the overprivileged and we have not effectively lifted up the underprivileged. Both of these manifestations of injustice have retarded happiness. No wise man has any intention of destroying what is known as the profit motive, because by the profit motive we mean the right by work to earn a decent livelihood for ourselves and for our families.

We have, however, a clear mandate from the people, that Americans must forswear that conception of the acquisition of wealth which, through excessive profits, creates undue private power over private affairs and, to our misfortune, over public affairs as well. In building toward this end we do not destroy ambition nor do we seek to divide our wealth into equal shares on stated occasions. We continue to recognize the greater ability of some to earn more than others. But we do assert that the ambition of the individual to obtain for him and his a proper security, a reasonable leisure, and a decent living throughout life, is an ambition to be preferred to the appetite for great wealth and great power.

I recall to your attention my message to the Congress last June in which I said: "Among our objectives I place the security of the men, women, and children of the Nation first." That remains our first and continuing task; and in a very real sense every major legislative enactment of this Congress should be a component part of it.

In defining immediate factors which enter into our quest, I have spoken to the Congress and the people of three great divisions:

1. The security of a livelihood through the better use of the national resources of the land in which we live.

2. The security against the major hazards and vicissitudes of life.

3. The security of decent homes.

I am now ready to submit to the Congress a broad program designed ultimately to establish all three of these factors of security—a program which because of many lost years will take many future years to fulfill.

A study of our national resources, more comprehensive than any previously made, shows the vast amount of necessary and practicable work which needs to be done for the development and preservation of our natural wealth for the enjoyment and advantage of our people in generations to come. The sound use of land and water is far more comprehensive than the mere planting of trees, building of dams, distributing of electricity or retirement of submarginal land. It recognizes that stranded populations, either in the country or the city, cannot have security under the conditions that now surround them.

To this end we are ready to begin to meet this problem—the intelligent care of population throughout our Nation, in accordance with an intelligent distribution of the means of livelihood for that population. A definite program for putting people to work, of which I shall speak in a moment, is a component part of this greater program of security of livelihood through the better use of our national resources.

Closely related to the broad problem of livelihood is that of security against the major hazards of life. Here also a comprehensive survey of what has been attempted or accomplished in many nations and in many States proves to me that the time has come for action by the National Government. I shall send to you, in a few days, definite recommendations based on these studies. These recommendations will cover the broad subjects of unemployment insurance and old-age insurance, of benefits for children, for mothers, for the handicapped, for maternity care, and for other aspects of dependency and illness where a beginning can now be made.

The third factor—better homes for our people—has also been the subject of experimentation and study. Here too, the first practical steps can be made through the proposals which I shall suggest in relation to giving work to the unemployed.

Whatever we plan and whatever we do should be in the light of these three clear objectives of security. We cannot afford to lose valuable time in haphazard public policies which cannot find a place in the broad outlines of these major purposes. In that spirit I come to an immediate issue made for us by hard and inescapable circumstance—the task of putting people to work. In the spring of 1933 the issue of destitution seemed to stand apart; today, in the light of our experience and our new national policy, we find we can put people to work in ways which conform to, initiate, and carry forward the broad principles of that policy.

The first objectives of emergency legislation of 1933 were to relieve destitution, to make it possible for industry to operate in a more rational and orderly fashion, and to put behind industrial recovery the impulse of large expenditures in Government undertakings. The purpose of the National Industrial Recovery Act to provide work for more people succeeded in a substantial manner within the first few months of its life, and the act has continued to maintain employment gains and greatly improved working conditions in industry.

The program of public works provided for in the Recovery Act launched the Federal Government into a task for which there was little time to make preparation and little American experience to follow. Great employment has been given and is being given by these works.

More than 2 billions of dollars have also been expended in direct relief to the destitute. Local agencies of necessity determined the recipients of this form of relief. With inevitable exceptions the funds were spent by them with reasonable efficiency, and as a result actual want of food and clothing in the great majority of cases has been overcome.

But the stark fact before us is that great numbers still remain unemployed.

A large proportion of these unemployed and their dependents have been forced on the relief rolls. The burden on the Federal Government has grown with great rapidity. We have here a human as well as an economic problem. When humane considerations are concerned, Americans give them precedence. The lessons of history, confirmed by the evidence immediately before me show conclusively that continued dependence upon relief induces a spiritual and moral disintegration fundamentally destructive to the national fiber. To dole out relief in this way is to administer a narcotic, a subtle destroyer of the human spirit. It is inimical to the dictates of sound policy. It is in violation of the traditions of America. Work must be found for able-bodied but destitute workers.

The Federal Government must and shall quit this business of relief.

I am not willing that the vitality of our people be further sapped by the giving of cash, of market baskets, of a few hours of weekly work cutting grass, raking leaves or picking up papers in the public parks. We must preserve not only the bodies of the unemployed from destitution but also their self-respect, their self-reliance and courage and determination. This decision brings me to the problem of what the Government should do with approximately 5 million unemployed now on the relief rolls.

About one million and a half of these belong to the group which in the past was dependent upon local welfare efforts. Most of them are unable for one reason or another to maintain themselves independently—for the most part, through no fault of their own. Such people, in the days before the great depression, were cared for by local efforts—by States, by counties, by towns, by cities, by churches, and by private welfare agencies. It is my thought that in the future they must be cared for as they were before. I stand ready through my own personal efforts, and through the public influence of the office that I hold, to help these local agencies to get the means necessary to assume this burden.

The security legislation which I shall propose to the Congress will, I am confident, be of assistance to local effort in the care of this type of cases. Local responsibility can and will be resumed, for after all, common sense tells us that the wealth necessary for this task existed and still exists in the local community, and the dictates of sound administration require that this responsibility be in the first instance a local one.

There are, however, an additional 3½ million employable people who are on relief. With them the problem is different and the responsibility is different. This group was the victim of a Nation-wide depression caused by conditions which were not local but national. The Federal Government is the only governmental agency with sufficient power and credit to meet this situation. We have assumed this task and we shall not shrink from it in the future. It is a duty dictated by every intelligent consideration of national policy to ask you to make it possible for the United States to give employment to all of these 3½ million employable people now on relief, pending their absorption in a rising tide of private employment.

It is my thought that with the exception of certain of the normal public building operations of the Government, all emergency public works shall be united in a single new and greatly enlarged plan.

With the establishment of this new system we can supersede the Federal Emergency Relief Administration with a coordinated authority which will be charged with the orderly liquidation of our present relief activities and the substitution of a national chart for the giving of work.

This new program of emergency public employment should be governed by a number of practical principles.

(1) All work undertaken should be useful—not just for a day, or a year, but useful in the sense that it affords permanent improvement in living conditions or that it creates future new wealth for the Nation.

(2) Compensation on emergency public projects should be in the form of security payments which should be larger than the amount now received as a relief dole, but at the same time not so large as to encourage the rejection of opportunities for private employment or the leaving of private employment to engage in Government work.

(3) Projects should be undertaken on which a large percentage of direct labor can be used.

(4) Preference should be given to those projects which will be self-liquidating in the sense that there is a reasonable expectation that the Government will get its money back at some future time.

(5) The projects undertaken should be selected and planned so as to compete as little as possible with private enterprises. This suggests that if it were not for the necessity of giving useful work to the unemployed now on relief, these projects in most instances would not now be undertaken.

(6) The planning of projects would seek to assure work during the coming fiscal year to the individuals now on relief, or until such time as private employment is available. In order to make adjustment to increasing private employment, work should be planned with a view to tapering it off in proportion to the speed with which the emergency workers are offered positions with private employers.

(7) Effort should be made to locate projects where they will serve the greatest unemployment needs as shown by present relief rolls, and the broad program of the National Resources Board should be freely used for guidance in selection. Our ultimate objective being the enrichment of human lives, the Government has the primary duty to use its emergency expenditures as much as possible to serve those who cannot secure the advantages of private capital.

Ever since the adjournment of the Seventy-third Congress, the administration has been studying from every angle the possibility and the practicability of new forms of employment. As a result of these studies I have arrived at certain very definite convictions as to the amount of money that will be necessary for the sort of public projects that I have described. I shall submit these figures in my Budget message. I assure you now they will be within the sound credit of the Government.

The work itself will cover a wide field, including clearance of slums, which for adequate reasons cannot be undertaken by private capital; in rural housing of several kinds, where, again, private capital is unable to function; in rural electrification; in the reforestation of the great watersheds of the Nation; in an intensified program to prevent soil erosion and to reclaim blighted areas; in improving existing road systems and in constructing national highways designed to handle modern traffic; in the elimination of grade crossings; in the extension and enlargement of the successful work of the Civilian Conservation Corps; in non-Federal work, mostly self-liquidating and highly useful to local divisions of government; and on many other projects which the Nation needs and cannot afford to neglect.

This is the method which I propose to you in order that we may better meet this present-day problem of unemployment. Its greatest advantage is that it fits logically and usefully into the long-range permanent policy of providing the three types of security which constitute as a whole an American plan for the betterment of the future of the American people.

I shall consult with you from time to time concerning other measures of national importance. Among the subjects that lie immediately before us are the consolidation of Federal regulatory administration over all forms of transportation, the renewal and clarification of the general purposes of the National Industrial Recovery Act, the strengthening of our facilities for the prevention, detection, and treatment of crime and criminals, the restoration of sound conditions in the public-utilities field through abolition of the evil features of holding companies, the gradual tapering off of the emergency credit activities of Government, and improvement in our taxation forms and methods.

We have already begun to feel the bracing effect upon our economic system of a restored agriculture. The hundreds of millions of additional income that farmers are receiving is finding its way into the channels of trade. The farmers' share of the national income is slowly rising. The economic facts justify the widespread opinion of those engaged in agriculture that our provision for maintaining a balanced production give at this time the most adequate remedy for an old and vexing problem. For the present, and especially in view of abnormal world conditions, agricultural adjustment with certain necessary improvements in methods should continue.

It seems appropriate to call attention at this time to the fine spirit shown during the past year by our public servants. I cannot praise too highly the cheerful work of the civil-service employees, and of those temporarily working for the Government. As for those thousands in our various public agencies spread throughout the country who, without compensation, agreed to take over heavy responsibilities in connection with our various loan agencies, and particularly in direct relief work, I cannot say too much. I do not think any country could show a higher average of cheerful and even enthusiastic teamwork than has been shown by these men and women.

I cannot with candor tell you that general international relationships outside the borders of the United States are improved. On the surface of things many old jealousies are resurrected, old passions aroused; new strivings for armament and power, in more than one land, rear their ugly heads. I hope that calm counsel and constructive leadership will provide the steadying influence and the time necessary for the coming of new and more practical forms of representative government throughout the world wherein privilege and power will occupy a lesser place and world welfare a greater.

I believe, however, that our own peaceful and neighborly attitude toward other nations is coming to be understood and appreciated. The maintenance of international peace is a matter in which we are deeply and unselfishly concerned. Evidence of our persistent and undeniable desire to prevent armed conflict has recently been more than once afforded.

There is no ground for apprehension that our relations with any nation will be otherwise than peaceful. Nor is there ground for doubt that the people of most nations seek relief from the threat and burden attaching to the false theory that extravagant armament cannot be reduced and limited by international accord.

The ledger of the past year shows many more gains than losses. Let us not forget that, in addition to saving millions from utter destitution, child labor has been for the moment outlawed, thousands of homes saved to their owners and most important of all, the morale of the nation has been restored. Viewing the year 1934 as a whole, you and I can agree that we have a generous measure of reasons for giving thanks.

It is not empty optimism that moves me to a strong hope in the coming year. We can, if we will, make 1935 a genuine period of good feeling, sustained by a sense of purposeful progress. Beyond the material recovery, I sense a spiritual recovery as well. The people of America are turning as never before to those permanent values that are not limited to the physical objectives of life. There are growing signs of this on every hand. In the face of these spiritual impulses we are sensible of the Divine Providence to which nations turn now, as always, for guidance and fostering care.

THIRD ANNUAL MESSAGE.

THE WHITE HOUSE, *January 3, 1936.*

MR. PRESIDENT, MR. SPEAKER, MEMBERS OF THE SENATE AND OF THE HOUSE OF REPRESENTATIVES:

We are about to enter upon another year of the responsibility which the electorate of the United States has placed in our hands. Having come thus far, it is fitting that we should pause to survey the ground which we have covered and the path which lies ahead.

On the 4th day of March 1933, on the occasion of taking the oath of office as President of the United States, I addressed the people of our country. Need I recall either the scene or the national circumstances attending the occasion? The crisis of that moment was almost exclusively a national one. In recognition of that fact, so obvious to the millions in the streets and in the homes of America, I devoted by far the greater part of that address to what I called, and the Nation called, critical days within our own borders.

You will remember that on that 4th day of March 1933, the world picture was an image of substantial peace. International consultation and widespread hope for the bettering of relations between the nations gave to all of us a reasonable expectation that the barriers to mutual confidence, to increased trade, and to the peaceful settlement of disputes could be progressively removed. In fact my only reference to the field of world policy in that address was in these words: "I would dedicate this Nation to the policy of the good neighbor—the neighbor who resolutely respects himself and, because he does so, respects the rights of others—a neighbor who respects his obligations and respects the sanctity of his agreements in and with a world of neighbors."

In the years that have followed that sentiment has remained the dedication of this Nation. Among the nations of the great Western Hemisphere the policy of the good neighbor has happily prevailed. At no time in the four and a half centuries of modern civilization in the Americas has there existed—in any year, any decade, or any generation in all that time—a greater spirit of mutual understanding, of common helpfulness, and of devotion to the ideals of self-government than exists today in the 21 American Republics and their neighbor, the Dominion of Canada. This policy of the good neighbor among the Americas is no longer a hope—no longer an objective remaining to be accomplished; it is a fact, active, present, pertinent, and effective. In this achievement every American nation takes an understanding part. There is neither war nor rumor of war nor desire for war. The inhabitants of this vast area, 250,000,000 strong, spreading more than 8,000 miles from the Arctic to the Antarctic, believe in and propose to follow the policy of the good neighbor; and they wish with all their heart that the rest of the world might do likewise.

The rest of the world—ah, there's the rub.

Were I today to deliver an inaugural address to the people of the United States I could not limit my comments on world affairs to one paragraph. With much regret I should be compelled to devote the greater part to world affairs. Since the summer of that same year of 1933 the temper and the purposes of the rulers of many of the great populations in Europe and Asia have not pointed the way either to peace or to good will among men. Not only have peace and good will among men grown more remote in those areas of the earth during this period, but a point has been reached where the people of the Americas must take cognizance of growing ill will, of marked trends toward aggression, of increasing armaments, of shortening tempers—a situation which has in it many of the elements that lead to the tragedy of general war.

On those other continents many nations, principally the smaller peoples, if left to themselves, would be content with their boundaries and willing to solve within themselves and in cooperation with their neighbors their individual problems, both economic and social. The rulers of those nations, deep in their hearts, follow these peaceful and reasonable aspirations of their peoples. These rulers must remain ever vigilant against the possibility today or tomorrow of invasion or attack by the rulers of other peoples who fail to subscribe to the principles of bettering the human race by peaceful means.

And within those other nations—those which today must bear the primary, definite responsibility for jeopardizing world peace—what hope lies? To say the least, there are grounds for pessimism. It is idle for us or for others to preach that the masses of the people who constitute those nations which are dominated by the twin spirits of autocracy and aggression are out of sympathy with their rulers, that they are allowed no opportunity to express themselves, that they would change things if they could.

That, unfortunately, is not so clear. It might be true that the masses of the people in those nations would change the policies of their governments if they could be allowed full freedom, full access to the processes of democratic government as we understand them. But they do not have that access: Lacking it they follow blindly and fervently the lead of those who seek autocratic power.

Nations seeking expansion, seeking the rectification of injustice springing from former wars, or seeking outlets for trade, for population, or even for their own peaceful contributions to the progress of civilization, fail to demonstrate that patience necessary to attain reasonable and legitimate objectives by peaceful negotiation or by an appeal to the finer instincts of world justice.

They have therefore impatiently reverted to the old belief in the law of the sword, or to the fantastic conception that they, and they alone, are chosen to fulfill a mission and that all the others among the billion and a half of human beings in the world must and shall learn from and be subject to them.

I recognize and you will recognize that these words which I have chosen with deliberation will not prove popular in any nation that chooses to fit this shoe to its foot. Such sentiments, however, will find sympathy and understanding in those nations where the people themselves are honestly desirous of peace but must constantly aline themselves on one side or the other in the kaleidoscopic jockeying for position that is characteristic of European and Asiatic relations today. For the peace-loving nations, and there are many of them, find that their very identity depends on their moving and moving again on the chessboard of international politics.

I suggested in the spring of 1933 that 85 or 90 percent of all the people in the world were content with the territorial limits of their respective nations and were willing further to reduce their armed forces if every other nation in the world would agree to do likewise.

That is equally true today, and it is even more true today that world peace and world good will are blocked by only 10 or 15 percent of the world's population. That is why efforts to reduce armies have thus far not only failed but have been met by vastly increased armaments on land and in the air and that is why even efforts to continue the existing limits on naval armaments into the years to come show such little current success.

But the policy of the United States has been clear and consistent. We have sought with earnestness in every possible way to limit world armaments and to attain the peaceful solution of disputes among all nations.

We have sought by every legitimate means to exert our moral influence against repression, against discrimination, against intolerance and autocracy, and in favor of freedom of expression, equality before the law, religious tolerance, and popular rule.

In the field of commerce we have undertaken to encourage a more reasonable interchange of the world's goods. In the field of international finance we have, so far as we are concerned, put an end to dollar diplomacy, to money grabbing, to speculation for the benefit of the powerful and rich, at the expense of the small and the poor.

As a consistent part of a clear policy, the United States is following a twofold neutrality toward any and all nations which engage in wars that are not of immediate concern to the Americas. First, we decline to encourage the prosecution of war by permitting belligerents to obtain arms, ammunition, or implements of war from the United States. Second, we seek to discourage the use by belligerent nations of any and all American products calculated to facilitate the prosecution of a war in quantities over and above our normal exports to them in time of peace.

I trust that these clear objectives thus unequivocally stated will be carried forward by cooperation between this Congress and the President.

I realize that I have emphasized to you the gravity of the situation which confronts the people of the world. This emphasis is justified because of its importance to civilization and therefore to the United States. Peace is jeopardized by the few and not by the many. Peace is threatened by those who seek selfish power. The world has witnessed similar eras—as in the days when petty kings and feudal barons were changing the map of Europe every fortnight, or when great emperors and great kings were engaged in a mad scramble for colonial empire.

We hope that we are not again at the threshold of such an era. But if face it we must, then the United States and the rest of the Americas can play but one role: Through a well-ordered neutrality to do naught to encourage the contest, through adequate defense to save ourselves from embroilment and attack, and through example and all legitimate encouragement and assistance to persuade other nations to return to the days of peace and good will.

The evidence before us clearly proves that autocracy in world affairs endangers peace and that such threats do not spring from those nations devoted to the democratic ideal. If this be true in world affairs, it should have the greatest weight in the determination of domestic policies.

Within democratic nations the chief concern of the people is to prevent the continuation or the rise of autocratic institutions that beget slavery at home and aggression abroad. Within our borders, as in the world at large, popular opinion is at war with a power-seeking minority.

That is no new thing. It was fought out in the Constitutional Convention of 1787. From time to time since then the battle has been continued, under Thomas Jefferson, Andrew Jackson, Theodore Roosevelt and Woodrow Wilson.

In these later years we have witnessed the domination of government by financial and industrial groups, numerically small but politically dominant in the 12 years that succeeded the World War. The present group of which I speak is, indeed, numerically small and, while it exercises a large influence and has much to say in the world of business, it does not, I am confident, speak the true sentiments of the less articulate but more important elements that constitute real American business.

I go back once more. In March 1933 I appealed to the Congress of the United States and to the people in a new effort to restore power to those to whom it rightfully belonged. The response to that appeal resulted in the writing of a new chapter in the history of popular government. You, the Members of the legislative branch, and I, the Executive, contended for and established a new relationship between government and people.

What were the terms of that new relationship? They were an appeal from the clamor of many private and selfish interests, yes, an appeal from the clamor of partisan interest, to the ideal of the public interest. Government became the representative and the trustee of the public interest. Our aim was to build upon essentially democratic institutions, seeking all the while the adjustment of burdens, the help of the needy, the protection of the weak, the liberation of the exploited, and the genuine protection of the people's property.

It goes without saying that to create such an economic constitutional order more than a single legislative enactment was called for. We had to build, you in the Congress and I, as the Executive, upon a broad base. Now, after 34 months of work, we contemplate a fairly rounded whole. We have returned the control of the Federal Government to the city of Washington.

To be sure, in so doing, we have invited battle. We have earned the hatred of entrenched greed. The very nature of the problem that we faced made it necessary to drive some people from power and strictly to regulate others. I made that plain when I took the oath of office in March 1933. I spoke of the practices of the unscrupulous money changers who stood indicted in the court of public opinion. I spoke of the rulers of the exchanges of mankind's goods, who failed through their own stubbornness and their own incompetence. I said that they had admitted their failure and had abdicated.

Abdicated? Yes, in 1933; but now with the passing of danger they forget their damaging admissions and withdraw their abdication.

They offer, they seek, let us put it that way, the restoration of their selfish power. They offer to lead us back round the same old corner into the same old dreary street.

Yet they are still determined groups that are intent upon that very thing. Rigorously held up to popular examination their true character presents itself. They steal the livery of great national constitutional ideals to serve discredited special interests. As guardians and trustees for great groups of individual stockholders they wrongfully seek to carry the property and the interests entrusted to them into the arena of partisan politics. They seek—this minority in business and industry—to control and often do control and use for their own purposes legitimate and highly honored business associations; they engage in vast propaganda to spread fear and discord among the people—they would "gang up" against the people's liberties.

The principle that they would instill into government if they succeed in seizing power is well shown by the principles which many of them have instilled into their own affairs: autocracy toward labor, toward stockholders, toward consumers, toward sentiment. Autocrats in smaller things, they seek autocracy in bigger things. "By their fruits ye shall know them."

If these gentlemen believe, as they say they believe, that the measures adopted by this Congress and its predecessor, and carried out by this administration, have hindered rather than promoted recovery, let them be consistent. Let them propose to this Congress the complete repeal of these measures. The way is open to such a proposal.

In other words, let action be positive and not negative. The way is open in the Congress of the United States for an expression of opinion by yeas and nays. Shall we say that values are restored and that the Congress will, therefore, repeal the laws under which we have been bringing them back? Shall we say that because national income has grown with rising prosperity we shall repeal existing taxes and thereby put off the day of approaching a balanced budget and of starting to reduce the national debt? Shall we abandon the reasonable support and regulation of banking? Shall we restore the dollar to its former gold content? Shall we say to the farmer, "The prices for your products are in part restored; now go and hoe your own row?" Shall we say to the home owners, "We have reduced your rates of interest—we have no further concern with how you keep your home or what you pay for your money; that is your affair"? Shall we say to the several millions of unemployed citizens who face the very problem of existence—yes, of getting enough to eat—"We will withdraw from giving you work; we will turn you back to the charity of your communities and to those men of selfish power who tell you that perhaps they will employ you if the Government leaves them strictly alone"? Shall we say to the needy unemployed, "Your problem is a local one except that perhaps the Federal Government, as an act of mere generosity, will be willing to pay to your city or to your county a few grudging dollars to help maintain your soup kitchens "? Shall we say to the children who have worked all day in the factory, " Child labor is a local issue and so are your starvation wages; something to be solved or left unsolved by the jurisdiction of 48 States "? Shall we say to the laborer, " Your right to organize, your relations with your employer have nothing to do with the public interest; if your employer will not even meet with you to discuss your problems and his, that is none of our affair "? Shall we say to the unemployed and the aged, " Social security lies not within the province of the Federal Government; you must seek relief elsewhere "? Shall we say to the men and women who live in conditions of squalor in country and in city, " The health and the happiness of you and your children are no concern of ours "? Shall we expose our population once more by the repeal of laws to protect them against the loss of their honest investments and against the manipulations of dishonest speculators? Shall we abandon the splendid efforts of the Federal Government to raise the health standards of the Nation and to give youth a decent opportunity through such means as the Civilian Conservation Corps?

Members of the Congress, let these challenges be met. If this is what these gentlemen want, let them say so to the Congress of the United States. Let them no longer hide their dissent in a cowardly cloak of generality. Let them define the issue. We have been specific in our affirmative action. Let them be specific in their negative attack.

But the challenge faced by this Congress is more menacing than merely a return to the past—bad as that would be. Our resplendent economic autocracy does not want to return to that individualism of which they prate, even though the advantages under that system went to the ruthless and the strong. They realize that in 34 months we have built up new instruments of public power. In the hands of a people's government this power is wholesome and proper. But in the hands of political puppets of an economic autocracy such power would provide shackles for the liberties of the people. Give them their way and they will take the course of every autocracy of the past—power for themselves, enslavement for the public.

And their weapon is the weapon of fear. I have said, " The only thing we have to fear is fear itself." That is as true today as it was in 1933. But such fear as they instill today is not a natural fear, a normal fear; it is a synthetic, manufactured, poisonous fear that is being spread subtly, expensively, and cleverly by the same people who cried in those other days, " Save us, save us, else we perish."

I am confident that the Congress of the United States well understands the facts and is ready to wage unceasing warfare against those who seek a continuation of that spirit of fear. The carrying out of the laws of the land as enacted by the Congress requires protection until final adjudication by the highest tribunal of the land. The Congress has the right and can find the means to protect its own prerogatives.

We are justified in our present confidence. Restoration of national income, which shows continuing gains for the third successive year, supports the normal and logical policies under which agriculture and industry are returning to full activity. Under these policies we approach a balance of the National Budget. National income increases; tax receipts, based on that income, increase without the levying of new taxes. That is why I am able to say to this, the second session of the Seventy-fourth Congress, that based on existing laws it is my belief that no new taxes, over and above the present taxes, are either advisable or necessary.

National income increases; employment increases. Therefore, we can look forward to a reduction in the number of those citizens who are in need. Therefore, also, we can anticipate a reduction in our appropriations for relief.

In the light of our substantial material progress, in the light of the increasing effectiveness of the restoration of popular rule, I recommend to the Congress that we advance; and that we do not retreat. I have confidence—confidence that you will not fail the people of the Nation whose mandate you have already so faithfully fulfilled.

I repeat, with the same faith and the same determination, my words of March 4, 1933—"We face the arduous days that lie before us in the warm courage of national unity; with a clear consciousness of seeking old and precious moral values; with a clean satisfaction that comes from the stern performance of duty by old and young alike. We aim at the assurance of a rounded and permanent national life. We do not distrust the future of essential democracy."

I cannot better end this Message on the state of the Union than by repeating the words of a wise philosopher at whose feet I sat many years ago:

What great crises teach all men whom the example and counsel of the brave inspire is this lesson: Fear not, view all the tasks of life as sacred, have faith in the triumph of the ideal, give daily all that you have to give, be loyal and rejoice whenever you find yourselves part of a great ideal enterprise. You at this moment have the honor to belong to a generation whose lips are touched by fire. You live in a land that now enjoys the blessings of peace. But let nothing human be wholly alien from you. The human race now passes through one of its great crises. New ideas, new issues—a new call for men to carry on the work of righteousness, of charity, of courage, of patience, and of loyalty * * *. However, memory brings back this moment to your minds, let it be able to say to you: That was a great moment. It was the beginning of a new era. * * * This world in its crisis called for volunteers, for men of faith in life, of patience in service, of charity and of insight. I responded to the call however I could. I volunteered to give myself to my Master—the cause of humane and brave living. I studied, I loved, I labored, unsparingly and hopefully, to be worthy of my generation.

FOURTH ANNUAL MESSAGE.

THE WHITE HOUSE, *January 6, 1937.*

To the Congress of the United States:

For the first time in our national history a President delivers his Annual Message to a new Congress within a fortnight of the expiration of his term of office. While there is no change in the Presidency this year, change will occur in future years. It is my belief that under this new constitutional practice the President should in every fourth year, insofar as seems reasonable, review the existing state of our national affairs and outline broad future problems, leaving specific recommendations for future legislation to be made by the President about to be inaugurated.

At this time, however, circumstances of the moment compel me to ask your immediate consideration of: First, measures extending the life of certain authorizations and powers which, under present statutes, expire within a few weeks; second, an addition to the existing Neutrality Act to cover specific points raised by the unfortunate civil strife in Spain; and, third, a deficiency appropriation bill for which I shall submit estimates this week.

In March 1933 the problems which faced our nation, and which only our national government had the resources to meet, were more serious even than appeared on the surface.

It was not only that the visible mechanism of economic life had broken down. More disturbing was the fact that long neglect of the needs of the underprivileged had brought too many of our people to the verge of doubt as to the successful adaptation of our historic traditions to the complex modern world. In that lay a challenge to our democratic form of government itself.

Ours was the task to prove that democracy could be made to function in the world of today as effectively as in the simpler world of a hundred years ago. Ours was the task to do more than to argue a theory. The times required the confident answer of performance to those whose instinctive faith in humanity made them want to believe that in the long run democracy would prove superior to more extreme forms of government as a process of getting action when action was wisdom, without the spiritual sacrifices which those other forms of government exact.

That challenge we met. To meet it required unprecedented activities under Federal leadership—to end abuses—to restore a large measure of material prosperity—to give new faith to millions of our citizens who had been traditionally taught to expect that democracy would provide continuously wider opportunity and continuously greater security in a world where science was continuously making material riches more available to man.

In the many methods of attack with which we met these problems, you and I, by mutual understanding and by determination to cooperate, helped to make democracy succeed by refusing to permit unnecessary disagreement to arise between two of our branches of government. That spirit of cooperation was able to solve difficulties of extraordinary magnitude and ramification with few important errors, and at a cost cheap when measured by the immediate necessities and the eventual results.

I look forward to a continuance of that cooperation in the next 4 years. I look forward also to a continuance of the basis of that cooperation—mutual respect for each other's proper sphere of functioning in a democracy which is working well, and a common-sense realization of the need for play in the joints of the machine.

On that basis, it is within the right of the Congress to determine which of the many new activities shall be continued or abandoned, increased or curtailed.

On that same basis, the President alone has the responsibility for their administration. I find that this task of Executive management has reached the point where our administrative machinery needs comprehensive overhauling. I shall, therefore, shortly address the Congress more fully in regard to modernizing and improving the executive branch of the Government.

That cooperation of the past 4 years between the Congress and the President has aimed at the fulfillment of a twofold policy—first, economic recovery through many kinds of assistance to agriculture, industry, and banking; and, second, deliberate improvement in the personal security and opportunity of the great mass of our people.

The recovery we sought was not to be merely temporary. It was to be a recovery protected from the causes of previous disasters. With that aim in view—to prevent a future similar crisis—you and I joined in a series of enactments—safe banking and sound currency, the guarantee of bank deposits, protection for the investor in securities, the removal of the threat of agricultural surpluses, insistence on collective bargaining, the outlawing of sweatshops, child labor and unfair trade practices, and the beginnings of security for the aged and the worker.

Nor was the recovery we sought merely a purposeless whirring of machinery. It is important, of course, that every man and woman in the country be able to find work, that every factory run, that business as a whole earn profits. But government in a democratic nation does not exist solely, or ever primarily, for that purpose.

It is not enough that the wheels turn. They must carry us in the direction of a greater satisfaction in life for the average man. The deeper purpose of democratic government is to assist as many of its citizens as possible—especially those who need it most—to improve their conditions of life, to retain all personal liberty which does not adversely affect their neighbors, and to pursue the happiness which comes with security and an opportunity for recreation and culture.

Even with our present recovery we are far from the goal of that deeper purpose. There are far-reaching problems still with us for which democracy must find solutions if it is to consider itself successful.

For example, many millions of Americans still live in habitations which not only fail to provide the physical benefits of modern civilization but breed disease and impair the health of future generations. The menace exists not only in the slum areas of the very large cities, but in many smaller cities as well. It exists on tens of thousands of farms, in varying degrees, in every part of the country.

Another example is the prevalence of an un-American type of tenant farming. I do not suggest that every farm family has the capacity to earn a satisfactory living on its own farm. But many thousands of tenant farmers—indeed most of them—with some financial assistance and with some advice and training, can be made self-supporting on land which can eventually belong to them. The nation would be wise to offer them that chance instead of permitting them to go along as they do now, year after year, with neither future security as tenants nor hope of ownership of their homes nor expectation of bettering the lot of their children.

Another national problem is the intelligent development of our social security system, the broadening of the services it renders, and practical improvement in its operation. In many nations where such laws are in effect success in meeting the expectations of the community has come through frequent amendment of the original statute.

And, of course, the most far-reaching and the most inclusive problem of all is that of unemployment and the lack of economic balance, of which unemployment is at once the result and the symptom. The immediate question of adequate relief for the needy unemployed who are capable of performing useful work I shall discuss with the Congress during the coming months. The broader task of preventing unemployment is a matter of long-range evolutionary policy. To that we must continue to give our best thought and effort. We cannot assume that immediate industrial and commercial activity which mitigates present pressures justifies the national government at this time in placing the unemployment problem in a filing cabinet of finished business.

Fluctuations in employment are tied to all other wasteful fluctuations in our mechanism of production and distribution. One of these wastes is speculation. In securities or commodities, the larger the volume of speculation the wider become the upward and downward swings, and the more certain the result that in the long run there will be more losses than gains in the underlying wealth of the community.

And, as is now well known to all of us, the same net loss to society comes from reckless overproduction and monopolistic underproduction of natural and manufactured commodities.

Overproduction, underproduction, and speculation are three evil sisters who distill the troubles of unsound inflation and disastrous deflation. It is to the interest of the Nation to have government help private enterprise to gain sound general price levels and to protect those levels from wide perilous fluctuations. We know now that if early in 1931 government had taken the steps which were taken 2 and 3 years later the depression would never have reached the depths of the beginning of 1933.

Sober second thought confirms most of us in the belief that the broad objectives of the National Recovery Act were sound. We know now that its difficulties arose from the fact that it tried to do too much. For example, it was unwise to expect the same agency to regulate the length of working hours, minimum wages, child labor, and collective bargaining on the one hand and the complicated questions of unfair trade practices and business controls on the other.

The statute of N. R. A. has been outlawed. The problems have not. They are still with us.

That decent conditions and adequate pay for labor and just return for agriculture can be secured through parallel and simultaneous action by 48 States is a proven impossibility. It is equally impossible to obtain curbs on monopoly, unfair trade practices, and speculation by State action alone. There are those who, sincerely or insincerely, still cling to State action as a theoretical hope. But experience with actualities makes it clear that Federal laws supplementing State laws are needed to help solve the problems which result from modern invention applied in an industrialized nation which conducts its business with scant regard to State lines.

During the past year there has been a growing belief that there is little fault to be found with the Constitution of the United States as it stands today. The vital need is not an alteration of our fundamental law but an increasingly enlightened view with reference to it. Difficulties have grown out of its interpretation; but rightly considered, it can be used as an instrument of progress and not as a device for prevention of action.

It is worth our while to read and re-read the preamble of the Constitution and Article I thereof which confers the legislative powers upon the Congress of the United States. It is also worth our while to read again the debates in the Constitutional Convention of one hundred and fifty years ago. From such reading, I obtain the very definite thought that the members of that Convention were fully aware that civilization would raise problems for the proposed new Federal Government, which they themselves could not even surmise; and that it was their definite intent and expectation that a liberal interpretation in the years to come would give to the Congress the same relative powers over new national problems as they themselves gave to the Congress over the national problems of their day.

In presenting to the Convention the first basic draft of the Constitution, Edmund Randolph explained that it was the purpose "to insert essential principles only, lest the operation of government should be clogged by rendering those provisions permanent and unalterable which ought to be accommodated to times and events."

With a better understanding of our purposes, and a more intelligent recognition of our needs as a nation, it is not to be assumed that there will be prolonged failure to bring legislative and judicial action into closer harmony. Means must be found to adapt our legal forms and our judicial interpretation to the actual present national needs of the largest progressive democracy in the modern world.

That thought leads to a consideration of world problems. To go no further back than the beginning of this century, men and women everywhere were seeking conditions of life very different from those which were customary before modern invention and modern industry and modern communications had come into being. The World War, for all of its tragedy, encouraged these demands and stimulated action to fulfill these new desires.

Many national governments seemed unable adequately to respond; and, often with the improvident assent of the masses of the people themselves, new forms of government were set up with oligarchy taking the place of democracy. In oligarchies, militarism has leapt forward, while in those nations which have retained democracy, militarism has waned.

I have recently visited three of our sister republics in South America. The very cordial receptions with which I was greeted were in tribute to democracy. To me the outstanding observation of that visit was that the masses of the peoples of all the Americas are convinced that the democratic form of government can be made to succeed and do not wish to substitute for it any other form of government. They believe that democracies are best able to cope with the changing problems of modern civilization within themselves, and that democracies are best able to maintain peace among themselves.

The Inter-American Conference, operating on these fundamental principles of democracy, did much to assure peace in this hemisphere. Existing peace machinery was improved. New instruments to maintain peace and eliminate causes of war were adopted. Wider protection of the interests of the American republics in the event of war outside the Western Hemisphere was provided. Respect for, and observance of, international treaties and international law were strengthened. Principles of liberal trade policies, as effective aids to the maintenance of peace were reaffirmed. The intellectual and cultural relationships among American republics were broadened as a part of the general peace program.

In a world unhappily thinking in terms of war, the representatives of 21 nations sat around a table, in an atmosphere of complete confidence and understanding, sincerely discussing measures for maintaining peace. Here was a great and a permanent achievement directly affecting the lives and security of the 250,000,000 human beings who dwell in this Western Hemisphere. Here was an example which must have a wholesome effect upon the rest of the world.

In a very real sense, the conference in Buenos Aires sent forth a message on behalf of all the democracies of the world to those nations which live otherwise. Because such other governments are perhaps more spectacular, it was high time for democracy to assert itself.

Because all of us believe that our democratic form of government can cope adequately with modern problems as they arise, it is patriotic as well as logical for us to prove that we can meet new national needs with new laws consistent with an historic constitutional framework clearly intended to receive liberal and not narrow interpretation.

The United States of America, within itself, must continue the task of making democracy succeed.

In that task the legislative branch of our Government will, I am confident, continue to meet the demands of democracy whether they relate to the curbing of abuses, the extension of help to those who need help, or the better balancing of our interdependent economies.

So, too, the executive branch of the Government must move forward in this task, and, at the same time, provide better management for administrative action of all kinds.

The judicial branch also is asked by the people to do its part in making democracy successful. We do not ask the courts to call nonexistent powers into being, but we have a right to expect that conceded powers or those legitimately implied shall be made effective instruments for the common good.

The process of our democracy must not be imperiled by the denial of essential powers of free government.

Your task and mine is not ending with the end of the depression. The people of the United States have made it clear that they expect us to continue our active efforts in behalf of their peaceful advancement.

In that spirit of endeavor and service I greet the Seventy-fifth Congress at the beginning of this auspicious new year.

FIFTH ANNUAL MESSAGE.

THE WHITE HOUSE, *January 3, 1938.*

MR. PRESIDENT, MR. SPEAKER, MEMBERS OF THE SENATE AND OF THE HOUSE OF REPRESENTATIVES:

In addressing the Congress on the state of the Union present facts and future hazards demand that I speak clearly and earnestly of the causes which underlie events of profound concern to all.

In spite of the determination of this Nation for peace, it has become clear that acts and policies of nations in other parts of the world have far-reaching effects, not only upon their immediate neighbors but also on us.

I am thankful that I can tell you that our Nation is at peace. It has been kept at peace despite provocations which in other days, because of their seriousness, could well have engendered war. The people of the United States and the Government of the United States have shown capacity for restraint and a civilized approach to the purposes of peace, while at the same time we maintain the integrity inherent in the sovereignty of 130,000,000 people, lest we weaken or destroy our influence for peace and jeopardize the sovereignty itself.

It is our traditional policy to live at peace with other nations. More than that, we have been among the leaders in advocating the use of pacific methods of discussion and conciliation in international differences. We have striven for the reduction of military forces.

But in a world of high tension and disorder, in a world where stable civilization is actually threatened, it becomes the responsibility of each nation which strives for peace at home and peace with and among others to be strong enough to assure the observance of those fundamentals of peaceful solution of conflicts which are the only ultimate basis for orderly existence.

Resolute in our determination to respect the rights of others and to command respect for the rights of ourselves, we must keep ourselves adequately strong in self-defense.

There is a trend in the world away from the observance both of the letter and the spirit of treaties. We propose to observe, as we have in the past, our own treaty obligations; but we cannot be certain of reciprocity on the part of others.

Disregard for treaty obligations seems to have followed the surface trend away from the democratic representative form of government. It would seem, therefore, that world peace through international agreements is most safe in the hands of democratic representative governments—or, in other words, peace is most greatly jeopardized in and by those nations where democracy has been discarded or has never developed.

I have used the words "surface trend," for I still believe that civilized man increasingly insists, and in the long run will insist, on genuine participation in his own government. Our people believe that over the years democracies of the world will survive, and democracy will be restored or established in those nations which today know it not. In that faith lies the future peace of mankind.

At home conditions call for my equal candor. Events of recent months are new proof that we cannot conduct a national government after the practice of 1787, or 1837 or 1887, for the obvious reason that human needs and human desires are infinitely greater, infinitely more difficult to meet than in any previous period in the life of our Republic. Hitherto it has been an acknowledged duty of government to meet these desires and needs; nothing has occurred of late to absolve the Congress, the courts, or the President from that task. It faces us—as squarely, as insistently—as in March 1933.

Much of trouble in our own lifetime has sprung from a long period of inaction, from ignoring what fundamentally was happening to us, and from a time-serving unwillingness to face facts as they forced themselves upon us.

Our national life rests on two nearly equal producing forces—agriculture and industry—each employing one-third of our citizens. The other third transports and distributes the products of the first two or performs special services for the whole.

The first great force—agriculture—and with it the production of timber, minerals, and other natural resources—went forward feverishly and thoughtlessly until Nature rebelled and we saw deserts encroach, floods destroy, trees disappear, and soil exhausted.

At the same time we have been discovering that vast numbers of our farming population live in a poverty more abject than that of many of the farmers of Europe whom we are wont to call peasants; that the prices of our products of agriculture are too often dependent on speculation by nonfarming groups; and that foreign nations, eager to become self-sustaining or ready to put virgin land under the plow, are no longer buying our surpluses of cotton and wheat and lard and tobacco and fruit as they had before.

Since 1933 we have knowingly faced a choice of three remedies. First, to cut our cost of farm production below that of other nations, an obvious impossibility in many crops today unless we revert to human slavery or its equivalent.

Second, to make the Government the guarantor of farm prices and the underwriter of excess farm production without limit, a course which would bankrupt the strongest government in the world in a decade.

Third, to place the primary responsibility directly on the farmers themselves, under the principle of majority rule, so that they may decide, with full knowledge of the facts of surpluses, scarcities, world markets, and domestic needs, what the planting of each crop should be in order to maintain a reasonably adequate supply which will assure a minimum adequate price under the normal processes of the law of supply and demand.

That means adequacy of supply but not glut. It means adequate reserves against the day of drought. It is shameless misrepresentation to call this a policy of scarcity. It is in truth insurance before the fact, instead of government subsidy after the fact.

Any such plan for the control of excessive surpluses and the speculation they bring has two enemies. There are those well-meaning theorists who harp on the inherent right of every free-born American to do with his land what he wants—to cultivate it well or badly; to conserve his timber by cutting only the annual increment thereof—or to strip it clean, let fire burn the slash, and erosion complete the ruin; to raise only one crop—and if that crop fails, to look for food and support from his neighbors or his Government.

That, I assert, is not an inherent right of citizenship. For if a man farms his land to the waste of the soil or the trees, he destroys not only his own assets but the Nation's assets. Or if by his methods he makes himself, year after year, a financial hazard of the community and the Government, he becomes not only a social problem but an economic menace. The day has gone by when it could be claimed that Government has no interest in such ill-considered practices and no right through representative methods to stop them.

The other group of enemies is perhaps less well-meaning. It includes those who for partisan purposes oppose each and every practical effort to help the situation, and also those who make money from undue fluctuations in crop prices.

I gladly note that measures which seek to initiate a Government program for a balanced agriculture are now in conference between the two Houses of the Congress. In their final consideration, I hope for a sound, consistent measure which will keep the cost of its administration within the figure of current Government expenditures in aid of agriculture. The farmers of this Nation know that a balanced output can be put into effect without excessive cost and with the cooperation of the great majority of them.

If this balance can be created by an all-weather farm program, our farm population will soon be assured of relatively constant purchasing power. From this will flow two other practical results: The consuming public will be protected against excessive food and textile prices, and the industries of the Nation and their workers will find a steadier demand for wares sold to the agricultural third of our people.

To raise the purchasing power of the farmer is, however, not enough. It will not stay raised if we do not also raise the purchasing power of that third of the Nation which receives its income from industrial employment. Millions of industrial workers receive pay so low that they have little buying power. Aside from the undoubted fact that they thereby suffer great human hardship, they are unable to buy adequate food and shelter, to maintain health or to buy their share of manufactured goods.

We have not only seen minimum-wage and maximum-hour provisions prove their worth economically and socially under Government auspices in 1933, 1934, and 1935, but the people of this country, by an overwhelming vote, are in favor of having the Congress—this

Congress—put a floor below which industrial wages shall not fall, and a ceiling beyond which the hours of industrial labor shall not rise.

Here again let us analyze the opposition. A part of it is sincere in believing that an effort thus to raise the purchasing power of lowest paid industrial workers is not the business of the Federal Government. Others give "lip service" to a general objective, but do not like any specific measure that is proposed. In both cases it is worth our while to wonder whether some of these opponents are not at heart opposed to any program for raising the wages of the underpaid or reducing the hours of the overworked.

Another group oppose legislation of this type on the ground that cheap labor will help their locality to acquire industries and outside capital, or to retain industries which today are surviving only because of existing low wages and long hours. It has been my thought that, especially during these past 5 years, this Nation has grown away from local or sectional selfishness and toward national patriotism and unity. I am disappointed by some recent actions and by some recent utterances which sound like the philosophy of half a century ago.

There are many communities in the United States where the average family income is pitifully low. It is in those communities that we find the poorest educational facilities and the worst conditions of health. Why? It is not because they are satisfied to live as they do. It is because those communities have the lowest per capita wealth and income; therefore, the lowest ability to pay taxes; and, therefore, inadequate functioning of local government.

Such communities exist in the East, in the Middle West, in the far West, and in the South. Those who represent such areas in every part of the country do their constituents ill-service by blocking efforts to raise their incomes, their property values and, therefore, their whole scale of living. In the long run, the profits from child labor, low pay and overwork enure not to the locality or region where they exist but to the absentee owners who have sent their capital into these exploited communities to gather larger profits for themselves. Indeed, new enterprises and new industries which bring permanent wealth will come more readily to those communities which insist on good pay and reasonable hours, for the simple reason that there they will find a greater industrial efficiency and happier workers.

No reasonable person seeks a complete uniformity in wages in every part of the United States; nor does any reasonable person seek an immediate and drastic change from the lowest pay to the highest pay. We are seeking, of course, only legislation to end starvation wages and intolerable hours; more desirable wages are and should continue to be the product of collective bargaining.

Many of those who represent great cities have shown their understanding of the necessity of helping the agricultural third of the Nation. I hope that those who represent constituencies primarily agricultural will not underestimate the importance of extending like aid to the industrial third.

Wage-and-hour legislation, therefore, is a problem which is definitely before this Congress for action. It is an essential part of economic recovery. It has the support of an overwhelming majority of our people in every walk of life. They have expressed themselves through the ballot box.

Again I revert to the increase of national purchasing power as an underlying necessity of the day. If you increase that purchasing power for the farmers and for the industrial workers—especially for those in both groups who have least of it today—you will increase the purchasing power of the final third of our population—those who transport and distribute the products of farm and factory, and those of the professions who serve all groups. I have tried to make clear to you, and through you to the people of the United States, that this is an urgency which must be met by complete and not by partial action.

If it is met—if the purchasing power of the Nation as a whole—in other words, the total of the Nation's income—can be still further increased—other happy results will flow from such increase.

We have raised the Nation's income from 38 billion dollars in the year 1932 to about 68 billion dollars in the year 1937. Our goal, our objective, is to raise it to 90 or 100 billion dollars.

We have heard much about a balanced Budget, and it is interesting to note that many of those who have pleaded for a balanced Budget as the sole need now come to me to plead for additional Government expenditures at the expense of unbalancing the Budget. As the Congress is fully aware, the annual deficit, large for several years, has been declining the last fiscal year and this. The proposed Budget for 1939, which I shall shortly send to the Congress, will exhibit a further decrease in the deficit, though not a balance between income and outgo.

To many who have pleaded with me for an immediate balancing of the Budget, by a sharp curtailment or even elimination of Government functions, I have asked the question, "What present expenditures would you reduce or eliminate?" And the invariable answer has been, "That is not my business—I know nothing of the details, but I am sure that it could be done." That is not what you or I would call helpful citizenship.

On only one point do most of them have a suggestion. They think that relief for the unemployed by the giving of work is wasteful, and when I pin them down I discover that at heart they are actually in favor of substituting a dole in place of useful work. To that neither I nor, I am confident, the Senators and Representatives in the Congress will ever consent.

I am as anxious as any banker or industrialist or businessman or investor or economist that the Budget of the United States Government be brought into balance as quickly as possible. But I lay down certain conditions which seem reasonable and which I believe all should accept.

The first condition is that we continue the policy of not permitting any needy American who can and is willing to work to starve because the Federal Government does not provide the work.

The second is that the Congress and the Executive join hands in eliminating or curtailing any Federal activity which can be eliminated or curtailed or even postponed without harming necessary Government functions or the safety of the Nation from a national point of view. The third is to raise the purchasing power of the Nation to the point that the taxes on this purchasing power—or, in other words, on the Nation's income—will be sufficient to meet the necessary expenditures of the National Government.

I have hitherto stated that, in my judgment, the expenditures of the National Government cannot be cut much below $7,000,000,000 a year without destroying essential functions or letting people starve. That sum can be raised and will be cheerfully provided by the American people, if we can increase the Nation's income to a point well beyond the present level.

This does not mean that as the Nation's income goes up the Federal expenditures should rise in proportion. On the contrary, the Congress and the Executive should use every effort to hold the normal Federal expenditures to approximately the present level, thus making it possible, with an increase in the Nation's income and the resulting increase in tax receipts, not only to balance future Budgets but to reduce the debt.

In line with this policy fall my former recommendations for the reorganization and improvement of the administrative structure of the Government, both for immediate Executive needs and for the planning of future national needs. I renew those recommendations.

In relation to tax changes, three things should be kept in mind. First, the total sum to be derived by the Federal Treasury must not be decreased as a result of any changes in schedules. Second, abuses by individuals or corporations designed to escape taxpaying by using various methods of doing business, corporate and otherwise—abuses which we have sought, with great success, to end—must not be restored. Third, we should rightly change certain provisions where they are proven to work definite hardship, especially on the small businessmen of the Nation. But, speculative income should not be favored over earned income.

It is human nature to argue that this or that tax is responsible for every ill. It is human nature on the part of those who pay graduated taxes to attack all taxes based on the principle of ability to pay. These are the same complainants who for a generation blocked the imposition of a graduated income tax. They are the same complainants who would impose the type of flat sales tax which places the burden of government more on those least able to pay and less on those most able to pay.

Our conclusion must be that while proven hardships should be corrected, they should not be corrected in such a way as to restore abuses already terminated or to shift a greater burden to the less fortunate.

This subject leads naturally into the wider field of the public attitude toward business. The objective of increasing the purchasing power of the farming third, the industrial third, and the service third of our population presupposes the cooperation of what we call capital and labor.

Capital is essential; reasonable earnings on capital are essential; but misuse of the powers of capital or selfish suspension of the employment of capital must be ended, or the capitalistic system will destroy itself through its own abuses.

The overwhelming majority of businessmen and bankers intend to be good citizens. Only a small minority have displayed poor citizenship by engaging in practices which are dishonest or definitely harmful to society. This statement is straightforward and true. No person in any responsible place in the Government of the United States today has ever taken any position contrary to it.

But, unfortunately for the country, when attention is called to, or attack is made on specific misuses of capital, there has been a deliberate purpose on the part of the condemned minority to distort the criticism into an attack on all capital. That is willful deception but it does not long deceive.

If attention is called to, or attack made on, certain wrongful business practices, there are those who are eager to call it "an attack on all business." That, too, is willful deception that will not long deceive.

Let us consider certain facts:

There are practices which most people believe should be ended. They include tax avoidance through corporate and other methods, which I have previously mentioned; excessive capitalization, investment write-ups, and security manipulations; price rigging and collusive bidding in defiance of the spirit of the antitrust laws by methods which baffle prosecution under the present statutes. They include high-pressure salesmanship which creates cycles of overproduction within given industries and consequent recessions in production until such time as the surplus is consumed; the use of patent laws to enable larger corporations to maintain high prices and withhold from the public the advantages of the progress of science; unfair competition which drives the smaller producer out of business locally, regionally, or even on a national scale; intimidation of local or State government to prevent the enactment of laws for the protection of labor by threatening to move elsewhere; the shifting of actual production from one locality or region to another in pursuit of the cheapest wage scale.

The enumeration of these abuses does not mean that business as a whole is guilty of them. Again, it is deception that will not long deceive to tell the country that an attack on these abuses is an attack on business.

Another group of problems affecting business, which cannot be termed specific abuses, gives us food for grave thought about the future. Generically such problems arise out of the concentration of economic control to the detriment of the body politic—control of other people's money, other people's labor, other people's lives.

In many instances such concentrations cannot be justified on the ground of operating efficiency, but have been created for the sake of securities profits, financial control, the suppression of competition, and the ambition for power over others. In some lines of industry a very small numerical group is in such a position of influence that its actions are of necessity followed by the other units operating in the same field.

That such influences operate to control banking and finance is equally true, in spite of the many efforts, through Federal legislation, to take such control out of the hands of a small group. We have but to talk with hundreds of small bankers throughout the United States to realize that, irrespective of local conditions, they are compelled in practice to accept the policies laid down by a small number of the larger banks in the Nation. The work undertaken by Andrew Jackson and Woodrow Wilson is not finished yet.

The ownership of vast properties or the organization of thousands of workers creates a heavy obligation of public service. The power should not be sought or sanctioned unless the responsibility is accepted as well. The man who seeks freedom from such responsibility in the name of individual liberty is either fooling himself or trying to cheat his fellow men. He wants to eat the fruits of orderly society without paying for them.

As a nation we have rejected any radical revolutionary program. For a permanent correction of grave weaknesses in our economic system we have relied on new applications of old democratic processes. It is not necessary to recount what has been accomplished in preserving the homes and livelihood of millions of workers on farms and in cities, in reconstructing a sound banking and credit system, in reviving trade and industry, in reestablishing security of life and property. All we need today is to look upon the fundamental, sound economic conditions to know that this business recession causes more perplexity than fear on the part of most people and to contrast our prevailing mental attitude with the terror and despair of 5 years ago.

Furthermore, we have a new moral climate in America. That means that we ask business and finance to recognize that fact, to cure such inequalities as they can cure without legislation but to join their Government in the enactment of legislation where the ending of abuses and the steady functioning of our economic system calls for Government assistance. The Nation has no obligation to make America safe for incompetent businessmen or for businessmen who fail to note the trend of the times and continue the use of machinery of economics and practices of finance as outworn as the cotton spindle of 1870.

Government can be expected to cooperate in every way with the business of the Nation provided the component parts of business abandon practices which do not belong to this day and age, and adopt price and production policies appropriate to the times.

In regard to the relationship of government to certain processes of business, to which I have referred, it seems clear to me that existing laws require reconstruction. I expect, therefore, to address the Congress in a special message on this subject, and I hope to have the help of business in the efforts of government to help business.

I have spoken of labor as another essential in the three great groups of the population in raising the Nation's income. Definite strides in collective bargaining have been made and the right of labor to organize has been nationally recognized. Nevertheless, in the evolution of the process difficult situations have arisen in localities and among groups. Unfortunate divisions relating to jurisdiction among the workers themselves have retarded production within given industries and have, therefore, affected related industries. The construction of homes and other buildings has been hindered in some localities not only by unnecessarily high prices for materials but also by certain hourly wage scales.

For economic and social reasons our principal interest for the near future lies along two lines: First, the immediate desirability of increasing the wages of the lowest-paid groups in all industry, and, second, in thinking in terms of regularizing the work of the individual worker more greatly through the year—in other words, in thinking more in terms of the worker's total pay for a period of a whole year rather than in terms of his remuneration by the hour or by the day.

In the case of labor as in the case of capital, misrepresentation of the policy of the Government of the United States is deception which will not long deceive. In both cases we seek cooperation. In every case power and responsibility must go hand in hand.

I have spoken of economic causes which throw the Nation's income out of balance; I have spoken of practices and abuses which demand correction through the cooperation of capital and labor with the Government. But no government can help the destinies of people who insist on putting sectional and class consciousness ahead of general weal. There must be proof that sectional and class interests are prepared more greatly than they are today to be national in outlook.

A government can punish specific acts of spoliation; but no government can conscript cooperation. We have improved some matters by way of remedial legislation. But where in some particulars that legislation has failed we cannot be sure whether it fails because some of its details are unwise or because it is being sabotaged. At any rate, we hold our objectives and our principles to be sound. We will never go back on them.

Government has a final responsibility for the well-being of its citizenship. If private cooperative endeavor fails to provide work for willing hands and relief for the unfortunate, those suffering hardship from no fault of their own have a right to call upon the Government for aid; and a government worthy of its name must make fitting response.

It is the opportunity and the duty of all those who have faith in democratic methods as applied in industry, in agriculture, and in business, as well as in the field of politics, to do their utmost to cooperate with government—without regard to political affiliation, special interests, or economic prejudices—in whatever program may be sanctioned by the chosen representatives of the people.

That presupposes on the part of the representatives of the people, a program, its enactment, and its administration.

Not because of the pledges of party programs alone, not because of the clear policies of the past 5 years, but chiefly because of the need of national unity in ending mistakes of the past and meeting the necessities of today, we must carry on.

I do not propose to let the people down.

I am sure the Congress of the United States will not let the people down.

SIXTH ANNUAL MESSAGE.

THE WHITE HOUSE, *January 4, 1939.*

To the Congress of the United States:

In reporting on the state of the Nation, I have felt it necessary on previous occasions to advise the Congress of disturbance abroad and of the need of putting our own house in order in the face of storm signals from across the seas. As this Seventy-sixth Congress opens there is need for further warning.

A war which threatened to envelop the world in flames has been averted, but it has become increasingly clear that peace is not assured.

All about us rage undeclared wars—military and economic. All about us grow more deadly armaments—military and economic. All about us are threats of new aggression—military and economic.

Storms from abroad directly challenge three institutions indispensable to Americans, now as always. The first is religion. It is the source of the other two—democracy and international good faith.

Religion, by teaching man his relationship to God, gives the individual a sense of his own dignity and teaches him to respect himself by respecting his neighbors.

Democracy, the practice of self-government, is a covenant among free men to respect the rights and liberties of their fellows.

International good faith, a sister of democracy, springs from the will of civilized nations of men to respect the rights and liberties of other nations of men.

In a modern civilization, all three—religion, democracy, and international good faith—complement each other.

Where freedom of religion has been attacked, the attack has come from sources opposed to democracy. Where democracy has been overthrown, the spirit of free worship has disappeared. And where religion and democracy have vanished, good faith and reason in international affairs have given way to strident ambition and brute force.

An ordering of society which relegates religion, democracy, and good faith among nations to the background can find no place within it for the ideals of the Prince of Peace. The United States rejects such an ordering and retains its ancient faith.

There comes a time in the affairs of men when they must prepare to defend not their homes alone but the tenets of faith and humanity on which their churches, their governments, and their very civilization are founded. The defense of religion, of democracy, and of good faith among nations is all the same fight. To save one we must now make up our minds to save all.

We know what might happen to us of the United States if the new philosophies of force were to encompass the other continents and invade our own. We, no more than other nations, can afford to be surrounded by the enemies of our faith and our humanity. Fortunate it is, therefore, that in this Western Hemisphere we have, under a common ideal of democratic government, a rich diversity of resources and of peoples functioning together in mutual respect and peace.

That hemisphere, that peace, and that ideal we propose to do our share in protecting against storms from any quarter. Our people and our resources are pledged to secure that protection. From that determination no American flinches.

This by no means implies that the American Republics disassociate themselves from the nations of other continents—*it does not mean* the Americas against the rest of the world. We as one of the Republics reiterate our willingness to help the cause of world peace. We stand on our historic offer to take counsel with all other nations of the world to the end that aggression among them be terminated, that the race of armaments cease and that commerce be renewed.

But the world has grown so small and weapons of attack so swift that no nation can be safe in its will to peace so long as any other single powerful nation refuses to settle its grievances at the council table.

For if any government bristling with implements of war insists on policies of force, weapons of defense give the only safety.

In our foreign relations we have learned from the past what not to do. From new wars we have learned what we must do.

We have learned that effective timing of defense, and the distant points from which attacks may be launched are completely different from what they were 20 years ago.

We have learned that survival cannot be guaranteed by arming after the attack begins—for there is new range and speed to offense.

We have learned that long before any overt military act, aggression begins with preliminaries of propaganda, subsidized penetration, the loosening of ties of good will, the stirring of prejudice, and the incitement to disunion.

We have learned that God-fearing democracies of the world which observe the sanctity of treaties and good faith in their dealings with other nations cannot safely be indifferent to international lawlessness anywhere. They cannot forever let pass, without effective protest, acts of aggression against sister nations—acts which automatically undermine all of us.

Obviously they must proceed along practical, peaceful lines. But the mere fact that we rightly decline to intervene with arms to prevent acts of aggression does not mean that we must act as if there were no aggression at all. Words may be futile, but war is not the only means of commanding a decent respect for the opinions of mankind. There are many methods short of war, but stronger and more effective than mere words, of bringing home to aggressor governments the aggregate sentiments of our own people.

At the very least, we can and should avoid any action, or any lack of action, which will encourage, assist, or build up an aggressor. We have learned that when we deliberately try to legislate neutrality, our neutrality laws may operate unevenly and unfairly—may actually give aid to an aggressor and deny it to the victim. The instinct of self-preservation should warn us that we ought not to let that happen any more.

And we have learned something else—the old, old lesson that probability of attack is mightily decreased by the assurance of an ever ready defense. Since 1931 world events of thunderous import have moved with lightning speed. During these 8 years many of our people clung to the hope that the innate decency of mankind would protect the unprepared who showed their innate trust in mankind. Today we are all wiser—and sadder.

Under modern conditions what we mean by "adequate defense"—a policy subscribed to by all—must be divided into three elements. First we must have armed forces and defenses strong enough to ward off sudden attack against strategic positions and key facilities essential to ensure sustained resistance and ultimate victory. Secondly, we must have the organization and location of those key facilities so that they may be immediately utilized and rapidly expanded to meet all needs without danger of serious interruption by enemy attack.

In the course of a few days I shall send you a special message making recommendations for those two essentials of defense against danger which we cannot safely assume will not come.

If these first two essentials are reasonably provided for, we must be able confidently to invoke the third element, the underlying strength of citizenship—the self-confidence, the ability, the imagination, and the devotion that give the staying power to see things through.

A strong and united nation may be destroyed if it is unprepared against sudden attack. But even a nation well armed and well organized from a strictly military standpoint, may, after a period of time, meet defeat if it is unnerved by self-distrust, endangered by class prejudice, by dissension between capital and labor, by false economy, and by other unsolved social problems at home.

In meeting the troubles of the world we must meet them as one people—with a unity born of the fact that for generations those who have come to our shores, representing many kindreds and tongues, have been welded by common opportunity into a united patriotism. If another form of government can present a united front in its attack on a democracy, the attack must be met by a united democracy. Such a democracy can and must exist in the United States.

A dictatorship may command the full strength of a regimented nation. But the united strength of a democratic nation can be mustered only when its people, educated by modern standards to know what is going on and where they are going, have conviction that they are receiving as large a share of opportunity for development, as large a share of material success and of human dignity, as they have a right to receive.

Our Nation's program of social and economic reform is therefore a part of defense as basic as armaments themselves.

Against the background of events in Europe, in Africa, and in Asia during these recent years, the pattern of what we have accomplished since 1933 appears in even clearer focus.

For the first time we have moved upon deep-seated problems affecting our national strength and have forged national instruments adequate to meet them.

Consider what the seemingly piecemeal struggles of these 6 years add up to in terms of realistic national preparedness.

We are conserving and developing natural resources—land, water, power, forests.

We are trying to provide necessary food, shelter, and medical care for the health of our population.

We are putting agriculture—our system of food and fiber supply—on a sounder basis.

We are strengthening the weakest spot in our system of industrial supply—its long-smoldering labor difficulties.

We have cleaned up our credit system so that depositor and investor alike may more readily and willingly make their capital available for peace or war.

We are giving to our youth new opportunities for work and education.

We have sustained the morale of all the population by the dignified recognition of our obligations to the aged, the helpless, and the needy.

Above all, we have made the American people conscious of their interrelationship and their interdependence. They sense a common destiny—and a common need of each other. Differences of occupation, geography, race, and religion no longer obscure the Nation's fundamental unity in thought and in action.

We have our difficulties, true—but we are a wiser and a tougher Nation than we were in 1929, or 1932.

Never have there been 6 years of such far-flung internal preparedness in our history. And all this has been done without any dictator's power to command, without conscription of labor or confiscation of capital, without concentration camps, and without a scratch on freedom of speech, freedom of the press or the rest of the Bill of Rights.

We see things now that we could not see along the way. The tools of government which we had in 1933 are outmoded. We have had to forge new tools for a new role of government in democracy—a role of new responsibility for new needs and increased responsibility for old needs, long neglected.

Some of these tools had to be roughly shaped and still need some machining down. Many of those who fought bitterly against the forging of these new tools welcome their use today. The American people, as a whole, have accepted them. The Nation looks to the Congress to improve the new machinery which we have permanently installed, provided that in the process the social usefulness of the machinery is not destroyed or impaired.

All of us agree that we should simplify and improve laws if experience and operation clearly demonstrate the need. For instance, all of us want better provision for our older people under our social security legislation. For the medically needy we must provide better care.

Most of us agree that for the sake of employer and employee alike we must find ways to end factional labor strife and employer-employee disputes.

Most of us recognize that none of these tools can be put to maximum effectiveness unless the executive processes of government are revamped—reorganized, if you will—into more effective combination. And even after such reorganization it will take time to develop administrative personnel and experience in order to use our new tools with a minimum of mistakes. The Congress, of course, needs no further information on this.

With this exception of legislation to provide greater Government efficiency, and with the exception of legislation to ameliorate our railroad and other transportation problems, the past three Congresses have met, in part or in whole, the pressing needs of the new order of things.

We have now passed the period of internal conflict in the launching of our program of social reform. Our full energies may now be released to invigorate the processes of recovery in order to preserve our reforms, and to give every man and woman who wants to work a real job at a living wage.

But time is of paramount importance. The deadline of danger from within and from without is not within our control. The hourglass may be in the hands of other nations. Our own hourglass tells us that we are off on a race to make democracy work, so that we may be efficient in peace and therefore secure in self-defense.

This time element forces us to still greater efforts to attain the full employment of our labor and our capital.

The first duty of our statesmanship today is to bring capital and manpower together.

Dictatorships do this by main force. By using main force they apparently succeed at it—for the moment. However, we abhor their methods, we are compelled to admit that they have obtained substantial utilization of all their material and human resources. Like it or not they have solved, for a time at least, the problem of idle men and idle capital. Can we compete with them by boldly seeking methods of putting idle men and idle capital together and, at the same time, remain within our American way of life, within the Bill of Rights, and within the bounds of what is, from our point of view, civilization itself?

We suffer from a great unemployment of capital. Many people have the idea that as a nation we are overburdened with debt and are spending more than we can afford. That is not so. Despite our Federal Government expenditures the entire debt of our national economic system, public and private together, is no larger today than it was in 1929, and the interest thereon is far less than it was in 1929.

The object is to put capital—private as well as public—to work.

We want to get enough capital and labor at work to give us a total turnover of business, a total national income, of at least eighty billion dollars a year. At that figure we shall have a substantial reduction of unemployment; and the Federal revenues will be sufficient to balance the current level of cash expenditures on the basis of the existing tax structure. That figure can be attained, working within the framework of our traditional profit system.

The factors in attaining and maintaining that amount of national income are many and complicated.

They include more widespread understanding among businessmen of many changes which world conditions and technological improvements have brought to our economy over the last 20 years—changes in the interrelationship of price and volume and employment, for instance—changes of the kind in which businessmen are now educating themselves through opportunities like the so-called monopoly investigation.

They include a perfecting of our farm program to protect farmers' income and consumers' purchasing power from alternate risks of crop gluts and crop shortages.

They include wholehearted acceptance of new standards of honesty in our financial markets.

They include reconcilement of enormous, antagonistic interests—some of them long in litigation—in the railroad and general transportation field.

They include the working out of new techniques—private, State, and Federal—to protect the public interest in and to develop wider markets for electric power.

They include a revamping of the tax relationships between Federal, State, and local units of government, and consideration of relatively small tax increases to adjust inequalities without interfering with the aggregate income of the American people.

They include the perfecting of labor organization and a universal ungrudging attitude by employers toward the labor movement, until there is a minimum of interruption of production and employment because of disputes, and acceptance by labor of the truth that the welfare of labor itself depends on increased balanced output of goods.

To be immediately practical, while proceeding with a steady evolution in the solving of these and like problems, we must wisely use instrumentalities, like Federal investment, which are immediately available to us.

Here, as elsewhere, *time* is the deciding factor in our choice of remedies.

Therefore, it does not seem logical to me—at the moment we seek to increase production and consumption—for the Federal Government to consider a drastic curtailment of its own investments.

The whole subject of Government investing and Government income is one which may be approached in two different ways.

The first calls for the elimination of enough activities of government to bring the expenses of government immediately into balance with income of government. This school of thought maintains that because our national income this year is only sixty billion dollars, ours is only a sixty-billion-dollar country; that government must treat it as such; and that without the help of government, it may some day, somehow, happen to become an eighty-billion-dollar country.

If the Congress decides to accept this point of view, it will logically have to reduce the present functions or activities of government by one-third. The Congress will have to accept the responsibility for such reduction; and the Congress will have to determine which activities are to be reduced.

Certain expenditures we cannot possibly reduce, such as the interest on the public debt. A few million dollars saved here or there in the normal or in curtailed work of the old Departments and Commissions will make no great saving in the Federal Budget. Therefore, the Congress would have to reduce drastically some of certain large items, such as aids to agriculture and soil conservation, veterans' pensions, flood control, highways, waterways, and other public works, grants for social and health security, Civilian Conservation Corps activities, relief for the unemployed, or national defense.

The Congress alone has the power to do all this, as it is the appropriating branch of the Government.

The other approach to the question of Government spending takes the position that this Nation ought not to be and need not be only a sixty-billion-dollar nation; that at this moment it has the men and the resources sufficient to make it at least an eighty-billion-dollar nation. This school of thought does not believe that it can become an eighty-billion-dollar nation in the near future if government cuts its operations by one-third. It is convinced that if we were to try it, we would invite disaster—that we would not long remain even a sixty-billion-dollar nation. There are many complicated factors with which we have to deal, but we have learned that it is unsafe to make abrupt reductions at any time in our net expenditure program.

By our common-sense action of resuming Government activities last spring we have reversed a recession and started the new rising tide of prosperity and national income which we are now just beginning to enjoy.

If Government activities are fully maintained, there is a good prospect of our becoming an eighty-billion-dollar country in a very short time. With such a national income, present tax laws will yield enough each year to balance each year's expenses.

It is my conviction that down in their hearts the American public—industry, agriculture, finance—wants this Congress to do whatever needs to be done to raise our national income to eighty billion dollars a year.

Investing soundly must preclude spending wastefully. To guard against opportunist appropriations, I have on several occasions addressed the Congress on the importance of permanent long-range planning. I hope, therefore, that following my recommendation of last year, a permanent agency will be set up and authorized to report on the urgency and desirability of the various types of government investment.

Investment for prosperity can be made in a democracy.

I hear some people say, "This is all so complicated. There are certain advantages in a dictatorship. It gets rid of labor trouble, of unemployment, of wasted motion, and of having to do your own thinking."

My answer is, "Yes; but it also gets rid of some other things which we Americans intend very definitely to keep—and we still intend to do our own thinking."

It will cost us taxes and the voluntary risk of capital to attain some of the practical advantages which other forms of government have acquired.

Dictatorship, however, involves costs which the American people will never pay: The cost of our spiritual values. The cost of the blessed right of being able to say what we please. The cost of freedom of religion. The cost of seeing our capital confiscated. The cost of being cast into a concentration camp. The cost of being afraid to walk down the street with the wrong neighbor. The cost of having our children brought up not as free and dignified human beings, but as pawns molded and enslaved by a machine.

If the avoidance of these costs means taxes on my income; if avoiding these costs means taxes on my estate at death, I would bear those

taxes willingly as the price of my breathing and my children breathing the free air of a free country, as the price of a living and not a dead world.

Events abroad have made it increasingly clear to the American people that dangers within are less to be feared than dangers from without. If, therefore, a solution of this problem of idle men and idle capital is the price of preserving our liberty, no formless selfish fears can stand in our way.

Once I prophesied that this generation of Americans had a rendezvous with destiny. That prophesy comes true. To us much is given; more is expected.

This generation will "nobly save or meanly lose the last best hope of earth * * * The way is plain, peaceful, generous, just—a way which if followed the world will forever applaud and God must forever bless."

SEVENTH ANNUAL MESSAGE.

THE WHITE HOUSE, *January 3, 1940.*

To the Congress of the United States:

As the Congress reassembles, the impact of wars abroad makes it natural to approach "the state of the Union" through a discussion of foreign affairs.

But it is important that those who hear and read this message should in no way confuse that approach with any thought that our Government is abandoning, or even overlooking, the great significance of its domestic policies.

The social and economic forces which have been mismanaged abroad until they have resulted in revolution, dictatorship, and war are the same as those which we here are struggling to adjust peacefully at home.

You are well aware that dictatorships—and the philosophy of force which justifies and accompanies dictatorships—have originated in almost every case in the necessity for drastic action to improve internal conditions where democratic action for one reason or another has failed to respond to modern needs and modern demands.

It was with farsighted wisdom that the framers of the Constitution brought together in one magnificent phrase three great concepts—"common defense," "general welfare," and "domestic tranquillity."

More than a century and a half later we still believe with them that our best defense is the promotion of our general welfare and domestic tranquillity.

In previous messages to the Congress I have repeatedly warned that, whether we like it or not, the daily lives of American citizens will, of necessity, feel the shock of events on other continents. This is no longer mere theory for it has been definitely proved by the facts of yesterday and today.

To say that the domestic well-being of 130,000,000 Americans is deeply affected by the well-being or the ill-being of the populations of other nations is only to recognize in world affairs the truth we all accept in home affairs.

If in any local unit—a city, county, State, or region—low standards of living are permitted to continue, the level of the civilization of the entire Nation will be pulled downward.

The identical principle extends to the rest of a civilized world. But there are those who wishfully insist, in innocence or ignorance, or both, that the United States of America as a self-contained unit can live happily and prosperously, its future secure, inside a high wall of isolation while, outside, the rest of civilization and the commerce and culture of mankind are shattered.

I can understand the feelings of those who warn the Nation that they will never again consent to the sending of American youth to fight on the soil of Europe. But, as I remember, nobody has asked them to consent—for nobody expects such an undertaking.

The overwhelming majority of our fellow citizens do not abandon in the slightest their hope and expectation that the United States will not become involved in military participation in the war.

I can also understand the wishfulness of those who oversimplify the whole situation by repeating that all we have to do is to mind our own business and keep the Nation out of war. But there is a vast difference between keeping out of war and pretending that this war is none of our business.

We do not have to go to war with other nations, but at least we can strive with other nations to encourage the kind of peace that will lighten the troubles of the world, and by so doing help our own Nation as well.

I ask that all of us everywhere think things through with the single aim of how best to serve the future of our own Nation. I do not mean merely its future relationship with the outside world. I mean its domestic future as well—the work, the security, the prosperity, the happiness, the life of all the boys and girls of the United States, as they are inevitably affected by such world relationships. For it becomes clearer and clearer that the future world will be a shabby and dangerous place to live in—even for Americans to live in—if it is ruled by force in the hands of a few.

Already the crash of swiftly moving events over the earth has made us all think with a longer view. Fortunately, that thinking cannot be controlled by partisanship. The time is long past when any political party or any particular group can curry and capture public favor by labeling itself the "peace party" or the "peace bloc." That label belongs to the whole United States and to every right thinking man, woman, and child within it.

For out of all the military and diplomatic turmoil, out of all the propaganda and counterpropaganda of the present conflicts, there are two facts which stand out and which the whole world acknowledges.

The first is that never before has the Government of the United States done so much as in our recent past to establish and maintain the policy of the good neighbor with its sister nations.

The second is that in almost every nation in the world today there is a true public belief that the United States has been, and will continue to be, a potent and active factor in seeking the reestablishment of peace.

In these recent years we have had a clean record of peace and good will. It is an open book that cannot be twisted or defamed. It is a record that must be continued and enlarged.

So I hope that Americans everywhere will work out for themselves the several alternatives which lie before world civilization, which necessarily includes our own.

We must look ahead and see the possibilities for our children if the rest of the world comes to be dominated by concentrated force alone—even though today we are a very great and a very powerful nation.

We must look ahead and see the effect on our own future if all the small nations throughout the world have their independence snatched from them or become mere appendages to relatively vast and powerful military systems.

We must look ahead and see the kind of lives our children would have to lead if a large part of the rest of the world were compelled to worship the god imposed by a military ruler, or were forbidden to worship God at all; if the rest of the world were forbidden to read and hear the facts—the daily news of their own and other nations—if they were deprived of the truth which makes men free.

We must look ahead and see the effect on our future generations if world trade is controlled by any nation or group of nations which sets up that control through military force.

It is, of course, true that the record of past centuries includes destruction of small nations, enslavement of peoples, and building of empires on the foundation of force. But wholly apart from the greater international morality which we seek today, we recognize the practical fact that with modern weapons and modern conditions, modern man can no longer live a civilized life if we are to go back to the practice of wars and conquests of the seventeenth and eighteenth centuries.

Summing up this need of looking ahead, and in words of common sense and good American citizenship, I hope that we will have fewer American ostriches in our midst. It is not good for the ultimate health of ostriches to bury their heads in the sand.

Only an ostrich would look upon these wars through the eyes of cynicism or ridicule.

Of course, the peoples of other nations have the right to choose their own form of government. But we in this Nation still believe that such choice should be predicated on certain freedoms which we think are essential everywhere. We know that we ourselves will never be wholly safe at home unless other governments recognize such freedoms.

Twenty-one American republics, expressing the will of 250,000,000 people to preserve peace and freedom in this hemisphere are displaying a unanimity of ideals and practical relationships which gives hope that what is being done here can be done on other continents. We in all the Americas are coming to the realization that we can retain our respective nationalities without, at the same time, threatening the national existence of our neighbors.

Such truly friendly relationships, for example, permit us to follow our own domestic policies with reference to our agricultural products, while at the same time we have the privilege of trying to work out mutual assistance arrangements for a world distribution of world agricultural surpluses.

And we have been able to apply the same simple principle to many manufactured products—surpluses of which must be sold in the world export markets if we would continue a high level of production and employment.

For many years after the World War blind economic selfishness in most countries, including our own, resulted in a destructive mine field of trade restrictions which blocked the channels of commerce among nations. This policy was one of the contributing causes of existing wars. It dammed up vast unsalable surpluses, helping to bring about unemployment and suffering in the United States and everywhere else.

To point the way to break up the log jam, our Trade Agreements Act was passed—based upon a policy of equality of treatment among nations and of mutually profitable arrangements of trade.

It is not correct to infer that legislative powers have been transferred from the Congress to the executive branch of the Government. Everybody recognizes that general tariff legislation is a congressional function, but we know that, because of the stupendous task involved in the fashioning and passing of a general law, it is advisable to provide at times of emergency some flexibility to make the general law adjustable to quickly changing conditions.

We are in such a time today. Our present trade-agreement method provides a temporary flexibility and is, therefore, practical in the best sense. It should be kept alive to serve our trade interests—agricultural and industrial—in many valuable ways during the existing wars.

But what is more important, the Trade Agreements Act should be extended as an indispensable part of the foundation of any stable and durable peace.

The old conditions of world trade made for no enduring peace; and when the time comes, the United States must use its influence to open up the trade channels of the world in order that no nation need feel compelled in later days to seek by force of arms what it can well gain by peaceful conference. For this purpose we need the Trade Agreements Act even more than when it was passed.

I emphasize the leadership which this Nation can take when the time comes for a renewal of world peace. Such an influence will be greatly weakened if this Government becomes a dog in the manger of trade selfishness.

The first President of the United States warned us against entangling foreign alliances. The present President of the United States subscribes to and follows that precept.

But trade cooperation with the rest of the world does not violate that precept in any way.

Even as through these trade agreements we prepare to cooperate in a world that wants peace, we must likewise be prepared to take care of ourselves if the world cannot attain peace.

For several years past we have been compelled to strengthen our own national defense. That has created a very large portion of our Treasury deficits. This year, in the light of continuing world uncertainty, I am asking the Congress for Army and Navy increases which are based not on panic but on common sense. They are not as great as enthusiastic alarmists seek. They are not as small as unrealistic persons claiming superior private information would demand.

As will appear in the Annual Budget tomorrow, the only important increase in any part of the Budget is the estimate for national defense. Practically all other important items show a reduction. Therefore, in the hope that we can continue in these days of increasing economic prosperity to reduce the Federal deficit, I am asking the Congress to levy sufficient additional taxes to meet the emergency spending for national defense.

Behind the Army and Navy, of course, lies our ultimate line of defense—"the general welfare" of our people. We cannot report, despite all the progress we have made in our domestic problems—despite the fact that production is back to 1929 levels—that all our problems are solved. The fact of unemployment of millions of men and women remains a symptom of a number of difficulties in our economic system not yet adjusted.

While the number of the unemployed has decreased, while their immediate needs for food and clothing—as far as the Federal Government is concerned—have been largely met, while their morale has been kept alive by giving them useful public work, we have not yet found a way to employ the surplus of our labor which the efficiency of our industrial processes has created.

We refuse the European solution of using the unemployed to build up excessive armaments which eventually result in dictatorships. We encourage an American way—through an increase of national income which is the only way we can be sure will take up the slack. Much progress has been made; much remains to be done.

We recognize that we must find an answer in terms of work and opportunity.

The unemployment problem today has become very definitely a problem of youth as well as of age. As each year has gone by hundreds of thousands of boys and girls have come of working age. They now form an army of unused youth. They must be an especial concern of democratic government.

We must continue, above all things, to look for a solution of their special problem. For they, looking ahead to life, are entitled to action on our part and not merely to admonitions of optimism or lectures on economic laws.

Some in our midst have sought to instill a feeling of fear and defeatism in the minds of the American people about this problem.

To face the task of finding jobs faster than invention can take them away—is not defeatism. To warble easy platitudes that if we will only go back to ways that have failed, everything will be all right—is not courage.

We met a problem of real fear and real defeatism in 1933. We faced the facts—with action, not with words.

The American people will reject the doctrine of fear, confident that in the thirties we have been building soundly a new order of things different from the order of the twenties. In this dawn of the decade of the forties, with our program of social improvement started, we must continue to carry on the processes of recovery so as to preserve our gains and provide jobs at living wages.

There are, of course, many other items of great public interest which could be enumerated in this message—the continued conservation of our natural resources, the improvement of health and of education, the extension of social security to larger groups, the freeing of large areas from restricted transportation discriminations, the extension of the merit system and many others.

Our continued progress in the social and economic field is important not only for the significance of each part of it but for the total effect which our program of domestic betterment has upon that most valuable asset of a nation in dangerous times—its national unity.

The permanent security of America in the present crisis does not lie in armed force alone. What we face is a set of world-wide forces of disintegration—vicious, ruthless, destructive of all the moral, religious, and political standards which mankind, after centuries of struggle, has come to cherish most.

In these moral values, in these forces which have made our Nation great, we must actively and practically reassert our faith.

These words—"national unity"—must not be allowed to become merely a high-sounding phrase, a vague generality, a pious hope, to which everyone can give lip service. They must be made to have real meaning in terms of the daily thoughts and acts of every man, woman, and child in our land during the coming year and the years that lie ahead.

For national unity is, in a very real and deep sense, the fundamental safeguard of all democracy.

Doctrines which set group against group, faith against faith, race against race, class against class, fanning the fires of hatred in men too despondent, too desperate to think for themselves, were used as rabble-rousing slogans on which dictators could ride to power. And once in power they could saddle their tyrannies on whole nations, and on their weaker neighbors.

This is the danger to which we in America must begin to be more alert. For the apologists for foreign aggressors, and equally those selfish and partisan groups at home who wrap themselves in a false mantle of Americanism to promote their own economic, financial, or political advantage, are now trying European tricks upon us, seeking to muddy the stream of our national thinking, weakening us in the face of danger, by trying to set our own people to fighting among themselves. Such tactics are what have helped to plunge Europe into war. We must combat them, as we would the plague, if American integrity and security are to be preserved. We cannot afford to face the future as a disunited people.

We must as a united people keep ablaze on this continent the flames of human liberty, of reason, of democracy, and of fair play as living things to be preserved for the better world that is to come.

Overstatement, bitterness, vituperation, and the beating of drums, have contributed mightily to ill feeling and wars between nations. If these unnecessary and unpleasant actions are harmful in the international field, they are also hurtful in the domestic scene. Peace among ourselves would seem to have some of the advantage of peace between us and other nations. And in the long run history amply demonstrates that angry controversy surely wins less than calm discussion.

In the spirit, therefore, of a greater unselfishness, recognizing that the world—including the United States of America—passes through perilous times, I am very hopeful that the closing session of the

Seventy-Sixth Congress will consider the needs of the Nation and of humanity with calmness, tolerance, and cooperative wisdom.

May the year 1940 be pointed to by our children as another period when democracy justified its existence as the best instrument of government yet devised by mankind.

EIGHTH ANNUAL MESSAGE.

THE WHITE HOUSE, *January 6, 1941.*

To the Congress of the United States:

I address you, the Members of the Seventy-seventh Congress, at a moment unprecedented in the history of the Union. I use the word "unprecedented," because at no previous time has American security been as seriously threatened from without as it is today.

Since the permanent formation of our Government under the Constitution, in 1789, most of the periods of crisis in our history have related to our domestic affairs. Fortunately, only one of these—the 4-year War between the States—ever threatened our national unity. Today, thank God, 130,000,000 Americans, in 48 States, have forgotten points of the compass in our national unity.

It is true that prior to 1914 the United States often had been disturbed by events in other continents. We had even engaged in two wars with European nations and in a number of undeclared wars in the West Indies, in the Mediterranean and in the Pacific for the maintenance of American rights, and for the principles of peaceful commerce. In no case, however, had a serious threat been raised against our national safety or our independence.

What I seek to convey is the historic truth that the United States as a nation has at all times maintained opposition to any attempt to lock us in behind an ancient Chinese wall while the procession of civilization went past. Today, thinking of our children and their children, we oppose enforced isolation for ourselves or for any part of the Americas.

That determination of ours was proved, for example, during the quarter century of wars following the French Revolution.

While the Napoleonic struggles did threaten interests of the United States because of the French foothold in the West Indies and in Louisiana, and while we engaged in the War of 1812 to vindicate our right to peaceful trade, it is, nevertheless, clear that neither France nor Great Britain nor any other nation was aiming at domination of the whole world.

In like fashion, from 1815 to 1914—99 years—no single war in Europe or in Asia constituted a real threat against our future or against the future of any other American nation.

Except in the Maximilian interlude in Mexico, no foreign power sought to establish itself in this hemisphere; and the strength of the British fleet in the Atlantic has been a friendly strength. It is still a friendly strength.

Even when the World War broke out in 1914, it seemed to contain only small threat of danger to our own American future. But, as time went on, the American people began to visualize what the downfall of democratic nations might mean to our own democracy.

We need not overemphasize imperfections in the Peace of Versailles. We need not harp on failure of the democracies to deal with problems of world reconstruction. We should remember that the peace of 1919 was far less unjust than the kind of "pacification" which began even before Munich, and which is being carried on under the new order of tyranny that seeks to spread over every continent today. The American people have unalterably set their faces against that tyranny.

Every realist knows that the democratic way of life is at this moment being directly assailed in every part of the world—assailed either by arms, or by secret spreading of poisonous propaganda by those who seek to destroy unity and promote discord in nations still at peace.

During 16 months this assault has blotted out the whole pattern of democratic life in an appalling number of independent nations, great and small. The assailants are still on the march, threatening other nations, great and small.

Therefore, as your President, performing my constitutional duty to "give to the Congress information of the state of the Union," I find it necessary to report that the future and the safety of our country and of our democracy are overwhelmingly involved in events far beyond our borders.

Armed defense of democratic existence is now being gallantly waged in four continents. If that defense fails, all the population and all the resources of Europe, Asia, Africa, and Australasia will be dominated by the conquerors. The total of those populations and their resources greatly exceeds the sum total of the population and resources of the whole of the Western Hemisphere—many times over.

In times like these it is immature—and incidentally untrue—for anybody to brag that an unprepared America, single-handed, and with one hand tied behind its back, can hold off the whole world.

No realistic American can expect from a dictator's peace international generosity, or return of true independence, or world disarmament, or freedom of expression, or freedom of religion—or even good business.

Such a peace would bring no security for us or for our neighbors. "Those who would give up essential liberty to purchase a little temporary safety deserve neither liberty nor safety."

As a nation we may take pride in the fact that we are soft-hearted; but we cannot afford to be soft-headed.

We must always be wary of those who with sounding brass and a tinkling cymbal preach the "ism" of appeasement.

We must especially beware of that small group of selfish men who would clip the wings of the American eagle in order to feather their own nests.

I have recently pointed out how quickly the tempo of modern warfare could bring into our very midst the physical attack which we must expect if the dictator nations win this war.

There is much loose talk of our immunity from immediate and direct invasion from across the seas. Obviously, as long as the British Navy retains its power, no such danger exists. Even if there were no British Navy, it is not probable that any enemy would be stupid enough to attack us by landing troops in the United States from across thousands of miles of ocean, until it had acquired strategic bases from which to operate.

But we learn much from the lessons of the past years in Europe—particularly the lesson of Norway, whose essential seaports were captured by treachery and surprise built up over a series of years.

The first phase of the invasion of this hemisphere would not be the landing of regular troops. The necessary strategic points would be occupied by secret agents and their dupes—and great numbers of them are already here, and in Latin America.

As long as the aggressor nation smaintain the offensive, they—not we—will choose the time and the place and the method of their attack.

That is why the future of all American Republics is today in serious danger.

That is why this annual message to the Congress is unique in our history.

That is why every member of the executive branch of the Government and every Member of the Congress face great responsibility—and great accountability.

The need of the moment is that our actions and our policy should be devoted primarily—almost exclusively—to meeting this foreign peril, for all our domestic problems are now a part of the great emergency.

Just as our national policy in internal affairs has been based upon a decent respect for the rights and dignity of all our fellow men within our gates, so our national policy in foreign affairs has been based on a decent respect for the rights and dignity of all nations, large and small. And the justice of morality must and will win in the end.

Our national policy is this:

First, by an impressive expression of the public will and without regard to partisanship, we are committed to all-inclusive national defense.

Second, by an impressive expression of the public will and without regard to partisanship, we are committed to full support of all those resolute peoples, everywhere, who are resisting aggression and are thereby keeping war away from our hemisphere. By this support, we express our determination that the democratic cause shall prevail; and we strengthen the defense and security of our own Nation.

Third, by an impressive expression of the public will and without regard to partisanship, we are committed to the proposition that principles of morality and considerations for our own security will never permit us to acquiesce in a peace dictated by aggressors and sponsored by appeasers. We know that enduring peace cannot be bought at the cost of other people's freedom.

In the recent national election there was no substantial difference between the two great parties in respect to that national policy. No issue was fought out on this line before the American electorate. Today, it is abundantly evident that American citizens everywhere are demanding and supporting speedy and complete action in recognition of obvious danger.

Therefore, the immediate need is a swift and driving increase in our armament production.

Leaders of industry and labor have responded to our summons. Goals of speed have been set. In some cases these goals are being reached ahead of time; in some cases we are on schedule; in other cases there are slight but not serious delays; and in some cases—and I am sorry to say very important cases—we are all concerned by the slowness of the accomplishment of our plans.

The Army and Navy, however, have made substantial progress during the past year. Actual experience is improving and speeding up our methods of production with every passing day. And today's best is not good enough for tomorrow.

I am not satisfied with the progress thus far made. The men in charge of the program represent the best in training, ability, and patriotism. They are not satisfied with the progress thus far made. None of us will be satisfied until the job is done.

No matter whether the original goal was set too high or too low, our objective is quicker and better results.

To give two illustrations:

We are behind schedule in turning out finished airplanes; we are working day and night to solve the innumerable problems and to catch up.

We are ahead of schedule in building warships; but we are working to get even further ahead of schedule.

To change a whole nation from a basis of peacetime production of implements of peace to a basis of wartime production of implements of war is no small task. And the greatest difficulty comes at the beginning of the program, when new tools and plant facilities and new assembly lines and shipways must first be constructed before the actual matériel begins to flow steadily and speedily from them.

The Congress, of course, must rightly keep itself informed at all times of the progress of the program. However, there is certain information, as the Congress itself will readily recognize, which, in the interests of our own security and those of the nations we are supporting, must of needs be kept in confidence.

New circumstances are constantly begetting new needs for our safety. I shall ask this Congress for greatly increased new appropriations and authorizations to carry on what we have begun.

I also ask this Congress for authority and for funds sufficient to manufacture additional munitions and war supplies of many kinds, to be turned over to those nations which are now in actual war with aggressor nations.

Our most useful and immediate role is to act as an arsenal for them as well as for ourselves. They do not need man power. They do need billions of dollars worth of the weapons of defense.

The time is near when they will not be able to pay for them in ready cash. We cannot, and will not, tell them they must surrender, merely because of present inability to pay for the weapons which we know they must have.

I do not recommend that we make them a loan of dollars with which to pay for these weapons—a loan to be repaid in dollars.

I recommend that we make it possible for those nations to continue to obtain war materials in the United States, fitting their orders into our own program. Nearly all of their matériel would, if the time ever came, be useful for our own defense.

Taking counsel of expert military and naval authorities, considering what is best for our own security, we are free to decide how much should be kept here and how much should be sent abroad to our friends who by their determined and heroic resistance are giving us time in which to make ready our own defense.

For what we send abroad, we shall be repaid, within a reasonable time following the close of hostilities, in similar materials, or, at our option, in other goods of many kinds which they can produce and which we need.

Let us say to the democracies: "We Americans are vitally concerned in your defense of freedom. We are putting forth our energies, our resources, and our organizing powers to give you the strength to regain and maintain a free world. We shall send you, in ever-increasing numbers, ships, planes, tanks, guns. This is our purpose and our pledge."

In fulfillment of this purpose we will not be intimidated by the threats of dictators that they will regard as a breach of international law and as an act of war our aid to the democracies which dare to resist their aggression. Such aid is not an act of war, even if a dictator should unilaterally proclaim it so to be.

When the dictators are ready to make war upon us, they will not wait for an act of war on our part. They did not wait for Norway or Belgium or the Netherlands to commit an act of war.

Their only interest is in a new one-way international law, which lacks mutuality in its observance, and, therefore, becomes an instrument of oppression.

The happiness of future generations of Americans may well depend upon how effective and how immediate we can make our aid felt. No one can tell the exact character of the emergency situations that we may be called upon to meet. The Nation's hands must not be tied when the Nation's life is in danger.

We must all prepare to make the sacrifices that the emergency—as serious as war itself—demands. Whatever stands in the way of speed and efficiency in defense preparations must give way to the national need.

A free nation has the right to expect full cooperation from all groups. A free nation has the right to look to the leaders of business, of labor, and of agriculture to take the lead in stimulating effort, not among other groups but within their own groups.

The best way of dealing with the few slackers or troublemakers in our midst is, first, to shame them by patriotic example, and, if that fails, to use the sovereignty of government to save government.

As men do not live by bread alone, they do not fight by armaments alone. Those who man our defenses, and those behind them who build our defenses, must have the stamina and courage which come from an unshakable belief in the manner of life which they are defending. The mighty action which we are calling for cannot be based on a disregard of all things worth fighting for.

The Nation takes great satisfaction and much strength from the things which have been done to make its people conscious of their individual stake in the preservation of democratic life in America. Those things have toughened the fiber of our people, have renewed their faith, and strengthened their devotion to the institutions we make ready to protect.

Certainly this is no time to stop thinking about the social and economic problems which are the root cause of the social revolution which is today a supreme factor in the world.

There is nothing mysterious about the foundations of a healthy and strong democracy. The basic things expected by our people of their political and economic systems are simple. They are—

Equality of opportunity for youth and for others.
Jobs for those who can work.
Security for those who need it.
The ending of special privilege for the few.
The preservation of civil liberties for all.
The enjoyment of the fruits of scientific progress in a wider and constantly rising standard of living.

These are the simple and basic things that must never be lost sight of in the turmoil and unbelievable complexity of our modern world. The inner and abiding strength of our economic and political systems is dependent upon the degree to which they fulfill these expectations.

Many subjects connected with our social economy call for immediate improvement.

As examples:

We should bring more citizens under the coverage of old-age pensions and unemployment insurance.

We should widen the opportunities for adequate medical care.

We should plan a better system by which persons deserving or needing gainful employment may obtain it.

I have called for personal sacrifice. I am assured of the willingness of almost all Americans to respond to that call.

A part of the sacrifice means the payment of more money in taxes. In my Budget message I recommend that a greater portion of this great defense program be paid for from taxation than we are paying today. No person should try, or be allowed, to get rich out of this program; and the principle of tax payments in accordance with ability to pay should be constantly before our eyes to guide our legislation.

If the Congress maintains these principles, the voters, putting patriotism ahead of pocketbooks, will give you their applause.

In the future days, which we seek to make secure, we look forward to a world founded upon four essential human freedoms.

The first is freedom of speech and expression—everywhere in the world.

The second is freedom of every person to worship God in his own way—everywhere in the world.

The third is freedom from want—which, translated into world terms, means economic understandings which will secure to every nation a healthy peacetime life for its inhabitants—everywhere in the world.

The fourth is freedom from fear—which, translated into world terms, means a world-wide reduction of armaments to such a point and in such a thorough fashion that no nation will be in a position to commit an act of physical aggression against any neighbor—anywhere in the world.

That is no vision of a distant millennium. It is a definite basis for a kind of world attainable in our own time and generation. That kind of world is the very antithesis of the so-called new order of tyranny which the dictators seek to create with the crash of a bomb.

To that new order we oppose the greater conception—the moral order. A good society is able to face schemes of world domination and foreign revolutions alike without fear.

Since the beginning of our American history we have been engaged in change—in a perpetual peaceful revolution—a revolution which goes on steadily, quietly adjusting itself to changing conditions—without the concentration camp or the quick-lime in the ditch. The world order which we seek is the cooperation of free countries, working together in a friendly, civilized society.

This Nation has placed its destiny in the hands and heads and hearts of its millions of free men and women; and its faith in freedom under the guidance of God. Freedom means the supremacy of human rights everywhere. Our support goes to those who struggle to gain those rights or keep them. Our strength is in our unity of purpose.

To that high concept there can be no end save victory.

NINTH ANNUAL MESSAGE

THE WHITE HOUSE, *January 6, 1942.*

Mr. Vice President, Mr. Speaker, Members of the Senate and of the House of Representatives, in fulfilling my duty to report upon the state of the Union, I am proud to say to you that the spirit of the American people was never higher than it is today—the Union was never more closely knit together—this country was never more deeply determined to face the solemn tasks before it.

The response of the American people has been instantaneous. It will be sustained until our security is assured.

Exactly 1 year ago today I said to this Congress: "When the dictators are ready to make war upon us, they will not wait for an act of war on our part * * *. They—not we—will choose the time and the place and the method of their attack."

We now know their choice of the time. A peaceful Sunday morning—December 7, 1941.

We know their choice of the place. An American outpost in the Pacific.

We know their choice of the method. The method of Hitler himself.

Japan's scheme of conquest goes back half a century. It was not merely a policy of seeking living room; it was a plan which included the subjugation of all the peoples in the Far East and in the islands of the Pacific, and the domination of that ocean by Japanese military and naval control of the western coasts of North, Central, and South America.

The development of this ambitious conspiracy was marked by the war against China in 1894; the subsequent occupation of Korea; the war against Russia in 1904; the illegal fortification of the mandated Pacific Islands following 1920; the seizure of Manchuria in 1931; and the invasion of China in 1937.

A similar policy of criminal conquest was adopted by Italy. The Fascists first revealed their imperial designs in Libya and Tripoli. In 1935 they seized Abyssinia. Their goal was the domination of all North Africa, Egypt, parts of France, and the entire Mediterranean world.

But the dreams of empire of the Japanese and Fascist leaders were modest in comparison with the gargantuan aspirations of Hitler and his Nazis. Even before they came to power in 1933, their plans for conquest had been drawn. Those plans provided for ultimate domination, not of any one section of the world, but of the whole earth and all the oceans on it.

With Hitler's formation of the Berlin-Rome-Tokyo alliance, all these plans of conquest became a single plan. Under this, in addition to her own schemes of conquest, Japan's role was to cut off our supply of weapons of war to Britain, Russia, and China—weapons which increasingly were speeding the day of Hitler's doom. The act of Japan at Pearl Harbor was intended to stun us—to terrify s to such an extent that we would divert our industrial and military strength to the Pacific area, or even to our own continental defense.

The plan failed in its purpose. We have not been stunned. We have not been terrified or confused. This reassembling of the Seventy-seventh Congress is proof of that; for the mood of quiet, grim resolution which here prevails, bodes ill for those who conspired and collaborated to murder world peace.

That mood is stronger than any mere desire for revenge. It expresses the will of the American people to make very certain that the world will never so suffer again.

Admittedly, we have been faced with hard choices. It was bitter, for example, not to be able to relieve the heroic and historic defenders of Wake Island. It was bitter for us not to be able to land a million men and a thousand ships in the Philippine Islands.

But this adds only to our determination to see to it that the Stars and Stripes will fly again over Wake and Guam; and that the brave people of the Philippines will be rid of Japanese imperialism; and will live in freedom, security, and independence.

Powerful and offensive actions must and will be taken in proper time. The consolidation of the United Nations' total war effort against our common enemies is being achieved.

That is the purpose of conferences which have been held during the past 2 weeks in Washington, in Moscow, and in Chungking. That is the primary objective of the declaration of solidarity signed in Washington on January 1, 1942, by 26 nations united against the Axis Powers.

Difficult choices may have to be made in the months to come. We will not shrink from such decisions. We and those united with us will make those decisions with courage and determination.

Plans have been laid here and in the other capitals for coordinated and cooperative action by all the United Nations—military action and economic action. Already we have established unified command of land, sea, and air forces in the southwestern Pacific theater of war. There will be a continuation of conferences and consultations among military staffs, so that the plans and operations of each will fit into a general strategy designed to crush the enemy. We shall not fight isolated wars—each nation going its own way. These 26 nations are united—not in spirit and determination alone, but in the broad conduct of the war in all its phases.

For the first time since the Japanese and the Fascists and the Nazis started along their bloodstained course of conquest they now face the fact that superior forces are assembling against them. Gone forever are the days when the aggressors could attack and destroy their victims one by one without unity of resistance. We of the United Nations will so dispose our forces that we can strike at the common enemy wherever the greatest damage can be done.

The militarists in Berlin and Tokyo started this war. But the massed, angered forces of common humanity will finish it.

Destruction of the material and spiritual centers of civilization—this has been and still is the purpose of Hitler and his Italian and Japanese chessmen. They would wreck the power of the British Commonwealth and Russia and China and the Netherlands—and then combine all their forces to achieve their ultimate goal, the conquest of the United States.

They know that victory for us means victory for freedom.

They know that victory for us means victory for the institution of democracy—the ideal of the family, the simple principles of common decency and humanity.

They know that victory for us means victory for religion.

And they could not tolerate that. The world is too small to provide adequate "living room" for both Hitler and God. In proof of that, the Nazis have now announced their plan for enforcing their new German, pagan religion throughout the world—the plan by which the Holy Bible and the Cross of Mercy would be displaced by Mein Kampf and the swastika and the naked sword.

Our own objectives are clear; the objective of smashing the militarism imposed by war lords upon their enslaved peoples—the objective of liberating the subjugated nations—the objective of establishing and securing freedom of speech, freedom of religion, freedom from want, and freedom from fear everywhere in the world.

We shall not stop short of these objectives—nor shall we be satisfied merely to gain them and then call it a day. I know that I speak for the American people—and I have good reason to believe I speak also for all the other peoples who fight with us—when I say that this time we are determined not only to win the war, but also to maintain the security of the peace which will follow.

But modern methods of warfare make it a task, not only of shooting and fighting, but an even more urgent one of working and producing.

Victory requires the actual weapons of war and the means of transporting them to a dozen points of combat.

It will not be sufficient for us and the other United Nations to produce a slightly superior supply of munitions to that of Germany, Japan, Italy, and the stolen industries in the countries which they have overrun.

The superiority of the United Nations in munitions and ships must be overwhelming—so overwhelming that the Axis nations can never hope to catch up with it. In order to attain this overwhelming superiority the United States must build planes and tanks and guns and ships to the utmost limit of our national capacity. We have the ability and capacity to produce arms not only for our own forces, but also for the armies, navies, and air forces fighting on our side.

And our overwhelming superiority of armament must be adequate to put weapons of war at the proper time into the hands of those men in the conquered nations, who stand ready to seize the first opportunity to revolt against their German and Japanese oppressors, and against the traitors in their own ranks, known by the already infamous name of "Quislings." As we get guns to the patriots in those lands, they, too, will fire shots heard round the world.

This production of ours in the United States must be raised far above its present levels, even though it will mean the dislocation of the lives and occupations of millions of our own people. We must raise our sights all along the production line. Let no man say it cannot be done. It must be done—and we have undertaken to do it.

I have just sent a letter of directive to the appropriate departments and agencies of our Government, ordering that immediate steps be taken:

1. To increase our production rate of airplanes so rapidly that in this year, 1942, we shall produce 60,000 planes, 10,000 more than the goal set a year and a half ago. This includes 45,000 combat planes—bombers, dive-bombers, pursuit planes. The rate of increase will be continued, so that next year, 1943, we shall produce 125,000 airplanes, including 100,000 combat planes.

2. To increase our production rate of tanks so rapidly that in this year, 1942, we shall produce 45,000 tanks; and to continue that increase so that next year, 1943, we shall produce 75,000 tanks.

3. To increase our production rate of anti-aircraft guns so rapidly that in this year, 1942, we shall produce 20,000 of them; and to continue that increase so that next year, 1943, we shall produce 35,000 anti-aircraft guns.

4. To increase our production rate of merchant ships so rapidly that in this year, 1942, we shall build 8,000,000 deadweight tons as compared with a 1941 production of 1,100,000. We shall continue that increase so that next year, 1943, we shall build 10,000,000 tons.

These figures and similar figures for a multitude of other implements of war will give the Japanese and Nazis a little idea of just what they accomplished in the attack on Pearl Harbor.

Our task is hard—our task is unprecedented—and the time is short. We must strain every existing armament-producing facility to the utmost. We must convert every available plant and tool to war production. That goes all the way from the greatest plants to the smallest—from the huge automobile industry to the village machine shop.

Production for war is based on men and women—the human hands and brains which collectively we call Labor. Our workers stand ready to work long hours; to turn out more in a day's work; to keep the wheels turning and the fires burning 24 hours a day, and 7 days a week. They realize well that on the speed and efficiency of their work depend the lives of their sons and their brothers on the fighting fronts.

Production for war is based on metals and raw materials—steel, copper, rubber, aluminum, zinc, tin, Greater and greater quantities of them will have to be diverted to war purposes. Civilian use of them will have to be cut further and still further—and, in many cases, completely eliminated.

War costs money. So far, we have hardly even begun to pay for it. We have devoted only 15 percent of our national income to national defense. As will appear in my Budget message tomorrow, our war program for the coming fiscal year will cost $56,000,000,000, or, in other words, more than one-half of the estimated annual national income. This means taxes and bonds and bonds and taxes. It means cutting luxuries and other nonessentials. In a word, it means an "all-out" war by individual effort and family effort in a united country.

Only this all-out scale of production will hasten the ultimate all-out victory. Speed will count. Lost ground can always be regained—lost time never. Speed will save lives; speed will save this Nation which is in peril; speed will save our freedom and civilization—and slowness has never been an American characteristic.

As the United States goes into its full stride, we must always be on guard against misconceptions which will arise naturally or which will be planted among us by our enemies.

We must guard against complacency. We must not underrate the enemy. He is powerful and cunning—and cruel and ruthless. He will stop at nothing which gives him a chance to kill and to destroy. He has trained his people to believe that their highest perfection is achieved by waging war. For many years he has prepared for this very conflict—planning, plotting, training, arming, fighting. We have already tasted defeat. We may suffer further set-backs. We must face the fact of a hard war, a long war, a bloody war, a costly war.

We must, on the other hand, guard against defeatism. That has been one of the chief weapons of Hitler's propaganda machine—used time and again with deadly results. It will not be used successfully on the American people.

We must guard against divisions among ourselves and among all the other United Nations. We must be particularly vigilant against racial discrimination in any of its ugly forms. Hitler will try again to breed mistrust and suspicion between one individual and another, one group and another, one race and another, one government and another. He will try to use the same technique of falsehood and rumor-mongering with which he divided France from Britain. He is trying to do this with us even now. But he will find a unity of will and purpose against him, which will persevere until the destruction of all his black designs upon the freedom and safety of the people of the world.

We cannot wage this war in a defensive spirit. As our power and our resources are fully mobilized, we shall carry the attack against the enemy—we shall hit him and hit him again wherever and whenever we can reach him.

We must keep him far from our shores, for we intend to bring this battle to him on his own home grounds.

American armed forces must be used at any place in all the world where it seems advisable to engage the forces of the enemy. In some cases these operations will be defensive, in order to protect key positions. In other cases, these operations will be offensive, in order to strike at the common enemy, with a view to his complete encirclement and eventual total defeat.

American armed forces will operate at many points in the Far East.

American armed forces will be on all the oceans—helping to guard the essential communications which are vital to the United Nations.

American land and air and sea forces will take stations in the British Isles—which constitute an essential fortress in this world struggle.

American armed forces will help to protect this hemisphere—and also bases outside this hemisphere, which could be used for an attack on the Americas.

If any of our enemies, from Europe or from Asia, attempt long-range raids by "suicide" squadrons of bombing planes, they will do so only in the hope of terrorizing our people and disrupting our morale. Our people are not afraid of that. We know that we may have to pay a heavy price for freedom. We will pay this price with a will. Whatever the price, it is a thousand times worth it. No matter what our enemies in their desperation may attempt to do to us—we will say, as the people of London have said, "We can take it". And what's more, we can give it back—and we will give it back—with compound interest.

When our enemies challenged our country to stand up and fight, they challenged each and every one of us. And each and every one of us has accepted the challenge—for himself and for the Nation.

There were only some 400 United States marines who in the heroic and historic defense of Wake Island inflicted such great losses on the enemy. Some of those men were killed in action; and others are now prisoners of war. When the survivors of that great fight are liberated and restored to their homes, they will learn that a hundred and thirty million of their fellow citizens have been inspired to render their own full share of service and sacrifice.

Our men on the fighting fronts have already proved that Americans today are just as rugged and just as tough as any of the heroes whose exploits we celebrate on the Fourth of July.

Many people ask, "When will this war end?" There is only one answer to that. It will end just as soon as we make it end, by our combined efforts, our combined strength, our combined determination to fight through and work through until the end—the end of militarism in Germany and Italy and Japan. Most certainly we shall not settle for less.

That is the spirit in which discussions have been conducted during the visit of the British Prime Minister to Washington. Mr. Churchill and I understand each other, our motives, and our purposes. Together, during the past 2 weeks, we have faced squarely the major military and economic problems of this greatest world war.

All in our Nation have been cheered by Mr. Churchill's visit. We have been deeply stirred by his great message to us. We wish him a safe return to his home. He is welcome in our midst, now and in days to come.

We are fighting on the same side with the British people, who fought along for long, terrible months, and withstood the enemy with fortitude and tenacity and skill.

We are fighting on the same side with the Russian people who have seen the Nazi hordes swarm up to the very gates of Moscow, and who with almost superhuman will and courage have forced the invaders back into retreat.

We are fighting on the same side as the brave people of China who for 4½ long years have withstood bombs and starvation and have whipped the invaders time and again in spite of superior Japanese equipment and arms.

We are fighting on the same side as the indomitable Dutch.

We are fighting on the same side as all the other governments in exile, whom Hitler and all his armies and all his Gestapo have not been able to conquer.

But we of the United Nations are not making all this sacrifice of human effort and human lives to return to the kind of world we had after the last World War.

We are fighting today for security, for progress and for peace, not only for ourselves, but for all men, not only for one generation but for all generations. We are fighting to cleanse the world of ancient evils, ancient ills.

Our enemies are guided by brutal cynicism, by unholy contempt for the human race. We are inspired by a faith which goes back through all the years to the first chapter of the Book of Genesis: "God created man in His own image."

We on our side are striving to be true to that divine heritage. We are fighting as our fathers have fought, to uphold the doctrine that all men are equal in the sight of God. Those on the other side are striving to destroy this deep belief and to create a world in their own image—a world of tyranny and cruelty and serfdom.

That is the conflict that day and night now pervades our lives. No compromise can end that conflict. There never has been—there never can be—successful compromise between good and evil. Only total victory can reward the champions of tolerance and decency and freedom and faith.

TENTH ANNUAL MESSAGE

THE WHITE HOUSE, *January 7, 1943.*

To the Congress of the United States:

The Seventy-eighth Congress assembles in one of the great moments in the history of this Nation. The past year was perhaps the most crucial for modern civilization; the coming year will be filled with violent conflict—yet with high promise of better things.

We must appraise the events of 1942 according to their relative importance; we must exercise a sense of proportion.

First in importance in the American scene has been the inspiring proof of the great qualities of our fighting men. They have demonstrated these qualities in adversity as well as in victory. As long as our flag flies over this Capitol, Americans will honor the soldiers, sailors, and marines who fought our first battles of this war against overwhelming odds—the heroes, living and dead, of Wake and Bataan and Guadalcanal, of the Java Sea and Midway and the North Atlantic convoys. Their unconquerable spirit will live forever.

By far the largest and most important developments in the whole strategic picture of 1942 were the events on the long fronts in Russia: First, the implacable defense of Stalingrad; and, second, the offensives by the Russian armies at various points which started in the latter part of November and which still roll on with great force and effectiveness.

The other major events of the year were the series of Japanese advances in the Philippines, the East Indies, Malaya, and Burma;

the stopping of the Japanese in the mid-Pacific, the South Pacific, and the Indian Oceans; the successful defense of the Near East by the British counterattack through Egypt and Libya; the American-British occupation of North Africa. Of continuing importance in the year 1942 were the unending, bitterly contested battles of the convoy routes and the gradual passing of air superiority from the Axis to the United Nations.

The Axis Powers knew that they must win the war in 1942—or eventually lose everything. I do not need to tell you that our enemies did not win this war in 1942.

In the Pacific area, our most important victory in 1942 was the air and naval battle off Midway Island. That action is historically important because it secured for our use communication lines stretching thousands of miles in every direction. In placing this emphasis on the battle of Midway, I am not unmindful of other successful actions in the Pacific, in the air, and on land and afloat—especially those on the Coral Sea and New Guinea and in the Solomon Islands. But these actions were essentially defensive. They were part of the delaying strategy that characterized this phase of the war.

During this period we inflicted steady losses upon the enemy—great losses of Japanese planes, naval vessels, transports, and cargo ships. As early as 1 year ago we set as a primary task in the war of the Pacific day-by-day and week-by-week destruction of more Japanese war material than Japanese industry could replace. Most certainly, that task has been and is being performed by our fighting ships and planes. A large part of this task has been accomplished by the gallant crews of our American submarines who strike on the other side of the Pacific at Japanese ships—right at the very mouth of the harbor of Yokohama.

We know that as each day goes by, Japanese strength in ships and planes is going down and down, and American strength in ships and planes is going up and up. The eventual outcome can be put on a mathematical basis. That will become evident to the Japanese people themselves when we strike at their own home islands, and bomb them constantly from the air.

In the attacks against Japan, we shall be joined with the heroic people of China, whose ideals of peace are so closely akin to our own. Even today we are flying as much lend-lease material into China as ever traversed the Burma Road, flying it over mountains 17,000 feet high, flying blind through sleet and snow. We shall overcome all the formidable obstacles, and get the battle equipment into China to shatter the power of our common enemy. From this war, China will realize the security, the prosperity, and the dignity which Japan has sought so ruthlessly to destroy.

The period of our defensive attrition in the Pacific is passing. Now our aim is to force the Japanese to fight. Last year, we stopped them. This year, we intend to advance.

In the European theater of war during this past year it was clear that our first task was to lessen the concentrated pressure on the Russian front by compelling Germany to divert part of her manpower and equipment to another theater of war.

After months of secret planning and preparation in the utmost detail, an enormous amphibious expedition was embarked for French North Africa from the United States and the United Kingdom in hundreds of ships. It reached its objectives with very small losses, and has already produced an important effect upon the whole situation of the war. It has opened to attack what Mr. Churchill well described as "the under-belly of the Axis", and it has removed the always dangerous threat of an Axis attack through West Africa against the South Atlantic Ocean and the continent of South America itself.

The well-timed and splendidly executed offensive from Egypt by the British Eighth Army was a part of the same major strategy of the United Nations.

Great rains and appalling mud and very limited communications have delayed the final battles of Tunisia. The Axis is reinforcing its strong positions. But I am confident that though the fighting will be tough, when the final Allied assault is made, the last vestige of Axis power will be driven from the south shores of the Mediterranean.

Any review of the year 1942 must emphasize the magnitude and diversity of the military activities in which this Nation has become engaged. As I speak to you, approximately one and a half million of our soldiers, sailors, marines, and fliers are in service outside our continental limits, all through the world. Our merchant seamen are carrying supplies to them and to our allies over every sea lane.

Few Americans realize the amazing growth of our air strength, though I am sure our enemy does. Day in and day out our forces are bombing the enemy and meeting him in combat on many different fronts over the world. And for those who question the quality of our aircraft and the ability of our fliers, I point to the fact that, in Africa, we are shooting down two enemy planes to every one we lose, and in the Pacific and in the Southwest Pacific we are shooting them down four to one.

We pay the tribute of the United States of America to the fighting men of Russia and China and Britain and the various members of the British Commonwealth—the millions of men who through the years of this war have fought our common enemies, and have denied to them the world conquest which they sought.

We pay tribute to the soldiers and fliers and seamen of others of the United Nations whose countries have been overrun by Axis hordes.

As a result of the Allied occupation of North Africa, powerful units of the French Army and Navy are going into action with the United Nations' forces. We welcome them as allies and as friends. They join with those Frenchmen who, since the dark days of June 1940 have been fighting valiantly for the liberation of their stricken country.

We pay tribute to the fighting leaders of our allies, to Winston Churchill, to Joseph Stalin, and to the Generalissimo Chiang Kai-shek. There is a very real unanimity between the leaders of the United Nations. This unity is effective in planning and carrying out the major strategy of this war, and in building up and maintaining the lines of supplies.

I cannot prophesy. I cannot tell you when or where the United Nations are going to strike next in Europe. But we are going to strike—and strike hard. I cannot tell you whether we are going to hit them in Norway, or through the Low Countries, or in France, or through Sardinia or Sicily, or through the Balkans, or through Poland —or at several points simultaneously. But I can tell you that no matter where and when we strike by land, we and the British and the

Russians will hit them from the air heavily and relentlessly. Day in and day out we shall heap tons upon tons of explosives on their war factories and utilities and seaports.

Hitler and Mussolini will understand the enormity of their miscalculation—that the Nazis would always have the advantage of superior air power as they did when they bombed Warsaw, Rotterdam, London, and Coventry. That superiority has gone—forever.

Yes—the Nazis and the Fascists have asked for it—and they are going to get it.

Our forward progress in this war has depended upon our progress on the production front.

There has been criticism of the management and conduct of our war production. Much of this self-criticism has had a healthy effect. It has spurred us on. It has reflected a normal American impatience to get on with the job. We are the kind of people who are never quite satisfied with anything short of miracles.

But there has been some criticism based on guesswork and even on malicious falsification of fact. Such criticism creates doubts and fears, and weakens our total effort.

I do not wish to suggest that we should be completely satisfied with our production progress—today, or next month, or ever. But I can report to you with genuine pride on what has been accomplished during 1942.

A year ago we set certain production goals for 1942 and 1943. Some people, including some experts, thought that we had pulled some big figures out of a hat just to frighten the Axis. But we had confidence in the ability of our people to establish new records. That confidence has been justified.

Of course, we realized that some production objectives would have to be changed—some adjusted upward, and others downward; some items would be taken out of the program completely, and others added. This was inevitable as we gained battle experience, and as technological improvements were made.

Our 1942 airplane production and tank production fell short, numerically, of the goals set a year ago. Nevertheless, we have plenty of reason to be proud of our record for 1942. We produced about 48,000 military planes—more than the airplane production of Germany, Italy, and Japan put together. Last month, December, we produced 5,500 military planes, and the rate is rapidly rising. Furthermore, as each month passes by, the averages of our types weigh more, take more man-hours to make, and have more striking power.

In tank production, we revised our schedule—and for good and sufficient reasons. As a result of hard experience in battle, we have diverted a portion of our tank-producing capacity to a stepped-up production of new, deadly field weapons, especially self-propelled artillery.

Here are some other production figures:

In 1942 we produced 56,000 combat vehicles, such as tanks and self-propelled artillery.

In 1942, we produced 670,000 machine guns, six times greater than our production in 1941 and three times greater than our total production during the year and a half of our participation in the First World War

We produced 21,000 antitank guns, six times greater than our 1941 production.

We produced ten and a quarter billion rounds of small arms ammunition, five times greater than our 1941 production and three times greater than our total production in the First World War.

We produced 181,000,000 rounds of artillery ammunition, 12 times greater than our 1941 production and 10 times greater than our total production in the First World War.

The arsenal of democracy is making good.

These facts and figures will give no aid and comfort to the enemy. On the contrary, I can imagine they will give him considerable discomfort. I suspect Hitler and Tojo will find it difficult to explain to the German and Japanese people just why it is that "decadent, inefficient democracy" can produce such phenomenal quantities of weapons and munitions—and fighting men.

We have given the lie to certain misconceptions—especially the one which holds that the various blocs or groups within a free country cannot forego their political and economic differences in time of crisis and work together toward a common goal.

While we have been achieving this miracle of production, during the past year our armed forces have grown from a little over 2,000,000 to 7,000,000. In other words, we have withdrawn from the labor force and the farms some 5,000,000 of our younger workers. And in spite of this, our farmers have contributed their share to the common effort by producing the greatest quantity of food ever made available during a single year in all our history.

Is there any person among us so simple as to believe that all this could have been done without creating some dislocations in our normal national life, some inconveniences, and even some hardships?

Who could have hoped to have done this without burdensome Government regulations which are a nuisance to everyone—including those who have the thankless task of administering them?

We all know that there have been mistakes—mistakes due to the inevitable process of trial and error inherent in doing big things for the first time. We all know that there have been too many complicated forms and questionnaires. I know about that. I have had to fill some of them out myself.

But we are determined to see to it that our supplies of food and other essential civilian goods are distributed on a fair and just basis—to rich and poor, management and labor, farmer and city dweller alike. And we are determined to keep the cost of living at a stable level. All this has required much information. The forms and questionnaires represent an honest and sincere attempt by honest and sincere officials to obtain this information.

We have learned by the mistakes that have been made.

Our experience will enable us during the coming year to improve the necessary mechanisms of wartime economic controls, and to simplify administrative procedures. But we do not intend to leave things so lax that loopholes will be left for cheaters, for chiselers, or for the manipulators of the "black market."

Of course, there have been inconveniences and disturbances—and even hardships. And there will be many, many more before we finally win. Yes, 1943 will not be an easy year for us on the home front. We shall feel in many ways in our daily lives the sharp pinch of total war.

Fortunately, there are only a few Americans who place appetite above patriotism. The overwhelming majority realize that the food we send abroad is for essential military purposes, for our own and Allied fighting forces, and for necessary help in areas that we occupy.

We Americans intend to do this great job together. In our common labors we must build and fortify the very foundation of national unity—confidence in one another.

It is often amusing, and it is sometimes politically profitable, to picture the city of Washington as a madhouse, with the Congress and the administration disrupted with confusion and indecision and general incompetence.

However—what matters most in war is results. And the one pertinent fact is that after only a few years of preparation and only 1 year of warfare, we are able to engage, spiritually as well as physically, in the total waging of total war.

Washington may be a madhouse—but only in the sense that it is the Capital City of a nation which is fighting mad. And I think that Berlin and Rome and Tokyo, which had such contempt for the obsolete methods of democracy, would now gladly use all they could get of that same brand of madness.

We must not forget that our achievements in production have been relatively no greater than those of the Russians and British and Chinese who have developed their war industries under the incredible difficulties of battle conditions. They have had to continue work through bombings and black-outs. They have never quit.

We Americans are in good, brave company in this war, and we are playing our own, honorable part in the vast common effort.

As spokesmen for the United States Government, you and I take off our hats to those responsible for our American production—to the owners, managers, and supervisors, to the draftsmen and engineers, to the workers—men and women—in factories and arsenals and shipyards and mines and mills and forests and railroads and highways.

We take off our hats to the farmers who have faced an unprecedented task of feeding not only a great nation but a great part of the world.

We take off our hats to all the loyal, anonymous, untiring men and women who have worked in private employment and in Government and who have endured rationing and other stringencies with good humor and good will.

We take off our hats to all Americans who have contributed magnificently to our common cause.

I have sought to emphasize a sense of proportion in this review of the events of the war and the needs of the war.

We should never forget the things we are fighting for. But, at this critical period of the war, we should confine ourselves to the larger objectives and not get bogged down in argument over methods and details.

We, and all the United Nations, want a decent peace and a durable peace. In the years between the end of the First World War and the beginning of the Second World War, we were not living under a decent or a durable peace.

I have reason to know that our boys at the front are concerned with two broad aims beyond the winning of the war; and their thinking and their opinion coincide with what most Americans here back home are mulling over. They know, and we know, that it would be inconceivable—it would, indeed, be sacrilegious—if this Nation and the world did not attain some real, lasting good out of all these efforts and sufferings and bloodshed and death.

The men in our armed forces want a lasting peace, and, equally, they want permanent employment for themselves, their families, and their neighbors when they are mustered out at the end of the war.

Two years ago I spoke in my annual message of Four Freedoms. The blessings of two of them—Freedom of Speech and Freedom of Religion—are an essential part of the very life of this Nation; and we hope that these blessings will be granted to all men everywhere.

The people at home and the people at the front—men and women—are wondering about the third freedom—Freedom from Want. To them it means that when they are mustered out, when war production is converted to the economy of peace, they will have the right to expect full employment—for themselves and for all able-bodied men and women in America who want to work.

They expect the opportunity to work, to run their farms, their stores, to earn decent wages. They are eager to face the risks inherent in our system of free enterprise.

They do not want a post-war America which suffers from undernourishment or slums—or the dole. They want no get-rich-quick era of bogus "prosperity" which will end for them in selling apples on a street corner, as happened after the bursting of the boom in 1929.

When you talk with our young men and women, you will find they want to work for themselves and their families; they consider they have the right to work; and they know that after the last war their fathers did not gain that right.

When you talk with our young men and women, you will find that with the opportunity for employment they want assurance against the evils of all major economic hazards—assurance that will extend from the cradle to the grave. This great Government can and must provide this assurance.

I have been told that this is no time to speak of a better America after the war. I am told it is a grave error on my part.

I dissent.

If the security of the individual citizen, or the family, should become a subject of national debate, the country knows where I stand.

I say this now to this Seventy-eighth Congress, because it is wholly possible that freedom from want—the right of employment and the right of assurance against life's hazards—will loom very large as a task of America during the coming 2 years.

I trust it will not be regarded as an issue—but rather as a task for all of us to study sympathetically, to work out with a constant regard for the attainment of the objective, with fairness to all and with injustice to none.

In this war of survival we must keep before our minds not only the evil things we fight against but the good things we are fighting for. We fight to retain a great past—and we fight to gain a greater future.

Let us remember that economic safety for the America of the future is threatened unless a greater economic stability comes to the rest of the world. We cannot make America an island in either a military or an economic sense. Hitlerism, like any other form of crime or disease, can grow from the evil seeds of economic as well as military feudalism.

Victory in this war is the first and greatest goal before us. Victory in the peace is the next. That means striving toward the enlargement of the security of man here and throughout the world—and, finally, striving for the fourth freedom—Freedom from fear.

It is of little account for any of us to talk of essential human needs, of attaining security, if we run the risk of another world war in 10 or 20 or 50 years. That is just plain common sense. Wars grow in size, in death and destruction, and in the inevitability of engulfing all nations, in inverse ratio to the shrinking size of the world as a result of the conquest of the air. I shudder to think of what will happen to humanity, including ourselves, if this war ends in an inconclusive peace, and another war breaks out when the babies of today have grown to fighting age.

Every normal American prays that neither he nor his sons nor his grandsons will be compelled to go through this horror again.

Undoubtedly a few Americans, even now, think that this Nation can end this war comfortably and then climb back into an American hole and pull the hole in after them.

But we have learned that we can never dig a hole so deep that it would be safe against predatory animals. We have also learned that if we do not pull the fangs of the predatory animals of this world, they will multiply and grow in strength—and they will be at our throats once more in a short generation.

Most Americans realize more clearly than ever before that modern war equipment in the hands of aggressor nations can bring danger overnight to our own national existence or to that of any other nation, or island, or continent.

It is clear to us that if Germany and Italy and Japan—or any one of them—remain armed at the end of this war, or are permitted to rearm, they will again, and inevitably, embark upon an ambitious career of world conquest. They must be disarmed and kept disarmed, and they must abandon the philosophy, and the teaching of that philosophy, which has brought so much suffering to the world.

After the First World War we tried to achieve a formula for permanent peace, based on a magnificent idealism. We failed. But, by our failure, we have learned that we cannot maintain peace at this stage of human development by good intentions alone.

Today the United Nations are the mightiest military coalition in history. They represent an overwhelming majority of the population of the world. Bound together in solemn agreement that they themselves will not commit acts of aggression or conquest against any of their neighbors, the United Nations can and must remain united for the maintenance of peace by preventing any attempt to rearm in Germany, in Japan, in Italy, or in any other nation which seeks to violate the Tenth Commandment—"Thou shalt not covet."

There are cynics and skeptics who say it cannot be done. The American people and all the freedom-loving peoples of this earth are now demanding that it must be done. And the will of these people shall prevail.

The philosophy of the Axis Powers is based on profound contempt for the human race. If, in the formation of our future policy, we were guided by the same cynical contempt, then we should be surrendering to the philosophy of our enemies, and our victory would turn to defeat.

The issue of this war is the basic issue between those who believe in mankind and those who do not—the ancient issue between those who put their faith in the people and those who put their faith in dictators and tyrants. There have always been those who did not believe in the people, who attempted to block their forward movement across history, to force them back to servility and suffering and silence.

The people have now gathered their strength. They are moving forward in their might and power—and no force, no combination of forces, no trickery, deceit, or violence, can stop them now. They see before them the hope of the world—a decent, secure, peaceful life for all men everywhere.

I do not prophesy when this war will end.

But I do believe that this year of 1943 will give to the United Nations a very substantial advance along the roads that lead to Berlin and Rome and Tokyo.

I tell you it is within the realm of possibility that this Seventy-eighth Congress may have the historic privilege of helping greatly to save the world from future fear.

Therefore, let us—all of us—have confidence, let us redouble our efforts.

A tremendeous, costly, long-enduring task in peace as well as in war is still ahead of us.

But, as we face that continuing task, we may know that the state of this Nation is good—the heart of this Nation is sound—the spirit of this Nation is strong—the faith of this Nation is eternal.

ELEVENTH ANNUAL MESSAGE

THE WHITE HOUSE, *January 11, 1944.*

To the Congress of the United States:

This Nation in the past 2 years has become an active partner in the world's greatest war against human slavery.

We have joined with like-minded people in order to defend ourselves in a world that has been gravely threatened with gangster rule.

But I do not think that any of us Americans can be content with mere survival. Sacrifices that we and our allies are making impose upon us all a sacred obligation to see to it that out of this war we and our children will gain something better than mere survival.

We are united in determination that this war shall not be followed by another interim which leads to new disaster—that we shall not repeat the tragic errors of ostrich isolationism—that we shall not repeat the excesses of the wild twenties when this Nation went for a joy ride on a roller coaster which ended in a tragic crash.

When Mr. Hull went to Moscow in October, and when I went to Cairo and Tehran in November, we knew that we were in agreement with our allies in our common determination to fight and win this war. But there were many vital questions concerning the future peace, and they were discussed in an atmosphere of complete candor and harmony.

In the last war such discussions, such meetings, did not even begin until the shooting had stopped and the delegates began to assemble at the peace table. There had been no previous opportunities for man-to-man discussions which lead to meetings of minds. The result was a peace which was not a peace.

That was a mistake which we are not repeating in this war.

And right here I want to address a word or two to some suspicious souls who are fearful that Mr. Hull or I have made "commitments" for the future which might pledge this Nation to secret treaties, or to enacting the role of Santa Claus.

To such suspicious souls—using a polite terminology—I wish to say that Mr. Churchill, and Marshal Stalin, and Generalissimo Chiang Kai-shek are all thoroughly conversant with the provisions of our Constitution. And so is Mr. Hull. And so am I.

Of course we made some commitments. We most certainly committed ourselves to very large and very specific military plans which require the use of all allied forces to bring about the defeat of our enemies at the earliest possible time.

But there were no secret treaties or political or financial commitments.

The one supreme objective for the future, which we discussed for each nation individually, and for all the United Nations, can be summed up in one word: Security.

And that means not only physical security which provides safety from attacks by aggressors. It means also economic security, social security, moral security—in a family of nations.

In the plain down-to-earth talks that I had with the Generalissimo and Marshal Stalin and Prime Minister Churchill, it was abundantly clear that they are all most deeply interested in the resumption of peaceful progress by their own peoples—progress toward a better life. All our Allies want freedom to develop their lands and resources, to build up industry, to increase education and individual opportunity, and to raise standards of living.

All our Allies have learned by bitter experience that real development will not be possible if they are to be diverted from their purpose by repeated wars—or even threats of war.

China and Russia are truly united with Britain and America in recognition of this essential fact:

The best interests of each nation, large and small, demand that all freedom-loving nations shall join together in a just and durable system of peace. In the present world situation, evidenced by the actions of Germany, Italy, and Japan, unquestioned military control over disturbers of the peace is as necessary among nations as it is among citizens in a community. And an equally basic essential to peace is a decent standard of living for all individual men and women and children in all nations. Freedom from fear is eternally linked with freedom from want.

There are people who burrow through our Nation like unseeing moles, and attempt to spread the suspicion that if other nations are encouraged to raise their standards of living, our own American standard of living must of necessity be depressed.

The fact is the very contrary. It has been shown time and again that if the standard of living of any country goes up, so does its purchasing power—and that such a rise encourages a better standard of living in neighboring countries with whom it trades. That is just plain common sense—and it is the kind of plain common sense that provided the basis for our discussions at Moscow, Cairo, and Tehran.

Returning from my journeyings, I must confess to a sense of letdown when I found many evidences of faulty perspectives here in Washington. The faulty perspective consists in overemphasizing lesser problems and thereby underemphasizing the first and greatest problem.

The overwhelming majority of our people have met the demands of this war with magnificent courage and understanding. They have accepted inconveniences; they have accepted hardships; they have accepted tragic sacrifices. And they are ready and eager to make whatever further contributions are needed to win the war as quickly as possible—if only they are given the chance to know what is required of them.

However, while the majority goes on about its great work without complaint, a noisy minority maintains an uproar of demands for special favors for special groups. There are pests who swarm through the lobbies of the Congress and the cocktail bars of Washington, representing these special groups as opposed to the basic interests of the Nation as a whole. They have come to look upon the war primarily as a chance to make profits for themselves at the expense of their neighbors—profits in money or in terms of political or social preferment.

Such selfish agitation can be highly dangerous in wartime. It creates confusion. It damages morale. It hampers our national effort. It muddies the waters and therefore prolongs the war.

If we analyze American history impartially, we cannot escape the fact that in our past we have not always forgotten individual and selfish and partisan interests in time of war—we have not always been united in purpose and direction. We cannot overlook the serious dissentions and the lack of unity in our War of the Revolution, in our War of 1812, or in our War Between the States, when the survival of the Union itself was at stake.

In the First World War we came closer to national unity than in any previous war. But that war lasted only a year and a half, and increasing signs of disunity began to appear during the final months of the conflict.

In this war, we have been compelled to learn how interdependent upon each other are all groups and sections of the population of America.

Increased food costs, for example, will bring new demands for wage increases from all war workers, which will in turn raise all prices of all things, including those things which the farmers themselves have to buy. Increased wages or prices will each in turn produce the same results. They all have a particularly disastrous result on all fixed income groups.

And I hope you will remember that all of us in this Government represent the fixed-income group just as much as we represent business owners, workers, and farmers. This group of fixed-income people includes teachers, clergy, policemen, firemen, widows and minors on fixed incomes, wives and dependents of our soldiers and sailors, and old-age pensioners. They and their families add up to one-quarter of our 130,000,000 people. They have few or no high-pressure representatives at the Capitol. In a period of gross inflation they would be the worst sufferers.

If ever there was a time to subordinate individual or group selfishness to the national good, that time is now. Disunity at home—bickerings, self-seeking partisanship, stoppages of work, inflation, business as usual, politics as usual, luxury as usual—these are the influences which can undermine the morale of the brave men ready to die at the front for us here.

Those who are doing most of the complaining are not deliberately striving to sabotage the national war effort. They are laboring under the delusion that the time is past when we must make prodigious sacrifices—that the war is already won and we can begin to slacken off. But the dangerous folly of that point of view can be measured by the distance that separates our troops from their ultimate objectives in Berlin and Tokyo—and by the sum of all the perils that lie along the way.

Over confidence and complacency are among our deadliest enemies. Last spring—after notable victories at Stalingrad and in Tunisia and against the U-boats on the high seas—over confidence became so pronounced that war production fell off. In 2 months, June and July, 1943, more than a thousand airplanes that could have been made and should have been made were not made. Those who failed to make them were not on strike. They were merely saying, "The war's in the bag—so let's relax."

That attitude on the part of anyone—government or management or labor—can lengthen this war. It can kill American boys.

Let us remember the lessons of 1918. In the summer of that year the tide turned in favor of the Allies. But this Government did not relax. In fact, our national effort was stepped up. In August 1918, the draft age limits were broadened from 21 to 31 to 18 to 45. The President called for "force to the utmost," and his call was heeded. And in November, only 3 months later, Germany surrendered.

That is the way to fight and win a war—all out—and not with half-an-eye on the battle fronts abroad and the other eye-and-a-half on personal, selfish, or political interests here at home.

Therefore, in order to concentrate all our energies and resources on winning the war, and to maintain a fair and stable economy at home, I recommend that the Congress adopt:

(1) A realistic tax law—which will tax all unreasonable profits, both individual and corporate, and reduce the ultimate cost of the war to our sons and daughters. The tax bill now under consideration by the Congress does not begin to meet this test.

(2) A continuation of the law for the renegotiation of war contracts—which will prevent exorbitant profits and assure fair prices to the Government. For 2 long years I have pleaded with the Congress to take undue profits out of war.

(3) A cost of food law—which will enable the Government (*a*) to place a reasonable floor under the prices the farmer may expect for his production; and (*b*) to place a ceiling on the prices a consumer will have to pay for the food he buys. This should apply to necessities only; and will require public funds to carry out. It will cost in appropriations about 1 percent of the present annual cost of the war.

(4) Early reenactment of the stabilization statute of October 1942. This expires June 30, 1944, and if it is not extended well in advance, the country might just as well expect price chaos by summer.

We cannot have stabilization by wishful thinking. We must take positive action to maintain the integrity of the American dollar.

(5) A national service law—which, for the duration of the war, will prevent strikes, and, with certain appropriate exceptions, will make available for war production or for any other essential services every able-bodied adult in this Nation.

These five measures together form a just and equitable whole. I would not recommend a national service law unless the other laws were passed to keep down the cost of living, to share equitably the burdens of taxation, to hold the stabilization line, and to prevent undue profits.

The Federal Government already has the basic power to draft capital and property of all kinds for war purposes on a basis of just compensation.

As you know, I have for 3 years hesitated to recommend a national service act. Today, however, I am convinced of its necessity. Although I believe that we and our allies can win the war without such a measure, I am certain that nothing less than total mobilization of all our resources of manpower and capital will guarantee an earlier victory, and reduce the toll of suffering and sorrow and blood.

I have received a joint recommendation for this law from the heads of the War Department, the Navy Department, and the Maritime Commission. These are the men who bear responsibility for the procurement of the necessary arms and equipment, and for the successful prosecution of the war in the field. They say:

"When the very life of the Nation is in peril the responsibility for service is common to all men and women. In such a time there can be no discrimination between the men and women who are assigned by the Government to its defense at the battlefront and the men and women assigned to producing the vital materials essential to successful military operations. A prompt enactment of a national service law would be merely an expression of the universality of this responsibility."

I believe the country will agree that those statements are the solemn truth.

National service is the most democratic way to wage a war. Like selective service for the armed forces, it rests on the obligation of each citizen to serve his nation to his utmost where he is best qualified.

It does not mean reduction in wages. It does not mean loss of retirement and seniority rights and benefits. It does not mean that any substantial numbers of war workers will be disturbed in their present jobs. Let these facts be wholly clear.

Experience in other democratic nations at war—Britain, Canada, Australia, and New Zealand—has shown that the very existence of national service makes unnecessary the widespread use of compulsory power. National service has proven to be a unifying moral force—based on an equal and comprehensive legal obligation of all people in a nation at war..

There are millions of American men and women who are not in this war at all. It is not because they do not want to be in it. But they want to know where they can best do their share National service provides that direction. It will be a means by which every man and woman can find that inner satisfaction which comes from making the fullest possible contribution to victory.

I know that all civilian war workers will be glad to be able to say many years hence to their grandchildren: "Yes, I, too, was in service in the great war. I was on duty in an airplane factory, and I helped make hundreds of fighting planes. The Government told me that in doing that I was performing my most useful work in the service of my country."

It is argued that we have passed the stage in the war where national service is necessary. But our soldiers and sailors know that this is not true. We are going forward on a long, rough road—and, in all journeys, the last miles are the hardest. And it is for that final effort—for the total defeat of our enemies—that we must mobilize our total resources. The national war program calls for the employment of more people in 1944 than in 1943.

It is my conviction that the American people will welcome this win-the-war measure which is based on the eternally just principle of "fair for one, fair for all."

It will give our people at home the assurance that they are standing four-square behind our soldiers and sailors. And it will give our enemies demoralizing assurance that we mean business—that we, 130,000,000 Americans, are on the march to Rome, Berlin, and Tokyo.

I hope that the Congress will recognize that, although this is a political year, national service is an issue which transcends politics. Great power must be used for great purposes.

As to the machinery for this measure, the Congress itself should determine its nature—but it should be wholly nonpartisan in its make-up.

Our armed forces are valiantly fulfilling their responsibilities to our country and our people. Now the Congress faces the responsibility for taking those measures which are essential to national security in this the most decisive phase of the Nation's greatest war.

Several alleged reasons have prevented the enactment of legislation which would preserve for our soldiers and sailors and marines the fundamental prerogative of citizenship—the right to vote. No amount of legalistic argument can becloud this issue in the eyes of these 10,000,000 American citizens. Surely the signers of the Constitution did not intend a document which, even in wartime, would be construed to take away the franchise of any of those who are fighting to preserve the Constitution itself.

Our soldiers and sailors and marines know that the overwhelming majority of them will be deprived of the opportunity to vote, if the voting machinery is left exclusively to the States under existing State laws—and that there is no likelihood of these laws being changed in time to enable them to vote at the next election. The Army and Navy have reported that it will be impossible effectively to administer 48 different soldier-voting laws. It is the duty of the Congress to remove this unjustifiable discrimination against the men and women in our armed forces—and to do it as quickly as possible.

It is our duty now to begin to lay the plans and determine the strategy for the winning of a lasting peace and the establishment of an American standard of living higher than ever before known. We cannot be content, no matter how high that general standard of living may be, if some fraction of our people—whether it be one-third or one-fifth or one-tenth—is ill-fed, ill-clothed, ill-housed, and insecure.

This Republic had its beginning, and grew to its present strength, under the protection of certain inalienable political rights—among them the right of free speech, free press, free worship, trial by jury, freedom from unreasonable searches and seizures. They were our rights to life and liberty.

As our Nation has grown in size and stature, however—as our industrial economy expanded—these political rights proved inadequate to assure us equality in the pursuit of happiness.

We have come to a clear realization of the fact that true individual freedom cannot exist without economic security and independence. "Necessitous men are not freemen." People who are hungry and out of a job are the stuff of which dictatorships are made.

In our day these economic truths have become accepted as self-evident. We have accepted, so to speak, a second Bill of Rights under which a new basis of security and prosperity can be established for all—regardless of station, race, or creed.

Among these are—

The right to a useful and remunerative job in the industries, or shops or farms or mines of the Nation;

The right to earn enough to provide adequate food and clothing and recreation;

The right of every farmer to raise and sell his products at a return which will give him and his family a decent living;

The right of every businessman, large and small, to trade in an atmosphere of freedom from unfair competition and domination by monopolies at home or abroad;

The right of every family to a decent home;

The right to adequate medical care and the opportunity to achieve and enjoy good health;

The right to adequate protection from the economic fears of old age, sickness, accident, and unemployment;

The right to a good education.

All of these rights spell security. And after this war is won we must be prepared to move forward, in the implementation of these rights, to new goals of human happiness and well-being.

America's own rightful place in the world depends in large part upon how fully these and similar rights have been carried into practice for our citizens. For unless there is security here at home there cannot be lasting peace in the world.

One of the great American industrialists of our day—a man who has rendered yeoman service to his country in this crisis—recently emphasized the grave dangers of "rightist reaction" in this Nation. All clear-thinking businessmen share his concern. Indeed, if such reaction should develop—if history were to repeat itself and we were to return to the so-called normalcy of the 1920's—then it is certain that even though we shall have conquered our enemies on the battlefields abroad, we shall have yielded to the spirit of fascism here at home.

I ask the Congress to explore the means for implementing this economic bill of rights—for it is definitely the responsibility of the Congress so to do. Many of these problems are already before committees of the Congress in the form of proposed legislation. I shall from time to time communicate with the Congress with respect to these and further proposals. In the event that no adequate program of progress is evolved, I am certain that the Nation will be conscious of the fact.

Our fighting men abroad—and their families at home—expect such a program and have the right to insist upon it. It is to their demands that this Government should pay heed rather than to the whining demands of selfish pressure groups who seek to feather their nests while young Americans are dying.

The foreign policy that we have been following—the policy that guided us at Moscow, Cairo, and Tehran—is based on the common sense principle which was best expressed by Benjamin Franklin on July 4, 1776: "We must all hang together, or assuredly we shall all hang separately."

I have often said that there are no two fronts for America in this war. There is only one front. There is one line of unity which extends from the hearts of the people at home to the men of our attacking forces in our farthest outposts. When we speak of our total effort, we speak of the factory and the field and the mine as well as of the battleground—we speak of the soldier and the civilian, the citizen and his Government.

Each and every one of us has a solemn obligation under God to serve this Nation in its most critical hour—to keep this Nation great—to make this Nation greater in a better world.

TWELFTH ANNUAL MESSAGE

THE WHITE HOUSE, *January 6, 1945.*

To the Congress of the United States:

In considering the state of the Union, the war and the peace that is to follow are naturally uppermost in the minds of all of us.

This war must be waged—it is being waged—with the greatest and most persistent intensity. Everything we are and have is at stake. Everything we are and have will be given. American men, fighting far from home, have already won victories which the world will never forget.

We have no question of the ultimate victory. We have no question of the cost. Our losses will be heavy.

We and our allies will go on fighting together to ultimate total victory.

We have seen a year marked, on the whole, by substantial progress toward victory, even though the year ended with a set-back for our arms, when the Germans launched a ferocious counterattack into Luxemburg and Belgium with the obvious objective of cutting our line in the center.

Our men have fought with indescribable and unforgettable gallantry under most difficult conditions, and our German enemies have sustained considerable losses while failing to obtain their objectives.

The high tide of this German effort was reached 2 days after Christmas. Since then we have reassumed the offensive, rescued the isolated garrison at Bastogne, and forced a German withdrawal along the whole line of the salient. The speed with which we recovered from this savage attack was largely possible because we have one supreme commander in complete control of all the Allied armies in France. General Eisenhower has faced this period of trial with admirable calm and resolution and with steadily increasing success. He has my complete confidence.

Further desperate attempts may well be made to break our lines, to slow our progress. We must never make the mistake of assuming that the Germans are beaten until the last Nazi has surrendered.

And I would express another most serious warning against the poisonous effects of enemy propaganda.

The wedge that the Germans attempted to drive in western Europe was less dangerous in actual terms of winning the war than the wedges which they are continually attempting to drive between ourselves and our allies.

Every little rumor which is intended to weaken our faith in our allies is like an actual enemy agent in our midst—seeking to sabotage our war effort. There are, here and there, evil and baseless rumors against the Russians—rumors against the British—rumors against our own American commanders in the field.

When you examine these rumors closley, you will observe that every one of them bears the same trade-mark—"Made in Germany."

We must resist this divisive propaganda—we must destroy it—with the same strength and the same determination that our fighting men are displaying as they resist and destroy the panzer divisions.

In Europe, we shall resume the attack and—despite temporary setbacks here or there—we shall continue the attack relentlessly until Germany is completely defeated.

It is appropriate at this time to review the basic strategy which has guided us through 3 years of war, and which will lead, eventually, to total victory.

The tremendous effort of the first years of this war was directed toward the concentration of men and supplies in the various theaters of action at the points where they could hurt our enemies most.

It was an effort—in the language of the military men—of deployment of our forces. Many battles—essential battles—were fought; many victories—vital victories—were won. But these battles and these victories were fought and won to hold back the attacking enemy, and to put us in positions from which we and our allies could deliver the final, decisive blows.

In the beginning our most important military task was to prevent our enemies—the strongest and most violently aggressive powers that ever have threatened civilization—from winning decisive victories. But even while we were conducting defensive, delaying actions, we were looking forward to the time when we could wrest the initiative from our enemies and place our superior resources of men and materials into direct competition with them.

It was plain then that the defeat of either enemy would require the massing of overwhelming forces—ground, sea, and air—in positions from which we and our allies could strike directly against the enemy homelands and destroy the Nazi and Japanese war machines.

In the case of Japan, we had to await the completion of extensive preliminary operations—operations designed to establish secure supply lines through the Japanese outer-zone defenses. This called for overwhelming sea power and air power—supported by ground forces strategically employed against isolated outpost garrisons.

Always—from the very day we were attacked—it was right militarily as well as morally to reject the arguments of those shortsighted people who would have had us throw Britain and Russia to the Nazi wolves and concentrate against the Japanese. Such people urged that we fight a purely defensive war against Japan while allowing the domination of all the rest of the world by nazi-ism and fascism.

In the European theater the necessary bases for the massing of ground and airpower against Germany were already available in Great Britain. In the Mediterranean area we could begin ground operations against major elements of the German Army as rapidly as we could put troops in the field, first in north Africa and then in Italy.

Therefore, our decision was made to concentrate the bulk of our ground and air forces against Germany until her utter defeat. That decision was based on all these factors; and it was also based on the realization that, of our two enemies, Germany would be more able to digest quickly her conquests, the more able quickly to convert the manpower and resources of her conquered territory into a war potential.

We had in Europe two active and indomitable allies—Britain and the Soviet Union—and there were also the heroic resistance movements in the occupied countries, constantly engaging and harassing the Germans.

We cannot forget how Britain held the line, alone, in 1940 and 1941; and at the same time, despite ferocious bombardment from the air, built up a tremendous armaments industry which enabled her to take the offensive at El Alamein in 1942.

We cannot forget the heroic defense of Moscow and Leningrad and Stalingrad, or the tremendous Russian offensives of 1943 and 1944 which destroyed formidable German armies.

Nor can we forget how, for more than 7 long years, the Chinese people have been sustaining the barbarous attacks of the Japanese and containing large enemy forces on the vast areas of the Asiatic mainland.

In the future we must never forget the lesson that we have learned—that we must have friends who will work with us in peace as they have fought at our side in war.

As a result of the combined effort of the Allied forces, great military victories were achieved in 1944: The liberation of France, Belgium, Greece, and parts of the Netherlands, Norway, Poland, Yugoslavia, and Czechoslovakia; the surrender of Rumania and Bulgaria; the invasion of Germany itself and Hungary; the steady march through the Pacific islands to the Philippines, Guam and Saipan; and the beginnings of a mighty air offensive against the Japanese islands.

Now, as this Seventy-ninth Congress meets, we have reached the most critical phase of the war.

The greatest victory of the last year was, of course, the successful breach on June 6, 1944, of the German "impregnable" sea wall of Europe and the victorious sweep of the Allied forces through France and Belgium and Luxemburg—almost to the Rhine itself.

The cross-channel invasion of the Allied armies was the greatest amphibious operation in the history of the world. It overshadowed all other operations in this or any other war in its immensity. Its success is a tribute to the fighting courage of the soldiers who stormed the beaches—to the sailors and merchant seamen who put the soldiers ashore and kept them supplied—and to the military and naval leaders who achieved a real miracle of planning and execution. And it is also a tribute to the ability of two nations, Britain and America, to plan together, and work together, and fight together in perfect cooperation and perfect harmony.

This cross-channel invasion was followed in August by a second great amphibious operation, landing troops in Southern France. In this, the same cooperation and the same harmony existed between the American, French, and other Allied forces based in north Africa and Italy.

The success of the two invasions is a tribute also to the ability of many men and women to maintain silence, when a few careless words would have imperiled the lives of hundreds of thousands, and would have jeopardized the whole vast undertakings.

These two great operations were made possible by success in the Battle of the Atlantic.

Without this success over German submarines, we could not have built up our invasion forces or air forces in Great Britain, nor could we have kept a steady stream of supplies flowing to them after they had landed in France.

The Nazis, however, may succeed in improving their submarines and their crews. They have recently increased their U-boat activity. The battle of the Atlantic—like all campaigns in this war—demands eternal vigilance. But the British, Canadian, and other Allied Navies, together with our own, are constantly on the alert.

The tremendous operations in Western Europe have overshadowed in the public mind the less spectacular but vitally important Italian front. Its place in the strategic conduct of the war in Europe has been obscured, and—by some people unfortunately—underrated.

It is important that any misconception on that score be corrected—now.

What the Allied forces in Italy are doing is a well-considered part in our strategy in Europe, now aimed at only one objective—the total defeat of the Germans. These valiant forces in Italy are continuing to keep a substantial portion of the German Army under constant pressure—including some 20 first-line German divisions and the necessary supply and transport and replacement troops—all of which our enemies need so badly elsewhere.

Over very difficult terrain and through adverse weather conditions, our Fifth Army and the British Eighth Army—reinforced by units from other United Nations, including a brave and well-equipped unit of the Brazilian Army—have, in the past year, pushed north through bloody Cassino and the Anzio beachhead, and through Rome until now they occupy heights overlooking the valley of the Po.

The greatest tribute which can be paid to the courage and fighting ability of these splendid soldiers in Italy is to point out that although their strength is about equal to that of the Germans they oppose, the Allies have been continuously on the offensive.

That pressure, that offensive, by our troops in Italy will continue.

The American people—and every soldier now fighting in the Apennines—should remember that the Italian front has not lost any of the importance which it had in the days when it was the only Allied front in Europe.

In the Pacific during the past year, we have conducted the fastest-moving offensive in the history of modern warfare. We have driven the enemy back more than 3,000 miles across the Central Pacific.

A year ago, our conquest of Tarawa was a little more than a month old.

A year ago, we were preparing for our invasion of Kwajalein, the second of our great strides across the Central Pacific to the Philippines.

A year ago, General MacArthur was still fighting in New Guinea almost 1,500 miles from his present position in the Philippine Islands.

We now have firmly established bases in the Mariana Islands, from which our Superfortresses bomb Tokyo itself—and will continue to blast Japan in ever-increasing numbers.

Japanese forces in the Philippines have been cut in two. There is still hard fighting ahead—costly fighting. But the liberation of the Philippines will mean that Japan has been largely cut off from her conquests in the East Indies.

The landing of our troops on Leyte was the largest amphibious operation thus far conducted in the Pacific.

Moreover, these landings drew the Japanese Fleet into the first great sea battle which Japan has risked in almost 2 years. Not since the night engagements around Guadalcanal in November-December 1942, had our Navy been able to come to grips with major units of the Japanese Fleet. We had brushed against their fleet in the first battle of the Philippine Sea in June 1944, but not until last October were we able really to engage a major portion of the Japanese Navy in actual combat. The naval engagement which raged for 3 days was the heaviest blow ever struck against Japanese sea power.

As a result of that battle, much of what is left of the Japanese Fleet has been driven behind the screen of islands that separates the Yellow Sea, the China Sea, and the Sea of Japan from the Pacific.

Our Navy looks forward to any opportunity which the lords of the Japanese Navy will give us to fight them again.

The people of this Nation have a right to be proud of the courage and fighting ability of the men in the armed forces—on all fronts. They also have a right to be proud of American leadership which has guided their sons into battle.

The history of the generalship of this war has been a history of teamwork and cooperation, of skill and daring. Let me give you one example out of last year's operations in the Pacific.

Last September Admiral Halsey led American naval task forces into Philippine waters and north to the East China Sea, and struck heavy blows at Japanese air and sea power.

At that time it was our plan to approach the Philippines by further stages, taking islands which we may call A, C, and E. However, Admiral Halsey reported that a direct attack on Leyte appeared feasible. When General MacArthur received the reports from Admiral Halsey's task forces, he also concluded that it might be possible to attack the Japanese in the Philippines directly—by passing islands, A, C, and E.

Admiral Nimitz thereupon offered to make available to General MacArthur several divisions which had been scheduled to take the intermediate objectives. These discussions, conducted at great distances, all took place in one day.

General MacArthur immediately informed the Joint Chiefs of Staff here in Washington that he was prepared to initiate plans for an attack on Leyte in October. Approval of the change in plan was given on the same day.

Thus, within the space of 24 hours, a major change of plans was accomplished which involved Army and Navy forces from two different theaters of operations—a change which hastened the liberation of the Philippines and the final day of victory—a change which saved lives which would have been expended in the capture of islands which are now neutralized far behind our lines.

Our over-all strategy has not neglected the important task of rendering all possible aid to China. Despite almost insuperable difficulties, we increased this aid during 1944. At present our aid to China must be accomplished by air transport—there is no other way. By the end of 1944, the Air Transport Command was carrying into China a tonnage of supplies three times as great as that delivered a year ago, and much more, each month, than the Burma Road ever delivered at its peak.

Despite the loss of important bases in China, the tonnage delivered by air transport has enabled General Chennault's Fourteenth Air Force, which includes many Chinese flyers, to wage an effective and aggressive campaign against the Japanese. In 1944 aircraft of the Fourteenth Air Force flew more than 35,000 sorties against the Japanese and sank enormous tonnage of enemy shipping, greatly diminishing the usefulness of the China Sea lanes.

British, Dominion, and Chinese forces together with our own have not only held the line in Burma against determined Japanese attacks but have gained bases of considerable importance to the supply line into China.

The Burma campaigns have involved incredible hardship, and have demanded exceptional fortitude and determination. The officers and men who have served with so much devotion in these far distant jungles and mountains deserve high honor from their countrymen.

In all of the far-flung operations of our own armed forces—on land, and sea and in the air—the final job, the toughest job, has been performed by the average, easy-going, hard-fighting young American, who carries the weight of battle on his own shoulders.

It is to him that we and all future generations of Americans must pay grateful tribute.

But—it is of small satisfaction to him to know that monuments will be raised to him in the future. He wants, he needs, and he is entitled to insist upon, our full and active support—now.

Although unprecedented production figures have made possible our victories, we shall have to increase our goals even more in certain items.

Peak deliveries of supplies were made to the War Department in December 1943. Due in part to cut-backs, we have not produced as much since then. Deliveries of Army supplies were down by 15 percent by July 1944, before the upward trend was once more resumed.

Because of increased demands from overseas, the Army Service Forces in the month of October 1944, had to increase its estimate of required production by 10 percent. But in November, 1 month later, the requirements for 1945 had to be increased another 10 percent, sending the production goal well above anything we have yet attained. Our armed forces in combat have steadily increased their expenditure of medium and heavy artillery ammunition. As we continue the decisive phases of this war, the munitions that we expend will mount day by day.

In October 1944, while some were saying the war in Europe was over, the Army was shipping more men to Europe than in any previous month of the war.

One of the most urgent immediate requirements of the armed forces is more nurses. Last April the Army requirement for nurses was set at 50,000. Actual strength in nurses was then 40,000. Since that time the Army has tried to raise the additional 10,000. Active recruiting has been carried on, but the net gain in 8 months has been only 2,000. There are now 42,000 nurses in the Army.

Recent estimates have increased the total number needed to 60,000. That means that 18,000 more nurses must be obtained for the Army alone and the Navy now requires 2,000 additional nurses.

The present shortage of Army nurses is reflected in undue strain on the existing force. More than a thousand nurses are now hospitalized, and part of this is due to overwork. The shortage is also indicated by the fact that 11 Army hospital units have been sent overseas without their complement of nurses. At Army hospitals in the United States there is only 1 nurse to 26 beds, instead of the recommended 1 to 15 beds.

It is tragic that the gallant women who have volunteered for service as nurses should be so overworked. It is tragic that our wounded men should ever want for the best possible nursing care.

The inability to get the needed nurses for the Army is not due to any shortage of nurses; 280,000 registered nurses are now practicing in this country. It has been estimated by the War Manpower Commission that 27,000 additional nurses could be made available to the armed forces without interfering too seriously with the needs of the civilian population for nurses.

Since volunteering has not produced the number of nurses required, I urge that the Selective Service Act be amended to provide for the induction of nurses into the armed forces. The need is too pressing to await the outcome of further efforts at recruiting.

The care and treatment given to our wounded and sick soldiers have been the best known to medical science. Those standards must be maintained at all costs. We cannot tolerate a lowering of them by failure to provide adequate nursing for the brave men who stand desperately in need of it.

In the continuing progress of this war we have constant need for new types of weapons, for we cannot afford to fight the war of today or tomorrow with the weapons of yesterday. For example, the American Army now has developed a new tank with a gun more powerful than any yet mounted on a fast-moving vehicle. The Army will need many thousands of these new tanks in 1945.

Almost every month finds some new development in electronics which must be put into production in order to maintain our technical superiority—and in order to save lives. We have to work every day to keep ahead of the enemy in radar. On D-day, in France, with our superior new equipment, we located and then put out of operation every warning set which the Germans had along the French coast.

If we do not keep constantly ahead of our enemies in the development of new weapons, we pay for our backwardness with the life's blood of our sons.

The only way to meet these increased needs for new weapons and more of them is for every American engaged in war work to stay on his war job—for additional American civilians, men and women, not engaged in essential work, to go out and get a war job. Workers who are released because their production is cut back should get another job where production is being increased. This is no time to quit or change to less essential jobs.

There is an old and true saying that the Lord hates a quitter. And this Nation must pay for all those who leave their essential jobs—or all those who lay down on their essential jobs for nonessential reasons. And—again—that payment must be made with the life's blood of our sons.

Many critical production programs with sharply rising needs are now seriously hampered by manpower shortages. The most important Army needs are artillery ammunition, cotton duck, bombs, tires, tanks, heavy trucks, and even B–29's. In each of these vital programs, present production is behind requirements.

Navy production of bombardment ammunition is hampered by manpower shortages; so is production for its huge rocket program. Labor shortages have also delayed its cruiser and carrier programs, and production of certain types of aircraft.

There is critical need for more repair workers and repair parts; this lack delays the return of damaged fighting ships to their places in the fleet, and prevents ships now in the fighting line from getting needed overhauling.

The pool of young men under 26 classified as I–A is almost depleted. Increased replacements for the armed forces will take men now deferred who are at work in war industry. The armed forces must have an assurance of a steady flow of young men for replacements. Meeting this paramount need will be difficult, and will also make it progressively more difficult to attain the 1945 production goals.

Last year, after much consideration, I recommended that the Congress adopt a national service act as the most efficient and democratic way of insuring full production for our war requirements. This recommendation was not adopted.

I now again call upon the Congress to enact this measure for the total mobilization of all our human resources for the prosecution of the war. I urge that this be done at the earliest possible moment.

It is not too late in the war. In fact, bitter experience has shown that in this kind of mechanized warfare where new weapons are constantly being created by our enemies and by ourselves, the closer we come to the end of the war, the more pressing becomes the need for sustained war production with which to deliver the final blow to the enemy.

There are three basic arguments for a national service law:

First, it would assure that we have the right numbers of workers in the right places at the right times.

Second, it would provide supreme proof to all our fighting men that we are giving them what they are entitled to, which is nothing less than our total effort.

And, third, it would be the final, unequivocal answer to the hopes of the Nazis and the Japanese that we may become half-hearted about this war and that they can get from us a negotiated peace.

National service legislation would make it possible to put ourselves in a position to assure certain and speedy action in meeting our manpower needs.

It would be used only to the extent absolutely required by military necessities. In fact, experience in Great Britain and in other nations at war indicates that use of the compulsory powers of national service is necessary only in rare instances.

This proposed legislation would provide against loss of retirement and seniority rights and benefits. It would not mean reduction in wages.

In adopting such legislation, it is not necessary to discard the voluntary and cooperative processes which have prevailed up to this time. This cooperation has already produced great results. The contribution of our workers to the war effort has been beyond measure. We must build on the foundations that have already been laid and supplement the measures now in operation, in order to guarantee the production that may be necessary in the critical period that lies ahead.

At the present time we are using the inadequate tools at hand to do the best we can by such expedients as manpower ceilings, and the use of priority and other powers, to induce men and women to shift from nonessential to essential war jobs.

I am in receipt of a joint letter from the Secretary of War and the the Secretary of the Navy, dated January 3, 1945, which says:

> With the experience of 3 years of war and after the most thorough consideration, we are convinced that it is now necessary to carry out the statement made by the Congress in the joint resolutions declaring that a state of war existed with Japan and Germany: That "to bring the conflict to a successful conclusion, all of the resources of the country are hereby pledged by the Congress of the United States."
>
> In our considered judgment, which is supported by General Marshall and Admiral King, this requires total mobilization of our manpower by the passage of a national war service law. The armed forces need this legislation to hasten the day of final victory, and to keep to a minimum the cost in lives.
>
> National war service, the recognition by law of the duty of every citizen to do his or her part in winning the war, will give complete assurance that the need for war equipment will be filled. In the coming year we must increase the output of many weapons and supplies on short notice. Otherwise we shall not keep our production abreast of the swiftly changing needs of war. At the same time it will be necessary to draw progressively many men now engaged in war production to serve with the armed forces, and their places in war production must be filled promptly. These developments will require the addition of hundreds of thousands to those already working in war industry. We do not believe that these needs can be met effectively under present methods.
>
> The record made by management and labor in war industry has been a notable testimony to the resourcefulness and power of America. The needs are so great, nevertheless, that in many instances we have been forced to recall soldiers and sailors from military duty to do work of a civilian character in war production, because of the urgency of the need for equipment and because of inability to recruit civilian labor.

Pending action by the Congress on the broader aspects of national service, I recommend that the Congress immediately enact legislation which will be effective in using the services of the 4,000,000 men now classified as IV–F in whatever capacity is best for the war effort.

In the field of foreign policy, we propose to stand together with the United Nations not for the war alone but for the victory for which the war is fought.

It is not only a common danger which unites us but a common hope. Ours is an association not of governments but of peoples—and the peoples' hope is peace. Here, as in England; in England, as in Russia; in Russia, as in China; in France, and through the continent of Europe, and throughout the world; wherever men love freedom, the hope and purpose of the people are for peace—a peace that is durable and secure.

It will not be easy to create this peoples' peace. We delude ourselves if we believe that the surrender of the armies of our enemies will make the peace we long for. The unconditional surrender of the armies of our enemies is the first and necessary step—but the first step only.

We have seen already, in areas liberated from the Nazi and the Fascist tyranny, what problems peace will bring. And we delude ourselves if we attempt to believe wishfully that all these problems can be solved overnight.

The firm foundation can be built—and it will be built. But the continuance and assurance of a living peace must, in the long run, be the work of the people themselves.

We ourselves, like all peoples who have gone through the difficult processes of liberation and adjustment, know of our own experience how great the difficulties can be. We know that they are not difficulties peculiar to any continent or any nation. Our own Revolutionary War left behind it, in the words of one American historian, "an eddy of lawlessness and disregard of human life." There were separatist movements of one kind or another in Vermont, Pennsylvania, Virginia, Tennessee, Kentucky, and Maine. There were insurrections, open or threatened, in Massachusetts and New Hampshire. These difficulties we worked out for ourselves as the peoples of the liberated areas of Europe, faced with complex problems of adjustment, will work out their difficulties for themselves.

Peace can be made and kept only by the united determination of free and peace-loving peoples who are willing to work together—willing to help one another—willing to respect and tolerate and try to understand one another's opinions and feelings.

The nearer we come to vanquishing our enemies the more we inevitably become conscious of differences among the victors.

We must not let those differences divide us and blind us to our more important common and continuing interests in winning the war and building the peace.

International cooperation on which enduring peace must be based is not a one-way street.

Nations like individuals do not always see alike or think alike, and international cooperation and progress are not helped by any nation assuming that it has a monopoly of wisdom or of virtue.

In the future world the misuse of power, as implied in the term "power politics," must not be a controlling factor in international relations. That is the heart of the principles to which we have subscribed. We cannot deny that power is a factor in world politics any more than we can deny its existence as a factor in national politics. But in a democratic world, as in a democratic nation, power must be linked with responsibility, and obliged to defend and justify itself within the framework of the general good.

Perfectionism, no less than isolationism or imperialism or power politics, may obstruct the paths to international peace. Let us not forget that the retreat to isolationism a quarter of a century ago was started not by a direct attack against international cooperation but against the alleged imperfections of the peace.

In our disillusionment after the last war we preferred international anarchy to international cooperation with nations which did not see and think exactly as we did. We gave up the hope of gradually achieving a better peace because we had not the courage to fulfill our responsibilities in an admittedly imperfect world.

We must not let that happen again, or we shall follow the same tragic road again—the road to a third world war.

We can fulfill our responsibilities for maintaining the security of our own country only by exercising our power and our influence to achieve the principles in which we believe and for which we have fought.

In August 1941 Prime Minister Churchill and I agreed to the principles of the Atlantic Charter, these being later incorporated into the Declaration by United Nations of January 1, 1942. At that time certain isolationists protested vigorously against our right to proclaim the principles—and against the very principles themselves. Today, many of the same people are protesting against the possibility of violation of the same principles.

It is true that the statement of principles in the Atlantic Charter does not provide rules of easy application to each and every one of this war-torn world's tangled situations. But it is a good and a useful thing—it is an essential thing—to have principles toward which we can aim.

And we shall not hesitate to use our influence—and to use it now—to secure so far as is humanly possible the fulfillment of the principles of the Atlantic Charter. We have not shrunk from the military responsibilities brought on by this war. We cannot and will not shrink from the political responsibilities which follow in the wake of battle.

I do not wish to give the impression that all mistakes can be avoided and that many disappointments are not inevitable in the making of peace. But we must not this time lose the hope of establishing an international order which will be capable of maintaining peace and realizing through the years more perfect justice between nations.

To do this we must be on our guard not to exploit and exaggerate the differences between us and our allies, particularly with reference to the peoples who have been liberated from Fascist tyranny. That is not the way to secure a better settlement of those differences or to secure international machinery which can rectify mistakes which may be made.

I should not be frank if I did not admit concern about many situations—the Greek and Polish for example. But those situations are not as easy or as simple to deal with as some spokesmen, whose sincerity I do not question, would have us believe. We have obligations, not necessarily legal, to the exiled governments, to the underground leaders, and to our major allies who came much nearer the shadows than we did.

We and our allies have declared that it is our purpose to respect the right of all peoples to choose the form of government under which they will live and to see sovereign rights and self-government restored to those who have been forcibly deprived of them. But with internal dissension, with many citizens of liberated countries still prisoners of war or forced to labor in Germany, it is difficult to guess the kind of self-government the people really want.

During the interim period, until conditions permit a genuine expression of the people's will, we and our allies have a duty, which we cannot ignore, to use our influence to the end that no temporary or provisional authorities in the liberated countries block the eventual exercise of the peoples' right freely to choose the government and institutions under which, as freemen, they are to live.

It is only too easy for all of us to rationalize what we want to believe, and to consider those leaders we like responsible and those we dislike irresponsible. And our task is not helped by stubborn partisanship, however, understandable on the part of opposed internal factions.

It is our purpose to help the peace-loving peoples of Europe to live together as good neighbors, to recognize their common interests and not to nurse their traditional grievances against one another.

But we must not permit the many specific and immediate problems of adjustment connected with the liberation of Europe to delay the establishment of permanent machinery for the maintenance of peace. Under the threat of a common danger, the United Nations joined together in war to preserve their independence and their freedom. They must now join together to make secure the independence and freedom of all peace-loving states, so that never again shall tyranny be able to divide and conquer.

International peace and well-being, like national peace and well-being, require constant alertness, continuing cooperation, and organized effort.

International peace and well-being, like national peace and well-being, can be secured only through institutions capable of life and growth.

Many of the problems of the peace are upon us even now while the conclusion of the war is still before us. The atmosphere of friendship and mutual understanding and determination to find a common ground of common understanding, which surrounded the conversations at Dumbarton Oaks, gives us reason to hope that future discussions will succeed in developing the democratic and fully integrated world security system toward which these preparatory conversations were directed.

We and the other United Nations are going forward, with vigor and resolution, in our efforts to create such a system by providing for it strong and flexible institutions of joint and cooperative action.

The aroused conscience of humanity will not permit failure in this supreme endeavor.

We believe that the extraordinary advances in the means of intercommunication between peoples over the past generation offer a practical method of advancing the mutual understanding upon which peace and the institutions of peace must rest, and it is our policy and purpose to use these great technological achievements for the common advantage of the world.

We support the greatest possible freedom of trade and commerce.

We Americans have always believed in freedom of opportunity, and equality of opportunity remains one of the principal objectives of our national life. What we believe in for individuals, we believe in also for nations. We are opposed to restrictions, whether by public act or private arrangement, which distort and impair commerce, transit and trade.

We have house cleaning of our own to do in this regard. But it is our hope, not only in the interest of our own prosperity but in the interest of the prosperity of the world, that trade and commerce and access to materials and markets may be freer after this war than ever before in the history of the world.

One of the most heartening events of the year in the international field has been the renaissance of the French people and the return of the French nation to the ranks of the United Nations. Far from having been crushed by the terror of Nazi domination, the French people have emerged with stronger faith than ever in the destiny of their country and in the soundness of the democratic ideals to which the French nation has traditionally contributed so greatly.

During her liberation, France has given proof of her unceasing determination to fight the Germans, continuing the heroic efforts of the resistance groups under the occupation and of all those Frenchmen throughout the world who refused to surrender after the disaster of 1940.

Today, French armies are again on the German frontier, and are again fighting shoulder to shoulder with our sons.

Since our landings in Africa, we have placed in French hands all the arms and material of war which our resources and the military situation permitted. And I am glad to say that we are now about to equip large new French forces with the most modern weapons for combat duty.

In addition to the contribution which France can make to our common victory, her liberation likewise means that her great influence will again be available in meeting the problems of peace.

We fully recognize France's vital interest in a lasting solution of the German problem and the contribution which she can make in achieving international security. Her formal adherence to the declaration by United Nations a few days ago and the proposal at the Dumbarton Oaks discussions, whereby France would receive one of the five permanent seats in the proposed Security Council, demonstrate the extent to which France has resumed her proper position of strength and leadership.

I am clear in my own mind that, as an essential factor in the maintenance of peace in the future, we must have universal military training after this war, and I shall send a special message to the Congress on this subject.

An enduring peace cannot be achieved without a strong America—strong in the social and economic sense as well as in the military sense.

In the state of the Union message last year I set forth what I considered to be an American economic bill of rights.

I said then, and I say now, that these economic truths represent a second bill of rights under which a new basis of security and prosperity can be established for all—regardless of station, race or creed.

Of these rights the most fundamental, and one on which the fulfillment of the others in large degree depends, is the "right to a useful and remunerative job in the industries or shops or farms or mines of the Nation." In turn, others of the economic rights of American citizenship, such as the right to a decent home, to a good education, to good medical care, to social security, to reasonable farm income, will, if fulfilled, make major contributions to achieving adequate levels of employment.

The Federal Government must see to it that these rights become realities—with the help of States, municipalities, business, labor, and agriculture.

We have had full employment during the war. We have had it because the Government has been ready to buy all the materials of war which the country could produce—and this has amounted to approximately half our present productive capacity.

After the war we must maintain full employment with Government performing its peacetime functions. This means that we must achieve a level of demand and purchasing power by private consumers—farmers, businessmen, workers, professional men, housewives—which is sufficiently high to replace wartime Government demands; and it means also that we must greatly increase our export trade above the pre-war level.

Our policy is, of course, to rely as much as possible on private enterprise to provide jobs. But the American people will not accept mass unemployment or mere makeshift work. There will be need for the work of everyone willing and able to work—and that means close to 60,000,000 jobs.

Full employment means not only jobs—but productive jobs. Americans do not regard jobs that pay substandard wages as productive jobs.

We must make sure that private enterprise works as it is supposed to work—on the basis of initiative and vigorous competition, without the stifling presence of monopolies and cartels.

During the war we have guaranteed investment in enterprise essential to the war effort. We should also take appropriate measures in peacetime to secure opportunities for new small enterprises and for productive business expansion for which finance would otherwise be unavailable.

This necessary expansion of our peacetime productive capacity will require new facilities, new plants, and new equipment.

It will require large outlays of money which should be raised through normal investment channels. But while private capital should finance this expansion program, the Government should recognize its responsibility for sharing part of any special or abnormal risk of loss attached to such financing.

Our full-employment program requires the extensive development of our natural resources and other useful public works. The undeveloped resources of this continent are still vast. Our river-watershed projects will add new and fertile territories to the United States. The Tennessee Valley Authority, which was constructed at a cost of $750,000,000—the cost of waging this war for less than 4 days—was a bargain. We have similar opportunities in our other great river basins. By harnessing the resources of these river basins, as we have in the Tennessee Valley, we shall provide the same kind of stimulus to enterprise as was provided by the Louisiana Purchase and the new discoveries in the West during the nineteenth century.

If we are to avail ourselves fully of the benefits of civil aviation, and if we are to use the automobiles we can produce, it will be necessary to construct thousands of airports and to overhaul our entire national highway system.

The provision of a decent home for every family is a national necessity, if this country is to be worthy of its greatness—and that task will itself create great employment opportunities. Most of our cities need extensive rebuilding. Much of our farm plant is in a state of disrepair. To make a frontal attack on the problems of housing and urban reconstruction will require thoroughgoing cooperation between industry and labor, and the Federal, State, and local governments.

An expanded social-security program, and adequate health and education programs, must play essential roles in a program designed to support individual productivity and mass purchasing power. I shall communicate further with the Congress on these subjects at a later date.

The millions of productive jobs that a program of this nature could bring are jobs in private enterprise. They are jobs based on the expanded demand for the output of our economy for consumption and investment. Through a program of this character we can maintain a national income high enough to provide for an orderly retirement of the public debt along with reasonable tax reduction.

Our present tax system geared primarily to war requirements must be revised for peacetime so as to encourage private demand.

While no general revision of the tax structure can be made until the war ends on all fronts, the Congress should be prepared to provide tax modifications at the end of the war in Europe, designed to encourage capital to invest in new enterprises and to provide jobs. As an integral part of this program to maintain high employment, we must, after the war is over, reduce or eliminate taxes which bear too heavily on consumption.

The war will leave deep disturbances in the world economy, in our national economy, in many communities, in many families, and in many individuals. It will require determined effort and responsible action of all of us to find our way back to peacetime, and to help others to find their way back to peacetime—a peacetime that holds the values of the past and the promise of the future.

If we attack our problems with determination we shall succeed. And we must succeed. For freedom and peace cannot exist without security.

During the past year the American people, in a national election, reasserted their democratic faith.

In the course of that campaign various references were made to "strife" between this administration and the Congress, with the implication, if not the direct assertion, that this administration and the Congress could never work together harmoniously in the service of the Nation.

It cannot be denied that there have been disagreements between the legislative and executive branches—as there have been disagreements during the past century and a half.

I think we all realize too that there are some people in this Capital City whose task is in large part to stir up dissension, and to magnify normal healthy disagreements so that they appear to be irreconcilable conflicts.

But—I think that the over-all record in this respect is eloquent: The Government of the United States of America—all branches of it—has a good record of achievement in this war.

The Congress, the Executive, and the Judiciary have worked together for the common good.

I myself want to tell you, the Members of the Senate and of the House of Representatives, how happy I am in our relationships and friendships. I have not yet had the pleasure of meeting some of the new Members in each House, but I hope that opportunity will offer itself in the near future.

We have a great many problems ahead of us and we must approach them with realism and courage.

This new year of 1945 can be the greatest year of achievement in human history.

Nineteen forty-five can see the final ending of the Nazi-Fascist reign of terror in Europe.

Nineteen forty-five can see the closing in of the forces of retribution about the center of the malignant power of imperialistic Japan.

Most important of all—1945 can and must see the substantial beginning of the organization of world peace. This organization must be the fulfillment of the promise for which men have fought and died in this war. It must be the justification of all the sacrifices that have been made—of all the dreadful misery that this world has endured.

We Americans of today, together with our allies, are making history—and I hope it will be better history than ever has been made before.

We pray that we may be worthy of the unlimited opportunities that God has given us.

Harry S. Truman

April 12, 1945 to January 20, 1953

FIRST ANNUAL MESSAGE.

Jan. 14, 1946

To the Congress of the United States:

A quarter century ago the Congress decided that it could no longer consider the financial programs of the various departments on a piecemeal basis. Instead it has called on the President to present a comprehensive Executive Budget. The Congress has shown its satisfaction with that method by extending the budget system and tightening its controls. The bigger and more complex the Federal Program, the more necessary it is for the Chief Executive to submit a single budget for action by the Congress.

At the same time, it is clear that the budgetary program and the general program of the Government are actually inseparable. The President bears the responsibility for recommending to the Congress a comprehensive set of proposals on all Government activities and their financing. In formulating policies, as in preparing budgetary estimates, the Nation and the Congress have the right to expect the President to adjust and coordinate the views of the various departments and agencies to form a unified program. And that program requires consideration in connection with the Budget, which is the annual work program of the Government.

Since our programs for this period which combines war liquidation with reconversion to a peacetime economy are inevitably large and numerous it is imperative that they be planned and executed with the utmost efficiency and the utmost economy. We have cut the war program to the maximum extent consistent with national security. We have held our peacetime programs to the level necessary to our national well-being and the attainment of our postwar objectives. Where increased programs have been recommended, the increases have been held as low as is consistent with these goals. I can assure the Congress of the necessity of these programs. I can further assure the Congress that the program as a whole is well within our capacity to finance it. All the programs I have recommended for action are included in the Budget figures.

For these reasons I have chosen to combine the customary Message on the State of the Union with the annual Budget Message, and to include in the Budget not only estimates for functions authorized by the Congress, but also for those which I recommend for its action.

I am also transmitting herewith the Fifth Quarterly Report of the Director of War Mobilization and Reconversion. It is a comprehensive discussion of the present state of the reconversion program and of the immediate and long-range needs and recommendations.

This constitutes, then, as complete a report as I find it possible to prepare now. It constitutes a program of government in relation to the Nation's needs.

With the growing responsibility of modern government to foster economic expansion and to promote conditions that assure full and steady employment opportunities, it has become necessary to formulate and determine the Government program in the light of national economic conditions as a whole. In both the executive and the legislative branches we must make arrangements which will permit us to formulate the Government program in that light. Such an approach has become imperative if the American political and economic system is to succeed under the conditions of economic instability and uncertainty which we have to face. The Government needs to assure business, labor, and agriculture that Government policies will take due account of the requirements of a full employment economy. The lack of that assurance would, I believe, aggravate the economic instability.

With the passage of a full employment bill which I confidently anticipate for the very near future, the executive and legislative branches of government will be empowered to devote their best talents and resources in subsequent years to preparing and acting on such a program.

I. FROM WAR TO PEACE—THE YEAR OF DECISION

In his last Message on the State of the Union, delivered one year ago, President Roosevelt said:

> This new year of 1945 can be the greatest year of achievement in human history.
>
> 1945 can see the final ending of the Nazi-Fascist reign of terror in Europe.
>
> 1945 can see the closing in of the forces of retribution about the center of the malignant power of imperialistic Japan.
>
> Most important of all—1945 can and must see the substantial beginning of the organization of world peace.

All those hopes, and more, were fulfilled in the year 1945. It was the greatest year of achievement in human history. It saw the end of the Nazi-Fascist terror in Europe, and also the end of the malignant power of Japan. And it saw the substantial beginning of world organization for peace. These momentous events became realities because of the steadfast purpose of the United Nations and of the forces that fought for freedom under their flags. The plain fact is that civilization was saved in 1945 by the United Nations.

Our own part in this accomplishment was not the product of any single service. Those who fought on land, those who fought on the sea, and those who fought in the air deserve equal credit. They were supported by other millions in the armed forces who through no fault of their own could not go overseas and who rendered indispensable service in this country. They were supported by millions in all levels of government, including many volunteers, whose devoted public service furnished basic organization and leadership. They were also supported by the millions of Americans in private life—men and women in industry, in commerce, on the farms, and in all manner of activity on the home front—who contributed their brains and their brawn in arming, equipping, and feeding them. The country was brought through four years of peril by an effort that was truly national in character.

Everlasting tribute and gratitude will be paid by all Americans to those brave men who did not come back, who will never come back—the 330,000 who died that the Nation might live and progress. All Americans will also remain deeply conscious of the obligation owed to that larger number of soldiers, sailors, and marines who suffered wounds and sickness in their service. They may be certain that their sacrifice will never be forgotten or their needs neglected.

The beginning of the year 1946 finds the United States strong and deservedly confident. We have a record of enormous achievements as a democratic society in solving problems and meeting opportunities as they developed. We find ourselves possessed of immeasurable advantages—vast and varied natural resources; great plants, institutions, and other facilities; unsurpassed technological and managerial skills; an alert, resourceful, and able citizenry. We have in the United States Government rich resources in information, perspective, and facilities for doing whatever may be found necessary to do in giving support and form to the widespread and diversified efforts of all our people.

And for the immediate future the business prospects are generally so favorable that there is danger of such feverish and opportunistic activity that our grave postwar problems may be neglected. We need to act now with full regard for pitfalls; we need to act with foresight and balance. We should not be lulled by the immediate alluring prospects into forgetting the fundamental complexity of modern affairs, the catastrophe that can come in this complexity, or the values that can be wrested from it.

But the long-range difficulties we face should no more lead to despair than our immediate business prospects should lead to the optimism which comes from the present short-range prospect. On the foundation of our victory we can build a lasting peace, with greater freedom and security for mankind in our country and throughout the world. We will more certainly do this if we are constantly aware of the fact that we face crucial issues and prepare now to meet them.

To achieve success will require both boldness in setting our sights and caution in steering our way on an uncharted course. But we have no luxury of choice. We must move ahead. No return to the past is possible.

Our Nation has always been a land of great opportunities for those people of the world who sought to become part of us. Now we have become a land of great responsibilities to all the people of all the world. We must squarely recognize and face the fact of those responsibilities. Advances in science, in communication, in transportation, have compressed the world into a community. The economic and political health of each member of the world community bears directly on the economic and political health of each other member.

The evolution of centuries has brought us to a new era in world history in which manifold relationships between nations must be formalized and developed in new and intricate ways.

The United Nations Organization now being established represents a minimum essential beginning. It must be developed rapidly and steadily. Its work must be amplified to fill in the whole pattern that has been outlined. Economic collaboration, for example, already charted, now must be carried on as carefully and as comprehensively as the political and security measures.

It is important that the nations come together as States in the Assembly and in the Security Council and in the other specialized assemblies and councils that have been and will be arranged. But this is not enough. Our ultimate security requires more than a process of consultation and compromise.

It requires that we begin now to develop the United Nations Organization as the representative of the world as one society. The United Nations Organization, if we have the will adequately to staff it and to make it work as it should, will provide a great voice to speak constantly and responsibly in terms of world collaboration and world well-being.

There are many new responsibilities for us as we enter into this new international era. The whole power and will and wisdom of our Government and of our people should be focused to contribute to and to influence international action. It is intricate, continuing business. Many concessions and adjustments will be required.

The spectacular progress of science in recent years makes these necessities more vivid and urgent. That progress has speeded internal development and has changed world relationships so fast that we must realize the fact of a new era. It is an era in which affairs have become complex and rich in promise. Delicate and intricate relationships, involving us all in countless ways, must be carefully considered.

On the domestic scene, as well as on the international scene, we must lay a new and better foundation for cooperation. We face a great peacetime venture; the challenging venture of a free enterprise economy making full and effective use of its rich resources and technical advances. This is a venture in which business, agriculture, and labor have vastly greater opportunities than heretofore. But they all also have vastly greater responsibilities. We will not measure up to those responsibilities by the simple return to "normalcy" that was tried after the last war.

The general objective, on the contrary, is to move forward to find the way in time of peace to the full utilization and development of our physical and human resources that were demonstrated so effectively in the war.

To accomplish this, it is not intended that the Federal Government should do things that can be done as well for the Nation by private enterprise, or by State and local governments. On the contrary, the war has demonstrated how effectively we can organize our productive system and develop the potential abilities of our people by aiding the efforts of private enterprise.

As we move toward one common objective there will be many and urgent problems to meet.

Industrial peace between management and labor will have to be achieved—through the process of collective bargaining—with Government assistance but not Government compulsion. This is a problem which is the concern not only of management, labor, and the Government, but also the concern of every one of us.

Private capital and private management are entitled to adequate reward for efficiency, but business must recognize that its reward results from the employment of the resources of the Nation. Business is a public trust and must adhere to national standards in the conduct of its affairs. These standards include as a minimum the establishment of fair wages and fair employment practices.

Labor also has its own new peacetime responsibilities. Under our collective bargaining system, which must become progressively more secure, labor attains increasing political as well as economic power, and this, as with all power, means increased responsibility.

The lives of millions of veterans and war workers will be greatly affected by the success or failure of our program of war liquidation and reconversion. Their transition to peacetime pursuits will be determined by our efforts to break the bottlenecks in key items of production, to make surplus property immediately available where it is needed, to maintain an effective national employment service, and many other reconversion policies. Our obligations to the people who won the war will not be paid if we fail to prevent inflation and to maintain employment opportunities.

While our peacetime prosperity will be based on the private enterprise system, Government can and must assist in many ways. It is the Government's responsibility to see that our economic system remains competitive, that new businesses have adequate opportunities, and that our national resources are restored and improved. Government must realize the effect of its operations on the whole economy. It is the responsibility of Government to gear its total program to the achievement of full production and full employment.

Our basic objective—toward which all others lead—is to improve the welfare of the American people. In addition to economic prosperity, this means that we need social security in the fullest sense of the term; the people must be protected from the fear of want during old age, sickness, and unemployment. Opportunities for a good education and adequate medical care must be generally available. Every family should have a decent home. The new economic bill of rights to which I have referred on previous occasions is a charter of economic freedom which seeks to assure that all who will may work toward their own security ana the general advancement; that we become a well-housed people, a well-nourished people, an educated people, a people socially and economically secure, an alert and responsible people.

These and other problems which may face us can be met by the cooperation of all of us in furthering a positive and well-balanced Government program—a program which will further national and international well-being.

II. THE FEDERAL PROGRAM

International Affairs

1. FOREIGN POLICY

The year 1945 brought with it the final defeat of our enemies. There lies before us now the work of building a just and enduring peace.

Our most immediate task toward that end is to deprive our enemies completely and forever of their power to start another war. Of even greater importance to the preservation of international peace is the need to preserve the wartime agreement of the United Nations and to direct it into the ways of peace.

Long before our enemies surrendered, the foundations had been laid on which to continue this unity in the peace to come. The Atlantic meeting in 1941 and the conferences at Casablanca, Quebec, Moscow, Cairo, Tehran, and Dumbarton Oaks each added a stone to the structure.

Early in 1945, at Yalta, the three major powers broadened and solidified this base of understanding. There fundamental decisions were reached concerning the occupation and control of Germany. There also a formula was arrived at for the interim government of the areas in Europe which were rapidly being wrested from Nazi control. This formula was based on the policy of the United States that people be permitted to choose their own form of government by their own freely expressed choice without interference from any foreign source.

At Potsdam, in July 1945, Marshal Stalin, Prime Ministers Churchill and Attlee, and I met to exchange views primarily with respect to Germany. As a result, agreements were reached which outlined broadly the policy to be executed by the Allied Control Council. At Potsdam there was also established a Council of Foreign Ministers which convened for the first time in London in September. The Council is about to resume its primary assignment of drawing up treaties of peace with Italy, Rumania, Bulgaria, Hungary, and Finland.

In addition to these meetings, and in accordance with the agreement at Yalta, the Foreign Ministers of Great Britain, the Soviet Union, and the United States conferred together in San Francisco last spring, in Potsdam in July, in London in September, and in Moscow in December. These meetings have been useful in promoting understanding and agreement among the three governments.

Simply to name all the international meetings and conferences is to suggest the size and complexity of the undertaking to prevent international war in which the United States has now enlisted for the duration of history.

It is encouraging to know that the common effort of the United Nations to learn to live together did not cease with the surrender of our enemies.

When difficulties arise among us, the United States does not propose to remove them by sacrificing its ideals or its vital interests. Neither do we propose, however, to ignore the ideals and vital interests of our friends.

Last February and March an Inter-American Conference on Problems of War and Peace was held in Mexico City. Among the many significant accomplishments of that Conference was an understanding that an attack by any country against any one of the sovereign American republics would be considered an act of aggression against all of them; and that if such an attack were made or threatened, the American republics would decide jointly, through consultations in which each republic has equal representation, what measures they would take for their mutual protection. This agreement stipulates that its execution shall be in full accord with the Charter of the United Nations Organization.

The first meeting of the General Assembly of the United Nations now in progress in London marks the real beginning of our bold adventure toward the preservation of world peace, to which is bound the dearest hope of men.

We have solemnly dedicated ourselves and all our will to the success of the United Nations Organization. For this reason we have sought to insure that in the peacemaking the smaller nations shall have a voice as well as the larger states. The agreement reached at Moscow last month preserves this opportunity in the making of peace with Italy, Rumania, Bulgaria, Hungary, and Finland. The United States intends to preserve it when the treaties with Germany and Japan are drawn.

It will be the continuing policy of the United States to use all its influence to foster, support, and develop the United Nations Organization in its purpose of preventing international war. If peace is to endure it must rest upon justice no less than upon power. The question is how justice among nations is best achieved. We know from day-to-day experience that the chance for a just solution is immeasurably increased when everyone directly interested is given a voice. That does not mean that each must enjoy an equal voice, but it does mean that each must be heard.

Last November, Prime Minister Attlee, Prime Minister MacKenzie King, and I announced our proposal that a commission be established within the framework of the United Nations to explore the problems of effective international control of atomic energy.

The Soviet Union, France, and China have joined us in the purpose of introducing in the General Assembly a resolution for the establishment of such a commission. Our earnest wish is that the work of this commission go forward carefully and thoroughly, but with the greatest dispatch. I have great hope for the development of mutually effective safeguards which will permit the fullest international control of this new atomic force.

I believe it possible that effective means can be developed through the United Nations Organization to prohibit, outlaw, and prevent the use of atomic energy for destructive purposes.

The power which the United States demonstrated during the war is the fact that underlies every phase of our relations with other countries. We cannot escape the responsibility which it thrusts upon us. What we think, plan, say, and do is of profound significance to the future of every corner of the world.

The great and dominant objective of United States foreign policy is to build and preserve a just peace. The peace we seek is not peace for twenty years. It is permanent peace. At a time when massive changes are occurring with lightning speed throughout the world, it is often difficult to perceive how this central objective is best served in one isolated complex situation or another. Despite this very real difficulty, there are certain basic propositions to which the United States adheres and to which we shall continue to adhere.

One proposition is that lasting peace requires genuine understanding and active cooperation among the most powerful nations. Another is that even the support of the strongest nations cannot guarantee a peace unless it is infused with the quality of justice for all nations.

On October 27, 1945, I made, in New York City, the following public statement of my understanding of the fundamental foreign policy of the United States. I believe that policy to be in accord with the opinion of the Congress and of the people of the United States. I believe that that policy carries out our fundamental objectives.

> 1. We seek no territorial expansion or selfish advantage. We have no plans for aggression against any other state, large or small. We have no objective which need clash with the peaceful aims of any other nation.
>
> 2. We believe in the eventual return of sovereign rights and self-government to all peoples who have been deprived of them by force.
>
> 3. We shall approve no territorial changes in any friendly part of the world unless they accord with the freely expressed wishes of the people concerned.
>
> 4. We believe that all peoples who are prepared for self-government should be permitted to choose their own form of government by their own freely expressed choice, without interference from any foreign source. That is true in Europe, in Asia, in Africa, as well as in the Western Hemisphere.
>
> 5. By the combined and cooperative action of our war allies, we shall help the defeated enemy states establish peaceful democratic governments of their own free choice. And we shall try to attain a world in which nazism, fascism, and military aggression cannot exist.
>
> 6. We shall refuse to recognize any government imposed upon any nation by the force of any foreign power. In some cases it may be impossible to prevent forceful imposition of such a government. But the United States will not recognize any such government.
>
> 7. We believe that all nations should have the freedom of the seas and equal rights to the navigation of boundary rivers and waterways and of rivers and waterways which pass through more than one country.
>
> 8. We believe that all states which are accepted in the society of nations should have access on equal terms to the trade and the raw materials of the world.
>
> 9. We believe that the sovereign states of the Western Hemisphere, without interference from outside the Western Hemisphere, must work together as good neighbors in the solution of their common problems.
>
> 10. We believe that full economic collaboration between all nations, great and small, is essential to the improvement of living conditions all over the world, and to the establishment of freedom from fear and freedom from want.
>
> 11. We shall continue to strive to promote freedom of expression and freedom of religion throughout the peace-loving areas of the world.

12. We are convinced that the preservation of peace between nations requires a United Nations Organization composed of all the peace-loving nations of the world who are willing jointly to use force, if necessary, to insure peace.

That is our foreign policy.

We may not always fully succeed in our objectives. There may be instances where the attainment of those objectives is delayed. But we will not give our full sanction and approval to actions which fly in the face of these ideals.

The world has a great stake in the political and economic future of Germany. The Allied Control Council has now been in operation there for a substantial period of time. It has not met with unqualified success. The accommodation of varying views of four governments in the day-to-day civil administration of occupied territory is a challenging task. In my judgment, however, the Council has made encouraging progress in the face of most serious difficulties. It is my purpose at the earliest practicable date to transfer from military to civilian personnel the execution of United States participation in the government of occupied territory in Europe. We are determined that effective control shall be maintained in Germany until we are satisfied that the German people have regained the right to a place of honor and respect.

On the other side of the world, a method of international cooperation has recently been agreed upon for the treatment of Japan. In this pattern of control, the United States, with the full approval of its partners, has retained primary authority and primary responsibility. It will continue to do so until the Japanese people, by their own freely expressed choice, choose their own form of government.

Our basic policy in the Far East is to encourage the development of a strong, independent, united, and democratic China. That has been the traditional policy of the United States.

At Moscow the United States, the Union of Soviet Socialist Republics, and Great Britain agreed to further this development by supporting the efforts of the national government and nongovernmental Chinese political elements in bringing about cessation of civil strife and in broadening the basis of representation in the Government. That is the policy which General Marshall is so ably executing today.

It is the purpose of the Government of the United States to proceed as rapidly as is practicable toward the restoration of the sovereignty of Korea and the establishment of a democratic government by the free choice of the people of Korea.

At the threshold of every problem which confronts us today in international affairs is the appalling devastation, hunger, sickness, and pervasive human misery that mark so many areas of the world.

By joining and participating in the work of the United Nations Relief and Rehabilitation Administration the United States has directly recognized and assumed an obligation to give such relief assistance as is practicable to millions of innocent and helpless victims of the war. The Congress has earned the gratitude of the world by generous financial contributions to the United Nations Relief and Rehabilitation Administration.

We have taken the lead, modest though it is, in facilitating under our existing immigration quotas the admission to the United States of refugees and displaced persons from Europe.

We have joined with Great Britain in the organization of a commission to study the problem of Palestine. The Commission is already at work and its recommendations will be made at an early date.

The members of the United Nations have paid us the high compliment of choosing the United States as the site of the United Nations headquarters. We shall be host in spirit as well as in fact, for nowhere does there abide a fiercer determination that this peace shall live than in the hearts of the American people.

It is the hope of all Americans that in time future historians will speak not of World War I and World War II, but of the first and last world wars.

2. FOREIGN ECONOMIC POLICY

The foreign economic policy of the United States is designed to promote our own prosperity, and at the same time to aid in the restoration and expansion of world markets and to contribute thereby to world peace and world security. We shall continue our efforts to provide relief from the devastation of war, to alleviate the sufferings of displaced persons, to assist in reconstruction and development, and to promote the expansion of world trade.

We have already joined the International Monetary Fund and the International Bank for Reconstruction and Development. We have expanded the Export-Import Bank and provided it with additional capital. The Congress has renewed the Trade Agreements Act which provides the necessary framework within which to negotiate a reduction of trade barriers on a reciprocal basis. It has given our support to the United Nations Relief and Rehabilitation Administration.

In accordance with the intentions of the Congress, lend-lease, except as to continuing military lend-lease in China, was terminated upon the surrender of Japan. The first of the lend-lease settlement agreements has been completed with the United Kingdom. Negotiations with other lend-lease countries are in progress. In negotiating these agreements, we intend to seek settlements which will not encumber world trade through war debts of a character that proved to be so detrimental to the stability of the world economy after the last war.

We have taken steps to dispose of the goods which on VJ-day were in the lend-lease pipe line to the various lend-lease countries and to allow them long-term credit for the purpose where necessary. We are also making arrangements under which those countries may use the lend-lease inventories in their possession and acquire surplus property abroad to assist in their economic rehabilitation and reconstruction. These goods will be accounted for at fair values.

The proposed loan to the United Kingdom, which I shall recommend to the Congress in a separate message, will contribute to easing the transition problem of one of our major partners in the war. It will enable the whole sterling area and other countries affiliated with it to resume trade on a multilateral basis. Extension of this credit will enable the United Kingdom to avoid discriminatory trade arrangements of the type which destroyed freedom of trade during the 1930's. I consider the progress toward multilateral trade which will be achieved by this agreement to be in itself sufficient warrant for the credit.

The view of this Government is that, in the longer run, our economic prosperity and the prosperity of the whole world are best served by the elimination of artificial barriers to international trade, whether in the form of unreasonable tariffs or tariff preferences or commercial quotas or embargoes or the restrictive practices of cartels.

The United States Government has issued proposals for the expansion of world trade and employment to which the Government of the United Kingdom has given its support on every important issue. These proposals are intended to form the basis for a trade and employment conference to be held in the middle of this year. If that conference is a success, I feel confident that the way will have been adequately prepared for an expanded and prosperous world trade.

We shall also continue negotiations looking to the full and equitable development of facilities for transportation and communications among nations.

The vast majority of the nations of the world have chosen to work together to achieve, on a cooperative basis, world security and world prosperity. The effort cannot succeed without full cooperation of the United States. To play our part, we must not only resolutely carry out the foreign policies we have adopted but also follow a domestic policy which will maintain full production and employment in the United States. A serious depression here can disrupt the whole fabric of the world economy.

3. OCCUPIED COUNTRIES

The major tasks of our Military Establishment in Europe following VE-day, and in the Pacific since the surrender of Japan, have been those of occupation and military government. In addition we have given much-needed aid to the peoples of the liberated countries.

The end of the war in Europe found Germany in a chaotic condition. Organized government had ceased to exist, transportation systems had been wrecked, cities and industrial facilities had been bombed into ruins. In addition to the tasks of occupation we had to assume all of the functions of government. Great progress has been made in the repatriation of displaced persons and of prisoners of war. Of the total of 3,500,000 displaced persons found in the United States zone only 460,000 now remain.

The extensive complications involved by the requirement of dealing with three other governments engaged in occupation and with the governments of liberated countries require intensive work and energetic cooperation. The influx of some 2 million German refugees into our zone of occupation is a pressing problem, making exacting demands upon an already overstrained internal economy.

Improvements in the European economy during 1945 have made it possible for our military authorities to relinquish to the governments of all liberated areas, or to the United Nations Relief and Rehabilitation Administration, the responsibility for the provision of food and other civilian relief supplies. The Army's responsibilities in Europe extend now only to our zones of occupation in Germany and Austria and to two small areas in northern Italy.

By contrast with Germany, in Japan we have occupied a country still possessing an organized and operating governmental system. Although severely damaged, the Japanese industrial and transportation systems have been able to insure at least a survival existence for the population. The repatriation of Japanese military and civilian personnel from overseas is proceeding as rapidly as shipping and other means permit.

In order to insure that neither Germany nor Japan will again be in a position to wage aggressive warfare, the armament-making potential of these countries is being dismantled and fundamental changes in their social and political structures are being effected. Democratic systems are being fostered to the end that the voice of the common man may be heard in the councils of his government.

For the first time in history the legal culpability of war makers is being determined. The trials now in progress in Nürnberg—and those soon to begin in Tokyo—bring before the bar of international justice those individuals who are charged with the responsibility for the sufferings of the past six years. We have high hope that this public portrayal of the guilt of these evildoers will bring wholesale and permanent revulsion on the part of the masses of our former enemies against war, militarism, aggression, and notions of race superiority.

4. DEMOBILIZATION OF OUR ARMED FORCES

The cessation of active campaigning does not mean that we can completely disband our fighting forces. For their sake and for the sake of their loved ones at home, I wish that we could. But we still have the task of clinching the victories we have won—of making certain that Germany and Japan can never again wage aggressive warfare, that they will not again have the means to bring on another world war. The performance of that task requires that, together with our allies, we occupy the hostile areas, complete the disarmament of our enemies, and take the necessary measures to see to it that they do not rearm.

As quickly as possible, we are bringing about the reduction of our armed services to the size required for these tasks of occupation and disarmament. The Army and the Navy are following both length-of-service and point systems as far as possible in releasing men and women from the service. The points are based chiefly on length and character of service, and on the existence of dependents.

Over 5 million from the Army have already passed through the separation centers.

The Navy, including the Marine Corps and the Coast Guard, has discharged over one and a half million.

Of the 12 million men and women serving in the Army and Navy at the time of the surrender of Germany, one-half have already been released. The greater part of these had to be brought back to this country from distant parts of the world

Of course there are cases of individual hardship in retention of personnel in the service. There will be in the future. No system of such size can operate to perfection. But the systems are founded on fairness and justice, and they are working at full speed. We shall try to avoid mistakes, injustices, and hardship—as far as humanly possible.

We have already reached the point where shipping is no longer the bottleneck in the return of troops from the European theater. The governing factor now has become the requirement for troops in sufficient strength to carry out their missions.

In a few months the same situation will exist in the Pacific. By the end of June, 9 out of 10 who were serving in the armed forces on VE-day will have been released. Demobilization will continue thereafter, but at a slower rate, determined by our military responsibilities.

Our national safety and the security of the world will require substantial armed forces, particularly in overseas service. At the same time it is imperative that we relieve those who have already done their duty, and that we relieve them as fast as we can. To do that, the Army and the Navy are conducting recruiting drives with considerable success.

The Army has obtained nearly 400,000 volunteers in the past four months, and the Navy has obtained 80,000. Eighty percent of these volunteers for the regular service have come from those already with the colors. The Congress has made it possible to offer valuable inducements to those who are eligible for enlistment. Every effort will be made to enlist the required number of young men.

The War and Navy Departments now estimate that by a year from now we still will need a strength of about 2 million, including officers, for the armed forces—Army, Navy, and Air. I have reviewed their estimates and believe that the safety of the Nation will require the maintenance of an armed strength of this size for the calendar year that is before us.

In case the campaign for volunteers does not produce that number, it will be necessary by additional legislation to extend the Selective Service Act beyond May 16, the date of expiration under existing law. That is the only way we can get the men and bring back our veterans. There is no other way. Action along this line should not be postponed beyond March, in order to avoid uncertainty and disruption.

Domestic Affairs

1. The Economic Outlook

Prophets of doom predicted that the United States could not escape a runaway inflation during the war and an economic collapse after the war. These predictions have not been borne out. On the contrary, the record of economic stabilization during the war and during the period of reconversion has been an outstanding accomplishment.

We know, however, that nothing is as dangerous as overconfidence, in war or in peace. We have had to fight hard to hold the line We have made strenuous efforts to speed reconversion. But neither the danger of a postwar inflation nor of a subsequent collapse in production and employment is yet overcome. We must base our policies not on unreasoning optimism or pessimism but upon a candid recognition of our objectives and upon a careful analysis of foreseeable trends.

Any precise appraisal of the economic outlook at this time is particularly difficult. The period of demobilization and reconversion is fraught with uncertainties. There are also serious gaps in our statistical information. Certain tendencies are, however, fairly clear and recognition of them should serve as background for the consideration of next year's Federal Program. In general, the outlook for business is good, and it is likely to continue to be good—provided we control inflation and achieve peace in management-labor relations.

Civilian production and employment can be expected to increase throughout the next year. This does not mean, however, that continuing full employment is assured. It is probable that demobilization of the armed forces will proceed faster than the increase in civilian employment opportunities. Even if substantial further withdrawals from the labor market occur, unemployment will increase temporarily. The extent to which this unemployment will persist depends largely on the speed of industrial expansion and the effectiveness of the policies of the Federal Government.

Along with extraordinary demand there are still at this time many critical shortages resulting from the war. These extraordinary demands and shortages may lead to a speculative boom, especially in the price of securities, real estate, and inventories.

Therefore, our chief worry still is inflation.

While we control this inflationary pressure we must look forward to the time when this extraordinary demand will subside. It will be years before we catch up with the demand for housing. The extraordinary demand for other durable goods, for the replenishment of inventories, and for exports may be satisfied earlier. No backlog of demand can exist very long in the face of our tremendous productive capacity. We must expect again to face the problem of shrinking demand and consequent slackening in sales, production, and employment. This possibility of a deflationary spiral in the future will exist unless we now plan and adopt an effective full employment program.

2. GENERAL POLICIES—IMMEDIATE AND LONG-RANGE

During the war, production for civilian use was limited by war needs and available manpower. Economic stabilization required measures to spread limited supplies equitably by rationing, price controls, increased taxes, savings bond campaigns, and credit controls. Now, with the surrender of our enemies, economic stabilization requires that policies be directed toward promoting an increase in supplies at low unit prices.

We must encourage the development of resources and enterprises in all parts of the country, particularly in underdeveloped areas. For example, the establishment of new peacetime industries in the Western States and in the South would, in my judgment, add to existing production and markets rather than merely bring about a shifting of production. I am asking the Secretaries of Agriculture, Commerce, and Labor to explore jointly methods for stimulating new industries, particularly in areas with surplus agricultural labor.

We must also aid small businessmen and particularly veterans who are competent to start their own businesses. The establishment and development of efficient small business ventures, I believe, will not take away from, but rather will add to, the total business of all enterprises.

Even with maximum encouragement of production, we cannot hope to remove scarcities within a short time. The most serious deficiencies will persist in the fields of residential housing, building materials, and consumers' durable goods. The critical situation makes continued rent control, price control, and priorities, allocations, and inventory controls absolutely essential. Continued control of consumer credit will help to reduce the pressure on prices of durable goods and will also prolong the period during which the backlog demand will be effective.

While we are meeting these immediate needs we must look forward to a long-range program of security and increased standard of living.

The best protection of purchasing power is a policy of full production and full employment opportunities. Obviously, an employed worker is a better customer than an unemployed worker. There always will be, however, some frictional unemployment. In the present period of transition we must deal with such temporary unemployment as results from the fact that demobilization will proceed faster than reconversion or industrial expansion. Such temporary unemployment is probably unavoidable in a period of rapid change. The unemployed worker is a victim of conditions beyond his control. He should be enabled to maintain a reasonable standard of living for himself and his family.

The most serious difficulty in the path of reconversion and expansion is the establishment of a fair wage structure.

The ability of labor and management to work together, and the wage and price policies which they develop, are social and economic issues of first importance.

Both labor and management have a special interest. Labor's interest is very direct and personal because working conditions, wages, and prices affect the very life and happiness of the worker and his family.

Management has a no less direct interest because on management rests the responsibility for conducting a growing and prosperous business.

But management and labor have identical interests in the long run. Good wages mean good markets. Good business means more jobs and better wages. In this age of cooperation and in our highly organized economy the problems of one very soon become the problems of all.

Better human relationships are an urgent need to which organized labor and management should address themselves. No government policy can make men understand each other, agree, and get along unless they conduct themselves in a way to foster mutual respect and good will.

The Government can, however, help to develop machinery which, with the backing of public opinion, will assist labor and management to resolve their disagreements in a peaceful manner and reduce the number and duration of strikes.

All of us realize that productivity—increased output per man—is in the long run the basis of our standard of living. Management especially must realize that if labor is to work wholeheartedly for an increase in production, workers must be given a just share of increased output in higher wages.

Most industries and most companies have adequate leeway within which to grant substantial wage increases. These increases will have a direct effect in increasing consumer demand to the high levels needed. Substantial wage increases are good business for business because they assure a large market for their products; substantial wage increases are good business for labor because they increase labor's standard of living; substantial wage increases are good business for the country as a whole because capacity production means an active, healthy, friendly citizenry enjoying the benefits of democracy under our free enterprise system.

Labor and management in many industries have been operating successfully under the Government's wage-price policy. Upward revisions of wage scales have been made in thousands of establishments throughout the Nation since VJ-day. It is estimated that about 6 million workers, or more than 20 percent of all employees in nonagricultural and nongovernmental establishments, have received wage increases since August 18, 1945. The amounts of increases given by individual employers concentrate between 10 and 15 percent, but range from less than 5 percent to over 30 percent.

The United States Conciliation Service since VJ-day has settled over 3,000 disputes affecting over 1,300,000 workers without a strike threat and has assisted in settling about 1,300 disputes where strikes were threatened which involved about 500,000 workers. Only workers directly involved, and not those in related industries who might have been indirectly affected, are included in these estimates.

Many of these adjustments have occurred in key industries and would have seemed to us major crises if they had not been settled peaceably.

Within the framework of the wage-price policy there has been definite success, and it is to be expected that this success will continue in a vast majority of the cases arising in the months ahead.

However, everyone who realizes the extreme need for a swift and orderly reconversion must feel a deep concern about the number of major strikes now in progress. If long continued, these strikes could put a heavy brake on our program.

I have already made recommendations to the Congress as to the procedure best adapted to meeting the threat of work stoppages in Nation-wide industries without sacrificing the fundamental rights of labor to bargain collectively and ultimately to strike in support of their position.

If we manage our economy properly, the future will see us on a level of production half again as high as anything we have ever accomplished in peacetime. Business can in the future pay higher wages and sell for lower prices than ever before. This is not true now for all companies, nor will it ever be true for all, but for business generally it is true.

We are relying on all concerned to develop, through collective bargaining, wage structures that are fair to labor, allow for necessary business incentives, and conform with a policy designed to "hold the line" on prices.

Production and more production was the byword during the war and still is during the transition from war to peace. However, when deferred demand slackens, we shall once again face the deflationary dangers which beset this and other countries during the 1930's. Prosperity can be assured only by a high level of demand supported by high current income; it cannot be sustained by deferred needs and use of accumulated savings.

If we take the right steps in time we can certainly avoid the disastrous excesses of runaway booms and headlong depressions. We must not let a year or two of prosperity lull us into a false feeling of security and a repetition of the mistakes of the 1920's that culminated in the crash of 1929.

During the year ahead the Government will be called upon to act in many important fields of economic policy from taxation and foreign trade to social security and housing. In every case there will be alternatives. We must choose the alternatives which will best measure up to our need for maintaining production and employment in the future. We must never lose sight of our long-term objectives: the broadening of markets—the maintenance of steadily rising demand. This demand can come from only three sources: consumers, businesses, or government.

In this country the job of production and distribution is in the hands of businessmen, farmers, workers, and professional people—in the hands of our citizens. We want to keep it that way. However, it is the Government's responsibility to help business, labor, and farmers do their jobs.

There is no question in my mind that the Government, acting on behalf of all the people, must assume the ultimate responsibility for the economic health of the Nation. There is no other agency that can. No other organization has the scope or the authority, nor is any other agency accountable, to all the people. This does not mean that the Government has the sole responsibility, nor that it can do the job alone, nor that it can do the job directly.

All the policies of the Federal Government must be geared to the objective of sustained full production and full employment—to raise consumer purchasing power and to encourage business investment. The programs we adopt this year and from now on will determine our ability to achieve our objectives. We must continue to pay particular attention to our fiscal, monetary, and tax policy, programs to aid business—especially small business—and transportation, labor-management relations and wage-price policy, social security and health, education, the farm program, public works, housing and resource development, and economic foreign policy.

For example, the kinds of tax measures we have at different times—whether we raise our revenue in a way to encourage consumer spending and business investment or to discourage it—have a vital bearing on this question. It is affected also by regulations on consumer credit and by the money market, which is strongly influenced by the rate of interest on Government securities. It is affected by almost every step we take.

In short, the way we handle the proper functions of government, the way we time the exercise of our traditional and legitimate governmental functions, has a vital bearing on the economic health of the Nation.

These policies are discussed in greater detail in the accompanying Fifth Quarterly Report of the Director of War Mobilization and Reconversion.

3. LEGISLATION HERETOFORE RECOMMENDED AND STILL PENDING

To attain some of these objectives and to meet the other needs of the United States in the reconversion and postwar period, I have from time to time made various recommendations to the Congress.

In making these recommendations I have indicated the reasons why I deemed them essential for progress at home and abroad. A few—a very few—of these recommendations have been enacted into law by the Congress. Most of them have not. I here reiterate some of them, and discuss others later in this Message. I urge upon the Congress early consideration of them. Some are more urgent than others, but all are necessary.

(1) Legislation to authorize the President to create **fact-finding boards** for the prevention of stoppages of work in Nation-wide industries after collective bargaining and conciliation and voluntary arbitration have failed—as recommended by me on December 3, 1945.

(2) Enactment of a satisfactory **full employment bill** such as the Senate bill now in conference between the Senate and the House—as recommended by me on September 6, 1945.

(3) Legislation to supplement the **unemployment insurance benefits** for unemployed workers now provided by the different States—as recommended by me on May 28, 1945.

(4) Adoption of a **permanent Fair Employment Practice Act**—as recommended by me on September 6, 1945.

(5) Legislation substantially raising the amount of **minimum wages** now provided by law—as recommended by me on September 6, 1945.

(6) Legislation providing for a comprehensive program for **scientific research**—as recommended by me on September 6, 1945.

(7) Legislation enacting a **health and medical care program**—as recommended by me on November 19, 1945.

(8) Legislation adopting the program of **universal training**—as recommended by me on October 23, 1945.

(9) Legislation providing an **adequate salary scale for all Government employees** in all branches of the Government—as recommended by me on September 6, 1945.

(10) Legislation making provision for **succession to the Presidency** in the event of the death or incapacity or disqualification of the President and Vice President—as recommended by me on June 19, 1945.

(11) Legislation for the **unification of the armed services**—as recommended by me on December 19, 1945.

(12) Legislation for the **domestic use and control of atomic energy**—as recommended by me on October 3, 1945.

(13) **Retention of the United States Employment Service** in the Federal Government for a period at least up to June 30, 1947—as recommended by me on September 6, 1945.

(14) **Legislation to increase unemployment allowances for veterans** in line with increases for civilians—as recommended by me on September 6, 1945.

(15) **Social security coverage for veterans** for their period of military service—as recommended by me on September 6, 1945.

(16) **Extension of crop insurance**—as recommended by me on September 6, 1945:

(17) Legislation permitting the **sale of ships** by the Maritime Commission at home and abroad—as recommended by me on September 6, 1945. I further recommend that this legislation include adequate authority for chartering vessels both here and abroad.

(18) Legislation to take care of the **stock piling of materials** in which the United States is naturally deficient—as recommended by me on September 6, 1945.

(19) Enactment of **Federal airport legislation**—as recommended by me on September 6, 1945.

(20) Legislation **repealing the Johnson Act** on foreign loans—as recommended by me on September 6, 1945.

(21) Legislation for the **development of the Great Lakes-St. Lawrence River Basin**—as recommended by me on October 3, 1945.

4. POLICIES IN SPECIFIC FIELDS

(a) *Extension of Price Control Act*

Today inflation is our greatest immediate domestic problem. So far the fight against inflation has been waged successfully. Since May 1943, following President Roosevelt's "hold the line" order and in the face of the greatest pressures which this country has ever seen, the cost of living index has risen only three percent. Wholesale prices in this same period have been held to an increase of two and one-half percent.

This record has been made possible by the vigorous efforts of the agencies responsible for this program. But their efforts would have been fruitless if they had not had the solid support of the great masses of our people. The Congress is to be congratulated for its role in providing the legislation under which this work has been carried out.

On VJ-day it was clear to all thinking people that the danger of inflation was by no means over. Many of us can remember vividly our disastrous experience following World War I. Then the very restricted wartime controls were lifted too quickly, and as a result prices and rents moved more rapidly upward. In the year and a half following the armistice, rents, food, and clothing shot to higher and still higher levels.

When the inevitable crash occurred less than two years after the end of the war, business bankruptcies were widespread. Profits were wiped out. Inventory losses amounted to billions of dollars. Farm income dropped by one-half. Factory pay rolls dropped 40 percent, and nearly one-fifth of all our industrial workers were walking the streets in search of jobs. This was a grim greeting, indeed, to offer our veterans who had just returned from overseas.

When I addressed the Congress in September, I emphasized that we must continue to hold the price line until the production of goods caught up with the tremendous demands. Since then we have seen demonstrated the strength of the inflationary pressures which we have to face.

Retail sales in the closing months of 1945 ran 12 percent above the previous peak for that season, which came in 1944. Prices throughout the entire economy have been pressing hard against the price ceilings. The prices of real estate, which cannot now be controlled under the law, are rising rapidly. Commercial rents are not included in the present price control law and, where they are not controlled by State law, have been increasing, causing difficulties to many businessmen.

It will be impossible to maintain a high purchasing power or an expanding production unless we can keep prices at levels which can be met by the vast majority of our people. Full production is the greatest weapon against inflation, but until we can produce enough goods to meet the threat of inflation the Government will have to exercise its wartime control over prices.

I am sure that the people of the United States are disturbed by the demands made by several business groups with regard to price and rent control.

I am particularly disturbed at the effect such thinking may have on production and employment. If manufacturers continue to hold back goods and decline to submit bids when invited—as I am informed some are doing—in anticipation of higher prices which would follow the end of price controls, we shall inevitably slow down production and create needless unemployment. On the other hand, there are the vast majority of American businessmen who are not holding back goods, but who need certainty about the Government pricing policy in order to fix their own long-range pricing policies.

Businessmen are entitled therefore to a clear statement of the policy of the Government on the subject. Tenants and housewives, farmers and workers—consumers in general—have an equal right.

We are all anxious to eliminate unnecessary controls just as rapidly as we can do so. The steps that we have already taken in many directions toward that end are a clear indication of our policy.

The present Price Control Act expires on June 30, 1946. If we expect to maintain a steady economy we shall have to maintain price and rent control for many months to come. The inflationary pressures on prices and rents, with relatively few exceptions, are now at an all-time peak. Unless the Price Control Act is renewed there will be no limit to which our price levels would soar. Our country would face a national disaster.

We cannot wait to renew the act until immediately before it expires. Inflation results from psychological as well as economic conditions. The country has a clear right to know where the Congress stands on this all-important problem. Any uncertainty now as to whether the act will be extended gives rise to price speculation, to withholding of goods from the market in anticipation of rising prices, and to delays in achieving maximum production.

I do not doubt that the Congress will be beset by many groups who will urge that the legislation that I have proposed should either be eliminated or modified to the point where it is nearly useless. The Congress has a clear responsibility to meet this challenge with courage and determination. I have every confidence that it will do so.

I strongly urge that the Congress now resolve all doubts and as soon as possible adopt legislation continuing rent and price control in effect for a full year from June 30, 1946.

(b) *Food subsidies*

If the price line is to be held, if our people are to be protected against the inflationary dangers which confront us, we must do more than extend the Price Control Act. In September we were hopeful that the inflationary pressures would by this time have begun to diminish. We were particularly hopeful on food. Indeed, it was estimated that food prices at retail would drop from 3 to 5 percent in the first six months following the end of the war.

In anticipation of this decline in food prices, it was our belief that food subsidies could be removed gradually during the winter and spring months, and eliminated almost completely by June 30 of this year. It was our feeling that the food subsidies could be dropped without an increase to the consumer in the present level of food prices or in the over-all cost of living.

As matters stand today, however, food prices are pressing hard against the ceilings. The expected decline in food prices has not occurred, nor is it likely to occur for many months to come. This brings me to the reluctant conclusion that food subsidies must be continued beyond June 30, 1946.

If we fail to take this necessary step, meat prices on July 1 will be from 3 to 5 cents higher than their average present levels; butter will be at least 12 cents a pound higher, in addition to the 5 cents a pound increase of last fall; milk will increase from 1 to 2 cents a quart; bread will increase about 1 cent a loaf; sugar will increase over 1 cent a pound; cheese, in addition to the increase of 4 cents now planned for the latter part of this month, will go up an additional 8 cents. In terms of percentages we may find the cost-of-living index for food increased by more than 8 percent, which in turn would result in more than a 3-percent increase in the cost of living.

If prices of food were allowed to increase by these amounts, I must make it clear to the Congress that, in my opinion, it would become extremely difficult for us to control the forces of inflation.

None of us likes subsidies. Our farmers, in particular, have always been opposed to them.

But I believe our farmers are as deeply conscious as any group in the land of the havoc which inflation can create. Certainly in the past eighteen months there has been no group which has fought any harder in support of the Government's price control program. I am confident that, if the facts are placed before them and if they see clearly the evils between which we are forced to choose, they will understand the reasons why subsidies must be continued.

The legislation continuing the use of food subsidies into the new fiscal year should be tied down specifically to certain standards. A very proper requirement, in my opinion, would be that subsidies be removed as soon as it is indicated that the cost of living will decline below the present levels.

(c) Extension of War Powers Act

The Second War Powers Act has recently been extended by the Congress for six months instead of for a year. It will now expire, unless further extended, on June 30, 1946. This act is the basis for priority and inventory controls governing the use of scarce materials, as well as for other powers essential to orderly reconversion.

I think that this Administration has given adequate proof of the fact that it desires to eliminate wartime controls as quickly and as expeditiously as possible. However, we know that there will continue to be shortages of certain materials caused by the war even after June 30, 1946. It is important that businessmen know now that materials in short supply are going to be controlled and distributed fairly as long as these war-born shortages continue.

I, therefore, urge the Congress soon to extend the Second War Powers Act. We cannot afford to wait until just before the act expires next June. To wait would cause the controls to break down in a short time, and would hamper our production and employment program.

(d) Small business and competition

A rising birth rate for small business, and a favorable environment for its growth, are not only economic necessities but also important practical demonstrations of opportunity in a democratic free society. A great many veterans and workers with new skills and experience will want to start in for themselves. The opportunity must be afforded them to do so. They are the small businessmen of the future.

Actually when we talk about small business we are talking about almost all of the Nation's individual businesses. Nine out of every ten concerns fall into this category, and 45 percent of all workers are employed by them. Between 30 and 40 percent of the total value of all business transactions are handled by small business.

It is obvious national policy to foster the sound development of small business. It helps to maintain high levels of employment and national income and consumption of the goods and services that the Nation can produce. It encourages the competition that keeps our free enterprise economy vigorous and expanding. Small business, because of its flexibility, assists in the rapid exploitation of scientific and technological discoveries. Investment in small business can absorb a large volume of savings that might otherwise not be tapped.

The Government should encourage and is encouraging small-business initiative and originality to stimulate progress through competition.

During the war, the Smaller War Plants Corporation assisted small concerns to make a maximum contribution to victory. The work of the Smaller War Plants Corporation is being carried on in peacetime by the Federal Loan Agency and the Department of Commerce. The fundamental approach to the job of encouraging small concerns must be based on:

1. Arrangements for making private and public financial resources available on reasonable terms.

2. Provision of technical advice and assistance to business as a whole on production, research, and management problems. This will help equalize competitive relationships between large and small companies, for many of the small companies cannot afford expensive technical research, accounting, and tax advice.

3. Elimination of trade practices and agreements which reduce competition and discriminate against new or small enterprises.

We speak a great deal about the free enterprise economy of our country. It is competition that keeps it free. It is competition that keeps it growing and developing. The truth is that we need far more competition in the future than we have had in the immediate past.

By strangling competition, monopolistic activity prevents or deters investment in new or expanded production facilities. This lessens the opportunity for employment and chokes off new outlets for idle savings. Monopoly maintains prices at artificially high levels and reduces consumption which, with lower prices, would rise and support larger production and higher employment. Monopoly, not being subject to competitive pressure, is slow to take advantage of technical advances which would lower prices or improve quality. All three of these monopolistic activities very directly lower the standard of living—through higher prices and lower quality of product—which free competition would improve.

The Federal Government must protect legitimate business and consumers from predatory and monopolistic practices by the vigilant enforcement of regulatory legislation. The program will be designed to have a maximum impact upon monopolistic bottlenecks and unfair competitive practices hindering expansion in employment.

During the war, enforcement of antimonopoly laws was suspended in a number of fields. The Government must now take major steps not only to maintain enforcement of antitrust laws but to encourage new and competing enterprises in every way. The deferred demand of the war years and the large accumulations of liquid assets provide ample incentive for expansion. Equalizing of business opportunity, under full and free competition, must be a prime responsibility in the reconversion period and in the years that follow. Many leading businessmen have recognized the importance of such action both to themselves and to the economy as a whole.

But we must do more than break up trusts and monopolies after they have begun to strangle competition. We must take positive action to foster new, expanding enterprises. By legislation and by administration we must take specific steps to discourage the formation or the strengthening of competition-restricting business. We must have an over-all antimonopoly policy which can be applied by all agencies of the Government in exercising the functions assigned to them—a policy designed to encourage the formation and growth of new and freely competitive enterprises.

Among the many departments and agencies which have parts in the program affecting business and competition, the Department of Commerce has a particularly important role. That is why I have recommended a substantial increase in appropriations for the next fiscal year for this Department.

In its assistance to industry, the Department of Commerce will concentrate its efforts on these primary objectives: Promotion of a large and well-balanced foreign trade; provision of improved technical assistance and management aids, especially for small enterprises; and strengthening of basic statistics on business operations, both by industries and by regions. To make new inventions and discoveries available more promptly to all businesses, small and large, the Department proposes to expand its own research activities, promote research by universities, improve Patent Office procedures, and develop a greatly expanded system of field offices readily accessible to the businesses they serve.

Many gaps exist in the private financial mechanism, especially in the provision of long-term funds for small- and medium-sized enterprises. In the peacetime economy the Reconstruction Finance Corporation will take the leadership in assuring adequate financing for small enterprises which cannot secure funds from other sources. Most of the funds should and will be provided by private lenders; but the Reconstruction Finance Corporation will share any unusual risks through guarantees of private loans, with direct loans only when private capital is unwilling to participate on a reasonable basis.

(*e*) *Minimum wage*

Full employment and full production may be achieved only by maintaining a level of consumer income far higher than that of the prewar period. A high level of consumer income will maintain the market for the output of our mills, farms, and factories, which we have demonstrated during the war years that we can produce. One of the basic steps which the Congress can take to establish a high level of consumer income is to amend the Fair Labor Standards Act to raise substandard wages to a decent minimum and to extend similar protection to additional workers who are not covered by the present act.

Substandard wages are bad for business and for the farmer. Substandard wages provide only a substandard market for the goods and services produced by American industry and agriculture.

At the present time the Fair Labor Standards Act prescribes a minimum wage of 40 cents an hour for those workers who are covered by the act. The present minimum wage represents an annual income of about $800 to those continuously employed for 50 weeks—clearly a wholly inadequate budget for an American family. I am in full accord with the proposal now pending in the Congress that the statutory minimum be raised immediately to 65 cents an hour, with further increases to 70 cents after one year and to 75 cents after two years. I also favor the proposal that the industry committee procedure be used to set rates higher than 65 cents per hour during the two-year interval before the 75-cent basic wage would otherwise become applicable.

The proposed minimum wage of 65 cents an hour would assure the worker an annual income of about $1,300 a year in steady employment. This amount is clearly a modest goal. After considering cost-of-living increases in recent years, it is little more than a 10-cent increase over the present legal minimum. In fact, if any large number of workers earn less than this amount, we will find it impossible to maintain the levels of purchasing power needed to sustain the stable prosperity which we desire. Raising the minimum to 75 cents an hour will provide the wage earner with an annual income of $1,500 if he is fully employed.

The proposed higher minimum wage levels are feasible without involving serious price adjustments or serious geographic dislocations.

Today about 20 percent of our manufacturing wage earners—or about 2 million—earn less than 65 cents an hour. Because wages in most industries have risen during the war, this is about the same as the proportion—17 percent— who were earning less than 40 cents an hour in 1941.

I also recommend that minimum wage protection be extended to several groups of workers not now covered. The need for a decent standard of living is by no means limited to those workers who happen to be covered by the act as it now stands. It is particularly vital at this period of readjustment in the national economy and readjustment in employment of labor to extend minimum wage protection as far as possible.

Lifting the basic minimum wage is necessary, it is justified as a matter of simple equity to workers, and it will prove not only feasible but also directly beneficial to the Nation's employers.

(*f*) *Agricultural programs*

The farmers of America generally are entering the crop year of 1946 in better financial condition than ever before. Farm mortgage debt is the lowest in 30 years. Farmers' savings are the largest in history. Our agricultural plant is in much better condition than after World War I. Farm machinery and supplies are expected to be available in larger volume, and farm labor problems will be less acute.

The demand for farm products will continue strong during the next year or two because domestic purchases will be supplemented by a high level of exports and foreign relief shipments. It is currently estimated that from 7 to 10 percent of the total United States food supply may be exported in the calendar year 1946.

Farm prices are expected to remain at least at their present levels in the immediate future, and for at least the next 12 months they are expected to yield a net farm income double the 1935–39 average and higher than in any year prior to 1943.

We can look to the future of agriculture with greater confidence than in many a year in the past. Agriculture itself is moving confidently ahead, planning for another year of big production, taking definite and positive steps to lead the way toward an economy of abundance.

Agricultural production goals for 1946 call for somewhat greater acreage than actually was planted in 1945. Agriculture is prepared to demonstrate that it can make a peacetime contribution as great as its contribution toward the winning of the war.

In spite of supplying our armed forces and our allies during the war with a fifth to a fourth of our total food output, farmers were still able to provide our civilians with 8 percent more food per capita than the average for the five years preceding the war. Since the surrender of Japan, civilian food consumption has risen still further. By the end of 1945 the amount of the increase in food consumption was estimated to be as high as 15 percent over the prewar average. The record shows that the people of this country want and need more food and that they will buy more food if only they have the jobs and the purchasing power. The first essential therefore in providing fully for the welfare of agriculture is to maintain full employment and a high level of purchasing power throughout the Nation.

For the period immediately ahead we shall still have the problem of supplying enough food. If we are to do our part in aiding the war-stricken and starving countries some of the food desires of our own people will not be completely satisfied, at least until these nations have had an opportunity to harvest another crop. During the next few months the need for food in the world will be more serious than at any time during the war. And, despite the large shipments we have already made, and despite what we shall send, there remain great needs abroad.

Beyond the relief feeding period, there will still be substantial foreign outlets for our farm commodities. The chief dependence of the farmer, however, as always, must be upon the buying power of our own people.

The first obligation of the Government to agriculture for the reconversion period is to make good on its price-support commitments. This we intend to do, with realistic consideration for the sound patterns of production that will contribute most to the long-time welfare of agriculture and the whole Nation. The period during which prices are supported will provide an opportunity for farmers individually to strengthen their position in changing over from a wartime to a peacetime basis of production. It will provide an opportunity for the Congress to review the needs of agriculture and make changes in national legislation where experience has shown changes to be needed. In this connection, the Congress will wish to consider legislation to take the place of the 1937 Sugar Act which expires at the end of this year. During this period we must do a thorough job of basic planning to the end that agriculture shall be able to contribute its full share toward a healthy national economy.

Our long-range agricultural policies should have two main objectives: First, to assure the people on the farms a fair share of the national income; and, second, to encourage an agricultural production pattern that is best fitted to the Nation's needs. To accomplish this second objective we shall have to take into consideration changes that have taken place and will continue to take place in the production of farm commodities—changes that affect costs and efficiency and volume.

What we seek ultimately is a high level of food production and consumption that will provide good nutrition for everyone. This cannot be accomplished by agriculture alone. We can be certain of our capacity to produce food, but we have often failed to distribute it as well as we should and to see that our people can afford to buy it. The way to get good nutrition for the whole Nation is to provide employment opportunities and purchasing power for all groups that will enable them to buy full diets at market prices.

Wherever purchasing power fails to reach this level we should see that they have some means of getting adequate food at prices in line with their ability to buy. Therefore, we should have available supplementary programs that will enable all our people to have enough of the right kind of food.

For example, one of the best possible contributions toward building a stronger, healthier Nation would be a permanent school-lunch program on a scale adequate to assure every school child a good lunch at noon. The Congress, of course, has recognized this need for a continuing school-lunch program and legislation to that effect has been introduced and hearings held. The plan contemplates the attainment of this objective with a minimum of Federal expenditures. I hope that the legislation will be enacted in time for a permanent program to start with the beginning of the school year next fall.

We have the technical knowledge and the productive capacity to provide plenty of good food for every man, woman, and child in the United States. It is time we made that possibility a reality.

(*g*) *Resource development*

The strength of our Nation and the welfare of the people rest upon the natural resources of the country. We have learned that proper conservation of our lands, including our forests and minerals, and wise management of our waters will add immensely to our national wealth.

The first step in the Government's conservation program must be to find out just what are our basic resources, and how they should be used. We need to take, as soon as possible, an inventory of the lands, the minerals, and the forests of the Nation.

During the war it was necessary to curtail some of our long-range plans for development of our natural resources, and to emphasize programs vital to the prosecution of the war. Work was suspended on a number of flood control and reclamation projects and on the development of our national forests and parks. This work must now be resumed, and new projects must be undertaken to provide essential services and to assist in the process of economic development.

The rivers of America offer a great opportunity to our generation in the management of the national wealth. By a wise use of Federal funds, most of which will be repaid into the Treasury, the scourge of floods and drought can be curbed, water can be brought to arid lands, navigation can be extended, and cheap power can be brought alike to the farms and to the industries of our land.

Through the use of the waters of the Columbia River, for example, we are creating a rich agricultural area as large as the State of Delaware. At the same time, we are producing power at Grand Coulee and at Bonneville which played a mighty part in winning the war and which will found a great peacetime industry in the Northwest. The Tennessee Valley Authority will resume its peacetime program of promoting full use of the resources of the Valley. We shall continue our plans for the development of the Missouri Valley, the Arkansas Valley, and the Central Valley of California.

The Congress has shown itself alive to the practical requirements for a beneficial use of our water resources by providing that preference in the sale of power be given to farmers' cooperatives and public agencies. The public power program thus authorized must continue to be made effective by building the necessary generating and transmission facilities to furnish the maximum of firm power needed at the wholesale markets, which are often distant from the dam sites.

These great developmental projects will open the frontiers of agriculture, industry, and commerce. The employment opportunities thus offered will also go far to ease the transition from war to peace.

(h) Public works

During the war even urgently needed Federal, State, and local construction projects were deferred in order to release resources for war production. In resuming public works construction, it is desirable to proceed only at a moderate rate, since demand for private construction will be abnormally high for some time. Our public works program should be timed to reach its peak after demand for private construction has begun to taper off. Meanwhile, however, plans should be prepared if we are to act promptly when the present extraordinary private demand begins to run out.

The Congress made money available to Federal agencies for their public works planning in the fiscal year 1946. I strongly recommend that this policy be continued and extended in the fiscal year 1947.

State and local governments also have an essential role to play in a national public works program. In my message of September 6, 1945, I recommended that the Congress vote such grants to State and local governments as will insure that each level of government makes its proper contribution to a balanced public construction program. Specifically, the Federal Government should aid State and local governments in planning their own public works programs, in undertaking projects related to Federal programs of regional development, and in constructing such public works as are necessary to carry out the various policies of the Federal Government.

Early in 1945 the Congress made available advances to State and local governments for planning public works projects, and recently made additional provision to continue these advances through the fiscal year 1946. I believe that further appropriations will be needed for the same purpose for the fiscal year 1947.

The Congress has already made provision for highway programs. It is now considering legislation which would expand Federal grants and loans in several other fields, including construction of airports, hospital and health centers, housing, water pollution control facilities, and educational plant facilities. I hope that early action will be taken to authorize these Federal programs.

With respect to public works of strictly local importance, State and local governments should proceed without Federal assistance except in planning. This rule should be subject to review when and if the prospect of highly adverse general economic developments warrants it.

All loans and grants for public works should be planned and administered in such a way that they are brought into accord with the other elements of the Federal Program.

Our long-run objective is to achieve a program of direct Federal and Federally assisted public works which is planned in advance and synchronized with business conditions. In this way it can make its greatest contribution to general economic stability.

(i) *National housing program*

Last September I stated in my message to the Congress that housing was high on the list of matters calling for decisive action.

Since then the housing shortage in countless communities, affecting millions of families, has magnified this call to action.

Today we face both an immediate emergency and a major postwar problem.

Since VJ-day the wartime housing shortage has been growing steadily worse and pressure on real estate values has increased. Returning veterans often cannot find a satisfactory place for their families to live, and many who buy have to pay exorbitant prices. Rapid demobilization inevitably means further overcrowding.

A realistic and practical attack on the emergency will require aggressive action by local governments, with Federal aid, to exploit all opportunities and to give the veterans as far as possible first chance at vacancies. It will require continuation of rent control in shortage areas as well as legislation to permit control of sales prices. It will require maximum conversion of temporary war units for veterans' housing and their transportation to communities with the most pressing needs; the Congress has already appropriated funds for this purpose.

The inflation in the price of housing is growing daily.

As a result of the housing shortage, it is inevitable that the present dangers of inflation in home values will continue unless the Congress takes action in the immediate future.

Legislation is now pending in the Congress which would provide for ceiling prices for old and new houses. The authority to fix such ceilings is essential. With such authority, our veterans and other prospective home owners would be protected against a skyrocketing of home prices. The country would be protected from the extension of the present inflation in home values which, if allowed to continue, will threaten not only the stabilization program but our opportunities for attaining a sustained high level of home construction.

Such measures are necessary stopgaps—but only stopgaps. This emergency action, taken alone, is good—but not enough. The housing shortage did not start with the war or with demobilization; it began years before that and has steadily accumulated. The speed with which the Congress establishes the foundation for a permanent, long-range housing program will determine how effectively we grasp the immense opportunity to achieve our goal of decent housing and to make housing a major instrument of continuing prosperity and full employment in the years ahead. It will determine whether we move forward to a stable and healthy housing enterprise and toward providing a decent home for every American family.

Production is the only fully effective answer. To get the wheels turning, I have appointed an emergency housing expediter. I have approved establishment of priorities designed to assure an ample share of scarce materials to builders of houses for which veterans will have preference. Additional price and wage adjustments will be made where necessary, and other steps will be taken to stimulate greater production of bottleneck items. I recommend consideration of every sound method for expansion in facilities for insurance of privately financed housing by the Federal Housing Administration and resumption of previously authorized low-rent public housing projects suspended during the war.

In order to meet as many demands of the emergency situation as possible, a program of emergency measures is now being formulated for action. These will include steps in addition to those already taken. As quickly as this program can be formulated, announcement will be made.

Last September I also outlined to the Congress the basic principles for the kind of decisive, permanent legislation necessary for a long-range housing program.

These principles place paramount the fact that housing construction and financing for the overwhelming majority of our citizens should be done by private enterprise. They contemplate also that we afford governmental encouragement to privately financed house construction for families of moderate income, through extension of the successful system of insurance of housing investment; that research be undertaken to develop better and cheaper methods of building homes; that communities be assisted in appraising their housing needs; that we commence a program of Federal aid, with fair local participation, to stimulate and promote the rebuilding and redevelopment of slums and blighted areas—with maximum use of private capital. It is equally essential that we use public funds to assist families of low income who could not otherwise enjoy adequate housing, and that we quicken our rate of progress in rural housing.

Legislation now under consideration by the Congress provides for a comprehensive attack jointly by private enterprise, State and local authorities, and the Federal Government. This legislation would make permanent the National Housing Agency and give it authority and funds for much needed technical and economic research. It would provide additional stimulus for privately financed housing construction. This stimulus consists of establishing a new system of yield insurance to encourage large-scale investment in rental housing and broadening the insuring powers of the Federal Housing Administration and the lending powers of the Federal savings and loan associations.

Where private industry cannot build, the Government must step in to do the job. The bill would encourage expansion in housing available for the lowest income groups by continuing to provide direct subsidies for low-rent housing and rural housing. It would facilitate land assembly for urban redevelopment by loans and contributions to local public agencies where the localities do their share.

Prompt enactment of permanent housing legislation along these lines will not interfere with the emergency action already under way. On the contrary, it would lift us out of a potentially perpetual state of housing emergency. It would offer the best hope and prospect to millions of veterans and other American families that the American system can offer more to them than temporary makeshifts.

I have said before that the people of the United States can be the best housed people in the world. I repeat that assertion, and I welcome the cooperation of the Congress in achieving that goal.

(j) Social security and health

Our Social Security System has just celebrated its tenth anniversary. During the past decade this program has supported the welfare and morale of a large part of our people by removing some of the hazards and hardships of the aged, the unemployed, and widows and dependent children.

But, looking back over 10 years' experience and ahead to the future, we cannot fail to see defects and serious inadequacies in our system as it now exists. Benefits are in many cases inadequate; a great many persons are excluded from coverage; and provision has not been made for social insurance to cover the cost of medical care and the earnings lost by the sick and the disabled.

In the field of old-age security, there seems to be no adequate reason for excluding such groups as the self-employed, agricultural and domestic workers, and employees of nonprofit organizations. Since many of these groups earn wages too low to permit significant savings for old age, they are in special need of the assured income that can be provided by old-age insurance.

We must take urgent measures for the readjustment period ahead. The Congress for some time has been considering legislation designed to supplement at Federal expense, during the immediate reconversion period, compensation payments to the unemployed. Again I urge the Congress to enact legislation liberalizing unemployment compensation benefits and extending the coverage. Providing for the sustained consumption by the unemployed persons and their families is more than a welfare policy; it is sound economic policy. A sustained high level of consumer purchases is a basic ingredient of a prosperous economy.

During the war, nearly 5 million men were rejected for military service because of physical or mental defects which in many cases might have been prevented or corrected. This is shocking evidence that large sections of the population are at substandard levels of health. The need for a program that will give everyone opportunity for medical care is obvious. Nor can there be any serious doubt of the Government's responsibility for helping in this human and social problem.

The comprehensive health program which I recommended on November 19, 1945, will require substantial additions to the Social Security System and, in conjunction with other changes that need to be made, will require further consideration of the financial basis for social security. The system of prepaid medical care which I have recommended is expected eventually to require amounts equivalent to 4 percent of earnings up to $3,600 a year, which is about the average of present expenditures by individuals for medical care. The pooling of medical costs, under a plan which permits each individual to make a free choice of doctor and hospital, would assure that individuals receive adequate treatment and hospitalization when they are faced with emergencies for which they cannot budget individually. In addition, I recommended insurance benefits to replace part of the earnings lost through temporary sickness and permanent disability.

Even without these proposed major additions, it would now be time to undertake a thorough reconsideration of our social security laws. The structure should be expanded and liberalized. Provision should be made for extending coverage credit to veterans for the period of their service in the armed forces. In the financial provisions we must reconcile the actuarial needs of social security, including health insurance, with the requirements of a revenue system that is designed to promote a high level of consumption and full employment.

(*k*) *Education*

Although the major responsibility for financing education rests with the States, some assistance has long been given by the Federal Government. Further assistance is desirable and essential. There are many areas and some whole States where good schools cannot be provided without imposing an undue local tax burden on the citizens. It is essential to provide adequate elementary and secondary schools everywhere, and additional educational opportunities for large numbers of people beyond the secondary level. Accordingly, I repeat the proposal of last year's Budget Message that the Federal Government provide financial aid to assist the States in assuring more nearly equal opportunities for a good education. The proposed Federal grants for current educational expenditures should be made for the purpose of improving the educational system where improvement is most needed. They should not be used to replace existing non-Federal expenditures, or even to restore merely the situation which existed before the war.

In the future we expect incomes considerably higher than before the war. Higher incomes should make it possible for State and local governments and for individuals to support higher and more nearly adequate expenditures for education. But inequality among the States will still remain, and Federal help will still be needed.

As a part of our total public works program, consideration should be given to the need for providing adequate buildings for schools and other educational institutions. In view of current arrears in the construction of educational facilities, I believe that legislation to authorize grants for educational facilities, to be matched by similar expenditures by State and local authorities, should receive the favorable consideration of the Congress.

The Federal Government has not sought, and will not seek, to dominate education in the States. It should continue its historic role of leadership and advice and, for the purpose of equalizing educational opportunity, it should extend further financial support to the cause of education in areas where this is desirable.

(l) *Federal Government personnel*

The rapid reconversion of the Federal Government from war to peace is reflected in the demobilization of its civilian personnel. The number of these employees in continental United States has been reduced by more than 500,000 from the total of approximately 2,900,000 employed in the final months of the war. I expect that by next June we shall have made a further reduction of equal magnitude and that there will be continuing reductions during the next fiscal year. Of the special wartime agencies now remaining, only a few are expected to continue actively into the next fiscal year.

At the same time that we have curtailed the number of employees, we have shortened the workweek by one-sixth or more throughout the Government and have restored holidays. The process of readjustment has been complicated and costs have been increased by a heavy turn-over in the remaining personnel—particularly by the loss of some of our best administrators. Thousands of war veterans have been reinstated or newly employed in the civil service. Many civilians have been transferred from war agencies to their former peacetime agencies. Recruitment standards, which had to be relaxed during the war, are now being tightened.

The elimination last autumn of overtime work for nearly all Federal employees meant a sharp cut in their incomes. For salaried workers, the blow was softened but by no means offset by the increased rates of pay which had become effective July 1. Further adjustments to compensate for increased living costs are required. Moreover, we have long needed a general upward revision of Federal Government salary scales at all levels in all branches—legislative, judicial, and executive. Too many in Government have had to sacrifice too much in economic advantage to serve the Nation.

Adequate salaries will result in economies and improved efficiency in the conduct of Government business—gains that will far outweigh the immediate costs. I hope the Congress will expedite action on salary legislation for all Federal employees in all branches of the Government. The only exception I would make is in the case of workers whose pay rates are established by wage boards; a blanket adjustment would destroy the system by which their wages are kept alined with prevailing rates in particular localities. The wage boards should be sensitive now, as they were during the war, to changes in local prevailing wage rates and should make adjustments accordingly.

I hope also that the Congress may see fit to enact legislation for the adequate protection of the health and safety of Federal employees, for their coverage under a system of unemployment compensation, and for their return at Government expense to their homes after separation from wartime service.

(m) *Territories, insular possessions, and the District of Columbia*

The major governments of the world face few problems as important and as perplexing as those relating to dependent peoples. This Government is committed to the democratic principle that it is for the dependent peoples themselves to decide what their status shall be. To this end I asked the Congress last October to provide a means by which the people of Puerto Rico might choose their form of government and ultimate status with respect to the United States. I urge, too, that the Congress promptly accede to the wishes of the people of Hawaii that the Territory be admitted to statehood in our Union, and that similar action be taken with respect to Alaska as soon as it is certain that this is the desire of the people of that great

Territory. The people of the Virgin Islands should be given an increasing measure of self-government.

We have already determined that the Philippine Islands are to be independent on July 4, 1946. The ravages of war and enemy occupation, however, have placed a heavy responsibility upon the United States. I urge that the Congress complete, as promptly and as generously as may be possible, legislation which will aid economic rehabilitation for the Philippines. This will be not only a just acknowledgment of the loyalty of the people of the Philippines, but it will help to avoid the economic chaos which otherwise will be their heritage from our common war. Perhaps no event in the long centuries of colonialism gives more hope for the pattern of the future than the independence of the Philippines.

The District of Columbia, because of its special relation to the Federal Government, has been treated since 1800 as a dependent area. We should move toward a greater measure of local self-government consistent with the constitutional status of the District. We should take adequate steps to assure that citizens of the United States are not denied their franchise merely because they reside at the Nation's Capital.

We have won a great war—we, the nations of plain people who hate war. In the test of that war we found a strength of unity that brought us through—a strength that crushed the power of those who sought by force to deny our faith in the dignity of man.

During this trial the voices of disunity among us were silent or were subdued to an occasional whine that warned us that they were still among us. Those voices are beginning to cry aloud again. We must learn constantly to turn deaf ears to them. They are voices which foster fear and suspicion and intolerance and hate. They seek to destroy our harmony, our understanding of each other, our American tradition of "live and let live." They have become busy again, trying to set race against race, creed against creed, farmer against city dweller, worker against employer, people against their own governments. They seek only to do us mischief. They must not prevail.

It should be impossible for any man to contemplate without a sense of personal humility the tremendous events of the 12 months since the last annual Message, the great tasks that confront us, the new and huge problems of the coming months and years. Yet these very things justify the deepest confidence in the future of this Nation of free men and women.

The plain people of this country found the courage and the strength, the self-discipline, and the mutual respect to fight and to win, with the help of our allies, under God. I doubt if the tasks of the future are more difficult. But if they are, then I say that our strength and our knowledge and our understanding will be equal to those tasks.

SECOND ANNUAL MESSAGE.

THE WHITE HOUSE, *January 6, 1947.*

MR. PRESIDENT, MR. SPEAKER, MEMBERS OF THE CONGRESS OF THE UNITED STATES:

I come before you today to report on the state of the Union and, in the words of the Constitution, to recommend such measures as I judge necessary and expedient.

I come also to welcome you as you take up your duties and to discuss with you the manner in which you and I should fulfill our obligations to the American people during the next 2 years.

The power to mold the future of this Nation lies in our hands—yours and mine—joined together.

If in this year, and in the next, we can find the right course to take as each issue arises, and if, in spite of all difficulties, we have the courage and the resolution to take that course, then we shall achieve a state of well-being for our people without precedent in history. And if we continue to work with the other nations of the world earnestly, patiently, and wisely, we can—granting a will for peace on the part of our neighbors—make a lasting peace for the world.

But, if we are to realize these ends, the Congress and the President, during the next 2 years, must work together. It is not unusual in our history that the majority of the Congress represents a party in opposition to the President's party. I am the twentieth President of the United States who, at some time during his term of office, has found his own party to be in the minority in one or both Houses of the Congress.

I realize that on some matters the Congress and the President may have honest differences of opinion. Partisan differences, however, did not cause material disagreements as to the conduct of the war. Nor, in the conduct of our international relations, during and since the war, have such partisan differences been material.

On some domestic issues we may, and probably shall, disagree. That in itself is not to be feared. It is inherent in our form of government. But there are ways of disagreeing; men who differ can still work together sincerely for the common good. We shall be risking the Nation's safety and destroying our opportunities for progress if we do not settle any disagreements in this spirit, without thought of partisan advantage.

General domestic economy

As the year 1947 begins, the state of our national economy presents great opportunities for all. We have virtually full employment. Our national production of goods and services is 50 percent higher than in any year prior to the war emergency. The national income in 1946 was higher than in any peacetime year. Our food production is greater than it has ever been. During the last 5 years, our productive facilities have been expanded in almost every field. The American standard of living is higher now than ever before and, when the housing shortage can be overcome, it will be even higher.

During the past few months we have removed at a rapid rate the emergency controls that the Federal Government had to exercise during the war. The remaining controls will be retained only so long as they are needed to protect the public. Private enterprise must be given the greatest possible freedom to continue the expansion of our economy.

In my proclamation of December 31, 1946, I announced the termination of hostilities. This automatically ended certain temporary legislation and certain Executive powers.

Two groups of temporary laws still remain: The first are those which by congressional mandate are to last during the "emergency"; the second are those which are to continue until the "termination of the war."

I shall submit to the Congress recommendations for the repeal of certain of the statutes which by their terms continue for the duration of the "emergency." I shall at the same time recommend that others within this classification be extended until the state of war has been ended by treaty or by legislative action. As to those statutes which continue until the state of war has been terminated, I urge that the Congress promptly consider each statute individually, and repeal such emergency legislation where advisable.

Now that nearly all wartime controls have been removed, the operation of our industrial system depends to a greater extent on the decisions of businessmen, farmers, and workers. These decisions must be wisely made with genuine concern for the public welfare. The welfare of businessmen, farmers, and workers depends upon the economic well-being of those who buy their products.

An important present source of danger to our economy is the possibility that prices might be raised to such an extent that the consuming public could not purchase the tremendous volume of goods and services which will be produced in 1947.

We all know that recent price increases have denied to many of our workers much of the value of recent wage increases. Farmers have found that a large part of their increased income has been absorbed by increased prices. While some of our people have received raises in income which exceed price increases, the great majority have not. Those persons who live on modest fixed incomes—retired persons living on pensions, for example—and workers whose incomes are relatively inflexible—such as teachers and other civil servants—have suffered hardship.

In the effort to bring about a sound and equitable price structure each group of our population has its own responsibilities.

It is up to industry not only to hold the line on existing prices, but to make reductions whenever profits justify such action.

It is up to labor to refrain from pressing for unjustified wage increases that will force increases in the price level.

And it is up to Government to do everything in its power to encourage high-volume production, for that is what makes possible good wages, low prices, and reasonable profits.

In a few days there will be submitted to the Congress the Economic Report of the President, and also the Budget Message. Those messages will contain many recommendations. Today I shall outline five major economic policies which I believe the Government should pursue during 1947. These policies are designed to meet our immediate needs and, at the same time, to provide for the long-range welfare of our free enterprise system:

First, promotion of greater harmony between labor and management.

Second, restriction of monopoly and unfair business practices; assistance to small business; and the promotion of the free competitive system of private enterprise.

Third, continuation of an aggressive program of home construction.

Fourth, the balancing of the budget in the next fiscal year, and the achieving of a substantial surplus to be applied to the reduction of the public debt.

Fifth, protection of a fair level of return to farmers in postwar agriculture.

Labor-management relations

The year just past—like the year after the First World War—was marred by labor-management strife.

Despite this outbreak of economic warfare in 1946, we are today producing goods and services in record volume. Nevertheless, it is essential to improve the methods for reaching agreement between labor and management and to reduce the number of strikes and lock-outs.

We must not, however, adopt punitive legislation. We must not, in order to punish a few labor leaders, pass vindictive laws which will restrict the proper rights of the rank and file of labor. We must not, under the stress of emotion, endanger our American freedoms by taking ill-considered action which will lead to results not anticipated or desired.

We must remember, in reviewing the record of disputes in 1946, that management shares with labor the responsibility for failure to reach agreements which would have averted strikes. For that reason we must realize that industrial peace cannot be achieved merely by laws directed against labor unions.

During the last decade and a half we have established a national labor policy in this country based upon free collective bargaining as the process for determining wages and working conditions.

This is still the national policy.

It should continue to be the national policy.

But as yet not all of us have learned what it means to bargain freely and fairly. Nor have all of us learned to carry the mutual responsibilities that accompany the right to bargain. There have been abuses and harmful practices which limit the effectiveness of our system of collective bargaining. Furthermore, we have lacked sufficient governmental machinery to aid labor and management in resolving differences.

Certain labor-management problems need attention at once and certain others, by reason of their complexity, need exhaustive investigation and study.

We should enact legislation to correct certain abuses and to provide additional governmental assistance in bargaining. But we should also concern ourselves with the basic causes of labor-management difficulties.

In the light of these considerations, I propose to you and urge your cooperation in effecting the following four-point program to reduce industrial strife:

Point No. 1 is the early enactment of legislation to prevent certain unjustifiable practices.

First, under this point, are jurisdictional strikes. In such strikes the public and the employer are innocent bystanders who are injured by a collision between rival unions. This type of dispute hurts production, industry, and the public—and labor itself. I consider jurisdictional strikes indefensible.

The National Labor Relations Act provides procedures for determining which union represents the employees of a particular employer. In some jurisdictional disputes, however, minority unions strike to compel employers to deal with them despite a legal duty to bargain with the majority union. Strikes to compel an employer to violate the law are inexcusable. Legislation to prevent such strikes is clearly desirable.

Another form of interunion disagreement is the jurisdictional strike involving the question of which labor union is entitled to perform a particular task. When rival unions are unable to settle such disputes themselves, provision must be made for peaceful and binding determination of the issues.

A second unjustifiable practice is the secondary boycott, when used to further jurisdictional disputes or to compel employers to violate the National Labor Relations Act.

Not all secondary boycotts are unjustified. We must judge them on the basis of their objectives. For example, boycotts intended to protect wage rates and working conditions should be distinguished from those in furtherance of jurisdictional disputes. The structure of industry sometimes requires unions, as a matter of self-preservation, to extend the conflict beyond a particular employer. There should be no blanket prohibition against boycotts. The appropriate goal is legislation which prohibits secondary boycotts in pursuance of unjustifiable objectives, but does not impair the union's right to preserve its own existence and the gains made in genuine collective bargaining.

A third practice that should be corrected is the use of economic force, by either labor or management, to decide issues arising out of the interpretation of existing contracts.

Collective-bargaining agreements, like other contracts, should be faithfully adhered to by both parties. In the most enlightened union-management relationships, disputes over the interpretation of contract terms are settled peacefully by negotiation or arbitration. Legislation should be enacted to provide machinery whereby unsettled disputes concerning the interpretation of an existing agreement may be referred by either party to final and binding arbitration.

Point No. 2 is the extension of the facilities within the Department of Labor for assisting collective bargaining.

One of our difficulties in avoiding labor strife arises from a lack of order in the collective-bargaining process. The parties often do not have a clear understanding of their responsibility for settling disputes through their own negotiations. We constantly see instances where labor or management resorts to economic force without exhausting the possibilities for agreement through the bargaining process. Neither the parties nor the Government have a definite yardstick for determining when and how Government assistance should be invoked. There is need for integrated governmental machinery to provide the successive steps of mediation, voluntary arbitration, and—ultimately in appropriate cases—ascertainment of the facts of the dispute and the reporting of them to the public. Such machinery would facilitate and expedite the settlement of disputes.

Point No. 3 is the broadening of our program of social legislation to alleviate the causes of workers' insecurity.

On June 11, 1946, in my message vetoing the Case bill, I made a comprehensive statement of my views concerning labor-management relations. I said then, and I repeat now, that the solution of labor-management difficulties is to be found not only in legislation dealing directly with labor relations but also in a program designed to remove the causes of insecurity felt by many workers in our industrial society. In this connection, for example, the Congress should consider the extension and broadening of our social security system, better housing, a comprehensive national health program, and provision for a fair minimum wage.

Point No. 4 is the appointment of a temporary joint commission to inquire into the entire field of labor-management relations.

I recommend that the Congress provide for the appointment of a temporary joint commission to undertake this broad study.

The President, the Congress, and management and labor have a continuing responsibility to cooperate in seeking and finding the solution of these problems. I, therefore, recommend that the commission be composed as follows: 12 to be chosen by the Congress from the members of both parties in the House and the Senate, and 8 representing the public, management, and labor, to be appointed by the President.

The commission should be charged with investigating and making recommendations upon certain major subjects, among others:

First, the special and unique problem of Nation-wide strikes in vital industries affecting the public interest. In particular, the Commission should examine into the question of how to settle or prevent such strikes without endangering our general democratic freedoms.

Upon a proper solution of this problem may depend the whole industrial future of the United States. The paralyzing effects of a Nation-wide strike in such industries as transportation, coal, oil, steel, or communications can result in national disaster. We have been able to avoid such disaster, in recent years, only by the use of extraordinary war powers. All those powers will soon be gone. In their place there must be created an adequate system and effective machinery in these vital fields. This problem will require careful study and a bold approach, but an approach consistent with the preservation of the rights of our people. The need is pressing. The commission should give this its earliest attention.

Second, the best methods and procedures for carrying out the collective-bargaining process. This should include the responsibilities of labor and management to negotiate freely and fairly with each other, and to refrain from strikes or lock-outs until all possibilities of negotiation have been exhausted.

Third, the underlying causes of labor-management disputes.

Some of the subjects presented here for investigation involve long-range study. Others can be considered immediately by the Commission and its recommendations can be submitted to the Congress in the near future.

I recommend that this commission make its first report, including specific legislative recommendations, not later than March 15, 1947.

Restriction of monopoly and promotion of private enterprise

The second major policy I desire to lay before you has to do with the growing concentration of economic power and the threat to free competition in private enterprise. In 1941 the Temporary National Economic Committee completed a comprehensive investigation into the workings of the national economy. The Committee's study showed that, despite half a century of antitrust law enforcement, one of the gravest threats to our welfare lay in the increasing concentration of power in the hands of a small number of giant organizations.

During the war, this long-standing tendency toward economic concentration was accelerated. As a consequence, we now find that to a greater extent than ever before, whole industries are dominated by one or a few large organizations which can restrict production in the interest of higher profits and thus reduce employment and purchasing power.

In an effort to assure full opportunity and free competition to business we will vigorously enforce the antitrust laws. There is much the Congress can do to cooperate and assist in this program.

To strengthen and enforce the laws that regulate business practices is not enough. Enforcement must be supplemented by positive measures of aid to new enterprises. Government assistance, research programs, and credit powers should be designed and used to promote the growth of new firms and new industries. Assistance to small business is particularly important at this time when thousands of veterans who are potential business and industrial leaders are beginning their careers.

We should also give special attention to the decentralization of industry and the development of areas that are now underindustrialized.

Housing

The third major policy is also of great importance to the national economy—an aggressive program to encourage home construction. The first Federal program to relieve the veterans' housing shortage was announced in February 1946. In 1946, 1,000,000 family housing units have been put under construction and more than 665,000 units have already been completed. The rate of expansion in construction has broken all records.

In the coming year the number of dwelling units built will approach, if not surpass, the top construction year of 1926. The primary responsibility to deliver housing at reasonable prices that veterans can afford rests with private industry and labor. The Government will continue to expedite the flow of key building materials, to limit nonresidential construction, and to give financial support where it will do the most good. Measures to stimulate rental housing and new types of housing construction will receive special emphasis.

To reach our long-range goal of adequate housing for all our people, comprehensive housing legislation is urgently required, similar to the nonpartisan bill passed by the Senate last year. At a minimum, such legislation should open the way for rebuilding the blighted areas of our cities and should establish positive incentives for the investment of billions of dollars of private capital in large-scale rental housing projects. It should provide for the improvement of housing in rural areas and for the construction, over a 4-year period, of half a million units of public low-rental housing. It should authorize a single peacetime Federal housing agency to assure efficient use of our resources on the vast housing front.

Fiscal affairs

The fourth major policy has to do with balancing the Budget. In a prosperous period such as the present one the Budget of the Federal Government should be balanced. Prudent management of public finance requires that we begin the process of reducing the debt. The Budget which I shall submit to you this week has a small margin of surplus. In the Budget Message I am making recommendations which, if accepted, will result in a substantially larger surplus which should be applied to debt retirement. One of these recommendations is that the Congress take early action to continue throughout the next fiscal year the war-excise-tax rates which, under the present law, will expire on June 30, 1947.

Expenditures relating to the war are still high. Considerable sums are required to alleviate world famine and suffering. Aid to veterans will continue at a peak level. The world situation is such that large military expenditures are required. Interest on the public debt and certain other costs are irreducible. For these reasons I have had to practice stringent economy in preparing the Budget, and I hope that the Congress will cooperate in this program of economy.

Agriculture

The fifth major policy has to do with the welfare of our farm population.

Production of food reached record heights in 1946. Much of our tremendous grain crop can readily be sold abroad and thus will become no threat in our domestic markets. But in the next few years American agriculture can face the same dangers it did after World War I. In the early twenties the Nation failed to maintain outlets for the new productive capacity of our agricultural plant. It failed to provide means to protect the farmer while he adjusted his acreage to peacetime demands.

The result we all remember too well. Farm production stayed up while demand and prices fell, in contrast with industry where prices stayed up and output declined. Farm surpluses piled up, and disaster followed.

We must make sure of meeting the problems which we failed to meet after the First World War. Present laws give considerable stability to farm prices for 1947 and 1948, and these 2 years must be utilized to maintain and develop markets for our great productive power.

The purpose of these laws was to permit an orderly transition from war to peace. The Government plan of support prices was not designed to absorb, at great cost, the unlimited surpluses of a highly productive agriculture.

We must not wait until the guaranties expire to set the stage for permanent farm welfare.

The farmer is entitled to a fair income.

Ways can be found to utilize his new skills and better practices, to expand his markets at home and abroad, and to carry out the objectives of a balanced pattern of peacetime production without either undue sacrifice by farm people or undue expense to the Government.

Health and general welfare

Of all our national resources, none is of more basic value than the health of our people. Over a year ago I presented to the Congress my views on a national health program. The Congress acted on several of the recommendations in this program—mental health, the health of mothers and children, and hospital construction. I urge this Congress to complete the work begun last year and to enact the most important recommendation of the program—to provide adequate medical care to all who need it, not as charity but on the basis of payments made by the beneficiaries of the program.

One administrative change would help greatly to further our national program in the fields of health, education, and welfare. I again recommend the establishment of a well-integrated department of welfare.

Veterans

Fourteen million World War II servicemen have returned to civilian life. The great majority have found their places as citizens of their communities and their Nation. It is a tribute to the fiber of our servicemen and to the flexibility of our economy that these adjustments have been made so rapidly and so successfully.

More than 2,000,000 of these veterans are attending schools or acquiring job skills through the financial assistance of the Federal Government. Thousands of sick and wounded veterans are daily receiving the best of medical and hospital care. Half a million have obtained loans, with Government guaranties, to purchase homes or farms or to embark upon new businesses. Compensation is being paid in almost 2,000,000 cases for disabilities or death. More than 3,000,000 are continuing to maintain their low-cost national service life insurance policies. Almost 7,000,000 veterans have been aided by unemployment and self-employment allowances.

Exclusive of mustering-out payments and terminal-leave pay, the program for veterans of all wars is costing over $7,000,000,000 a year—one-fifth of our total Federal Budget. This is the most far-reaching and complete veterans' program ever conceived by any nation.

Except for minor adjustments I believe that our program of benefits for veterans is now complete. In the long run the success of the program will not be measured by the number of veterans obtaining financial aid or by the number of dollars we spend. History will judge us not by the money we spend, but by the further contribution we enable our veterans to make to their country. In considering any additional legislation, that must be our criterion.

Civil rights

We have recently witnessed in this country numerous attacks upon the constitutional rights of individual citizens as a result of racial and religious bigotry. Substantial segments of our people have been prevented from exercising fully their right to participate in the election of public officials, both locally and nationally. Freedom to engage in lawful callings has been denied.

The will to fight these crimes should be in the heart of every one of us.

For the Federal Government that fight is now being carried on by the Department of Justice to the full extent of the powers that have been conferred upon it. While the Constitution withholds from the Federal Government the major task of preserving the peace in the several States, I am not convinced that present legislation reaches the limit of Federal power to protect the civil rights of its citizens.

I have, therefore, by Executive order, established the President's Committee on Civil Rights to study and report on the whole problem of federally secured civil rights, with a view to making recommendations to the Congress.

Natural resources

In our responsibility to promote the general welfare of the people, we have always to consider the natural resources of our country. They are the foundation of our life. In the development of the great river systems of America there is the major opportunity of our generation to contribute to the increase of the national wealth. This program is already well along; it should be pushed with full vigor.

I must advise the Congress that we are rapidly becoming a "have not" nation as to many of our minerals. The economic progress and the security of our country depend upon an expanding return of mineral discovery and upon improved methods of recovery. The Federal Government must do its part to meet this need.

Foreign affairs

Progress in reaching our domestic goals is closely related to our conduct of foreign affairs. All that I have said about maintaining a sound and prosperous economy and improving the welfare of our people has greater meaning because of the world leadership of the United States. What we do, or fail to do, at home affects not only ourselves but millions throughout the world. If we are to fulfill our responsibilities to ourselves and to other peoples, we must make sure that the United States is sound economically, socially, and politically. Only then will we be able to help bring about the elements of peace in other countries—political stability, economic advancement, and social progress.

Peace treaties for Italy, Bulgaria, Rumania, and Hungary have finally been prepared. Following the signing of these treaties next month in Paris, they will be submitted to the Senate for ratification. This Government does not regard the treaties as completely satisfactory. Whatever their defects, however, I am convinced that they are as good as we can hope to obtain by agreement among the principal wartime allies. Further dispute and delay would gravely jeopardize political stability in the countries concerned for many years.

During the long months of debate on these treaties, we have made it clear to all nations that the United States will not consent to settlements at the expense of principles we regard as vital to a just and enduring peace. We have made it equally clear that we will not retreat to isolationism. Our policies will be the same during the forthcoming negotiations in Moscow on the German and Austrian treaties, and during future conferences on the Japanese treaty.

The delay in arriving at the first peace settlements is due partly to the difficulty of reaching agreement with the Soviet Union on the terms of settlement. Whatever differences there may have been between us and the Soviet Union, however, should not be allowed to obscure the fact that the basic interests of both nations lie in the early making of a peace under which the peoples of all countries may return, as free men and women, to the essential tasks of production and reconstruction. The major concern of each of us should be the promotion of collective security, not the advancement of individual security.

Our policy toward the Soviet Union is guided by the same principles which determine our policies toward all nations. We seek only to uphold the principles of international justice which have been embodied in the Charter of the United Nations.

We must now get on with the peace settlements. The occupying powers should recognize the independence of Austria and withdraw their troops. The Germans and the Japanese cannot be left in doubt and fear as to their future; they must know their national boundaries, their resources, and what reparations they must pay. Without trying to manage their internal affairs, we can insure that those countries do not rearm.

International relief and displaced persons

The United States can be proud of its part in caring for peoples reduced to want by the ravages of war, and in aiding nations to restore their national economies. We have shipped more supplies to the hungry peoples of the world since the end of the war than all other countries combined.

However, insofar as admitting displaced persons is concerned, I do not feel that the United States has done its part. Only about 5,000 of them have entered this country since May 1946. The fact is that the executive agencies are now doing all that is reasonably possible under the limitation of existing law and established quotas. Congressional assistance in the form of new legislation is needed. I urge the Congress to turn its attention to this world problem, in an effort to find ways whereby we can fulfill our responsibilities to these thousands of homeless and suffering refugees of all faiths.

International trade

World economic cooperation is essential to world political cooperation. We have made a good start on economic cooperation through the International Bank, the International Monetary Fund, and the Export-Import Bank. We must now take other steps for the reconstruction of world trade and we should continue to strive for an international trade system as free from obstructions as possible.

Atomic energy

The United States has taken the lead in the endeavor to put atomic energy under effective international control. We seek no monopoly for ourselves or for any group of nations. We ask only that there be safeguards sufficient to insure that no nation will be able to use this power for military purposes. So long as all governments are not agreed on means of international control of atomic energy, the shadow of fear will obscure the bright prospects for the peaceful use of this enormous power.

In accordance with the Atomic Energy Act of 1946, the Commission established under that law is assuming full jurisdiction over our domestic atomic-energy enterprise. The program of the Commission will, of course, be worked out in close collaboration with the military services in conformity with the wish of the Congress, but it is my fervent hope that the military significance of atomic energy will steadily decline. We look to the Commission to foster the development of atomic energy for industrial use and scientific and medical research. In the vigorous and effective development of peaceful uses of atomic energy rests our hope that this new force may ultimately be turned into a blessing for all nations.

Military policy

In 1946 the Army and Navy completed the demobilization of their wartime forces. They are now maintaining the forces which we need for national defense and to fulfill our international obligations.

We live in a world in which strength on the part of peace-loving nations is still the greatest deterrent to aggression. World stability can be destroyed when nations with great responsibilities neglect to maintain the means of discharging those responsibilities.

This is an age when unforeseen attack could come with unprecedented speed. We must be strong enough to defeat, and thus to forestall, any such attack. In our steady progress toward a more rational world order the need for large armed forces is progressively declining, but the stabilizing force of American military strength must not be weakend until our hopes are fully realized. When a system of collective security under the United Nations has been established, we shall be willing to lead in collective disarmament, but, until such a system becomes a reality, we must not again allow our weakness to invite attack.

For these reasons we need well-equipped, well-trained armed forces and we must be able to mobilize rapidly our resources in men and material for our own defense, should the need arise.

The Army will be reduced to 1,070,000 officers and men by July 1, 1947. Half of the Army will be used for occupation duties abroad and most of the remainder will be employed at home in the support of these overseas forces.

The Navy is supporting the occupation troops in Europe and in the Far East. Its fundamental mission—to support our national interests wherever required—is unchanged. The Navy, including the Marine Corps, will average 571,000 officers and men during the fiscal year 1948.

We are encountering serious difficulties in maintaining our forces at even these reduced levels. Occupation troops are barely sufficient to carry out the duties which our foreign policy requires. Our forces at home are at a point where further reduction is impracticable. We should like an Army and a Navy composed entirely of long-term volunteers, but in spite of liberal inducements the basic needs of the Army are not now being met by voluntary enlistments.

The War Department has advised me that it is unable to make an accurate forecast at the present time as to whether it will be possible to maintain the strength of the Army by relying exclusively on volunteers. The situation will be much clearer in a few weeks, when the results of the campaign for volunteers are known. The War Department will make its recommendation as to the need for the extension of Selective Service in sufficient time to enable the Congress to take action prior to the expiration of the present law on March 31. The responsibility for maintaining our armed forces at the strength necessary for our national safety rests with the Congress.

The development of a trained citizen reserve is also vital to our national security. This can best be accomplished through universal training. I have appointed an Advisory Commission on Universal Training to study the various plans for a training program and I expect that the recommendations of the Commission will be of benefit to the Congress and to me in reaching decisions on this problem.

The cost of the Military Establishment is substantial. There is one certain way by which we can cut costs and at the same time enhance our national security. That is by the establishment of a single department of national defense. I shall communicate with the Congress in the near future with reference to the establishment of a single department of national defense.

National security does not consist only of an army, a navy, and an air force. It rests on a much broader base. It depends on a sound economy of prices and wages, on a prosperous agriculture, on satisfied and productive workers, on a competitive private enterprise free from monopolistic repression, on continued industrial harmony and production, on civil liberties and human freedoms—on all the forces which create in our men and women a strong moral fiber and spiritual stamina.

But we have a higher duty and a greater responsibility than the attainment of national security. Our goal is collective security for all mankind.

If we can work in a spirit of understanding and mutual respect, we can fulfill this solemn obligation which rests upon us.

The spirit of the American people can set the course of world history. If we maintain and strengthen our cherished ideals, and if we share our great bounty with war-stricken people over the world, then the faith of our citizens in freedom and democracy will spread over the whole earth and free men everywhere will share our devotion to these ideals.

Let us have the will and the patience to do this job together.

May the Lord strengthen us in our faith.

May He give us wisdom to lead the peoples of the world in His ways of peace.

THIRD ANNUAL MESSAGE

THE WHITE HOUSE, *January 7, 1948.*

MR. PRESIDENT, MR. SPEAKER, MEMBERS OF THE EIGHTIETH CONGRESS:

We are here today to consider the state of the Union.

On this occasion, above all others, the Congress and the President should concentrate their attention not upon party but upon country, not upon the things which divide us but upon those which bind us together—the enduring principles of our American system, and our common aspirations for the future welfare and security of the people of the United States.

The United States has become great because we, as a people, have been able to work together for great objectives even while differing about details.

The elements of our strength are many. They include our democratic government, our economic system, our great natural resources. But these are only partial explanations.

The basic source of our strength is spiritual. For we are a people with a faith. We believe in the dignity of man. We believe that he was created in the image of the Father of us all.

We do not believe that men exist merely to strengthen the state or to be cogs in an economic machine. We do believe that governments are created to serve the people and that economic systems exist to minister to their wants. We have a profound devotion to the welfare and rights of the individual as a human being.

The faith of our people has particular meaning at this time in history because of the unsettled and changing state of the world.

The victims of war in many lands are striving to rebuild their lives, and are seeking assurance that the tragedy of war will not occur again. Throughout the world new ideas are challenging the old. Men of all nations are reexamining the beliefs by which they live. Great scientific and industrial changes have released new forces which will affect the future course of civilization.

The state of our Union reflects the changing nature of the modern world. On all sides there is heartening evidence of great energy, of capacity for economic development, and, even more important, capacity for spiritual growth. But accompanying this great activity there are equally great questions, great anxieties, great aspirations. They represent the concern of an enlightened people that conditions should be so arranged as to make life more worth while.

We must devote ourselves to finding answers to these anxieties and aspirations. We seek answers which will embody the moral and spiritual elements of tolerance, unselfishness, and brotherhood upon which true freedom and opportunity must rest.

As we examine the state of our Union today, we can benefit from viewing it on a basis of the accomplishments of the last decade and our goals for the next. How far have we come during the last 10 years and how far can we go during the next 10?

It was 10 years ago that the determination of dictators to wage war upon mankind became apparent. The years that followed brought untold death and destruction.

We shared in the human suffering of the war, but we were fortunate enough to escape most of war's destruction. We were able through these 10 years to expand the productive strength of our farms and factories.

More important, however, is the fact that these years brought us new courage and new confidence in the ideals of our free democracy. Our deep belief in freedom and justice was reinforced in the crucible of war.

On the foundations of our greatly strengthened economy and our renewed confidence in democratic values we can continue to move forward.

There are some who look with fear and distrust upon planning for the future; yet our great national achievements have been attained by those with vision. Our Union was formed, our frontiers were pushed back, and our great industries were built by men who looked ahead.

I propose that we look ahead today toward those goals for the future which have the greatest bearing upon the foundations of our democracy and the happiness of our people.

I do so, confident in the thought that with clear objectives and with firm determination we can, in the next 10 years, build upon the accomplishments of the past decade to achieve a glorious future. Year by year, beginning now, we must make a substantial part of this progress.

Our first goal is to secure fully the essential human rights of our citizens.

The United States has always had a deep concern for human rights. Religious freedom, free speech, and freedom of thought are cherished realities in our land. Any denial of human rights is a denial of the basic beliefs of democracy and of our regard for the worth of each individual.

Today, however, some of our citizens are still denied equal opportunity for education, for jobs and economic advancement, and for the expression of their views at the polls. Most serious of all, some are denied equal protection under our laws. Whether discrimination is based on race, or creed, or color, or land of origin, it is utterly contrary to American ideals of democracy.

The recent report of the President's Committee on Civil Rights points the way to corrective action by the Federal Government and by State and local governments. Because of the need for effective Federal action, I shall send a special message to the Congress on this important subject.

We should also consider our obligation to assure the fullest possible measure of civil rights to the people of our Territories and possessions. I believe that the time has come for Alaska and Hawaii to be admitted to the Union as States.

Our second goal is to protect and develop our human resources.

The safeguarding of the rights of our citizens must be accompanied by an equal regard for their opportunities for development and their protection from economic insecurity. In this Nation the ideals of freedom and equality can be given specific meaning in terms of health, education, social security, and housing.

Over the past 12 years we have erected a sound framework of social-security legislation. Many millions of our citizens are now protected against the loss of income which can come with unemployment, old age, or the death of wage earners. Yet our system has gaps and inconsistencies; it is only half finished.

We should now extend unemployment compensation, old-age benefits, and survivors' benefits to millions who are not now protected. We should also raise the level of benefits.

The greatest gap in our social-security structure is the lack of adequate provision for the Nation's health. We are rightly proud of the high standards of medical care we know how to provide in the United States. The fact is, however, that most of our people cannot afford to pay for the care they need.

I have often and strongly urged that this condition demands a national health program. The heart of the program must be a national system of payment for medical care based on well-tried insurance principles. This great Nation cannot afford to allow its citizens to suffer needlessly from the lack of proper medical care.

Our ultimate aim must be a comprehensive insurance system to protect all our people equally against insecurity and ill health.

Another fundamental aim of our democracy is to provide an adequate education for every person.

Our educational systems face a financial crisis. It is deplorable that in a nation as rich as ours there are millions of children who do not have adequate schoolhouses or enough teachers for a good elementary or secondary education. If there are educational inadequacies in any State, the whole Nation suffers. The Federal Government has a responsibility for providing financial aid to meet this crisis.

In addition, we must make possible greater equality of opportunity to all our citizens for an education. Only by so doing can we insure that our citizens will be capable of understanding and sharing the responsibilities of democracy.

The Government's programs for health, education, and security are of such great importance to our democracy that we should now establish an executive department for their administration.

Health and education have their beginning in the home. No matter what our hospitals or schools are like, the youth of our Nation are handicapped when millions of them live in city slums and country shacks. Within the next decade we must see that every American family has a decent home. As an immediate step we need the long-range housing program which I have recommended on many occasions. This should include financial aids designed to yield more housing at lower prices. It should provide public housing for low-income families, and vigorous development of new techniques to lower the cost of building.

Until we can overcome the present drastic housing shortage, we must extend and strengthen rent control.

We have had, and shall continue to have, a special interest in the welfare of our veterans. Over 14,000,000 men and women who served in the armed forces in World War II have now returned to civilian life. Over 2,000,000 veterans are being helped through school; millions have been aided while finding jobs, and have been helped in buying homes, in obtaining medical care, and in adjusting themselves to physical handicaps.

All but a very few veterans have successfully made the transition from military life to their home communities. The success of our veterans' program is proved by this fact. This Nation is proud of the eagerness shown by our veterans to become self-reliant and self-supporting citizens.

Our third goal is to conserve and use our natural resources so that they can contribute most effectively to the welfare of our people.

The resources given by nature to this country are rich and extensive. The material foundations of our growth and economic development are the bounty of our fields, the wealth of our mines and forests, and the energy of our waters. As a nation, we are coming to appreciate more each day the close relationship between the conservation of these resources and the preservation of our national strength.

Yet we are doing far less than we know how to do to make use of our resources without destroying them. Both the public and private use of these resources must have the primary objective of maintaining and increasing these basic supports for an expanding future.

We must continue to take specific steps toward this goal. We must vigorously defend our natural wealth against those who would misuse it for selfish gain.

We need accurate and comprehensive knowledge of our mineral resources and must intensify our efforts to develop new supplies and to acquire stock piles of scarce materials.

We need to protect and restore our land—public and private—through combatting erosion and rebuilding the fertility of the soil.

We must expand our reclamation program to bring millions of acres of arid land into production, and to improve water supplies for additional millions of acres. This will provide new opportunities for veterans and others, particularly in the West, and aid in providing a rising living standard for a growing population.

We must protect and restore our forests by sustained-yield forestry and by planting new trees in areas now slashed and barren.

We must continue to erect multiple-purpose dams on our great rivers—not only to reclaim land, but also to prevent floods, to extend our inland waterways, and to provide hydroelectric power. This public power must not be monopolized for private gain. Only through well-established policies of transmitting power directly to its market and thus encouraging widespread use at low rates can the Federal Government assure the people of their full share of its benefits. Additional power—public and private—is needed to raise the ceilings now imposed by power shortages on industrial and agricultural development.

We should achieve the wise use of resources through the integrated development of our great river basins. We can learn much from our Tennessee Valley experience. We should no longer delay in applying the lessons of that vast undertaking to our other great river basins.

Our fourth goal is to lift the standard of living for all our people by strengthening our economic system and sharing more broadly among our people the goods we produce.

The amazing economic progress of the past 10 years points the way for the next 10.

Today 14,000,000 more people have jobs than in 1938.

Our yearly output of goods and services has increased by two-thirds.

The average income of our people, measured in dollars of equal purchasing power, has increased—after taxes—by more than 50 percent.

In no other 10 years have farmers, businessmen, and wage earners made such great gains.

We may not be able to expand as rapidly in the next decade as in the last, because we are now starting from full employment and very high production, but we can increase our annual output by at least one-third above the present level. We can lift our standard of living to nearly double what it was 10 years ago.

If we distribute these gains properly, we can go far toward stamping out poverty in our generation.

To do this, agriculture, business, and labor must move forward together.

Permanent farm prosperity and agricultural abundance will be achieved only as our whole economy grows and prospers. The farmer can sell more food at good prices when the incomes of wage earners are high and when there is full employment. Adequate diets for every American family, and the needs of our industries at full production, will absorb a farm output well above our present levels.

Although the average farmer is now better off than ever before, farm families as a whole have only begun to catch up with the standards of living enjoyed in the cities. In 1946 the average income of farm people was $779, contrasted with an average income of $1,288 for nonfarm people. Within the next decade we should eliminate elements of inequality in these living standards.

To this end our farm program should enable the farmer to market his varied crops at fair price levels and to improve his standard of living.

We need to continue price supports for major farm commodities on a basis which will afford reasonable protection against fluctuations in the levels of production and demand, The present price-support program must be reexamined and modernized.

Crop insurance should be strengthened and its benefits extended in order to protect the farmer against the special hazards to which he is subject.

We also need to improve the means for getting farm products into the markets and into the hands of consumers. Cooperatives which directly or indirectly serve this purpose must be encouraged—not discouraged. The school-lunch program should be continued and adequately financed.

We need to go forward with the rural electrification program to bring the benefits of electricity to all our farm population.

We can, and must, aid and encourage farmers to conserve their soil resources and restore the fertility of land that has suffered from neglect or unwise use.

All of these are practical measures upon which we should act immediately to enable agriculture to make its full contribution to our prosperity.

We must also strengthen our economic system within the next decade by enlarging our industrial capacity within the framework of our free enterprise system.

We are today far short of the industrial capacity we need for a growing future. At least $50,000,000,000 should be invested by industry to improve and expand our productive facilities over the next few years. But this is only the beginning. The industrial application of atomic energy and other scientific advances will constantly open up further opportunities for expansion. Farm prosperity and high employment will call for an immensely increased output of goods and services.

Growth and vitality in our economy depend on vigorous private enterprise. Free competition is the key to industrial development, full production and employment, fair prices, and an ever improving standard of living. Competition is seriously limited today in many industries by the concentration of economic power and other elements of monopoly. The appropriation of sufficient funds to permit proper enforcement of the present antitrust laws is essential. Beyond that we should go on to strengthen our legislation to protect competition.

Another basic element of a strong economic system is the well-being of wage earners.

We have learned that the well-being of workers depends on high production and consequent high employment. We have learned equally well that the welfare of industry and agriculture depends on high incomes for our workers.

The Government has wisely chosen to set a floor under wages; but our 40-cent minimum wage is inadequate and obsolete. I recommend lifting the minimum wage to 75 cents an hour.

In general, however, we must continue to rely on our sound system of collective bargaining to set wage scales. Workers' incomes should increase at a rate consistent with the maintenance of sound price, profit, and wage relationships and with increasing productivity.

The Government's part in labor-management relations is now largely controlled by the terms of the Labor-Management Relations Act of 1947. I made my attitude clear on this act in my veto message to the Congress last June. Nothing has occurred since to change my opinion of this law. As long as it remains the law of the land, however, I shall carry out my constitutional duty to administer it.

As we look ahead we can understand the crucial importance of restraint and wisdom in arriving at new labor-management contracts. Work stoppages would result in a loss of production—a loss which could bring higher prices for our citizens and could also deny the necessities of life to the hard-pressed peoples of other lands. It is my sincere hope that the representatives of labor and of industry will bear in mind that the Nation as a whole has a vital stake in the success of their bargaining efforts.

If we surmount our current economic difficulties, we can move ahead to a great increase in our national income which will enable all our people to enjoy richer and fuller lives.

All of us must advance together. One-fifth of our families now have average annual incomes of less than $850. We must see that our gains in national income are made more largely available to those with low incomes, whose need is greatest. This will benefit us all through providing a stable foundation of buying power to maintain prosperity.

Business, labor, agriculture, and Government, working together, must develop the policies which will make possible the realization of the full benefits of our economic system.

Our fifth goal is to achieve world peace based on principles of freedom and justice and the equality of all nations.

Twice within our generation, world wars have taught us that we cannot isolate ourselves from the rest of the world.

We have learned that the loss of freedom in any area of the world means a loss of freedom to ourselves—that the loss of independence by any nation adds directly to the insecurity of the United States and all free nations.

We have learned that a healthy world economy is essential to world peace—that economic distress is a disease whose evil effects spread far beyond the boundaries of the afflicted nation.

For these reasons the United States is vigorously following policies designed to achieve a peaceful and prosperous world.

We are giving, and will continue to give, our full support to the United Nations. While that Organization has encountered unforeseen and unwelcome difficulties, I am confident of its ultimate success. We are also devoting our efforts toward world economic recovery and the revival of world trade. These actions are closely related and mutually supporting.

We believe that the United States can be an effective force for world peace only if it is strong. We look forward to the day when nations will decrease their armaments; yet, so long as there remains serious opposition to the ideals of a peaceful world, we must maintain strong armed forces.

The passage of the National Security Act by the Congress at its last session was a notable step in providing for the security of this country. A further step which I consider of even greater importance is the early provision for universal training. There are many elements in a balanced national security program, all interrelated and necessary, but universal training should be the foundation for them all. A favorable decision by the Congress at an early date is of world importance. I am convinced that such action is vital to the security of this Nation and to the maintenance of its leadership.

The United States is engaged today in many international activities directed toward the creation of lasting peaceful relationships among nations.

We have been giving substantial aid to Greece and Turkey to assist these nations in preserving their integrity against foreign pressures. Had it not been for our aid, their situation today might well be radically different. The continued integrity of those countries will have a powerful effect upon other nations in the Middle East and Europe struggling to maintain their independence while they repair the damages of war.

The United States has special responsibilities with respect to the countries in which we have occupation forces: Germany, Austria, Japan, and Korea. Our efforts to reach agreements on peace settlements for these countries have so far been blocked, but we shall continue to exert our utmost efforts to obtain satisfactory settlements for each of these nations.

Many thousands of displaced persons, still living in camps overseas, should be allowed entry into the United States. I again urge the

Congress to pass suitable legislation at once so that this Nation may do its share in caring for homeless and suffering refugees of all faiths. I believe that the admission of these persons will add to the strength and energy of this Nation.

We are moving toward our goal of world peace in many ways, but the most important efforts which we are now making are those which support world economic reconstruction. We are seeking to restore the world trading system which was shattered by the war and to remedy the economic paralysis which grips many countries.

To restore world trade we have recently taken the lead in bringing about the greatest reduction of world tariffs that has ever occurred. The extension of the provisions of the Reciprocal Trade Agreements Act, which made this achievement possible, is of extreme importance. We must also go on to support the International Trade Organization, through which we hope to obtain worldwide agreement on a code of fair conduct in international trade.

Our present major effort toward economic reconstruction is to support the program for recovery developed by the countries of Europe. In my recent message to the Congress, I outlined the reasons why it is wise and necessary for the United States to extend this support.

I want to reaffirm my belief in the soundness and promise of this proposal. When the European economy is strengthened, the product of its industry will be of benefit to many other areas of economic distress. The ability of free men to overcome hunger and despair will be a moral stimulus to the entire world.

We intend to work also with other nations in achieving world economic recovery. We shall continue our cooperation with the nations of the Western Hemisphere. A special program of assistance to China, to provide urgent relief needs and to speed reconstruction, will be submitted to the Congress.

Unfortunately, not all governments share the hope of the people of the United States that economic reconstruction in many areas of the world can be achieved through cooperative effort among nations. In spite of these differences, we will go forward with our efforts to overcome economic paralysis.

No nation by itself can carry these programs to success; they depend upon the cooperative and honest efforts of all participating countries. Yet the leadership is inevitably ours.

I consider it of the highest importance that the Congress should authorize support for the European recovery program for the period from April 1, 1948, to June 30, 1952, with an initial amount for the first 15 months of 6.8 billion dollars. I urge the Congress to act promptly on this vital measure of our foreign policy on this decisive contribution to world peace.

We are following a sound, constructive, and practical course in carrying out our determination to achieve peace.

We are fighting poverty, hunger, and suffering.

This leads to peace—not war.

We are building toward a world where all nations, large and small alike, may live free from the fear of aggression.

This leads to peace—not war.

Above all else we are striving to achieve a concord among the peoples of the world based upon the dignity of the individual and the brotherhood of man.

This leads to peace—not war.

We can go forward with confidence that we are following sound policies, both at home and with other nations, which will lead us toward our great goals for economic, social, and moral achievement.

As we enter the new year, we must surmount one major problem which affects all our goals. That is the problem of inflation.

Already inflation in this country is undermining the living standards of millions of families. Food costs too much. Housing has reached fantastic price levels. Schools and hospitals are in financial distress. Inflation threatens to bring on disagreement and strife between labor and management.

Worst of all, inflation holds the threat of another depression, just as we had a depression after the unstable boom following the First World War.

When I announced last October that the Congress was being called into session, I described the price increases which had taken place since June 1946. Wholesale prices had increased 40 percent, and retail prices had increased 23 percent.

Since October prices have continued to rise. Wholesale prices have gone up at an annual rate of 18 percent. Retail prices have gone up at an annual rate of 10 percent.

The events which have occured since I presented my 10-point anti-inflation program to the Congress on November 17 have made it even clearer that all 10 points are essential.

High prices must not be our means of rationing.

We must deal effectively and at once with the high cost of living.

We must stop the spiral of inflation.

I trust that within the shortest possible time the Congress will make available to the Government the weapons that are so desperately needed in the fight against inflation.

One of the most powerful anti-inflationary factors in our economy today is the excess of Government revenues over expenditures.

Government expenditures have been and must continue to be held to the lowest safe levels. Since VJ-day Federal expenditures have been sharply reduced. They have been cut from more than 63 billion dollars in the fiscal year 1946 to less than 38 billion dollars in the present fiscal year. The number of civilian employees has been cut nearly in half—from 3¾ million down to 2 million.

On the other hand, Government revenues must not be reduced. Until inflation has been stopped there should be no cut in taxes that is not offset by additions at another point in our tax structure.

Certain adjustments should be made within our existing tax structure that will not affect total receipts, yet will adjust the tax burden so that those least able to pay will have their burden lessened by the transfer of a portion of it to those best able to pay.

Many of our families today are suffering hardship because of the high cost of living. At the same time profits of corporations reached an all-time record in 1947. Corporate profits totaled 17 billion dollars after taxes. This compared with 12.5 billion dollars in 1946, the previous high year.

Because of this extraordinarily high level of profits, corporations can well afford to carry a larger share of the tax load at this time.

During this period, in which the high cost of living is bearing down on so many of our families, tax adjustments should be made to ease their burden. The low-income group particularly is being pressed very hard. To this group a tax adjustment would result in a saving that could be used to buy the necessities of life.

I recommend therefore that, effective January 1, 1948, a cost of living tax credit be extended to our people consisting of a credit of $40 to each individual taxpayer and an additional credit of $40 for each dependent. Thus the income tax of a man with a wife and two children would be reduced $160. The credit would be extended to all taxpayers, but it would be particularly helpful to those in the low-income group.

It is estimated that such a tax credit would reduce the Federal revenue by 3.2 billion dollars. This reduction should be made up by increasing the tax on corporate profits in an amount that will produce this sum—with appropriate adjustment for small corporations.

This is the proper method of tax relief at this time. It gives relief to those who need it most without cutting the total tax revenue of the Government.

When the present danger of inflation has passed we should consider tax reduction based upon a revision of our entire tax structure.

When we have conquered inflation, we shall be in a position to move forward toward our chosen goals.

As we do so let us keep ever before us our high purposes.

We are determined that every citizen of this Nation shall have an equal right and equal opportunity to grow in wisdom and in stature and to take his place in the control of his Nation's destiny.

We are determined that the productive resources of the Nation shall be used wisely and fully for the benefit of all.

We are determined that the democratic faith of our people and the strength of our resources shall contribute their full share to the attainment of enduring peace in the world.

It is our faith in human dignity that underlies these purposes. It is this faith that keeps us a strong and vital people.

This is a time to remind ourselves of these fundamentals. For today the whole world looks to us for leadership.

This is the hour to rededicate ourselves to the faith in mankind that makes us strong.

This is the hour to rededicate ourselves to the faith in God that gives us confidence as we face the challenge of the years ahead.

FOURTH ANNUAL MESSAGE.

THE WHITE HOUSE, *January 5, 1949.*

MR. PRESIDENT, MR. SPEAKER, MEMBERS OF THE CONGRESS:

I am happy to report to this Eighty-first Congress that the state of the Union is good. Our Nation is better able than ever before to meet the needs of the American people, and to give them their fair chance in the pursuit of happiness. It is foremost among the nations of the world in the search for peace.

During the last 16 years, the American people have been creating a society which offers new opportunities for every man to enjoy his share of the satisfactions of life.

In this society, we are conservative about the values and principles which we cherish; but we are forward-looking in protecting those values and principles and in extending their benefits. We have rejected the discredited theory that the fortunes of the Nation should be in the hands of a privileged few. We have abandoned the trickle-down concept of national prosperity. Instead, we believe that our economic system should rest on a democratic foundation and that wealth should be created for the benefit of all.

The recent election shows that the American people are in favor of this kind of society and want to go on improving it.

The American people have decided that poverty is just as wasteful and just as unnecessary as preventable disease. We have pledged our common resources to help one another in the hazards and struggles of individual life. We believe that no unfair prejudice or artificial distinction should bar any American from an education, or from good health, or from a job that he is capable of performing.

The attainment of this kind of society demands the best efforts of every citizen in every walk of life, and it imposes increasing responsibilities on the Government.

The Government must work with industry, labor, and the farmers in keeping our economy running at full speed. The Government must see that every American has a chance to obtain his fair share of our increasing abundance. These responsibilities go hand in hand.

We cannot maintain prosperity unless we have a fair distribution of opportunity and a widespread consumption of the products of our factories and farms.

Our Government has undertaken to meet these responsibilities.

We have made tremendous public investments in highways, hydroelectric power projects, soil conservation, and reclamation. We have established a system of social security. We have enacted laws protecting the rights and the welfare of our working people and the income of our farmers. These Federal policies have paid for themselves many times over. They have strengthened the material foundations of our democratic ideals. Without them, our present prosperity would be impossible.

Reinforced by these policies, our private-enterprise system has reached new heights of production. Since the boom year of 1929, while our population has increased by only 20 percent, our agricultural production has increased by 45 percent, and our industrial production has increased by 75 percent. We are turning out far more goods and more wealth per worker than we have ever done before.

This progress has confounded the gloomy prophets, at home and abroad, who predicted the downfall of American capitalism. The American people, going their own way, confident in their own powers, have achieved the greatest prosperity the world has ever seen.

But, great as our progress has been, we still have a long way to go.

As we look around the country, many of our shortcomings stand out in bold relief.

We are suffering from excessively high prices.

Our production is still not large enough to satisfy our demands.

Our minimum wages are far too low.

Small business is losing ground to growing monopoly.

Our farmers still face an uncertain future. And too many of them lack the benefits of our modern civilization.

Some of our natural resources are still being wasted.

We are acutely short of electric power, although the means for developing such power are abundant.

Five million families are still living in slums and firetraps. Three million families share their homes with others.

Our health is far behind the progress of medical science. Proper medical care is so expensive that it is out of reach of the great majority of our citizens.

Our schools, in many localities, are utterly inadequate.

Our democratic ideals are often thwarted by prejudice and intolerance.

Each of these shortcomings is also an opportunity—an opportunity for the Congress and the President to work for the good of the people.

Our first great opportunity is to protect our economy against the evils of boom and bust.

This objective cannot be attained by Government alone. Indeed, the greater part of the task must be performed by individual efforts under our system of free enterprise. We can keep our present prosperity, and increase it, only if free enterprise and free government work together to that end.

We cannot afford to float along carelessly on a postwar boom until it collapses. And it is not enough merely to prepare to weather a recession if it comes. Instead, Government and business must work together constantly to achieve more and more jobs and more and more production—which mean more and more prosperity for all the people.

The business cycle is man-made; and men of good will, working together, can smooth it out.

So far as business is concerned, it should plan for steady, vigorous expansion—seeking always to increase its output, lower its prices, and avoid the vices of monopoly and restriction. So long as business does this, it will be contributing to continued prosperity, and it will have the help and encouragement of the Government.

The Employment Act of 1946 pledges the Government to use all its resources to promote maximum employment, production, and purchasing power. This means that the Government is firmly committed to protect business and the people against the dangers of recession and against the evils of inflation. This means that the Government must adapt its plans and policies to meet changing circumstances.

At the present time, our prosperity is threatened by inflationary pressures at a number of critical points in the economy. The Government must be in a position to take effective action at these danger spots. To that end, I recommend that the Congress enact legislation for the following purposes:

First, to continue the power to control consumer credit and enlarge the power to control bank credit.

Second, to grant authority to regulate speculation on the commodity exchanges.

Third, to continue export-control authority and to provide adequate machinery for its enforcement.

Fourth, to continue the priorities and allocation authority in the field of transportation.

Fifth, to authorize priorities and allocations for key materials in short supply.

Sixth, to extend and strengthen rent control.

Seventh, to provide stand-by authority to impose price ceilings for scarce commodities which basically affect essential industrial production or the cost of living, and to limit unjustified wage adjustments which would force a break in an established price ceiling.

Eighth, to authorize an immediate study of the adequacy of production facilities for materials in critically short supply, such as steel; and, if found necessary, to authorize Government loans for the expansion of production facilities to relieve such shortages, and furthermore to authorize the construction of such facilities directly if action by private industry fails to meet our needs.

The Economic Report, which I shall submit to the Congress shortly, will discuss in detail the economic background for these recommendations.

One of the most important factors in maintaining prosperity is the Government's fiscal policy. At this time, it is essential not only that the Federal budget be balanced, but also that there be a substantial surplus to reduce inflationary pressures, and permit a sizable reduction in the national debt, which now stands at $252,000,000,000. I recommend, therefore, that the Congress enact new tax legislation to bring in an additional $4,000,000,000 of Government revenue. This should come principally from additional corporate taxes. A portion should come from revised estate and gift taxes. Consideration should be given to raising personal income-tax rates in the middle and upper brackets.

If we want to keep our economy running in high gear, we must be sure that every group has the incentive to make its full contribution to the national welfare. At present, the working men and women of the Nation are unfairly discriminated against by a statute that abridges their rights, curtails their constructive efforts, and hampers our system of free collective bargaining. That statute is the Labor-Management Relations Act of 1947, sometimes called the Taft-Hartley Act.

That act should be repealed.

The Wagner Act should be reenacted. However, certain improvements, which I recommended to the Congress 2 years ago, are needed. Jurisdictional strikes and unjustifiable secondary boycotts should be prohibited. The use of economic force to decide issues arising out of the interpretation of existing contracts should be prevented. Without endangering our democratic freedoms, means should be provided for settling or preventing strikes in vital industries which affect the public interest.

The Department of Labor should be rebuilt and strengthened, and those units properly belonging within that Department should be placed in it.

The health of our economy and its maintenance at high levels further require that the minimum wage fixed by law should be raised to at least 75 cents an hour.

If our free-enterprise economy is to be strong and healthy we must reinvigorate the forces of competition. We must assure small business the freedom and opportunity to grow and prosper. To this purpose, we should strengthen our antitrust laws by closing those loopholes that permit monopolistic mergers and consolidations.

Our national farm program should be improved—not only in the interest of the farmers, but for the lasting prosperity of the whole Nation. Our goals should be abundant farm production and parity of income for agriculture. Standards of living on the farm should be just as good as anywhere else.

Farm price supports are an essential part of our program to achieve these ends. Price supports should be used to prevent farm price declines which are out of line with general price levels, to facilitate adjustments in production to consumer demands, and to promote good land use. Our price-support legislation must be adapted to these objectives. The authority of the Commodity Credit Corporation to provide adequate storage space for crops should be restored.

Our program for farm prosperity should also seek to expand the domestic market for agricultural products, particularly among low-income groups, and to increase and stabilize foreign markets.

We should give special attention to extending modern conveniences and services to our farms. Rural electrification should be pushed forward. And in considering legislation relating to housing, education, health, and social security, special attention should be given to rural problems.

Our growing population and the expansion of our economy depend upon the wise management of our land, water, forest, and mineral wealth. In our present dynamic economy, the task of conservation is not to lock up our resources but to develop and improve them. Failure, today, to make the investments which are necessary to support our progress in the future would be false economy.

We must push forward with the development of our rivers for power, irrigation, navigation, and flood control. We should apply the lessons of our Tennessee Valley experience to our other great river basins.

I again recommend that action be taken by the Congress to approve the St. Lawrence seaway and power project.

We must adopt a program for the planned use of the petroleum reserves under the sea, which are—and must remain—vested in the Federal Government. We must extend our programs of soil conservation. We must place our forests on a sustained-yield basis, and encourage the development of new sources of vital minerals.

In all this we must make sure that the benefits of these public undertakings are directly available to the people. Public power should be carried to consuming areas by public transmission lines where necessary to provide electricity at the lowest possible rates. Irrigation waters should serve family farms and not land speculators.

The Government has still other opportunities to help raise the standard of living of our citizens. These opportunities lie in the fields of social security, health, education, housing, and civil rights.

The present coverage of the social-security laws is altogether inadequate, and benefit payments are too low. One-third of our workers are not covered. Those who receive old-age and survivors' insurance benefits receive an average payment of only $25 a month. Many others who cannot work because they are physically disabled are left to the mercy of charity. We should expand our social-security program, both as to size of benefits and extent of coverage, against the economic hazards due to unemployment, old age, sickness, and disability.

We must spare no effort to raise the general level of health in this country. In a nation as rich as ours, it is a shocking fact that tens of millions lack adequate medical care. We are short of doctors, hospitals, and nurses. We must remedy these shortages. Moreover, we need—and we must have without further delay—a system of prepaid medical insurance which will enable every American to afford good medical care.

It is equally shocking that millions of our children are not receiving a good education. Millions of them are in overcrowded, obsolete buildings. We are short of teachers, because teachers' salaries are too low to attract new teachers, or to hold the ones we have. All these school problems will become much more acute as a result of the tremendous increase in the enrollment in our elementary schools in the next few years. I cannot repeat too strongly my desire for prompt Federal financial aid to the States to help them operate and maintain their school systems.

The governmental agency which now administers the programs of health, education, and social security should be given full departmental status.

The housing shortage continues to be acute. As an immediate step, the Congress should enact the provisions for low-rent public housing, slum clearance, farm housing, and housing research which I have repeatedly recommended. The number of low-rent public housing units provided for in the legislation should be increased to 1,000,000 units in the next 7 years. Even this number of units will not begin to meet our need for new housing.

Most of the houses we need will have to be built by private enterprise, without public subsidy. By producing too few rental units and too large a proportion of high-priced houses, the building industry is rapidly pricing itself out of the market. Building costs must be lowered.

The Government is now engaged in a campaign to induce all segments of the building industry to concentrate on the production of lower-priced housing. Additional legislation to encourage such housing will be submitted.

The authority which I have requested, to allocate materials in short supply and to impose price ceilings on such materials, could be used, if found necessary, to channel more materials into homes large enough for family life at prices which wage earners can afford.

The driving force behind our progress is our faith in our democratic institutions. That faith is embodied in the promise of equal rights and equal opportunities which the founders of our Republic proclaimed to their countrymen and to the whole world.

The fulfillment of this promise is among the highest purposes of government. The civil-rights proposals I made to the Eightieth Congress I now repeat to the Eighty-first Congress. They should be enacted in order that the Federal Government may assume the leadership and discharge the obligations clearly placed upon it by the Constitution.

I stand squarely behind those proposals.

Our domestic programs are the foundation of our foreign policy. The world today looks to us for leadership because we have so largely realized, within our borders, those benefits of democracy for which most of the peoples of the world are yearning.

We are following a foreign policy which is the outward expression of the democratic faith we profess. We are doing what we can to encourage free states and free peoples throughout the world, to aid the suffering and afflicted in foreign lands, and to strengthen democratic nations against aggression.

The heart of our foreign policy is peace. We are supporting a world organization to keep peace and a world economic policy to create prosperity for mankind. Our guiding star is the principle of international cooperation. To this concept we have made a national commitment as profound as anything in history. To it we have pledged our resources and our honor.

Until a system of world security is established upon which we can safely rely, we cannot escape the burden of creating and maintaining armed forces sufficient to deter aggression. We have made great progress in the last year in the effective organization of our armed forces, but further improvements in our national security legislation are necessary. Universal training is essential to the security of the United States.

During the course of this session I shall have occasion to ask the Congress to consider several measures in the field of foreign policy. At this time, I recommend that we restore the Reciprocal Trade Agreements Act to full effectiveness, and extend it for 3 years. We should also open our doors to displaced persons without unfair discrimination.

It should be clear by now to all nations that we are not seeking to freeze the status quo. We have no intention of preserving the injustices of the past. We welcome the constructive efforts being made by many nations to achieve a better life for their citizens. In the European recovery program, in our good-neighbor policy, and in the United Nations, we have begun to batter down those national walls which block the economic growth and the social advancement of the peoples of the world.

We believe that if we hold resolutely to this course the principle of international cooperation will eventually command the approval even of those nations which are now seeking to weaken or subvert it.

We stand at the opening of an era which can mean either great achievement or terrible catastrophe for ourselves and all mankind.

The strength of our Nation must continue to be used in the interest of all our people rather than a privileged few. It must continue to be used unselfishly in the struggle for world peace and the betterment of mankind the world over.

This is the task before us.

It is not an easy one. It has many complications, and there will be strong opposition from selfish interests.

I hope for cooperation from farmers, from labor, and from business. Every segment of our population and every individual have a right to expect from our Government a fair deal.

They have a right to expect that the Congress and the President will work in the closest cooperation with one objective—the welfare of the people of this Nation as a whole.

In the months ahead I know that I shall be able to cooperate with this Congress.

I am confident that the Divine Power which has guided us to this time of fateful responsibility and glorious opportunity will not desert us now.

With that help from Almighty God which we have humbly acknowledged at every turning point in our national life we shall be able to perform the great tasks which He now sets before us.

FIFTH ANNUAL MESSAGE

THE WHITE HOUSE, *January 4, 1950.*

MR. PRESIDENT, MR. SPEAKER, MEMBERS OF THE CONGRESS:

A year ago I reported to this Congress that the state of the Union was good. I am happy to be able to report to you today that the state of the Union continues to be good. Our Republic continues to increase in the enjoyment of freedom within its borders, and to offer strength and encouragement to all those who love freedom throughout the world.

During the past year we have made notable progress in strengthening the foundations of peace and freedom, abroad and at home.

We have taken important steps in securing the North Atlantic community against aggression. We have continued our successful support of European recovery. We have returned to our established policy of expanding international trade through reciprocal agreement. We have strengthened our support of the United Nations.

While great problems still confront us, the greatest danger has receded—the possibility which faced us 3 years ago that most of Europe and the Mediterranean area might collapse under totalitarian pressure. Today, the free peoples of the world have new vigor and new hope for the cause of peace.

In our domestic affairs, we have made notable advances toward broader opportunity and a better life for all our citizens.

We have met and reversed the first significant downturn in economic activity since the war. In accomplishing this, Government programs for maintaining employment and purchasing power have been of tremendous benefit. As the result of these programs, and the wisdom and good judgment of our businessmen and workers, major readjustments have been made without widespread suffering.

During the past year, we have also made a good start in providing housing for low-income groups; we have raised minimum wages; we have gone forward with the development of our natural resources; we have given greater assurance of stability to the farmer; and we have improved the organization and efficiency of our Government.

Today, by the grace of God, we stand a free and prosperous nation with greater possibilities for the future than any people have ever had before.

We are now, in this year of 1950, nearing the midpoint of the twentieth century.

The first half of this century will be known as the most turbulent and eventful period in recorded history. The swift pace of events promises to make the next 50 years decisive in the history of man on this planet.

The scientific and industrial revolution which began two centuries ago has, in the last 50 years, caught up the peoples of the globe in a common destiny. Two world-shattering wars have proved that no corner of the earth can be isolated from the affairs of mankind.

The human race has reached a turning point. Man has opened the secrets of nature and mastered new powers. If he uses them wisely, he can reach new heights of civilization. If he uses them foolishly, they may destroy him.

Man must create the moral and legal framework for the world which will insure that his new powers are used for good and not for evil. In shaping the outcome, the people of the United States will play a leading role.

Among all the great changes that have occurred in the last 50 years, none is more important than the change in the position of the United States in world affairs. Fifty years ago we were a country devoted largely to our own internal affairs. Our industry was growing, and we had new interests in the Far East and in the Caribbean, but we were primarily concerned with the development of vast areas of our own continental territory.

Today our population has doubled. Our national production has risen from about 50 billion dollars, in terms of today's prices, to the staggering figure of 255 billion dollars a year. We have a more productive economic system and a greater industrial potential than any other nation on the globe. Our standard of living is an inspiration for all other peoples. Even the slightest changes in our economic and social life have their effect on other countries all around the world.

Our tremendous strength has brought with it tremendous responsibilities. We have moved from the outer edge to the center of world affairs. Other nations look to us for a wise exercise of our economic and military strength, and for vigorous support of the ideals of representative government and a free society. We will not fail them.

Our objective in the world is peace. Our country has joined with others in the task of achieving peace. We know now that this is not an easy task, or a short one. But we are determined to see it through. Both of our great political parties are committed to working together—and I am sure they will continue to work together—to achieve this end. We are prepared to devote our energy and our resources to this task, because we know that our own security and the future of mankind are at stake.

Our success in working with other nations to achieve peace depends largely on what we do at home. We must preserve our national strength. Strength is not simply a matter of arms and force. It is a matter of economic growth, and social health, and vigorous institutions, public and private. We can achieve peace only if we maintain our productive energy, our democratic institutions, and our firm belief in individual freedom.

Our surest guide in the days that lie ahead will be the spirit in which this great Republic was founded. We must make our decisions in the conviction that all men are created equal, that they are equally entitled to life, liberty, and the pursuit of happiness, and that the duty of government is to serve these ends.

This country of ours has experienced many blessings, but none greater than its dedication to these principles. At every point in our history these ideals have served to correct our failures and shortcomings, to spur us on to greater efforts, and to keep clearly before us the primary purpose of our existence as a nation. They have enshrined for us, as a principle of government, the moral imperative to do justice, and the divine command to men to love one another.

These principles give meaning to all that we do.

In foreign policy they mean that we can never be tolerant of oppression or tyranny. They mean that we must throw our weight on the side of greater freedom and a better life for all peoples. These principles confirm us in carrying out the specific programs for peace which we have already begun.

We shall continue to give our wholehearted support to the United Nations. We believe that this organization can ultimately provide the framework of international law and morality without which mankind cannot survive. It has already set up new standards for the conduct of nations in the Declaration of Human Rights and the Convention on Genocide. It is moving ahead to give meaning to the concept of world brotherhood through a wide variety of cultural, economic, and technical activities.

The events of the past year again showed the value of the United Nations in bringing about the peaceful adjustment of tense international controversies. In Indonesia and in Palestine the efforts of the United Nations have put a stop to bloodshed and paved the way to peaceful settlements.

We are working toward the time when the United Nations will control weapons of mass destruction and will have the forces to preserve international law and order. While the world remains unsettled, however, and as long as our own security and the security of the free world require, we will maintain a strong and well-balanced defense organization. The Selective Service System is an essential part of our defense plans, and it must be continued.

Under the principles of the United Nations Charter we must continue to share in the common defense of free nations against aggression. At the last session this Congress laid the basis for this joint effort. We now must put into effect the common defense plans that are being worked out.

We shall continue our efforts for world economic recovery, because world prosperity is the only sure foundation for permanent peace.

As an immediate means to this end we must continue our support of the European recovery program. This program has achieved great success in the first 2 years of operation, but it has not yet been completed. If we were to stop this program now, or cripple it, just because it is succeeding, we should be doing exactly what the enemies of democracy want us to do. We should be just as foolish as a man who, for reasons of false economy, failed to put a roof on this house after building the foundation and the walls.

World prosperity also requires that we do all we can to expand world trade. As a major step in this direction we should promptly join the International Trade Organization. The purpose of this organization, which the United States has been foremost in creating, is to establish a code of fair practice, and an international authority for adjusting differences in international commercial relations. It is an effort to prevent the kind of anarchy and irresponsibility in world trade which did so much to bring about the world depression in the 1930's.

An expanding world economy requires the improvement of living standards and the development of resources in areas where human poverty and misery now prevail. Without such improvement, the recovery of Europe and the future of our own economy will not be secure. I urge that the Congress adopt the legislation now before it to provide for increasing the flow of technical assistance and capital investment to underdeveloped regions.

It is more essential now than ever, if the ideals of freedom and representative government are to prevail in these areas, and particularly in the Far East, that their people experience, in their own lives, the benefits of scientific and economic advances. This program will require the movement of large amounts of capital from the industrial nations, and particularly from the United States, to productive uses in the underdeveloped areas of the world. Recent world events make prompt action imperative.

This program is in the interest of all peoples; and it has nothing in common with either the old imperialism of the last century or the new imperialism of the Communists.

Our aim for a peaceful, democratic world of free peoples will be achieved in the long run, not by force of arms, but by an appeal to the minds and hearts of men. If the peace policy of the democratic nations is to be successful, they must demonstrate that the benefits of their way of life can be increased and extended to all nations and all races.

In the world today we are confronted with the danger that the rising demand of people everywhere for freedom and a better life may be corrupted and betrayed by the false promises of communism. In its ruthless struggle for power, communism seizes upon our imperfections, and takes advantage of the delays and set-backs which the democratic nations experience in their effort to secure a better life for their citizens. This challenge to us is more than a military challenge. It is a challenge to the honesty of our profession of the democratic faith; it is a challenge to the efficiency and stability of our economic system; it is a challenge to our willingness to work with other peoples for world peace and world prosperity.

For my part I welcome the challenge. I believe that our country, at this crucial point in world history, will meet that challenge successfully. I believe that, in cooperation with the other free nations of the world, we shall extend the full benefits of the democratic way of life to millions who do not now enjoy them, and preserve mankind from dictatorship and tyranny.

I believe that we shall succeed in our struggle for peace, because I have seen the success we have had in our own country in following the principles of freedom. Over the last 50 years the ideals of liberty and equal opportunity to which our Nation is dedicated have been increasingly realized in the lives of our people.

The ideal of equal opportunity no longer means simply the opportunity which a man has to advance beyond his fellows. Some of our citizens do achieve greater success than others as a reward for individual merit and effort, and this is as it should be. At the same time our country must be more than a land of opportunity for a select few. It must be a land of opportunity for all of us. In such a land all can grow and prosper together.

The simple truth that we can all go forward together is often questioned by selfish or short-sighted persons. It is strange that this is so, for this proposition is so clearly demonstrated by our national history. During the last 50 years, for example, our Nation has grown enormously in material well-being. This growth has come about, not by concentrating the benefits of our progress in the hands of a few, but by increasing the wealth of the great body of our citizens.

In the last 50 years the income of the average family has increased so greatly that its buying power has doubled. The average hours of work have declined from 60 to 40 a week, while the hourly production of the average worker has tripled. Average wages, allowing for price changes, have increased from about 45 cents an hour to $1.40 an hour.

We have accomplished what to earlier ages of mankind would have been a miracle—we work shorter hours, we produce more, and we live better.

Increasing freedom from poverty and drudgery has given a fuller meaning to American life. Our people are better educated; we have more opportunities for travel and recreation and enjoyment of the arts. We enjoy more personal liberty in the United States today than ever before.

If we can continue in the spirit of cooperative adventure which has marked the recent years of our progress, we can expect further scientific advances, further increases in our standard of living, and a still wider enjoyment of democratic freedom.

No one, of course, can foretell the future exactly. However, if we assume that we shall grow as fast in the future as we have grown in the past, we can get a good idea of how much our country should grow over the next 50 years.

At present our total national production is $255,000,000,000 a year. Our working population and our output per worker are increasing. If our productive power continues to increase at the same rate as it has increased for the past 50 years, our total national production 50 years from now will be nearly four times as much as it is today. Allowing for the expected growth in population, this would mean that the real income of the average family in the year 2000 A. D. would be about three times what it is today.

These are estimates of what we can do in the future, but we can reach these heights only if we follow the right policies. We have learned by bitter experience that progress is not automatic—that wrong policies lead to depression and disaster. We cannot achieve these gains unless we have a stable economy and avoid the catastrophes of boom and bust that have set us back in the past.

These gains cannot be achieved unless our businessmen maintain their spirit of initiative and enterprise and operate in a competitive economic system. They cannot be achieved unless our working men and women and their unions help to increase productivity and obtain for labor a fair share of the benefits of our economic system. They cannot be achieved unless we have a stable and prosperous agriculture. They cannot be achieved unless we conserve and develop our natural resources in the public interest. Our system will not work unless our people are healthy, well-educated, and confident of the future. It will not work unless all citizens can participate fully in our national life.

In achieving these gains, the Government has a special responsibility to help create and maintain the conditions which will permit the growth we know is possible. Foremost among these conditions is the need for a fair distribution of our increasing prosperity among all the great groups of our population who help to bring it about—business, labor, and agriculture.

Businessmen must continue to have the incentives necessary for investment and for the development of new lines of enterprise. In the future growth of this country lie possibilities for hundreds of thousands of new and independent businesses. As our national production increases, as it doubles and redoubles in the next 50 years, the number of independent and competing enterprises should also increase. If the number does not increase, our constantly growing economy will fall under the control of a few dominant economic groups whose powers will be so great that they will be a challenge to democratic institutions.

To avoid this danger, we must curb monopoly and provide aids to independent business so that it may have the credit and capital to compete in a system of free enterprise. I recommend that the Congress complete action at this session on the pending bill to close the loopholes in the Clayton Act which now permit monopolistic mergers. I also hope before this session is over to transmit to the Congress a series of proposals to strengthen the antimonopoly laws, to assist small business, and to encourage the growth of new enterprises.

In the case of labor free collective bargaining must be protected and encouraged. Collective bargaining is not only a fundamental economic freedom for labor; it is also a strengthening and stabilizing influence for our whole economy.

The Federal statute now governing labor relations is punitive in purpose and one-sided in operation. This statute is, and always has been, inconsistent with the practice of true and effective collective bargaining. It should be repealed and replaced by a law that is fair to all and in harmony with our democratic ideals.

A full understanding of the problems of modern labor relations is of such importance that I recommend the establishment of a Labor Extension Service to encourage educational activities in this field.

Another essential for our continued growth is a stable and prosperous agriculture. For many years we have been building a program to give the farmer a reasonable measure of protection against the special hazards to which he is exposed. That program was improved at the last session of the Congress. However, our farm legislation is still not adequate.

Although the Congress has properly declared as a matter of national policy that safeguards must be maintained against slumps in farm prices, there are serious shortcomings in the methods now available for carrying out this policy. Mandatory price supports should be provided for the commodities not now covered which are major sources of farm income.

Moreover, we should provide a method of supporting farm income at fair levels which will, at the same time, avoid piling up unmanageable surpluses and allow consumers to obtain the full benefit of our abundant agricultural production. A system of production payments gives the greatest promise of accomplishing this purpose. I recommend that the use of such a system be authorized.

One of the most important factors in our continued growth is the construction of more good, up-to-date housing. In a country such as ours there is no reason why decent homes should not be within the reach of all. With the help of various Government programs we have made great progress in the last few years in increasing the number of homes.

Despite this increase there is still an acute shortage of housing for the lower- and middle-income groups, especially in large metropolitan areas. We have laid the ground work for relieving the plight of lower-income families in the Housing Act of 1949. To aid middle-income families, I recommend that the Congress enact new legislation authorizing a vigorous program to help cooperatives and other nonprofit groups build housing which these families can afford.

Rent control has done a great deal to prevent the housing shortage from having had worse effects during this period of postwar adjustment. Rent control is still necessary to prevent widespread hardship and sharp curtailment of the buying power of millions of consumers in metropolitan areas. I recommend, therefore, that rent control be continued for another year.

If we are to achieve a better life for all, the natural resources of the country must be regarded as a public trust. We must use our precious assets of soil, water, forest, and grassland in such a way that they become constantly more productive and more valuable. Government investment in the conservation and development of our resources is necessary to the future economic expansion of the country.

We need to enlarge the production and transmission of public power. This is true not only in those regions which have already received great benefits from Federal power projects, but also in regions such as New England where the benefits of large-scale public power development have not yet been experienced.

In our hydroelectric and irrigation undertakings, as well as in our other resource programs, we must continue policies to assure that their benefits will be spread among the many and not restricted to a favored few.

Important resource legislation which should be passed at this session includes the authorization of the St. Lawrence seaway and power project and the establishment of the Columbia Valley Administration.

Through wise Government policies and Government expenditures for the conservation and development of our natural resources we can be sure of transmitting to our children and our children's children a country far richer and more productive than the one we know today.

The value of our natural resources is constantly being increased by the progress of science. Research is finding new ways of using such natural assets as minerals, sea water, and plant life. In the peaceful development of atomic energy, particularly, we stand on the threshold of new wonders. The first experimental machines for producing useful power from atomic energy are now under construction. We have made only the first beginnings in this field, but in the perspective of history they may loom larger than the first airplane, or even the first tools that started man on the road to civilization.

To take full advantage of the increasing possibilities of nature, we must equip ourselves with increasing knowledge. Government has a responsibility to see that our country maintains its position in the advance of science. As a step toward this end, the Congress should complete action on the measure to create a National Science Foundation.

Another duty of the Government is to promote the economic security, the health, and the education of its citizens. By so doing we strengthen both our economy and the structure of our society. In a nation as rich as ours all citizens should be able to live in decency and health.

Our social security system should be developed into the main reliance of our people for basic protection against the economic hazards of old age, unemployment, and illness. I earnestly hope that the Congress will complete action at this session on legislation to increase the benefits and extend the coverage of old-age and survivors insurance. The widespread movement to provide pensions in private industry dramatizes the need for improvements in the public insurance system.

I also urge that the Congress strengthen our unemployment compensation law to meet present-day needs more adequately. The economic downturn of the past year was the first real test that our system of unemployment insurance has had to meet. That test has proved the wisdom of the system, but it has also made strikingly apparent the need for improving its operation and increasing its coverage and its benefits.

In the field of health, there are immense opportunities to extend to more of our people the benefits of the amazing advances in medical science. We have made a good beginning in expanding our hospitals, but we must go on to remedy the shortages of doctors, nurses, and public health services, and to establish a system of medical insurance which will enable all Americans to afford good medical care.

We must take immediate steps to strengthen our educational system. In many parts of our country young people are being handicapped for life because of a poor education. The rapidly increasing number of children of school age, coupled with the shortage of qualified teachers, makes this problem more critical each year. I believe that the Congress should no longer delay in providing Federal assistance to the States so that they can maintain adequate schools.

As we go forward in achieving greater economic security and greater opportunity for all our people, we should make every effort to extend the benefits of our democratic institutions to every citizen. The religious ideals which we profess, and the heritage of freedom which we have received from the past, clearly place that duty upon us.

I again urge the Congress to enact the civil rights proposals I made in February 1948. These are proposals for the enactment of Federal statutes which will protect all our people in the exercise of their democratic rights and their search for economic opportunity, grant statehood to Alaska and Hawaii, provide a greater measure of self-government for our island possessions, and accord home rule to the District of Columbia. Some of those proposals have been before the Congress for a long time. Those who oppose them, as well as those who favor them, should recognize that it is the duty of the elected representatives of the people to let these proposals come to a vote.

Our democratic ideals, as well as our own best interests, require that we do our fair share in providing homes for the unfortunate victims of war and tyranny. In so doing we shall add strength to our democracy through the abilities and skills which these men and women will bring here. I urge the prompt enactment by the Congress of the legislation now before it to extend and broaden the existing displaced persons law and remove its discriminatory features.

The measures I am recommending to the Congress concerning both our foreign and our domestic policies represent a carefully considered program to meet our national needs. It is a program which necessarily requires large expenditures of funds. More than 70 percent of the Government's expenditures are required to meet the costs of past wars and to work for world peace. This is the dominant factor in our fiscal policy. At the same time the Government must make substantial expenditures which are necessary to the growth and expansion of the domestic economy.

At present, largely because of the ill-considered tax reduction of the Eightieth Congress, the Government is not receiving enough revenue to meet its necessary expenditures.

To meet this situation I am proposing that Federal expenditures be held to the lowest levels consistent with our international requirements and the essential needs of economic growth and the well-being of our people. At the same time we must guard against the folly of attempting budget slashes which would impair our prospects for peace or cripple the programs essential to our national strength.

The budget recommendations I shall shortly transmit to the Congress show that we can expect a substantial improvement in our fiscal position over the next few years, as the cost of some of the extraordinary postwar programs declines, and as Government revenue rises as a result of growth in employment and national income. To further improve our fiscal outlook, we should make some changes in our tax system which will reduce present inequities, stimulate business activity, and yield a moderate amount of additional revenue. I expect to transmit specific recommendations to the Congress on this subject at an early date.

The fiscal policy I am recommending is the quickest and safest way of achieving a balanced budget.

As we move forward into the second half of the twentieth century we must always bear in mind the central purpose of our national life. We do not seek material prosperity for ourselves because we love luxury; we do not aid other nations because we wish to increase our power. We have not devised programs for the security and well-being of our people because we are afraid or unwilling to take risks. This is not the meaning of our past history or our present course.

We work for a better life for all, so that all men may put to good use the great gifts with which they have been endowed by their Creator. We seek to establish those material conditions of life in which, without exception, men may live in dignity, perform useful work, serve their communities, and worship God as they see fit.

These may seem simple goals, but they are not little ones. They are worth a great deal more than all the empires and conquests of history. They are not to be achieved by military aggression or political fanaticism. They are to be achieved by humbler means—by hard work, by a spirit of self-restraint in our dealings with one another, and by a deep devotion to the principles of justice and equality.

It should make us truly thankful, as we look back to the beginnings of this country, that we have come so far along the road to a better life for all. It should make us humble to think, as we look ahead, how much farther we have to go to accomplish, at home and abroad, the objectives that were set out for us at the founding of this Nation.

As we approach the halfway mark in the twentieth century, we should ask for continued strength and guidance from that Almighty Power who has placed before us such great opportunities for the good of mankind in the years to come.

SIXTH ANNUAL MESSAGE.

THE WHITE HOUSE, *January 8, 1951*.

MR. PRESIDENT, MR. SPEAKER, MEMBERS OF THE CONGRESS:

This Eighty-second Congress faces as grave a task as any Congress in the history of our Republic.

The actions you take will be watched by the whole world. These actions will measure the ability of a free people, acting through their chosen representatives and their free institutions, to meet a deadly challenge to their way of life.

We can meet this challenge foolishly or wisely. We can meet it timidly or bravely, shamefully or honorably.

I know that the Eighty-second Congress will meet this challenge in a way worthy of our great heritage. I know that your debates will be earnest, responsible, and to the point. I know that from these debates there will come the great decisions needed to carry us forward.

At this critical time, I am glad to say that our country is in a healthy condition. Our democratic institutions are sound and strong. We have more men and women at work than ever before. We are able to produce more than ever before—in fact, far more than any country ever produced in the history of the world.

I am confident that we can succeed in the great task that lies before us.

We will succeed, but we must all do our part. We must all act together as citizens of this great Republic.

As we meet here today, American soldiers are fighting a bitter campaign in Korea.

We pay tribute to their courage, devotion, and gallantry.

Our men are fighting, alongside their United Nations allies, because they know, as we do, that the aggression in Korea is part of the attempt of the Russian Communist dictatorship to take over the world, step by step.

Our men are fighting a long way from home, but they are fighting for our lives and our liberties. They are fighting to protect our right to meet here today—our right to govern ourselves as a free nation.

The threat of world conquest by Soviet Russia endangers our liberty and endangers the kind of world in which the free spirit of man can survive. This threat is aimed at all peoples who strive to win or defend their own freedom and national independence.

Indeed, the state of our Nation is in great part the state of our friends and allies throughout the world. The gun that points at them points at us also.

The threat is a total threat and the danger is a common danger.

All free nations are exposed and all are in peril. Their only security lies in banding together. No one nation can find protection in a selfish search for a safe haven from the storm.

The free nations do not have any aggressive purpose. We want only peace in the world—peace for all countries. No threat to the security of any nation is concealed in our plans or programs.

We had hoped that the Soviet Union, with its security assured by the Charter of the United Nations, would be willing to live and let live. But, I am sorry to say, that has not been the case.

The imperialism of the Czars has been replaced by the even more ambitious, more crafty, and more menacing imperialism of the rulers of the Soviet Union.

This new imperialism has powerful military forces. It is keeping millions of men under arms. It has a large air force and a strong submarine force. It has complete control of the men and equipment of its satellities. It has kept its subject peoples and its economy in a state of perpetual mobilization.

The present rulers of the Soviet Union have shown that they are willing to use this power to destroy the free nations and win domination over the whole world.

The Soviet imperialists have two ways of going about their destructive work. They use the method of subversion and internal revolution, and they use the method of external aggression. In preparation for either of these methods of attack, they stir up class strife and disorder. They encourage sabotage. They put out poisonous propaganda. They deliberately try to prevent economic improvement.

If their efforts are successful, they foment a revolution, as they did in Czechoslovakia and China, and as they tried unsuccessfully to do in Greece. If their methods of subversion are blocked, and if they think they can get away with outright warfare, they resort to external aggression. This is what they did when they loosed the armies of their puppet states against the Republic of Korea, in an evil war by proxy.

We of the free world must be ready to meet both of these methods of Soviet action. We must not neglect one or the other.

The free world has power and resources to meet these two forms of aggression—resources that are far greater than those of the Soviet dictatorship. We have skilled and vigorous peoples, great industrial strength, and abundant sources of raw materials. And, above all, we cherish liberty. Our common ideals are a great part of our strength. These ideals are the driving force of human progress.

The free nations believe in the dignity and worth of man.

We believe in independence for all nations.

We believe that free and independent nations can band together into a world order based on law. We have laid the cornerstone of such a peaceful world in the United Nations.

We believe that such a world order can and should spread the benefits of modern science and industry, better health and education, more food and rising standards of living—throughout the world.

These ideals give our cause a power and vitality that Russian communism can never command.

The free nations, however, are bound together by more than an ideal. They are a real community bound together also by the ties of self-interest and self-preservation. If they should fall apart, the results would be fatal to human freedom.

Our own national security is deeply involved with that of the other free nations. While they need our support, we equally need theirs. Our national safety would be gravely prejudiced if the Soviet Union were to succeed in harnessing to its war machine the resources and the manpower of the free nations on the borders of its empire.

If western Europe were to fall to Soviet Russia, it would double the Soviet supply of coal and triple the Soviet supply of steel. If the free countries of Asia and Africa should fall to Soviet Russia, we would lose the sources of many of our most vital raw materials, including uranium, which is the basis of our atomic power. And Soviet command of the manpower of the free nations of Europe and Asia would confront us with military forces which we could never hope to equal.

In such a situation the Soviet Union could impose its demands on the world, without resort to conflict, simply through the preponderance of its economic and military power. The Soviet Union does not have to attack the United States to secure domination of the world. It can achieve its ends by isolating us and swallowing up all our allies. Therefore, even if we were craven enough—and I do not believe that we could be—I say even if we were craven enough to abandon our ideals, it would be disastrous for us to withdraw from the community of free nations.

We are the most powerful single member of this community, and we have a special responsibility. We must take the leadership in meeting the challenge to freedom and in helping to protect the rights of independent nations.

This country has a practical, realistic program of action for meeting this challenge.

First, we shall have to extend economic assistance, where it can be effective. The best way to stop subversion by the Kremlin is to strike at the roots of social injustice and economic disorder. People who have jobs, homes, and hopes for the future will defend themselves against the underground agents of the Kremlin. Our programs of economic aid have done much to turn back communism.

In Europe the Marshall plan has had electrifying results. As

European recovery progressed, the strikes led by the Kremlin's agents in Italy and France failed. All over western Europe the Communist Party took worse and worse beatings at the polls.

The countries which have received Marshall plan aid have been able, through hard work, to expand their productive strength—in many cases, to levels higher than ever before in their history. Without this strength they would be completely incapable of defending themselves today. They are now ready to use this strength in helping to build a strong combined defense against aggression.

We shall need to continue some economic aid to European countries. This aid should now be specifically related to the building of their defenses.

In other parts of the world, our economic assistance will need to be more broadly directed toward economic development. In the Near East, in Africa, in Asia, we must do what we can to help people who are striving to advance from misery, poverty, and hunger. We must also continue to help the economic growth of our good neighbors in this hemisphere. These actions will bring greater strength for the free world. They will give many people a real stake in the future and reason to defend their freedom. They will mean increased production of the goods they need and the materials we need.

Second, we shall need to continue our military assistance to countries which want to defend themselves.

The heart of our common defense effort is the North Atlantic community. The defense of Europe is the basis for the defense of the whole free world—ourselves included. Next to the United States, Europe is the largest workshop of the world. It is also a homeland of great religious beliefs shared by many of our citizens—beliefs which are now threatened by the tide of atheistic communism.

Strategically, economically, and morally the defense of Europe is part of our own defense.

That is why we have joined with the countries of Europe in the North Atlantic Treaty, pledging ourselves to work with them.

There has been much discussion recently over whether the European countries are willing to defend themselves. Their actions are answering this question.

Our North Atlantic Treaty partners have strict systems of universal military training. Several have recently increased the term of service. All have taken measures to improve the quality of training. Forces are being trained and expanded as rapidly as the necessary arms and equipment can be supplied from their factories and ours. Our North Atlantic Treaty partners, together, are building armies bigger than our own.

None of the North Atlantic Treaty countries, including our own country, has done enough yet. But real progress is being made.

Together, we have worked out defense plans. The military leaders of our own country took part in working out these plans, and are agreed that they are sound and within our capabilities.

To put these plans into action, we sent to Europe last week one of our greatest military commanders, Gen. Dwight D. Eisenhower.

General Eisenhower went to Europe to assume command of the united forces of the North Atlantic Treaty countries, including our own forces in Germany.

The people of Europe have confidence in General Eisenhower. They know his ability to put together a fighting force of allies. His mission is vital to our security. We should all stand behind him, and give him every bit of help we can.

Part of our job will be to reinforce the military strength of our European partners by sending them weapons and equipment as our military production expands.

Our program of military assistance extends to the nations of the Near East and the Far East which are trying to defend their freedom. Soviet communism is trying to make these nations into colonies, and to use their people as cannon fodder in new wars of conquest. We want their people to be free men and to enjoy peace.

Our country has always stood for freedom for the peoples of Asia. Long, long ago we stood for the freedom of the peoples of Asia. Our history shows this. We have demonstrated it in the Philippines. We have demonstrated it in our relations with Indonesia, India, and China. We hope to join in restoring the people of Japan to membership in the community of free nations.

It is in the Far East that we have taken up arms, under the United Nations, to preserve the principle of independence for free nations. We are fighting to keep the forces of Communist aggression from making a slave state out of Korea.

Korea has tremendous significance for the world. It means that free nations, acting through the United Nations, are fighting together against aggression.

We will understand the importance of this best if we look back into history. If the democracies had stood up against the invasion of Manchuria in 1931, or the attack on Ethiopia in 1935, or the seizure of Austria in 1938, if they had stood together against aggression on those occasions as the United Nations has done, the whole history of our time would have been different.

The principles for which we are fighting in Korea are right and just. They are the foundations of collective security and of the future of free nations. Korea is not only a country undergoing the torment of aggression; it is also a symbol. It stands for right and justice in the world against oppression and slavery. The free world must always stand for these principles—and we will stand with the free world.

As the third part of our program, we will continue to work for peaceful settlements of international disputes. We will support the United Nations and remain loyal to the great principles of international cooperation laid down in its Charter.

We are willing, as we have always been, to negotiate honorable settlements with the Soviet Union. But we will not engage in appeasement.

The Soviet rulers have made it clear that we must have strength as well as right on our side. If we build our strength—and we are building it—the Soviet rulers may face the facts and lay aside their plans to take over the world.

That is what we hope will happen, and that is what we are trying to bring about.

That is the only realistic road to peace.

These are the main elements of the course our Nation must follow as a member of the community of free nations. These are the things we must do to preserve our security and help create a peaceful world. But they will be successful only if we increase the strength of our own country.

Here at home we have some very big jobs to do. We are building much stronger military forces—and we are building them fast. We are preparing for full wartime mobilization, if that should be necessary. And we are continuing to build a strong and growing economy, able to maintain whatever effort may be required for as long as necessary.

We are building our own Army, Navy, and Air Force to an active strength of nearly 3½ million men and women. We are stepping up the training of the reserve forces, and establishing more training facilities, so that we can rapidly increase our active forces far more on short notice.

We are going to produce all the weapons and equipment that such an armed force will need. Furthermore, we will make weapons for our allies, and weapons for our own reserve supplies. On top of this, we will build the capacity to turn out on short notice arms and supplies that may be needed for a full-scale war.

Fortunately, we have a good start on this because of our enormous plant capacity and because of the equipment on hand from the last war. For example, many combat ships are being returned to active duty from the "mothball fleet" and many other can be put into service on very short notice. We have large reserves of arms and ammunition and thousands of workers skilled in arms production.

In many cases, however, our stocks of weapons are low. In other cases, those on hand are not the most modern. We have made remarkable technical advances. We have developed new types of jet planes and powerful new tanks. We are concentrating on producing the newest types of weapons and producing them as fast as we possibly can.

This production drive is more selective than the one we had during World War II, but it is just as urgent and intense. It is a big program and it is a costly one.

Let me give you two concrete examples: Our present program calls for expanding the aircraft industry so that it will have the capacity to produce 50,000 modern military planes a year. We are preparing the capacity to produce 35,000 tanks a year. We are not now ordering that many planes or that many tanks, and we hope that we never have to, but we mean to be able to turn them out if we need them.

The planes we are producing now are much bigger—and much better—than the planes we had during the last war.

We used to think that the B–17 was a huge plane, and the block-buster it carried a huge load. But the B–36 can carry five of those block-busters in its belly, and it can carry them five times as far. Of course, the B–36 is much more complicated to build than the B–17, and far more expensive. One B–17 costs about $275,000, while now one B–36 costs about 3½ million dollars.

I ask you to remember that what we are doing is to provide the best and most modern military equipment in the world for our fighting forces.

This kind of defense production program has two parts.

The first part is to get our defense production going as fast as possible. We have to convert plants and channel materials to defense production.

This means heavy cuts in the civilian use of copper, aluminum, rubber, and other essential materials. It means shortages in various consumer goods.

The second part is to increase our capacity to produce and to keep our economy strong for the long pull. We do not know how long Communist aggression will threaten the world.

Only by increasing our output can we carry the burden of preparedness for an indefinite period in the future. This means that we will have to build more power plants, and more steel mills, grow more cotton, mine more copper, and expand our capacity in many other ways.

The Congress will need to consider legislation, at this session, affecting all the aspects of our mobilization job. The main subjects on which legislation will be needed are—

First, appropriations for our military build-up.

Second, extension and revision of the Selective Service Act.

Third, military and economic aid to help build up the strength of the free world.

Fourth, revision and extension of the authority to expand production and to stabilize prices, wages, and rents.

Fifth, improvement of our agricultural laws, to help obtain the kinds of farm products we need for the defense effort.

Sixth, improvement of our labor laws to help provide stable labor-management relations and to make sure that we have steady production in this emergency.

Seventh, housing and training of defense workers, and the full use of all our manpower resources.

Eighth, means for increasing the supply of doctors, nurses, and other trained medical personnel critically needed for the defense effort.

Ninth, aid to the States to meet the most urgent needs of our elementary and secondary schools. Some of our plans will have to be deferred for the time being. But we should do all we can to make sure our children are being trained as good and useful citizens in these critical times ahead.

Tenth, a major increase in taxes to meet the cost of the defense effort.

The economic report and the budget message will discuss these subjects further. In addition, I shall send to the Congress special messages containing detailed recommendations on legislation needed at this session.

In the months ahead, the Government must give priority to activities that are urgent—like military procurement and atomic energy and power development. It must practice rigid economy in its nondefense activities. Many of the things we would normally do must be curtailed or postponed.

But in a long-term defense effort like this one, we cannot neglect the measures needed to maintain a strong economy and a healthy democratic society.

The Congress, therefore, should give continued attention to the measures which our country will need for the long pull. And it should act upon such legislation as promptly as circumstances permit.

To take just one example—we need to continue and complete the work of rounding out our system of social insurance. We still need to improve our protection against unemployment and old age. We still need to provide insurance against loss of earnings through sickness, and against the high costs of modern medical care.

Above all, we must remember that the fundamentals of our strength rest upon the freedoms of our people. We must continue our efforts to achieve the full realization of our democratic ideals. We must uphold freedom of speech and freedom of conscience in our land. We must assure equal rights and equal opportunities to all our citizens.

As we go forward this year in the defense of freedom, let us keep clearly before us the nature of our present effort.

We are building up our strength, in concert with other free nations, to meet the danger of aggression that has been turned loose on the world. The strength of the free nations is the world's best hope of peace.

I ask the Congress for unity in these crucial days.

Make no mistake about my meaning. I do not ask, or expect, unanimity. I do not ask for an end to debate. Only by debate can we arrive at decisions which are wise, and which reflect the desires of the American people. We do not have dictatorship in this country, and we will never have one in this country.

When I request unity, what I am really asking for is a sense of responsibility on the part of every Member of this Congress. Let us debate the issues, but let every man among us weigh his words and deeds. There is a sharp difference between harmful criticism and constructive criticism. If we are truly responsible as individuals, I am sure that we will be unified as a government.

Let us keep our eyes on the issues and work for the things we all believe in.

Let each of us put our country ahead of our party, and ahead of our own personal interests.

I had the honor to be a Member of the Senate during World War II, and I know from experience that unity of purpose and of effort is possible in the Congress without any lessening of the vitality of our two-party system.

Let us all stand together as Americans. And let us stand together with all men everywhere who believe in human liberty.

Peace is precious to us. It is the way of life we strive for with all the strength and wisdom we possess. But more precious than peace are freedom and justice. We will fight, if fight we must, to keep our freedom and to prevent justice from being destroyed.

These are the things that give meaning to our lives, and which we acknowledge to be greater than ourselves.

This is our cause—peace, freedom, justice.

We will pursue this cause with determination and humility, asking divine guidance that in all we do we may follow God's will.

SEVENTH ANNUAL MESSAGE.

THE WHITE HOUSE, *January 9, 1952.*

MR. PRESIDENT, MR. SPEAKER, MEMBERS OF THE CONGRESS:

I have the honor to report to the Congress on the state of the Union.

At the outset, I should like to speak of the necessity for putting first things first as we work together this year for the good of our country.

The United States and the whole free world are passing through a period of grave danger. Every action you take here in Congress, and every action I take as President, must be measured against the test of whether it helps to meet that danger.

This will be a Presidential election year—the kind of year in which politics plays a larger part in our lives than usual. That is perfectly proper. But we have a great responsibility to conduct our political fights in a manner that does not harm the national interest.

We can find plenty of things to differ about without destroying our free institutions and without abandoning our bipartisan foreign policy for peace.

When everything is said and done, all of us—Republicans and Democrats alike—all of us are Americans; and we are all going to sink or swim together.

We are moving through a perilous time. Faced with a terrible threat of aggression, our Nation has embarked upon a great effort to help establish the kind of world in which peace shall be secure. Peace is our goal—not peace at any price, but a peace based on freedom and justice. We are now in the midst of our effort to reach that goal. On the whole, we have been doing very well.

Last year, 1951, was a year in which we threw back aggression, added greatly to our military strength, and improved the chances for peace and freedom in many parts of the world.

This year, 1952, is a crucial year in the defense effort of the whole free world. If we falter, we can lose all the gains that we have made. If we drive ahead, with courage and vigor and determination, we can by the end of 1952 be in a position of much greater security. The way will be dangerous for years ahead, but if we put forth our best efforts this year—and next year—we can be "over the hump" in our effort to build strong defenses.

When we look at the record of the past year, 1951, we find important things on both the credit and the debit side of the ledger. We have made great advances. At the same time we have run into new problems which must be overcome.

Let us look at the credit side first.

Peace depends upon the free nations sticking together, and making a combined effort to check aggression and prevent war. In this respect 1951 was a year of great achievement.

In Korea the forces of the United Nations turned back the Chinese

Communist invasion, and did it without widening the area of conflict. The action of the United Nations in Korea has been a powerful deterrent to a third world war. However, the situation in Korea remains very hazardous. The outcome of the armistice negotiations is still uncertain.

In Indochina and Malaya our aid has helped our allies to hold back the Communist advance, although there are signs of further trouble in that area.

In 1951 we strengthened the chances of peace in the Pacific region by the treaties with Japan and by defense arrangements with Australia, New Zealand, and the Philippines.

In Europe combined defense has become a reality. The free nations have created a real fighting force. This force is not yet as strong as it needs to be; but it is already a real obstacle to any attempt by hostile forces to sweep across Europe to the Atlantic.

In 1951 we also moved to strengthen the security of Europe by the agreement to bring Greece and Turkey into the North Atlantic Treaty.

The United Nations, the world's great hope for peace, has come through a year of trial stronger and more useful than ever. The free nations have stood together in blocking Communist attempts to tear up the Charter.

At the present session of the United Nations in Paris, we, together with the British and the French, offered a plan to reduce and control all armaments under a foolproof inspection system. This is a concrete, practical proposal for disarmament.

But what happened? Vishinsky laughed at it. Listen to what he said: "I could hardly sleep at all last night * * *. I could not sleep because I kept laughing." The world will be a long time forgetting the spectacle of that fellow laughing at disarmament.

Disarmament is not a joke. Vishinsky's laughter met with shock and anger from people all over the world. And, as a result, Mr. Stalin's representative received orders to stop laughing and start talking.

If the Soviet leaders were to accept this proposal, it would lighten the burden of armaments and permit the resources of the earth to be devoted to the good of mankind. But until the Soviet Union accepts a sound disarmament proposal, and joins in peaceful settlements, we have no choice except to build up our defenses.

During this past year we added more than a million men and women to our Armed Forces. The total is now nearly 3½ million. We have made rapid progress in the field of atomic weapons. We have turned out 16 billion dollars worth of military supplies and equipment, three times as much as the year before.

Economic conditions in the country are good. There are 61 million people on the job; wages, farm incomes, and business profits are at high levels. Total production of goods and services in our country has increased 8 percent over the last year, about twice the normal rate of growth.

Perhaps the most amazing thing about our economic progress is the way we are increasing our basic capacity to produce. For example, we are now in the second year of a 3-year program which will double our output of aluminum, increase our electric-power supply by 40 percent, and increase our steel-making capacity by 15 percent. We can then produce 120 million tons of steel a year, as much as the rest of the world put together.

This expansion will mean more jobs and higher standards of living for all of us in the years ahead. At the present time it means greater strength for us and for the rest of the free world in the fight for peace.

Now, I must turn to the debit side of the ledger for the past year.

The outstanding fact to note on the debit side of the ledger is that the Soviet Union in 1951 continued to expand its military production and increase its already excessive military power.

It is true that the Soviets have run into increasing difficulties. Their hostile policies have awakened stern resistance among free men throughout the world. And, behind the iron curtain the Soviet rule of force has created growing political and economic stresses in the satellite nations.

Nevertheless, the grim fact remains that the Soviet Union is increasing its armed might. It is still producing more war planes than the free nations. It has set off two more atomic explosions. The world still walks in the shadow of another world war.

And here at home our defense preparations are far from complete.

During 1951 we did not make adequate progress in building up civil defense against atomic attack. This is a major weakness in our plans for peace, since inadequate civilian defense is an open invitation to surprise attack. Failure to provide adequate civilian defense has the same effect as adding to the enemy's supply of atom bombs.

In the field of defense production we have run into difficulties and delays in designing and producing the latest types of airplanes and tanks. Some machine tools and metals are still in extremely short supply.

In other free countries the defense build-up has created severe economic problems. It has increased inflation in Europe and has endangered the continued recovery of our allies.

In the Middle East political tensions and the oil controversy in Iran are keeping the region in a turmoil. In the Far East the dark threat of Communist imperialism still hangs over many nations.

This, very briefly, is the good side and the bad side of the picture.

Taking the good and bad together, we have made real progress this last year along the road to peace. We have increased the power and unity of the free world. And, while we were doing this, we have avoided world war on the one hand and appeasement on the other. This is a hard road to follow, but the events of the last year show that it is the right road to peace.

We cannot expect to complete the job overnight. The free nations may have to maintain for years the larger military forces needed to deter aggression. We must build steadily, over a period of years, toward political solidarity and economic progress among the free countries in all parts of the world.

Our task will not be easy; but, if we go at it with a will, we can look forward to steady progress. On our side are all the great resources of freedom; the ideals of religion and democracy, the aspiration of people for a better life, and the industrial and technical power of a free civilization.

These advantages outweigh anything the slave world can produce.

The only thing that can defeat us is our own state of mind. We can lose if we falter.

The middle period of a great national effort like this is a very difficult time. The way seems long and hard. The goal seems far distant. Some people get discouraged. That is only natural.

But if there are any among us who think we ought to ease up in the fight for peace, I want to remind them of three things—just three things.

First: The threat of world war is still very real. We had one Pearl Harbor; let's not get caught off guard again. If you don't think the threat of Communist armies is real, talk to some of our men back from Korea.

Second: If the United States had to try to stand alone against a Soviet-dominated world, it would destroy the life we know and the ideals we hold dear. Our allies are essential to us, just as we are essential to them. The more shoulders there are to bear the burden the lighter it will be.

Third: The things we believe in most deeply are under relentless attack. We have the great responsibility of saving the basic moral and spiritual values of our civilization. We have started out well, with a program for peace that is unparalleled in history. If we believe in ourselves and the faith we profess, we will stick to the job.

This is a time for courage, not for grumbling and mumbling.

Now, let us take a look at the things we have to do.

The thing that is uppermost in the minds of all of us is the situation in Korea. We must—and we will—keep up the fight there until we get the kind of armistice that will put an end to the aggression and protect the safety of our forces and the security of the Republic of Korea. Beyond that, we shall continue to work for a settlement in Korea that upholds the principles of the United Nations. We went into Korea because we knew that Communist aggression had to be met firmly if freedom was to be preserved in the world. We went into the fight to save the Republic of Korea, a free country, established under the United Nations. These are our aims. We will not give up until we attain them.

Meanwhile, we must continue to strengthen the forces of freedom throughout the world.

I hope the Senate will take early and favorable action on the Japanese peace treaty, on our security pacts with Pacific countries, and on the agreement to bring Greece and Turkey into the North Atlantic Treaty.

We are also negotiating an agreement with the German Federal Republic under which it can play an honorable and equal part among nations and take its place in the defense of Western Europe.

But treaties and plans are only the skeleton of our defense structure. The sinew and muscle of defense forces and equipment must be provided.

In Europe we must go on helping our friends and allies to build up their military forces. This means we must send weapons in large volume to our European allies. I have directed that weapons for Europe be given a very high priority. Economic aid is necessary, too, to supply the margin of difference between success and failure in making Europe a strong partner in our joint defense.

In the long run we want to see Europe freed from any dependence on our aid. Our European allies want that just as much as we do. The steps that are now being taken to build European unity should help bring that about. Five European countries are pooling their coal and steel production under the Schuman plan. Work is going forward on the merger of European national forces on the Continent into a single army. These great projects should become realities in 1952.

We should do all we can to help and encourage the move toward a strong and united Europe.

In Asia the new Communist empire is a daily threat to millions of people. The peoples of Asia want to be free to follow their own way of life. They want to preserve their culture and their traditions against communism just as much as we want to preserve ours. They are laboring under terrific handicaps: poverty, ill health, feudal systems of land ownership, and the threat of internal subversion or external attack. We can and must increase our help to them.

That means military aid, especially to those places like Indochina, which might be hardest hit by some new Communist attack.

It also means economic aid, both technical know-how and capital investment.

This last year we made available millions of bushels of wheat to relieve famine in India. But far more important, in the long run, is the work Americans are doing in India to help the Indian farmers themselves raise more grain. With the help of our technicians, Indian farmers, using simple inexpensive means, have been able since 1948 to double the crops in one area in India. One farmer there raised 63 bushels of wheat to the acre, where 13 bushels had been the average before.

This is our Point IV program at work. It is working—not only in India, but in Iran, Paraguay, Liberia—in 33 countries around the globe. Our technical missionaries are out there. We need more of them. We need more funds to speed their efforts, because there is nothing of greater importance in all our foreign policy. There is nothing that shows more clearly what we stand for and what we want to achieve.

My friends of the Congress, less than one-third of the expenditure for the cost of World War II would have created the developments necessary to feed the whole world so we would not have stomach-communism, and unless we fight that battle and win it we cannot win the cold war or a hot one either.

We have recently lost a great public servant who was leading this effort to bring opportunity and hope to the people of half the world. Dr. Henry Bennett and his associates died in the line of duty on a Point IV mission. It is up to us to carry on the great work for which they gave their lives.

During the coming year we must not forget the suffering of the people who live behind the iron curtain. In those areas minorities are being oppressed, human rights violated, religion persecuted. We should continue to expose those wrongs. We should continue and expand the activities of the Voice of America, which brings our message of hope and truth to those peoples and other peoples throughout the world.

I have just had an opportunity to discuss many of these world problems with Prime Minister Churchill. We have had a most satisfactory series of meetings. We thoroughly reviewed the situation in Europe, the Middle East, and the Far East. We both look forward to steady progress toward peace through the cooperative action and teamwork of the free nations.

Turning from our foreign policies, let us now consider the jobs we have here at home as part of our program for peace.

The first of these jobs is to move ahead full steam on our defense program.

Our objective is to have a well-equipped, active defense force large enough—in concert with the forces of our allies—to deter aggression and to inflict punishing losses on the enemy immediately if we should be attacked. This active force must be backed by adequate reserves, and by the plants and tools to turn out the tremendous quantities of new weapons that would be needed if war came. We are not building an active force adequate to carry on a full-scale war, but we are putting ourselves in a position to mobilize very rapidly if we have to.

This year I shall recommend some increases in the size of the active force we are building, with particular emphasis on air power. This means we shall have to continue large-scale production of planes and other equipment for a longer period of time than we had originally planned.

Planes and tanks and other weapons—what the military call "hard goods"—are now beginning to come off the production lines in volume. Deliveries of hard goods now amount to about a billion and a half dollars worth a month. A year from now we expect this rate to be doubled.

We shall have to hold a high rate of military output for about a year after that. In 1954 we hope to have enough equipment so that we can reduce the production of most military items substantially. The next 2 years should therefore be the peak period of defense production.

Defense needs will take a lot of our steel, aluminum, copper, nickel, and other scarce materials. This means smaller production of some civilian goods. The cut-backs will be nothing like those during World War II, when much civilian production was completely stopped, but there will be considerably less of some goods than we have been used to these past 2 or 3 years.

A very critical part of our defense job this year is to keep down inflation.

We can control inflation if we make up our minds to do it.

On the Executive side of the Government, we intend to hold the line on prices just as tightly as the law allows. We will permit only those wage increases which are clearly justified under sound stabilization policies; and we will see to it that industries absorb cost increases out of earnings wherever feasible, before they are authorized to raise prices. We will do that, at any rate, except where the recent amendments to the law specifically require us to give further price increases.

The Congress has a tremendous responsibility in this matter. Our stabilization law was shot full of holes at the last session. This year it will be one of the main tasks before the Congress to repair the damage and enact a strong anti-inflation law.

As a part of our program to keep our country strong, we are determined to preserve the financial strength of the Government. This means high taxes over the next few years. We must see to it that these taxes are shared among the people as fairly as possible. I expect to discuss these matters in the economic report and the budget message which will soon be presented to the Congress.

Our tax laws must be fair. And we must make absolutely certain they are administered fairly, without fear or favor of any kind for anybody. To this end, steps have already been taken to remedy weaknesses which have been disclosed in the administration of the tax laws. In addition, I hope the Congress will approve my reorganization plan for the Bureau of Internal Revenue. We must do everything necessary in order to make just as certain as is humanly possible that every taxpayer receives equal treatment under the law.

To carry the burden of defense, we must have a strong, productive, and expanding economy here at home. We cannot neglect those things that have made us the great and powerful Nation we are today.

Our strength depends upon the health, the morale, the freedom of our people. We can take on the burden of leadership in the fight for world peace because, for nearly 20 years, the Government and the people have been working together for the general welfare. We have given more and more of our citizens a fair chance at decent, useful, productive lives. That is the reason we are as strong as we are today.

This Government of ours—the Congress and the Executive both—must keep on working to bring about a fair deal for all Americans. Some people will say that we haven't the time or the money this year for measures for the welfare of the people. But if we want to win the fight for peace, this is a part of the job we cannot ignore.

We will have to give up some things; we will have to go forward on others at a slower pace. But, so far as I am concerned, I do not think we can give up the things that are vital to our national strength.

I believe most people in this country will agree with me on that.

I think most farmers understand that soil conservation and rural electrification and agricultural research are not frills or luxuries, but real necessities in order to boost our farm production.

I think most workers understand that decent housing and good working conditions are not luxuries, but necessities if the working men and women of this country are to continue to outproduce the rest of the world.

I think our businessmen know that scientific research and transportation services and more steel mills and power projects are not luxuries, but necessities to keep our business and our industry in the forefront of industrial progress.

I think everybody knows that social insurance and better schools and health services are not frills, but necessities in helping all Americans to be useful and productive citizens, who can contribute their full share in the national effort to protect and advance our way of life.

We cannot do all we want to in times like these—we have to choose the things that will contribute most to defense—but we must continue to make progress if we are to be a strong Nation in the years ahead.

Let me give you some examples.

We are going right ahead with urgently needed work to develop our natural resources, to conserve our soil and to prevent floods. We are going to produce essential power and build the lines we have to have to transmit it to our farms and factories. We are going to encourage exploration for new mineral deposits.

We are going to keep on building essential highways and taking the other steps that will assure the Nation an adequate transportation system on land, on the sea, and in the air.

We must move right ahead this year to see that defense workers and soldiers' families get decent housing at rents they can afford to pay.

We must begin our long-deferred program of Federal aid to education, to help the States meet the present crisis in the operation of our schools. And we must help with the construction of schools in areas where they are critically needed because of the defense effort.

We urgently need to train more doctors and other health personnel through aid to medical education. We also urgently need to expand the basic public-health services in our home communities, especially in defense areas. The Congress should go ahead with these two measures immediately.

I have set up an impartial commission to make a thorough study of the Nation's health needs. One of the things this Commission is looking into is how to bring the cost of modern medical care within the reach of all our people. I have repeatedly recommended national health insurance as the best way to do this. So far as I know, it is still the best way. If there are any better answers, I hope this Commission will find them. But of one thing I am sure: something must be done, and be done soon.

This year we ought to make a number of urgently needed improvements in our social-security law. For one thing, benefits under old-age and survivors insurance should be raised $5 a month above the present average of $42. For another thing, the States should be given special aid to help them increase public-assistance payments. By doing these things now, we can ease the pressure of living costs for people who depend on those fixed payments.

We should also make some cost-of-living adjustments for those receiving veterans' compensation for death or disability incurred in the service of our country. In addition, now is the time to start a sensible program of readjustment benefits for our veterans who have seen service since the fighting broke out in Korea.

Another thing the Congress should do at this session is to strengthen our system of farm price supports to meet the defense emergency. The "sliding scale" in the price-support law should not be allowed to penalize farmers for increasing production to meet defense needs. We should also find a new and less-costly method for supporting perishable commodities than the law now provides.

We need to act promptly to improve our labor law. The Taft-Hartley Act has many serious and far-reaching defects. Experience has demonstrated this so clearly that even the sponsors of the act now admit it needs to be changed. A fair law—fair to both management and labor—is indispensable to sound labor relations and to full, uninterrupted production. I intend to keep on working for a fair law until we get one.

As we build our strength to defend freedom in the world, we ourselves must extend the benefits of freedom more widely among all our own people. We need to take action toward the wider enjoyment of civil rights. Freedom is the birthright of every American.

The executive branch has been making real progress toward full equality of treatment and opportunity in the Armed Forces, in the civil service, and in private firms working for the Government. Further advances require action by the Congress, and I hope that means will be provided to give the Members of the Senate and the House a chance to vote on them.

I am glad to hear that home rule for the District of Columbia will be the first item of business before the Senate. I hope that it, as well as statehood for Hawaii and Alaska, will be adopted promptly.

All these measures I have been talking about—measures to advance the well-being of our people—demonstrate to the world the forward movement of our free society.

This demonstration of the way free men govern themselves has a more powerful influence on the people of the world, on both sides of the iron curtain, than all the trick slogans and pie-in-the-sky promises of the Communists.

But our shortcomings, as well as our progress, are watched from abroad. And there is one shortcoming I want to speak plainly about.

Our kind of government above all others cannot tolerate dishonesty among its public servants.

Some dishonest people worm themselves into almost every human organization. It is all the more shocking, however, when they make their way into a government such as ours, which is based on the principle of justice for all. Such unworthy public servants must be weeded out. I intend to see to it that Federal employees who have been guilty of misconduct are punished for it. I also intend to see to it that the honest and hard-working majority of our Federal employees are protected against partisan slander and malicious attack.

I have already made some recommendations to the Congress to help accomplish these purposes. I intend to submit further recommendations to this end. I will welcome the cooperation of the Congress in this effort.

I also think that the Congress can do a great deal to strengthen confidence in our institutions by applying rigorous standards of moral integrity in its own operations—and by finding an effective way to control campaign expenditures—and by protecting the rights of individuals in congressional investigations.

To meet the crisis which now hangs over the world, we need many different kinds of strength: Military, economic, political, and moral. And of all these, I am convinced that moral strength is the most vital.

When you come right down to it, it is the courage and the character of our Nation—and of each one of us as individuals—that will really decide how well we meet this challenge.

We are engaged in a great undertaking at home and abroad—the greatest, in fact, that any nation has ever been privileged to embark upon. We are working night and day to bring peace to the world and to spread the democratic ideals of justice and self-government to all people. Our accomplishments are already remarkable. We ought to be full of pride in what we are doing, and full of confidence and hope in the outcome. No nation ever had greater resources, or greater energy, or nobler traditions to inspire it.

And yet, day in and day out, we see a long procession of timid and fearful men who wring their hands and cry out that we have lost the way; that we don't know what we are doing; that we are bound to fail. Some say we should give up the struggle for peace, and others say we should have a war and get it over with. That is a terrible statement, but I have heard it. They want us to forget the great objective of preventing another world war—the objective for which our soldiers have been fighting in the hills of Korea.

If we are to be worthy of all that has been done for us by our soldiers in the field, we must be true to the ideals for which they are fighting. We must reject the counsels of defeat and despair. We must have the determination to complete the great work for which our men have laid down their lives.

In all we do we should remember who we are and what we stand for. We are Americans. Our forefathers had far greater obstacles than we have, and much poorer chances of success. They did not lose heart, or turn aside from their goals. In that darkest of all winters in American history, at Valley Forge, George Washington said: "We must not, in so great a contest, expect to meet with nothing but sunshine." With that spirit they won their fight for freedom.

We must have that same faith and vision. In the great contest in which we are engaged today we cannot expect to have fair weather all the way. But it is a contest just as important for this country and for all men as the desperate struggle that George Washington fought through to victory.

Let us prove, again, that we are not merely sunshine patriots and summer soldiers. Let us go forward, trusting in the God of Peace, to win the goals we seek.

EIGHTH ANNUAL MESSAGE.

THE WHITE HOUSE, *January 7, 1953.*

To the Congress of the United States:

I have the honor to report to the Congress on the state of the Union.

This is the eighth such report that, as President, I have been privileged to present to you and to the country. On previous occasions it has been my custom to set forth proposals for legislative action in the coming year. But that is not my purpose today. The presentation of a legislative program falls properly to my successor, not to me, and I would not infringe upon his responsibility to chart the forward course. Instead, I wish to speak of the course we have been following the past 8 years and the position at which we have arrived.

In just 2 weeks General Eisenhower will be inaugurated as President of the United States and I will resume, most gladly, my place as a private citizen of this Republic. The Presidency last changed hands 8 years ago this coming April. That was a tragic time: a time of grieving for President Roosevelt—the great and gallant human being who had been taken from us; a time of unrelieved anxiety to his successor, thrust so suddenly into the complexities and burdens of the Presidential office.

Not so this time. This time we see the normal transition under our democratic system. One President, at the conclusion of his term, steps back to private life; his successor, chosen by the people, begins his tenure of the office. And the Presidency of the United States continues to function without a moment's break.

Since the election I have done my best to assure that the transfer from one administration to another shall be smooth and orderly. From General Eisenhower and his associates I have had friendly and understanding collaboration in this endeavor. I have not sought to thrust upon him—nor has he sought to take—the responsibility which must be mine until 12 o'clock noon on January 20. But together I hope and believe we have found means whereby the incoming President can obtain the full and detailed information he will need to assume the responsibility the moment he takes the oath of office.

The President-elect is about to take up the greatest burdens, the most compelling responsibilities, given to any man. And I, with you and all Americans, wish for him all possible success in undertaking the tasks that will so soon be his.

What are these tasks? The President is Chief of State, elected representative of all the people, national spokesman for them and to them. He is Commander in Chief of our Armed Forces. He is charged with the conduct of our foreign relations. He is Chief Executive of the Nation's largest civilian organization. He must select and nominate all top officials of the executive branch and all Federal judges. And, on the legislative side, he has the obligation and the opportunity to recommend and to approve or veto legislation. Besides all this, it is to him that a great political party turns naturally for leadership, and that, too, he must provide as President.

This bundle of burdens is unique; there is nothing else like it on the face of the earth. Each task could be a full-time job. Together they would be a tremendous undertaking in the easiest of times.

But our times are not easy; they are hard—as hard and complex, perhaps, as any in our history. Now the President not only has to carry on these tasks in such a way that our democracy may grow and flourish and our people prosper, but he also has to lead the whole free world in overcoming the Communist menace—and all this under the shadow of the atomic bomb.

This is a huge challenge to the human being who occupies the Presidential office. But it is not a challenge to him alone, for in reality he cannot meet it alone. The challenge runs not just to him but to his whole administration, to the Congress, to the country.

Ultimately, no President can master his responsibilities, save as his fellow citizens—indeed, the whole people—comprehend the challenge of our times and move, with him, to meet it.

It has been my privilege to hold the Presidential office for nearly 8 years now, and much has been done in which I take great pride. But this is not personal pride. It is pride in the people, in the Nation. It is pride in our political system and our form of government—balky sometimes, mechanically deficient perhaps, in many ways, but enormously alive and vigorous; able through these years to keep the Republic on the right course, rising to the great occasions, accomplishing the essentials, meeting the basic challenge of our times.

There have been misunderstandings and controversies these past

8 years, but through it all the President of the United States has had that measure of support and understanding without which no man could sustain the burdens of the Presidential office, or hope to discharge its responsibilities.

For this I am profoundly grateful—grateful to my associates in the executive branch, most of them nonpartisan civil servants; grateful, despite our disagreements, to the Members of the Congress on both sides of the aisle; grateful especially to the American people, the citizens of this Republic, governors of us all.

We are still so close to recent controversies that some of us may find it hard to understand the accomplishments of these past 8 years. But the accomplishments are real and very great, not as the President's, not as the Congress', but as the achievements of our country and all the people in it.

Let me remind you of some of the things we have done since I first assumed my duties as President of the United States.

I took the oath of office on April 12, 1945. In May of that same year the Nazis surrendered. Then, in July, that great white flash of light, man-made at Alamogordo, heralded swift and final victory in World War II and opened the doorway to the atomic age.

Consider some of the great questions that were posed for us by sudden, total victory in World War II. Consider also how well we, as a Nation, have responded.

Would the American economy collapse after the war? That was one question. Would there be another depression here—a repetition of 1921 or 1929? The free world feared and dreaded it. The Communists hoped for it and built their policies upon that hope.

We answered that question—answered it with a resounding "No."

Our economy has grown tremendously. Free enterprise has flourished as never before. Sixty-two million people are now gainfully employed, compared with fifty-one million 7 years ago. Private businessmen and farmers have invested more than $200 billion in new plant and equipment since the end of World War II. Prices have risen further than they should have done—but incomes, by and large, have risen even more, so that real living standards are now considerably higher than 7 years ago. Aided by sound Government policies, our expanding economy has shown the strength and flexibility for swift and almost painless reconversion from war to peace, in 1945 and 1946; for quick reaction and recovery—well before Korea—from the beginnings of recession in 1949. Above all, this live and vital economy of ours has now shown the remarkable capacity to sustain a great mobilization program for defense, a vast outpouring of aid to friends and allies all around the world—and still to produce more goods and services for peaceful use at home than we have ever known before.

This has been our answer, up to now, to those who feared or hoped for a depression in this country.

How have we handled our national finances? That was another question arising at war's end. In the administration of the Government, no problem takes more of the President's time, year in and year out, than fashioning the budget, and the related problem of managing the public debt.

Financing World War II left us with a tremendous public debt, which reached $279 billion at its peak in February 1946.

Beginning in July 1946, when war and reconversion financing had ended, we have held quite closely to the sound standard that in times of high employment and high national income the Federal budget should be balanced and the debt reduced.

For the four fiscal years from July 1, 1946, to June 30, 1950, we had a net surplus of $4.3 billion. Using this surplus, and the Treasury's excess cash reserves, the debt was reduced substantially, reaching a low point of $251 billion in June 1949, and ending up at $257 billion on June 30, 1950.

In July of 1950 we began our rapid rearmament, and for 2 years held very close to a pay-as-we-go policy. But in the current fiscal year, and the next, rising expenditures for defense will substantially outrun receipts. This will pose an immediate and serious problem for the new Congress.

Now let me turn to another question we faced at the war's end. Would we take up again, and carry forward, the great projects of social welfare—so badly needed, so long overdue—that the New Deal had introduced into our national life? Would our Government continue to have a heart for the people, or was the progress of the New Deal to be halted in the aftermath of war as decisively as the progress of Woodrow Wilson's New Freedom had been halted after the First World War?

This question, too, we have answered. We have answered it by doubling old-age insurance benefits and extending coverage to 10,000,000 more people. We have answered it by increasing our minimum wage. We have answered by the 3,000,000 privately constructed homes, that the Federal Government has helped finance since the war, and the 155,000 units of low-rent public housing placed under construction since 1949.

We have answered with the 42,000 new hospital beds provided since 1946 through the joint efforts of the Federal Government and local communities.

We have answered by helping 8,000,000 veterans of World War II to obtain advanced education, 196,000 to start in business, and 64,000 to buy farms.

We have answered by continuing to help farmers obtain electric power, until today nearly 90 percent of our farms have power line electric service.

In these and other ways we have demonstrated, up to now, that our democracy has not forgotten how to use the powers of the Government to promote the people's welfare and security.

Another of the big postwar questions was this: What we would do with the Nation's natural resources—its soils and water, forests and grasslands. Would we continue the strong conservation movement of the 1930's, or would we, as we did after the First World War, slip back into the practices of monopoly, exploitation, and waste?

The answer is plain. All across our country the soil conservation movement has spread, aided by Government programs, enriching private and public lands, preserving them from destruction, improving them for future use. In our river basins we have invested nearly $5 billion of public funds in the last 8 years—invested them in projects to control floods, irrigate farmlands, produce low-cost power and get it to the housewives and farmers and businessmen who need it. We have been vigilant in protecting the people's property—lands and forests and oil and minerals.

We have had to fight hard against those who would use our resources for private greed; we have met set-backs; we have had to delay work because of defense priorities but, on the whole, we can be proud of our record in protecting our natural heritage and in using our resources for the public good.

Here is another question we had to face at the war's close: Would we continue, in peace as well as war, to promote equality of opportunity for all our citizens, seeking ways and means to guarantee for all of them the full enjoyment of their civil rights?

During the war we achieved great economic and social gains for millions of our fellow citizens who had been held back by prejudice. Were we prepared, in peacetime, to keep on moving toward full realization of the democratic promise? Or would we let it be submerged, wiped out, in postwar riots and reaction, as after World War I?

We answered these questions in a series of forward steps at every level of Government and in many spheres of private life. In our Armed Forces, our civil service, our universities, our railway trains, the residential districts of our cities, in stores and factories all across the Nation, in the polling booths as well, the barriers are coming down. This is happening, in part, at the mandate of the courts; in part, at the insistence of Federal, State, and local governments; in part, through the enlightened action of private groups and persons in every region and every walk of life.

There has been a great awakening of the American conscience on the issues of civil rights. And all this progress—still far from complete but still continuing—has been our answer, up to now, to those who questioned our intention to live up to the promises of equal freedom for us all.

There was another question posed for us at the war's end, which equally concerned the future course of our democracy: Could the machinery of government and politics in this Republic be changed, improved, adapted rapidly enough to carry through, responsibly and well, the vast, new, complicated undertakings called for in our time?

We have answered this question, too; answered it by tackling the most urgent, most specific, problems which the war experience itself had brought into sharp focus. The reorganization of the Congress in 1946; the unification of our armed services, beginning in 1947; the closer integration of foreign and military policy through the National Security Council created that same year; and the Executive reorganizations, before and after the Hoover-Acheson Commission report in 1949—these are landmarks in our continuing endeavor to make government an effective instrument of service to the people.

I come now to the most vital question of all, the greatest of our concerns: Could there be built in the world a durable structure of security, a lasting peace for all the nations, or would we drift, as after World War I, toward another terrible disaster—a disaster which this time might be the holocaust of atomic war?

That is still the overriding question of our time. We cannot know the answer yet; perhaps we will not know it finally for a long time to come. But day and night, these past 8 years, we have been building for peace, searching out the way that leads most surely to security and freedom and justice in the world for us and all mankind.

This, above all else, has been the task of our Republic since the end of World War II, and our accomplishment so far should give real pride to all Americans. At the very least a total war has been averted, each day up to this hour. And at the most we may already have succeeded in establishing conditions which can keep that kind of war from happening, for as far ahead as man can see.

The Second World War radically changed the power relationships of the world. Nations once great were left shattered and weak; channels of communication, routes of trade, political and economic ties of many kinds were ripped apart.

And in this changed, disrupted, chaotic situation, the United States and the Soviet Union emerged as the two strongest powers of the world. Each had tremendous human and natural resources, actual or potential, on a scale unmatched by any other nation.

Nothing could make plainer why the world is in its present state—and how that came to pass—than an understanding of the diametrically opposite principles and policies of these two great powers in a war-ruined world.

For our part, we in this Republic were—and are—free men, heirs of the American Revolution, dedicated to the truths of our Declaration of Independence:

> * * * that all men are created equal, that they are endowed by their Creator with certain unalienable Rights * * * That to secure these rights, Governments are instituted among Men, deriving their just powers from the consent of the governed, * * *.

Our postwar objective has been in keeping with this great idea. The United States has sought to use its preeminent position of power to help other nations recover from the damage and dislocation of the war. We held out a helping hand to enable them to restore their national lives and to regain their positions as independent, self-supporting members of the great family of nations. This help was given without any attempt on our part to dominate or control any nation. We did not want satellites but partners.

The Soviet Union, however, took exactly the opposite course.

Its rulers saw in the weakened condition of the world not an obligation to assist in the great work of reconstruction, but an opportunity to exploit misery and suffering for the extension of their power. Instead of help, they brought subjugation. They extinguished, blotted out, the national independence of the countries that the military operations of World War II had left within their grasp.

The difference stares at us from the map of Europe today. To the west of the line that tragically divides Europe we see nations continuing to act and live in the light of their own traditions and principles. On the other side we see the dead uniformity of a tyrannical system imposed by the rulers of the Soviet Union. Nothing could point up more clearly what the global struggle between the free world and the Communists is all about.

It is a struggle as old as recorded history; it is freedom versus tyranny.

For the dominant idea of the Soviet regime is the terrible conception that men do not have rights but live at the mercy of the state.

Inevitably this idea of theirs—and all the consequences flowing from it—collided with the efforts of free nations to build a just and peaceful world. The "cold war" between the Communists and the free world is nothing more or less than the Soviet attempt to checkmate and defeat our peaceful purposes, in furtherance of their own dread objective.

We did not seek this struggle; God forbid. We did our utmost to avoid it. In World War II we and the Russians had fought side by side, each in our turn attacked and forced to combat by the aggressors. After the war we hoped that our wartime collaboration could be maintained, that the frightful experience of Nazi invasion, of devastation in the heart of Russia, had turned the Soviet rulers away from their old proclaimed allegiance to world revolution and Communist dominion. But instead they violated, one by one, the solemn agreements they had made with us in wartime. They sought to use the rights and privileges they had obtained in the United Nations; to frustrate its purposes and cut down its powers as an effective agent of world progress and the keeper of the world's peace.

Despite this outcome the efforts we made toward peaceful collaboration are a source of our present strength. They demonstrated that we believed what we proclaimed, that we actually sought honest agreements as the way to peace. Our whole moral position, our leadership in the free world today, is fortified by that fact.

The world is divided, not through our fault or failure, but by Soviet design. They, not we, began the cold war. And because the free world saw this happen—because men know we made the effort and the Soviet rulers spurned it—the free nations have accepted leadership from our Republic in meeting and mastering the Soviet offensive.

It seems to me especially important that all of us be clear, in our own thinking, about the nature of the threat we have faced—and will face for a long time to come. The measures we have devised to meet it take shape and pattern only as we understand what we were, and are, up against.

The Soviet Union occupies a territory of 8,000,000 square miles. Beyond its borders, east and west, are the nearly 5,000,000 square miles of the satellite states—virtually incorporated into the Soviet Union—and of China, now its close partner. This vast land mass contains an enormous store of natural resources sufficient to support an economic development comparable to our own.

That is the Stalinist world. It is a world of great natural diversity in geography and climate, in distribution of resources, in population, language, and living standards, in economic and cultural development. It is a world whose people are not all convinced Communists by any means. It is a world where history and national traditions, particularly in its borderlands, tend more toward separation than unification, and run counter to the enforced combination that has been made of these areas today.

But it is also a world of great man-made uniformities, a world that bleeds its population white to build huge military forces; a world in which the police are everywhere and their authority unlimited; a world where terror and slavery are deliberately administered both as instruments of government and as means of production; a world where all effective social power is the state's monopoly—yet the state itself is the creature of the Communist tyrants.

The Soviet Union, with its satellites, and China are held in the tight grip of Communist Party chieftains. The party dominates all social and political institutions. The party regulates and centrally directs the whole economy. In Moscow's sphere, and in Peiping's, all history, philosophy, morality, and law are centrally established by rigid dogmas, incessantly drummed into the whole population and subject to interpretation, or to change, by none except the party's own inner circle.

And, lest their people learn too much of other ways of life, the Communists have walled off their world, deliberately and uniformly, from the rest of human society.

That is the Communist base of operation in their cold war. In addition they have at their command hundreds and thousands of dedicated foreign Communists, people in nearly every free country who will serve Moscow's ends. Thus the masters of the Kremlin are provided with deluded followers all through the free world, whom they can manipulate, cynically and quite ruthlessly, to serve the purposes of the Soviet state.

Given their vast internal base of operations, and their agents in foreign lands, what are the Communist rulers trying to do?

Inside their homeland the Communists are trying to maintain and modernize huge military forces. And, simultaneously, they are endeavoring to weld their whole vast area and population into a completely self-contained, advanced industrial society. They aim, some day, to equal or better the production levels of Western Europe and North America combined—thus shifting the balance of world economic power, and war potential, to their side.

They have a long way to go, and they know it. But they are prepared to levy upon living generations any sacrifice that helps strengthen their armed power, or speed industrial development.

Externally the Communist rulers are trying to expand the boundaries of their world, whenever and wherever they can. This expansion they have pursued steadfastly since the close of World War II, using any means available to them.

Where the Soviet Army was present, as in the countries of Eastern Europe, they have gradually squeezed free institutions to death.

Where postwar chaos existed in industrialized nations, as in Western Europe, the local Stalinists tried to gain power through political processes, politically inspired strikes, and every available means for subverting free institutions to their evil ends.

Where conditions permitted, the Soviet rulers have stimulated and aided armed insurrection by Communist-led revolutionary forces, as in Greece, Indochina, the Philippines, and China, or outright aggression by one of their satellites, as in Korea.

Where the forces of nationalism, independence, and an economic change were at work throughout the great sweep of Asia and Africa, the Communists tried to identify themselves with the cause of progress, tried to picture themselves as the friends of freedom and advancement—surely one of the most cynical efforts of which history offers record.

Thus everywhere in the free world the Communists seek to fish in troubled waters, to seize more countries, to enslave more millions of human souls. They were, and are, ready to ally themselves with any group, from the extreme left to the extreme right, that offers them an opportunity to advance their ends.

Geography gives them a central position. They are both a European and an Asian power, with borders touching many of the most sensitive and vital areas in the free world around them. So situated, they can use their armies and their economic power to set up simultaneously a whole series of threats, or inducements, to such widely dispersed places as Western Germany, Iran, and Japan. These pressures and attractions can be sustained at will, or quickly shifted from place to place.

Thus the Communist rulers are moving, with implacable will, to create greater strength in their vast empire, and to create weakness and division in the free world, preparing for the time their false creed teaches them must come: The time when the whole world outside their sway will be so torn by strife and contradictions that it will be ripe for the Communist plucking.

This is the heart of the distorted Marxist interpretation of history. This is the glass through which Moscow and Peiping look out upon the world, the glass through which they see the rest of us. They seem really to believe that history is on their side. And they are trying to boost "history" along, at every opportunity, in every way they can.

I have set forth here the nature of the Communist menace confronting our Republic and the whole free world. This is the measure of the challenge we have faced since World War II—a challenge partly military and partly economic, partly moral and partly intellectual, confronting us at every level of human endeavor and all around the world.

It has been and must be the free world's purpose not only to organize defenses against aggression and subversion, not only to build a structure of resistance and salvation for the community of nations outside the iron curtain, but in addition to give expression and opportunity to the forces of growth and progress in the free world, to so organize and unify the cooperative community of free men that we will not crumble but grow stronger over the years, and the Soviet Empire, not the free world, will eventually have to change its ways or fall.

Our whole program of action to carry out this purpose has been directed to meet two requirements.

The first of these had to do with security. Like the pioneers who settled this great continent of ours, we have had to carry a musket while we went about our peaceful business. We realized that if we and our allies did not have military strength to meet the growing Soviet military threat, we would never have the opportunity to carry forward our efforts to build a peaceful world of law and order—the only environment in which our free institutions could survive and flourish.

Did this mean we had to drop everything else and concentrate on armies and weapons? Of course it did not; side by side with this urgent military requirement, we had to continue to help create conditions of economic and social progress in the world. This work had to be carried forward alongside the first, not only in order to meet the nonmilitary aspects of the Communist drive for power, but also because this creative effort toward human progress is essential to bring about the kind of world we as freemen want to live in.

These two requirements—military security and human progress—are more closely related in action than we sometimes recognize. Military security depends upon a strong economic underpinning and a stable and hopeful political order; conversely, the confidence that makes for economic and political progress does not thrive in areas that are vulnerable to military conquest.

These requirements are related in another way. Both of them depend upon unity of action among the free nations of the world. This, indeed, has been the foundation of our whole effort, for the drawing together of the free people of the world has become a condition essential not only to their progress but to their survival as free people.

This is the conviction that underlies all the steps we have been taking to strengthen and unify the free nations during the past 7 years.

What have these steps been? First of all, How have we gone about meeting the requirement of providing for our security against this world-wide challenge?

Our starting point, as I have said on many occasions, has been and remains the United Nations.

We were prepared, and so were the other nations of the free world, to place our reliance on the machinery of the United Nations to safeguard peace. But before the United Nations could give full expression to the concept of international security embodied in the Charter, it was essential that the five permanent members of the Security Council honor their solemn pledge to cooperate to that end. This the Soviet Union has not done.

I do not need to outline here the dreary record of Soviet obstruction and veto and the unceasing efforts of the Soviet representatives to sabotage the United Nations. It is important, however, to distinguish clearly between the principle of collective security embodied in the Charter and the mechanisms of the United Nations to give that principle effect. We must frankly recognize that the Soviet Union has been able, in certain instances, to stall the machinery of collective security. Yet it has not been able to impair the principle of collective security. The free nations of the world have retained their allegiance to that idea. They have found the means to act despite the Soviet veto, both through the United Nations itself and through the application of this principle in regional and other security arrangements that are fully in harmony with the Charter and give expression to its purposes.

The free world refused to resign itself to collective suicide merely because of the technicality of a Soviet veto.

The principle of collective measures to forestall aggression has found expression in the Treaty of Rio de Janeiro, the North Atlantic Treaty, now extended to include Greece and Turkey, and the several treaties we have concluded to reinforce security in the Pacific area.

But the free nations have not this time fallen prey to the dangerous illusion that treaties alone will stop an aggressor. By a series of vigorous actions, as varied as the nature of the threat, the free nations have successfully thwarted aggression or the threat of aggression in many different parts of the world.

Our country has led or supported these collective measures. The aid we have given to people determined to act in defense of their freedom has often spelled the difference between success and failure.

We all know what we have done, and I shall not review in detail the steps we have taken. Each major step was a milepost in the developing unity, strength, and resolute will of the free nations.

The first was the determined and successful effort made through the United Nations to safeguard the integrity and independence of Iran in 1945 and 1946.

Next was our aid and support to embattled Greece, which enabled her to defeat the forces threatening her national independence.

In Turkey cooperative action resulted in building up a bulwark of military strength for an area vital to the defenses of the entire free world.

In 1949 we began furnishing military aid to our partners in the North Atlantic Community and to a number of other free countries.

The Soviet Union's threats against Germany and Japan, its neighbors to the west and to the east, have been successfully withstood. Free Germany is on its way to becoming a member of the peaceful community of nations, and a partner in the common defense. The Soviet effort to capture Berlin by blockade was thwarted by the courageous Allied airlift. An independent and democratic Japan has been brought back into the community of free nations.

In the Far East the tactics of Communist imperialism have reached heights of violence unmatched elsewhere, and the problem of concerted action by the free nations has been at once more acute and more difficult.

Here, in spite of outside aid and support, the free Government of China succumbed to the Communist assault. Our aid has enabled the free Chinese to rebuild and strengthen their forces on the island of Formosa. In other areas of the Far East—in Indochina, Malaya, and the Philippines—our assistance has helped sustain a stanch resistance against Communist insurrectionary attacks.

The supreme test, up to this point, of the will and determination of the free nations came in Korea, when Communist forces invaded the Republic of Korea, a state that was in a special sense under the protection of the United Nations. The response was immediate and resolute. Under our military leadership the free nations for the first time took up arms, collectively, to repel aggression.

Aggression was repelled, driven back, punished. Since that time Communist strategy has seen fit to prolong the conflict, in spite of honest efforts by the United Nations to reach an honorable truce. The months of deadlock have demonstrated that the Communists cannot achieve by persistence, or by diplomatic trickery, what they failed to achieve by sneak attack. Korea has demonstrated that the free world has the will and the endurance to match the Communist effort to overthrow international order through local aggression.

It has been a bitter struggle and it has cost us much in brave lives and human suffering, but it has made it plain that the free nations will fight side by side, that they will not succumb to aggression or intimidation, one by one. This, in the final analysis, is the only way to halt the Communist drive to world power.

At the heart of the free world's defense is the military strength of the United States.

From 1945 to 1949 the United States was sole possessor of the atomic bomb. That was a great deterrent and protection in itself.

But when the Soviets produced an atomic explosion—as they were bound to do in time—we had to broaden the whole basis of our strength. We had to endeavor to keep our lead in atomic weapons. We had to strengthen our Armed Forces generally and to enlarge our productive capacity—our mobilization base. Historically, it was the Soviet atomic explosion in the fall of 1949, 9 months before the aggression in Korea, which stimulated the planning for our program of defense mobilization.

What we needed was not just a central force that could strike back against aggression. We also needed strength along the outer edges of the free world, defenses for our allies as well as for ourselves, strength to hold the line against attack as well as to retaliate.

We have made great progress on this task of building strong defenses. In the last 2½ years we have more than doubled our own defenses, and we have helped to increase the protection of nearly all the other free nations.

All the measures of collective security, resistance to aggression, and the building of defenses, constitute the first requirement for the survival and progress of the free world. But, as I have pointed out, they are interwoven with the necessity of taking steps to create and maintain economic and social progress in the free nations. There can be no military strength except where there is economic capacity to back it. There can be no freedom where there is economic chaos or social collapse. For these reasons our national policy has included a wide range of economic measures.

In Europe the grand design of the Marshall plan permitted the people of Britain and France and Italy and a half dozen other countries, with help from the United States, to lift themselves from stagnation and find again the path of rising production, rising incomes, rising standards of living. The situation was changed almost overnight by the Marshall plan; the people of Europe have a renewed hope and vitality, and they are able to carry a share of the military defense of the free world that would have been impossible a few years ago.

Now the countries of Europe are moving rapidly toward political and economic unity, changing the map of Europe in more hopeful ways than it has been changed for 500 years. Customs unions, European economic institutions like the Schuman plan, the movement toward European political integration, the European Defense Community, all are signs of practical and effective growth toward greater common strength and unity. The countries of Western Europe, including the free Republic of Germany are working together, and the whole free world is the gainer.

It sometimes happens, in the course of history, that steps taken to meet an immediate necessity serve an ultimate purpose greater than may be apparent at the time. This, I believe, is the meaning of what has been going on in Europe under the threat of aggression. The free nations there, with our help, have been drawing together in defense of their free institutions. In so doing they have laid the foundations of a unity that will endure as a major creative force beyond the exigencies of this period of history. We may, at this close range, be but dimly aware of the creative surge this movement represents, but I believe it to be of historic importance. I believe its benefits will survive long after Communist tyranny is nothing but an unhappy memory.

In Asia and Africa the economic and social problems are different, but no less urgent. There hundreds of millions of people are in ferment, exploding into the twentieth century, thrusting toward equality and independence and improvement in the hard conditions of their lives.

Politically, economically, socially, things cannot and will not stay in their prewar mold in Africa and Asia. Change must come, is coming, fast. Just in the years I have been President, 12 free nations, with more than 600,000,000 people, have become independent: Burma, Indonesia, the Philippines, Korea, Israel, Libya, India, Pakistan and Ceylon, and the three Associated States of Indochina, now members of the French Union. These names alone are testimony to the sweep of the great force which is changing the face of half the world.

Working out new relationships among the peoples of the free world would not be easy in the best of times. Even if there were no Communist drive for expansion, there would be hard and complex problems of transition from old social forms, old political arrangements, old economic institutions to the new ones our century demands—problems of guiding change into constructive channels, of helping new nations grow strong and stable. But now, with the Soviet rulers striving to exploit this ferment for this own purposes, the task has become harder and more urgent—terribly urgent.

In this situation we see the meaning and the importance of the Point IV program, through which we can share our store of know-how and of capital to help these people develop their economies and reshape their societies. As we help Iranians to raise more grain, Indians to reduce the incidence of malaria, Liberians to educate their children better, we are at once helping to answer the desires of the people for advancement, and demonstrating the superiority of freedom over communism. There will be no quick solution for any of the difficulties of the new nations of Asia and Africa—but there may be no solution at all if we do not press forward with full energy to help these countries grow and flourish in freedom and in cooperation with the rest of the free world.

Our measures of economic policy have already had a tremendous effect on the course of events. Eight years ago the Kremlin thought postwar collapse in Western Europe and Japan—with economic dislocation in America—might give them the signal to advance. We demonstrated they were wrong. Now they wait with hope that the economic recovery of the free world has set the stage for violent and disastrous rivalry among the economically developed nations, struggling for each other's markets and a greater share of trade. Here is another test that we shall have to meet and master in the years immediately ahead. And it will take great ingenuity and effort—and much time—before we prove the Kremlin wrong again. But we can do it. It is true that economic recovery presents its problems, as does economic decline, but they are problems of another order. They are the problems of distributing abundance fairly, and they can be solved by the process of international cooperation that has already brought us so far.

These are the measures we must continue. This is the path we must follow. We must go on, working with our free associates, building an international structure for military defense and for economic, social, and political progress. We must be prepared for war, because war may be thrust upon us. But the stakes in our search for peace are immensely higher than they have ever been before.

For now we have entered the atomic age, and war has undergone a technological change which makes it a very different thing from what it used to be. War today between the Soviet Empire and the free nations might dig the grave not only of our Stalinist opponents but of our own society, our world as well as theirs.

This transformation has been brought to pass in the 7 years from Alamogordo to Eniwetok. It is only 7 years, but the new force of atomic energy has turned the world into a very different kind of place.

Science and technology have worked so fast that war's new meaning may not yet be grasped by all the peoples who would be its victims; nor, perhaps, by the rulers in the Kremlin. But I have been President of the United States, these 7 years, responsible for the decisions which have brought our science and our engineering to their present place. I know what this development means now. I know something of what it will come to mean in the future.

We in this Government realized, even before the first sucessful atomic explosion, that this new force spelled terrible danger for all mankind unless it were brought under international control. We promptly advanced proposals in the United Nations to take this new source of energy out of the arena of national rivalries; to make it impossible to use as a weapon of war. These proposals, so pregnant with benefit for all humanity, were rebuffed by the rulers of the Soviet Union.

The language of science is universal; the movement of science is always forward into the unknown. We could not assume that the Soviet Union would not develop the same weapon, regardless of all our precautions, nor that there were not other and even more terrible means of destruction lying in the unexplored field of atomic energy.

We had no alternative, then, but to press on, to probe the secrets of atomic power to the uttermost of our capacity, to maintain, if we could, our initial superiority in the atomic field. At the same time we sought persistently for some avenue, some formula, for reaching an agreement with the Soviet rulers that would place this new form of power under effective restraints—that would guarantee no nation would use it in war. I do not have to recount here the proposals we made, the steps taken in the United Nations, striving at least to open a way to ultimate agreement. I hope and believe that we will continue to make these efforts so long as there is the slightest possibility of progress. All civilized nations are agreed on the urgency of the problem and have shown their willingness to agree on effective measures of control—all save the Soviet Union and its satellites. But they have rejected every reasonable proposal.

Meanwhile, the progress of scientific experiment has outrun our expectations. Atomic science is in the full tide of development; the unfolding of the innermost secrets of matter is uninterrupted and irresistible. Since Alamogordo we have developed atomic weapons with many times the explosive force of the early models, and we have produced them in substantial quantities. And recently in the thermonuclear tests at Eniwetok, we have entered another stage in the world-shaking development of atomic energy. From now on man moves into a new era of destructive power, capable of creating explosions of a new order of magnitude, dwarfing the mushroom clouds of Hiroshima and Nagasaki.

We have no reason to think that the stage we have now reached in the release of atomic energy will be the last. Indeed, the speed of our scientific and technical progress over the last 7 years shows no signs of abating. We are being hurried forward, in our mastery of the atom, from one discovery to another, toward yet unforeseeable peaks of destructive power.

Inevitably, until we can reach international agreement, this is the path we must follow. And we must realize that no advance we make is unattainable by others; that no advantage in this race can be more than temporary.

The war of the future would be one in which man could extinguish millions of lives at one blow, demolish the great cities of the world, wipe out the cultural achievements of the past—and destroy the very structure of a civilization that has been slowly and painfully built up through hundreds of generations.

Such a war is not a possible policy for rational man. We know this, but we dare not assume that others would not yield to the temptation science is now placing in their hands.

With that in mind, there is something I would say to Stalin: You claim belief in Lenin's prophecy that one stage in the development of Communist society would be war between your world and ours. But Lenin was a preatomic man, who viewed society and history with preatomic eyes. Something profound has happened since he wrote. War has changed its shape and its dimension. It cannot now be a "stage" in the development of anything save ruin for your regime and your homeland.

I do not know how much time may elapse before the Communist rulers bring themselves to recognize this truth. But when they do, they will find us eager to reach understandings that will protect the world from the danger it faces today.

It is no wonder that some people wish that we had never succeeded in splitting the atom. But atomic power, like any other force of nature, is not evil in itself. Properly used, it is an instrumentality for human betterment. As a source of power, as a tool of scientific inquiry, it has untold possibilities. We are already making good progress in the constructive use of atomic power. We could do much more if we were free to concentrate on its peaceful uses exclusively.

Atomic power will be with us all the days of our lives. We cannot legislate it out of existence. We cannot ignore the dangers or the benefits it offers.

I believe that man can harness the forces of the atom to work for the improvement of the lot of human beings everywhere. That is our goal. As a nation, as a people, we must understand this problem; we must handle this new force wisely through our democratic processes. Above all we must strive, in all earnestness and good faith, to bring it under effective international control. To do this will require much wisdom and patience and firmness. The awe-inspiring responsibility in this field now falls on a new administration and a new Congress. I will give them my support, as I am sure all our citizens will, in whatever constructive steps they may take to make this newest of man's discoveries a source of good and not of ultimate destruction.

We cannot tell when or whether the attitude of the Soviet rulers may change. We do not know how long it may be before they show a willingness to negotiate effective control of atomic energy and honorable settlements of other world problems. We cannot measure how deep-rooted are the Kremlin's illusions about us. We can be sure, however, that the rulers of the Communist world will not change their basic objectives lightly or soon.

The Communist rulers have a sense of time about these things wholly unlike our own. We tend to divide our future into short spans, like the 2-year life of this Congress, or the 4 years of the next Presidential term. They seem to think and plan in terms of generations. And there is, therefore, no easy, short-run way to make them see that their plans cannot prevail.

This means there is ahead of us a long hard test of strength and stamina between the free world and the Communist domain; our politics and our economy, our science and technology against the best they can do; our liberty against their slavery; our voluntary concert of free nations against their forced amalgam of "people's republics"; our strategy against their strategy; our nerve against their nerve.

Above all, this is a test of the will and the steadiness of the people of the United States.

There has been no challenge like this in the history of our Republic. We are called upon to rise to the occasion as no people before us.

What is required of us is not easy. The way we must learn to live, the world we have to live in, cannot be so pleasant, safe, or simple as most of us have known before or confidently hoped to know.

Already we have had to sacrifice a number of accustomed ways of working and of living, much nervous energy, material resources, even human life. Yet if one thing is certain in our future, it is that more sacrifice still lies ahead.

Were we to grow discouraged now, were we to weaken and slack off, the whole structure we have built, these past 8 years, would come apart and fall away. Never then, no matter by what stringent means, could our free world regain the ground, the time, the sheer momentum, lost by such a move. There can and should be changes and improvements in our programs, to meet new situations, serve new needs. But to desert the spirit of our basic policies, to step back from them now, would surely start the free world's slide toward the darkness that the Communists have prophesied—toward the moment for which they watch and wait.

If we value our freedom and our way of life and want to see them safe, we must meet the challenge and accept its implications, stick to our guns, and carry out our policies.

I have set out the basic conditions, as I see them, under which we have been working in the world, and the nature of our basic policies. What, then, of the future? The answer, I believe, is this: As we continue to confound Soviet expectations, as our world grows stronger, more united, more attractive to men on both sides of the iron curtain, then inevitably there will come a time of change within the Communist world. We do not know how that change will come about, whether by deliberate decision in the Kremlin, by coup d'état, by revolution, by defection of satellites, or perhaps by some unforeseen combination of factors such as these.

But if the Communist rulers understand they cannot win by war, and if we frustrate their attempts to win by subversion, it is not too much to expect their world to change its character, moderate its aims, become more realistic and less implacable, and recede from the cold war they began.

Do not be deceived by the strong face, the look of monolithic power that the Communist dictators wear before the outside world. Remember their power has no basis in consent. Remember they are so afraid of the free world's ideas and ways of life, they do not dare to let their people know about them. Think of the massive effort they put forth to try to stop our Campaign of Truth from reaching their people with its message of freedom.

The masters of the Kremlin live in fear their power and position would collapse were their own people to acquire knowledge, information, comprehension about our free society. Their world has many elements of strength, but this one fatal flaw: the weakness represented by their iron curtain and their police state. Surely a social order at once so insecure and so fearful, must ultimately lose its competition with our free society.

Provided just one thing—and this I urge you to consider carefully—provided that the free world retains the confidence and the determination to outmatch the best our adversary can accomplish and to demonstrate for uncertain millions on both sides of the iron curtain the superiority of the free way of life.

That is the test upon all the free nations; upon none more than our own Republic.

Our resources are equal to the task. We have the industry, the skills, the basic economic strength. Above all we have the vigor of free men in a free society. We have our liberties. And, while we keep them, while we retain our democratic faith, the ultimate advantage in this hard competition lies with us, not with the Communists.

But there are some things that could shift the advantage to their side. One of the things that could defeat us is fear—fear of the task we face, fear of adjusting to it, fear that breeds more fear, sapping our faith, corroding our liberties, turning citizen against citizen, ally against ally. Fear could snatch away the very values we are striving to defend.

Already the danger signals have gone up. Already the corrosive process has begun. And every diminution of our tolerance, each new act of enforced conformity, each idle accusation, each demonstration of hysteria, each new restrictive law, is one more sign that we can lose the battle against fear.

The Communists cannot deprive us of our liberties—fear can. The Communists cannot stamp out our faith in human dignity—fear can. Fear is an enemy within ourselves; and, if we do not root it out, it may destroy they very way of life we are so anxious to protect.

To beat back fear, we must hold fast to our heritage as freemen. We must renew our confidence in one another, our tolerance, our sense of being neighbors, fellow citizens. We must take our stand on the Bill of Rights. The inquisition, the star chamber, have no place in a free society.

Our ultimate strength lies not alone in arms, but in the sense of moral values and moral truths that give meaning and vitality to the purposes of free people. These values are our faith, our inspiration, the source of our strength, and our indomitable determination.

We face hard tasks, great dangers. But we are Americans and we have faced hardships and uncertainty before; we have adjusted before to changing circumstances. Our whole history has been a steady training for the work it is now ours to do.

No one can lose heart for the task, none can lose faith in our free ways, who stops to remember where we began, what we have sought, and what accomplished, all together as Americans.

I have lived a long time and seen much happen in our country. And I know, out of my own experience, that we can do what must be done.

When I think back to the country I grew up in—and then look at what our country has become—I am quite certain that having done so much, we can do more.

After all, it has been scarcely 15 years since most Americans rejected out-of-hand the wise counsel that aggressors must be "quarantined." The very concept of collective security, the foundation stone of all our actions now, was then strange doctrine, shunned and set aside. Talk about adapting; talk about adjusting; talk about responding as a people to the challenge of changed times and circumstances—there has never been a more spectacular example than this great change in America's outlook on the world.

Let all of us pause now, think back, consider carefully the meaning of our national experience. Let us draw comfort from it and faith and confidence in our future as Americans.

The Nation's business is never finished. The basic questions we have been dealing with, these 8 years past, present themselves anew. That is the way of our society. Circumstances change and current questions take on different forms, new complications, year by year. But underneath the great issues remain the same—prosperity, welfare, human rights, effective democracy, and, above all, peace.

Now we turn to the inaugural of our new President. And in the great work he is called upon to do he will have need for the support of a united people, a confident people, with firm faith in one another and in our common cause. I pledge him my support as a citizen of our Republic, and I ask you to give him yours.

To him, to you, to all my fellow citizens, I say, Godspeed!

May God bless our country and our cause.

Dwight D. Eisenhower

January 20, 1953 to January 20, 1961

FIRST ANNUAL MESSAGE.

THE WHITE HOUSE, *February 2, 1953.*

MR. PRESIDENT, MR. SPEAKER, MEMBERS OF THE EIGHTY-THIRD CONGRESS:

For the warmth of your reception my deep and grateful thanks.

I welcome the honor of appearing before you to deliver my first message to the Congress.

It is manifestly the joint purpose of the congressional leadership and of this administration to justify the summons to governmental responsibility issued last November by the American people.

The grand labors of this leadership will involve—

Application of America's influence in world affairs with such fortitude and such foresight that it will deter aggression and eventually secure peace;

Establishment of a national administration of such integrity and such efficiency that its honor at home will ensure respect abroad;

Encouragement of those incentives that inspire creative initiative in our economy, so that its productivity may fortify freedom everywhere; and

Dedication to the well-being of all our citizens and to the attainment of equality of opportunity for all, so that our Nation will ever act with the strength of unity in every task to which it is called.

The purpose of this message is to suggest certain lines along which our joint efforts may immediately be directed toward realization of these four ruling purposes.

The time that this administration has been in office has been too brief to permit preparation of a detailed and comprehensive program of recommended action to cover all phases of the responsibilities that devolve upon our country's new leaders. Such a program will be filled out in the weeks ahead of us as, after appropriate study, I shall submit additional recommendations for your consideration. Today can provide only a sure and substantial beginning.

II

Our country has come through a painful period of trial and disillusionment since the victory of 1945. We anticipated a world of peace and cooperation. The calculated pressures of aggressive communism have forced us, instead, to live in a world of turmoil.

From this costly experience we have learned one clear lesson. We have learned that the free world cannot indefinitely remain in a posture of paralyzed tension. To do so leaves forever to the aggressor the choice of time and place and means to cause greatest hurt to us at least cost to himself.

This administration has, therefore, begun the definition of a new, positive foreign policy. This policy will be governed by certain basic ideas. They are these:

First. Our foreign policy must be clear, consistent, and confident. This means that it must be the product of genuine, continuous cooperation between the executive and the legislative branches of this Government. It must be developed and directed in the spirit of true bipartisanship. And I assure you, Members of this Congress, I mean that fully, earnestly, and sincerely.

Second. The policy we embrace must be a coherent global policy The freedom we cherish and defend in Europe and in the Americas is no different from the freedom that is imperiled in Asia.

Third. Our policy, dedicated to making the free world secure, will envision all peaceful methods and devices—except breaking faith with our friends. We shall never acquiesce in the enslavement of any people in order to purchase fancied gain for ourselves. I shall ask the Congress at a later date to join in an appropriate resolution making clear that this Government recognizes no kind of commitment contained in secret understandings of the past with foreign governments which permit this kind of enslavement.

Fourth. The policy we pursue will recognize the truth that no single country, even one so powerful as ours, can alone defend the liberty of all nations threatened by Communist aggression from without or subversion within. Mutual security means effective mutual cooperation. For the United States, this means that, as a matter of common sense and national interest, we shall give help to other nations in the measure that they strive earnestly to do their full share of the common task. No wealth of aid could compensate for poverty of spirit. The heart of every free nation must be honestly dedicated to the preserving of its own independence and security.

Fifth. Our policy will be designed to foster the advent of practical unity in Western Europe. The nations of that region have contributed notably to the effort of sustaining the security of the free world. From the jungles of Indochina and Malaya to the northern shores of Europe, they have vastly improved their defensive strength. Where called upon to do so, they have made costly and bitter sacrifices to hold the line of freedom.

But the problem of security demands closer cooperation among the nations of Europe than has been known to date. Only a more closely integrated economic and political system can provide the greatly increased economic strength needed to maintain both necessary military readiness and respectable living standards.

Europe's enlightened leaders have long been aware of these facts. All the devoted work that has gone into the Schuman plan, the European Army, and the Strasbourg Conference has testified to their vision and determination. These achievements are the more remarkable when we realize that each of them has marked a victory—for France and Germany alike—over the divisions that in the past have brought tragedy to these two great nations and to the world.

The needed unity of Western Europe manifestly cannot be manufactured from without; it can only be created from within. But it is right and necessary that we encourage Europe's leaders by informing them of the high value we place upon the earnestness of their efforts toward this goal. Real progress will be conclusive evidence to the American people that our material sacrifices in the cause of collective security are matched by essential political, economic, and military accomplishments in Western Europe.

Sixth. Our foreign policy will recognize the importance of profitable and equitable world trade.

A substantial beginning can and should be made by our friends themselves. Europe, for example, is now marked by checkered areas of labor surplus and labor shortage, of agricultural areas needing machines and industrial areas needing food. Here and elsewhere we can hope that our friends will take the initiative in creating broader markets and more dependable currencies, to allow greater exchange of goods and services among themselves.

Action along these lines can create an economic environment that will invite vital help from us.

Such help includes—

First, revising our customs regulations to remove procedural obstacles to profitable trade. I further recommend that the Congress take the Reciprocal Trade Agreements Act under immediate study and extend it by appropriate legislation. This objective must not ignore legitimate safeguarding of domestic industries, agriculture, and labor standards. In all executive study and recommendations on this problem labor and management and farmers alike will be earnestly consulted.

Second, doing whatever our Government can properly do to encourage the flow of private American investment abroad. This involves, as a serious and explicit purpose of our foreign policy, the encouragement of a hospitable climate for such investment in foreign nations.

Third, availing ourselves of facilities overseas for the economical production of manufactured articles which are needed for mutual defense and which are not seriously competitive with our own normal peacetime production.

Fourth, receiving from the rest of the world, in equitable exchange for what we supply, greater amounts of important raw materials which we do not ourselves possess in adequate quantities.

III

In this general discussion of our foreign policy, I must make special mention of the war in Korea.

This war is, for Americans, the most painful phase of Communist aggression throughout the world. It is clearly a part of the same calculated assault that the aggressor is simultaneously pressing in Indochina and in Malaya, and of the strategic situation that manifestly embraces the island of Formosa and the Chinese Nationalist forces there. The working out of any military solution to the Korean war will inevitably affect all these areas.

The administration is giving immediate increased attention to the development of additional Republic of Korea forces. The citizens of that country have proved their capacity as fighting men and their eagerness to take a greater share in the defense of their homeland. Organization, equipment, and training will allow them to do so. Increased assistance to Korea for this purpose conforms fully to our global policies.

In June 1950, following the aggressive attack on the Republic of Korea, the United States Seventh Fleet was instructed both to prevent attack upon Formosa and also to insure that Formosa should not be used as a base of operations against the Chinese Communist mainland.

This has meant, in effect, that the United States Navy was required to serve as a defensive arm of Communist China. Regardless of the situation in 1950, since the date of that order the Chinese Communists have invaded Korea to attack the United Nations forces there. They have consistently rejected the proposals of the United Nations Command for an armistice. They recently joined with Soviet Russia in rejecting the armistice proposal sponsored in the United Nations by the Government of India. This proposal had been accepted by the United States and 53 other nations.

Consequently there is no longer any logic or sense in a condition that required the United States Navy to assume defensive responsibilities on behalf of the Chinese Communists. This permitted those Communists, with greater impunity, to kill our soldiers and those of our United Nations allies in Korea.

I am, therefore, issuing instructions that the Seventh Fleet no longer be employed to shield Communist China. Permit me to make crystal clear, this order implies no aggressive intent on our part. But we certainly have no obligation to protect a nation fighting us in Korea.

IV

Our labor for peace in Korea and in the world imperatively demands the maintenance by the United States of a strong fighting service ready for any contingency.

Our problem is to achieve adequate military strength within the limits of endurable strain upon our economy. To amass military power without regard to our economic capacity would be to defend ourselves against one kind of disaster by inviting another.

Both military and economic objectives demand a single national military policy, proper coordination of our armed services, and effective consolidation of certain logistics functions.

We must eliminate waste and duplication of effort in the armed services.

We must realize clearly that size alone is not sufficient. The biggest force is not necessarily the best force—we want the best.

We must not let traditions or habits of the past stand in the way of developing an efficient military force. All members of our forces must be ever mindful that they serve under a single flag and for a single cause.

We must effectively integrate our armament programs and plan them in such careful relation to our industrial facilities that we assure the best use of our manpower and our materials.

Because of the complex technical nature of our military organization and because of the security reasons involved, the Secretary of Defense must take the initiative and assume the responsibility for developing plans to give our Nation maximum safety at minimum cost. Accordingly, the new Secretary of Defense and his civilian and military associates will, in the future, recommend such changes in present laws affecting our defense activities as may be necessary in order to clarify responsibility and improve the total effectiveness of our defense effort.

This effort must always conform to policies laid down in the National Security Council.

The statutory function of the National Security Council is to assist the President in the formulation and coordination of significant domestic, foreign, and military policies required for the security of this Nation. In these days of tension it is essential that this central body have the vitality to perform effectively its statutory role. I propose to see that it does so.

Careful formulation of policies must be followed by clear understanding of them by all peoples. A related need, therefore, is to make more effective all activities of the Government related to international information.

I have recently appointed a committee of representative and informed citizens to survey this subject and to make recommendations in the near future for legislative, administrative, or any other action.

A unified and dynamic effort in this whole field is essential to the security of the United States and of the other peoples in the community of free nations. There is but one sure way to avoid global war—and that is to win the cold war.

While retaliatory power is one strong deterrent to a would-be aggressor, another powerful deterrent is defensive power. No enemy is likely to attempt an attack foredoomed to failure.

Because the building of a completely impenetrable defense against attack is still not possible, total defensive strength must include civil defense preparedness. Because we have incontrovertible evidence that Soviet Russia possesses atomic weapons, this kind of protection becomes sheer necessity.

Civil defense responsibilities primarily belong to the State and local governments, including recruiting, training, and organizing volunteers to meet any emergency. The immediate job of the Federal Government is to provide leadership, to supply technical guidance, and to continue to strengthen its civil defense stockpile of medical, engineering, and related supplies and equipment. This work must go forward without lag.

V

I have referred to the inescapable need for economic health and strength if we are to maintain adequate military power and exert influential leadership for peace in the world.

Our immediate task is to chart a fiscal and economic policy that can:

First, reduce the planned deficits and then balance the budget, which means, among other things, reducing Federal expenditures to the safe minimum;

Second, meet the huge costs of our defense;

Third, properly handle the burden of our inheritance of debt and obligations;

Fourth, check the menace of inflation;

Fifth, work toward the earliest possible reduction of the tax burden;

Sixth, make constructive plans to encourage the initiative of our citizens.

It is important that all of us understand that this administration does not and cannot begin its task with a clean slate. Much already has been written on the record, beyond our power quickly to erase or to amend. This record includes our inherited burden of indebtedness and obligations and deficits.

The current year's budget, as you know, carries a 5.9 billion dollar deficit; and the budget, which was presented to you before this administration took office, indicates a budgetary deficit of 9.9 billion for the fiscal year ending June 30, 1954. The national debt is now more than 265 billion dollars. In addition, the accumulated obligational authority of the Federal Government for future payment totals over 80 billion dollars. Even this amount is exclusive of large contingent liabilities, so numerous and extensive as to be almost beyond description.

The bills for the payment of nearly all of the 80 billion dollars of obligations will be presented during the next 4 years. These bills, added to the current costs of government we must meet, make a formidable burden.

The present authorized Government-debt limit is 275 billion dollars. The forecast presented by the outgoing administration with the fiscal year 1954 budget indicates that—before the end of the fiscal year and at the peak of demand for payments during that year—the total Government debt may approach and even exceed that limit. Unless budgeted deficits are checked, the momentum of past programs will force an increase of the statutory debt limit.

Permit me this one understatement: To meet and to correct this situation will not be easy.

Permit me this one assurance: Every department head and I are determined to do everything we can to resolve it.

The first order of business is the elimination of the annual deficit. This cannot be achieved merely by exhortation. It demands the concerted action of all those in responsible positions in the Government and the earnest cooperation of the Congress.

Already, we have begun an examination of the appropriations and expenditures of all departments in an effort to find significant items that may be decreased or canceled without damage to our essential requirements.

Getting control of the budget requires also that State and local governments and interested groups of citizens restrain themselves in their demands upon the Congress.

A balanced budget is an essential first measure in checking further depreciation in the buying power of the dollar. This is one of the critical steps to be taken to bring an end to planned inflation. Our purpose is to manage the Government's finances so as to help and not hinder each family in balancing its own budget.

Reduction of taxes will be justified only as we show we can succeed in bringing the budget under control. As the budget is balanced and inflation checked, the tax burden that today stifles initiative can and must be eased.

Until we can determine the extent to which expenditures can be reduced, it would not be wise to reduce our revenues.

Meanwhile, the tax structure as a whole demands review. The Secretary of the Treasury is undertaking this study immediately. We must develop a system of taxation which will impose the least possible obstacle to the dynamic growth of the country. This includes particularly real opportunity for the growth of small businesses. Many readjustments in existing taxes will be necessary to serve these objectives and also to remove existing inequities. Clarification and simplification in the tax laws as well as the regulations will be undertaken.

In the entire area of fiscal policy—which must, in its various aspects, be treated in recommendations to the Congress in coming weeks—there can now be stated certain basic facts and principles.

First. It is axiomatic that our economy is a highly complex and sensitive mechanism. Hasty and ill-considered action of any kind could seriously upset the subtle equation that encompasses debts, obligations, expenditures, defense demands, deficits, taxes, and the general economic health of the Nation. Our goals can be clear, our start toward them can be immediate—but action must be gradual.

Second. It is clear that too great a part of the national debt comes due in too short a time. The Department of the Treasury will undertake—indeed has undertaken—at suitable times a program of extending part of the debt over longer periods and gradually placing greater amounts in the hands of longer-term investors.

Third. Past differences in policy between the Treasury and the Federal Reserve Board have helped to encourage inflation. Henceforth, I expect that their single purpose shall be to serve the whole Nation by policies designed to stabilize the economy and encourage the free play of our people's genius for individual initiative.

In encouraging this initiative, no single item in our current problems has received more thoughtful consideration by my associates, and by the many individuals called into our counsels, than the matter of price and wage control by law.

The great economic strength of our democracy has developed in an atmosphere of freedom. The character of our people resists artificial and arbitrary controls of any kind. Direct controls, except those on credit, deal not with the real causes of inflation but only with its symptoms. In times of national emergency, this kind of control has a role to play. Our whole system, however, is based upon the assumption that, normally, we should combat wide fluctuations in our price structure by relying largely on the effective use of sound fiscal and monetary policy, and upon the natural workings of economic law.

Moreover, American labor and American business can best resolve their wage problems across the bargaining table. Government should refrain from sitting in with them unless, in extreme cases, the public welfare requires protection.

We are, of course, living in an international situation that is neither an emergency demanding full mobilization, nor is it peace. No one can know how long this condition will persist. Consequently, we are forced to learn many new things as we go along—clinging to what works, discarding what does not.

In all our current discussions on these and related facts, the weight of evidence is clearly against the use of controls in their present forms. They have proved largely unsatisfactory or unworkable. They have not prevented inflation; they have not kept down the cost of living. Dissatisfaction with them is wholly justified. I am convinced that now—as well as in the long run—free and competitive prices will best serve the interests of all the people, and best meet the changing, growing needs of our economy.

Accordingly, I do not intend to ask for a renewal of the present wage and price controls on April 30, 1953. In the meantime, steps will be taken to eliminate controls in an orderly manner, and to terminate special agencies no longer needed for this purpose. It is obviously to be expected that the removal of these controls will result in individual price changes—some will move up, some down. But a maximum of freedom in market prices as well as in collective bargaining is characteristic of a truly free people.

I believe also that material and product controls should be ended, except with respect to defense priorities and scarce and critical items essential for our defense. I shall recommend to the Congress that legislation be enacted to continue authority for such remaining controls of this type as will be necessary after the expiration of the existing statute on June 30, 1953.

I recommend the continuance of the authority for Federal control over rents in those communities in which serious housing shortages exist. These are chiefly the so-called defense areas. In these and all areas the Federal Government should withdraw from the control of rents as soon as practicable. But before they are removed entirely, each legislature should have full opportunity to take over, within its own State, responsibility for this function.

It would be idle to pretend that all our problems in this whole field of prices will solve themselves by mere Federal withdrawal from direct controls.

We shall have to watch trends closely. If the freer functioning of our economic system, as well as the indirect controls which can be appropriately employed, prove insufficient during this period of strain and tension, I shall promptly ask this Congress to enact such legislation as may be required.

In facing all these problems—wages, prices, production, tax rates, fiscal policy, deficits—everywhere we remain constantly mindful that the time for sacrifice has not ended. But we are concerned with the encouragement of competitive enterprise and individual initiative precisely because we know them to be our Nation's abiding sources of strength.

VI

Our vast world responsibility accents with urgency our people's elemental right to a government whose clear qualities are loyalty, security, efficiency, economy, and integrity.

The safety of America and the trust of the people alike demand that the personnel of the Federal Government be loyal in their motives and reliable in the discharge of their duties. Only a combination of both loyalty and reliability promises genuine security.

To state this principle is easy; to apply it can be difficult. But this security we must and we shall have. By way of example, all principal new appointees to departments and agencies have been investigated at their own request by the Federal Bureau of Investigation.

Confident of your understanding and cooperation, I know that the primary responsibility for keeping out the disloyal and the dangerous rests squarely upon the executive branch. When this branch so conducts itself as to require policing by another branch of the Government, it invites its own disorder and confusion.

I am determined to meet this responsibility of the Executive. The heads of all executive departments and agencies have been instructed to initiate at once effective programs of security with respect to their personnel. The Attorney General will advise and guide the departments and agencies in the shaping of these programs, designed at once to govern the employment of new personnel and to review speedily any derogatory information concerning incumbent personnel.

To carry out these programs, I believe that the powers of the executive branch under existing law are sufficient. If they should prove inadequate, the necessary legislation will be requested.

These programs will be both fair to the rights of the individual and effective for the safety of the Nation. They will, with care and justice, apply the basic principle that public employment is not a right but a privilege.

All these measures have two clear purposes: Their first purpose is to make certain that this Nation's security is not jeopardized by false servants. Their second purpose is to clear the atmosphere of that unreasoned suspicion that accepts rumor and gossip as substitutes for evidence.

Our people, of course, deserve and demand of their Federal Government more than security of personnel. They demand, also, efficient and logical organization, true to constitutional principles.

I have already established a Committee on Government Organization. The Committee is using as its point of departure the reports of the Hoover Commission and subsequent studies by several independent agencies. To achieve the greater efficiency and economy which the Committee analyses show to be possible, I ask the Congress to extend the present Government Reorganization Act for a period of 18 months or 2 years beyond its expiration date of April 1, 1953.

There is more involved here than realining the wheels and smoothing the gears of administrative machinery. The Congress rightfully expects the Executive to take the initiative in discovering and removing outmoded functions and eliminating duplication.

One agency, for example, whose head has promised early and vigorous action to provide greater efficiency is the Post Office. One of the oldest institutions of our Federal Government, its service should be the best. Its employees should merit and receive the high regard and esteem of the citizens of the Nation. There are today in some areas of the postal service, both waste and incompetence to be corrected. With cooperation of the Congress, and taking advantage of its accumulated experience in postal affairs, the Postmaster General will institute a program directed at improving service while at the same time reducing costs and decreasing deficits.

In all departments, dedication to these basic precepts of security and efficiency, integrity, and economy can and will produce an administration deserving of the trust the people have placed in it.

Our people have demanded nothing less than good, efficient government. They shall get nothing less.

VII

Vitally important are the water and minerals, public lands and standing timber, forage and wildlife of this country. A fast-growing population will have vast future needs in these resources. We must more than match the substantial achievements in the half-century since President Theodore Roosevelt awakened the Nation to the problem of conservation.

This calls for a strong Federal program in the field of resource development. Its major projects should be timed, wherever possible to assist in leveling off peaks and valleys in our economic life. Soundly planned projects already initiated should be carried out. New ones will be planned for the future.

The best natural resources program for America will not result from exclusive dependence on Federal bureaucracy. It will involve a partnership of the States and local communities, private citizens, and the Federal Government, all working together. This combined effort will advance the development of the great river valleys of our Nation and the power that they can generate. Likewise, such a partnership can be effective in the expansion throughout the Nation of upstream storage; the sound use of public lands; the wise conservation of minerals; and the sustained yield of our forests.

There has been much criticism, some of it apparently justified, of the confusion resulting from overlapping Federal activities in this entire field of resource-conservation. This matter is being exhaustively studied and appropriate reorganization plans will be developed.

Most of these particular resource problems pertain to the Department of the Interior. Another of its major concerns is our country's island possessions. Here, one matter deserves attention. The platforms of both political parties promised immediate statehood to Hawaii. The people of that Territory have earned that status. Statehood should be granted promptly with the first election scheduled for 1954.

VIII

One of the difficult problems which face the new administration is that of the slow, irregular decline of farm prices. This decline, which has been going on for almost 2 years, has occurred at a time when most nonfarm prices and farm costs of production are extraordinarily high.

Present agricultural legislation provides for the mandatory support of the prices of basic farm commodities at 90 percent of parity. The Secretary of Agriculture and his associates will, of course, execute the present act faithfully and thereby seek to mitigate the consequences of the downturn in farm income.

This price-support legislation will expire at the end of 1954.

So we should begin now to consider what farm legislation we should develop for 1955 and beyond. Our aim should be economic stability and full parity of income for American farmers. But we must seek this goal in ways that minimize governmental interference in the farmers' affairs, that permit desirable shifts in production, and that encourage farmers themselves to use initiative in meeting changing economic conditions.

A continuing study reveals nothing more emphatic than the complicated nature of this subject. Among other things, it shows that the prosperity of our agriculture depends directly upon the prosperity of the whole country—upon the purchasing power of American consumers. It depends upon the opportunity to ship abroad large surpluses of particular commodities and, therefore, upon sound economic relationships between the United States and many foreign countries. It involves research and scientific investigation, conducted on an extensive scale. It involves special credit mechanisms and marketing, rural electrification, soil conservation, and other programs.

The whole complex of agricultural programs and policies will be studied by a Special Agricultural Advisory Commission, as I know it will, by appropriate committees of the Congress. A nonpartisan group of respected authorities in the field of agriculture has already been appointed as an interim advisory group.

The immediate changes needed in agricultural programs are largely budgetary and administrative in nature. New policies and new programs must await the completion of the far-reaching studies which have already been launched.

IX

The determination of labor policy must be governed not by the vagaries of political expediency but by the firmest principles and convictions. Slanted partisan appeals to American workers, spoken as if they were a group apart, necessitating a special language and treatment, are an affront to the fullness of their dignity as American citizens.

The truth in matters of labor policy has become obscured in controversy. The very meaning of economic freedom as it affects labor has become confused. This misunderstanding has provided a climate of opinion favoring the growth of governmental paternalism in labor relations. This tendency, if left uncorrected, could end only by producing a bureaucratic despotism. Economic freedom is, in fact, the requisite of greater prosperity for every American who earns his own living.

In the field of labor legislation, only a law that merits the respect and support of both labor and management can help reduce the loss of wages and of production through strikes and stoppages, and thus add to the total economic strength of the Nation.

We have now had 5 years' experience with the Labor Management Act of 1947, commonly known as the Taft-Hartley law. That experience has shown the need for some corrective action, and we should promptly proceed to amend that act.

I know that the Congress is already proceeding with renewed studies of this subject. Meanwhile, the Department of Labor is at once beginning work to devise further specific recommendations for your consideration.

In the careful working out of legislation, I know you will give thoughtful consideration—as will we in the executive branch—to the views of labor, of management, and of the general public. In this process, it is only human that each of us should bring forward the argument of self-interest. But if all conduct their arguments in the overpowering light of national interest—which is enlightened self-interest—we shall get the right answers. I profoundly hope that every citizen of our country will follow with understanding your progress in this work. The welfare of us all is involved.

Especially must we remember that the institutions of trade unionism and collective bargaining are monuments to the freedom that must prevail in our industrial life. They have a century of honorable achievement behind them. Our faith in them is proven, firm, and final.

Government can do a great deal to aid the settlement of labor disputes without allowing itself to be employed as an ally of either side. Its proper role in industrial strife is to encourage the processes of mediation and conciliation. These processes can successfully be directed only by a government free from the taint of any suspicion that it is partial or punitive.

The administration intends to strengthen and to improve the services which the Department of Labor can render to the worker and to the whole national community. This Department was created—just 40 years ago—to serve the entire Nation. It must aid, for example, employers and employees alike in improving training programs that will develop skilled and competent workers. It must enjoy the confidence and respect of labor and industry in order to play a significant role in the planning of America's economic future. To that end, I am authorizing the Department of Labor to establish promptly a tripartite advisory committee consisting of representatives of employers, labor, and the public.

X

Our civil and social rights form a central part of the heritage we are striving to defend on all fronts and with all our strength.

I believe with all my heart that our vigilant guarding of these rights is a sacred obligation binding upon every citizen. To be true to one's own freedom is, in essence, to honor and respect the freedom of all others.

A cardinal ideal in this heritage we cherish is the equality of rights of all citizens of every race and color and creed.

We know that discrimination against minorities persists despite our allegiance to this ideal. Such discrimination—confined to no one section of the Nation—is but the outward testimony to the persistence of distrust and of fear in the hearts of men.

This fact makes all the more vital the fighting of these wrongs by each individual, in every station of life, in his every deed.

Much of the answer lies in the power of fact, fully publicized; of persuasion, honestly pressed; and of conscience, justly aroused. These are methods familiar to our way of life, tested and proven wise.

I propose to use whatever authority exists in the office of the President to end segregation in the District of Columbia, including the Federal Government, and any segregation in the Armed Forces.

Here in the District of Columbia, serious attention should be given to the proposal to develop and to authorize, through legislation, a system to provide an effective voice in local self-government. While consideration of this proceeds, I recommend an immediate increase of two in the number of District Commissioners to broaden representation of all elements in our local population. This will be a first step toward insuring that this Capital provide an honored example to all communities of our Nation.

In this manner, and by the leadership of the office of the President exercised through friendly conferences with those in authority in our States and cities, we expect to make true and rapid progress in civil rights and equality of employment opportunity.

There is one sphere in which civil rights are inevitably involved in Federal legislation. This is the sphere of immigration.

It is a manifest right of our Government to limit the number of immigrants our Nation can absorb. It is also a manifest right of our Government to set reasonable requirements on the character and the numbers of the people who come to share our land and our freedom.

It is well for us, however, to remind ourselves occasionally of an equally manifest fact: we are—one and all—immigrants or the sons and daughters of immigrants.

Existing legislation contains injustices. It does, in fact, discriminate. I am informed by Members of the Congress that it was realized, at the time of its enactment, that future study of the proper basis of determining quotas would be necessary.

I am therefore requesting the Congress to review this legislation and to enact a statute which will at one and the same time guard our legitimate national interests and be faithful to our basic ideas of freedom and fairness to all.

In another but related area—that of social rights—we see most clearly the new application of old ideas of freedom.

This administration is profoundly aware of two great needs born of our living in a complex industrial economy. First, the individual citizen must have safeguards against personal disaster inflicted by forces beyond his control; second, the welfare of the people demands effective and economical performance by the Government of certain indispensable social services.

In the light of this responsibility, certain general purposes and certain concrete measures are plainly indicated now.

There is urgent need for greater effectiveness in our programs, both public and private, offering safeguards against the privations that too often come with unemployment, old age, illness, and accident. The provisions of the old-age and survivors insurance law should promptly be extended to cover millions of citizens who have been left out of the social-security system. No less important is the encouragement of privately sponsored pension plans. Most important of all, of course, is renewed effort to check the inflation which destroys so much of the value of all social-security payments.

Our school system demands some prompt, effective help. During each of the last 2 years, more than 1½ million children have swelled the elementary and secondary school population of the country. Generally, the school population is proportionately higher in States with low per capita income. This whole situation calls for careful congressional study and action. I am sure you share my conviction that the firm conditions of Federal aid must be proved need and proved lack of local income.

One phase of the school problem demands special attention. The school population of many districts has been greatly increased by the swift growth of defense activities. These activities have added little or nothing to the tax resources of the communities affected. Legislation aiding construction of schools in these districts expires on June 20. This law should be renewed; and, likewise, the partial payments for current operating expenses for these particular school districts should be made, including the deficiency requirement of the current fiscal year.

Public interest similarly demands one prompt specific action in protection of the general consumer. The Food and Drug Administration should be authorized to continue its established and necessary program of factory inspections. The invalidation of these inspections by the Supreme Court of December 8, 1952, was based solely on the fact that the present law contains inconsistent and unclear provisions. These should be promptly corrected.

I am well aware that beyond these few immediate measures there remains much to be done. The health and housing needs of our people call for intelligently planned programs. Involved are the solvency of the whole security system; and its guarding against exploitation by the irresponsible.

To bring clear purpose and orderly procedure into this field, I anticipate a thorough study of the proper relationship among Federal, State, and local programs. I shall shortly send you specific recommendations for establishing an appropriate commission, together with a reorganization plan defining new administrative status for all Federal activities in health, education, and social security.

I repeat that there are many important subjects of which I make no mention today. Among these is our great and growing body of veterans. America has traditionally been generous in caring for the disabled—and the widow and the orphan of the fallen. These millions remain close to all our hearts. Proper care of our uniformed citizens and appreciation of the past service of our veterans are part of our accepted governmental responsibilities.

XI

We have surveyed briefly some problems of our people and a portion of the tasks before us.

The hope of freedom itself depends in real measure upon our strength, our heart, and our wisdom.

We must be strong in arms. We must be strong in the source of all our armament, our productivity. We all—workers and farmers, foremen and financiers, technicians and builders—all must produce, produce more, and produce yet more.

We must be strong, above all, in the spiritual resources upon which all else depends. We must be devoted with all our heart to the values we defend. We must know that each of these values and virtues applies with equal force at the ends of the earth and in our relations with our neighbor next door. We must know that freedom expresses itself with equal eloquence in the right of workers to strike in the nearby factory, and in the yearnings and sufferings of the peoples of Eastern Europe.

As our heart summons our strength, our wisdom must direct it.

There is, in world affairs, a steady course to be followed between an assertion of strength that is truculent and a confession of helplessness that is cowardly.

There is, in our affairs at home, a middle way between untrammeled freedom of the individual and the demands for the welfare of the whole Nation. This way must avoid government by bureaucracy as carefully as it avoids neglect of the helpless.

In every area of political action, freemen must think before they can expect to win.

In this spirit must we live and labor: confident of our strength, compassionate in our heart, clear in our mind.

In this spirit, let us together turn to the great tasks before us.

SECOND ANNUAL MESSAGE.

THE WHITE HOUSE, *January 7, 1954.*

MR. PRESIDENT, MR. SPEAKER, MEMBERS OF THE 83D CONGRESS:

It is a high honor again to present to the Congress my views on the state of the Union and to recommend measures to advance the security, prosperity, and well-being of the American people.

All branches of this Government—and I venture to say both of our great parties—can support the general objective of the recommendations I make today, for that objective is the building of a stronger America. A nation whose every citizen has good reason for bold hope; where effort is rewarded and prosperity is shared; where freedom expands and peace is secure—that is what I mean by a stronger America.

Toward this objective a real momentum has been developed during this administration's first year in office. We mean to continue that momentum and to increase it. We mean to build a better future for this Nation.

Much for which we may be thankful has happened during the past year.

First of all we are deeply grateful that our sons no longer die on the distant mountains of Korea. Although they are still called from our homes to military service, they are no longer called to the field of battle.

The Nation has just completed the most prosperous year in its history. The damaging effect of inflation on the wages, pensions, salaries, and savings of us all has been brought under control. Taxes have begun to go down. The cost of our Government has been reduced and its work proceeds with some 183,000 fewer employees; thus the discouraging trend of modern governments toward their own limitless expansion has in our case been reversed. The cost of armaments becomes less oppressive as we near our defense goals; yet we are militarily stronger every day. During the year, creation of the new Cabinet Department of Health, Education, and Welfare symbolized the Government's permanent concern with the human problems of our citizens.

Segregation in the Armed Forces and other Federal activities is on the way out. We have also made progress toward its elimination in the District of Columbia. These are steps in the continuing effort to eliminate interracial difficulty.

Some developments beyond our shores have been equally encouraging. Communist aggression, halted in Korea, continues to meet in Indochina the vigorous resistance of France and the Associated States, assisted by timely aid from our country. In West Germany, in Iran, and in other areas of the world, heartening political victories have been won by the forces of stability and freedom. Slowly but surely the free world gathers strength. Meanwhile, from behind the Iron Curtain there are signs that tyranny is in trouble and reminders that its structure is as brittle as its surface is hard.

There has been in fact a great strategic change in the world during the past year. That precious intangible, the initiative, is becoming ours. Our policy, not limited to mere reaction against crises provoked by others, is free to develop along lines of our choice not only abroad but also at home. As a major theme for American policy during the coming year, let our joint determination be to hold this new initiative and to use it.

We shall use this initiative to promote three broad purposes: First, to protect the freedom of our people; second, to maintain a strong, growing economy; third, to concern ourselves with the human problems of the individual citizen.

Only by active concern for each of these purposes can we be sure that we are on the forward road to a better and a stronger America. All my recommendations today are in furtherance of these three purposes.

I

FOREIGN AFFAIRS

American freedom is threatened so long as the world Communist conspiracy exists in its present scope, power, and hostility. More closely than ever before, American freedom is interlocked with the freedom of other people. In the unity of the free world lies our best chance to reduce the Communist threat without war. In the task of maintaining this unity and strengthening all its parts, the greatest responsibility falls naturally on those who, like ourselves, retain the most freedom and strength.

We shall, therefore, continue to advance the cause of freedom on foreign fronts.

In the Far East we retain our vital interest in Korea. We have negotiated with the Republic of Korea a mutual security pact, which develops our security system for the Pacific and which I shall promptly submit to the Senate for its consent to ratification. We are prepared to meet any renewal of armed aggression in Korea. We shall maintain indefinitely our bases in Okinawa. I shall ask the Congress to authorize continued material assistance to hasten the successful conclusion of the struggle in Indochina. This assistance will also bring closer the day when the Associated States may enjoy the independence already assured by France. We shall also continue military and economic aid to the Nationalist Government of China.

In south Asia, profound changes are taking place in free nations which are demonstrating their ability to progress through democratic methods. They provide an inspiring contrast to the dictatorial methods and backward course of events in Communist China. In these continuing efforts, the free peoples of south Asia can be assured of the support of the United States.

In the Middle East, where tensions and serious problems exist, we will show sympathetic and impartial friendship.

In Western Europe our policy rests firmly on the North Atlantic Treaty. It will remain so based as far ahead as we can see. Within its organization, the building of a united European community, including France and Germany, is vital to a free and self-reliant Europe. This will be promoted by the European Defense Community which offers assurance of European security. With the coming of unity to Western Europe, the assistance this Nation can render for the security of Europe and the free world will be multiplied in effectiveness.

In the Western Hemisphere we shall continue to develop harmonious and mutually beneficial cooperation with our neighbors. Indeed, solid friendship with all our American neighbors is a cornerstone of our entire policy.

In the world as a whole, the United Nations, admittedly still in a state of evolution, means much to the United States. It has given uniquely valuable services in many places where violence threatened. It is the only real world forum where we have the opportunity for international presentation and rebuttal. It is a place where the nations of the world can, if they have the will, take collective action for peace and justice. It is a place where the guilt can be squarely assigned to those who fail to take all necessary steps to keep the peace. The United Nations deserves our continued firm support.

FOREIGN ASSISTANCE AND TRADE

In the practical application of our foreign policy, we enter the field of foreign assistance and trade.

Military assistance must be continued. Technical assistance must be maintained. Economic assistance can be reduced. However, our economic programs in Korea and in a few other critical places of the world are especially important, and I shall ask Congress to continue them in the next fiscal year.

The forthcoming budget message will propose maintenance of the Presidential power of transferability of all assistance funds and will ask authority to merge these funds with the regular defense funds. It will also propose that the Secretary of Defense have primary responsibility for the administration of foreign military assistance in accordance with the policy guidance of the Secretary of State.

The fact that we can now reduce our foreign economic assistance in many areas is gratifying evidence that its objectives are being achieved. By continuing to surpass her prewar levels of economic activity, Western Europe gains self-reliance. Thus our relationship enters a new phase which can bring results beneficial to our taxpayers and our allies alike, if still another step is taken.

This step is the creation of a healthier and freer system of trade and payments within the free world—a system in which our allies can earn their own way and our own economy can continue to flourish. The free world can no longer afford the kinds of arbitrary restraints on trade that have continued ever since the war. On this problem I shall submit to the Congress detailed recommendations, after our Joint Commission on Foreign Economic Policy has made its report.

ATOMIC ENERGY PROPOSAL

As we maintain our military strength during the coming year and draw closer the bonds with our allies, we shall be in an improved position to discuss outstanding issues with the Soviet Union. Indeed we shall be glad to do so whenever there is a reasonable prospect of constructive results. In this spirit the atomic energy proposals of the United States were recently presented to the United Nations General Assembly. A truly constructive Soviet reaction will make possible a new start toward an era of peace, and away from the fatal road toward atomic war.

DEFENSE

Since our hope is peace, we owe ourselves and the world a candid explanation of the military measures we are taking to make that peace secure.

As we enter this new year, our military power continues to grow. This power is for our own defense and to deter aggression. We shall not be aggressors, but we and our allies have and will maintain a massive capability to strike back.

Here are some of the considerations in our defense planning:

First, while determined to use atomic power to serve the usages of peace, we take into full account our great and growing number of nuclear weapons and the most effective means of using them against an aggressor if they are needed to preserve our freedom. Our defense will be stronger if, under appropriate security safeguards, we share with our allies certain knowledge of the tactical use of our nuclear weapons. I urge the Congress to provide the needed authority.

Second, the usefulness of these new weapons creates new relationships between men and materials. These new relationships permit economies in the use of men as we build forces suited to our situation in the world today. As will be seen from the budget message on January 21, the airpower of our Navy and Air Force is receiving heavy emphasis.

Third, our Armed Forces must regain maximum mobility of action. Our strategic reserves must be centrally placed and readily deployable to meet sudden aggression against ourselves and our allies.

Fourth, our defense must rest on trained manpower and its most economical and mobile use. A professional corps is the heart of any security organization. It is necessarily the teacher and leader of those who serve temporarily in the discharge of the obligation to help defend the Republic. Pay alone will not retain in the career service of our Armed Forces the necessary numbers of long-term personnel. I strongly urge, therefore, a more generous use of other benefits important to service morale. Among these are more adequate living quarters and family housing units and medical care for dependents.

Studies of military manpower have just been completed by the National Security Training Commission and a committee appointed by the Director of the Office of Defense Mobilization. Evident weaknesses exist in the state of readiness and organization of our Reserve Forces. Measures to correct these weaknesses will be later submitted to the Congress.

Fifth, the ability to convert swiftly from partial to all-out mobilization is imperative to our security. For the first time, mobilization officials know what the requirements are for 1,000 major items needed for military uses. These data, now being related to civilian requirements and our supply potential, will show us the gaps in our mobilization base. Thus we shall have more realistic plant-expansion and stockpiling goals. We shall speed their attainment. This Nation is at last to have an up-to-date mobilization base—the foundation of a sound defense program.

Another part of this foundation is, of course, our continental transport system. Some of our vital heavy materials come increasingly from Canada. Indeed our relations with Canada, happily always close, involve more and more the unbreakable ties of strategic interdependence. Both Nations now need the St. Lawrence seaway for security as well as for economic reasons. I urge the Congress promptly to approve our participation in its construction.

Sixth, military and nonmilitary measures for continental defense must be and are being strengthened. In the current fiscal year we are allocating to these purposes an increasing portion of our effort, and in the next fiscal year we shall spend nearly a billion dollars more for them than in 1953.

An indispensable part of our continental security is our civil defense effort. This will succeed only as we have the complete cooperation of State governors, mayors, and voluntary citizen groups. With their help we can advance a cooperative program which, if an attack should come, would save many lives and lessen destruction.

The defense program recommended in the 1955 budget is consistent with all of the considerations which I have just discussed. It is based on a new military program unanimously recommended by the Joint Chiefs of Staff and approved by me following consideration by the National Security Council. This new program will make and keep America strong in an age of peril. Nothing should bar its attainment.

The international and defense policies which I have outlined will enable us to negotiate from a position of strength as we hold our resolute course toward a peaceful world. We now turn to matters which are normally characterized as domestic, well realizing that what we do abroad affects every problem at home—from the amount of taxes to our very state of mind.

INTERNAL SECURITY

Under the standards established for the new employee security program, more than 2,200 employees have been separated from the Federal Government. Our national security demands that the investigation of new employees and the evaluation of derogatory information respecting present employees be expedited and concluded at the earliest possible date. I shall recommend that the Congress provide additional funds where necessary to speed these important procedures.

From the special employment standards of the Federal Government I turn now to a matter relating to American citizenship. The subversive character of the Communist Party in the United States has been clearly demonstrated in many ways, including court proceedings. We should recognize by law a fact that is plain to all thoughtful citizens—that we are dealing here with actions akin to treason—that when a citizen knowingly participates in the Communist conspiracy he no longer holds allegiance to the United States.

I recommend that Congress enact legislation to provide that a citizen of the United States who is convicted in the courts of hereafter conspiring to advocate the overthrow of this Government by force or violence be treated as having, by such act, renounced his allegiance to the United States and forfeited his United States citizenship.

In addition, the Attorney General will soon appear before your committees to present his recommendations for needed additional legal weapons with which to combat subversion in our country and to deal with the question of claimed immunity.

II

STRONG ECONOMY

I turn now to the second great purpose of our Government: Along with the protection of freedom, the maintenance of a strong and growing economy.

The American economy is one of the wonders of the world. It undergirds our international position, our military security, and the standard of living of every citizen. This administration is determined to keep our economy strong and to keep it growing.

At this moment we are in transition from a wartime to a peacetime economy. I am confident that we can complete this transition without serious interruption in our economic growth. But we shall not leave this vital matter to chance. Economic preparedness is fully as important to the Nation as military preparedness.

Subsequent special messages and the economic report on January 28 will set forth plans of the administration and its recommendations for congressional action. These will include flexible credit and debt management policies; tax measures to stimulate consumer and business spending; suitable lending, guaranteeing, insuring, and grant-in-aid activities; strengthened old-age and unemployment insurance measures; improved agricultural programs; public-works plans laid well in advance; enlarged opportunities for international trade and investment. This mere enumeration of these subjects implies the vast amount of study, coordination, and planning, to say nothing of authorizing legislation, that altogether make our economic preparedness complete.

If new conditions arise that require additional administrative or legislative action, the administration will still be ready. A government always ready, as this is, to take well-timed and vigorous action, and a business community willing, as ours is, to plan boldly and with confidence, can between them develop a climate assuring steady economic growth.

THE BUDGET

I shall submit to the Congress on January 21 the first budget prepared by this administration, for the period July 1, 1954, through June 1955.

This budget is adequate to the current needs of the Government. It recognizes that a Federal budget should be a stabilizing factor in the economy. Its tax and expenditure programs will foster individual initiative and economic growth.

Pending the transmittal of my budget message, I shall mention here only a few points about our budgetary situation.

First, one of our initial acts was to revise, with the cooperation of the Congress, the budget prepared before this administration took office. Requests for new appropriations were greatly reduced. In addition, the spending level provided in that budget for the current fiscal year has been reduced by about $7,000,000,000. In the next fiscal year we estimate a further reduction in expenditures of more than $5,000,000,000. This will reduce the spending level over the 2 fiscal years by more than $12,000,000,000. We are also reducing further our requests for new appropriations.

Second, despite the substantial loss of revenue in the coming fiscal year, resulting from tax reductions now in effect and tax adjustments which I shall propose, our reduced spending will move the new budget closer to a balance.

Third, by keeping new appropriation requests below estimated revenues, we continue to reduce the tremendous accumulation of unfinanced obligations incurred by the Government under past appropriations.

Fourth, until those claims on our Government's revenues are further reduced, the growth in the public debt cannot be entirely stopped. Because of this—because the Government's bills have to be paid every month, while the tax money to pay them comes in with great unevenness within the fiscal year—and because of the need for flexibility to manage this enormous debt, I find it necessary to renew my request for an increase in the statutory debt limit.

TAXES

The new budget provides for a lower level of taxation than has prevailed in preceding years. Six days ago individual income taxes were reduced and the excess-profits tax expired. These tax reductions are justified only because of the substantial reductions we already have made and are making in governmental expenditures. As additional reductions in expenditures are brought gradually but surely into sight, further reductions in taxes can and will be made. When budget savings and sound governmental financing are assured, tax burdens should be reduced so that taxpayers may spend their own money in their own way.

While we are moving toward lower levels of taxation we must thoroughly revise our whole tax system. The groundwork for this revision has already been laid by the Committee on Ways and Means of the House of Representatives, in close consultation with the Department of the Treasury. We should now remove the more glaring tax inequities, particularly on small taxpayers; reduce restraints on the growth of small business; and make other changes that will encourage initiative, enterprise, and production. Twenty-five recommendations toward these ends will be contained in my budget message.

Without attempting to summarize these manifold reforms, I can here illustrate their tendency. For example, we propose more liberal tax treatment for dependent children who work, for widows or widowers with dependent children, and for medical expenses. For the business that wants to expand or modernize its plant, we propose liberalized tax treatment of depreciation, research and development expenses, and retained earnings.

Because of the present need for revenue the corporation income tax should be kept at the current rate of 52 percent for another year, and the excise taxes scheduled to be reduced on April 1, including those on liquor, tobacco, gasoline, and automobiles, should be continued at present rates.

Immediate extension of the Renegotiation Act of 1951 is also needed to eliminate excessive profits and to prevent waste of public funds in the purchase of defense materials.

AGRICULTURE

The well-being of our 160 million people demands a stable and prosperous agriculture. Conversely, every farmer knows he cannot prosper unless all America prospers. As we seek to promote increases in our standard of living, we must be sure that the farmer fairly shares in that increase. Therefore, a farm program promoting stability and prosperity in all elements of our agriculture is urgently needed.

Agricultural laws now in effect successfully accomplished their wartime purpose of encouraging maximum production of many crops. Today, production of these crops at such levels far exceeds present demand. Yet the laws encouraging such production are still in effect. The storage facilities of the Commodity Credit Corporation bulge with surplus stocks of dairy products, wheat, cotton, corn, and certain vegetable oils; and the Corporation's presently authorized borrowing authority—$6,750,000,000—is nearly exhausted. Some products, priced out of domestic markets, and others, priced out of world markets, have piled up in Government hands. In a world in which millions of people are hungry, destruction of food would, of course, be unconscionable. Yet surplus stocks continue to threaten the market and, in spite of the acreage controls authorized by present law, surpluses will continue to accumulate.

We confront two alternatives: The first is to impose still greater acreage reductions for some crops and apply rigid Federal controls over the use of the diverted acres. This will regiment the production of every basic agricultural crop. It will place every producer of those crops under the domination and control of the Federal Government in Washington. This alternative is contrary to the fundamental interests not only of the farmer but of the Nation as a whole. Nor is it a real solution to the problem facing us.

The second alternative is to permit the market price for these agricultural products gradually to have a greater influence on the planning of production by farmers, while continuing the assistance of the Government. This is the sound approach. To make it effective, surpluses existing when the new program begins must be insulated from the normal channels of trade for special uses. These uses would include school-lunch programs, disaster relief, emergency assistance to foreign friends, and of particular importance the stockpiling of reserves for a national emergency.

Building on the agricultural laws of 1948 and 1949, we should establish a price-support program with enough flexibility to attract the production of needed supplies of essential commodities and to stimulate the consumption of those commodities that are flooding American markets. Transition to modernized parity must be accomplished gradually. In no case should there be an abrupt downward change in the dollar level or in the percentage level of price supports.

Next Monday I shall transmit to the Congress my detailed recommendations embodying this approach. They have been developed through the cooperation of innumerable individuals vitally interested in agriculture. My special message on Monday will briefly describe the consultative and advisory processes to which this whole program has been subjected during the past 10 months.

I have chosen this farm program because it will build markets, protect the consumers' food supply, and move food into consumption instead of into storage. It is a program that will remove the threat to the farmer of these overhanging surpluses, a program, also, that will stimulate production when a commodity is scarce and encourage consumption when nature is bountiful. Moreover, it will promote the individual freedom, responsibility, and initiative which distinguish American agriculture. And, by helping our agriculture achieve full parity in the market, it promises our farmers a higher and steadier financial return over the years than any alternative plan.

CONSERVATION

Part of our Nation's precious heritage is its natural resources. It is the common responsibility of Federal, State, and local governments to improve and develop them, always working in the closest harmony and partnership.

All Federal conservation and resource development projects are being reappraised. Sound projects now under way will be continued. New projects in which the Federal Government has a part must be economically sound, with local sharing of cost wherever appropriate and feasible. In the next fiscal year work will be started on 23 projects that meet these standards. The Federal Government will continue to construct and operate economically sound flood-control, power, irrigation, and water-supply projects wherever these projects are beyond the capacity of local initiative, public or private, and consistent with the needs of the whole Nation.

Our conservation program will also take into account the important role played by farmers in protecting our soil resources. I recommend enactment of legislation to strengthen agricultural conservation and upstream flood-prevention work, and to achieve a better balance with major flood-control structures in the downstream areas.

Recommendations will be made from time to time for the adoption of—

A uniform and consistent water resources policy;

A revised public lands policy; and

A sound program for safeguarding the domestic production of critical and strategic metals and minerals.

In addition we shall continue to protect and improve our national forests, parks, monuments, and other natural and historic sites, as well as our fishery and wildlife resources. I hope that pending legislation to improve the conservation and management of publicly owned grazing lands in national forests will soon be approved by the Congress.

NATIONAL HIGHWAYS

To protect the vital interest of every citizen in a safe and adequate highway system, the Federal Government is continuing its central role in the Federal aid highway program. So that maximum progress can be made to overcome present inadequacies in the interstate highway system, we must continue the Federal gasoline tax at 2 cents per gallon. This will require cancellation of the one-half cent decrease which otherwise will become effective April 1, and will maintain revenues so that an expanded highway program can be undertaken.

When the Commission on Intergovernmental Relations completes its study of the present system of financing highway construction, I shall promptly submit it for consideration by the Congress and the governors of the States.

POST OFFICE

It is apparent that the substantial savings already made, and to be made, by the Post Office Department cannot eliminate the postal deficit. I recommend, therefore, that the Congress approve the bill now pending in the House of Representatives providing for the adjustment of certain postal rates. To handle the long-term aspects of this, I also recommend that the Congress create a permanent commission to establish fair and reasonable postal rates from time to time in the future.

III

HUMAN PROBLEMS

Along with the protection of freedom and maintenance of a strong and growing economy, this administration recognizes a third great purpose of government: concern for the human problems of our citizens. In a modern industrial society, banishment of destitution and cushioning the shock of personal disaster on the individual are proper concerns of all levels of government, including the Federal Government. This is especially true where remedy and prevention alike are beyond the individual's capacity.

LABOR AND WELFARE

Of the many problems in this area, those I shall first discuss are of particular concern to the members of our great labor force, who with their heads, hearts, and hands produce so much of the wealth of our country.

Protection against the hazards of temporary unemployment should be extended to some 6½ millions of workers, including civilian Federal workers, who now lack this safeguard. Moreover, the Secretary of Labor is making available to the States studies and recommendations in the fields of weekly benefits, periods of protection, and extension of coverage. The economic report will consider the related matter of minimum wages and their coverage.

The Labor Management Relations Act of 1947 is basically a sound law. However, 6 years of experience have revealed that in some respects it can be improved. On January 11 I shall forward to the Congress suggestions for changes designed to reinforce the basic objectives of the act.

Our basic social-security program, the old-age and survivors insurance system, to which individuals contribute during their productive years and receive benefits based on previous earnings, is designed to shield them from destitution. Last year I recommended extension of the social-insurance system to include more than 10,000,000 additional persons. I ask that this extension soon be accomplished. This and other major improvements in the insurance system will bring substantial benefit increases and broaden the membership of the insurance system, thus diminishing the need for Federal grants-in-aid for such purposes. A new formula will therefore be proposed, permitting progressive reduction in such grants as the need for them declines.

Federal grant-in-aid welfare programs, now based on widely varying formulas, should be simplified. Concrete proposals on 14 of them will be suggested to the appropriate committees.

The program for rehabilitation of the disabled especially needs strengthening. Through special vocational training, this program presently returns each year some 60,000 handicapped individuals to productive work. Far more disabled people can be saved each year from idleness and dependence if this program is gradually increased. My more detailed recommendations on this and the other social-insurance problems I have mentioned will be sent to the Congress on January 14.

HEALTH

I am flatly opposed to the socialization of medicine. The great need for hospital and medical services can best be met by the initiative of private plans. But it is unfortunately a fact that medical costs are rising and already impose severe hardships on many families. The Federal Government can do many helpful things and still carefully avoid the socialization of medicine.

The Federal Government should encourage medical research in its battle with such mortal diseases as cancer and heart ailments, and should continue to help the States in their health and rehabilitation programs. The present Hospital Survey and Construction Act should be broadened in order to assist in the development of adequate facilities for the chronically ill, and to encourage the construction of diagnostic centers, rehabilitation facilities, and nursing homes. The war on disease also needs a better working relationship between Government and private initiative. Private and nonprofit hospital and medical insurance plans are already in the field, soundly based on the experience and initiative of the people in their various communities.

A limited Government reinsurance service would permit the private and nonprofit insurance companies to offer broader protection to more of the many families which want and should have it. On January 18 I shall forward to the Congress a special message presenting this administration's health program in its detail.

EDUCATION

Youth—our greatest resource—is being seriously neglected in a vital respect. The Nation as a whole is not preparing teachers or building schools fast enough to keep up with the increase in our population.

The preparation of teachers as, indeed, the control and direction of public education policy, is a State and local responsibility. However, the Federal Government should stand ready to assist States which demonstrably cannot provide sufficient school buildings. In order to appraise the needs, I hope that this year a conference on education will be held in each State, culminating in a national conference. From these conferences on education, every level of government—from the Federal Government to each local school board—should gain the information with which to attack this serious problem.

HOUSING

The details of a program to enlarge and improve the opportunities for our people to acquire good homes will be presented to the Congress by special message on January 25.

This program will include—

Modernization of the home mortgage insurance program of the Federal Government;

Redirection of the present system of loans and grants-in-aid to cities for slum clearance and redevelopment;

Extension of the advantages of insured lending to private credit engaged in this task of rehabilitating obsolete neighborhoods;

Insurance of long-term, mortgage loans, with small down payment for low-income families; and, until alternative programs prove more effective,

Continuation of the public housing program adopted in the Housing Act of 1949.

If the individual, the community, the State and Federal Governments will alike apply themselves, every American family can have a decent home.

VETERANS' ADMINISTRATION

The internal reorganization of the Veterans' Administration is proceeding with my full approval. When completed, it will afford a single agency whose services, including medical facilities, will be better adapted to the needs of those 20,000,000 veterans to whom this Nation owes so much.

SUFFRAGE

My few remaining recommendations all relate to a basic right of our citizens—that of being represented in the decisions of the Government.

I hope that the States will cooperate with the Congress in adopting uniform standards in their voting laws that will make it possible for our citizens in the Armed Forces overseas to vote.

In the District of Columbia the time is long overdue for granting national suffrage to its citizens and also applying the principle of local self-government to the Nation's Capital. I urge the Congress to move promptly in this direction and also to revise District revenue measures to provide needed public-works improvements.

The people of Hawaii are ready for statehood. I renew my request for this legislation in order that Hawaii may elect its State officials and its representatives in Washington along with the rest of the country this fall.

For years our citizens between the ages of 18 and 21 have, in time of peril, been summoned to fight for America. They should participate in the political process that produces this fateful summons. I urge Congress to propose to the States a constitutional amendment permitting citizens to vote when they reach the age of 18.

CONCLUSION

I want to add one final word about the general purport of these many recommendations.

Our Government's powers are wisely limited by the Constitution; but quite apart from those limitations there are things which no government can do or should try to do.

A government can strive, as ours is striving, to maintain an economic system whose doors are open to enterprise and ambition—those personal qualities on which economic growth largely depends. But enterprise and ambition are qualities which no government can supply. Fortunately no American government need concern itself on this score; our people have these qualities in good measure.

A government can sincerely strive for peace, as ours is striving, and ask its people to make sacrifices for the sake of peace. But no government can place peace in the hearts of foreign rulers. It is our duty then to ourselves and to freedom itself to remain strong in all those ways—spiritual, economic, military—that will give us maximum safety against the possibility of aggressive action by others.

No government can inoculate its people against the fatal materialism that plagues our age. Happily, our people, though blessed with more material goods than any people in history, have always reserved their first allegiance to the kingdom of the spirit, which is the true source of that freedom we value above all material things.

But a government can try, as ours tries, to sense the deepest aspirations of the people, and to express them in political action at home and abroad. So long as action and aspiration humbly and earnestly seek favor in the sight of the Almighty, there is no end to America's forward road; there is no obstacle on it she will not surmount in her march toward a lasting peace in a free and prosperous world.

THIRD ANNUAL MESSAGE.

THE WHITE HOUSE, *Jan. 6, 1955*

MR. PRESIDENT, MR. SPEAKER, LADIES AND GENTLEMEN OF THE CONGRESS:

My friends, first, I do most sincerely thank you from the bottom of my heart for the cordiality of your welcome, and I extend cordial greetings to the 84th Congress. We shall have much to do together; I am sure that we shall get it done—and, that we shall do it in harmony and good will. And here I am certain you will permit me this morning a personal allusion. The district where I was born has been represented in this Congress for more years than he cares to remember, I suppose, by our distinguished Speaker. Today is his birthday, and I want to join with the rest of you in felicitating him and in wishing him many happy returns of the day.

Now, ladies and gentlemen, at the outset, I believe it would be well to remind ourselves of this great fundamental of our national life: our common belief that every human being is divinely endowed with dignity and with worth and inalienable rights. This faith, with its corollary—that to grow and flourish people must be free—shapes the interests and the aspirations of every American.

From this deep faith have evolved three main purposes of our Federal Government:

First, to maintain justice and freedom among ourselves and to champion them for others so that we may work effectively for enduring peace;

Second, to help keep our economy vigorous and expanding, thus sustaining our international strength and assuring better jobs, better living, better opportunities for every citizen; and

Third, to concern ourselves with the human problems of our people so that every American may have the opportunity to lead a healthy, productive and rewarding life.

It is under these three headings that I shall present to you today, ladies and gentlemen, the thoughts that I believe appropriate to this occasion.

Now, foremost among these broad purposes of government is our support of freedom, justice, peace.

It is of the utmost importance, then, that each of us understand the true nature of the world struggle now taking place.

It is not a struggle merely of economic theories, or of forms of government, or of military power. The issue is the true nature of man. Either man is the creature whom the Psalmist described as "a little lower than the angels," crowned with glory and honor, holding "dominion over the works" of his Creator; or, man is a soulless, animated machine to be enslaved, used and consumed by the state for its own glorification.

It is, therefore, a struggle which goes to the roots of the human spirit, and its shadow falls across the long sweep of man's destiny. This prize, so precious, so fraught with ultimate meaning, is the true object of the contending forces in the world.

In the past year, there has been progress justifying hope for the ultimate rule of freedom and justice in the world. Free nations are collectively stronger than at any time in recent years.

Just as nations of this hemisphere, in the historic Caracas and Rio Conferences, have closed ranks against imperialistic communism and strengthened their economic ties, so free nations elsewhere have forged new bonds of unity.

Recent agreements between Turkey and Pakistan have laid a foundation for increased strength in the Middle East. With our understanding support, Egypt and Britain, Yugoslavia and Italy, Britain and Iran have resolved dangerous differences. The security of the Mediterranean has been enhanced by an alliance among Greece, Turkey, and Yugoslavia. Agreements in Western Europe have paved the way for unity to replace past divisions which have undermined Europe's economic and military vitality. The defense of the West appears likely at last to include a free, democratic Germany, participating as an equal in the councils of NATO.

In Asia and the Pacific, the pending Manila Pact supplements our treaties with Australia, New Zealand, the Philippines, Korea and Japan and our prospective treaty with the Republic of China. These pacts stand as solemn warning that future military aggression and subversion against the free nations of Asia will meet united response. The Pacific Charter, also adopted at Manila, is a milestone in the development of human freedom and self-government in the Pacific area.

Under the auspices of the United Nations, there is promise of progress in our country's plan for the peaceful use of atomic energy.

Finally, today the world is at peace. It is, to be sure, an insecure peace. Yet all humanity finds hope in the simple fact that for an appreciable time there has been no active battlefield on earth. This same fact inspires us to work all the more effectively with other nations for the well-being, the freedom, the dignity, of every human on earth. In the ultimate achievement of this great purpose lies the only sure promise of security and permanent peace for any nation, including our own.

These developments are heartening. But sobering problems remain.

The massive military machines and ambitions of the Soviet-Communist bloc still create uneasiness in the world. All of us are aware of the continuing reliance of the Soviet Communists on military force, of the power of their weapons, of their present resistance to realistic armament limitation, and of their continuing effort to dominate or intimidate free nations on their periphery. Their steadily growing power includes an increasing strength in nuclear weapons. This power, combined with the proclaimed intentions of the Communist leaders to communize the world, is the threat confronting us today.

To protect our nations and our peoples from the catastrophe of a nuclear holocaust, free nations must maintain countervailing military power to persuade the Communists of the futility of seeking to advance their ends through aggression. If Communist rulers understand that America's response to aggression will be swift and decisive—that never shall we buy peace at the expense of honor or faith—they will be powerfully deterred from launching a military venture engulfing their own peoples and many others in disaster. Now this, of course, is a form of world stalemate. But in this stalemate each of us—every American—may and must exercise his high duty to strive in every honorable way for enduring peace.

The military threat is but one menace to our freedom and security. We must not only deter aggression; we must also frustrate the effort of Communists to gain their goals by subversion. To this end, free nations must maintain and reinforce their cohesion, their internal security, their political and economic vitality, and their faith in freedom.

In such a world, America's course is clear:

We must strengthen the collective defense under the United Nations Charter and gird ourselves with sufficient military strength and productive capacity to discourage resort to war and protect our Nation's vital interests.

We must continue to support and strengthen the United Nations. At this moment, by vote of the United Nations General Assembly, its Secretary General is in Communist China on a mission of deepest concern to all Americans: seeking the release of our never-to-be-forgotten American aviators and all other United Nations prisoners wrongfully detained by the Communist regime.

We must also encourage the efforts being made in the United Nations to limit armaments and to harness the atom to peaceful use.

We must expand international trade and investment and assist friendly nations whose own best efforts are still insufficient to provide the strength essential to the security of the free world.

We must be willing to use the processes of negotiation whenever they will advance the cause of just and secure peace.

In respect to all these matters, we must, through a vigorous information program, keep the peoples of the world truthfully advised of our actions and purposes. This problem has been attacked with new vigor during the past months. I urge that the Congress give its earnest attention to the great advantages that can accrue to our country through the successful and expanded operations of this information program.

We must carry forward our educational exchange program.

Now, to advance these many efforts, the Congress must act in this session on appropriations, legislation, and treaties. Today I shall mention especially our foreign economic and military programs.

The recent economic progress in many free nations has been heartening. The productivity of labor and the production of goods and services are increasing in ever-widening areas. There is a growing will to improve the living standards of all men. This progress is important to all our people. It promises us allies who are strong and self-reliant; it promises a growing world market for the products of our mines, our factories, our farms.

But only through steady effort can we continue this progress. Barriers still impede trade and the flow of capital needed to develop each nation's human and material resources. Wise reduction of these barriers is a long-term objective of our foreign economic policy—a policy of an evolutionary and selective nature, assuring broad benefits to our own and to other peoples.

We must gradually reduce certain tariff obstacles to trade. These actions should, of course, be accompanied by a similar lowering of trade barriers by other nations, so that we may move steadily together toward economic advantage for all. We must further simplify our customs procedures. We must facilitate the flow of capital and continue technical assistance, both directly and through the United Nations. This must go to less developed countries to strengthen their independence and raise their living standards. Many another step must be taken in the free world to release forces of private initiative.

On January 10, by special message, I shall submit specific recommendations for carrying forward the legislative phases of our foreign economic policy.

Our many efforts to build a better world include the maintenance of our military strength. This is a vast undertaking. Over 4 million Americans—servicemen and civilians—are on the rolls of the Defense Establishment. During the past 2 years, by attacking duplication and overstaffing, by improved procurement and inventory controls, by concentrating on the essentials, many billions of dollars have been saved on these defense activities. I should like to mention certain fundamentals underlying this vast program.

First, I repeat that a realistic limitation of armaments and an enduring, just peace remain our national goals; we maintain powerful military forces because there is no present alternative—they are forces designed for deterrent and defensive purposes, able instantly to strike back with destructive power in response to any attack.

Second, we must stay alert to the fact that undue reliance on one weapon or preparation for only one kind of warfare simply invites an enemy to resort to another. We must, therefore, keep in our Armed Forces balance and flexibility adequate to our needs.

Third, to keep our Armed Forces abreast of the advances of science, our military planning must be flexible enough to utilize the new weapons and techniques which flow ever more speedily from our research and development programs. The forthcoming military budget therefore emphasizes modern airpower in the Air Force, Navy, and Marine Corps and increases the emphasis on new weapons, especially those of rapid and destructive striking power.

It seeks continuous modernization of our Army. It accelerates the continental defense program and the buildup of military reserve forces. It continues a vigorous program of stockpiling strategic materials and strengthening our mobilization base. It provides for reduction of forces in certain categories and their expansion in others, to fit them to the military realities of our time. These emphases in our defense planning have been made at my personal direction after long and thoughtful—even prayerful—study. In my judgment, they will give our Nation a defense accurately adjusted to the national need.

Fourth, pending a world agreement on armament limitation, we must continue to expand our supplies of nuclear weapons for our land, naval, and air forces. We shall continue our encouraging progress, at the same time, in the peaceful use of atomic power.

Fifth, in the administration of these costly programs, we demand the utmost efficiency. We must assure our people not only of adequate protection but also of a defense that can and will be resolutely carried forward from year to year until the threat of aggression has disappeared.

To help maintain this kind of armed strength and to improve its efficiency, I urge the enactment of several important measures.

The first concerns the Selective Service Act which expires next June 30. For the foreseeable future, our standing forces must remain much larger than voluntary methods can sustain. We must, therefore, extend the statutory authority to induct men for 2 years of military service.

The second kind of measure concerns the rapid turnover of our most experienced servicemen. This process seriously weaknes the combat readiness of our Armed Forces and is unnecessary and extravagantly expensive. To encourage more trained servicemen to remain in uniform, I shall, on the 13th of this month, propose a number of measures to increase the attractions of a military career. These measures will include more adequate medical care for dependents, survivors' benefits, more and better housing, and selective adjustments in military pay and allowances.

And, third, I shall present a program to rebuild and strengthen the civilian components of our Armed Forces. Because it will go far in assuring fair and equitable participation in military service, it is of particular importance to our combat veterans. In keeping with our historic military policy, the program is designed to build civilian reserves capable of effective military service in an emergency in lieu of maintaining active forces in excess of the Nation's immediate need.

Through this program the individual will be able to discharge one of his obligations to the Nation; equally, the Nation will be able to discharge one of its obligations to a potential future serviceman; namely, to give him the greatest possible chance of survival in time of war.

An effective defense requires continuance of our aggressive attack on subversion at home. In this effort we have, in the past 2 years, made real progress. FBI investigations have been reinforced by a new Internal Security Division in the Department of Justice; the security activities of the Immigration and Naturalization Service have been revitalized; an improved security system is in effect throughout the Government; the Department of Justice and the FBI have been armed with new legal weapons forged by the 83d Congress.

We shall continue to ferret out and to destroy Communist subversion.

We shall, in the process, carefully preserve our traditions and the basic rights of every American citizen.

Our civil defense program is also a key element in the protection of our country. We are developing cooperative methods with State governors, mayors, and voluntary citizen groups, in building the civil defense. The significance of this organization in time of war is obvious; its swift assistance in disaster areas last year proved its importance in time of peace.

An industry capable of rapid expansion and essential materials and facilities available in time of emergency are indispensable. I urge, therefore, a 2-year extension of the Defense Production Act and title II of the First War Powers Act of 1941. These are cornerstones of our program for the development of an adequate mobilization base.

At this point, I should like to make this additional observation.

Our quest for peace and freedom necessarily presumes that we who hold positions of public trust, must rise above self and section—that we must subordinate to the general good our partisan and our personal pride and prejudice. Tirelessly, with united purpose, we must fortify the material and spiritual foundations of this land of freedom. As never before, there is need for unhesitating cooperation among the branches of our Government.

At this time the executive and legislative branches are under the management of different political parties. This fact places both parties on trial before the American people.

In less perilous days of the past, division of governmental responsibility among our great parties has at times produced indecision approaching futility. We must not let this happen in our time. We must avoid a paralysis of the will for peace and international security.

Now in the traditionally bipartisan areas—military security and foreign relations—I can report to you that I have already, with the present leaders of this Congress, exchanged assurances of unreserved cooperation. Yet, the security of our country requires more than maintenance of military strength and success in foreign affairs; these vital matters are in turn dependent upon concerted and vigorous action in a number of supporting programs.

I say, therefore, to the 84th Congress:

In all areas basic to the strength of America, there will be—to the extent I can insure them—cooperative, constructive relations between the executive and legislative branches of this Government. Let the general good be our yardstick on every great issue of our time. In that pledge I should include, also, the similar pledge of every head of department or independent agency in this Government.

Our efforts to defend our freedom and to secure a just peace are, of course, inseparable from the second great purpose of our Government: to help maintain a strong, growing economy—an economy vigorous and free, in which there are ever-increasing opportunities, just rewards for effort, and a stable prosperity that is widely shared.

In the past 2 years, many important governmental actions helped our economy adjust to conditions of peace. Controls were removed from wages, prices, and materials. Tax revisions encouraged increased private spending and employment. Federal expenditures were sharply reduced, making possible a record tax cut. These actions, together with flexible monetary and debt management policies, helped to halt inflation and stabilize the value of the dollar. A program of partnership in resource development was begun. Social security and unemployment insurance laws were broadened. New laws started the process of balancing farm production with farm markets. Shipbuilding and stockpiling programs strengthened key sectors of the economy, while improving our mobilization base. A new housing law brought impressive progress in an area fundamental to our economic strength and closed loopholes in the old law that permitted dishonest manipulation. Many of these programs are just beginning to exert their stimulating effect upon the whole economy and upon specific communities and industries throughout the country.

1954 was one of the most prosperous years in our history. Business activity surges with new strength. Production is rising. Employment is high. Toward the end of last year average weekly wages in manufacturing were higher than ever before. Personal income after taxes is at a record level. So is consumer spending. Construction activity is reaching new peaks. Export demand for our goods is strong. State and local government expenditures on public works are rising. Savings are high, and credit is readily available.

So, today, the transition to a peacetime economy is largely behind us. The economic outlook is good.

Now the many promising factors I have mentioned do not guarantee sustained economic expansion; but, they do give us a strong position from which to carry forward our economic growth. If we as a people act wisely, our annual national output can rise within a decade from its present level of about $360 billion to $500 billion, measured in dollars of stable buying power.

The budget message on January 17, the economic report on the 20th of the month, and several special messages will set forth in detail programs to foster the growth of our economy and to protect the integrity of the people's money. Today I discuss these only in general terms.

Government efficiency and economy remain essential to progress toward a balanced budget. More than $10 billion were cut from the spending program first proposed in the budget of January 9, 1953. So expenditures of that year were $6½ billion below those of the previous year. In the current fiscal year, Government spending will be nearly $4½ billion less than in the fiscal year ending last June 30. New spending authority has been held below expenditures, reducing, thus, Government obligations accumulated over the years.

Last year we had a large tax cut and, for the first time in 75 years a basic revision of tax laws. It is now clear that defense and other essential Government costs must remain at a level precluding further tax reductions this year. Although excise and corporation income taxes must, therefore, be continued at their present rates, further tax cuts will be possible when justified by lower expenditures and by revenue increases arising from the Nation's economic growth. I am hopeful that such reductions can be made next year.

At the foundation of our economic growth are the raw materials and energy produced from our minerals and fuels, lands and forests, and water resources. With respect to them, I believe that the Nation must adhere to three fundamental policies: first, to develop, wisely use, and to conserve basic resources from generation to generation; second, to follow the historic pattern of developing these resources primarily by private citizens under fair provisions of law, including restraints for proper conservation; and third, to treat resource development as a partnership undertaking—a partnership in which the participation of private citizens and State and local governments is as necessary as is Federal participation.

This policy has encouraged local public bodies and private citizens to plan their own power sources. Increasing numbers of applications to the Federal Power Commission to conduct surveys and prepare plans for power development are evidence of local response.

The Federal Government and local and private organizations have been encouraged to coordinate their developments. This is important because Federal hydroelectric developments supply but a very small fraction of the Nation's power needs. Such partnership projects as Priest Rapids in Washington, the Coosa River development in Alabama, the Markham Ferry in Oklahoma already have the approval of this Congress. This year justifiable projects of a similar nature will again have administration support.

Now, of course, the Federal Government must shoulder its own partnership obligations by undertaking projects of such complexity and size that their success requires Federal development. In keeping with this principle I again urge the Congress to approve the development of the upper Colorado River Basin to conserve and assure better use of precious water essential to the future of the West.

In addition, the 1956 budget will recommend appropriations to start 6 new reclamation projects, and more than 30 new Corps of Engineers projects of varying size. Going projects and investigations of potential new resource developments will be, of course, continued.

A great need in this broad field is a nationwide comprehensive water resources policy firmly based in law. Such a policy is under preparation and when completed will be submitted to the Congress for its consideration.

Continued vigilance will be maintained over our fisheries, wildlife resources, the national parks and forests, and the public lands; and we shall continue to encourage an orderly development of the Nation's mineral resources.

A modern highway system is essential to meet the needs of our growing population, our expanding economy, and our national security. We are accelerating our highway-improvement program under existing State and Federal laws and authorizations. But this effort will not, in itself, assure our people of an adequate system. This problem has been carefully considered by the conference of State governors and by a special Advisory Committee on a National Highway Program, composed of leading private citizens. I have received the recommendations of the governors' conference, and will shortly receive the views of the special committee. Aided by their findings, I plan to submit on January 27 recommendations which will meet our most pressing national highway needs.

In further recognition of the importance of transportation to our economic strength and security, the administration, through a Cabinet committee, is thoroughly examining existing Federal transportation policies to determine their effect on the adequacy of transportation services. This is the first such comprehensive review ever undertaken directly by the executive branch of the Government in modern times. We are not only examining major problems facing the various modes of transport; we are also studying closely the interrelationships of civilian and Government requirements for transportation. Legislation will be recommended to correct such policy deficiencies as we find.

The Nation's public-works activities are tremendous in scope. It is estimated that more than $12 billion will be expended in 1955 for the development of land, water, and other resources; control of floods, and navigation and harbor improvements; construction of roads, schools, and municipal water supplies, and disposal of domestic and industrial wastes. Many of the Federal, State, and local agencies responsible for this work are highly efficient. But public-works activities are closely interrelated and have a substantial influence on the growth of the country. Moreover, in times of threatening economic contraction, they may become a valuable sustaining force. Efficient planning and execution of the Nation's public works require the coordination of Federal activities and effective cooperation with State and local governments.

The Council of Economic Advisers, through its public works planning section, has made important advances during the past year in effecting this coordination and cooperation. To give more emphasis and continuity to this essential coordination, I shall request the Congress to appropriate funds for the support of an Office of Coordinator of Public Works in the Executive Office of the President.

Now a most significant element in our growing economy is an agriculture that is stable, prosperous, and free. The problems of our agriculture have evolved over many years and cannot be solved overnight; nevertheless, governmental actions last year hold great promise of fostering a better balance between production and markets and, consequently, a better and more stable income for farmers.

Through vigorous administration and new authority provided by the 83d Congress, surplus farm products are now moving into consumption. From February 1953 through November 1954 the rate of increase in Government-held surpluses has been greatly reduced by our moving into use more than $2,300,000,000 worth of Government-owned farm commodities. Domestic consumption remains high, and farm exports will be higher than last year. As a result of the flexibility provided by the Agricultural Act of 1954, we can move toward less restrictive acreage controls.

Thus, farm production is gradually adjusting to markets, markets are being expanded, and stocks are moving into use. We can now look forward to an easing of the influences depressing farm prices, to reduced Government expenditures for purchase of surplus products, and to less Federal intrusion into the lives and plans of our farm people.

Agricultural programs have been redirected toward better balance, greater stability and sustained prosperity. We are headed in the right direction. I urgently recommend to the Congress that we continue resolutely on this road.

Greater attention must be directed to the needs of low-income farm families. Twenty-eight percent of our farm-operator families have net cash incomes of less than $1,000 per year. I shall later submit recommendations designed to assure the steady alleviation of their most pressing concerns.

Because drought also remains a serious agricultural problem, I shall recommend legislation to strengthen Federal disaster assistance programs. This legislation will seek an improved appraisal of need, better adjustment of the various programs to local conditions, and a more equitable sharing of costs between the States and the Federal Government.

The prosperity of our small-business enterprises is an indispensable element in the maintenance of our economic strength. Creation of the Small Business Administration and tax laws facilitating small-business expansion are but two of the many steps this Government has taken to encourage smaller enterprises. I recommend that Congress extend the Small Business Act of 1953 now due to expire next June.

We come now to the third great purpose of our Government—its concern for the health, productivity, and well-being of all our people.

Every citizen wants to give full expression to his God-given talents and abilities and to have the recognition and respect accorded under our great traditions. Americans want a good standard of living—not simply to accumulate possessions, but to fulfill a legitimate aspiration for an environment in which their families may live meaningful and happy lives. Our people are committed, therefore, to the creation and preservation of opportunity for every citizen, opportunity to lead a more rewarding life. They are equally committed to the alleviation of unavoidable misfortune and distress among their fellow citizens.

The aspirations of most of our people can best be fulfilled through their own enterprise and initiative, without Government interference. This administration, therefore, follows two simple rules: First, the Federal Government should perform an essential task in this field only when it cannot otherwise be adequately performed; and, second, in performing that task, our Government must not impair the self-respect, the freedom, and the incentive of the individual. So long as these two rules are observed, the Government can and must fully meet its obligations without creating a dependent population or a domineering bureaucracy.

During the past 2 years, notable advances were made in these functions of government. Protection of old-age and survivors insurance was extended to an additional 10 million of our people by action of Congress. Legislation was enacted to provide unemployment-insurance protection to some 4 million additional Americans. Stabilization of living costs and the halting of inflation protected the value of pensions and savings. A broad program now helps to bring good homes within the reach of the great majority of our people. With the States, we are providing more clinics, hospitals, and nursing homes for patients with chronic illnesses. Also, with the States, we have begun a fruitful expansion in the restoration of disabled persons to employment and to useful lives. In the areas of Federal responsibility, we have made historic progress in eliminating from among our people demeaning practices based on race or color.

All of us may be proud of these achievements during the past 2 years. Yet essential Federal tasks remain to be done.

As part of our efforts to provide decent, safe, and sanitary housing for low-income families, we must carry forward the housing program authorized during the past Congress. We must also authorized contracts for a firm program of 35,000 additional public housing units in each of the next 2 fiscal years. This program will meet the most pressing obligations of the Federal Government into the 1958 fiscal year for planning and building public housing. By that time the private building industry, aided by the Housing Act of 1954, will have had the opportunity to assume its full role in providing adequate housing for low-income families.

The health of our people is one of our most precious assets. Knowledge available to combat disease and disability should be fully used. Otherwise, we as a people are guilty not only of neglect of human suffering but also of wasting our national strength.

Advances in medical care are not available to enough of our citizens. Our Nation must do more to reduce the impact of accident and disease. Two fundamental problems confront us:

First, high and ever-rising costs of health services; second, serious gaps and shortages in those services.

By special message on January 24, I shall propose a coordinated program to strengthen and improve existing health services. This program will continue to reject socialized medicine. It will emphasize individual and local responsibility. Under it the Federal Government will neither dominate nor direct, but it will serve as a helpful partner.

The recommendations will include a Federal health reinsurance service to encourage the development of better voluntary health insurance coverage by private organizations. I shall recommend measures to improve the medical care of that group of our citizens who, because of need, receive Federal-State public assistance.

To reduce the gaps in medical services, I shall propose—

New measures to facilitate construction of needed health facilities and help reduce shortages of trained health personnel;

Vigorous steps to combat the misery and national loss involved in mental illness;

Improved services for crippled children and for maternal and child health;

Better consumer protection under our existing pure food and drug laws; and, finally,

Strengthened programs to combat the increasingly serious pollution of our rivers and streams and the growing problems of air pollution.

Last year's expansion of social-security coverage and the new program of improved medical care for public-assistance recipients together suggest modification of the formula for Federal sharing in old-age-assistance payments. I recommend modification of the formula where such payments will, in the future, supplement benefits received under the old-age and survivors insurance system.

It is the right of every American, from childhood on, to have access to knowledge. In our form of society, this right of the individual takes on a special meaning. The education of all our citizens is therefore imperative to the maintenance and invigoration of America's free institutions.

Today, we face grave educational problems. Up-to-date analyses of these problems and their solutions are being carried forward through the individual State conferences, and the White House conferences to be completed this year.

However, such factors as population growth, additional responsibilities of schools, and increased and longer school attendance have produced an unprecedented classroom shortage. This shortage is of immediate concern to all our people. Affirmative action must be taken now.

Without impairing in any way the responsibilities of our States, our localities, communities, or families, the Federal Government should serve as an effective agent in dealing with this problem. I shall forward a special message to the Congress on February 15, presenting a program dealing with this shortage.

To help the States do a better job, we must strengthen their resources for preventing and dealing with juvenile delinquency. I shall propose Federal legislation to assist the States in dealing with this nationwide problem. We shall carry forward the vigorous efforts of the administration to improve the international control of traffic in narcotics and, in cooperation with State and local agencies, to combat narcotic addiction in our own country.

I should like to speak to you now of additional matters of importance to all our people, and especially to our wage earners.

During the past year certain industrial changes and the readjustment of the economy to conditions of peace brought unemployment and other difficulties to various localities and industries. These problems are engaging our most earnest attention. But for the overwhelming majority of our working people, the past year has meant good jobs. Moreover, the earnings and savings of our wage earners are no longer depreciating in value. Because of cooperative relationships between labor and management, fewer working days were lost through strikes in 1954 than in any year in the past decade.

The outlook for our wage earners can be made still more promising by several legislative actions.

First, in the past 5 years we have had economic growth which will support an increase in the Federal minimum wage. In the light of present economic conditions, I recommend its increase to 90 cents an hour. I also recommend that many others, at present excluded, be given the protection of a minimum wage.

Second, I renew my recommendation of last year for amendment of the Labor Management Relations Act of 1947 to further the basic objectives of that statute. I especially call to the attention of the Congress amendments dealing with the right of economic strikers to vote in representation elections and the need for equalizing the obligation under the act to file disclaimers of Communist affiliation.

Third, the administration will propose other important measures, including occupational safety, workmen's compensation for longshoremen and harbor workers, and the "8-hour laws" applicable to

Federal contractors. Legislation will also be proposed respecting nonoccupational disability insurance and unemployment compensation in the District of Columbia.

On January 11 I shall propose a pay adjustment plan for civilian employees outside the postal field service to correct inequities and increase individual pay rates. I shall also recommend voluntary health insurance on a contributory basis for Federal employees and their dependents. In keeping with the Group Life Insurance Act passed in the 83d Congress, this protection should be provided on the group-insurance principle and purchased from private facilities. Also on January 11 I shall recommend a modern pay plan, including pay increases, for postal field employees. As part of this program, and to carry forward our progress toward elimination of the large annual postal deficit, I shall renew my request for an increase in postal rates. Again I urge that in the future the fixing of rates be delegated to an impartial, independent body.

Needed improvements in survivor, disability, and retirement benefits for Federal personnel have been extensively considered by an appropriate committee. The committee's proposals would strengthen and improve benefits for our career people in Government. I endorse their broad objectives. Full contributory coverage under old-age and survivors insurance should be made available to all Federal personnel, just as in private industry. For career military personnel, the protection of the old-age and survivors insurance system would be an important and long-needed addition, especially to their present unequal and inadequate survivorship protection. The military retirement pay system should remain separate and unchanged. Certain adjustments in the present civilian personnel retirement systems will be needed. However, these systems also are a basic part of a total compensation and should be separately and independently retained.

I also urge the Congress to approve a long overdue increase in the salaries of Members of Congress and of the Federal judiciary. In my opinion, this raise should be substantial because I believe it should be to a level commensurate with their heavy responsibilities.

Our concern for the individual in our country requires that we consider several additional problems.

We must continue the program to help our Indian citizens improve their lot and make their full contribution to national life.

Two years ago I advised the Congress of injustices under existing immigration laws. Through humane administration, the Department of Justice is doing what it legally can to alleviate hardships. Clearance of aliens before arrival has been initiated and, except for criminal offenders, the imprisonment of aliens awaiting admission or deportation has been stopped. Certain provisions of law, however, have the effect of compelling action in respect to aliens which are inequitable in some instances and discriminatory in others. These provisions should be corrected in this session of the Congress.

As the complex problems of Alaska are resolved, that Territory should be expected to achieve statehood. In the meantime, there is no justification for deferring the admission to statehood of Hawaii. I again urge approval of this measure.

We have three splendid opportunities to demonstrate the strength of our belief in the right of suffrage. First, I again urge that a constitutional amendment be submitted to the States to reduce the voting age for Federal elections. Second, I renew my request that the principle of self-government be extended and the right of suffrage granted to the citizens of the District of Columbia. Third, I again recommend that we work with the States to preserve the voting rights of citizens in the Nation's service overseas.

In our determination to keep faith with those who in the past have met the highest call of citizenship, we now have under study the system of benefits for veterans and for surviving dependents of deceased veterans and servicemen. Studies will be undertaken to determine the need for measures to ease the readjustment to civilian life of men required to enter the Armed Forces for 2 years of service.

In the advancement of the various activities which will make our civilization endure and flourish, the Federal Government should do more to give official recognition to the importance of the arts and other cultural activities. I shall recommend the establishment of a Federal Advisory Commission on the Arts within the Department of Health, Education, and Welfare, to advise the Federal Government on ways to encourage artistic and cultural endeavor and appreciation. I shall also propose that awards of merit be established whereby we can honor our fellow citizens who make great contributions to the advancement of our civilization and of this country.

Every citizen rightly expects efficient and economical administration of these many governmental programs I have outlined today. I strongly recommend extension of the Reorganization Act, and the law establishing the Commission on Intergovernmental Relations, both of which expire this spring. Thus, the Congress will assure continuation of the excellent progress recently made in improving Government organization and administration. In this connection we are looking forward with great interest to the reports which will soon be going to the Congress from the Commission on Organization of the Executive Branch of the Government. I am sure that these studies, made under the chairmanship of former President Herbert Hoover with the assistance of more than 200 distinguished citizens, will be of great value in paving the way toward more efficiency and economy in the Government.

And now, I return to the point at which I began—the faith of our people.

The many programs here summarized are, I believe, in full keeping with their needs, interests, and aspirations. The obligations upon us are clear:

> To labor earnestly, patiently, prayerfully, for peace, for freedom, for justice, throughout the world;
>
> To keep our economy vigorous and free, that our people may lead fuller, happier lives;
>
> To advance, not merely by our words but by our acts, the determination of our Government that every citizen shall have opportunity to develop to his fullest capacity.

As we do these things, before us is a future filled with opportunity and with hope. That future will be ours if, in our time, we keep alive the patience, the courage, the confidence in tomorrow, the deep faith of the millions who, in years past, made and preserved us this Nation.

A decade ago, in the death and desolation of European battlefields, I saw the courage and resolution, I felt the inspiration, of American youth. In these young men I felt America's buoyant confidence and irresistible will to do. In them I saw, too, a devout America, humble before God.

And so, I know in my heart—and I believe that all Americans know—that, despite the anxieties of this divided world, our faith, and the cause in which we all believe, will surely prevail.

And now, my friends, my apologies for the length of this address, and thank you for your great courtesy.

FOURTH ANNUAL MESSAGE

THE WHITE HOUSE, *January 5, 1956.*

To the Congress of the United States:

The opening of this new year must arouse in us all grateful thanks to a kind Providence whose protection has been ever present and whose bounty has been manifold and abundant. The state of the Union today demonstrates what can be accomplished under God by a free people; by their vision, their understanding of national problems, their initiative, their self-reliance, their capacity for work, and by their willingness to sacrifice whenever sacrifice is needed.

In the past 3 years, responding to what our people want their Government to do, the Congress and the Executive have done much in building a stronger, better America. There has been broad progress in fostering the energies of our people, in providing greater opportunity for the satisfaction of their needs, and in fulfilling their demands for the strength and security of the Republic.

Our country is at peace. Our security posture commands respect. A spiritual vigor marks our national life. Our economy, approaching the $400 billion mark, is at an unparalleled level of prosperity. The national income is more widely and fairly distributed than ever before. The number of Americans at work has reached an all-time high. As a people, we are achieving ever higher standards of living—earning more, producing more, consuming more, building more, and investing more than ever before.

Virtually all sectors of our society are sharing in these good times.

Our farm families, if we act wisely, imaginatively, and promptly to strengthen our present farm programs, can also look forward to sharing equitably in the prosperity they have helped to create.

War in Korea ended 2½ years ago. The collective security system has been powerfully strengthened. Our defenses have been reinforced at sharply reduced costs. Programs to expand world trade and to harness the atom for the betterment of mankind have been carried forward. Our economy has been freed from governmental wage and price controls. Inflation has been halted; the cost of living stabilized.

Government spending has been cut by more than $10 billion. Nearly 300,000 positions have been eliminated from the Federal payroll. Taxes have been substantially reduced. A balanced budget is in prospect. Social security has been extended to 10 million more Americans and unemployment insurance to 4 million more. Unprecedented advances in civil rights have been made. The long-standing and deep-seated problems of agriculture have been forthrightly attacked.

This record of progress has been accomplished with a self-imposed caution against unnecessary and unwise interference in the private affairs of our people, of their communities, and of the several States.

If we of the executive and legislative branches, keeping this caution ever in mind, address ourselves to the business of the year before us—and to the unfinished business of last year—with resolution, the outlook is bright with promise.

Many measures of great national importance recommended last year to the Congress still demand immediate attention—legislation for school and highway construction; health and immigration legislation; water-resources legislation; legislation to complete the implementation of our foreign economic policy; such labor legislation as amendments of the Labor-Management Relations Act, extension of the Fair Labor Standards Act to additional groups not now covered, and occupational safety legislation; and legislation for construction of an atomic-powered exhibit vessel.

Many new items of business likewise require our attention—measures that will further promote the release of the energies of our people; that will broaden opportunity for all of them; that will advance the Republic in its leadership toward a just peace; measures, in short, that are essential to the building of an ever-stronger, ever-better America.

Every political and economic guide supports a valid confidence that wise effort will be rewarded by an even more plentiful harvest of human benefit than we now enjoy. Our resources are too many, our principles too dynamic, our purposes too worthy, and the issues at stake too immense for us to entertain doubt or fear. But our responsibilities require that we approach this year's business with a sober humility.

A heedless pride in our present strength and position would blind us to the facts of the past, to the pitfalls of the future. We must walk ever in the knowledge that we are enriched by a heritage earned in the labor and sacrifice of our forebears; that, for our children's children, we are trustees of a great Republic and a time-tested political system; that we prosper as a cooperating member of the family of nations.

In this light the administration has continued work on its program for the Republic, begun 3 years ago. Because the vast spread of national and human interests is involved within it, I shall not in this message attempt its detailed delineation. Instead, from time to time during this session, there will be submitted to the Congress specific recommendations within specific fields. In the comprehensive survey required for their preparation, the administration is guided by enduring objectives. The first is—

THE DISCHARGE OF OUR WORLD RESPONSIBILITY

Our world policy and our actions are dedicated to the achievement of peace with justice for all nations.

With this purpose, we move in a wide variety of ways and through many agencies to remove the pall of fear; to strengthen the ties with our partners and to improve the cooperative cohesion of the free world; to reduce the burden of armaments; and to stimulate and inspire action among all nations for a world of justice and prosperity and peace. These national objectives are fully supported by both our political parties.

In the past year our search for a more stable and just peace has taken varied forms. Among the most important were the two Conferences at Geneva, in July and in the fall of last year. We explored the possibilities of agreement on critical issues that jeopardize the peace.

The July meeting of heads of government held out promise to the world of moderation in the bitterness, of word and action, which tends to generate conflict and war. All were in agreement that a nuclear war would be an intolerable disaster which must not be permitted to occur. But in October, when the Foreign Ministers met again, the results demonstrated conclusively that the Soviet leaders are not yet willing to create the indispensable conditions for a secure and lasting peace.

Nevertheless, it is clear that the conflict between international communism and freedom has taken on a new complexion.

We know the Communist leaders have often practiced the tactics of retreat and zigzag. We know that Soviet and Chinese communism still poses a serious threat to the free world. And in the Middle East recent Soviet moves are hardly compatible with the reduction of international tension.

Yet Communist tactics against the free nations have shifted in emphasis from reliance on violence and the threat of violence to reliance on division, enticement, and duplicity. We must be well prepared to meet the current tactics which pose a dangerous though less obvious threat. At the same time, our policy must be dynamic as well as flexible, designed primarily to forward the achievement of our own objectives rather than to meet each shift and change on the Communist front. We must act in the firm assurance that the fruits of freedom are more attractive and desirable to mankind in the pursuit of happiness than the record of communism.

In the face of Communist military power, we must, of course, continue to maintain an effective system of collective security. This involves two things—a system which gives clear warning that armed aggression will be met by joint action of the free nations, and deterrent military power to make that warning effective. Moreover, the awesome power of the atom must be made to serve as a guardian of the free community and of the peace.

In the last year the free world has seen major gains for the system of collective security: The accession to the North Atlantic Treaty Organization and Western European Union of the sovereign Federal German Republic; the developing cooperation under the Southeast Asia Collective Defense Treaty; and the formation in the Middle East of the Baghdad Pact among Turkey, Iraq, Iran, Pakistan, and the United Kingdom. In our own hemisphere, the inter-American system has continued to show its vitality in maintaining peace and a common approach to world problems. We now have security pacts with more than 40 other nations.

In the pursuit of our national purposes, we have been steadfast in our support of the United Nations, now entering its second decade with a wider membership and ever-increasing influence and usefulness. In the release of our 15 fliers from Communist China, an essential prelude was the world opinion mobilized by the General Assembly, which condemned their imprisonment and demanded their liberation. The successful Atomic Energy Conference held in Geneva under United Nations auspices and our atoms-for-peace program have been practical steps toward the worldwide use of this new energy source. Our sponsorship of such use has benefited our relations with other countries. Active negotiations are now in progress to create an international agency to foster peaceful uses of atomic energy.

During the past year the crucial problem of disarmament has moved to the forefront of practical political endeavor. At Geneva, I declared the readiness of the United States to exchange blueprints of the military establishments of our Nation and the U. S. S. R. to be confirmed by reciprocal aerial reconnaissance. By this means, I felt mutual suspicions could be allayed and an atmosphere developed in which negotiations looking toward limitation of arms would have improved chances of success.

In the United Nations Subcommittee on Disarmament last fall this proposal was explored, and the United States also declared itself willing to include reciprocal ground inspection of key points. By the overwhelming vote of 56 to 7, the United Nations on December 16 endorsed these proposals an gave them a top priority. Thereby, the issue is placed squarely before the bar of world opinion. We shall persevere in seeking a general reduction of armaments under effective inspection and control, which are essential safeguards to insure reciprocity and protect the security of all.

In the coming year much remains to be done.

While maintaining our military deterrent, we must intensify our efforts to achieve a just peace. In Asia we shall continue to give help to nations struggling to maintain their freedom against the threat of Communist coercion or subversion. In Europe we shall endeavor to increase not only the military strength of the North Atlantic Alliance but also its political cohesion and unity of purpose. We shall give such assistance as is feasible to the recently renewed effort of Western European nations to achieve a greater measure of integration, such as in the field of peaceful uses of atomic energy.

In the Near East we shall spare no effort in seeking to promote a fair solution of the tragic dispute between the Arab States and Israel, all of whom we want as our friends. The United States is ready to do its part to assure enduring peace in that area. We hope that both sides will make the contributions necessary to achieve that purpose. In Latin America we shall continue to cooperate vigorously in trade and other measures designed to assist economic progress in the area.

Strong economic ties are an essential element in our free world partnership. Increasing trade and investment help all of us prosper together. Gratifying progress has been made in this direction, most recently by the 3-year extension of our trade-agreements legislation.

I most earnestly request that the Congress approve our membership in the Organization for Trade Cooperation, which would assist the carrying out of the General Agreement on Tariffs and Trade to which we have been a party since 1948. Our membership in the OTC will provide the most effective and expeditious means for removing discriminations and restrictions against American exports and in making our trade agreements truly reciprocal. United States membership in the Organization will evidence our continuing desire to cooperate in promoting an expanded trade among the free nations. Thus the Organization, as proposed, is admirably suited to our own interests and to those of like-minded nations in working for steady expansion of trade and closer economic cooperation. Being strictly an administrative entity, the Organization for Trade Cooperation cannot, of course, alter the control by Congress of the tariff, import, and customs policies of the United States.

We need to encourage investment overseas by avoiding unfair tax duplications, and to foster foreign trade by further simplification and improvement of our customs legislation.

We must sustain and fortify our Mutual Security Program. Because the conditions of poverty and unrest in less developed areas make their people a special target of international communism, there is a need to help them achieve the economic growth and stability necessary to preserve their independence against Communist threats and enticements.

In order that our friends may better achieve the greater strength that is our common goal, they need assurance of continuity in economic assistance for development projects and programs which we approve and which require a period of years for planning and completion. Accordingly, I ask Congress to grant limited authority to make longer-term commitments for assistance to such projects, to be fulfilled from appropriations to be made in future fiscal years.

These various steps will powerfully strengthen the economic foundation of our foreign policy. Together with constructive action abroad, they will maintain the present momentum toward general economic progress and vitality of the free world.

In all things, change is the inexorable law of life. In much of the world the ferment of change is working strongly; but grave injustices are still uncorrected. We must not, by any sanction of ours, help to perpetuate these wrongs. I have particularly in mind the oppressive division of the German people, the bondage of millions elsewhere, and the exclusion of Japan from United Nations membership.

We shall keep these injustices in the forefront of human consciousness and seek to maintain the pressure of world opinion to right these vast wrongs in the interest both of justice and secure peace.

Injustice thrives on ignorance. Because an understanding of the truth about America is one of our most powerful forces, I am recommending a substantial increase in budgetary support of the United States Information Agency.

The sum of our international effort should be this: The waging of peace, with as much resourcefulness, with as great a sense of dedication and urgency, as we have ever mustered in defense of our country in time of war. In this effort, our weapon is not force. Our weapons are the principles and ideas embodied in our historic traditions, applied with the same vigor that in the past made America a living promise of freedom for all mankind.

To accomplish these vital tasks, all of us should be concerned with the strength, effectiveness, and morale of our State Department and our Foreign Service.

Another guide in the preparation of the administration's program is—

THE CONSTANT IMPROVEMENT OF OUR NATIONAL SECURITY

Because peace is the keystone of our national policy, our defense program emphasizes an effective flexible type of power calculated to deter or repulse any aggression and to preserve the peace. Short of war, we have never had military strength better adapted to our needs with improved readiness for emergency use. The maintenance of this strong military capability for the indefinite future will continue to call for a large share of our national budget. Our military programs must meet the needs of today. To build less would expose the Nation to aggression. To build excessively, under the influence of fear, could defeat our purposes and impair or destroy the very freedom and economic system our military defenses are designed to protect.

We have improved the effectiveness and combat readiness of our forces by developing and making operational new weapons and by integrating the latest scientific developments, including new atomic weapons, into our military plans. We continue to push the production of the most modern military aircraft. The development of long-range missiles has been on an accelerated basis for some time. We are moving as rapidly as practicable toward nuclear-powered aircraft and ships. Combat capability, especially in terms of firepower, has been substantially increased. We have made the adjustments in personnel permitted by the cessation of the Korean war, the buildup of our allies and the introduction of new weapons. The services are all planning realistically on a long-term basis.

To strengthen our continental defenses the United States and Canada, in the closest cooperation, have substantially augmented early warning networks. Great progress is being made in extending surveillance of the Arctic, the Atlantic, and the Pacific approaches to North America.

In the last analysis our real strength lies in the caliber of the men and women in our Armed Forces, Active and Reserve. Much has been done to attract and hold capable military personnel, but more needs to be done. This year, I renew my request of last year for legislation to provide proper medical care for military dependents and a more equitable survivors' benefit program. The administration will prepare additional recommendations designed to achieve the same objectives, including career incentives for medical and dental officers and nurses, and increases in the proportion of Regular officers.

Closely related to the mission of the Defense Department is the task of the Federal Civil Defense Administration. A particular point of relationship arises from the fact that the key to civil defense is the expanded continental defense program, including the distant early warning system. Our Federal civil-defense authorities have made progress in their program, and now comprehensive studies are being conducted jointly by the Federal Civil Defense Administration, the States, and critical target cities to determine the best procedures that can be adopted in case of an atomic attack. We must strengthen Federal assistance to the States and cities in devising the most effective common defense.

We have a broad and diversified mobilization base. We have the facilities, materials, skills, and knowledge rapidly to expand the production of things we need for our defense whenever they are required. But mobilization base requirements change with changing technology and strategy. We must maintain flexibility to meet new requirements. I am requesting, therefore, that the Congress once again extend the Defense Production Act.

Of great importance to our Nation's security is a continuing alertness to internal subversive activity within or without our Government. This administration will not relax its efforts to deal forthrightly and vigorously in protection of this Government and its citizens against subversion, at the same time fully protecting the constitutional rights of all citizens.

A third objective of the administration is—

FISCAL INTEGRITY

A public office is, indeed, a public trust. None of its aspects is more demanding than the proper management of the public finances. I refer now not only to the indispensable virtues of plain honesty and trustworthiness but also to the prudent, effective, and conscientious use of tax money. I refer also to the attitude of mind that makes efficient and economical service to the people a watchword in our Government.

Over the long term, a balanced budget is a sure index to thrifty management—in a home, in a business, or in the Federal Government. When achievement of a balanced budget is for long put off in a business or home, bankruptcy is the result. But in similar circumstances a government resorts to inflation of the money supply. This inevitably results in depreciation of the value of the money and an increase in the cost of living. Every investment in personal security is threatened by this process of inflation, and the real values of the people's savings, whether in the form of insurance, bonds, pension, and retirement funds or savings accounts, are thereby shriveled.

We have made long strides these past 3 years in bringing our Federal finances under control. The deficit for fiscal year 1953 was almost $9½ billion. Larger deficits seemed certain—deficits which would have depreciated the value of the dollar and pushed the cost of living still higher. But Government waste and extravagance were searched out. Nonessential activities were dropped. Government expenses were carefully scrutinized. Total spending was cut by $14 billion below the amount planned by the previous administration for the fiscal year 1954.

This made possible—and it was appropriate in the existing circumstances of transition to a peacetime economy—the largest tax cut in any year in our history. Almost $7½ billion were released and every taxpayer in the country benefited. Almost two-thirds of the savings went directly to individuals. This tax cut also helped to build up the economy, to make jobs in industry, and to increase the production of the many things desired to improve the scale of living for the great majority of Americans.

The strong expansion of the economy, coupled with a constant care for efficiency in Government operations and an alert guard against waste and duplication, has brought us to a prospective balance between income and expenditure. This is being done while we continue to strengthen our military security.

I expect the budget to be in balance during the fiscal year ending June 30, 1956.

I shall propose a balanced budget for the next fiscal year ending June 30, 1957.

But the balance we are seeking cannot be accomplished without the continuing everyday effort of the executive and legislative branches to keep expenditures under control. It will also be necessary to continue all of the present excise taxes without any reduction and the corporation-income taxes at their present rates for another year beyond next April 1.

It is unquestionably true that our present tax level is very burdensome and, in the interest of long term and continuous economic growth, should be reduced when we prudently can. It is essential, in the sound management of the Government's finances, that we be mindful of our enormous national debt and of the obligation we have toward future Americans to reduce that debt whenever we can appropriately do so. Under conditions of high peacetime prosperity, such as now exist, we can never justify going further into debt to give ourselves a tax cut at the expense of our children. So, in the present state of our financial affairs, I earnestly believe that a tax cut can be deemed justifiable only when it will not unbalance the budget, a budget which makes provision for some reduction, even though modest, in our national debt. In this way we can best maintain fiscal integrity.

A fourth aim of our program is—

TO FOSTER A STRONG ECONOMY

Our competitive enterprise system depends on the energy of free human beings, limited by prudent restraints in law, using free markets to plan, organize, and distribute production, and spurred by the prospect of reward for successful effort. This system has developed our resources. It has marvelously expanded our productive capacity. Against the record of all other economic systems devised through the ages, this competitive system has proved the most creative user of human skills in the development of physical resources, and the richest rewarder of human effort.

This is still true in this era when improved living standards and rising national requirements are accompanied by swift advances in technology and rapid obsolescence in machines and methods. Typical of these are the strides made in construction of plants to produce electrical energy from atomic power and of laboratories and installations for the application of this new force in industry, agriculture, and the healing arts. These developments make it imperative—to assure effective functioning of our enterprise system—that the Federal Government concern itself with certain broad areas of our economic life. Most important of these is—

Agriculture

Our farm people are not sharing as they should in the general prosperity. They alone of all major groups have seen their incomes decline rather than rise. They are caught between two millstones—

rising production costs and declining prices. Such harm to a part of the national economy so vitally important to everyone is of great concern to us all. No other resource is so indispensable as the land that feeds and clothes us. No group is more fundamental to our national life than our farmers.

In successful prosecution of the war, the Nation called for the utmost effort of its farmers. Their response was superb; their contribution unsurpassed. Farmers are not now to be blamed for the mountainous, price-depressing surpluses produced in response to wartime policies and laws that were too long continued. War markets are not the markets of peacetime. Failure to recognize that basic fact by the timely adjustment of wartime legislation brought its inevitable result in peacetime—surpluses, lower prices, and lower incomes for our farmers.

The dimensions of Government responsibility are as broad and complex as the farm problem itself. We are here concerned not only with our essential continuing supplies of food and fiber, but also with a way of life. Both are indispensable to the well-being and strength of the Nation. Consideration of these matters must be above and beyond politics. Our national farm policy, so vital to the welfare of farm people and all of us, must not become a field for political warfare. Too much is at stake.

Our farm people expect of us, who have responsibility for their Government, understanding of their problems and the will to help solve them. Our objective must be to help bring production into balance with existing and new markets, at prices that yield farmers a return for their work in line with what other Americans get.

To reach this goal, deep-seated problems must be subjected to a stepped-up attack. There is no single easy solution. Rather, there must be a many-sided assault on the stubborn problems of surpluses, prices, costs, and markets; and a steady, persistent, imaginative advance in the relationship between farmers and their Government.

In a few days, by special message, I shall lay before the Congress my detailed recommendations for new steps that should be taken promptly to speed the transition in agriculture and thus assist our farmers to achieve their fair share of the national income.

Basic to this program will be a new attack on the surplus problem—for even the best-conceived farm program cannot work under a multibillion-dollar weight of accumulated stocks.

I shall urge authorization of a soil-bank program to alleviate the problem of diverted acres and an overexpanded agricultural plant. This will include an acreage reserve to reduce current and accumulated surpluses of crops in most serious difficulty, and a conservation reserve to achieve other needed adjustments in the use of agricultural resources. I shall urge measures to strengthen our surplus disposal activities.

I shall propose measures to strengthen individual commodity programs, to remove controls where possible, to reduce carryovers, and to stop further accumulations of surpluses. I shall ask the Congress to provide substantial new funds for an expanded drive on the research front to develop new markets, new crops, and new uses. The rural development program to better the lot of low-income farm families deserves full congressional support. The Great Plains program must go forward vigorously. Advances on these and other fronts will pull down the price-depressing surpluses and raise farm income.

In this time of testing in agriculture we should all together, regardless of party, carry forward resolutely with a sound and forward-looking program on which farm people may confidently depend, now and for years to come.

I shall briefly mention four other subjects directly related to the well-being of the economy, preliminary to their fuller discussion in the Economic Report and later communications.

Resources conservation

I wish to reemphasize the critical importance of the wise use and conservation of our great natural resources of land, forests, minerals, and water and their long-range development consistent with our agricultural policy. Water in particular now plays an increasing role in industrial processes, in the irrigation of land, in electric power, as well as in domestic uses. At the same time, it has the potential of damage and disaster.

A comprehensive legislative program for water conservation will be submitted to the Congress during the session. The development of our water resources cannot be accomplished overnight. The need is such that we must make faster progress and without delay. Therefore, I strongly recommend that action be taken at this session on such wholly Federal projects as the Colorado River storage project and the Fryingpan-Arkansas project; on the John Day partnership project, and other projects which provide for cooperative action between the Federal Government and non-Federal interests; and on legislation, which makes provision for Federal participation in small projects under the primary sponsorship of agencies of State and local government.

During the past year the areas of our national parks have been expanded, and new wildlife refuges have been created. The visits of our people to the parks have increased much more rapidly than have the facilities to care for them. The administration will submit recommendations to provide more adequate facilities to keep abreast of the increasing interest of our people in the great outdoors.

Disaster assistance

A modern community is a complex combination of skills, specialized buildings, machines, communications, and homes. Most importantly, it involves human lives. Disaster in many forms—by flood, frost, high winds, for instance—can destroy on a massive scale in a few hours the labor of many years.

Through the past 3 years the administration has repeatedly moved into action wherever disaster struck. The extent of State participation in relief activities, however, has been far from uniform and, in many cases, has been either inadequate or nonexistent. Disaster-assistance legislation requires overhauling, and an experimental program of flood-damage indemnities should be undertaken. The administration will make detailed recommendations on these subjects.

Area redevelopment

We must help deal with the pockets of chronic unemployment that here and there mar the Nation's general industrial prosperity. Economic changes in recent years have been often so rapid and far-reaching that areas committed to a single local resource or industrial activity have found themselves temporarily deprived of their markets and their livelihood.

Such conditions mean severe hardship for thousands of people as the slow process of adaptation to new circumstances goes on. This process can be speeded up. Last year I authorized a major study of the problem to find additional steps to supplement existing programs for the redevelopment of areas of chronic unemployment. Recommendations will be submitted, designed to supplement, with Federal technical and loan assistance, local efforts to get on with this vital job. Improving such communities must, of course, remain the primary responsibility of the people living there and of their States. But a soundly conceived Federal partnership program can be of real assistance to them in their efforts.

Highway legislation

Legislation to provide a modern, interstate highway system is even more urgent this year than last, for 12 months have now passed in which we have fallen further behind in road construction needed for the personal safety, the general prosperity, the national security of the American people. During the year, the number of motor vehicles has increased from 58 million to 61 million. During the past year over 38,000 persons lost their lives in highway accidents, while the fearful toll of injuries and property damage has gone on unabated.

In my message of February 22, 1955, I urged that measures be taken to complete the vital 40,000-mile interstate system over a period of 10 years at an estimated Federal cost of approximately $25 billion. No program was adopted.

If we are ever to solve our mounting traffic problem, the whole interstate system must be authorized as one project, to be completed approximately within the specified time. Only in this way can industry efficiently gear itself to the job ahead. Only in this way can the required planning and engineering be accomplished without the confusion and waste unavoidable in a piecemeal approach. Furthermore, as I pointed out last year, the pressing nature of this problem must not lead us to solutions outside the bounds of sound fiscal management. As in the case of other pressing problems, there must be an adequate plan of financing. To continue the drastically needed improvement in other national highway systems, I recommend the continuation of the Federal aid highway program.

Aside from agriculture and the four subjects specifically mentioned, an integral part of our efforts to foster a strong and expanding free economy is keeping open the door of opportunity to new and small enterprises, checking monopoly, and preserving a competitive environment. In this past year the steady improvement in the economic health of small business has reinforced the vitality of our competitive economy. We shall continue to help small business concerns to obtain access to adequate financing and to competent counsel on management, production, and marketing problems.

Through measures already taken, opportunities for small-business participation in Government procurement programs, including military procurement, are greatly improved. The effectiveness of these measures will become increasingly apparent. We shall continue to make certain that small business has a fair opportunity to compete and has an economic environment in which it may prosper.

In my message last year I referred to the appointment of an advisory committee to appraise and report to me on the deficiencies as well as the effectiveness of existing Federal transportation policies. I have commended the fundamental purposes and objectives of the committee's report. I earnestly recommend that the Congress give prompt attention to the committee's proposals.

Essential to a prosperous economic environment for all business, small and large—for agriculture and industry and commerce—is efficiency in Government. To that end, exhaustive studies of the entire governmental structure were made by the Commission on Intergovernmental Relations and the Commission on the Organization of the Executive Branch of the Government—the reports of these Commissions are now under intensive review and already in the process of implementation in important areas.

One specific and most vital governmental function merits study and action by the Congress. As part of our program of promoting efficiency in Government and getting the fiscal situation in hand, the Post Office Department in the past 3 years has been overhauled. Nearly 1,000 new post offices have been provided. Financial practices have been modernized, and transportation and operating methods are being constantly improved. A new wage and incentive plan for the half-million postal employees has been established. Never before has the postal system handled so much mail so quickly and so economically.

The Post Office Department faces two serious problems: First, much of its physical plant—post offices and other buildings—is obsolete and inadequate. Many new buildings and the modernization of present ones are essential if we are to have improved mail service. The second problem is the Department's fiscal plight. It now faces an annual deficit of one-half billion dollars.

Recommendations on postal facilities and on additional postal revenues will be submitted to the Congress.

A final consideration in our program planning is—

THE RESPONSE TO HUMAN CONCERNS

A fundamental belief shines forth in this Republic. We believe in the worth and dignity of the individual. We know that if we are to govern ourselves wisely, in the tradition of America, we must have the opportunity to develop our individual capacities to the utmost.

To fulfill the individual's aspirations in the American way of life, good education is fundamental. Good education is the outgrowth of good homes, good communities, good churches, and good schools. Today our schools face pressing problems—problems which will not yield to swift and easy solutions, or to any single action. They will yield only to a continuing, active, informed effort by the people toward achieving better schools.

This kind of effort has been spurred by the thousands of conferences held in recent months by half a million citizens and educators in all parts of the country, culminating in the White House Conference on Education. In that Conference, some 2,000 delegates, broadly representative of the Nation, studied together the problems of the Nation's schools.

They concluded that the people of the United States must make a greater effort through their local, State, and Federal Governments to improve the education of our youth. This expression from the people must now be translated into action at all levels of government.

So far as the Federal share of responsibility is concerned, I urge that the Congress move promptly to enact an effective program of Federal assistance to help erase the existing deficit of school classrooms. Such a program, which should be limited to a 5-year period, must operate to increase rather than decrease local and State support of schools and to give the greatest help to the States and localities with the least financial resources. Federal aid should in no way jeopardize the freedom of local school systems. There will be presented to the Congress a recommended program of Federal assistance for school construction.

Such a program should be accompanied by action to increase services to the Nation's schools by the Office of Education and by legislation to provide continuation of payments to school districts where Federal activities have impaired the ability of those districts to provide adequate schools.

Under the 1954 amendments to the old-age and survivors' insurance program, protection was extended to some 10 million additional workers, and benefits were increased. The system now helps protect 9 out of 10 American workers and their families against loss of income in old age or on the death of the breadwinner. The system is sound. It must be kept so. In developing improvements in the system, we must give the most careful consideration to population and social trends, and to fiscal requirements. With these considerations in mind, the administration will present its recommendations for further expansion of coverage and other steps which can be taken wisely at this time.

Other needs in the area of social welfare include increased child-welfare services, extension of the program of aid to dependent children, intensified attack on juvenile delinquency, and special attention to the problems of mentally retarded children. The training of more skilled workers for these fields and the quest for new knowledge through research in social welfare are essential. Similarly the problems of our aged people need our attention.

The Nation has made dramatic progress in conquering disease—progress of profound human significance which can be greatly accelerated by an intensified effort in medical research. A well-supported, well-balanced program of research, including basic research, can open new frontiers of knowledge, prevent and relieve suffering, and prolong life. Accordingly I shall recommend a substantial increase in Federal funds for the support of such a program. As an integral part of this effort, I shall recommend a new plan to aid construction of non-Federal medical research and teaching facilities and to help provide more adequate support for the training of medical research manpower.

Finally, we must aid in cushioning the heavy and rising costs of illness and hospitalization to individuals and families. Provision should be made, by Federal reinsurance or otherwise, to foster extension of voluntary health insurance coverage to many more persons, especially older persons and those in rural areas. Plans should be evolved to improve protection against the costs of prolonged or severe illness. These measures will help reduce the dollar barrier between many Americans and the benefits of modern medical care.

The administration health program will be submitted to the Congress in detail.

The response of Government to human concerns embraces, of course, other measures of broad public interest, and of special interest to our working men and women. The need still exists for improvement of the Labor Management Relations Act. The recommendations I submitted to the Congress last year take into account not only the interests of labor and management but also the public welfare. The needed amendments should be enacted without further delay.

We must also carry forward the job of improving the wage-hour law. Last year I requested the Congress to broaden the coverage of the minimum wage. I repeat that recommendation, and I pledge the full resources of the executive branch to assist the Congress in finding ways to attain this goal. Moreover, as requested last year, legislation should be passed to clarify and strengthen the 8-hour laws for the benefit of workers who are subject to Federal wage standards on Federal and federally assisted construction and other public works.

The administration will shortly propose legislation to assure adequate disclosure of the financial affairs of each employee pension and welfare plan and to afford substantial protection to their beneficiaries in accordance with the objectives outlined in my message of January 11, 1954. Occupational safety still demands attention, as I pointed out last year, and legislation to improve the Longshoremen's and Harbor Workers' Compensation Act is still needed. The improvement of the District of Columbia unemployment insurance law and legislation to provide employees in the District with nonoccupational disability insurance are no less necessary now than 12 months ago. Legislation to apply the principle of equal pay for equal work without discrimination because of sex is a matter of simple justice. I earnestly urge the Congress to move swiftly to implement these needed labor measures.

In the field of human needs, we must carry forward the housing program, which is contributing so greatly to the well-being of our people and the prosperity of our economy. Home ownership is now advanced to the point where almost 3 of every 5 families in our cities, towns, and suburbs own the houses they live in.

For the housing program, most of the legislative authority already exists. However, a firm program of public housing is essential until the private building industry has found ways to provide more adequate housing for low-income families. The administration will propose authority to contract for 35,000 additional public housing units in each of the next 2 fiscal years for communities which will participate in an integrated attack on slums and blight.

To meet the needs of the growing number of older people, several amendments to the National Housing Act will be proposed to assist the private homebuilding industry as well as charitable and nonprofit organizations.

With so large a number of the American people desiring to modernize and improve existing dwellings, I recommend that the title I program for permanent improvements in the home be liberalized.

I recommend increases in the general FHA mortgage insurance authority; the extension of the FHA military housing program; an increase in the authorization for urban planning grants; in the special assistance authority of the Federal National Mortgage Association; and continued support of the college housing program in a way that will not discourage private capital from helping to meet the needs of our colleges.

The legislation I have recommended for workers in private industry should be accompanied by a parallel effort for the welfare of Government employees. We have accomplished much in this field, including a contributory life-insurance program; equitable pay increases and a fringe benefits program, covering many needed personnel policy changes, from improved premium pay to a meaningful incentive award program.

Additional personnel-management legislation is needed in this session. As I stated last year, an executive pay increase is essential to efficient governmental management. Such an increase, together with needed adjustments in the pay for the top career positions, is also necessary to the equitable completion of the Federal-pay program initiated last year. Other legislation will be proposed, including legislation for prepaid group health insurance for employees and their dependents, and to effect major improvements in the civil-service retirement system.

All of us share a continuing concern for those who have served this Nation in the Armed Forces. The Commission on Veterans' Pensions is at this time conducting a study of the entire field of veterans' benefits, and will soon submit proposed improvements.

We are proud of the progress our people have made in the field of civil rights. In executive-branch operations throughout the Nation, elimination of discrimination and segregation is all but completed. Progress is also being made among contractors engaged in furnishing Government services and requirements. Every citizen now has the opportunity to fit himself for and to hold a position of responsibility in the service of his country. In the District of Columbia, through the voluntary cooperation of the people, discrimination and segregation are disappearing from hotels, theaters, restaurants, and other facilities.

It is disturbing that in some localities allegations persist that Negro citizens are being deprived of their right to vote and are likewise being subjected to unwarranted economic pressures. I recommend that the substance of these charges be thoroughly examined by a bipartisan commission created by the Congress. It is hoped that such a commission will be established promptly so that it may arrive at findings which can receive early consideration.

The stature of our leadership in the free world has increased through the past 3 years because we have made more progress than ever before in a similar period to assure our citizens equality in justice, in opportunity, and in civil rights. We must expand this effort on every front. We must strive to have every person judged and measured by what he is, rather than by his color, race, or religion. There will soon be recommended to the Congress a program further to advance the efforts of the Government, within the area of Federal responsibility, to accomplish these objectives.

One particular challenge confronts us. In the Hawaiian Islands, East meets West. To the islands, Asia and Europe and the Western Hemisphere, all the continents, have contributed their peoples and their cultures to display a unique example of a community that is a successful laboratory in human brotherhood.

Statehood, supported by the repeatedly expressed desire of the islands' people and by our traditions, would be a shining example of the American way to the entire earth. Consequently, I urgently request this Congress to grant statehood for Hawaii. Also, in harmony with the provisions I last year communicated to the Senate and House Committees on Interior and Insular Affairs, I trust that progress toward statehood for Alaska can be made in this session.

Progress is constant toward full integration of our Indian citizens into normal community life. During the past 2 years the administration has provided school facilities for thousands of Indian children previously denied this opportunity. We must continue to meet the needs of increased numbers of Indian children. Provision should also be made for the education of adult Indians whose schooling in earlier years was neglected.

In keeping with our responsibility of world leadership and in our own self-interest, I again point out to the Congress the urgent need for revision of the immigration and nationality laws. Our Nation has always welcomed immigrants to our shores. The wisdom of such a policy is clearly shown by the fact that America has been built by immigrants and the descendants of immigrants. That policy must be continued realistically with present day conditions in mind.

I recommend that the number of person admitted to this country annually be based not on the 1920 census but on the latest, the 1950 census. Provision should be made to allow for greater flexibility in the use of quotas, so, if one country does not use its share the vacancies may be made available for the use of qualified individuals from other countries.

The law should be amended to permit the Secretary of State and the Attorney General to waive the requirements of fingerprinting on a reciprocal basis for persons coming to this country for temporary visits. This and other changes in the law are long overdue and should be taken care of promptly. Detailed recommendations for revision of the immigration laws will be submitted to the Congress.

I am happy to report substantial progress in the flow of immigrants under the Refugee Relief Act of 1953; however, I again request this Congress to approve without further delay the urgently needed amendments to that act which I submitted in the last session. Because of the high prosperity in Germany and Austria, the number of immigrants from those countries will be reduced. This will make available thousands of unfilled openings which I recommend be distributed to Greece and Italy and to escapees from behind the Iron Curtain.

Once again I ask the Congress to join with me in demonstrating our belief in the right of suffrage. I renew my request that the principle of self-government be extended and the right of suffrage granted to the citizens of the District of Columbia.

To conclude: the vista before us is bright. The march of science, the expanding economy, the advance in collective security toward a just peace—in this threefold movement our people are creating new standards by which the future of the Republic may be judged.

Progress, however, will be realized only as it is more than matched by a continuing growth in the spiritual strength of the Nation. Our dedication to moral values must be complete in our dealings abroad and in our relationships among ourselves. We have single-minded devotion to the common good of America. Never must we forget that this means the well-being, the prosperity, the security of all Americans in every walk of life.

To the attainment of these objectives, I pledge full energies of the administration, as in the session ahead, it works on a program for submission to you, the Congress of the United States.

FIFTH ANNUAL MESSAGE.

THE WHITE HOUSE, *January 10, 1957.*

To the Congress of the United States:

I appear before the Congress today to report on the state of the Union and the relationships of the Union to the other nations of the world. I come here, firmly convinced that at no time in the history of the Republic have circumstances more emphatically underscored the need, in all echelons of government, for vision and wisdom and resolution.

You meet in a season of stress that is testing the fitness of political systems and the validity of political philosophies. Each stress stems in part from causes peculiar to itself. But every stress is a reflection of a universal phenomenon.

In the world today, the surging and understandable tide of nationalism is marked by widespread revulsion and revolt against tyranny, injustice, inequality, and poverty. As individuals, joined in a common hunger for freedom, men and women and even children pit their spirit against guns and tanks. On a larger scale, in an ever more persistent search for the self-respect of authentic sovereignty and the economic base on which national independence must rest, peoples sever old ties; seek new alliances; experiment, sometimes dangerously, in their struggle to satisfy these human aspirations.

Particularly, in the past year, this tide has changed the pattern of attitudes and thinking among millions. The changes already accomplished foreshadow a world transformed by the spirit of freedom. This is no faint and pious hope. The forces now at work in the minds and hearts of men will not be spent through many years. In the main, today's expressions of nationalism are, in spirit, echoes of our forefathers' struggle for independence.

This Republic cannot be aloof to these events heralding a new epoch in the affairs of mankind.

Our pledged word, our enlightened self-interest, our character as a nation commit us to a high role in world affairs: a role of vigorous leadership, ready strength, sympathetic understanding.

The state of the Union, at the opening of the 85th Congress, continues to vindicate the wisdom of the principles on which this Republic is founded. Proclaimed in the Constitution of the Nation and in many of our historic documents, and founded in devout religious convictions, these principles enunciate:

A vigilant regard for human liberty.
A wise concern for human welfare.
A ceaseless effort for human progress.

Fidelity to these principles, in our relations with other peoples, has won us new freindships and has increased our opportunity for service within the family of nations. The appeal of these principles is universal, lighting fires in the souls of men everywhere. We shall continue to uphold them against those who deny them and in counseling with our friends.

At home the application of these principles to the complex problems of our national life has brought us to an unprecedented peak in our economic prosperity and has exemplified in our way of life the enduring human values of mind and spirit.

Through the past 4 years these principles have guided the legislative programs submitted by the Administration to the Congress. As we attempt to apply them to current events, domestic and foreign, we must take into account the complex entity that is the United States of America; what endangers it; what can improve it.

The visible structure is our American economy itself. After more than a century and a half of constant expansion, it is still rich in a wide variety of natural resources. It is first among nations in its people's mastery of industrial skills. It is productive beyond our own needs of many foodstuffs and industrial products. It is rewarding to all our citizens in opportunity to earn and to advance in self-realization and in self-expression. It is fortunate in its wealth of educational and cultural and religious centers. It is vigorously dynamic in the limitless initiative and willingness to venture that characterize free enterprise. It is productive of a widely shared prosperity.

Our economy is strong, expanding, and fundamentally sound. But in any realistic appraisal, even the optimistic analyst will realize that in a prosperous period the principal threat to efficient functioning of a free enterprise system is inflation. We look back on 4 years of prosperous activities during which prices, the cost of living, have been relatively stable—that is, inflation has been held in check. But it is clear that the danger is always present, particularly if the Government might become profligate in its expenditures or private groups might ignore all the possible results on our economy of unwise struggles for immediate gain.

This danger requires a firm resolution that the Federal Government shall utilize only a prudent share of the Nation's resources, that it shall live within its means, carefully measuring against need alternative proposals for expenditures.

Through the next 4 years, I shall continue to insist that the executive departments and agencies of Government search out additional ways to save money and manpower. I urge that the Congress be equally watchful in this matter.

We pledge the Government's share in guarding the integrity of the dollar. But the Government's efforts cannot be the entire campaign against inflation, the thief that can rob the individual of the value of the pension and social security he has earned during his productive life. For success, Government's efforts must be paralleled by the attitudes and actions of individual citizens.

I have often spoken of the purpose of this administration to serve the national interest of 170 million people. The national interest must take precedence over temporary advantages, which may be secured by particular groups at the expense of all the people.

In this regard I call on leaders in business and in labor to think well on their responsibility to the American people. With all elements of our society, they owe the Nation a vigilant guard against the inflationary tendencies that are always at work in a dynamic economy operating at today's high levels. They can powerfully help counteract or accentuate such tendencies by their wage and price policies.

Business in its pricing policies should avoid unnecessary price increases, especially at a time like the present when demand in so many areas presses hard on short supplies. A reasonable profit is essential to the new investments that provide more jobs in an expanding economy. But business leaders must, in the national interest, studiously avoid those price rises that are possible only because of vital or unusual needs of the whole Nation.

If our economy is to remain healthy, increases in wages and other labor benefits, negotiated by labor and management, must be reasonably related to improvements in productivity. Such increases are beneficial, for they provide wage earners with greater purchasing power. Except where necessary to correct obvious injustices, wage increases that outrun productivity, however, are an inflationary factor. They make for higher prices for the public generally and impose a particular hardship on those whose welfare depends on the purchasing power of retirement income and savings. Wage negotiations should also take cognizance of the right of the public generally to share in the benefits of improvements in technology.

Freedom has been defined as the opportunity for self-discipline. This definition has a special application to the areas of wage and price policy in a free economy. Should we persistently fail to discipline ourselves, eventually there will be increasing pressure on Government to redress the failure. By that process freedom will step by step disappear. No subject on the domestic scene should more attract the concern of the friends of American working men and women and of free business enterprise than the forces that threaten a steady depreciation of the value of our money.

* * *

Concerning developments in another vital sector of our economy—agriculture—I am gratified that the long slide in farm income has been halted and that further improvement is in prospect. This is heartening progress. Three tools that we have developed—improved surplus disposal, improved price-support laws, and the soil bank—are working to reduce price-depressing Government stocks of farm products. Our concern for the well-being of farm families demands that we constantly search for new ways by which they can share more fully in our unprecedented prosperity. Legislative recommendations in the field of agriculture are contained in the budget message.

Our soil, water, mineral, forest, fish, and wildlife resources are being conserved and improved more effectively. Their conservation and development are vital to the present and future strength of the Nation. But they must not be the concern of the Federal Government alone. State and local entities and private enterprise should be encouraged to participate in such projects.

I would like to make special mention of programs for making the best uses of water, rapidly becoming our most precious natural resource, just as it can be, when neglected, a destroyer of both life and wealth. There has been prepared and published a comprehensive water report developed by a Cabinet committee and relating to all phases of this particular problem.

In the light of this report, there are two things I believe we should keep constantly in mind: The first is that each of our great river valleys should be considered as a whole. Piecemeal operations within each lesser drainage area can be self-defeating or, at the very least, needlessly expensive. The second is that the domestic and industrial demands for water grow far more rapidly than does our population.

The whole matter of making the best use of each drop of water from the moment it touches our soil until it reaches the oceans, for such purposes as irrigation, flood control, power production, and domestic and industrial uses clearly demands the closest kind of cooperation and partnership between municipalities, States, and the Federal Government. Through partnership of Federal, State, and local authorities in these vast projects we can obtain the economy and efficiency of development and operation that springs from a lively sense of local responsibility.

Until such partnership is established on a proper and logical basis of sharing authority, responsibility, and costs, our country will never have both the fully productive use of water that it so obviously needs and protection against disastrous flood.

If we fail in this, all the many tasks that need to be done in America could be accomplished only at an excessive cost, by the growth of a stifling bureaucracy and, eventually, with a dangerous degree of centralized control over our national life.

In all domestic matters, I believe that the people of the United States will expect of us effective action to remedy past failure in meeting critical needs.

High priority should be given the school construction bill. This will benefit children of all races throughout the country—and children of all races need schools now. A program designed to meet emergency needs for more classrooms should be enacted without delay. I am hopeful that this program can be enacted on its own merits, uncomplicated by provisions dealing with the complex problems of integration. I urge the people in all sections of the country to approach these problems with calm and reason, with mutual understanding and good will, and in the American tradition of deep respect for the orderly processes of law and justice.

I should say here that we have much reason to be proud of the progress our people are making in mutual understanding—the chief buttress of human and civil rights. Steadily we are moving closer to the goal of fair and equal treatment of citizens without regard to race or color. But unhappily much remains to be done.

Last year the administration recommended to the Congress a four-point program to reinforce civil rights. That program included—

(1) Creation of a bipartisan commission to investigate asserted violations of civil rights and to make recommendations;

(2) Creation of a civil rights division in the Department of Justice in charge of an Assistant Attorney General;

(3) Enactment by the Congress of new laws to aid in the enforcement of voting rights; and

(4) Amendment of the laws so as to permit the Federal Government to seek from the civil courts preventive relief in civil rights cases.

I urge that the Congress enact this legislation.

* * *

Essential to the stable economic growth we seek is a system of well-adapted and efficient financial institutions. I believe the time has come to conduct a broad national inquiry into the nature, performance, and adequacy of our financial system, both in terms of its direct service to the whole economy and in terms of its function as the mechanism through which monetary and credit policy takes effect.

I believe the Congress should authorize the creation of a commission of able and qualified citizens to undertake this vital inquiry. Out of their findings and recommendations the administration would develop and present to the Congress any legislative proposals that might be indicated for the purpose of improving our financial machinery.

In this message it seems unnecessary that I should repeat recommendations involving our domestic affairs that have been urged upon the Congress during the past 4 years, but which, in some instances, did not reach the stage of completely satisfactory legislation.

The administration will, through future messages either directly from me or from heads of the departments and agencies, transmit to the Congress specific recommendations. These will involve our financial and fiscal affairs; our military and civil defenses; the administration of justice; our agricultural economy; our domestic and foreign commerce; the urgently needed increase in our postal rates; the development of our natural resources; our labor laws, including our labor-management relations legislation; and vital aspects of the health, education, and welfare of our people. There will be special recommendations dealing with such subjects as atomic energy, the furthering of public works, the continued efforts to eliminate Government competition with the businesses of taxpaying citizens.

A number of legislative recommendations will be mentioned specifically in my forthcoming budget message, which will reach you within the week. That message will also recommend such sums as are needed to implement the proposed action.

* * *

Turning to the international scene:

The existence of a strongly armed imperialistic dictatorship poses a continuing threat to the free world's and thus to our own Nation's security and peace. There are certain truths to be remembered here.

First, America alone and isolated cannot assure even its own security. We must be joined by the capability and resolution of nations that have proved themselves dependable defenders of freedom. Isolation from them invites war. Our security is also enhanced by the immeasurable interest that joins us with all peoples who believe that peace with justice must be preserved, that wars of aggression are crimes against humanity.

Another truth is that our survival in today's world requires modern, adequate, dependable military strength. Our Nation has made great strides in assuring a modern defense, so armed in new weapons, so deployed, so equipped, that today our security force is the most powerful in our peacetime history. It can punish heavily any enemy who undertakes to attack us. It is a major deterrent to war.

By our research and development more efficient weapons—some of amazing capabilities—are being constantly created. These vital efforts we shall continue. Yet we must not delude ourselves that safety necessarily increases as expenditures for military research or forces in being go up. Indeed, beyond a wise and reasonable level, which is always changing and is under constant study, money spent on arms may be money wasted on sterile metal or inflated costs, thereby weakening the very security and strength we seek.

National security requires far more than military power. Economic and moral factors play indispensable roles. Any program that endangers our economy could defeat us. Any weakening of our national will and resolution, any diminution of the vigor and initiative of our individual citizens, would strike a blow at the heart of our defenses.

The finest military establishment we can produce must work closely in cooperation with the forces of our friends. Our system of regional pacts, developed within the Charter of the United Nations, serves to increase both our own security and the security of other nations.

This system is still a recent introduction on the world scene. Its problems are many and difficult, because it insists on equality among its members and brings into association some nations traditionally divided. Repeatedly in recent months, the collapse of these regional alliances has been predicted. The strains upon them have been at times indeed severe. Despite these strains our regional alliances have proved durable and strong, and dire predictions of their disintegration have proved completely false.

With other free nations, we should vigorously prosecute measures that will promote mutual strength, prosperity, and welfare within the free world. Strength is essentially a product of economic health and social well-being. Consequently, even as we continue our programs of military assistance, we must emphasize aid to our friends in building more productive economies and in better satisfying the natural demands of their people for progress. Thereby we shall move a long way toward a peaceful world.

A sound and safeguarded agreement for open skies, unarmed aerial sentinels, and reduced armament would provide a valuable contribution toward a durable peace in the years ahead. And we have been persistent in our efforts to reach such an agreement. We are willing to enter any reliable agreement which would reverse the trend toward ever more devastating nuclear weapons; reciprocally provide against the possibility of surprise attack; mutually control the outer-space missile and satellite development; and make feasible a lower level of armaments and armed forces and an easier burden of military expenditures. Our continuing negotiations in this field are a major part of our quest for a confident peace in this atomic age.

This quest requires as well a constructive attitude among all the nations of the free world toward expansion of trade and investment, that can give all of us opportunity to work out economic betterment.

An essential step in this field is the provision of an administrative agency to insure the orderly and proper operation of existing arrangements under which multilateral trade is now carried on. To that end I urge congressional authorization for United States membership in the proposed Organization for Trade Cooperation, an action which will speed removal of discrimination against our export trade.

We welcome the efforts of a number of our European friends to achieve an integrated community to develop a common market. We likewise welcome their cooperative effort in the field of atomic energy.

To demonstrate once again our unalterable purpose to make of the atom a peaceful servant of humanity, I shortly shall ask the Congress to authorize full United States participation in the International Atomic Energy Agency.

World events have magnified both the responsibilities and the opportunities of the United States Information Agency. Just as, in recent months, the voice of communism has become more shaken and confused, the voice of truth must be more clearly heard. To enable our Information Agency to cope with these new responsibilities and opportunities, I am asking the Congress to increase appreciably the appropriations for this program and for legislation establishing a career service for the Agency's overseas Foreign Service officers.

The recent historic events in Hungary demand that all free nations share to the extent of their capabilities in the responsibility of granting asylum to victims of Communist persecution. I request the Congress promptly to enact legislation to regularize the status in the United States of Hungarian refugees brought here as parolees. I shall shortly recommend to the Congress by special message the changes in our immigration laws that I deem necessary in the light of our world responsibilities.

The cost of peace is something we must face boldly, fearlessly. Beyond money, it involves changes in attitudes, the renunciation of old prejudices, even the sacrifice of some seeming self-interest.

Only 5 days ago I expressed to you the grave concern of your Government over the threat of Soviet aggression in the Middle East. I asked for congressional authorization to help counter this threat. I say again that this matter is of vital and immediate importance to the Nation's and the free world's security and peace. By our proposed programs in the Middle East, we hope to assist in establishing a climate in which constructive and long-term solutions to basic problems of the area may be sought.

From time to time, there will be presented to the Congress requests for other legislation in the broad field of international affairs. All requests will reflect the steadfast purpose of this administration to pursue peace, based on justice. Although in some cases details will be new, the underlying purpose and objectives will remain the same.

All proposals made by the administratin in this field are based on the free world's unity. This unity may not be immediately obvious unless we examine link by link the chain of relationships that binds us to every area and to every nation. In spirit the free world is one, because its peoples uphold the right of independent existence for all nations. I have already alluded to their economic interdependence. But their interdependence extends also into the field of security.

First of all, no reasonable man will question the absolute need for our American neighbors to be prosperous and secure. Their security and prosperity are inextricably bound to our own. And we are, of course, already joined with these neighbors by historic pledges.

Again, no reasonable man will deny that the freedom and prosperity and security of Western Europe are vital to our own prosperity and security. If the institutions, the skills, the manpower of its peoples were to fall under the domination of an aggressive imperialism, the violent change in the balance of world power and in the pattern of world commerce could not be fully compensated for by any American measures, military or economic.

But these people, whose economic strength is largely dependent on free and uninterrupted movement of oil from the Middle East, cannot prosper—indeed, their economies would be severely impaired—should that area be controlled by an enemy and the movement of oil be subject to its decisions.

Next, to the eastward, are Asiatic and far eastern peoples, recently returned to independent control of their own affairs or now emerging into sovereign statehood. Their potential strength constitutes new assurance for stability and peace in the world—if they can retain their independence. Should they lose freedom and be dominated by an aggressor, the worldwide effects would imperil the security of the free world.

In short, the world has so shrunk that all free nations are our neighbors. Without cooperative neighbors, the United States cannot maintain its own security and welfare, because—

First, America's vital interests are worldwide, embracing both hemispheres and every continent.

Second, we have community of interest with every nation in the free world.

Third, interdependence of interests requires a decent respect for the rights and the peace of all peoples.

These principles motivate our actions within the United Nations. There, before all the world, by our loyalty to them, by our practice of them, let us strive to set a standard to which all who seek justice and who hunger for peace can rally.

May we at home, here at the seat of government, in all the cities and towns and farmlands of America, support these principles in a personal effort of dedication. Thereby each of us can help establish a secure world order in which opportunity for freedom and justice will be more widespread, and in which the resources now dissipated on the armaments of war can be released for the life and growth of all humanity.

When our forefathers prepared the immortal document that proclaimed our independence, they asserted that every individual is endowed by his Creator with certain inalienable rights. As we gaze back through history to that date, it is clear that our Nation has striven to live up to this declaration, applying it to nations as well as to individuals.

Today we proudly assert that the Government of the United States is still committed to this concept, both in its activities at home and abroad.

The purpose is divine; the implementation is human.

Our country and its Government have made mistakes—human mistakes. They have been of the head, not of the heart. And it is still true that the great concept of the dignity of all men, alike created in the image of the Almighty, has been the compass by which we have tried and are trying to steer our course.

So long as we continue by its guidance, there will be true progress in human affairs, both among ourselves and among those with whom we deal.

To achieve a more perfect fidelity to it, I submit, is a worthy ambition as we meet together in these first days of this, the 1st session of the 85th Congress.

SIXTH ANNUAL MESSAGE.

THE WHITE HOUSE, *January 9, 1958.*

Mr. President, Mr. Speaker, Members of the 85th Congress: It is again my high privilege to extend personal greetings to the Members of the 85th Congress.

All of us realize that, as this new session begins, many Americans are troubled about recent world developments which they believe may threaten our Nation's safety. Honest men differ in their appraisal of America's material and intellectual strength, and the dangers that confront us. But all know these dangers are real.

The purpose of this message is to outline the measures that can give the American people a confidence—just as real—in their own security.

I am not here to justify the past, gloss over the problems of the present, or propose easy solutions for the future.

I am here to state what I believe to be right and what I believe to be wrong; and to propose action for correcting what I think wrong.

I

There are two tasks confronting us that so far outweigh all others that I shall devote this year's message entirely to them.

The first is to insure our safety through strength.

As to our strength, I have repeatedly voiced this conviction: We now have a broadly based and efficient defensive strength, including a great deterrent power, which is, for the present, our main guaranty against war; but, unless we act wisely and promptly, we could lose that capacity to deter attack or defend ourselves.

My profoundest conviction is that the American people will say, as one man: No matter what the exertions or sacrifices, we shall maintain that necessary strength.

But we could make no more tragic mistake than merely to concentrate on military strength.

For if we did only this, the future would hold nothing for the world but an age of terror.

And so our second task is to do the constructive work of building a genuine peace. We must never become so preoccupied with our desire for military strength that we neglect those areas of economic development, trade, diplomacy, education, ideas, and principles where the foundations of real peace must be laid.

II

The threat to our safety, and to the hope of a peaceful world, can be simply stated. It is Communist imperialism.

This threat is not something imagined by critics of the Soviets. Soviet spokesmen, from the beginning, have publicly and frequently declared their aim to expand their power, one way or another, throughout the world.

The threat has become increasingly serious as this expansionist aim has been reinforced by an advancing industrial, military, and scientific establishment.

But what makes the Soviet threat unique in history is its all-inclusiveness. Every human activity is pressed into service as a weapon of expansion. Trade, economic development, military power, arts, science, education, the whole world of ideas—all are harnessed to this same chariot of expansion.

The Soviets are, in short, waging total cold war.

The only answer to a regime that wages total cold war is to wage total peace.

This means bringing to bear every asset of our personal and national lives upon the task of building the conditions in which security and peace can grow.

III

Among our assets, let us first briefly glance at our military power.

Military power serves the cause of security by making prohibitive the cost of any aggressive attack.

It serves the cause of peace by holding up a shield behind which the patient constructive work of peace can go on.

But it can serve neither cause if we make either of two mistakes. The one would be to overestimate our strength, and thus neglect crucially important actions in the period just ahead. The other would be to underestimate our strength. Thereby we might be tempted to become irresolute in our foreign relations, to dishearten our friends, and to lose our national poise and perspective in approaching the complex problems ahead.

Any orderly balance sheet of military strength must be in two parts. The first is the position as of today. The second is the position in the period ahead.

As of today: our defensive shield comprehends a vast complex of ground, sea, and air units, superbly equipped and strategically deployed around the world. The most powerful deterrent to war in the world today lies in the retaliatory power of our Strategic Air Command and the aircraft of our Navy. They present to any potential attacker who would unleash war upon the world the prospect of virtual annihilation of his own country.

Even if we assume a surprise attack on our bases, with a marked reduction in our striking power, our bombers would immediately be on their way in sufficient strength to accomplish this mission of retaliation. Every informed government knows this. It is no secret.

Since the Korean armistice, the American people have spent $225 billion in maintaining and strengthening this overall defensive shield.

This is the position as of today.

Now as to the period ahead: Every part of our Military Establishment must and will be equipped to do its defensive job with the most modern weapons and methods. But it is particularly important to our planning that we make a candid estimate of the effect of long-range ballistic missiles on the present deterrent power I have described.

At this moment, the consensus of opinion is that we are probably somewhat behind the Soviets in some areas of long-range ballistic missile development. But it is my conviction, based on close study of all relevant intelligence, that if we make the necessary effort, we will have the missiles, in the needed quantity and in time, to sustain and strengthen the deterrent power of our increasingly efficient bombers. One encouraging fact evidencing this ability is the rate of progress we have achieved since we began to concentrate on these missiles.

The intermediate ballistic missiles, Thor and Jupiter, have already been ordered into production. The parallel progress in the intercontinental ballistic missile effort will be advanced by our plans for acceleration. The development of the submarine-based Polaris missile system has progressed so well that its future procurement schedules are being moved forward markedly.

When it is remembered that our country has concentrated on the development of ballistic missiles for only about a third as long as the Soviets, these achievements show a rate of progress that speaks for itself. Only a brief time back, we were spending at the rate of only about $1 million a year on long-range ballistic missiles. In 1957 we spent more than $1 billion on the Atlas, Titan, Thor, Jupiter, and Polaris programs alone.

But I repeat, gratifying though this rate of progress is, we must still do more.

Our real problem, then, is not our strength today; it is rather the vital necessity of action today to insure our strength tomorrow.

* * *

What I have just said applies to our strength as a single country. But we are not alone. I have returned from the recent NATO meeting with renewed conviction that, because we are a part of a worldwide community of free and peaceful nations, our own security is immeasurably increased.

By contrast, the Soviet Union has surrounded itself with captive and sullen nations. Like a crack in the crust of an uneasily sleeping volcano, the Hungarian uprising revealed the depth and intensity of the patriotic longing for liberty that still burns within these countries.

The world thinks of us as a country which is strong, but which will never start a war. The world also thinks of us as a land which has never enslaved anyone and which is animated by humane ideals. This friendship, based on common ideals, is one of our greatest sources of strength.

It cements into a cohesive security arrangement the aggregate of the spiritual, military, and economic strength of all those nations which, with us, are allied by treaties and agreements.

* * *

Up to this point, I have talked solely about our military strength to deter a possible future war.

I now want to talk about the strength we need to win a different kind of war—one that has already been launched against us.

It is the massive economic offensive that has been mounted by the Communist imperialists against free nations.

The Communist imperialist regimes have for some time been largely frustrated in their attempts at expansion based directly on force. As a result, they have begun to concentrate heavily on economic penetration, particularly of newly developing countries, as a preliminary to political domination.

This nonmilitary drive, if underestimated, could defeat the free world regardless of our military strength. This danger is all the greater precisely because many of us fail or refuse to recognize it. Thus, some people may be tempted to finance our extra military effort by cutting economic assistance. But at the very time when the economic threat is assuming menacing proportions, to fail to strengthen our own effort would be nothing less than reckless folly.

Admittedly, most of us did not anticipate the psychological impact upon the world of the launching of the first earth satellite. Let us not make the same kind of mistake in another field, by failing to anticipate the much more serious impact of the Soviet economic offensive.

As with our military potential, our economic assets are more than equal to the task. Our independent farmers produce an abundance of food and fiber. Our free workers are versatile, intelligent, and hard working. Our businessmen are imaginative and resourceful. The productivity, the adaptability of the American economy is the solid foundation stone of our security structure.

We have just concluded another prosperous year. Our output was once more the greatest in the Nation's history. In the latter part of the year, some decline in employment and output occurred, following the exceptionally rapid expansion of recent years. In a free economy, reflecting as it does the independent judgments of millions of people, growth typically moves forward unevenly. But the basic forces of growth remain unimpaired. There are solid grounds for confidence that economic growth will be resumed without an extended interruption. Moreover, the Federal Government, constantly alert to signs of weakening in any part of our economy, always stands ready, with its full power, to take any appropriate further action to promote renewed business expansion.

If our history teaches us anything, it is this lesson: so far as the economic potential of our Nation is concerned, the believers in the future of America have always been the realists.

I count myself as one of this company.

Our long-range problem, then, is not the stamina of our enormous engine of production. Our problem is to make sure that we use these vast economic forces confidently and creatively, not only in direct military defense efforts, but likewise in our foreign policy, through such activities as mutual economic aid and foreign trade.

In much the same way, we have tremendous potential resources on other nonmilitary fronts to help in countering the Soviet threat: education, science, research, and, not least, the ideas and principles by which we live. And in all these cases the task ahead is to bring these resources more sharply to bear upon the new tasks of security and peace in a swiftly changing world.

IV

There are many items in the administration's program, of a kind frequently included in a state of the Union message, with which I am not dealing today. They are important to us and to our prosperity. But I am reserving them for treatment in separate communications because of my purpose today of speaking only about matters bearing directly upon our security and peace.

I now place before you an outline of action designed to focus our resources upon the two tasks of security and peace.

In this special category I list eight items requiring action. They are not merely desirable. They are imperative.

1. DEFENSE REORGANIZATION

The first need is to assure ourselves that military organization facilitates rather than hinders the functioning of the Military Establishment in maintaining the security of the Nation.

Since World War II, the purpose of achieving maximum organizational efficiency in a modern defense establishment has several times occasioned action by the Congress and by the executive.

The advent of revolutionary new devices, bringing with them the problem of overall continental defense, creates new difficulties, reminiscent of those attending the advent of the airplane half a century ago.

Some of the important new weapons which technology has produced do not fit into any existing service pattern. They cut across all services, involve all services, and transcend all services, at every stage from development to operation. In some instances they defy classification according to branch of service.

Unfortunately, the uncertainties resulting from such a situation, and the jurisdictional disputes attending upon it, tend to bewilder and confuse the public and create the impression that service differences are damaging the national interest.

Let us proudly remember that the members of the Armed Forces give their basic allegiance solely to the United States. Of that fact all of us are certain. But pride of service and mistaken zeal in promoting particular doctrine has more than once occasioned the kind of difficulty of which I have just spoken.

I am not attempting today to pass judgment on the charge of harmful service rivalries. But one thing is sure. Whatever they are, America wants them stopped.

Recently I have had under special study the never-ending problem of efficient organization, complicated as it is by new weapons. Soon my own conclusions will be finalized. I shall promptly take such executive action as is necessary and, in a separate message, I shall present appropriate recommendations to the Congress.

Meanwhile, without anticipating the detailed form that a reorganization should take, I can state its main lines in terms of objectives:

A major purpose of military organization is to achieve real unity in the Defense Establishment in all the principal features of military activity. Of all these, one of the most important to our Nation's security is strategic planning and control. This work must be done under unified direction.

The defense structure must be one which, as a whole, can assume, with top efficiency and without friction, the defense of America. The Defense Establishment must therefore plan for a better integration of its defensive resources, particularly with respect to the newer weapons now building and under development. These obviously require full coordination in their development, production, and use. Good organization can help assure this coordination.

In recognition of the need for single control in some of our most advanced development projects, the Secretary of Defense has already decided to concentrate into one organization all the antimissile and satellite technology undertaken within the Department of Defense.

Another requirement of military organization is a clear subordination of the military services to duly constituted civilian authority.

This control must be real; not merely on the surface.

Next there must be assurance that an excessive number of compartments in organization will not create costly and confusing compartments in our scientific and industrial effort.

Finally, to end interservice disputes requires clear organization and decisive central direction, supported by the unstinted cooperation of every individual in the Defense Establishment, civilian and military.

2. ACCELERATED DEFENSE EFFORT

The second major action item is the acceleration of the defense effort in particular areas affected by the fast pace of scientific and technological advance.

Some of the points at which improved and increased effort are most essential are these:

We must have sure warning in case of attack. The improvement of warning equipment is becoming increasingly important as we approach the period when long-range missiles will come into use.

We must protect and disperse our striking forces and increase their readiness for instant reaction. This means more base facilities and standby crews.

We must maintain deterrent retaliatory power. This means, among other things, stepped-up long-range missile programs; accelerated programs for other effective missile systems; and, for some years, more advanced aircraft.

We must maintain freedom of the seas. This means nuclear submarines and cruisers; improved antisubmarine weapons; missile ships; and the like.

We must maintain all necessary types of mobile forces to deal with local conflicts, should there be need. This means further improvements in equipment, mobility, tactics, and firepower.

Through increases in pay and incentive, we must maintain in the Armed Forces the skilled manpower modern military forces require.

We must be forward looking in our research and development to anticipate and achieve the unimagined weapons of the future.

With these and other improvements, we intend to assure that our vigilance, power, and technical excellence keep abreast of any realistic threat we face.

3. MUTUAL AID

Third: We must continue to strengthen our mutual security efforts.

Most people now realize that our programs of military aid and defense support are an integral part of our own defense effort. If the foundations of the free world structure were progressively allowed to crumble under the pressure of Communist imperialism, the entire house of freedom would be in danger of collapse.

As for the mutual economic assistance program, the benefit to us is threefold. First, the countries receiving this aid become bulwarks against Communist encroachment as their military defenses and economies are strengthened. Nations that are conscious of a steady improvement in their industry, education, health, and standard of living are not apt to fall prey to the blandishments of Communist imperialists.

Second, these countries are helped to reach the point where mutually profitable trade can expand between them and us.

Third, the mutual confidence that comes from working together on constructive projects creates an atmosphere in which real understanding and peace can flourish.

To help bring these multiple benefits, our economic aid effort should be made more effective.

In proposals for future economic aid, I am stressing a greater use of repayable loans, through the development loan fund, through funds generated by sale of surplus farm products, and through the Export-Import Bank.

While some increase in Government funds will be required, it remains our objective to encourage shifting to the use of private capital sources as rapidly as possible.

One great obstacle to the economic aid program in the past has been, not a rational argument against it on the merits, but a catchword: "giveaway program."

The real fact is that no investment we make in our own security and peace can pay us greater dividends than necessary amounts of economic aid to friendly nations.

This is no "giveaway."

Let's stick to facts.

We cannot afford to have one of our most essential security programs shot down with a slogan.

4. MUTUAL TRADE

Fourth: Both in our national interest, and in the interest of world peace, we must have a 5-year extension of the Trade Agreements Act with broadened authority to negotiate.

World trade supports a significant segment of American industry and agriculture. It provides employment for 4½ million American workers. It helps supply our ever-increasing demand for raw materials. It provides the opportunity for American free enterprise to develop on a worldwide scale. It strengthens our friends and increases their desire to be friends. World trade helps to lay the groundwork for peace by making all free nations of the world stronger and more self-reliant.

America is today the world's greatest trading nation. If we use this great asset wisely to meet the expanding demands of the world, we shall not only provide future opportunities for our own business, agriculture, and labor, but in the process strengthen our security posture and other prospects for a prosperous, harmonious world.

As President McKinley said, as long ago as 1901: "Isolation is no longer possible or desirable * * * The period of exclusiveness is past."

5. SCIENTIFIC COOPERATION WITH OUR ALLIES

Fifth: It is of the highest importance that the Congress enact the necessary legislation to enable us to exchange appropriate scientific and technical information with friendly countries as part of our effort to achieve effective scientific cooperation.

It is wasteful in the extreme for friendly allies to consume talent and money in solving problems that their friends have already solved—all because of artificial barriers to sharing. We cannot afford to cut ourselves off from the brilliant talents and minds of scientists in friendly countries. The task ahead will be hard enough without handcuffs of our own making.

The groundwork for this kind of cooperation has already been laid in discussions among NATO countries. Promptness in following through with legislation will be the best possible evidence of American unity of purpose in cooperating with our friends.

6. EDUCATION AND RESEARCH

Sixth: In the area of education and research, I recommend a balanced program to improve our resources, involving an investment of about a billion dollars over a 4-year period. This involves new activities by the Department of Health, Education, and Welfare designed principally to encourage improved teaching quality and student opportunities in the interests of national security. It also provides a fivefold increase in sums available to the National Science Foundation for its special activities in stimulating and improving science education.

Scrupulous attention has been paid to maintaining local control of educational policy, spurring the maximum amount of local effort, and to avoiding undue stress on the physical sciences at the expense of other branches of learning.

In the field of research, I am asking for substantial increases in basic research funds, including a doubling of the funds available to the National Science Foundation for this purpose.

But Federal action can do only a part of the job. In both education and research, redoubled exertions will be necessary on the part of all Americans if we are to rise to the demands of our times. This means hard work on the part of State and local governments, private industry, schools and colleges, private organizations and foundations, teachers, parents, and—perhaps most important of all—the student himself, with his bag of books and his homework.

With this kind of all-inclusive campaign, I have no doubt that we can create the intellectual capital we need for the years ahead, invest it in the right places—and do all this, not as regimented pawns, but as free men and women.

7. SPENDING AND SAVING

Seventh: To provide for this extra effort for security, we must apply stern tests of priority to other expenditures, both military and civilian.

This extra effort involves, most immediately, the need for a supplemental defense appropriation of $1.3 billion for fiscal year 1958.

In the 1959 budget, increased expenditures for missiles, nuclear ships, atomic energy, research and development, science and education, a special contingency fund to deal with possible new technological discoveries, and increases in pay and incentives to obtain and retain competent manpower add up to a total increase over the comparable figures in the 1957 budget of about $4 billion.

I believe that, in spite of these necessary increases, we should strive to finance the 1959 security effort out of expected revenues. While we now believe that expected revenues and expenditures will roughly balance, our real purpose will be to achieve adequate security, but always with the utmost regard for efficiency and careful management.

This purpose will require the cooperation of Congress in making careful analysis of estimates presented, reducing expenditure on less essential military programs and installations, postponing some new civilian programs, transferring some to the States, and curtailing or eliminating others.

Such related matters as the national debt ceiling and tax revenues will be dealt with in later messages.

8. WORKS OF PEACE

My last call for action is not primarily addressed to the Congress and people of the United States. Rather, it is a message from the people of the United States to all other peoples, especially those of the Soviet Union.

This is the spirit of what we would like to say:

"In the last analysis, there is only one solution to the grim problems that lie ahead. The world must stop the present plunge toward more and more destructive weapons of war, and turn the corner that will start our steps firmly on the path toward lasting peace.

"Our greatest hope for success lies in a universal fact: the people of the world, as people, have always wanted peace and want peace now.

"The problem, then, is to find a way of translating this universal desire into action.

"This will require more than words of peace. It requires works of peace."

Now, may I try to give you some concrete examples of the kind of works of peace that might make a beginning in the new direction.

For a start our people should learn to know each other better. Recent negotiations in Washington have provided a basis in principle for greater freedom of communication and exchange of people. I urge the Soviet Government to cooperate in turning principle into practice by prompt and tangible actions that will break down the unnatural barriers that have blocked the flow of thought and understanding between our people.

Another kind of work of peace is cooperation on projects of human welfare. For example, we now have it within our power to eradicate from the face of the earth that age-old scourge of mankind: malaria. We are embarking with other nations in an all-out 5-year campaign to blot out this curse forever. We invite the Soviets to join with us in this great work of humanity.

Indeed, we would be willing to pool our efforts with the Soviets in other campaigns against the diseases that are the common enemy of all mortals—such as cancer and heart disease.

If people can get together on such projects, is it not possible that we could then go on to a full-scale cooperative program of science for peace?

We have as a guide and inspiration the success of our atoms-for-peace proposal, which in only a few years, under United Nations auspices, became a reality in the International Atomic Energy Agency.

A program of science for peace might provide a means of funneling into one place the results of research from scientists everywhere and from there making it available to all parts of the world.

There is almost no limit to the human betterment that could result from such cooperation. Hunger and disease could increasingly be driven from the earth. The age-old dream of a good life for all could, at long last, be translated into reality.

But of all the works of peace, none is more needed now than a real first step toward disarmament.

Last August the United Nations General Assembly, by an overwhelming vote, approved a disarmament plan that we and our allies sincerely believed to be fair and practical. The Soviets have rejected both the plan, and the negotiating procedure set up by the United Nations. As a result, negotiation on this supremely important issue is now at a standstill.

But the world cannot afford to stand still on disarmament. We must never give up the search for a basis of agreement.

Our allies from time to time develop differing ideas on how to proceed. We must concert these convictions among ourselves. Thereafter, any reasonable proposal that holds promise for disarmament and reduction of tension must be heard, discussed, and, if possible, negotiated.

But a disarmament proposal, to hold real promise, must at the minimum have one feature: reliable means to insure compliance by all. It takes actions and demonstrated integrity on both sides to create and sustain confidence. And confidence in a genuine disarmament agreement is vital, not only to the signers of the agreement, but also to the millions of people all over the world who are weary of tensions and armaments.

I say once more, to all peoples, that we will always go the extra mile with anyone on earth if it will bring us nearer a genuine peace.

CONCLUSION

These, then, are the ways in which we must funnel our energies more efficiently into the task of advancing security and peace.

These actions demand and expect two things of the American people: sacrifice, and a high degree of understanding. For sacrifice to be effective it must be intelligent. Sacrifice must be made for the right purpose and in the right place—even if that place happens to come close to home.

After all, it is no good demanding sacrifice in general terms one day, and the next day, for local reasons, opposing the elimination of some unneeded Federal facility.

It is pointless to condemn Federal spending in general, and the next moment condemn just as stongly an effort to reduce the particular Federal grant that touches one's own interest.

And it makes no sense whatever to spend additional billions on military strength to deter a potential danger, and then, by cutting aid and trade programs, let the world succumb to a present danger in economic guise.

My friends of the Congress: The world is waiting to see how wisely and decisively a free representative government will now act.

I believe that this Congress possesses and will display the wisdom promptly to do its part in translating into law the actions demanded by our Nation's interests. But, to make law effective, our kind of government needs the full voluntary support of millions of Americans for these actions.

I am fully confident that the response of the Congress and of the American people will make this time of test a time of honor. Mankind then will see more clearly than ever that the future belongs, not to the concept of the regimented atheistic state, but to the people—the God-fearing peace-loving people of all the world.

SEVENTH ANNUAL MESSAGE.

THE WHITE HOUSE, *January 9, 1959.*

Members of the 86th Congress and friends: First I should like to assure the delegation of our newest State, Alaska, of my satisfaction that it now begins its participation with all of you in the work of Congress for the benefit of the United States.

May I voice the hope that before my term of office is ended I shall have the opportunity and the great satisfaction of seeing the 50th star in our national flag.

Members of the Congress, this is the moment when Congress and the Executive annually begin their cooperative work to build a better America.

One basic purpose unites us: To promote strength and security, side by side with liberty and opportunity.

* * *

As we meet today, in the 170th years of the Republic, our Nation must continue to provide—as indeed all other free governments have had to do throughout time—a satisfactory answer to a question as old as history. It is: Can Government based upon liberty and the God-given rights of man, permanently endure when ceaselessly challenged by a dictatorship, hostile to our mode of life, and controlling an economic and military strength of great and growing power?

For us the answer has always been found, and is still found in the devotion, the vision, the courage and the fortitude of our people.

Moreover, this challenge we face, not as a single powerful nation, but as one that has in recent decades reached a position of recognized leadership in the free world.

We have arrived at this position of leadership in an era of remarkable productivity and growth. It is also a time when man's power of mass destruction has reached fearful proportions.

Possession of such capabilities helps create world suspicion and tension. We, on our part, know that we seek only a just peace for all, with aggressive designs against no one. Yet we realize that there is uneasiness in the world because of a belief on the part of peoples that through arrogance, miscalculation, the fear of attack, catastrophic war could be launched. Keeping the peace in today's world more than ever calls for the utmost in the Nation's resolution, wisdom, steadiness and unremitting effort.

We cannot build peace through desire alone. Moreover, we have learned the bitter lesson that international agreements, historically considered by us as sacred, are regarded in Communist doctrine and in practice to be mere scraps of paper. The most recent proof of their disdain of international obligations, solemnly undertaken, is their announced intention to abandon their responsibilities respecting Berlin.

As a consequence of these actions we can have no confidence in any treaty to which Communists are a party except where such a treaty provides within itself for self-enforcing mechanisms. Indeed, the demonstrated disregard of the Communists of their own pledges is one of the greatest obstacles to world success in substituting the rule of law for rule by force.

Yet step by step we must strengthen the institutions of peace—a peace that rests upon justice—a peace that depends upon a deep knowledge and clear understanding by all peoples, including our own, of the consequences of failure in this great purpose.

I

To achieve this peace we seek to prevent war at any place and in any dimension. If, despite our best efforts, a local dispute should flare into armed hostilities, the next problem would be to keep the conflict from spreading, and so compromising freedom. In support of these objectives we maintain forces of great power and flexibility.

Our formidable air striking forces are a powerful deterrent to general war. Large and growing portions of these units can depart from their bases in a matter of minutes.

Similar forces are included in our naval fleets.

Ground and other tactical formations can move with swiftness and precision, when requested by friendly and responsible governments, to help curb threatened aggression. The stabilizing influence of this capacity has been dramatically demonstrated more than once over the past year.

Our military and related scientific progress has been highly gratifying.

Great strides have been made in the development of ballistic missiles. Intermediate range missiles are now being deployed in operational units. The Atlas intercontinental ballistic missile program has been marked by rapid development as evidenced by recent successful tests. Missile training units have been established and launching sites are far along in construction.

New aircraft that fly at twice the speed of sound are entering our squadrons.

We have successfully placed five satellites in orbit, which have gathered information of scientific importance never before available. Our latest satellite illustrates our steady advance in rocketry and foreshadows new developments in world-wide communications.

Warning systems constantly improve.

Our atomic submarines have shattered endurance records and made historic voyages under the North Polar Sea.

A major segment of our national scientific and engineering community is working intensively to achieve new and greater developments. Advance in military technology requires adequate financing but, of course, even more, it requires talent and time.

All this I give only as a matter of history, as a record of our progress in space and ballistic missile fields in no more than 4 years of intensive effort. At the same time we clearly recognize that some of the recent Soviet accomplishments in this particular technology are indeed brilliant.

Under the law enacted last year the Department of Defense is being reorganized to give the Secretary of Defense full authority over the Military Establishment. Greater efficiency, more cohesive effort, and speedier reaction to emergencies are among the many advantages we are already noting from these changes.

These few highlights point up our steady military gains. We are rightfully gratified by the achievements they represent. New and greater developments preoccupy the major portion of the Nation's scientists. But we must remember that these imposing armaments are purchased at great cost.

National security programs account for nearly 60 percent of the entire Federal budget for this coming fiscal year.

Modern weapons are exceedingly expensive.

The overall cost of introducing Atlas into our Armed Forces will average $35 million per missile on the firing line.

This year we are investing an aggregate of close to $7 billion in missile programs alone.

Other billions go for research, development, test, and evaluation of new weapons systems.

Our latest atomic submarines will cost $50 million each, while some special types will cost three times as much.

We are now ordering fighter aircraft which are priced at 50 times as much as the fighters of World War II.

We are buying certain bombers that cost their weight in gold, exactly.

These sums are tremendous, even when compared with the marvelous resiliency and capacity of our economy.

Such expenditures demand both balance and perspective in our planning for defense. At every turn, we must weigh, judge, and select. Needless duplication of weapons and forces must be avoided.

We must guard against feverish building of vast armaments to meet glibly predicted moments of so-called maximum peril. The threat we face is not sporadic or dated; it is continuous. Hence we must not be swayed in our calculations either by groundless fear or by complacency. We must avoid extremes, for vacillation between extremes is inefficient, costly, and destructive of morale. In these days of unceasing technological advance, we must plan our defense expenditures systematically and with care, fully recognizing that obsolescence compels the never-ending replacement of older weapons with new ones.

The defense budget for the coming year has been planned on the basis of these principles and considerations. Over these many months I have personally participated in its development.

The aim is a sensible posture of defense. The secondary aim is increased efficiency and avoidance of waste. Both are achieved by this budgetary plan.

Working by these guidelines I believe with all my heart that America can be as sure of the strength and efficiency of her Armed Forces as she is of their loyalty. I am equally sure that the Nation will thus avoid useless expenditures which, in the name of security, might tend to undermine the economy and, therefore, the Nation's safety.

* * *

Our own vast strength is only a part of that required for dependable security. Because of this we have joined with nearly 50 other nations in collective security arrangements. In these common undertakings each nation is expected to contribute what it can in sharing the heavy load. Each supplies part of a strategic deployment to protect the forward boundaries of freedom.

Constantly we seek new ways to make more effective our contribution to this system of collective security. Recently I have asked a committee of eminent Americans of both parties to reappraise our military assistance programs and the relative emphasis which should be placed on military and economic aid.

I am hopeful that preliminary recommendations of this committee will be available in time to assist in shaping the mutual security program for the coming fiscal year.

Any survey of the free world's defense structure cannot fail to impart a feeling of regret that so much of our effort and resources must be devoted to armaments. At Geneva and elsewhere we continue to seek technical and other agreements that may help to open up, with some promise, the issues of international disarmament. America will never give up the hope that eventually all nations can, with mutual confidence, drastically reduce these nonproductive expenditures.

II

The material foundation of our national safety is a strong and expanding economy. This we have—and this we must maintain. Only with such an economy can we be secure and simultaneously provide for the well-being of our people.

A year ago the Nation was experiencing a decline in employment and in output. Today that recession is fading into history, and this without gigantic, hastily improvised public works projects or untimely tax reductions. A healthy and vigorous recovery has been underway since last May. New homes are being built at the highest rate in several years. Retail sales are at peak levels. Personal income is at an alltime high.

The marked forward thrust of our economy reaffirms our confidence in competitive enterprise. But—clearly—wisdom and prudence in both the public and private sectors of the economy are always necessary.

The outlook is this: 1960 commitments for our Armed Forces, the Atomic Energy Commission and military assistance, exceed $47 billion. In the foreseeable future they are not likely to be significantly lower. With an annual population increase of 3 million, other governmental costs are bound to mount.

After we have provided wisely for our military strength, we must judge how to allocate our remaining Government resources most effectively to promote our well-being and our economic growth.

Federal programs that will benefit all citizens are moving forward.

Next year we will be spending increased amounts on health programs—

On Federal assistance to science and education;
On the development of the Nation's water resources;
On the renewal of urban areas; and
On our vast system of Federal-aid highways.

Each of these additional outlays is being made necessary by the surging growth of America.

Let me illustrate. Responsive to this growth, Federal grants and long-term loans to assist 14 major types of capital improvements in our cities will total over $2 billion in 1960, and this figure is double the expenditure of 2 years ago. The major responsibility for development in these fields rests in the localities, even though the Federal Government will continue to do its proper part in meeting the genuine needs of a burgeoning population.

But the progress of our economy can more than match the growth of our needs. We need only to act wisely and confidently.

Here, I hope you will permit me to digress long enough to express something that is much on my mind.

As I said in the beginning, the basic question facing us today is more than mere survival—the military defense of national life and territory. It is the preservation of a way of life.

We must meet the world challenge and at the same time permit no stagnation in America.

Unless we progress, we regress.

We can successfully sustain security and remain true to our heritage of freedom if we clearly visualize the tasks ahead and set out to perform them with resolution and vigor. We must first define these tasks and then understand what we must do to perform them.

If progress is to be steady we must have long-term guides extending far ahead, certainly 5, possibly even 10 years. They must reflect the knowledge that before the end of 5 years we will have a population of more than 190 million. They must be goals that stand high, and so inspire every citizen to climb always toward mounting levels of moral, intellectual, and material strength. Every advance toward them cannot do other than serve to stir pride in individual and national achievements.

To define these goals, I intend to mobilize help from every available source.

We need more than politically ordained national objectives if we are to challenge the best efforts of free men and women. A group of selfless, able and devoted individuals, outside of Government, could effectively participate in making the necessary appraisal of the potentials of our future.

The result would be the establishment of national goals that would not only spur us on the our finest efforts, but also would meet the stern test of practicality.

The Committee I plan will comprise educators and representatives of labor, management, finance, the professions, and every other kind of useful activity.

Such a study would update and supplement, in the light of continuous changes in our society and its economy, the monumental work of the Committee on Recent Social Trends which was appointed in 1931 by President Hoover. Its report has stood the test of time and has had a beneficial influence on national development.

The new Committee would be concerned, among other things, with the living standards of our people, their health and education, their better assurance of life and liberty, and their greater opportunities. It would also be concerned with methods to meet such goals and what levels of government—local, State, or Federal—might or should be particularly concerned.

As one example, consider our schools, operated under the authority of local communities and States. In their capacity and in their quality they conform to no recognizable standards. In some places facilities are ample, in others meager. Pay of teachers ranges between wide limits, from the adequate to the shameful. As would be expected, quality of teaching varies just as widely. But to our teachers we commit the most valuable possession of the Nation and of the family—our children.

We must have teachers of competence. To obtain and hold them we need standards. We need a national goal. Once established I am certain that public opinion would compel steady progress toward its accomplishment.

Such studies would be helpful, I believe, to government at all levels and to all individuals. The goals so established could help us see our current problems in perspective. They will spur progress.

We do not forget, of course, that our Nation's progress and fiscal integrity are interdependent and inseparable. We can afford everything we clearly need, but we cannot afford one cent of waste. We must examine every item of governmental expense critically. To do otherwise would betray our Nation's future.

Thrift is one of the characteristics that have made this Nation great; why should we ignore it now?

We must avoid any contribution to inflationary processes which could disrupt sound growth in our economy.

Prices have displayed a welcome stability in recent months and, if we are wise and resolute, we will not tolerate inflation in the years to come. But history makes clear the risks inherent in any failure to deal firmly with the basic causes of inflation. Two of the most important of these causes are the wage-price spiral and continued deficit financing.

Inflation would reduce job opportunities, price us out of world markets, shrink the value of savings, and penalize the thrift so essential to finance a growing economy.

Inflation is not a Robin Hood, taking from the rich to give to the poor. Rather, it deals most cruelly with those who can least protect themselves. It strikes hardest those millions of our citizens whose incomes do not quickly rise with the cost of living. When prices soar, the pensioner and the widow see their security undermined, the man of thrift sees his savings melt away; the white-collar worker, the minister, and the teacher see their standards of living dragged down.

Inflation can be prevented. But this demands statesmanship on the part of business and labor leaders and of government at all levels.

We must encourage the self-discipline, the restraint necessary to curb the wage-price spiral and, except only in critical emergencies, we must meet current costs from current revenue.

To minimize the danger of future soaring prices and to keep our economy sound and expanding, I shall present to the Congress certain proposals.

First, I shall submit a balanced budget for the next year, a year expected to be the most prosperous of our entire history. It is a realistic budget with wholly attainable objectives.

If we cannot live within our means during such a time of rising prosperity, the hope for fiscal integrity will fade; and if we persist in living beyond our means we make it difficult for every family in our land to balance its own household budget. But to live within our means would be a tangible demonstration to ourselves and to others of the self-discipline needed to assure a stable dollar.

The Constitution entrusts the Executive with many functions, but the Congress—and the Congress alone—has the power of the purse. Ultimately upon Congress rests responsibility for determining the scope and amount of Federal spending.

By working together, the Congress and the Executive can keep a balance between income and outgo. If this is done there is real hope that we can look forward to a time in the foreseeable future when needed tax reforms can be accomplished.

In this hope, I am requesting the Secretary of the Treasury to prepare appropriate proposals for revising, at the proper time, our tax structure, to remove inequities and to enhance incentives for all Americans to work, to save, and to invest. Such recommendations will be made as quickly as our fiscal condition permits. These prospects will be brightened if 1960 expenditures do not exceed the levels recommended.

Second, I shall recommend to the Congress that the Chief Executive be given the responsibility either to approve or to veto specific items of appropriations and authorization bills. I assure you gentlemen that I know this recommendation has been made time and again by every President that has appeared in this Hall for many years, but I say this, it still is one of the most important corrections that could be made in our annual expenditure program, because this would save tax dollars.

Third, to reduce Federal operations in an area where private enterprise can do the job, I shall recommend legislation for greater flexibility in extending Federal credit, and in improving the procedures under which private credits are insured or guaranteed. Present practices have needlessly added large sums to Federal expenditures.

Fourth, action is required to make more effective use of the large Federal expenditures for agriculture and to achieve greater fiscal control in this area.

Outlays of the Department of Agriculture for the current fiscal year, for the support of farm prices on a very few farm products, will exceed $5 billion. That is a sum equal to approximately two-fifths of the net income of all farm operators in the United States.

By the end of this fiscal year it is estimated that there will be in Government hands surplus farm products worth about $9 billion. And by July 1, 1959, Government expenditures for storage, interest, and handling of its agricultural inventory will reach a rate of $1 billion a year.

This level of expenditure for farm products could be made willingly for a temporary period if it were leading to a sound solution of the problem. But unfortunately this is not true. We need new legislation.

In the past I have sent messages to the Congress requesting greater freedom for our farmers to manage their own farms and greater freedom for markets to reflect the wishes of producers and consumers. Legislative changes that followed were appropriate in direction but did not go far enough.

The situation calls for prompt and forthright action. Recommendation for action will be contained in a message to be transmitted to the Congress shortly.

* * *

These fiscal and related actions will help create an environment of price stability for economic growth. However, certain additional measures are needed.

I shall ask Congress to amend the Employment Act of 1946 to make it clear that Government intends to use all appropriate means to protect the buying power of the dollar.

I am establishing a continuing Cabinet group on price stability for economic growth to study governmental and private policies affecting costs, prices, and economic growth. It will strive also to build a better public understanding of the conditions necessary for maintaining growth and price stability.

Studies are being undertaken to improve our information on prices, wages, and productivity.

I believe all citizens in all walks of life will support this program of action to accelerate economic growth and promote price stability.

III

I take up next certain aspects of our international situation and our progress to strengthen it.

America's security can be assured only within a world community of strong, stable, independent nations, in which the concepts of freedom, justice, and human dignity can flourish.

There can be no such thing as Fortress America. If ever we were reduced to the isolation implied by that term, we would occupy a prison, not a fortress. The question whether we can afford to help other nations that want to defend their freedom but cannot fully do so from their own means, has only one answer: We can and we must, as we have been doing so since 1947.

Our foreign policy has long been dedicated to building a permanent and just peace.

During the past 6 years our free world security arrangements have been bolstered and the bonds of freedom have been more closely knit. Our friends in Western Europe are experiencing new internal vitality, and are increasingly more able to resist external threats.

Over the years the world has come to understand clearly that it is our firm policy not to countenance aggression. In Lebanon, Taiwan, and Berlin our stand has been clear, right, and expressive of the determined will of a united people.

Acting with other free nations we have undertaken the solemn obligation to defend the people of free Berlin against any effort to destroy their freedom. In the meantime we shall constantly seek meaningful agreements to settle this and other problems, knowing full well that not only the integrity of a single city but the hope of all free peoples is at stake.

We need, likewise, to continue helping to build the economic base so essential to the free world's stability and strength.

The International Monetary Fund and the World Bank have both fully proven their worth as instruments of international financial cooperation. Their Executive Directors have recommended an increase in each member country's subscription. I am requesting the Congress for immediate approval of our share of these increases.

We are now negotiating with representatives of the 20 Latin American Republics for the creation of an inter-American financial institution. Its purpose would be to join all the American Republics in a common institution which would promote and finance development in Latin America. One great result of this would be to make more effective use of capital from the World Bank, the Export-Import Bank, and private sources.

Private enterprise continues to make major contributions to economic development in all parts of the world. But we have not yet marshaled the full potential of American business for this task, particularly in countries which have recently attained their independence. I shall present to this Congress a program designed to encourage greater participation by private enterprise in economic development abroad.

Further, all of us know that to advance the cause of freedom we must do much more than help build sound economies. The spiritual, intellectual, and physical strength of people throughout the world will in the last analysis determine their willingness and their ability to resist communism.

To give a single illustration of our many efforts in these fields: We have been a participant in the effort that has been made over the past few years against one of the great scourges of mankind—disease. Through the mutual security program public health officials are being trained by American universities to serve in less developed countries. We are engaged in intensive malaria eradication projects in many parts of the world in this work. America's major successes in our own country prove the feasibility of success everywhere.

By these and other means we shall continue and expand our campaign against the afflictions that now bring needless suffering and death to so many of the world's people. We wish to be part of a great shared effort toward the triumph of health.

I think most of us would agree that America is best described by one word, "freedom."

If we hope to strengthen freedom in the world we must be ever mindful of how our own conduct reacts elsewhere. No nation has ever been so floodlighted by world opinion as the United States is today. Everything we do is carefully scrutinized by other peoples throughout the world. The bad is seen along with the good.

Because we are human we err. But as free men we are also responsible for correcting the errors and imperfections of our ways.

Last January I made comprehensive recommendations to the Congress for legislation in the labor-management field. To my disappointment, Congress failed to act. The McClellan committee disclosures of corruption, racketeering, and abuse of trust and power in labor-management affairs have aroused America and amazed other peoples. Its disclosures emphasize the need for improved local law enforcement and the enactment of effective Federal legislation to protect the public interest and to insure the rights and economic freedoms of millions of American workers. Halfhearted measures will not do. I shall recommend prompt enactment of legislation designed—

To safeguard workers' funds in union treasuries against misuse of any kind whatsoever;

To protect the rights and freedoms of individual union members, including the basic right to free and secret elections of officers;

To advance true and responsible collective bargaining;

To protect the public and innocent third parties from unfair and coercive practices, such as boycotting and blackmail picketing.

The workers and the public must have these vital protections.

In other areas of human rights—freedom from discrimination in voting, in public education, in access to jobs, and in other respects—the world is likewise watching our conduct.

The image of America abroad is not improved when schoolchildren, through closing of some of our schools and through no fault of their own, are deprived of their opportunity for an education.

The government of a free people has no purpose more noble than to work for the maximum realization of equality of opportunity under law. That is the concept under which our founding papers were written. This is not the sole responsibility of any one branch of our Government. The judicial arm, which has the ultimate authority for interpreting the Constitution, has held that certain State laws and practices discriminate upon racial grounds and are unconstitutional. Whenever the supremacy of the Constitution of the United States is challenged, I shall continue to take every proper action necessary to uphold it.

One of the fundamental concepts of our constitutional system is that it guarantees to every individual, regardless of race, religion, or national origin, the equal protection of the laws. Those of us who are privileged to hold public office have a solemn obligation to make meaningful this inspiring objective. We can fulfill that obligation by our leadership in teaching, persuading, demonstrating, and in enforcing the law.

We are now making noticeable progress in the field of civil rights—we are moving forward toward achievement of equality of opportunity for all people everywhere in the United States. In the interest of the Nation and of each of its citizens, that progress must continue.

Legislative proposals of the administration in this field will be submitted to the Congress early in the session. All of us should help to make clear that the Government is united in the common purpose of giving support to the law and the decisions of the courts.

* * *

Finally, by moving steadily toward the goal of greater freedom under law, for our own people, we shall be the better prepared to work for the cause of freedom under law throughout the world.

All peoples are sorely tired of the fear, destruction, and the waste of war. As never before, the world knows the human and material costs of war and seeks to replace force with a genuine rule of law among nations.

It is my purpose to intensify efforts during the coming 2 years in seeking ways to supplement the procedures of the United Nations and other bodies with similar objectives, to the end that the rule of law may replace the rule of force in the affairs of nations. Measures toward this end will be proposed later, including a reexamination of our own relation to the International Court of Justice.

And lastly, let us remind ourselves that Marxist scripture is not new; it is not the gospel of the future. Its basic objective is dictatorship, old as history. What is new is the shining prospect that man can build a world where all can live in dignity.

We seek victory—not over any nation or people—but over the

ancient enemies of us all; victory over ignorance, poverty, disease, and human degradation wherever they may be found.

We march in the noblest of causes—human freedom.

If we make ourselves worthy of America's ideals, if we do not forget that our Nation was founded on the premise that all men are creatures of God's making, the world will come to know that it is free men who carry forward the true promise of human progress and dignity.

EIGHTH ANNUAL MESSAGE.

THE WHITE HOUSE, *January 7, 1960.*

MR. PRESIDENT, MR. SPEAKER, MEMBERS OF THE 86TH CONGRESS, MY FELLOW CITIZENS:

Seven years ago I entered my present office with one long-held resolve overriding all others. I was then, and remain now, determined that the United States shall become an ever more potent resource for the cause of peace—realizing that peace cannot be for ourselves alone, but for peoples everywhere. This determination is, I know, shared by the entire Congress—indeed, by all Americans.

My purpose today is to discuss some features of America's position, both at home and in her relations to others.

First, I point out that for us, annual self-examination is made a definite necessity by the fact that we now live in a divided world of uneasy equilibrium, with our side committed to its own protection and against aggression by the other.

With both sections of this divided world in possession of unbelievably destructive weapons, mankind approaches a state where mutual annihilation becomes a possibility. No other fact of today's world equals this in importance—it colors everything we say, plan, and do.

There is demanded of us vigilance, determination, and the dedication of whatever portion of our resources that will provide adequate security, especially provide a real deterrent to aggression. These things we are doing.

All these facts emphasize the importance of striving incessantly for a just peace.

Only through the strengthening of the spiritual, intellectual, economic, and defensive resources of the free world can we, in confidence, make progress toward this goal.

Second, we note that recent Soviet deportment and pronouncements suggest the possible opening of a somewhat less strained period in the relationships between the Soviet Union and the rest of the world. If these pronouncements be genuine, there is brighter hope of diminishing the intensity of past rivalry and eventually of substituting persuasion for coercion. Whether this is to become an era of lasting promise remains to be tested by actions.

Third, we now stand in the vestibule of a vast new technological age—one that, despite its capacity for human destruction, has an equal capacity to make poverty and human misery obsolete. If our efforts are wisely directed—and if our unremitting efforts for dependable peace begin to attain some success—we can surely become participants in creating an age characterized by justice and rising levels of human well-being.

Over the past year the Soviet Union has expressed an interest in measures to reduce the common peril of war.

While neither we nor any other free world nation can permit ourselves to be misled by pleasant promises until they are tested by performance, yet we approach this apparently new opportunity with the utmost seriousness. We must strive to break the calamitous cycle of frustrations and crises which, if unchecked, could spiral into nuclear disaster; the ultimate insanity.

Though the need for dependable agreements to assure against resort to force in settling disputes is apparent to both sides yet as in other issues dividing men and nations, we cannot expect sudden and revolutionary results. But we must find some place to begin.

One obvious road on which to make a useful start is in the widening of communication between our two peoples. In this field there are, both sides willing, countless opportunities—most of them well known to us all—for developing mutual understanding, the true foundation of peace.

Another avenue may be through the reopening, on January 12, of negotiations looking to a controlled ban on the testing of nuclear weapons. Unfortunately, the closing statement from the Soviet scientists who met with our scientists at Geneva gives the clear impression that their conclusions have been politically guided. Those of the British and American scientific representatives are their own freely formed, individual and collective opinions. I am hopeful that, as new negotiations begin, truth—not political opportunism—will guide the deliberations.

Still another field may be found in the field of disarmament, in which the Soviets have professed a readiness to negotiate seriously. They have not, however, made clear the plans they may have, if any, for mutual inspection and verification—the essential condition for any extensive measure of disarmament.

There is one instance where our initiative for peace has recently been successful. A multilateral treaty signed last month provides for the exclusively peaceful use of Antarctica, assured by a system of inspection. It provides for free and cooperative scientific research in that continent, and prohibits nuclear explosions there pending general international agreement on the subject. I shall transmit its text to the Senate for consideration and approval in the near future. The treaty is a significant contribution toward peace, international cooperation, and the advancement of science.

The United States is always ready to participate with the Soviet Union in serious discussion of these or any other subjects that may lead to peace with justice.

Certainly it is not necessary to repeat that the United States has no intention of interfering in the internal affairs of any nation; by the same token we reject any attempt to impose its system on us or on other peoples by force or subversion.

This concern for the freedom of other peoples is the intellectual and spiritual cement which has allied us with more than 40 other nations in a common defense effort. Not for a moment do we forget that our own fate is firmly fastened to that of these countries; we will not act in any way which would jeopardize our solemn commitments to them.

We and our friends are, of course, concerned with self-defense. Growing out of this concern is the realization that all people of the free world have a great stake in the progress, in freedom, of the uncommitted and newly emerging nations. These peoples, desperately hoping to lift themselves to decent levels of living must not, by our neglect, be forced to seek help from, and finally become virtual satellites of, those who proclaim their hostility to freedom.

Their natural desire for a better life must not be frustrated by withholding from them necessary technical and investment assistance. This is a problem to be solved not by America alone, but also by every nation cherishing the same ideals and in position to provide help.

In recent years America's partners and friends in Western Europe and Japan have made great economic progress. Their newly found economic strength is eloquent testimony to the striking success of the policies of economic cooperation which we and they have pursued.

The international economy of 1960 is markedly different from that of the early postwar years. No longer is the United States the only major industrial country capable of providing substantial amounts of the resources so urgently needed in the newly developing countries.

To remain secure and prosperous themselves, wealthy nations must extend the kind of cooperation to the less fortunate members that will inspire hope, confidence, and progress. A rich nation can for a time, without noticeable damage to itself, pursue a course of self-indulgence, making its single goal the material ease and comfort of its own citizens—thus repudiating its own spiritual and material stake in a peaceful and prosperous society of nations. But the enmities it will incur, the isolation into which it will descend, and the internal moral, spiritual, economic, and political softness that will be engendered, will, in the long term, bring it to disaster.

America did not become great through softness and self-indulgence. Her miraculous progress and achievements flow from other qualities far more worthy and substantial—

Adherence to principles and methods consonant with our religious philosophy;

A satisfaction in hard work;

The readiness to sacrifice for worthwhile causes;

The courage to meet every challenge;

The intellectual honesty and capacity to recognize the true path of her own best interests.

To us and to every nation of the free world, rich or poor, these qualities are necessary today as never before if we are to march together to greater security, prosperity, and peace.

I believe the industrial countries are ready to participate actively in supplementing the efforts of the developing nations to achieve progress.

The immediate need for this kind of cooperation is underscored by the strain in our international balance of payments. Our surplus from foreign business transactions has in recent years fallen substantially short of the expenditures we make abroad to maintain our military establishments overseas, to finance private investment, and to provide assistance to the less developed nations. In 1959 our deficit in balance of payments approached $4 billion.

Continuing deficits of anything like this magnitude would, over time, impair our own economic growth and check the forward progress of the free world.

We must meet this situation by promoting a rising volume of exports and world trade. Further, we must induce all industrialized nations of the free world to work together to help lift the scourge of poverty from less fortunate nations. This will provide for better sharing of this burden and for still further profitable trade.

New nations, and others struggling with the problems of development, will progress only, regardless of any outside help, if they demonstrate faith in their own destiny and possess the will and use their own resources to fulfill it. Moreover, progress in a national transformation can be only gradually earned; there is no easy and quick way to follow from the ox cart to the jet plane. But, just as we drew on Europe for assistance in our earlier years, so now do those new and emerging nations that have this faith and determination deserve help.

Over the last 15 years, 20 nations have gained political independence. Others are doing so each year. Most of them are woefully lacking in technical capacity and in investment capital; without free-world support in these matters they cannot effectively progress in freedom.

Respecting their need, one of the major focal points of our concern is the south Asian region. Here, in two nations alone, are almost 500 million people, all working, and working hard, to raise their standards, and, in doing so, to make of themselves a strong bulwark against the spread of an ideology that would destroy liberty.

I cannot express to you the depth of my conviction that, in our own and free-world interests, we must cooperate with others to help these people achieve their legitimate ambitions, as expressed in their different multiyear plans. Through the World Bank and other instrumentalities, as well as through individual action by every nation in position to help, we must squarely face this titanic challenge.

All of us must realize, of course, that development in freedom by the newly emerging nations, is no mere matter of obtaining outside financial assistance. An indispensable element in this process is a strong and continuing determination on the part of these nations to exercise the national discipline necessary for any sustained development period. These qualities of determination are particularly essential because of the fact that the process of improvement will necessarily be gradual and laborious rather than revolutionary. Moreover, everyone should be aware that the development process is no short-term phenomenon. Many years are required for even the most favorably situated countries.

I shall continue to urge the American people, in the interests of their own security, prosperity, and peace, to make sure that their own part of this great project be amply and cheerfully supported. Free-world decisions in this matter may spell the difference between world disaster and world progress in freedom.

Other countries, some of which I visited last month, have similar needs.

A common meeting ground is desirable for those nations which are prepared to assist in the development effort. During the past year I have discussed this matter with the leaders of several western nations.

Because of its wealth of experience, the Organization for European Economic Cooperation could help with initial studies needed. The goal is to enlist all available economic resources in the industrialized free world—especially private investment capital. But I repeat that this help, no matter how great, can be lastingly effective only if it is used as a supplement to the strength of spirit and will of the people of the newly developing nations.

By extending this help we hope to make possible the enthusiastic enrollment of these nations under freedom's banner. No more startling contrast to a system of sullen satellites could be imagined. If we grasp this opportunity to build an age of productive partnership between the less fortunate nations and those that have already achieved a high state of economic advancement, we will make brighter the outlook for a world order based upon security, freedom, and peace. Otherwise, the outlook could be dark indeed. We face what may be a turning point in history, and we must act decisively.

As a nation we can successfully pursue these objectives only from a position of broadly based strength.

No matter how earnest is our quest for guaranteed peace, we must maintain a high degree of military effectiveness at the same time we are engaged in negotiating the issue of arms reduction. Until tangible and mutually enforceable arms reduction measures are worked out, we will not weaken the means of defending our institutions.

America possesses an enormous defense power. It is my studied conviction that no nation will ever risk general war against us unless we should be so foolish as to neglect the defense forces we now so powerfully support. It is worldwide knowledge that any nation which might be tempted today to attack the United States, even though our country might sustain great losses, would itself promptly suffer a terrible destruction. But I once again assure all peoples and all nations that the United States, except in defense, will never turn loose this destructive power.

During the past year our long-range striking power, unmatched today in manned bombers, has taken on new strength as the Atlas intercontinental ballistic missile has entered the operational inventory. In 14 recent test launchings, at ranges of over 5,000 miles, Atlas has been striking on an average within 2 miles of the target. This is less than the length of a jet runway—well within the circle of total destruction. Incidentally, there was an Atlas firing last night. From all reports so far received, its performance conformed to the high standards I have described. Such performance is a great tribute to American scientists and engineers, who in the past 5 years have had to telescope time and technology to develop these long-range ballistic missiles, where America had none before.

This year, moreover, growing numbers of nuclear-powered submarines will enter our active forces, some to be armed with Polaris missiles. These remarkable ships and weapons, ranging the oceans, will be capable of accurate fire on targets virtually anywhere on earth. Impossible to destroy by surprise attack, they will become one of our most effective sentinels for peace.

To meet situations of less than general nuclear war, we continue to maintain our carrier forces, our many service units abroad, our always ready Army strategic forces and Marine Corps divisions, and the civilian components. The continuing modernization of these forces is a costly but necessary process, and is scheduled to go forward at a rate which will steadily add to our strength.

The deployment of a portion of these forces beyond our shores, on land and sea, is persuasive demonstration of our determination to stand shoulder-to-shoulder with our allies for collective security. Moreover, I have directed that steps be taken to program our military assistance to these allies on a longer range basis. This is necessary for a sounder collective defense system.

Next I refer to our program in space exploration, which is often mistakenly supposed to be an integral part of defense research and development.

We note that, first, America has made great contributions in the past 2 years to the world's fund of knowledge of astrophysics and space science. These discoveries are of present interest chiefly to the scientific community; but they are important foundation stones for more extensive exploration of outer space for the ultimate benefit of all mankind.

Second, our military missile program, going forward so successfully, does not suffer from our present lack of very large rocket engines, which are so necessary in distant space exploration. I am assured by experts that the thrust of our present missiles is fully adequate for defense requirements.

Third, the United States is pressing forward in the development of large rocket engines to place vehicles of many tons into space for exploration purposes.

Fourth, in the meantime, it is necessary to remember that we have only begun to probe the environment immediately surrounding the earth. Using launch systems presently available, we are developing satellites to scout the world's weather; satellite relay stations to facilitate and extend communications over the globe; for navigation aids to give accurate bearings to ships and aircraft; and for perfecting instruments to collect and transmit the data we seek. This is the area holding the most promise for early and useful applications of space technology.

Fifth, we have just completed a year's experience with our new space law. I believe it deficient in certain particulars and suggested improvements will be submitted to the Congress shortly.

The accomplishment of the many tasks I have alluded to requires the continuous strengthening of the spiritual, intellectual, and economic sinews of American life. The steady purpose of our society is to assure justice, before God, for every individual. We must be ever alert that freedom does not wither through the careless amassing of restrictive controls or the lack of courage to deal boldly with the giant issues of the day.

A year ago, when I met with you, the Nation was emerging from an economic downturn, even though the signs of resurgent prosperity were not then sufficiently convincing to the doubtful. Today our surging strength is apparent to everyone; 1960 promises to be the most prosperous year in our history.

Yet we continue to be afflicted by nagging disorders.

Among current problems that require solution participated in by citizens as well as Government are—

The need to protect the public interest in situations of prolonged labor-management stalemate;

The persistent refusal to come to grips with a critical problem in one sector of American agriculture;

The continuing threat of inflation, together with the persisting tendency toward fiscal irresponsibility;

In certain instances the denial to some of our citizens of equal protection of the law.

Every American was disturbed by the prolonged dispute in the steel industry and the protracted delay in reaching a settlement.

We are all relieved that a settlement has at last been achieved in that industry. Percentagewise, by this settlement the increase to the steel companies in employment costs is lower than in any prior wage settlement since World War II. It is also gratifying to note that despite the increase in wages and benefits several of the major steel producers have announced that there will be no increase in steel prices at this time. The national interest demands that in the period of industrial peace which has been assured by the new contract, both management and labor make every possible effort to increase efficiency and productivity in the manufacture of steel so that price increases can be avoided.

One of the lessons of this story is that the potential danger to the entire Nation of longer and greater strikes must be met. To insure against such possibilities we must of course depend primarily upon the good commonsense of the responsible individuals. It is my intention to encourage regular discussions between management and labor outside the bargaining table, to consider the interest of the public as well as their mutual interest in the maintenance of industrial peace, price stability, incentive for continuous investment, and economic growth. Both the Executive and the Congress will, I know, be watching developments with keenest interest.

To me, it seems almost absurd that the United States should recognize the need, and so earnestly to seek, for cooperation among the nations unless we can achieve voluntary, dependable, abiding cooperation among the important segments of our own free society. Without such cooperation we cannot prosper.

Failure to face up to basic issues in areas other than those of labor-management can cause serious strains on the firm freedom supports of our society.

Agriculture is one of these areas.

Our basic farm laws were written 27 years ago, in an emergency effort to redress hardship caused by a worldwide depression. They were continued—and their economic distortions intensified—during World War II in order to provide incentives for production of food needed to sustain a war-torn world.

Today our farm problem is totally different. It is that of effectively adjusting to the changes caused by a scientific revolution. When the original farm laws were written, an hour's farm labor produced only one-fourth as much wheat as at present. Farm legislation is woefully out of date, ineffective, and expensive.

For years we have gone on with an outmoded system which not only has failed to protect farm income, but also has produced soaring, threatening surpluses. Our farms have been left producing for war while America has long been at peace.

Once again I urge Congress to enact legislation that will gear production more closely to markets, make costly surpluses more manageable, provide greater freedom in farm operations, and steadily achieve increased net farm incomes.

Another issue that we must meet squarely is that of living within our means. This requires restraint in expenditure, constant reassessment of priorities, and the maintenance of stable prices.

To do so we must prevent inflation. Here is an opponent of so many guises that it is sometimes difficult to recognize. But our clear need is to stop continuous and general price rises—a need that all of us can see and feel.

To prevent steadily rising costs and prices calls for stern self-discipline by every citizen. No person, city, State, or organized group can afford to evade the obligation to resist inflation, for every single American pays its crippling tax.

Inflation's ravages do not end at the water's edge. Increases in prices of the goods we sell abroad threaten to drive us out of markets that once were securely ours. Whether domestic prices, so high as to be noncompetitive, result from demands for too-high profit margins or from increased labor costs that outrun growth in productivity, the final result is seriously damaging to the Nation.

We must fight inflation as we would a fire that imperils our home. Only by so doing can we prevent it from destroying our salaries, savings, pensions, and insurance, and from gnawing away the very roots of a free, healthy economy and the Nation's security.

One major method by which the Federal Government can counter inflation and rising prices is to insure that its expenditures are below its revenues. The debt with which we are now confronted is about $290 billion. With interest charges alone now costing taxpayers about $9½ billion, it is clear that this debt growth must stop. You will be glad to know that despite the unsettling influences of the recent steel strike, we estimate that our accounts will show, on June 30, this year, a favorable balance of approximately $200 million.

I shall present to the Congress for 1961 a balanced budget. In the area of defense, expenditures continue at the record peacetime levels of the last several years. With a single exception, expenditures in every major category of health, education, and welfare will be equal or greater than last year. In space expenditures the amounts are practically doubled. But the overall guiding goal of this budget is national need—not response to specific group, local or political insistence.

Expenditure increases, other than those I have indicated, are largely accounted for by the increased cost of legislation previously enacted. I repeat, this budget will be a balanced one. Expenditures will be $79,800 million. The amount of income over outgo described in the budget as a surplus to be applied against our national debt is $4,200 million.

Personally, I do not feel that any amount can be properly called a surplus as long as the Nation is in debt; I prefer to think of such an item as a reduction of our children's inherited mortgage. And once we have established such payments as normal practices we can profitably make improvements in our tax structure and thereby truly reduce the heavy burdens of taxation. In any event this one reduction will save taxpayers each year approximately $200 million in interest costs.

This favorable balance will help ease pressures in our credit and capital markets. It will enhance the confidence of people all over the world in the strength of our economy and our currency and in our individual and collective ability to be fiscally responsible.

In the management of the huge public debt the Treasury is unfortunately not free of artificial barriers. Its ability to deal with the difficult problems in this field has been weakened greatly by the unwillingness of the Congress to remove archaic restrictions. The need for a freer hand in debt management is even more urgent today because the costs of the undesirable financing practices which the Treasury has been forced into are mounting. Removal of this roadblock has high priority in my legislative recommendations.

Still another issue relates to civil rights measures.

In all our hopes and plans for a better world we all recognize that provincial and racial prejudices must be combatted. In the long perspective of history, the right to vote has been one of the strongest pillars of a free society. Our first duty is to protect this right against all encroachment. In spite of constitutional guarantees, and notwithstanding much progress of recent years, bias still deprives some persons in this country of equal protection of the laws.

Early in your last session I recommended legislation which would help eliminate several practices discriminating against the basic rights of Americans. The Civil Rights Commission has developed additional constructive recommendations. I hope that these will be among the matters to be seriously considered in the current session. I trust that Congress will thus signal to the world that our Government is striving for equality under law for all our people.

Each year and in many ways our Nation continues to undergo profound change and growth.

In the past 18 months we have hailed the entry of two more States of the Union—Alaska and Hawaii. We salute these two western stars.

Our vigorous expansion, which we all welcome as a sign of health and vitality, is many-sided. We are, for example, witnessing explosive growth in metropolitan areas.

By 1975 the metropolitan areas of the United States will occupy twice the territory they do today. The roster of urban problems with which they must cope is staggering. They involve water supply, cleaning the air, adjusting local tax systems, providing for essential educational, cultural, and social services, and destroying those conditions which breed delinquency and crime.

In meeting these, we must, if we value our historic freedoms, keep within the traditional framework of our Federal system with powers divided between the National and State Governments. The uniqueness of this system may confound the casual observer, but it has worked effectively for nearly 200 years.

I do not doubt that our urban and other perplexing problems can be solved in the traditional American method. In doing so we must realize that nothing is really solved, indeed ruinous tendencies are set in motion by yielding to the deceptive bait of the "easy" Federal tax dollar.

Our educational system provides a ready example. All recognize the vital necessity of having modern school plants, well-qualified and adequately compensated teachers, and of using the best possible teaching techniques and curriculums.

We cannot be complacent about educating our youth. But the route to better trained minds is not through the swift administration of a Federal hypodermic or sustained financial transfusion. The educational process, essentially a local and personal responsibility, cannot be made to leap ahead by crash, centralized governmental action.

The administration has proposed a carefully reasoned program for helping eliminate current deficiencies. It is designed to stimulate classroom construction, not by substitution of Federal dollars for State and local funds, but by incentives to extend and encourage State and local efforts. This approach rejects the notion of Federal domination or control. It is workable, and should appeal to every American interested in advancement of our educational system in the traditional American way. I urge the Congress to take action upon it.

There is one other subject concerning which I renew a recommendation I made in my state of the Union message last January. I then advised the Congress of my purpose to intensify our efforts to replace force with a rule of law among nations. From many discussions abroad, I am convinced that purpose is widely and deeply shared by other peoples and nations of the world.

In the same message I stated that our efforts would include a reexamination of our own relation to the International Court of Justice. The Court was established by the United Nations to decide international legal disputes between nations. In 1946 we accepted the Court's jurisdiction, but subject to a reservation of the right to determine unilaterally whether a matter lies essentially within domestic jurisdiction. There is pending before the Senate a resolution which would repeal our present self-judging reservation. I support that resolution and urge its prompt passage. If this is done, I intend to urge similar acceptance of the Court's jurisdiction by every member of the United Nations.

Here perhaps it is not amiss for me to say a personal word to the Members of the Congress, in this my final year of office, a word about the institutions we respectively represent and the meaning which the relationships between our two branches has for the days ahead.

I am not unique as a President in having worked with a Congress controlled by the opposition party—except that no other President ever did it for quite so long. Yet in both personal and official relationships we have weathered the storms of the past 5 years. For this I am deeply grateful.

My deep concern in the next 12 months, before my successor takes office, is with our joint congressional-executive duty to our own and to other nations. Acting upon the beliefs I have expressed here today, I shall devote my full energies to the tasks at hand, whether these involve travel for promoting greater world understanding, negotiations to reduce international discord, or constant discussions and communications with the Congress and the American people on issues both domestic and foreign.

In pursuit of these objectives, I look forward to, and shall dedicate myself to, a close and constructive association with the Congress.

Every minute spent in irrelevant interbranch wrangling is precious time taken from the intelligent initiation and adoption of coherent policies for our national survival and progress.

We seek a common goal—brighter opportunity for our own citizens and a world peace with justice for all.

Before us and our friends is the challenge of an ideology which, for more than four decades, has trumpeted abroad its purpose of gaining ultimate victory over all forms of government at variance with its own.

We realize that however much we repudiate the tenets of imperialistic communism, it represents a gigantic enterprise. Its leaders compel its subjects to subordinate their freedom of action and spirit and personal desires for some hoped-for advantage in the future.

The Communists can present an array of material accomplishments over the past 15 years that lends a false persuasiveness to many of their glittering promises to the uncommitted peoples.

The competition they provide is formidable. We so recognize it.

But in our scale of values we place freedom first. Our whole national existence and development have been geared to that basic concept and is responsible for the position of free-world leadership to which we have succeeded. It is the highest prize that any nation can possess; it is one that communism can never offer. And America's record of material accomplishment in freedom is written not only in the unparalleled prosperity of our own Nation, but in the many billions we have devoted to the reconstruction of free-world economies wrecked by World War II and in the effective help of many more billions we have given in saving the independence of many others threatened by outside domination. Assuredly we have the capacity for handling the problems in the new era of the world's history we are now entering.

But we must use that capacity intelligently and tirelessly, regardless of personal sacrifice.

The fissure that divides our political planet is deep and wide.

We live, moreover, in a storm of semantic disorder in which old labels no longer faithfully describe.

Police states are called "people's democracies."

Armed conquest of free people is called "liberation."

Such slippery slogans make difficult the problem of communicating true faith, facts, and beliefs.

We must make clear our peaceful intentions, our aspirations for a better world. To do so, we must use language to enlighten the mind, not as the instrument of the studied innuendo and distorter of truth.

And we must live by what we say.

On my recent visit to distant lands I found one statesman after another eager to tell me of the elements of their government that had been borrowed from our American Constitution, and from the indestructible ideals set forth in our Declaration of Independence.

As a nation we take pride that our own constitutional system, and the ideals which sustain it have been long viewed as a fountainhead of freedom.

By our every word and action we must strive to make ourselves worthy of this trust, ever mindful that an accumulation of seemingly minor encroachments upon freedom gradually could break down the entire fabric of a free society.

So persuaded, we shall get on with the task before us.

So dedicated, and with faith in the Almighty, humanity shall one day achieve the unity in freedom to which all men have aspired from the dawn of time.

NINTH ANNUAL MESSAGE

THE WHITE HOUSE, *January 12, 1961.*

To the Congress of the United States:

Once again it is my constitutional duty to assess the state of the Union.

On each such previous occasion during these past 8 years I have outlined a forward course designed to achieve our mutual objective—a better America in a world of peace. This time my function is different.

The American people, in free election, have selected new leadership which soon will be entrusted with the management of our Government. A new President shortly will lay before you his proposals to shape the future of our great land. To him, every citizen, whatever his political beliefs, prayerfully extends best wishes for good health and for wisdom and success in coping with the problems that confront our Nation.

For my part, I should like, first, to express to you of the Congress, my appreciation of your devotion to the common good and your friendship over these difficult years. I will carry with me pleasant memories of this association in endeavors profoundly significant to all our people.

We have been through a lengthy period in which the control over the executive and legislative branches of Government has been divided between our two great political parties. Differences, of course, we have had, particularly in domestic affairs. But in a united determination to keep this Nation strong and free and to utilize our vast resources for the advancement of all mankind, we have carried America to unprecedented heights.

For this cooperative achievement I thank the American people and those in the Congress of both parties who have supported programs in the interest of our country.

I should also like to give special thanks for the devoted service of my associates in the executive branch and the hundreds of thousands of career employees who have implemented our diverse Government programs.

My second purpose is to review briefly the record of these past 8 years in the hope that, out of the sum of these experiences, lessons will emerge that are useful to our Nation. Supporting this review are detailed reports from the several agencies and departments, all of which are now or will shortly be available to the Congress.

Throughout the world the years since 1953 have been a period of profound change. The human problems in the world grow more acute hour by hour; yet new gains in science and technology continually extend the promise of a better life. People yearn to be free, to govern themselves; yet a third of the people of the world have no freedom, do not govern themselves. The world recognizes the catastrophic nature of nuclear war; yet it sees the wondrous potential of nuclear peace.

During the period, the United States has forged ahead under a constructive foreign policy. The continuing goal is peace, liberty, and well-being—for others as well as ourselves. The aspirations of all peoples are one—peace with justice in freedom. Peace can only be attained collectively as peoples everywhere unite in their determination that liberty and well-being come to all mankind.

Yet while we have worked to advance national aspirations for freedom, a divisive force has been at work to divert that aspiration into dangerous channels. The Communist movement throughout the world exploits the natural striving of all to be free and attempts to subjugate men rather than free them. These activities have caused and are continuing to cause grave troubles in the world.

Here at home these have been times for careful adjustment of our economy from the artificial impetus of a hot war to constructive growth in a precarious peace. While building a new economic vitality without inflation, we have also increased public expenditures to keep abreast of the neeeds of a growing population and its attendant new problems, as well as our added international responsibilities. We have worked toward these ends in a context of shared responsibility—conscious of the need for maximum scope to private effort and for State and local, as well as Federal, governmental action.

Success in designing and executing national purposes, domestically and abroad, can only come from a steadfast resolution that integrity in the operation of Government and in our relations with each other be fully maintained. Only in this way could our spiritual goals be fully advanced.

FOREIGN POLICY

On January 20, 1953, when I took office, the United States was at war. Since the signing of the Korean armistice in 1953, Americans have lived in peace in highly troubled times.

During the 1956 Suez crisis, the U.S. Government strongly supported United Nations action—resulting in the ending of the hostilities in Egypt.

Again in 1958, peace was preserved in the Middle East despite new discord. Our Government responded to the request of the friendly Lebanese Government for military help, and promptly withdrew American forces as soon as the situation was stabilized.

In 1958 our support of the Republic of China during the all-out bombardment of Quemoy restrained the Communist Chinese from attempting to invade the offshore islands.

Although, unhappily, Communist penetration of Cuba is real and poses a serious threat, Communist-dominated regimes have been deposed in Guatemala and Iran. The occupation of Austria has ended and the Trieste question has been settled.

Despite constant threats to its integrity, West Berlin has remained free.

Important advances have been made in building mutual security arrangements—which lie at the heart of our hopes for future peace and security in the world. The Southeast Asia Treaty Organization has been established; the NATO alliance has been militarily strengthened; the Organization of American States has been further developed as an instrument of inter-American cooperation; the Anzus treaty has strengthened ties with Australia and New Zealand, and a mutual security treaty with Japan has been signed. In addition, the CENTO Pact has been concluded, and while we are not officially a member of this alliance we have participated closely in its deliberations.

The atoms-for-peace proposal to the United Nations led to the creation of the International Atomic Energy Agency. Our policy has been to push for enforcible programs of inspection against surprise attack, suspension of nuclear testing, arms reduction, and peaceful use of outer space.

The United Nations has been vigorously supported in all of its actions, including the condemnations of the wholesale murder of the people of Tibet by the Chinese Communists and the brutal Soviet repression of the people of Hungary, as well as the more recent U.N. actions in the Congo.

The United States took the initiative in negotiating the significant treaty to guarantee the peaceful use of vast Antarctica.

The U.S. Information Agency has been transformed into a greatly improved medium for explaining our policies and actions to audiences overseas, answering the lies of Communist propaganda, and projecting a clearer image of American life and culture.

Cultural, technological, and educational exchanges with the Soviet Union have been encouraged, and a comprehensive agreement was made which authorized, among other things, the distribution of our Russian language magazine Amerika and the highly successful American exhibition in Moscow.

This country has continued to withhold recognition of Communist China and to oppose vigorously the admission of this belligerent and unrepentant nation into the United Nations. Red China has yet to demonstrate that it deserves to be considered a peace-loving nation.

With Communist imperialism held in check, constructive actions were undertaken to strengthen the economies of free world nations. The U.S. Government has given sturdy support to the economic and technical assistance activities of the U.N. This country stimulated a doubling of the capital of the World Bank and a 50-percent capital increase in the International Monetary Fund. The Development Loan Fund and the International Development Association were established. The United States also took the lead in creating the Inter-American Development Bank.

Vice President Nixon, Secretaries of State Dulles and Herter, and I traveled extensively through the world for the purpose of strengthening the cause of peace, freedom, and international understanding. So rewarding were these visits that their very success became a significant factor in causing the Soviet Union to wreck the planned summit conference of 1960.

These vital programs must go on. New tactics will have to be developed, of course, to meet new situations, but the underlying principles should be constant. Our great moral and material commitments to collective security, deterrence of force, international law, negotiations that lead to self-enforcing agreements, and the economic interdependence of free nations should remain the cornerstone of a foreign policy that will ultimately bring permanent peace with justice in freedom to all mankind. The continuing need of all free nations today is for each to recognize clearly the essentiality of an unbreakable bond among themselves based upon a complete dedication to the principles of collective security, effective cooperation and peace with justice.

NATIONAL DEFENSE

For the first time in our Nation's history we have consistently maintained in peacetime, military forces of a magnitude sufficient to deter and if need be to destroy predatory forces in the world.

Tremendous advances in strategic weapons systems have been made in the past 8 years. Not until 1953 were expenditures on long-range ballistic missile programs even as much as a million dollars a year; today we spend 10 times as much each day on these programs as was spent in all of 1952.

No guided ballistic missiles were operational at the beginning of 1953. Today many types give our Armed Forces unprecedented effectiveness. The explosive power of our weapons systems for all purposes is almost inconceivable.

Today the United States has operational Atlas missiles which can strike a target 5,000 miles away in a half hour. The Polaris weapons system became operational last fall and the Titan is scheduled to become so this year. Next year, more than a year ahead of schedule, a vastly improved ICBM, the solid-propellant Minuteman, is expected to be ready.

Squadrons of accurate intermediate range ballistic missiles are now operational. The Thor and Jupiter IRBM's based in forward areas can hit targets 1,500 miles away in 18 minutes.

Aircraft which fly at speeds faster than sound were still in a developmental stage 8 years ago. Today American fighting planes go twice the speed of sound. And either our B–58 medium-range jet bomber or our B–52 long-range jet bomber can carry more explosive power than was used by all combatants in World War II—Allies and Axis combined.

Eight years ago we had no nuclear-powered ships. Today 49 nuclear warships have been authorized. Of these, 14 have been commissioned, including 3 of the revolutionary Polaris submarines. Our nuclear submarines have cruised under the North Pole and circumnavigated the earth while submerged. Sea warfare has been revolutionized, and the United States is far and away the leader.

Our tactical air units overseas and our aircraft carriers are alert; Army units, guarding the frontiers of freedom in Europe and the Far East, are in the highest state of readiness in peacetime history; our Marines, a third of whom are deployed in the Far East, are constantly prepared for action; our Reserve Establishment has maintained high standards of proficiency, and the Ready Reserve now numbers over 2½ million citizen-soldiers.

The Department of Defense, a young and still evolving organization, has twice been improved and the line of command has been shortened in order to meet the demands of modern warfare. These major reorganizations have provided a more effective structure for unified planning and direction of the vast Defense Establishment. Gradual improvements in its structure and procedures are to be expected.

U.S. civil defense and nonmilitary defense capacity has been greatly strengthened and these activities have been consolidated in one Federal agency.

The defense forces of our allies now number 5 million men, several thousand combatant ships, and over 25,000 aircraft. Programs to strengthen these allies have been consistently supported by the administration. U.S. military assistance goes almost exclusively to friendly nations on the rim of the Communist world. This American contribution to nations who have the will to defend their freedom, but insufficient means, should be vigorously continued. Combined with our allies, the free world now has a far stronger shield than we could provide alone.

Since 1953, our defense policy has been based on the assumption that the international situation would require heavy defense expenditures for an indefinite period to come, probably for years. In this protracted struggle, good management dictates that we resist overspending as resolutely as we oppose underspending. Every dollar uselessly spent on military mechanisms decreases our total strength and, therefore, our security. We must not return to the crash-program psychology of the past when each new feint by the Communists was responded to in panic. The "bomber gap" of several years ago was always a fiction, and the "missile gap" shows every sign of being the same.

The Nation can ill afford to abandon a national policy which provides for a fully adequate and steady level of effort, designed for the long pull; a fast adjustment to new scientific and technological advances; a balanced force of such strength as to deter general war, to effectively meet local situations and to retaliate to attack and destroy the attacker; and a strengthened system of free world collective security.

THE ECONOMY

The expanding American economy passed the half-trillion-dollar mark in gross national product early in 1960. The Nation's output of goods and services is now nearly 25 percent higher than in 1952.

In 1959, the average American family had an income of $6,520, 15 percent higher in dollars of constant buying power than in 1952, and the real wages of American factory workers have risen 20 percent during the past 8 years. These facts reflect the rising standard of individual and family well-being enjoyed by Americans.

Our Nation benefits also from a remarkable improvement in general industrial peace through strengthened processes of free collective bargaining. Time lost since 1952 because of strikes has been half that lost in the 8 years prior to that date. Legislation now requires that union members have the opportunity for full participation in the affairs of their unions. The administration supported the Landrum-Griffin Act, which I believe is greatly helpful to the vast bulk of American labor and its leaders, and also is a major step in getting racketeers and gangsters out of labor-management affairs.

The economic security of working men and women has been strengthened by an extension of unemployment insurance coverage to 2.5 million ex-servicemen, 2.4 million Federal employees, and 1.2 million employees of small businesses, and by a strengthening of the Railroad Unemployment Insurance Act. States have been encouraged to improve their unemployment compensation benefits, so that today average weekly benefits are 40 percent higher than in 1953.

Determined efforts have improved workers' safety standards. Enforceable safety standards have been established for longshoremen and ship repair workers; Federal safety councils have been increased from 14 to over 100; safety awards have been initiated, and a national construction safety program has been developed.

A major factor in strengthening our competitive enterprise system, and promoting economic growth, has been the vigorous enforcement of antitrust laws over the last 8 years and a continuing effort to reduce artificial restraints on competition and trade and enhance our economic liberties. This purpose was also significantly advanced in 1953 when, as one of the first acts of this administration, restrictive wage and price controls were ended.

An additional measure to strengthen the American system of competitive enterprise was the creation of the Small Business Administration in 1953 to assist existing small businesses and encourage new ones. This agency has approved over $1 billion in loans, initiated a new program to provide long-term capital for small businesses, aided in setting aside $3½ billion in Government contracts for award to small business concerns, and brought to the attention of individual businessmen, through programs of information and education, new developments in management and production techniques. Since 1952, important tax revisions have been made to encourage small businesses.

Many major improvements in the Nation's transportation system have been made:

> After long years of debate, the dream of a great St. Lawrence Seaway, opening the heartland of America to ocean commerce, has been fulfilled.
>
> The new Federal Aviation Agency is fostering greater safety in air travel.
>
> The largest public construction program in history—the 41,000-mile National System of Interstate and Defense Highways—has been pushed rapidly forward. Twenty-five percent of this system is now open to traffic.

Efforts to help every American build a better life have included also a vigorous program for expanding our trade with other nations. A 4-year renewal of the Reciprocal Trade Agreements Act was passed in 1958, and a continuing and rewarding effort has been made to persuade other countries to remove restrictions against our exports. A new export expansion program was launched in 1960, inaugurating improvement of export credit insurance and broadening research and information programs to awaken Americans to business opportunities overseas. These actions and generally prosperous conditions abroad have helped push America's export trade to a level of $20 billion in 1960.

Although intermittent declines in economic activity persist as a problem in our enterprise system, recent downturns have been moderate and of short duration. There is, however, little room for complacency. Currently our economy is operating at high levels, but unemployment rates are higher than any of us would like, and chronic pockets of high unemployment persist. Clearly, continued sound and broadly shared economic growth remains a major national objective toward which we must strive through joint private and public efforts.

If Government continues to work to assure every American the fullest opportunity to develop and utilize his ability and talent, it will be performing one of its most vital functions, that of advancing the welfare and protecting the dignity, rights, and freedom of all Americans.

GOVERNMENT FINANCE AND ADMINISTRATION

In January 1953 the consumer's dollar was worth only 52 cents in terms of the food, clothing, shelter, and other items it would buy compared to 1939. Today the inflationary spiral which had raised the cost of living by 36 percent between 1946 and 1952 has all but ceased and the value of the dollar virtually stabilized.

In 1954 we had the largest tax cut in history, amounting to $7.4 billion annually, of which over 62 percent went to individuals mostly in the small income brackets.

This administration has directed constant efforts toward fiscal responsibility. Balanced budgets have been sought when the economy was advancing, and a rigorous evaluation of spending programs has been maintained at all times. Resort to deficit financing in prosperous times could easily erode international confidence in the dollar and contribute to inflation at home. In this belief, I shall submit a balanced budget for fiscal 1962 to the Congress next week.

There has been a firm policy of reducing Government competition with private enterprise. This has resulted in the discontinuance of some 2,000 commercial industrial installations and in addition the curtailment of approximately 550 industrial installations operated directly by Government agencies.

Also an aggressive surplus disposal program has been carried on to identify and dispose of unneeded Government-owned real property. This has resulted in the addition of a substantial number of valuable properties to local tax rolls, and a significant monetary return to the Government.

Earnest and persistent attempts have been made to strengthen the position of State and local governments and thereby to stop the dangerous drift toward centralization of governmental power in Washington.

Significant strides have been made in increasing the effectiveness of Government. Important new agencies have been established, such as the Department of Health, Education, and Welfare, the Federal Aviation Agency, and the National Aeronautics and Space Administration. The Council of Economic Advisers was reconstituted.

The operation of our postal system has been modernized to get better and more efficient service. Modernized handling of local mail now brings next-day delivery to 168 million people in our population centers, expanded carrier service now accommodates 9.3 million families in the growing suburbs, and 1.4 million families have been added to the rural delivery service. Commonsense dictates that the postal service should be on a self-financing basis.

The concept of a trained and dedicated Government career service has been strengthened by the provision of life and health insurance benefits, a vastly improved retirement system, a new merit promotion program, and the first effective incentive awards program. With no sacrifice in efficiency, Federal civilian employment since 1953 has been reduced by over a quarter of a million persons.

I am deeply gratified that it was under the urging of this administration that Alaska and Hawaii became our 49th and 50th States.

AGRICULTURE

Despite the difficulties of administering congressional programs which apply outmoded prescriptions and which aggravate rather than solve problems, the past 8 years brought notable advances in agriculture.

Total agricultural assets are approximately $200 billion—up $36 billion in 8 years.

Farmowner equities are at the near record high of $174 billion.

Farmownership is at a record high with fewer farmers in a tenant and sharecropper status than at any time in our Nation's history.

The food-for-peace program has demonstrated how surplus of American food and fiber can be effectively used to feed and clothe the needy abroad. Aided by this humanitarian program, total agricultural exports have grown from $2.8 billion in 1953 to an average of about $4 billion annually for the past 3 years. For 1960, exports are estimated at $4.5 billion, the highest volume on record. Under the food-for-peace program, the largest wheat transaction in history was consummated with India in 1960.

The problems of low-income farm families received systematic attention for the first time in the rural development program. This program has gone forward in 39 States, yielding higher incomes and a better living for rural people most in need.

The Rural Electrification Administration has helped meet the growing demand for power and telephones in agricultural areas. Ninety-seven percent of all farms now have central station electric power. Dependence upon Federal financing should no longer be necessary.

The Farm Credit Administration has been made an independent agency more responsive to the farmer's needs.

The search for new uses for our farm abundance and to develop new crops for current needs has made major progress. Agricultural research appropriations have increased by 171 percent since 1953.

Farmers are being saved approximately $80 million a year by the repeal in 1956 of Federal taxes on gasoline used in tractors and other machinery.

Since 1953, appropriations have been doubled for county agents, home agents and the Extension Service.

Eligibility for social security benefits has been extended to farmers and their families.

Yet in certain aspects our agricultural surplus situation is increasingly grave. For example, our wheat stocks now total 1.3 billion bushels. If we did not harvest 1 bushel of wheat in this coming year, we would still have all we could eat, all we could sell abroad, all we could give away, and still have a substantial carryover. Extraordinary costs are involved just in management and disposal of this burdensome surplus. Obviously important adjustments must still come. Congress must enact additional legislation to permit wheat and other farm commodities to move into regular marketing channels in an orderly manner and at the same time afford the needed price protection to the farmer. Only then will agriculture again be free, sound, and profitable.

NATURAL RESOURCES

New emphasis has been placed on the care of our national parks. A 10-year development program of our national park system—Mission 66—was initiated and 633,000 acres of park land have been added since 1953.

Appropriations for fish and wildlife operations have more than doubled. Thirty-five new refuges, containing 11,342,000 acres, have been added to the national wildlife management system.

Our Nation's forests have been improved at the most rapid rate in history.

The largest sustained effort in water resources development in our history has taken place. In the field of reclamation alone, over 50 new projects, or project units, have been authorized since 1953—including the billion dollar Colorado River storage project. When all these projects have been completed they will have a storage capacity of nearly 43 million acre-feet—an increase of 50 percent over the Bureau of Reclamation's storage capacity in mid-1953. In addition, since 1953 over 450 new navigation flood control and multiple-purpose projects of the Corps of Engineers have been started, costing nearly $6 billion.

Soil and water conservation has been advanced as never before. One hundred forty-one projects are now being constructed under the watershed protection program.

Hydroelectric power has been impressively developed through a policy which recognizes that the job to be done requires comprehensive development by Federal, State, and local governments and private enterprise. Teamwork is essential to achieve this objective.

The Federal Columbia River power system has grown from 2 multipurpose dams with a 2.6 million kilowatt capacity to 17 multipurpose projects completed or under construction with an ultimate installed capacity of 8.1 million kilowatts. After years of negotiation, a Columbia River storage development agreement with Canada now opens the way for early realization of unparalleled power, flood-control, and resource conservation benefits for the Pacific Northwest. A treaty implementing this agreement will shortly be submitted to the Senate.

A farsighted and highly successful program for meeting urgent water needs is being carried out by converting salt water to fresh water. A 75-percent reduction in the cost of this process has already been realized.

Continuous resource development is essential for our expanding economy. We must continue vigorous, combined Federal, State and private programs, at the same time preserving to the maximum extent possible our natural and scenic heritage for future generations.

EDUCATION, SCIENCE, AND TECHNOLOGY

The National Defense Education Act of 1958 is already a milestone in the history of American education. It provides broad opportunities for the intellectual development of all children by strengthening courses of study in science, mathematics, and foreign languages, by developing new graduate programs to train additional teachers, and by providing loans for young people who need financial help to go to college.

The administration proposed on numerous occasions a broad new 5-year program of Federal aid to help overcome the classroom shortage in public elementary and secondary schools. Recommendations were also made to give assistance to colleges and universities for the construction of academic and residential buildings to meet future enrollment increases.

This administration greatly expanded Federal loans for building dormitories for students, teachers, and nurses training, a program assisting in the construction of approximately 200,000 living accommodations during the past 8 years.

There has been a vigorous acceleration of health, resource, and education programs designed to advance the role of the American Indian in our society. Last fall, for example, 91 percent of the Indian children between the ages of 6 and 18 on reservations were enrolled in school. This is a rise of 12 percent since 1953.

In the field of science and technology, startling strides have been made by the new National Aeronautics and Space Administration. In little more than 2 years, NASA has successfully launched meteorological satellites, such as Tiros I and Tiros II, that promise to revolutionize methods of weather forecasting; demonstrated the feasibility of satellites for global communications by the successful launching of Echo I; produced an enormous amount of valuable scientific data, such as the discovery of the Van Allen radiation belt; successfully launched deep-space probes that maintained communication over the greatest range man has ever tracked; and made real progress toward the goal of manned space flights.

These achievements unquestionably make us preeminent today in space exploration for the betterment of mankind. I believe the present organizational arrangements in this area, with the revisions proposed last year, are completely adequate for the tasks ahead.

Americans can look forward to new achievements in space exploration. The near future will hold such wonders as the orbital flight of an astronaut, the landing of instruments on the moon, the launching of the powerful giant Saturn rocket vehicles, and the reconnaissance of Mars and Venus by unmanned vehicles.

The application of atomic energy to industry, agriculture, and medicine has progressed from hope and experiment to reality. American industry and agriculture are making increasing use of radioisotopes to improve manufacturing, testing, and crop raising. Atomic energy has improved the ability of the healing professions to combat disease, and holds promise for an eventual increase in man's lifespan.

Education, science, technology, and balanced programs of every kind—these are the roadways to progress. With appropriate Federal support, the States and localities can assure opportunities for achieving excellence at all levels of the educational system; and with the Federal Government continuing to give wholehearted support to basic scientific research and technology, we can expect to maintain our position of leadership in the world.

CIVIL RIGHTS

The first consequential Federal civil rights legislation in 85 years was enacted by Congress on recommendation of the administration in 1957 and 1960.

A new Civil Rights Division in the Department of Justice has already moved to enforce constitutional rights in such areas as voting and the elimination of Jim Crow laws.

Greater equality of job opportunity in Federal employment and employment with Federal contractors has been effectively provided through the President's Committees on Government Contracts and Government Employment Practices.

The Civil Rights Commission has undertaken important surveys in the fields of housing, voting, and education.

Segregation has been abolished in the Armed Forces, in Veterans' hospitals, in all Federal employment, and throughout the District of Columbia—administratively accomplished progress in this field that is unmatched in America's recent history.

This pioneering work in civil rights must go on. Not only because discrimination is morally wrong, but also because its impact is more than national—it is worldwide.

HEALTH AND WELFARE

Federal medical research expenditures have increased more than fourfold since 1954.

A vast variety of the approaches known to medical science has been explored to find better methods of treatment and prevention of major diseases, particularly heart diseases, cancer, and mental illness.

The control of air and water pollution has been greatly strengthened.

Americans now have greater protection against harmful, unclean, or misrepresented foods, drugs, or cosmetics through a strengthened Food and Drug Administration and by new legislation which requires that food additives be proved safe for human consumption before use.

A newly established Federal Radiation Council, along with the Department of Health, Education, and Welfare, analyzes and coordinates information regarding radiological activities which affect the public health.

Medical manpower has been increased by Federal grants for teaching and research.

Construction of new medical facilities has been stepped up and extended to include nursing homes, diagnostic and treatment centers, and rehabilitation facilities.

The vocational rehabilitation program has been significantly expanded. About 90,000 handicapped people are now being rehabilitated annually so they are again able to earn their own living with self-respect and dignity.

New legislation provides for better medical care for the needy aged, including those older persons, who, while otherwise self-sufficient, need help in meeting their health care costs. The administration recommended a major expansion of this effort.

The coverage of the Social Security Act has been broadened since 1953 to make 11 million additional people eligible for retirement, disability or survivor benefits for themselves or their dependents, and the social security benefits have been substantially improved.

Grants to the States for maternal and child welfare services have been increased.

The States, aided by Federal grants, now assist some 6 million needy people through the programs of old-age assistance, aid to dependent children, aid to the blind, and aid to the totally and permanently disabled.

HOUSING AND URBAN DEVELOPMENT

More houses have been built during the past 8 years—over 9 million—than during any previous 8 years in history.

An historic new approach—urban renewal—now replaces piecemeal thrusts at slum pockets and urban blight. Communities engaged in urban renewal have doubled and renewal projects have more than tripled since 1953. An estimated 68 projects in 50 cities will be completed by the end of the current fiscal year; another 577 projects will be underway, and planning for 310 more will be in process. A total of $2 billion in Federal grants will ultimately be required to finance these 955 projects.

New programs have been initiated to provide more and better housing for elderly people. Approximately 25,000 units especially designed for the elderly have been built, started, or approved in the past 3 years.

For the first time, because of Federal help and encouragement, 90 metropolitan areas and urban regions and 1,140 smaller towns throughout the country are making comprehensive development plans for their future growth and development.

American communities have been helped to plan water and sanitation systems and schools through planning advances for 1,600 public works projects with a construction cost of nearly $2 billion.

Mortgage insurance on individual homes has been greatly expanded. During the past 8 years, the Federal Housing Administration alone insured over 2½ million home mortgages valued at $27 billion, and in addition, insured more than 10 million property improvement loans.

The Federal Government must continue to provide leadership in order to make our cities and communities better places in which to live, work, and raise families, but without usurping rightful local authority, replacing individual responsibility, or stifling private initiative.

IMMIGRATION

Over 32,000 victims of Communist tyranny in Hungary were brought to our shores, and at this time our country is working to assist refugees from tyranny in Cuba.

Since 1953, the waiting period for naturalization applicants has been reduced from 18 months to 45 days.

The administration also has made legislative recommendations to liberalize existing restrictions upon immigration while still safeguarding the national interest. It is imperative that our immigration policy be in the finest American tradition of providing a haven for oppressed peoples and fully in accord with our obligation as a leader of the free world.

VETERANS

In discharging the Nation's obligation to our veterans, during the past 8 years there have been:

The readjustment of World War II veterans was completed, and the 5 million Korean conflict veterans were assisted in achieving successful readjustment to civilian life;

Increases in compensation benefits for all eligible veterans with service-connected disabilities;

Higher non-service-connected pension benefits for needy veterans;

Greatly improved benefits to survivors of veterans dying in or as a result of service;

Authorization, by Presidential directive, of an increase in the number of beds available for sick and disabled veterans;

Development of a 12-year, $900 million construction program to modernize and improve our veterans hospitals;

New modern techniques brought into the administration of veterans' affairs to provide the highest quality service possible to those who have defended us.

CONCLUSION

In concluding my final message to the Congress, it is fitting to look back to my first—to the aims and ideals I set forth on February 2, 1953: To use America's influence in world affairs to advance the cause of peace and justice, to conduct the affairs of the executive branch with integrity and efficiency, to encourage creative initiative in our economy, and to work toward the attainment of the well-being and equality of opportunity of all citizens.

Equally, we have honored our commitment to pursue and attain specific objectives. Among them, as stated 8 years ago: strengthening of the mutual security program; development of world trade and commerce; ending of hostilities in Korea; creation of a powerful deterrent force; practicing fiscal responsibility; checking the menace of inflation; reducing the tax burden; providing an effective internal security program; developing and conserving our natural resources; reducing governmental interference in the affairs of the farmer;

strengthening and improving services by the Department of Labor, and the vigilant guarding of civil and social rights.

I do not close this message implying that all is well—that all problems are solved. For progress implies both new and continuing problems and, unlike Presidential administrations, problems rarely have terminal dates.

Abroad, there is the continuing Communist threat to the freedom of Berlin, an explosive situation in Laos, the problems caused by Communist penetration of Cuba, as well as the many problems connected with the development of the new nations in Africa. These areas, in particular, call for delicate handling and constant review.

At home, several conspicuous problems remain: promoting higher levels of employment, with special emphasis on areas in which heavy unemployment has persisted; continuing to provide for steady economic growth and preserving a sound currency; bringing our balance of payments into more reasonable equilibrium and continuing a high level of confidence in our national and international financial systems; eliminating heavily excessive surpluses of a few farm commodities; and overcoming deficiencies in our health and educational programs.

Our goal always has been to add to the spiritual, moral, and material strength of our Nation. I believe we have done this. But it is a process that must never end. Let us pray that leaders of both the near and distant future will be able to keep the Nation strong and at peace, that they will advance the well-being of all our people, that they will lead us on to still higher moral standards, and that, in achieving these goals, they will maintain a reasonable balance between private and governmental responsibility.

John F. Kennedy

January 20, 1961 to November 22, 1963

FIRST ANNUAL MESSAGE

THE WHITE HOUSE, *January 30, 1.*

MR. SPEAKER, MR. VICE PRESIDENT, AND MEMBERS OF THE CONGRESS:

It is a pleasure to return from whence I came. You are among my oldest friends in Washington, and the House is my oldest home.

It was here, more than 14 years ago, that I first took the oath of Federal office. It was here, for 14 years, that I gained both knowledge and inspiration from members of both parties in both Houses—from your wise and generous leaders—and from the pronouncements which I can vividly recall, sitting then where you sit now—including the programs of two great Presidents, the undimmed eloquence of Churchill, the soaring idealism of Nehru, the steadfast words of General de Gaulle. To speak from this same historic rostrum is a sobering experience; to be back among so many friends is a happy one.

I am confident that friendship will continue. Our Constitution wisely assigns both joint and separate roles to each branch of the Government; and a President and a Congress who hold each other in mutual respect will neither permit nor attempt any trespass. For my part, I shall withhold from neither the Congress nor the people any fact or report, past, present, or future, which is necessary for an informed judgment of our conduct and hazards. I shall neither shift the burden of Executive decisions to the Congress, nor avoid responsibility for the outcome of those decisions.

I speak today in a hour of national peril and national opportunity. Before my term has ended, we shall have to test anew whether a nation organized and governed such as ours can endure. The outcome is by no means certain. The answers are by no means clear. All of us together—this administration, this Congress, this Nation—must forge those answers.

But today, were I to offer—after little more than a week in office—detailed legislation to remedy every national ill, the Congress would rightly wonder whether the desire for speed had replaced the duty of responsibility.

My remarks, therefore, will be limited. But they will also be candid. To state the facts frankly is not to despair the future nor indict the past. The prudent heir takes careful inventory of his legacies, and gives a faithful accounting to those whom he owes an obligation of trust. And, while the occasion does not call for another recital of our blessings and assets, we do have no greater asset than the willingness of a free and determined people, through its elected officials, to face all problems frankly and meet all dangers free from panic or fear.

I

The present state of our economy is disturbing. We take office in the wake of 7 months of recession, 3½ years of slack, 7 years of diminished economic growth, and 9 years of falling farm income.

Business bankruptcies have reached their highest level since the great depression. Since 1951 farm income has been squeezed down by 25 percent. Save for a brief period in 1958, insured unemployment is at the highest peak in our history. Of some 5½ million Americans who are without jobs, more than 1 million have been searching for work for more than 4 months. And during each month some 150,000 workers are exhausting their already meager jobless benefit rights.

Nearly one-eighth of those who are without jobs live almost without hope in nearly 100 especially depressed and troubled areas. The rest include new school graduates unable to use their talents, farmers forced to give up their part-time jobs that had balanced their budgets, skilled and unskilled workers laid off in such important industries as metals, machinery, automobiles, and apparel.

Our recovery from the 1958 recession, moreover, was anemic and incomplete. Our gross national product never regained its full potential. Unemployment never returned to normal levels. Maximum use of our national industrial capacity was never restored.

In short, the American economy is in trouble. The most resourceful industrialized country on earth ranks among the last in economic growth. Since last spring our economic growth rate actually receded. Business investment is in a decline. Profits have fallen below predicted levels. Construction is off. A million unsold automobiles are in inventory. Fewer people are working—and the average workweek has shrunk well below 40 hours. Yet prices have continued to rise—so that now too many Americans have *less* to spend for items that cost them *more* to buy.

Economic prophecy is at best an uncertain art—as demonstrated by the prediction 1 year ago from this same podium that 1960 would be "the most prosperous year in our history." Nevertheless, forecasts of continued slack and only slightly reduced unemployment throughout 1961 and 1962 have been made with alarming unanimity—and this administration does not intend to stand helplessly by.

We cannot afford to waste idle hours and empty plants while awaiting the end of a recession. We must show the world what a free economy can do—to reduce unemployment, to put unused capacity to work, to spur new productivity, and to foster higher economic growth within a range of sound fiscal policies and relative price stability.

I will propose to the Congress within the next 14 days measures to improve unemployment compensation through temporary increases in amount and duration on a self-supporting basis—to provide more food to the families of the unemployed, and aid to their needy children—to redevelop our areas of chronic labor surplus—to expand the services of the U.S. Employment Offices—to stimulate housing and construction—to secure more purchasing power for our lowest paid workers by raising and expanding the minimum wage—to offer tax incentives for sound plant investment—to increase the development of our natural resources—to encourage price stability—and to take other steps aimed at insuring a prompt recovery and paving the way for increased long-range growth. This is not a partisan program concentrating on our weaknesses—it is, I hope, a national program to realize our strength.

II

Efficient expansion at home, stimulating the new plant and technology that can make our goods more competitive, is also the key to the international balance-of-payments problem. Laying aside all alarmist talk and panicky solutions, let us put that knotty problem in its proper perspective.

It is true that, since 1958, the gap between the dollars we spend or invest abroad and the dollars returned to us here has substantially widened. This overall deficit in our balance of payments increased by nearly $11 billion in the last 3 years—and holders of dollars abroad converted them to gold in such quantity as to cause a total outflow of nearly $5 billion of gold from our gold reserve. The 1959 deficit was caused in large part by the failure of our exports to penetrate foreign markets—the result both of restrictions on our goods and our own uncompetitive prices. The 1960 deficit, on the other hand, was more the result of an increase in private capital outflow seeking new opportunity, higher return, or speculative advantage abroad.

Meanwhile this country has continued to bear more than its share of the West's military and foreign aid obligations. Under existing policies, another deficit of $2 billion is predicted for 1961—and individuals in those countries whose dollar position once depended on these deficits for improvement now wonder aloud whether our gold reserves will remain sufficient to meet our gold obligations.

All this is cause for concern—but it is not cause for panic. For our monetary and financial position remains exceedingly strong. Including our drawing rights in the International Monetary Fund and the gold reserve held as backing for our currency and Federal Reserve deposits, we have some $22 billion in total gold stocks and other international monetary reserves available—and I now pledge that their full strength stands behind the value of the dollar for use if needed.

Moreover, we hold large assets abroad—the total owed this Nation far exceeds the claims upon our reserves—and our exports once again substantially exceed our imports.

In short, we need not—and we shall not—take any action to increase the dollar price of gold from $35 an ounce—to impose exchange controls—to reduce our antirecession efforts—to fall back on restrictive trade policies—or to weaken our commitments around the world.

This administration will not distort the value of the dollar in any fashion—and this is a commitment.

Prudence and good sense do require, however, that new steps be taken to ease the payments deficit and prevent any gold crisis. Our success in world affairs has long depended in part upon foreign confidence in our ability to pay. A series of Executive orders, legislative remedies, and cooperative efforts with our allies will get underway immediately—aimed at attracting foreign investment and travel to this country—promoting American exports, at stable prices and with more liberal governmental guarantees and financing—curbing tax and customs loopholes that encourage undue spending of private dollars abroad—and (through OECD, NATO, and otherwise) sharing with our allies all efforts to provide for the common defense of the free world and the hopes for growth of the less developed lands. While the current deficit lasts, ways will be found to ease our dollar outlays abroad without placing the full burden on the families of men whom we have asked to serve our flag overseas. In short, whatever is required will be done to back up all our efforts abroad, and to make certain that, in the future as in the past, the dollar is as "sound as a dollar."

III

But more than our exchange of international payments is out of balance. The current Federal budget for fiscal 1961 is almost certain to show a net deficit. The budget already submitted for fiscal 1962 will remain in balance only if the Congress enacts all the revenue measures requested—and only if an earlier and sharper upturn in the economy than my economic advisers now think likely produces the tax revenues estimated. Nevertheless, a new administration must of necessity build on the spending and revenue estimates already submitted. Within that framework, barring the development of urgent national defense needs or a worsening of the economy, it is my current intention to advocate a program of expenditures which, including revenues from a stimulation of the economy, will not of and by themselves unbalance the earlier budget.

However, we will do what must be done. For our national household is cluttered with unfinished and neglected tasks. Our cities are being engulfed in squalor. Twelve long years after Congress declared our goal to be "a decent home and a suitable environment for every American family," we still have 25 million Americans living in substandard homes. A new housing program under a new Housing and Urban Affairs Department will be needed this year.

Our classrooms contain 2 million more children than they properly have room for, taught by 90,000 teachers not properly qualified to teach. One-third of our most promising high school graduates are financially unable to continue the development of their talents. The war babies of the 1940's, who overcrowded our schools in the 1950's, are now descending in the 1960's upon our colleges—with two college students for every one 10 years from now—and our colleges are ill prepared. We lack the scientists, the engineers, and the teachers our world obligations require. We have neglected oceanography, saline water conversion, and the basic research that lies at the root of all technological progress. Federal grants for both higher and public school education can no longer be delayed.

Medical research has achieved new wonders—but these wonders are too often beyond the reach of too many people, owing to a lack of income (particularly among the aged), a lack of hospital beds, a lack of nursing homes, and a lack of doctors and dentists. Measures to provide health care for the aged under social security, and to increase the supply of both facilities and personnel, must be undertaken this year.

Our supply of clean water is dwindling. Organized and juvenile crimes cost the taxpayers millions of dollars each year, making it essential that we have improved enforcement and new legislative safeguards. The denial of constitutional rights to some of our fellow Americans on account of race—at the ballot box and elsewhere—disturbs the national conscience, and subjects us to the charge of world opinion that our democracy is not equal to the high promise of our heritage. Morality in private business has not been sufficiently spurred by morality in public business. A host of problems and projects in all 50 States, thought not possible to include in this message, deserves—and will receive—the attention of both the Congress and the executive branch. On most of these matters, messages will be sent to the Congress within the next 2 weeks.

IV

But all these problems pale when placed beside those which confront us around the world. No man entering upon this office, regardless of his party, regardless of his previous service in Washington, could fail to be staggered upon learning—even in this brief 10-day period—the harsh enormity of the trials through which we must pass in the next 4 years. Each day the crises multiply. Each day their solution grows more difficult. Each day we draw nearer the hour of maximum danger, as weapons spread and hostile forces grow stronger. I feel I must inform the Congress that our analyses over the last 10 days make it clear that—in each of these principal areas of crisis—the tide of events has been running out and time has not been our friend.

In Asia, the relentless pressures of the Chinese Communists menace the security of the entire area—from the borders of India and South Viet Nam to the jungles of Laos, struggling to protect its newly won independence. We seek in Laos what we seek in all Asia, and, indeed, in all the world—freedom for the people and independence for their government. This Nation shall persevere in our pursuit of these objectives.

In Africa, the Congo has been brutally torn by civil strife, political unrest, and public disorder. We shall continue to support the heroic efforts of the United Nations to restore peace and order—efforts which are now endangered by mounting tensions, unsolved problems, and decreasing support from many member states.

In Latin America, Communist agents seeking to exploit that region's peaceful revolution of hope have established a base on Cuba, only 90 miles from our shores. Our objection with Cuba is not over the people's drive for a better life. Our objection is to their domination by foreign and domestic tyrannies. Cuban social and economic reform should be encouraged. Questions of economic and trade policy can always be negotiated. But Communist domination in this hemisphere can never be negotiated.

We are pledged to work with our sister Republics to free the Americas of all such foreign domination and all tyranny, working toward the goal of a free hemisphere of free governments, extending from Cape Horn to the Arctic Circle.

In Europe our alliances are unfulfilled and in some disarray. The unity of NATO has been weakened by economic rivalry and partially eroded by national interest. It has not yet fully mobilized its resources nor fully achieved a common outlook. Yet no Atlantic power can meet on its own the mutual problems now facing us in defense, foreign aid, monetary reserves, and a host of other areas; and our close ties with those whose hopes and interests we share are among this Nation's most powerful assets.

Our greatest challenge is still the world that lies beyond the cold war—but the first great obstacle is still our relations with the Soviet Union and Communist China. We must never be lulled into believing that either power has yielded its ambitions for world domination—ambitions which they forcefully restated only a short time ago. On the contrary, our task is to convince them that aggression and subversion will not be profitable routes to pursue those ends. Open and peaceful competition—for prestige, for markets, for scientific achievement, even for men's minds—is something else again. For if freedom and communism were to compete for man's allegiance in a world at peace, I would look to the future with ever increasing confidence.

To meet this array of challenges—to fulfill the role we cannot avoid on the world scene—we must reexamine and revise our whole arsenal of tools.

One must not overshadow the other. On the Presidential coat of arms, the American eagle holds in his right talon the olive branch, while in his left is held a bundle of arrows. We intend to give equal attention to both.

First, we must strengthen our military tools. We are moving into a period of uncertain risk and great commitment in which both the military and diplomatic possibilities require a free world force so powerful as to make any aggression clearly futile. Yet in the past, lack of a consistent, coherent military strategy, the absence of basic assumptions about our national requirements and the faulty estimates and duplication arising from interservice rivalries have all made it difficult to assess accurately how adequate—or inadequate—our defenses really are.

I have, therefore, instructed the Secretary of Defense to reappraise our entire defense strategy—our ability to fulfill our commitments—the effectiveness, vulnerability, and dispersal of our strategic bases, forces, and warning systems—the efficiency and economy of our operation and organization—the elimination of obsolete bases and installations—and the adequacy, modernization, and mobility of our present conventional and nuclear forces and weapons systems in the light of present and future dangers. I have asked for preliminary conclusions by the end of February—and I shall then recommend whatever legislative, budgetary, or executive action is needed in the light of these conclusions.

In the meantime, I have asked the Defense Secretary to initiate immediately three new steps clearly needed now:

(*a*) I have directed prompt action to increase our airlift capacity. Obtaining additional air transport mobility—and obtaining it now—will better assure the ability of our conventional forces to respond, with discrimination and speed, to any problem at any spot on the globe at any moment's notice. In particular it will enable us to meet any deliberate effort to avoid or divert our forces by starting limited wars in widely scattered parts of the globe.

(*b*) I have directed prompt action to step up our Polaris submarine program. Using unobligated shipbuilding funds now (to let contracts originally scheduled for the next fiscal year) will build and place on station—at least 9 months earlier than planned—substantially more units of a crucial deterrent—a fleet that will never attack first, but possess sufficient powers of retaliation, concealed beneath the seas, to discourage any aggressor from launching an attack on our security.

(*c*) I have directed prompt action to accelerate our entire missile program. Until the Secretary of Defense's reappraisal is completed, the emphasis here will be largely on improved organization and decision making—on cutting down the wasteful duplications and time lag that have handicapped our whole family of missiles. If we are to keep the peace, we need an invulnerable missile force powerful enough to deter any aggressor from even threatening an attack he would know could not destroy enough of our own force to prevent his own destruction. For as I said upon taking the oath of office: "Only when our arms are sufficient beyond doubt can we be certain beyond doubt that they will never be employed."

Secondly, we must improve our economic tools. Our role is essential and unavoidable in the construction of a sound and expanding economy for the entire non-Communist world, helping other nations build the strength to meet their own problems, to satisfy their own aspirations, and to surmount their own dangers. The problems in achieving this goal are towering and unprecedented—the response must be towering and unprecedented as well, much as lend-lease and the Marshall plan were in earlier years, which brought such fruitful results.

(*a*) I intend to ask the Congress for authority to establish a new and more effective program for assisting the economic, educational, and social development of other countries and continents. That program must stimulate and take more effectively into account the contributions of our allies, and provide central policy direction fo· all our own programs that now so often overlap, conflict, or diffuse our energies, and resources. Such a program, compared to past programs, will require—

more flexibility for short-run emergencies;

more commitment to long-term development;

new attention to education at all levels;

greater emphasis on the recipient nations' role, their effort and their purpose, with greater social justice for their own people, with broader distribution and participation of their people, and more efficient public administration and more efficient tax systems of their own.

and orderly planning for national and regional development instead of a piecemeal approach.

(*b*) I hope the Senate will take early action approving the convention establishing the Organization for Economic Cooperation and Development. This will be an important instrument in sharing with our allies this development effort—working toward the time when each nation will contribute in proportion to its own ability to pay. For, while we are prepared to assume our full share of these huge burdens, we cannot and must not be expected to bear them alone.

(*c*) To our sister Republics to the south, we have pledged a new alliance for progress—alianza para progreso. Our goal is a free and prosperous Latin America, realizing for all its states and their citizens a degree of economic and social progress that matches their historic contributions of culture, intellect, and liberty. To start this Nation's role at this time in that alliance of neighbors, I am recommending the following:

That the Congress appropriate in full the $500 million fund pledged by the Act of Bogotá, to be used not as an instrument of the cold war, but as a first step in the sound development of the Americas.

That a new Inter-Departmental Task Force be established under the leadership of the Department of State, to coordinate at the highest level all policies and programs of concern to the Americas.

That our delegates to the OAS, working with those of other members, strengthen that body as an instrument to preserve the peace and to prevent foreign domination anywhere in the hemisphere.

That, in cooperation with other nations, we launch a new hemispheric attack on illiteracy and inadequate educational opportunities at all levels; and, finally,

That a food-for-peace mission be sent immediately to Latin America to explore ways in which our vast food abundance can be used to help end hunger and malnutrition in certain areas of suffering in our own hemisphere.

(*d*) This administration is expanding its new food-for-peace program in every possible way. The product of our abundance must be more effectively used to relieve hunger and help economic growth in all corners of the globe. I have asked the director of this program to recommend additional ways in which these surpluses can advance the interests of world peace—including the establishment of world food reserves.

(*e*) An even more valuable national asset is our reservoir of dedicated men and women—not only on our college campuses but in every age group—who have indicated their desire to contribute their skills, their efforts, and a part of their lives to the fight for world order. We can mobilize this talent through the formation of a National Peace Corps, enlisting the services of all those with the desire and capacity to help foreign lands meet their urgent needs for trained personnel.

(*f*) Finally, while our attention is centered on the development of the non-Communist world, we must never forget our hopes for the ultimate freedom and welfare of the eastern European peoples. In order to be prepared to help reestablish historic ties of friendship, I am asking the Congress for increased discretion to use economic tools in this area whenever this is found to be clearly in the national interest. This will require amendment of the Mutual Defense Assistance Control Act along the lines I proposed as a member of the Senate, and upon which the Senate voted last summer. Meanwhile, I hope to explore with the Polish Government the possibility of using our frozen Polish funds on projects of peace that will demonstrate our abiding friendship and interest in the people of Poland.

Third, we must sharpen our political and diplomatic tools—the means of cooperation and agreement on which an enforceable world order must ultimately rest.

(*a*) I have already taken steps to coordinate and expand our disarmament effort—to increase our programs of research and study—and to make arms control a central goal of our national policy under my personal direction. The deadly arms race, and the huge resources it absorbs, have too long overshadowed all else we must do. We must prevent that arms race from spreading to new nations, to new nuclear powers, and to the reaches of outer space. We must make certain that our negotiators are better informed and better prepared—to formulate workable proposals of our own and to make sound judgments about the proposals of others.

I have asked the other governments concerned to agree to a reasonable delay in the talks on a nuclear test ban—and it is our intention to resume negotiations prepared to reach a final agreement with any nation, that is equally willing to agree to an effective and enforceable treaty.

(*b*) We must increase our support of the United Nations as an instrument to end the cold war instead of an arena in which to fight it. In recognition of its increasing importance and the doubling of its membership—

we are enlarging and strengthening our own mission to the U.N.

we shall help insure that it is properly financed.

we shall work to see that the integrity of the office of the Secretary-General is maintained.

And I would address a special plea to the smaller nations of the world—to join with us in strengthening this organization, which is far more essential to their security than it is to ours—the only body in the world today where no nation need be powerful to be secure, where every nation has an equal voice, and where any nation can exert influence not according to the strength of its armies but according to the strength of its ideas. It deserves the support of all.

(*c*) Finally, this administration intends to explore promptly all possible areas of cooperation with the Soviet Union and other nations "to invoke the wonders of science instead of its terrors." Specifically, I now invite all nations—including the Soviet Union—to join with us in developing a weather prediction program, in a new communications satellite program, and in preparation for probing the distant planets of Mars and Venus, probes which may someday unlock the deepest secrets of the universe.

Today this country is ahead in the science and technology of space, while the Soviet Union is ahead in the capacity to lift large vehicles into orbit. Both nations would help themselves as well as other nations by removing these endeavors from the bitter and wasteful competition of the cold war. The United States would be willing to join with the Soviet Union and the scientists of all nations in a greater effort to make the fruits of this new knowledge available to all—and, beyond that, in an effort to extend farm technology to hungry nations—to wipe out disease—to increase exchanges of scientists and their knowledge—and to make our own laboratories available to technicians of other lands who lack the facilities to pursue their own work. Where nature makes natural allies of us all, we can demonstrate that beneficial relations are possible even with those with whom we most deeply disagree—and this must someday be the basis of world peace and world law.

V

I have commented on the state of the domestic economy, our balance of payments, our Federal and social budget and the state of the world. I would like to conclude with a few remarks about the state of the executive branch. We have found it full of honest and useful public servants—but their capacity to act decisively at the exact time action is needed has too often been muffled in the morass of committees, timidities, and fictitious theories which have created a growing gap between decision and execution, between planning and reality. In a time of rapidly deteriorating situations at home and abroad, this is bad for the public service and particularly bad for the country; and we mean to make a change.

I here pledge myself and my colleagues in the Cabinet to a continuous encouragement of initiative, responsibility, and energy in serving the public interest. Let every public servant know, whether his post is high or low, that a man's rank and reputation in this administration will be determined by the size of the job he does, and not by the size of his staff, his office, or his budget. Let it be clear that this administration recognizes the value of daring and dissent—that we greet healthy controversy as the hallmark of healthy change. Let the public service be a proud and lively career. And let every man and woman who work in any area of our National Government, in any branch, at any level, be able to say with pride and honor in future years: "I served the U.S. Government in that hour of our Nation's need."

For only through complete dedication by us all to the national interest can we bring our country through the troubled years that lie ahead. Our problems are critical. The tide is unfavorable. The news will be worse before it is better. And while hoping and working for the best, we should prepare ourselves for the worst.

We cannot escape our dangers—neither must we let them drive us to panic or narrow isolation. In many areas of the world where the balance of power already rests with our adversary, the forces of freedom are sharply divided. It is one of the ironies of our time that the techniques of a harsh and repressive system should be able to instill discipline and ardor in its servants—while the blessings of liberty have too often stood for privilege, materialism, and a life of ease.

But I have a different view of liberty.

Life in 1961 will not be easy. Wishing it, predicting it, even asking for it, will not make it so. There will be further setbacks before the tide is turned. But turn it we must. The hopes of all mankind rest upon us—not simply upon those of us in this Chamber, but upon the peasant in Laos, the fisherman in Nigeria, the exile from Cuba, the spirit that moves every man and Nation who shares our hopes for freedom and the future. And in the final analysis, they rest most of all upon the pride and perseverance of our fellow American citizens.

In the words of the great President whose birthday we honor today, closing his final state-of-the-Union message 16 years ago: "We pray that we may be worthy of the unlimited opportunities that God has given us."

SECOND ANNUAL MESSAGE.

Jan. 11, 1962

MR. VICE PRESIDENT—MY OLD COLLEAGUE FROM MASSACHUSETTS AND YOUR NEW SPEAKER, JOHN MCCORMACK—MEMBERS OF THE 87TH CONGRESS—LADIES AND GENTLEMEN:

This week we begin anew our joint and separate efforts to build the American future. But, sadly, we build without a man who linked a long past with the present and looked strongly to the future. "Mister Sam" Rayburn is gone. Neither this House nor the Nation is the same without him.

Members of the Congress, the Constitution makes us not rivals for power but partners for progress. We are all trustees for the American people, custodians of the American heritage. It is my task to report the state of the Union—to improve it is the task of us all.

In the past year, I have traveled not only across our own land but to other lands—to the North and the South, and across the seas. And I have found—as I am sure you have, in your travels—that people everywhere, in spite of occasional disappointments, look to us—not to our wealth or power, but to the splendor of our ideals. For our Nation is commissioned by history to be either an observer of freedom's failure or the cause of its success. Our overriding obligation in the months ahead is to fulfill the world's hopes by fulfilling our own faith.

I. STRENGTHENING THE ECONOMY

That task must begin at home. For if we cannot fulfill our own ideals here we cannot expect others to accept them. And when the youngest child alive today has grown to the cares of manhood, our position in the world will be determined first of all by what provisions we make today—for his education, his health, and his opportunities for a good home and a good job and a good life.

At home, we began the year in the valley of recession—we completed it on the high road of recovery and growth. With the help of new congressionally approved or administratively increased stimulants to our economy, the number of major surplus labor areas has declined from 101 to 60; nonagricultural employment has increased by more than a million jobs; and the average factory workweek has risen to well over 40 hours. At year's end the economy, which Mr. Khrushchev once called a "stumbling horse," was racing to new records in consumer spending, labor income, and industrial production.

We are gratified—but we are not satisfied. Too many unemployed are still looking for the blessings of prosperity. As those who leave our schools and farms demand new jobs automation takes old jobs away. To expand our growth and job opportunities, I urge on the Congress three measures:

(1) First, the Manpower Training and Development Act, to stop the waste of able-bodied men and women who want to work, but whose only skill has been replaced by a machine, or moved with a mill,

or shut down with a mine;

(2) Second, the Youth Employment Opportunities Act, to help train and place not only the 1 million young Americans who are both out of school and out of work, but the 26 million young Americans entering the labor market in this decade; and

(3) Third, the 8-percent tax credit for investment in machinery and equipment, which, combined with planned revisions of depreciation allowances, will spur our modernization, our growth and our ability to compete abroad.

Moreover—pleasant as it may be to bask in the warmth of recovery—let us not forget that we have suffered three recessions in the last 7 years. The time to repair the roof is when the sun is shining—by filling three basic gaps in our antirecession protection. We need:

(1) First, Presidential standby authority, subject to congressional veto, to adjust personal income tax rates downward within a specified range and time, to slow down an economic decline before it has dragged us all down.

(2) Second, Presidential standby authority, upon a given rise in the rate of unemployment, to accelerate Federal and federally aided capital improvement programs; and

(3) Third, a permanent strengthening of our unemployment compensation system—to maintain for our fellow citizens searching for a job and cannot find it, their purchasing power and their living standards without constant resort—as we have seen in recent years by Congress and the administrations—to temporary supplements.

If we enact this six-part program, we can show the whole world that a free economy need not be an unstable economy—that a free system need not leave men unemployed—and that a free society is not only the most productive but the most stable form of organization yet fashioned by man.

II. Fighting Inflation

But recession is only one enemy of a free economy—inflation is another. Last year, 1961, despite rising production and demand, consumer prices held almost steady—and wholesale prices declined. This is the best record of overall price stability of any comparable period of recovery since the end of World War II.

Inflation too often follows in the shadow of growth—while price stability is made easy by stagnation or controls. But we mean to maintain both stability and growth in a climate of freedom.

Our first line of defense against inflation is the good sense and public spirit of business and labor—keeping their total increases in wages and profits in step with productivity. There is no single statistical test to guide each company and each union. But I strongly urge them—for their country's interest, and for their own—to apply the test of the public interest to these transactions.

Within this same framework of growth and wage-price stability:

This administration has helped keep our economy competitive by widening the access of small business to credit and Government contracts, and by stepping up the drive against monopoly, price fixing, and racketeering.

We will submit a Federal pay reform bill aimed at giving our classified, postal, and other employees new pay scales more comparable to those of private industry;

We are holding the fiscal 1962 budget deficit far below the level incurred after the last recession in 1958; and, finally, I am submitting for fiscal 1963 a balanced Federal budget.

This is a joint responsibility, requiring congressional cooperation on appropriations, and on three sources of income in particular:

(1) First, an increase in postal rates, to end the postal deficit.

(2) Secondly, passage of the tax reforms previously urged, to remove unwarranted tax preferences, and to apply to dividends and to interest the same withholding requirements we have long applied to wages; and

(3) Third, extension of the present excise and corporation tax rates, except for those changes—which will be recommended in a message—affecting transportation.

III. Getting America Moving

But a stronger nation and economy require more than a balanced budget. They require progress in those programs that spur our growth and fortify our strength.

CITIES

A strong America depends on its cities—America's glory, and sometimes America's shame. To substitute sunlight for congestion, and progress for decay, we have stepped up existing urban renewal and housing programs, and launched new ones—redoubled the attack on water pollution—speeded aid to airports, hospitals, highways, and our declining mass transit systems—and secured new weapons to combat organized crime, racketeering, and youth delinquency, assisted by the coordinated and hard-hitting efforts of our investigative services: The FBI, Internal Revenue, the Bureau of Narcotics, and many others. We shall need further anticrime, mass transit, and transportation legislation—and new tools to fight air pollution. And with all this effort underway, both equity and commonsense require that our Nation's urban areas—containing three-fourths of our population—sit as equals at the Cabinet table. I urge a new Department of Urban Affairs and Housing.

AGRICULTURE AND RESOURCES

A strong America also depends on its farms and natural resources. American farmers took heart in 1961—from a billion dollar rise in farm income—and from a hopeful start on reducing the farm surpluses. But we are still operating under a patchwork accumulation of old laws, which cost us $1 billion a year in CCC carrying charges alone, yet fail to halt rural poverty or boost farm earnings.

Our task is to master and turn to fully fruitful ends the magnificent productivity of our farms and farmers. The revolution on our own countryside stands in the sharpest contrast to the repeated farm failures of the Communist nations, and is a source of pride to us all. Since 1950 our agricultural output per man-hour has actually doubled. Without new, realistic measures, it will someday swamp our farmers and our taxpayers in a national scandal or a farm depression.

I will, therefore, submit to the Congress a new comprehensive farm program—tailored to fit the use of our land and the supplies of each crop to the long-range needs of the sixties—and designed to prevent chaos in the sixties with a program of commonsense.

We also need for the sixties—if we are to bequeath our full national estate to our heirs—a new long-range conservation and recreation program—expansion of our superb national parks and forests—preservation of our authentic wilderness areas—new starts on water and power projects as our population steadily increases—and expanded REA generation and transmission loans.

CIVIL RIGHTS

But America stands for progress in human rights as well as economic affairs, and a strong America requires the assurance of full and equal rights to all its citizens, of any race or of any color. This administration has shown as never before how much could be done through the full use of Executive powers—through the enforcement of laws already passed by the Congress—through persuasion, negotiation, and litigation, to secure the constitutional rights of all: the right to vote, the right to travel without hindrance across State lines, and the right to free public education.

I issued last March a comprehensive order to guarantee the right to equal employment opportunity in all Federal agencies and contractors. The Vice President's Committee thus created has done much, including the voluntary "plans for progress" which, in all sections of the country, are achieving a quiet but striking success in opening up to all races new professional, supervisory, and other job opportunities.

But there is much more to be done—by the Executive, by the courts, and by the Congress. Among the bills now pending before you, on which the executive departments will comment in detail, are appropriate methods of strengthening these basic rights which have our full support. The right to vote, for example, should no longer be denied through such arbitrary devices on a local level, sometimes abused, such as literacy tests and poll taxes. As we approach the 100th anniversary next January, of the Emancipation Proclamation, let the acts of every branch of the Government—and every citizen—portray that "righteousness does exalt a nation."

HEALTH AND WELFARE

Finally, a strong America cannot neglect the aspirations of its citizens—the welfare of the needy, the health care of the elderly, the education of the young. For we are not developing the Nation's wealth for its own sake. Wealth is the means—and people are the ends. All our material riches will avail us little if we do not use them to expand the opportunities of our people.

Last year, we improved the diet of needy people—provided more hot lunches and fresh milk to schoolchildren—built more college dormitories—and, for the elderly, expanded private housing, nursing homes, health services, and social security. But we have just begun.

To help those least fortunate of all, I am recommending a new public welfare program, stressing services instead of support, rehabilitation instead of relief, and training for useful work instead of prolonged dependency.

To relieve the critical shortage of doctors and dentists—and this is a matter which concerns us all—and expand research, I urge action to aid medical and dental colleges and scholarships and to establish new National Institutes of Health.

To take advantage of modern vaccination achievements, I am proposing a mass immunization program, aimed at the virtual elimination of such ancient enemies of our children as polio, diphtheria, whooping cough, and tetanus.

To protect our consumers from the careless and the unscrupulous, I shall recommend improvements in the food and drug laws—strengthening inspection and standards, halting unsafe and worthless products, preventing misleading labels, and cracking down on the illicit sale of habit-forming drugs.

But in matters of health, no piece of unfinished business is more important or more urgent than the enactment under the social security system of health insurance for the aged.

For our older citizens have longer and more frequent illnesses, higher hospital and medical bills and too little income to pay them. Private health insurance helps some—but its cost is high and its coverage limited. Public welfare cannot help those too proud to seek relief but hard pressed to pay their own bills. Nor can their children or grandchildren always sacrifice their own health budgets to meet this constant drain.

Social security has long helped to meet the hardships of retirement, death, and disability. I now urge that its coverage be extended without further delay to provide health insurance for the elderly.

EDUCATION

Equally important to our strength is the quality of our education. Eight million adult Americans are classified as functionally illiterate. This is a disturbing figure reflected in selective service rejection rates—welfare rolls and crime rates. And I shall recommend plans for a massive attack to end this adult illiteracy.

I shall also recommend bills to improve educational quality, to stimulate the arts, and, at the college level, to provide Federal loans for the construction of academic facilities and federally financed scholarships.

If this Nation is to grow in wisdom and strength, then every able highschool graduate should have the opportunity to develop his talents. Yet nearly half lack either the funds or the facilities to attend college. Enrollments are going to double in our colleges in the short space of 10 years. The annual cost per student is skyrocketing to astronomical levels—now averaging $1,650 a year, although almost half of our families earn less than $5,000. They cannot afford such costs—but this Nation cannot afford to maintain its military power and neglect its brainpower.

But excellence in education must begin at the elementary level. I sent to the Congress last year a proposal for Federal aid to public school construction and teachers salaries. I believe that bill, which passed the Senate and received House committee approval, offered the minimum amount required by our needs and—in terms of across-the-board aid—the maximum scope permitted by our Constitution. I therefore see no reason to weaken or withdraw that bill: and I urge its passage at this session.

"Civilization," said H. G. Wells, "is a race between education and catastrophe." It is up to you in this Congress to determine the winner of that race.

These are not unrelated measures addressed to specific gaps or grievances in our national life. They are the pattern of our intentions and the foundation of our hopes.

"I believe in democracy," said Woodrow Wilson, "because it releases the energy of every human being." The dynamic of democracy is the power and the purpose of the individual; and the policy of this administration is to give to the individual the opportunity to realize his own highest possibilities.

Our program is to open to all the opportunity for steady and productive employment, to remove from all the handicap of arbitrary or irrational exclusion, to offer to all the facilities for education and health and welfare, to make society the servant of the individual and the individual the source of progress, and thus to realize for all the full promise of American life.

IV. Our Goals Abroad

All of these efforts at home give meaning to our efforts abroad. Since the close of the Second World War, a global civil war has divided and tormented mankind. But it is not our military might, or our higher standard of living, that has most distinguished us from our adversaries. It is our belief that the state is the servant of the citizen and not his master.

This basic clash of ideas and wills is but one of the forces reshaping our globe—swept as it is by the tides of hope and fear, by crises in the headlines today that become mere footnotes tomorrow. Both the successes and the setbacks of the past year remain on our agenda of unfinished business. For every apparent blessing contains the seeds of danger—every area of trouble gives out a ray of hope—and the one unchangeable certainty is that nothing is certain or unchangeable.

Yet our basic goal remains the same: a peaceful world community of free and independent states—free to choose their own future and their own system, so long as it does not threaten the freedom of others.

Some may choose forms and ways that we would not choose for ourselves—but it is not for us that they are choosing. We can welcome diversity—the Communist cannot. For we offer a world of choice—they offer the world of coercion. And the way of the past shows clearly enough that freedom, not coercion, is the wave of the future. At times our goal has been obscured by crisis or endangered by conflict—but it draws sustenance from five basic sources of strength:

the moral and physical strength of the United States;
the united strength of the Atlantic community;
the regional strength of our hemispheric relations;
the creative strength of our efforts in the new and developing nations; and
the peace-keeping strength of the United Nations.

V. Our Military Strength

Our moral and physical strength begins at home as already discussed. But it includes our military strength as well. So long as fanaticism and fear brood over the affairs of men, we must arm to deter others from aggression.

In the past 12 months our military posture has steadily improved. We increased the previous defense budget by 15 percent—not in the expectation of war but for the preservation of peace. We more than doubled our acquisition rate of Polaris submarines—we doubled the production capacity for Minuteman missiles—and increased by 50 percent the number of manned bombers standing ready on 15-minute alert. This year the combined force levels planned under our new Defense budget—including nearly 300 additional Polaris and Minuteman missiles—have been precisely calculated to insure the continuing strength of our nuclear deterrent.

But our strength may be tested at many levels. We intend to have at all times the capacity to resist nonnuclear or limited attacks—as a complement to our nuclear capacity, not as a substitute. We have rejected any all-or-nothing posture which would leave no choice but inglorious retreat or unlimited retaliation.

Thus we have doubled the number of ready combat divisions in the Army's strategic reserve—increased our troops in Europe—built up the Marines—added a new sealift and airlift capacity—modernized our weapons and ammunition—expanded our antiguerrilla forces—and increased the active fleet by more than 70 vessels and our tactical air forces by nearly a dozen wings.

Because we needed to reach this higher long-term level of readiness more quickly, 155,000 members of the Reserve and National Guard were activated under the act of this Congress. Some disruptions and distress were inevitable. But the overwhelming majority bear their burdens—and their Nation's burdens—with admirable and traditional devotion.

In the coming year, our reserve programs will be revised—two Army divisions will, I hope, replace those Guard divisions on duty—and substantial other increases will boost our Air Force fighter units, the procurement of equipment, and our continental defense and warning efforts. The Nation's first serious civil defense shelter program is underway, identifying, marking, and stocking 50 million spaces; and I urge your approval of Federal incentives for the construction of public fallout shelters in schools and hospitals and similar centers.

VI. The United Nations

But arms alone are not enough to keep the peace—it must be kept by men. Our instrument and our hope is the United Nations—and I see little merit in the impatience of those who would abandon this imperfect world instrument because they dislike our imperfect world. For the troubles of a world organization merely reflect the troubles of the world itself. And if the organization is weakened, these troubles can only increase. We may not always agree with every detailed action taken by every officer of the United Nations, or with every voting majority. But as an institution, it should have in the future, as it has had in the past since its inception, no stronger or more faithful member than the United States of America.

In 1961, the peace-keeping strength of the United Nations was reinforced. And those who preferred or predicted its demise, envisioning a troika in the seat of Hammarskjold—or Red China inside the Assembly—have seen instead a new vigor, under a new Secretary General and a fully independent Secretariat. In making plans for a new forum and principles on disarmament—for peace-keeping in outer space—for a decade of development effort—the U.N. fulfilled its charter's lofty aims.

Eighteen months ago the tangled, turbulent Congo presented the U.N. with its gravest challenge. The prospect was one of chaos—or certain big-power confrontation, with all its hazards and all of its risks, to us and to others. Today the hopes have improved for peaceful conciliation within a united Congo. This is the objective of our policy in this important area.

No policeman is universally popular—particularly when he uses his stick to restore law and order on his beat. Those members who are willing to contribute their votes and their views—but very little else—have created a serious deficit by refusing to pay their share of special U.N. assessments. Yet they do pay their annual assessments to retain their votes—and a new U.N. bond issue, financing special operations for the next 18 months, is to be repaid with interest from these regular assessments. This is clearly in our interest. It will not only keep the U.N. solvent, but require all voting members to pay their fair share of its activities. Our share of special operations has long been much higher than our share of the annual assessment—and the bond issue will in effect reduce our disproportionate obligation, and for these reasons, I am urging Congress to approve our participation.

With the approval of this Congress, we have undertaken in the past year a great new effort in outer space. Our aim is not simply to be first on the moon, any more than Charles Lindbergh's real aim was to be the first to Paris. His aim was to develop the techniques of our own country and other countries in the field of air and the atmosphere, and our objective in making this effort, which we hope will place one of our citizens on the moon, is to develop in a new frontier of science, commerce, and cooperation, the position of the United States and the free world.

This Nation belongs among the first to explore it, and among the first, if not the first, we shall be. We are offering our know-how and our cooperation to the U.N. Our satellites will soon be providing other nations with improved weather observations. And I shall soon send to the Congress a measure to govern the financing and operation of an international communications satellite system, in a manner consistent with the public interest and our foreign policy.

But peace in space will help us naught once peace on earth is gone. World order will be secured only when the whole world has laid down these weapons which seem to offer present security but threaten the future survival of the human race. That armistice day seems very far away. The vast resources of this planet are being devoted more and more to the means of destroying, instead of enriching, human life.

But the world was not meant to be a prison in which man awaits his execution. Nor has mankind survived the tests and trials of thousands of years to surrender everything—including its existence—now. This Nation has the will and the faith to make a supreme effort to break the logjam on disarmament and nuclear tests—and we will persist until we prevail, until the rule of law has replaced the ever-dangerous use of force.

VII. Latin America

I turn now to a prospect of great promise: our hemispheric relations. The alliance for progress is being rapidly transformed from proposal to program. Last month in Latin America I saw for myself the quickening of hope, the revival of confidence, and the new trust in our country—among workers and farmers as well as diplomats. We have pledged our help in speeding their economic, educational, and social progress. The Latin American Republics have in turn pledged a new and strenuous effort of self-help and self-reform.

To support this historic undertaking, I am proposing—under the authority contained in the bills of the last session of the Congress—a special long-term alliance for progress fund of $3 billion. Combined with our food for peace, Export-Import Bank, and other resources, this will provide more than $1 billion a year in new support for the alliance. In addition, we have increased twelvefold our Spanish and Portuguese-language broadcasting in Latin America, and improved hemispheric trade and defense. And while the blight of communism has been increasingly exposed and isolated in the Americas, liberty has scored a gain. The people of the Dominican Republic, with our firm encouragement and help, and those of our sister Republics of this hemisphere, are safely passing the treacherous course from dictatorship through disorder toward democracy.

VIII. The New and Developing Nations

Our efforts to help other new or developing nations, and to strengthen their stand for freedom, have also made progress. A newly unified Agency for International Development is reorienting our foreign assistance to emphasize long-term development loans instead of grants, more economic aid instead of military, individual plans to meet the individual needs of the nations, and new standards on what they must do to marshal their own resources.

A newly conceived Peace Corps is winning friends and helping people in 14 countries—supplying trained and dedicated young men and women, to give these new nations a hand in building a society, and a glimpse of the best that is in our country. If there be a problem here, it is that we cannot supply the spontaneous and mounting demand.

A newly expanded food for peace program is feeding the hungry of many lands with the abundance of our productive farms—providing lunches for children in school, wages for economic development, relief for the victims of flood and famine, and a better diet for millions whose daily bread is their chief concern.

These programs help people; and, by helping people, they help freedom. The views of their governments may sometimes be very different from ours—but events in Africa, the Middle East and Eastern Europe teach us never to write off any nation as lost to the Communists. That is the lesson of our time. We support the independence of those newer or weaker states whose history, geography, economy or lack of power impels them to remain outside "entangling alliances"—as we did for more than a century. For the independence of nations is a bar to the Communists' "grand design"—it is the basis of our own.

In the past year, for example, we have urged a neutral and independent Laos—regained there a common policy with our major allies—and insisted that a cease fire precede negotiations. While a workable formula for supervising its independence is still to be achieved, both the spread of war—which might have involved this country also—and a Communist occupation have thus far been prevented.

A satisfactory settlement in Laos would also help to achieve and safeguard the peace in Vietnam—where the foe is increasing his tactics of terror—where our own efforts have been stepped up—and where the local government has initiated new programs and reforms to broaden the base of resistance. The systematic aggression now bleeding that country is not a "war of liberation"—for Vietnam is already free. It is a war of attempted subjugation—and it will be resisted.

IX. The Atlantic Community

Finally, the united strength of the Atlantic Community has flourished in the last year under severe tests. NATO has increased both the number and the readiness of its air, ground, and naval units—both its nuclear and nonnuclear capabilities. Even greater efforts by all its members are still required. Nevertheless, our unity of purpose and will has been, I believe, immeasurably strengthened.

The threat to the brave city of Berlin remains. In these last 6 months the Allies have made it unmistakably clear that our presence in Berlin, our free access thereto, and the freedom of 2 million West Berliners would not be surrendered either to force or through appeasement—that, to maintain those rights and obligations, we are prepared to talk, when appropriate, and to fight, if necessary. Every member of NATO stands with us in a common commitment to preserve this symbol of freeman's will to remain free.

I cannot now predict the course of future negotiations over Berlin. I can only say that we are sparing no honorable effort to find a peaceful and mutually acceptable resolution of this problem. I believe such a resolution can be found, and with it an improvement in our relations with the Soviet Union, if only the leaders in the Kremlin will recognize the basic rights and interests involved, and the interest of all mankind in peace.

But the Atlantic Community is no longer concerned with purely military aims. As its common undertakings grow at an ever-increasing pace, we are, and increasingly will be, partners in aid, trade, defense, diplomacy, and monetary affairs.

The emergence of the new Europe is being matched by the emergence of new ties across the Atlantic. It is a matter of undramatic daily cooperation in hundreds of workaday tasks: of currencies kept in effective relation, of development loans meshed together, of standardized weapons, and concerted diplomatic positions. The Atlantic Community grows, not like a volcanic mountain, by one mighty explosion, but like a coral reef, from the accumulating activity of all.

Thus, we in the free world are moving steadily toward unity and cooperation, in the teeth of that old Bolshevik prophecy, and at the very time when extraordinary rumbles of discord can be heard across the Iron Curtain. It is not free societies which bear within them the seeds of inevitable disunity.

X. Our Balance of Payments

On one special problem, of great concern to our friends, and to us, I am proud to give the Congress an encouraging report. Our efforts to safeguard the dollar are progressing. In the 11 months preceding last February 1, we suffered a net loss of nearly $2 billion in gold. In the 11 months that followed, the loss was just over half a billion dollars. And our deficit in our basic transactions with the rest of the world—trade, defense, foreign aid, and capital, excluding volatile short-term flows—has been reduced from $2 billion for 1960 to about one-third that amount for 1961. Speculative fever against the dollar is ending—and confidence in the dollar has been restored.

We did not—and could not—achieve these gains through import restrictions, troop withdrawals, exchange controls, dollar devaluation, or choking off domestic recovery. We acted not in panic but in perspective. But the problem is not yet solved. Persistently large deficits would endanger our economic growth and our military and defense commitments abroad. Our goal must be a reasonable equilibrium in our balance of payments. With the cooperation of the Congress, business, labor, and our major allies, that goal can be reached.

We shall continue to attract foreign tourists and investments to our shores, to seek increased military purchases here by our allies, to maximize foreign aid procurement from American firms, to urge increased aid from other fortunate nations to the less fortunate, to seek tax laws which do not favor investment in other industrialized nations or tax havens, and to urge coordination of allied fiscal and monetary policies so as to discourage large and disturbing capital movements.

Above all, if we are to pay for our commitments abroad, we must expand our exports. Our businessmen must be export-conscious and export-competitive. Our tax policies must spur modernization of our plants—our wage and price gains must be consistent with productivity to hold the line on prices—our export credit and promotion campaigns for American industries must continue to expand.

But the greatest challenge of all is posed by the growth of the European Common Market. Assuming the accession of the United Kingdom, there will arise across the Atlantic a trading partner behind a single external tariff similar to ours with an economy which nearly equals our own. Will we in this country adapt our thinking to these new prospects and patterns—or will we wait until events have passed us by?

This is the year to decide. The Reciprocal Trade Act is expiring. We need a new law—a wholly new approach—a bold new instrument of American trade policy. Our decision could well affect the unity of the West, the course of the cold war and the economic growth of our Nation for a generation to come.

If we move decisively, our factories and farms can increase their sales to their richest, fastest growing market. Our exports will increase. Our balance-of-payments position will improve. And we will have forged across the Atlantic a trading partnership with vast resources for freedom.

If, on the other hand, we hang back in deference to local economic pressures, we will find ourselves cut off from our major allies. Industries—and I believe this is most vital—industries will move their plants and jobs and capital inside the walls of the Common Market, and jobs, therefore, will be lost here in the United States, if they cannot otherwise compete for its consumers.

Our farm surpluses will pile up, and our balance of trade, as you all know, to Europe, Common Market, in farm products, is nearly 3 or 4 to 1 in our favor, amounting to one of the best earners of dollars in our balance-of-payments structure, and without entrance to this market, without the ability to enter it, our farm surpluses will pile up in the Middle West, tobacco in the South, and other commodities, which have gone through Western Europe for 15 years.

Our balance-of-payments position will worsen. Our consumers will lack a wider choice of goods at lower prices. And millions of American workers—whose jobs depend on the sale or the transportation or the distribution of exports or imports, or whose jobs will be endangered by the movement of our capital to Europe, or whose jobs can be maintained only in an expanding economy—these millions of workers in your home States and mine will see their real interests sacrificed.

Members of the Congress, the United States did not rise to greatness by waiting for others to lead. This Nation is the world's foremost manufacturer, farmer, banker, consumer, and exporter. The Common Market is moving ahead at an economic growth rate twice ours. The Communist economic offensive is underway. The opportunity is ours—the initiative is up to us—and I believe that 1962 is the time.

To seize that initiative, I shall shortly send to the Congress a new 5-year trade expansion action, far-reaching in scope but designed with great care to make certain that its benefits to our people far outweigh any risks. The bill will permit the gradual elimination of tariffs here in the United States and in the Common Market on those items in which we together supply 80 percent of the world's trade—mostly items in which our own ability to compete is demonstrated by the fact that we sell abroad, in these items, substantially more than we import. This step will make it possible for our major industries to compete with their counterparts in Western Europe for access to European consumers.

On the other hand, the bill will permit a gradual reduction of duties up to 50 percent—permit bargaining by major categories—and provide for appropriate and tested forms of assistance to firms and employees adjusting to import competition. We are not neglecting the safeguards provided by peril points, an escape clause, or the national security amendment. Nor are we abandoning our non-European friends or our traditional most-favored-nation principle. On the contrary, the bill will provide new encouragement for their sale of tropical agricultural products, so important to our friends in Latin America, who have long depended upon the European Common Market who now find themselves faced with new challenges which we must join with them in overcoming.

Concessions, in this bargaining, must of course be reciprocal, not unilateral. The Common Market will not fulfill its own high promise unless its outside tariff walls are low. The dangers of restriction or timidity in our own policy have counterparts for our friends in Europe. For together we face a common challenge: to enlarge the prosperity of freemen everywhere—and to build in partnership a new trading community in which all free nations may gain from the productive energy of free competitive effort.

These various elements in our foreign policy lead, as I have said, to a single goal—the goal of a peaceful world of free and independent states. This is our guide for the present and our vision for the future—a free community of nations, independent but interdependent, uniting north and south, east and west, in one great family of man, outgrowing and transcending the hates and fears that rend our age.

We will not reach that goal today, or tomorrow. We may not reach it in our own lifetime. But the quest is the greatest adventure of our century. We sometimes chafe at the burden of our obligations, the complexity of our decisions, the agony of our choices. But there is no comfort or security for us in evasion, no solution in abdication, no relief in irresponsibility.

A year ago, in assuming the tasks of the Presidency, I said that few generations, in all history, had been granted the role of being the great defender of freedom in its hour of maximum danger. This is our good fortune; and I welcome it now as I did a year ago. For it is the fate of this generation—of you in the Congress and of me as President—to live with a struggle we did not start, in a world we did not make. But the pressures of life are not always distributed by choice. And while no nation has ever faced such a challenge, no nation has ever been so ready to seize the burden and glory of freedom. And in this high endeavor may God watch over the United States of America.

THIRD ANNUAL MESSAGE.

Jan. 14, 1963

MR. VICE PRESIDENT, MR. SPEAKER, MEMBERS OF THE 88TH CONGRESS:

I congratulate you all—not merely on your electoral victory but on your selected role in history. For you and I are privileged to serve the great Republic in what could be the most decisive decade of its life. The choices we make, for good or ill, will affect the wellfare of generations yet unborn.

Little more than a hundred weeks ago I assumed the office of President of the United States. In seeking the help of the Congress and my countrymen, I pledged no easy answers. I pledged—and asked—only toil and dedication. These the Congress and the people have given in good measure. And today, having witnessed in recent months a heightened respect for our national purpose and power, having seen the courageous calm of a united people in a perilous hour, and having observed a steady improvement in the opportunities and well-being of our citizens, I can report to you that the state of this old but youthful Union is good.

In the world beyond our borders, steady progress has been made in building a world of order. The people of West Berlin remain free and secure. A settlement, though still precarious, has been reached in Laos. The spearpoint of aggression has been blunted in South

Vietnam. The end of agony may be in sight in the Congo. The doctrine of troika is dead. And, while danger continues, a deadly threat has been removed from Cuba.

At home, the recession is behind us. Well over a million more men and women are working today than were working 2 years ago. The average factory workweek is once again more than 40 hours; our industries are turning out more goods than ever before; and more than half of the manufacturing capacity that lay silent and wasted 100 weeks ago is humming with activity.

In short, both at home and abroad, there may now be a temptation to relax. For the road has been long, the burden heavy, and the pace consistently urgent.

But we cannot be satisfied to rest here. This is the side of the hill, not the top. The mere absence of war is not peace. The mere absence of recession is not growth. We have made a beginning—but we have only begun.

Now the time has come to make the most of our gains—to translate the renewal of our national strength into the achievement of our national purpose.

II

America has enjoyed 22 months of uninterrupted economic recovery. But recovery is not enough. If we are to prevail in the long run, we must expand the longrun strength of our economy. We must move along the path to a higher rate of growth and full employment.

For this would mean tens of billions of dollars more each year in production, profits, wages, and public revenues. It would mean an end to the persistent slack which has kept unemployment at or above 5 percent for 61 out of 62 months—and an end to the growing pressures for such restrictive measures as the 35-hour week, which alone could increase hourly labor costs by as much as 14 percent, start a new wage-price spiral of inflation, and undercut our efforts to compete with other nations.

To achieve these greater gains, one step, above all, is essential—the enactment this year of a substantial reduction and revision in Federal income taxes.

For it is increasingly clear—to those in Government, business, and labor who are responsible for our economy's success—that our obsolete tax system exerts too heavy a drag on private purchasing power, profits, and employment. Designed to check inflation in earlier years, it now checks growth instead. It discourages extra effort and risk. It distorts the use of resources. It invites recurrent recessions, depresses our Federal revenues, and causes chronic budget deficits.

Now, when the inflationary pressures of the war and postwar years no longer threaten, and the dollar commands new respect—now, when no military crisis strains our resources—now is the time to act. We cannot afford to be timid or slow. For this is the most urgent task confronting the Congress in 1963.

In an early message, I shall propose a permanent reduction in tax rates which will lower liabilities by $13.5 billion. Of this, $11 billion results from reducing individual tax rates, which now range between 20 and 91 percent to a more sensible range of 14 to 65 percent, with a split in the present first bracket. Two and one-half billion dollars results from reducing corporate tax rates, from 52 percent—which gives the Government today a majority interest in profits—to the permanent pre-Korean level of 47 percent. This is in addition to the more than $2 billion cut in corporate tax liabilities resulting from last year's investment credit and depreciation reform.

To achieve this reduction within the limits of a manageable budgetary deficit, I urge: First, that these cuts be phased over 3 calendar years, beginning in 1963 with a cut of some $6 billion at annual rates; second, that these reductions be coupled with selected structural changes, beginning in 1964, which will broaden the tax base, and unfair or unnecessary preferences, remove or lighten certain hardships, and in the net offset some $3.5 billion of the revenue loss; and third, that budgetary receipts at the outset be increased by $1.5 billion a year, without any change in tax liabilities, by gradually shifting the tax payments of large corporations to a more current time schedule. This combined program, by increasing the amount of our national income, will in time result in still higher Federal revenues. It is a fiscally responsible program—the surest and soundest way of achieving in time a balanced budget in a balanced full employment economy.

This net reduction in tax liabilities of $10 billion will increase the purchasing power of American families and business enterprises in every tax bracket, with the greatest increase going to our low-income consumers. It will, in addition, encourage the initiative and risk taking on which our free enterprise system depends: induce more investment, production, and capacity use; help provide the 2 million new jobs we need every year; and reinforce the American principle of additional reward for additional effort.

I do not say that a measure for tax reduction and reform is the only way to achieve these goals.

> No doubt a massive increase in Federal spending could also create jobs and growth—but, in today's setting, private consumers, employers, and investors should be given a full opportunity first.
>
> No doubt a temporary tax cut could provide a spur to our economy—but a longrun problem compels a longrun solution.
>
> No doubt a reduction in either individual or corporation taxes alone would be of great help—but corporations need customers and jobseekers need jobs.
>
> No doubt tax reduction without reform would sound simpler and more attractive to many—but our growth is also hampered by a host of tax inequities and special preferences which have distorted the flow of investment.
>
> And, finally, there are no doubt some who would prefer to put off a tax cut in the hope that ultimately an end to the cold war would make possible an equivalent reduction in Government expenditures—but that end is not in view and to wait for it would be costly and self-defeating.

In submitting a tax program which will, of course, temporarily increase the deficit but can, I believe, ultimately end it, and in recognition of the need to control expenditures, I will shortly submit a fiscal 1964 administrative budget which, while allowing for needed rises in defense, space and fixed interest charges, holds total expenditures for all other purposes below this year's level.

This requires the reduction or postponement of many desirable programs, the absorption of a large part of last year's Federal pay raise through personnel and other economies, the termination of certain installations and projects, and the substitution in several programs of private for public credit. But I am convinced that the enactment this year of tax reduction and tax reform overshadows all other domestic problems in this Congress. For we cannot lead for long the cause of peace and freedom, if we ever cease to set the pace at home.

III

Tax reduction alone, however, is not enough to strengthen our society, to provide opportunities for the 4 million new Americans who are born every year, to improve the lives of the 32 million Americans who still live on the outskirts of poverty.

The quality of American life must keep pace with the quantity of American goods.

This country cannot afford to be materially rich and spiritually desperately poor.

Therefore, by holding down the budgetary cost of existing programs to keep within the limitations I have set, it is both possible and imperative to adopt other new measures that we cannot afford to postpone.

These measures are based on a series of fundamental premises, grouped under four related headings:

First, we need to strengthen our Nation by investing in our youth:

The future of any country which is dependent on the will and wisdom of its citizens is damaged, and irreparably damaged, whenever any of its children are not educated to the fullest extent of his capacity, from grade school through graduate school. Today, an estimated 4 out of every 10 students in the fifth grade will never finish high school—and that is a waste we cannot afford.

In addition, there is no reason why 1 million young Americans, out of school and out of work, should all remain unwanted and often untrained on our city streets when their energies can be put to good use.

Finally, the oversea success of our Peace Corps volunteers, most of them young men and women carrying skills and ideals to needy people, suggests the merit of a similar corps serving our own community needs: in mental hospitals, on Indian reservations, in centers for the aged or for young delinquents, in schools for the illiterate or the handicapped. As the idealism of our youth has served world peace, so can it serve the domestic tranquillity.

Second, we need to strengthen our Nation by safeguarding its health:

Our working men and women—instead of being forced to ask for help from public charity once they are old and ill—should start contributing now to their own retirement health program through the social security system.

Moreover, all our miracles of medical research will count for little if we cannot reverse the growing nationwide shortage of doctors, dentists, and nurses, and the widespread shortages of nursing homes and modern urban hospital facilities. Merely to keep the present ratio of doctors and dentists from declining any further, this country must over the next 10 years increase the capacity of our medical schools by 50 percent and our dental schools by 100 percent.

Finally, and of deep concern, I believe that the abandonment of the mentally ill and the mentally retarded to the grim mercy of custodial institutions too often inflicts on them and their families a needless cruelty which this Nation should not endure. The incidence of mental retardation in the United States of America is three times as high as that of Sweden, for example—and that figure can and must be reduced.

Third, we need to strengthen our Nation by protecting the basic rights of its citizens:

The right to competent counsel must be assured to every man accused of crime in Federal court, regardless of his means.

And the most precious and powerful right in the world, the right to vote in a free American election, must not be denied to any citizen on grounds of his race or his color.

I wish that all qualified Americans permitted to vote were willing to vote; but surely, in this centennial year of the Emancipation, all those who are willing to vote should always be permitted.

Fourth, we need to strengthen our Nation by making the best and the most economical use of its resources and facilities:

Our economic health depends on having healthy transportation arteries; and I believe the way to a more modern, economical choice of national transportation service is through increased competition and decreased regulation. Local mass transit, faring even worse, is as essential a community service as highways. Nearly three-fourths of our citizens live in urban areas, which occupy only 2 percent of our land, and if local transit is to survive and relieve the congestion of these cities, it needs Federal stimulation and assistance.

Next, this Government is in the storage and stockpile business to the melancholy tune of $16 billion. We must continue to support farm income, but we should not pile more farm surpluses on top of the $7.5 billion worth we already own. We must maintain a stockpile of strategic materials, but the $8.5 billion worth we have acquired—for reasons both good and bad—is much more than we need; and we should be empowered to dispose of the excess in ways which will not cause market disruption.

Finally, our already overcrowded national parks and recreation areas will have twice as many visitors 10 years from now. If we do not plan today for the future growth of these and other great natural assets—not only parks and forests but wildlife and wilderness preserves, and water projects of all kinds—our children and their children will be poorer in every sense of the word. Proposals will be made to the Congress in the coming days to meet these challenges.

These are not domestic concerns alone. For upon our achievement of greater vitality and strength at home hang our fate and future in the world: our ability to sustain and supply the security of free men and nations; our ability to command their respect for our leadership; our ability to expand our trade without threat to our balance of payments; and our ability to adjust to the changing demands of cold war competition and challenge.

We shall be judged more by what we do at home than what we preach abroad. Nothing we could do to help the developing countries would help them half as much as a booming American economy, which consumes their raw materials. And nothing our opponents could do to encourage their own ambitions would encourage them half so much as a lagging U.S. economy. These domestic tasks do not divert our energy from our security—they provide the very foundation for freedom's survival and success.

IV

Turning to the world outside, it was only a few years ago—in southeast Asia, Africa, Eastern Europe, Latin America, even in outer space—that communism sought to convey the image of a unified, confident, and expanding empire, closing in on a sluggish America and a free world in disarray. But few people would hold to that picture today.

In these past months, we have reaffirmed the scientific and military superiority of freedom. We have doubled our efforts in space, to assure us of being first in the future. We have undertaken the most far-reaching defense improvements in the peacetime history of this country. And we have maintained the frontiers of freedom from Vietnam to West Berlin.

But complacency or self-congratulation can imperil our security as much as the weapons of our adversary. A moment of pause is not a promise of peace. Dangerous problems remain from Cuba to the South China Sea. The world's prognosis prescribes not a year's vacation, but a year of obligation and opportunity.

Four special avenues of opportunity stand out: The Atlantic alliance, the developing nations, the new Sino-Soviet difficulties, and the search for worldwide peace.

V

First, how fares the grand alliance? Free Europe is entering into a new phase of its long and brilliant history. The era of colonial expansion has passed; the era of national rivalries is fading; and a new era of interdependence and unity is taking shape. Defying the old prophecies of Marx, consenting to what no conqueror could ever compel, the free nations of Europe are moving toward a unity of purpose and power and policy in every sphere of activity.

For 17 years this movement has had our consistent support, both political and economic. Far from resenting the new Europe, we regard her as a welcome partner, not a rival. For the road to world peace and freedom is still very long, and there are burdens which only full partners can share—in supporting the common defense, in expanding world trade, in alining our balance of payments, in aiding the emergent nations, in concerting political and economic policies, and in welcoming to our common effort other industrialized nations, notably Japan, whose remarkable economic and political development of the 1950's permits it now to play on the world scene a major constructive role.

No doubt differences of opinion will continue to get more attention than agreements on action, as Europe moves from independence to more formal interdependence. But these are honest differences among honorable associates—more real and frequent, in fact, among our West European Allies than between them and the United States. For the unity of freedom has never relied on uniformity of opinion, fortunately. But the basic agreement of this alliance on fundamental issues continues.

The first task of the alliance remains the common defense. Last month Prime Minister Macmillan and I laid plans for a new stage in our long cooperative effort, one which aims to assist in the wider task of framing a common nuclear defense for the whole alliance.

The Nassau agreement recognizes that the security of the West is indivisible, and so must be our defense. But it also recognizes that this is an alliance of proud and sovereign nations, and works best when we do not forget it. It recognizes further that the nuclear defense of the West is not a matter for the present nuclear powers alone, that France will be such a power in the future, and that ways must be found without increasing the hazards of nuclear diffusion, to increase the role of our other partners in planning, manning, and directing a truly multilateral nuclear force within an increasingly intimate NATO alliance. Finally, the Nassau agreement recognizes that nuclear defense is not enough, that the agreed NATO levels of conventional strength must be met, and that the NATO alliance cannot afford to be in a position of having to answer every threat with nuclear weapons or nothing.

We remain too near the Nassau decisions, and too far from their final realization, to know their final place in history. But I believe that, for the first time, the door is open for the nuclear defense of the alliance to become a source of confidence, instead of a cause of contention.

The next most pressing concern of the alliance is our common economic goals of trade and growth. This Nation continues to be concerned about its balance-of-payments deficit, which, despite its decline, remains a stubborn and troublesome problem. We believe, moreover, that closer economic ties among all free nations are essential to prosperity and peace. And neither we nor the members of the Common Market are so affluent that we can long afford to shelter high cost farms or factories from the winds of foreign competition, or to restrict the channels of trade with other nations of the free world. If the Common Market should now move toward protectionism and restrictionism, it would undermine its own basic principles. This Government means to use the authority conferred on it last year by the Congress to encourage trade expansion on both sides of the Atlantic and around the world.

VI

Second, what of the developing and nonalined nations? They were shocked by the Soviets' sudden and secret attempt to transform Cuba into a nuclear striking base, and by Communist China's arrogant invasion of India. They have been reassured by our prompt assistance to India, by our support through the United Nations of the Congo's unification, by our patient search for disarmament, and by the improvement in our treatment of citizen and visitors whose skins do not happen to be white. And as the older colonialism recedes, and the neocolonialism of the Communist Powers stands out more starkly than ever, they realize more clearly that the issue in the world struggle is not communism versus capitalism, but coercion versus free choice.

They realize that the longing for independence is the same the world over, whether it is the independence of West Berlin or Vietnam. They realize that such independence runs athwart all Communist ambitions but is in keeping with our own—and that our approach to their needs is resilient and resourceful, while the Communists rely on ancient doctrines and old dogmas.

Nevertheless it is hard for any nation to focus on an external or subversive threat to its independence when its energies are drained in daily combat with the forces of poverty and despair. It makes little sense for us to assail, in speeches and resolutions, the horrors of communism, to spend $50 billion a year to prevent its military advance, and then to begrudge spending, largely on American products, less than one-tenth of that amount to help other nations strengthen their independence and cure the social chaos in which communism always has thrived.

I am proud—and I think most Americans are proud—of a mutual defense and assistance program, evolved with bipartisan support in three administrations, which has, with all of its recognized problems, contributed to the fact that not a single one of the nearly 50 U.N. members to gain independence since the Second World War has succumbed to Communist control.

I am proud of a program and of a country that has helped to arm and feed and clothe millions of people on the frontlines of freedom.

I am especially proud that this country has put forward for the 1960's a vast cooperative effort to achieve economic growth and social progress throughout the Americas—the Alliance for Progress.

I do not underestimate the difficulties that we face in this mutual effort among our close neighbors, but the free states of this hemisphere, working in close collaboration, have begun to make this Alliance a reality. Today it is feeding one out of every four school-age children in Latin America an extra food ration from our farm surplus. It has distributed 1.5 million schoolbooks and is building 17,000 classrooms. It has helped resettle tens of thousands of farm families on land they can call their own. It is stimulating our good neighbors to more self-help and reform—fiscal, social, institutional, and land reforms. It is bringing housing and hope and health to millions who were previously forgotten. The men and women of this hemisphere know that the Alliance would not succeed if it were only another name for U.S. handouts—that it can succeed only as the Latin American nations themselves devote their best effort to fulfilling its goals.

The story is the same in Africa, in the Middle East, in Asia. Wherever nations are willing to help themselves, we stand ready to help them build new bulwarks of freedom. We are not purchasing votes for the cold war; we have gone to the aid of imperiled nations, neutrals and allies alike. What we do ask—and all that we ask—is that our help be used to the best advantage, and that their own efforts not be diverted by needless quarrels with other independent nations.

Despite all its past achievements, the continued progress of the mutual assistance program requires a persistent discontent with present progress. We have been reorganizing this program to make it a more effective and efficient instrument, and that process will continue this year.

But free world development will still be an uphill struggle. Governmental aid can only supplement the role of private investment, trade expansion, and commodity stabilization, and, above all, internal self-improvement. The processes of growth are gradual—bearing fruit in a decade, not in a day. Our successes will neither be quick nor dramatic. But if these programs were ever to be ended, our failures in a dozen countries would be sudden and would be certain.

Neither money nor technical assistance, however, can be our only weapon against poverty. In the end, the crucial effort is one of purpose, requiring not only the fuel of finance but the torch of idealism. And nothing carries the spirit of American idealism and expresses our hopes better and more effectively to the far corners of the earth than the Peace Corps.

A year ago, less than 900 Peace Corps volunteers were on the job. A year from now they will number more than 9,000—men and women, aged 18 to 79, willing to give 2 years of their lives to helping people in other lands.

There are, in fact, nearly 1 million Americans serving their country and the cause of freedom in oversea posts, a record no other people can match. Surely those of us who stay at home should be glad to help indirectly—by supporting our aid programs; by opening our doors to foreign visitors and diplomats and students; and by proving, day by day, by deed as well as by word, that we are a just and generous people.

VII

Third, what comfort can we take from the increasing strains and tensions within the Communist bloc? Here hope must be tempered with caution. For the Soviet-Chinese disagreement is over means, not ends. A dispute over how to bury the West is no grounds for Western rejoicing.

Nevertheless, while a strain is not a fracture, it is clear that the forces of diversity are at work inside the Communist camp, despite all the iron disciplines of regimentation and all the iron dogmatisms of ideology. Marx is proven wrong once again: for it is the closed Communist societies, not the free and open societies, which carry within themselves the seeds of internal disintegration.

This disarray of the Communist empire has been heightened by two other formidable forces. One is the historic force of nationalism and the yearning of all men to be free. The other is the gross inefficiency of their economies. For a closed society is not open to ideas of progress, and a police state finds it cannot command the grain to grow.

New nations asked to choose between two competing systems need only compare conditions in East and West Germany, Eastern and Western Europe, North and South Vietnam. They need only compare the disillusionment of Communist Cuba with the promise of a hemisphere Alliance for Progress. And all the world knows that no successful system builds a wall to keep its people in and freedom out, and that the wall of shame dividing Berlin is a symbol of Communist failure.

VIII

Finally, what can we do to move from the present pause toward enduring peace? Again I would counsel caution. I foresee no spectacular reversal in Communist methods or goals. But if all these trends and developments can persuade the Soviet Union to walk the path of peace, then let her know that all free nations will join with her. But until that choice is made, and until the world can develop a reliable system of international security, the free peoples have no choice but to keep their arms near.

This country, therefore, continues to require the best defense in the world—a defense which is suited to the sixties. This means, unfortunately, a rising defense budget—for there is no substitute for adequate defense, and no "bargain basement" way of achieving it. It means the expenditure of more than $15 billion this year on nuclear weapons systems alone, a sum which is about equal to the combined defense budgets of our European allies.

But it also means improved air and missile defenses, improved civil defense, a strengthened antiguerrilla capacity and, of prime importance, more powerful and flexible nonnuclear forces. For threats of massive retaliation may not deter piecemeal aggression—and a line of destroyers in a quarantine, or a division of well-equipped men on a border, may be more useful to our real security than the multiplication of awesome weapons beyond all rational need.

But our commitment to national safety is not a commitment to expand our Military Establishment indefinitely. We do not dismiss disarmament as an idle dream. For we believe that, in the end, it is the only way of assuring the security of all without impairing the interests of any. Nor do we mistake honorable negotiation for appeasement. While we shall never weary in the defense of freedom, neither shall we abandon the pursuit of peace.

In this quest the United Nations requires our full and continued support. Its value in serving the cause of peace has been shown anew in its role in the West New Guinea settlement, in its use as a forum for the Cuban crisis, and in its task of unification in the Congo. Today the United Nations is primarily the protector of the small and the weak, and a safety valve for the strong. Tomorrow it can form the framework for a world of law—a world in which no nation dictates the destiny of another, and in which the vast resources now devoted to destructive means will serve constructive ends.

In short, let our adversaries choose. If they choose peaceful competition, they shall have it. If they come to realize that their ambitions cannot succeed—if they see that their "wars of liberation" and subversion will ultimately fail; if they recognize that there is more security in accepting inspection than in permitting new nations to master the black arts of nuclear weapons and war; and if they are willing to turn their energies, as we are, to the great unfinished tasks of our own peoples—then, surely, the areas of agreement can be very wide indeed: a clear understanding about Berlin, stability in southeast Asia, an end to nuclear testing, new checks on surprise or accidental attack, and, ultimately, general and complete disarmament.

IX

For we seek not the worldwide victory of one nation or system but a worldwide victory of men. The modern globe is too small, its weapons too destructive—they multiply too fast—and its disorders too contagious to permit any other kind of victory.

To achieve this end the United States will continue to spend a greater portion of its national production than any other people in the free world. For 15 years no other free nation has demanded so much of itself. Through hot wars and cold, through recession and prosperity, through the ages of the atom and outer space, the American people have neither faltered nor has their faith flagged. If at times our actions seem to make life difficult for others, it is only because history has made life difficult for us all.

But difficult days need not be dark. I think these are proud and memorable days in the cause of peace and freedom. We are proud, for example, of Maj. Rudolf Anderson who gave his life over the island of Cuba. We salute Sp. James Allen Johnson who died on the border of South Korea. We pay honor to Sgt. Gerald Pendell who was killed in Vietnam. They are among the many who in this century, far from home, have died for our country. Our task now, and the task of all Americans, is to live up to their commitments.

My friends, I close on a note of hope. We are not lulled by the momentary calm of the sea or the somewhat clearer skies above. We know the turbulence that lies below, and the storms beyond the horizon this year. Now the winds of change appear to be blowing more strongly than ever, in the world of communism as well as our own. For 175 years we have sailed with those winds at our back, and with the tides of human freedom in our favor. We steer our ship with hope, as Thomas Jefferson said, "leaving fear astern."

Today we still welcome those winds of change—and we have every reason to believe that our tide is running strong. With thanks to Almighty God for seeing us through a perilous passage, we ask His help anew in guiding the good ship Union.

Lyndon B. Johnson

November 22, 1963 to –

FIRST ANNUAL MESSAGE.

Jan. 8, 1964

MR. SPEAKER, MR. PRESIDENT, MEMBERS OF THE HOUSE AND SENATE, MY FELLOW AMERICANS:

I will be brief, for our time is necessarily short and our agenda is already long.

Last year's congressional session was the longest in peacetime history. With that foundation, let us work together to make this year's session the best in the Nation's history.

Let this session of Congress be known as the session which did more for civil rights than the last hundred sessions combined; as the session which enacted the most far-reaching tax cut of our time; as the session which declared all out war on human poverty and unemployment in these United States; as the session which finally recognized the health needs of all of our older citizens; as the session which reformed our tangled transportation and transit policies; as the session which achieved the most effective, efficient foreign aid program ever; and as the session which helped to build more homes, and more schools, and more libraries, and more hospitals than any single session of Congress in the history of our Republic. All this and more can and must be done. It can be done by this summer.

And it can be done without any increase in spending. In fact, under the budget that I shall shortly submit, it can be done with an actual reduction in Federal expenditures and Federal employment.

We have in 1964 a unique opportunity and obligation to prove the success of our system; to disprove those cynics and critics at home and abroad who question our purpose and our competence.

If we fail, if we fritter and fumble away our opportunity in needless, senseless quarrels between Democrats and Republicans, or between the House and the Senate, or between the South and the North, or between the Congress and the administration, then history will rightfully judge us harshly. But if we succeed, if we can achieve these goals by forging in this country a greater sense of union, then, and only then, can we take full satisfaction in the state of the Union.

Here in the Congress, you can demonstrate effective legislative leadership by discharging the public business with clarity and dispatch—voting each important proposal up or voting it down but at least bringing it to a fair and a final vote.

Let us carry forward the plans and programs of John Fitzgerald Kennedy—not because of our sorrow or sympathy, but because they are right.

In his memory today, I especially ask all members of my own political faith, in this election year, to put your country ahead of your party, and to always debate principles—never debate personalities.

For my part, I pledge a progressive administration which is efficient, and honest, and frugal.

The budget to be submitted to the Congress shortly is in full accord with this pledge. It will cut our deficit in half, from $10 billion to

$4.9 billion. It will be, in proportion to our national output, the smallest budget since 1951. It will call for a substantial reduction in Federal employment, a feat accomplished only once before in the last 10 years. While maintaining the full strength of our combat defenses, it will call for the lowest number of civilian personnel in the Department of Defense since 1950.

It will call for total expenditures of $97.9 billion—compared to $98.4 for the current year, a reduction of more than $500 million. It will call for new obligational authority of $103.8 billion—a reduction of more than $4 billion below last year's request of $107.9 billion.

But it is not a standstill budget—for America cannot afford to stand still. Our population is growing. Our economy is more complex. Our people's needs are expanding. But by closing down obsolete installations, by curtailing less urgent programs, by cutting back where cutting back seems to be wise, by insisting on a dollar's worth for a dollar spent, I am able to recommend in this reduced budget the most Federal support in history for education, for health, for retraining the unemployed, and for helping the economically and the physically handicapped.

This budget, and this year's legislative program, are designed to help each and every American citizen fulfill his basic hopes: His hopes for a fair chance to make good, his hopes for fairplay from the law, his hopes for a full-time job on full-time pay, his hopes for a decent home for his family in a decent community, his hopes for a good school for his children with good teachers, and his hopes for security when faced with sickness or unemployment or old age.

Unfortunately many Americans live on the outskirts of hope—some because of their poverty, and some because of their color, and all too many because of both. Our task is to help replace their despair with opportunity.

This administration today here and now declares unconditional war on poverty in America. I urge this Congress and all Americans to join with me in that effort.

It will not be a short or easy struggle—no single weapon or strategy will suffice—but we shall not rest until that war is won. The richest nation on earth can afford to win it. We cannot afford to lose it; $1,000 invested in salvaging an unemployable youth today can return $40,000 or more in his lifetime. Poverty is a national problem, requiring improved national organization and support. But this attack, to be effective, must also be organized at the State and local level and must be supported and directed by State and local efforts.

For the war against poverty will not be won here in Washington. It must be won in the field—in every private home, in every public office, from the courthouse to the White House.

The program I shall propose will emphasize this cooperative approach to help that one-fifth of all American families with incomes too small to even meet their basic needs.

Our chief weapons in a more pinpointed attack will be better schools, and better health, and better homes, and better training, and better job opportunities to help more Americans—especially young Americans—escape from squalor and misery and unemployment rolls where other citizens help to carry them. Very often a lack of jobs and money is not the cause of poverty but the symptom.

The cause may lie deeper—in our failure to give our fellow citizens a fair chance to develop their own capacities—in a lack of education and training, in a lack of medical care and housing, in a lack of decent communities in which to live and bring up their children.

But whatever the cause, our joint Federal-local effort must pursue poverty, pursue it wherever it exists, in city slums and small towns, in sharecropper shacks or in migrant worker camps, on Indian reservations, among whites as well as Negroes, among the young as well as the aged, in the boomtowns and in the depressed areas.

Our aim is not only to relieve the symptoms of poverty but to cure it; and, above all, to prevent it. No single piece of legislation, however, is going to suffice. We will launch a special effort in the chronically distressed areas of Appalachia. We must expand our small but our successful area redevelopment program. We must enact youth employment legislation to put jobless, aimless, hopeless youngsters to work on useful projects. We must distribute more food to the needy through a broader food stamp program. We must create a National Service Corps to help the economically handicapped of our own country as the Peace Corps now helps those abroad. We must modernize our unemployment insurance and establish a high-level Commission on Automation. If we have the brainpower to invent these machines, we have the brainpower to make certain that they are a boon and not a bane to humanity. We must extend the coverage of our minimum wage laws to more than 2 million workers now lacking this basic protection of purchasing power. We must, by including special school aid funds as part of our education program, improve the quality of teaching and training and counseling in our hardest hit areas. We must build more libraries in every area, and more hospitals and nursing homes under the Hill-Burton Act, and train more nurses to staff them. We must provide hospital insurance for our older citizens, financed by every worker and his employer under social security contributing no more than $1 a month during the employee's working career to protect him in his old age in a dignified manner, without cost to the Treasury, against the devastating hardship of prolonged or repeated illness. We must, as a part of a revised housing and urban renewal program, give more help to those displaced by slum clearance, provide more housing for our poor and our elderly, and seek as our ultimate goal in our free enterprise system a decent home for every American family. We must help obtain more modern mass transit within our communities as well as low-cost transportation between them. Above all, we must release $11 billion of tax reduction into the private spending stream to create new jobs and new markets in every area of this land.

These programs are obviously not for the poor or the underprivileged alone. Every American will benefit by the extension of social security to cover the hospital costs of their aged parents. Every American community will benefit from the construction or modernization of schools, libraries, hospitals, and nursing homes; from the training of more nurses; and from the improvement of urban renewal and public transit. And every individual American taxpayer and every corporate taxpayer will benefit from the earliest possible passage of the pending tax bill—from both the new investment it will bring and the new jobs that it will create.

That tax bill has been thoroughly discussed for a year. Now we need action. The new budget clearly allows it. Our taxpayers surely deserve it. Our economy strongly demands it. And every month of delay dilutes its benefits in 1964 for consumption, for investment, and for employment. For until the bill is signed, its investment incentives cannot be deemed certain, and the withholding rate cannot be reduced—and the most damaging and devastating thing you can do to any businessman in America is to keep him in doubt and to keep him guessing on what our tax policy is. And I say that we should now reduce to 14 percent instead of 15 percent our withholding rate. I, therefore, urge the Congress to take final action on this bill by the 1st of February if at all possible. For however proud we may be of the unprecedented progress of our free enterprise economy over the last 3 years, we should not and we cannot permit it to pause. In 1963, for the first time in history, we crossed the 70 million job mark—but we will soon need more than 75 million jobs. In 1963, our gross national product reached the $600 billion level—$100 billion higher than when we took office. But it easily could and it should be still $30 billion higher today than it is. Wages and profits and family income are also at their highest levels in history—but I would remind you that 4 million workers and 13 percent of our industrial capacity are still idle today. We need a tax cut now to keep this country moving.

For our goal is not merely to spread the work. Our goal is to create more jobs. I believe the enactment of a 35-hour week would sharply increase costs, would invite inflation, would impair our ability to compete, and merely share instead of creating employment. But I am equally opposed to the 45- or 50-hour week in those industries where consistently excessive use of overtime causes increased unemployment. So, therefore, I recommend legislation authorizing the creation of tripartite industry committees to determine, on an industry-by-industry basis, as to where a higher penalty rate for overtime would increase job openings without unduly increasing costs—and authorizing the establishment of such higher rates.

Let me make one principle of this administration abundantly clear: All of these increased opportunities—in employment, in education, in housing, and in every field—must be open to Americans of every color. As far as the writ of Federal law will run, we must abolish not some but all racial discrimination.

For this is not merely an economic issue—or a social, political, or international issue. It is a moral issue; and it must be met by the passage this session of the bill now pending in the House.

All members of the public should have equal access to facilities open to the public. All members of the public should be equally eligible for Federal benefits that are financed by the public. All members of the public should have an equal chance to vote for public officials, and to send their children to good public schools, and to contribute their talents to the public good.

Today Americans of all races stand side by side in Berlin and in Vietnam. They died side by side in Korea. Surely they can work and eat and travel side by side in their own country.

We must also lift by legislation the bars of discrimination against those who seek entry into our country, particularly those with much-needed skills and those joining their families. In establishing preferences, a nation that was built by the immigrants of all lands can ask those who now seek admission: "What can you do for our country?" But we should not be asking: "In what country were you born?"

For our ultimate goal is a world without war, a world made safe for diversity, in which all men, goods, and ideas can freely move across every border and every boundary.

We must advance toward this goal in 1964 in at least 10 different ways, not as partisans but as patriots.

First, we must maintain—and our reduced defense budget will maintain—that margin of military safety and superiority obtained through 3 years of steadily increasing both the quality and the quantity of our strategic, our conventional, and our antiguerrilla forces. In 1964 we will be better prepared than ever before to defend the cause of freedom—whether it is threatened by outright aggression or by the infiltration practiced by those in Hanoi and Havana who ship arms and men across international borders to foment insurrection. And we must continue to use that strength, as John Kennedy used it in the Cuban crisis and for the test ban treaty, to demonstrate both the futility of nuclear war and the possibilities of lasting peace.

Second, we must take new steps—and we shall make new proposals at Geneva—toward the control and the eventual abolition of arms. Even in the absence of agreement we must not stockpile arms beyond our needs or seek an excess of military power that could be provocative as well as wasteful. And it is in this spirit that in this fiscal year we are cutting back our production of enriched uranium by 25 percent. We are shutting down four plutonium piles. We are closing many nonessential military installations. And it is in this spirit that we today call on our adversaries to do the same.

Third, we must make increased use of our food as an instrument of peace, making it available—by sale, or trade, or loan, or donation—to hungry people in all nations which tell us of their needs and accept proper conditions of distribution.

Fourth, we must assure our preeminence in the peaceful exploration of outer space, focusing on an expedition to the moon in this decade—in cooperation with other powers if possible, alone if necessary.

Fifth, we must expand world trade. Having recognized in the act of 1962 that we must buy as well as sell, we now expect our trading partners to recognize that we must sell as well as buy. We are willing to give them competitive access to our market—asking only that they do the same for us.

Sixth, we must continue, through such measures as the interest equalization tax as well as the cooperation of other nations, our recent progress toward balancing our international accounts.

This administration must and will preserve the present gold value of the dollar.

Seventh, we must become better neighbors with the free states of the Americas—working with the councils of the OAS, with a stronger Alliance for Progress, and with all the men and women of this hemisphere who really believe in liberty and justice for all.

Eighth, we must strengthen the ability of free nations everywhere to develop their independence and raise their standard of living—and thereby frustrate those who prey on poverty and chaos. To do this, the rich must help the poor—and we must do our part. We must achieve a more rigorous administration of our development assistance, with larger roles for private investors, for other industrialized nations, for international agencies, and for the recipient nations themselves.

Ninth, we must strengthen our Atlantic and Pacific partnerships, maintain our alliances, and make the United Nations a more effective instrument for national independence and international order.

Tenth, and finally, we must develop with our allies new means of bridging the gap between the East and the West, facing danger boldly wherever danger exists, but being equally bold in our search for new agreements which can enlarge the hopes of all while violating the interests of none.

In short, I would say to the Congress that we must be constantly prepared for the worst and constantly acting for the best. We must be strong enough to win any war, and we must be wise enough to prevent one.

We shall neither act as aggressors nor tolerate acts of aggression. We intend to bury no one—and we do not intend to be buried. We can fight, if we must, as we have fought before—but we pray that we will never have to fight again.

My good friends and my fellow Americans, in these last 7 sorrowful weeks we have learned anew that nothing is so enduring as faith and nothing is so degrading as hate.

John Kennedy was a victim of hate, but he was also a great builder of faith—faith in our fellow Americans, whatever their creed or their color or their station in life; and faith in the future of man, whatever his divisions and differences.

This faith was echoed in all parts of the world. On every continent and in every land to which Mrs. Johnson and I traveled, we found faith and hope and love toward this land of America and toward our people.

So I ask you now, in the Congress and in the country, to join with me in expressing and fulfilling that faith, in working for a nation—a nation that is free from want and a world that is free from hate—a world of peace and justice, and freedom and abundance, for our time and for all time to come.

SECOND ANNUAL MESSAGE.

Jan. 4, 1965

Mr. Speaker, Mr. President, Members of Congress, My Fellow Americans:

On this Hill, which was my home, I am stirred by old friendships.

Though total agreement between the Executive and the Congress is impossible, total respect is important.

I am proud to be among my colleagues of the Congress whose legacy to their trust is their loyalty to their Nation.

I am not unaware of the inner emotions of the new Members of this body.

Twenty-eight years ago, I felt as you do now. You will soon learn that you are among men whose first love is their country, men who try each day to do what they believe is right.

* * *

We are entering the third century of the pursuit of American union.

Two hundred years ago, in 1765, nine assembled colonies first joined together to demand freedom from arbitrary power.

For the first century we struggled to hold together the first continental union of democracy in the history of man. One hundred years ago, in 1865, following a terrible test of blood and fire, the compact of union was finally sealed.

For a second century we labored to establish a unity of purpose and interest among the many groups which make up the American community.

That struggle has often brought pain and violence. It is not yet over. But we have achieved a unity of interest among our people unmatched in the history of freedom.

And now, in 1965, we begin a new quest for union. We seek the unity of man with the world he has built—with the knowledge that can save or destroy him—with the cities which can stimulate or stifle him—with the wealth and machines which can enrich or menace his spirit.

We seek to establish a harmony between man and society which will allow each of us to enlarge the meaning of his life and all of us to elevate the quality of our civilization.

This is the search we begin tonight.

State of the World

But the unity we seek cannot realize its full promise in isolation. For today the state of the Union depends, in large measure, upon the state of the world.

Our concern and interest, compassion and vigilance, extend to every corner of a dwindling planet.

Yet, it is not merely our concern but the concern of all freemen. We will not, and should not, assume it is the task of Americans alone to settle all the conflicts of a torn and troubled world.

Let the foes of freedom take no comfort from this. For in concert with other nations, we shall help men defend their freedom.

Our first aim remains the safety and well-being of our own country.

We are prepared to live as good neighbors with all, but we cannot be indifferent to acts designed to injure our interests, our citizens, or our establishments abroad. The community of nations requires mutual respect. We shall extend it—and we shall expect it.

In our relations with the world we shall follow the example of Andrew Jackson who said: "I intend to ask for nothing that is not clearly right and to submit to nothing that is wrong." And he promised, "the honor of my country shall never be stained by an apology from me for the statement of truth or the performance of duty." That was our policy in the 1830's and that is our policy today.

Our own freedom and growth have never been the final goal of the American dream.

We were never meant to be an oasis of liberty and abundance in a worldwide desert of disappointed dreams. Our Nation was created to help strike away the chains of ignorance and misery and tyranny wherever they keep man less than God means him to be.

We are moving toward that destiny, never more rapidly than in the last 4 years.

In this period we have built a military power strong enough to meet any threat and destroy any adversary. And that superiority will continue to grow so long as this office is mine—and you sit on Capitol Hill.

In this period no new nation has become Communist, and the unity of the Communist empire has begun to crumble.

In this period we have resolved in friendship our disputes with our neighbors of the hemisphere, and joined in an Alliance for Progress toward economic growth and political democracy.

In this period we have taken more steps toward peace—including the test ban treaty—than at any time since the cold war began.

In this period we have relentlessly pursued our advances toward the conquest of space.

Most important of all, in this period, the United States has re-emerged into the fullness of its self-confidence and purpose. No longer are we called upon to get America moving. We are moving. No longer do we doubt our strength or resolution. We are strong and we have proven our resolve.

No longer can anyone wonder whether we are in the grip of historical decay. We know that history is ours to make. And if there is great danger, there is now also the excitement of great expectations.

America and the Communist Nations

Yet we still live in a troubled and perilous world. There is no longer a single threat. There are many. They differ in intensity and danger. They require different attitudes and different answers.

With the Soviet Union we seek peaceful understandings that can lessen the danger to freedom.

Last fall I asked the American people to choose that course.

I will carry forward their command.

If we are to live together in peace, we must come to know each other better.

I am sure the American people would welcome a chance to listen to the Soviet leaders on our television—as I would like the Soviet people to hear our leaders.

I hope the new Soviet leaders can visit America so they can learn about this country at firsthand.

In Eastern Europe restless nations are slowly beginning to assert their identity. Your Government, assisted by leaders in labor and business, is exploring ways to increase peaceful trade with these countries and the Soviet Union. I will report our conclusions to the Congress.

In Asia, communism wears a more aggressive face.

We see that in Vietnam.

Why are we there?

We are there, first, because a friendly nation has asked us for help against Communist aggression. Ten years ago we pledged our help. Three Presidents have supported that pledge. We will not break it.

Second, our own security is tied to the peace of Asia. Twice in one generation we have had to fight against aggression in the Far East. To ignore aggression would only increase the danger of a larger war.

Our goal is peace in southeast Asia. That will come only when aggressors leave their neighbors in peace.

What is at stake is the cause of freedom. In that cause we shall never be found wanting.

The Non-Communist World

But communism is not the only source of trouble and unrest. There are older and deeper sources—in the misery of nations and in man's irrepressible ambition for liberty and a better life.

With the free Republics of Latin America I have always felt—and my country has always felt—special ties of interest and affection. It will be the purpose of this administration to strengthen these ties. Together we share and shape the destiny of the new world. In the coming year I hope to pay a visit to Latin America. And I will steadily enlarge our commitment to the Alliance for Progress as the instrument of our war against poverty and injustice in the hemisphere.

In the Atlantic community we continue to pursue our goal of 20 years—a Europe growing in strength, unity, and cooperation with America. A great unfinished task is the reunification of Germany through self-determination.

This European policy is not based on any abstract design. It is based on the realities of common interests and common values, common dangers and common expectations. These realities will continue to have their way—especially in our expanding trade and our common defense.

Free Americans have shaped the policies of the United States. And because we know these realities, those policies have been, and will be, in the interest of Europe.

Free Europeans must shape the course of Europe. And, for the same reasons, that course has been, and will be, in our interest and the interest of freedom.

I found this truth confirmed in my talks with European leaders in the last year. I hope to repay these visits to some of our friends in Europe this year.

In Africa and Asia we are witnessing the turbulent unfolding of new nations and continents.

We welcome them to the society of nations.

We are committed to help those seeking to strengthen their own independence, and to work most closely with those governments dedicated to the welfare of all their people.

We seek not fidelity to an iron faith but a diversity of belief as varied as man himself. We seek not to extend the power of America but the progress of humanity. We seek not to dominate others but to strengthen the freedom of all.

I will seek new ways to use our knowledge to help deal with the explosion in world population and the growing scarcity in world resources.

Finally, we renew our commitment to the continued growth and effectiveness of the United Nations. The frustrations of the U.N. are a product of the world we live in, not of the institution which gives them voice. It is far better to throw these differences open to the assembly of nations than permit them to fester in silent danger.

These are some of the goals of the American Nation in the world.

For ourselves we seek neither praise nor blame, gratitude nor obedience.

We seek peace.

We seek freedom.

We seek to enrich the life of man.

For that is the world in which we will flourish.

That is the world we mean for all men to have.

* * *

Toward the Great Society

World affairs will continue to call upon our energy and courage.

But today we can turn increased attention to the character of American life.

We are in the midst of the greatest upward surge of economic well-being in the history of any nation.

Our flourishing progress has been marked by price stability unequalled in the world. Our balance-of-payments deficit has declined and the soundness of our dollar is unquestioned. I pledge to keep it that way. I urge business and labor to cooperate to that end.

We worked for two centuries to climb this peak of prosperity. But we are only at the beginning of the road to the Great Society. Ahead now is a summit where freedom from the wants of the body can help fulfill the needs of the spirit.

We built this Nation to serve its people.

We want to grow and build and create, but we want progress to be the servant and not the master of man.

We do not intend to live—in the midst of abundance—isolated from neighbors and nature, confined by blighted cities and bleak suburbs, stunted by a poverty of learning and an emptiness of leisure.

The Great Society asks not only how much, but how good; not only how to create wealth, but how to use it; not only how fast we are going, but where we are headed.

It proposes as the first test for a nation: the quality of its people.

This kind of society will not flower spontaneously from swelling riches and surging power.

It will not be the gift of Government or the creation of Presidents.

It will require of every American, for many generations, both faith in the destination and the fortitude to make the journey.

Like freedom itself, it will always be challenge and not fulfillment.

Tonight we accept that challenge.

A National Agenda

I propose we begin a program in education to insure every American child the fullest development of his mind and skills.

I propose we begin a massive attack on crippling and killing diseases.

I propose we launch a national effort to make the American city a better and more stimulating place to live.

I propose we increase the beauty of America and end the poisoning of our rivers and the air we breathe.

I propose we carry out a new program to develop regions of our country now suffering from distress and depression.

I propose we make new efforts to control and prevent crime and delinquency.

I propose we eliminate every remaining obstacle to the right and opportunity to vote.

I propose we honor and support the achievements of thought and the creations of art.

I propose we make an all-out campaign against waste and inefficiency.

THE TASK

Our basic task is threefold:

—to keep our economy growing;

—to open for all Americans the opportunities now enjoyed by most Americans;

—to improve the quality of life for all.

In the next 6 weeks I will submit special messages with detailed proposals for national action in each of these areas.

Tonight I would like briefly to explain some of my major recommendations in the three main areas of national need.

I. A Growing Economy

BASIC POLICIES

First, we must keep our Nation prosperous. We seek full employment opportunity for every American. I will present a budget designed to move the economy forward. More money will be left in the hands of the consumer by a substantial cut in excise taxes. We will continue along the path toward a balanced budget in a balanced economy.

I confidently predict—what every economic sign now tells us—the continued flourishing of the American economy.

But we must remember that fear of a recession can contribute to the fact of a recession. The knowledge that our Government will, and can, move swiftly will strengthen the confidence of investors and business.

Congress can reinforce this confidence by insuring that its procedures permit rapid action on temporary income tax cuts. And special funds for job-creating public programs should be made available for immediate use if recession threatens.

Our continued prosperity demands continued price stability. Business, labor, and the consumer all have a high stake in keeping wages and prices within the framework of the guideposts that have already served the Nation so well.

Finding new markets abroad for our goods depends on the initiative of American business. But we stand ready—with credit and other help—to assist the flow of trade which will benefit the entire Nation.

ON THE FARMS

Our economy owes much to the efficiency of our farmers. We must continue to assure them the opportunity to earn a fair reward. I have instructed the Secretary of Agriculture to lead a major effort to find new approaches to reduce the heavy cost of our farm programs and to direct more of our effort to the small farmer who needs help most.

INCREASED PROSPERITY

We can help insure continued prosperity through—

—a regional recovery program to assist development of stricken areas left behind by our national progress;

—further efforts to provide our workers with the skills demanded by modern technology, for the laboring man is an indispensable force in the American system;

—extension of the minimum wage to more than 2 million unprotected workers;

—improvement and modernization of the unemployment compensation system.

As pledged in our 1960 and 1964 Democratic platforms, I will propose to Congress changes in the Taft-Hartley Act including section 14–B. I will do so hoping to reduce conflicts that for several years have divided Americans in various States.

In a country that spans a continent, modern transportation is vital to continued growth.

TRANSPORTATION FOR GROWTH

I will recommend heavier reliance on competition in transportation and a new policy for our merchant marine.

I will ask for funds to study high-speed rail transportation between urban centers. We will begin with test projects between Boston and Washington. On high-speed trains, passengers could travel this distance in less than 4 hours.

II. Opportunity for All

Second, we must open opportunity to all our people.

Most Americans tonight enjoy a good life. But far too many are still trapped in poverty, idleness, and fear.

Let a just nation throw open to them the city of promise:

—*to the elderly*, by providing hospital care under social security and by raising benefit payments to those struggling to maintain the dignity of their later years;

—*to the poor*, through doubling the war against poverty this year;

—to Negro Americans, through enforcement of the civil rights law and elimination of barriers to the right to vote;

—to those in other lands seeking the promise of America, through an immigration law based on the work a man can do and not where he was born or how he spells his name.

III. To Enrich the Life of All

Our *third* goal is to improve the quality of American life.

THROUGH EDUCATION

We begin with learning.

Every child must have the best education our Nation can provide.

Thomas Jefferson said no nation can be both ignorant and free. Today no nation can be both ignorant and great.

In addition to our existing programs, I will recommend a new program for schools and students with a first-year authorization of $1,500 million.

It will help at every stage along the road to learning.

For the preschool years we will help needy children become aware of the excitement of learning.

For the primary and secondary school years we will aid public schools serving low-income families and assist students in both public and private schools.

For the college years we will provide scholarships to high school students of the greatest promise and greatest need and guaranteed low-interest loans to students continuing their college studies.

New laboratories and centers will help our schools lift their standards of excellence and explore new methods of teaching. These centers will provide special training for those who need and deserve special treatment.

THROUGH BETTER HEALTH

Greatness requires not only an educated people but a healthy people.

Our goal is to match the achievements of our medicine to the afflictions of our people.

We already carry on a large program for research and health.

In addition, regional medical centers can provide the most advanced diagnosis and treatment for heart disease, cancer, stroke, and other major diseases.

New support for medical and dental education will provide the trained men to apply our knowledge.

Community centers can help the mentally ill and improve health care for school-age children from poor families, including services for the mentally retarded.

THROUGH IMPROVING THE WORLD WE LIVE IN

The city

An educated and healthy people require surroundings in harmony with their hopes.

In our urban areas the central problem today is to protect and restore man's satisfaction in belonging to a community where he can find security and significance.

The first step is to break old patterns—to begin to think, work, and plan for the development of entire metropolitan areas. We will take this step with new programs of help for basic community facilities and neighborhood centers of health and recreation.

New and existing programs will be open to those cities which work together to develop unified long-range policies for metropolitan areas.

We must also make important changes in our housing programs if we are to pursue these same basic goals.

A Department of Housing and Urban Development will be needed to spearhead this effort in our cities.

Every citizen has the right to feel secure in his home and on the streets of his community.

To help control crime, we will recommend programs—

—to train local law enforcement officers;

—to put the best techniques of modern science at their disposal:

—to discover the causes of crime and better ways to prevent it.

I will soon assemble a panel of outstanding experts to search out answers to the national problem of crime and delinquency.

The beauty of America

For over three centuries the beauty of America has sustained our spirit and enlarged our vision. We must act now to protect this heritage. In a fruitful new partnership with the States and cities the next decade should be a conservation milestone. We must make a massive effort to save the countryside and establish—as a green legacy for tomorrow—more large and small parks, more seashores and open spaces than have been created during any period in our history.

A new and substantial effort must be made to landscape highways and provide places of relaxation and recreation wherever our roads run.

Within our cities imaginative programs are needed to landscape streets and transform open areas into places of beauty and recreation.

We will seek legal power to prevent pollution of our air and water before it happens. We will step up our effort to control harmful wastes, giving first priority to the cleanup of our most contaminated rivers. We will increase research to learn more about control of pollution.

We hope to make the Potomac a model of beauty and recreation for the entire country—and preserve unspoiled stretches of some of our waterways with a wild rivers bill.

More ideas for a beautiful America will emerge from a White House Conference on Natural Beauty which I will soon call.

Art and science

We must also recognize and encourage those who can be pathfinders for the Nation's imagination and understanding.

To help promote and honor creative achievements, I will propose a National Foundation on the Arts.

To develop knowledge which will enrich our lives and insure our progress, I will recommend programs to encourage basic science, particularly in the universities—and to bring closer the day when the oceans will supply our growing need for fresh water.

IV. The Government

For government to serve these goals it must be modern in structure, efficient in action, and ready for any emergency.

I am currently reviewing the structure of the executive branch. I hope to reshape and reorganize it to meet more effectively the tasks of today.

Wherever waste is found, I will eliminate it.

Last year we saved almost $3½ billion by eliminating waste.

I intend to do better this year.

And I will soon report to you on our progress and on new economies we plan to make.

Even the best of government is subject to the worst of hazards.

I will propose laws to insure the necessary continuity of leadership should the President become disabled or die.

In addition, I will propose reforms in the electoral college—leaving undisturbed the vote by States—but making sure no elector can substitute his will for that of the people.

* * *

Last year I spoke to you after 33 years of public service—most of them on this Hill.

This year I speak after 1 year as President of the United States.

Many of you in this Chamber are among my oldest friends. We have shared many happy moments and many hours of work. And we have watched many Presidents together. Yet, only in the White House can you finally know the full weight of this Office.

The greatest burden is not running the huge operations of government—or meeting daily troubles, large and small—or even working with the Congress.

A President's hardest task is not to *do* what is right, but to *know* what is right.

Yet the Presidency brings no special gift of prophecy or foresight. You take an oath—step into an office—and must then help guide a great democracy.

The answer was waiting for me in the land where I was born.

It was once barren land. The angular hills were covered with scrub cedar and a few live oaks. Little would grow in the harsh caliche soil. And each spring the Pedernales River would flood the valley.

But men came and worked and endured and built.

Today that country is abundant with fruit, cattle, goats, and sheep. There are pleasant homes, and lakes, and the floods are gone.

Why did men come to that once forbidding land?

They were restless, of course, and had to be moving on. But there was more than that. There was a dream—a dream of a place where a freeman could build for himself, and raise his children to a better life—a dream of a continent to be conquered, a world to be won, a nation to be made.

Remembering this, I knew the answer.

A President does not shape a new and personal vision of America.

He collects it from the scattered hopes of the American past.

It existed when the first settlers saw the coast of a new world, and when the first pioneers moved westward.

It has guided us every step of the way.

It sustains every President. But it is also your inheritance and it belongs equally to the people we serve.

It must be interpreted anew by each generation for its own needs; as I have tried, in part, to do today.

It shall lead us as we enter this third century of the search for "a more perfect Union."

This, then, is the state of the Union: Free, restless, growing, and full of hope.

So it was in the beginning.

So it shall always be, while God is willing, and we are strong enough to keep the faith.

THIRD ANNUAL MESSAGE.

JANUARY 12, 1966.

Mr. Speaker, Mr. President, Members of the House and Senate, My Fellow Americans:

I come before you tonight to report on the state of the Union for the third time. I come here to thank you and to add my tribute once more to the Nation's gratitude for this, the 89th Congress.

This Congress has already reserved for itself an honored chapter in the history of America.

Our Nation tonight is now engaged in a brutal and bitter conflict in Vietnam. Later on I want to discuss that struggle in some detail with you. It just must be the center of our concerns. But we will not permit those who fire upon us in Vietnam to win a victory over the desires and the intentions of all of the American people. This Nation is mighty enough, its society is healthy enough, its people are strong enough to pursue our goals in the rest of the world while still building a great society here at home. And that is what I have come here to ask of you tonight.

I recommend that you provide the resources to carry forward with full vigor the great health and education programs that you enacted into law last year.

I recommend that we prosecute with vigor and determination our war on poverty.

I recommend that you give a new and daring direction to our foreign aid program designed to make a maximum attack on hunger and disease and ignorance in those countries that are determined to help themselves, and to help those nations that are trying to control population growth.

I recommend that you make it possible to expand trade between the United States and Eastern Europe and the Soviet Union.

I recommend to you a program to rebuild completely on a scale never before attempted entire central and slum areas of several of our cities in America.

I recommend that you attack the wasteful and degrading poisoning of our rivers, and as the cornerstone of this effort clean completely entire large river basins.

I recommend that you meet the growing menace of crime in the streets by building up law enforcement and by revitalizing the entire Federal system from prevention to probation.

I recommend that you take additional steps to insure equal justice to all of our people by effectively enforcing nondiscrimination in Federal and State jury selection by making it a serious Federal crime to obstruct public and private efforts to secure civil rights and by outlawing discrimination in the sale of rental housing.

I recommend that you help me modernize and streamline the Federal Government by creating a new Cabinet level Department of Transportation and reorganizing several existing agencies.

In turn I will restructure our civil service in the top grades so that men and women can easily be assigned to jobs where they are most needed, and ability will be both required, as well as rewarded.

I will ask you to make it possible for Members of the House of Representatives to work more effectively in the service of the Nation through a constitutional amendment extending the term of a Congressman to 4 years concurrent with that of the President.

Because of Vietnam we cannot do all that we should or all that we would like to do. We will ruthlessly attack waste and inefficiency. We will make sure that every dollar is spent with the thrift and with the commonsense which recognizes how hard the taxpayer worked in order to earn it.

We will continue to meet the needs of our people by continuing to develop the Great Society.

Last year alone the wealth that we produced increased $47 billion, and it will soar again this year to a total over $720 billion. Because our economic policies have produced rising revenues, if you approve every program that I recommend tonight our total budget deficit will be one of the lowest in many years. It will be only $1.8 billion next year.

Total spending in the administrative budget will be $112.8 billion. Revenues next year will be $111 billion. On a cash basis, which is the way that you and I keep our family budget, the Federal budget next year will actually show a surplus.

That is to say, that if we include all the money that your Government will take in and all the money that your Government will spend, your Government next year will collect one-half billion dollars more than it will spend in the year 1967.

I have not come here tonight to ask for pleasant luxuries and for idle pleasures. I have come here to recommend that you, the representatives of the richest nation on earth, you the elected servants of the people who live in abundance unmatched on this globe, you bring the most urgent decencies of life to all of your fellow Americans.

There are men who cry out that we must sacrifice. Well, let us rather ask them, who will they sacrifice? Are they going to sacrifice the children who seek the learning, or the sick who need medical care, or the families who dwell in squalor that are now brightened by the hope of home? Will they sacrifice opportunity for the distressed, the beauty of our land, the hope of our poor?

Time may require further sacrifices, and if it does, then we will make them. But we will not heed those who wring it from the hopes of the unfortunate here in a land of plenty.

I believe that we can continue the Great Society while we fight in Vietnam. But if there are some who do not believe this, then in the name of justice let them call for the contribution of those who live in the fullness of our blessing, rather than try to strip it from the hands of those that are most in need.

And let no one think that the unfortunate and the oppressed of this land sit stifled and alone in their hope tonight! Hundreds of their servants and their protectors sit before me tonight here in this great Chamber.

The Great Society leads us along three roads—growth and justice and liberation.

First is growth—the national prosperity which supports the well-being of our people and which provides the tools of our progress.

I can report to you tonight what you have seen for yourselves already in almost every city and countryside. This Nation is flourishing. Workers are making more money than ever, with after-tax income in the past 5 years up 33 percent; in the last year alone up 8 percent. More people are working than ever before in our history, an increase last year of 2½ million jobs. Corporations have greater after-tax earnings than ever in history. For the past 5 years those earnings have been up over 65 percent. Last year alone, they had a rise of 20 percent. Average farm income is higher than ever. Over the past 5 years, it is up 40 percent. Over the past year, it was up 22 percent alone.

I was informed this afternoon by the distinguished Secretary of the Treasury that his preliminary estimates indicate that our balance of payments deficit has been reduced from $2.8 billion in 1964 to $1.3 billion or less in 1965.

This achievement has been made possible by the patriotic voluntary cooperation of businessmen and bankers working with your Government.

We must now work together with increased urgency to wipe out this balance-of-payments deficit altogether in the next year.

As our economy surges toward new heights we must increase our vigilance against the inflation which raises the cost of living and which lowers the savings of every family in this land. It is essential to prevent inflation that we ask both labor and business to exercise price and wage restraint, and I do so again tonight.

I believe it desirable because of increased military expenditures that you temporarily restore the automobile and certain telephone excise tax reductions made effective only 12 days ago. Without raising taxes or even increasing the total tax bill, we should move to improve our withholding system so that Americans can more realistically pay as they go; speed up the collection of corporate taxes; and make other necessary simplifications of the tax structure at an early date. I hope these measures will be adequate, but if the necessities of Vietnam require it, I will not hesitate to return to the Congress for additional appropriations or additional revenues if they are needed.

The second road is justice. Justice means that a man's hope should not be limited by the color of his skin.

I propose legislation to establish unavoidable requirements for nondiscriminatory jury selection in Federal and State courts, and to give the Attorney General the power necessary to enforce those requirements.

I propose:

Legislation to strengthen the authority of Federal courts to try those who murder, attack, or intimidate either civil rights workers or others exercising their constitutional rights and to increase penalties to a level equal to the nature of the crime.

Legislation resting on the fullest constitutional authority of the Federal Government to prohibit racial discrimination in the sale or rental of housing.

For that other nation, within a nation, the poor whose distress has now captured the conscience of America, I will ask Congress not only to continue but to speed up the war on poverty, and in so doing we will provide the added energy of achievement with the increased efficiency of experience to improve the life of our rural Americans and our farm population. We will plan for the future through the establishment of several new community development districts, improved education through the use of Teachers Corps teams, better health measures, physical examinations and adequate and available medical resources.

For those who labor I propose to improve unemployment insurance, to expand minimum wage benefits, and by the repeal of section 14(b) of the Taft-Hartley Act to make the labor laws in all our States equal to the laws of the 31 States which do not have tonight right-to-work measures.

I also intend to ask the Congress to consider measures which without improperly invading State and local authority will enable us effectively to deal with strikes which threaten irreparable damage to the national interest.

The third path is the path of liberation. It is to use our success for the fulfillment of our lives. A great nation is one which breeds a great people.

A great people flower not from wealth and power but from a society which spurs them to the fullness of their genius—that alone is a great society.

Yet slowly, painfully on the edge of victory has come the knowledge that shared prosperity is not enough. In the midst of abundance modern man walks oppressed by forces which menace and confine the quality of his life and which individual abundance alone will not overcome.

We can subdue and we can master these forces by bringing increased meaning to our lives if all of us, Government and citizens, are bold enough to change old ways, daring enough to assault new dangers and if the dream is dear enough to call forth the limitless capacities of this great people.

This year we must continue to improve the quality of American life.

Let us fulfill and improve the great health and education programs of last year, extending special opportunities to those who risk their lives in our Armed Forces.

I urge the House of Representatives to complete action on three programs already passed by the Senate—the Teachers Corps, the rent assistance, and home rule for the District of Columbia.

In some of our urban areas we must help rebuild entire sections and neighborhoods containing in some cases as many as a hundred thousand people. Working together private enterprise and Government must press forward with the task of providing homes and shops, parks and hospitals, and all the other necessary parts of a flourishing community where people can come to live the good life.

I will offer other proposals to stimulate and to reward planning for the growth of entire metropolitan areas.

Of all the reckless devastations of our national heritage none is really more shameful than the continued poisoning of our rivers and our air.

We must undertake a cooperative effort to end pollution in several river basins, making additional funds available to help draw the plans and construct the plants that are necessary to make the waters of our entire river systems clean and make them a source of pleasure and beauty for all of our people.

To attack and to overcome growing crime and lawlessness I think we must have a stepped-up program to help modernize and strengthen our local police forces.

Our people have a right to feel secure in their homes and on their streets, and that right just must be secured.

Nor can we fail to arrest destruction of life and property on our highways.

I will propose a Highway Safety Act of 1966 to seek an end to this mounting tragedy.

We must also act to prevent the deception of the American consumer, requiring all packages to state clearly and truthfully their contents; all interest and credit charges to be fully revealed; and keeping harmful drugs and cosmetics away from our stores.

It is the genius of our Constitution that under its shelter of enduring institutions and rooted principles there is ample room for the rich fertility of American political invention.

We must change to master change, and I propose to take steps to modernize and streamline the executive branch, to modernize the relations between city and State and Nation.

A new Department of Transportation is needed to bring together our transportation activities. The present structure, 35 Government agencies spending $5 billion yearly, makes it almost impossible to serve either the growing demands of this great Nation or the needs of the industry or the right of the taxpayer to full efficiency and real frugality.

And I will propose in addition a program to construct and flight test a new supersonic transport airplane that will fly three times the speed of sound, in excess of 2,000 miles per hour.

I propose to examine our Federal system, the relation between city, State, Nation, and the citizens themselves. We need a commission of the most distinguished scholars and men of public affairs to do this job, and I will ask them to move on to develop a creative federalism to best use the wonderful diversity of our institutions and our people to solve the problems and to fulfill the dreams of the American people.

And as the process of election becomes more complex and more costly we must make it possible for those without personal wealth to enter public life without being obligated to a few large contributors.

Therefore, I will submit new legislation to revise the present unrealistic restriction on contribution to prohibit the endless proliferation of committees, bringing local and State committees under the act, to attach strong teeth and severe penalties to the requirement of full disclosure of contribution, and to broaden the participation of the people through added tax incentive, to stimulate small contributions to the party and to the candidate of their choice.

To strengthen the work of Congress I strongly urge an amendment to provide a 4-year term for Members of the House of Representatives which should not begin before 1972.

The present 2-year term requires most Members of Congress to divert enormous energies to an almost constant process of campaigning, depriving this Nation of the fullest measure of both their skill and their wisdom. Today, too, the work of government is far more complex than in our early years, requiring more time to learn and more time to master the technical tasks of legislating. And a longer term will serve to attract more men of the highest quality to political life. The Nation, the principle of democracy, and I think each congressional district, will all be better served by a 4-year term for Members of the House, and I urge your swift action.

Tonight the cup of peril is full in Vietnam.

That conflict is not an isolated episode, but another great event in the policy that we have followed with strong consistency since World War II.

The touchstone of that policy is the interest of the United States. But nations sink when they see that interest only through a narrow glass.

In a world that has grown small and dangerous, pursuit of narrow aims could bring decay and even disaster.

An America that is mighty beyond description, yet living in a hostile or despairing world, would be neither safe nor free to build a civilization to liberate the spirit of man.

In this pursuit we helped rebuild Western Europe. We gave our aid to Greece and Turkey, and we defended the freedom of Berlin.

In this pursuit we have helped new nations toward independence, we have extended a helping hand to the Peace Corps and carried forward the largest program of economic assistance in the world.

In this pursuit we worked to build a hemisphere of democracy and of social justice.

In this pursuit we have defended against Communist aggression—in Korea under President Truman, in the Formosa Straits under President Eisenhower, in Cuba under President Kennedy, and again in Vietnam.

Tonight Vietnam must hold the center of our attention, but across the world problems and opportunities crowd in on the American Nation. I will discuss them fully in the months to come, and I will follow the five continuing lines of policy that America has followed under its last four Presidents.

The first principle is strength.

Tonight I can tell you that we are strong enough to keep all of our commitments. We will need expenditures of $58.3 billion for the next fiscal year to maintain this necessary defense might.

While special Vietnam expenditures for the next fiscal year are estimated to increase by $5.8 billion, I can tell you that all the other expenditures put together in the entire Federal budget will rise this coming year by only six-tenths of a billion dollars. This is true because of the stringent cost conscious economy program inaugurated in the Defense Department and followed by the other departments of Government.

A second principle of policy is the effort to control, to reduce, and to ultimately eliminate the modern engines of destruction.

We will vigorously pursue existing proposals—and seek new ones—to control arms and stop the spread of nuclear weapons.

A third major principle of our foreign policy is to help build those associations of nations which reflect the opportunities and the necessities of the modern world.

By strengthening the common defense, by stimulating world commerce, by meeting new hopes, these associations serve the cause of a flourishing world.

We will take new steps this year to help strengthen the Alliance for Progress, the unity of Europe, the community of the Atlantic, the regional organizations of developing continents, and that supreme association, the United Nations.

We will work to strengthen economic cooperation, to reduce barriers to trade, and to improve international finance.

A fourth enduring strand of policy has been to help improve the life of man.

From the Marshall plan to this very moment tonight that policy has rested on the claims of compassion and the certain knowledge that only a people advancing in expectation will build secure and peaceful lands.

This year I propose major new directions in our program of foreign assistance to help those countries who will help themselves.

We will conduct a worldwide attack on the problems of hunger and disease and ignorance.

We will place the matchless skill and the resources of our own great America in farming and in fertilizers at the service of those countries committed to develop a modern agriculture.

We will aid those who educate the young in other lands and we will give children in other continents the same head start that we are trying to give our own children. To advance these ends, I will propose the International Education Act of 1966.

I will also propose the International Health Act of 1966 to strike at disease by a new effort to bring modern skills and knowledge to the uncared for, those suffering in the world, and by trying to wipe out smallpox and malaria and control yellow fever over most of the world during this next decade, to help countries trying to control population growth by increasing our research, and we will earmark funds to help their efforts.

In the next year, from our foreign aid sources we propose to dedicate $1 billion to these efforts, and we call on all who have the means to join us in this work in the world.

The fifth and most important principle of our foreign policy is support of national independence, the right of each people to govern themselves and to shape their own institutions.

For a peaceful world order will be possible only when each country walks the way that it has chosen to walk for itself.

We follow this principle by encouraging the end of colonial rule.

We follow this principle abroad as well as at home by continued hostility to the rule of the many by the few, or the oppression of one race by another.

We follow this principle by building bridges to Eastern Europe. I will ask the Congress for authority to remove the special tariff restrictions which are a barrier to increasing trade between the East and the West.

The insistent urge toward national independence is the strongest force of today's world in which we live.

In Africa and Asia and Latin America it is shattering the designs of those who would subdue others to their ideas or their will.

It is eroding the unity of what was once a Stalinist empire.

In recent months a number of nations have cast out those who would subject them to the ambitions of mainland China.

History is on the side of freedom and is on the side of societies as shaped from the genius of each people. History does not favor a single system or belief unless force is used to make it so.

And that is why it has been necessary for us to defend this basic principle of our policy—to defend it in Berlin and in Korea and in Cuba and tonight in Vietnam. For tonight, as so many nights before, young Americans struggle and young Americans die in a distant land.

Tonight, as so many nights before, the American Nation is asked to sacrifice the blood of its children and the fruits of its labor for the love of its freedom.

How many times in my lifetime and in yours have the American people gathered as they do now to hear their President tell them of conflict and tell them of danger?

Each time they have answered, they have answered with all the effort that the security and freedom of this Nation required, and they do again tonight in Vietnam.

Not too many years ago Vietnam was a peaceful if troubled land. In the north was an independent Communist government. In the south a people struggled to build a nation with the friendly help of the United States.

There were some in South Vietnam who wished to force Communist rule on their own people, but their progress was slight. Their hope of success was dim. Then little more than 6 years ago North Vietnam decided on conquest, and from that day to this soldiers and supplies have moved from north to south in a swelling stream that is swallowing the remnants of revolution and aggression.

And as the assault mounted, our choice gradually became clear. We could leave, abandoning South Vietnam to its attackers and to certain conquest, or we could stay and fight beside the people of South Vietnam.

We stayed. And we will stay until aggression has stopped.

We will stay because a just nation cannot leave to the cruelty of its enemies a people who have staked their lives and independence on America's solemn pledge—a pledge which has grown through the commitments of three American Presidents.

We will stay because in Asia and around the world are countries whose independence rests in large measure on confidence in America's word and in America's protection. To yield to force in Vietnam would weaken that confidence, would undermine the independence of many lands, and would whet the appetite of aggression. We would have to fight in one land and then we would have to fight in another or abandon much of Asia to the domination of Communists.

And we do not intend to abandon Asia to conquest.

Last year the nature of the war in Vietnam changed again. Swiftly increasing numbers of armed men from the North crossed the borders to join forces that were already in the South. Attack and terror increased, spurred and encouraged by the belief that the United States lacked the will to continue and that their victory was near.

Despite our desire to limit conflict, it was necessary to act to hold back the mounting aggression to give courage to the people of the South and to make our firmness clear to the North. Thus, we began limited air action against military targets in North Vietnam. We increased our fighting force to its present strength tonight of 190,000 men.

These moves have not ended the aggression, but they have prevented its success. The aims of the enemy have been put out of reach by the skill and bravery of Americans and their allies, and by the enduring courage of the South Vietnamese who, I can tell you, lost eight men last year for every one of ours.

The enemy is no longer closer to victory. Time is no longer on his side. There is no cause to doubt the American commitment.

Our decision to stand firm has been matched by our desire for peace.

In 1965 alone we had 300 private talks for peace in Vietnam with friends and adversaries throughout the world.

Since Christmas your Government has labored again with imagination and endurance to remove any barrier to peaceful settlement. For 20 days now we and our Vietnamese allies have dropped no bombs in North Vietnam.

Able and experienced spokesmen have visited in behalf of America more than 40 countries. We have talked to more than a hundred governments, all 113 that we have relations with and some that we do not. We talked to the United Nations, and we called upon all of its members to make any contribution that they could toward helping gain peace.

In public statements and in private communications to adversaries and to friends in Rome and Warsaw, in Paris and Tokyo, in Africa and throughout this hemisphere, America has made her position abundantly clear.

We seek neither territory nor bases, economic domination or military alliance in Vietnam. We fight for the principle of self-determination that the people of South Vietnam should be able to choose their own course, choose it in free elections without violence, without terror.

and without fear. The people of all Vietnam should make a free decision on the great question of reunification.

And this is all we want for South Vietnam. It is all the people of South Vietnam want. And if there is a single nation on this earth that desires less than this for its people, then let its voice be heard. We have also made it clear from Hanoi to New York that there are no arbitrary limits to our search for peace. We stand by the Geneva Agreements of 1954 and 1962. We will meet at any conference table. We will discuss any proposals—4 points or 14 or 40—and we will consider the views of any group. We will work for a cease fire now, or once discussions have begun.

We will respond if others reduce their use of force and we will withdraw our soldiers once South Vietnam is securely guaranteed the right to shape its own future.

We have said all this and we have asked and hoped and we have waited for a response.

So far we have received no response to prove either success or failure.

We have carried our quest for peace to many nations and peoples because we share this planet with others whose future, in large measure, is tied to our own action and whose counsel is necessary to our own hopes.

We have found understanding and support, and we know they wait with us tonight for some response that could lead to peace.

I wish tonight that I could give you a blueprint for the course of this conflict over the coming months, but we just cannot know what the future may require. We may have to face long, hard combat or a long, hard conference or even both at once.

Until peace comes, or if it does not come, our course is clear. We will act as we must to help protect the independence of the valiant people of South Vietnam. We will strive to limit the conflict, for we wish neither increased destruction nor do we want to invite increased danger.

But we will give our fighting men what they must have, every gun and every dollar and every decision, whatever the cost or whatever the challenge.

And we will continue to help the people of South Vietnam care for those that are ravaged by battle, create progress in the villages, and carry forward the healing hopes of peace as best they can amidst the uncertain terrors of war.

And let me be absolutely clear. The days may become months and the months may become years, but we will stay as long as aggression commands us to battle.

There may be some who do not want peace, whose ambitions stretch so far that war in Vietnam is but a welcome and convenient episode in an immense design to subdue history to their will. But for others it must now be clear that the choice is not between peace and victory. It lies between peace and the ravages of a conflict from which they can only lose.

The people of Vietnam, North and South, seek the same things, the shared needs of man—the needs for food and shelter and education—the chance to build and work and till the soil free from the arbitrary horrors of battle—the desire to walk in the dignity of those who master their own destiny. For many painful years, in war and revolution and infrequent peace, they have struggled to fulfill those needs.

It is a crime against mankind that so much courage and so much will and so many dreams must be flung on the fires of war and death.

To all of those caught up in this conflict we therefore say again tonight: Let us choose peace, and with it the wondrous works of peace, and beyond that, the time when hope reaches toward consummation, and life is the servant of life.

In this work we plan to discharge our duty to the people whom we serve.

This is the state of the Union.

But over it all—wealth and promise—and expectation—lies our troubling awareness of American men at war tonight.

How many men who listen to me tonight have served their Nation in other wars? How very many are not here to listen?

War in Vietnam is not like these other wars; yet, finally, war is always the same. It is young men dying in the fullness of their promise. It is trying to kill a man that you do not even know well enough to hate.

Therefore, to know war is to know that there is still madness in this world.

Many of you share the burden of this knowledge tonight with me. But there is a difference. For, finally, I must be the one to order our guns to fire—against all the most inward pulls of my desire. For we have children to teach, and we have sick to be cured, and we have men to be freed. There are poor to be lifted up and there are cities to be built and there is a world to be helped.

Yet, we will do what we must.

I am hopeful and I will try the best I can with everything I have to end this battle and to return our sons to their desires.

Yet, as long as others will challenge America's security and test the dearness of our belief with fire and steel, then we must stand or see the promise of two centuries tremble. I believe tonight that you do not want me to try that risk. And from that belief, your President summons his strength for the trials that lie ahead in the days to come.

The work must be our work now. Scarred by the weaknesses of man, with whatever guidance God may offer us, we must nevertheless, and alone, with our mortality, strive to ennoble the life of man on earth.

Thank you and goodnight.

Index

Index

The Presidents are listed first and chronologically within each subject category.

C

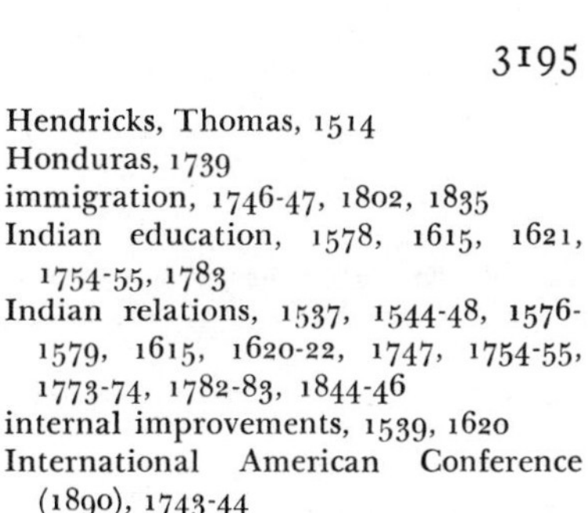

D

G

H

I

J

K

L

M

O

Q

R

S

T

U

V